HISTORY OF GREECE

CLASSICAL TEXTS AND STUDIES NO. 3

In the same series

No. 1: *Fasti Umbrici: études sur le vocabulaire et le rituel des Tables eugubines*
by Willy Alfred Borgeaud

No. 2: *Le calendrier romain: recherches chronologiques*
by Pierre Brind'Amour

Hermann Bengtson

HISTORY OF GREECE

FROM THE BEGINNINGS TO THE BYZANTINE ERA

Translated and Updated by Edmund F. Bloedow

University of Ottawa Press

Printed and bound in Canada

ISBN 0-7766-0210-1 (clothbound)
ISBN 0-7766-0111-3 (paperback)

This work was translated from the fourth edition of Hermann Bengtson's *Griechische Geschichte*, published by C.H. Beck in 1969.

Canadian Cataloguing in Publication Data

Bengtson, Hermann, 1909-
History of Greece

(Classical texts and studies ; 3)
Translation of: *Griechische Geschichte*. 4th ed.
Bibliography: p.
ISBN 0-7766-0210-1 (bound) —
ISBN 0-7766-0111-3 (pbk.)

1. Greece — History — To 146 B.C. 2. Greece — History — 146 B.C.-323 A.D. I. Bloedow, Edmund F. (Edmund Frederick), 1930- . II. Title. III. Series.

DF214.B4613 1988 938 C88-090281-7

This book has been published with the help of a grant from the Faculty of Arts, University of Ottawa

UNIVERSITÉ D'OTTAWA
UNIVERSITY OF OTTAWA

Contents

Illustrations

Translator's Preface

The idea for this translation originated some time ago, but only now has it been possible to bring it to fulfilment. A one-volume *History of Greece* in English, by a master in the field, which not only continues beyond the death of Alexander the Great but also includes both the Hellenistic period and the Roman Empire and, in addition, provides a critical evaluation of the ancient sources as well as citations of the modern literature, has long been a *desideratum* (nor does there appear to be any immediate prospect of such an undertaking).

This translation is based on the fourth German edition (1969). Although the translation itself was completed in 1974, it was thought desirable to bring the modern research up to date. On both the translation and updating the translator worked in close collaboration with the author, and in the latter aspect there was mutual exchange of material, as the idea was to publish the English edition to coincide with the appearance of the fifth German edition (1977). Due to technical problems, however, the English edition could not appear at that point and, because of the time which then elapsed, it was considered appropriate to bring the research up to date once more. Unfortunately, it has not been possible to incorporate this updated research into the original format, and so it is included in a separate section. It is hoped that the presence of the new material will compensate for the consequent inconvenience. Since Professor Bengtson's *Griechische Geschichte* is designed not only for undergraduates but also for graduate students and for scholars, the same principles were followed in adding new research as were adopted in the German editions.

I should like to thank Professor Bengtson for his assistance with the translation and for the material which he generously made available to me. Indeed part of the intent of my translation is as a gesture of honour to him, as a *discipulus magistro*. My thanks are also due in no small measure to others, but to none more than to my wife, Audrey Newnham, and to Jennifer Wilson, who have rendered an immeasurable service in the arduous task of reading the proofs. The opportunity to use the excellent facilities of the various libraries in Munich, made possible by two grants from the Humanities Research Fund of the University of Ottawa, in 1973 and 1985, was invaluable for the task of updating the research. The text was originally edited by Professor Alan Samuel, who also designed the format and undertook the abbreviations. The battle plans have been adapted from Kromayer-Veith's *Schlachtenatlas* by Dorothy Woermke and Shelley Laskin.

Edmund F. Bloedow
Ottawa, May 1988

Preface to the First Edition

The latest (fifth) edition (1914) of Robert v. Pöhlmann's *Griechische Geschichte und Quellenkunde* is long out of print. My teacher Walter Otto, who from 1920 until the time of his death (1 Nov. 1941) was editor of the *Handbuch der Altertumswissenschaft*, unfortunately did not get as far as carrying out his plan of writing a new *Greek History* within the framework of the *Handbuch* series. But the more diverse research has become during the last decades, the more the need has arisen for a comprehensive work of this kind, and one which in particular took into account the latest research and the latest archaeological finds.

The kindness of the Publisher, who granted me—apart from the inevitable setting of certain limits in respect of its length—complete freedom in every detail, allowed me to carry out my own plan of the format which I had envisaged for years: for me there had never been any doubt that a comprehensive treatment of Greek History must include, in addition to the classical period, also the Hellenistic and, besides this, the Roman era of the Hellenic people as well. The times in which Greek histories end with Chaeroneia (338 B.C.) are over, and it scarcely requires special pleading for the fact that this book includes a detailed treatment of the Hellenistic Age, of the Hellenistic states and a sketch of Hellenistic civilisation.

But equally necessary was a basic sketch of the historical developments of the Greeks during the Roman Empire. There is no denying that the Greeks and Hellenic culture once more, during the Byzantine Empire, did play, even though in new forms, an extremely important rôle, one, namely, within the perspective of world history, the effects of which continued deep within the history of modern Europe. But anyone who wishes to understand developments in Byzantium cannot overlook the history of the Greeks during the climax of the Roman Empire. This very era affords extensive scope for future research, and for me it would be satisfaction if the preliminary sketch in this book were soon to be followed by new, detailed studies which would not only correct the picture contained therein but also render it out of date as a whole.

These introductory remarks indicate that Pöhlmann's *Grundriss* has been replaced by a completely new work, not a "political textbook" as such, rather a genuine handbook, a working tool. The real object of the book is to preserve continuity of research in this field and by the exposition of what has been achieved provide fellow-scholars and a future generation with a basis for further research.

What is offered in this *Greek History* may be described as that which one could expect from the author on the basis of his previous research: it is predominantly a *political* Greek History. Apart from the fact that the time has not yet come for a fully-balanced cultural history, namely, one that devotes equal attention to all periods of the Greeks, one should bear in mind that this book constitutes one unit within the larger framework of the *Handbuch der Altertumswissenschaft*, which contains comprehensive studies of Greek literature, Greek religion and Greek archaeological monuments, and will perhaps, when the time is ripe for it, also include a treatment of Greek culture. By inserting summaries between sections, however, I have attempted at least to suggest the outlines of the spiritual and general cultural developments, and this in particular for those periods, such as the so-called archaic, the Hellenistic and the Roman eras, which are generally less well known than the classical period of the Greeks. It is to be hoped that these initial suggestions can be built upon and carried further at some future date.

In the bibliographical references an attempt has been made to include a certain wealth of material: but should one or another important study not be mentioned, this does not always suggest that it was unknown to the author. It was only natural that the available space dictated certain limits. Some material may unfortunately also have been overlooked, and it would be in the interests of the matter if fellow-scholars would support me by sending their work in the future even more so than in the past, although I am extremely thankful for the many who have already done so. I have also dropped the plan, in the introduction of this work, to give an overview of the general research tools in the field of Greek History. Whoever wishes information in this area, can find the essential material, although arranged from a different perspective, in my *Einfuhrung in die Alte Geschichte* (Munich 1949).

The text of the present *Greek History* was written during a time when conditions for scholarly research were anything other than suitable, in the period from the autumn of 1946 to the spring of 1949. What it means—not to speak at all of other difficulties—not to have one's own books at one's disposal at a time when in Munich not a single Library was functioning can only be appreciated by those who during the war worked under similar circumstances.

Of the number of friends and assistants who remained loyal to me even during difficult years I should like to mention in particular the names of M. P. Nilsson and Günther Klaffenbach. I am grateful for the invitation, on Nilsson's initiative, to go to Sweden, which made it possible to consult a number of studies not available here in Munich. In addition Professor Nilsson kindly allowed me to consult the manuscript of Vol. II of his *Geschichte der griechischen Religion*. I am no less grateful for a number of suggestions by correspondence. Günther Klaffenbach assisted in the task, not easy, of reading the proofs, and while doing so was able to suggest various corrections and additions which have improved the book and thereby will also profit scholarship. Apart from this he insisted on checking out a large number of references, an act of friendship for which I am deeply grateful.

I also wish to express my warmest thanks to the Publisher, the C. H. Bech'sche Verlagsbuchhandlung, with whom I have enjoyed the most cordial relations for years. It is thanks to the Publisher alone that in the past years I have been able to devote myself to scholarly research. In addition I wish to acknowledge my special gratitude to Dr. Heinrich Beck and his assistant, Dr. Georg Sund, for their willingness to accede to my plans to provide the book with various maps and appendices.

Munich, August 1950 — Hermann Bengtson

Preface to the Second Edition

The request of the Publisher to undertake a new edition of the *Greek History* did not take me by surprise or unprepared. Since the book first appeared almost 10 years ago I have attempted to evaluate the latest research, and wherever I was convinced that the conclusions were correct I entered them in my working copy.

By going through the new material and research of the last decade it became evident that there were no grounds for a fundamental revision of the work, although numerous corrections in respect of details were warranted.

It cannot be the task of a handbook simply to compile the research that has been carried out: it is much more important to make a critical analysis of the latest studies: such a, necessarily subjective, judgment appears, in my view, to be better than none at all: the user of a handbook may rightly demand not to be left in the lurch in this respect.

I should gladly have adopted—to take but one instance—a more positive view of the decipherment of Linear B by Ventris and his collaborators than that expressed within the frame of this book. But as things stand at the moment a cautious attitude is more in place than the opposite: until we find ourselves on solid ground a consideration, even a hypothetical one, of the results of the decipherment does not recommend itself: *grammatici certant, adhuc sub iudice lis est.*—In citing the secondary literature I have kept within bounds, and, wherever possible, avoided exclusively accumulating bibliographies—the terror of so many recent publications. If old and new, what is out of date and what is lasting are cited in a variegated mixture, the user is only too often led astray. It is the duty of a handbook to emphasise what is valuable, record what is useful and leave the rest aside.

In surveying the achievements in the field of Greek History during the last decade one is struck by the fact that certain areas, for instance, the Pentecontaetia, have enjoyed particular interest, while others, indeed very worthy of being studied, have remained almost untouched. The latter applies also to the history of the Greeks during the Roman Empire. I may take this opportunity to voice once more the petition that this very important sector of Hellenic History not be overlooked.

The revised manuscript was submitted to the Publisher in July and September 1959. But since the actual printing took place while I was Rector of the University certain delays were unavoidable.

I am happy to be able to acknowledge here the help of my pupils: Dr. Hatto H. Schmitt assisted in reading the proofs, and Manfred Janke reorganised the Index.

Würzburg, June 1960 Hermann Bengtson

Preface to the Fourth Edition

In preparing this new edition I have endeavoured to take account of the most recent research, in so far as I was aware of it, and to bring the bibliography up to date. The area which has received most attention during the immediate past has been Greek Prehistory and Protohistory. In the other areas of Greek History less work has been done, although here too there was some material that warranted inclusion. I hope that the book's usefulness has been increased, especially through the new bibliographical references. The type has been reset.

I wish to thank my pupils who assisted in reading the proofs and with the printing: Thomas Fischer, Dr. Werner Huss, Wolfgang Orth and Ralf Urban. The last named also prepared the Index.

Munich, December 1968 — Hermann Bengtson

HISTORY OF GREECE

1
THE EARLY AGES OF GREECE

THE IMMIGRATION INTO GREECE

Greece is not a land of opulence and plenty.[1] The extent of cultivable land is slight and the country as a whole is dominated by the barren Karst range, whose forests had in part already fallen prey to fire in antiquity. Drastic changes in temperature, combined with considerable variations in climate from one region to another, and the ever recurring drought of the summer months do not make for an easy life in this sun-drenched land. Nothing falls into the lap of the inhabitants of Greece without toil, and often all human efforts prove in vain when the Earthshaker Poseidon brandishes his trident. The country faces towards the East, and it is on the frequently and deeply indented east coast that land and sea interpenetrate to the greatest degree. Here the best harbours are found. Most of the rivers flow eastwards, into the Thracian and Aegean Seas. In contrast, conditions for seafaring in the west are much less favourable. Only the long Gulf of Corinth offers ships adequate shelter from the storms of the Adriatic, and the harbours in northwest Greece and on the west coast of the Peloponnesus never attained more than local importance.

Rugged mountains divide Greece from the backbone of the Balkan Peninsula, and traffic generally moves along the river valleys, the large gateways from north to south. From the Pindus, which separates Thessaly from Epirus and serves as a virtual wall between peoples, to Mount Taygetus in the southern Peloponnesus, one mountain chain links into another. Because of its mountains, the country is split up into a large number of small and even minute geographical units, between which immediate communication is often difficult. There is room for larger and more densely settled areas only in Thessaly, Attica and to some extent in the plains of the Alpheius, Pamisus and Eurotas rivers. Islands, which extend from the east coast of Greece to Asia Minor and to Crete, have always facilitated communications with Greece. The fortunes of the inhabitants of the Greek Peninsula are governed by the omnipresence of the sea.[2] The sea moulds the history of the country in terms of the past, the present and the future.

No information and no epic poem reaches back into the primitive times of the Greek people. Even the awareness that their place of origin was outside Hellas had become lost to the Greeks in historical times. They frequently regarded themselves as autochthonous–sprung from the soil–but their view that the "Pelasgians" and "Carians" were former inhabitants stands in clear contradiction to this. What modern scholars profess to know about primitive times in Hellas rests on conclusions drawn from studies in prehistory, comparative philology and the topography of settlements. Taken individually these studies differ in importance and reliability, but viewed as a whole they do permit us to frame a correct picture of the early period of Greece.

The immigration of the Indo-European forefathers of the Greeks into the country which took its name from them is undoubtedly connected with the migrations in the Middle Danube-Carpathian region. Propelled by tribes which poured into this region from the north or northeast, the former inhabitants of the Hungarian plain were forced to move southwards. The emigrants were groups of the original Indo-Europeans, who originated in the vast area between the Baltic Sea and the interior of Asia.[3] The change from sedentary life to migration reshaped their way of life and ethnic composition. Many adventurers of foreign extraction may have attached themselves to the migrants, and since migrating demanded proven leaders, the immediate result was a considerable strengthening and focussing of power. Hitherto, in more tranquil times, powerful leaders would scarcely have been needed. The religion of this people from whom the forefathers of the Greeks stemmed shows a mixture of fetishistic and animistic ideas, combined with elements from nature worship. They perceived in the sky god, whom the later Greeks worshipped under the venerable name of Zeus pater, an embodiment of omnipotent nature, with whose powers their life was most intimately bound up. They also worshipped the sky god as the patron of human order, the family and the state. Their state was composed of clans or brotherhoods, and united members of one tribe and one language.

The Indo-Europeans in the Hungarian plain possessed a peasant culture, had the plough and the loom, and cattle, sheep and goats for livestock and wealth. Their herds and flocks accompanied them during their migrations, so that they maintained a continuous rhythm of temporary nomadic life alternating with sedentary existence. The unique position of Greek within the context of the large Indo-European family of languages[4] does not link the Greek people sufficiently with any other into a narrower grouping, so that the theory of Graeco-Italic connection[5], once held by some scholars, has long since been rightly abandoned.

The Indo-Europeans took possession of Hellas so early in prehistoric times that the dating of this crucial event will to some degree remain uncertain so long as it is impossible to establish it conclusively with the aid of synchronous evidence from outside Greece. It is at least certain, however, that the Indo-European migration, the first for which there is evidence in Greece, must have occurred before the Dorian invasion of the Peloponnesus (twelfth century B.C.), and very probably even before the first flowering of Mycenaean culture (second half of the sixteenth century B.C.). A catastrophe at the end of the Early Helladic period (about 1900

B.C.)[6] brought the destruction of a large number of settlements on the Greek mainland, in a wide zone from western Greece to the Argolid. It is highly probable,[7] but not yet certainly established, that this catastrophe is to be traced back to the immigration of the Indo-Europeans.

Internal developments in Greece are illuminated by archaeological finds,[8] which show Neolithic culture reaching back to the sixth millennium. Peak Neolithic culture is designated as "Sesklo culture," since Sesklo, in Thessaly, is the principal site of the discoveries. It is found most concentrated in the region of Thessaly (about 150 settlements) and in the district around Corinth. Towards the west it extends beyond Corfu as far as the Italian region of Molfetta in Apulia. Unfortified settlements with rectangular and oblong mud huts are characteristic of Sesklo culture. The pottery, at first employing white and later coloured ornamental designs, is primitive but cannot deny influences from Western Asia.[9] There are stone tools, as well as some made of obsidian from the island of Melos.

The "Dimini" culture, immediately preceding the Early Helladic period (before the middle of the third millennium),[10] shows fortified settlements, which suggest more troubled times. Band Ceramic motifs show that the Dimini people had foreign connections, with a point of origin in the region of Transylvania.[11] In other respects, however, Dimini culture was overshadowed by that of Asia Minor, to wit Troy I, Poliochni and Thermi (on Lesbos). Some have argued for additional immigrants from the north,[12] but conclusive evidence is lacking. The case depends primarily on the appearance of the megaron, a rectangular room with its hearth as focal point. But this architectural feature also appears as the so-called double megaron not only in the Sesklo culture, but also in Troy I (about 3200-2600 B.C. according to Blegen; about 2700-1900 B.C. according to Milojčić and others), and it is not impossible that this type of construction developed independently in the region of the Aegean and Anatolia, without northern connections.[13]

Early Helladic culture (c. 2500-1900 B.C.), with its characteristic *urfirnis* pottery, was a distinctly peasant culture. Its area included, in addition to Thessaly, primarily central Greece (Phocis, Boeotia, Attica) and the northern Peloponnesus (Argolis, Corinth). The hill of Tiryns, with its large circular structure, shows itself as the seat of a warlike ruling family even in this early period. The village form of settlement predominated in the Cyclades, while the dense population of Attica (Hagios Kosmas) and Aegina shows distinctively Mediterranean characteristics.[14]

It is particularly in language that the former Mediterranean inhabitants of Greece have left visible traces behind. Comparative philology has recognised some place-names, like those ending in *-nthos* and *-ssos* as non-Indo-European, and postulates a link with the previous inhabitants, whose settlements must have extended over Hellas, the Cyclades and south-west Asia Minor.[15] The names Corinthos, Zacynthos, Ilissos, Cephissos and similar forms are pre-Indo-European. Names like these are found most often in Attica and in the Argolid, but also appear in central Greece and on the islands.[16] Names for many plants and metals, and terms taken from the sphere of navigation and fishing are evidence that the pre-Indo-European population had a distinctive civilising influence on the life and thinking of the immigrants.

Scholars designate the pre-Indo-European population of Hellas as "Aegean." The later Greeks called these people Carians, Leleges or Pelasgians.[17] There is no evidence about the process of interchange and cultural exchange between the immigrating Indo-Europeans from the north and the original inhabitants. The fact that the Greeks accepted certain features from the life and language of the old Mediterranean civilisation appears to indicate a lengthy period of adjustment and exchange, in which the new inhabitants of the country were the recipients and the original population the donors. From this cultural and anthropological fusion of old Mediterranean and new Indo-European elements the Greek people emerged in the second millennium.

The first Indo-European immigration into Hellas—probably at the beginning of the Middle Helladic period—was no uniform event. It was a gradual ebb and flow of tribes and tribal segments, a continual reversal of war and peace, internal struggles and peaceful co-existence. Of decisive importance was the gradual establishment of the Indo-Europeans as political leaders over the highly civilised Mediterranean inhabitants. The great structural differences among the Greek dialects suggest that these did not develop on Hellenic soil, but were brought in by the immigrants.[18] Three major dialect groups emerge: the Ionian, Arcado-Aeolic (often given the comprehensive name Achaean) and Doric-North-West Greek.[19] Earlier scholars repeatedly attempted to use dialect studies for the history of the Greek tribes—futile endeavours, since language and national characteristics are of different dimensions and belong in different categories. In consequence, all theories which attempt to date the immigrations of the Greek tribes chronologically are, in so far as they have been based on dialect studies, from the very outset built on sand. The only certain fact is that the bearers of the Doric-North-West Greek dialects did not set foot on Greek soil until the end of the Late Helladic period.

With regard to the distribution of the great dialect groups before Doric-North-West Greek appeared, Ionic was spoken not only in Attica and on Euboea but originally also in the Argolid, other parts of the Peloponnesus and Boeotia. Arcado-Aeolic ("Achaean") is found in Thessaly and throughout the entire Peloponnesus. Here, as in Boeotia, it more or less asserted itself over Ionic, an event which may none the less be connected with the migrations and imposition of the speakers of Arcado-Aeolic over those who spoke Ionic.

The first half of the second millennium B.C., which marks a decisive turning point, indeed a new beginning for Hellas, was an era of great upheaval for the entire Mediterranean world, and especially for the East. The effects of the first great Indo-European migration were felt deep within the heart of Anatolia and as far as northern Mesopotamia, indeed as far as India. In the course of the migration, the forefathers of the Hittites reached central Anatolia—whether from the west across the Bosporus or the Hellespont or from the east across the Caucasus is difficult to determine. Their initial appearance falls in the nineteenth century B.C.[20] After a period of isolated city-states, the so-called first empire of the Hatti rose under the ruler Tabarna (Labarna), in about 1600 B.C. The fusion of the immigrant Indo-European ruling class with the Anatolian population was completed within a few generations, and this fusion moulded the genuine native type of Asia Minor, the so-called Hittites (Hatti). Their close ties with the soil are manifested in the Anatolian deities, which the immigrants took over.

About half a century before Labarna, Hammurabi,[21] the great law-giver of the ancient Orient, was the Babylonian ruler. After the most brilliant period, under the great conquerors Sargon and Naramsin of Akkad (at the end of the third millennium), an era of decline followed in Babylon. During this so-called Neo-Sumerian period, the great number of small city-states re-emerged. After this, the immigrant Semitic Amorites from the west brought about a significant rejuvenation in Babylon, contributing very decisively to the flowering of Babylonian culture in the time of Hammurabi. In this period Babylonia became a culturally leading power of the greatest importance in Western Asia. Its culture was eagerly adopted by the neighbouring peoples, and the Hittites even took over the Babylonian cuneiform script.

Egypt, the third major power of the second millennium B.C., after the end of the powerful Middle Kingdom (c. 1950-1680 B.C.) fell prey to the Hyksos,[22] a homogeneous or heterogeneous people whose anthropological character has not as yet been established for certain. Characteristic features of the Hyksos are the feudal structure of their state and the use of warriors in horse-drawn chariots. These Asiatic rulers made the Delta city of Auaris the capital of their empire, which in addition to Egypt probably also included large sections of Syria. The Hyksos empire thereby paralleled that of the Hurrians, who appeared at approximately the same time in Upper Mesopotamia and whose ruling class contained Indo-European, more specifically Aryan, names.[23] It was not until after more than one hundred years of foreign domination that the rulers of the Eighteenth Dynasty of Egypt (Ahmose) finally threw off the yoke of the Hyksos from the necks of the Egyptians (c. 1560 B.C.) and thereby paved the way for the great expansion of the New Kingdom.[24]

About the middle, but certainly before the end of the second millennium B.C., the Indo-Europeans for the first time forced their way over the mountains of the Hindu Kush into the Punjab. Their arrival coincided with the decline of the ancient civilisation of Mohenjo Daro and Harappa.

Viewed as a whole, the Indo-European migrations in the second millennium embraced the wide regions from the Apennine peninsula and the Balkans to central Asia. The fact that the Hittite kingdom of central Anatolia became oriented towards the southeast, in the direction of northern Syria and northern Mesopotamia, was of fundamental importance for further developments in Greece. The old, highly developed cultures in the region of the Near East must have constituted a far greater attraction for the Hittites than did the West, on which the Hittite kingdom turned its back, as it were. Moreover, to what degree the Hittites exerted a political influence on western Asia Minor is uncertain, since the historical geography of Anatolia for the time of the Hittites still presents many unsolved difficulties. At all events the existence of a great Anatolian empire, controlling connections between Mesopotamia, Syria and the West through possession of the Taurus passes, was of crucial importance for the political, economic and cultural developments of the peripheral countries of the Aegean. The Hittite kingdom loomed on the Greek horizon in the Mycenaean period as the model of a great empire. In the sphere of civilisation, however, the influence from Asia Minor is overlapped by the much stronger stimulus of Minoan Crete, whose first period of efflorescence coincided precisely with the beginning of the Middle Helladic period (c. 1900 B.C.), while the second climax in Minoan culture was approximately simultaneous with the Early Mycenaean period (Late Helladic I).

Innumerable monuments permit us to form a colourful picture of ancient Cretan culture. The Cretan writing symbols have remained mute up to the present day, despite all the mental acumen which has been brought to bear upon them, since a Creto-Egyptian or Creto-cuneiform bilingual source is lacking. The imposing Minoan heritage which the excavations have brought to light is so overwhelmingly abundant and varied that with its discovery a new world has been opened up to scholars, a world which rivals the ancient highly developed cultures of Egypt and Mesopotamia.

MINOAN CULTURE

In view of its fortunate location and its mild climate the ancients termed Crete, the largest island in the eastern Mediterranean, the "isle of the blessed." Lying at the intersection of many sea routes between Egypt, Syria, Asia Minor, Greece and the West, in the course of its history the island was exposed to the most varied influences from foreign cultures. In turn it radiated these in all directions. Like a concave mirror, Crete united many rays into a powerful beam shining with a strong light through the darkness of the early period of Aegean history. The names of Crete and Mycenae are symbols of an epoch in early Greek history which began about 1700 and ended in the twelfth century B.C. At first the Greeks readily yielded to the overwhelming influence of Cretan culture. This state of affairs changed from approximately 1400 B.C. onwards, when the Hellenes, having now become aware of their own strength, boldly launched forth on the seas towards the south and east. In a 'Viking era' a new spirit evolved in Greece, with a new attitude to the world around.

The first period of flowering in Cretan art began in Early Minoan III, about 2200 B.C., with a powerful stimulus from the north through the influence of Band Ceramic motifs.[25] The period saw construction of the great palaces of Cnossus and Phaestus, buildings which posterity has made the symbols of Minoan culture. The first period of Cretan culture came to an abrupt end in a great catastrophe at the close of the eighteenth or the beginning of the seventeenth century, at approximately the same time as the Hyksos established their rule over Egypt. This first destruction was, however, of only ephemeral significance. In Cnossus, Phaestus and Mallia, new and more spacious palaces emerged out of the ruins. Once more the island experienced a period of distinct cultural efflorescence, in which the peculiarly modern and charming character reflects the buoyant spirit of the Cretan personality. All fell into total ruin again about 1400 B.C., and with this the legend-enveloped empire of the Cretan king Minos sank forever into the sea of oblivion.

A map of the Cretan settlements in the Minoan period presents an informative picture:[26] While the East and the interior, especially the fertile plain of the Mesara, show numerous settlements, the West is almost bare. Although this may in part be conditioned by the state in which scholarship currently finds itself, the orientation of the island towards the east, south and north becomes clearly evident, a characteristic as true for the early as for the later periods of Cretan history.

The Neolithic era in Crete goes back to the first half of the sixth millennium. Later the inhabitants, related to the "Carian" population of early Greece and western Asia Minor,[27] settled in open villages with an unmistakable tendency to advance towards the sea, especially on the east coast. Here too we find the fishermen's huts, while a distinctly peasant culture developed in the agricultural plain of the Mesara. After modest beginnings Cretan culture grew until, from the end of the third millennium onwards, it attained wonderful strength and vitality. This has been designated as the "Kamares period," named from the pottery found in the Kamares cave on the southern slopes of Mount Ida. It is polychrome pottery, with a great many patterns, lines, curves and motifs from the plant world, on a dark glazed background. Vessels of eggshell thinness, which manifestly developed as an imitation of metal ware,[28] are a particular feature.

A characteristic court culture evolved in the environment of the older palaces of Cnossus and Phaestus in central Crete at the beginning of Middle Minoan I (approximately 2000 B.C.), and at the same time life concentrated primarily in the urban settlements. This inaugurated an era, aristocratic in character, which marked the end of the older predominantly peasant culture. The palaces were also economic centres, with oil mills and workshops of every description. The emergence of a new mode of life was above all a characteristic feature. Not battles and war, but sensuous enjoyment appears as the goal of existence. The character of this *bon vivant* period was still further reinforced by an external security so well established that the palaces were never fortified by walls and bastions. And as the Cretans became aware of their strength, the Cretan name (Keftiu, Kaphtor) enjoyed a good reputation in Egypt, Babylonia and Syria. At that time, however, Greece still meant nothing to the Cretans. The peasant population of Hellas had no need of the treasures which Minoan culture was able to offer.

Chronologically, the Kamares period coincides approximately with the Twelfth Egyptian Dynasty of the Middle Kingdom (c. 1950-c. 1750 B.C.).

Cretan craftsmen may have journeyed to the land of the Nile at that time, for Cretan pottery has been found in the Fayûm and in distant Upper Egypt. Ardent exchange developed between Crete and the Near East. Babylonian cylinder-seals—in particular from the period of Hammurabi—are to be found in great numbers in Cretan palaces. The French excavations at Mari on the Middle Euphrates (Tell Hariri)[29] leave little doubt along which route trade moved. Merchant vessels sailed back and forth between Crete (Kaphtor) and Ras Shamra (Ugarit) in north Syria,[30] and from Ras Shamra the road led into the Euphrates Valley and to Babylon. Contacts between the Cretan and Egyptian cultures were of a still closer nature. The idea of hieroglyphic writing came from the land of the Nile, although there was no lack of pictographic preliminary stages in the development of the Cretan script on the island itself.[31] Papyrus, the indispensable material for writing, was the particular commodity which came from Egypt. In the field of art and architecture the Cretans learned the complex technique of ceiling decoration from the Egyptians and passed it on to the Greek mainland, to the palaces of Tiryns and Mycenae. A greater Cretan dependence on Egypt is, however, scarcely probable.

When the first highly developed culture of Crete perished by sudden catastrophe towards the end of the eighteenth century or shortly thereafter, the first great Indo-European migration had already given the world a new aspect. Eduard Meyer regarded the discovery of an alabaster lid bearing the name of the Hyksos king Chian in the charred ruins of the palace of Cnossus[32] as evidence for the destruction of the older Cretan palaces by the plundering hordes of Hyksos. He considered King Chian to be a "world ruler" whose empire embraced Egypt, Crete and Babylonia.[33] The evidence for such a theory is, however, far from adequate,[34] and it is much more probable that a devastating earthquake, so frequent on Crete, reduced the cities to ruins.[35] Once before, the palace of Cnossus had fallen victim to a similar catastrophe.

Crete soon recovered. Peace at home and freedom from foreign danger allowed the palaces to rise in new splendour. During this time a hegemony emerged under the leadership of Cnossus. With at least 50,000 inhabitants,[36] this city stood as undisputed head of all Cretan settlements. A great many new villas of the vassals and royal dignitaries sprang up alongside the palaces. A new naturalistic style in art, born in the court environment, demonstrates with lively modernity the sensuous and optimistic life of the happy island.

The fact that the most impressive and most characteristic works of the new style have been found outside Crete, in the shaft graves of Mycenae and in the vaulted tomb of Vaphio (Amyclae in Laconia), shows that Cretan art was particularly esteemed abroad. Frescoes from the palace of Cnossus, such as the crocus picker in a Cretan "magic garden," the lively representations of athletic contests and wonderful inlaid work like the dagger blade depicting a hunting scene in an Egyptian papyrus thicket,[37] are unsurpassed in the entire art of antiquity. The colourful reflection of a life bordering on fantasy mirrored in the picturesque frescoes and works of art such as the harvester vase from Hagia Triada bear witness to keen observation and open-mindedness. A gradual decline becomes evident in the so-called palace style, and when in approximately 1500 B.C. (?) the palaces were again destroyed (perhaps as the result of another great earthquake),[38] Minoan culture was a spent force. Meanwhile in Greece the seeds which were scattered abroad by the example of Cretan artistic creativity had taken root.

Minoan culture, which reached its indisputable acme about the middle of the sixteenth century, expressed Cretan life itself in the growth of cities and especially palaces. The central figure in Cretan society was the woman, the lady, as in the era of the mediaeval singers. The peculiar Western character of this culture[39] lends to Cretan life an element of over-refinement, indeed of morbidity, which is completely foreign to the national character of the Greeks. This applies most of all to the cultural leaders of Crete; the significance of the populace is not known. The dense residential quarters of the settlements (for instance, in Gournia), have the extensive agglutinative character distinctive of the Mediterranean, such as may still be observed in the settlements of eastern Crete. In the Minoan period this was the type of settlement at Pseira, Mochlos, Palaikastro and to some degree also in Mallia and Cnossus. Alongside these dense residential quarters, characterised by a close network of houses, there emerged in a great many places regular quarters of villas, especially in the immediate vicinity of the palaces. The villas appear to have been the residences of the landed aristocracy, vassals and functionaries of the rulers: wealthy classes who formed the splendid framework of court life. Festivals were celebrated and bull fights, boxing and wrestling contests performed for them. The world of this society apparently knew nothing of the hard struggle for life; rather everything was sublimated and geared to refined pleasure.

The Cretan script grew out of the needs of the court and the general administration.[40] Everywhere and in all ages in which it appears, writing is the symbol of bureaucracy. On Crete a direct line of development leads from the older pictographic preliminary stages to Cretan hieroglyphic writing, and from this to the "Linear Script" as represented by two advanced systems (Linear A and B). Apart from these there are also additional systems, of which Linear H is to be regarded as the mother of the now famous Linear B (E. Grumach). Linear B appears only in the later Palace of Cnossus, and presumably was a script created especially for the needs of the court. Inventories and calculations in a decimal system seem to constitute the chief contents of the clay tablets. Both linear systems have forty-eight symbols in common, whereas the court calligraphy had an additional sixteen new characters. It is a syllabic script, from which Cyprian writing (known from the seventh and subsequent centuries) developed into the Greek language.[41] Apart from this late acceptance the Cretan script died out. It did not exert a deeper influence on Mycenaean culture—despite the discovery of many clay tablets bearing the Cretan script (probably an inventory register) in the so-called 'Palace of Nestor' in Ano Englianos and in Mycenae (v.i.p. 367).

Cretan religion was a different matter.[42] It contributed essentially to the moulding of the Greek gods and daemons, for the former population of Hellas was ethnically related to the Cretans and the native culture had again and again asserted itself over the immigrants. The close connection between Cretan religion and nature is of particular note, and the predominance of the feminine element is also very important. The "Magna Mater" as well as the snake goddess and the mistress of beasts played an important rôle. Offerings were brought to them in grottoes, caves and also in the chapels of the palaces. Horns and the double axe were the principal cult symbols. The origin of the horns of consecration is uncertain, while the double axe is found in Asia Minor among the Hittites and in Upper Mesopotamia as an attribute of the Hurrian thunder god Teshub. The double axe outlasted the whole of antiquity as a symbol of Jupiter Dolichenus. Cretan religion also included a large number of daemons and monsters, similar to those of the Hittites, and column and tree cults. In many instances, however, the substance and nature of Cretan religion remains shrouded in darkness.

Of far-reaching historical importance were the close relations between Crete and the Greek mainland, ties which reached their indisputable climax in the sixteenth century. However much the Greeks absorbed from Crete, the highly developed Cretan civilisation did not succeed in transforming the Greek personality. Minoan civilisation certainly taught the Greeks to utilise this culture in refining their own way of life, but in general it was restricted to outward appropriation; the treasures of Crete were not able to vanquish the souls of the Greeks.

MYCENAEAN CULTURE

The migration of the Indo-Europeans into Greece, like that of the Hittites into central Anatolia, has left no visible archaeological traces behind. This is perhaps evidence that the immigrants became completely dependent on the higher civilisation of the original Mediterranean population of the country. At first the material conditions of life in Greece remained unaltered,[43] the culture of the entire Middle Helladic period (c. 1900-1550 B.C.) being distinctly peasant.[44] The simple grey Minyan ware (also called Orchomenus ware), or the yellow Minyan pottery, which shows no traces of foreign influence, is characteristic of this epoch. The peasant population of the country held tenaciously to its own established traditions even after the immigration of the Indo-European tribes, and within a short time succeeded in assimilating the new inhabitants of the country. No connections existed with regions outside Greece; the new problem of adjustment and equalisation with the Indo-Europeans initially claimed all the energies of the indigenous inhabitants.

Something of the material life of the period came to light with the discovery of a shaft grave complex outside the fortress of Mycenae by J.

Papadimitriu in 1951, one of the great surprises of recent years. The greater number of these graves (about twenty-five to date) still belong to the end of the Middle Helladic period, earlier than the shaft graves discovered by Schliemann in the grave circle within the fortress (v.i.p. 14). The funerary offerings in the newly discovered shaft graves do not bear comparison with those from the Schliemann graves, but none the less show an abundance of wealth, above all in weapons. Like later examples, the grave stelae which were erected on mounds show hunting scenes, though still without chariots.

At the beginning of the so-called Late Helladic era, that is, approximately in the middle of the sixteenth century, the predominantly peasant culture of the Middle Helladic period yielded to a new way of life. Delight in war, hunting and the possession of costly bronze weapons, and the introduction of war chariots are evidence of a new warlike spirit, marking a complete break with the past. It is highly probable that the Indo-Europeans had now, doubtless after a long period of incubation, finally asserted themselves in the social sphere as the ruling class. The strong fortresses, the centres of the powerful warlike nobles, symbolise the new way of life. We now find ruling over the broad masses of the common people an élite military aristocracy whose ideals—fighting, feuds, court festivities—differ fundamentally from the peasant population. The heroic period derived its name from Mycenae,[45] the fortress in the "furthermost nook of steed-nourishing Argos."[46] Alongside Mycenae we find Tiryns, an almost immediate neighbour, and other fortresses on the hills of Nauplia and Midea. In fact, the Argolid was in general very densely populated.[47] In Attica, the most important fortress was the Acropolis in Athens, fortified by Cyclopean walls, the so-called *Pelargikon*.[48] The culture of the earlier Mycenaean period was for the most part restricted to the east of Greece. In the west, discoveries have only been made in those regions where immigration by sea was convenient; for instance, at Pylos-Kakovatos and at Messenian Pylos. The principal region was in central Greece and in the Peloponnesus.

However little the influence of the highly developed Minoan civilisation on Hellas can be denied, especially in the sixteenth century, the monumental structures of the Mycenaean period clearly manifest a completely different spirit, warlike and heroic, which does not have the slightest element in common with Cretan ideals. While Cretan society seems to have devoted itself to the fleeting attraction of the moment, the Greeks built structures for eternity. Mighty stone walls of polygonal masonry towering into mountains and meticulously fortified gates reinforced by stone bastions attest the warlike spirit of the ruling families. At the centre of the fortress was the palace, with its large stately hall, rectangular in form with its principal feature the *megaron* with hearth. In the *megaron* the ruler of the fortress ate the common meal with his vassals. Any stranger or suppliant who sought refuge at the hearth was under the protection of the highest deity, Zeus who welcomes the stranger.[49] The inner unity and balance of the entire structure of the palace, with its corridors and apartments for the servants built around the *megaron* with its open halls, showed a distinct contrast to the Mediterranean way of building found in Crete, where the most diverse types of rooms in the palaces were grouped around the large central court in such a manner that all semblance of a systematic arrangement was lost (cf. the so-called labyrinth). As in their architecture, so in their attire (*chiton*) the Indo-Europeans adhered to the past in Hellas. The same holds true for their language, even though many Aegean words were absorbed into it.

Unmistakable heights in Greek development were attained in the later sixteenth and early part of the fourteenth centuries, while in contrast the fifteenth century was a period of retrogression. Just in this era, under Minoan influence, foreign infiltration into Mycenaean culture reached its culmination. Heinrich Schliemann's excavations at Mycenae, Tiryns and Orchomenus have revealed a lively picture of Mycenaean culture. The discovery of the shaft graves at Mycenae (1876) was epoch-making. In six graves sunk deep into the soft rock, Schliemann found a positively fabulous number of funerary gifts of gold jewellery and splendid weapons. The martial character of the funerary offerings marks these shaft graves[50] as the burial places of the ruling family in Mycenae, and the nine men (as well as eight women and two small children) buried in them may represent a ruling dynasty. Five of the men wore golden masks over their faces—the first attempt at portraiture on European soil! Of interest is the thesis that from the masks various types of beard are to be assumed, as in the sixth century B.C. masks of the dead from Trebenishte on Lake Ochrida and the northern finds from the Hallstatt (La-Tène) period.[51] The vast number of extremely costly articles excludes the possibility that they were manufactured by domestic craftsmen. The lords of Mycenae must have brought back from their plundering expeditions the magnificent golden diadems and gold foil which was then made into figurines and ornaments in large quantities. For the preservation of these costly objects, such as the bronze swords and daggers which the warriors had once brandished or which they had taken from the enemy, we are indebted to the custom of placing the booty as a "death portion" for the occupant along with the body in the grave.[52] If the conspicuous wealth in weapons is evidence of a spirit completely different from the Minoans, this is even more manifest in the artless, almost crudely executed stone grave stelae.[53] Some of them have been preserved, though partially in fragments. The dead person is depicted in the centre of the relief, standing on a light two-wheeled chariot—the first time that the chariot is portrayed in Hellas. In contrast to Crete, the woman was of no account whatsoever in the public life of Mycenae, even though the jewellery placed in the grave along with the woman suggests that she shared in the royal pageant.

A change from burial in shaft graves to interment in vaulted tombs took place at the turn of the sixteenth century.[54] These tombs had gigantic dimensions. The vault (actually an apparent vault) of the so-called "Treasury of Atreus" (built about 1350 B.C.)[55] has a diameter of 14½ metres, a magnificent architectural achievement. It was only overshadowed in the time of imperial Rome by the genuine dome of the Pantheon built by

Hadrian, with a diameter three times as great. The vaulted tombs express a new spirit and a new era in which the urge towards the monumental and the immense forcefully establishes itself.[56] The Lion Gate at Mycenae, also undoubtedly not built until 1350 B.C. (Late Helladic III),[57] with its singular feature, the Cretan column flanked by two lions facing each other, has no counterpart in Hellas. The heraldic rendering points to the ancient Orient, perhaps to Hattusas (Boghazköy), the capital of the Hittite kingdom.[58] The builders of the vaulted tombs enclosed the terrain of the grave shafts within a circular double wall (so-called grave circle), a feature which seems to imply northern connections.[59] In this way the burial place of the dead henceforth became separated from the realm of the living. The vaulted tombs at Mycenae have been plundered, whereas those at Vaphio (Laconia)—only to a small degree—and above all the graves at Dendra (Midea),[60] in the Argolid, have retained their treasures. Again a large number of costly weapons, gold drinking cups and jewellery shows the harmonising of a northern spirit with Mediterranean civilisation. Furthermore, the polychrome frescoes from Mycenae and Tiryns, depicting primarily battles and hunting scenes,[61] are a creation of the same spirit.

The political structure of Greece in the Mycenaean period has often been argued, and widely varying opinions have been given. It is doubtful that a union of larger areas can have taken place anywhere but in the Argolid and Boeotia. In the Argolid, Mycenae, whose relationship to Tiryns is admittedly puzzling, appears for some time to have held a hegemonial position, while in Boeotia the masters of the great fortress of Gha (Gla) in the later Lake Copaïs played a leading rôle. The "knights" of the surrounding fortresses may have been vassals recognising the sovereignty of these rulers. The union of parts of the Argolid and Boeotia was no doubt possible only through bitter coercion. The result is manifested in the building of an extensive road system in the Argolid[62] and in the draining of the Copaïs region by the so-called "dikes of the Minyans."[63] Only a rigorous central power could have planned and executed such projects, which required a large number of foreign slaves, obtained from abroad on military and plundering expeditions, and an equal amount of domestic forced labour. These projects constitute achievements which parallel the creations of the ancient Orient—the pyramids and ziggurats. The monumental tombs immortalised the fame of the ruling families, whose memory survived in the cult of the dead, a cult continuing partially into the historical period. Although certain details may have been copied from the ancient Orient, the execution and design manifest a unique "northern" spirit which was generally characteristic of the creations from the Mycenaean period.

Greek heroic legend tells of the rule in Argos of Agamemnon, to whose forefathers Zeus granted the sceptre of rule. In the Heracles legend, Eurystheus, king of Mycenae, ruled over all the neighbouring population. These legends and the existence of the central sanctuary of Hera of Prosymna between Mycenae and Tiryns may reflect the reminiscence of a perhaps only very transitory political union of the Argolid in the Mycenaean period. Perhaps the legend recounting the expedition of the "Seven against Thebes" contains a historical reminiscence of a feud between the prince of Mycenae and the lords of Thebes. But nothing in this regard is certain. Lasting and larger political formations are also improbable, primarily because all the necessary conditions were lacking, especially the creation of a "bureaucracy." In like manner the knowledge of the Cretan script, proven by recent finds, can have extended to only a narrow circle. In consequence the theory of a great Achaean empire, held in particular by Eduard Meyer and Martin P. Nilsson, has slight probability.[64] The assumption that oriental ideas could have contributed to the notion of the "divine right" of the Mycenaean ruler—Homer calls the king "god-loved"[65]—is equally unfounded. In greater enterprises of war there may have been a "military king," but in time of peace everyone went his own way. Thus the fragmentation of Greece into an endless number of small and even minute territories would appear to have been a historical fact as early as the Mycenaean period.[66]

During the first half of the second millennium the Minoans held undisputed sovereignty over the Aegean and the entire eastern Mediterranean. Minoan bases were to be found on many islands, including Aegina, Thera, Melos and perhaps also Samos.[67] The picture, however, gradually changes with the appearance of the Mycenaean Greeks on the seas. The rich treasures of the shaft graves and vaulted tombs bear witness to the success of their plundering expeditions by sea.[68] Mycenaean mastery of the seas did not, however, reach its climax until after the overthrow of the Cretan thalassocracy (c. 1400 B.C.). But it was of only relatively short duration, for entirely new power formations followed in the wake of the great Aegean migration in the twelfth century.

The decisive expansion of the Mycenaeans falls in the fourteenth and thirteenth centuries. Mycenaean potsherds are to be found in the Cyclades and Mycenaean settlements on Rhodes, and the sphere of Mycenaean trade in the east extended to Syria, where Ras Shamra, Minet el Beïda and Byblus constitute important places of discovery of Mycenaean pottery—Mycenaean objects reached the heart of Egypt, and in the west as far as southern Italy and Sicily.[69] Research into the differentiation of the material and its allocation to specific places of origin is unfortunately still in its initial stages,[70] so that the individual events, the routes of early Greek trade and commercial colonisation remain shrouded in darkness. The radius of Greek trade did indeed touch on the sphere of interest of the Hittite kingdom, but in actual fact hardly overlapped with it. The diffusion of Mycenaean pottery is essentially restricted to those regions which lay west and south of the Hittite kingdom. The finds do not give any grounds to conclude that there was extensive colonisation and settlement. There will undoubtedly have been Mycenaean factories on Rhodes and Cyprus as well as on the coast of north Syria, but colonists in large numbers appear to have settled only on Cyprus, where the term "Achaean coast" (Strabo XIV 682) testifies to the presence of the Achaeans. On Rhodes, Achaea, the name for the fortress of Ialysus, is reminiscent of the

Achaean expansion.[71] There can indeed be no doubt that "Achaeans" was the inclusive name for the Greeks in the Mycenaean period.[72]

The world-wide distribution of Mycenaean pottery, stretching far beyond the radius of the Minoan finds in the region of the Mediterranean, is only understandable on the assumption of an extensive trade. This in turn presupposes the existence of a sizeable fleet which ruled the seas and kept the sea routes open. In Ugarit (Ras Shamra) Mycenaean pottery appears suddenly in approximately 1400 B.C.[73] The wares came largely from Cyprian workshops, suggesting not only the adoption of Mycenaean models, but in all probability also the settling of Greek craftsmen on Cyprus. An extensive commercial expansion of this nature is inconceivable without political direction. From approximately 1400 B.C. onwards Hellas was substantially overpopulated, for the barrenness of the soil and the lack of intensive methods of agriculture precluded feeding the inhabitants at home. In consequence the boldest and most enterprising individuals were lured out on the seas to adventures abroad; Crete, the islands of the Aegean, Rhodes and Cyprus formed their immediate destinations, but served also as the intermediate points en route to the Near East. The merchant who transported Greek oil and wine abroad, and with these the articles of Greek pottery, was followed by the Greek craftsman, the potter, the goldsmith, the architect and the shipwright. The Greeks took with them to the East their burial customs and features from the mainland way of life. Even Greek religion found admittance into Ras Shamra, as finds of Mycenaean idols have proven. It is not improbable that the presence of Greek conquerors on the island of Crete is reflected in the vaulted tombs there, of which a particularly stately example has been found in Kephala (west of Isopata) near Cnossus.[74]

Anatolia proper, however, remained closed to the Achaeans, apart from a narrow coastal strip in the extreme south-west.[75] Yet the country of *Ahhijawa* (or *Ahhija*), a name which phonetically bears a resemblance to Achaeans, is often mentioned on Hittite cuneiform tablets from the period of the great conqueror Subbilulyuma (c. 1365 B.C.).[76] From the point of view of comparative philology a solution to this problem does not seem possible. The "great *Ahhijawa* empire" invented by Emil Forrer through ingenious combinations has vanished again. The careful investigation of Hittite documents, chiefly by Ferdinand Sommer, has proven Forrer's theory to be untenable, especially with regard to the equation of names.[77] The country of *Ahhijawa* will most probably have to be sought primarily in the south-east, in Cilicia,[78] and in view of the current state of scholarship the "*Ahhijawa* question" is practically insoluble. Perhaps it is possible to regard the inhabitants of *Ahhijawa* as the "Hypachaeans" of Herodotus (VII 91) and as the *Aqaivasa* of Egyptian inscriptions, namely as one and the same Anatolian (non-Greek) people.[79] But the great *Ahhijawa* empire, which allegedly paralleled the states of the ancient Orient and extended over parts of Greece, the islands and parts of the Anatolian coast, never existed.[80]

The superiority of the Mycenaean Greeks over their opponents rested on the existence of a class of noble single warriors who went into battle in chariots. Protected by the immense tower shield and armed with spear and short sword, the warrior went out to meet the enemy on foot. He was assisted by the "companions," the "followers," who also gathered for the common meal in the house of the feudal lord. The latter regarded it as his honour to entertain them and to give them their due share of the booty. In great feuds several princes united together by acknowledging one of their number as *hegemon* and by a formal oath pledging themselves to follow him. When the feud came to an end the military federation broke up in the same manner as it had come into existence.

Our knowledge of the principal features of political and social life in the Mycenaean period rests on, apart from the monuments, primarily those poems which have come down to us under the name of Homer, to wit the *Iliad* and the *Odyssey*. In the investigation basic to this subject M. P. Nilsson (*Homer and Mycenae* [1933]), following in the footsteps of others, succeeded in distinguishing the earlier from the later elements in the Homeric epics. Nilsson was especially successful in showing that Greek heroic legend has its roots in the Mycenaean era.[81] A number of elements in Homer are also Mycenaean, even though in the poems they have been fused with later material into an intrinsic unity. It is primarily the cult of the dead that goes back to the Mycenaean period, continuing in the vaulted tomb at Menidi in Attica even until the fifth century B.C.[82]

The central problem in Greek religion during the earliest times is the attitude of the Indo-Europeans to the religious beliefs of the Mediterranean population of ancient Greece. If the evidence is reliable, then Minoan religion exerted a profound influence on the minds of the Greek inhabitants. The representation of various deities—Artemis as Britomartis, Dictynna and Aphaea—is Minoan. The "palace goddess," later worshipped under the name of Athena, likewise originated from the Minoan world. The diffusion of Minoan ideas among the broad masses of the ordinary people is reflected in the adoption of Minoan cult objects and cult forms on the mainland. The fact that there are no cult figures in human form would indeed appear to suggest that the Greeks continued to cultivate their Indo-European heritage.[83] The gods were worshipped in sacred groves, in caves and on the mountain heights, and recently, temples and sanctuaries have been discovered.

In many instances the immigrants made the customs of the native population their own. Whether this assumption also holds good with respect to burial customs remains uncertain. In the Mycenaean period burial was the sole prevailing form of interment in Greece, although traces of burning in Mycenaean graves permit us to suppose that the funerary offerings, often very costly, were consigned to the fire.[84] But certain alone is the fact that cremation was much more widespread in central Europe than in the south.[85] Traces of animal and human sacrifices have hitherto been found only in isolated cases (for instance in Midea).

"Mycenaean religion is the mother of Greek religion just as the

Mycenaean people are the forefathers of the historical Greeks" (Nilsson). It is important to bear this in mind when examining the historical continuity revealed in the fact that certain Mycenaean places of worship were retained by the Greeks in the historical period. The Telesterium of Eleusis, the continuity of the cult at Delphi, in the sanctuary of Calaureia, in Tegea, Elateia and in the temple of Aphaea on Aegina are evidence for this.[86] Not even the upheavals precipitated by the Aegean migration succeeded in rupturing everywhere the connections between Hellenic life and the Mycenaean period. This continuity lives on in the Homeric epics, which give in outline a picture of that heroic age which poetic tradition alone has preserved—after it no longer retained a place on earth.

2
MIGRATION AND TRANSITION

ARRIVAL OF THE DORIANS

The period of the Great Migration began before 1200 B.C. in the region of the Mediterranean. The upheavals which it precipitated are perceptible in almost the entire world of the eastern Mediterranean, from the Apennine peninsula to Mesopotamia, and from Hungary to the frontiers of Egypt. In the history of civilisation the Great Migration constitutes the decisive turning point from the Bronze Age to the Iron Age, which began at approximately the same time throughout the whole Aegean. Once again the Hungarian plain received the first stimulus for the migration of a people and the pressure imposed upon the Hungarian Plain intensified in neighbouring areas. The ancestors of the Illyrians and other peoples in the second half of the second millennium found themselves being pushed southwards.[1] Nothing certain is known about the cause of their migration, and the conjecture that they wanted to gain control of the iron monopolised by the Hittites[2] is strictly hypothetical. The southward migration of the early Illyrians and other tribes shows in its effects on neighbouring peoples, as the migrants forced the Thracians eastwards into Asia Minor, Greek tribes southwards into the Peloponnesus and thence into Crete and the Sporades. The immigration too of a large group of Italics from the north into the Apennine peninsula was touched off by Illyrian pressure.[3] Seen in general, it is a repetition of events at the beginning of the second millennium. Indo-European peoples, breaking out from a centre of unrest after a longer period of sedentary life, once more set the world in motion.

Retreating before the pressure of the Thracian tribes, segments of the Phrygians remained behind in Europe (the Bryges). In the course of seeking a new home in Mysia and on the western plateau of Anatolia they absorbed Illyrian elements. The so-called buckle pottery, originally at home in the region of Macedonia and Thrace, makes its appearance in Asia Minor with the coming of the Thracian tribes and represents a typical feature of the national character of the Thracian people.[4] It is not inconceivable that in approximately 1200 B.C. Troy (to wit Troy VII A) succumbed to the invading Thracian hordes and not, as was earlier thought, Troy VI (W. Dörpfeld), which was much more likely destroyed by an earthquake, as the researches of C. Blegen have shown.[5]

The advance of the Illyrians affected not only the Thracians, but also the Dorians in northern Greece (in the Pindus region?). The southward movement of the Dorians, the so-called "Dorian Migration," inaugurated a new epoch in Greek history and brought the final Indo-Europeanisation of Hellas. To deny the historicity of the "Dorian Migration"[6] is a serious error of modern hypercritical scholars, who exclude a historically founded knowledge of the formation of the Greek people in the second millennium. Of course, only the archaeological and dialect-geographical evidence comes into question, and not the later historians like Herodotus and Thucydides nor poets such as Tyrtaeus and Pindar.[7] The term "Dorian Migration" embraces developments from early Greek history extending over many decades, perhaps over a century or an even longer period.

The fact that Dorian partially overlay the older dialects suggests that the Dorian element assimilated both the new immigrant Indo-Europeans at the beginning of the second millennium and the native population of Greece which fused with them over the following centuries. The remoulding of the ethnic picture becomes visible above all on the east coast of the Peloponnesus, where the Arcadian element was forced into the mountainous interior of the peninsula by the warlike Dorians—the name *Dorieis* is a shortened form of *dorimachoi*, "spear fighters."[8]

By the time of the Dorian Migration ancient Achaean culture was long past its climax. Even before the arrival of the vigorous northern stock the old centres in the Argolid showed clear symptoms of decline. The sun was setting for the heroic age of Mycenae, so that a mere push from the outside was all that was needed to overthrow this decrepit world. Efforts to reinforce the fortifications of Mycenae in the thirteenth century had proved vain, and the troubled time brought construction of a refuge on the hill of Tiryns.[9] However, other regions in the Peloponnesus, such as the district of Achaea, did not experience a time of actual flowering until the Late Mycenaean period.

The ravages of the Dorian Migration extended over a wide area of Greece. In addition to the great centres in the Argolid,[10] Korakou and Zygouries-Kleonai in Corinthia sank in ruins, with Crete and the islands in the southern Aegean, including Melos and Phylakopi, also affected. The direction of the Dorian advance clearly points from north to south; the conjecture that the Dorians first seized control of Crete and the southern Cyclades and then crossed over to the mainland[11] is impossible.

A faint memory of the Dorian Migration is reflected in the legend of the "return of the Heraclidae." The names in the legend—the Heraclid Hyllus, Dymas, Pamphylus, and the two sons of King Aegimius—manifestly reflect an attempt to explain the origin of the Dorian tribes, the Hylli, Dymani and Pamphyli.[12] The name Hylli is Illyrian, Dymas is the legendary ancestor of the original Dorian *phyle* or tribe, and Pamphylus symbolises ethnic elements composed of Dorian and other tribes. That the tiny district of Doris at Mount Oeta was the point of departure of the Dorian Migration is a fabrication of later times. The Dorians were intermingled with Illyrian elements, which incidentally also reappear among the Macedonians and Thracians. Whether the Philistines, who in the course of the

Great Migration reached the portals of Egypt, are to be regarded as also having a touch of Illyrian blood[13] remains questionable. At all events a warning must be sounded even today against "Panillyrism," which has from time to time become fashionable. The hordes of migrating Dorians did not set foot in Attica, and the legendary sacrificial death of King Codrus of Athens[14] perhaps reflects the defence against them.

The Dorian Migration transformed the tribal groupings in mainland Greece completely. At the end of the migration period the Dorians emerged as the ruling element in the east and south of the Peloponnesus, chiefly in Argos but later also in Laconia. The national characteristics of the Achaeans gradually became fused with the Dorians, as the Mediterranean population of the country had once become blended with the Indo-Europeans.[15] The Dorians to a considerable degree reinvigorated the Indo-European element with new blood, as did the "North-West Greeks" who in the course of the Great Migration penetrated into northern and central Greece (Thessaly, Aetolia, Phocis) and into the northern Peloponnesus (Achaea, Elis). The Thessalians in part drove out the Aeolian population of the region, and reduced others to the status of dependents. In Boeotia, on the other hand, it is more probable that a peaceful equalisation was reached between the old Aeolian and the new North-West Greeks, an event which is perhaps reflected in the Boeotian mixed dialect on the frontier between the two language groups.

The Dorians and the North-West Greeks were not solely responsible for the decline of Mycenaean culture.[16] The once flourishing civilisation of the Mycenaean Greeks was at the time only a shadow of its former greatness, and an inevitable decline continued into the so-called Sub-Mycenaean era, indeed even further into the Geometric period, as finds from the Athenian necropolis at the Eridanus show. The concurrence of the decline in Mycenaean culture and the upheavals of the Dorian Migration in the twelfth century made for a decisive break in early Greek history.

As the migration went on, the Dorians crossed the sea and made their way to Crete, to the southern Cyclades and Sporades, and even to the mainland of Asia Minor, into south-west Caria and ultimately to Pamphylia.[17] The Dorians thus followed in the footsteps of the Achaeans. The occupation of Crete is of particular importance. The original inhabitants (Cydonians and Eteocretans)[18] were confined to the extreme western and eastern parts of the island, while the Achaean elements may have become submerged in the Dorians. Thus a wide Dorian zone stretches from the Peloponnesus across the Aegean as far as Anatolia. Larger political formations failed to develop, just as they had formerly under the Achaeans.

From the point of view of world history, the invasion of Thracian tribes into Asia Minor was even more important than the penetration of the Dorians and North-West Greeks into Hellas. Soon after 1200 B.C. the Hittite kingdom in Anatolia sank in the maelstrom of the Great Migration, after lasting almost five hundred years.[19] There is now much evidence to suggest that the Hittite kingdom was destroyed by the invasion of foreign peoples coming from the sea. The same holds true for Ugarit (Ras Shamra), as recent finds of clay tablets have shown.[20] That the fall of the Hittite kingdom was linked with the migration of the sea peoples is also shown by the account of Ramses III in Medinet Habu:[21] "No country withstood their armies, beginning with the Hatti: Kedi, Carchemish, Arvad, Alashiya were devastated." The inscription reveals the progress of the assault by the sea peoples from Asia Minor through Cilicia (Kedi), Syria and Phoenicia against the eastern frontier of Egypt. Cyprus (Alashiya) alone lay outside the land route.

The invasion was no doubt a joint enterprise by land and by sea. The Puluseta, Zakkari, Shakalsha, Danuna and Washesh are cited by the Egyptian Pharaoh as sea peoples. The Harris Papyrus gives the Sherdana in place of the Shakalsha. The identification of these peoples is uncertain, apart from the Puluseta, the Philistines. They all, however, belong in the area of the Aegean, although Greeks are not mentioned among them.[22] This avalanche rolling down on Egypt was brought to a halt at the doors of the land of the Nile by Ramses III. The movement had exhausted itself just in time to save Egypt. The Philistines settled in the land which from them acquired the name of Palestine.

The Great Aegean Migration precipitated a complete ethnological reshaping of the ancient world. The Hittite kingdom was wiped out, but its civilisation survived for centuries in the small states of northern Syria and inner Anatolia. A system of medium and small states, which came under the influence of the Aramaic element, rose in the intermediate zone between Asia Minor and Mesopotamia. The predominant factor, however, arising out of the ruins in the twelfth century was the emergence of Assur, the Middle Assyrian empire under Tiglathpilesar I, which during its expansion collided with the Phrygians at the upper reaches of the Euphrates. In addition to Assur the city-states of Phoenicia experienced a significant rise.[23] In the following centuries ships from Tyre penetrated deep into the west as far as southern Spain, and from there brought home the valuable tin from Britain and silver from Spain. In the period from about 1000 to 800 B.C. the Phoenicians filled the gap left by the elimination of Cretan sea power and the decline of the Achaeans. At the same time, the Etruscans[24] made their appearance in the Mediterranean, their ships moving approximately the same time as those of the Phoenicians and reaching the coast of later Etruria or Toscana (their point of departure in the Aegean world was perhaps Mysia). From their contact with the eastern cultures they transplanted a piece of oriental civilisation into the West. Individual ethnic segments may have remained behind in the Aegean, for instance, on Lemnos.

THE RESHAPING OF THE GREEK WORLD (c. 1100-800 B.C.)

After the great Aegean Migration the Greek world sank into almost impenetrable darkness, which leaves us practically no historical information.[25] In consequence, events of incalculable importance in determining the ethnic and political character of the Greek world at the beginning of the first millennium are unknown. The changes in continental Hellas brought by the Dorians and the North-West Greek tribes and the events which led to the colonisation of the west coast of Anatolia are perceptible only in rough outline, and then only on the basis of evidence obtained from ethnic regroupings.

In material culture the period of the Aegean Migration also marks a decisive break in Hellas. Here the Iron Age begins about 1100 B.C.,[26] and about the same time, namely in the eleventh century, the first cinerary graves appeared in larger numbers in Greece, in the Athenian necropolis at the Eridanus and in Ialysus on Rhodes. But the break with the past was not complete, for the overwhelming majority of Greeks, including the Dorians, continued to bury their dead.[27] Worthy of particular attention is the increasing recurrence of weapons as funerary offerings, in contrast to the Mycenaean period, when weapons are found only in the stately graves of the rulers. In an earlier era craftsmanship in arms was restricted to the narrow circle of the military nobility, whereas now it would appear to embrace a broader class of free commoners.

The epoch-making event of the second transition period, the colonisation of the west coast of Asia Minor, is connected with the migrations which the Aegean Migration also touched off in Hellas. The view that it was principally an "evasion movement" on the part of the North-Achaeans (Aeolians) in Thessaly and the Ionians in Attica and on Euboea, compressed together by the immigrating Dorians and North-West Greeks, is too simplistic. At the very least, the chronological evidence cancels out an immediate connection between the colonisation and the Dorian Migration. However, both, the Dorian Migration and the colonisation of the west coast of Asia Minor, are two different aspects of a single, great historical phenomenon—those movements which received their impetus from the Aegean Migration. Although finds of Mycenaean sherds on Anatolian soil show trade relations between Hellas and the west coast of Asia Minor in the Late Helladic period, they are not plentiful enough to show a Late Mycenaean colonisation—except at Miletus.[28] As long as the Hittite empire remained intact, the west coast of Asia Minor in general remained closed to the Hellenes. Archaeological finds suggest that the Ionian colonisation began shortly after the Dorian Migration, probably about 1000 B.C. or even somewhat earlier.[29] The Greek occupation of the Cyclades preceded the colonisation, but probably to some degree also paralleled it.

Members of all Greek tribes took part in the expeditions to the coast of Asia Minor. From the motherland they took with them their customs, their legends and the festivals of their gods, and in addition in many instances the place names with which they had become familiar. From north to south along the coast of Asia Minor one found the Aeolians, the Ionians and the Dorians adjoining one another in a manner corresponding precisely to conditions on the east coast of the motherland. Certain places, like the peninsula of Mimas, the island of Chios and the cities of Phocaea and Smyrna, were a prolonged bone of contention between the

Aeolians and the Ionians, but at the end of the eighth century the Ionians, not inconsiderably reinforced by immigrants from the homeland, asserted themselves and took over the hegemony among the Greek tribes in Asia Minor. Already in the eighth century the Ionians united together into a politico-religious amphictyony. This federation, the "commonwealth of the Ionians," was headed by an elective duke (*basileus*) appointed by the entire body of the federation, somewhat comparable to the Etruscan *lucumo* or the Thessalian *tagos*.[30] The sanctuary of Poseidon Heliconius on the peninsula of Mycale formed the centre of the Ionian federation. The Dorian communities assembled around the Triopium sanctuary of Apollo at Cnidus, and the Aeolians perhaps around the temple of Apollo at Gryneum. All attempts on the part of the Greeks to penetrate further into the interior proved unsuccessful. The manner in which the settling of the coastal regions of Asia Minor transpired is illustrated by the *Iliad*, which may reflect the reminiscence of an abortive expedition against Troy (not settled by Aeolian colonists before 700 B.C.). A host of warriors landed on the shores of the Scamander Plain, and using the naval encampment as its base, fought for the Trojan fortress of Ilium which was courageously defended by its inhabitants. The lot of the conquered was a hard one—the male population put to the sword or reduced to slavery, and the women become the booty of the victors.

In the new homeland, in the midst of a foreign environment, the Greek colonists for the first time became truly conscious of their own national identity. Consequently, on the soil of Asia Minor, in the centuries after the turn of the millennium, the first inclinations towards a feeling of Greek solidarity developed. The *Iliad* is the finest expression of this. Of far greater importance, however, for the political development of the Greek people was the *polis*, which first emerged on the soil of Asia Minor, perhaps in connection with urban-like settlements of the Anatolians.[31] The unbridgeable gulf between the Hellenes and the native population of Anatolia and the danger of sudden destruction continuously hovering over the new settlements from the very beginning forced the colonists to take refuge within the walls of fortified settlements. Closely packed within a fortification wall, the Hellenes adopted a form of life which had been alien to them in Greece, where village settlements prevailed. Asia Minor formed an urban life, greatly confined but correspondingly more intensive, which produced that spirit and political mentality characteristic of the Greeks during the historical period. They developed a patriotism that bound them to the narrower motherland, the *polis*, and the new political communities showed an unusual intensification of internal political life, features in this heightened form unique in the ancient world.

There were, however, drawbacks to developments in the colonial region. The Greeks underestimated the political power factor, and by considering only their own communities they gradually lost the standard by which to determine their relationship to differently oriented forms of government. Above all, they had no sense of the significance of large territories as the basis for political expansion. Developments in Asia

Minor, especially in Ionia, present a unique phenomenon, which must be explained by special geographical as well as political conditions. It preceded developments on the mainland by a considerable period, probably by several centuries. It is therefore highly probable that Greece received decisive stimuli from the colonial region, not only in cultural but also in political life.[32]

The culture of the transition period from 1100 to 800 B.C. has a peculiar double layer. The great upheavals caused by the Aegean Migration were followed by a considerable material impoverishment, so that Greek civilisation suffered a setback for centuries. In the cultural field the splitting up of the Mycenaean *koine*—unity—into many branches is especially significant. Each branch took on a notable life of its own, a surprising parallel to developments in political life in Hellas and in the colonial regions of Asia Minor. The transition from the Sub-Mycenaean to the Protogeometric period, and later, from approximately 900 B.C., to the Geometric style, marks a fundamental change not only in artistic taste but also in the attitude of the Greek individual to the world. Circular and straight lines now predominate, and the human figure, represented in elongated, angular forms, became to some extent an abstraction. It was an era of hard times reflected in art, with war and fighting its chief themes—the genuine expression of a restless age. The first great products of the Greek mind, the invention of alphabetic writing and the creation of the Homeric epics, are only apparent contrasts to the material poverty of the culture of the transition period. Man becomes conscious of his energies and capabilities most of all in times not blessed with material abundance. It is just in periods of decline that the human spirit is capable of creating works whose full meaning only later generations are able to comprehend. It was from the close contacts between the Greeks and Phoenicians that the Hellenes obtained the Phoenician consonantal alphabet. This event, epoch-making for the history of civilisation in the entire West, seems to have occurred in the ninth or, at the earliest, in the tenth century, perhaps on the soil of Asia Minor.[33]

With the decline of Minoan and Mycenaean culture the Phoenicians became the masters of the eastern Mediterranean (v.s.p. 24). In the Homeric epics they appear as cunning merchants, daring seafarers and wily kidnappers.[34] Their wares are exceptionally prized: "made in Phoenicia" ("Sidon") is synonymous with outstanding quality, and this above all in respect to metal products and variegated "Sidonian" fabrics. In fact Phoenician craftsmanship actually attained outstanding achievements in imitating Assyrian, Egyptian and Hittite art.[35] Indeed, recent finds of splendid gold bowls with lively animal scenes call for revision of previous conclusions about the alleged lack of originality in indigenous Phoenician art. Indisputable Phoenician influence can be detected in Greek art of the Late Geometric period (eighth century).[36] Evidence of extensive contacts between the Aegean world and Phoenicia is provided not only by a large number of foreign words in Greek of Phoenician derivation but also by the appearance of Semitic deities in the Aegean, especially Phoenician gods—the Cabiri of Samothrace[37] and the much disputed Melicertes at the Isthmus, who is scarcely to be divorced from Melkart. The Phoenicians were not, incidentally, the original creators in the realm of language, as the Greeks and for a long time modern scholars thought they were. Unbroken contact with Egyptian culture since the days of the Old Kingdom (cf. Byblus finds) also acted as an important stimulus on the Phoenicians and Syrians in moulding their language. The alphabet from Ras Shamra (in northern Syria) of the thirteenth or fourteenth century B.C. on the basis of phonetic elements presents a developed alphabetical script employing cuneiform symbols.[38] It was thus the invention of an individual genius, in a region where the most varied influences from Egypt, Mesopotamia, Asia Minor and the Aegean intersected.

More recent finds and studies have shown that the Minoan script was used in Hellas during the Mycenaean period (v.i.p. 367). It in no way, however, embraced wide circles but was a "secret script" of the few who were capable of learning it. How different the writing which the Greeks took over from the Phoenicians! The Greek alphabet sprang from the mind of a single genius who, also acquainted with the peculiarities of Phoenician, brilliantly coped with the characteristics of the Greek language. This individual developed the Phoenician consonantal script into a complete phonetic script—the first purely phonetic script in the history of civilisation![39] Four symbols—*Aleph, He, Iod, Ayin*—were taken from the twenty-two consonants of the Phoenician alphabet[40] to designate the Greek vowels A,E,I,O, by employing the "acrophonetic" principle; the northern Semitic *Waw* was used to reproduce the U, while the V was a later invention. In the employment of sibilants, for which the Semites had no less than four sounds at their disposal, as well as in the use of the so-called supplementary letters (xi, phi, chi, psi) the earliest Greek alphabets have extensive differences in details, reflected in the separate development of the various local alphabets. The alphabet which most closely resembles the original is that of Crete and the one native to the southern Cyclades (the so-called "green" alphabet), in which the supplementary letters are absent.[41] Of all the Greek phonetic alphabets that of Chalcis on Euboea acquired by far the greatest importance. From the Chalcidian colony of Cyme in southern Italy (Cumae) the alphabet of Chalcis became the mother of all Italic systems and probably also of the Etruscan alphabet.

As the Hymettus sherds from Attica and Corinthian ostraca have shown,[42] the art of writing was widespread in Hellas as early as the eighth century B.C. During this period people began to keep lists of athletic victors, and artists recorded their names and signatures. In fact the Greek script, because it was easy to learn, from the very outset was known to the entire population, or at least a broad section of the educated circles—in contrast to the writing systems in the ancient Orient, all of which were exclusively within the reach of only a small class of priests and professional scribes. This was of fundamental importance for the development of Hellenic cultural life, for neither tradition nor special interests of a certain class could influence or control the cultural development of the Hellenic people.

The creation of the great epics paralleled the invention of alphabetic writing in the transition period. The Homeric poems were predominant in Greek cultural life from the archaic to the Byzantine period. Their importance in national Greek education and the inexhaustible treasure of practical poesy stored within their pages (E. Bethe) render them one of the greatest achievements of the Greek mind, all the more amazing since they mark the very beginning of Greek literature. Greek heroic epic, from whose creations only the two most important poems—the *Iliad* and the *Odyssey*—are extant, was no doubt the product of a long development over centuries, with beginnings in the time of the Dorian Migration. Their development reached a critical stage when the cultivation of heroic songs passed from the nobility to the class of professional singers, at first the Aeodists and then to the Rhapsodists, who celebrated in song the fame of their ancestors at the courts of the ruling aristocracy. It is scarcely a coincidence that the Homeric epics arose on Greek soil—in Ionia. The Greek aristocratic clans were, in Ionia more than elsewhere, intent on cultivating traditions which linked them with the life of the Greek people in its entirety. The geographical proximity of the Greek motherland, with which the closest ties were continuously maintained, fostered these efforts.

Modern scholars agree that the present forms of the *Iliad* and the *Odyssey* are the result of a long development. Their composition shows hiatuses and joinings, irregularities and secondary "crampings," and even outright contradictions. It is inevitable to conclude that a number of poets shared in the creation of these epics, but their individual contributions can probably never be satisfactorily established. Ever since Professor F. A. Wolf at the University of Halle in his *Prolegomena ad Homerum* (1795) raised the question of the origin of the epics, to wit the "Homeric question," it has never come to rest: *adhuc sub iudice lis est*.[43]

This is not the place to enter into a discussion of the complicated course of Homeric scholarship.[44] The *historical* problem is that in the *Iliad* and the *Odyssey*, but more especially in the *Iliad*, we find two worlds fused together by poetic fancy. The Greek heroic period—Mycenaean—is inseparable from the ninth or eighth century world of the poet who moulded the *Iliad* in accordance with a unified plan and left his own imprint on it. Many objects from material culture[45] point to the Mycenaean period, such as the "cup of Nestor" described in the *Iliad*, of which a counterpart was found in the fourth shaft grave at Mycenae.[46] Moreover the statements in the Catalogue of Ships (*Iliad* II 484 ff.) do not essentially contradict the geographical distribution of settlements in the Mycenaean period.[47] A great many later elements are joined together with earlier ones: the use of writing, the tower shield which has been identified with the so-called Dipylon shield (a long shield in the shape of a figure 8),[48] the description of the shield of Achilles with orientalising motifs[49]—these and many more doubtless belong in the post-Mycenaean period. The twofold style in the *Iliad* and the *Odyssey* also corresponds to the juxtaposition of the old and the new in the depiction of the material culture.[50] The embellishing epithets, which in many places have become rigid formulae, and the appearance of Aeolic forms disclose an intellectual world which poetic tradition has artistically fused with the present.

Both epics, the *Iliad* and the *Odyssey*, younger by several generations,[51] derive from a knightly sphere. They point to a world of nobility, warlike and proud of their ancestors, whose ideals consist of fighting and victory, and insatiable striving for booty and delight in agonistic feats. The individual who gave the *Iliad* its distinctive inner and outer form and rendered it an unsurpassable work of art was a member of this knightly world. As the famous verses depicting the fate of the Aeneadae dwelling in the Troad until about 700 B.C. reveal, he felt himself to be part of the ruling dynasty, and he may have recited his poems at the court of these rulers.[52]

The Homeric poems laid the foundations on which Greek national feeling arose. All Greek tribes without exception acknowledged their kinship to Homer. The statement of Herodotus (II 53) that Homer and Hesiod gave the Hellenes their gods is entirely true. As the imagination of the poet lent the individual gods their form, so they entered into Hellenic religion, and it was a result of the Homeric poems that this aristocratic world of the gods, the counterpart to Mycenaean conditions in Greece, triumphed over the innumerable local deities throughout Greece. In contrast to the latter, this Homeric world attained genuine panhellenic recognition. The fact that in Hellenic religion the world of the gods always appears as something tangible, as something ever present in the life of the individual, rests on the influence of the Homeric poems. In the creation of a legendary realm[53] embracing all Greek tribes the notion of Greek unity became evident for the first time in the transition period. It is not by accident that it was born in the young colonial region of western Asia Minor. In an era when the *polis* set about to become the symbol of political life among the Greeks the world of the great epics kept alive the memory of those mythical times in which heroes from all Greek tribes fought for the fortress of Troy. Thus the Homeric poems not only gave the Greeks a literary medium but also became an effective catalyst in Greek national consciousness and in a common Greek religiosity.

The Greek world of the transition period derived its character from the dominating position of the Hellenic nobility. What the nobility gained at that time, the monarchy lost. After the period of land acquisition was over, it was no longer imperative for the monarchy to maintain rigorous control and to unite the Greek tribes and tribal splinters.[54] Now the great problems arising from the regrouping of the Greek people no longer existed, problems which it had only been possible to solve in unison and under centralised leadership. It is therefore no wonder that the nobility, supported by their land and by a following of a great many smallholders and serfs (as, for instance, in Thessaly), gradually seized complete control of power and within a short time entirely governed the whole of public life. The elimination of the monarchy, which took place, probably by evolution, in the whole of the Greek world before the beginning of the second great colonisation (middle of the eighth century), was in fact the most important consequence of the rise of the noble families. In those places where the monarchy was retained—Laconia, Argos, Arcadia, Elis and also the frontier regions of the Greek world like Macedonia—its political powers became limited, although this did not prevent certain monarchs in a later period from trespassing beyond their prescribed rights. It was, however, exclusively the nobility in the Assembly—comprised of those capable of bearing arms—who now determined the course of public life. The common man was forced to comply with the decisions of the nobles. The Homeric poems accurately reflect these conditions. The Athenian Dipylon vases[55] bear witness to the splendour and power of the Hellenic nobility, above all in the magnificent funeral scenes depicted on them. Otherwise the entire Greek world resounded with the din of fighting and war. These wars were in fact conducted principally for booty and fame. Gold, bronze, iron and women were the prizes of the victors, and attention has rightly been drawn to the enormous passion for booty which runs like a red thread through the epics.[56] Even the greatest Homeric heroes boast of stealing cattle, and piracy was generally regarded as a legitimate means of acquiring wealth. No one thought piracy dishonourable, unless the plundering expeditions were directed against the members of one's own tribe or one's confederates. Whoever went abroad possessed no rights, and only he who had many friends among the members of his class succeeded in asserting himself.

The great increase in the population of the Greek motherland, above all the Dorians but also the other tribes, soon made it evident that the newly-won country had become too small. Since an intensification in crop raising by a change in the primitive methods of agriculture was out of the question, conditions at the end of the transition period increasingly drove the Greeks in the direction of a new expansion. It was, besides other causes, the striving for new areas of settlement that led to the second great colonisation period about the middle of the eighth century.

THE CHRONOLOGY OF GREEK HISTORY TO THE BEGINNING OF THE EIGHTH CENTURY B.C.

The chronology of early Greek history rests on connections between Greece and the outside world—to the ancient Orient, to Crete and to Asia Minor. The accuracy of the dates in the chronology[57] of the early history of Greece is without guarantee,[58] and, moreover, attempts by modern scholars to date historical developments at the end of the second millennium B.C. with the aid of family trees and genealogies have failed.[59] A genuine chronological tradition begins to take shape gradually in Greece only after alphabetic writing had become known. The first evidence is provided by the catalogue of Olympian victors and the Spartan Ephor lists (see p. 396f.), but all dates from early Greek history before the eighth century B.C. can only be regarded as approximate. This applies above all to the chronological collocations for the second half of the third millennium, and still applies to the entire second millennium, for which not a single astronomically confirmed date in Greece is available. Events of fundamental importance for Greek history, such as the Dorian Migration and the colonisation of the west coast of Asia Minor, can, for instance, be dated only to the nearest century.

F. Schachermeyr, V. Milojčić and F. Matz have done research into early Greek chronology within the framework of Aegean chronology.[60] For the connections between Creto-Mycenaean culture and Egypt the work of D. Fimmen is still useful,[61] despite the great amount of new material which has since accumulated.[62] Connections with contemporary developments in Anatolia are established by the chronology of Troy, the details of which have not as yet been conclusively established,[63] as well as by the throne succession in the Hittite empire.[64] The chronology of the Hittite empire has now been established on a new base date through the redating of Hammurabi, the most famous king of the First Dynasty of Babylon. A cuneiform tablet from the French excavations in Mari (Tell Hariri) on the Middle Euphrates shows that Hammurabi was a contemporary of the Assyrian king Samsiadad I, whose reign is to be placed, on the basis of a newly discovered king list of Chorsabad, in approximately 1729-1697;[65] Hammurabi therefore belongs to the period about 1700 B.C. (c. 1728-1686).[66] This new dating is also important for connections between Mesopotamia and Crete, which emerge from the cuneiform texts found in Mari. The conquest of Babylon by a surprise plundering campaign of the Hittite king Mursilis I (according to the so-called "Short Chronology," earlier dated to 1758 B.C.) has been computed to 1531 B.C. by Cornelius.[67] This eliminates the gap of more than 200 years between the Old and the New Hittite empire—a gap assumed between approximately 1650 and 1400 B.C.—or shrinks it into a few decades between the death of Mursilis I and the accession of Telepinus, now dated to approximately 1480 B.C., or somewhat earlier (c. 1500 B.C.).

Egyptian chronology is of equally fundamental importance for the chronology of the Aegean. The researches of O. Neugebauer[68] and A. Scharff[69] have shown that the "earliest date in world history" established by Eduard Meyer in his day, 19 July 4241 B.C., allegedly the date of the introduction of the Egyptian calendar, is untenable. The history of ancient Egypt does not really begin until approximately 3000 B.C., and probably not even until 2900 or shortly thereafter. Its beginnings—King Menes and the First Dynasty—are approximately contemporaneous with the Jamdat Nasr period in Mesopotamia and the Early Dynastic period,[70] which in other respects needs to be re-established with new specific dates.

Egyptian chronology especially provides us with the key for determining the chronological sequence of the Cretan layers. The schematic division of Cretan chronology into Early Minoan (EM), Middle Minoan (MM) and Late Minoan (LM) by Sir Arthur Evans, the outstanding British excavator of Cnossus, with its breakdown into three respective subdivisions (EM I-III, MM I-III, LM I-III), cannot be discarded, as inopportune as it may be. The scheme is needed because the same division has been adopted for Hellas, with the chronology of early Greek history divided by A. J. B. Wace and C. W. Blegen into the successive stages of Early Helladic I-III, Middle Helladic I-III and Late Helladic I-III, and is generally accepted today.

The beginning of the Bronze Age in Crete (Early Minoan I) must, on the basis of the discoveries of Egyptian stone vessels, probably be placed in the Third Dynasty—approximately 2400 B.C.[71] Early Minoan (I-III) itself is approximately contemporary with the Sixth to the Tenth Dynasties of Egypt, falling approximately in the time from 2400 to 2000 B.C. In the Aegean the Bronze Age begins with the Middle Minoan (and the Middle Helladic) period. Finds from the so-called Kamares period (MM II) in Egypt (Kahun, Abydus, Harageh)[72] from the time of the Twelfth Dynasty (earlier computed to about 1995-1788 B.C., but now to be lowered by several decades) make it possible to date the beginning of Middle Minoan II to about 1800 B.C.[73] The third stage of the Middle Minoan period (MM III) is dated, *inter alia*, by the discovery of an alabaster lid bearing the cartouche of the Hyksos king, Chian, found in the charred ruins of the older Palace of Cnossus, which was destroyed in the seventeenth century.[74] Late Minoan I starts at the beginning (or probably later, about the middle) of the sixteenth century. This dating is confirmed by the Minoan connections with the period of the shaft graves in Hellas, for Mycenaean weapons of this period have been found in Egypt in the tomb of Ahhotep, the mother of Ahmose, the victor over the Hyksos.[75] On the basis of Minoan finds in Kahun and Egyptian stone vessels in Isopata on Crete,[76] the period from approximately 1450 to 1400 B.C. has been assigned to Late Minoan II. The later Cretan palaces were destroyed about 1400 B.C. (or shortly thereafter) (v.i.p. 9).

Egyptian chronology is equally determinative for dating the "Aegean Migration." Merneptah's victory over the Libyans (1227 B.C. according to Ed Meyer) inaugurates the period of unrest, and information from the eighth year of Ramses III (soon after 1200 B.C.)[77] shows that the Hittite empire has already collapsed (v.i.p. 23 f.).

Our discussion of the chronology of the Greek mainland in the Helladic period may be restricted to a very brief outline. Finds from Hagios Kosmas in Attica, from Aegina and above all from Asine have established the period about 2000 B.C. as the end of the Early Helladic period (thus Blegen, Persson, Schachermeyr *et al.*). In view of the shortening of Cretan chronology, however, this date will in all probability have to be lowered somewhat, but by no means later than 1900 B.C. The Dimini period precedes the Early Helladic without essentially overlapping with it, and will have to be placed before the middle of the third millennium B.C. It belongs to the Late Neolithic. The older Neolithic period, represented by the finds from Sesklo in Thessaly, belongs in the first half of the third millennium or still earlier; its offshoots extend almost to the end of this millennium (cf. the chart in Matz, *Ägäis*, 180). Agreement has not as yet been reached with regard to the subdivision of Early Helladic into its three phases (I-III); for this, new data must be awaited. In the Middle Helladic period (c. 1900-c.1550 B.C.), and in fact probably at the beginning of that period, the Indo-Europeans migrated into Greece (v.i.p. 4). The Late Helladic period (c. 1550-c. 1150 B.C.) is synonymous with the Mycenaean period of Greek history. On the basis of the results from the German excavations in the Cerameicus in Athens the end of this period can now be dated to about 1150 B.C. (Matz: 1100 B.C.).[78] It was followed by the so-called Sub-Mycenaean period, marking a clear cultural regression, and, probably towards the end of the second millennium, the Protogeometric era,[79] which goes on into the Geometric style, a style which sets the fashion from the beginning of the ninth down into the eighth century B.C. The dates for the periods of the second millennium can by their very nature be regarded as only approximate, with corrections expected in the future. On the whole, however, it is at least possible now to regard the chronology of the second millennium as reasonably reliable in broad outline.

With the history of Greece from the immigration of the Indo-Europeans up to the threshold of the eighth century B.C. discernible only in outline, important events like the conflict of the immigrants with the Mediterranean population of the country remain shrouded in almost total darkness. There are no clues to the numerical relationship between the Indo-Europeans and the former inhabitants. However, the distinct flowering of Mycenaean culture is definite evidence for the profound influence of the new ethnic element which succeeded in asserting itself as the decisive factor in Hellas about the middle of the second millennium. In particular, the immigrants attained undisputed leadership in political affairs. The Dorian Migration, finally, was no less than revolutionary in importance. It shaped the ethnic character of Greece to the pattern which remained almost unaltered to the end of antiquity—in other words, for a millennium and a half. The migrations and the profound upheavals brought about by the immigration of the Indo-Europeans at the beginning of the second millennium and the later coming of the North-West Greeks and Dorians precipitated longer periods of cultural stagnation, indeed of regression. It is no wonder that the centuries from 1900 to 1550 and from 1100 to 800 B.C. are all but empty pages in Greek history. But even in this earliest and darkest period of Greek history these new people on Greek soil showed their ability to assimilate and adapt foreign culture. This applies not only to the connections between the Hellenes and the highly developed Minoan culture, but equally also to their relations with the Near East, contacts which led to the Greeks' adapting the North-Phoenician consonantal alphabet.

As early as the second millennium B.C. a basic feature of Greek history emerges—that the destiny of the Hellenes is closely interwoven with the sea which surrounds them. The history of the Hellenic people finds its actual fulfilment in colonisation. The Achaeans, as well as the Ionian, Aeolian and Dorian tribes—the former at the end of the Mycenaean period, the latter in connection with the Dorian Migration—crossed the sea and founded new settlements outside the narrow confines of the motherland, so that by the beginning of the first millennium the Aegean had become a Greek sea. The earliest periods disclose the hallmark of the whole of Greek history: the extensive political isolation of the individual tribes and tribal splinters, which lack not only all national cohesion but even a common name for all members of the Greek people. Thus the outlines of later developments are already evident at the cradle of the Greek people. The thrust of their history is not a policy of power politics based on the unification of their energies, but much more an intensifying of political life in internal affairs, in activating the capacities of the Greek individual in the interests of a cultural mission. From the point of view of world history, this was of great importance and ultimately gave shape to an era in the ancient world that was determined by the Greek mind.

3
THE GREEK COLONISATION (800-500 BC)

THE BEGINNING OF GREEK INDIVIDUALISM

After the dark transition period came the era of the great Hellenic colonisation, a decisive turning point in Greek history. It is no accident that the first written documents of history come almost at the same time as the launching forth of the Greeks into the expanse of the Mediterranean. There are magistrate lists, registers of victors and similar catalogues, which may have originated from contact with the world of the ancient Orient. In the period of the great colonisation the individual personality for the first time emerges from the broad mass of the nameless populace. From now on the individual makes his appearance in politics, literature and art, and Hellenic history loses some of its collective character. For the first time in two and a half millennia of Greek history the creative personality moves into the foreground. Poetry boasts such outstanding names as Hesiod and Archilochus, Alcaeus and Sappho, Anacreon and Simonides, and western science begins with Thales of Miletus and the Ionian natural philosophers. The Athenian statesman Solon, his contemporary Pittacus of Mytilene and the great tyrants Periander, Peisistratus and Polycrates embody the constructive Greek genius in political life. They are the first individuals of flesh and blood which the political history of Europe produces. Polycrates of Samos and the sons of Peisistratus in Athens granted a home in their courts to literature, and the poets Ibycus and Anacreon sojourned at the court of the Samian ruler, while at Athens Lasus of Hermione, Pratinas, Simonides and Onomacritus the seer lent splendour to the court of the Peisistratidae. We see foreshadowed here the patronage of letters as later practised by the Ptolemies, and by Augustus and his successors in Rome and Constantinople. The world of the spirit bridges the multiplicity of Hellenic tribes and states, and creates a larger, ideal homeland in which all Greeks share. This unity of Hellenic cultural life is the counterpart to the extensive political fragmentation in Archaic Greece. The unity of the Hellenic mind is symbolised in the figures of the "Seven Sages," who come from all parts of the Greek world, who belong to the entire Hellenic people and whose personalities reflect the first generation of individuals.

Religion also forms part of the foundation of Greek unity which, through cult observations, became intimately interwoven with the political life of the Greek people. In addition to the Olympian gods, whose personalities were stamped by Hesiod and Homer, the vast number of local deities had a life of their own—a colourful reflection of the scope of the Hellenic mind, animating the country with figures of a supernatural character. Of all the sacred places, Delphi, with its oracle of Apollo, who had immigrated from the East and had become naturalised in Hellas, exerted the profoundest influence on the souls of the Greeks. The ethics which the Delphic god proclaimed became the guiding principles in the moral life of the Hellenic nobility, and contributed decisively towards the moulding of Greek humanism. At Delphi the first steps were taken in regulating the Hellenic calendar system, a system which in its immensely variegated character was a true image of the Hellenic world of politics. As early as the sixth century the Delphic Oracle enjoyed extensive recognition outside as well as within Greece. It was primarily the prophetic inspiration of the Pythia which contributed to this. At an unknown, but certainly early, date it forced into the background the oracle by lot, which up to that time had been exclusively consulted.

The formation of a "church" or an ecclesiastical hierarchy did not, however, take place in Hellas at any time.[1] The Hellenic mind, whose free sway manifests itself so impressively at the end of the archaic period in the Ionian natural philosophers, never submitted to dogma. The strength of Greek individualism reveals itself in religion, in the expanding Orphic teachings and the cult of Dionysus. These currents, of which the Orphic derives from the East and the worship of Dionysus from Thrace, at the end of the archaic period gripped the imagination of most of the population. Their mysteries offered the seeking individual a new, personal relationship to the divine, which belief in the Olympian gods could not do. In addition, the cult of Dionysus was promoted by the tyrants, chiefly Peisistratus, as a genuine peasant religion of the rural population. The religion of Dionysus has had the most extensive influence on Western man, in that Attic tragedy emerged from its cultic performances. After the initial steps in the time of Peisistratus, a generation or so later, tragedy, primarily under Aeschylus, attained the form which became the classical model.

In the realm of the pictorial arts the archaic period marks a new beginning. During the preceding Geometric era Hellenic art was split up into numerous, separate branches, a development parallel to the political fragmentation of Greece in the transitional period. In this respect there is little change from what had existed, although abundant stimuli streamed into Greece from Egypt, Mesopotamia and Asia Minor—evidence of growing intercourse and increasing exchange between Greece and the ancient cultures of the Near East. The then classical art of the Old Kingdom of Egypt was chiefly responsible for directing Greek art along new paths. And how the Greeks knew in what way to make the stimulus from the Orient bear fruit! The development of numismatic art which, along with coinage, they took over from the Lydians in the seventh century, the enlivening and re-forming of glyptic art derived from Mesopotamian culture, and the *interpretatio Graeca* of the pose of the Egyptian sphinx—these and many additional artistic motifs testify to the strong re-creative vitality of the Greek genius in the encounter between the Occident and the Orient. Evidence for this spirit of individualism is the fact that the creative artists now acknowledge their works by imprinting their signatures on them, a practice unknown in the Orient.

Many monumental structures also owe their origin to Eastern stimulus. Some were erected on Greek soil after the beginning of the seventh century, but more in the course of the sixth. The Heraeum of Samos, the temple of Zeus built by the Peisistratidae in Athens, the Artemisium dedicated to the great Anatolian mother goddess at Ephesus, the temple of Apollo at Didyma near Miletus, the sanctuary of Apollo at Selinus in Sicily—all these came from a new way of thinking, in which the striving towards monumentality forges its way into the foreground. Never again did the Greeks build such a large number of temples as in this period—unerring evidence for the religious emotions embracing wide sectors of the people and the rulers.

The Greeks derived weights and measures, and astronomical knowledge such as the zodiac and the sun-dial from ancient Babylon, with the Ionians the initial recipients. Coinage came from Lydia, and in the field of music the Greeks learned from the Lydians and Phrygians in Asia Minor. The myth of the five ages of the world in Hesiod's *Works and Days* (vss. 106 ff.) is based on the oriental notion of the cyclical course of world history. Oriental stimuli may also have contributed to the origin of animal fables. The connections which can be traced between the Hittite epic of *Cumarbi* and Hesiod's *Theogony* have attracted a great deal of attention, and even if we may not as yet know through what media Anatolian mythology became transferred to Greece, the connections can no longer be denied; in this respect too *ex Oriente lux, ex Oriente dei* is applicable.

What the Greeks received they soon returned to the East, in manifold measure. In the sixth century Greek engineers, physicians and artists spread around the entire world. In particular the Greeks contributed very substantially to the rise of the later Achaemenid empire. Thus the annexing of the narrow coastal strip in Asia Minor settled by Greeks was epoch-making not only for the Hellenisation of the Lydians but later also in terms of Graeco-Persian relations.

THE ORIENT AND THE RISE OF THE GREEK STATES

Greek history in the archaic period was closely interwoven with the contemporary history of the Near East. The fate of Ionia in particular is indivisibly bound up with the whole of Anatolia. In addition, Greek colonisation, beginning approximately in the middle of the eighth century, included precisely the frontier areas of Western Asia, as well as Cyrenaica and the south coast of the Black Sea, and the settling of Greek merchants and mercenaries in Egypt in the seventh century for the first time also established a close contact between the land of the Pharaohs and Hellas. About 600 B.C. the area encompassed by the Greek colonisation extended from Spain to the Caucasus, and from southern Russia to Egypt. It was a colonial expansion of vast extent, and leaves the notable achievements of the Phoenicians far behind. The fact that the existence of the Greeks, especially of the Ionians, was continuously inter-related with the powers of Western Asia makes it necessary to outline Near Eastern history and look more closely at east-west relations.

After the destruction of the Hittite empire (soon after 1200 B.C.) there emerged in Anatolia the kingdom of the Indo-European Phrygians.[2] The central region of the realm lay at the sources of the Sangarius. Ruled by a warlike, landed aristocracy whose members as powerful landowners dominated a large number of vassals, the Phrygians soon attempted to expand their territory towards the east. At the end of the twelfth century they came into conflict with the Middle Assyrian empire at the Upper Euphrates, which halted their expansion. Not until the time of King Midas and his contemporary, the Assyrian Sargon II (722-705 B.C.), do we have evidence for new, fluctuating battles at the bend in the Euphrates, in Cilicia and Cataonia. These regions had close political and religious ties with the Greeks. As once the Indo-European Hittites, so the Phrygians and the Hellenes also accepted Anatolian deities into their pantheon, above all the Magna Mater, in whose image emerged the Ephesian Artemis.[3] Ionian mediation also brought many connections between the Phrygians and the Greek motherland, and Midas the ruler of Phrygia was also among the founders of the sanctuary of Delphian Apollo.[4]

The Lydians, in the region of the Hermus, at first also fell under the shadow of the emergent Phrygian kingdom. The rise of the Lydian nation is linked with Gyges, the founder of the Mermnad dynasty (the first half of the seventh century).[5] For two and a half centuries the Lydians controlled the history of Asia Minor. In contrast to the Phrygian kingdom, which crystallised around Gordium and the old priestly city of Pessinus, the centre of Lydian power lay closer to the Aegean Sea. Sardis, with its elevated fortress, and regarded as impregnable, was the capital of the Lydian kings. In the course of less than a century the Lydians succeeded in extending their rule over the whole of Asia Minor west of the Halys.[6] Only the principality of Cilicia, which under its native ruler, the Syennesis controlled the important Taurus passes, succeeded in asserting itself as an independent state. Cilicia also brought parts of Cappadocia and perhaps even of Pamphylia under its sovereignty (about 600 B.C.).[7]

The great landed proprietors constituted the backbone of the Lydian state, and their ranks provided the feudal army of the king. In general the Lydian kingdom was distinctly feudal in character, a feature which marked the central district of Lydia until the Hellenistic, indeed even into the Roman, period. As long as the energies of the Lydians were wholly claimed by building up their power they constituted no danger to the Greeks in western Asia Minor. In addition, the invasions (about 675 B.C.) of the Cimmerians, an Iranian people originating from the steppes of southern Russia,[8] put the newly-founded kingdom of Gyges to a severe

MAP I

The Greek World c. 800 B.C.

Illyria
Thrace
Epirus
Lemnos
Tendeos
Troy (Ilium)
Aeolians
Thessaly
Iolcis
Lesbos
Pitane
Gryneum
Lydia
Cyme
Myrina
Phocaea
Larisa
Smyrna
Sardis
Herm
Leucas
Aetolia
Euboea
Scyros
Phocis
Chalcis
Cephallenia
Boeotia
Chios
Clazomenae
Thebes
Teus
Achaea
Attica
Erythrae
Colophon
Corinth
Lebedus
Ephesus
Zacynthus
Elis
Arcadia
Athens
Andros
Notium
Argolis
Ionians
Priene
Maeand
Samos
Myus
Argos
Miletus
Messenia
Paros
Sparta
Naxos
Halicarnassus
Laconia
Cos
Cnidus
Melos
Dorians
Thera
Rhode
Cydonia
Gortyn
Crete
Mediterranean
Ionians
Dorians
North-West Greeks
Aeolians
Arcadians
Achaeans
The ethnic affinity of the inhabitants of Messenia is disputed.
Thessaly and Boeotia with a North-West Greek component.
Places with finds from the Mycenaean period in Asia Minor are underlined.

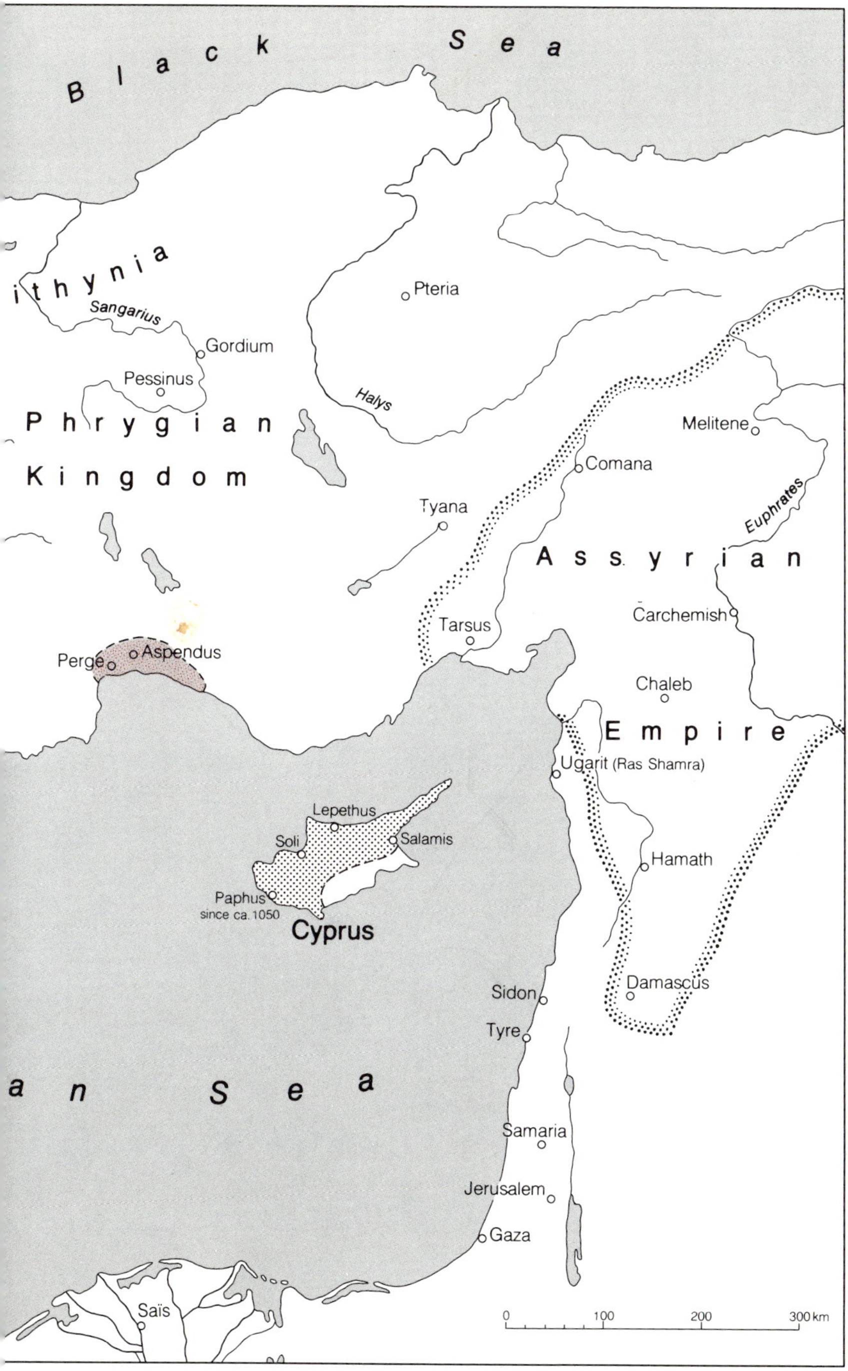
Black Sea
ithynia
Sangarius
Gordium
Pessinus
Phrygian Kingdom
Pteria
Halys
Tyana
Melitene
Comana
Euphrates
Assyrian Empire
Carchemish
Tarsus
Perge
Aspendus
Chaleb
Ugarit (Ras Shamra)
Lepethus
Soli
Salamis
Hamath
Paphus
since ca. 1050
Cyprus
Sidon
Damascus
Tyre
an Sea
Samaria
Jerusalem
Gaza
Saïs
0
100
200
300 km

test. The booty which the roving barbarians hoped to find in the Artemisium of Ephesus lured them as far as the east coast of the Aegean Sea. The Artemisium went up in flames, and a number of Greek cities suffered severe plunderings. The war poems of Callinus of Ephesus herald the terror with which the violent barbarians threatened Ionia.[9] The Phrygian kingdom did not survive the Cimmerian invasion, but the Lydian kingdom, thanks to the energy of Ardys, successor to Gyges, succeeded in recovering within a short time. Under Ardys and his successors, Sadyattes and Alyattes, the Lydians began to cast their gaze west. Fighting between the advancing Lydians, whose upper classes incidentally soon became extensively Hellenised, and the disunited Ionians now continued without interruption. Decisive victories were however denied to *this* generation of Lydian kings, although Alyattes succeeded in bringing Smyrna under his power.[10] The city withdrew from the Ionian alliance and thereby lost her rights as a city, which she was not to regain until Lysimachus granted them back to her. In the conflict between the Lydians under Alyattes and the Medes under Cyaxares at the Halys—the five-year war finally ended in 585 B.C. with an alliance negotiated by the Cilician Syennesis—a new grouping of powers appeared in the East, which also demanded tribute from the Lydians.

No less far-reaching in their effect on the Greek world in the colonisation period were the repercussions from political developments in Western Asia. The formation of a power centre in the Near East under the Assyrians prevented the colonial expansion of the Greeks on the coasts of Syria and Phoenicia, and not until the collapse of Assyrian domination in Egypt did the gates of the land of the Nile open to the Greeks.

The history of Western Asia after the catastrophe of the Aegean migration is characterised by disintegration—almost actual atomisation—in the political realm, a striking parallel to simultaneous developments in Greece. In northern Syria, where from earliest times the strong cultural currents and the aspirations of power politics from north, south and east intersected, a particularly large number of small and medium-sized states emerged. All these combined elements from the Hittites and their civilisation with a progressively increasing Aramaic colouring. This political fragmentation provided the conditions for the rise of the Assyrian empire[11] in the ninth century. In contrast to the temporary expansion of the so-called Middle Assyrian empire (at the end of the twelfth-eleventh century), the extension of Assyrian power was now of longer duration. Under Assurnasirpal (883-859 B.C.) the Assyrian empire was by far the most powerful state in the entire world. A large number of smaller but highly organised provinces grouped themselves around the central region of the empire, the so-called Arbelitis beyond the Tigris, where Calah rose as a magnificent second capital alongside Assur on this side of the river. The governors of these provinces united in a single person both military and civil powers and thereby guaranteed a rigorous administration. Assur's pride was its formidable army, an outstanding power instrument in the far-reaching plans of the Assyrian kings. Far and wide, no wall was able to withstand the onslaughts of the Assyrian blockading machines, and the system of transplanting complete nations and tribes, practised with consummate skill already at that time, was suited as no other to suppress all resistance.

The initial climax of Assyrian power under Assurnasirpal was at first followed by a regression, and then, under Shalmanassar IV (782-772 B.C.), by an unmistakable decline. The aspiring state of Urartu (between Lake Van and Lake Urmia) emerged as a dangerous rival to the Assyrians, and temporarily pushed its sphere of power far towards the west. Under Sarduris I (c. 830 B.C.) the rulers of Melitene and Commagene were among the vassals of the new major power of the north. After the usurper Tiglathpilesar III (745-727 B.C.) acceded to the throne the Assyrians went over to an offensive on all fronts. The Aramaic kingdom of Damascus was conquered, Babylonia joined in personal union with the crown of Assur, and under Sargon II (722-705 B.C.) the northern kingdom of Israel with the capital of Samaria was also subjugated. The late "Hittite empire" of Carchemish in 717 B.C. also fell as booty to the Assyrians. Its location between the fords of the Euphrates and the Taurus passes gave it exceptionally great strategic and economic importance.

The first contacts between Assyrians and Greeks for which historical evidence is available occurred during the reign of Sargon II. In 712 B.C. the Assyrians eliminated a Greek adventurer—the cuneiform inscription calls him *Iamâni*, the "Ionian"—who had set himself up as ruler in the Philistine city of Ashdod.[12] Two years later in Babylon Sargon II received tribute from seven city-kings of Cyprus. Finally, a late but trustworthy source attests a conflict between Assyrians and Greeks in the plain of Cilicia during the reign of Sennacherib (705-681 B.C.), the successor to Sargon,[13] revealing the policy of the Assyrian empire reaching out towards the west.

The conquest of Egypt by Assarhaddon in 671 B.C. marks the outward climax of Assyrian power. Its territory extended from the Armenian highlands to deep within the Sudan, and from central Anatolia to the Persian Gulf. The central region of the empire, divided into small, tightly organised provinces, controlled a wide arc of vassal states which were held in check by constant fear of the Assyrian army. Under Assurbanipal (668-629? B.C.), the successor to Assarhaddon—to whom posterity is indebted for the treasures of his palace-library in Nineveh (Kuyunjik)—Cyrus I, the Achaemenid ruler of Parsumash, also found himself as vassal of the Assyrian king.[14]

While the Assyrian empire developed into a world power, Egypt experienced a period of distinct decline. Under the rule of the Theban priestly kings and the Libyan generals the harmonious balance of the classes disappeared, and the mercenary army became a canker in the state, consuming its best energies.

Just as at the time of the later Ptolemies, mercenaries were settled at various points throughout the country. The military profession was hereditary from father to son, and while the other classes, which had likewise developed into castes, were now nothing more than burden-bearers in the service of the state, the soldiery regarded itself as the highest class in the kingdom.[15] The old feeling for sensuous pleasure and receptivity of everything beautiful in literature and art, so characteristic of the Egyptians, suffered a barbarisation. Under the Ethiopian rulers of the XXVth Dynasty (from the end of the eighth century) a large number of local, urban rulers displaced the central government, above all in Lower and Central Egypt where there was no hierarchical centre like the priestly state of Ammon of Thebes.

By adroitly taking advantage of the crisis into which the Assyrians had been precipitated by the Cimmerians, the nome prince Psammetichus of Saïs (663-609 B.C.) evicted the Assyrian garrisons from Egypt,[16] helped by Greek and Carian mercenaries. Then, in addition to the Hellenic mercenaries garrisoned in Daphne, Pelusium and perhaps also in Elephantine, many Greek traders and merchants entered the land of the Nile. The Milesians were the first granted permission by Psammetichus I to settle a fortified colony at the mouth of the Bolbitinian branch of the Nile.[17] The founding, moreover, of the Greek city of Naucratis is probably to be dated as early as the second half of the seventh century,[18] for discoveries of Greek pottery in the Delta begin as early as 650 B.C., and the first Attic vases appear in Naucratis before the turn of the century. The ambitious plans of Necho, the successor to Psammetichus I, opened up a great field to Egyptian trade. Necho planned to build a canal through the Isthmus of Sinai—one of the many canal enterprises in antiquity—but for the time being it remained uncompleted.[19] If the information in a papyrus from the period of the Roman Empire may be trusted,[20] the first Greek settlement in Rhacotis falls in the time of Psammetichus II (593 B.C.?), and would then constitute the germ cell of Alexandria, founded in 331 B.C.

In the last two decades of the seventh century the international situation in Western Asia underwent a fundamental change. With the rise of the Indo-European Medes under the Deiocid house, and above all during the reign of Cyaxares the son of Phraortes, and with the founding of the Neo-Babylonian empire by Nabopolassar (626 B.C.), a power coalition began to take shape. The Assyrian empire ultimately succumbed to this. As the chronology study by C. J. Gadd (published in 1923) has shown,[21] the royal city of Assur was conquered by the united Medes and Chaldaeans in 614 B.C., and ancient Nineveh in 612 B.C. The last Assyrian king, Sin-sar-iskun, died in the flames of his palace, and the Assyrian royal capitals were so completely destroyed that their location was not found until approximately one hundred years ago by modern excavators.

The fall of Assur and Nineveh ended a great epoch in Near Eastern history. The fall in 610 B.C. of the kingdom of Harran (Carrhae) in Upper Mesopotamia, an Assyrian right of the younger son, with the ruler Assuruballit, had no historical significance. After the fall of Nineveh, however, the whole world breathed a sigh of relief from the cruel terror which had weighed down upon it for centuries. The exuberant joy of the subject peoples vented itself in moving jubilation. In spite of the undeniable negative side, however, the great achievements of the hard Assyrian nation must not be overlooked.[22] In the Assyrian state, the first complete embodiment of the power-state on earth, Western Asia had for centuries possessed a power which established order out of the divisive chaos of nations, united them into a whole, and imposed its will on it. One may well suppose that the peoples of Western Asia resisted the Assyrian efforts to fuse them into a "levelled down" medley of nations and to erase their peculiarities in customs and language, in order to make them, as the Assyrian inscriptions put it, "of one mouth."[23]

The booty was divided between the victors. Upper Mesopotamia and Syria fell to the Neo-Babylonian (Chaldaean) kingdom, while the Medes, holding the region of the upper Tigris, became dangerous neighbours to the Chaldaeans and also to the Lydians, following the conquest of the former central territory of Urartu. After the victory of the Neo-Babylonians over Pharaoh Necho (605 B.C.) in the struggle for Syria, a balance of power emerged in the Near East, a Neo-Babylonian-Median dualism that would sooner or later have to be decided.

The events in Western Asia had their effects on the Greeks. In Ionia, in particular, there must have been precise knowledge of political and economic conditions in Western Asia. Here too the fall of the Assyrian empire was regarded as a great turning point in history, and even half a century or so after the fall of Nineveh the Milesian Phocylides praised the small, ordered *polis* in contrast to the mighty but irrationally ruled Nineveh.[24]

GREECE AND THE POLIS

In contrast to Western Asia, Greece in the eighth and seventh centuries had an almost unlimited number of small states. They emerged from the splitting up of the tribal alliances after land acquisition in Greece had come to an end. Not only geographical conditions but also the particularistic nature of the Hellenes contributed significantly to developments in this direction. It is characteristic of the small polities that within their respective territory there was at any given time only one urban settlement, and this settlement gave the state its name.[25] Originally there was no constitutional difference between the city and the rural area, but the city, the polis, into which the political and religious life concentrated itself, gradually acquired an increasing preponderance over the rural area. The polis, the first constitutional state in the history of the West, arose (probably influenced by the more rapid developments in the colonial region of Asia Minor, v.i.p. 26) on the soil of the Greek motherland probably at the very time that the Assyrian empire reached its culmination in the eighth century as the incarnation of the power-state on earth.[26] As fundamental as the difference was between the legal position of subjects and rulers of the state in the East and the West, in the idea of the divine as the basis of the state they coincided. Among the Assyrians it was the imperial deity Assur, who from a city god had become the ruler of the world. The Assyrian king acted as his representative on earth, and in the royal inscriptions he gives account to the god for all his conduct. Among the Greeks the great plurality of city deities were the divine monarchs, the ideal rulers of the polis. In the cult of the city god the political realm is united with the religious world. For the polis—in ideal form—is a community of justice, religion and in many cases also of economics.[27]

The outward characteristic of the polis is its territorial limitation, which produced an extraordinary concentration of political, religious, intellectual and economic life within the realm of the many small states. It forced the various "community states" to observe moderation in foreign policy and to unite with other states when extensive goals were to be reached. The community states were not large, although the Lacedaemonian and the Attic territories—uncharacteristic since they developed under special conditions—were sizeable: Laconia together with Messenia encompassed approximately 3276 square miles, Attica about 995 square miles. Even the area of community states such as Argos (546 sq. m.) and Corinth (343 sq. m.) is still greater than the general average. In Phocis there were, for instance, no fewer than twenty-two independent states in an area of only about 643 square miles, which approximates an average of 27 to 29 square miles. In Crete (3315 sq.m.) there probably existed a hundred states,[28] Rhodes (569 sq. m.) had three down to the end of the fifth century, and Lesbos (783 sq. m.) as many as six. On the smaller islands, however, there was as a rule only one community state.[29]

Larger states developed on the Greek mainland during the dark centuries following the Dorian Migration only in those regions where the geographical conditions and geomorphological features promoted unification: in the plain of the Peneius and its tributaries in Thessaly, in the Attic *akte*—promontory—projecting far to the south, in the Argolid cut off from the rest of the Peloponnesus and in the Eurotas valley in the plain between Mount Taygetus and Mount Parnon—all regions in the east of Greece. In contrast to this the west maintained a state of extensive political fragmentation. The same applies across the Aegean to the Ionians, who were confined to a narrow fringe of the Anatolian seaboard. Pressure from the kingdoms of the Phrygians and Lydians prevented their development into larger powers.

The formation of all other Greek polities was overshadowed by the rise of the Spartan military state in the eighth and seventh centuries. This was a singular phenomenon, explicable only on the basis of interwoven historical, geographical and social conditions. When the Dorian hordes inundated the valley of Lacedaemon at the beginning of the first millennium the former rulers of the country, the Achaeans, succeeded in retaining only a few settlements. The stronghold of Amyclae, lying as an outer fort at the entrance to the Eurotas, held out for a longer time.[30] In this region a peaceful settlement was ultimately reached between Dorians and Achaeans, and the Amyclaeans were accepted as equal members into the Dorian political union. The centre of the new state was the open settlement of Sparta. The founding of this completely unfortified town presupposes the conquest and pacification of the entire surrounding territory.

Divided among the Dorian warriors in the form of property lots, with the more fertile parts of the Eurotas Valley awarded to the eminent Spartan lords, the less coveted frontier areas became the possession of the remaining conquerors. The size of the original Spartan hide amounted to seventy-five acres,[31] but this figure cannot be regarded as certain. The masses of the pre-Dorian inhabitants, who had previously paid taxes to the ruling Achaean families, were reduced by the conquerors to the level of quasi state slaves called Helots.[32] These Helots tilled the land for the new masters, whose life was concentrated in Sparta. The crop yields made it possible for the Dorian ruling class to devote themselves exclusively to war, hunting, athletic exercises and the conducting of political council meetings.

By the eighth century the rapid increase in the Spartan ruling class precipitated a chronic need for land, which dominated the whole of Spartan life and Spartan politics until the middle of the sixth century. Conquest or colonisation alone could alleviate the distress. Confident in their military superiority, the Spartans chose the path of conquest. In two major wars, the gravity of which is evident in the war poems of Tyrtaeus, they conquered the grain land of Messenia beyond Mount Taygetus, whose central region was formed by the plain of the Pamisus. Although the tradition of the so-called Messenian wars is in great measure legendary,[33] it is certain that the First Messenian War, which probably falls in the last third of the eighth century,[34] was unusually protracted. The Messenians allegedly did not abandon the stronghold of Ithome and give up their resistance until the twentieth year of the war.[35] The Helotisation by the victorious Spartans forced a terrible fate upon the valiant Messenian people, amounting to total enslavement and loss of their land as private property. But Sparta had gained the land which it needed for the sustenance of its citizens. By the end of the First Messenian War it was by far the largest and most powerful state in the whole of the Peloponnesus.

The great Helot revolt in Messenia which broke out about the middle of the seventh century precipitated a very serious crisis for the Spartans; on many occasions they found themselves on the verge of total defeat. In addition, the Messenians had found powerful allies in the Peloponnesus: the Pisans, who temporarily evicted the Eleans from the presidency of the Olympian games,[36] the Arcadians under King Aristocrates of Orchomenus and above all the Argives. Besides this, Sparta found herself in the midst of a serious internal crisis, with a widespread cry for a land redistribution.[37] And the halo of Spartan invincibility had lost a great deal of its sheen after a number of defeats at the hands of the insurgents. The severe afflictions of the time are reflected in the war poems of Tyrtaeus. Finally, thoroughly unnerved by a Spartan victory at the "Great Foss," the Messenians withdrew into the inaccessible fortress of Hira.[38] Legend has woven a wreath of heroic exploits around Aristomenes the leader of the Messenian insurgents, and he became the model for the national gang-leader such as the Peloponnesus produced again and again. The fall of

Hira sealed the doom of Messenian liberty. The Spartan squires returned home, but in the *Perioikoi* communities in the north and south they set up strong military bases which held the country as if in iron clamps.

The central figure in the Peloponnesian alliance against Sparta was King Pheidon of Argos. As recent scholarship has shown, he belongs in the middle of the seventh century.[39] The statement by Herodotus (VI 127), that Pheidon gave measures to the Peloponnesians—a contention which in later sources (Ephorus) was expanded by adding the invention of weights and coinage—is obviously not correct as transmitted.[40] The fact, however, that the Argive ruler is associated with basic transactions in the field of economics argues for his historical importance, but the "Argive empire" assumed by a number of earlier scholars[41] is merely a creation of fancy.

The district of Cynuria, situated between Mount Parnon and the Argolid Gulf and once part of the area where Ionian tribes had settled, became the bone of contention between Sparta and Argos. After protracted and fluctuating battles it ultimately remained in Spartan hands.[42] Thyreatis, lying at their northern frontier, was also taken from the Argives, but not until the middle of the sixth century.[43] The efforts of Sparta against Arcadia, however, were less successful, although in view of the extensive fragmentation of that country, it appeared to offer the best prospects for a decisive victory. All Spartan bravery proved in vain before the walls of Tegea, which had emerged from a *synoikismos* ("settling together") with the neighbouring communities. A treaty was concluded (middle of the sixth century) in which the Tegeans pledged to hand over all Messenian exiles in their territory and to render military service in the Spartan army.[44]

The Spartan-Tegean treaty marks a decisive turning point in Spartan foreign policy. Hitherto the rapid growth in population had forced the Spartans increasingly along the path of conquest, whereas now, and indeed for the entire future, Sparta appeared to be saturated. The population curve had passed its zenith.[45]

In central Greece only the district of Attica developed, under the political aegis of Athens, into a unitary state. Legend attributes the origin of the Attic polity to the *synoikismos* effected by the mythical hero Theseus. Certain cultic traditions suggest that the Attic unitary state was preceded by a period of particularism.[46] Under the leadership of the ruling family living on the Acropolis in Athens, the other districts of Attica—the "Central Plain," the Marathon *Tetrapolis* and the *Akte* (including Thoricus and Sunium)—joined with Athens. This took place over a long period, and had come to an end in the eighth century.[47] The annexation of the priestly state of Eleusis, however, probably did not come about until some time in the seventh century (?).[48] As a polis Athens was a completely singular phenomenon in Hellas—the total merging of a whole territory into one "city state" so that both town and country are fused together. The politically wise Athenian leaders concentrated all political life within their city, and at the same time gave the nobility of the surrounding districts of Attica their share in political affairs, to create at this early date a new, unique political form—a "community state."

Despite the formation of the community state, the old Hellenic tribes in many districts still retained some degree of importance in practical politics. In the Peloponnesus the Arcadians, the Achaeans and the Eleans continued to assemble in their long accustomed centres to take counsel on common matters under the protection of Zeus. Decrees of the Eleans are preserved in inscriptions from Olympia.[49] Above all in central Greece among the Aetolians and Acarnanians, but also among a number of smaller tribes like the Aenianians, the Dolopes, Phocians and others, the institutions of the old tribal states remained in vogue. In Aetolia and Acarnania the village form of settlement prevailed until the fifth and fourth centuries. It is no wonder that the tribal states scarcely took part in the political life of the Greeks, for they lacked that feature which characterised the community state—rigorous central authority and the subordinating of all political life to a numerically restricted ruling class. Developments in Boeotia illustrate how disastrous the lack of an actual central authority could be. The antagonism among the leading communities, above all between Thebes and Orchomenus, for centuries frustrated the political union of the country, while an ideal unity at the tribal level was emphasised by united observation of the cult of Athena Itonia at Coroneia and of Poseidon at Onchestus. All other Greek tribal states were overshadowed in importance, however, by the federal state of Thessaly,[50] which apparently began when the district of Thessaliotis, the central region, united with the cantons of Pelasgiotis, Hestiaeotis and Phthiotis into a "*tetrarchia*" (in the eighth century B.C.?). The federation was headed by the *tagos*,[51] an elective duke, who was of little importance in time of peace, but in time of war became the commander-in-chief of the entire Thessalian army. The political influence of Thessaly soon affected its neighbours, the Magnesians, Perrhaebians, Aenianians and Dolopes. A predominant position in the Amphictyony of Anthela and later, from about 600 B.C., in the Delphic Amphictyony, made the Thessalian federation the most important political formation in Hellas, apart from Sparta, by about 600 B.C. The rivalries among the cantons and the powerful Thessalian noble families, however, prevented Thessaly from playing its rôle in Greek history before the fourth century.

At the beginning of the seventh century (?) the Macedonians, under their king, Perdiccas I, forged their way from the mountains into the plain of the Haliacmon and advanced as far as the Aegean coast.[52] The rocky nest of Aegae became the centre of the Macedonian monarchy, and even later, after the country had a new capital in Pella, it remained the burial place of Macedonian kings. The Macedonians, by taking possession of the coastal district on the lower courses of the Haliacmon, brought to a close the era of land acquisition in Greece. About two generations before this the second great colonial expansion of the Greeks had begun with a vigorous prelude in both East and West.

In the archaic period the Greek world presents a general picture of widespread fragmentation. Particularistic elements are everywhere surging to the foreground, and the tribal states have lost their importance in terms of practical politics. Sparta represents the most important power formation on Greek soil, its power resting on the brutal suppression of the Messenians. Despite the indisputable preponderance of centrifugal forces, certain unifying tendencies must not be overlooked; these indeed lacked force in the political life of the Greeks, but were the more significant in terms of the identity of the Greek people. The feeling of solidarity on the part of all people speaking the Greek language was born during this period. Through colonisation and extensive commercial relations, the mutuality of language fostered the environment in which the Greeks became acquainted. It was not only the Greeks of Ionia but the colonists of all Greek tribes, finding themselves in a foreign environment, in a foreign land and among people speaking a foreign language, who became conscious of the community of their Greek language, Greek customs and Greek way of life.[53] How it came about that the small district of Hellas in southern Thessaly gave the entire country its name is unknown.[54] It is scarcely coincidental that the term Hellene appears for the first time in the works of Archilochus[55] (middle of the seventh century), who had seen many lands and had participated in the colonisation itself. The sanctuary in Naucratis, in Egypt, built by the united efforts of nine cities (in the time of Amasis, 569-526 B.C.), was called the *Hellenion*. Votive inscriptions there read "to the 'gods of the Hellenes'," further evidence for the formation of a common Greek consciousness in foreign countries.[56] Nor was there, moreover, a lack of panhellenic institutions in the motherland itself. The Delphic oracle of Apollo attained general Greek importance. As early as the eighth century it was eagerly consulted on political matters (cf. the remarks on the Great Rhetra, v.i.p. 66 f.). The influence of the Delphic priesthood was responsible for achieving general recognition in Greece for the eight-year intercalary cycle (*oktaëteris*) originating from Babylon, probably in the latter part of the seventh century. This established an important element of unity among the numerous Greek calendar systems.[57] In view of the fact that the festivals of the gods could be fixed with certainty for all Hellas it was now possible for the first time to lay the foundations for unity at least in the religious sphere. The federation of the surrounding states which had grouped themselves around the ancient sanctuary of Demeter of Anthela at Thermopylae formed the germ cell of the Delphic Amphictyony. It was not until this sanctuary had declined that the Delphic Amphictyony attained greater importance (about the seventh century).[58] Although it already encompassed all states in central Greece in approximately 600 B.C., its influence on Greek politics remained very modest. This is scarcely to be wondered at in view of the fact that all members, large as well as small, had equal voting powers, so that the large state of Thessaly could on occasion find itself forced to bow to the veto of the small Ozolian Locris and Phocis. The smaller the degree of unanimity that could be achieved in the political sphere, the more did the members of the Amphictyony concern themselves with the administration of the sanctuary and with questions pertaining to the cult and sacred rites. It was the Delphic Amphictyony which achieved the recognition of certain obligations in international law by its members in time of war. Cutting off the water supply of an enemy and destroying a federal city were regarded as forbidden[59]—principles which excellently reflect the spirit of the "agonistic" era, although in actual fact they may have been disregarded time and again.

Olympia competed with Delphi in panhellenic importance. From the beginning of the eighth century the youth met here every four years for athletic contests, at first just from the Peloponnesus but from the beginning of the sixth century from other parts of the Hellenic world, including even Ionia and the colonies of southern Italy.[60] There was a sacred armistice throughout the entire Greek world connected with the Olympian festival,[61] so that the contestants and visitors could travel to Olympia and return home again in safety. Greek origin and free birth were the conditions for participation in the games. The umpires of the games bore the title of *Hellanodikai.* As one of the few panhellenic institutions of early Greece, the Olympian games doubtless contributed their share to the formation of a Greek national consciousness, and this the more so since athletic contests for their own sake were completely unknown in the ancient Orient. That the Greeks neither then nor later attained political unity becomes understandable if one calls to mind the parallel from the modern Olympic games.

The gradual moulding of a Greek national feeling in the archaic period is inseparably and reciprocally connected above all with the great Hellenic colonisation, which began about the middle of the eighth century. This latter movement led the Greeks out of the narrow limits of their homeland and made Greek ways, Greek culture and Greek customs a determining factor in the ancient world.

THE EXPANSION OF THE GREEKS IN THE MEDITERRANEAN WORLD (750-550 B.C.)

The second period of Greek expansion in the Mediterranean began about the middle of the eighth century, almost half a millennium after the end of the Achaean colonisation. It was carried out by members of all classes of the Greek people, from the nobility to the landless peasants. In its origin and course it is ultimately a phenomenon which defies all historical explanation. Whatever the causes, it is above all the expression of a fundamentally new outlook on life, for which the frontiers of the homeland had become too constricted. It is therefore no accident that the man who first appears before us in his individuality, Archilochus of Paros, was an active participant and sufferer in this movement. In contrast to the Achaean expansion, its dimensions in terms of area and demo-political considerations extended almost infinitely. When the colonisation gradually abated about the middle of the sixth century after a period of two hundred years, flourishing Hellenic colonies extended over almost the entire basin of the Mediterranean. Only in the East did the great empires of Western Asia prevent the Greeks from settling on the coast of Syria.

The expansion is the more amazing in view of the fact that in planning and execution it was undertaken by individual Greek communities and individual Greek personalities, without any central supervision.[62] The initiative came from the Greek communities, the poleis, or from certain groups within the population. Of far-reaching consequence for the history of the Western world was this transplanting abroad of Greek political institutions, especially the community state, the polis. In a foreign environment it most demonstrated its vitality. Through the great colonisation the Greeks for the first time became a leading people in the ancient world and the destiny of the Greek people was henceforth inseparably interwoven with that of East and West.

The leadership of this great mass movement was undertaken by the Greek nobility. From their numbers came the founders, the *oikistai*, of the new colonial towns. The multitudes of emigrants assembled in the harbour cities of the motherland, in Chalcis, Eretria, Megara and Corinth. In Asia the prime coloniser was Miletus, which actually attained a monopolising position in the seventh century. The community which provided the ships in general also sent out the *oikistos*, and after his death the colonists ascribed heroic honours to him. The close ties between the mother-city and the colony are first and foremost documented in the religious sphere. Tribe-divisions, the names of magistrates, the calendar system, the cult of the city gods—all migrated from the metropolis into the new homeland, where the bonds with the mother-city were piously cultivated. Of cardinal importance was the fact that the majority of *apoikiai*—colonies—were autonomous communities independent of the polis which sent them out. In general, the distinctive political individualism of the Greeks prevented the colony from being ruled by the mother-city. Exceptions to this may be found in the colonial empire of Periander (c. 600 B.C.), and in the relationship of the later Syracusan colonies to their mother-city.[63]

The causes for emigrating[64] are to be found in the internal conditions of the Greek motherland. In the first place there is the (relative) overpopulation of Hellas, a periodically recurring phenomenon in Greek history. For the archaic period it is attested by various documents. Hesiod, for instance (*Works and Days* 376), counselled that the family be restricted to a single child! It is moreover known that the exposure of new-born infants was generally practised in Greece.[65] Places such as Thessaly, Boeotia and Attica—even at first—probably participated in the emigration. They too must have channelled their surplus population abroad through the great harbours. In addition to overpopulation, serious social conflicts, like the internal struggles in cities like Megara, Corinth, Athens and Mytilene, must also have prompted many thousands to leave their homelands. Opposition to the tyrants too by a certain sector of the citizenry repeatedly drove people of all classes from their country.

Trade and a search for new arable land were from the very outset connected. To date, reliable evidence for the important extension of Greek navigation and Greek trade in the period immediately preceding the colonisation exists only for the West. In no less than thirty different places in the area from Apulia to Marseilles, archaeological finds have brought to light evidence for Greek imports in the eighth and seventh centuries, above all in the form of Greek vases. The vases came from almost the entire Greek world—from Crete, from the Cyclades, from Boeotia and Corinth. Certain features suggest the idea that even in the first half of the ninth century Greek artists found themselves in Etruria, in Falerii and Tarquinii, and that there was even a perceptible first Hellenisation of Etruscan arts and crafts.[66] Knowledge of the geography of the west and the north reflected in the *Odyssey* and in the legend of the Argonauts is confirmed by archaeological evidence, and it is no accident that naval battles and ships are the predominant motifs on Attic Dipylon vases. The colonisation was preceded by a period of discoveries, with merchant captains from Chalcis playing an outstanding rôle in the West.[67]

What we today regard as the second colonisation was in fact a vast number of frequently unverifiable specific events, plans, endeavours, successes and failures. K. J. Beloch[68] assumed a systematically progressive movement based in southern Italy and spreading over Sicily and the entire West, and moving from the occupation of the Propontic coast along the shores of the Black Sea. However, this not only runs counter to the evidence but also overlooks the many different and often interrelated factors that were involved in the colonial foundations. The considerations governing the choice of location for founding settlements were as varied as the reasons which motivated the Greeks to leave their homes.[69] One may have been moved abroad by the urge into distant unknown places, another by dire affliction or the hope of acquiring fabulous treasures and riches from commercial enterprises. The new cities were sited for the economic importance of the hinterland, the quality of the soil for agriculture, the attitude of the native population to foreigners, the protected character of a given place, the communications with traffic routes, and various other factors which are in part imponderable.

The fact that the direction of the Greek colonial expansion was primarily towards the west and north of the Mediterranean is explained by the international situation. In the East, in Western Asia, the empire under Tiglathpilesar III was then continuously expanding. The clash between Greeks and Assyrians in the plain of Cilicia during the reign of Sennacherib (v.s.p. 42) shows that Assyria had placed a barrier to the Greeks in the East. In Syria only very sporadic commercial colonies are to be found—at the mouth of the Orontes[70] and perhaps also at Tell Sukas.[71] They served to expedite immediate exchange between Hellas and Western Asia while avoiding the land route through Anatolia.

In contrast to this the conditions for a colonial expansion in the West were all the more favourable. Here there was no political power such as the Assyrian empire. The Italic tribes, in themselves discordant, and the Etruscans, who originated from the east, were particularly open to Greek trade and Greek civilisation. An important general condition for colonisation was provided by the great progress in nautical skill, the gradual increase in the size and cargo capacity of ships and finally by the geographical information about the western world which had been obtained by Greek voyagers since the end of the Mycenaean period.

Sailing through the straits of Messina the Chalcidians were the first to reach Campania, a district that was fertile and favoured by nature. In a region similar to the motherland in climate and vegetation they founded the city of Cyme (Cumae), about the middle of the eighth century at the latest.[72] Before this they had in all probability established a base on the off-shore island of Ischia.[73] No other Hellenic colony in the West was destined to such far-reaching cultural significance as Cyme, the first Chalcidian settlement. It probably furnished the Etruscans, and through them the Romans, with the alphabet of Chalcis. If today we regard the letter X as "ks" and do not read it with the Greeks as "k," we are following Chalcidian practice. Cyme no doubt also introduced the Greek gods to the Italics, who then received them into their pantheon.[74] Colonists from Cyme (Cumae) were responsible for founding Neapolis (c. 600 B.C.), which later far outstripped the mother-city.

The east coast of Sicily was also a goal of the Chalcidian voyagers. At the foot of Mount Aetna the settlement of Naxos emerged (founded according to tradition in 735 B.C.).[75] In the fertile hill-country, sloping as far as the Symaethus River, Chalcidians founded the colony of Catana. Greek settlers from Chalcis also established themselves on the small island of Ortygia, the germ cell of Syracuse, later founded by Corinth.[76] In Sicily, in addition to the Corinthians, the Megarians notably followed in the footsteps of the Chalcidians. They assured the pre-eminence of the Dorian element over the Ionian on the island. While Megara Hyblaea retained the reminiscence of the mother-city by its name, Syracuse, a colony of Corinth, became the most powerful city in Sicily.[77] In general the great commercial metropolis of Corinth, supported by her possession of the island of Corcyra, succeeded in creating for herself a superior position in the west in the seventh century. Corinth's success came primarily because Chalcis had become entangled in a dispute with her rival Eretria over the Lelantine plain (c. 700-650 B.C.).[78]

At first, however, the Chalcidians still continued to set the pace in the West. They gained a strong foothold on both sides of the straits—Zancle on Sicily and Rhegium at the southern tip of Italy were Chalcidian settlements.[79] With the stronghold of Mylae and the colony of Himera, founded by Zancle, the Chalcidians established strong bases for themselves on the northern coast of Sicily. In contrast to this the Dorians prevailed in the south, settling Acrae and Casmenae in the middle of the seventh century and Camarina about 600 B.C. Of the eastern Greeks the Rhodians alone took part in the Sicilian colonisation and were responsible for Gela, founded approximately 688 B.C., and Acragas, a colony of Gela, about 580 B.C. The attempt to gain a foothold in the extreme west, in Lilybaeum, was frustrated, primarily because of the opposition of the Elymians. The Dorian colonists, however, found a new home on the desolate Lipari islands. The interior of Sicily, however, was beyond the energies of the Hellenes. Here the native population asserted itself—in the east the Siculi, in the west the Sicani. Both soon entered into ardent cultural and economic exchange with the Greeks. The western tip of the island remained Punic. The Carthaginians maintained their bases in Motye, Panormus (Palermo) and Solus, and above all cultivated close connections with the Elymians, who had immigrated from the area of the Aegean.[80] Some have said that Chalcidians founded a colony in Tunis but evidence for it is far from adequate.[81]

The Greek colonisation in southern Italy presents an essentially different picture. Here commercial considerations were not the determining factor. Rather the need for land forced thousands of emigrants out of the north of the Peloponnesus and Locris to the fertile plains of southern Italy. Thus many settlements appeared in the Gulf of Tarentum, where even the smallest coastal plain was exploited, and when there was no more land on the east coast the Greeks pushed directly across Italy to the western sea. Here on the west coast, from Rhegium (Reggio di Calabria) to Poseidonia (Paestum), was a string of flourishing Hellenic colonial towns. Croton, Sybaris and Metapontum were settlements of Achaean colonists, whereas Locri Epizephyrii by its name indicates that the settlers originated from Locris. Tarentum, founded by the legendary Parthenians (c. 700 B.C.),[82] was the only colony Sparta ever founded. Of the settlements in southern Italy Croton and Sybaris conquered an extensive territory. In the end Sybaris allegedly ruled over four Italic peoples and twenty-five cities, but the 300,000 armed troops which she could allegedly throw into the field[83] is definitely a considerable exaggeration. Today the great Doric temples[84] on the coast at Poseidonia (Paestum), a colonial town of Sybaris, with their stark beauty still bear witness to the power and the determination of the Hellenes in southern Italy. With the excavation of the Heraeum at the mouth of the Silarus another great temple was brought to light, whose archaic metopes with their legendary representations constitute one of the great surprises of western Greek sculpture.[85]

In addition to the Ionians it is above all the Hellenes of southern Italy, and among them the Achaean element from the Peloponnesus, who emerge as the political and cultural leaders among sixth century Greeks. Modern theories which attempt to explain the efflorescence in all spheres of life of the Greeks in southern Italy on the basis of the Italic element as the determining influence in the Greek colonial towns from the very beginning are completely erroneous.[86] If anywhere, it is here that Greek culture and Greek intellectual life shed the rays of their influence on the world around, which in turn readily accepted the gifts of a higher civilisation, especially that of the Greek language. Up to the present day in certain localities of south Bruttium, at the slopes of the Aspromonte, the southern spurs of the Sila mountains and in the district between Lecce and Otranto the Greek dialect has preserved undeniable elements of "Dorian" (that is, pre-Byzantine) Graecisms,[87] which are to be traced back to the one-time Greek population of the country! In the sixth century the term "Magna Graecia" came into use for southern Italy. It is possible that it was intended to designate the contrast between the expan-

MAP II

The Great Greek Colonisation (750-550 B.C.)

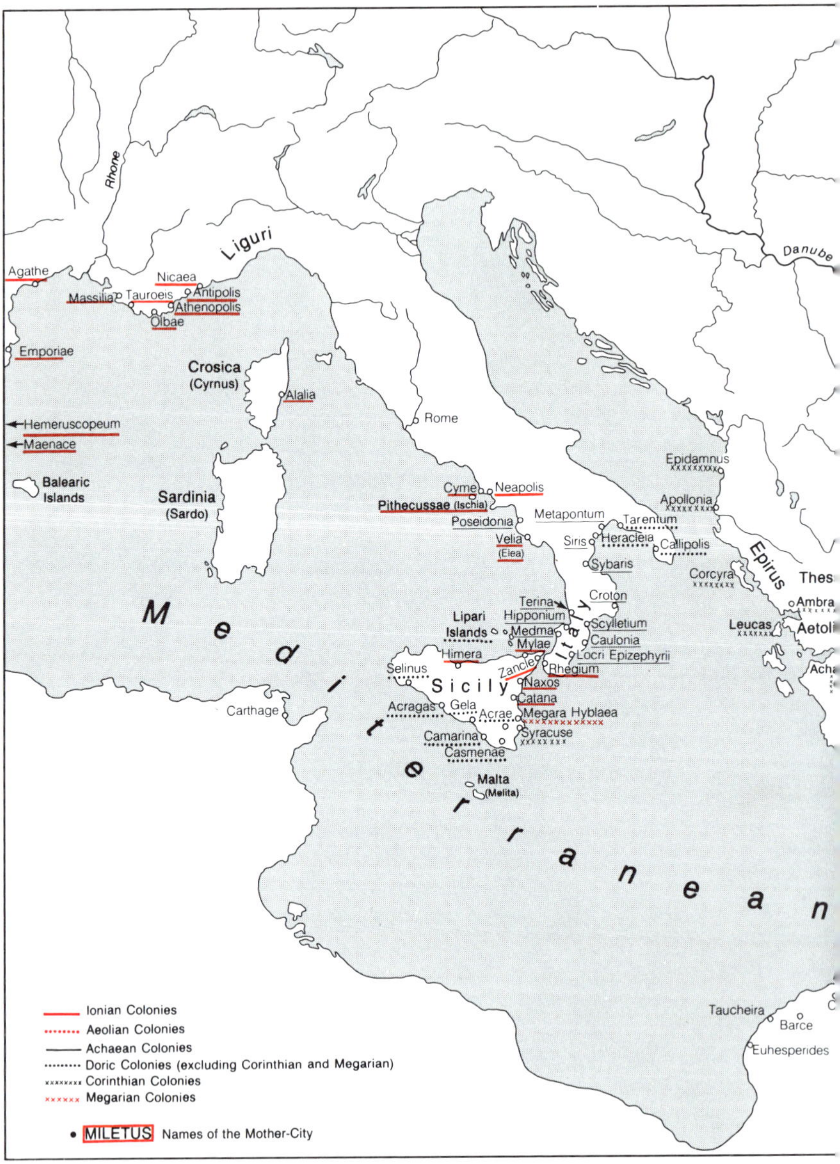

Rhone
Liguri
Danube
Agathe
Nicaea
Massilia
Tauroeis
Antipolis
Athenopolis
Olbae
Emporiae
Crosica
(Cyrnus)
Alalia
Rome
Hemeruscopeum
Maenace
Balearic
Islands
Sardinia
(Sardo)
Epidamnus
Cyme
Neapolis
Apollonia
Pithecussae (Ischia)
Metapontum
Tarentum
Poseidonia
Siris
Heracleia
Callipolis
Velia
(Elea)
Epirus
Sybaris
Corcyra
Thes
Croton
Terina
Ambra
Lipari
Islands
Hipponium
Medma
Scylletium
Leucas
Aetol
Caulonia
Mylae
Italy
Locri Epizephyrii
Himera
Zancle
Rhegium
Selinus
Sicily
Naxos
Acha
Catana
Carthage
Acragas
Gela
Acrae
Megara Hyblaea
Syracuse
Camarina
Casmenae
Malta
(Melita)
Mediterranean
Taucheira
Barce
Euhesperides
Ionian Colonies
Aeolian Colonies
Achaean Colonies
Doric Colonies (excluding Corinthian and Megarian)
Corinthian Colonies
Megarian Colonies
MILETUS Names of the Mother-City

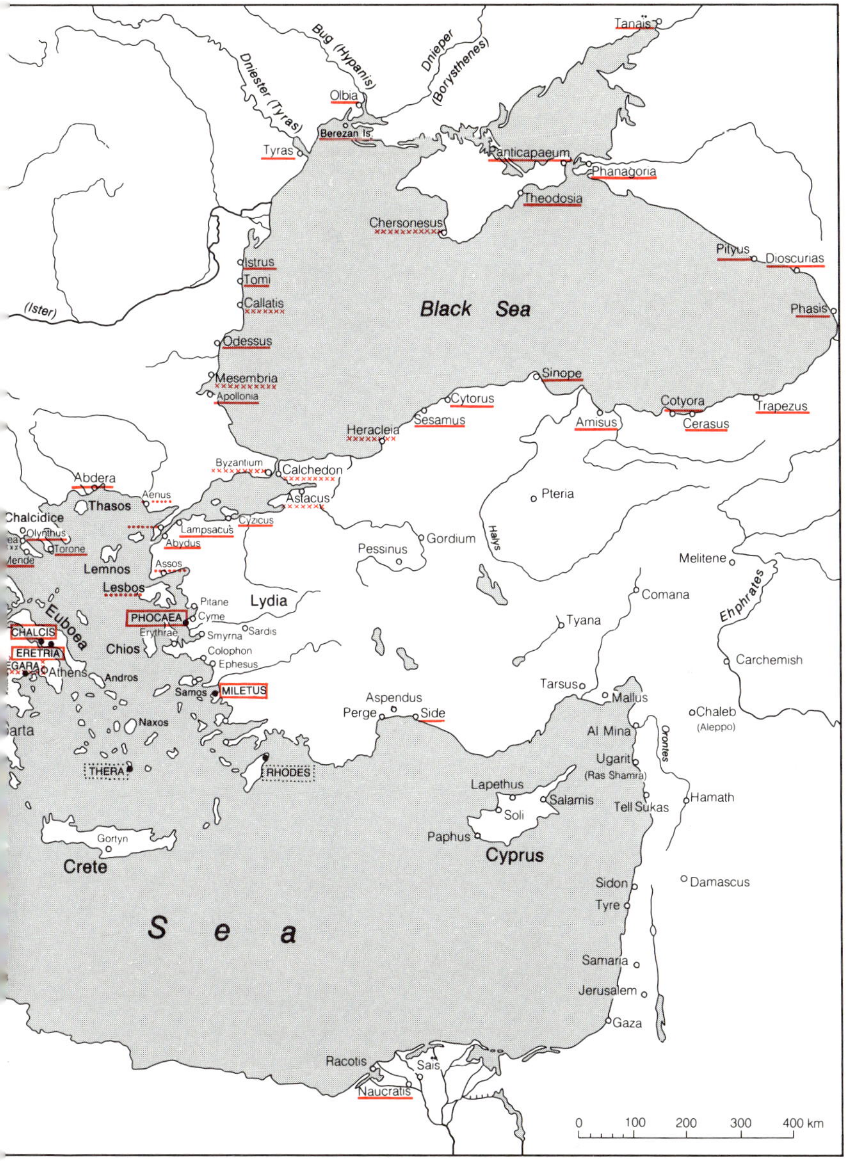

Tanais
Bug (Hypanis)
Dnieper
(Borysthenes)
Dniester (Tyras)
Olbia
Berezan Is.
Tyras
Panticapaeum
Phanagoria
Theodosia
Chersonesus
Istrus
Tomi
Callatis
(Ister)
Black Sea
Pityus
Dioscurias
Phasis
Odessus
Mesembria
Apollonia
Sinope
Cytorus
Sesamus
Heracleia
Amisus
Cotyora
Cerasus
Trapezus
Byzantium
Calchedon
Abdera
Aenus
Astacus
Pteria
Chalcidice
Thasos
Olynthus
Torone
Mende
Cyzicus
Lampsacus
Abydus
Gordium
Halys
Pessinus
Melitene
Lemnos
Assos
Lesbos
Euboea
Pitane
Cyme
Lydia
PHOCAEA
Erythrae
Smyrna
Sardis
Comana
Euphrates
Tyana
CHALCIS
ERETRIA
Chios
Colophon
Ephesus
Athens
Andros
Carchemish
Samos
MILETUS
Tarsus
Mallus
Aspendus
Perge
Side
Naxos
Chaleb
(Aleppo)
Al Mina
Orontes
THERA
RHODES
Ugarit
(Ras Shamra)
Lapethus
Salamis
Soli
Tell Sukas
Hamath
Gortyn
Crete
Paphus
Cyprus
Sidon
Damascus
Tyre
Sea
Samaria
Jerusalem
Gaza
Racotis
Sais
Naucratis
0
100
200
300
400 km

sive territory encompassed by the colonial region in southern Italy and the much more constricted conditions in the motherland.[88] It was also in southern Italy that the name *Graeci* was coined for the Hellenes—in some way connected with the Boeotian Graei.[89]

Probably in the middle or towards the end of the seventh century a Greek ship, that of Colaeus of Samos, after sailing beyond the "Pillars of Hercules" (Straits of Gibraltar), for the first time reached the open ocean and ancient Tartessus, a colony of the Iberi and the centre of the active tin trade maintained with the British Isles.[90] The Phocaeans above all took advantage of the connections with the distant West.[91] In the vicinity of the estuary of the Rhône they established the colony of Massalia (c. 600 B.C.). Its favourable location at the terminus of the great trade artery leading up the Rhône soon made it the largest and wealthiest Greek city of the western Mediterranean.[92] Its cultural influence penetrated deep into the hinterland; the Helvetii in the time of Caesar used the Greek alphabet because of the influence of the Massaliots. Traces of ancient Phocaean Graecisms also appear to be preserved in a number of dialects of southern France.[93] Along the coast of southern France as far as the Pyrenees there emerged a great many factories, established by Massalia as bases for trade with Spain. Maenace, the forerunner of Malaga, the most westerly settlement of the Greeks, was also a colonial town of the Massaliots.[94] The colonies along the sea between the Rhône and the Maritime Alps, including Nicaea (Nizza), served to carry on trade with Italy. The Phocaeans also set foot on Corsica (Cyrnus), and it almost appeared as if the western basin of the Mediterranean were about to become a landlocked sea of the Phocaeans and the Massaliots, when the coalition between the Etruscans and the Carthaginians put an end to Greek expansion with the naval battle of Alalia (c. 540 B.C.).

Greeks of almost all tribes took part in the colonisation of the West, whereas the settling of the Black Sea coasts was, according to tradition, the work of a single city, Miletus, which allegedly founded more than ninety colonial towns on the Pontus and Propontis.[95] With an initial advance into the area of the Black Sea in about the middle of the eighth century Miletus founded the commercial factories of Sinope, Trapezus and perhaps also Amisus.[96] These, however, together with Cyzicus at the Propontis, were precipitated into such affliction by the Cimmerian invasion that they had to be abandoned. The actual colonisation of the Pontus by Milesian *apoikiai* began in the course of the seventh century. Considerations of trade policy combined with the search for agricultural land. The main object was to open up the rich hinterland of southern Russia, with its trade routes connecting it equally with the Baltic amber district and with central Asia, and to establish communications with metal-rich Iberia at the Caucasus and with the region of Lake Van. The estuary branches of the large rivers in southern Russia were, like the Propontis (Sea of Marmara), famous for their wealth in fish. The inland regions provided grain as well as flax and wool in abundance, and Scythian slaves were no less eagerly sought, finding their way to Ionia on Milesian ships. The Scythians, a people of Iranian origin,[97] inhabiting the steppes of southern Russia, were friendly towards the Greeks. The distinguished Scythian nobles in particular gladly welcomed Greek art objects. Milesian vases and splendid articles of goldsmith work have been found in many tumuli (kurgans) of southern Russia. The Greek settlers for their part were impressed by the Scythian way of life, by their dress and manner of fighting, so that in many places a Graeco-Scythian civilisation was beginning to emerge. One of the oldest Milesian colonies was situated on the island of Berezan at the mouth of the Dnieper (Borysthenes). Here excavations have disclosed a large number of articles; the settlement had to be abandoned by the Greeks on account of floods.[98] It was Olbia, however, at the mouth of the Bug (Hypanis), founded at the end of the seventh century, that developed into the most important city in southern Russia.[99] Less famous and less important was the colony of Tyras (Akkerman) on the Dniester.[100] There were numerous Hellenic settlements in the Crimea,[101] the Tauric Chersonesus. The Greek settlers were particularly attracted by the mild climate and the fertile soil, which in sheltered places made even viticulture possible. In addition to Chersonesus, founded as a colony of Heracleia Pontica (a daughter-city of Megara) and which never renounced its Dorian character, Theodosia (Feodosia) and Panticapaeum (Kertch)[102] emerged here as *apoikiai* of Miletus. Across the straits on the Taman peninsula Tean settlers founded Phanagoreia about 540 B.C. At the mouth of the Don, Tanaïs sprang up as the most northerly and easterly Greek city, at the ancient frontier between Europe and Asia.

The west coast of the Pontus also became fringed with flourishing colonies: Istrus, Tomis (Constantsa), Odessus and Apollonia were cities planted by Miletus. The Milesians were, however, forced to share the possession of the Propontic coasts and the straits with the Dorian Megarians, who had arrived here before them and had founded Chalcedon and Byzantium, the former as early as the first half of the seventh century, the latter later.[103] Milesians meanwhile settled in Abydus at the Hellespont, on the island of Proconnesus and in Cius. It is not impossible that Megara and Miletus concluded a sort of *entente cordiale* in the seventh century.[104]

Even the inhospitable south coast of Thrace, inhabited by war-like tribes, became the goal of colonial endeavours in the seventh and sixth centuries. The Parians landed on the densely forested island of Thasos[105] and penetrated its hinterland (c. 680 B.C.). One thousand colonists are said to have taken part in the expedition.[106] Archilochus participated in the later battles with the natives, and trenchantly calls the colonists "the woe of all Greece." Subsequently a closer relationship continued to exist between Paros and Thasos, a circumstance to be assumed as usual between a mother-city and an *apoikia*.[107] Like many another settlement the colony of Abdera, founded by Clazomenae about 650 B.C., fell victim to attacks by Thracian tribes. Teans who had abandoned their homeland on account of the Persians resettled in the place and within a very short time it began to flourish and actively participated in the cultural life of the Greek people. Settlers from Chalcis on Euboea gave

Chalcidice its name,[108] while Potidaea was an *apoikia* of Corinth, from the time of the sea-ruling Periander. It remained the only Corinthian base in the area of the Aegean. The principal region of colonial expansion by the powerful city of the Isthmus lay in the West, in Sicily and on the coasts of the Ionian Sea—in Acarnania, Epirus and Illyria. Here many Corinthian colonies were founded, including Ambracia, Apollonia and Epidamnus, partly established in association with the daughter-city Corcyra.

In North Africa the most important Greek settlements were Cyrene in Libya and Naucratis on the Canopitic branch of the Nile.[109] After reaching the small island of Platea, colonists from Thera (c. 630 B.C.) penetrated into the interior of Libya, and in a region rich in resources they laid the foundations for the city of Cyrene.[110] In contrast to the colonies founded almost exclusively under the leadership of the Greek aristocracy, in Cyrene the monarchy, taken over from the mother-city of Thera, was continued. Its close connection with the sanctuary of Libyan Ammon in the Oasis of Siwah, its wealth in horses and sheep, its export of curative silphium plants, its daughter-cities founded in the sixth century on the plateau of Barca and on the nearby coast (Barce, Taucheira, Euhesperides)—all these enabled Cyrene to develop into an imposing power in Libya, one which even could assert itself against Egypt.

The second colonisation marks a crucial turning point in the political and cultural life of the Greek people. By giving to their settlements the form of "community state" wherever they established a new homeland, the Greeks carried the idea of the autonomous, self-sufficient polis abroad into distant lands and continents. In this period the polis first superseded the tribal state and for the first time became the prevailing and characteristic political form throughout the Greek world. Overcoming the constricted conditions of the motherland and constant association with foreign cultures and peoples—Scythians and inhabitants of Asia Minor, Thracians and Illyrians, Sicels and Italics, Ligurians and Iberians, Libyans and Egyptians—whetted the sensitivity of the Greeks to their own and to things foreign. It taught them to regard themselves as a single great community in language and culture, customs and religion, in the face of which tribal differences receded more and more into the background. Greek culture and Greek religion migrated to foreign lands and the Greeks repeatedly recognised in foreign deities attributes with which they were familiar in their own gods. As high as the Greeks in many places towered over the natives, whom they called "*Barbaroi*" for their non-Greek language, they none the less established many lasting ties with the native aristocracies through intermarriage, as in Scythia and Libya.[111] A thousand bonds, however, united the colonists with their homeland. It was the particular pride of the overseas communities to send their youth to the great Olympian festival in the motherland. Cyrene and the Sicilian communities in particular were able to boast of an imposing number of Olympian victors. The world had now become larger for the Greeks than in earlier times. Antimenidas, the brother of Alcaeus of Lesbos, together with other associates, served King Nebuchadnezzar of Babylon as mercenaries (Alcaeus fr. 50 Diehl). Cuneiform texts from the south fortress of Babylon contain the names of Ionian craftsmen,[112] and during the reign of Psammetichus II (at the beginning of the sixth century) Carian and Greek mercenaries immortalised themselves on the Colossi of Abu Simbel in Nubia.[113]

Here and there distinctively archaic features in culture and way of life appear, in contrast to the rapid growth of the colonial towns. Thus through the mediation of Ionian colonists typical elements of Mycenaean (!) civilisation recur in southern Russia, as, for instance, the vaulted tombs and large quantities of gold jewellery used as funerary offerings.[114] Gold masks have been found in Scythian royal tombs from even as late as the third century A.D.

The frequent question whether the Greek settlements were agricultural or commercial colonies is in this general form incorrectly formulated. It is much more relevant to consider each individual case by itself.[115] And in forming any conclusion on the harbours of antiquity[116] it must not be overlooked that in many cases, due to the small size and limited draught of the ships, a flat shore would have been adequate as a landing place. The differentiation made between warships and merchant vessels beginning about 700 B.C. suggests, *inter alia*, that a certain intensification in trade took place during the archaic period, but it is clearly not until the time of Peisistratus and Polycrates that we meet a real leap in Greek overseas trade.[117] Only then, in the middle of the sixth century, that is, in conjunction with the spread of coinage, trade assumed those forms which determined the economic character of the Greek world until deep into the fourth century. An extensive overseas trade in particularly valuable goods, however, is attested as early as the seventh century by finds of Corinthian vases in Italy and Milesian vases in southern Russia. And more recent investigations[118] have proven the existence of Attic black-figure vases for the first half of the sixth century in the regions from Massalia to central Anatolia, from southern Russia to Naucratis, regardless of whether these vases were carried there aboard Attic, Corinthian or other ships.

4
POLITICS AND SOCIETY IN THE COLONISATION PERIOD

THE ARISTOCRACY AND THE LAND

The internal development of Greece and of Greek society during the period of the great colonisation felt essentially no decisive influence from forces outside Greece. Aristocracy yielded to the timocratic hoplite polis, and this to a quasi-democratic form of state as, for instance, in Chios (soon after 600 B.C.) or later in Athens at the end of the sixth century. The shifts came from internal social conflicts as well as military exigencies, and all these led to the broadening of the class base of military service. As later in ancient Republican Rome, so in Greece the constitution and the military organisation mutually determined each other. In many cases the development was directed by prominent individuals, powerful tyrants and lawgivers like Zaleucus, Charondas, Dracon and Solon. Although there were differences in timing of the internal developments of the various Greek communities, with the Ionian cities most progressive—certain basic features can be combined into a total general picture. This picture represents most of Greece, but the specific development of Sparta and Athens diverges most from it.

The Greek economy in the archaic period was based on agrarian principles, with all but primitive forms. The two-field system, which continued in Greece down into the fourth century B.C., meant that each year a disproportionately large amount of land remained untilled. The iron ploughshare was unknown to Hesiod and, as during the migration period, in the entire west of Greece pasturing prevailed. The introduction of coinage into the Greek world, at first in Ionia[1] in the seventh century and then in certain communities of the motherland like Aegina, Corinth and Athens, from approximately 600 B.C. onwards, did little to alter the basic agrarian character of the economy. The smaller coin denominations necessary to a more animated local and inter-local trade did not exist. The gradual absorption of small and medium farmers by the large landowners and widespread enslavement by debt were characteristic phenomena of the age. For the first time in Greek history slavery assumed economic importance. The first Greek state to employ slaves purchased abroad was Chios, but a gradual increase in slavery for farming and industry is also evident in the rest of Greece.[2] It developed into disastrous proportions. Discerning tyrants like Periander of Corinth attempted to curb the growth of slavery, but in general they had little success, as later developments show.

By the eighth century political leadership was exclusively in the hands of the Greek nobility (v.s.p. 30 f.). Monarchy was supplanted in almost the whole of the Greek world by the rule of the noble families, the Bacchiads in Corinth, the Penthilids in Mytilene and the Basilids in Ephesus and Erythrae. In certain communities the perpetual monarchy was replaced by a limited, annual kingship, as, for instance, in Nisaean Megara and Athens. In Athens the hereditary monarchy yielded to a limited ten-year monarchy about the middle of the eighth century, and this in turn to the annual archonship in 683/2 B.C. (the beginning of the Attic archon lists).[2] A concomitant of the change in terminology—*archon* instead of *basileus*—was an essential reduction in authority. To assist the archon the polemarch (military colonel) was placed in charge of warfare, and the six-member board of *thesmothetai* (lawgivers) in charge of justice. The king (*basileus*), whose honour, rendered sacred by tradition, one did not venture to eliminate completely, together with the queen (*basilinna*), retained only his sacred functions (cf. the *rex sacrorum* in Rome). But in contrast to Rome, the monarchy was never outlawed anywhere in Greece, evidence that the transition from monarchy to aristocracy proceeded along evolutionary lines.

The rule of the Greek nobility, resting on the superior economic and social position of the aristocracy, was a distinctly caste rule.[4] First and foremost the noble families united in their control the greatest amount of land.[5] A special characteristic of the noble class was horse raising—"horse feeders" was the epithet which the proud nobles of Chalcis and Euboea assumed for themselves. Armed with sword and lance and protected by shield and costly armour, the nobles went mounted into battle; they dismounted for combat in order to make trial of their opponents in agonistic fashion, since the use of long-range weapons such as arrows and slings was prohibited in this type of fighting.[6] The panhellenic involvement of the nobility becomes most conspicuous in the Lelantine War, the ten-year struggle in the first half of the seventh century between Chalcis and Eretria over the wide fertile plain on the island of Euboea.[7] The nobles of Chalcis were supported by auxiliaries from Thessaly and Samos, while Eretria received assistance from Miletus.

In this kind of fighting the army of the free commoners could not prevail against the heavily armed horse, and as a consequence the broad masses figured neither in war nor in the Council. In many places the small farmers sank to the level of serfs of the large landowners, and it is possible that widespread serfdom[8] in Greece had some of its roots in the confiscation of land leased to peasants. Greek aristocratic society to a great degree looked down upon the masses with arrogant disdain. The nickname "Dustyfoots"[9] was coined for that part of the population in Epidaurus excluded from the number of full-blooded citizens, who were limited to only 180 members. Hesiod of Ascra (c. 700 B.C.) has portrayed the many troubles and adverse circumstances characterising the every-day life of the small farmers of Boeotia. It was a hopeless life, filled with toil and disappointments, and only an unshakeable faith in divine justice could comfort people in the face of the adversities of earthly existence. The hard struggle of the peasants for survival had its counterpart in the life of the aristocracy, which consisted of contests, chariot races, hunting and leisure. It is no accident that in the seventh century the games at Olympia, and later also the Pythian, Nemean and Isthmian games, acquired panhellenic significance.[10] Here the nobility, allied by extensive marriage ties and hospitality, gathered in order to realise their ideals of life in athletic contests. The fame of the Olympian games was at the same time the fame of the aristocracy. The political exclusiveness of the ruling aristocratic caste is illustrated in the restriction of full-blooded citizenship to a closed number, often to the "thousand" or the "hundred houses."[11] These terms derive originally from the military sphere, and confirm the view of Aristotle, who maintains that the aristocratic *politeia* is embodied in the military caste.[12]

When the monarchy was abolished all the important offices in the state fell to the nobles. The fact, however, that the aristocracy assumed complete control of the legal system had particularly important consequences. The Eupatrids in Athens, as Plutarch states (*Life of Theseus* 25), were the experts on divine matters (that is, they held the priestly offices), they furnished the archons, were teachers of the laws and interpreters of divine and earthly justice. In many instances the result was the formation of a regular class justice under which the broad masses, the free commoners, including primarily the small farmers, suffered greatly. In the simile of the hawk and the nightingale Hesiod gave pointed expression to these unjust conditions. The affliction of the small farmer in Boeotia, who is not given his due, is reflected in the expression of the "gift-devouring kings."[13] The term refers to the aristocratic judges who abused the rights of the ordinary man. The latter could appeal only to the wrath of Zeus.

There are, however, some brighter features to the Greek aristocracy in the eighth and seventh centuries. The direction given to the many efforts in colonisation brought great fame to the nobility, who furnished the leaders for the masses of land-seeking peasants.[14] In many Greek communities, a Council composed of members from the aristocracy was of great political importance. This Council, like the Areopagus at Athens, introduced a degree of constancy into the fluctuating political life, providing a stabilising counterpart to annually changing officers.

On the whole, however, the aristocratic state in the archaic period, which reached its climax in the first half of the seventh century, was characterised by distinctly conservative features. The actual cause of its decline was its inability to adapt itself to new conditions of life, like the transformation of the Hellenic economy in the colonisation period. Although this transformation was very slow, it was all the more certain. The aristocratic state, based essentially on landed property, was left behind by commercial developments. These developments first resulted in a state organised around a broader military base, and later more democratic political forms, which in many cases passed through the intermediate stage of tyranny.

The decisive turn in developments was precipitated by the military system. At the beginning of the seventh century a change in tactics brought about the compact unit of the combatting phalanx,[15] and before 600 B.C. that had become the prevailing form in almost all Greek states. If in the past the individual warriors from among the nobles had, despite their small numbers, decided the issue of battle, now the circle of active combatants had become greatly extended. What was most important, the issue was now decided by the mass of hoplites welded together into the phalanx, by whose unflinching discipline the attacks of not only the individual warriors but also of the chariot squadrons were crushed. The advanced level of metalwork now enabled the Greeks to manufacture those weapons which the masses of the armed foot required: spear and sword, round shield (though protecting the breast only, it was all the lighter to manipulate), armour and bronze greaves. The phalanx tactics resulted in a complete transformation in the science of war, and beyond this no less altered the previous way of life. If the nobles at one time fought for fame and booty,[16] the task of the hoplites was to fulfil their duty. They had to keep their position in the ranks and were not allowed to forsake their comrades, not even if it should cost them their lives, for the destruction of the phalanx was certain if the enemy succeeded in piercing the ranks. Uninterrupted training and the strictest discipline, based on a strong feeling of solidarity, moulded the phalanx into an extremely efficient tactical body such as western warfare had not hitherto known. Sparta was the first important state which, due to the crisis caused by the Second Messenian War, changed from individual warriors to the phalanx tactics. Other Greeks, acting in accordance with the laws of historical development, followed the Spartans. In Sparta the introduction of the phalanx tactics led to a distinctive military state, while in many other places throughout Greece it brought the formation of the "hoplite politeia," represented by those citizens who were capable of equipping themselves.

An example of the new military system is the so-called class division of Solon. With its grouping of the citizens, however, into three principal classes—*hippeis, zeugitai, thetes*—it is certainly pre-Solonian and belongs to the last decades of the seventh century.[17] In this division the phalanx, composed of the *zeugitai*, the masses of citizen farmers,[18] already appears alongside the *hippeis* who formed the aristocratic corps of horse. Those citizens who owned no property, the *thetes*, followed the army as light-armed troops, javelin-throwers and slingers, as craftsmen and baggage supervisors. What Solon did was to employ the existing military class division as the basis for a political classification of the Athenian citizen body.

Another essential element in the gradual democratisation of the aristocracy was the codification of current law. Although a Near Eastern stimulus (via Ionia?) can scarcely be ignored, Greek legislation in the seventh and sixth centuries is none the less a genuine product of the Hellenic mind. Still, with the codification of law, which now replaced a form of justice hitherto transmitted only orally, a foreign element entered into Hellenic cultural life. The Greeks understood how to assimilate this new foreign element into their culture, as they did in so many other cases. Thus they not only laid the foundation for European law but also paved the way for an epoch-making development in western law and legal thinking for all time to come. That the life of the state as well as that of the individual citizen could be regulated and governed by expressly created laws was a genuinely Hellenic idea. The individual clauses of the laws governing luxury, sensuality, extravagance, and even the law governing funerals, which were becoming ever more pompous, reveal the stirrings of a democratic spirit, a spirit which openly challenged the very life forms of the aristocracy. It is consequently no wonder that the opposition of the nobles, who had control of justice, could be broken only after serious internal struggles.

What was thought to be known in antiquity about such lawgivers as Zaleucus of Locri in southern Italy (before the middle of the seventh century), Charondas of Sicilian Catana (sixth century?) and Dracon of Athens (c. 624 B.C.),[19] partly belongs in the realm of legend. There is nothing, however, to justify explaining the lawgivers completely as mythical figures, in the way that hypercritical scholars have done.[20] The recording of the so-called Code of Gortyn (on Crete) is of particular importance for the knowledge of ancient Greek law. Although the extant epigraphical version admittedly dates back only to the first half of the fifth century, it nevertheless reflects considerably older legal institutions. There are, moreover, original fragments of older statutes, preserved on the walls of the temple of Apollo Pythius in Gortyn.

The Greek law codes reproduce current law based on custom, naturally with more or less important modifications by the lawgivers. Behind the individual clauses, chiefly in criminal law, may be seen the aim to fix penalties legally and thus remove them from the realm of judicial arbitrary decisions. In many cases educative designs are unmistakable. New laws pertaining to obligations, the right of succession and slavery were particularly numerous. Penalties were actually of inhuman severity. According to the code of Dracon, the penalty for theft in Athens was death.[21] If anyone fell into arrears with his debts, he, together with his family, became the property of his creditor. Dracon's differentiation between murder and unintentional killing (homicide) was a great step forward. Murder was penalised by death, manslaughter by banishment. The time in which the relations of the murdered person pursued the principle of revenge was now a thing of the past, and so private blood feuds, which had often led to shocking murder, were eliminated by state administration of justice. This too was a further indication that the idea of the state was gaining ground, gradually overcoming family ties. Sparta, however, took no part in codification of law, in contrast to kindredly Dorian Crete. The alleged provisions of Lycurgus included the prohibition to have recourse to written laws.[22]

THE GREEK TYRANTS

Greek tyranny emerged from the internal quarrels and party factions of the ruling noble class. It embodies the breakthrough of the individual personality into the field of politics. The term *tyrannis* is certainly non-Greek, perhaps Aegean (?).[23] The word appears for the first time in Greek literature in Archilochus (fr. 22 Diehl). From approximately the middle of the seventh century the great tyrants controlled Greek history for almost an entire century, at first in the Greek states of the Isthmus (Corinth, Megara, Sicyon), and then in Ionia.[24] Athens actually did not undergo her period of tyranny until the middle and second half of the sixth century, with Peisistratus and his house (v.i.p. 80 ff.)

The tyrants gave to the Greek state what it most required: a centralised, resolute control of supreme power in both internal and foreign policy, which had previously become fragmented and in many cases the tool of aristocratic family interests. In consequence tyranny marks a considerable activation of energy and power in the Hellenic states, on a scale hitherto unknown. The tyrants aimed not only to rule over the citizen body of their own polis but in addition, indeed above all, to subjugate other communities. To attain this objective they strove to consolidate their own positions through political alliances and by establishing economic relations with foreign states. All Greek tyrants without exception pursued a distinct family policy which skilfully combined the interests of the states dependent on them. The tyrants understood even better than the nobility how to achieve mutual support through intermarriage and how to establish a community of interests among the ruling personalities.

The picture of early tyranny displays great variety and diversity.[25] Even the later hatred against the tyrants did not succeed in wiping out the memory of the great figures from the early period. In Ionian Miletus *tyrannis* came to power with Thrasybulus in the struggle against the Lydians at the turn of the seventh century.[26] In contrast to this, the Ephesian despot Melas was the son-in-law of Alyattes, king of Lydia. In Samos the *tyrannis* of Damoteles came from bitter fighting among the noble land owners, and was, however, soon overthrown (c. 600 B.C.). In Mytilene on Lesbos Pittacus, as *aisymnetes* and recognised arbiter,[27] ultimately restored order after vigorous inner conflicts, following the *tyrannis* of Melanchrus, Myrsilus and Meleager.

In the motherland the cities of the Isthmus fell to tyrants in the seventh century. In Sicyon the family of the Orthagorids ruled for almost a whole century;[28] under Cleisthenes it reached the climax of its power.[29] Aristocratic suitors from the entire Hellenic world contested for Cleisthenes' daughter Agariste, and in the end the Alcmeonid Megacles from Athens escorted her home (c. 575 B.C.).[30] In Corinth the tyrant Cypselus took the helm after the overthrow of the aristocratic oligarchy of the Bacchiads (according to tradition, in 657 B.C.).[31] Under his son, Periander,[32] Corinth reached the indisputable climax of its economic and political power in the archaic period. About the turn of the seventh century the ceramic industry in Corinth began to undergo a vigorous growth (for which the discoveries of the Americans in the Cerameicus of the city and those of British excavations in the Corinthian harbour Perachora provide the best evidence[33]). Distinctly imperialistic features, otherwise foreign in early Greek history, appear in the position of the Corinthian colonies. They remained in strict political association with the mother-city, as may be seen in the colonies on the coast of Epirus and Illyria. Corinth coerced her colony Corcyra—according to Thucydides (I, 13.4) the war between Corinth and Corcyra about 600 B.C. was the first naval battle between Greeks—controlled the colony of Potidaea on Chalcidice and subjected Epidaurus. Eduard Meyer has not unjustifiably called Periander the most powerful ruler in the Greek world about 600 B.C.

The tyrants paid particular attention to economics, although they were hardly great tradesmen, manufacturers and royal merchants.[34] Apart from the limited scope and restricted intensity of Hellenic economic life in the archaic period, the economy was still without doubt predominantly agrarian (v.s.p. 59 f.). By prohibiting the purchase of slaves and by making idleness liable to punishment,[35] Periander no doubt intended to secure the profitableness of free labour, to promote private and state prosperity and to divert the citizens from futile schemes. The tyrant put an end to the eternal feuding between the landowners and the proletariat which fluctuated between city and country by forbidding the seasonal influx of farm labourers into the city. It is no accident that the imposing old Doric sculptures from Corcyra belong to the era of Periander.[36] This island, an important intermediate station for Corinthian trade with the West, also shared significantly in the flowering of the mother-city.

The tyrants in many cases acted as champions of the broad masses of the *demos*—the people. Thus, when viewed from the vantage point of a later period, *tyrannis* actually assumes the appearance of an "anticipated democracy" (Jacob Burckhardt). This applies, for instance, both to the Orthagorids and to Theagenes of Megara,[37] whom the poorer section of the population had raised to power. In many cases the tyrants (as Peisistratus later in Attica) promoted rural cults, such as that of Dionysus, who as patron of viniculture enjoyed particular veneration among the rural population. The hostile attitude of the tyrants to the nobility is shown, for example, in the edict issued by Cleisthenes in Sicyon forbidding the reciting of the Homeric poems. This measure struck at the very roots of aristocratic education. The conflicts between the tyrants and the noble families steadily increased the number of Greek exiles.[38] They were to be found everywhere and, constituting an element of unrest, were always ready to return to their native cities at times of upheaval and there to meet violence with violence. Military service led many of them into distant lands, for they were willing to risk their lives in the interests of anyone who could pay for their services.

In the west of the Greek world tyranny also struck firm roots, at first in Sicily, namely in Leontini (Panaetius about 615 B.C.). The most important figure among the western despots, however, was Phalaris of Agrigentum (c. 570 B.C.);[39] his brutality was on the lips of all. (The once so famous letters of Phalaris have been irrefutably proven spurious by the British philologist Richard Bentley in his researches from 1697 and 1699—the first major accomplishment of Classical Philology.)[40] It was of great importance to Greek history that Athens did not come under the rule of tyrants until late, and Sparta on the other hand not at all. Sparta and Athens are also the only Greek states whose internal development in the period of the colonisation can be traced in its main features, though the evidence even for this is very fragmentary.

EARLY SPARTA

The peculiar character of the Spartan political system was the result of a gradual development, *not* the work of a single legislator. Although a certain number of scholars[41] hold the mythical figure Lycurgus and the ephor Cheilon responsible for the fundamental transformation of the Spartan state in the sixth century, neither can reliably be associated with any changes whatsoever. The form of the Spartan constitution towards the end of the sixth century is the result of a century-long "state of siege," in which the few Spartans found themselves confronted by the vast number of conquered subjects. The basic features of Spartan political life are named in the Great Rhetra, the oldest document of Greek history, which stems from at least the beginning of the seventh century, perhaps even from the end of the eighth (v.i.p. 411 f.). These are the dual monarchy, the "Council of Elders" composed of thirty members (including the two kings), and the military assembly, the *Apella*. In the early period all political decisions of any importance came from the co-operation of these three. The origin of the peculiar dual kingship, which was hereditary in the houses of the Agiads and the Eurypontids, is shrouded in darkness,[42] although there are certain, partially valid parallels elsewhere in Greece.[43] The "Council of Elders," perhaps composed of the heads of the most prominent families in the early period (cf. the Roman *patres*), acted as advisors to the kings who, like the Roman consuls, both possessed the royal *imperium*—power. The Council also had certain powers in the field of criminal law. The position of the members corresponds approximately to "the first of the Macedonians," who not infrequently appear alongside the military assembly in Macedonia.[44]

The Great Rhetra[45] reflects the reduction of the power of the kings in favour of the people. It marks the end of a period of internal conflict in the course of which the Spartan military monarchy lost its predominant position. The exact date is unknown; it is in particular completely impossible to connect a reported response of the Delphic oracle with the alleged incorporation of Amyclae into the Spartan commonwealth early in the eighth century, as has been suggested. The special importance of the Great Rhetra lies in the fact that it gives to the *damos*, that is, to the military community of the Spartiates, the final decision in all matters. Establishing regular intervals for summoning the *Apella*—the assembly—suggests that this was not the case before. Subordinate to the provision to hold regular meetings of the assembly is the command of the Great Rhetra to establish a sanctuary to Zeus Syllanius and Athena Syllania, to form tribes and obes and to inaugurate a *Gerousia*—the Council of Elders—with a membership of thirty (including the *archagetai*, the kings). The *Gerousia* was an innovation. It has been said—but there is doubt here—that its establishment was a curtailment of the rights of the military assembly.[46] The epithets of Zeus and Athena have not as yet been clarified.[47] In view of the lack of concrete statements in the Rhetra, all conjectures with regard to the "forming of tribes and obes" would appear to be built on sand. Since the original Dorian tribes (*Hylleis, Dymanes, Pamphyloi*) are attested by Tyrtaeus (fr. 1, Diehl) as special divisions of the Spartan army as late as the Second Messenian War, this reference can only be associated with a reorganisation of *these* tribes. The obes are connected with the villages of which the unfortified Sparta was composed, and they formed the original class of Spartan full-blooded citizens whose life was concentrated in Sparta.

Sparta itself emerged from the union of five villages, including Amyclae, which lay about one hour's travelling distance from the city. This event took place about 800 B.C. at the latest. The Great Rhetra does not mention the ephors. Originally they were religious dignitaries, "observers of the heavens,"[48] and did not become political magistrates until the Spartan state had advanced along the path of democratisation. Ultimately they could even call the kings to account. As exponents of the *damos* they increasingly curbed the power of the kings, particularly from the sixth century onwards, until they had restricted them essentially to military command. The beginning of the ephor lists (754/3 B.C.) dates the rise of the ephorate in the eighth century.[49] Whether the number of five ephors is to be connected with the five villages of Sparta remains doubtful.[50]

Although the number of citizens in the early period was indeed considerable (c. 9000-10,000 capable of bearing arms), it none the less constituted only a small minority in comparison with the numerically much greater pre-Dorian population in Laconia. Through the subjugation of Messenia the numerical relationship became even less favourable for the Spartans. There was, besides the Spartiates, the full-blooded citizens, the large number of Lacedaemonian residents—*perioikoi*. These were distributed over approximately one hundred towns, and lived chiefly in the mountainous fringeland of Laconia and in the south and north of Messenia.[51] The *perioikoi* too were Dorians[52] and, like the Spartans, members of the state of the Lacedaemonians. Their contingents formed the largest part of the Spartan army, but they were excluded from participation in the *Apella* and from the Spartan system of state education. The situation of the *helots*,[53] the masses of the pre-Dorian population of Laconia, and of the ethnically heterogeneous population of Messenia was entirely different. As a type of state slave,[54] they were bound to the soil and obliged to pay taxes to the Spartan lords. The ground rent imposed upon them—in Messenia half the total harvest[55]—enabled the Spartan lords in Sparta, far from their property, to lead a military camp life, maintaining and continuously increasing Spartan military strength.

The foundation of the state was the Spartan system of education—the *agoge*. There was almost nothing private about the life of a full-blooded Spartan citizen, a way of life fundamentally different from that of all other Greeks. Spartan society has at all times, even in antiquity, been regarded as something foreign and unnatural. Primitive forms of life from the migration period and the pressure of constant readiness for battle on the part of the Spartan troops led to a distinctive military communal life—to which no counterpart may be found in the whole of ancient history.[56] Like the Spartan state, the specific forms of Spartan community life were the result of a longer development. It is not impossible that the serious peril of the Second Messenian War at the end of the seventh century contributed decisively to the formation of the *agoge*.

A unique contrast may be noted between the moulding of the military form of life and the openness of the Spartans towards the achievements of foreign cultures in the seventh and also partly in the sixth centuries B.C. A great many finds of archaic miniature works of art in the Eurotas Valley, monumental structures such as the temple of Artemis Orthia (c. 600 B.C.) and the throne of Apollo from Amyclae,[57] the presence of numerous poets, including the musician Terpander of Lesbos and the lyric poet Alcman of Sardis (seventh century), the celebration of joyful festivals of the gods,[58] above all the Carneia and the Hyacinthia[59]—all this testifies to the fact that Sparta ardently participated in the rich cultural life of the time and was especially open to the eastern stimulating influence of Lydia[60] and Ionia. Enthusiastic Spartan participation in the Olympian games from the end of the eighth to the middle of the sixth century also shows Spartan association with the life of the whole of Greece.

From approximately the end of the seventh century onwards, gloomy shades begin to appear in the colourful picture. The population decreased, and to match, the Spartan government increased their determination to maintain Sparta's position in the Peloponnesus, even at the price of everything that had brought wealth and splendour to its citizens. The achievements of the Spartans in the military sphere were the more significant. Continual training and constant readiness welded the Spartan army into a powerful instrument, small in numbers but all the more flexible. It was an army such as the ancient world had seen before only among the Assyrians. The war poems of Tyrtaeus proclaim the change from the tactics of the individual warrior to the compact phalanx, but the conversion to hoplite tactics was probably not completed until the latter part of the seventh century. Equality on the battlefield, such as the phalanx demanded, must result in equal rights in civil life. In consequence the Spartans, who shared in the common meal proudly called themselves the "Equals," even though the economic differences between individuals may still have been extremely important.

Anyone who could not afford his contribution of the amount required for providing the common meal[61] fell into the throngs of the "Inferiors,"[62] excluded from the community of full-blooded citizens. By establishing the whole system of education on a military foundation, including gymnastics, the ideal of unconditional fulfilment of duty, obedience and the renouncing of possessions was instilled into Spartans during boyhood.[63] Torn from home and parents at the age of seven, a boy grew up under the supervision of older youths. At fourteen he moved up into the class of *Eirenes*,[64] and at twenty into the community of warriors, which from then on constituted his sphere of life. Marriage and family, for which little room remained, in the main served only to produce new blood. In consequence paederasty was cultivated the more ardently in Sparta and in fact even became a recognised element in Spartan life.

The dark side of the Spartan state first became evident in the sixth century with the most rigid supervision of the Helots through the institution of a secret service, the expulsion of all foreigners, prohibition of gold and silver coins (in their place the famous iron money circulated in Sparta as small change), the refusal to participate in the cultural life of Greece—these measures gave Sparta nothing less than the appearance of a "reactionary military and police state" (U. Wilcken).

ATHENS

How completely different were internal developments in Athens! Through the Solonian reforms and the *tyrannis* of Peisistratus and his sons, Athens achieved an *isonomia*—"equality under the laws"—allowing the individual citizen extensive scope for his varied capabilities. The Athenians evolved a constitution which later generations called "democracy," rather than a military state. At the earliest point to which we can penetrate into the history of Athens we find a distinct aristocratic state with all political and religious authority in the hands of the great noble families. In consequence, until late in the seventh century, the history of Athens and Attica is less the history of a state than that of the great noble families—the Alcmeonids, Medontids, Eteobutads, Lycomids, Philaids and many others.[65] Because our sources are limited—apart from the archon lists there were no contemporary records in either the seventh or the sixth century—general social developments can be traced in outline only, partly through inferences from institutions of a later period.

Towards the end of the seventh century the greatest amount of cultivable land is found in the hands of the great noble families, a phenomenon stabilising almost all economic power in the hands of the nobility. The broad mass of the population, the free wage earners (thetes) and a considerable number of the former small farmers found themselves in strict dependence on the great noble landowners. They were either bound under obligation as debtors or else had sunk to the status of bondsmen. For the use of land they had to hand over to their landlords a tax amounting to a sixth part of the harvest (the so-called *hektemoroi*, a term which in later times was no longer understood, since the institution was apparently abolished by Solon).[66] The cruel severity of the obligation law —inability to pay brought the enslavement of the person and family of the debtor—must have contributed substantially to an intolerable accentuation of social conflicts in Attica.

When the young Olympian victor Cylon,[67] supported by a mercenary force which his father-in-law, the tyrant Theagenes of Megara, had placed at his disposal, made an attempt to establish a tyranny in Athens (in the year 636 or 632 B.C.), he failed, and ultimately not least because the Attic small farmers remained loyal to the noble families. Cylon escaped, but his followers were torn from the altars and killed, on the orders of the ruling archon Megacles, of the family of the Alcmeonids, an outrage for which the Alcmeonidae and Athens were to pay dearly.

With the codification of current law in Athens by Dracon (about 624 B.C.) one of the most important demands of the broad masses was met.[68] The idea of the state was gaining ground. It is uncertain whether there was a constitutional reform connected with the legislation of Dracon. What we find concealed in the so-called "Code of Dracon" in the *Constitution of Athens* of Aristotle (§4) is undoubtedly the reflection of later ideas, particularly the oligarchic endeavours of the year 411 B.C., so that it cannot be regarded as authentic.[69] It was not Dracon but the young Solon, a generation later, who directed internal developments at Athens along new lines. He is not only the first person of flesh and blood in Attic history but the first statesman on European soil deserving this name.

Solon's life and work[70] fell in a time of crisis in the Greek world. About 600 B.C. trade and industry began to flourish. The gradual spread of coinage in Greece marked a notable change in the prevailing agrarian economy.[71] Not until then did Athens engage in the great movement of Greek colonial expansion. The first attempt to assure herself of a particularly favourable base for maritime trade on the Asiatic coast of the Hellespont, at Sigeum, led to fighting with the Mytilenaeans towards the end of the seventh century.[72] About 600 B.C. the war was ended temporarily by the arbitration of Periander. The Athenians retained Sigeum, while the Mytilenaeans kept Achilleum, an outer fort, which prevented the Athenians from enjoying direct access to the Hellespont. Relations between Athens and neighbouring Megara were also tense. Both struggled for decades to gain possession of Salamis, until Peisistratus ultimately won the island for Athens.[73] The first steps on the road to maritime expansion by Athens were the most difficult, for she was not able to make up the great head-start which the others had gained. Corinth and Megara in particular had so consolidated their position by extensive trade relations that in contrast to them Athens at first played only a comparatively secondary rôle. Towards the close of the seventh century she could as yet by no means be considered a sea power. (The meaning of the forty-eight Naucraries into which Attica was divided is controversial. Perhaps they derived from a division of Attica into districts to protect the coast against pirates.[74])

For Athens to become active in foreign politics, a reorganisation of

1. Dimini.

2. Troy. Section of the fortification walls of Troy VI.

3. Cnossus. Site of the palace. View towards the west.

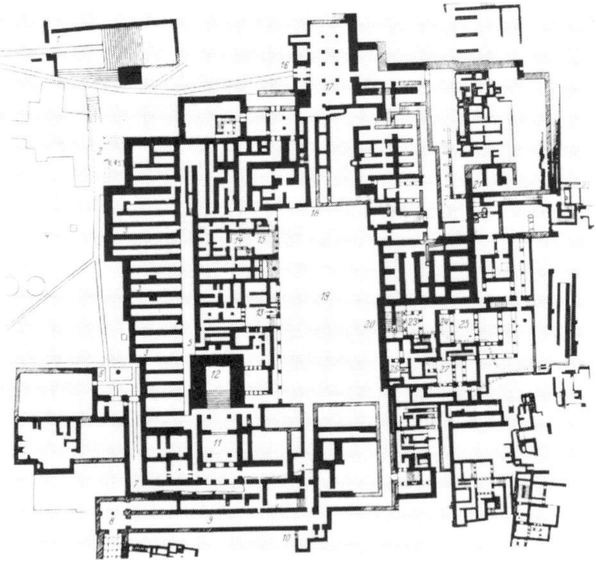

4. Cnossus. Plan of the palace.

5. Fresco painting from Akrotiri, Thera. Boxing boys. National Museum, Athens.

6. Fresco painting from Akrotiri, Thera. Swallows in flight. National Museum, Athens.

7. Mycenae. View of the palace (foreground) and the upper Argolid.

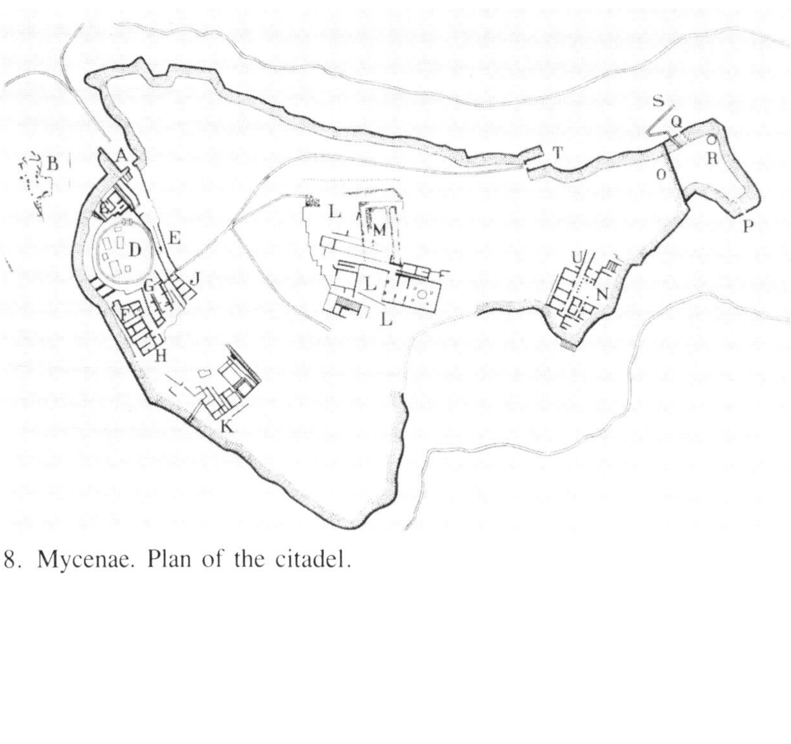

8. Mycenae. Plan of the citadel.

9. Linear B Tablet from Cnossus.

10. Amphora by Exekias. Achilles and Ajax playing a game. Vatican, Rome.

11. Mycenae. The lion gate (detail).

12. Mycenae. Entrance to the so-called Treasury of Atreus.

13. Tiryns. Mycenaean fortification wall.

14. Lower Pindus range (in Arcadia). View towards the west.

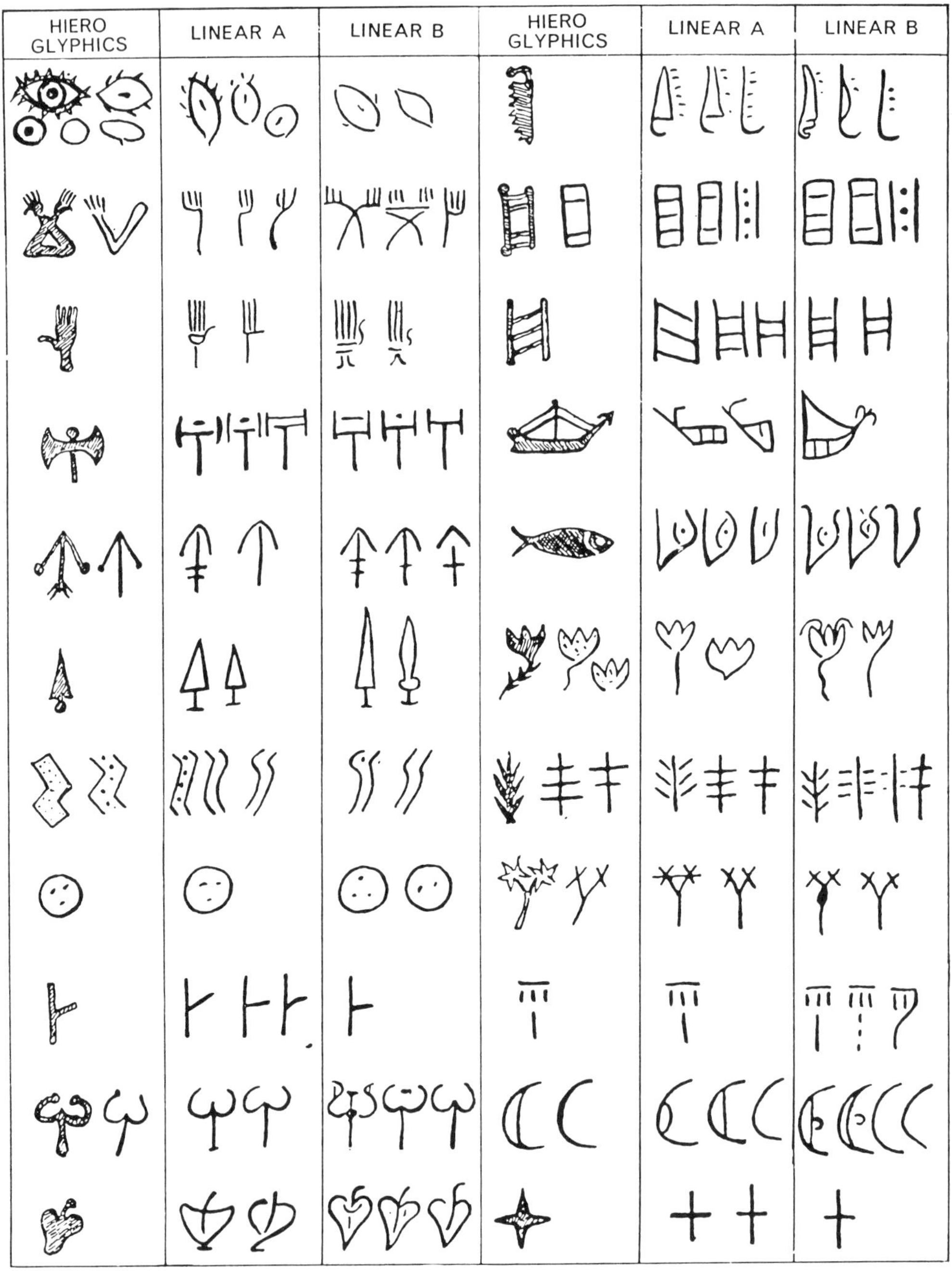

15a. Development of writing in the Bronze Age Aegean. After Evans.

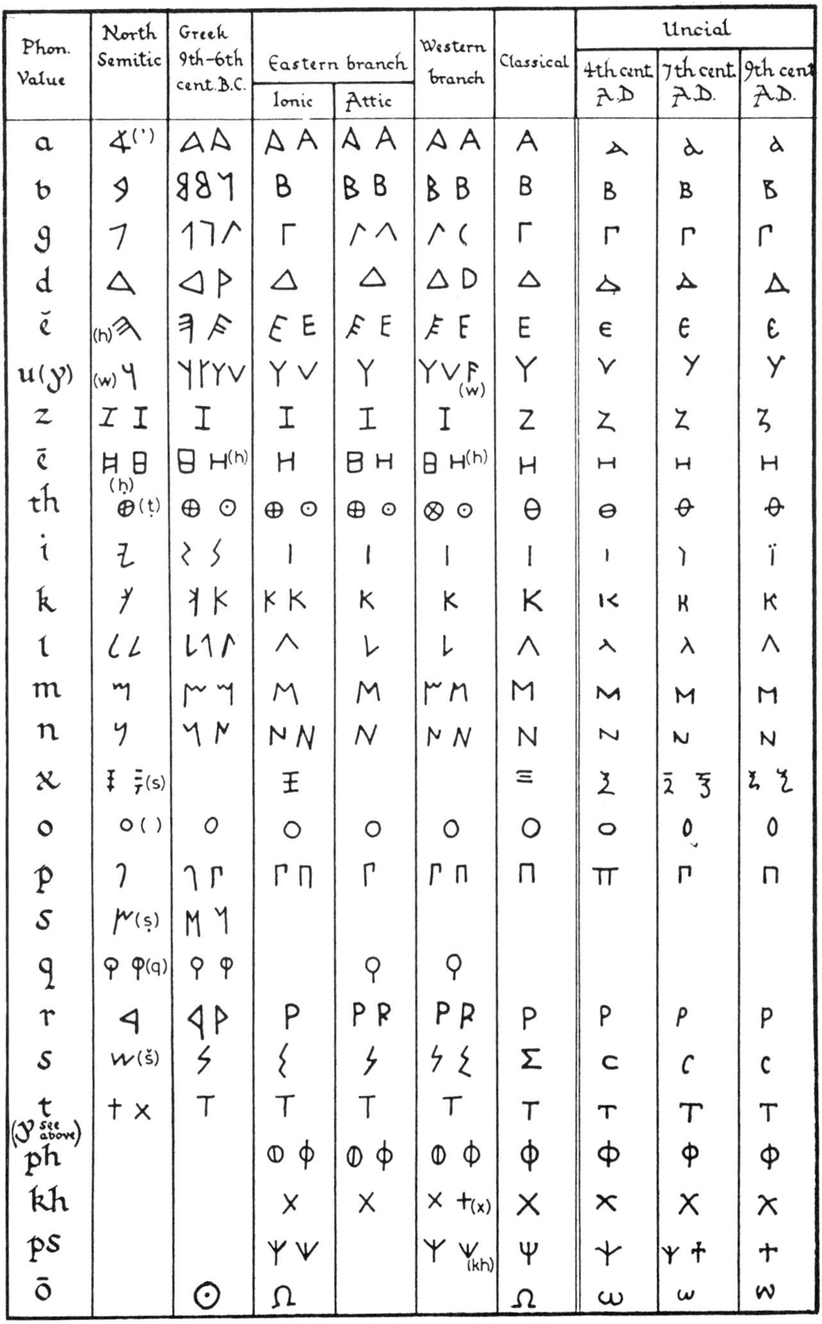

Phon. Value
North Semitic
Greek 9th–6th cent. B.C.
Eastern branch
Ionic
Attic
Western branch
Classical
Uncial
4th cent. A.D.
7th cent. A.D.
9th cent. A.D.
a
b
g
d
ĕ
u(y)
z
ē
th
i
k
l
m
n
x
o
p
s
q
r
s
t
(y see above)
ph
kh
ps
ō

15b. Development of the Greek alphabet. After Diringer.

16. Argos. View from the Acropolis.

17. Chigi Vase. Hoplites in phalanx formation. c. 640 B.C. Villa Giulia, Rome.

18. Messenia. Hellenistic masonry at Ithome.

19. The Isthmus of Corinth and Megara. View towards the north from the Acrocorinth.

20. Olympia. Temple of Hera.

internal affairs was needed. To his credit, Solon, who stemmed from the old royal clan of the Medontidae, drew attention in his impressive elegies to the necessity for an equalisation of the classes. His poem, the so-called Eunomia,[75] was in particular, a call to harmony. It contains a ring of Hesiodic motifs of the just and unjust polis. It was the victory in the struggle for Salamis that bore Solon to power. In 594 B.C. he was elected "arbiter" between the classes,[76] with plenary powers. His position corresponds to that of an *aisymnetes* (for instance, Pittacus of Mytilene). Solon's reorganisation[77] consisted of three acts, which must be clearly distinguished from one another. He freed the citizens from debt, he reformed the coinage, weights and measures, and he set up legislation, the last including his reform of the constitution. His "shaking off the burdens" was regarded as particularly revolutionary by his contemporaries, but the substance of it is now disputed. It is clear that Solon prohibited the enslavement of debtors for all time, and by giving the law retroactive force he struck at the very roots of enslavement by debt, which was then widespread in Attica and the source of so many social abuses. Solon prided himself (fr. 24 Diehl) on the removal of the mortgage stones,[78] which everywhere raised their heads in the black soil of Attica, and on the transformation into free ownership of the soil which had hitherto been enslaved. Thus what Solon carried out was in a sense a "freeing of the farmers." Later at all events *hektemoroi* were no longer found. Under Solon they appear to have become owners of the land which they tilled, in return for the payment of a land tax. By setting a definite limit to the amount of property one could own[79] Solon encouraged the preservation of the small and medium farmers. The *seisachtheia*—shaking off the debts—as a whole meant an exceptionally pronounced encroachment on private property, probably greater than Attica or any part of Greece had felt in the past. Thousands of property owners suffered severe losses, but an even greater number of bondsmen succeeded in again becoming free owners of land. Solon's agrarian reform placed the Attic state on a completely new economic and social foundation, and severely shook the dominating position of the nobility. Furthermore, the Solonian reform presupposes a firmly rooted concept of the state in Athens. The principle of every genuinely constitutional state, that the interests of the group come before those of the individual, was realised by Solon and acknowledged by the majority of Athenian citizens, even the nobility.

Later tradition in part (Androtion) incorrectly connects Solon's reform of the coinage, weights[80] and measures with the *seisachtheia*. The details of these changes remain obscure,[81] and the only certainty is that Solon departed from the Peloponnesian (Aeginetan) currency and turned to the Euboic-Ionian standard.[82] The class division carried out by Solon on the basis of the existing military constitution (v.s.p. 62) was of far-reaching consequence. By making agricultural production the basis of the class division Solon sharply demarcated the individual classes from one another. The *hippeis* had to produce at least three hundred bushels (or measures), while the *zeugitai*, to wit the masses of the hoplite corps, two hundred annually. Those who fell below this figure belonged to the *thetes*. The "Five-Hundred-Bushellers" were expressly selected from among the *hippeis* and gathered into a special class.[83] The transfer of the military constitution to the political sphere was only a consequence of the general development at the end of the seventh century, but it meant a radical departure from the principles of the old aristocratic state. No longer birth but property, and property in the form of land, was the deciding factor in the gradation of the political rights of the individual citizen. The most important magistracies were reserved exclusively for members of the special class, the "Five-Hundred-Bushellers" (*pentakosiomedimnoi*). They alone could become archons and treasurers, while the other offices were open to the *hippeis* and *zeugitai* but not to the *thetes*. The *thetes* were, however, admitted to the Assembly and to the Popular Court,[84] which as a court of appeal formed the highest judicial body in Athens.

Solon's class division, based on production, signified the decisive turn in the direction of timocracy. It is unlikely that Solon should have excused from the costs of public responsibilities the wealthy citizens who did not own property. In order to include this group their wealth was converted into drachms, a measure which Ulrich Wilcken has correctly dated to the Solonian period.[85]

Solon's legislation[86] in no way constitutes a uniform system. The divisions which he effected had their point of departure much more in the sphere of action of the various magistrates. It replaced the Code of Dracon, except that the laws pertaining to bloodshed were retained. Through the medium of Attic law in the first Maritime League, Solon's laws actually attained universal significance. They survived further in Hellenistic[87] and Roman law, and through the Justinian codification (*Digesta* XLVII 22,4) and the acceptance of Roman law in the Middle Ages the ordinances pertaining to guilds even found entrance into modern European law. Two basic ideas emerge in Solon's laws: the attempt to encourage the emancipation of the individual from the clan and place him within the higher unity of the state, and an effort to promote trade and craftsmanship. The first idea reveals itself in the ordinance allowing a childless person to make a will. Of greater importance for the future was the introduction of the so-called "popular appeal." Anyone, not merely kin, could now bring a public indictment against an individual if he were of the opinion that someone had been unjustly treated.[88]

By prohibiting the export of all agricultural products apart from oil Solon promoted the Attic economy. Grain was scarce and even at that time some had to be imported. Meanwhile Attic olive oil and, with it, Attic vases were conquering increasing markets. The law that no one in his old age could demand support from his sons unless he had permitted them to learn a trade and Solon's attempt to draw foreign tradesmen to Athens[89] underline the growing importance of craftsmanship in the city about the turn of the century. It would seem that in this the legislator followed the stimulus from Ionia, the most advanced part of the Greek world.

Solon did not leave behind him a written constitution, a "constitutional-basic-law."[90] In view of the inability of the Greeks to draw a distinction between law and constitution, however, his legislation certainly overlapped with many aspects of the political constitution. Aristotle's statement that Solon introduced the election of the archons by lot deserves no countenance.[91] On the other hand Solon did establish the Council of the Four Hundred, to which one hundred members from each of the four phylae were elected by lot.[92] As in the case of the Popular Council of Chios it created a counterweight to the aristocratic Council of the Areopagus which stemmed from the time of the monarchy. This latter Council supervised the affairs of the state and was designated as "guardian of the laws" (Plut., *Sol.* 19). Of far-reaching political importance, finally, was the amnesty which again opened the gates of the city to the Alcmeonidae, who had been banished on account of the outrage connected with Cylon.[93]

Solon's laws were recorded on revolving wooden tablets. Excerpts from them (or supplements) were inscribed on stone columns in the Royal Hall.[94] There can be no question that the publicity of Solonian law presupposes that the majority of Athenian citizens could read.

Solon's work has been variously judged by posterity. The Greeks of the fourth century B.C. regarded him, along with Cleisthenes, as the father of Attic democracy—a view which is certainly not justified in the light of circumstances in Athens about 600 B.C., even though it may have some element of truth. Among more recent scholars, U. v. Wilamowitz thought that Solon could not be called a great statesman: "That he was a great statesman his conscience would have denied, just as we must deny it."[95] In contrast to this view it should be emphasised that Solon's reorganisation, combining a sure feeling for tradition with an energetic re-formation, appears unquestionably to be the creation of a genuine, important statesman. With an eye to the future, Solon prepared the way for the later economic and social development of Athens. He stands at the head of the development which leads through Peisistratus, Cleisthenes and Themistocles to Pericles, and laid the foundations for that Attic state which in the fifth century took over the leadership of Greece. Even more, Solon created on the Greek mainland the first modern state which actually deserves this name. With Solon's creation the idea of the state begins in Europe. His achievement had weaknesses, the greatest being the lack of a definite central authority. The annually changing archonship, the *Ekklesia* subjected to external influence and oscillating opinions, the Areopagus dethroned by Solon and the new Council of Four Hundred existed competitively alongside one another—a situation which with various changes in specific details remained characteristic of Attic democracy from the cradle to the grave.

As customarily happens to reformers, Solon enjoyed unreserved recognition from only a part of his fellow-citizens. His action had been too radical for the wealthy nobility, while the unpropertied masses saw their hopes disappointed for a new distribution of land. Within a decade the office of eponymous archon twice remained vacant. The archon Damasias finally attempted to establish himself as tyrant, for two years and two months retained his office (582-580 B.C.), and was then overthrown. The office of eponymous archon was replaced by a ten-man commission, which consisted of five Eupatrids, three *agroikoi* (non-noble large landowners) and two *demiourgoi* (craftsmen).[96] In the following decades internal conflicts at Athens continued. From this came the formation of local groups,[97] which were exploited for political ends by ambitious leaders. Lycurgus, probably a member of the old noble Eteobutadae, led the "people of the Plain," predominantly the conservative element of the propertied nobility dwelling in the Cephisus Valley, with their followers. The Alcmeonid Megacles led the "people of the Coast," inhabiting the promontory of Sunium. The "hill dwellers,"[98] the poorer population from Mount Parnes to Brilessus, the most radical group, regarded Peisistratus of Brauron as their leader. Just as more than a generation before, in the seventh century, Athens and Attica again presented the picture of a clan-state in upheaval, due to the personal rivalries of the noble families. The idea of the state which Solon's reorganisation had established was again in greatest jeopardy. Still, the economic conditions were different from those in the pre-Solonian era. Trade and commerce were growing, a situation which decisively contributed to the ultimate victory of Peisistratus.

In contrast to Attic timocracy and the Spartan military state, the patriarchal aristocracy was still firmly rooted in the remainder of Greece during the first half of the sixth century, particularly in Thessaly and also in parts of the Peloponnesus. It is highly probable that the spirit of democracy was not restricted to the Greek mainland, for an inscription from Chios,[99] probably dating from the first half of the sixth century, names a Popular Council, which apparently formed a counterweight to the Aristocratic Council. But it is just as certain that in actual fact it was not the *demos* but the tyrants who controlled and governed political developments. Violent conflicts flared up again and again between the despots and the nobles, as, for instance, in Lesbos. Thus in the first half of the sixth century B.C. the conflict between the powerful individual and the state as a whole was at its height. In Sparta alone did the idea of the state and the distinct form of state education absorb all individual striving on the part of the citizens.

5
THE GROWTH OF POWER

THE PERSIAN EMPIRE

The political phenomenon which characterises the Mediterranean world in the middle of the sixth century is the rise of major powers in both East and West. The Indo-European Persian empire in the East and the Carthaginian colonial empire in the western Mediterranean ended the prevailing balance of power and created a great new era. Both very soon drew the Greek world into their orbit. Thus Greek history in the second half of the sixth century, forms a prelude to the great conflict between Greeks and Persians at the beginning of the fifth century. If the Greeks were able to withstand the powerful pressure from east and west, they owed this to the fact that in the Spartan hegemony in the Peloponnesus and in the Syracusan state in the West they had pioneers in the struggle for freedom, under whose leadership the rest of the Hellenes succeeded in uniting against the common foe.

About the middle of the sixth century, the Persians, under the leadership of the Achaemenid Cyrus II (559-530 B.C.), cast off the supremacy of the Medes. Only conflicting reports of the events in the interior of Iran reached Ionia—reports which were later woven together into a wreath of stories around the personalities of Astyages (*Istuwegu*), king of the Medes, Mandane, his daughter, and Cyrus, his son-in-law. The expansion of the Persians within a few decades is a unique phenomenon in the history of the ancient world. The personality of Cyrus, the founder of the empire, the peculiar political and social character of the Persian state and not least the generally favourable international situation in the Near East—all coincided to provide the climate for expansion. Croesus, the king of Lydia, Nabonid, the ruler of Chaldaea, and Amasis of Egypt united together against Cyrus the Achaemenid.[1] With the protection which this coalition afforded in the rear. Croesus in 547 (?) launched the attack with an invasion of Cappadocia, which since 585 B.C. had been within the Iranian sphere of interests. The Persian counter-attack forced the Lydians rapidly to clear the country which had just been won and to withdraw to the west across the Halys, hitherto the frontier between the Lydian and Persian realms. A decisive victory for Cyrus at Sardis (the Lydian cavalry is said to have been thrown into confusion by the Persian camel riders) forced the Lydians to their knees. After a brief siege of the capital Croesus found himself a prisoner of the Persian king. Cyrus sent him to Media and gave him a city in which to live (still in the autumn of 547 B.C.?).[2] The Greeks, like the Delphic oracle, had been fully convinced that Croesus was invincible, but now their world, along with the whole eastern Mediterranean, came under the shadow of the overwhelming Persian victory. The first to feel the change in the international situation was Ionia. Under Mazares and Harpagus the Persians proceeded to subjugate most of the coastal cities of Ionia. Only powerful Miletus was allowed to renew the alliance which it had once formed with the Lydians. The reorganisation of Asia Minor concluded with the creation of the satrapies of Sardis and Dascylium, which incorporated the Greeks of Ionia and Aeolis. The inhabitants of Phocaea and Teos had previously abandoned their cities and taken to the sea. The Phocaeans at first found a new home in distant Alalia on Corsica, and later in Elea in southern Italy. The Teans settled in Abdera on the Thracian coast and in Phanagoreia on the Cimmerian Bosporus. Bias of Priene allegedly counselled his compatriots at a congress of the Ionian League to evacuate all cities and to found a new Ionia in the western Sea. This counsel—if it is actually historical—was not followed.

Persian rule was not anything basically new for the Greeks in Asia Minor. The new masters, however, who secured the country through garrisons and military colonies, were much more outsiders than the Lydians, with whom the Greeks had had an active cultural and material exchange. The Greek coast of Asia Minor had been a jewel for the kings of Lydia, and they had always been conscious of its worth. The Persian king, distant in Susa or Ecbatana, entrusted Asia Minor and the Greeks in that region to the rule of his satraps who acted as all but absolute lords. The king of Persia was far away; only seldom did complaints from his subjects in the West reach his ears.

In 539 B.C. Cyrus conquered the Neo-Babylonian kingdom, and in October that year the Babylonians welcomed him jubilantly as he made his entry into the sacred city of the god Marduk. This also indirectly created a new situation for the Greeks in Asia Minor, for it changed the pattern of trade routes from the East. It is probable that by the time Babylonia fell, the large commercial metropolises of Phoenicia acknowledged the sovereignty of Cyrus, and thus formed part of the new country joined in personal union with the Persian empire, "Babylon and the Region Beyond-the-River" (that is, the Euphrates). In 534 B.C. Cyrus for the first time placed this region under a governor, named Gubaru.[3] Trade in goods from the East now made its way along the ancient caravan routes through the Syro-Arabian desert to the harbours of Phoenicia, which, closer to the East, were distinctly favoured.[4]

The founder of the Persian empire devoted the last years of his life to battles against the Sacae, the nomads of the steppes in the north-east of Iran who repeatedly poured over the open frontiers of the empire with their cavalry hordes.[5] Cyrus the Great was killed in the region of the Lower Oxus in 530 B.C. His son Cambyses (530-522 B.C.) completed his father's work by conquering Egypt (525 B.C.). With all the rights and titles of the Egyptian sovereign, Cambyses became successor to Psammetichus III, the last Pharaoh of the land. In Manetho's list (third century B.C.) the Persian kings are included as a special Dynasty—the XXVIIth. As in the case of the Neo-Babylonian kingdom, so Egypt was now joined in personal union with the crown of Persia.

At the end of Cambyses' reign the Persian empire was shaken by the revolt of one of the Magi, Gaumata (Greek Smerdis). Gaumata posed as Bardya (the "pseudo Bardya"), the son of Cyrus who had been killed by Cambyses, and rapidly gained a following through popular measures like a general tax remission. Cambyses died in Syria on the return journey from Egypt and, as it seems, of a natural death (522 B.C.). Out of the disorders in the fluctuating struggle lasting for more than a year, Darius, the son of Hystaspes (Vistaspa) and stemming from a collateral line of the Achaemenids, emerged as victor over Gaumata and a number of other pretenders (end of 521 B.C.).[6] His reign began a new era in the history of the Achaemenid empire. Darius I (522-486 B.C.) gave to the empire, whose foundations had been laid by Cyrus, that inner and outer form under which it became the most important power in the ancient world for almost two centuries.

Within its frontiers, stretching from the Indus in the east to the Aegean in the west and from the mountains of the Caucasus to torrid Nubia, the Persian world empire embraced a vast number of peoples and tribes of the most diverse levels of culture. The Aryans comprised the aristocratic element, primarily the inhabitants of the ancestral Achaemenid country of Persis.[7] But from the time of Cyrus on, the Medes and the Elamites had also occupied a special position and were shown preference in being drawn into the administration of the vast empire. The king formed the head of the realm; with pride he confessed himself to be a worshipper of the god Ahuramazda, the chief deity of the Persians, to whom ruler and subjects presented their burnt offerings on altars under the open heavens. An inscription of unusual importance, found in Persepolis and dating to the time of Xerxes the son of Darius,[8] shows that the kings of Persia were adherents of the religion propagated by Zoroaster, as primarily represented by the priestly caste of the Magi.[9] By acknowledging a Supreme Being who demanded from his devotees the proof of moral conduct, the Persian religion of the Achaemenidae towers far above most of the religions of the Near East. On the other hand, the attitude of the Persians towards the religions of other peoples was one of almost unsurpassed tolerance. Between the king and the Persian nobles there was a relationship of loyalty based on moral obligation, which found expression in unconditional obedience and in the dutiful allegiance of the vassal peoples to the sovereign feudal lord. To serve the king was the noblest duty of a Persian, and riding, shooting with the bow and telling the truth he learned from his youth.

After suppressing the great revolt, Darius carried out (in 518 B.C.?) a reorganisation of the vast empire. The whole territory of the realm was divided into twenty tax districts (called *nomoi* by Herodotus). At the same time Darius retained the satrapies as administrative units. They are the most characteristic expression of the old feudal structure of the Persian empire established by Cyrus the Great. The number of satrapies varied from time to time, as is reflected in the epigraphical lists of countries drawn up by Darius and Xerxes. In contrast to the satrapies, the tax districts, which were in part identical with the former and in part overlapped with them, are the expression of a more absolutist system of government modelled on the ancient oriental empires, like the Assyrian and Neo-Babylonian. Darius introduced the so-called chancery Aramaic as the official language of the administration.[10] Documents in this language have been found in Elephantine on the southern frontier of Egypt and in districts of India as well as in Lydia. In the monumental inscriptions, including the great inscription from Behistun, there is, in addition to the Old-Persian text written in a new cuneiform script, also a Babylonian and an Elamite version. In Persepolis an archive was found consisting of some 5000-7000 clay tablets written in the Elamite language[11]—further evidence for the special position of Elam and its ancient culture within the Persian empire.

By sending out Persian officers, soldiers and civil servants, Persian colonies emerged everywhere throughout the empire. The most important officials were the satraps. Their name (*sathrapavan*, "protectors of the government") is no doubt of Median origin. With their courts, palaces and zoos, the capitals of the satraps were copies in miniature of the court of the Great King. Certain satrapies (as, for instance, Dascylium in northern Asia Minor) remained in a sort of hereditary possession of the same family for generations. The concentration of all military and civil power in one person granted a satrap extensive independence, even from the capital of the empire. This, in addition to the important dynastic power of the provincial governors, was the most important cause of the many satrap revolts, of which there was no end from about the middle of the fifth century onwards. Supervisory organs, the "Eyes" and the "Ears" of the Great King, formed a certain counterweight to the independence of the satraps. The negative side of the system admittedly came to light all too soon: reciprocal spying and denunciations ultimately became an every day occurrence.

The Persian imperial army was composed of the garrisons of the imperial fortresses as well as of the levies which the Great King summoned to active duty in time of war. In addition, there were the contingents of the innumerable subject peoples under the command of the satraps or the local princes. These troops varied greatly in armament and importance in action. The core of the entire army was formed by the Persian foot—the ten thousand "Immortals". From their number, 1000 under the command of the chiliarch, the *hazarapatis*, served as the king's bodyguard, while their commander, upon relinquishing his original military authority, rose to the position of first minister of the empire—to "Grand Vizier."[12] From the provinces the tribute flowed into the central treasury (*ganzaka*) created by Darius, in all probability modelled on Assyrian lines.

The large-scale extension of the road network in the empire, probably on the model of the Assyrians,[13] served primarily administrative purposes but indirectly also to promote trade and commerce. With its 111 posting stations the "Royal Road" was a symbol of the greatness and efficiency of the empire. It led from Ephesus, via Sardis to Gordium on the

Sangarius, and from there to Pteria in Cappadocia. After crossing the Armenian mountains and following the course of the Tigris it went through Arbeletis and ultimately reached Susa. The monumental buildings of Darius and Xerxes[14] were a particularly characteristic expression of the grandeur of the vast world empire. For the construction of the imperial palace at Susa Darius enlisted the peoples of the entire realm: Babylon provided the clay bricks, Syria the cedars of Lebanon, Lydia and Bactria supplied gold, Egypt silver, Nubia ivory, while the Ionians and Carians worked as craftsmen and artists on the citadel.[15]

Economic conditions in the various countries of the empire differed greatly. While coinage had to a certain extent prevailed as the basis of the economy in Lydia since the seventh century, ingots of precious metals were used as standards in the Near East and in Egypt. In addition, bartering in natural goods prevailed throughout the entire realm, and in the eastern satrapies it predominated without restriction. By creating an imperial currency Darius I brought order into the chaotic conditions. The "Daric," a gold coin bearing the image of the Great King in the pose of a kneeling bowman, with its weight of 8.42 grammes, corresponded to half the weight of the Phocaean stater, the denomination most extensively used in Ionia, and on the other hand corresponded to 1/60 of the Babylonian mina. This coin of Darius therefore established a certain bridge in trade between East and West, and created the conditions for economic unity in the Persian empire. In order to open up new channels for trade, the sea captain Scylax of Caryanda in Caria undertook an exploratory expedition down the Cabul and Indus rivers. Sailing westwards along the coast, then south around the Arabian peninsula into the Red Sea, he ultimately reached Suez, allegedly twenty-nine months after setting sail.[16] A supplement to this brilliant nautical achievement—not until the expedition of Nearchus in the time of Alexander do we encounter anything approximately comparable to it—was the completion of the canal from the Nile Delta through the wadi Tumîlât to the Red Sea, which had already been inaugurated by the Egyptian king Necho.

The rulers of the empire of the Achaemenids regarded themselves as the successors to the Old Babylonian and Assyrian world rulers and demonstrated their claim to it in their titles. Darius I repeatedly called himself "king of the lands of all tribes."[17] Political and military exigencies forced the Great King to extend his frontiers continually in order to ensure the security of the inhabitants of the empire. When the Persian colossus, after the annexation of Asia Minor, had advanced to the east coast of the Aegean Sea, security demanded control also of the island states of the Aegean (some of which, like Samos and Chios, had possessions on the Anatolian mainland), the Hellenic cities on the shores of the Black Sea and ultimately Greece itself. The Greek communities of the motherland and of Ionia were so closely interwoven in both politics and economics that the annexing of the Greek-inhabited regions of Asia Minor forced a westward thrust by the Persians. Internal conditions in Greece itself must also have enticed the Persians to such action. For wherever one might look, discord, quarrelling and party conflicts prevailed among the nobility, the *demos* and the tyrants. A union of the innumerable states appeared completely impossible, and it was reasonable to assume that they would easily fall prey to a strong foreign power.

On the other hand the vast expanse of the Persian empire in itself must have appeared as something alien to the Greeks. Nor did they ever put forth an effort to discover the moral strength on which the empire was based or to acquire a deeper understanding for the peculiar feudalistic nature of the relationship between the Great King and his vassals. For the Greeks it was much more the negative aspects of Persian rule which always remained the characteristic ones, chiefly the oriental favouritism at the court of the Great King and the "Byzantine" forms of Persian court ceremonies, which could not be reconciled with the Greek concept of freedom. Furthermore, the Greeks detested the frequent examples of arbitrary administration by the satraps in Asia Minor and the encouragement which the Persians gave to the despotic rulers in the Ionian cities, rulers who like the Persians held to the idea of loyal allegiance. As communities of free citizens the Ionian poleis were a foreign element in a vast empire in which the will of the Great King alone decided the weal and the woe of millions of his subjects. It was not from the antithesis between freedom and bondage but from the mutual inability to understand each other and from the inner differences of their national characters that the struggle in world history between the Greeks and the Persians was born.

GREECE AND THE WEST ON THE EVE OF THE PERSIAN WAR

The most important cosmopolitan power on the Greek mainland was the so-called Peloponnesian League, under the hegemony of Sparta.[18] It had developed on the basis of special alliances between Sparta and various Peloponnesian states in the course of the second half of the sixth century —Tegea (v.s.p. 404 n.44), Mantineia, Orchomenus, Corinth and beyond the peninsula, Megara and Aegina. On the strength of her unequivocal military superiority Sparta, as the hegemonial power, held the absolute leadership in the Alliance. The various members, whose sovereignty remained unaffected, were obliged to serve with two thirds of their military strength when Sparta summoned them. As a power formation Sparta's Peloponnesian League overshadowed all other Greek states, even Thessaly, to say nothing whatever of Athens. In Thessaly the noble families, the Aleuads of Larisa, the Scopads of Crannon and the ruler Antiochus of Pharsalus, held a predominant position. Simonides of Ceos celebrated their fame and their kingly munificence in song.[19]

Athens began a new era in her history in 561/60 B.C. with the tyranny of Peisistratus. Leader of the faction of the hill dwellers (v.s.p. 74), he had particularly distinguished himself in the struggle against Megara.[20] On the laurels of his military victory he rose to *tyrannis*. For his personal protection he was granted a bodyguard comprised of club-bearers,[21] and with their aid took possession of the Acropolis and thereby became master of Athens.

The first phase of his absolute rule[22] was very brief. The tyrant was forced to yield to the united opposition of the *pediakoi* and the *paralioi*, and withdraw from the country; the Alcmeonid Megacles, however, soon recalled him. But the coalition between Peisistratus and the Alcmeonidae—it was consolidated by the marriage of the tyrant to the daughter of Megacles—did not last long. Peisistratus now was banished for the second time. Using the great resources he had built up, especially the revenues from the gold mines in Macedonia and Thrace, and by connections with the Eretrian nobility, the tyrant returned to Athens for the second time. In this instance he led a mercenary force which routed the Athenian contingent at Pallene. Amidst the jubilation of the Athenian population he entered the city and to his death (528/7 B.C.) held the reins of government.

The rule of Peisistratus rested on illegal force.[23] It robbed the Athenian people of their *palladium*—the right to decide their own welfare. That large sections of the Attic population, particularly the masses of small farmers, favoured the tyrant does not contradict this. Peisistratus made it his particular concern to promote the interests of the farmers. He granted them advance payments for the operation of agriculture (probably seed loans),[24] and introduced deme judges and thereby placed rural justice on a new foundation.[25] The efforts of the tyrant in social matters were a necessary supplement to the Solonian programme, serving to promote the strong middle class which from this time onwards was a determining factor in Athens.

The endeavours of Peisistratus to consolidate his tyranny through power bases outside the context of the Athenian polis were especially pronounced. His gold mines at Mount Pangaeum and around Rhaecelus provided him with the financial resources for maintaining mercenary troops, including a great many Thracians and possibly even Scythians. Since there were not sufficient revenues for large expenditures, primarily for his building programme, the tyrant found himself compelled to introduce an income tax (a land-produce tax) of 5% (?), which the Athenians regarded as particularly oppressive.

Peisistratus' will to power urged Athens on the path of expansion. His foreign policy is inseparably linked with the general rise in trade about the middle of the sixth century and with the spread of coinage.[26] Finds have been made of Attic coins which Peisistratus struck, bearing the image of Athena the goddess of the city and her insignia the owl, instead of the heraldic emblem of the Eupatrids. The spread of these coins over the wide area from Egypt to Athos, from Tarentum to Chios and Cos,[27] and the even greater diffusion of Attic black-figure vases[28] document the sudden rise in Attic maritime trade. Athens now held a competitive position alongside Aegina and Corinth, the great rivals of the motherland, and soon outstripped them. In the sixth century Attic trade also reached Etruria, as vase inscriptions from Caere show. There may actually have been an Attic colony in this place,[29] although this still requires clarification. The distinct commercial character of Athenian colonisation in the time of Peisistratus produced the new settlement of Sigeum as well as the colonisation of the Thracian Chersonese carried out under the elder Miltiades from the family of the Philaidae.[30] In Sigeum Peisistratus, following the example of the Cypselids, set up Hegisistratus, one of his sons, as regent, and the despatching of the Athenian colony to the Chersonese had support from Peisistratus. The exit of the Hellespont, through which ships laden with grain from southern Russia had to pass, was now under Athenian control.

The tyrant anchored his rule in Athens by a particularly skilful and elaborate system of alliances.[31] He not only cultivated close relationships with the "society of tyrants," with Lygdamis of Naxos and Polycrates of Samos, but also had connections with the mounted nobility of Thessaly, with Eretria and Argos. Nor was the Macedonian monarchy, nor even Sparta itself, which later assumed such a hostile attitude towards the tyrants,[32] absent from the allies of Peisistratus. Only the Delphic priesthood withheld support from the tyrant.

Peisistratus died a natural death in 528/7 B.C. and was succeeded by his two sons Hippias and Hipparchus. Of the two, Hipparchus the younger came more into prominence both as ruler and as a private individual.[33] In truth it was the quasi-monarchical rule of a tyrant family in which the energetic Hippias and the artistically inclined Hipparchus excellently complemented each other. The fate which hovered over the head of every tyrant first struck Hipparchus; in the great Panathenaic festival of 514 B.C. he fell victim to a murderous attack by a number of young Athenians, among them Harmodius and Aristogeiton, allegedly on account of a personal grievance.[34] The Athenian democracy celebrated the tyrant-slayers both in picture and in song, and their deed became the symbol of Athenian liberty. The daggers which snatched Hipparchus away also struck at the heart of the tyranny of Hippias. The thirst for freedom could no longer be suppressed, regardless of the degree to which Hippias might tighten the reins. The Delphic oracle commanded the Spartans to end their relationship with the Peisistratidae. After an unsuccessful attempt to gain a solid foothold in Phalerum the Peloponnesian forces under the command of the Spartan king Cleomenes I appeared before the gates of Athens. Blockaded on the Acropolis, Hippias capitulated and sought refuge in Sigeum (510 B.C.). Ultimately, the Persian advance towards the west destroyed the economic foundations of the tyranny.[34a]

Even before the overthrow of the Peisistratidae, Polycrates of Samos, probably the most important of the older Greek tyrants, had met his end through execution. The craftiness of the Persian satrap Oroetes of Sardis, who lured the Aeacid into Persian territory in Asia Minor, brought about his end (c. 522 B.C.). Polycrates had at one time gained control of Samos with the aid of Lygdamis of Naxos, and succeeded in wielding power even against his own brothers.[35] In addition to a mercenary army he also had command of a respectable fleet such as the Aegean had hitherto not seen. Like the Peisistratidae, he gathered to his court a great many artists and poets, including Ibycus and Anacreon. His construction works became famous: the architect Eupalinus of Megara built a vast aqueduct, Rhoecus of Samos erected the Heraeum, with its great dimensions, and besides this Polycrates built a large quay. Polycrates had trade relations with the entire Greek world. (A late but not unreliable source[36] lists Epirus, Lacedaemon, Scyros, Naxos, Miletus, Attica and Sicily.) He was also on close friendly terms with Amasis of Egypt.[37] His death at the hands of the Persians marks the beginning of a new era. He had succeeded in asserting himself in the face of an expedition by the Lacedaemonians and the Corinthians (c. 524 B.C.) but in the long run he was no match for the expansion of the Persian world empire. After his death his former private secretary Maeandrius seized control of Samos, but was eliminated by a Persian expedition, which placed the rule of Samos in the hands of Polycrates' brother Syloson as the vassal of Persia (before 513/12 B.C.). Thus Samos too was now part of the Persian empire.

The Scythian expedition of King Darius I about 513/12 B.C., aimed at securing the open northern frontier of the empire against the continual invasion of the Scythian cavalry tribes, marks an epoch in the relations between Hellas and the Persian empire.[38] Darius had conceived the gigantic plan of subjugating the entire Pontic-Caspian steppes from the Danube to the Jaxartes (Syr-darya). But he seriously underestimated the enormous distances involved[39] and did not take into account the difficulties of conducting a war in the roadless and waterless regions of the south Russian steppes. Darius evidently wanted to attack the Scythians in the rear, by striking from the west, that is, from the Lower Danube. The preparations corresponded with the magnitude of the plan—construction of a huge floating-bridge across the Bosporus, and the raising of large contingents among the satraps and vassals. The Ionian Mandrocles designed the bridge, and the Ionian tyrants, headed by Histiaeus of Miletus, provided contingents. The expedition was conducted as a combined operation of the army and fleet. After bridging the Danube just above the Delta Darius moved with the main body of his army into the Bessarabian steppes. The Scythians, however, consistently avoided a pitched battle. It was the waterless steppes that forced the Persians to retreat, probably without ever having crossed a single major river in south Russia. The bridge across the Danube had remained intact; the counsel of the younger Miltiades (the ruler of the Thracian Chersonese and among the vassals of the king), to break up the bridge, had been rejected by the Ionians.[40]

Darius failed to achieve the object of the expedition, that is, to secure his northern frontier.[41] But the campaign resulted in the subjugation of the Greek cities on the Propontis—Byzantium, Chalcedon *et al.* Some of these had revolted when they heard the news of the failure of the Scythian expedition, and had therefore to be brought into submission by the Persian fleet under Otanes. The Persians thus secured an important bridgehead on European soil, in which the principality of the younger Miltiades on the Gallipoli peninsula was also incorporated. After the Persians had annexed the southern coast of Thrace with its rich gold mines on the Strymon and at Mount Pangaeum, and had accepted the submission of Amyntas king of Macedonia, the Persian empire stretched from the northern shores of the Aegean to the Lower Danube. A new satrapy was created out of the newly won territory of Thrace, and was secured by bases in Doriscus and Eion.

Despite the undeniable setback in prestige from the abortive Scythian expedition, the great Persian colossus advancing ever closer to Greece made a tremendous impression. The Persian expansion, which Herodotus regarded as the cause of the Persian wars, now cast its shadow over Greece and beyond it into the western Mediterranean. An exile from Tarentum hoped to be restored to his native city by Darius.[42] This and the voyage of the Greek physician Democedes of Croton to the West,[43] together with Persian officers, in Sidonian ships, demonstrate the world-wide dimensions of Achaemenid western policy.

In the West the Carthaginians and the Etruscans had set a limit to Greek colonial expansion in the second half of the sixth century. In central Italy the Etruscan Inter-City League had in the course of the seventh century developed into the leading power, with its influence extending from the Po Valley (Felsina-Bologna) in the north to Campania in the south. As the League, however, lacked inner solidarity, the Etruscans themselves were unable to assimilate other peoples, which prevented Etruscan culture, greatly influenced by Greek civilisation, from penetrating Italy. Outside its central territory Etruscan rule, which itself was restricted to a very thin upper class, was only ephemeral. This was the case in Rome too, which at the end of the sixth century broke away from the Etruscans and struck a separate course.

Far more important for the western Greeks, however, was the Carthaginian expansion. According to tradition the city of Carthage[44] (Carthage means "New Town") was founded by Phoenicians from Tyre in 814/13 B.C. It was restricted to a narrow strip of land in modern Tunisia, for which the inhabitants had to pay a ground rent to the Libyans until some time in the fifth century. In the course of the seventh and sixth centuries the city grew into the most important commercial centre among the Phoenician colonies in North Africa. The other Phoenician cities in the West submitted to her rule, Utica alone maintaining a separate status. Situated where all the most important sea-routes intersected, Carthage became the centre of a large commercial empire. Her factories extended from Gades in southern Spain, via Pithecusae, Sardinia, Sicily and Malta to Syrtis Major (Arae Philaenorum). It was not until much later that the Carthaginian traders, who had settled primarily on islands and promontories (Thucydides VI 2), were followed by the Carthaginian armies. It would seem that the sea battle of Alalia off Corsica (c. 540 B.C.), in which the united fleets of the Carthaginians and Etruscans fought against the Phocaeans and which ended with such extraordinarily heavy losses for the Greeks, marked a crucial turning point in the policy of the aspiring commercial metropolis. From this time onwards armies of Carthaginian citizens and foreign mercenaries fought in western Sicily, on Sardinia and in Africa. The ancient Iberian metropolis of Tartessus probably was destroyed by the

Carthaginians about 500 B.C. and thereafter the Straits of Gibraltar were closed to the Greeks. The Carthaginians were indisputable masters at concluding treaties. The Etruscans, Massaliots, Cyrenaeans and the Romans (first treaty in 508/7 B.C.) were their partners, and respect for the prohibited zones of the Carthaginians in the western sea was again and again impressed upon them.

By about 600 B.C., Greek colonial expansion in the West had already passed its climax. What had been gained by struggle had now to be maintained by tenacious fighting. Massalia, however, actually pushed her colonies even as far as Spain in the sixth century. Cyme, the oldest of all Greek cities in the West, repulsed the assault of the Etruscans and their allies, the Umbrians and Daunians (c. 525 B.C.). One Aristodemus was the saviour of the city, and he later set himself up as tyrant and in the manner of the despotic rulers of those times adorned Cyme with magnificent buildings. In order to finance these and to pay his mercenaries he confiscated the possessions of a great many aristocrats. He created the necessary backbone for his rule by enfranchising slaves.[45]

In spite of all this the sixth century ended with a severe setback for the Greeks in Magna Graecia: in 511/10 B.C. Sybaris fell victim to the greed of her neighbouring city Croton and was totally destroyed.[46] Political and economic conflicts ended in this terrible catastrophe, the convulsions of which were felt as far away as Ionia (Miletus). Even apart from this the Greek cities were often involved in conflicts with each other, with repeated feuds often involving a large number of cities.[47]

In southern Italy the sect of the Pythagoreans acquired particular importance at the end of the sixth century. Their founder, Pythagoras, had abandoned his home in Samos during the tyranny of Polycrates. In Magna Graecia, as philosopher, mathematician and reformer of religion and morals, he exerted a profound influence, which soon benefited the rule of the aristocrats in Croton and Metapontum. Pythagoras died in Metapontum soon after the turn of the century.[48] Croton's particular fame rested on the international reputation of her physicians (Democedes) and her able-bodied youths, who took part in the Olympian games with enthusiasm and great success. All this could not, however, conceal the fact that the great days of the Greeks in southern Italy were, at the turn of the century, irretrievably a thing of the past, at a time when the tyranny of Hippocrates of Gela, the germ cell of the powerful Syracuso-Gelan double-state, was becoming consolidated.

The overthrow of Hippias (510 B.C.) marked a turning point in the internal and foreign developments of the Attic state. The Cleisthenic reform and events in foreign politics placed Athens in the political limelight. The Alcmeonid Cleisthenes, himself a noble, was designing political reform, but met stubborn opposition from the majority of Attic noble families led by Isagoras. Under the tyrants the nobles had remained in the country, whereas the Alcmeonidae had been forced, at least temporarily, to go into exile.[49] It was not until Isagoras and the Spartan king Cleomenes I had, after being blockaded on the Acropolis, voluntarily capitulated, that Cleisthenes could proceed with his reforms (508/7 B.C.). They seem to have been carried out only gradually, a reorganisation[50] stemming from the exigencies of current politics. That they pointed towards the future shows they sprang from the mind of a genuine statesman. The reforms had become necessary to destroy the newly formed exclusive factions in the state and to prevent them from ever recurring again. The factions chiefly concerned were the large landowners of the central plain, the people of the coast who engaged predominantly in commerce and fishing, and the small farmers from the hill-country of north-east Attica, who had once helped Peisistratus to power. The special interests of these groups, which partly coincided with the efforts of the noble clans and partly conflicted with them, threatened to undermine national feeling and to make the state the victim of class passions. In order to prevent this, Cleisthenes created a territorial division of Attica and Athens to split up the city, the interior and the coast each into ten triple units (*trittyes*). Each *trittys* from the three zones was now (allegedly as the lot ordained) fused together into one *phyle*—tribe. The geographical location of the *trittys* was of no significance.[51] The ten local *phylae*, created to "mix the demos", replaced the old four gentilic tribes, which from now on retained importance only in the religious sphere. (It must not be overlooked that even before Cleisthenes Attica had, in addition to the gentilic division of the nobility,[52] a local division, which embraced the entire population: the four clan-*phylae* were then divided into a total of twelve *trittyes* and forty-eight naucraries.[53])

In this field the reform of Cleisthenes was thorough. By the creation of an exclusively territorial division the gentilic associations were completely broken up. From now on the deme, the "community," formed the smallest autonomous administrative unit. It was established not only in the urban district of Athens but equally in the rural parts, headed by the *demarch*. Upon the demes, originally probably one hundred (due to cleavages the number later became considerably larger), devolved the keeping of the citizen lists, the nominal register, and the direction of local self-government in finance and religion. The fully-enfranchised Athenian citizen now officially named himself only according to the deme in which he lived at the time of the reorganisation;[54] the Attic people had thus emerged from the influence of the noble families and their adherents by the fusion of the urban and rural districts.

The new *trittyes* had no particular function. The ten local *phylae*, named after Attic heroes, each furnished a hoplite regiment in the phalanx, headed by one elected *strategos*—general—and in addition one squadron of horse. Until some time in the fifth century the *strategoi* were subordinate to the polemarch,[55] the military commander of the army. The Solonian Council of the Four Hundred was replaced by the Council of the Five Hundred.[56] Each *phyle* had to furnish fifty councillors, taken from the various demes, in proportion to the number of citizens in a particular deme. This is "perhaps the first example of representation proportionate to the population which history records" (K. J. Beloch).

The 500 members of the Council divided themselves according to their membership in the ten *phylae* into ten sections (*prytaneis*), each consisting of fifty *bouleutai*—councillors. Each section (*prytaneia*) served as superintending executive for a tenth part of the year.[57] During this time the councillors from that particular *prytaneia* were housed in the *Prytaneion*. A part of the members, including the daily rotating *epistates* (the president), remained day and night in the state building, the *Tholos*, so named after its circular shape.[58] Since every bill submitted to the *Ekklesia* had to be deliberated on beforehand by the *Boulé*, the Council was the most important organ in the whole state machinery. In order to prevent the recurrence of tyranny, Cleisthenes invented ostracism, the "*ostrakon* court." Each year, in the sixth *prytaneia*, the question was put in the *Ekklesia* whether an ostracism should be conducted. If the answer were positive, a vote was taken in the eighth *prytaneia*, and if 6000 votes were recorded, the citizen with the highest count had to withdraw from Attica for a period of ten years, but without damage to his honour or property. An ostracism was conducted for the first time in 487 B.C.—evidence that the power of the nobility had been completely broken.[59]

In view of the great strain on Athens in foreign politics, especially from Sparta who twice intervened in Athens within a very short space of time (508 and 506 B.C.), it seems amazing that the Cleisthenic reforms could have been carried out at all. It was of great consequence that Athens turned to Persia. Out of fear of its Greek opponents, the city submitted itself to Artaphernes the satrap of Sardis (c. 507 B.C.) in exchange for assurances of a Persian alliance.[60] When the Athenians retained the upper hand in the conflict with the Boeotians and Chalcidians in 506 B.C.[61] they tried to dispel the shadow of the great Persian colossus by repudiating the envoys of the Great King. A dangerous game was being played in Athens!

In contrast to the Spartan military state in Laconia, in Attica *isonomia* had arisen. It was an alien phenomenon in the aristocratically-governed community-states of Greece. Athens' break from isolation was due to political developments abroad. It was the Persian peril which brought the Greeks of all tribes together. Not only Sparta, the leader of Greece, but along with her Athens also stood the crucial test in the struggle for Hellenic freedom.

6
THE PERSIAN WARS

THE IONIAN REVOLT (500 or 499—494 BC)

The revolt of the Ionian Greeks against Persian rule in 500 (or 499) B.C. marks the beginning of a new era. For the first time in its history the Persian world empire encountered the national opposition of a particular people, a resistance which forced the Persians to enlist sizeable land and sea forces and which was only suppressed after more than five years of bitter fighting. The fact that the revolt of the Ionians in Asia Minor was the first in a long chain of open rebellions in the Achaemenid empire is sufficient to mark the general historical importance of the event. It is of much less importance that the Ionian struggle for freedom can be traced back also to economic causes and certainly also to personal motives on the part of Ionian political leaders. To attribute a thorough lack of moral will-power, discipline and strategy to the Ionians[1] is a gross exaggeration, and even if such an assertion were in its entirety justified, it would still in no way detract from the general significance of the great event.

The deeper causes of the revolt lay in the Persian policy towards the Greeks of Asia Minor. Following their feudalistic system of government the Persians had placed trusted Greek agents of the Great King at the helm everywhere in the Greek cities within their sphere of power. In the eyes of the citizens in the Greek cities these men were nothing other than tyrants who fettered the independent life of the poleis. The dynasts of these cities, on the other hand, had the backing of the Persian satraps and the pro-Persian circles among the citizens—and of the latter there was no lack in Ionia.

It is understandable that the Persians and their partisans should be held responsible for the economic recession which Ionian trade had suffered during the last quarter of the sixth century. The conquest of Egypt by Cambyses (525 B.C.) meant that Greek, especially Ionian, trade with the land of the Nile was severely impaired; the decline of the Greek trade centre Naucratis speaks a very clear language.[2] In addition, Darius I had, subsequent to the Scythian expedition (513/12 ? B.C.), laid hands on the straits between Asia and Europe, and the Persians controlled Greek northern trade with the region of the Black Sea. This was of extremely vital importance to a city like Miletus, and finally, the destruction of Sybaris (511/10 B.C.), with whom it was on friendly terms, constituted another serious blow to this great Ionian metropolis. This event threatened to ruin the prosperity of Miletus completely for it meant the loss of its western market. No wonder that on the news of the destruction of Sybaris the Milesians shaved their heads as a sign of mourning (Herod. VI 21).[3] But it was not economic but political motives which were crucial in the revolt, however keenly the economic recession was felt by the Ionians. The encroachment on communal autonomy by the Persian administration and by the tyrants whom the Persians supported was most resented. Only a Greek could appreciate what it meant that his own destiny was no longer determined by the *Ekklesia* of his native city but by the satraps or by the Great King of Persia in distant Susa.

If we are to believe Herodotus, the revolt was kindled by the personal motives of Aristagoras, the tyrant of Miletus. Encouraged by Naxian exiles, Aristagoras allegedly sought and gained the support of Artaphernes, the satrap of Sardis, for a combined expedition against the Cycladic island of Naxos. The aim of the tyrant of Miletus was without a doubt to establish a large sphere of power for himself in the Aegean. Artaphernes, the satrap of Sardis, supported the enterprise by commanding the other Ionian cities to provide ships for transporting Persian land forces. The "viceroy of the Great King in Asia Minor" for the first time appeared on the scene as the standard-bearer of an extensive western policy. This western policy continued as long as the Persian empire remained intact and rendered the deputy of the Great King in Sardis the most important personality in the Achaemenid empire for the Greeks. When contrary to expectation the city of Naxos could not be subjugated, the large-scale expedition turned out to be a failure.[4] Both the satrap and the tyrant were no doubt incriminated in the eyes of the Great King. Herodotus (V 35) would have us believe that Aristagoras saw in a revolt of the Ionians the last hope of saving himself from the wrath of the Persians. He abdicated the tyranny in Miletus, and shortly thereafter the dynasts who had been put in place by the Persians were also driven out of other Ionian communities. From Miletus the revolt spread until it embraced the entire coast of Asia Minor. Everywhere *strategoi*, elected to take charge of the anticipated military operations, displaced the tyrants. That the movement in Asia Minor could spread so rapidly shows that the soil had been well prepared for a revolt. Aristagoras would have regarded it as most prudent not to act in opposition to the general feeling, which had spread through most classes of the population.[5]

But the expulsion of the tyrants and the ejection of the Persian garrisons was not sufficient. The main issue now was to work out a common war plan and to look about for allies. At this crucial stage the political weakness of the Ionian Greeks became conspicuous. There was neither a uniform supreme command nor a common strategy. Even at the Congress of the Ionians in Miletus, where the decision to revolt was taken, the widely travelled Hecataeus is said to have drawn attention to the vast dimensions of the Persian empire (on the basis of a map drawn by himself?) and to have counselled against the revolt. His advice was rejected, and his counsel to melt down the votive offerings of the temple at Didyma and to use the funds therefrom for equipping a fleet is also said to have fallen on deaf ears.[6]

The revolt took the Persians completely by surprise, and threatened a vital spot in the empire—the north-west frontier. It was with a view to securing this frontier that Darius I had established the satrapy of Thrace (v.s.p. 83). For the Greeks in Asia Minor everything depended on appealing to the "brethren" of the motherland for aid. The Spartan hoplites were urgently needed, as well as the fleets of the Greek maritime cities Corinth, Aegina and Athens. In the winter of 500/499 B.C. (or 499/8) Aristagoras betook himself to Greece, but the results of his mission were disappointing. In the Peloponnesus the decisive struggle between Lacedaemon and Argos was impending, so Sparta failed the Ionians.[7] Of the maritime cities only Athens decided to send aid across the Aegean, in the form of a squadron of twenty ships. The Athenians feared the restoration of Hippias by the Persians and perhaps hoped to gain the islands of Lemnos and Imbros.[8] Five Eretrian ships joined those of Athens—that was all Hellas had to offer the Ionians in Asia.

Operations in Asia Minor began with a surprising thrust of the Ionians against Sardis, the centre of Persian power in Anatolia.[9] The city went up in flames and even the national sanctuary of the Lydians, the temple of Cybele, was reduced to ashes. The Persian garrison, however, held out on the Acropolis. Anticipating the approaching Persian reinforcements, the Ionians retreated to the coast; at Ephesus they were defeated for the first time.[10] The flames of the burning city of Sardis, however, became the signal for the suppressed peoples in Asia Minor, for the Greeks at the Hellespont, the Carians, the Lycians and even for the Graeco-Oriental mixed population on the island of Cyprus—all now joined the revolt. On the other hand the Athenians abandoned their Ionian brethren at Ephesus and returned home (498 B.C.).

The Persian counter-measures suggest a large-scale strategy: first the important island of Cyprus, lying at the intersection of many traffic routes, was reconquered (497 B.C.). The next Persian thrust was directed against the straits, designed to regain control over the important sea routes for the Persians. The Greek cities at the Dardanelles, on the Sea of Marmara and in Aeolis were soon subdued. Aristagoras gave the cause of freedom up as lost and, no longer feeling safe in Miletus, fled to Thracian Myrcinus on the Strymon, with which the Great King had once presented Histiaeus, the father-in-law of Aristagoras and his predecessor in the Milesian tyranny. In Thrace Aristagoras fell in battle against the Edonians in 496 B.C.

In order to complete the military victories with the weapons of diplomacy Histiaeus, who had been summoned to the court of the Great King in Susa prior to the revolt, was despatched to Ionia by Darius I. Histiaeus, however, betrayed the confidence of the Persian king, sympathising openly with the insurgents. The Ionians on the other hand mistrusted him, as demonstrated by Miletus' refusing to open her gates to him. In consequence nothing remained for him but to seek his fortune on his own. Accordingly, as a free-booter from Byzantium and later from Lesbos he carried on his mischief at the straits, until on a plundering expedition in

Aeolis he fell into the hands of the Persians, who ended his life by crucifixion (493 B.C.).[11]

The struggle for the freedom of Ionia had meanwhile entered its final phase, with the blockading of Miletus by the Persian fleet. Quarrels, open betrayal and criminal negligence sealed the doom of the Ionians in the battle off the island of Lade (495 or 494 B.C.).[12] After blockading Miletus both by sea and by land the Persians took it by storm (494 B.C.). The city, the most costly pearl in the crown of Ionian communities, was apparently in large measure destroyed. It did not succeed in regaining its former importance until some time in the Hellenistic period.[13] Following the example given to the peoples of the Near East by the Assyrians, the Persians deported the Milesians into the interior of the vast empire and settled them in the region of the Lower Tigris. Ionians and Carians are later found as craftsmen in the construction of the palace of Darius in Susa. The highly famous temple of Didymian Apollo before the gates of Miletus was destroyed,[14] and the treasures and the priesthood dragged off. A bronze votive offering from Didyma (an astragal) was rediscovered by French excavators in Susa.[15] The wealthy islands of Chios and Lesbos were severely affected and a number of cities on the Propontis sank into dust and ashes. The rule of the Persian satraps was re-established, the tribute system re-introduced—albeit without any increase in the rate of assessment. That all the tyrants were re-instated, however, is out of the question.[16]

Persian control had some benefits. The Persians set up organised legal procedure between members of the different communities, and so made provision for security under law, absent before because of the innumerable quarrels in Greek internal affairs. The country was resurveyed and recorded in land-registers, a measure which in later times Alexander and the Seleucids used as a model. Ionian cultural life was apparently not decisively affected by the unhappy sequel to the revolt. Hecataeus of Miletus, who enjoyed an equal reputation among Greeks and Persians,[17] was then at the height of his creative powers, and along with him the philosopher Heracleitus of Ephesus. Both remained in their homeland, whereas Xenophanes of Colophon, after a long life of wandering, settled in Elea (Velia) in southern Italy. Thus the spirit of Old Ionia survived, at home and abroad, despite the destruction of Ionian freedom.

The suppression of the revolt brought an expedition of the Persian Mardonius to Thrace and Macedonia to re-establish Persian authority in this region.[18] At the beginning of 492 B.C. the Persian army and fleet, fresh from the victory at Lade, set out from their bases in Cilicia. In Thrace the Persian land forces suffered serious losses at the hands of the native population, especially the Bryges. The fleet suffered shipwreck on the return voyage by the autumn storms off Mount Athos in Chalcidice. The losses in this reverse were also considerable; the figures given by tradition—300 ships and 20,000 men—admittedly warrant no countenance. But the object of the expedition had been achieved. The Thracian satrapy was again securely in Persian hands and Macedonia was once more a vassal state of Persia (Herod. VI 44).

Recent scholarship, chiefly on the authority of K. J. Beloch, has accepted the view that the expedition of Mardonius was not directed against Hellas itself,[19] as Georg Busolt, Eduard Meyer and others, following Herodotus, had maintained.[20] Greek tradition regarding the so-called first Persian expedition of 492 B.C. is in fact a legend. It owes its origin to a retrospective view, with the later invasions of Darius (490 B.C.) and Xerxes (480 B.C.) in mind.

HELLAS AND PERSIA TO THE BATTLE OF MARATHON (500-490 B.C.)

The Greeks of the motherland had participated hardly at all in the Ionian struggle for freedom in Asia Minor. In Sparta the impending conflict with Argos and the aversion of the Lacedaemonians to overseas expeditions, and in Athens the fluctuations in internal affairs, prevented them from rendering effective aid to the Ionians. Attic politics in the post-Cleisthenic period were taken up with the conflict between the Alcmeonidae and the pro-tyrannic party.[21] Neither "party" was unfriendly towards the Persians; the supporters of *tyrannis* even hoped that the Persians would restore Hippias, then living in Sigeum. That a relation or supporter of the Peisistratidae, Hipparchus son of Charmus,[22] succeeded in being elected as eponymous archon in Athens for the year 496 B.C. is evidence that there was no longer any question of a resentment towards the tyrannophiles. When the tragedian Phrynichus presented the *Sack of Miletus* on the stage and deeply moved the audience by portraying the capture of the great Ionian sister-city, the Attic authorities prosecuted the poet and imposed a fine on him. Behind Phrynichus, however, there stood the Lycomid Themistocles, son of Neocles and whose mother was a woman of Acarnania.[23] His election to the archonship in 493 B.C.[24] marks a decisive change in public opinion at Athens. The fate of the Ionians in Asia Minor had opened the eyes of the Athenians to what they could expect from the Persians. Unless a fleet were built it seemed useless to entertain any idea of resisting the world power of the East. In order to man the fleet a large cross-section of the population would have to be enlisted to serve on the ships. As archon Themistocles' first measure was a proposal for the construction of a military harbour with the necessary docks and arsenals in the bay of Piraeus—hitherto the beach at Phalerum had sufficed for the shallow vessels. But at the time nothing more than the initial steps towards building a fleet was achieved. The great reputation of the Philaid Miltiades, who returned from the Chersonese in 493 B.C., temporarily forced Themistocles into the background again; not until ten years later did he resume his plans for building the fleet, and only then could he carry them through to completion (v.i.p. 96 f.).

Miltiades, abortively accused of tyranny in the Chersonese by his opponents (the Alcmeonidae?), was regarded by the Athenians as the proper leader for the impending struggle. The strategy was to conduct the battle in the traditional manner, namely with the hoplite phalanx. Aristeides of Alopece, also a declared opponent of the Alcmeonidae, was on close terms with Miltiades.

The leading power in Greece, however, was Sparta, the leader of the Peloponnesian League, a defensive alliance to which Athens incidentally did not belong.[25] The fluctuating foreign policy of Sparta reflects the latent conflict between the monarchy and the ephorate. The former, in the person of Cleomenes I, pursued an active and expansive foreign policy, while the latter sought to reduce the prerogatives of the kings and committed itself to cautious reserve in foreign affairs. It was King Cleomenes I who overthrew Argos, the last serious enemy of Sparta in the Peloponnesus. In the violent battle of Sepeia the forces of the Peloponnesian League emerged victorious over the Argives (c. 494 B.C.).[26] Tiryns and Mycenae thereupon went over to the side of Sparta, while Argos moved to the verge of destruction by serious internal conflicts.[27] As a result the Argives ceased to be serious rivals of Sparta. The conflict between Cleomenes I and Damaratus, however, prevented the Spartans from fully exploiting their victory. With the aid of the Delphic oracle Cleomenes forced the deposition of his partner in the crown, on the grounds of illegitimate birth, whereupon Damaratus went to the court of the Persian king. Impenetrable darkness obscures the end of the life of Cleomenes (488 B.C.?);[28] Leonidas acceded to the throne as his successor.

The policy of Darius towards the Greeks in the crucial decade between 500 and 490 B.C. displays all the elements characteristic of later Persian policy. By forming close personal relations with part of the Greek aristocracy the Persians sought to prepare the ground for a gradual political penetration of Greece. The Great King accepted a number of Hellenic nobles, for instance, Metiochus, son of the younger Miltiades, and the banished Spartan king Damaratus, into the circle of the eminent Persian imperial nobility, and presented them with land. The Persians also displayed a deliberate veneration for the Delphic oracle and its priesthood. But particularly close connections existed between the Persians and the Thessalians, especially with the family of the Aleuadae, relations which found expression in the coins of Larisa on the Persian standard.[29]

The statement of Herodotus (VI 48), that the Persian king sent heralds to Greece in 491 B.C. to demand that the Hellenes submit themselves to the Persians, warrants no belief.[30] About this time Athens was involved in a conflict with her neighbour, the powerful maritime city of Aegina and mistress of the Saronic Gulf.[31] Sparta's peremptory order put an end to the dissension which had already lasted for some time, forcing the Aeginetans to produce hostages but leaving Athens with her back free for the impending attack of the Persians.

The destination of the Persian expedition which put out to sea in the summer of 490 B.C. under the command of Datis, an experienced Median officer—the fleet being under the admiralty of Artaphernes, son of the satrap of Sardis bearing the same name—was Eretria and Athens. Both cities were to be punished for helping the Ionians. This was, however, only a pretext for establishing conditions which would make for Persian supremacy over Greece: Sparta was to be isolated and the remaining states split up into a series of impotent groups. The number of warships (allegedly 600 triremes) is conventional and certainly exaggerated. The landing troops conveyed across on transports must be reckoned at approximately 20,000.[32]

As the Persian fleet sailed through the Aegean most of the Cyclades surrendered. Naxos was punished for its conduct in 500 B.C. Datis, the actual leader of the expedition, presented a solemn offering to Apollo at Delos.[33] After landing on Euboea the first devastating blow struck the city of Eretria. Her fate was sealed by treachery; the inhabitants were dragged off and resettled far away in Ardericca in Susiana, a colony visited more than a generation later by Herodotus (Herod. VI 119).

On the advice of Hippias the Persians landed at the Plain of Marathon in Attica. In the choice of this location, political (the small farmers of this district were regarded as particularly friendly towards the tyrants) and strategical considerations appear to have been equally decisive. In addition, it was only possible to deploy the Persian cavalry successfully on level ground. In the face of the Persian invasion the Athenians were thrown back entirely on their own resources. A highly dangerous situation, which was further accentuated by the existence of a strong pro-tyrannic group within the walls of the city! An appeal for help to Sparta, the *prostates* of Hellas, was, it is true, not in vain but, whatever the reasons may have been,[34] the Spartan auxiliary corps arrived too late in Attica. In contrast to this the Plataeans, who were on friendly terms with Athens, helped as much as they could. The total forces numbered about 10,000, that is, numerically they were considerably inferior to the Persian landing corps. Although Athens was protected by a fortification wall,[35] it was nevertheless decided, on the proposal of Miltiades in the *Ekklesia*, to meet the Persians in the field,[36] in order to prevent them from advancing any further along the road leading from Marathon to Athens[37]—a resolution of extraordinary boldness, which staked everything on one card. The Athenians took up their position on the north-east slopes of Agrieliki[38] and remained there for a number of days opposing the Persians, who in awareness of their superiority repeatedly offered battle. It was Miltiades, one of the ten generals, who prevailed upon the polemarch Callimachus to accept. The actual course of the battle is disputed, for topographical problems also create a number of difficulties.[39] It is certain, however, that it was a pitched battle and not a rear-guard action by the Persians.[40] In all probability the Persians and not the Athenians led the attack (contrary to Herodotus).[41] Once having resolved to parry the Persian attack, the phalanx of the Athenian hoplites on approaching the enemy traversed the last two hundred yards "at the double" in order to avoid the hail of arrows from the Persians. While the centre had to yield to the Persian core, the strong wings put the enemy to flight, and then by wheeling inward, completed the victory. The triumph was not, however, completely followed up, probably because the heavily armed troops were too exhausted. The Persians, who by a delaying action, continued their resistance at a small brook (the Charadra) and before their ships, succeeded in re-embarking most of their landing corps. The attempt to sail round the point of Sunium and to take Athens by a surprise attack had to be abandoned by Datis, for the victorious Attic troops had rushed south in forced marches and encamped in the Gymnasium of Cynosarges in order to protect the city.[42]

Although the battle of Marathon (September 490 B.C.)[43] did not decide the issue in the struggle between the Persians and the Greeks, it was none the less of the greatest importance. It was a victory of better Athenian arms and the superiority of Greek tactics. The stimulus to morale which the Greeks—not the Athenians only—received by this victory can scarcely be overestimated. Marathon is inseparably linked with the name of Miltiades, the first important general of the West. It was he who brought about the decisive vote and he it was who prevailed upon Callimachus to accept battle. Miltiades must, however, share the renown of the victory with Callimachus, who met his death on the battlefield. Callimachus' name unjustifiably sank into oblivion, and not until the victory statue was discovered bearing an inscription dedicated to Callimachus' memory by his relatives has his share in the victory been brought into its proper light.[44]

THE BUILDING OF THEMISTOCLES' FLEET AND PERSIAN MOBILISATION

The victory at Marathon created the conditions for the naval expedition of Miltiades against the western Cyclades (spring 489 B.C.).[45] Following some initial successes, however, the enterprise came to a standstill before the walls of Paros and had to be abandoned. Miltiades was arraigned in Athens and on the plea of having "deceived" the people was sentenced to pay an enormous fine. His death soon after cleared the way for his opponents.

After the removal of Miltiades fate overtook a number of leading men from the circle of the tyrannophiles and the Alcmeonidae in Athens. In these circumstances the Athenians for the first time resorted to the ostracism which had been created two decades earlier by Cleisthenes. The first victim of the lot of banishment was Hipparchus, son of Charmus (487 B.C.), next the Alcmeonid Megacles (486 B.C.), and his brother-in-law, Xanthippus (484 B.C.). In 482 B.C. Aristeides was also forced to go into exile. These ostracisms[46] show a certain systematic policy, and new ostraca show that Themistocles was the driving force behind at least a part of them. The Lycomid may also have been influential in the decisive reform of the constitution in 487/6 B.C. Although all details concerning it remain shrouded in darkness,[47] it nevertheless marks a step forward in the development towards full democracy. The archonship was annulled as an elective office and the nine archons—now members of the second class, the *hippeis*, also became eligible for the archonship—were now chosen by a combined system of pre-election and sortition. The individual Attic demes elected fifty candidates in advance from each *phyle*, and then from this number the nine archons were chosen by lot. The archonship thereby lost its position of supremacy. It was displaced by the *strategia*—office of general—which continued to be an elective office. The polemarch, who at Marathon had

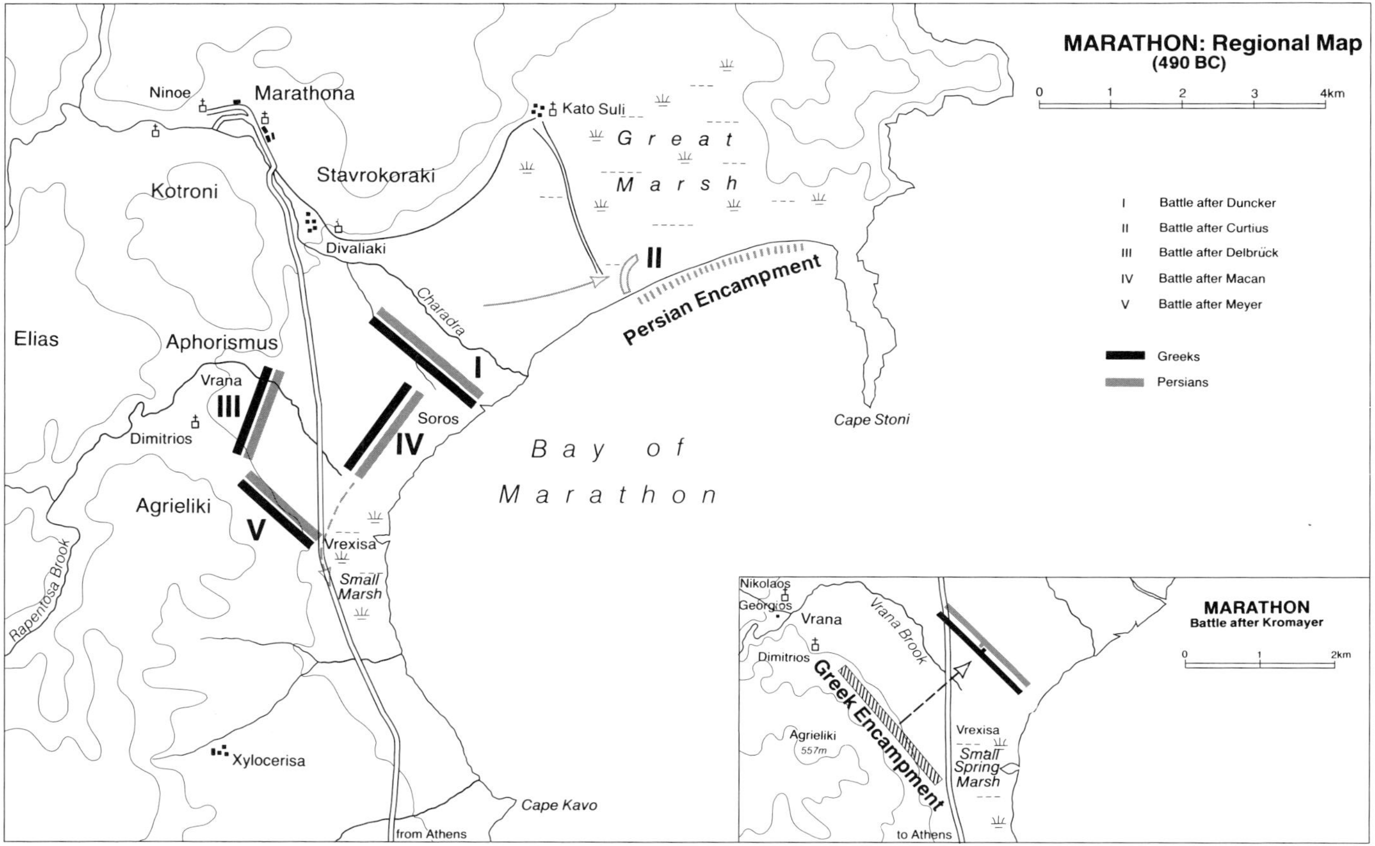
MARATHON: Regional Map
(490 BC)
0 1 2 3 4km
I Battle after Duncker
II Battle after Curtius
III Battle after Delbrück
IV Battle after Macan
V Battle after Meyer
Greeks
Persians
Ninoe
Marathona
Kato Suli
Great Marsh
Stavrokoraki
Kotroni
Divaliaki
Charadra
Persian Encampment
Elias
Aphorismus
Vrana
Dimitrios
Soros
Cape Stoni
Bay of Marathon
Agrieliki
Vrexisa
Small Marsh
Rapentosa Brook
Xylocerisa
Cape Kavo
from Athens
MARATHON
Battle after Kromayer
0 1 2km
Nikolaos
Georgios
Vrana
Vrana Brook
Dimitrios
Greek Encampment
Agrieliki
557m
Vrexisa
Small Spring Marsh
to Athens

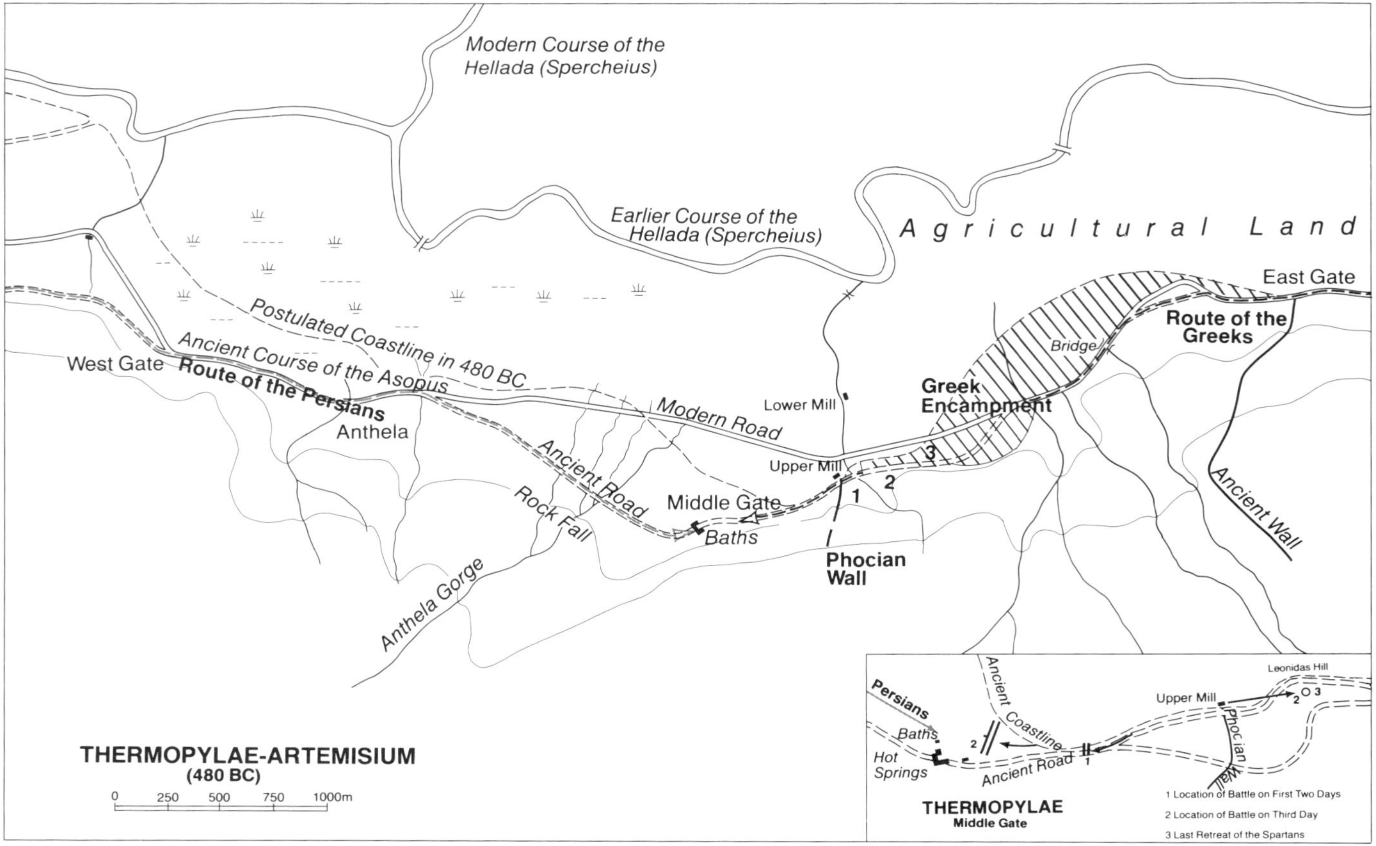

Modern Course of the
Hellada (Spercheius)
Earlier Course of the
Hellada (Spercheius)
Agricultural Land
East Gate
Route of the
Greeks
Bridge
Greek
Encampment
Ancient Wall
Lower Mill
Upper Mill
1
2
3
Phocian
Wall
Middle Gate
Baths
Postulated Coastline in 480 BC
Ancient Course of the Asopus
West Gate
Route of the Persians
Anthela
Modern Road
Ancient Road
Rock Fall
Anthela Gorge
THERMOPYLAE-ARTEMISIUM
(480 BC)
0
250
500
750
1000m
Persians
Baths
Hot
Springs
Ancient Coastline
Ancient Road
Upper Mill
Leonidas Hill
Phocian Wall
THERMOPYLAE
Middle Gate
1 Location of Battle on First Two Days
2 Location of Battle on Third Day
3 Last Retreat of the Spartans

been commander-in-chief of the entire forces, now lost all importance, whereas the *strategoi* immediately took over a number of administrative and financial powers, and gradually rose to become the most important representatives of the Attic state. The claim that the office of an *epistrategos* was created[48] is not supported by our sources.

The banishment of his political opponents removed the last impediments to Themistocles' plans for a fleet. The protracted conflict between Athens and Aegina, the latter then at the height of its power, was an inducement to building sea power. A dispute broke out afresh in 488/7 B.C. and ended in a deep humiliation for Athens.[49] Besides political, there were also economic considerations behind the design. In particular, protection of the grain ships may have played a certain part in the plan to build a navy.[50] News of the vast Persian mobilisation and the construction of the canal at Athos on the Chalcidian peninsula overcame the last elements of resistance at Athens. A radical political reshaping of the Athenian state was inseparably connected with the building of the fleet. In order to man the ships it was necessary to have recourse to the broad masses of the fourth class, the *thetes*. They too were now obliged to contribute their full share to the defense of the state. The realisation that now full citizen rights could no longer be withheld from the *thetes* did not deter Themistocles or his friends. The solving of problems in internal politics would have to wait until after the impending struggle. In order to finance the building programme, which began in 482 B.C., funds were obtained, on the proposal of Themistocles, from the revenues of the state silver mines at Laurium, now increased appreciably by a new mine that had just been opened.[51] In order to equip the warships the most prosperous Athenian citizens were obliged to make personal contributions (the system of *trierarchia*). In the opinion of Eduard Meyer[52] the building of the fleet more than doubled the military strength of Athens within a few years, and this despite the fact that the intended number of 200 triremes was not reached.[53] Athens now became the strongest sea-power of the Greek motherland, and far outstripped her rivals, even Corinth and Aegina. On only one other occasion does ancient history attest the building of a fleet of as much importance as that which Themistocles built in less than two years:[54] the creation of Roman sea-power during the initial years of the First Punic War. The Athenian fleet assumed a position of equality alongside the hoplite army of the Peloponnesian League, the core of which was formed by the Lacedaemonians, and thus the foundations of Athenian-Spartan dualism were laid, even before the beginning of the great Persian War.

Persian mobilisation was delayed by internal disturbances. In 486/5 B.C., that is, only seven years after the suppression of the Ionian Revolt, the Egyptians rebelled against Persian domination. This is the more notable, for it was precisely the Egyptians—so far as we know—who had little reason to complain about Achaemenid rule. For almost two years the land of the Nile remained independent, until in 484 B.C. Xerxes, the successor of Darius I (who died in 486 B.C.), reconquered it. Xerxes also abolished once and for all the special position of Egypt. The country, which had previously stood in personal union with the Persian crown, was now reduced to the level of the other satrapies, and thereby lost its prerogatives.[55] The Babylonians also revolted at almost the same time as the Egyptians; datings on the basis of cuneiform inscriptions give the names of native usurpers.[56] The answer of Xerxes to this was the removal of the special monarchy of Babylon, an event which is, however, probably not to be dated until 479 or 478 B.C., in the period following the Greek expedition, that is, after the Babylonians had revolted for the second time.[57]

In their dimensions the preparations which Xerxes had been making since 483 B.C. to make Persia ready for the campaign against Greece far surpass anything of like nature in the past. They give an imposing picture of the strength and organisation of the Achaemenid world empire, which at the time stood at the height of its power. Traces of the canal at Athos have been discovered by modern archaeology.[58] In order to ensure the provisioning of the army numerous magazines were set up in Macedonia and Thrace. Special importance was attached to close co-operation between the army and fleet and troops were enlisted from all parts of the empire. It was no frontier war which Xerxes intended to conduct; on the contrary, he planned an expedition of conquest on the grandest scale. It is therefore impossible that with these designs he had only the small country of Greece in mind. It is, rather, probable that the conquest of Greece was to be only the first stage on the way to incorporating the entire south-east of Europe into the Persian empire. What had been prepared by the Scythian expedition of Darius I and by the expedition of Mardonius, this Xerxes wanted to complete.

XERXES' CAMPAIGN AGAINST GREECE (480 B.C.)

In the autumn of 481 B.C. Persian mobilisation was essentially completed. Of all the powers within the frontiers of the Greek world besides the Peloponnesian League under the hegemony of Sparta, only the Syracusan realm of Gelon could constitute a danger to Persian design if it should throw its weight into the scales in favour of the Hellenes of the motherland. A Persian-Carthaginian treaty, the reality of which ought not to be doubted, recognised this.[59] Thus the military strategy of Xerxes embraced almost the entire Mediterranean. Creating a far-sighted policy, the Achaemenid king displayed both foresight and the ability to gauge the strength of his opponents. Taking counsel from eminent Persians and from Greek emigrants,[60] he quickly seized the opportunities presented by the general situation. If fortune favoured, Xerxes could be certain of sovereignty over the entire territory of the Greek-inhabited Mediterranean.

At the beginning of June, 480 B.C., the hordes of the Persian army crossed the Hellespont between Abydus and Sestos on two floating bridges constructed by the Greek Harpalus.[61] From here they proceeded along the coastal route to the region of Therma in Macedonia.

The problem of the size of the Persian army is practically insoluble. That the fantastic figures of Herodotus—he places the number of the entire forces at more than five million, of which 1,700,000 were combatant foot and 80,000 horse—are not believable, has long been generally recognised by scholars.[62] In a penetrating study, based on the possibilities of furnishing supplies and the time required to cross the Hellespont, General E. v. Fischer arrived at the conclusion that the army of Xerxes cannot have numbered more than 50,000 combatants.[63] But this figure leaves unexplained the fear of the Greeks in the face of the advancing Persian army—unless we are to conclude that rumour had exaggerated the size of the army into gigantic proportions. The British general Sir Frederick Maurice has arrived at higher figures (a total of 175,000 combatants).[64] The number of ships given by Aeschylus, 1207 (*Persae* 341 ff.), has had an able advocate in A. Köster.[65]

Heralds, commissioned to summon the Greeks to subject themselves to Persia, went in advance of the Persian army. In view of the impending Persian invasion an unusually pessimistic mood prevailed in Greece, accentuated by the Delphic oracle, which foretold destruction and ruin.[66] To yield to Persia, however, was completely out of the question for the two leading states of Sparta and Athens, and their attitude brought a number of other Greek poleis into the defensive struggle. Many states, however, remained aloof. Argos in particular assumed a neutral position, Corcyra was doubtful, while the Sicilian ruler Gelon made his help subject to conditions which the Greeks of the motherland were not in a position to fulfil.[67] In Thessaly and Boeotia an open pro-Median mood prevailed. Pindar praised the blessings of peace[68]—in the face of the greatest war in Greek history.

At a congress of the Greek states which were resolved to defend themselves against the Persians and had joined together into an alliance, a general peace was proclaimed throughout Hellas in the autumn of 481 B.C. All feuds were to cease and all exiles to return to their own communities.[69] Those Greeks who showed themselves sympathetic towards the Persian cause were threatened with destruction and a tenth of their property was to pass into the possession of Apollo at Delphi.[70] For the first time in Greek history a military alliance[71] took as its rôle the consolidating of all anti-Persian resources in the motherland. It was the great crisis of the time which prompted the Greeks to forget divisions and to call to mind unifying elements—their common origin and their common national identity.

Themistocles[72] drew up the military strategy, in co-operation with the Spartan ephors. The decision was to take place on the seas, with the hope of the Greeks resting in the young Athenian fleet. No one dared risk a decisive battle with the masses of Persian land forces. The rôle of the Greek army was to co-operate with their own naval forces by holding up the advance of the Persian army until the Greek fleet had succeeded in inflicting a decisive defeat on the Persians at a favourable place. Even the initial measures showed the basic idea of Greek strategy. The Greeks initially took up a greatly advanced forward line of defence in the defile of Tempe south of Mount Olympus.[73] Since it could be easily circumvented from the west, it had shortly to be abandoned, perhaps also in view of the uncertain attitude of the Thessalians, who later openly went over to the side of the Persians. In contrast to Tempe, Thermopylae offered the very advantages which the Greeks required in the face of Persian superiority. The passes prevented the Persian army from fanning out, while at sea the narrow sound of the Euripus made it impossible to overwhelm the co-operating Greek fleet. If the advance of the Persian land forces could be held up for a limited time at Thermopylae, then the Greek fleet could, if conditions were favourable, possibly force a decision. The contingent which took up its position at Thermopylae under the command of the Spartan king Leonidas, consisted of 4000 Peloponnesians (including 300 Spartiates), 700 Thespians, levies of Phocians and Opuntic Locrians and 400 Thebans, whose heart was actually on the side of the Persians. The corps was only about 7000, but ought to have been adequate to carry out the limited-time assignment.[74]

The Greek fleet, with a total of 270 ships, took up its position off the north-west tip of Euboea, at Cape Cephala. Its assignment was to wipe out the Persian naval power in the sound between the island of Euboea and the mainland, and thereby force the army of Xerxes to retreat. On the voyage southwards the Persians sustained heavy losses in a storm at the south-east tip of the Magnesian peninsula (off Cape Sepias) and 400 ships at anchor off the steep coast were destroyed.

According to Herodotus (VIII 15) the battles of Thermopylae and of Artemisium[75] took place on the same day—in mid-summer 480 B.C.—a statement which research by August Köster has now confirmed as correct. On the fifth day after arriving at Thermopylae the Persians began a frontal attack against the Greek position.[76] It was on this day that the sea battle of Artemisium was launched. The Greeks had taken up their position before the second of three gates (defiles) situated one behind the other. For two days the Persian assault remained completely ineffectual, but on the third day Persian contingents under Hydarnes slipped around the Greek position to the south with the aid of local guides,[77] surprised the incautious Phocian detachment which had been stationed to guard the back path, and appeared in Leonidas' rear. Despite the fact that the Persians had circumvented his position, Leonidas had to try to hold the Persians back at least until the last southbound Greek warship had passed the western tip of Euboea, in a narrow channel which was in places little more than fifteen yards wide and which could easily be sealed off. Otherwise the costly Greek fleet would be lost and the war decided. In spite of all the criticism which has been levelled against his conduct, Leonidas carried out the rôle assigned to him in an exemplary manner.[78] The Spartan king permitted a considerable number of the contingents to retire southwards, while he himself kept 700 Thespians and 300 Spartiates with him. Crowded together on one hill, they perished to the last man. The sacrifice was not in vain. The feat of Leonidas gave the Greeks a shining example of duty fulfilled in their struggle for freedom.

On the crucial third day the Persian admiralty (after confirmation of the destruction of the squadron despatched southwards to circumvent the Greek detachment) attempted a reckless frontal attack to break through the Greek blocking force lying off Euboea and the little island of Argyronesi, and sail in the direction of the Euripus. The Greeks, with heavy losses, held their ground against the enormous pressure, until news of the fall of Thermopylae fundamentally altered the entire strategic situation. The Greek fleet consequently disengaged itself from the enemy on the following day, and without being noticed by the latter withdrew through the Euripus into the Saronic Gulf. Despite serious losses the Persians could regard the double battle of Thermopylae and Artemisium as a strategic victory. The goal, access to central Greece, had been achieved. The Greeks did indeed look upon Artemisium as at least a tactical success,[79] but taken in conjunction with Thermopylae the naval engagement was no doubt a defeat. It was of decisive importance in terms of further operations.

After the fall of Thermopylae the whole of central Greece lay open to the Persians, who advanced burning cities and villages. Thebes, which had fought only half-heartedly for the cause of freedom, was spared. By openly aligning itself with the Medes, Delphi was able to save the treasures of the sanctuary.[80] The population of Attica had to be evacuated; alone on the Acropolis a weak garrison remained behind.[81] After a siege it was subdued by the Persians and the citadel systematically ravished.

While the Greeks were still feverishly working on the fortification of the narrow isthmus, the last defensive position in Greece, the Hellenic fleet under the admiralty of the Spartan Eurybiades took up a new position off the island of Salamis. In total it consisted of slightly more than 300 vessels, with Athens contributing by far the greatest contingent, followed by Corinth and Aegina.[82] In selecting the battle site the view of Themistocles prevailed. Themistocles alone rejected the concept of fighting the war on land, and was the first to champion the autonomy of the fleet and the idea that the war must be decided on the seas. The design to induce the Persians to accept battle at the spot of Themistocles' choice is revealed in his secret message to Xerxes, the authenticity of which ought not to be called in question. It is attested by Aeschylus in his *Persae*, produced only eight years after the event. Let Xerxes attack forthwith, as the Greeks have resolved to take flight,[83] was Themistocles' message.

The crucial battle was fought in the narrowest place in the sound of Salamis, in the waters between Mount Aegaleus, the island of Psyttaleia (Lipsokutala) and the peninsula of Cynosura projecting eastwards, that is, in the exact place where Themistocles wanted to have the Persians.[84]

The Persian plan for the battle of Salamis shows certain similarities to the tactics employed in the battle of Artemisium. Again a circumventing squadron was despatched, ordered to sail southwards around Salamis in order to block the straits between the island and Megara,[85] so that the Greek fleet would have been caught in a *cul de sac*. In addition, the island of Psyttaleia (Lipsokutala) was occupied by a Persian landing corps, which was to haul up the Greek wrecks. The Persian fleet fought with its front facing southwards, in its rear the heights of Mount Aegaleus, from which Xerxes viewed the impressive drama unfolding at his feet. The Persian right was probably at Hagios Georgios. The Phoenicians fought at Hagios Georgios, while the Ionian contingent, adjacent to Psyttaleia, held the left wing. The Greek front faced northwards, with the Aeginetans on the right wing and the Athenians on the left. The course of the fateful battle still presents numerous difficulties, but it may be regarded as certain that the decision was effected by a surprise flank attack from the west by the Athenians (perhaps after sailing round the island of Hagios Georgios?)—a manoeuvre which crowded the Persian vessels, already in very close formation, even closer together and encumbered their manoeuvrability.[86] The Persians none the less put up a fierce fight. Their troops on Psyttaleia were cut down by Attic hoplites and archers under Aristeides. After twelve hours of fighting the battle ended in total victory for the Greeks, and the Persian vessels which escaped destruction sailed back to the wharf at Phalerum. The Persians could not now contemplate a continuation of operations on land. Without even an attack against the Isthmus, Xerxes led his land forces back to Athens.

In seeking the causes of the Persian defeat it must not be overlooked[87] that the ships of the Persians were more seaworthy and more manoeuvrable than those of the Greeks. In addition, the Phoenicians and Ionian mariners had a better knowledge of the sea than the Greeks of the mother-country, and had a distinct feeling of superiority towards their opponents. On the other hand the Persian fleet was still suffering from the severe losses of the three-day storm off Cape Sepias before the battle of Artemisium. Besides this, nautical inadequacy, limited familiarity with Greek waters, inefficiency on the part of the Persian admirals from the Persian aristocracy, slavish adherence to a policy of land warfare—all these factors combine to explain the serious defeat. In addition, at Salamis the Greeks were fighting for their homeland and for freedom, whereas the Persians were merely induced by a reward from the hand of the Great King, provided he were favourably inclined. The irrational element proved to be the decisive factor. Thanks to the brilliant strategy of Themistocles,[88] it triumphed over numerical superiority and greater experience.

The battle of Salamis (end of September 480 B.C.) ended the campaigns that year. The triumphal march of Xerxes from Olympus to the Isthmus of Corinth had been brought to a standstill.[89] The Greeks were not, however, in a position to take full strategic advantage of the victory which they had gained. Thus the suggestion of Themistocles to make a naval thrust against the Hellespont was rejected by the Peloponnesians.[90] The threat to Greece posed by the main body of the Persian army wintering in Thessaly under the command of Mardonius remained. The Great King betook himself to Sardis in order to be near at hand for the opening of a new campaign against Greece planned for the following spring. The message of Themistocles to Xerxes advising him to retreat can scarcely have been definitive in Xerxes' decision to withdraw from

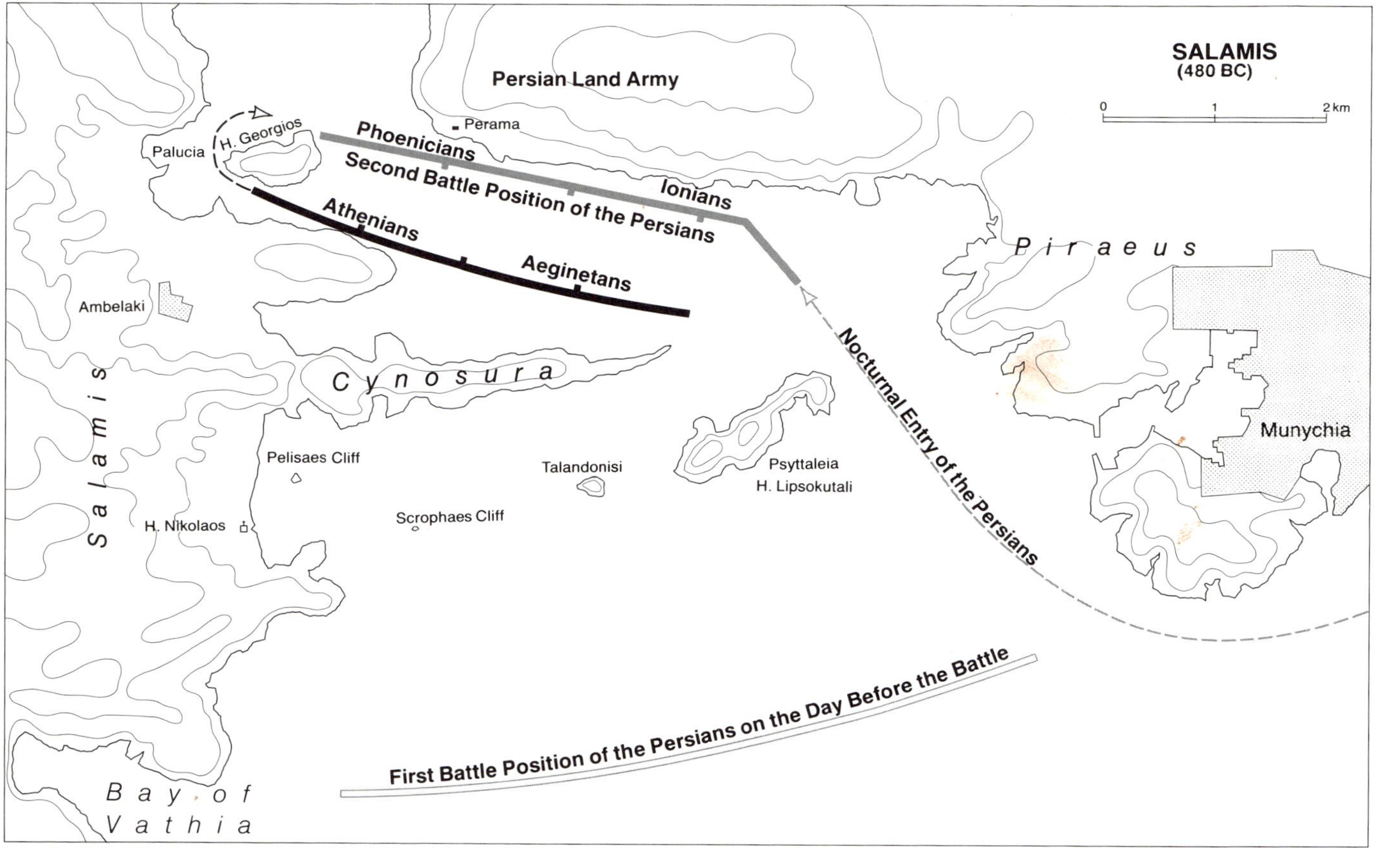
SALAMIS
(480 BC)
0
1
2 km
Persian Land Army
Perama
Phoenicians
Second Battle Position of the Persians
Ionians
Palucia
H. Georgios
Athenians
Aeginetans
Piraeus
Munychia
Ambelaki
Cynosura
Salamis
Nocturnal Entry of the Persians
Pelisaes Cliff
Talandonisi
Psyttaleia
H. Lipsokutali
H. Nikolaos
Scrophaes Cliff
First Battle Position of the Persians on the Day Before the Battle
Bay of
Vathia

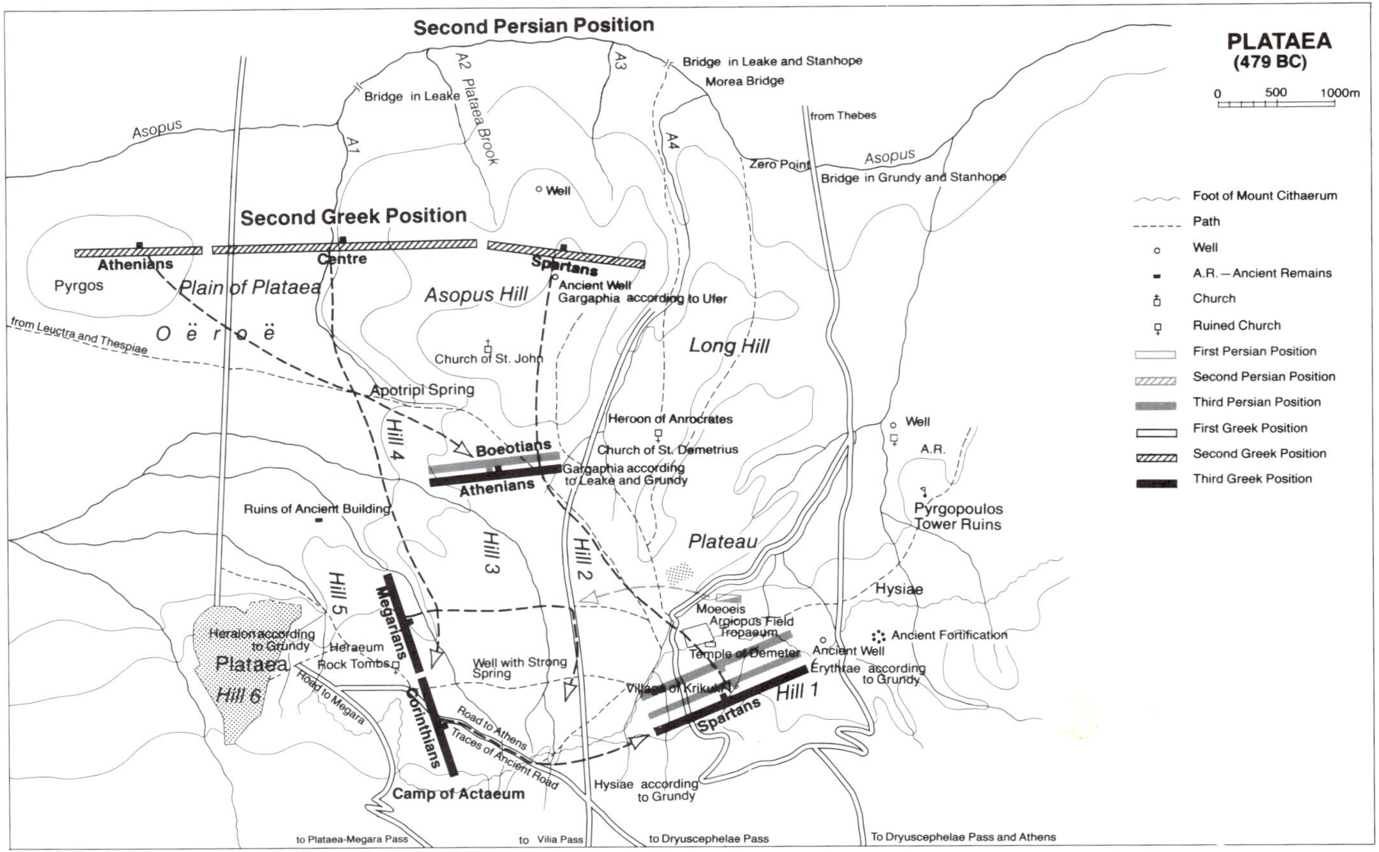
PLATAEA
(479 BC)
0 500 1000m
Foot of Mount Cithaerum
Path
Well
A.R. – Ancient Remains
Church
Ruined Church
First Persian Position
Second Persian Position
Third Persian Position
First Greek Position
Second Greek Position
Third Greek Position
Second Persian Position
Second Greek Position
Bridge in Leake
A2 Plataea Brook
A3
Bridge in Leake and Stanhope
Morea Bridge
from Thebes
Asopus
A1
A4
Zero Point
Bridge in Grundy and Stanhope
Well
Athenians
Centre
Spartans
Pyrgos
Plain of Plataea
Asopus Hill
Ancient Well
Gargaphia according to Ufer
from Leuctra and Thespiae
Oëroë
Church of St. John
Long Hill
Apotripi Spring
Heroon of Anrocrates
Church of St. Demetrius
Hill 4
Boeotians
Athenians
Gargaphia according to Leake and Grundy
Well
A.R.
Ruins of Ancient Building
Hill 3
Hill 2
Plateau
Pyrgopoulos Tower Ruins
Hill 5
Megarians
Hysiae
Moeoeis
Argiopus Field
Tropaeum
Ancient Fortification
Heraion according to Grundy
Heraeum
Rock Tombs
Temple of Demeter
Ancient Well
Plataea
Well with Strong Spring
Erythrae according to Grundy
Hill 6
Village of Krikuki
Hill 1
Road to Megara
Corinthians
Road to Athens
Traces of Ancient Road
Spartans
Hysiae according to Grundy
Camp of Actaeum
to Plataea-Megara Pass
to Vilia Pass
to Dryuscephelae Pass
To Dryuscephelae Pass and Athens

Greece, for this second message of the Athenian is probably an unhistorical duplication of the first one before the battle.[91]

The deep impression made by the Persian defeat is reflected in the revolts which broke out not only in Chalcidice but also in the heart of the Persian empire, in Babylonia. While Olynthus was soon brought into subjection again, Potidaea continued to hold out.[92] Its citizens therefore justifiably appear on the Serpent Column at Delphi among their fellow-combatants in the struggle for freedom. In Babylon the magnificent temple of Bel-Marduk was destroyed by the Persians and the special monarchy of Babel abolished. It was this Babylonian revolt of 479 B.C. that frustrated the designs of Xerxes to resume the Greek campaign with fresh troops.[93]

Greek operations after the battle of Salamis were practically meaningless. Contributions were collected from the Cyclades in order to punish them for their pro-Median attitude. The land thrust planned by the Spartan Cleombrotus across the Isthmus into central Greece never took place. Had it been conducted and failed, it would have jeopardised everything which had hitherto been achieved. It was far more important to keep the Greek army intact because the decisive battle on land was still to come.

THE GREEK VICTORIES AT MYCALE AND PLATAEA (479 B.C.)

While Themistocles was in Sparta during the winter of 480/79 B.C., the common strategy of the allied states was drawn up. Once more only half-measures were taken. The Spartan king Leotychidas' naval demonstration to protect the Cyclades was completely devoid of results. On the other hand the versatile Mardonius generated an energetic diplomacy from his headquarters in Thessaly, aiming to split the Hellenic block and trying above all to win Athens over. In the spring of 479 B.C. the Macedonian king, Alexander I, appeared in Athens as his negotiator. He had far-reaching Persian offers to convey, provided the Athenians declared themselves willing to join an alliance.[94]

In the winter of 480/79 B.C., however, a political change of great consequence took place in Athens. Xanthippus, who by marriage was related to the Alcmeonidae, and Aristeides were elected generals in place of Themistocles. In Athens there was apparently dissatisfaction with the results of Themistocles' negotiations at the Congress in Sparta. In the summer of 479 B.C. the countryside of Attica and the city of Athens had once more to be evacuated in the face of the Persian army advancing from the north.[95] While the population sought refuge on Salamis the Persians completed the destruction of Athens. Sparta could no longer turn a deaf ear to the urgent pleas from Athens. Pausanias, the guardian of the young king Pleistarchus, son of Leonidas, led the Peloponnesian forces across the Isthmus. He was joined by the contingents of the Greek confederates from Athens, Plataea, Megara, Aegina, from Corinth and her colonies, all in all about 30,000—this was about the limit that free Greece was able to put into the field. Mardonius had withdrawn to Boeotia and waited for the enemy in the district of Plataea, with about 40,000–50,000 troops.[96]

The peculiar course of the battle at Plataea[97] is only understandable if we assume that the various Greek contingents fought out the struggle in a certain isolation, without paying much attention to the orders of Pausanias the commander-in-chief. The actual battle took place in the region north of Plataea (west of the road leading from Thebes to Athens) in the district of the Asopus brook. When Pausanias gave a command to retreat, with the intention of defending the important Dryus-Cephalae Pass, complete confusion in the Greek army followed, for the Athenians under Aristeides refused to comply. On the contrary, they advanced even further north, deeper into the river bed.[98] In this precarious situation the Persian attack struck the Greeks, but was repulsed by the Spartan phalanx. Again the Greek lance triumphed over the Persian bow. Mardonius fell, along with a large number of Persians. Nothing certain is known about the fighting of the Athenian contingent. Pausanias could justly claim the glory of the victory,[99] for he had mastered the situation despite failure by part of the army. The Hellenes erected an altar to Zeus on the battlefield and founded a penteteric (recurring every four years) "salvation" festival, and entrusted its supervision to the Plataeans. Their district was proclaimed inviolable by the confederates.[100]

It still remained to settle accounts with Thebes, the stronghold of Medism on Greek soil. In spite of their strong fortifications the Thebans lost courage and handed over the pro-Persian elements, whom Pausanias ordered to be put to death at the Isthmus. This marked the end of the campaign on the Greek side. For almost one and a half centuries—until Chaeroneia (338 B.C.)—no foreign enemy set foot on Greek soil. The Greeks now, however, abandoned the defensive policy which they had been forced to adopt in the face of Xerxes' invasion. Thus Plataea forms a decisive turning point in Greek history, historically no less important than Alexander's crossing into Asia in 334 B.C.

Although the season was already well advanced, the victory of Plataea was followed up by a Greek naval expedition to Ionia under the command of the Spartan king Leotychidas.[101] At the promontory of Mycale, on the plain at the mouth of the Maeander, he came upon the Persian naval encampment, and stormed it with a superior Greek landing force.[102] The Persian ships went up in flames and some of the Persians met their death in the surrounding hills at the hands of the Ionians.[103] Mycale was the signal to the Ionians for a general revolt from Persia. Everywhere the tyrants and Persian garrisons, by now already weak, were driven out.[104]

To protect themselves from the Persians in the future, the Ionians requested admission into the Hellenic Alliance, provided Sparta as *hegemon* was prepared to take over the protection of the Ionians. The Spartans, in clear recognition of the political possibilities, declined, urging the Ionians to resettle in Greece instead. The Spartans proposed to give the Ionians the Greek cities which had joined the Persians, a plan which in practical terms would have been impossible to carry out. Only the islands of Lesbos, Chios and Samos were accepted into the Hellenic Symmachy, viz. through Athenian intercession. But Athens herself formed separate treaties with certain communities in Ionia and at the Hellespont,[105] treaties which establish the germ of the first Attic Maritime League.

In the Delphic Amphictyony an epilogue still took place (autumn of 479 or spring of 478 B.C.): the Spartans demanded the exclusion of all those states which had not participated in the struggle against the Persians. Themistocles opposed this proposal and thereby saved the Amphictyony.

With the capture of Sestos at the Hellespont the naval campaign came to a conclusion. This is the last event which Herodotus related in his *Histories*. On land the defensive struggle of the Greeks saw an even later terminus. In 477 B.C.[106] the Spartan king Leotychidas undertook an expedition to Thessaly, primarily to punish the pro-Median nobility, but gained no decisive victory. In fact, he had no choice but to leave the Aleuadae in possession of their sovereignty over Larisa. The Greeks sought to explain this failure on the assumption that Leotychidas had been bribed.[107]

Salamis and Plataea decided the Greek struggle for freedom. Even though the Persian wars did not come to an official conclusion until a full generation later, with the Peace of Callias (449 B.C.), the Greek victories at Salamis and Plataea mark a great turning point in ancient history. The struggle for freedom was not merely a question of material existence for the Hellenes—that defeat would mean enslavement and deportation the Greeks knew only too well. The war was fought for much more fundamental matters, the most priceless possessions of the Greek individual and the Greek people: external and internal freedom, human dignity and political autonomy—in short everything that gave worth and abundance to life among the Hellenes, both individually and collectively. Anyone who could read the signs of the times, who was aware of the fate that awaited the Ionian brethren in Asia Minor, knew that the dark clouds of Persian despotism would also envelop the Greek motherland if the Greeks did not join together in a united defense.

Certainly the Persians too, the leading people in the Achaemenid world empire, possessed ideals whose worth did not escape the Greeks: the loyalty of the vassals to their hereditary master, unconditional devotion of the Persian individual to the ruling house, the pride of the nobles in the distinctive Aryan manner, delight in knightly contests and championing justice and truth. Close association with the old cultures of Western Asia, above all of the Babylonians, had by no means been without effect on the Persians. Under Near Eastern influence religion and morals, thinking and feeling had undergone a crucial change within half a century. The new generation which had taken over the helm no longer found its way back to the simple patriarchal conditions like those of the time of Cyrus the Great. The Great King and the Persian individual subject were separated by a great gulf which grew steadily wider; it must have been the ways in which ruler and subjects dealt with each other that would have appeared particularly alien to the Greeks, indeed even offensive. The same holds true for the tyranny of bureaucracy which had moved into Ionia in the wake of the Persian satraps.

The great afflictions caused by the Persians kindled the flames of a feeling of Hellenic solidarity for the first time in Greek history. If the Athenians, as Herodotus relates (VIII 144), answered the proposal for an alliance from the Persian Mardonius in 479 B.C. with the remark that it was not for them to become traitors to that which was Hellenic, which manifested itself in their common origin and language, in their common sanctuaries and sacrifices and in their common customs, this answer excellently reflects the spirit of the times, be it historical or not. If there was one Greek state that comprehended the significance of the struggle for freedom in its deepest sense, it was Athens. Her inhabitants had twice been forced to leave their native soil, and the Athenian political leaders, in placing their fleet unconditionally under Spartan admiralty, demonstrated to all that the cause of the nation must take precedence over the prerogatives of the individual communities. The Greeks, however, even after the victories of Salamis and Plataea, were still far removed from any practical realisation of the idea of panhellenism in the life of the individual communities. The reality of the resolution to establish a common striking force of 10,000 hoplites and 1000 horse for the continuation of the struggle after the battle of Plataea, a resolution which appears to anticipate the organisation of the Corinthian League of 338/7 B.C., is at all events not entirely free of doubt.[108]

In terms of world history, the ramifications of the Greek triumph over the Persians are almost incalculable. By repulsing the assault of the East the Hellenes charted the political and cultural development of the West for an entire century. With the triumphant struggle for liberty by the Greeks, Europe was first born, both as a concept and as a reality. The human values for which the Greeks staked their lives are still the highest in the life of Western man. The freedom which permitted Greek culture to rise to the classical models in art, drama, philosophy and historiography, this Europe owes to those who fought at Salamis and Plataea, to Themistocles no less than to Pausanias. The Greeks defended not only political freedom but also the intellectual autonomy which characterises Western man. If we regard ourselves today as free thinking people, it is the Greeks who created the conditions for this.

Measured against the vastness of the Persian world empire, Hellas was a country of only second or third rank, which, split up into a large number of smaller states, seemed hardly likely to play a political rôle of importance. The example of the Greek struggle for freedom proves that the history of the human spirit is not bound by geography and power-politics. It rests more on the achievements of the creative genius than on the collective factor of the masses, although the statesman needs the group to accomplish his plans. It is surely no accident that the Persian empire, apart from the rulers who immortalised their deeds in magnificent monumental inscriptions, cannot attest a single individual personality whose achievements have become evident in any field of the human spirit. How soon, in spite of indisputable talents, did the Persians succumb to the embrace of the Orient! The end of Persian culture is marked by a levelling off, not by individualisation as in Greece. In contrast to this, Hellas, through her physicians and learned men, for many centuries rechannelled new strength and new life into the Persian empire. In return for this it received nothing, or at any rate little, and in most cases only material goods. The Greek spirit, however, truly became leaven in an entire world, in both the Occident and the Orient.

THE WESTERN GREEKS FROM 500 to 480 B.C.

The principal feature of Sicilian history at the turn of the sixth century is tyranny. It emerged for the most part from social revolutions, which at times were even further accentuated by tribal conflicts, as, for instance, by the struggle between the landowners (*gamoroi*) and the Sicilian bondsmen in Syracuse. *Tyrannis* in Sicily greatly activated the energies of the Hellenes and united them. As champions of the Hellenes against Carthaginian aggression the tyrants inaugurated a new epoch in the history of the western Greeks. For the first time the idea of the polis was not only supplemented, but to a certain degree even yielded to the idea of the territorial state. By recognising the political and economic power inherent in a territory extending as far as possible, the Sicilian tyrants were the creators of a new political concept, which anticipated developments in the East by more than a century. Political power was admittedly purchased at a high price. The life and liberty of their fellow-citizens were of little account to the despotic rulers, who aimed to establish a dynastic power, anchored as securely as possible by political marriages. Thus the Sicilian rulers Anaxilaus of Rhegium, Hippocrates of Gela, his successor, Gelon, and Terillus of Himera ruthlessly destroyed the idyll of small states characteristic of Sicily. They led the Sicilian polis out of an era of powerlessness and set new national goals for the Greeks of Sicily. Only in this way could they crush the Carthaginian peril which threatened to suppress the Greeks of the West.

Of the Sicilian tyrannies, that of Cleander in Gela on the south coast of Sicily (from 505 B.C. onwards) is of particular historical importance, for it was the beginning of the later Syracuso-Gelan double-state of the Deinomenidae. Cleander's brother, Hippocrates, established a military monarchy in Gela, with its chief support in a strong mercenary contingent. Only by pursuing a path of conquest could it ensure its survival. By subjugating a number of Sicel communities in the interior of the island and by incorporating the Chalcidian colonies of Callipolis, Naxos and Leontini into his sphere of rule, Hippocrates extended his dominions as far as the further side of Mount Aetna. Like a wide band the Gelan state stretched directly across the entire island, cutting it into two parts, into a greater western and a smaller eastern part.

After a decisive victory over the Syracusans at the Helorus river, Hippocrates forced them to withdraw from Camarina. His successor,

Gelon,[109] son of Deinomenes, who after the death of Hippocrates in 491 B.C. (?) seized the helm from the sons of the tyrant, succeeded in crowning the work of his father by joining Syracuse to the emergent east Sicilian territorial state. When certain banished *gamoroi* from Syracuse in Casmenae appealed for help, he restored them to their native city, but once having set his foot in the door did not withdraw it again. The annexation of Syracuse (c. 485 B.C.) to the emerging state of the Deinomenidae, hitherto ruled from Gela, was one of the most outstanding events in Sicilian history. In contrast to Gela, Syracuse with its suitable harbour and its possibilities for expansion on the plateau of Epipolae, was destined to become the capital of a Sicilian state. By resettling inhabitants from Megara Hyblaea, Sicilian Euboea, Gela and Camarina, by the construction of strong fortifications, the settlement of Syracusan Achradina and by building a navy—about the same time as Themistocles raised Athens to the leading sea power in the Hellenic East—the Deinomenid Gelon laid the foundations for the subsequent greatness of Syracuse. In the city he himself held the nominally constitutional office of *strategos* with plenary powers,[110] but the entire family of the Deinomenidae shared in the government. Thus Gelon's younger brother, Hieron, was governor in Gela. As the next oldest member of the dynasty, the succession in the *tyrannis* fell to him. That the entire state was regarded as the possession of the house of the tyrants, bequeathed as private property, was a genuine patrimonial notion, which was later adopted by the Hellenistic rulers. The outward form of self-government by the citizens, however, remained intact in Syracuse under Gelon (and probably in the remaining cities as well). The *Ekklesia* still continued to meet but had assumed a different aspect, for on the injunction of the tyrant a great many mercenaries, chiefly Arcadians, were forced into the citizen-body, an event which also seems to be an anticipation of later Hellenistic practices.

The second important tyrant state arose at the beginning of the fifth century B.C. at the Sicilian straits. Its nucleus was the city of Rhegium (Reggio di Calabria). Its ruler, Anaxilaus (494-476 B.C.), extended his power over Sicilian Zancle (Dancle)[111] as well. For this he enlisted the help of banished Samians and Milesians who had abandoned their home after the battle of Lade. Anaxilaus, however, soon became dissatisfied with them and called in settlers from Messenia, after whom Zancle was renamed as Messana (today Messina).[112] The ruler welded Rhegium and Messana together into a single state, which among other things struck common coins.

Gelon found a valuable confederate in the state of Theron of Acragas, whose territory, after Terillus of Himera (483/2 B.C.) had been expelled, extended from the Libyan to the Tyrrhenian Sea. By reciprocal marriage ties a close bond was formed between the two rulers. The preponderance of the coalition between Gelon and Theron prompted the remaining tyrants to appeal to that power which was most interested in preventing an extensive unification of Sicily, Carthage.

Terillus' appeal for help gave the Carthaginians the long and intensely desired pretext to frustrate the progressive unification of the island under the leadership of the Deinomenidae. It was no accident that the Carthaginian attack coincided with the offensive of Xerxes against the Greek motherland. Both acts of aggression had been synchronised as the result of a single large-scale plan,[113] which had set as its goal the political destruction of the Hellenes in East and West. This was one of the "most grandiose political alliances which simultaneously hurled the hordes of Asia on Hellas and the Phoenicians on Sicily in order with one blow to wipe liberty and civilisation off the face of the earth" (Th. Mommsen). A large mercenary army composed of Libyans, Phoenicians, Sardinians, Corsicans, Iberians and Ligurians landed on Sicilian soil at Panormus (Palermo) under the command of Hamilcar, to recapture Himera from Theron. The united command of the Greek forces was under Gelon, with Theron subordinating himself to him. In the battle at the Himeras river, the course of which can no longer be reconstructed,[114] the Greeks were victorious, with Hamilcar ending his life in the flames (480 B.C.). From the Carthaginian booty and war reparations the victor Gelon erected a large number of temples and sent magnificent votive offerings to the panhellenic sanctuaries at Delphi and Olympia.[115] From the battle of Himera onwards Gelon was the most powerful ruler in the West; Pindar[116] proclaimed his renown and placed the Sicilian victory on a level with the battles of Salamis and Plataea.

Thus the history of the western Greeks in the period of the great Persian wars ended with a victory of universal historical importance. In the West too it was the great individual personality that successfully fought for and defended the liberty of the Hellenes. The Syracuso-Gelan double-state of Gelon, which after Gelon's death in 478 B.C. passed into the hands of Hieron, took its place alongside Sparta and Athens, the leading states of the motherland. Under Hieron Syracuse became the cultural centre of the Hellenic West.

7
FIFTY CRUCIAL YEARS

THE IMPORTANCE OF THE GREEK POLIS

Greek history from the Persian wars to Philip II of Macedonia is the story of the rise and decline of the polis. During this period the polis developed into an organism with the most intensive and active political life at home and the greatest openness to cultural influence from abroad. It is no accident that in this period Greek cultural life reached the first summit in European history. Philosophy, drama and historiography took the forms which have remained the classical models ever since. In the political realm, however, the highly negative aspects of Greek life also became apparent, as the various city states were unable to unite into larger powers. This disunity cannot be attributed solely to the lack of administrative conditions suitable to control and penetration of larger areas. Since each and every polis, even the smallest, jealously guarded its own autonomy, any steps towards the formation of an empire were extremely difficult to start and in the long run were doomed to failure. If it is true that the era of the great Persian wars for the first time made the Greeks conscious of their national kinship, it is also true that Sparto-Athenian dualism fostered precisely the factors which made for division in the political life of the Greeks. The internal disunity of Hellas was the soil in which Persian intervention celebrated its triumphs from the end of the Peloponnesian War on. Even the idea of a panhellenic peace treaty, promulgated in Hellas from the beginning of the fourth century onwards, could not advance beyond promising beginnings to invigorate national feeling to any decisive degree.

The era of the polis was a vital stage in the internal development of the Hellenic people. It was during this time that the Greek citizen became a "political animal." Although important individual personalities, primarily from the circles of the Hellenic noble families, had in large measure determined the politics of the city states in the sixth century, now the full citizen-body appears as the ruling factor of the Greek states. It united itself behind the person of a leader and granted him constitutional powers to carry out his plans. The clan followers of the archaic period were replaced by political followers. The political objectives of the state now had unconditional priority over those of the clan, a change in the political psyche which soon was to develop along similar lines in Rome. The importance of the period of the Greek polis in world history, however, lies in the fact that for one and a half centuries Greece was able to stand as an autonomous factor within the framework of world events. Between the battle of Plataea (479 B.C.) and Chaeroneia (338 B.C.) no foreign army set foot on Greek soil. No matter how marked the changes in Hellenic politics may have become in Greece, above all since the end of the Peloponnesian War, internal developments at the political and cultural level remained almost entirely unaffected by foreign factors. Regarded as a whole, the history of Greece in the fifth century is a clear demonstration that the influence and universal importance of a people are not necessarily dependent on the extent of geographical territory, nor on the numbers of subject peoples, nor even on great individual personalities. Much more do they depend on political maturity and insight on the part of broadly based classes in the citizen-body, which here for the first time in world history appear as the standard-bearers of political responsibility. It is the thorough-going intensification of political and cultural life which lends importance to this era, far surpassing all other periods in Greek history.

Politics during the period from 478 to 431 B.C. were dominated by the conflict between Athens and Persia and the growing Attic-Spartan dualism. This was the period of the birth of the most important power ever founded and directed by a Greek polis—the Attic Maritime League. Athens and the League of which she was the *hegemon*, and no longer Sparta, were the standard-bearers of the national war against Persia. That war, after great initial successes for the Greeks, ended in 449 B.C. with the Treaty of Callias. During this era political developments in Greece were not determined by the individual polis but much more by the large federal organisations, the Peloponnesian League and the Attic Maritime League. World politics showed a certain balance of power between East and West, a circumstance determined to a great extent by the internal disturbances which kept the Persian empire quiet.

The most important event in internal politics during the Pentecontaetia was the creation of the radical Athenian democracy by Ephialtes and Pericles. Carrying the idea of *isonomia* to the fullest limits ultimately threw the gates wide open to the rule of the demagogues. The negative consequences did not immediately become evident because of Pericles, who after the death of Ephialtes (461 B.C.) became the dominating figure in Athenian politics. Under his aegis Attic democracy presented the world with the finest and most enduring gift of which any state, a community of rulers and ruled, is capable. In the works of great masters in poetry and art it gave the West the classical models for all time, models which even today still constitute an integral part of European culture. The concentration of political and cultural life in Athens, the centre of the Attic Maritime League, did indeed have its negative side. It caused a cultural recession among the League members, in many cases even ruin. Artists left the cities of Ionia for the West; the times of the sixth century in which cities like Cnidus, Siphnos and Clazomenae erected their magnificent treasuries at Delphi were irretrievably a thing of the past.

In addition to the Greek motherland, where Sparta appears less and less in international politics, primarily because of a declining trend in population, there was the Hellenic West—Sicily and Magna Graecia. With the overthrow of the tyrants in Sicily a new era began in the West, characterised by internal disturbances, fighting among the individual Greek communities, and above all by the awakening native Sicel and Italic tribes. The energies of these native peoples were still too greatly fragmented to match those of the western Hellenes, but a new era was knocking at the doors of the Greek cities, warning them to unite, if they did not want to lose their most priceless possessions: liberty and control over their own destiny.

THE FOUNDING OF THE ATTIC MARITIME LEAGUE. THE ERA OF CIMON (478-463 B.C.)

In the first fifteen years after the expedition of Xerxes, Athens rose to the status of a great power. In the Attic Maritime League Athens created an instrument equal in power to the Peloponnesian League under Spartan hegemony. In these years the Spartan-Athenian conflict became a historical fact, breaking into the open for the first time over the construction of the Long Walls at Athens.

The building of the Long Walls, inspired by Themistocles, was to turn Athens into a strong fortress and render the city impregnable to all external foes. The construction of the Long Walls was in a certain sense the extension of the Athenian navy, the creation of Themistocles. Together they establish the superior strategic position of Athens and distinguish it from all other Greek states until the end of the Peloponnesian War. Themistocles' plan met with opposition not only from the closest neighbours of Athens, chiefly Aegina, but also from Sparta. While Themistocles betook himself to Sparta in order to give the confederate pacifying assurances[1] (winter 479/8 B.C.), the Athenians built a circular wall approximately four miles in length as quickly as they could. They used a stone base with superstructure of clay bricks, and every feasible kind of material. Even grave stelae were built into the wall.[2] After completing the city wall at Athens fortifications were begun at Piraeus, with construction there ending in the course of the seventies. According to the design of Themistocles, Athens was to become a mighty land and sea fortress, but only towards the end of the sixties was the enterprise crowned with the construction of the North Wall and the Phalerum Wall. City and harbour were thereby transformed into a single fortification.

In the first years after Mycale (479 B.C.) Pausanias of Sparta played a peculiar rôle. After a united Greek naval expedition to Cyprus had ended with the conquest of many Cypriote communities and their joining the Hellenic Alliance (winter 478 B.C.), the imperious conduct of Pausanias at the siege of the stronghold of Byzantium led to the direct insubordination of Ionian contingents. When Byzantium had been captured, Sparta had to recall the king (477 B.C.). The conduct of Pausanias—he had engaged a bodyguard comprised of Persians and Egyptians and in addition had adopted Median dress and manners—marks him as a great individualist who ignored the boundaries set by the Spartan state. Far from his homeland, he sought to establish on his own initiative a position of power for himself. That he conspired with the Persians in this enterprise, as he was later accused of having done when brought to trial in Sparta, is in no way proven.[3] He was not condemned at the time, and later returned to Byzantium on his own initiative, where he succeeded in asserting himself for a short time as an independent ruler (probably until 476 B.C.).

Sparta's withdrawal from the naval war cleared the way for Athens in the Aegean. The Ionian Greeks saw in Athens' fleet the only instrument capable of preventing the return of Persian rule. In 478/7 B.C. (under the archonship of Timosthenes) a number of Ionian and Aeolian communities, along with many islands, united under the hegemony of Athens.[4] This was the birth of the famous Attic Maritime League, in whose organisation Themistocles and above all Aristeides distinguished themselves. This was a separate alliance within the framework of the great Panhellenic Alliance led by Sparta, and took as its rôle the continuation of the Persian War and the protection of the Hellenes in Asia Minor from Persian aggression.

In its outward form this new federation was a defensive-offensive alliance in perpetuity.[5] The larger members of the League, especially the islands of Chios, Samos and Lesbos, were obliged to contribute warships. Those who had no fleet were to pay contributions into the League treasury, located in the temple of Apollo and Artemis on Delos. These contributions—originally not tribute but compensatory payments—were assessed by Aristeides at a total of 460 talents.[6] This sum remained unaltered for over fifty years, until after the beginning of the Peloponnesian War (425 B.C.), even though the principles of levying the contributions may have shifted considerably with many communities joining the League and many changes in their economic resources. It seems that the incomes of the various states and their agricultural production provided a basis for the first assessment.[7] The sum of 460 talents is low, for the first Persian satrapy in Asia Minor at one time contributed 520 talents to the Great King. The individual states were generally reassessed every four years.[8] The League treasury was administered by the board of *hellenotamiai*, officials who were appointed by the Athenian *demos*.[9] The League held its sessions on Delos, and each member of the League, regardless of its size or economic resources, had only one vote. This was true even of Athens, but because she was the hegemon she could control the resolutions of the League assembly. It was to prove a serious disadvantage to the member-states that the League had been formed in perpetuity; Athens later used this agreement with brutality to suppress all efforts at emancipation. The League at the height of its power embraced the entire Aegean, from the Ionian-Aeolic coast of Asia Minor to Euboea and from Chalcidice to Rhodes. It was not established overnight, for new members joined as late as the fifties, and the number of members fluctuated greatly. The fragmentary nature of the so-called Tribute Lists makes an accurate estimate

MAP III

The Persian Empire and the Greek World c. 480 B.C.

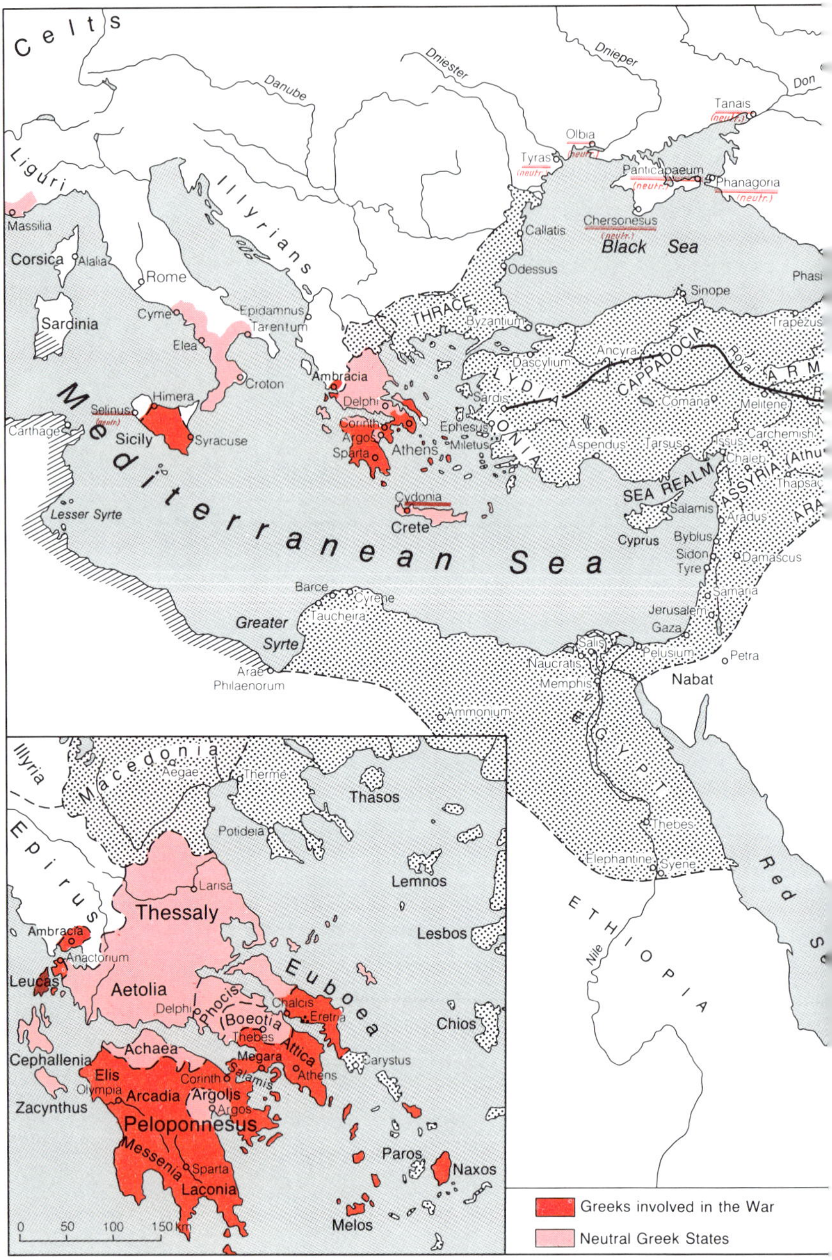
Celts
Danube
Dniester
Dnieper
Don
Tanais
(neutr.)
Olbia
(neutr.)
Tyras
(neutr.)
Panticapaeum
(neutr.)
Phanagoria
(neutr.)
Chersonesus
(neutr.)
Liguri
Illyrians
Massilia
Corsica
Alalia
Rome
Sardinia
Cyme
Epidamnus
Tarentum
Elea
Croton
Callatis
Black Sea
Odessus
Sinope
Phasi
Trapezus
THRACE
Byzantium
Dascylium
Ancyra
CAPPADOCIA
Royal
LYDIA
Sardis
Comana
Melitene
IONIA
Ephesus
Miletus
Aspendus
Tarsus
Issus
Carchemish
Chalebi
ASSYRIA
Thapsac
SEA REALM
Salamis
Aradus
Cyprus
Byblus
Sidon
Tyre
Damascus
Samaria
Jerusalem
Gaza
Salis
Pelusium
Petra
Nabat
Naucratis
Memphis
Ammonium
EGYPT
Thebes
Elephantine
Syene
Red Sea
ETHIOPIA
Nile
Ambracia
Delphi
Corinth
Argos
Sparta
Athens
Cydonia
Crete
Mediterranean Sea
Himera
Selinus
(neutr.)
Sicily
Syracuse
Carthage
Lesser Syrte
Greater Syrte
Barce
Cyrene
Taucheira
Arae Philaenorum
Illyria
Macedonia
Aegae
Therme
Thasos
Potideia
Epirus
Larisa
Thessaly
Lemnos
Ambracia
Anactorium
Lesbos
Leucas
Aetolia
Euboea
Delphi
Phocis
Chalcis
Eretria
Boeotia
Thebes
Chios
Achaea
Megara
Attica
Carystus
Cephallenia
Elis
Olympia
Corinth
Salamis
Athens
Arcadia
Argolis
Argos
Zacynthus
Peloponnesus
Messenia
Sparta
Laconia
Paros
Naxos
Melos
0
50
100
150 km
Greeks involved in the War
Neutral Greek States

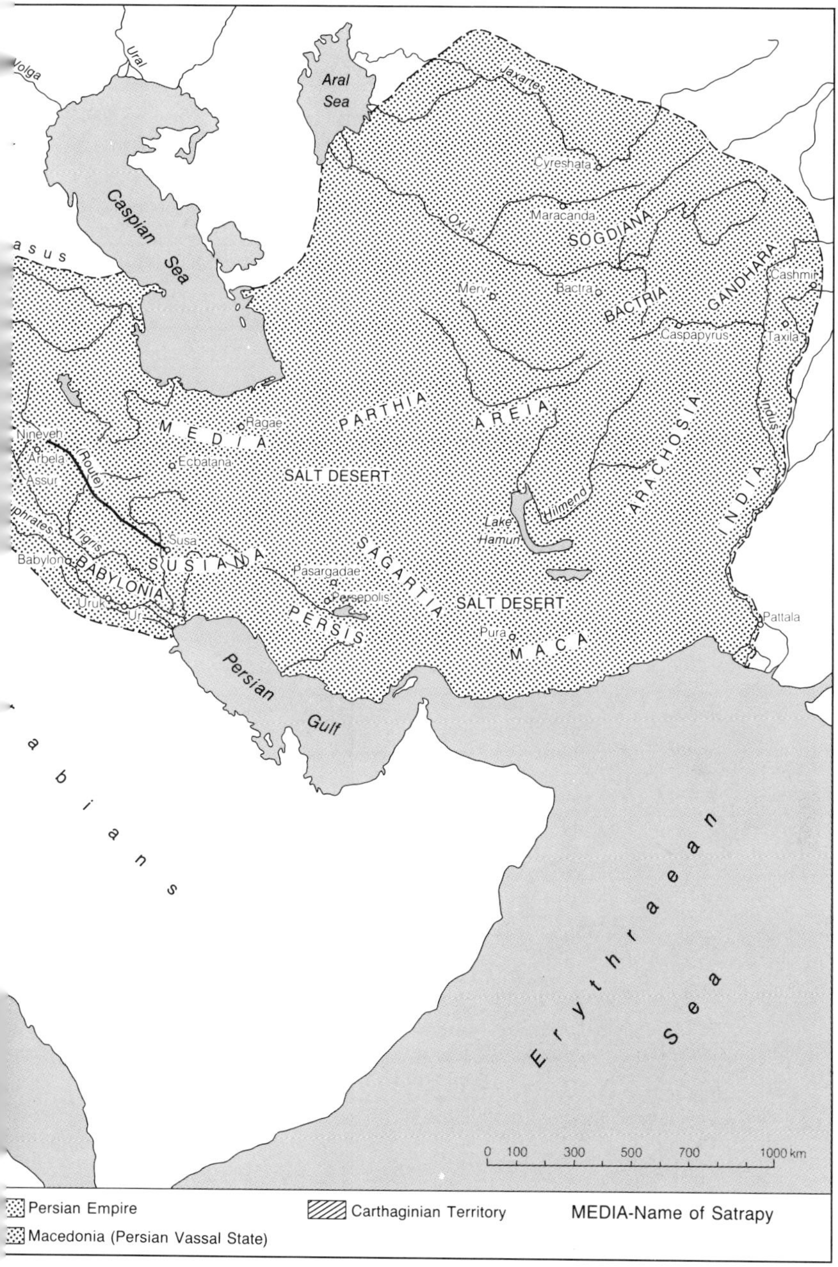
Ural
Volga
Aral Sea
Jaxartes
Caspian Sea
Cyreshata
Maracanda
Oxus
SOGDIANA
GANDHARA
Cashmir
Merv
Bactra
BACTRIA
Caspapyrus
Taxila
PARTHIA
AREIA
ARACHOSIA
Indus
Nineveh
Ragae
MEDIA
Arbela
(Route)
Ecbatana
Assur
SALT DESERT
Hilmend
INDIA
Lake Hamun
Tigris
Susa
Babylon
SUSIANA
SAGARTIA
BABYLONIA
Pasargadae
Persepolis
SALT DESERT
Uruk
Ur
PERSIS
Pura
Pattala
MACA
Persian Gulf
Erythraean Sea
0 100 300 500 700 1000 km
Persian Empire
Macedonia (Persian Vassal State)
Carthaginian Territory
MEDIA-Name of Satrapy

impossible. Although we have evidence for more than 400 cities in the Attic Maritime League in 425 B.C., this number represents a great many more than we can assume for 478/7 B.C.

In continuing the offensive war against Persia the Athenians found the Spartan confederates a valuable protection in the rear, which first made possible the concentration of Athenian power against the East. The modern theory that Sparta concluded a special peace treaty with the Persians through the mediation of Pausanias living in Byzantium[10] finds no support in our sources! Not the least reason for its improbability is the fact that Sparta's appeal to Athens for help in the Third Messenian War bears witness to the existence of the Panhellenic Symmachy still at the end of the sixties.[11]

Athenian policy in the seventies reflects the conflict between Themistocles and Cimon. While the victor of Salamis, perceiving with clear foresight an approaching conflict with the Spartan confederate, turned his eyes to the future and sought to increase the position of Athens as much as possible, without any consideration whatsoever for Sparta, the conservatively disposed Cimon,[12] son of Miltiades, supported a policy of trustful co-operation with the Spartans. This position also found expression in his personal attitude towards Sparta and in his sympathies with the Spartan way of life.[13] Both men, however, were agreed that the Persian War must be continued at all costs. In Athens in those years the performance of Aeschylus' *Persae* (472 B.C.), and prior to this the *Phoenissae* of Phrynichus (476 B.C.), kept alive the memory of the great past, when the Athenian fleet had fought for and attained the liberty of Hellas.

Cimon too embodied the great towering noble personality, but in contrast to his forerunners of the sixth century B.C. his individuality merged with the state. Cimon's kingly munificence is attested by the buildings in the Agora and the Cimon Gardens.[14] His wealth obliged him, and his noble birth and his military competence destined him, to become *strategos* of the Attic state. Indeed, through family traditions he identified himself with Athenian aims. His private life may have included certain features understandable only in terms of the traditions of the nobility—in particular the close personal loyalty between Cimon and the fellow-members of his deme, and equally his double-marriage and the appearance of his sister Elpinice in public life. Nevertheless, as statesman and general he was the "arm of the Attic State" (H. Berve), which employed him to conduct foreign policy against the Persians and, should it be necessary, also against the confederates.

In 476 B.C.[15] Cimon succeeded in driving Pausanias out of the stronghold of Byzantium. Sparta had not lifted a finger on Pausanias' behalf. It may be that his dominating position at the straits made him a nuisance not only to Attic trade but also to the rest of the Hellenes. Cimon sailed with the fleet from Byzantium to Eion and Scyros, and in 475 B.C.[16] conquered both, as well as Carystus. But Doriscus in Thrace still remained a Persian base for years.

It was not until the latter part of the seventies that the Persians energetically concentrated on greater mobilisation. In order to take up the offensive war the Persians stationed a large Phoenician fleet in Pamphylia, while awaiting further reinforcements. The Athenians under Cimon anticipated the Persian attack. After occupying Lycian Phaselis and forcing it to join the Attic Maritime League, Cimon fought a violent joint naval and land battle at the mouth of the Eurymedon river. The Persian naval encampment fell into Athenian hands, and a new Persian fleet was defeated.[17] With this great victory at the Eurymedon[18] (in the first half of the sixties),[19] Persian domination in the waters between Cyprus and Asia Minor was broken, and the Aegean was transformed into a Greek lake. As at Salamis, so also at the Eurymedon the spirit of Greek seamanship showed itself superior to the great technical skill of the Phoenician crews. The victory belonged to the League; it was simultaneously the proving ground of the Attic Maritime Alliance, which in the following decades—until the Peace of Callias (449 B.C.)—also appears as the most important opponent of the Persian empire. Themistocles had struggled for the liberty of the Greeks at Salamis; with the victory of Cimon at the Eurymedon Athens became a major power.

In the development of the first Maritime League the battle of the Eurymedon marks a notable turning point. It is most probable that the great majority of Lycian and Carian communities, and perhaps also various Ionian cities (Ephesus?), joined the Alliance at that time.[20] On the other hand the view grew stronger among some League members that with the elimination of the immediate Persian peril the protection of the Athenian fleet was no longer necessary. Tutelage under the hegemonial power was found to be irksome, especially since Athens employed her dominant position in the League to secure significant economic advantages for herself at the cost of the League members. Even before the battle of Eurymedon Naxos had seceded and had been brought into subjection again. It was the first example of open opposition to the Attic Alliance.

In 465 B.C. Cimon directed an expedition against the Persian dominions in the Thracian Chersonese.[21] Another enterprise, carried out at particularly great expenditure, was aimed at the plain of the Lower Strymon,[22] that region with certain connections to Athens since the time of the Peisistratidae. If the rich Thracian hinterland could be successfully penetrated politically and economically, then a new expansive field would be opened to Attic trade. The occupation of the plain at the Nine Ways (*Enneahodoi*) with 10,000 colonists led to a serious conflict with the wealthy island of Thasos, which had drawn a considerable part of its revenues from the Thracian hinterland. Thasos revolted, and Cimon blockaded it both by land and by sea (465 B.C.)[23] The defeat which the Attic settlers encountered in battle against the Thracian Edones at Drabescus put an end to Attic expansion on the Strymon (464 B.C.),[24] but the hopes of the Thasians for armed Spartan intervention were disappointed. The great earthquake in 464 B.C. which completely destroyed the city of Sparta, with great loss of life, made active Spartan intervention impossible. After a blockade of two years Thasos was forced to lay down its arms. The conditions of capitulation were the surrendering of the fleet, the razing of the walls and the loss of its mainland possessions along with the Thasian share in the gold mines at Pangaeum. The prosperity of the island was destroyed for many years, an admonishing example to the rest of the League members.

It was of far-reaching importance for developments in the entire ancient world that the state of war between Athens and Persia had now lasted without interruption for more than an entire generation—since the Attic fleet had intervened in the Ionian Revolt. This must inevitably lead to an increasingly sharper division between East and West, not only in economic but also in cultural life. The ties which had once linked the Greek motherland and Ionia with the Orient had been severed. Both worlds went their separate ways, with forms determined by their own laws, laws that were of crucial importance for future developments.

THE END OF PAUSANIAS AND THEMISTOCLES. THE GREAT HELOT REVOLT. THE CONSUMMATION OF ATTIC DEMOCRACY

While the Attic Maritime League under the hegemony of Athens continued the struggle against the Persians, and while Sparta, with her dominant position in the Peloponnesus seriously threatened, was entangled in bitter struggles with her neighbours, the Greeks expelled from their midst precisely those individuals to whom more than any others they owed their liberty—Themistocles and Pausanias, the victors of Salamis and Plataea. The event, symbolising the triumph of the state over the great individual personalities, is evidence of the transformation in Hellenic political thinking during the seventies and sixties of the fifth century. The ever increasing efforts of the Athenian citizen-body to govern itself were irreconcilable with the superiority possessed by Themistocles, a position which he held on the strength of his achievements and the following in the state devoted to him. No less was the autocratic conduct of Pausanias incompatible with the Spartan political system, of which the ephors considered themselves to be the chosen protectors. It was no accident that in Athens the fall of Themistocles was followed by the extreme democracy, and in Sparta the death of Pausanias was followed by the rule of the ephorate for several centuries. Both states, Athens as well as Sparta, stood at a crucial turning point in their histories, in internal and in foreign policy: from now on their paths diverged, and after the ostracism of Cimon (461 B.C.), there was no statesman to be found in either polis who could have brought the states together to accept a common policy in the interests of all Hellas.

With growing anti-Laconian movement throughout the Peloponnesus, Sparta found herself confronted with an unusually acute situation internally and abroad. The Spartans nevertheless, despite inferior numbers and considerable losses in the battles of Tegea and Dipaea, once more retained the upper hand over the Tegeans, Argives and Arcadians (at the end of the seventies?).[25] Sparta's hegemony in the Peloponnesus was particularly shaken by a democratic movement in confederate Elis. Here ten tribes and a Council of Five Hundred were introduced (c. 470 B.C.), apparently on the Attic model. The rule of the aristocratic families was thereby broken, and these were the very families whose proven friendship with the Lacedaemonians had hitherto constituted the guarantee of the close Spartan-Elian alliance. These serious conflicts in the Peloponnesus in large measure lay behind Sparta's inactivity in foreign politics in the theatre of the East during the first two decades after Plataea.

Upon being driven out of Byzantium in 476 B.C., Pausanias fled into the Troad and settled in the stronghold of Colonae, apparently with the tacit consent of the Persian satrap of Phrygia. Themistocles was ostracised in 471 B.C.,[26] and went from Athens to Argos. From there he is alleged to have incited the anti-Spartan movement in the Peloponnesus. Pausanias surprisingly (in 469 B.C.?) once more complied with the command of the ephors to return to Sparta, and there the victor of Plataea was cast into prison. No evidence could be adduced to substantiate the charge of treasonable connections with the Persians. It was instead the imprudence of Pausanias which led to his ruin: he carried on intrigue with the Helots and thereby undermined the very foundations of the Spartan state.[27] He was denounced to the ephors and died by starvation after fleeing for asylum into the temple of Athena Chalcioecus (467 B.C. ?).[28] Only a few years before this the Spartan king Leotychidas had been found guilty of bribery, on the basis of old accusations prompted by his conduct during the Thessalian campaign of 477 B.C., and died in banishment at Tegea.[29] The victory of the ephorate was complete, but at a very high price.

The indictment brought against Themistocles, now living in exile, was that he had conspired with Pausanias. The charge was treason ("Medism"). On the basis of incriminating evidence, allegedly found in the papers of Pausanias, the ephors demanded that steps be taken against Themistocles. In Athens an Alcmeonid (Leobotes), supported by Cimon, brought forward an indictment in the form of the *eisangelia*.[30] Themistocles did not appear in person for the trial but defended himself in writing. He was condemned to death and placed under *atimia*, proscription, in the entire area of the Confederacy. Even if both Athens and Sparta were persuaded of Themistocles' guilt, the condemnation of the great statesman and *strategos* on the grounds of Medism nevertheless remains an enormous miscarriage of justice. Themistocles had to flee in most heroic fashion to escape the bailiffs, from Argos to Corcyra,[30a] from there to King Admetus of the Molossians, then to Macedonia and from Pydna across the Aegean to Ephesus. The Persian king Artaxerxes I—he had acceded the throne of the Achaemenidae in 465/4 B.C. after the murder of Xerxes[31]—welcomed him most courteously at his court and gave him hereditary tenure over the cities of Magnesia on the Maeander, Myus, Lampsacus and a number of smaller towns in the Troad.[32] Themistocles continued to live in Magnesia until the beginning of the fifties. It was the tragedy of his life that his fellow-citizens at Athens were unable to follow his ideas. Thus the eminent statesman who ventured to set about solving political problems, the real significance of which only future generations were to recognise, found no support in the struggle for power in internal politics. His followers proved too weak against his many influential opponents, and were unable to prevent his downfall.[33]

The terrible catastrophe caused by the earthquake in Sparta (summer 464 B.C.), which to all appearances substantially decimated those capable of bearing arms,[34] was the signal for a large-scale Helot revolt in Messenia (the so-called Third Messenian War). A number of *perioikoi* towns also joined the movement against Sparta.[35] The hatred of the Messenians accruing for long centuries unleashed itself in dreadful atrocities against the Spartan lords, atrocities which probably find their parallel only in the great Peasant War in Germany. Still Spartan discipline this time too gained the upper hand. As in the First Messenian War (v.s.p. 46), the insurgents withdrew to Mount Ithome. The Spartans, realising that they were not capable of carrying out an effective siege, appealed to Athens for help. Here, in Cimon's absence, the radical faction had taken over the helm of the state and their chief exponent, Ephialtes, vigorously opposed the idea of sending any aid. Nevertheless Cimon, who, after the unsuccessful indictment by his opponents (the name of Pericles appears among them for the first time), had once more been elected as *strategos*, succeeded in gaining a decision to send an auxiliary corps of 4000 hoplites. The Spartans, however, soon sent the Athenians back home again, on the grounds that they were no longer required (autumn 462 B.C.). In Athens this affront led to an end to the Alliance which had been formed in the face of Xerxes' invasion. With that, the bond which had held Athens and Sparta together since 481 B.C. was severed. The growing division between the two largest states of Greece found symbolic expression in this act. Mount Ithome had still to be invested for some time; in 460/59 B.C. the Messenians capitulated under guaranteed withdrawal,[36] and were settled by the Athenians in Naupactus.

While Cimon was still absent in Messenia, a fundamental change in the constitution was introduced at Athens by Ephialtes (in the summer of 462 B.C.). It was directed chiefly against the preponderant position of the ancient aristocratic council of the nobility, the Areopagus of ex-archons.[37] The Areopagus lost all its political rights, and retained only jurisdiction in cases of homicide and a certain supervision of religious matters. The Council, the committees of the Popular Court and the Assembly now stepped into the ensuing gap. The Council, which in addition to supervision of the majority of "magistrates" also exercised extensive authority in criminal law, had to deliberate in advance on all legislation put before the *Ekklesia*, with or without its own recommending verdict (so-called *probouleuma*). The committees of the Popular Court (*Heliaea*), composed of 6000 appointed by lot, adjudicated upon the discharge of magistrates at the end of their term of office. By introducing prosecution for unconstitutional conduct, every citizen without exception now had the right to bring an indictment against anyone who proposed an enactment which to him appeared contrary to law. It had prorogative force. After the murder of Ephialtes (461 B.C.), Pericles[38] assumed the leadership of the democratic cause and carried the reform further. He introduced daily payments for the jurors, later also for the members of the Council, and for all "magistrates" appointed by lot.[39] In 458/7 B.C. the *zeugitae*, the third class, were for the first time admitted to the archonship. The *thetes* as such, however, never acquired the right to be elected to any office.

Never in history—in the judgment of Eduard Meyer—was self-government by the *demos* put into practice so strongly as in the reform of the constitution by Ephialtes in Athens. The *demos* was now sovereign in the courts and sovereign in the whole of public life. The reforms were borne along on an over-exaggerated mistrust of the free, independent personality, which was now tolerated only as an executive organ or a corrective of the constitution. And yet its elimination from public life was by no means achieved. The overthrow of Ephialtes was the birth of the demagogues, who now, raised aloft on the waves of a fickle popular favour, entered into the mainstream of public life. But now only that individual who made politics his life-time occupation could successfully gain insight into the complexity of foreign affairs and the functioning of a well ordered administration of finance. The prerequisite to the life of politics was economic independence such as only the wealthy nobility possessed. It is therefore not surprising that this class also appeared as the leaders in the next generation (until the beginning of the Peloponnesian War). In general Attic democracy,[40] which excluded broad masses from political rights, in particular the many metics and slaves, was in reality always the rule of an aristocratic minority, those enjoying full citizen rights. The political insight of this minority and their willingness to sacrifice themselves for the commonwealth, as manifested in the *leitourgia*—public duties—should not be overlooked.

The reformer Ephialtes had to pay for his success with his life, his murder probably the act of a political hotspur.[41] His death and the banishment of Cimon cleared the way for a superior statesman—Pericles.

ATHENS IN THE TIME OF PERICLES

A characteristic view of Pericles in the modern era of Classicism is that of Adolf Schmidt, one time historian and philologist at the University of Jena. The Athenian statesman is seen not only as the representative of a short period in time and of a small state, the Attic republic, nor indeed as just the most important representative of a great people and its history, but as the actual representative of an entire period in world history and of a universal stage in the development of mankind. For this scholar Pericles stands at the zenith of the whole of antiquity, or the classical period, and his person and work represent one of those extensive and lofty cultural waves destined to lead mankind towards its highest cultural goals. In contrast to this view more recent scholarship, inaugurated by Julius Beloch (*Die attische Politik seit Perikles* [1884]) has in many instances reached a highly self-contradictory verdict on the achievements of the Attic statesman. While Beloch's critical mind recognised Pericles neither as a statesman nor as a military general and left only the important "parliamentarian," a much more favourable evaluation prevails among scholars of the present day, and rightly so.[42] The singular harmony between the Periclean political form and the Periclean "culture policy" must reflect primarily upon that individual whose organising mind succeeded in combining the individual threads into an organic whole. Seldom in world history has a state understood how to interweave the accomplishment of a high cultural rôle with its political mission as well as Athens did during the generation before the Peloponnesian War. By its almost superhuman magnificence the Attic state was certainly striving to document its leading position and its predominant power in Hellas. Still, this splendour was not merely the transient expression of outward striving for power but much more "the fulfilment of a cultural mission springing from the innermost soul of the Greek genius and valid for all time" (E. Hohl). That the Athenian people attacked with zeal the growing responsibilities of their political hegemony is the work of Pericles. His rousing enthusiasm gave form and expression to the ideas, and realised the plans of the architects and artists by providing funds from the contributions of the League members. That the structures with which Pericles adorned Athens show a uniform monumentality, inner unity and perfect harmony, is due to his indefatigable, creative mind which erected a monument for all time.

The Periclean townscape of Athens was principally determined by the immense fortifications at Piraeus as well as by great buildings, mostly on the citadel of the Acropolis. The monumental structures have determined the aspect of Athens for all time, and even down to our own day the venerable ruins still attest the vigour of spirit which at one time brought their beauty into existence.

The Attic auxiliary corps had hardly been sent back home from Messenia by the Spartans (462 B.C.) when the Themistoclean fortification plan became a reality. Athens, now joined to Piraeus and Phalerum by the so-called North Wall and the Phalerum Wall, was transformed into an enormous citadel, regarded as impregnable in terms of the siegecraft of those times. Later the third unit was added, the "Middle" Wall, running parallel with the Piraeus Wall. In case of an enemy invasion the space within the Long Walls between the city and Piraeus was large enough to absorb the entire population of Attica. The times in which one had to flee to Salamis and Troezen were forever past once the Long Walls were as good as completed in 445 B.C., after fifteen years of construction.[43] Piraeus with its three harbour coves was strongly fortified, reinforced with bastions and towers, and equipped with arsenals and wharfs, and with boat houses to accommodate the triremes. It was the strongest naval base in the Greek world; only Syracuse had anything similar to exhibit.

After building the fortifications, Athens turned to monumental architecture in the city and on the Acropolis.[44] The two Persian occupations (480 and 479 B.C.) had left little of the ancient splendour of Peisistratid Athens standing. Many temples stood in semi-ruins, their walls blackened by smoke. Cimon's kingly munificence had initiated the building of a more beautiful Athens. After the victory at Eion (476/5 B.C.) he built the so-called Hermes Hall, while his brother-in-law, Peisianax, erected the Stoa Poecile and decorated it with paintings by the leading artists of his day, Polygnotus, Micon and Panaenus. In Cimon's time the Theseum was also built; it housed the bones said to be of Theseus, conveyed from Scyros to Athens.

This was all, however, only a prelude to the building activity of Pericles, which was based on the contributions of the League members to the League treasury. With the idea of adorning the citadel Pericles resumed the plans of the Peisistratidae, only on a much greater scale. Great retaining walls were built to extend the area of the Acropolis. In the fill, the so-called "Persian rubble," modern excavators have found a great many archaic works of art and Old Attic inscriptions. On the Acropolis the landmark temple of Pallas Athena, the Parthenon, was built by Ictinus and Callicrates. Construction first began after the Peace of Callias (449 B.C.) on the foundations of the old sanctuary. It was built of the reddish shimmering Pentelic marble. In 438 B.C. the majestic statue of the goddess from the hand of Pheidias celebrated its entry into the *naos* of the Temple.[45] The Parthenon frieze, depicting the Panathenaic procession, proclaimed the greatness and glory of Athens, whose citizens moulded the Attic national festival into a celebration renowned throughout the entire world. The entrance to the Acropolis was the Propylaea of Mnesicles, a monumental gateway with five portals and columns uniting Doric and Ionic forms.[46] Across from the Parthenon rose the new sanctuary of Athena Polias, usually called the Erechtheum, after the Attic hero Erechtheus. Construction of this temple in all probability also began under Pericles, but it did not reach completion until the end of the fifth century. With the Theseum (probably a sanctuary of Hephaestus), located on the elevation of the Agora (north-west of the Acropolis), and with the Odeon, erected for musical performances at the south-east foot of the Acropolis, Athens acquired a whole series of magnificent structures in a very few years. The construction programme, with its costly marble, shed splendour over the narrow alleys of new dwellings hastily erected after the Persian conflagration, and turned Athens into a marvel of the ancient world.

The Periclean building programme made unusually high demands on finances. From the tribute of the members of the Attic Maritime League and out of the money from the members of the great Alliance against Persia, who themselves were sinking to the level of subjects, there arose a new Athens displaying to every visitor the universality of her worth. For the population of Athens[47] the building programme created an inexhaustible source of employment and income for many years. Plutarch (*Pericles* 12) gives a colourful picture of the many crafts and trade branches which were employed on the buildings: carpenters, sculptors, masons, bronze pourers, dyers, goldsmiths, workers in ivory, painters, embroiderers, engravers, transport contractors, both by sea and by land, and workers in the marble quarries—all found remunerative employment here. And every trade, adds Plutarch, had its army of day labourers and helpers, and thus every age group and every vocation received its share in employment and prosperity. Detailed research into the cost of living in ancient times (G. Glotz) has shown that at no time in antiquity was it ever lower than during this period. Even the working slave in the time of Pericles fared better than the free lower ranking "official" and better than the qualified free labourer during the whole of later antiquity[48]—a particularly impressive confirmation of our ancient sources, in which the era of Pericles appears as the Golden Age of antiquity.

The new relationship of Athens to her history found expression in historical paintings: large frescoes, paintings depicting the battle of the Amazons, the destruction of Troy and the battles of Marathon and Oenoe (v.i.p. 126), adorned the Stoa Poecile and portrayed the greatness of past and present vividly before the eyes of the Athenians.

As Athens gained her predominant political and economic position in the late fifth century, the Attic dialect, primarily through the creations of the Athenian dramatists, gained considerable ground over the Ionian, which had hitherto prevailed in the realm of historiography and science (for instance, in medicine). But it was not until the glory of Athens had begun to fade that the Attic dialect became a literary medium. The oldest monument of Attic prose is the pseudo-Xenophontic *Constitution of Athens*, an anonymous pamphlet probably from the first years of the Peloponnesian War. As Pheidias (c. 500-420 B.C.), the creator of the seated figure of Zeus at Olympia and the statue of Athena Promachus, left the imprint of his character on the art of this epoch, so the Attic stage was dominated by Sophocles who, through Cimon's arbitration, for the first time won the prize at the Great Dionysia in 468 B.C. in competition with the older Aeschylus. While the life of Aeschylus extended down to the Periclean era (died 456 B.C.), Sophocles is its actual cultural representative. The personalities in his tragedies are people of that time who have become flesh and blood, even though they may to a large extent lack individuality—in this respect comparable to the herms. Like the historian Herodotus of Halicarnassus, the philosopher Anaxagoras of Clazomenae, the town planner Hippodamus of Miletus, the creator of the first ideal state, so Sophocles and Pheidias belonged to the circle of Pericles and Aspasia—Aspasia, the Ionia-born lady-friend of Pericles who avidly shared in the work of the Attic statesman.[49]

The culture of Periclean Athens belonged to a large cross-section of her population. Every Athenian could probably write, and it was self-evident that the boys of the wealthy and middle classes should attend the *Gymnasium*. In early youth at school the Athenian learned Homer, Hesiod and the Lyric poets by heart, while Homeric verses formed the models for elementary instruction used by the writing master. The verses of the wise Solon and the aristocratically proud Theognis were sung on festive occasions. When the plays of Sophocles went on stage before an audience numbering in the thousands in the Theatre of Dionysus, the dramatist and the actors could count on having a public capable of appreciating the finer points of dramatic technique and not a few literary allusions. And yet in one point Attic society differed fundamentally from that of, for instance, the Renaissance. Attic women were excluded from it, even though Euripides was able to portray the feminine soul with the most delicate empathy.

From the fall of Cimon and after the violent death of Ephialtes (461 B.C.) Pericles was the centre of the Attic state. After the ostracism of his opponent Thucydides, son of Melesias (443 B.C.), he was elected *strategos* year after year. The formal basis of his dominating position was the *strategia*. The actual basis was his personal authority among the Attic people, in which he far surpassed his fellow-generals. The nature of his position has been described in the famous words of Thucydides (II 65.9): "the Athenian constitution is a democracy in name only, in reality it is the rule of the foremost man."[50] Pericles governed the citizen-body in the *Ekklesia* by the outstanding gift of oratory, which again and again brought the masses back under his spell.[51]

Under Pericles the Attic state saw a gradual transformation from a productivity state to a welfare state, which was to have unusually serious consequences. The introduction of payment for offices, a consequence of the consummated democracy of Ephialtes, gradually corrupted at least part of the citizens, and these, after becoming accustomed to public welfare, rejected the idea of productive employment.[52] In order to make provision for the poorer landless classes of the Attic population, but also because of political aims within the League, the Athenians sent out colonies—*apoikiai*—and cleruchies. While the *apoikiai* were established as independent communities with their own citizenship on the model of the older colonies in the archaic period,[53] the *kleruchiai* remained bound by closest political ties with the Attic state. The cleruchs retained their Attic citizenship and their territory was part of the Attic state. Such cleruchies were, among other places, on Naxos, Andros, Lesbos, in Oreus on Euboea,[54] in the Thracian Chersonese and in Amphipolis, partly with Attic garrisons under *phrourarchoi*. The great dimensions of the Attic sphere of power also drew the west and north of the Hellenic world into their orbit. The leading personalities of the time participated in the founding of the panhellenic colony of Thurii in southern Italy in 444/3 B.C. (in the vicinity of the ruins of Sybaris)[55]: the Sophist Protagoras of Abdera, the philosopher Empedocles of Agrigentum, the historian Herodotus of Halicarnassus, the architect Hippodamus of Miletus who designed the layout of the city. With the founding of this colony Athenian policy cast its shadow as far as southern Italy. There Athens, as shown by the renewal of treaties with Rhegium and Leontini (433 B.C.), emerged as the rival of Corinthian commercial power, for Corinth, on the basis of her close ties with Syracuse, regarded western trade as her monopoly. With the expedition to the Pontus (middle of the thirties) Pericles advanced into the Bosporic empire,[56] which controlled the corn exports from southern Russia. The world-wide trade connections of Athens and the colourful abundance of her imports are portrayed by the comic poet Hermippus in his *Phormophoroi* (performed before 425 B.C.),[57] but the information he gives also applies to the decade preceding the Peloponnesian War:

"From Cyrene ships bring us Silphium stalks and beef hides, from the Hellespont tuna fish and pickled fish of all kinds, from Italy barley and rib pieces of beef. Syracuse provides swine and cheese, Egypt sails and papyrus rolls, Syria incense, Crete cypress wood for the gods, in Libya ivory can be purchased in abundance, while from Rhodes come raisins and dried figs, pears and fat sheep from Euboea, slaves from Phrygia, mercenaries from Arcadia, good-for-nothing rascals from Pagasae, chestnuts and almonds are delivered by Paphlagonia, dates and fine flour by Phoenicia and rugs and coloured pillows by Carthage."

In two areas the internal policy of Pericles was to prove dangerous, in fact even disastrous: his policy dealing with the franchise and his administration of finance. The more radical Attic democracy became, the more intolerant it was towards the large cross-section of those who were not full citizens. The democracy more and more feared that a relatively large number of citizens formally enjoying equal rights might dilute some of the advantages which the emergent welfare state had to offer to the poorer elements in the citizen-body through payment for offices and corn distribution. The *demos* was blind to the damage which the exclusion of that so-vital class must bring in its wake. Thus a measure brought in by Pericles in 451/50 B.C. excluded from the number of fully enfranchised citizens, sons born of non-Attic mothers,[58] a measure which would have been unthinkable and incapable of implementation in the aristocratic state.

The heavy burden on finances caused by the steadily increasing building activity made it completely impossible to form a suitable reserve fund within the state treasury in the years between 454 and 434 B.C. The high cost of the war from 460 B.C. onwards, particularly the Cypriote and Egyptian expedition, must have completely devoured the League contributions. What else remained but to fall back on the treasure of Athena Polias which up till then had been dead capital? It was only with the finance decree of Callias (434 B.C.), much discussed by modern scholars, that the Athenians first tried to form a reserve of hidden assets by proposing to add 3000 talents to the treasure of Athena. In case of emergency, that is, in case of war, which already loomed on the horizon—one could fall back on this resource.[59] The treasure of Athena contained 6000 talents when the Peloponnesian War began (Thuc. II 13.3).[60] In the regulations of the decree of Callias it is necessary to see simultaneously a diplomatic stroke of Pericles, that is, an attempt by the statesman to shield himself from the accusation that he had squandered millions on his buildings. But what had been neglected over a number of decades could not be made up within a matter of a few years. The indictment at the end of the Pentecontaetia, the era which had brought Athens to unexpected heights, carries the ominous word "neglect."[61]

THE ATTIC MARITIME LEAGUE AND SPARTAN HEGEMONY UP TO THE EVE OF THE PELOPONNESIAN WAR

The Spartan gesture of sending back the Attic auxiliary corps from Mount Ithome in the autumn of 462 B.C. marks the final break between the two confederates. Direct repercussions in foreign politics did not follow for the time being, because of the general situation. In particular, the Persian War was still claiming the energies of Athens and her Alliance. The Persians admittedly remained completely inactive in the West. During the reign of Artaxerxes I (465-425 B.C.) the vast empire was recovering from a low ebb in its development, shaken by dangerous revolts which affected the Bactrians, Syrians and Egyptians. The revolt of the native princes Inaros and Amyrtaeus in the western Nile Delta and the decisive victory of the insurgents over the Persian satrap Achaemenes at Papremis[62] prompted the Athenians to intervene in Egypt. In the background were considerations of power politics and trade. Egypt, the richest grainland along with Sicily and southern Russia, and with its valuable papyrus, offered extensive scope to Athenian trade, provided only that Athens understood how to open up the country.[63] With the capture of the Persian stronghold of Memphis the enterprise, which had begun with a victory for the Athenians on the Nile, assumed a highly promising character (460 B.C.).[64] The Persian garrison in the citadel of Memphis, however, succeeded in holding out.

Sparta was saddled with the Messenian revolt until 460/59 B.C. Argos, Sparta's inveterate foe, chose this moment to attack Mycenae, forced her to capitulate through starvation and sent the population into slavery, with Sparta unable to rescue her ally. In the battle of Oenoe (on the road from Argos to Mantineia) the Spartan army was defeated by the Argives and Athenian volunteers (460 B.C.?). The Athenians regarded the battle as an important victory, for the Spartan halo of invincibility on the open battlefield had been destroyed![65] The annexation of Mantineia and Megara to Athens reflects the competitive strength of democratic ideas. For Athens, the Megarian treaty admittedly brought the open enmity of commercially powerful Corinth, who for her part united with Aegina, the mistress of the Saronic Gulf and the old rival of Athens. After severe reverses, explicable in terms of the strain on Athenian resources by the coincident Egyptian expedition, Athens succeeded in blockading Aegina, in the spring of 459 B.C.

In spite of severe losses,[66] Athens had asserted herself everywhere in the field.[67] Sparta, her principal adversary, who directed the course of anti-Athenian policy in Greece from afar, had not as yet been engaged in open battle. It was not until the urgent plea for help from the Dorians of Oeta that a large Spartan contingent of the Peloponnesian League first made its appearance in central Greece.[68] Only now did Sparta, shored up by a treaty with the Boeotians, feel strong enough to force the issue at the place where Athens could be struck in her most vulnerable spot. Sparta's victory over Athens and her allies at Tanagra (summer 457 B.C.)[69] did not, however, achieve any lasting political results. The Spartan forces withdrew again and two months later the battle of Oenophyta re-established Athenian domination in Boeotia.[70] A consequence of this state of affairs was the capitulation of Aegina (456 B.C.). Subjected to severe conditions, she was compelled to enter the Attic Maritime League.[71] With brutal force Athens destroyed the potential of the city, so that artistic life in Aegina was soon completely extinguished.

The year 455 B.C. marks the indisputable summit of Athenian power during the Pentecontaetia. The entire area from the Isthmus of Corinth to the Malian Gulf was under Attic control. Thessaly was, at least nominally, dependent on Athens, and the Dorian commercial cities Aegina, Megara and Troezen were members of the League. The Aegean had become an Athenian sea. The expedition of Tolmides was an expression of the increased will-to-power. In 455 B.C. after landing in Laconia and inflicting considerable damage on the Spartans, he sailed around the southern tip of the Peloponnesus.[72] Through the annexation of Achaea, that "happy country without a history," Athens set foot on the northern Peloponnesus and from the time of the settlement of Messenian Helots in Naupactus held the entrance to the Corinthian Gulf under her supervision. The great Dorian commercial city at the Isthmus sustained its severest blow, however, when Tolmides broke into the Corinthian colonial empire in the Ionian Sea. Here Zacynthus and Cephallenia joined Athens. The political leadership of Athens was already casting its eyes towards the distant west,[73] when the turn of events in Egypt forced direct attention to the east.

In Egypt the Persian Megabyzus, after suppressing the Babylonian revolt, co-operating with a large Phoenician fleet, won a great victory over the Egyptians and their Athenian allies in the Delta (456 B.C.). The Athenians were besieged on the island of Prosopitis in the Nile for a year and a half, and finally all but a few survivors were destroyed by the Persians (454 B.C.).[74] Inaros was taken prisoner by the Persians. Amyrtaeus on the other hand continued the opposition against the Persians with his loyal followers in the western Delta. The consequences of the defeat on Prosopitis, the first which Athens had suffered in decades at the hands of the Persians, were incalculable. She lost Cyprus, and in extreme consternation the League treasury (on the proposal of the Samians)[75] was transferred from Delos to Athens (summer 454 B.C.). Still, neither Persia nor Sparta was in a position to take advantage of the situation. The events produced a five-year truce between Sparta and Athens, in 453 B.C., after a second Athenian expedition into the western sea (under the command of Pericles).[76] As a price for this truce Athens had to abandon her ally, Argos, who now for her part formed a thirty-years' peace treaty with Sparta, in 451 B.C. (?).[77] Only now had the Spartans again become masters in their own house, the Peloponnesus.

Cimon's return from exile once more fanned the Persian War into flame. A large League force of 200 vessels appeared off Cyprus and gained a signal victory over the Persians at Cyprian Salamis (450 B.C.); it was celebrated by the Athenians as one of their greatest feats,[78] although it too failed to bring about a decision in the struggle which had now lasted for more than thirty years. Cimon himself did not, however, live to witness it; he had died shortly before at the blockading of Citium. The recall of the fleet from Cyprian and Egyptian waters by Pericles and the despatching of the wealthy Callias to Susa[79] signify a new epoch in Attic policy towards Persia. After tough negotiations the parties finally came to terms in the spring of 449 B.C.,[80] on the basis of a delimitation of their respective spheres of interest. No Persian vessel would in future be permitted to enter the Aegean. The eastern entrance to the Bosporus in the north and the Lycian city of Phaselis in the south were the demarcation points on the coasts. In western Asia Minor a demilitarised zone a horse's run, that is three days' march wide, was established at the Aegean. Persian troops were not allowed to set foot in it. A formal peace treaty was not concluded, however, since the Persian king still held to his former claim that all living people within the sphere of his dominions were his subjects. The treaty[81] was nevertheless ratified by a binding declaration of King Artaxerxes I. In the Peace of Callias the Athenians did not cover themselves with glory, but merely secured *de facto* recognition of the *status quo* in Asia Minor.

The peace treaty was to be crowned by a Congress with the entire Greek world in attendance, including Sparta, which Pericles planned to convene in Athens. Since Athens had in the Peace of Callias given up her great national mission of prosecuting the Persian War, the Periclean peace programme was of decisive importance if Athens was to maintain her claims to the leadership in Greece alongside Sparta. The programme called for the preservation of peace, the security of the seas and the restoration of the temples which had been destroyed by the Persians.[82] Sparta was not, however, prepared to endorse the plan, and the design consequently miscarried. The date of the Congress is disputed: either the year 448-447 B.C. or the first years after 446 B.C. will have to be regarded as possible alternatives.[83]

The overthrow of the Boeotian oligarchy meant a severe reverse for Athens (summer 447 B.C.?). The Athenians, defeated at Coroneia, were consequently forced to withdraw from the whole of Boeotia, except for Plataea. On Theban initiative a Boeotian League was formed, consisting of eleven districts, each of which furnished sixty *bouleutai* for the federal Council, and 1000 hoplites and 100 horse for the federal army—an example of early Greek representative government.[84] In the following year (446 B.C.) Euboea and Megara seceded from Athens, and only by bribing the Spartan king Pleistoanax and his advisor Cleandridas was Pericles able to induce the army of the Peloponnesian League, hastening to Megara's assistance, to withdraw.[85] This now gave Pericles a free hand in Euboea. Chalcis and Histiaea were severely punished, and an Attic cleruchy (Oreus) established in Histiaea. The Thirty-Years' Treaty concluded between Athens and Sparta (446/5 B.C.) brought a lull in the great struggle between the two Greek rivals. The Peace confirmed the *status quo*. Athens had to relinquish her influence in central Greece and in the Peloponnesus, but her supremacy over Aegina remained unaltered.[86]

As for the outward composition and the inner form of the Attic Maritime League, these were subject to continual changes ever since the League was established in 478/7 B.C. The Peace of Callias (449 B.C.), which did indeed eliminate the Persian War but not the danger from the world empire, was also of fundamental importance for the development of the League. From the sixties onwards, the steadily increasing preponderance of Attic supremacy had again and again induced various League members to try to evade the oppressive rule of Athens (v.s.p. 116). It is thus out of the question that the "Peace of Callias" first brought about the internal transformation of the League from an Alliance into the "Empire" of Athens. Nor does the division of the League's members into districts,[87] first apparent in the Tribute Lists of 446/5 B.C., prove anything with reference to this question. It is rather of greater importance that, as it seems, the payment of the League contributions was either completely suspended[88] in the year of the "Peace of Callias" (449/8 B.C.) or made by only a small number of the League members[89]—clear evidence for the repercussions which the Treaty had on the League. The political and economic superiority of Athens had its counterpart in the leading rôle Attic culture played in the League, by the advancement of the Attic dialect and script, as well as by the Athenian judicial system. The currency of the League members was in part displaced by Attic coins. The issues of the League members, above all the islands, show considerable gaps from about 450 B.C. onwards, no doubt a result of the Attic coinage law. It was only in the Peloponnesian War that the rebellious members of the League more and more resumed the striking of their own coins.[90]

In 450/49 B.C. Athens intervened in the internal affairs of Miletus, and also did so in Samos in favour of the democratic faction in 442 B.C.,[91] interventions which mark a very decisive encroachment on the autonomy of the League members. The "fellow-combatants" in many cases became "subjects" of Athens. A fragment from an inscription[92] shows how meticulously Athens supervised the tribute payments of the League members. Each member was given a seal for the tribute accounts. The point is that the complete subjugation of Samos after the Samian revolt (441-439 B.C.)[93] demonstrated to the League members what they could expect from Athens if they dared to resist. For the political penetration of the League, however, Athens completely lacked the prime prerequisites, above all a trained bureaucracy, which was non-existent in Greece and which only the Persian empire possessed. An impediment of equal importance was the lack of any feeling for empire among the League members. With the political and material preponderance of Athens this could not arise. It was the Hellenic feeling for liberty that stood in the way of the transformation of the League into an Attic "province."

The last years before the Peloponnesian War saw a growing opposition to Pericles in Athens. The chief opponent to Pericles, Thucydides (son of Melesias), who personally took up the cause of the League members, had already fallen victim to ostracism in 443 B.C.[94] The growing opposition, however, is attested in comedy and in lawsuits against the followers of the "Olympian." Anaxagoras, Pheidias and Aspasia were successively indicted.[95] But there cannot have been any serious undermining of the leading position of Pericles in the thirties.[96]

THE WESTERN GREEKS DURING THE PENTECONTAETIA: THE AWAKENING OF THE SICELS AND ITALICS

While in the East the war continued against the Persians for a full thirty years after the Greek victories of Salamis and Plataea, in the West the battle of Himera (480 B.C.) brought to Sicily seventy years of peace from the Carthaginians. The period was an especially favourable one for the cultural development of the western Greeks. After the death of Gelon (478 B.C.) his brother Hieron seized control of the Syracuso-Gelan double-state. In Syracuse he surrounded himself with a splendid "Court of the Muses."[97] His guests were the most eminent poets of the day: Pindar and Bacchylides, Simonides and Aeschylus temporarily sojourned in Syracuse and celebrated the renown of the ruler in verse and in song. From his victory over the Etruscans at Cyme (Cumae) Hieron emerged as the saviour of the western Greeks from the Etruscan peril. Pindar (*Pyth.* I 140) rightly maintains that Hieron "from their fleet-running ships did hurl the young warriors of the Etruscans into the sea, drawing back Hellas from grievous bondage." For the beginning of the Roman state too, Hieron's victory was important. It ultimately secured Rome's independence.

The full flowering of the Sicilian tyranny after the victories over Carthage and the Etruscans did not, however, succeed in blinding the Greeks to its weakness, its illegitimacy. Even though Hieron, Anaxilaus and Theron maintained large mercenary armies, and although they made splendid cities almost spring up out of the ground (Hieron, for instance, founded Doric Aetna),[98] resettled citizens at will and constructed bastions and magnificent buildings, nowhere did they succeed in firmly anchoring their rule. Thrasybulus was not able to retain his hold on the *tyrannis* in Syracuse and over the dominions of the Deinomenidae for even a year after the death of his brother Hieron (466 B.C.). The revolt of the Syracusans set ablaze the struggle for freedom in the whole of Sicily. The last tyranny to fall was that of Rhegium-Messana, in 461 B.C. The philosopher Empedocles was chiefly responsible for the reorganisation of the state of Acragas. He coined the classical maxim on the way of life his Greek compatriots pursued, which as no other describes the character of the colonial Hellenes in the West: "the Agrigentines revel as if tomorrow they must die, but build as if they would live forever."[99] The period after the victory of Himera in fact saw the building of a surprisingly large number of magnificent temples in Acragas, Syracuse, Selinus, and Himera. Of these, the Olympieum at Acragas, with its great dimensions, is a particularly impressive architectural achievement.[100]

Freedom had scarcely been won back again when internal strife in the Sicilian communities once more raised its head.[101] Syracuse, Gela, Acragas, Himera, Rhegium—all were torn asunder by internal quarrels. Under these conditions the mercenaries, favoured by the tyrants, formed dangerous concentrations of unrest, especially in Syracuse. A completely new

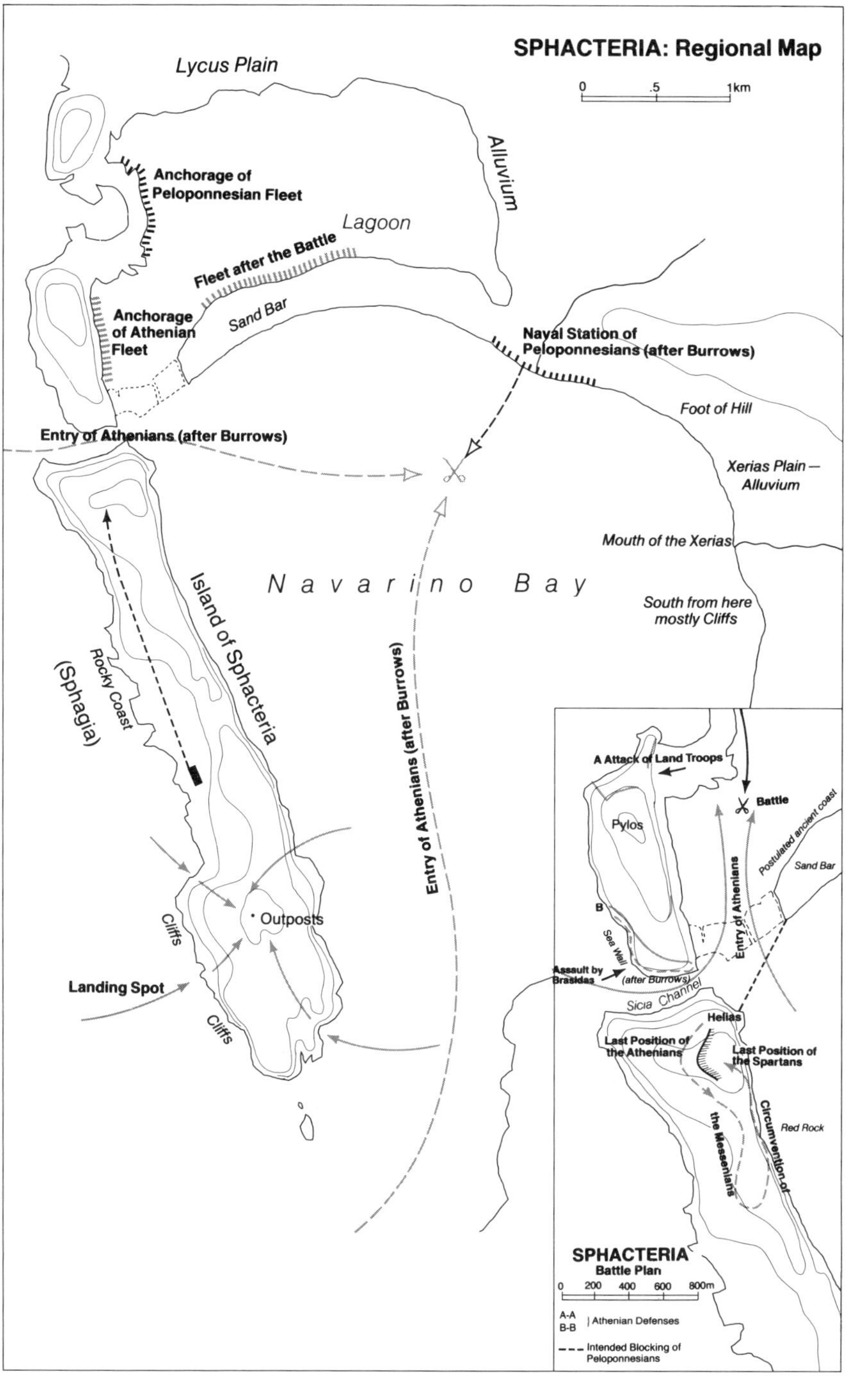

SPHACTERIA: Regional Map
0
.5
1km
Lycus Plain
Alluvium
Anchorage of
Peloponnesian Fleet
Lagoon
Fleet after the Battle
Sand Bar
Anchorage
of Athenian
Fleet
Naval Station of
Peloponnesians (after Burrows)
Foot of Hill
Entry of Athenians (after Burrows)
Xerias Plain —
Alluvium
Mouth of the Xerias
Navarino Bay
South from here
mostly Cliffs
Island of Sphacteria
Rocky Coast
(Sphagia)
Entry of Athenians (after Burrows)
Outposts
Cliffs
Landing Spot
Cliffs
A Attack of Land Troops
Battle
Pylos
Postulated ancient coast
Sand Bar
Entry of Athenians
B
Sea Wall
Assault by
Brasidas
(after Burrows)
Sicia Channel
Helias
Last Position of
the Athenians
Last Position of
the Spartans
Red Rock
Circumvention of
the Messenians
SPHACTERIA
Battle Plan
0
200
400
600
800m
A-A
B-B
Athenian Defenses
Intended Blocking of
Peloponnesians

element in the picture of Sicilian history was the awakening of the native Sicilian people, who found a national leader in Ducetius.[102] The Sicels wanted to drive the Greeks completely off the island. Ducetius founded the capital of the Sicilian federal state at Palice, and sought to advance from the interior towards the sea. A turn in events only came when Ducetius was defeated by the combined forces of Syracuse and Acragas. He was compelled to seek refuge in Syracuse from his own followers, and from there the Syracusans sent him abroad into honourable detention at Corinth (451 or 450 B.C.). Although the Sicel did return once more to his homeland, he never exerted any further influence on political developments in the island. Much more did the Syracusans succeed in re-establishing their hegemony. Towards the end of the thirties Syracuse again emerged as by far the strongest power in Sicily, indeed in the entire Greek West.[103]

The external history of Magna Graecia in the fifth century is only discernible in broad outline. On all sides the Greeks were involved in vigorous defensive struggles against the awakening peoples of ancient Italy. Tarentum and Rhegium suffered a terrible defeat at the hands of the Iapygians (473 B.C.).[104] In the realm of internal affairs the demos rose up in many cities against the aristocratic ruling class provided by the Pythagoreans. On all sides there was civil war, theft, murder, plundering—a distressing picture of Hellenic disunity.[105] The little town of Elea (later Velia) on the west coast of Lucania was like an oasis in the desert. Within its walls lived the most prominent Greek thinkers, Parmenides and Zenon. In a magnificent didactic poem Parmenides immortalised his natural philosophy, which, together with the postulation of an aethereal fire and "lightless darkness," exhibits a peculiar dualistic character. His doctrine of the zones, based on the notion of a globular earth, was of great importance to the scientific study of man. Thus the little polis of Elea is an example of the potential of the Hellenic mind when it found suitable soil to foster it.

In contrast to the Hellenic communities in southern Italy, Massalia was a stronghold of peace and security in the fifth century. With her great commercial connections, extending westwards deep into the interior of Spain, in the north along the Rhône towards the north of France and the area of the Rhine, and in the east far into the Italian districts, Massalia was the most important maritime city in the West alongside Carthage. Particularly close ties existed between this western Greek colony and the emergent Roman state, ties which are explicable in terms of the common struggle against the Etruscans. When the Romans dedicated a golden tripod to Apollo at Delphi after they conquered Veii (396 B.C.), they set it up in the treasury of the Massaliots. Just as the legend of the founding of Rome was moulded by the Greeks, in like manner it was to the Hellenes that Rome owed its freedom from Etruscan rule. Greek victories stood at the cradle of the Roman state, and only the permeation of Roman society by Hellenic culture made it possible for Rome to rise to world dominion in subsequent centuries.

8
THE PELOPONNESIAN WAR

INTRODUCTION

The summit of achievement by classical Greece during the time of Pericles was followed by the crisis of the Peloponnesian War, which lasted for almost thirty years.[1] The world-wide extent of the war—from the Greek mainland east across the Aegean and through Macedonia and Thrace as far as Asia Minor, west across the Ionian Sea as far as Sicily and southern Italy—marks it as the greatest event in Greek history since the military campaign of Xerxes against Greece. The Persian empire and the Hellenic West were drawn into its orbit, making the war an extremely important event, no less than a turning point in the history of the ancient world. It is more than symbolic that the account of the war was written by Thucydides, the greatest historian of antiquity.

Not Sparta but the Persian empire emerged as victor from the world-wide struggle. The fourth century began as a Persian and ended as a Macedonian century. The enormous amount of energy released by this war both inside and outside Hellas had disruptive and destructive repercussions in many fields, above all in the political and economic realms. As a result of the war Greece, which since Salamis and Plataea had become the centre of the world, was gradually forced to the periphery of affairs, while the East, under Persia, and the West, particularly under the empire of Dionysius I of Syracuse, rose to the foreground. The wheels of the Greek polis gradually ground to a halt. Athens' creation, the Maritime League, had failed to stand the crucial test. An excess of freedom and the inability to achieve a satisfactory balance between liberty and traditional ties destroyed the power not only of Athens and her domain but of Greece as well.

The war's crisis did not pass without leaving its mark on the Greek individual. The swelling waves of hatred and dreadful cruelty, often victimising defenceless prisoners and inhabitants of conquered cities, cast a dark shadow over the bright picture of the Hellenic character portrayed by the undying works of art in the fifth century. The inexhaustible creative vitality of the Hellenic mind, however, even in the darkest years of the great war, is nothing less than astonishing. Most of the works of Euripides († 406 B.C.) and the majority of the political comedies of Aristophanes, who appeared for the first time in 427 B.C., belong to the period of the war. They attest a flourishing intellectual life in Athens, in which the annual performances of tragedies and comedies continued unabated, although the wharfs and workshops in the city and Piraeus resounded with the din of military preparations. Nor did the chisels and saws of the builders come to a complete standstill. Construction on the so-called Erechtheum continued and in the expenditures for the war the treasurers did not forget to immortalise the deductions for the citizens, metics and slaves.

In the first years of the war the "new thought" of the Sophists came to Athens in the person of the eloquent Gorgias, the ambassador from Leontini. The teachings of the Sophists were a decisive factor in moulding the character of the new Hellenic personality. They actually brought about a revolution in Greek culture, their effects perceptible in every sphere of life, and not least in politics. For all the negative consequences, the positive must not be overlooked: the Sophists laid the foundations for scientific thinking. By placing man at the centre of things they inaugurated a new way of looking at the world. The study of the nature of man which pervades this period is a thoroughly modern feature. The new scientific spirit emerges from the writings of the physician Hippocrates of Cos, the founder of the new science of medicine (born c. 460 B.C.) and the writings of his like-minded circle. Above all, the treatise on the "Sacred Illness" and the booklet on climate are impressive witnesses of genuine scientific thinking, which would no longer be satisfied with metaphysical explanations. It is therefore no accident that the terminology in the *History* of Thucydides shows undeniable echoes of the Hippocratic Corpus.

Nowhere, however, does the new Hellenic spirit reveal itself so clearly as in the sphere of religious belief. The openness of the Hellenic mind towards foreign influences manifests itself in the naturalisation of numerous foreign deities in Greece. Thracian Bendis, Phrygian Sabazius, Libyan Ammon and many others became recognised in Hellas, even though politics may often have paved the way for religion. In all ages, however, affliction teaches men to pray, and thus in the Peloponnesian War too the faithful in large multitudes turned to the mystery cults in order to find comfort and hope.

On the other hand the new Greek, moulded by the war and its ruthlessness, very often ignored the bounds of right, ethos and good faith. Autocrats like Alcibiades and Lysander ruled the political stage, while the masses were no less gripped by a power mania. In the Popular Assemblies feelings of revenge often triumphed over emotions of sober reflection. In particular the attitude of the Attic demos shows that the sovereign people is hardly an instrument of infallible political insight. The brighter shades, however, are not entirely lacking in the gloomy picture. The great humanity of Socrates, with the courage of his convictions, the faithful and patient fulfilment of duty by so many nameless thousands and the great readiness for sacrifice on the part of Athens cannot be gainsaid by posterity. It is a tragic fate that fulfills itself in the Attic-Spartan power struggle. The inability of victorious Sparta to build a new and free Hellas and the preponderance of Persian power sealed the decline of the Greek people. It took Alexander of Macedonia more than two generations later to arouse the Greeks to new life.

EVENTS LEADING UP TO THE PELOPONNESIAN WAR

In his *History*, Thucydides takes issue with the view that Pericles instigated the so-called Peloponnesian War in order to overcome difficulties in internal politics. The eminent historian perceived the more fundamental causes, which he differentiated from the external reasons. He understood the Athenian-Spartan dualism as well as the antithesis in the internal policies pursued by the two leading states in Greece. The majority of modern scholars have followed Thucydides, with the sole exception of K. J. Beloch, who has championed the view which Thucydides attacks, blaming Pericles, a view which we find put forward primarily in contemporary comedy. The course of events, however, up to the outbreak of open hostilities in the spring of 431 B.C. is conclusive evidence for the correctness of Thucydides' view. If there is anything certain it is this: Pericles did not seek the war, although he certainly did not avoid it once the rupture seemed irreparable and when events permitted no other choice to the Attic statesman without a deep and pointless humiliation for Athens.

The flames of the great war were kindled by the discord between the commercial powers, Athens and Corinth. The queen-city of the Isthmus, relying upon the extensive colonial possessions on the islands and coast of the Ionian Sea which she held in strict political and economic dependence, had been almost undisputed mistress of communications between Greece and the West in the sixth century. In the rich island of Corcyra she possessed an important intermediate base from which Corintho-Corcyraean trade encompassed almost the whole of the West—Sicily, southern Italy and the entire Apennine peninsula. Only after the great victories over Persia did Corinth first encounter serious competition from the growing Athenian trade in the West. Discoveries of Attic vases in Italy and treaties which Athens concluded with cities of the Greek West, and not least the founding of Thurii (v.s.p. 124), bear witness to this trade.

Corinth, with her incomparable strategic location on two seas, could also have taken a leading part in eastern trade had not her activity in the East been seriously curtailed by the rivalry of Aegina and Megara. In the course of the Pentecontaetia the rapid rise of Athens forced Corinth to assume a new position. In the so-called first Peloponnesian War, Corinth, by lending her active support to the weaker Aeginetans, found herself on the side of the enemy of Athens. Athens countered this by concluding a treaty with Achaea and above all by taking control of Naupactus, the "Athenian Gibraltar" in the Corinthian Gulf (v.s.p. 119). By this stroke Pericles threatened the commercial metropolis of Corinth mortally. If she wished to avoid ruin, the once so-proud queen of the Ionian Sea had to strain every nerve to extricate herself from the strangling tentacles.

In contrast to Corinth, whose vital interests were being threatened, Sparta, the hegemonial power in the Peloponnesian League, was anything but disposed towards a war. The decreasing population, the spectre of the dreaded recurrence of a Helot revolt, limited financial and economic resources and the relaxed state of the Peloponnesian League, in comparison with the strictly organised Attic Maritime League—all these factors crippled Sparta's initiative. She did not choose the war, but was forced into it by Corinth and her allies.

About the middle of the thirties, when the din from the Samian revolt had been muffled, dark clouds began to gather on the horizon of the Ionian Sea. The enmity between Corinth and her daughter-city Corcyra produced a regular war, in which the supremacy of the western sea was at stake.[2] Internal quarrels between the oligarchic and democratic factions in the Corcyraean colony of Epidamnus (now Durazzo) summoned both states to intervene. The Corinthians, who rejected Corcyra's proposal for arbitration, sustained a devastating defeat in a sea battle at the promontory of Leucimme (at the southern tip of Corcyra). Epidamnus surrendered to the Corcyraeans, and the Corinthian garrison was taken prisoner (435 B.C.). While Corinth, supported by Leucas and Ambracia, feverishly rearmed, Corcyra sent an appeal for help to Athens and requested a defensive alliance.[3] After considerable vacillation, the Attic *Ekklesia* succeeded in reaching an affirmative decision. In mid-summer 433 B.C., in the vicinity of the Sybota islands (in the straits between Corcyra and the mainland), 150 Corinthian and 110 Corcyraean triremes confronted each other. The intervention of the Attic auxiliary squadron, which had at first assumed an attitude of reserve, prevented the Corinthians from taking full advantage of the victory they had won.[4]

In Potidaea on Chalcidice too, Athenian and Corinthian interests clashed. As a Corinthian colony founded by Periander, Potidaea had proved to be a strong fortress of Hellenic freedom in the north. It had joined the Attic Maritime League, without however forfeiting its ties with the mother-city, which annually despatched the leading magistrates to Potidaea. When the Corcyraean conflict was at its height, in the summer of 433 B.C., Pericles demanded that Potidaea hand over the Corinthian *Epidamiourgoi* and raze the South Wall running directly across the peninsula of Pallene. Potidaea, relying on the treaty with the Macedonian king Perdiccas II, countered the Athenian demands with an open revolt (about May 432 B.C.); the Bottiaeans and the Chalcidians also joined the insurgents.[5] The height of the conflict was marked by the "Megarian *psephisma*," closing all the harbours of the Maritime League to the Megarians, the allies of Corinth and rivals of Athens—a devastating blow to Megarian trade (432 B.C.). Pericles' contemporaries regarded this *psephisma*—he justified it by insignificant incidents such as appear everywhere and always in times of crisis—as the actual cause of the war, but incorrectly, for the *psephisma* was merely the expression of one among many differences which had arisen between Athens and the Peloponnesians. This is also how Thucydides (I 67) presents it. When Megara complained, the Spartan *Apella* and then a session of the Peloponnesian League decided that Athens had violated the Thirty Years' Peace. War had become inevitable.

The winter of 432/1 B.C. was taken up with shadow negotiations. Both

MAP IV

Greece on the Eve of the Peloponnesian War (431 B.C.)

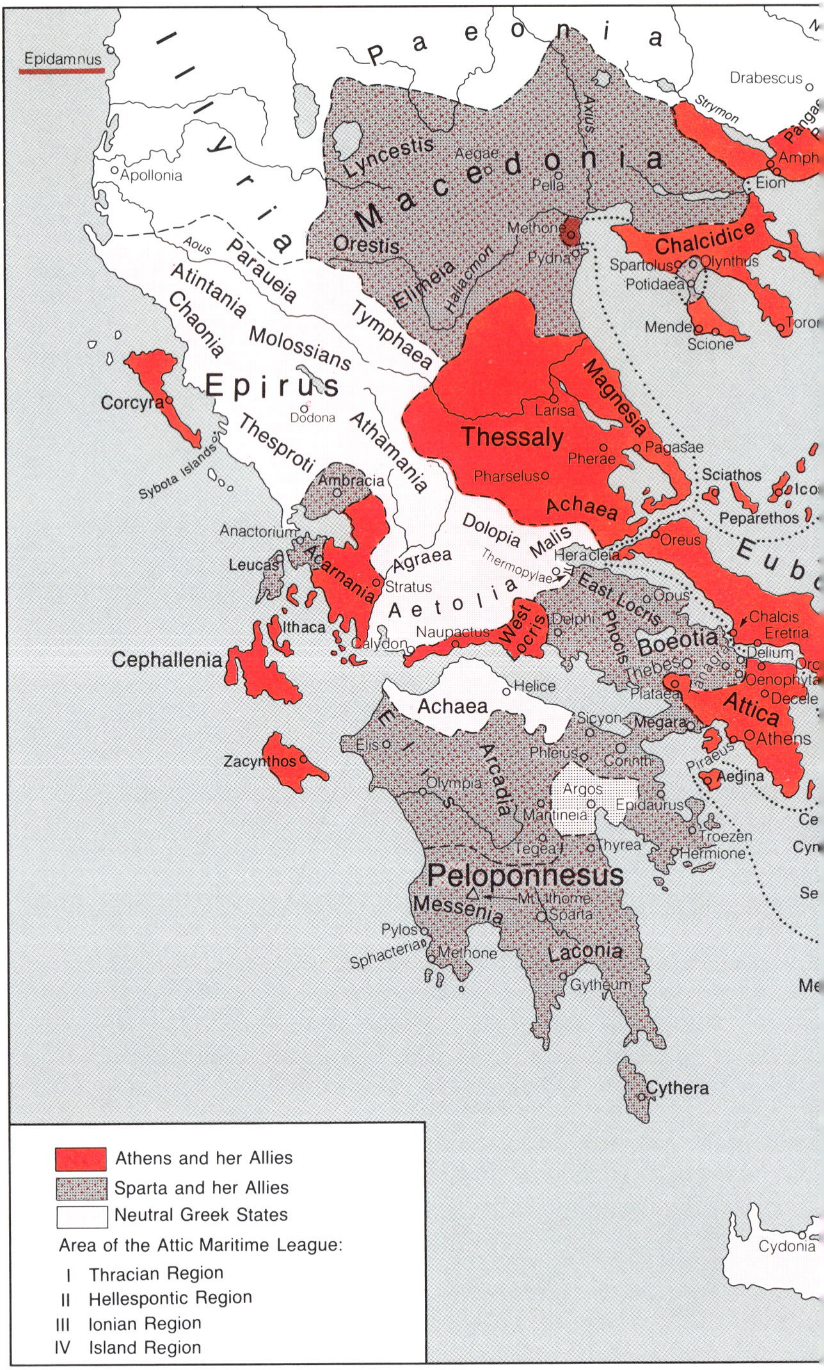

Epidamnus
Illyria
Paeonia
Macedonia
Drabescus
Strymon
Axius
Lyncestis
Aegae
Pella
Amph
Eion
Apollonia
Methone
Pydna
Chalcidice
Olynthus
Spartolus
Potidaea
Mende
Scione
Toron
Aous
Paraueia
Orestis
Elimeia
Haliacmon
Atintania
Chaonia
Molossians
Tymphaea
Epirus
Corcyra
Dodona
Magnesia
Larisa
Thessaly
Pherae
Pagasae
Pharselus
Achaea
Sciathos
Peparethos
Thesproti
Athamania
Sybota Islands
Ambracia
Anactorium
Dolopia
Malis
Oreus
Euboea
Leucas
Acarnania
Agraea
Stratus
Thermopylae
Heraclea
East Locris
Opus
Aetolia
Ithaca
Delphi
Phocis
Chalcis
Eretria
Boeotia
Delium
Cephallenia
Calydon
Naupactus
West Locris
Thebes
Tanagra
Oenophyta
Decele
Plataea
Attica
Helice
Achaea
Sicyon
Megara
Elis
Athens
Zacynthos
Phleius
Corinth
Piraeus
Aegina
Olympia
Arcadia
Argos
Epidaurus
Mantineia
Troezen
Hermione
Tegea
Thyrea
Peloponnesus
Mt. Ithome
Messenia
Sparta
Pylos
Sphacteria
Methone
Laconia
Gytheum
Cythera
Cydonia
Athens and her Allies
Sparta and her Allies
Neutral Greek States
Area of the Attic Maritime League:
I Thracian Region
II Hellespontic Region
III Ionian Region
IV Island Region

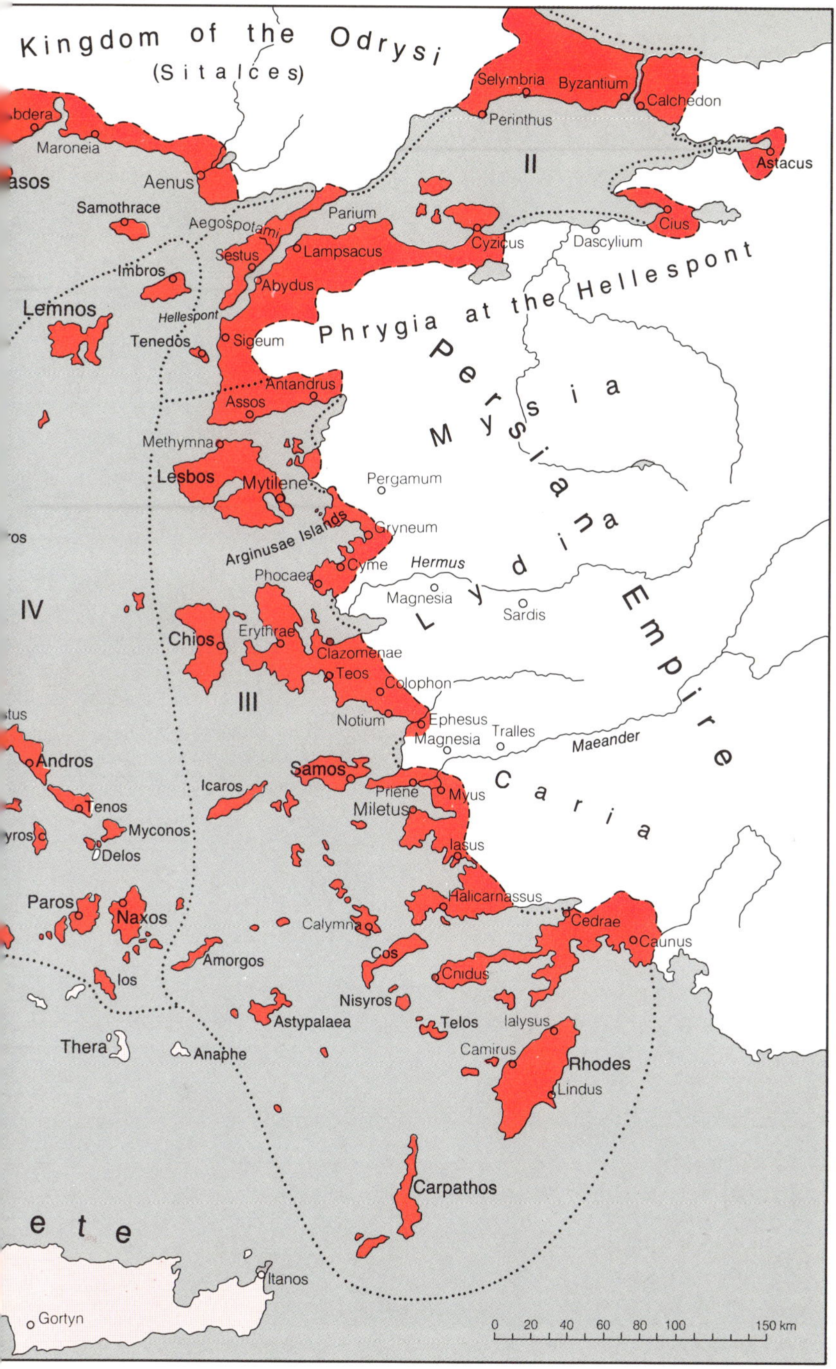

Kingdom of the Odrysi
(Sitalces)
Selymbria
Byzantium
Calchedon
Perinthus
Astacus
II
Maroneia
Aenus
Samothrace
Aegospotami
Parium
Cius
Sestus
Lampsacus
Cyzicus
Dascylium
Imbros
Abydus
Phrygia at the Hellespont
Lemnos
Hellespont
Tenedos
Sigeum
Persian Empire
Antandrus
Assos
Mysia
Methymna
Lesbos
Mytilene
Pergamum
Arginusae Islands
Gryneum
Cyme
Hermus
Phocaea
Lydia
Magnesia
Sardis
IV
Chios
Erythrae
Clazomenae
Teos
Colophon
III
Notium
Ephesus
Magnesia
Tralles
Maeander
Andros
Samos
Icaros
Priene
Myus
Caria
Tenos
Miletus
Myconos
Delos
Iasus
Paros
Naxos
Halicarnassus
Calymna
Cedrae
Caunus
Amorgos
Cos
Cnidus
Ios
Nisyros
Astypalaea
Telos
Ialysus
Thera
Anaphe
Camirus
Rhodes
Lindus
Carpathos
Itanos
Gortyn
0 20 40 60 80 100 150 km

parties, above all Sparta, sought by diplomatic means to gain a favourable starting point and to convince public opinion in Greece of the justice of their cause. Sparta was decidedly more successful in this than her Athenian opponent. When Sparta ultimately demanded of Athens that she banish the Alcmeonidae, heavily laden with a curse—by which she meant Pericles—and that she restore to the members of the Attic League their autonomy,[6] she was preparing for war with propaganda. The autonomy of the Hellenes was proclaimed as the aim of the war, with the sure expectation that this slogan would find a response in the Maritime League. Pericles, however, remained unmoved in the face of the Peloponnesian demands. When the antagonists rejected his proposal on the basis of the Peace Treaty of 446/5 B.C., it was clear to all the world who wanted the war. Corinth and her allies were the ones who swept Sparta along by threats that help would be found elsewhere—an allusion to Argos, who did not belong to the Peloponnesian League.

THE ARCHIDAMIAN WAR (431-421 B.C.)[7]

The adversaries in the decisive conflict of arms were fundamentally different in their structure and military strength. Athens, indisputably the greatest sea power in the eastern Mediterranean, had at her disposal the wealthy resources from the entire area of the Maritime League. In the Ionian Sea she possessed Zacynthus and Corcyra, while in the West, in Sicily and southern Italy, Segesta, Leontini and Rhegium were important allies. In central Greece the Messenians in Naupactus, the Acarnanians, the Amphilochians and above all the Thessalians were on the side of Athens. By land, however, the city was surrounded by enemies on all sides. Megara, Corinth and the Boeotians were merely waiting for a favourable moment to attack their hated neighbour. In the Peloponnesus Argos and Achaea alone remained neutral, all other states enlisting their contingents in the army of the Peloponnesian League, which was further strengthened by additions from Phocis and the East Locrians. Thus in the war almost the entire Hellenic world from Ionia to Sicily was divided into two camps.[8]

The land forces of the Peloponnesian League had a strength of 40,000, against which Athens could put into the field only about 13,000 hoplites, plus 1200 horse and 1600 archers, the last of only limited effectiveness. The Attic land reserves, with a strength of 16,000, served only for defensive action and for garrison troops.[9] The situation by sea was completely different. The large fleet of 300 Attic triremes, further strengthened by warships from Chios, Lesbos and Corcyra, had no counterpart in the Mediterranean. The Athenian ships were manned by the *thetes*, metics and slaves from Athens, as well as by recruits from within the Maritime League, all available in adequate numbers. The Peloponnesian League had no financial reserves whatever at its disposal, not even a war chest, but depended rather on contributions from the League members in money and in kind.[10] Athens, on the other hand, had strong financial resources in the tribute from the League which flowed in regularly, and in the reserve fund established on Callias' initiative. Altogether the Attic state treasury may, however, have already exceeded its record level in consequence of the high expenditures for Pericles' magnificent building programme.[11]

The strategy of Pericles rested on the difference in the military strength of the opponents by land and by sea. The countryside of Attica was to be sacrificed—except for a number of garrisons on the Boeotian border[12]—and the entire Attic population was to withdraw within the Long Walls. A blockade of the gigantic Athens-Piraeus double-fortress would be completely ineffective so long as the Athenian flag remained sovereign on the seas. Landing sorties in the region of the Peloponnesus were planned as counterstrokes by Attic naval forces. Periclean strategy deliberately forfeited impressive outward successes. On the other hand, however, its execution made the greatest demands on the population in terms of morale and discipline, and that precisely from the non-combatant elements. Never could such a plan have sprung from the mind of a statesman and *strategos* who instigated the war to win cheap laurels.[13]

The war began in the spring of 431 B.C. with a surprise attack of the Thebans on Plataea. From time immemorial Plataea had enjoyed very close ties with Athens. Scarcely three hours' distance away, it presented a permanent threat to Thebes. The Theban hoplites who forced their way into Plataea were overwhelmed, and 180 were executed. A warning from Athens arrived too late. Within two months of this bloody prelude, the Peloponnesian army invaded Attica under the command of the Spartan king Archidamus. Despite the faltering of morale among the Attic population crowded together within the Long Walls, for whom temples and rapidly constructed barracks had to suffice as emergency dwellings, Pericles held to his strictly defensive strategy, with the result that the Peloponnesians withdrew after only one month. As a counterstroke, Athens despatched a squadron against the Peloponnesus. The fleet was repulsed in Methone by Brasidas, but then sailed into the Ionian Sea and brought Cephallenia over to the side of Athens, as well as Sollium in Acarnania. With the eviction of the Aeginetans—they were replaced by Attic cleruchs—Pericles made a clean sweep of things in the Saronic Gulf. On the other hand the plundering expedition in the region of Megara was nothing but an act of revenge, and did nothing whatever to alter the military situation.

Nor did the invasion by the Peloponnesians in the spring of 430 B.C., which caused particularly severe devastation in Attica, bring any turn in events. But in the summer of 430 B.C. a dreadful epidemic originating in the Near East broke out in the overcrowded city and in the Athenian fleet. It was the so-called "plague," the course of which Thucydides (II 48-54) has described with such incomparable vividness. The character of the disease is still disputed today.[14] In four years the epidemic carried off no less than a third of the Attic population. In the wake of the fear of death, despondency and despair gained the upper hand over all political reason among the crowded population. A guilty person was sought, and found—in Pericles. Charged with embezzlement, he was insultingly deposed from the *strategia* (autumn 430 B.C.), an office which he had held for fifteen consecutive years.

The lawsuit and condemnation of Pericles[15] mark a new phase in the war. It was now a matter of life and death. The prosecution of the war was intensified on both sides, and the Peloponnesians killed every Athenian who fell into their hands in order to maintain a full-scale quarantine.

Potidaea, after two years of heroic defense, capitulated in the spring of 429 B.C., bringing noticeable relaxation for Athens in the north. A treaty concluded between Athens and the powerful Thracian king Sitalces[16] established a strong support for Athenian rule in the north, chiefly in respect of oscillating Macedonia.[17] But the great hopes which Athens placed in Sitalces were not destined to see fulfilment.[18] Even so, the Thracian king remained a noteworthy ally, for his dominions embraced the wide area between the Strymon, the Black Sea and the Lower Danube, and thus offered Athenian trade tremendous possibilities. Large-scale successes in the north, however, were not forthcoming. The blockading force freed by the surrender of Potidaea suffered a serious defeat at Spartolus in a battle with the Chalcidians and Bottiaeans. In terms of military history, this was the first time that light armed troops and horse triumphed over hoplites. The revolution in fighting tactics which was brought about a generation later, primarily by Iphicrates, is already foreshadowed here.

In contrast to developments in the north, in the west the naval expedition of Phormion (autumn 429 B.C.) ended in a double victory for Athens.[19] The Peloponnesians failed to remove the strangling naval fortress of Naupactus. The Athenian fleet continued to maintain the blockade of the Peloponnesus: prices rose and the flow of grain from Sicily ceased, with the result that not only the Corinthians but also the Peloponnesians discovered what it meant to be at war with Athens.

In the spring elections of 429 B.C. Pericles was reinstated, but he was a broken man. He had lost his two legitimate sons in the plague, and he himself was to become its victim a few months later. No one in Athens possessed his great political experience, or the ability to keep a tight rein on the multiple threads of strategy, diplomacy and finance. Pericles never had outstanding collaborators,[20] and it is not completely without justification that Beloch has accused him of surrounding himself with intellectual nonentities. The helm was now taken over by Eucrates, Lysicles (a friend of Pericles) and Cleon, the "Tanner," a demagogue of the very first order—figures who came from the class of great businessmen and who, in contrast to the rural population which had in many cases been deprived of house and home, were determined to continue the war at any price. Cleon had earlier bitterly opposed the Periclean war policy, but after the death of his rival became its greatest exponent, the type of "stick-it-out politician," such as almost every long and hard-fought war in history produces. Violently attacked in comedy, above all by Eupolis and Aristophanes, and portrayed with surpassing irony a generation later by Thucydides,[21] Cleon, despite all his energy,[22] appears as the genuine grave-digger of Athenian greatness. Nicias, son of Niceratus, emerged as Cleon's rival. Nicias rose to prominence on the strength of his position as *strategos*.[23] In general, after the death of Pericles the paths of military professionals diverged from those of the demagogues, on the whole to the advantage of military interests.

Due to the effects of the plague neither side was active in prosecuting the war in 429 B.C. A surprise attack on Piraeus by the enterprising Brasidas came to nothing. In 428 B.C. the revolt of the wealthy island of Lesbos, with the capital city of Mytilene, brought a crisis for Athens. Only by enlisting all her energies, her financial and military resources,[24] including Attic cleruchs from abroad, could Athens maintain a siege of Mytilene. The city was ultimately forced into unconditional surrender through starvation (summer 427 B.C.). In the Athenian *Ekklesia* Cleon proposed a terrible punishment for the insurgents. The whole adult male population was to be executed, the women and children sold into slavery and the land distributed among Attic cleruchs. Not until the following day did the Athenians avail themselves of more sober reflection. The ultimate sentence was harsh enough. Mytilene had to atone for her disaffection with the loss of her territory, and no less than 1000 citizens who had been most seriously implicated were executed. This unprecedented act of murder, which was expressly commanded by the Attic *Ekklesia*, has seemed so atrocious that some earlier scholars have attempted to eliminate it from the historical record or to reduce its magnitude.[25] The Peloponnesians were not a step behind their adversaries in brutality. In Plataea, which capitulated shortly after Mytilene, over 200 Plataeans and Athenians were put to the sword (autumn 427 B.C.).

In the prosecution of the war, foreign military events were interwoven with internal party struggles, like, for instance, the suppression of an oligarchic revolution in Corcyra with Athenian help (mid-summer 427 B.C.). For the position of Athens in the West the control of this island in the Ionian Sea at just that time was of greatest importance, since events in Sicily had taken a turn which made direct intervention by Athens seem opportune. Syracuse was predominant, as she had created for herself a notable alliance in the Dorian communities of Gela, Selinus, Messana, Himera and Locri Epizephyrii. This elicited the formation of a counter-coalition composed in the main of Ionian-Chalcidian cities (Naxos, Catana, Leontini, Rhegium and a single Dorian polis Camarina) and of Sicels, a coalition that was not, however, a match for the adversaries. Then in the autumn of 427 B.C. Athens despatched a small fleet under Laches to Sicily (the so-called first Sicilian expedition of the Athenians).[26] Athens had already been allied with Rhegium and Leontini for years.[27] The treaty with Segesta was renewed by Laches and it would seem that Halicyae threw herself into the arms of the Athenians (427/6 or at the latest 426/5 B.C.).[28]

The year 426 B.C. brought little progress for the Peloponnesians. Their establishment of a military garrison of Heracleia Trachis (at the northern exit of Thermopylae) was the only event which assumed any strategic

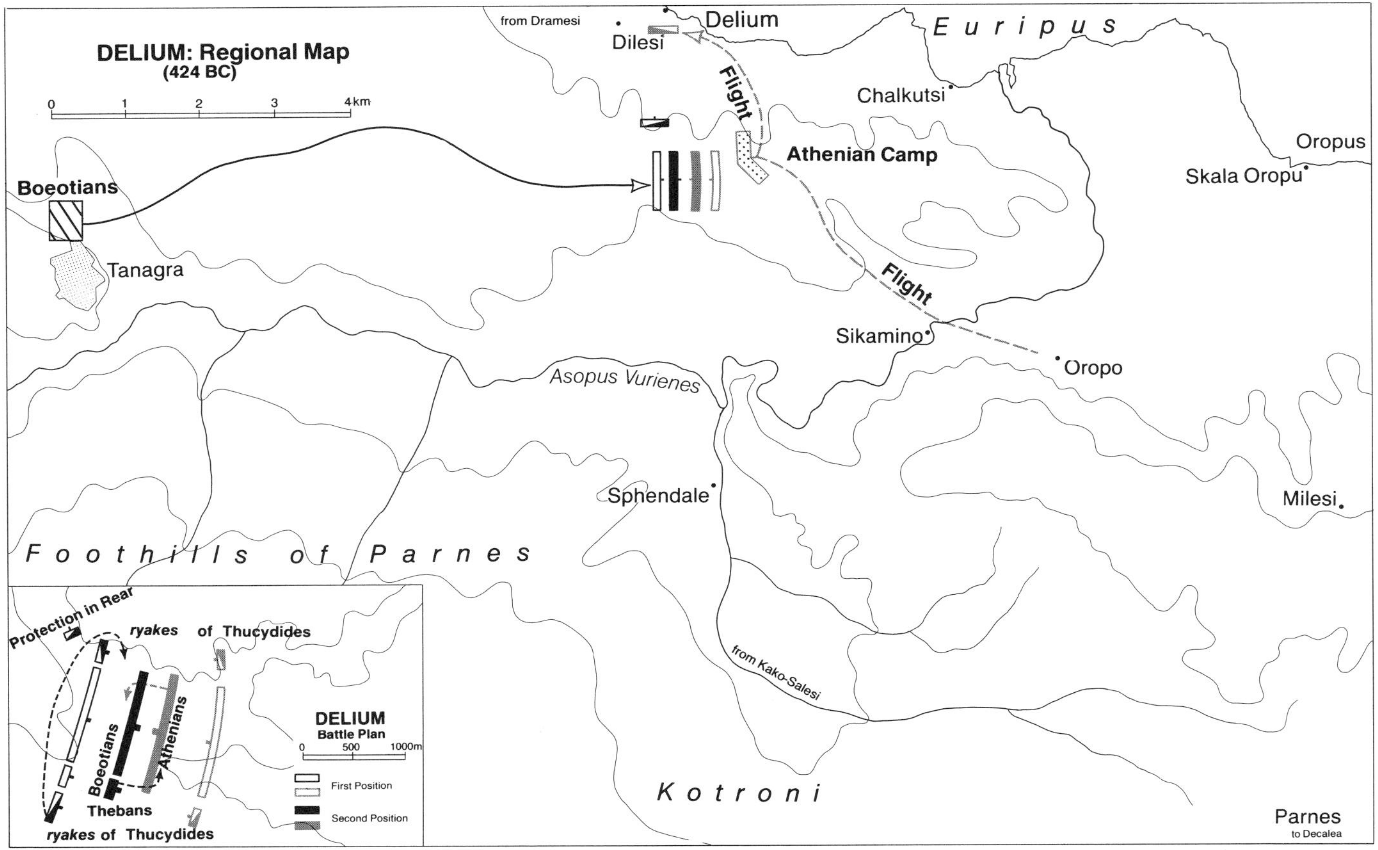
DELIUM: Regional Map
(424 BC)
0 1 2 3 4km
Boeotians
Tanagra
from Dramesi
Dilesi
Delium
Euripus
Flight
Chalkutsi
Athenian Camp
Oropus
Skala Oropu
Flight
Sikamino
Oropo
Asopus Vurienes
Sphendale
Milesi
Foothills of Parnes
from Kako-Salesi
Kotroni
Parnes
to Decalea
Protection in Rear
ryakes of Thucydides
Boeotians
Athenians
Thebans
ryakes of Thucydides
DELIUM
Battle Plan
0 500 1000m
First Position
Second Position

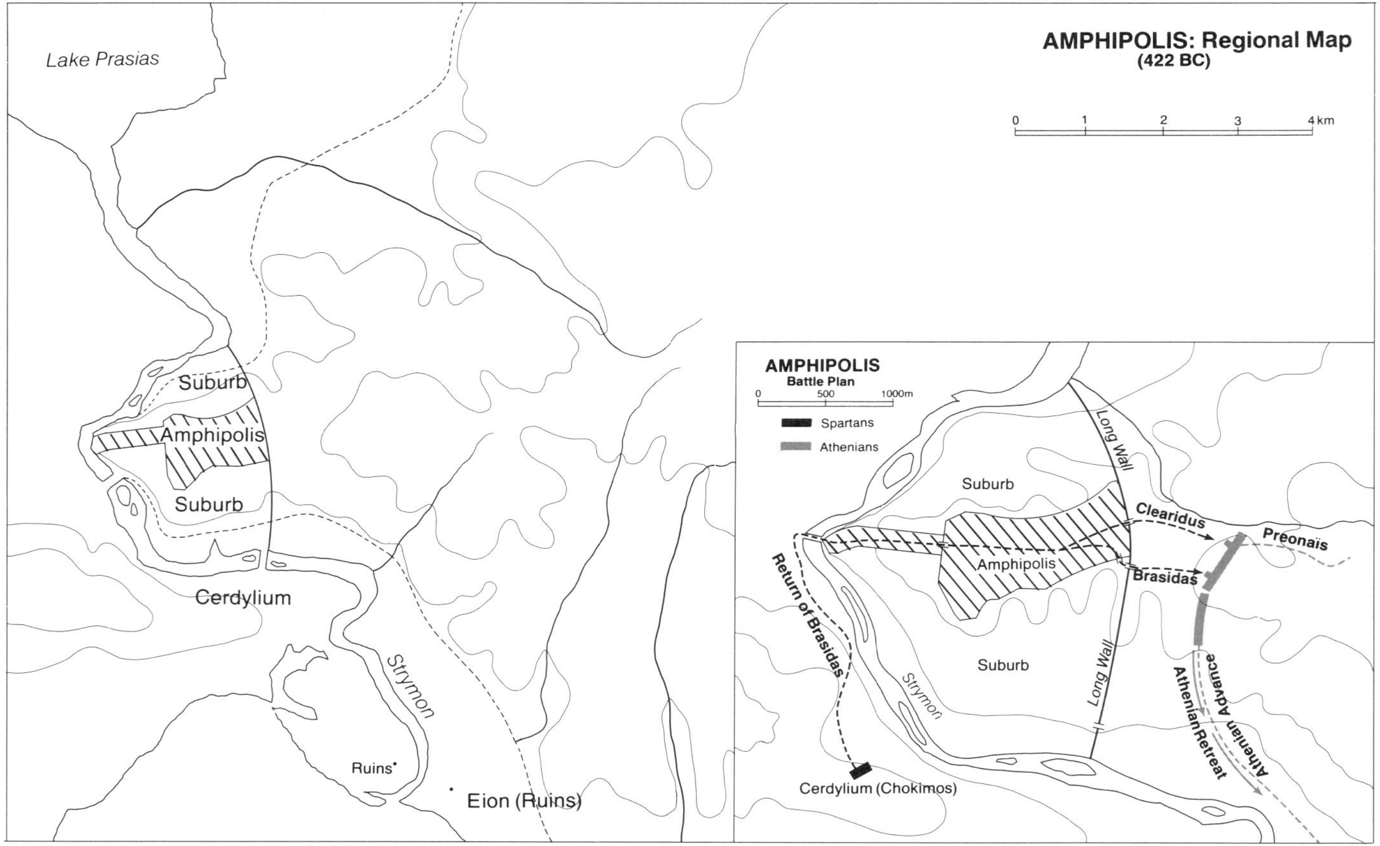
AMPHIPOLIS: Regional Map
(422 BC)
0
1
2
3
4 km
Lake Prasias
Suburb
Amphipolis
Suburb
Cerdylium
Strymon
Ruins
Eion (Ruins)
AMPHIPOLIS
Battle Plan
0
500
1000m
Spartans
Athenians
Suburb
Long Wall
Clearidus
Preonais
Amphipolis
Brasidas
Return of Brasidas
Suburb
Long Wall
Strymon
Athenian Advance
Athenian Retreat
Cerdylium (Chokimos)

importance, providing a base for operations against central Greece. In Athens an internal change of great consequence took place: not a single one of the former generals was re-elected. Instead, Cleon, already *hellenotamias* since 427/6 B.C., and with him the war party, took over the helm. This change brought considerably increased activity in Attic politics.

In April of 425 B.C., the Athenians sent a second and larger squadron to Sicily, joined by one Demosthenes, who had been elected *strategos* for 425/4 B.C. Well trained in military matters he perceived in the harbour of Pylos on the west coast of the Peloponnesus an ideal place from which to exert decisive pressure on the enemy.[29] From Pylos it would be possible to make connections with the Messenians and thereby conjure up the spectre of a new Messenian war against Sparta. The landing at Pylos was a complete success. All attacks of the Peloponnesians, both by land and by sea, were repulsed, and 420 Lacedaemonian hoplites, a tenth of the total Spartan forces, were cut off on the offshore island of Sphacteria after they had landed. Under the pressure of this catastrophe Sparta was prepared to enter peace negotiations, and obtained an armistice in the theatre of Pylos. Sparta's offer included not only re-establishing the Thirty Years' Peace of 446/5 B.C., but even a defensive-offensive alliance. Cleon, however, rejected the offer. In a moving session of the *Ekklesia*, the course of which Thucydides has described in unsurpassed prose, Nicias forced Cleon to take over the command at Pylos. Cleon, however, relied completely on Demosthenes, and the second day after his arrival forced the Lacedaemonians who had been cut off—still almost 300 hoplites—into unconditional surrender (August 425 B.C.)

To the indisputable credit of Cleon, under the influence of the surprising success at Sphacteria which brought him extraordinary honours, including accommodation in the *Prytaneion* for life and a seat of honour in the theatre, he pressed for the reorganisation of the tribute payments among the members of the League. The so-called Cleon Assessment of 425/4 B.C.[30] fixed the tribute anew. Instead of the amount set by Aristeides, totaling 460 talents, paid for over half a century, the total sum was now raised to 1460 talents.[31] Since the financial reserves of Athens were exhausted, there was no other alternative. Let the members of the League therefore pay, so long as the Athenian fleet, that costly arm of the *demos*, continued to rule the seas. By increasing reimbursement in the *Heliaea* from two to three obols per day Cleon put the Attic masses strongly in debt to him.

With the occupation of the island of Cythera (424 B.C.) by Nicias, naval operations made unusually favourable progress for Athens. The blockade of the Peloponnesus was now almost complete and it appeared to be only a matter of time until Sparta would be forced to her knees. In this hour of peril Brasidas,[32] son of Tellis, became the saviour of Sparta. At Methone (in the first year of the war), then at Pylos, he had distinguished himself with unusual prudence and bravery. Now he was entrusted with the command of a small force which Sparta despatched to aid the Chalcidians in 424 B.C. After an admirable march across the

Isthmus—whereby Megara, except for the harbour of Nisaea, was wrested from Athens—through Boeotia, via Heracleia Trachis and through Thessaly, Brasidas arrived at the frontiers of Macedonia. The king, Perdiccas II, had already prepared the ground in advance through diplomacy.[33] Brasidas understood how to strike the Achilles' heel of the Attic empire. The first of the Chalcidian communities to join him were Acanthus and Stageira. He captured Amphipolis in the region of the Strymon, which the *strategos* Thucydides (the subsequent historian of the war) was incapable of defending, holding only the harbour-city of Eion. Brasidas thus dealt a severe blow to Athenian prestige in the north of the Aegean. The gold mines in the district of Mount Pangaeum fell into his hands and the revolt of the cities in the region of Thrace assumed wider dimensions (autumn 424 B.C.).

In general the year 424 B.C. was an unfortunate one for Athens. A large-scale concentric attack on Boeotia by the Athenians failed. While retreating, the Attic phalanx was completely defeated at Delium by a surprise flank attack of the Boeotians who were arrayed twenty-five deep on the right wing.[34] It was the only major battle of the entire ten-year Archidamian War and in it the Athenians were defeated—further evidence for the correctness of Periclean strategy. For the first time the Boeotians employed the tactics of the "oblique phalanx," which was later developed by Epameinondas with such great success and completely revolutionised Greek military science (v.i.p. 170). Incidentally, Athenian influence also took a negative turn in the West, in Sicily. In the face of the Attic reinforcements which the squadron of Sophocles and Eurymedon brought from Pylos to Sicily, the Greeks there settled their quarrel at the Congress of Gela (424 B.C.). The Syracusan Hermocrates[35] had spread at the session the inflaming slogan "Sicily for the Siceliots." Attic aid was no longer required, and the Athenian fleet returned home.[36] In 424/3 B.C. a revision of the Attic citizen list was, it seems, undertaken, since there was a larger amount of grain available for distribution.[37]

The many lawsuits against Attic *strategoi* (Laches, Eurymedon, Sophocles, Thucydides)[38] reveal the nervous mood of the Athenians. There was dissatisfaction with the conduct of the war. The war party lost ground and in 423 B.C. the peace for which the multitudes were longing actually appeared to be in sight—a one-year truce which Laches brought about.[39] After the death of Artaxerxes I the Athenians renewed the Peace of Callias (424 or at the latest 423 B.C.),[40] so that no immediate danger threatened from the east. Rapid developments on Chalcidice, however, destroyed the prospects for peace. A dispute arose over Scione, which had seceded from Athens in the very days when the armistice was being signed. The Athenians insisted that it be returned, while the Spartans were only willing to allow the appointment of a special court of arbitration. Thus the war continued, and Cleon, the new hero of the Attic democracy, now also reaped victories in the north.[41] In the winter of 423/2 B.C. Nicias brought the ever-oscillating Macedonian king Perdiccas II over to the side of Athens and put him under obligation with a treaty to deliver ship timber from the forests of his dominions.[42] Cleon succeeded in taking Torone and other cities in Thrace, including Galepsus, but in a reconnaissance thrust against Amphipolis he left himself seriously exposed.[43] Six hundred Athenians, and Cleon himself, were left dead on the battlefield; the fallen of the enemy included Brasidas. The citizens of Amphipolis erected a monument to him in the market place and conferred heroic honours on him.

The deaths of Cleon and Brasidas removed the chief obstacles to an understanding. In Athens the peace party of Nicias gained the upper hand, and Sparta, because she expected serious difficulties with her inveterate foe, Argos, in the near future—the end of the Thirty Years' Peace loomed on the horizon—was no less prepared to negotiate for peace. Sparta demanded that the prisoners of Sphacteria be returned and Pylos, Cythera and Methana evacuated. For her part, however, she was prepared to restore to the Athenians all communities which had seceded from the Attic Alliance and had gone over to the Peloponnesian side during the war. Despite opposition from the Athenian radicals, the "lamp manufacturer" Hyperbolus and Peisander, in April 421 B.C., after an ultimatum from Sparta gave her demands the necessary force, a peace of fifty years was concluded between the Athenians and Lacedaemonians and their respective allies.[44]

The "Peace of Nicias" was without question an important victory for Athens.[45] The aim with which Pericles had entered the war, to wit the maintenance of the *status quo*, had been attained. In contrast to this the Peloponnesian slogan concerning the freedom and autonomy of the Hellenes had proven to be merely empty words. The Attic countryside admittedly lay devastated and Athens had not recovered from the serious loss of life suffered by the plague. Large cracks had appeared in the structure of the Maritime League, especially in the region of Thrace. Time would tell whether Athens would be able to counter the centrifugal forces affecting certain members of the League, not just with armed force, but preferably through some imaginative reorganising. This was particularly necessary in view of the fact that the struggle between Athens and Sparta had not as yet been decided.

THE ERA OF THE PEACE OF NICIAS (421-414 B.C.)
THE GREAT SICILIAN EXPEDITION OF ATHENS (415-413 B.C.)

The obligations which had been accepted with the Peace of Nicias were not fulfilled by either party, for neither was willing nor able to do so. Of the members of the Peloponnesian League, Corinth, Megara, Elis and Boeotia did not even ratify the treaty. The Spartan *harmostes*—governor—of Amphipolis, Clearidas, refused to hand over the city to the vengeance of Athens. The only action he was prepared to take was to clear the coastal cities of Thrace. The Athenians answered with reprisals: they continued to occupy Cythera and refused to permit the prisoners of Sphacteria to return home to Lacedaemonia. Corinth felt the greatest dissatisfaction. She had regained neither Corcyra nor Potidaea, and had not won back Sollium or Anactorium, because the Acarnanians retained possession of the bases. The crisis in the Peloponnesian League drove Sparta into the arms of the Athenians. In the spring of 421 B.C. an Attic-Spartan defensive alliance was concluded for a period of fifty years.[46] This only accentuated the mistrust of the other Peloponnesians and led to an open revolt within the Peloponnesian League. Elis and Mantineia withdrew from the alliance and formed a separate league with Corinth, Argos and the Chalcidians,[47] so that Sparta was now as good as isolated in the Peloponnesus. As always, the driving force behind these machinations was Corinth. She turned the growing democratic movement in the Peloponnesus to her own account and astutely played it off against the aristocratic Sparta. Sparta had once employed similar tactics against Athens and her Maritime League, and now ideological differences were mobilised against the Lacedaemonian claim to hegemony. It was only a very weak substitute for ground lost in the Peloponnesus when Spartan diplomacy succeeded in concluding a treaty with Boeotia in the winter of 421/20 B.C.[48]

Open dissatisfaction with the hollow peace resulted in a complete reversal of Attic policy. People no longer wanted to have anything to do with Nicias and his Peace. The horrors of the ten-year war had been forgotten too quickly. The radical faction with its leaders Hyperbolus and Alcibiades consequently gained the upper hand. Alcibiades was son of Cleinias and his mother was an Alcmeonid.[49] After the death of his father, Alcibiades grew up in the house of Pericles. His outstanding talents, mental and physical, appear to have destined him to a career of fame. In his youth, however, he had learned neither to master himself nor to restrain his passions, not even as a result of his company with Socrates. His indisputable talents would therefore have destructive consequences, the more so because his entire conduct was determined by ungovernable ambition. He was only too well aware that in his mental powers he far surpassed his contemporaries in Athens, and it is no wonder that even sober thinking politicians all too often allowed themselves to become blinded by the captivating charm of his personality and the undeniable brilliance of his genius. The political aim of Alcibiades was the total isolation of Sparta. To this end a league was formed with Argos, Mantineia and Elis, initially on the basis of a defensive alliance for a period of one hundred years (summer 420 B.C.).[50] This alliance, like the Argive-Epidaurian conflict of the following year, in which both Athens and Sparta intervened, already foreshadowed coming developments. These developments were however, delayed because Alcibiades, defeated in the *strategoi* elections in the spring of 418 B.C., did not return to the helm.

The struggle for hegemony in the Peloponnesus between Sparta and Argos culminated in the battle of Mantineia (418 B.C.). Although reinforced by an Attic auxiliary corps, the Argives and the forces of the new separate league were no match for the phalanx of the Lacedaemonians under the command of King Agis. It was the greatest battle fought on

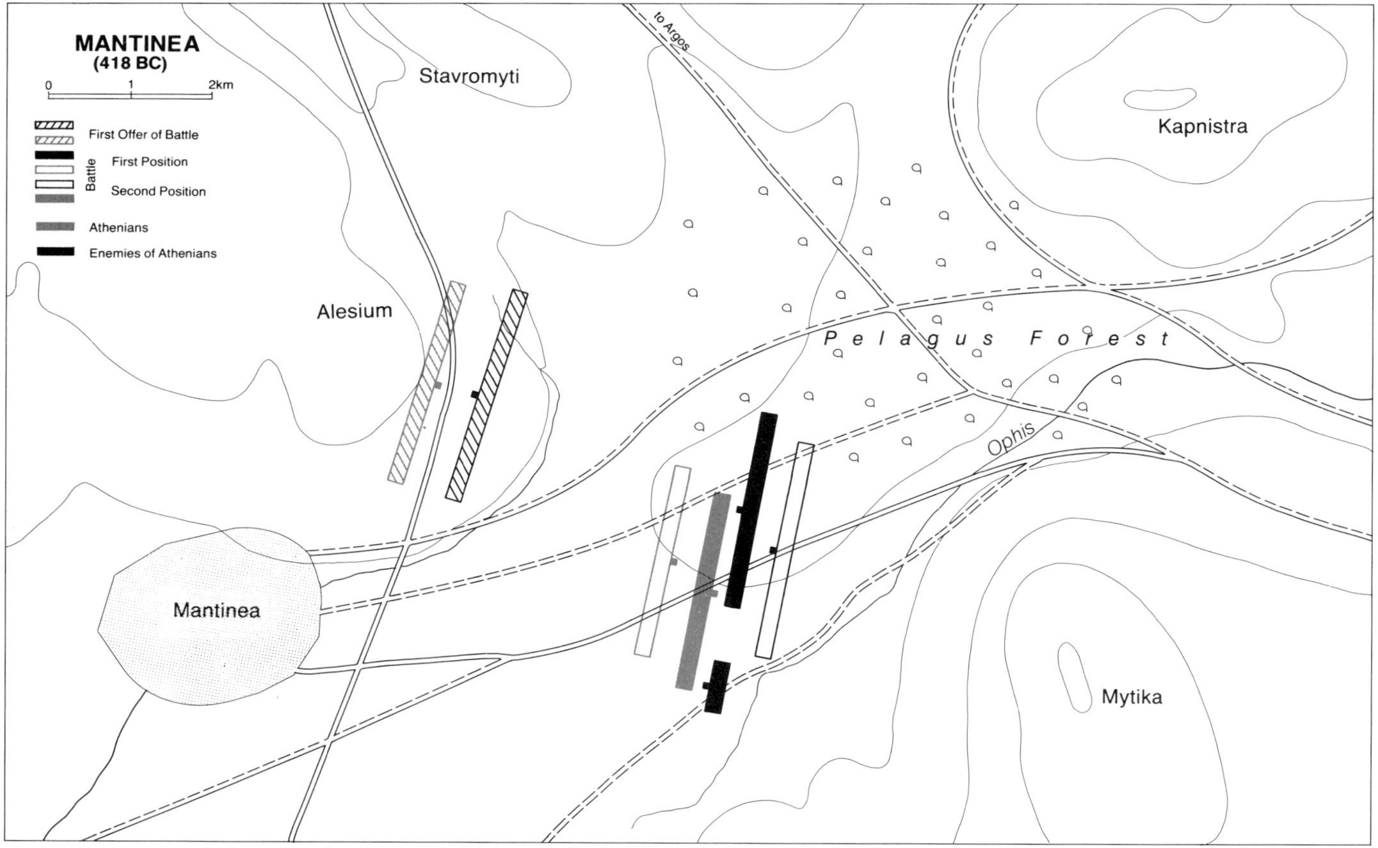
MANTINEA
(418 BC)
0
1
2km
First Offer of Battle
Battle
First Position
Second Position
Athenians
Enemies of Athenians
Stavromyti
to Argos
Kapnistra
Alesium
Pelagus Forest
Ophis
Mantinea
Mytika

Greek soil since Plataea.[51] As a result Sparta re-established her hegemony unequivocally in the Peloponnesus. Argos, Mantineia and Achaea joined the Peloponnesian League;[52] Elis alone kept aloof. The separate league, with its leaning upon Athens, had vanished and with it the illusions entertained at Athens, who had been bewitched by Alcibiades.

In Athens everything depended on the outcome of the political duel between Alcibiades and Nicias[53]—it was a question of war or peace. In this state of affairs an attempt was made to resolve the issue by resorting to an institution which should long since have been relegated to the rubbish heap of Attic democracy—ostracism. Alcibiades succeeded in taking the teeth out of this institution now levelled against him by achieving the sheer impossible—by bringing Nicias his opponent over to his side and entering into an alliance with him. The third individual, Hyperbolus, who actually bore the brunt of the weapon, was sentenced to exile by the institution (spring 417 B.C.?).[54] Ostracism had thereby demonstrated its complete uselessness so drastically that it was never again used in Athens.

Nicias and Alcibiades, elected *strategoi* for the year 417/16 B.C., both strove for rapid successes abroad. While Nicias in 417 B.C. achieved little in Thrace, Teisias and Cleomedes laid the island of Melos at the feet of Athens. Disregarding the neutrality of the island, they took it by force; those citizens who did not suffer the fate of execution were placed on the slave market. The Athenian expedition against Dorian Melos was a demonstration of brutal force, as Thucydides has shown in his famous "Melian Dialogue."[55] Sparta, however, refused to be lured out of her attitude of reserve either by this provocation or by plundering skirmishes on the part of the Athenian garrison in Pylos. It is possible that Sparta's passive attitude was in part determined by renewed quarrels with Argos. Moreover, Argos had again entered into league relationship with Athens (spring 416 B.C.).[56]

The crucial turning point in the fate not only of Athens but also of the whole of Greece came about through the events in the West, in Sicily. The Peace Congress of Gela (424 B.C.) had only put a temporary end to the quarrels among the Greek communities of the island. Dorian Syracuse subjugated Ionian Leontini, the ally of Athens, and incorporated the territory of the city into the Syracusan state. Thereupon Segesta, who was involved in a dispute with Selinus, relying on her treaty with Athens, appealed to the great protective power in the Greek motherland. If the help which Athens finally sent assumed such major proportions that it precipitated certain misgivings even on the part of the Athenian allies in Sicily, this came from the policy for which Alcibiades was chiefly responsible. For the Greeks of the motherland Sicily had always been regarded as the "Golden West." The incomparably greater economic opportunities, the wealth of Sicilian fields for corn and cattle, the splendour of proud temples and rich votive offerings—all these turned the island into a fairyland which offered its treasures to anyone who was willing to avail himself of them. The Athenian fleet had unlimited control of the maritime route to the western sea. The quarrels among the Sicilian poleis presented a superior outside power with an ideal opportunity for successful intervention.

For the man in the street at Athens there was no doubt whatever that the expansion of Athenian power in Sicily would double, indeed even triple, the standard of living for each individual citizen. Alcibiades deliberately nurtured the blind confidence of the multitudes, and this for selfish reasons. The Sicilian command which he sought was to become the basis of a position of great personal power, such as only the vastness of the West could offer. On the model of the tyrants, Alcibiades entered no fewer than seven teams in the Olympian games of 416 B.C. The members of Athens' League had compliantly contributed towards furnishing his magnificent tent, and as the Sicilian rulers Gelon and Hieron had once requested of Pindar, so Alcibiades now solicited a victory paean from Euripides.[57] Thus the brilliant appearance of the young lion swept the great masses along with him, except for a very few pessimists.[58] The Attic *Ekklesia* resolved (415 B.C.) to go to the aid of Segesta and attend to re-establishing the autonomy of Leontini. The contingent sent to help the Sicilian allies, under the command of Nicias, Lamachus and Alcibiades, consisted of 134 triremes with a crew of 25,000 (in addition to 6400 landing troops).[59] The three generals were invested with special plenary powers for directing operations and for concluding treaties.[60] The die had been cast. Athens turned her back on Hellas and cast her eyes towards the West, in the hope that unlimited resources of Sicilian power would later bring Greece into subjection.[61]

Political excitement in Athens had reached an unprecedented pitch. Immediately before the departure of the Sicilian fleet the tremendous tension unleashed itself in the *Hermae* sacrilege[62]—the smashing of some sacred statues of the god Hermes. This piece of youthful villainy, which the superstitious multitudes regarded as a bad omen, was never fully explained in its motivation. There is some evidence to support the view that the perpetrators, who in outrageous arrogance mutilated the *Hermae* in the dead of night, came from the circles of the oligarchic clubs. Alcibiades was also among those denounced. He was accused of having profaned the sacred Mysteries of Eleusis in the house of a friend. No clear evidence was produced and the investigation was postponed until the return of the expedition, although Alcibiades urgently pressed for the matter to be cleared up.

Sicily, including even the Athenian allies, gave the great fleet only a cool reception. The lack of any clear military strategy on the part of the Attic generals was to prove disastrous. Lamachus advocated the idea of first storming the bulwark of the western Dorians—Syracuse. Alcibiades was opposed to this, arguing that it was better to annex the smaller communities first in order to gain a base for operations. Any hope of advancing more rapidly along these lines, however, was self-delusion. The only one to join willingly was the Chalcidian colony of Naxos. Catana had to be taken by force. Nothing was more damaging to the course of the operations than the recall of Alcibiades. Through impeachment by

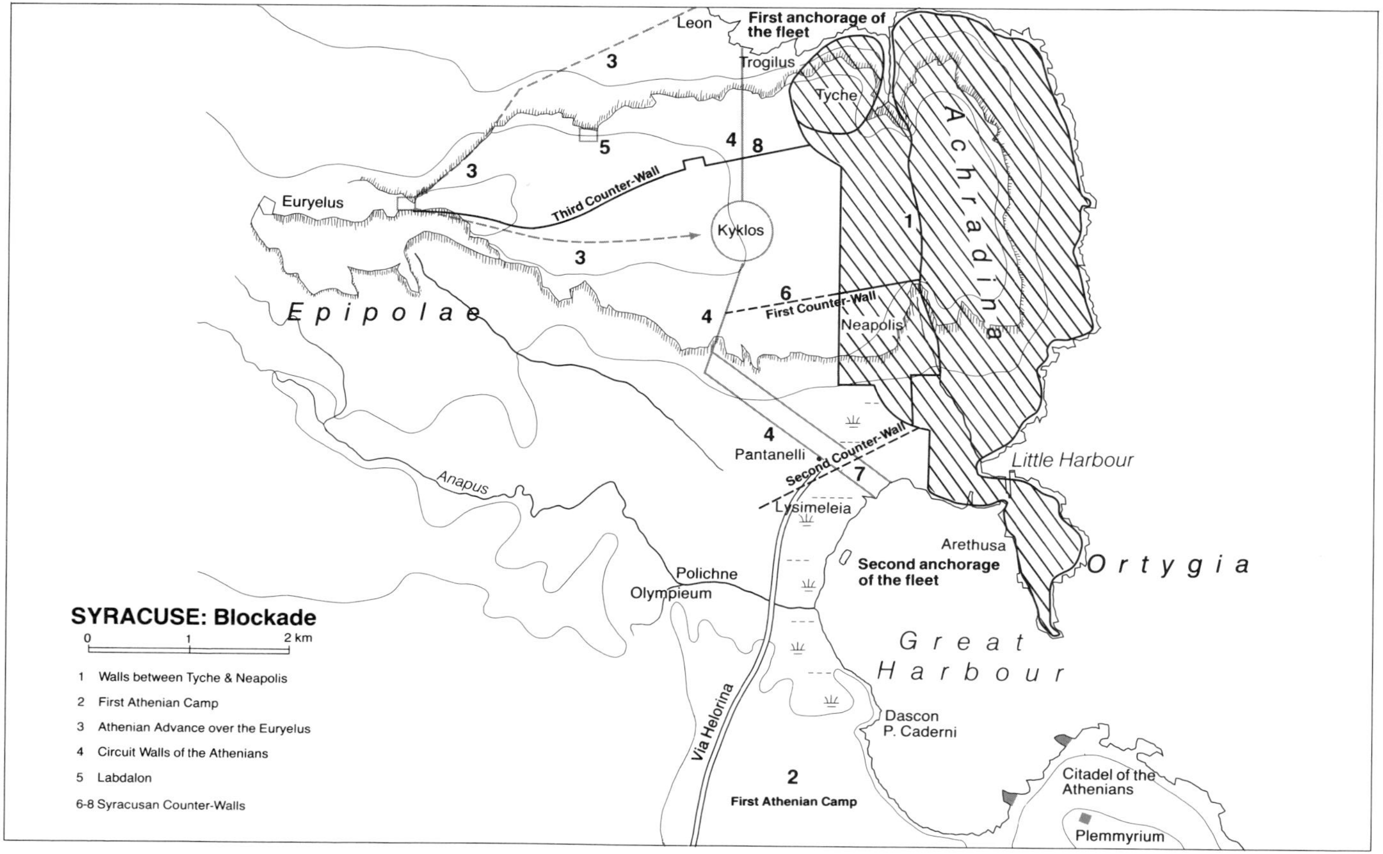
Leon
First anchorage of the fleet
Trogilus
Tyche
Achradina
Euryelus
Third Counter-Wall
Kyklos
First Counter-Wall
Neapolis
Epipolae
Pantanelli
Second Counter-Wall
Little Harbour
Anapus
Lysimeleia
Arethusa
Second anchorage of the fleet
Ortygia
Polichne
Olympieum
Great Harbour
Via Helorina
Dascon
P. Caderni
First Athenian Camp
Citadel of the Athenians
Plemmyrium
SYRACUSE: Blockade
0
1
2 km
1 Walls between Tyche & Neapolis
2 First Athenian Camp
3 Athenian Advance over the Euryelus
4 Circuit Walls of the Athenians
5 Labdalon
6-8 Syracusan Counter-Walls

Thessalus son of Cimon, who charged him with complicity in the *Hermae* sacrilege, Alcibiades was summoned back to Athens to plead his case before law. At Thurii he succeeded in escaping from his own trireme, and without delay betook himself to Elis and from there to Lacedaemonia.[63] Thus Alcibiades, the hero of the Attic democracy, became a traitor to his country, his feelings of personal revenge more important than the life and welfare of his native city, which he had launched on the greatest adventure of its history.

With Alcibiades' withdrawal the heart went out of the great Sicilian enterprise. After random isolated attempts the Athenians ultimately (late Autumn 415 B.C.) succeeded in effecting a landing in the Great Harbour of Syracuse. From an initial encounter Nicias emerged as victor over the forces of the city. Thereupon Hermocrates, the leading statesman of Syracuse, sent an urgent plea for help to Corinth and Sparta, the great protectors of the western Dorians, urging them to prosecute the war against Athens in Hellas.

In May 414 B.C. the Athenians landed for the second time in the area of Syracuse, on this occasion in the north of the city. Seizing the heights of Epipolae and constructing a wall from there to the Great Harbour, they cut the city off from the hinterland. The besieged inhabitants built counter walls, attempting to extricate themselves from the pincer grip. When the peril in the city had reached its most crucial point Sparta despatched Gylippus, an experienced officer, to Sicily. He landed at Himera and with the aid of auxiliary troops from the Sicilian communities fought his way through the inadequately controlled Athenian blockading line and entered the city. As the besieged were inspired with new courage by his arrival, in the same measure did the morale of the Athenians sink. Discipline in the blockading forces fell off, particularly among the great masses of inactive naval crews whose ranks had become noticeably thin through defections. When Gylippus regained control of the dominating Epipolae and built a new large counter wall from Achradina to Euryalus, the blockade had been shattered. The Athenian forces found themselves exposed to continuous assaults from the city and from the interior. The situation was further aggravated by the loss of the naval base at Plemmyrium. In these straits Nicias despatched home a plea for help. The dismal news, which reached Athens in the late autumn of 414 B.C., with one blow destroyed the web of illusions which up to that time not even the darkest rumours had been able to tear asunder. Not until December 414 B.C. were ten triremes sent to the West under Eurymedon, and several months later another sixty-five under Demosthenes. The decision to send them was not an easy one for the Athenians to take, for, since the summer of 414 B.C., the war between Athens and Sparta had broken out afresh. The hollow Peace of Nicias had come to an end, and general war had ensued from the Sicilian adventure.

In the spring of 413 B.C. the army of the Peloponnesian League once more crossed the frontier into Attica, for the first time in twelve years. The Spartan king Agis, on the advice of Alcibiades, set up a permanent camp at Deceleia, just twelve miles from Athens, and ravished the north of Attica with fire and sword. In Attica commercial activity came to a standstill, the state slaves in large numbers deserted the mines, and over the city itself hovered the Damocles sword of a Spartan attack. Nervousness and fear gripped the multitudes whose Sicilian hopes had been so brutally crushed.

Shortly thereafter, in the late summer of 413 B.C., the great Sicilian expedition of Athens ended in a dreadful catastrophe. The arrival of new reinforcements had for the moment considerably improved the position of the Athenians at Syracuse, but in an unfortunate surprise attack at night on Epipolae Demosthenes suffered a decisive defeat (July 413 B.C.). The crisis was further accentuated by disagreement between Nicias and Demosthenes. Costly weeks were allowed to slip by in complete inactivity. Finally Nicias, who feared prosecution in Athens, declared himself ready to break up the blockade, which had long since become utterly pointless. Due to an eclipse of the moon—on 27 August 413 B.C.—the procrastinating, superstitious Nicias put off for a whole month the departure of the fleet which was lying at anchor. The fate of the expedition was accordingly sealed. The Syracusans cut off all possible departure for the fleet from the Great Harbour. An attempt to break through failed, and the advice of Demosthenes to make another attempt on the following day was, despite the agreement of Nicias, not followed.

There was consequently no alternative but to withdraw into the interior. All the ships had to be abandoned. But even in the execution of this strategy, for which there were few prospects, there was further delay due to the irresolution of Nicias when Hermocrates released a news flash that all avenues and roads to the interior were already blocked. If ever there was a time in the history of warfare, it was Nicias' behaviour here that demonstrates the correctness of the military principle that missing opportunities and failure to act are incomparably more serious than an error in tactics. The retreat of the Athenians, whose number Thucydides has probably set too high at 40,000 turned into a "*Via Dolorosa*"—Way of Grief. It was no army that finally set out in a south-westerly direction along the road via Elorus to Camarina, but an undisciplined multitude mostly of untrained naval crews, completely lacking in self-confidence, without orderly command, without supplies, without water and continuously threatened by the enemy. It was not long before the main force lost contact with those in the rear. First Demosthenes was compelled to surrender with 6000 of the last detachments, and two days later the same fate overtook the main force under Nicias at the Assinarus river.[64] The prisoners were thrown into the stone quarries of Achradina. Those who did not die within the next two months from hunger and exposure were sold into slavery. Gylippus the Spartan would gladly have spared Nicias and Demosthenes, but the Syracusans were hot for their blood.[65]

The destruction of the Athenian army in the stone quarries of Syracuse was, in its dimensions and consequences, the most devastating catastrophe that ever befell a Greek army. It was caused by insufficient knowledge of the actual situation in Sicily as well as by the military incompetence of Nicias.[66] The importance of the defeat for the future course of the great war was incalculable. It forms the crux of the war, as Thucydides has already delineated it.

THE DECELEIAN AND THE IONIAN WAR (414-404 B.C.)

The disaster of the Athenian expedition was a turning point not only in the history of Greece but also in that of the entire ancient world. For fifty years after this event, political developments in Hellas were strongly influenced by the Persian empire, whose foreign policy, directed by the western satraps, became ever more active. In 424/3 B.C. the Athenians, by concluding the so-called Epilycus Treaty, renewed the so-called "Peace of Callias,"[67] in perpetuity, with Darius II Ochus, who had acceded to the Achaemenid throne after the death of Artaxerxes I (425/4 B.C.) and after a very short interim reign of Xerxes II and of Sogdianus. No danger now threatened the Attic empire from the side of Persia. Athens made a highly imprudent and dangerous move in 414 B.C., openly supporting the Carian dynast Amorges who had seceded from the Persians.[68] It was the general weakening of the Athenian position that induced the Persians to abandon their passivity in Asia Minor. Darius II ordered Tissaphernes, the satrap of Lydia and military commander of the whole of Asia Minor and Pharnabazus, the satrap of Phrygia, to collect the outstanding tribute from the Greek cities in Asia Minor. Persia regarded the Treaty of Callias as annulled, openly assumed a hostile attitude towards Athens, and paid subsidies to the Spartans. The Spartans for their part now abandoned the Greeks of Asia Minor to the Persians (summer 412 B.C.).[69] In consequence, the island of Chios and the cities of Mytilene and Methymna on Lesbos revolted from Athens. In Asia Minor too (Miletus) Athenian supremacy began to crumble (412 B.C.). In Athens itself difficulties were mounting. Financial reserves were almost completely exhausted, so that there appeared to be no other alternative but (probably in the course of 413 B.C.) to supplement the tribute, which was now coming in only irregularly, by adding a five per cent tax on all imports and exports carried by sea within the compass of the Maritime League.[70] In 412 B.C. it was even necessary to draw on the last emergency reserve fund of 1000 talents. In addition, reverses in foreign politics gave a considerable impetus to underground movements. The democracy had to accept the responsibility for what happened in Sicily; it was no wonder that the *hetaireiai*—political clubs—of the oligarchic faction became feverishly active.

The oligarchs were led by four individuals: Antiphon, one of the most outstanding advocates (*logographoi*) of his day, Peisander, a one time radical democrat and intimate friend of Cleon, Phrynichus and Theramenes of Steiria. The first "move to the right" was the election of ten *probouloi* in 413 B.C. They formed the supreme authority in Athens and took over some of the powers of the Council.[71] The oligarchic movement was given particular weight through its connections with Alcibiades. After initially working against his native city from Ionia in the interests of

Sparta, he completely changed his attitude and put out feelers towards the Athenian fleet lying at anchor off Samos, whose officers had already been strongly influenced by the oligarchic movement. The offer of Alcibiades to effect a treaty with the king of Persia, should a change in the constitution take place at Athens in the interests of the oligarchy, made a deep impression in Athens. The great hopes of the Athenians were, however, disappointed. In 411 B.C. Tissaphernes and Pharnabazus renewed their treaty with Sparta. The Phoenician fleet could not, however, be enlisted, perhaps because a revolt had broken out in Egypt.[72]

In 411 B.C. the democracy, that is, what was still left of it, collapsed, undermined from within and without. Its overthrow began in May with the establishment of a commission of thirty, which included the ten *probouloi*. In the *Ekklesia*, which convened on 8 June under unusual circumstances—not on the Pnyx as previously but at Colonus outside Athens—a general attack was launched against the democracy. Peisander brought in a proposal to abolish all payment for offices, the life-blood of the democracy, and to restrict the ruling citizen body to 5000. These were to be consulted on political decisions, above all with regard to concluding treaties, in case the Council—it was to be composed of 400 appointed members with unlimited power—thought this the right thing to do.[73] The aim of the overthrow was therefore not a rule of the 5000 but a dictatorship of the Four Hundred.[74] The event was no more and no less than a revolution, as shown by the account which Thucydides (VIII 65) gives of the oligarchic terror, even though Aristotle using oligarchic sources and documentary evidence, creates the illusion of a quiet evolution.[75] The democracy of Athens, however, was buried approximately one hundred years after Cleisthenes laid its foundations.

If the Athenians thought they could create a better platform for foreign policy through the oligarchic revolution, they made a fundamental error. In Samos a revolt of the *demos* against the aristocratic *geomoroi* ended in the restoration of the democracy in 412 B.C.,[76] while Athens for her part at that time restored to the Samians the autonomy which they had lost when they broke away in the time of Pericles (v.i.p. 129.). The revolution on the island was not without repercussions on the Athenian fleet lying at anchor off Samos. The oligarchic movement, directed in the main by the naval officers, was suppressed before it could really come into the open. New generals were elected, including Thrasyllus and the subsequently so famous Thrasybulus. In consequence the fleet, the instrument of Athenian power, stood as the bulwark of the democracy, in opposition to the native city governed by the oligarchy!

While efforts were being made in Samos to win the good offices of Alcibiades for arbitration between the fleet and the homeland, the Attic oligarchy saw that its final hour had come. In order to stay in power Antiphon and his friends strove to conclude a peace with Sparta on any terms. The fortifying of Eëtioneia at Piraeus, however, aroused the probably not entirely unfounded suspicion among the people that there was a design afoot to admit the Peloponnesians within the harbour in order to

21. Delphi. View towards the north. Modern village (left) and the ancient sanctuary (right).

22. Delphi. Omphalos, symbolising the centre of the earth.

23. The Aegean Sea.

24. Kylix by Exekias. Dionysus crossing the sea. Staatliche Antikensammlungen, Munich.

25. Solon.
Ny Carlsberg
Glyptotek,
Copenhagen.

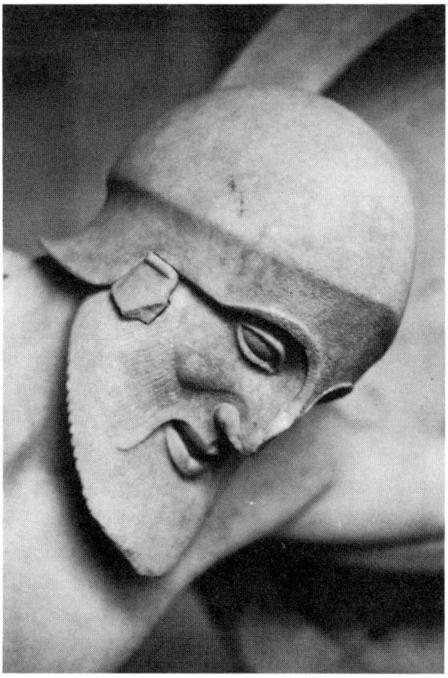

26. Wounded warrior.
Detail from the West
Pediment of the Temple
of Aphaia on Aegina.
Glyptothek, Munich.

27. Sardis.
The Acropolis.

28. Croesus on the funeral pyre.
Amphora by Myron. Louvre,
Paris.

29. Pasargadae. Tomb of Cyrus the Great.

30. Persepolis. Palace of Xerxes.

31. Persepolis. Palace of Xerxes. The Great King seated on his throne supported by his subjects.

32. Persepolis. Palace of Xerxes. Detail of frieze: Subject nations bringing tribute.

33. Samos. The plain containing the Heraeum and the Sacred Way. View towards the west.

34. Samos. Heraeum. Part of the base of a column from the Temple of Hera.

35. Samos. Section of Polycrates' city wall.

36. Samos.
Griffin protome.

37. Athens. Aerial view of the Acropolis.

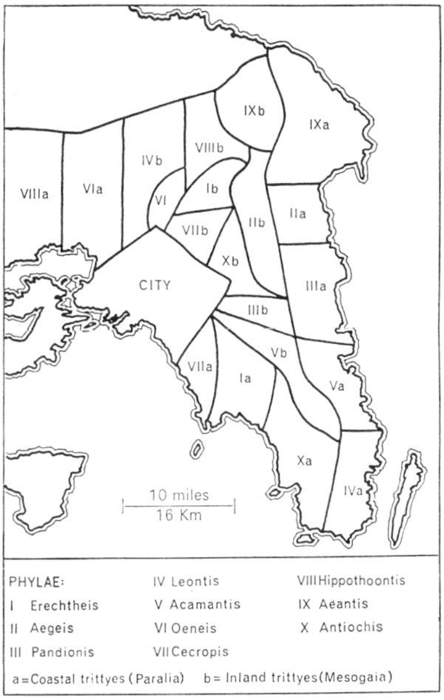

38. The Cleisthenic division of Attica.

39. Peplos Kore. Acropolis Museum, Athens.

40. Bronze statue (detail) of Poseidon or Zeus, found off Artemisium. National Museum, Athens.

41. Delphi. Tholos.

42. Section of the (bronze) Serpent Column erected at Delphi by the Greek allies after the Persian Wars. Hippodrome, Istanbul.

43. Herodotus. Metropolitan Museum of Art, New York.

44. Temple of Apollo at Bassae, Arcadia.

terrorise the populace. In the whirl of events piling up one after another in the summer of 411 B.C.—the revolt of Euboea was followed by the loss of the Dardanelles and important Byzantium, so that the corn ships from the Pontus did not arrive in Athens[77]—the rule of the Four Hundred, the extreme oligarchy, collapsed. The democratic and oligarchic factions now reached a compromise. After evicting the Four Hundred the ruling power was assumed by the 5000 citizens "who could equip themselves with arms." They formed a Council which, divided into four sections, took over the direction of state affairs on the principle of rotation. This was the constitution of Theramenes, created on the Boeotian model. It may be identified with the "future constitution" recorded by Aristotle (*Constitution of Athens* 30), which at the time was laid before the *demos* in the first extraordinary session of the *Ekklesia* at Colonus.[78] It, however, remained in effect for only eight months.

There was meanwhile no end to the number of reverses which Athens suffered in foreign affairs. In addition to the loss of Euboea and almost the entire area of the Hellespont came the revolt of the island of Thasos, economically one of the most productive members in the League, as well as the defection of Abdera (autumn 411 B.C.). The days of Athenian supremacy on the seas were a thing of the past. Persian subsidies enabled Sparta to maintain an efficient fleet, with the needed backbone provided by an excellent Syracusan contingent under the command of Hermocrates. Only extraordinary measures and men with new ideas could now save Athens, and so the Athenians turned their eyes towards Alcibiades, whom the naval crews at Samos had elected *strategos* and who conducted himself like a sovereign there. Under Thrasybulus the Athenians were victorious—though with heavy losses—over the Spartan fleet towards the end of the highly eventful year of 411 B.C., in two encounters, at Cynossema and Abydus. The turn in events, however, was brought about by the naval battle of Cyzicus (May 410 B.C.). The strategy of Alcibiades outmanoeuvred and achieved the total defeat of Sparta. Not a single Spartan ship escaped, and the Spartan admiral Mindarus fell in battle.[79] This brought the re-establishment of Athenian naval supremacy at the straits. Across from Byzantium a garrison was stationed to impose a tariff on all traffic from the Pontus, revenues which greatly helped Athenian finances.

The defeat at Cyzicus struck Sparta like a thunderbolt. Under the pressure of the complete loss of the costly fleet she was willing to accept the previous *status quo* in return for peace; Deceleia was to be exchanged for Pylos and Cythera. Cleophon bears the responsibility for the rejection of the favourable overtures.[80] Shortly thereafter the rule of the Five Thousand, which had otherwise rested on a weak footing, collapsed, and with it the moderate oligarchic constitution of Theramenes disappeared.[81] In July 410 B.C. the old Council of Five Hundred again took over the direction of state affairs and the Popular Court of the *Heliaea* once more began to sit. For the first time in Athenian history it was resolved to codify the whole sum of current law, and the task was entrusted to a special commission. This is the first known attempt in antiquity to embrace the constitution and public, private and religious law of a state through a comprehensive codification.[82] The attempt, however, came to nothing, because individual members of the commission proved to be corrupt and prolonged the affair out of selfish motives. In order to ensure the livelihood of those citizens who did not fill any public office and who did not serve in the army or fleet, Cleophon introduced the so-called *diobelia*, a genuine "state pension."[83] In addition, relief works were created; for instance, construction began on the Erechtheum. In the long run the *diobelia* imposed an intolerable burden on Attic finances, especially since the League members by every possible means increasingly sought to evade the payment of tribute.

Under the influence of brilliant foreign successes—Chalcedon, Selymbria[84] and even Byzantium had been regained by Alcibiades, and besides this an armistice was reached with Pharnabazus the satrap of Phrygia (409 B.C.)[85]—Alcibiades was elected *strategos* for the year 408/7 B.C. At the *Plynteria*[86] of 408 B.C. he celebrated his triumphal entry into his native city, from which he had departed seven years before at the head of the proud Sicilian fleet. Officially acquitted from all accusations and after being presented with an honorary gift as a substitute for his confiscated property, Alcibiades was given unlimited command both on land and on sea as *generalissimo*.[87] When he thereupon conducted the sacred procession on land from Athens to Eleusis under the protection of the armed forces—the procession could not be staged hitherto due to the Spartan garrison—his reputation had reached dizzy heights. He was regarded as the saviour of the fatherland.

Alcibiades was not, however, able to keep up his triumphal progress at the Hellespont and in Ionia. The general situation had undergone such a fundamental change that even Alcibiades was no longer able to arrest the fate of Athens. In the person of Lysander the Spartan government finally came upon the general they required for the fleet, that costly instrument of war. Lysander, who did not hesitate in the least in employing any means against the enemy, was in his personal life frugal and, something to which great weight was attached by the Greeks, completely above bribery.[88] Impelled by burning ambition, he consumed his energies in the service of his country. It was Lysander who injected into the mind of the Great King of Persia the notion that only a complete victory by Sparta, and not the re-establishing of the former balance of power in Greece, corresponded to the true interests of the Persian empire. The resolute Spartan statesman understood particularly well how to win Cyrus the Younger, from 408 B.C. onwards viceroy of Sardis, completely for his cause.

Lysander was called upon to undergo the first test of his competence as *strategos* in the battle of Notium (spring 407 B.C.). The defeat of the Athenians at the same time sealed the doom of Alcibiades. The angry *demos* deposed him from his command. The former *generalissimo* of Athens betook himself to his fortresses in the Thracian Chersonese and there led the life of an independent grand lord. After the fall of Athens (404 B.C.) he fled to the court of the Persian satrap Pharnabazus who, at the instigation of Lysander, had him put to death. Thus Alcibiades, the violent type of man, for whom there was nothing sacred in life, himself met a violent end. The oscillating fortunes of his extraordinary life have repeatedly drawn posterity's attention. Thus the emperor Hadrian visited the town of Melissa in Phrygia where Alcibiades had been murdered and honoured the memory of the famous Athenian by erecting a statue to him.

Just as Alcibiades was replaced by Conon, so Callicratidas, a Spartan of the old school, succeeded Lysander after the latter had ended his one-year term in the *nauarchia*—sea command. Although Callicratidas fell out with Cyrus the Younger, so that the Persian subsidies stopped, the Spartan offensive by sea scored a brilliant success. After losing Teos and Methymna (on Lesbos), Conon was blockaded with his ships inside the harbour of Mytilene. This terrible crisis once more aroused the former energies of the Athenians. By making the greatest sacrifices and with the help of the faithful Samos, a fleet of 150 triremes was once more assembled.[89] At Arginusae (at the southern entrance to the sound of Lesbos) the Spartans were decisively defeated, and more than seventy of Callicratidas' ships fell into Athenian hands (August 406 B.C.). The grief caused by the grave casualties among the crews—mostly Athenian citizens—led to the Arginusae lawsuit in Athens. The *Ekklesia*—not the regular law court—in a tumultuous trial condemned to death *en bloc* six generals, including the son of Pericles, because they had failed to save the shipwrecked crews. A number of *prytaneis*, including Socrates, had objected to the illegal prosecution—without success.[90] The condemnation of the generals was a warning for Athens and her citizens, who had passed a sentence running counter to all laws of reason. In order to complete the misfortune a new offer for peace from Sparta on the current *status quo* was abruptly rejected in Athens on the objection of Cleophon.[91] For how could Sparta have met Athenian demands to restore the cities which had seceded from Athens, even if she had had the honest intention of doing so? In 406 B.C., when the Athenians found themselves in the most dire straits, ambassadors journeyed to Sicily in order to take up negotiations with Carthage. If hopes were set on this mission, our knowledge of which is derived from inscriptions,[92] they never saw fulfilment.

The decision in the war was brought about by the Spartan fleet. Its operations were directed by Lysander, who had been appointed flag officer for the nauarch Aracus. The combination of the occupation of Deceleia in Attica and the blocking of the Dardanelles led to the economic ruin of Athens. Added to this was the defeat in the naval battle of Aegospotami (mid-summer 405 B.C.).[93] With this engagement the greatness of Athens sank into the grave. Thousands of prisoners fell into the hands of the Spartans, among them 3000-4000 Athenians, who were put to death to atone for previous Athenian atrocities.[94] Conon, whose culpable irresponsibility had contributed to the Spartan victory, fled to Cyprus. The remainder of the once so proud Attic Maritime League collapsed; the Hellespontine and Thracian communities joined the side of the victor. The

Samians alone remained loyal and as a reward received the tardy gift of Attic citizenship.[95]

The loss of the last fleet sealed the fate of Athens. While Lysander crossed the Saronic Gulf with 150 ships, the Spartan land forces united under the command of Kings Agis and Pausanias (II) in a strong encampment at the Academy, immediately before the gates of the city. The land forces withdrew again in the winter but the blockade continued. In Athens all hope faded; the Athenians were prepared to negotiate and even to give up the Attic empire—provided Samos and the cleruchies were left in their hands, as the latter were completely indispensable for the livelihood of the citizens. When the Spartans, however, demanded that the Long Walls be razed to a distance of ten stades and all former Attic dominions be renounced, with the exception of Lemnos, Imbros and Scyros, the mood in the beleaguered city changed again. Under the influence of Cleophon all discussion on these conditions was forbidden. Theramenes thereupon went to Lysander, allegedly to obtain more favourable terms, but in reality, to wait for a change of disposition in Athens. In actual fact Cleophon within a short space had had his day. He was eliminated by an indictment for violation of military duty. Theramenes went as plenipotentiary ambassador to Sparta.[96]

In establishing peace terms, Sparta opposed the intensely bitter enemies of Athens, led by Corinth and Thebes who urged the razing of the city. Sparta had no interest in destroying Athens, but the peace terms were extremely severe. Athens lost all her foreign possessions; all fortifications, including the Long Walls, were to be razed; the entire fleet, apart from twelve vessels, was to be surrendered and all banished citizens allowed to return. In addition, Athens was to be under obligation to Spartan military service,[97] that is, she was compelled to join the Peloponnesian League. The day after the return of Theramenes[98] the Athenian *Ekklesia* ratified the conditions—there was no other alternative. On 16 *Munichion* (end of April) 404 B.C. the victor Lysander and his fleet entered Piraeus. With the subjection of Samos, who laid down her arms after a siege of several months, the Great War came to an end. Athens and the Attic empire lay at the victor's feet.

9
THE DECLINE OF THE GREEK POLIS

INTRODUCTION

The end of the Peloponnesian War exposed the great crisis in the Hellenic world in all spheres of life—political, economic and social. The war had brought acute casualties and extensive devastation of fertile farm and garden land, especially in Attica, but also in parts of the Peloponnesus. Broad sectors of the population had become poverty stricken, and hovering over all like a nightmare was the threat of arbitrary injustice. It reached its climax in the despotic acts of the Thirty in Athens. All these factors were, however, only a symptom of the malaise which had seized the Hellenic state, the polis. This crisis eventually brought the end of this kind of government. At the close of the fourth century it is no longer the polis but the Hellenistic monarchies on the Macedonian model which appear as the standard-bearers of world affairs, whereas the polis forever lost its significance. The fundamental change for the Greeks, the turning from a political rôle to the ethical, the cultural realm is prefigured in the life of Plato. In fact, what Hellas lost in the political sphere it won back two-fold in the cultural. In the fourth century Plato and Aristotle established the universal supremacy of the Greek mind, at the time when Hellas was sinking into political impotence and had become the plaything of foreign powers, especially of the Persian empire.

Because Sparta, the victor of the Great War, did not possess any constructive ideas for remoulding the Hellenic world, the decline of Athens left a vacuum that could not be filled. Spartan rule in particular lacked a great national idea, like that of the Maritime League under the leadership of Athens, championing the defensive struggle of the Hellenes against the Persians. And the ephemeral Theban hegemony (371-362 B.C.), which followed the Spartan, rested at bottom solely on the exploitation of a singular situation in power politics by the genius of Epameinondas and Pelopidas. It was therefore no more than a short interlude. The centre of gravity in world affairs had by the end of the fifth century shifted to the East. From there Persian gold poured into Greece. In the West, in Sicily, the free Hellenes had in the face of the great Carthaginian crisis bowed to the cruel hand of the Syracusan ruler Dionysius I. This tyrant was indisputably the greatest figure among the Greeks in the first generation after the end of the Peloponnesian War. In Sicily and in western Anatolia peculiarly modern features in political life and culture anticipate the developments of coming centuries.

The fourth century is overshadowed by the death of Socrates of Athens (399 B.C.). At a time when political, social and ethical bonds increasingly slackened and dissolved, Socrates, who was accused of introducing new daemonic doctrines and of corrupting the youth, paid for his personal convictions with his life. In an era when the masses no longer possessed any ideals, when the educated embraced the relativism of the Sophists, Socrates, as master of his students, as their instructor and inspirer to truth, taught them ethical intellectualism—the knowledge of the essence of virtue and its practical realisation, understanding and action, merged together into a single whole. For Socrates theory and practice formed an indivisible unity. The incomparable influence which he exerted on the contemporary and future world is to be explained by the deep moral seriousness of his personality. This influence most affected his students, of whom Plato (427-347 B.C.) became the herald of the moral greatness of his teacher.

Plato himself first appeared as a writer of tragedies. His experience of Socrates, however, directed his endeavours into a new field, which moulded him into one of the greatest teachers of mankind. Through the Academy, which he had founded after returning from his first Sicilian expedition (c. 387 B.C.)—it was located in the fields outside Athens and named after the hero Academus—Plato laid the foundations for developing scientific method. In addition, Plato created an imposing dualistic world view. Over against the corporeal world, the world of becoming, he set another world, the world of true being, embodied in independent realities, the "Forms." Under the influence of Orphic-Pythagorean teachings, Plato took over the doctrine of the immortality of the soul, and so directed the thinking of the worldly Greek to that which is eternal and imperishable. It was the greatest revolution in Western thought before the appearance of Jesus Christ. It was Plato's personal fate, however, to be forcibly excluded from activity in practical politics in his native city, to which in his old age he gave such vivid expression (*Seventh Letter* 325). The Greek city-state had outlived itself: for precisely the best citizens it no longer had any room. The spirit consequently fled into the world of the unreal, into utopia, and in this realm Plato's writings on political theory, his *Republic* and *Laws*, gained eternal significance.

The more interest in political life waned, the more the hopes of the multitudes concentrated on the great personalities which the fourth century produced in almost unparalleled abundance. Lysander and Dionysius I, Euagoras and Agesilaus—they are the theme of historiography as well as of contemporary journalism. And the glorification of the individual personality again and again brought to the fore the idea that only the rule of the powerful individual could save Hellas from political impotence. Isocrates and Xenophon erected monuments to men of the sword. The Sicilian tyrant had no lack of admirers, and it is no accident that Lysander was the first Hellene to have divine honours ascribed to him.

Before the Greek polis disappeared as a power factor, Greek political thinking created the idea of a general peace embracing all Greeks, which if loosely applied could have contributed decisively to the political reshaping of the Hellenic states. But the general situation prevented this. Even so, the panhellenic notion of such a peace was one of the most important common manifestations of the fourth century, which saw such a profusion of struggles in Greek internal affairs.

GREECE AFTER THE PELOPONNESIAN WAR (404-400 B.C.)

With the downfall of Athens, Spartan rule displaced the first Attic Maritime League, and thus a coarse, indeed even violent, system took the place of an organism that had been delicately linked together.[1] Sparta's hegemony rested on her alliance with Persia, whose gold had created the Spartan fleet and undermined the rule of the Athenians. In other respects, however, Sparta was completely unsuited to take over Athenian supremacy, even to a limited degree. She possessed neither a population of size sufficient to govern such large territories and to permit political penetration of the dependent states,[2] nor any ideal or economic bond to unite the Peloponnesian League with the Greeks of the motherland, Thrace and Asia Minor. For no good reason, Sparta committed serious errors which soon stifled all sympathy for the victor: Lysander deprived Chios of her fleet, and the other Athenian allies, who had once groaned under the burden of the contributions to the Maritime League, all too soon discovered that Sparta was no less oppressive than the former hegemonial power. In addition, Sparta everywhere supported oligarchic minorities by establishing so-called *dekarchiai* (ten-man executives).[3] She sought to confirm these by posting military garrisons under Spartan officers (*harmostai*), and so generated much ill feeling. The autonomy which Sparta had promised and of which many had dreamed after the defeat of Athens all too soon manifested itself as a mere shadow. Hellas had not become more free; on the contrary, in many cases there was much less freedom than ever before. Insecurity on the seas also became a problem, for after the disappearance of the Athenian sea police the waters soon became the playground of pirates.

The rise of the Lacedaemonian state did not fail to leave its mark on the Spartans themselves. Broad sectors of the population were corrupted by the influx of precious metals. The Spartans, forbidden by law to own precious metals, deposited them outside the frontiers of the country, in such places as Tegea and Delphi. Cases of bribery were the order of the day. Serious social tensions arose from the imbalance between the depleted number of full-blooded citizens and the great masses of impoverished Spartans (the so-called *hypomeiones*), tensions which culminated in the conspiracy of Cinadon. However, his plot to overthrow the conditions governing the ownership of property was discovered and the revolutionaries were punished by execution (398 B.C.).[4]

After the fall of Athens Lysander became the "uncrowned king of Hellas" (Ed. Meyer). The Greeks lavished extravagant honours on him.

The Samians changed the name of the festival of Hera to the *Lysandreia*, altars were erected to him, sacrifices brought for him and in Greek temples his statues took their place alongside those of the Olympian gods. Lysander was the first Greek to be elevated by his contemporaries to the realm of the divine, a forerunner of the Hellenistic idea of god incarnate.[5] In this respect too he ranged far beyond the limits set by the Spartan state for the individual citizen.

In Athens the peace treaty envisaged the re-establishment of the "constitution inherited from the fathers," a provision to which the oligarchs naturally gave their own interpretation. Under the pressure of Lysander's fleet Attic democracy went to the grave in mid-summer of 404 B.C.—for the second time within seven years (v.s.p. 150). After the oligarchs had initially formed a "committee on procedure," consisting of five ephors,[6] a government commission of thirty citizens was appointed. Theramenes and the highly gifted but violent Critias (Plato's uncle) were its exponents. Instead of working out the new constitution, the Thirty, with the connivance of Lysander, seized control of power in Athens. A Spartan garrison under the command of a harmost took possession of the Acropolis and within a short time the rule of the Thirty[7] disclosed itself as a reign of terror. With the help of denunciations all undesirable elements were swept out of the way. No less than 1500 Athenian citizens were put to death by execution, while many others, including Thrasybulus, only saved their lives by flight.[8] Thebes, Argos, Megara and other places granted them asylum. The terror of the Thirty eventually collapsed (the timid metic Lysias has given his own excellent eyewitness account) but first turned against its own followers, the moderate wing under the leadership of Theramenes. Although Theramenes impressively defended himself, he was executed. In order to suppress every element of criticism, they did not even hesitate to forbid the teaching of rhetoric!

Salvation came to the city from without. A small band of Athenian exiles and emigrants under Thrasybulus launched a sudden raid from Boeotia and took possession of the garrison of Phyle at the foothills of Parnassus.[9] After defeating the Spartan garrison and after taking Munichia, Thrasybulus controlled Piraeus, the vital artery to Athens. Critias and his colleague Charmides fell in street fighting. The rule of the Thirty disintegrated (end of 404 or beginning of 403 B.C.).[10] They were replaced by a Board of Ten comprised of the moderate faction,[11] as represented by Theramenes. A settlement between democrats and oligarchs, however, was still far from being realised. Lysander proceeded to oppose Thrasybulus and blockaded Piraeus. At this juncture the Spartan king Pausanias II, who had been despatched by the ephors, appeared in Attica at the head of an army. Lysander was compelled to submit to him, and after the Spartans had, in an engagement against the democrats,[12] demonstrated that they were resolved to take serious action, the quarrelling parties in Athens and Piraeus were ready to settle their differences. A general amnesty ensued (under the archonship of Eucleides, 403/2 B.C.).[13] The only ones excluded from it were members of the Board of "Thirty" and the "Ten." In September 403 B.C. the democrats marched from Piraeus into the city, and the Council of Five Hundred once more began to function. The oligarchic interlude had come to an end; Athens was again a democracy. A complete reconciliation did not, however, come about until 401/0 B.C., when the separate state of Eleusis,[14] which had been formed by the radical oligarchs in 403 B.C., rejoined the Attic state.

The most important event, however, in the first years after the war was the fall of Lysander (end of 403 B.C.?).[15] His position of unlimited power had long been a thorn in the flesh of the ephors. It is therefore not surprising that in Sparta one was only too glad to lend an ear to the complaints which were pouring in from every side about Lysander and his harmosts. All attempts of the once so-powerful Lysander to regain his former leading position through intrigues in Sparta and the roundabout means of the great panhellenic sanctuaries of Dodona, Delphi and even the oracle of Ammon in Libya proved vain. Once again the idea of the state in Sparta triumphed over the powerful individual personality.

Lysander's fall was synonymous with Sparta's reduction of activity in the sphere of power politics. The new line ran, "a return to traditional Peloponnesian policy." On Sparta's doorstep Elis, the only state in the peninsula which did not belong to the Peloponnesian League, was, after repeated campaigns, forced into submission (402-400 B.C.). Elis lost half her territory but retained the directorship of the Olympian games.[16] Sparta's hegemony in the Peloponnesus therefore appeared more securely established than ever. The future, however, was to demonstrate that Sparta could not abandon the Aegean world to its own fate. In particular, the Greek cities of Asia Minor and their relationship to Persia urgently demanded a fundamental clarification. Sparta had pawned them off for gold to the Persian king, who up till then had, however, lacked the power to assert his supremacy effectually in Ionia. The result was a state of suspense which in the long run became completely unbearable.

THE EXPEDITION OF CYRUS THE YOUNGER (401-400 B.C.)
THE SPARTAN-PERSIAN WAR IN WESTERN ASIA MINOR (400-394 B.C.)

Under Artaxerxes II, who acceded to the Achaemenid throne in 404 B.C. as successor to his father Darius II, the decline of the Persian empire became clearly evident. On the one hand there was no end to the harem intrigues in Susa, while on the other the empire sustained a severe blow by the revolt of Egypt, which in 404 B.C., under the Delta prince Amyrtaeus, regained its independence and maintained it for a full sixty years. In addition, the authority of the central government, which had already suffered a deep decline, was very seriously threatened by the incessant quarrels among the centrifugal forces, the satraps. With their vast territorial dominions and surrounded by thousands of vassals, the satraps acted almost as absolute rulers in their own territories,[17] without paying much heed to the orders of the Great King in distant Susa. In Asia Minor the discord between the young prince Cyrus, a brother of Artaxerxes II, and the one time absolute satrap Tissaphernes led to such chaotic conditions as to make a mockery of any ordered imperial administration. Cyrus, the viceroy (*karanos*) of Asia Minor since 408 B.C. and ultimately confirmed as such by his brother, pursued a reckless dynastic policy in the satrapies of Lydia, Greater Phrygia and Cappadocia by attempting to extend his own territory at the expense of the neighbouring satrapies. He thus became involved in a dispute with Tissaphernes over the important city of Miletus. In reality, however, he had set his aims much higher—control of the vast Achaemenid empire which had been denied him at the death of his father Darius II.

The conditions necessary for the enterprise were created by recruiting Greek mercenaries, everywhere available for little money in the years after the end of the Great War, and by engineering a secret alliance between Cyrus and Sparta.[18] The Spartans despatched an auxiliary force under Cheirisophus which joined the army of Cyrus in Cilicia. The Spartan fleet also took part in the operations.[19] The enterprise was launched on the pretext of a local action against the insurgent Pisidians. With the consent of the Cilician Syennesis, Cyrus succeeded in crossing the important Taurus passes,[20] and encountered no opposition in northern Syria. The Great King, Artaxerxes II, who had been warned by Tissaphernes, marshalled the contingents of the East in Babylonia. They could in no way compare with the Greek hoplites and peltasts in the army of Cyrus. In the autumn of 401 B.C. they joined battle at the town of Cunaxa (north of Babylon).[21] Cyrus, who rashly stormed the centre of the army of the Great King and wounded his brother with his own hand, when already feeling himself to be the victor, was killed in the turmoil. The expedition accordingly became pointless. The return march of the Greeks, who had been robbed of their leaders by the guile of Tissaphernes,[22] up the Tigris, through the inclement mountain regions of Armenia to the Black Sea, which they reached at Trapezus, is a page of imperishable renown in the annals of Greek military history. Never has the military and moral superiority of the Greeks over the far greater numbers of Asiatics become so clearly evident as in this march from Babylonia to the Black Sea. It is a feat which, in its psychological effects, can only be compared with Thermopylae.

The return of the 8600 mercenaries (that is how many had survived from 13,000) was inconvenient to not a few, especially the Spartans. They found themselves most embarrassingly compromised in the eyes of the Great King, and denied any association with the "*Kyrioi*." Xenophon's design to found a colony at the Pontus and in Bithynia ran aground in the face of opposition from the satrap Pharnabazus.[23] The rest of the Ten Thousand—the tale of their exploits was on the lips of all—were pushed off to Thrace where they entered the pay of Seuthes, a dethroned chieftain.[24] This marked the end of a venture which had shaken the great Persian empire to its very foundations.

The death of Cyrus the Younger and the return of Tissaphernes to Asia Minor in 400 B.C. made the position of the Greek cities in Asia Minor a burning question. Tissaphernes, who had once signed the treaty for Persian subsidies with the Spartans (v.s.p. 149), began to carry out the decree which handed the Hellenes of Asia Minor over to the Great King. It was not merely a matter of prestige that determined this action. Should Persia take possession of the Ionian harbours, she would, with her fleet, be in a position to exercise control over the Aegean, which had become a territory without a ruler after the collapse of Athens and her Maritime League. The Ionian appeal for help confronted the Spartans with the choice between the Persian alliance and the liberty of the Ionians. The Spartans gave the Greeks in Ionia assurances of their assistance (400 B.C.).[25]

The force which the Spartans despatched to Asia Minor under the command of Thribon numbered little more than 5000 and was consequently inadequate for major operations. It did not achieve more than minor successes, but it did succeed in at least securing the cities of Aeolis from Persian attack. Pharnabazus and Tissaphernes, the Persian satraps, were at odds with each other. Each prosecuted the war on his own, in accordance with his own aims, until a truce was concluded in 397 B.C. between them and the Spartan Dercylidas. It was not until the command was taken over by Agesilaus, who in 399 B.C. had, with the aid of Lysander, acceded to the throne, that the Spartans conducted the war more actively. Agesilaus behaved like the successor of Agamemnon, seeking to give the war with the satraps a panhellenic character. The military expedition of the new Agamemnon was launched with the offering of a sacrifice at Aulis—as before the expedition against Troy—incidentally a notable example of the practical significance of mythology in the life of the Greeks. No convincing victories were, however, scored after the landing of Agesilaus at Ephesus. At the Pactolus river, before the gates of Sardis, he engaged in battle with the Persian horse,[26] but the Spartan attempt to take the city failed.

The Persians hoped that the naval war would decide the issue, and built a fleet of significant size at Cyprus, an enterprise in which the Athenian Conon played an important rôle as advisor to Euagoras, king of Salamis. Success did not come at first, since Conon had been shut up and blockaded within the harbour of Caunus in Caria (396 B.C.). The rivalry between the Persian leaders freed the Spartans from their most dangerous opponent, Tissaphernes, when he was slain by the chiliarch Tithraustes who had been sent to Asia Minor. Thus the war in western Anatolia remained essentially what it had been: a series of plundering excursions, camping in winter quarters, armistices which were not as a rule ratified and attempts at reciprocal deception. In these circumstances the brunt was born by the Ionians, upon whom devolved the burden of provisioning the Spartan troops. In other respects the Spartans had an easy time of it militarily. Agesilaus, who exploited the disunity between Tithraustes and Pharnabazus, drove the Persian hordes before him and collected a vast amount of booty. At this juncture events in the Greek motherland necessitated the recall of the Spartan forces from Asia Minor to Greece.

THE REVOLT OF THE GREEKS AGAINST SPARTA AND THE KING'S PEACE (395-386 B.C.)

During the first years of the fourth century Persian policy, with extensive employment of gold, succeeded in effectively inciting the Greeks against the violent Spartan system of government. In the employ of the satrap Pharnabazus, Timocrates of Rhodes journeyed to Greece where he poured Persian gold into Thebes, Corinth, Argos and Athens, so that nothing more than a slight gesture was needed to precipitate a general revolt of the Greeks against Spartan despotism. The conflict that the Persians wanted was kindled by the antagonism between the Locrians[27] and Phocians (395 B.C.).

Behind the Locrians stood Thebes, the leading power of the Boeotian League, with its peculiar representative constitution (*Hellenika* of Oxyrhynchus XI). The Boeotian *koinon* was composed of eleven "districts," each of which had to furnish one boeotarch, as well as sixty members to the Federal Council, and a contingent of 1000 hoplites and 100 horse to the federal army. Thebes itself (together with a few smaller communities) consisted of four "districts." The Phocians found support in Sparta. Athens, on whose attitude much depended, concluded a defensive alliance with Boeotia.[28] Spartan operations at first met with little success. In the attempt to take Haliartus at Lake Copaïs, Lysander was defeated by the Boeotian force and himself remained dead on the battlefield (autumn 395 B.C.). In consequence of this reverse the Spartan allies in central Greece, as well as Corinth, Argos and the Chalcidians, joined the side of the enemy. The Spartan king Pausanias (II) arrived too late in Haliartus, and surrendered Boeotia without a stroke of the sword. When faced with condemnation in Sparta he fled the country to Tegea. The Spartans consequently had no alternative but to recall Agesilaus from Asia. Persian policy had fully achieved its object. Before Agesilaus arrived in Greece the army of the Peloponnesian League had retained the upper hand in a fierce battle at the little stream of Nemea near Corinth (July 394 B.C.).[29] It was reserved for Agesilaus, after a victorious engagement at Coroneia (August 394 B.C.), to re-establish Spartan supremacy in Boeotia.[30]

The issue was, however, decided not on Greek soil but in Asia Minor, where the decision must inevitably take place. With Cyprian, Rhodian and Phoenician ships, the Athenian Conon and the Persian satrap Pharnabazus scored a decisive victory over the Spartan nauarch Peisander at Cnidus (beginning of August 394 B.C.). After a brief glory of just ten years the Spartan "maritime empire" sank beneath the waves in the waters of Cnidus. In Asia Minor and the Aegean the consequences of the Spartan defeat were incalculable.[31] Everywhere the Spartan garrisons were driven out, together with the hated harmosts. A number of Greek cities opened their gates to the Persians and only at the Hellespont was Dercylidas able to uphold Spartan rule.

The success of Persia was nothing less than overwhelming. It was the greatest and most momentous Persian victory since the defeat of the

Athenian expeditionary force on Prosopitis in the Nile (v.s.p. 127), indeed the greatest Persian victory ever over Greeks. For the first time since the days of Xerxes the Persian fleet ventured to make an appearance off the coast of Greece, advanced against the Peloponnesus, and using Cythera as a base, opened a vigorous pirate war against Greek merchantmen. In the following year, 393 B.C. (spring or summer), Conon returned to Athens. Here his conduct after Aegospotami had been forgotten, and as the envoy of the Great King he received honours of unusual distinction.[32] Persian gold was used to rebuild the Piraeus ring and the Long Walls.[33] In addition, a number of treaties were concluded with Chios, Mytilene, Cos, Cnidus and Eteocarpathus among others.[34] Finally, the old cleruchies of Lemnos, Imbros and Scyros, of such vital importance for the sustenance of the impoverished Attic population, were reunited with the Attic state. Besides this, Persian subsidies made it possible to increase the daily pay in the *Ekklesia* from 1 to 3 obols. In other respects it was exclusively Persian interests that were decisive in bringing about the restoration of Athens. The tool in the hands of the Persians, however, was Conon—nothing shows more clearly the gulf between those times when a Pericles determined Athenian policy towards Persia.

At the beginning of 392 B.C. a democratic revolution broke out in Corinth, followed by a political alliance with Argos.[35] As an early attempt to overcome the narrow limits of the polis the short-lived Corinthian-Argive double-state (it was dissolved again after the Peace of Antalcidas in 386 B.C.) deserves special notice. The union at the Isthmus and in the Argolid created a notable counterweight to Spartan hegemony, and it scarcely requires proof that this development too was decisively promoted by Persian gold.

Sparta sustained a severe blow when one of her contingents, on being taken by a surprise attack by Athenian peltasts under the command of Iphicrates, was defeated and suffered many casualties (end of 392 B.C.).[36] The defeat was the sign of a coming change in Hellenic military science. The future belonged not to the heavily armed and cumbersome phalanx of hoplites but to the "peltasts" armed with light shields, lance and javelin, that is, the mercenaries who, in contrast to the citizen militia, found themselves in constant training. In conjunction with the external change in Greek military policy the theory of warfare developed into a separate discipline during the first half of the fourth century B.C.[37] Siege techniques (*poliorketika*) too were finally raised to the level of a science by Dionysius I of Syracuse and Philip II of Macedonia. They did not, however, come into their own until after the time of Alexander the Great.

The peace negotiations begun in 392 B.C. (before the destruction of the Lacedaemonian *mora*) between Athens and Sparta reveal the Persian shadow hovering over Greece. Andocides, who went to Sparta as one of the plenipotentiary envoys of Athens, has left an official, though not untendentious, account of the event in his "Peace Oration" (*Or.* III).[38] The controversial point was the principle of the autonomy of the various Greek states, on account of which Sparta had entered the Peloponnesian

War and which she was now championing with unusual tenacity. Sparta was prepared to accept not only the rebuilding of the Long Walls at Athens, the enlarging of the Athenian fleet, but even the union of the old Attic cleruchies of Lemnos, Imbros and Scyros with Athens (which would have amounted to a nullification of the Peace of 404 B.C.), provided only that Athens declare herself prepared to acknowledge the Spartan demand for the autonomy of all Greek states. In these negotiations the concept of a peace embracing all Greeks without exception, was for the first time thrown into the debate by Sparta.[39] In the course of the fourth century that concept was to acquire central importance in Hellenic politics. The idea of a general peace was nourished by a deep and widespread longing for peace and to a large extent coincided with the mood of the times. But in Athens the Spartan offer was rejected. The fact of the matter was that the theatre in which the fate of Greece was to be decided had long since shifted to the other side of the Aegean. The key to the situation lay in the hands of the Great King of Persia, with whom Sparta was still in a state of war. In order to reach a settlement with the Persians the Spartans sent Antalcidas, son of Leon,[40] to the satrap Tiribazus at Sardis. As a price for the Persian peace Sparta offered to relinquish all Asia Minor, which amounted to a complete capitulation to the Great King. The Peace Congress, however, which had been summoned in Sardis, in which ambassadors from Athens, Boeotia and Argos also participated, ran aground on the question of Asia Minor. In contrast to the remaining Greeks the Athenians hesitated to abandon their Ionian kinsmen to the Persians.[41] The change of front by the satrap of Sardis—Tiribazus had taken Conon prisoner but he had escaped and died at the court of Euagoras of Salamis on Cyprus—did not meet with the applause of the central administration of Persia, which, as before, continued to regard Sparta as the more dangerous enemy. The result was a sudden important change of government in Asia Minor. The predominant position of the viceroy of Sardis was eliminated, and Tiribazus recalled. Ionia, which had up to this time been governed jointly with Lydia, now received its own satrap in the person of Struthas, and Lydia was placed under the control of Autophradates and Caria under the native dynast Hecatomnus of Mylasa. The revival of the Spartan-Persian conflict once more kindled the flames of war in Asia Minor. The despatching of Thibron of Sparta across the Aegean, however, ended in a serious setback: his army was attacked by the satrap Struthas and Thibron himself slain (391 B.C.).

Of far greater consequence, however, was the change which took place in the state of affairs in the Aegean. In 389 B.C. a triple alliance was concluded between the Cyprian dynast Euagoras (who had emancipated himself from the Persian empire), the Egyptian king Acoris and the Athenians[42]—which was very favourable to Athens in particular. Her fleet, under the command of Thrasybulus, achieved surprising successes in 389 B.C. Thasos, Samothrace, the Thracian Chersonese, Byzantium and Chalcedon were won, and Halicarnassus and Clazomenae came over to the side of Athens.[43] It was no wonder that the triumphal entry of Thrasybulus into Athens raised the most daring hopes! The Athenians were expecting wonders and a life of leisure and luxury, as the second *Pluto* of Aristophanes (performed in 388 B.C.) portrays.[44] When the tense expectations were disappointed, the ill-feeling of the multitudes vented itself on Thrasybulus. He, however, evaded responsibility, and met his death on a plundering expedition in Pamphylia.

The Spartans had for their part taken possession of the island of Aegina and from there launched a pirate war against Attic ships. Since it was at first impossible to block the straits, Sparta seized Athens by the throat. The threat continued until the end of the war, and even Piraeus was not safe from Spartan assaults.

The issue of the war was finally decided in Asia Minor. Tiribazus had returned to Sardis about 388 B.C., after Struthas had been recalled. Sparta immediately took advantage of this sudden change in Asia Minor. Once more Antalcidas journeyed to Sardis, and from there, together with Tiribazus, proceeded to Susa and the court of the Great King.[45] The conditions which the king of Persia set for peace and an alliance with Sparta included the relinquishing to Persia of the mainland of Asia Minor, including Cyprus and Clazomenae, and the autonomy of all Greek cities, with the exception of the old Attic cleruchies. These demands met with stubborn opposition on the part of the enemies of Sparta. If they were accepted, then Athens would lose everything she had just won through Thrasybulus. Argos would have to renounce union with Corinth and Thebes her hegemony in the Boeotian League—in other words, all significant power formations in Hellas which could somehow form a counterweight to Sparta would be destroyed. On the other hand there were not a few Greeks who gladly welcomed the principle of autonomy which the Persians demanded. On the whole, however, the opposition prevailed and it was not until Antalcidas blockaded the straits with a powerful fleet[46]—it had been built with the aid of the satraps of Asia Minor and Dionysius I of Syracuse who was allied with Sparta—and the spectre of starvation stood at the gates of Athens that they were prepared to yield.

The envoys from all the Greek states who had taken part in the war and had now assembled in Sardis in 387 B.C. were presented with a decree by Tiribazus, the representative of the Great King. The text, preserved in the *Hellenica* of Xenophon, (V I.31) reads: "Artaxerxes the Great King deems it right that the cities of Asia, and, of the islands, Clazomenae and Cyprus, belong to him,[47] but that the remaining Greek cities, small as well as great, be autonomous, except Lemnos, Imbros and Scyros, which, as in olden times, are to be in the possession of Athens." Anyone who refused to accept these conditions faced the threat of war, according to another clause. In other respects the decree is actually an excerpt from the peace conditions which had been agreed upon in Susa between Persia and Sparta, which the Persians made the basis of a general peace embracing all Greeks. The sense of power of the oriental Great King shows in the form in which it was published, an edict, a dictated peace, as Isocrates characterised it at a later date (*Panegyr*. 176).[48]

The Spartans were appointed executors of the peace which the Great

King "imposed" on the Greeks.[49] Under their supervision a general peace Congress was held at Sparta in 386 B.C. Here the Greeks declared themselves willing to accept the conditions, although the Corinthians and Thebans only did so after vigorous resistance. The Great King, by joining in the oath when the decree was issued, became the "guarantor of the peace" (Isoc., *Panegyr.* 175). In order to carry out the principle of autonomy in Hellas, Sparta brought into effect a general peace among the Greeks,[50] a peace which was therefore partly the result of the King's Peace.[51] Earlier scholars have attempted to explain the absence of a time limit in the King's Peace in terms of the diplomatic practices of the Orient, but the eastern basis is by no means certain, for there are also Greek treaties which were concluded in perpetuity.

The King's Peace marked the nadir in Greek history. The Peace served to split Hellas up into impotent fragmentary states, and the Great King assumed the rôle of guarantor of this state of affairs. The great power of the East forced the Greeks into subjection. Impotence and bondage seemed to have become the lot of the Hellenes, and in fact the subsequent half century up to the founding of the Corinthian League in 338/7 B.C. was overshadowed by the dark clouds of the King's Peace. At one time when the Greeks were assembled at the great Olympian festival the highly gifted Gorgias of Leontini had delivered a searing speech against the Persians and warning the Hellenes to unite, and in the *Epitaphios* in honour of the Athenians who fell in the Corinthian War he had reminded them of the victories over the barbarians. Of this spirit there was no longer a breath to be traced in a Greece which had forgotten her glorious past.

SPARTA AND THEBES IN THE STRUGGLE FOR SUPREMACY; THE SECOND ATHENIAN MARITIME LEAGUE (386-371 B.C.)

The King's Peace stabilised conditions in Asia Minor, so that a new period of economic prosperity began for the Ionians. The effects of this economic boom extended to the Greek mainland and deep within Anatolia. On the other hand, the edict of the Great King was a terrible blow to Greek freedom. The only state which received any benefit from the provisions of the King's Peace was Sparta. Her hegemony in the Peloponnesian League, which respected the autonomy of the League members, was in no way affected by the Peace. It was no wonder that Sparta, under the leadership of the Ephorate and Agesilaus, did everything possible to strengthen her position even further in Hellas. The times in which world affairs were determined in Greece, as in the days of Pericles, were indeed irretrievably a thing of the past, and there was no question that any significant shift in power in Hellas could only come about if it were tolerated or fostered by Persia. In 385 B.C. Mantineia was forced into the Lacedaemonian League. The city was split up into five independent districts, each of which had to contribute its contingent to the League army.[52] In Phleius too Sparta asserted her will and forced the restoration of the oligarchic exiles.[53]

Sparta's hegemony in central Greece rested principally on the alliance which she had concluded with the various communities of Boeotia, whereby the principle of autonomy was employed against Thebes in favour of Spartan supremacy. When Thebes refused to render military service to Sparta in the Olynthian War in 382 B.C., the Lacedaemonian Phoebidas, probably on a secret order from the ephors, took possession of the Cadmeia—the citadel—in Thebes. The Theban oligarchs assisted him in this.[54] Ismenias, a sworn enemy of Sparta—he had once been responsible for Persian gold flowing in Greece—was executed, his death justified on the grounds that he had become traitor to the Hellenic cause.[55] Phoebidas' incursion into Thebes set off such a wave of indignation throughout Greece that the Spartan government was forced to dissociate itself publicly from the matter. They imposed a fine on Phoebidas, but the garrison on the Cadmeia remained.

In the same year (382 B.C.) Sparta intervened in the conflict between the Chalcidian League and Macedonia, with the Spartans and the Macedonian king Amyntas III as protectors of the various Chalcidian communities, joining forces against the now-dominant Olynthus. An army of 10,000 men marched through Greece towards the north. After a long siege Olynthus, the head of the Chalcidian League, was forced to capitulate in 379 B.C. The Chalcidian state was dissolved and Amyntas regained unlimited sovereignty in Macedonia.

Sparta's success in the north marked the height of her power in the fourth century B.C. It was, in fact, the final climax of her power. Far away from her home base, Sparta emerged as arbiter in distant Chalcidice and there too enforced her principle of autonomy of the individual states. As early as 382 B.C. Sparta had created for herself an extensive organisation in Hellas, a territorial division into districts along military lines. It is an excellent reflection of the power of Spartan hegemony. The ten districts under Spartan military service encompassed the whole of Greece, from the southern tip of the Peloponnesus to Thrace in the north. Seven of them came from the Peloponnesus: the first was exclusively Lacedaemonia, the second and third encompassed Arcadia, the fourth Elis, the fifth Achaea, the sixth Corinth and Megara, the seventh Sicyon, Phleius and the coastal cities of the Argolid. The eighth was composed of Acarnania, the ninth of Phocis and Locris, while the tenth district incorporated Boeotia before 379 B.C. but later Olynthus and Sparta's allies in Thrace. It would seem that each district had to contribute 1000 foot to the League army. The furnishing of troops could, however, be discharged by paying the equivalent in money, in which case one member of the horse was equal to four hoplites and one hoplite to two peltasts.

In Diodorus' survey (XV 31) for the year 378 B.C. there is no longer any mention of Thebes. In 379 B.C. important changes had taken place in Thebes, the first signs of a new power emerging in Greece and the first cracks in Sparta's League organisation. Theban exiles, who had found asylum and active support in Athens,[56] overthrew the oligarchic Spartan puppet régime in Thebes and forced the Spartan garrison on the Cadmeia to capitulate under terms of withdrawing freely, in the winter of 379 B.C.

The impression which this created in Sparta was nothing less than shattering. The officers who had been in command on the Cadmeia were executed or punished with heavy fines and an abortive attempt was made to retrieve the situation by despatching the Spartan king Cleombrotus. Thebes remained lost to Sparta and the cornerstone of Spartan rule in central Greece had been knocked out.

The liberation of Thebes from Spartan domination created the conditions for the founding of an Attic Maritime League in 377 B.C., precisely one hundred years after the first Attic Maritime League had been established by Aristeides and Themistocles. The new union was based on individual treaties which Athens concluded from 384/3 B.C. onwards—the first one with Chios.[57] Athens formally called on the Hellenes, the Barbarians on the mainland and any Islanders who were not subject to the Great King.[58] Most of the islands in the Aegean, the Greek cities on the Thracian coast and later also communities in the Ionian Sea joined. At the height of its development the League included 70 members, considerably smaller than the first Maritime League. The so-called second Attic Maritime League did not, in accordance with the stipulations of the King's Peace, encroach upon the autonomy of the League members. Athens herself assumed a position of parity with, not, as in the previous century, superiority over, the other members. In the *Synhedrion*, the Federal Assembly, which met in Athens, each League member had one vote, but a valid resolution required agreement between the *Synhedrion* and Athens, that is, the resolutions of the *Synhedrion* required the endorsement of the Athenian *Ekklesia*. The members of the League paid contributions—but not tribute.[59] Athens had to furnish by far the largest contingent of the fleet and to take over the executive in the region encompassed by the League.

In Athens a new generation took over the helm during the years after the King's Peace. The leading statesman, Callistratus of Aphidnae, played the same role in the organisation of the second Maritime League as Aristeides of Alopece had once in the first Attic Maritime League. Like the latter, he showed outstanding ability in the field of finance.[60] At his side were, as mercenary commanders, Chabrias, a friend of Plato, and Iphicrates, a highly competent tactician. Timotheus, son of Conon, by reason of his great wealth also exerted an important influence in Athens. The new figures were men of action and able to stand their ground in the line of battle. They were far removed from onesided political doctrinairism, and in consequence were particularly suited to be standard-bearers of an impartial Attic policy.

Thebes, in the years after the liberation of the Cadmeia (379 B.C.), became the school of warfare and politics. Her position, which neither the expeditions of Agesilaus nor of Cleombrotus to Boeotia (377 and 376 B.C.) could shake, rested on her hegemony in the Boeotian League, which now once more made itself felt in the outside world.[61] The head of the government was formed by the seven (no longer eleven) boeotarchs, and an Assembly of all Boeotians convened in Thebes. There was even a Boeotian federal fleet, but that did not attain any major importance.

MAP V

Greece in 362 B.C .

Paeonia
Illyrians
Lake Ochrida
Lyncestis
Orestis
Macedonia
Elimeia
Tymphaea
Haliacmon
Axius
Strymon
Bisaltia
Edon
Aegae
Pella
Alorus
Beroea
Methone
Pydna
Dion
Therma
Arethusa
Apollonia
Galep
Stageir
Aca
Dion
Amp
Chalcidice
Olynthus
Mecyberna
Potidaea
Mende
Apollonia
Aous
Parauaea
Epirus
Atintania
Chaonians
Phoenice
Molossians
Thesprotians
Corcyra
Passaron
Dodona
Cassopia
Ambracia
Athamania
Dolopia
Perrhaebia
Gyrton
Gonnus
Thessaly
Magnesia
Tricca
Larisa
Crannon
Scotussa
Pherae
Pharsalus
Pagassae
Halus
Sciathos
Peparethos
Achaea
Echinus
Mallis
Aenianians
Oreus
Euboea
Nicaea
Heracleia
Thermopylae
Amphilochians
Argos
Agraea
Acarnania
Leucas
Alysia
Agrinium
Stratus
Thermus
Aetolia
Amphissa
Locris
Elateia
Opus
Phocis
Chaeroneia
Chalcis
Eretria
Haliartus
Thebes
Tanagra
Oropus
Lebadeia
Boeotia
Delphi
Leuctra
Plataea
Ithaca
Cephallenia
Calydon
Naupactus
Same
Pale
Pronni
Cranaeae
Patrae
Aegium
Dyme
Achaea
Cyllene
Pellene
Sicyon
Megara
Eleusis
Athens
Piraeus
Salamis
Cleitor
Corinth
Elis
Phleius
Zacynthus
Orchomenus
Mantineia
Aegina
Epidaurus
Olympia
Heraea
Arcadia
Argos
Calaureia
Troezen
Lepreon
Tegea
Megalopolis
Hermione
Thyrea
Cyparissia
Ithome
Messene
Sparta
Laconia
Pylos
Corone
Methone
Asine
Gytheum
Cythera
Neapolis
Tarentum
Metapontum
Heracleia
Hydrus
Elea
Callepolis
Laus
Thurii
Sybaris
Terina
Croton
Carthaginian Territory
Lipari Islands
Hipponium
Medma
Locri
Dionysius
Panormus
Messene
Cephaloedium
Kingdom of Dionysius
Catana
Acragas
Syracuse
Gela
Helorus
0 50 100 km
Athens and the Second Attic Maritime Alliance
The Attic cleruchies are underlined
Boeotia an
Sparta an

Kingdom of Cotys
Heraeum Teichus
Selymbria
Byzantium
Calchedon
Perinthus
Nestus
Maroneia
Abdera
Hebrus
Aenus
Thasos
Ganus
Proconnesus
Cius
Myrlea
Dascylium
Cardia
Crithote
Parium
Priapus
Cyzicus
Samothrace
Alopeconnesus
Lampsacus
Satrapy of Dascylium
Imbros
Abydus
Eleus
Hellespont
Lemnos
Sigeum
Ilium
Hephaesteia
Myrina
Scepsis
Tenedos
Ceprene
Mysia
Antandrus
Assos
Adramyttium
Persian Empire
Methymna
Antissa
Lesbos
Mytilene
Pergamum
Pyrrha
Atarneus
Elaea
Satrapy of Orontes
Satrapy of Sardis
Scyros
Cyme
Phocaea
Magnesia
Hermus
Sardis
Chios
Erythrae
Clazomenae
Teos
Colophon
Lebedus
Notium
Ephesus
Tralles
Maeander
Magnesia
Andros
Samos
Priene
Satrapy of Maussolus
Alabanda
Icaros
Ceos
Tenos
Myconos
Syros
Delos
Cynthos
Iasus
Mylasa
Leros
Myndus
Halicarnassus
Seriphos
Paros
Naxos
Calymnos
Cos
Caunus
Siphnos
Amorgos
Cnidus
Sicinos
Ios
Nisyros
Syme
Melos
Astypalaea
Rhodes
Telos
Camirus
Thera
Anaphe
Chalce
Rhodes
0 20 40 60 80 km
Chalcidian League
Macedonia
Independent Greek cities
Empire of Dionysius

With the naval victory of Chabrias over the Peloponnesian fleet in the sound between Naxos and Paros (376 B.C.), the Athenians gained complete naval supremacy in the Aegean. The successes of Chabrias on the Thracian coast (375 B.C.) were crowned by a treaty with the Macedonian king Amyntas III, who was avidly cultivated as a supplier of wood, so important for ship-building.[62]

Besides development of the second Athenian League, the years between 370 and 360 B.C. were marked by the rise of an important state in the north. Thessaly had in the past been the scene of continual fighting among the powerful noble families, and so had played only a passing rôle within the mainstream of political events. But now, in the person of the great tyrant Jason of Pherae,[63] one time student of the Sophist Gorgias of Leontini, the country had a highly competent leader whose iron hand could force the warring factions of the country to unite. The task was completed in 372 B.C., two years after Polydamas the tetrarch of Pharsalus had submitted to Jason.[64] No other power in Greece could put into the field an army comparable to that of Thessaly–8000 horse and 20,000 foot. Allied with the king of Macedonia and with Athens–Jason was temporarily a member of the second Attic Maritime League[65]–and supported by loyal vassals, the Thessalian *tagos* (Duke) could draw even closer to the idea of a Persian war and thereby win the applause of Isocrates and the Greek patriots.

In 375/4 B.C. a peace congress had met at Sparta. It was a Spartan-Athenian effort; both parties watched the rise of Thebes with jealous eyes. It is noteworthy that foreign powers too, namely Dionysius I and the Great King of Persia,[66] had a hand in the enterprise. From this effort came the proclamation of a general panhellenic peace.[67] Despite its brief duration, it merits attention because it is to be traced back to Hellenic initiative. The intervention of the Athenian Timotheus in the internal affairs of Zacanthus gave the Spartans the desired opportunity to regard the peace as violated, particularly since they had found the peace inconvenient. In Athens a lawsuit was brought against Timotheus, but he was acquitted. Jason of Pherae and Alcetas the king of Epirus had personally thrown their weight behind Timotheus in Athens.[68] His recall marked the end of Athenian successes in foreign affairs. When Iphicrates, his successor in command, liberated Corcyra from a Peloponnesian blockade, the oarsmen of the Athenian fleet had to hire themselves out to the Corcyraeans as farm labourers in order to save their lives!

When Thebes, who nominally belonged to the Maritime League, destroyed Plataea, the League ally of Athens (374/3 or 373/2 B.C.),[69] the old antagonists Athens and Sparta once more patched up their differences. At the instigation of the Great King of Persia another general peace congress took place at Sparta, in the summer of 371 B.C.,[70] at which Dionysius I of Syracuse and Amyntas III of Macedonia were also represented. Once more the stipulations of the King's Peace, asserting the autonomy of the Greek states, served as the basis of the negotiations. Athens had her Maritime League recognized, and even obtained, the endorsement of her claims to Amphipolis and the Thracian Chersonese. In the peace charter Thebes also figured among the member states of the Maritime League. A vigorous dispute arose between Thebes and the Spartan king Agesilaus over the supplementary demand of the boeotarch Epameinondas to have the word "Thebans" in the text replaced by the term "Boeotians" (which would have amounted to official recognition of the Boeotian League).[71] Since Epameinondas refused to yield, the day after the peace was signed, it was already nothing more than an empty document.

At the Congress in Sparta, Epameinondas for the first time stepped onto the stage of history.[72] What the ancients professed to know about his early life before 371 B.C. belongs to the realm of legend. It is only certain that he was a disciple of the Pythagorean Lysis of Tarentum. An aristocrat in his demeanour, from the top of his head to the sole of his foot, he made no secret of his aversion to democracy, but despite this he served his native polis faithfully. On close friendly terms with the somewhat younger Pelopidas,[73] making no personal claims, and above bribery, Epameinondas is one of the most agreeable figures of the fourth century. His historical importance lies in the sphere of military strategy.[74] In this field he was one of the most daring innovators of all time. Before his time Greek strategy depended on the parallel phalanx: by means of a reinforced right wing, the opponents sought to envelop each other and, after outflanking the enemy, to turn his flank from the wing, a tactic which continually reappears in many variations. By employing the tactic of combined forces, Epameinondas contributed to the breakthrough of a new idea—the "oblique battle formation." It was no longer the right wing (as still at Delium in 424 B.C.) but the left wing, up to fifty deep, which now decided a battle.[75] The idea of Epameinondas, most effectively employed in the battle of Leuctra (371 B.C.), marked a new epoch in military strategy. The times in which Sparta's army decided every battle with the thrust of the right wing were irretrievably a thing of the past.

The decision in the struggle for the supremacy of Greece came no more than twenty days after the end of the Peace Congress at Sparta. Sparta issued an ultimatum to Thebes to the effect that she restore autonomy to the Boeotian communities. Thebes resolutely refused to comply. Thereupon the Lacedaemonian forces in Phocis under King Cleombrotus received the order to move into Boeotia. By means of a clever tactical manoeuvre Cleombrotus outwitted the Boeotians who were stationed south of Lake Copaïs, detoured around Mount Helicon in the south, and appeared in Crëusis. Turning northwards from here he marched to Leuctra, seven miles west of Thebes. Epameinondas had only 7000 troops to throw into the field against 10,000 of Cleombrotus, but the battle ended, thanks to the new tactics of Epameinondas, in a complete defeat of the Spartans.[76] The Lacedaemonian right wing was no match for the onset of the Boeotians who, fifty deep and sixty broad, formed almost a square block, and in whose front ranks the "Sacred Band" fought under Pelopidas. All heroic valour on the part of the Spartans proved in vain. Of the 700 Spartiates more than half lay strewn on the battlefield, Cleombrotus

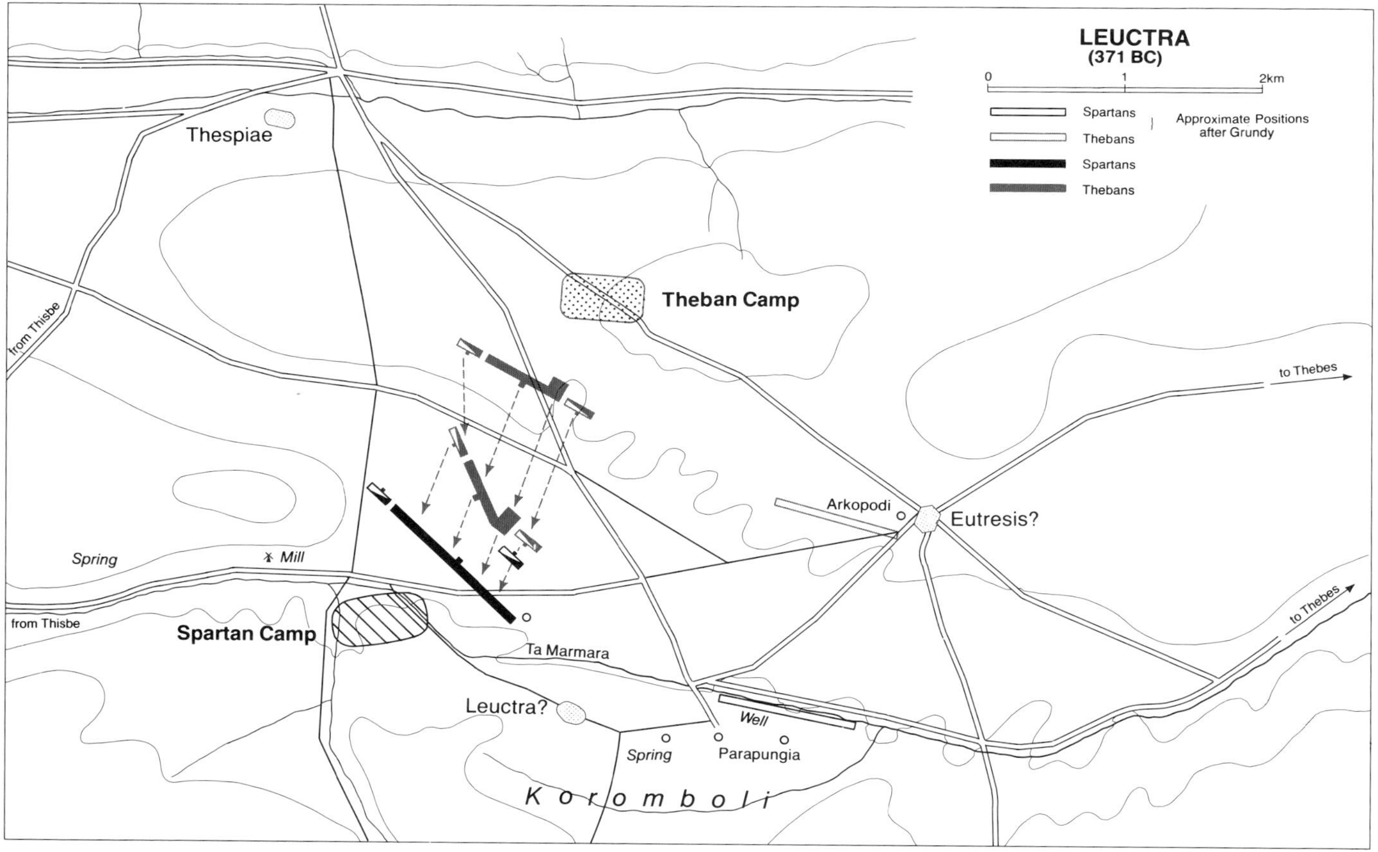
LEUCTRA
(371 BC)
0
1
2km
Spartans
Thebans
Approximate Positions after Grundy
Spartans
Thebans
Thespiae
Theban Camp
from Thisbe
to Thebes
Arkopodi
Eutresis?
Spring
Mill
from Thisbe
Spartan Camp
Ta Marmara
to Thebes
Leuctra?
Well
Spring
Parapungia
Koromboli

among them. Sparta never recovered from this shattering blow. The remainder of the Lacedaemonian forces (the left wing had not engaged in the battle at all) withdrew to a fortified camp in the hills. By requesting the Boeotians to deliver up the fallen, they acknowledged defeat. Through the arbitration of Jason of Pherae, the ally of the Boeotians, Sparta obtained a military truce,[77] and the remainder of the army withdrew to safety beyond Mount Cithaeron. In Sparta itself the victory of Epameinondas precipitated the utmost dismay and dejection. Athens too, who had reckoned with a sure victory for Sparta, was bitterly disappointed.

Leuctra is one of the most important turning points in Greek history. In this battle the Spartan sword was shattered. What the King's Peace had envisaged, the fragmentation of Greece into a number of minute, impotent states, this the battle of Leuctra completed. Thus in the decade after Leuctra, in the period of the Theban Hegemony (371-362 B.C.), Greek history fell under the shadow of the domination of foreign powers to an even greater degree than had been the case since the time when the King's Peace was imposed.

THE ERA OF THE THEBAN HEGEMONY (371-362 B.C.)

After the battle of Leuctra there was only a single power left besides Boeotia to take a leading position among the Greek states—Thessaly, under the tyrant Jason of Pherae. Jason had taken possession of the stronghold Heracleia at Mount Oeta and thereby held the key to central Greece. He entertained plans to appear with the Thessalian levies at Delphi for the celebration of the Pythian games of 370 B.C. It seemed as if a conflict with Boeotia had become inevitable, when the dagger of conspirators snatched the tyrant away, and plunged Thessaly into internal confusion.[78]

Boeotia's growing importance is reflected in a number of alliances which embraced the whole of central Greece. The West and East Locrians, the Phocians, Malians, Aenianians, the communities of Euboea, the Acarnanians and even the Aetolians[79] went over to the Boeotian League. The fact that a number of Boeotian allies were simultaneously members of the Maritime League brought increasing friction between Athens and Thebes. At a second peace congress in the highly eventful year of 371 B.C., in which almost all Greek states participated, including Sparta, Athens had the stipulations of autonomy in the King's Peace expanded under oath into a common peace. This gesture was directed against Thebes, but remained void of any practical effect.[80]

The dominating feature of Greek history between Leuctra (371 B.C.) and Mantineia (362 B.C.) is the attempt of Thebes to expand her influence in the Peloponnesus, to shatter the Lacedaemonian military alliance and to deal Sparta her death blow. The invasion of the Peloponnesus by Boeotian armies reflects the completely altered character of the internal situation in Greece. Sparta, once the hegemonial power of Hellas, now found herself forced into an exclusively defensive position and involved in a life and death struggle, in which she could scarcely stand her ground entirely on her own weak resources. Within the context of world affairs this struggle between Sparta and Thebes was virtually of no importance whatever. Thebes too, despite the genius of Epameinondas and Pelopidas, to whom she owed her ascendency, was merely a pawn in the Persian political game, just as Sparta had been in the years following the King's Peace.

In the Peloponnesus the Spartan defeat brought on a period of internal disorder.[81] On all sides the hitherto suppressed democratic movement raised its head. Murder, banishments and confiscation, such as Greece had not previously seen on this scale, characterised the new era, both anti-aristocratic and anti-Spartan. The Peloponnesian state shook to its very foundations, and all subversive forces pushed their way to the surface, playing an outrageous game with the lives and property of the citizens. Thus in Argos no fewer than 1000 citizens were literally cut down with clubs.[82]

Under the leadership of Mantineia the Arcadians united into a federal state in 370 B.C.,[83] a move undeniably directed against Sparta. The young state had to seek support where it was to be found—in Thebes. For Epameinondas this plea for help from the Arcadians was the desired pretext to finish off Sparta once and for all. On the first of four Peloponnesian campaigns the Boeotian forces, together with their allies, advanced into the Eurotas Valley, but were not able to cross the river, which was greatly swollen from the winter rains (370/69 B.C.). Of far greater importance was the Messenian revolt in the spring of 369 B.C., incited by Epameinondas, and the founding of a Messenian state independent of Sparta. Sparta thereby not only lost a third, and indeed the most fertile part, of her territory, but was robbed of the very foundations of her existence,[84] for the Spartan form of life was based essentially on the diligence and villeinage of the Helots. The city of Messene at Mount Ithome formed the centre of the new state.[85] Under the protection of Boeotian arms a gigantic *synoikismos*—union—took place at the same time in Arcadia. The capital of Megalopolis was founded through the "settling together" of thirty-nine communities. It was laid out as a bulwark blocking the Spartan road from the Eurotas to the Alpheius. With its gigantic dimensions Megalopolis is the precursor of the Hellenistic city foundations, which were also carried out by means of *synoikismoi*. In the centre of the polis a huge roofed hall (the *Thersileion*) was erected.[86] It was designed to accommodate the Assembly of the Arcadian League, the "*Myrioi*" (Ten Thousand). The League struck its own coins and commanded a League army, to which 5000 Arcadians were recruited annually. Thus the first expedition of Epameinondas to the Peloponnesus had completely wrecked the Spartan system. Wherever one looked in Sparta, one was confronted with mortal foes, and the loss of the fertile Messenian countryside raised the spectre of dire need everywhere in the land.

The success of Epameinondas in the Peloponnesus led to closer ties between Sparta and Athens. At the beginning of 369 B.C. an alliance was concluded.[87] Dionysius I too sent aid to Sparta in the form of 2000 Celtic and Iberian mercenaries. The second expedition of Epameinondas to the

Peloponnesus (spring 369 B.C.)[88] was void of any decisive success. In the boeotarch elections Epameinondas and Pelopidas were not in the running, and in fact they were prosecuted (autumn 369 B.C.).[89]

The death of Jason of Pherae (370 B.C.) gave Thebes a free hand in the north. Internal disorder, not only in Thessaly but also in Macedonia, offered a favourable pretext for the intervention of foreign powers. In Thessaly, Jason's brothers Polydorus and Polyphron succeeded him in power, and both, through assassination, met the same end as Jason. The Aleuads thereupon summoned foreign powers to intervene. Alexander II, king of Macedonia, seized the cities of Crannon and Larisa.[90] Macedonia, however, was itself not sufficiently consolidated to be able to rule Thessaly. An attempt by the Theban Pelopidas to arbitrate between Alexander II and Ptolemy of Alorus, the pretender to the throne, came to nothing.[91] The king, Alexander II, was murdered by Ptolemy—at the instigation of his own mother (Eurydice) (369/8 B.C.). As guardian of the young prince Perdiccas (III), brother of Alexander, Ptolemy seized control. In Athens, Iphicrates supported the queen mother Eurydice,[92] the widow of Amyntas III. Thebes for her part joined the side of Ptolemy. Philip, the younger brother of Perdiccas, found himself, along with other young Macedonians, in Thebes as a pledge of loyalty of the new regent in Macedonia.[93]

Things did not go well for Pelopidas in Thessaly. The Theban was no match for the new tyrant, Alexander of Pherae, a nephew of Polyphron. The Thessalian despot captured Pelopidas and his colleague Ismenias, and it was not until 367 B.C. that the diplomacy of Epameinondas was able to move him to release Pelopidas.

From the spring of 368 B.C. onwards a peace congress met at Delphi. Persian gold, which the satrap Ariobarzanes had through agents lavished on Greece, was again involved. Since Sparta refused to yield, the Congress became stalled on the question of Messenia. More success was achieved in the negotiations that were taken up in 367 B.C. under the aegis of the Great King in Susa. Pelopidas emerged as victor from the "competitive grovelling" (Beloch) in the efforts to gain the favour of Artaxerxes II. In the treaty which was concluded between Persia and the Boeotians the most important provision had reference to the independence of Messenia (this was a mortal blow for Sparta). The treaty also provided for the cession of the district of Triphylia by the Arcadians to Elis, the autonomy of Amphipolis and finally the dismantling of the Athenian fleet, which was a thorn in the flesh for the Persians.[94] An evil fate now awaited the envoys of Athens and Sparta, who had submitted to the Persian edict. The Spartan Antalcidas put an end to his life on the return journey, while the Athenian Timagoras was accused at home and paid for the failure of his mission with his life.[95] Thebes alone had attained the object of her desires. Her hegemony in Hellas, which was based on the old Theban-Persian alliance, appeared to be more firmly established than ever. No one in Hellas ventured even to entertain the idea of resisting the powerful edict of the Great King, although the evidence of decline in the Achaemenid empire had now become evident to the eyes of all the world in the revolts of the western satrapies,[96] and also in the fact that Egypt continued to assert her independence as much as ever.

The Theban success in Susa and the annexation of the frontier city of Oropus by the Boeotians (in 366 B.C.)[97] resulted in a complete reorientation of Athenian policy.[98] Athens had vainly sought aid from Sparta. The policy advocated by Callistratus to link up with Persia and Sparta had revealed itself as a chimera. Athens now turned about face. She concluded a defensive alliance with the Arcadian League, so that, nominally still in league with Sparta, she found herself obligated to render help to the Spartans against the Arcadians and to the Arcadians against Sparta, depending on which of the two Athenian allies was regarded as the victim of aggression.

The time was still not ripe for a general peace in Hellas. In 366 B.C. a separate peace was concluded in Thebes between the Boeotians and a number of states in the north of the Peloponnesus (Corinth, Phleius, Epidaurus [?].[99] Spartan aloofness made a deep impression in Greece. In Athens Isocrates in his *Archidamos* supported the Spartan position. The sympathies which a powerful Sparta had at one time frivolously thrown away under Lysander she won back during these years—but it was now too late. When the Spartan government despatched King Agesilaus across the sea to Asia Minor to assist the insurgent satrap Ariobarzanes in his struggle against the Carian dynast Maussollus and the Lydian satrap Autophradates, they did so to replenish the empty treasury in Sparta. The gold of Ariobarzanes weighed heavier than the Spartan iron currency.

Furthermore, violating the declaration made at the founding of the new Maritime League, to refrain from any fresh annexation of territory, Timotheus seized from the Persians the important island of Samos (365 B.C.), on which 2000 Athenian cleruchs were settled.[100] In the Thracian Chersonese too (Sestos, Crithote), and even in Byzantium the Athenians once more gained a foothold. Of importance were the successes of Timotheus in the north. He admittedly did not succeed in taking Amphipolis, but instead took Pydna and Methone, both supremely important as gateways to the Macedonian hinterland. The communities of Torone and Potidaea declared their secession from the Chalcidian League, and Potidaea became an Attic cleruchy,[101] a second Samos. Athens had long since left the road of "league" policy. She dreamed of a new Attic empire, the rise of which appeared to be favoured by the chaotic conditions in Greece and above all by the paralysis of Persian initiative.

In Thessaly the Boeotians had meanwhile stepped up their influence. Pelopidas had fallen in a victorious battle at Cynoscephalae,[102] but the power of Alexander of Pherae was still restricted to his own tetrarchy and he himself was obliged to render military service to the Boeotians. In order to be able to enter the larger scene of Greek politics, however, the land power of Boeotia required access to the sea and an efficient navy. It was Epameinondas who, perhaps with the aid of a Carthaginian,[103] inaugurated the change in policy. The harbour of Larymna in Locris was annexed; Macedonia supplied timber for ship-building. Of utmost importance for the Boeotian plans, however, was the island of Euboea with its strategic harbours. The first naval expedition of Epameinondas (364 B.C.) was directed against the straits. Byzantium immediately went over to him, and Chios and Rhodes, the most important member states of the Attic Maritime League, also changed sides.[104] Lasting success was, however, denied Epameinondas, because it was impossible to maintain the success of the first and only naval campaign.[105] An open break with Athens, incidentally, did not ensue.

The whole misery of Hellenic petty politics came into the open through the confused state of affairs in the Peloponnesus. Elis and Arcadia quarrelled over the district of Triphylia, whereby Elis joined the side of Sparta, while Athens sent a contingent of horse to aid the Arcadians (365 B.C.). Pisatis was created as a state independent of Elis, through the goodwill of Arcadia, and it received the charge of the Olympian games. During the celebration of the Olympian festival in 364 B.C. a battle broke out between Arcadians and Eleans in the midst of the sacred territory. The Arcadians did not shrink from plundering the temple treasures of Olympia, for their generals needed money to pay the federal levies. There was no other alternative but to take out a forced temple loan. This sacrilege, however, did not prove a blessing for the Arcadians. Fanned by the old enmity between Tegea and Mantineia, an open split resulted in the League. While Megalopolis and Tegea remained steadfast in league with Boeotia, the remainder of the Arcadians, under the leadership of Mantineia, concluded an alliance with Elis, Achaea and Phleius, which Athens joined (362 B.C.).[106] Due to the fact that Mantineia and Sparta became allied,[107] the Boeotians now found themselves confronted by a strong coalition in the Peloponnesus. Since 370/69 B.C., when Epameinondas had first set foot on Peloponnesian soil, times had decisively changed.

It was the new grouping of powers that once more summoned Epameinondas in 362 B.C.—for the fourth time—into the Peloponnesus. As in the first expedition, he made an attack on Sparta, which was, however, just as unsuccessful as the assault against Mantineia. Trusting in his military forces, the largest which he had ever held under his command, Epameinondas pressed for a decision. It came on the plateau of Mantineia, on the twelfth of *Scirophorion* 362 B.C.[108] With approximately equal numbers on each side, the shock of the Boeotian troops once more proved overwhelming against the right wing of the Spartans and Mantineians. "Like a trireme" (Xenophon) the Boeotians pierced the enemy lines. But when Epameinondas fell in the fray among the foremost ranks, the Boeotians again saw the victory that was already all but within their grasp slip from their fingers.

The total exhaustion of the protagonists led to peace in 362/1 B.C. A common peace followed, from which only Sparta once more remained aloof. The independence of Messenia was reaffirmed and the division of Arcadia into a northern league under Mantineia and a southern league (with Tegea and Megalopolis) was recognised. Otherwise the border war between Sparta and Messenia continued for years to come. Sparta's power was, however, not great enough to regain control of Messenia.

There is an interesting modern theory relating to the peace of 362/1

B.C.[109] This was allegedly the first peace which the Greeks concluded in the fourth century, independent of any influence from foreign powers. The fact that the Greeks at that time rejected an invitation from the insurgent western satraps to take part in the struggle against the King of Persia[110] manifests, it is argued, a new outlook, which differs fundamentally from that of the recent decades after the King's Peace. Greece allegedly returned to herself. Such a conclusion is, however, completely incorrect. It especially overlooks the state of exhaustion in which Hellas found itself after Mantineia. If the Greeks hesitated to assist the satraps against the Great King, this is nothing other than the admission of their own weakness. It was so acute that the Hellenes were not even able to take the slightest advantage of the fact that conditions in the Persian empire were becoming more and more chaotic.[111]

Xenophon's *Hellenica* end with the battle of Mantineia. This is not entirely without justification, for Mantineia indeed marks the end of that era in Greek history which was characterised by the polis. Hegemonial formations in Hellas are now a thing of the past. The polis was incapable of developing from within itself the resources which were so urgently required in Greece to reshape conditions politically, socially and economically. Ever since the beginning of the Peloponnesian War the Greeks had spent themselves in ceaseless internecine struggles, and thus threw the doors wide open to the intervention of foreign powers, especially the Persian empire. With the collapse of Spartan hegemony in the Peloponnesus and the ephemeral power of Thebes, under Persian favour, the fate of the Greeks appeared to be sealed once and for all. Even the notion of a panhellenic "general peace" which had moved into the foreground since the beginning of the fourth century, had not succeeded in altering the political aspect of the country.

In the decades after Mantineia, political thinking still moved along old lines. The idea of the "general peace" consequently did not become a constructive element in the political life of the Greeks. It had been, and continued to be, no more than the expression of a deep and genuine longing for peace in a country embarrassed by unending wars stretching over many decades. The concept of the sovereign polis was indeed not irreconcilable with the idea of a general peace in Hellas, but the obsession with autonomy, the pride of the Greek city-states, made the emergence of larger power formations extremely difficult from the very outset, and in many cases actually impossible. Thus it was in the last instance due to its inherent features that the Greek polis collapsed as a factor in world history. Despite all, however, its importance in the history of civilisation remains great. As a society of rulers and ruled it constitutes the highest and most intricately developed form of Western political thinking. Through the concentration of political and cultural energy within the most restricted space it attained achievements in all spheres of cultural life, achievements which are unique and incomparable. In the Hellenic polis western man for the first time became aware of his mission and his destiny, to be the standard-bearer of the idea of political and personal freedom in a world separated from oriental despotism of the Persian type. The political self-awareness of the Greeks and their great civilising achievements laid the foundations for that culture which forms an imperishable possession of the West. Only because they had passed through the school of the polis did the Greeks become the salt of the earth in the Hellenistic period. But through the Hellenes—as once in the time of the great colonisation during the archaic period—Greek customs, Greek religion and Greek thinking found a new home in distant lands. The Hellenic polis had to sink into impotence so that the Greek mind could conquer a new world for itself. What had once been sown in Hellas bore fruit a thousandfold in the great expanses of the East.

THE EMPIRE OF DIONYSIUS I AND HIS SUCCESSORS IN SICILY. TIMOLEON (406-337 B.C.)

The history of the Greek West in the first third of the fourth century falls under the shadow of the dominating figure of Dionysius I of Syracuse. While the poleis of the Greek motherland suffered shipwreck on the rocks of ceaseless wars, there arose simultaneously on Sicilian soil a state which broke loose from the narrow limits of the polis and became a territorial state. Under Dionysius I the western Greeks took over the leadership among the Hellenes, a highly important shift in the balance of political power in the Mediterranean, which brings the decline of the Greek motherland into even sharper focus.

In 409 B.C., only four years after the catastrophe of the Sicilian expedition of Athens, calamity once more befell Sicily. For seventy years, since Gelon had defeated the Carthaginians in the battle of Himera (480 B.C.), Sicily had been secure from Punic danger. But at the end of the fifth century Segesta, involved in a quarrel with Selinus, appealed to the Carthaginians for help (410 B.C.). The Carthaginians under Hannibal levelled the unfortunate Selinus to the ground (409 B.C.), and Himera too was completely destroyed.[112] The vast temple ruins still bear witness today to the magnificence of the city in the fifth century. In Himera no fewer than 3000 Greeks fell victim to Hamilcar's mania (v.s.p. 108 f.), an act of brutality which sent a terrifying shudder throughout the Greek West. A large-scale Carthaginian offensive resulted in the overthrow of Acragas (406 B.C.); Gela and Camarina also had to be cleared by the Greeks. While in Hellas Persian gold and the Spartan sword were putting an end to Athens and her Maritime League, the dark clouds of a Carthaginian invasion hovered over Sicily—of all the important communities on the island Syracuse alone succeeded in repelling the Carthaginians. The great successes of Carthage are ultimately explicable in terms of the altered situation ensuing from the destruction of the great Athenian fleet in the harbour of Syracuse in 413 B.C. Not Syracuse but Carthage reaped the greatest benefits from the disaster of Athens.

In these circumstances Dionysius became the saviour of Sicily. After removing the board of multiple generals he was elected sole *strategos* with plenary powers, at the age of twenty-five (406 B.C.),[113] and so had the supreme command of the Carthaginian War. The plenipotentiary *strategia* was the bridge by which Dionysius rose to tyranny (405 B.C.). After bringing the war against the Carthaginians to an end in the same year with a relatively favourable peace—not only was Carthage compelled to acknowledge the independence of Syracuse, but in addition the freedom of Messana and Leontini, as well as that of all the Sicels, was affirmed[114]—he was the leading figure in the Syracusan state. He had meanwhile been careful not to alter the democratic forms, nor did he prevent the *Ekklesia* from passing its resolutions. Later Attic decrees mention Dionysius as "ruler of Sicily,"[115] and this could in fact have been the later official title.

In order to meet the Carthaginians in a future war with prospects of victory, the tyrant of Syracuse built gigantic fortifications on the island of Ortygia and in the fort of Euryalus. By incorporating Epipolae into Syracuse the Sicilian metropolis now became the largest city in the entire Greek world. In addition, Dionysius created many factories for the manufacture of weapons, produced an array of modern siege equipment, and built tetraconters and penteconters, so that he ultimately had at his command a war fleet of 300 vessels. There was nothing to match it anywhere else in the entire world. These achievements could only be realised by ruthlessly harnessing the financial resources of the territory over which he had control.[116]

In 397 B.C., Dionysius declared war on the Carthaginians, aiming to clear Sicily of the foreigners, who controlled more than half the island—the entire south coast and the north coast as far as Himera. The declaration of war brought a wild outbreak of Hellenic national hatred against the Carthaginians, and the many Semitic merchants in the Greek cities of Sicily had to pay dearly for the sins once committed by the Carthaginian armies.[117] All the Greek cities joined Syracuse in the first year of the war, and that year ended with the Greek conquest of the strongly fortified Carthaginian arsenal Motye on the western tip of Sicily.[118] In the following year (396 B.C.) the landing of Himilco at Panormus brought about a turn in events. The Carthaginians regained control of Motye and Eryx; Dionysius was compelled to retreat to Syracuse, with his fleet sustaining serious losses in a battle at Catana. Dionysius was only saved (summer 396 B.C.) by the outbreak of a serious plague in the Carthaginian army, which had blockaded Syracuse. A successful sally from the city dealt the Carthaginians a shattering blow, and their fleet was also destroyed. It was not, however, until four years later, in 392 B.C., that a peace treaty was concluded with Carthage, after numerous reverses for the Greeks. The whole of Sicily, except for the north-west, was now under the rule of Dionysius, the liberator of the western Greeks from Punic oppression.[119]

Rule over Sicily cannot stop at the straits. Dionysius, who already stood in treaty relationship with Locri, regarded the South Italian League—Croton, Caulonia, Sybaris (on the Traïs), Thurii, Hipponium, Tarentum and others—the greatest obstacle to his plans for southern Italy. So he concluded an alliance with the Italic Lucanians and decisively defeated the forces of the League in 388 B.C. at the Eleporus River. In the ensuing peace it would seem that the Isthmus of Catanzaro became the northern boundary of the Syracusan sphere of influence.[120] This practically signified the death sentence for the autonomy of the isolated Rhegium. The city was forced to capitulate in 386 B.C., after a dreadful period of suffering, and Dionysius was now firmly established on both sides of the straits of Messina.

In the years during which the Italian mainland was being devastated by the Celtic raids, the ruler of Sicily proceeded to establish a powerful colonial empire in the Adriatic. He founded a colony and a naval base on the island of Issa (Lissa), and built the harbours of Ancon (Ancona) and Adria (at the mouth of the Po) on Italian soil. Where the flags of Corinth and Corcyra had once flown, there Syracusan ships now sailed. In 384 B.C. the fleet attacked the coast of Etruria, and plundered the temple of Leucothea in Pyrgi, the harbour city of Caere. A base was also established on the southern tip of Corsica (Porto Vecchio?).

The achievement of Dionysius appears all the greater if one bears in mind that it was attained in the face of opposition from a large part of the Syracusan citizenry and from the Greek cities of southern Italy. And so, when war broke out again between Dionysius and Carthage in 382 B.C., these communities joined the Carthaginian side. This renewed conflict ended in a considerable reverse for the western Greeks.[121] They lost Selinus, Heraclea Minoa and Thermae to the Carthaginians, so that the Himeras and Halycus rivers formed the frontier between the Greek and Carthaginian territory on the island. Even the last Carthaginian war, precipitated by Dionysius in 368 B.C., did nothing to alter the situation.[122] Only the intervention of Rome, more than a century later, was to create new conditions in Sicily.

The recognition which his great achievements in war and peace should have won him was, during his life time, denied Dionysius, the saviour of the Sicilian Greeks. The elder Scipio rightly placed him alongside the great figure of Agathocles (Polyb. XV 35). His rule, however, showed the more offensive features of *tyrannis*. Dionysius surrounded himself with a bodyguard, created an efficient secret police, and however much he strove to realise in his personal life the ideal of irreproachable conduct[123] – it was not empty gesture when he named his daughters *Arete* (Goodness), *Dikaiosyne* (Justice) and *Sophrosyne* (Wisdom)—in the eyes of the Greeks his rule remained what it in reality was, a tyranny with the stain of illegitimacy. His achievements as a statesman too, great as they were, ultimately remained incomplete. He did not succeed in completely forcing Carthage out of Sicily. Thus the hostility between Hellenes and Carthaginians continued, and the successor of Dionysius took it over as a heritage.

Dionysius II (367-357 B.C.) possessed neither the talents of his father nor his sense of duty.[124] At first he was under the influence of Dion, the brother-in-law of the elder Dionysius, but later, after Dion's banishment (366 B.C.), he turned to Philistus. On Dion's advice Plato was invited to the Syracusan court, in the hope of realising here in the young, malleable ruler the ideal state on earth. The utopia, however, came to grief on the hard rocks of reality. The banished Dion returned to Syracuse in 357 B.C. with Carthaginian help, and (as *strategos* with plenary powers) restored order. Dionysius II, who had at first asserted himself on the fortress of Ortygia, fled to Locri in southern Italy. Dion himself, neither a statesman nor a strong personality, followed the path of tyranny and in 354 B.C. fell victim to a mercenary conspiracy. The death of Dion was followed by new disorders, until Dionysius II in 347 B.C. succeeded in gaining control of power in Syracuse for the second time. In other respects Sicily presented a bleak picture of Hellenic disunity and impotence in those days. In many cities local tyrannies mushroomed out of the ground, as in Leontini, Catana, Tauromenium, Messana and Agyrium. It seemed as if chaos itself were about to break out and spread over the Sicilian Hellenes after the elimination of Syracusan hegemony. In Syracuse the leaders of the party which had been banished by Dionysius II turned for help to the mother-city of Corinth. The latter sent Timoleon as arbiter to Syracuse (344 B.C.). Landing at Tauromenium, he was greeted by the tyrant Andromachus as the saviour of Sicily. Even Dionysius II went over to him, renouncing the *tyrannis*. In Syracuse Hicetas, the opponent of the tyrant, attempted to assert himself with Carthaginian support, but in vain. The brilliant victory of Timoleon over the Carthaginians at the Crimisus River (342 B.C.) restored the political supremacy of the Hellenes throughout the island. In the peace of 339 B.C. the old frontiers at the Himeras and Halycus rivers were confirmed. After the victory over the foreign enemy Timoleon turned to the task of restoring order to the internal conditions in the Greek cities in Sicily. All tyrannies were abolished, with the single exception of Andromachus of Tauromenium, who had once welcomed Timoleon on his arrival. In the historian Timaeus, the son of Andromachus, Timoleon found the enthusiastic herald of his exploits in Sicily.

In 337 B.C. the work of restoring internal peace had been concluded, for the Greek communities had united to form a federal union headed by Syracuse. Timoleon, on his own volition, abdicated his extraordinary position, the plenipotentiary *strategia* with which he had been invested, and spent the remainder of his days in Syracuse. He is one of the most peculiar personalities of his time, one of the last great figures which the Greeks of the fourth century produced, a man who devoted his entire energies to his ideals and who gave Sicily the foreign and domestic peace which the island so urgently needed.

In southern Italy no comparable saviour emerged for the Greeks. Tarentum, finding itself harassed by the Lucanians, turned to Sparta for help. From 342 B.C. onwards the Spartan king Archidamus III found himself on Italian soil with a mercenary army, and he was killed at Mandonium in a battle against the allied Lucanians and Messapians (338 B.C.). It was an open question how long the Greeks in southern Italy could still assert themselves against the awakening world of Italic peoples.

10
PHILIP II OF MACEDONIA

THE BEGINNING OF A NEW ERA

The definitive break between the old and the new era, of crucial importance in the life of the Greek people, falls in the middle of the fourth century B.C. Only a few years after the Greek states had sunk into political impotence at the battle of Mantineia (362 B.C.) there arose on the edge of the Greek world that power which was destined to take over the political hegemony of the Hellenes: the Macedonian monarchy under Philip II (359-336 B.C.). In the middle of the fourth century the great change among the Hellenes became evident in all spheres—in politics, economics and no less in cultural life. While the old fades away in death, new beginnings become everywhere apparent. On the whole the picture which Greece presents in this transitional period is heterogeneous and full of paradox: in place of order we find political chaos in Hellas, and in the place of intelligent planning, in many instances, arbitrary action. The life of the polis comes increasingly under the shadow of the evolution of business, and it is very significant that a number of leading Attic politicians, for instance, Eubulus and Lycurgus, emerged as experts in finance. There is unmistakably a certain increase in maritime trade, a development reflected in a large number of commercial treaties and in the Greek banking system.

The social antagonism between the rich and the poor, which was becoming more and more accentuated, was a principal factor contributing to the political decline of the Greek states. While the wealthy were burdened with the unpleasant *leitourgiai*—civic duties—(*choregia, trierarchia*)—the poorer elements in the population rapidly accustomed themselves to nourishment from public funds. The highest duties of the state now included the responsibility of ensuring the livelihood of its citizens, a factor which did not remain without repercussions in foreign politics.[1] Radicals saw salvation in a completely new land division. The social unrest which shook Greece to its very foundations is revealed in a wave of banishments and confiscations.[2] Hellas produced a fluctuating proletariat from the many homeless exiles, who fomented new anarchic movements. Recruits from these masses made up the mercenary armies, which became an essential characteristic of the fourth century. While the citizen now regarded military service only as a burden, the mercenaries pursued it as a professional trade. There were no longer any military events in Hellas nor even in Asia in which Greek mercenaries did not take a decisive part.

Not only the wars of the fifth century but also above all the great plague, which broke out in 430 B.C., had cut greatly into the population in various parts of Greece. The first half of the fourth century B.C. was also predominantly a time of war.[3] Despite this there was an increasing population growth, a phenomenon also to be traced to the fewer war casualties: warfare had become more humane. Thus it turns out that in the fourth century Greece in increasing measure suffered from a relative overpopulation and an acute need for land. Time and again plans for colonisation were activated. Xenophon wanted to found a new home at the Black Sea for his companions in arms, and Isocrates dreamed of all Asia Minor up to the Taurus as a sphere for Greek colonisation (*Philippos* 120). The Greek people urgently required a region which could absorb their surplus energies if they were not to suffer domestic ruin in internecine war.

The internal situation was in fact not unfavourable for an expansion of the Hellenes, especially towards the east. The Persian empire, for instance, found itself in a state of progressive decline in the first half of the fourth century. Satrap revolts, continuing for years, broke out in Asia Minor, and as a result local native dynasties emerged. With the aid of mercenaries which they had acquired these dynasts practically made themselves independent of the Great King. Thus the one time so powerful Achaemenid empire had become a "colossus with feet of clay." Moreover, its economic importance was no longer what it had been under the rulers of the fifth century, for the rich grainland of Egypt had succeeded in asserting its independence throughout the first half of the fourth century, from 404/3 to 342 B.C.

The limits of the potential of Hellas remained, inherent within the system of small states which was the antithesis to the international colonisation plans of the Greek patriots. There was nevertheless, even in the first half of this century, no lack of attempts to find new means of overcoming the impotence of the countless individual states. The union of the Arcadians and the Aetolians into federal states was a first step along a road which other Greek tribes took in the period after Alexander the Great. Thus at the end of the history of a free Hellas there was a return to those political conditions which had once formed the point of departure during the acquisition of land (v.s.p. 4 f.). It appeared as if the tribal state, in the form of a federal state, was to become the symbol of a new epoch in the political life of Hellas. Through the idea of the general panhellenic peace, not only the widespread longing for peace but also the common identity of the Greeks was kept alive.

This panhellenic idea finds its journalistic form of expression primarily in the orations of Isocrates. Contemporary rhetoric shows a predilection for examples taken from panhellenic mythology: when Isocrates compared the Macedonian king Philip II with the Hellenic shepherd of the people, Agamemnon, the implications were readily understood in Hellas. It is a mistake when modern historical research in part considerably underestimates the psychological preparation of panhellenic thinking ensuing from contemporary rhetoric.[4]

The new era made itself known above all in an accentuated cult of the great personalities, who were often elevated to the status of god incarnate. Divine honours had already been ascribed to the Spartan Lysander. Clearchus the tyrant of Heracleia Pontica (he was murdered in 352 B.C., after a rule of twelve years) declared himself to be the son of Zeus and demanded corresponding honours from his subjects—a true forerunner of Macedonian Alexander. And the example of the Syracusan physician Menecrates, who adopted the practice of signing his letters as "Menecrates Zeus," demonstrates how thin the line between the divine and the mortal had become in that period, even though in this instance the pathological must not be overlooked.

Greek intellectual life too found new forms. While the Hellenic poets and artists, actors and singers had gone on pilgrimages to the courts of the great Sicilian tyrants, now the splendour of the royal courts all round Hellas drew them into their orbit. At the end of the fifth century Euripides and Zeuxis the painter sojourned in the Macedonian capital of Pella, both as guests of King Archilaus (413-399 B.C.). Upon the death of Maussollus, the dynast of Caria (353 B.C.), his sister Artemisia invited tenders among Greek men of letters to write his obituary. Far away from the Greek motherland, in Heracleia on the Pontic Sea, the tyrant Clearchus created the first public library. At this time Athens still continued to be the undisputed centre of Hellenic learning, although many new centres of culture, which received their light from that great centre of learning, arose on the periphery of the Greek world. The *Academy* of Plato sent its disciples into all the world, and they turned up from Sicily to the Greek cities of the Pontus. Greek learning and Greek thought permeated the vast dimensions of the inhabited world. Even at the Persian court and in the Persian empire Greek scholars and artists, and above all physicians, were welcome guests.

The new era is reflected in a new attitude of the individual to the world around. Antiphon the tragedian, living at the court of Dionysius I in Syracuse, characterised this new emotional attitude to life with the telling statement: "whatever is too powerful by nature, this we subdue by art." Dionysius, moreover, was the first ruler to enlist the scientific research of learned men for practical inventions. Two names stand at the head of a new epoch, indeed actually at the beginning of Greek, and thereby of western, science: Eudoxus of Cnidus († c. 355 B.C.) and Aristotle of Stageira (384-322 B.C.), both coming from Plato's school, the *Academy*. As mathematician and astronomer, physician and philosopher, geographer and physicist, as well as practical politician, all combined in one person, Eudoxus attained great fame. Thus the famous "elements" of Euclid's geometry (c. 300 B.C.) rest essentially on his researches, and in astronomy his doctrine of the spheres acquired general recognition. In his extensive universality Eudoxus was a genuine forerunner of the great Hellenistic scholars and it is scarcely fortuitous that his *Phainomena*, which were rendered into verse by Aratus at the injunction of the Macedonian king Antigonus Gonatas, became a favourite book of the educated reading public in the Hellenistic period.

When Eudoxus died Aristotle was still sitting at the feet of Plato. After the death of the latter (347 B.C.) Aristotle took his departure from Athens. During his life of wandering he visited the court of the dynast Hermias of Atarneus in Asia Minor; Mytilene, Assos, and the Macedonian capital of Pella and little Miëza were all places of sojourn. Not until 335/4 B.C. did he return to Athens, where he founded his school, the *Peripatos*. Here, surrounded by a great many students, he became the centre of Hellenic intellectual life. It was Aristotle who consummated the decisive change from speculation to empirical research. By including his students as systematic collaborators in collecting and screening subject matter, Aristotle became the originator of western science, the creator of the idea of scientific organisation. In almost all fields of human knowledge—it was only from medicine that he, the son of a physician, remained aloof—with the aid of his students he collected a vast amount of material and in part at least discussed it in comprehensive treatises. The collecting of 158 political constitutions—of these the *Constitution of Athens*, which was discovered on a papyrus less than a hundred years ago, has become the most famous—a complete list of victors at the Pythian games, the records of dramatic performances in Athens, research in the field of physics, meteorology, zoology and botany—these and many other writings testify to the scope and energy of his ceaselessly inquiring, organising and critical mind. By including epistemological and ethical problems in his research Aristotle united in his person, when at the height of his powers, almost the entire world of knowledge. Thus he stands as a genuine universal scholar at the inception of western learning, which after his death disintegrated into a large number of separate branches. It was not until almost two millennia later that a similarly supereminent universal figure arose in the West, in the person of Leibniz.

The rapid growth of Hellenic intellectual life in the fourth century B.C. is reflected in the emergence of a new ideal in learning. The statement of Isocrates (*Panegyr.* 50), that only he is a Hellene who has taken part in Attic education, betrays a cosmopolitan outlook. Underlying this statement is the conviction of the absolute superiority of Attic education. Thus the concept of "Hellenic" did not become broader. With the shedding of national ties it became an ideal of learning. Together with the latter the idea of "humanity" was born, but this too was embodied only in certain individuals and not in the many. At the same time the concept of classical arose. From 386 B.C. onwards it became the practice in Athens to have an older play performed with the new tragedies; in 339 B.C. the same demand was also realised with regard to comedies.

About the middle of the fourth century the contours of a new development began to take shape—a gradually emerging but progressively expanding assimilation of Hellenism with the cultural world of the East. On the heels of the Greek merchants who settled in the coastal cities of Phoenicia, on Cyprus and in Egypt, Greek culture also entered the countries of ancient civilisation.[5] No less in Cyprus than in the peripheral zone of Asia Minor an unusual Graeco-Eastern hybrid culture emerged. In

Egypt the tomb of Petosiris at Hermopolis Magna shows unmistakable evidence of Greek influence,[6] and the discovery of the oldest Greek papyrus containing the *Persae* of Timotheus in Abusir-el-Meleq is evidence for the existence of Greek literature in the Egyptian countryside at least as early as the last third of the fourth century. The emergence of a new type of city in Carian Halicarnassus anticipates later developments. Through the union of six neighbouring communities the native dynast Maussollus considerably enlarged the city and then adorned it with magnificent buildings designed by Greek architects. The Maussolleum which his sister-wife Artemisia erected was regarded as one of the seven wonders of the world. With its royal fortress and a military and commercial harbour, and the design of its princely palace, Halicarnassus appears as a precursor of Ptolemaic Alexandria. The time was ripe for a widespread acceptance of Greek culture and Greek civilisation in the vast regions of the East.[7] Seen in this light, Alexander appears as the great executor of the universal law which in its basic features is foreshadowed as early as 360/59 B.C. It is really the middle of the fourth century that saw the beginning of this new period, an era which Johann Gustav Droysen called the period of Hellenism.

Droysen, following primarily the approach of Joh. Drusius (*Adnotationes ad Nov. Test.*, 1612) and J. G. Herder, used the term "Hellenism"—contrary to the meaning of the Greek term[8]—for an epoch in which he saw the principal feature to be the fusing of Greek and Oriental elements.[9] It must be admitted that this terminology is not very fortunate. Apart from the fact that a linguistic misconception generated the idea of this epoch, its characterisation as the fusion of Hellenic and oriental cultures appears to be too much of a generalisation. At all events it is in itself insufficient to account for the complex historical phenomena of the period.[10] Therefore, although Droysen on the basis of his fusion theory logically at first also included in the term "Hellenism" the entire pagan-Greek period of the Roman Empire,[11] the chronological interpretation of the term is preferable, though in the version which begins the epoch not with Alexander but a generation earlier, that is, about 360 B.C. At all events the time of Augustus forms the terminus of Hellenism. Apart from the fact that this interpretation has long since been generally adopted by scholars, it is completely justified in that the period from 360 to 30 B.C. possesses a specific character of its own, whether we consider the art, literature, philosophy or political life of the Greeks.

MACEDONIA BEFORE PHILIP II

With King Philip the Macedonian people take over the helm in the history of antiquity, and with Alexander's conquest of the Persian empire they attain world dominion. A young people and without a history, they owe their rise to the great ruler Philip II. It was he who accustomed this people of shepherds and peasants to urban life, who subdued the belligerent barbarian neighbours, opened up access to the sea and the country itself to Hellenic culture. For the Greeks, however, the Macedonians always remained *barbaroi*, never recognised by the Hellenes as cultural equals, not even when on the crest of world dominion.

In the cultural gulf between Greeks and Macedonians the question of Macedonian national origin was never of more than secondary importance in antiquity. For modern scholars the evidence from names[12]—there is not a single sentence extant from the language of the Old Macedonians—tilts the scales in favour of the view that includes the Macedonians among the Greeks. The names of places and months and most personal names are wholly Greek. The theory, therefore, advocated by the student of Indo-European comparative linguistics, P. Kretschmer,[13] that the Macedonians were of Graeco-Illyrian hybrid stock, is not to be regarded as very probable. So the majority of modern historians, admittedly with the noteworthy exception of Julius Kaerst,[14] have argued correctly for the Hellenic origin of the Macedonians. They should be included in the group of North-West Greek tribes.[15] This does not, however, discount the statement of Thucydides (II 99) that the Macedonians were related to the Epirotes from possibly having an element of truth. From the point of view of history it is more important that a century of isolation in the country which bears their name moulded the Macedonians into a distinctive social, political and anthropological unit, developing their essential features from within, and without domination by Hellenic influence. Thus the character of the Macedonian people had long since been moulded when, in the great power struggle between Athens and Philip, the hate-filled orations of Demosthenes repeatedly emphasised the divisive features between Greeks and Macedonians.

The earlier development of the Macedonian people is shrouded in all but total darkness. In the earliest times Thraco-Phrygian tribes settled in the land, and crossed over to Asia Minor in the course of the great Aegean migration at the end of the second millennium. The southern districts of Elimeia and Orestis on the upper reaches of the Haliacmon at the Thessalian border formed the germ-cell of the Macedonian state. Pushing northwards from here the Macedonians took possession of Eordaea, and turned Aegae, perched on a lofty, dominating cliff, into the centre of the state. The first Macedonian king was Perdiccas I, who probably lived in the early part of the seventh century (?), but it is only with his fifth successor, Amyntas I, towards the end of the sixth century, that historical research finds itself on solid footing. It was Amyntas I who offered Hippias a place of asylum in Anthemus when he was banished from Athens.[16] At that time the Macedonians had already crossed the Axius and were on the verge of advancing eastwards into the area of the lower reaches of the Strymon.

The outstanding figure in Macedonian history in the fifth century is Alexander I, to whom posterity had given the epithet "Philhellene" (he ruled from about 495 to 450/49 B.C.).[17] This king strove to bring his people into union with Hellenic culture. By tracing the Macedonian royal house of the Argeads back to Peloponnesian Argos he favoured the pseudo-genealogical inclinations of the Greeks, and his reward was admittance to the Olympian games. The royal house of Macedonia thereby became recognised as legitimately Hellenic. The first, most important, step towards closer ties between Macedonians and Greeks had been taken. It was Alexander I who carried out a decisive military reform, placing the masses of peasants as infantry under the honourable name of *Pezhetairoi*, the "Companions on Foot," alongside the military nobility on horse, the "Companions" of the king.[18]

While Alexander's successor Perdiccas II[19] understood how to navigate the country skilfully through the Archidamian War, his son Archelaus I (414/13-400/399 B.C.) gave Macedonia for the first time a major rôle in the mainstream of Greek political life. In the view of Thucydides[20] Archelaus contributed more to the internal development of the royal kingdom and the organisation of the Macedonian army than his eight predecessors combined. He regained control of Pydna, established the relationship of the kingship with the princes of Elimeia and Orestis in Upper Macedonia on a new foundation, and finally, and in this a precursor of Philip II, intervened more vigorously in the internal affairs of Thessaly (400/399 B.C.?).[21] By a number of important economic measures, road construction, and by joining Macedonia to the Persian system of coinage he considerably increased the prosperity of the country. The division of Lower Macedonia into districts, which rested on a military basis, is perhaps to be traced back to this ruler. The particular characteristic of this division makes the districts around an urban centre form the cantons from which the military forces were drawn for the individual regiments.[22]

Great was the fame of the king as protector of the Muses! At his court in Pella resided a number of eminent artists, including the epic poet Choerilus, the musician Timotheus of Miletus and the tragedian Agathon. It was at Pella that Euripides wrote his *Bacchae* and extolled the royal patron in the play *Archelaus*, in which he also portrayed the founding of Macedonia.[23] The royal palace was adorned with the paintings of Zeuxis, and an invitation was extended to Socrates urging him to come to Pella. After the death of Archelaus—like his grandfather, Alexander Philhellene, he was murdered—the country sank into confusion and throne disputes, which filled the first decades of the fourth century. On her eastern flank the Chalcidian League, powerful and expanding on all fronts, emerged as a dangerous rival to Macedonia, while in the west the Illyrians[24] became more and more active and through their incursions repeatedly created serious trouble for Macedonia. It was Spartan intervention in the north in the years between 382 and 379 B.C. (v.s.p. 167) that liberated the Macedonian king Amyntas III (393-370 B.C.) from the extremely critical situation in which he found himself in the wake of Chalcidian expansion.[25]

The Macedonian state, which appears in the official documents under the term "the Macedonians," was a typically feudal state with a monarchical head. The immediate rule of the Macedonian kings extended only over Lower Macedonia, that is, over the coastal districts of Pieria, Emathia and Mygdonia. In contrast to this, Upper Macedonia, that district from which the Macedonians launched forth on their conquests, namely Lyncestis, Orestis and Tymphaea, had its own princes, who only submitted to the king as sovereign when he decided to make his power felt.

Although it extended to the sea in Pieria, Macedonia was a typical inland state, for the most important harbours—Pydna and Methone—were in the hands of the Hellenes.[26] The economy of the country was distinctly agrarian, with forests of particular importance to the country's economy. A number of commercial treaties attest that Macedonia, as a producer of shipbuilding timber, pitch and tar, was a welcome partner and ally among the Greeks.

The patriarchal kingship of the Macedonians, a military monarchy, reaches back to the early period of Macedonian history. As late as the time of Alexander the Great, he, as king, was military commander, priest and judge of his people. In time of war the king sought his chief support in the nobility, whose members, as the Myrmidons of Achilles, bear the distinguished name of *Hetairoi* ("Companions") of the king. The institution of the Macedonian military assembly,[27] composed of those capable of bearing arms, also stems from early times. It confirmed the new king by acclamation, no doubt also intervened in regulating the succession in case of disturbances, and ultimately formed the final court for cases of high treason. The military assembly, even though in altered form, long survived in the Hellenistic states.

Franz Hampl has developed his own theories about the relationship of the Macedonian king to his people.[28] According to Hampl the king occupied a position over and above the state; he alone determined foreign policy, while the state as such did not participate in this field. The territorial acquisitions of the Macedonian kings must therefore (according to Hampl) be regarded as the personal property of the king. Hampl's hypothesis, however, which rests on *inter alia* the alleged omission of the king's title in treaties with foreign powers, lacks foundation; it is conclusively refuted by epigraphical evidence.[29] In Macedonia the king represented the people, while the inner unity and uniformity of the kingship and the people gave the great rulers Philip and Alexander the support and strength they required to establish Macedonian world sovereignty.[30]

THE FIRST YEARS OF PHILIP'S REIGN (359-354 B.C.)

Philip of Macedonia was the youngest son of Amyntas III and Eurydice. The years from fifteen to seventeen, important for his personal development, he had spent as a hostage in Thebes.[31] After returning home in 365 B.C. his brother, King Perdiccas III (365-359 B.C.), conferred a fiefdom upon him.[32] Shortly before this Perdiccas had succeeded in ridding himself of Ptolemy of Alorus, who as guardian of the young king and husband of Eurydice had retained power for four years (369/8-365 B.C.).[33] The most important achievement of Perdiccas III, however, was his gaining of the important harbour city Amphipolis. A Macedonian garrison secured it against attack from the Athenian fleet.[34] The event marked a turning point of far-reaching consequences in Macedonian policy. It is true that Amphipolis was not a member of the second Attic Maritime League, but the Peace Congress at Sparta (371 B.C.) had confirmed the city as a possession of Athens. During the reign of Perdiccas the Attic statesman Callistratus came to Macedonia, after his banishment (361/0 B.C.), and carried out a tariff reorganisation.[35] Everything that had been achieved was, however, jeopardised by a threat to the country from the west. In a fierce battle against the Illyrians in 359 B.C. the young king, Perdiccas III, fell with thousands of his soldiers.[36] The Paeonians and Thracians too now regarded this as an opportunity to ravage the unfortunate country by incursions from north and east. In the land itself pretenders to the throne emerged on the scene: Pausanias, the earlier opponent of Ptolemy of Alorus, Archelaus (a son of Amyntas III from his first marriage with Gygaea), Argaeus—these all strove for the crown, and the saying, "woe to the country whose king is a child!" appeared to have become fearfully true.

In the general confusion Philip, as guardian of his young nephew Amyntas, the son of Perdiccas III, seized the reins of government. By cunning and by force he eliminated his foreign and domestic foes. By formally renouncing control of Amphipolis, Philip succeeded in winning Athens, who had favoured the pretender Argaeus, over to his side. An official peace treaty[37] was concluded, in accordance with which Athens agreed to hand Pydna over to Philip in exchange for Amphipolis, the former standing in treaty relationship with Athens. In a great battle in Upper Macedonia Philip routed the Illyrians (358 B.C.). They were forced to abandon their eastern border district at Lake Ochrida to Macedonia, and thereby secured Macedonia's exposed western frontier.[38] The independence of the Upper Macedonian vassal principalities of Elimeia and Orestis now also came to an end.[39] An important step had thereby been taken on the road towards a Macedonian centralised state.

Philip genuinely merited the royal title which the military assembly conferred on him.[40] After Alexander I Philhellene and Archelaus he became the great organiser of the Macedonian army. Through continuous training and in many campaigns he welded the Macedonian national army into a flexible instrument for power. The neighbouring states had nothing comparable to range against it. The core was now formed by the phalanx of the *Pezhetairoi*. No opponent far and wide could match the onslaught of the solid wall of tree-length spears. The horse, composed of the *Hetairoi* and regularly posted on the wings, was moulded into a decisive striking force in battle. With this reorganisation of the army Philip turned the feudal state into the Macedonian national state—a completely new element in the history of the Western world.

The rise of the Macedonian monarchy ran parallel with the decline of Athens and her Maritime League. The suggestions for reform which Isocrates made in his *Areiopagitikos* (357 B.C.) fell on deaf ears[41]—Isocrates recommended the restoration of the constitution inherited from the fathers and the re-establishment of the Areopagus, that is, an expressly oligarchic-conservative programme modelled on the constitution of Theramenes. Within the framework of the Maritime League a separate confederation came into existence in the same year, on the initiative of the Carian dynast Maussollus. Chios, Rhodes, Byzantium and later Cos also joined. These states seceded from Athens, who in spite of desperate exertion could not bring them to heel again.[42] When Athens complied with a peace in 355 B.C.,[43] the one time so proud second Maritime League was nothing more than a shadow of its former greatness, the number of members had deteriorated to a third and the League itself was restricted to the Cyclades, Euboea, the islands in the northern Aegean and a number of cities on the Thracian coast.[44]

The weakness of Athens became Philip's opportunity. To begin with he threw himself against Amphipolis, under the pretext of subduing the city in the interests of Athens. Amphipolis was taken by storm (357 B.C.) and from then on, as an important point on the lower reaches of the Strymon, became an integral part of the Macedonian monarchy as long as it existed.[45] In order to regain possession of Amphipolis Athens was to hand over Pydna. Since Athens was not in a position to do so, Philip forthwith also took possession of this city (winter 357/6 B.C.).[46] Ever quick to retort, he countered Athens' declaration of war by concluding an alliance with the Chalcidians, the most important power in the north apart from Macedonia.[47] In doing so he gave the Chalcidian League not only the district of Anthemus but also the territory of Potidaea, conquered and destroyed by him in 356 B.C. and whose Attic cleruchs he abruptly sent home.

The plea for help from the Thasian colony of Crenides on the northern slopes of Mount Pangaeum, with its rich deposits in gold, gave Philip the desired opportunity to move towards the east. He despatched new colonists to Crenides, whereupon the place was refounded under the name of Philippi.[48] Here for the first time in Greek history a human name appeared as the designation for a city. Philippi stands at the head of a development which extends to the cities of Alexander and to those founded by his successors. The rich yields from the gold mines of Pangaeum—allegedly more than 1000 talents annually[49]—established Philip's policy on a new foundation. Macedonian gold soon began to compete with Persian, and it did not take long before the *Philippeios* forced the *Daric* out of circulation among the Greeks.[50] When the princes Cetriporis of Thrace, Lyppeius of Paeonia and Grabus of Illyria united into a northern league directed against Philip, which Athens incidentally also joined (356 B.C.),[51] the political and strategic superiority of Macedonia became drastically evident. The king of Paeonia became a vassal of Philip, the Illyrians were defeated by Parmenion, Philip's most important assistant, and in the east the Macedonians reached the Nestus, which subsequently formed the border against free Thrace. When Philip finally captured the Greek city of Methone in the summer of 354 B.C.,[52] Macedonia stood at the great crossroads of her policy. She had burst her fetters and had been successful all along the line in gaining access to the sea. The first phase of Macedonian expansion had ended.

GREECE AND MACEDONIA IN THE TIME OF THE THIRD SACRED WAR (356-346 B.C.)

While Philip was beleaguering Methone, central Greece was ablaze. The conflict between the Phocians on the one hand and the Boeotians and

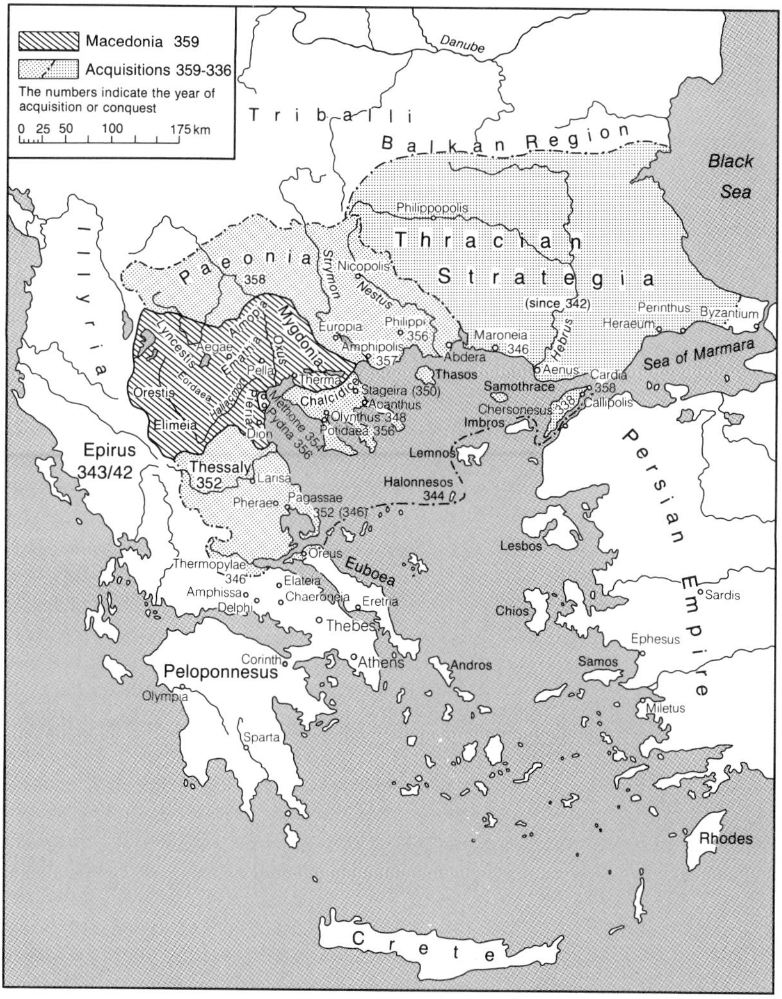

MAP VI The Rise of Macedonia under Philip II (359-336 B.C.)

Thessalians on the other had kindled the flames of a dangerous war which spread increasingly to other parts of Hellas. The question at issue was the hegemony of the Pylaean-Delphic Amphictyony and therefore the leadership of the whole of central Greece. The Amphictyony, to which twelve Greek tribes belonged—each member had two votes in the Council of the *Amphictyones*—was under the determining influence of Thebes. Thebes faced a rival in the Phocians, who had refused to render military service to Boeotia at Mantineia. And the Phocians had not forgotten that the Delphic sanctuary had been theirs up to the Second Sacred War (448 B.C.). In the spring of 356 B.C.[53] the Boeotians brought accusations against a number of leading Phocians, allegedly for sacrilegious crimes at Delphi, and gained their condemnation. The Phocians warded off this thrust by taking possession of Delphi, both the town and the sacred precinct (summer 356 B.C.), after they had protected themselves by an alliance with Sparta. Under the leadership of Philomelus, who as *strategos* with plenary powers[54] took over the helm of the state, they defeated the Locrians of Amphissa who were attempting to prevent the Phocians from taking possession of Delphi. In consequence Delphi was completely delivered up to the Phocians. As the *Naopoioi* lists show,[55] the Phocians and their allies now controlled the sacred precinct. When Philomelus amassed a mercenary army of 10,000 troops with the aid of the rich temple treasures, the minute country of Phocis became the strongest military power in the whole of Greece. After Philomelus fell in a battle at Neon against the Boeotians (autumn 354 B.C.), Onomarchus replaced him as leader of the country. He struck coins in his own name[56] and in other respects conducted himself as political leader of Phocis. Under him it reached the climax of its power—a strange phenomenon, which only proves how impotent the former leading states of Greece had become.

Spilling over into Thessaly, the Sacred War spread to wider areas. While the tyrants of Pherae favoured Onomarchus, the Aleuadae sent an appeal for help to King Philip. Success at first eluded the Macedonian king. Onomarchus twice defeated the Macedonians and asserted his position in Thessaly (summer 353 B.C.).[57] His victories were the more significant in view of the fact that Boeotia, the other antagonist, was greatly weakened. The Boeotian League had plunged into the chaos of the satrap revolts in Asia Minor with a sizeable force under the command of Pammenes, and notably as the ally of the insurgent Artabazus. In consequence of the autocratic conduct of Pammenes, the expedition ended in total failure for the Boeotians.[58]

The struggle for power in Greece was decided in the spring of 352 B.C. on Thessalian soil. Philip emerged victorious over Onomarchus on the Crocus field (probably the plain at the Gulf of Pagasae).[59] The Phocian tyrant lay dead on the battlefield, while the Macedonian king had no less than 3000 prisoners hurled as temple robbers into the sea—a terrifying punishment which had a profound effect upon the Greeks. Even after his victory Philip still remained the elected federal commander of the Thessalian militia.[60] Macedonian ships were stationed at Pagasae, a number of Thessalian communities received garrisons, and from Thessalian tariffs Philip received a substantial increase in revenues. Thus Macedonia established its supremacy over the important country of Thessaly. Philip's attempt, however, to intervene in central Greece failed. The king found the passes at Thermopylae blocked by a large force of the Phocian confederates—among these no less than 5000 Athenian hoplites—and wisely turned back (summer 352 B.C.).

As great as the successes of Philip were in the south, the greatest and most difficult tasks had not as yet been carried out. More than anything else the relationship between Macedonia and the Chalcidian League, whose dominions were a foreign body within the Macedonian kingdom, called for a fundamental revision. No one could doubt that in the struggle between the king and the League there was more involved than clearing up frontier incidents. It was much more the question of the degree to which the Hellenic polis was prepared to submit to the will of a monarch without at the same time essentially renouncing its distinctive character. The question of Macedonian expansion towards the east also remained unresolved. The Nestus did not constitute a natural frontier for an emerging power such as Macedonia—the goal must be the straits between Europe and Asia. But anyone active at the Hellespont must inevitably come into conflict with Athens and Persia. Whatever the plans of Philip may have included, he could no longer do without an efficient navy, and this could only be furnished by the Greeks, and above all by the Athenians. Philip must therefore have turned his eyes towards Greece already.

But it is unlikely that Philip's ultimate goal was to establish an empire embracing the entire backbone of the Balkan peninsula.[61] Be that as it may, it is at all events certain that the Macedonian deferred the conflict with Greece, chiefly with Athens, as long as possible. In Hellas he initially pursued a policy of peaceful penetration, without being very scrupulous in the means he employed. The fact that he was ultimately forced into open conflict is to be attributed primarily to the implacable opposition of Demosthenes. The great orator mobilised the energies of the Hellenes against the monarch from the north, above all by shifting the theatre in the power struggle to the ideological sphere and in this way decisively accentuating the conflict, and in fact even making the differences between Philip and the Greeks unbridgeable.

In Athens the longing for a stable peace had understandably gained ground in the wake of the unfortunate sequel to the Confederate War (357-355 B.C.). Xenophon's *Poroi* bear witness to this increasing tendency. At the helm of Athenian policy was the clear-headed Eubulus, a man free of all extravagances and who had been president of the treasury of the *Theoricon* since 354 B.C., the key position in the administration of the state. It was as follower of Eubulus that Demosthenes rose to prominence.[62] His maiden speeches, especially those on the *Symmoriai*,[63] are closely linked with the policy of Eubulus.[64] At first Demosthenes had no reason to oppose Philip. A decisive change in his position is first noticeable in the *First Philippic*, delivered in 349 B.C. But even this oration is still a far cry from the Macedonian-hater that Demosthenes was to become after the Peace of Philocrates (346 B.C.). His support of Peloponnesian Megalopolis[65] demonstrates how inaccurately the Athenian orator judged the general power situation in Greece as late as 352 B.C. Through an act of intervention in the Peloponnesus Demosthenes hoped to bind the confederates to Athens, especially Argos, Messenia and Sicyon, who had been left in the lurch by the Boeotians. Eubulus immediately recognised this political utopia for what it was, a difference of opinion which resulted in an open break between the two statesmen.

The weather side of Athens, however, lay not towards the south but the north, at the straits. Although Athens had concluded an alliance with the regional prince Cersobleptes,[66] she nevertheless openly favoured his rival Amadocus and the Hellenic cities of Perinthus and Byzantium, because a certain balance of power lay in her interests. In 352 B.C. Chares re-established Attic sovereignty in the Thracian Chersonese: Sestos was taken by storm and the peninsula settled with Attic cleruchs. At this juncture Philip's Thracian campaign (end of 352 B.C.?),[67] which within a short time took him as far as Heraeum Teichus, created a completely new situation. The Thracian regional princes Amadocus and Cersobleptes hastened to conclude a treaty with the Macedonian. Although illness prevented Philip from taking full advantage of his successes, the Thracian territory between the Nestus and the Black Sea (apart from the Chersonese) was subsequently a Macedonian sphere of influence.

A further severe blow was inflicted on Athens by Philip's move against the Chalcidian League. Stageira was captured and destroyed in 350 B.C.[68] In addition, Philip's privateers roamed the sea and inflicted significant damage on Attic trade. In a great political speech, the *First Philippic*, Demosthenes openly took issue with Philip for the first time, in the spring of 349 B.C. The refusal of the Olynthians to respect Philip's demand to release his half-brothers Arrhidaeus and Menelaus, who had fled thither,[69] finally gave the king the long-sought after pretext he required to attack the Chalcidians. He marched into their territory and subdued one city after another. Athens now—at the eleventh hour—concluded a formal treaty with the Chalcidians[70] and sent auxiliary expeditions under Chares and Charidemus to the north.[71] They were, however, totally ineffectual. Philip was more successful, and what is more, he brought about the defection of the entire island of Euboea from Athens (except for Carystus).[72] In 348 B.C. Olynthus fell into Philip's hands. It would seem that the city was totally destroyed and Macedonian cleruchs settled in its territory.[73] The remaining Chalcidian cities lost their autonomy and were incorporated into the Macedonian state. A large number of Philip's "Companions" were settled in the newly won dominions. The importance of gaining Chalcidice for Macedonia can scarcely be overestimated, and not only in a material sense. The incorporating of an ancient centre of Hellenic culture into the Macedonian state created new conditions for an encounter between Greeks and Macedonians, and there can be no question that it was the Macedonians who were the beneficiaries.

Despite his repeatedly insisting, though entirely in vain, on an active prosecution of the war in the north by Athens, Demosthenes was not to blame for Philip's great successes. He now propounded the view that Athens required peace above all else, in order to consolidate and regenerate her energies for the crucial struggle which he foresaw against King Philip. Thus an Athenian embassy, sent to the court of the Macedonian king in Pella at the beginning of 346 B.C., included not only Aeschines and Philocrates but Demosthenes himself.[74] Through his captivating amiability Philip succeeded in winning Aeschines over entirely to his side. From then onwards Aeschines appears as a convinced opponent of Demosthenes. Philip insisted that a peace be concluded on the basis of the current possessions, that is, it was to include Macedonia and her allies on the one side and Athens and her allies on the other, but apart from Phocis and Halus (Thessaly). When a counter embassy from Macedonia under Antipater and Parmenion journeyed to Athens, the *Ekklesia*, after heated debate, accepted the terms in principle but demanded that the provision (discreditable to Athens) dealing with Phocis and Halus be deleted.[75] Before a ratification of the terms by Philip could be attained the versatile statesman conducted a lightning campaign into Thrace where he forced the annexation of Cersobleptes to Macedonia as a new vassal prince.[76] After this Philip took an oath on the peace in Pella in the form in which the Athenian Assembly had demanded.[77] For Demosthenes and his friends the Peace of 346 B.C. ("Peace of Philocrates") was only a breathing space. Immediately after the return of the embassy to Athens Demosthenes took issue with his fellow envoys, accusing them of pro-Macedonian sympathies whereby they had allegedly damaged Athenian interests.

While the Phocians ignored Athens' demand that they withdraw from Delphi, Philip with resolute hand took control of Thermopylae. Since the temple treasures were declining, further resistance on the part of the Phocians proved futile. After a treaty of capitulation had been concluded, which ensured the mercenaries free withdrawal, Macedonian garrisons moved into the fortified places of the country.[78] Philip had thereby gained a solid foothold in the heart of Greece (July 346 B.C.).

In the Amphictyonic Council the two votes of the Phocian temple robbers were conferred upon Philip personally.[79] Now at last the Macedonian king was accepted into the community of Greeks. From now on the representatives of Philip sat alongside the envoys of the Greek tribes—this too a proclamation of a new epoch which was to receive its character from the great individual personalities. The reorganisation of the Delphic Amphictyony was crowned by a general peace, although initially it applied only to the members of the Amphictyony.[80]

Philip's successes did not permit the Macedonian enemies in Athens, headed by Demosthenes, to sleep. On the initiative of the great orator Athens refused to send sacred envoys to Delphi for the celebration of the Pythian games—a stroke which was a match for any snub Philip might conceive.[81] When the Macedonian king proceeded to make an inquiry in Athens, Demosthenes once more mounted the stage, with his "Peace Oration": let the Athenians become well aware how bitter it will be should they have to bow to foreign tyranny! Aeschines and the other Macedonian sympathisers had no easy task in dealing with the inflamed passions of the multitudes. They, however, found an excellent ally in the aged orator and pamphleteer Isocrates. He had just released his tract *Philippos* to the entire world, urging Philip as benefactor[82] of the Hellenes to bring an end to the discord in Hellas and enlist the energies of the Greeks in a national war against Persia! For untold thousands who were consuming each other in an internecine war within the narrow limits of the homeland there would be a vast region and new undreamed of possibilities for economic development in Asia Minor. What Isocrates wrote was read from one end of the Hellenic world to the other (K. J. Beloch), and the fact that public opinion in Greece gradually became more and more receptive to Philip's plans is to be credited to this great orator and political theoretician. The future belonged to those ideas which he never tired of propagating in his pamphlets, even though their realisation assumed a different form from that which Isocrates had envisaged. While Isocrates became the herald of Attic culture in the world of his day, Demosthenes continued to believe with growing fanaticism in the great political mission of his native Athens. Her glorious past conferred upon her the right, indeed even placed her under obligation, to conduct herself in a way worthy of her ancestors and to take over the hegemony of Hellas which was her exclusive charge. A ruinous conflict runs through the life of Demosthenes —an unbridgeable gulf between willing and doing. In good faith the passionate patriot overestimated the moral and material energies of Athens, and it was on this miscalculation that he suffered shipwreck.

FROM THE PEACE OF PHILOCRATES TO THE DEATH OF PHILIP II (346-336 B.C.)

King Philip no less than Demosthenes welcomed the Peace of Philocrates. It was only now that the sovereign could carry out the organisation of the country which had become so urgent, and the securing of his frontiers against the belligerent neighbours to the west.[83] In hard-fought battles, which in the Drilon Valley took Philip close to the Adriatic, he routed the Illyrians under Pleuratus (344 B.C.). Exposing himself to considerable danger, as he was wont to do, the king sustained a spear wound on this campaign.[84] The Illyrian enterprise was followed by a reorganisation of conditions in Thessaly. When the establishment of a *dekadarchia*, that is, the institution of a *koinon* of ten communities, had proved impractical (344 B.C.), it was replaced by a *tetrarchia*, a "quadripartite rulership" (342 B.C.). From now on Thessaly appears divided into four districts with each having a town as a regional capital; at the head of these subdivisions were *tetrarchai*, "district commissioners," appointed under Philip's approval.[85] It is uncertain whether the Macedonian king was elected as archon of Thessaly in 334 B.C. or not until two years later[86]—he deliberately avoided the title of *tagos*. For almost a century and a half, up to the battle of Cynoscephalae (197 B.C.), Thessaly remained in closest association with Macedonia and her royal house, the Argeads and the Antigonids—and this with almost no interruption.

Demosthenes too did not remain idle. After an "agitation tour" in the Peloponnesus (344 B.C.), with the intent of stirring up feeling against Macedonia, he launched forth on a new course in 344/3 B.C. He now proceeded to play the Persian card.[87] Athens, however, shrank from concluding a formal alliance with the Great King, Artaxerxes III. To the displeasure of the great orator a Persian embassy had to return without having accomplished its purpose.

Under the leadership of Python of Byzantium a Macedonian embassy arrived in Athens simultaneously with the Persian envoys. Philip wanted to eliminate a few "flaws" from the Peace of Philocrates and above all to prevail upon the Athenians to acknowledge the conditions of the Peace in all details.[88] If Athens had complied with these demands, it would have involved the formal renunciation of Amphipolis, Pydna and Potidaea—no wonder, therefore, that the Athenians could not be induced to concur. In the oscillating quarrel a pamphlet by Speusippus, the head of the Platonic Academy, took up the issue in favour of the Macedonian king, attempting to justify Philip's claims to Amphipolis and Chalcidice with the favourite mythological arguments. Negotiations between Athens and Philip dragged on until the summer of 342 B.C. without any settlement being reached.

The Macedonian king meanwhile established his political policy on a new footing by means of a treaty of friendship and non-aggression with Persia (summer 343 B.C.). It would seem that the astute statesman gained a free hand in Thrace by pledging not to intervene in Asia Minor.[89] The most important result was, however, that Philip now had his back free, so that the decisive struggle for the hegemony of Greece could begin. By intervening in the Epirote throne disputes in favour of the young Molossian Alexander,[90] Philip further secured his western flank (winter 343/2 B.C.), a most important move with respect to Thessaly.

In the winter of 343/2 B.C. Egypt saw an event of international historical significance, which cast its shadow as far as Greece and Macedonia. The Persian king Artaxerxes III Ochus marched into the old coronation city of Memphis as victor over Egypt. The sixty-year rebellion of the country was suppressed, and Egypt once more became part of the Achaemenid empire.[91]

The altered situation in world affairs brought about by the resurgence of the Persian empire at first induced Philip to give way to Athens. He put forward the proposal to expand the Peace of Philocrates into a general peace (spring 342 B.C.). The Athenians, however, were already in a state of war hysteria (this is evident from the oration of Hegesippus *On Halonnesus* and from the *Third Philippic* of Demosthenes), and therefore rejected Philip's proposal. When Philip thereupon turned his attention to Thrace (June 342 B.C.) there could be no doubt about the approaching decision in the struggle for the hegemony of Hellas. This time Philip made a clean sweep of things in Thrace. He forced the regional princes Cersobleptes and Teres to submit, and organised the entire country between the Nestus and the Black Sea into a Macedonian "province." The king also appointed a *strategos* as governor, manifestly on the model of the Persian satrapies.[92] Military colonies consolidated the conquest. With its wealth in population and natural resources Thrace meant an important expansion of Macedonian power. It was no wonder that the king now set his aims higher. In 342 B.C. he concluded a treaty with the dynast Hermias of Atarneus.[93] It was expected, and not without justification, that Philip would launch an offensive across the straits into Asia, and Hermias was prepared to pave the way for the king by offering him his principality as a bridgehead in Aeolis.[94] It is admittedly difficult to determine with certainty what Philip was actually aiming at in terms of Persia. That the internal weakness of the Achaemenid empire did not escape the keen eye of the Macedonian—despite the important success in Egypt—must be regarded as certain. It is, however, improbable that he would have taken up the struggle before the situation in Greece had been settled.

Philip's advance against the straits caused his opponents in Athens to become active. In an inflammatory war oration, the *Third Philippic*, Demosthenes demanded an increase in mobilisation and propaganda on the part of the neutrals. A defensive alliance was concluded with Byzantium and Abydus. To the disappointment of Demosthenes, however, Chios and Rhodes refused to show their colours. Persia too could be induced even less to assume a pro-Athenian attitude, as Hermias of Atarneus had meanwhile been treacherously taken into Persian custody by Mentor[95] and the acute danger of a Macedonian invasion eliminated.

Philip's attack on Perinthus set the machinery in motion. The city, which now lay within the Macedonian sphere of power, was to be forced into subjection. Philip's aggression enabled Demosthenes to score a surprising success in foreign policy: a Hellenic league under Athenian leadership came into existence.[96] The rôle of this alliance, essentially defensive in character, was to repel the impending Macedonian assault. Boeotia, however, the most important land power in Greece, remained aloof from the alliance. Despite the fact that Philip employed new siege tactics, he was unable to take Perinthus.[97] The city obtained aid from Byzantium and from Arsites, the Persian satrap of the territory across the Hellespont. Although Philip in marching through the Thracian Chersonese became guilty of violating the sovereignty of Athenian territory—he actually admitted it in his correspondence to Athens[98]—the latter did not as yet move to the attack. It was not until the king brought the conflict to a head by capturing a large Athenian grain fleet at the Bosporus[99] that the stele bearing the Treaty of Philocrates was knocked over in Athens. The war which Demosthenes wanted had begun (autumn 340 B.C.).

The great naval superiority of his opponents caused Philip no little concern. His own fleet found itself confined within the Black Sea and thus cut off from operations. Athenian ships under the command of Chares blocked the southern entrance to the Bosporus. When the Macedonians launched a blockade of Byzantium which was also without success, the king made a surprising decision, to conduct a campaign against the Scythians on the Lower Danube, with a view to restoring the self-confidence of his army (339 B.C.). Philip returned as victor. On the return march, however, he once more sustained a serious wound in a battle against the Triballi.[100]

In order to drive a wedge between Athens and Boeotia Philip made use of the Delphic Amphictyony, and especially the Locrians of Amphissa. They intended to submit a complaint in the Amphictyony accusing Athens of hanging up two undedicated golden shields in the temple during the Third Sacred War. The diplomatic adroitness of Demosthenes, however, succeeded in frustrating the designs of the king. Athens, who anticipated the complaint with a counter accusation against Amphissa,[101] resolutely refused to take part in the federal execution now resolved upon against the Locrians. The declaration of the Sacred War against Amphissa finally gave Philip the desired opportunity to intervene in central Greece. At the regular autumn Pythian festival (October/November 339 B.C.) the members of the Amphictyony conferred the command of the war upon the Macedonian king. Philip now acted with lightning speed. Marching via Heracleia he penetrated into the Cephisus Valley, and after circumventing the bulwark of Nicaea (at Thermopylae), held by the Boeotians, took control of Elateia.[102] When news reached Athens in November 339 B.C. that Philip was already south of Thermopylae, the effect was like a thunderbolt and even created a state of panic. Demosthenes has impressively portrayed the effect of this news in his *De Corona* (169 ff.). It was not Athens, however, but Thebes who was immediately most threatened. Although the Macedonians still continued to entertain the hope that they might draw the Boeotians over to their side, the latter had already anticipated the decision by occupying Nicaea. Only now, when it was all but too late, a formal alliance was concluded between Athens and Boeotia. The Boeotians were invested with the chief command of the land forces, while the naval command was to alternate between both. Athens pledged to assume two thirds of the war expenditures. The oncoming winter brought military operations on both sides almost to a complete standstill. But in place of this both parties carried on diplomatic warfare the more energetically.

While Philip's promises to the East Locrians and the Phocians fell on good ground, Demosthenes brought into existence, on the basis of the Hellenic alliance (v.s.p. 197), a large coalition which extended over the whole of central Greece, parts of the Peloponnesus (Megara, Achaea) and many islands. As a tribute of well merited recognition the great patriot was presented with the golden garland.

The first blow of the Macedonian lion struck the mercenaries under Chares and Proxenus at Amphissa. They were taken by a surprise attack and devastatingly defeated. The confederates found themselves gradually forced out of Phocis. Delphi and even the important city of Naupactus fell into Macedonian hands. In order to prevent their being outflanked, the Greeks withdrew to Chaeroneia. Here, more for political than for strategic reasons, they took up their position for the decisive battle against the Macedonian king. It was no longer possible to maintain the unity of the confederates by a purely defensive strategy. The Greeks needed a

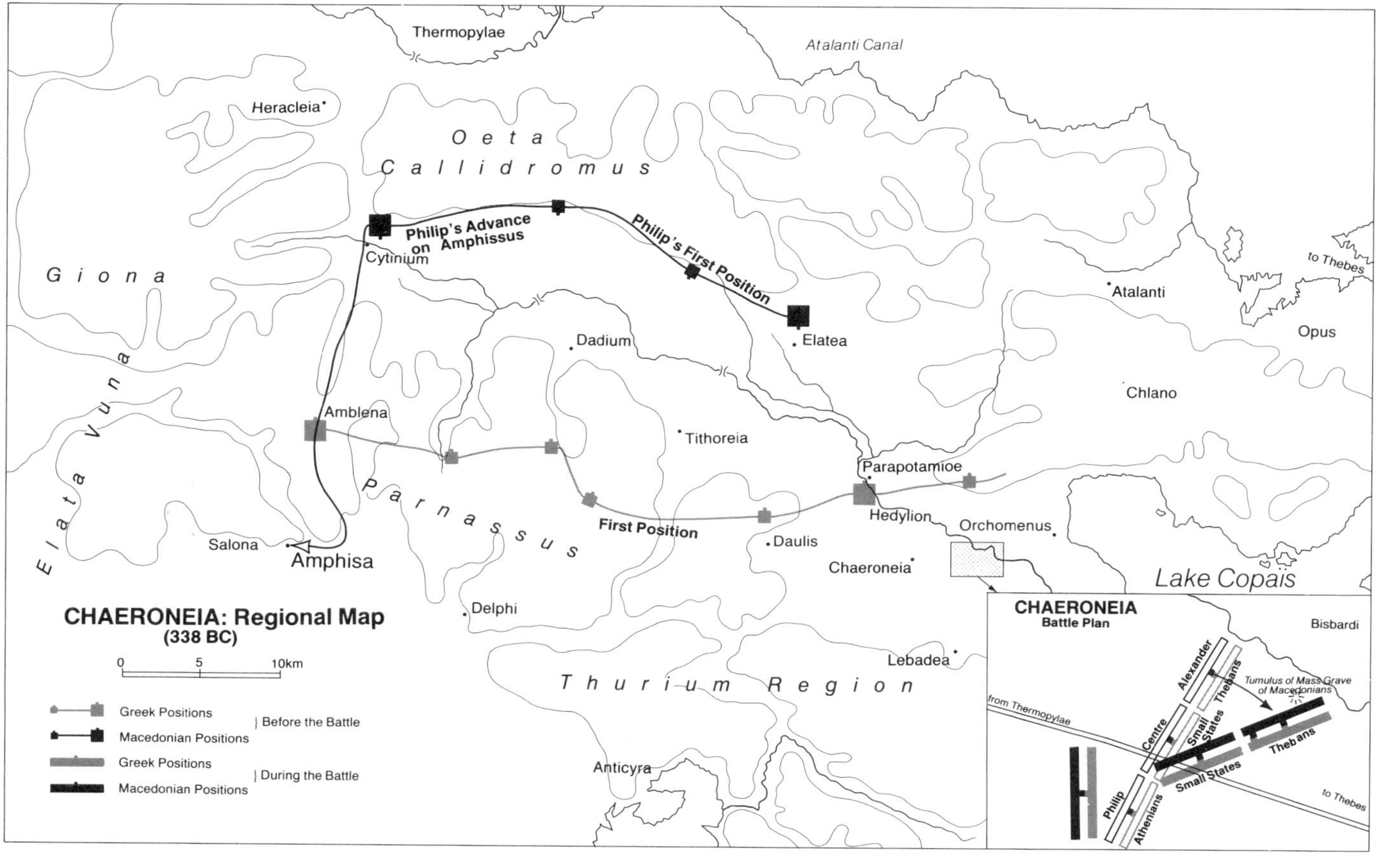

Thermopylae
Atalanti Canal
Heracleia
Oeta
Callidromus
Philip's Advance on Amphissus
Philip's First Position
Cytinium
Giona
to Thebes
Atalanti
Opus
Elatea
Dadium
Chlano
Elata Vuna
Amblena
Tithoreia
Parapotamioe
Parnassus
Hedylion
First Position
Orchomenus
Daulis
Salona
Amphisa
Chaeroneia
Lake Copais
Delphi
CHAERONEIA: Regional Map
(338 BC)
0
5
10km
Lebadea
Thurium Region
Greek Positions
Macedonian Positions
Before the Battle
Greek Positions
Macedonian Positions
During the Battle
Anticyra
CHAERONEIA
Battle Plan
Bisbardi
Alexander
Thebans
Tumulus of Mass Grave of Macedonians
from Thermopylae
Centre
Small States
Thebans
Small States
Philip
Athenians
to Thebes

decisive military victory. Thus the battle which decided the fate of Hellas was fought in the Cephisus Valley at Chaeroneia (2 August 338 B.C.).[103] The position of the confederates was not unfavourably chosen. The right wing faced towards the Cephisus, while the left was south of the city of Chaeroneia. In this way they blocked not only the roads leading through the Cephisus Valley to Coroneia and Thebes, but also the road over the Cerata Pass towards Lebadeia. Both armies had a strength of approximately 30,000. Philip directed his main thrust against the Boeotians, on the right wing of the Greeks, while with his own right he carried out a feigned retreat. Alexander, son of Philip, pierced the Boeotian phalanx. The Theban Sacred Band remained man for man on the battlefield, and when the Greek centre was shattered and the left wing circumvented, complete disorder ensued, with the individual contingents seeking to rescue themselves by taking flight.

The victory of the Macedonians symbolised the rise of the inherently stable monarchy over the loose coalition of Greek city-states. The Greeks, remembering their great past, believed themselves to be fighting for the honour and greatness of Hellas. In reality, however, they were trusting in a forlorn hope, an error illuminated by heroic splendour. Ulrich Wilcken has rightly stated[104] that for such a famous city as Athens it was a law of honour and self-respect not to give up the leading position in Greece to a stronger power without a struggle. Thus Chaeroneia reconciles us to certain weaknesses and inadequacies which plagued the Greek polis, weaknesses from which not even a Demosthenes was free. Although the struggle between monarchy and polis still continues throughout the succeeding chapters of Greek history, at Chaeroneia the decision fell in favour of the former, and opened a new chapter in Hellenic history.

Philip refrained from persecuting the Greeks. He knew how to use moderation in victory and kept his greater aim in view—the unification of the Hellenes under the hegemony of Macedonia for conducting the Persian War. Thebes alone felt the full weight of the victor's blow. A Macedonian garrison took possession of the Cadmeia, and the opponents of Philip were either banished or executed. Theban supremacy in central Greece had come to an end once and for all.[105] In Athens, after initial impetuosity, reason prevailed. The extended hand of Philip was accepted and a peace concluded with him, a peace particularly supported by Phocion, Aeschines and Demades. Demosthenes had left Athens by ship. The city itself was treated with easy terms. The integrity of her territory remained guaranteed, except for the Thracian Chersonese, which Philip took into his possession. The Maritime League was dissolved.[106] Despite the conclusion of a formal treaty with Macedonia, opinion in Athens was divided. The highly esteemed Isocrates had urged Philip, in his *Panathenaikos* (published in 339 B.C.), to assume the hegemony of Hellas, alluding in it to the position of Agamemnon as panhellenic leader. In his third letter, written immediately after Chaeroneia,[107] the orator and political writer, now almost one hundred years old, put forward the view that it was now in the power of the Macedonian king to compel the Greeks to follow him. "When you have subdued the Persian," wrote Isocrates to Philip, "nothing else remains for you but to become a god." The Hellenistic idea of divine kingship is here foreshadowed.[108] Still the old spirit had not yet been quenched in Athens. In the winter of 338 B.C., no one else but Demosthenes was permitted to deliver the "Funeral Oration" over the fallen, the *Epitaphios*. The speech rings with the bitter complaint over the lost greatness of the city and of the flower of the Athenian youth who fell at Chaeroneia. It is the "funeral dirge on the lost freedom of Hellas" (F. R. Wüst).

Philip's march across the Isthmus into the Peloponnesus restored order in Greece. While Corinth and Megara concluded peace at once, the Spartans refused to submit to the will of the Macedonians. They lost in particular Cynuria and found themselves confined to the small district between Parnon and Taygetus. The neighbouring states such as Megalopolis, Tegea, Messenia and Argos were the prime beneficiaries.[109] Sparta was consequently removed from the ranks of the leading powers in Greece, conclusively and for all time.

At Philip's summons ambassadors from all Greek poleis (with the exception of the resentful Sparta) made their way to Corinth in the winter of 338 B.C. The aim of the "constituent assembly" was to create a large panhellenic alliance, such as had not been seen hitherto in this form in Hellas. The concluding of a "general peace" shows a conscious link with the ideas of the fourth century.[110] This "general peace" was of utmost importance for the public life of Greece. It forbade all quarrels between Greek states, as well as the altering of existing constitutions by means of force. The treaty also made provisions for free navigation, and privateering was outlawed. The principle of non-interference in the autonomy of the various states was in practice admittedly violated on occasion. Thus the presence of Macedonian garrisons on the Cadmeia of Thebes, on Acrocorinth and in Chalcis on Euboea was justified on grounds of concern for public security.

The individual members participated in the League organ, the so-called *Synhedrion*, in the form of a representative system according to their respective importance. The larger states, especially the state leagues, had single votes, while the smaller ones, combined with others, had block votes. Philip himself had no seat in the *Synhedrion*. Taken legally, the Hellenic Alliance was an association in which "the followers of a hegemonial power united together into a league in the form of a federation" (Triepel).

A second act was to join to the "general peace" the establishing of a *symmachia*, a mutual defensive-offensive alliance between Philip and the united Hellenes of the Panhellenic League, concluded in perpetuity.[111] The life-long hegemony of Philip over the Greeks was an integral part of the *Symmachia*.

The system organised on these lines had turned out completely contrary to the dream of Isocrates. Philip's genius welded the alliance into an instrument which considerably increased the military strength of Macedonia. It was no wonder that the Greeks themselves were little enthused over the reorganisation. Far from seeing in the alliance of Corinth the realisation of a political ideal, they regarded the presence of Macedonian garrisons as nothing less than a sign of bondage. All who, like the Greeks, looked upon the autonomous polis as an unshakeable ideal must certainly have felt the intervention of a superior power from outside Hellas as bitter coercion. Wherever the Macedonian king issued orders, there the Greek polis was forced to maintain silence. Even settling the many internal tensions by means of quarrelling was taken away from the Greeks.

The "constituent session" of the Corinthian Congress was followed in the spring of 337 B.C. by a "war session." In this session Philip submitted the proposal for conducting the Persian War. By astutely propagating the idea of retaliation—the Greeks were to demand requital for the temples once destroyed by Xerxes—the Macedonian proclaimed the conflict of arms as a war of revenge.[112] For the prosecution of the great struggle thus planned the *Synhedrion* conferred special plenary powers on the Macedonian king, finding expression in the title bestowed on Philip as "plenipotentiary *strategos*."[113]

With this the die had been cast. A strong Macedonian vanguard under the command of Parmenion and Attalus crossed the Hellespont in the following year (336 B.C.). The attack of the Macedonians struck the Persian empire at a most critical moment. The energetic king Artaxerxes III had died in 338 B.C. After his younger son Arses had occupied the throne of the Achaemenidae as a figurehead for two years, Darius III Codomannus, from a collateral line of the royal house, seized the throne with the help of the eunuch Bagoas. The Macedonian peril, however, passed the Persian empire by. In the summer of 336 B.C., at the wedding celebrations of the daughter of the Macedonian king, Cleopatra, to King Alexander of Epirus, the dagger of an assassin eliminated Philip. The motives for the assassination were alleged to have been of a personal nature, but the evidence supports the view that a plot between Philip's wife Olympias[114] and prominent Macedonians from the aristocracy lay at the root of the matter.[115]

The death of Philip II in Aegae in 336 B.C. snuffed out the life of a man who in every respect was an integrated person. He was indisputably one of the greatest rulers of antiquity, and there is much truth in the statement of Theopompus (frg. 27), that Europe (namely the Balkan Peninsula) had never produced as mighty a man as Philip the son of Amyntas. Brilliant as an organiser and reckless as a general—he had repeatedly endangered himself and sustained a great many wounds—a competent and astute diplomat who never hesitated to attain by devious means what he could not otherwise achieve, the Macedonian king towers far above all his contemporaries. No one was a match for him in politics; the moving complaints and the angry outbursts by Greek statesmen at Philip's perfidiousness speak an unequivocal language. But where there is much light there is also much darkness. In his personal life Philip had not learned to exercise moderation—he resembled Caesar in the fascinating charm he exerted over people within his sphere, and not least over women. His impetuosity ultimately precipitated his ruin. His achievement, to wit the consolidating of the Balkan Peninsula, including Hellas, under Macedonian sovereignty, is a feat comparable to the labours of Heracles; no king after Philip ever achieved the like again. Thus Philip laid the foundations for the work of his great son Alexander and created the conditions for a new epoch in the history of civilisation.

11
ALEXANDER THE GREAT

ALEXANDER IN GREECE

Of great importance in the life of Alexander was the spiritual heritage from his mother Olympias, a princess from the royal house of the Aeacidae in Epirus. Unless all the evidence is deceptive, Alexander (born 356 B.C.) owed to his mother that daemonic and unfathomable nature which was repeatedly such a source of trouble to himself and to those associated with him. As far as we can tell the young prince was entirely under the influence of his mother and never enjoyed a close relationship with his father. Alexander's instructors were the orator Anaximenes of Lampsacus and, after 343/2 B.C., Aristotle of Stageira.[1] It was primarily Aristotle who introduced the eager prince to the Greeks and their culture, especially to Homer, for whose *Iliad* the prince had a rapturous enthusiasm which stimulated him to an excessive cult of Achilles. Even when the paths of teacher and pupil separated after three years the crown prince never forgot the deep impression which the supereminent mind of this Hellene had made upon him. He later stated that to Philip he owed the fact that he was alive, but to Aristotle the knowledge of the good life. And it was to King Alexander that his one time instructor later addressed the works *Alexander or For the Colonists* and *On Monarchy*.

While taking part in Philip's campaign against Byzantium (340/39 B.C.) as "regent of the kingdom" the crown prince, at the age of sixteen, founded his first Alexander city—Alexandropolis in Thrace.[2] Philip's marriage to Cleopatra widened the rift between father and son even more. Alexander departed from Macedonia with his mother, and the subsequent reconciliation mediated by the Corinthian Demaratus was never more than superficial, although the prince was in no way implicated in Philip's assassination (336 B.C.). Alexander's accession to the throne—the work of Philip's generals, Antipater in particular—was followed by a genuine Balkan massacre of whatever enemies of the new king and members of the royal family could constitute a danger to Alexander. Amyntas, Philip's nephew (v.s.p. 189), and the Lyncestians, closely associated with him, and Attalus, Cleopatra's uncle, who at the time was in command of the Macedonian vanguard in Asia—they were all eliminated and Cleopatra abandoned to the revenge of Olympias.[3]

Hellas was in a state of ferment. Thebes, Aetolia and the Peloponnesus constituted centres of unrest, while the Macedonian garrison was driven out of Ambracia. In Athens too, upon whom all eyes were now focussed, the anti-Macedonian movement of Demosthenes and Lycurgus steadily gained ground. The remodelling of the Attic military system—from now on every citizen upon reaching *ephebeia* had to complete a two-year period of military service—was ultimately directed against Macedonia. They had not gotten over Chaeroneia. The recently discovered Attic *tyrannis* law of Eucrates[4] appears to indicate that in 337/6 B.C. there was a genuine fear in Athens, perhaps not without reason, that a *tyrannis* (supported by the Macedonian king?) would be established. Alexander meanwhile secured the most important Greek positions of power. Thessaly conferred upon him the honour of general of the federal army and the Delphic Amphictyony recognised him as *hegemon* of Hellas. In accordance with the conditions of the defensive-offensive alliance concluded between Philip and the Greeks a regular renewal of the Corinthian League was not required. Thus at Corinth Alexander was only invested with a special command of the Persian War which had now become his aim (336 B.C.).[5]

Alexander's first campaign against the peoples beyond the northern frontier of Macedonia, the Thracians, Triballi and Getae, vividly demonstrates the unusual energy, vitality and the strategic and tactical competence of the king.[6] Without his trusted advisers Parmenion and Antipater, Alexander advanced beyond Philippopolis, either over the Shipka Pass or over the Kajan or Koja Balkan Pass, and from there probably via Silistria to the Lower Danube. After crossing the river, a venture which Arrian explains in terms of Alexander's "yearning,"[7] the king offered sacrifice to Zeus, Heracles and the river god, on the north bank of the stream, as he was to do later on the Indus at the other end of the world. After victorious battles in Albania against the Illyrian prince Cleitus, Alexander received news of open rebellion in Greece. The rumour had spread that the king was dead, and that the Persian gold which Darius III Codomannus poured out lavishly provided the final straw in accentuating the hostility of the Greeks towards the Macedonians. In Thebes the Macedonian garrison on the Cadmeia found itself beleaguered and the Athenians, Arcadians and Eleans more or less openly joined the Thebans. After forced marches which brought Alexander in thirteen days from the Illyrian border (Pelium) to Onchestus in Boeotia, the king appeared in central Greece, defeated the Thebans and forced his way into the city (autumn 335 B.C.). He left the punishment of the Thebans to the *Synhedrion* of the allies—the total destruction of the city,[8] the selling of the population into slavery, and the fugitive Thebans wandering about the whole of Hellas to be treated as having no rights. This was nothing short of a Draconian sentence, and it made a deep impression on the Greeks. Athens assumed an unworthy attitude. She congratulated the king not only on his safe return from the Balkan campaign but even on putting down the Theban rebellion. Alexander knew how to exercise moderation. Of his open opponents in Athens only Charidemus had to give way. There can hardly be any doubt that Alexander's attitude was determined by the admiration for Attic culture which Aristotle had instilled in him. In addition, political considerations prompted him to avoid anything that would engender unnecessary bitterness among the Greeks. But above all else, the longer he considered them the more he became preoccupied with his plans for the Persian War, the execution of which his father had entrusted to him.

In Asia Minor the situation for the Macedonian advance guard under Parmenion, later under Calas, had become precarious. The Rhodian mercenary commander Memnon, whom the Great King had invested with the chief military command in the western coastal provinces of the empire, demonstrated that he was a *strategos* of notable qualities. Ultimately only the bridgeheads of Rhoeteum and Abydus remained in Macedonian hands.

From the point of view of finance, Alexander's position before he set out on his Asian campaign was anything but bright. The Macedonian state treasury was empty. The king is said to have had only seventy talents for the maintenance of his army and was consequently forced to take out a "war loan" of 200 talents.[9] His confidence in victory was not, however, dampened by financial difficulties. Alexander was convinced that he would find all the necessary provisions for his army in the land of the Great King. The best sources[10] give the number of Alexander's Macedonian army at 30,000 foot and 5000 horse, with the core formed by Philip's seasoned veterans, the *Pezhetairoi* of the phalanx. All in all the Corinthian League furnished only 7000 foot, 600 horse and 160 triremes—a disproportionately small contingent,[11] a number to a certain extent explicable in terms of Alexander's limited confidence in the trustworthiness of the Hellenes. Since the Hellenic fleet was more than doubly inferior to Persian naval strength,[12] Alexander would be compelled to force a decision in the war on land. At least one fourth of the Macedonian forces remained at home in order to protect the country from Illyrian and Thracian invasions and to give Macedonian rule in Greece the backbone it needed. Antipater, the trusted paladin of Philip, was placed in command of the 12,000 foot and 1500 horse. He was appointed governor of Macedonia and simultaneously acted as representative of Alexander, the *hegemon* of the Panhellenic League, with the title "*strategos* of Europe."[13]

FROM THE HELLESPONT TO PERSEPOLIS (334-331 B.C.)

Darius III Codomannus, who stemmed from a collateral line of the Achaemenid royal house and in 336 B.C. acceded to the throne of Cyrus and Darius the Great, was a ruler of entirely average stamp, without the striking talents and qualities which the administration of the vast empire required during that period of crisis.[14] The Achaemenid empire, imposing in its enormous dimensions, its inexhaustible man power and its fabulous material resources, had for two centuries united the nations of the Near and Middle East into a large political community of one common destiny. It was now no more than a "colossus with feet of clay."[15] The central government of Persia did not succeed in fusing the many peoples and tribes together into an organic whole. Nor could it control the strong feudalistic and centrifugal tendencies of the satraps, who had large territories, especially in the regions of Asia Minor. A large number of Persian subjects were, however, content to live under the patriarchal rule of the Great King and consequently had no cause to look to a foreign power for their "freedom." On the Iranian plateau, moreover, there was still a great deal of ancient vitality in the Persian tribe which had at one time brought the world to its knees. The anaesthetising effect of the old oriental cultures, especially that of ancient Babylon, which had corrupted the Iranian ruling class in the west of the empire, had not as yet penetrated into these remoter areas. The wars of the two preceding generations had not affected the core of the empire, and the expedition of the Ten Thousand had been merely episodic. Was it any wonder that the Persians could be lulled into complete security and into disregard for the news of mobilisation in Macedonia and Greece? Europe was far away and court flunkies in Susa made certain that unpleasant news did not reach the ears of the ruler of the world. In addition, the Great King possessed in the highly trained Greek mercenaries troops with which any opponent in the world could be confronted. The Egyptian expedition of Artaxerxes III had proven this only a few years hitherto.

Alexander completed his preparations in the spring of 334 B.C. Unimpeded by the Persians and supported by the Hellenic fleet, the army crossed from Sestos to Abydus. On reaching the Asiatic mainland the king hurled his spear ashore from his ship and thus symbolically took possession of this new continent.[16] While visiting the hallowed site of Ilium, where he had a wreath placed on the tomb of Achilles and a conciliatory sacrifice offered for Priam, the romantic tendencies of the youthful ruler, the new Achilles, came to the surface.[17]

On the Persian side the war in Asia Minor was at first the concern of the satraps, who were directly affected by it. No commander-in-chief had been appointed. The advice of the astute Memnon of Rhodes, to lure Alexander into the vast interior, leaving evacuated areas in a state of desolation while at the same time launching an offensive in the Macedonian rear and bringing the war into Greece, was counsel that faded away unheeded. The Persian satraps (Spithridates of Lydia, Arsites, satrap of Hellespontic Phrygia, Atizyes of Greater Phrygia and Mithrobuzanes of Cappadocia) did not want to abandon their territories to the conqueror without a struggle and consequently assembled their forces at Zeleia (south of the Propontis = Sea of Marmara). In the encounter at the Granicus River (c. May/June 334 B.C.) the Persians were decisively defeated, not only by reason of the verve of Alexander but also by their own tactical blunders. The Greek mercenaries fighting on the Persian side were, apart from a few survivors, completely crushed.[18]

From the booty Alexander sent 300 panoplies to Athens and dedicated them to Athena. The inscription, which does not mention the royal title nor the Macedonians, reads: "Alexander son of Philip and the Hellenes (except the Spartans), taken from the *barbaroi* who dwell in Asia."[19] Alexander, the panhellenic federal commander, emphasised the common Greek character of the Persian War. The real situation was, however, very

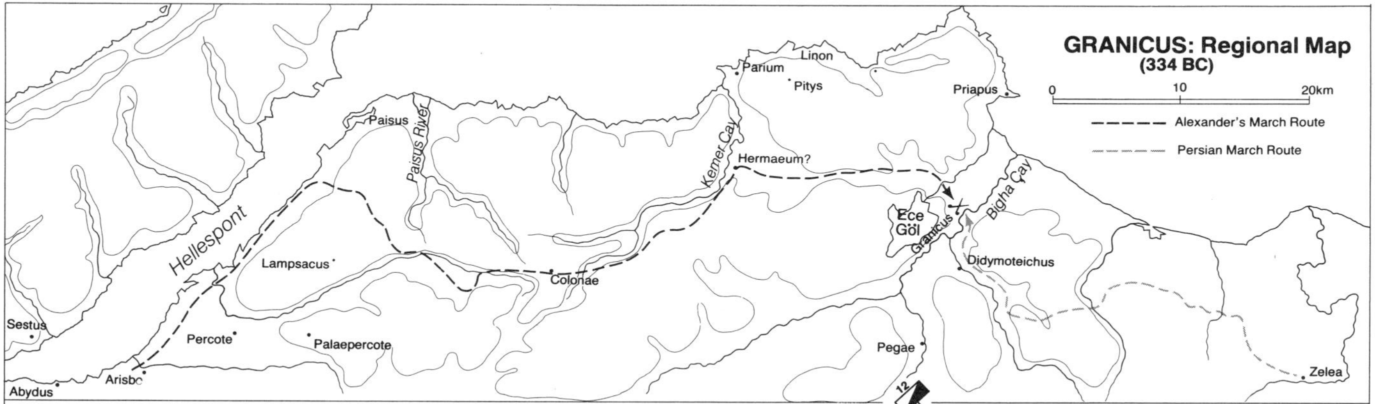
GRANICUS: Regional Map
(334 BC)
0 10 20km
Alexander's March Route
Persian March Route
Hellespont
Sestus
Abydus
Arisbe
Percote
Lampsacus
Palaepercote
Paisus
Paisus River
Colonae
Kemer Çay
Hermaeum?
Parium
Linon
Pitys
Priapus
Ece Göl
Granicus
Bigha Çay
Didymoteichus
Pegae
Zelea

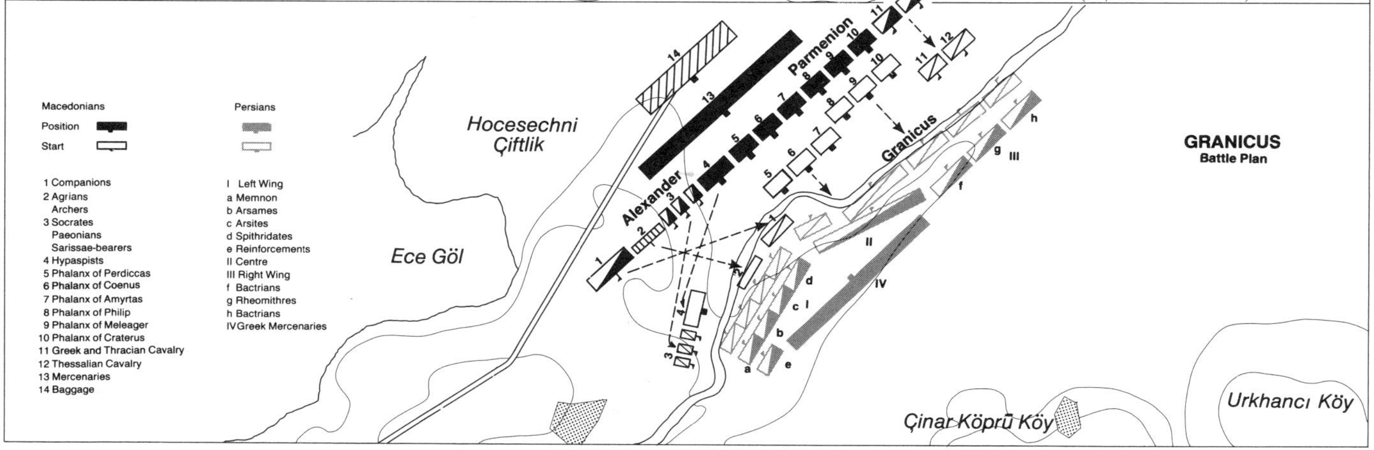
GRANICUS
Battle Plan
Macedonians
Position
Start
Persians
1 Companions
2 Agrians
Archers
3 Socrates
Paeonians
Sarissae-bearers
4 Hypaspists
5 Phalanx of Perdiccas
6 Phalanx of Coenus
7 Phalanx of Amyrtas
8 Phalanx of Philip
9 Phalanx of Meleager
10 Phalanx of Craterus
11 Greek and Thracian Cavalry
12 Thessalian Cavalry
13 Mercenaries
14 Baggage
I Left Wing
a Memnon
b Arsames
c Arsites
d Spithridates
e Reinforcements
II Centre
III Right Wing
f Bactrians
g Rheomithres
h Bactrians
IV Greek Mercenaries
Hocesechni Çiftlik
Ece Göl
Alexander
Parmenion
Granicus
Çinar Köprü Köy
Urkhancı Köy

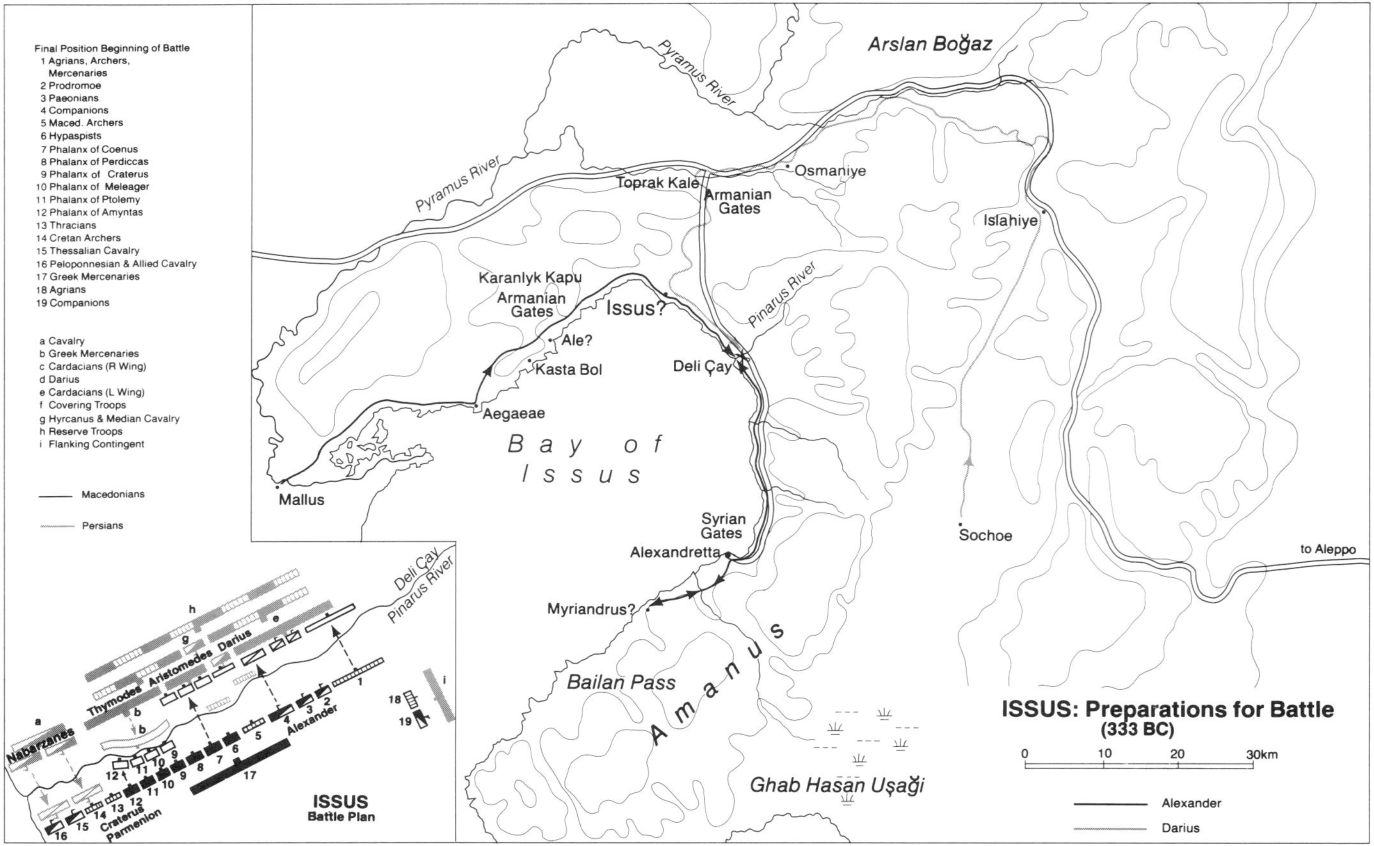
ISSUS: Preparations for Battle
(333 BC)
0 10 20 30km
Alexander
Darius
Arslan Boğaz
Pyramus River
Pyramus River
Toprak Kale
Armanian Gates
Osmaniye
Islahiye
Karanlyk Kapu
Armanian Gates
Issus?
Pinarus River
Ale?
Kasta Bol
Deli Çay
Aegaeae
Bay of Issus
Mallus
Syrian Gates
Alexandretta
Myriandrus?
Sochoe
to Aleppo
Bailan Pass
Amanus
Ghab Hasan Uşaği
Final Position Beginning of Battle
1 Agrians, Archers, Mercenaries
2 Prodromoe
3 Paeonians
4 Companions
5 Maced. Archers
6 Hypaspists
7 Phalanx of Coenus
8 Phalanx of Perdiccas
9 Phalanx of Craterus
10 Phalanx of Meleager
11 Phalanx of Ptolemy
12 Phalanx of Amyntas
13 Thracians
14 Cretan Archers
15 Thessalian Cavalry
16 Peloponnesian & Allied Cavalry
17 Greek Mercenaries
18 Agrians
19 Companions
a Cavalry
b Greek Mercenaries
c Cardacians (R Wing)
d Darius
e Cardacians (L Wing)
f Covering Troops
g Hyrcanus & Median Cavalry
h Reserve Troops
i Flanking Contingent
Macedonians
Persians
Deli Çay
Pinarus River
Nabarzanes
Thymodes
Aristomedes
Darius
Alexander
Craterus
Parmenion
ISSUS
Battle Plan

different from the propaganda. By proclaiming the Macedonian Calas as governor of Lesser Phrygia and at the same time retaining the title of Persian satrap, Alexander demonstrated to all the world that he regarded himself as legal successor to the Great King in the Asiatic territory "won by the spear."

Further operations in Asia Minor were dictated by the exigencies imposed upon Alexander by the inferiority of the Hellenic fleet. In order to take the naval bases from the Persians Alexander had no alternative but to proceed by land, in order to undercut their fleet by conquering the coasts and harbours. To begin with, Sardis, the old capital city of the Lydian kingdom, capitulated along with its allegedly impregnable citadel, and that without a stroke of the sword. By restoring to the Lydians their ancient laws and presenting them with their freedom,[20] Alexander demonstrated that he had come as the liberator of the nations from Persian rule.[21] By showing respect for the national characteristics of foreign peoples and attempting to win them over to his side, he established links with the founders of the Achaemenid empire, Cyrus the Great and Darius I. Federalism and not coercive centralism was his strategy.

With the capture of Ephesus, one of the most important harbour cities on the west coast of Anatolia—here the pro-Persian oligarchs were driven out and democracy re-established—and the annexation of almost all the remaining cities in Ionia and Aeolis, a burning question arose: in what form were these communities to be incorporated into the dominions occupied by Alexander? Earlier scholars—with the notable exception of J. G. Droysen—held the view that the Greek cities of Asia Minor were incorporated into the Corinthian League.[22] The observation, however, that Alexander did not conclude a regular treaty with a single Greek city in Asia Minor, as well as the fact that freedom and autonomy, the chief pillars of the polis, were "granted" to the Greek communities of Asia Minor, clearly points in another direction. It can scarcely be disputed that the Hellenes of Asia Minor in fact became subjects of the conqueror.[23] That a certain measure of communal autonomy was conceded to the poleis does not stand in contradiction to this. A final and fundamental reorganisation of the relationship of the Greek cities to the new ruler was not, however, undertaken, nor indeed even contemplated by Alexander, since military exigencies forced everything else into the background. In particular the question whether Alexander united the Greek cities of Asia Minor into city leagues, or if the reconstruction of these old sacred alliances, the Ionian, Aeolian and perhaps also the Ilian leagues, began later with Antigonus Monophthalmus, remains disputed.[24] But it is certain that in his lifetime it was precisely the Ionian communities who ascribed divine honours to Alexander and dedicated a cult to him—measures which were undoubtedly prompted by the rejoicing over their liberation from Persian sovereignty.[25]

At the fortified city of Miletus Alexander for the first time encountered more tenacious resistance. The Persian fleet was, however, unable to relieve the beleaguered city, since the Hellenic fleet had cut off access to the harbour. Miletus was ultimately taken by storm; the name of Alexander appears in the *Stephanephoroi* lists of 334/3 B.C. With this event the campaign of 334 B.C. came to a close. The Hellenic fleet was disbanded and part of the Macedonian army was sent home on leave. Alexander had meanwhile appointed Asander, the brother of Parmenion, satrap of Lydia and Ionia, and separated civil authority from matters of finance by placing the latter in the hands of a special official.

With the exception of Halicarnassus, which did not fall until some time later, and only after a protracted siege, the entire west coast of Asia Minor was now in the hands of the Macedonian king. He had liberated the Greeks of this region from Persian rule and formed close ties with the native peoples, the Lydians and Carians. Alexander entrusted the rule of Caria to Ada the native dynast, and even had himself adopted by her[26]—further evidence of his regard for native customs. For the peoples of Asia Minor Alexander came not as oppressor but as liberator. In the winter of 334/3 B.C. he continued his march through Lycia and Pamphylia, and did not set up winter quarters until he arrived at Gordium on the Sangarius, the old capital of the Phrygian kingdom.[27]

What no one before him had been able to accomplish, the Macedonian had achieved within a few months. He stood in the heart of Asia Minor, the contingents of the Persian satraps scattered before him and Persian rule in Anatolia virtually collapsed. The greatest stroke of good fortune for Alexander, however, was the end of the man who formed the very soul of the resistance to the Macedonian—the death of Memnon at the siege of Mytilene. The successors of the great Rhodian *strategos* did still score certain victories, but the recall of the Greek mercenaries from the fleet by Darius was decisive, as it downgraded the Aegean to a second-rate theatre of the war. This occurred at approximately the same time as Alexander was preparing to leave Gordium. He proceeded via Ankyra (Ankara) to the Taurus, after appointing a native (Sabictas) as satrap of southern Cappadocia. Alexander never did set foot in northern Cappadocia, the so-called Pontus. It remained—as did Armenia later—a gap in the emerging empire of Alexander.

After Alexander had subdued Cilicia and crossed over the Amanus passes leading to Syria, a battle at Issus on the Syrian coastal plain in the vicinity of modern Alexandretta (November 333 B.C.) decided the fate of Asia Minor. Inadequate reconnaissance on the part of the Macedonians and the Persians resulted in both armies moving parallel past each other over different passes—the Macedonians southwards, the Persians northwards—so that the Great King finally appeared unexpectedly in Issus in Alexander's rear. Thus the armies engaged with fronts reversed.[28] When the decision hung in the balance Darius lost his nerve in the face of the cavalry onset led by Alexander himself. He prematurely gave the battle up as lost and took to flight. Through reckless pursuit until nightfall Alexander succeeded in piercing the enemy forces. Only two divisions succeeded in escaping, one unbroken detachment of Greek mercenaries to the east across the Euphrates, another, a larger one, towards the south. In the camp not only the baggage but also the mother, the wife and the children of the Great King were taken prisoner by Alexander.

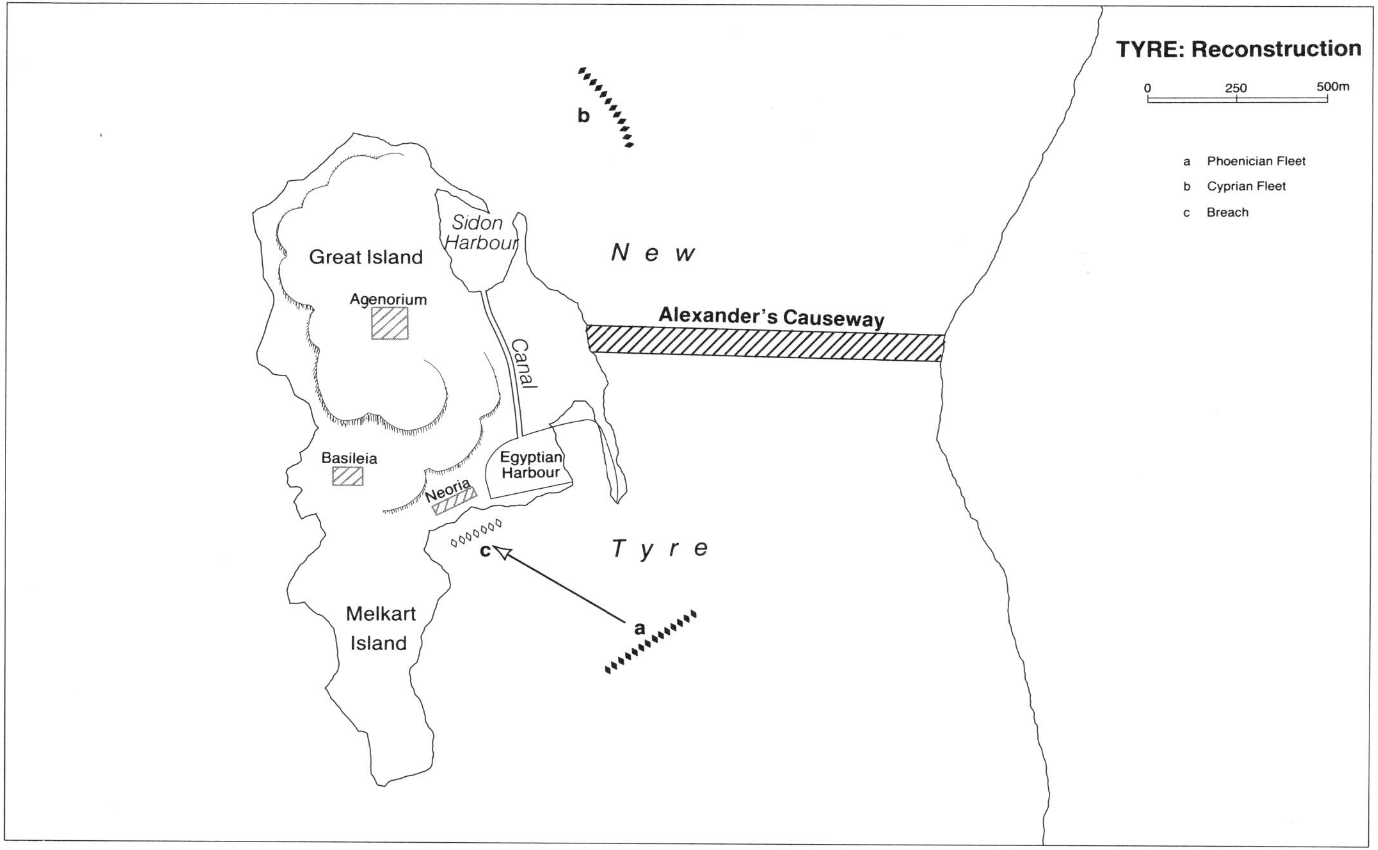
TYRE: Reconstruction
0
250
500m
a Phoenician Fleet
b Cyprian Fleet
c Breach
b
New
Tyre
Alexander's Causeway
Great Island
Agenorium
Sidon Harbour
Canal
Egyptian Harbour
Basileia
Neoria
c
a
Melkart Island

The victory made a powerful impression on public opinion, and most of all in Hellas. Here anti-Macedonian feeling, primarily on the part of a figure such as Demosthenes, had reckoned with the decisive defeat of Alexander. The significance which Alexander attached to this victory is reflected in the answer which he gave to Darius when the latter requested that he hand over his family and proposed a treaty of friendship and an alliance. The Macedonian demanded of the Achaemenid that when writing to him in the future he address him as "King of Asia,"[29] that is, the proud victor laid claim, already at this time, to sovereignty over the entire Achaemenid empire.

After this great victory Alexander continued to pursue his original plan, to force the Persians to retreat from the seas. The principle was, just as before, conquest of the coastal provinces. While the maritime cities of Phoenicia, namely Aradus, Byblus and Sidon, went over to the side of the victor, wealthy and powerful Tyre refused to admit Alexander within its walls. The request of the king to present in the new city an official sacrifice to Melkart, the chief deity of the city (by the Greek interpretation he was on a par with Heracles, the progenitor of the Macedonian royal house),[30] was rejected by the Tyrians. The governor of the city alone was authorised to perform such an offering, and Tyre wanted to remain neutral. There consequently remained no alternative but to blockade the ancient metropolis. It was one of the most difficult exploits of Alexander's entire campaign. In the determination and energy which it demanded of Alexander it is, according to the view of E. Schramm, unrivalled by any other siege in world history. To provide a base for his siege works Alexander constructed a causeway across the more than 800 yards between the ancient city on the mainland and the island on which the new city of Tyre was situated. Not until the Cyprian and Phoenician ships at Sidon went over to the side of the besieger was the blockade from the sea successful. The decisive breach was made from the sea and the city was taken by storm (c. August 332 B.C.).[31] At Tyre the king received new peace proposals from Darius. In addition to a large ransom for the Achaemenid womenfolk the Persian once more offered the Macedonian a treaty of friendship, the hand of his daughter in marriage and the Euphrates as frontier. Once more Alexander declined.[32]

Count York von Wartenburg has declared Alexander's expedition to Egypt a fundamental error in strategy.[33] This enterprise allegedly took the conqueror far afield from his real objective and gave Darius the opportunity to cut off his lines of communication for the second time (that the Persian king did not understand how to take advantage of this favourable situation is another matter). But this fails to appreciate the fact that the basic strategy of Alexander, to gain control of the coast and to secure his base of operations,[34] would have remained incomplete without the conquest of the land of the Nile. On his march through South Syria—that Alexander visited Jerusalem at this time is a legend[35]—he encountered strong opposition only in Gaza. Egypt itself was handed over to him, without a battle, by the satrap Mazaces. There the bitterest memories still prevailed in the wake of the victorious reconquest of the country a decade earlier by Artaxerxes III Ochus. Thus the Macedonian was in general welcomed as liberator, and the priests at Memphis placed the double crown of the land on his head.[36] In full awareness of the Egyptian tradition, Alexander appeared in Egypt not as the legal successor to the Achaemenids but as successor to the long line of native Pharaohs. National characteristics, customs, and the peculiar Egyptian religion he treated with great understanding and distinctive tolerance, as he had done with regard to the Lydians and Carians in Asia Minor.

During his sojourn on the coast Alexander laid the corner-stone of the city which today still bears his name—Alexandria (beginning of 331 B.C.).[37] The location of the site could not have been better chosen. The city lay on the western estuary-branch of the Nile where the offshore island of Pharos made the construction of an excellently protected harbour possible, and Lake Mareotis an equally excellent inland harbour. Here the prevailing easterly current of the Mediterranean drives the vast amount of silt and sediment which the Nile carries with it towards the east. While all other harbours on the Nile estuaries are continuously in danger of silting up, Alexandria is entirely free of this. The city took the form of an extended rectangle drawn up on the ground plan of Hippodamus, under the direction of the architect Deinocrates of Rhodes. Alexandria, combining all the advantages of an ideal sea and river harbour, within a short time rose to become the most important transshipping point in Egypt. Under the early Ptolemies it became the largest trading centre in the Mediterranean alongside Carthage. In addition to the Hellenes, natives and other non-Greek elements from the very outset acquired a home in the city.[38]

Once more it was the irrational in the nature of the young king, his "yearning," which prompted him to undertake the difficult expedition into the Oasis of Ammon at Siwah.[39] According to our best source (Ptolemy), he wanted to obtain certainty with respect to his divine origin.[40] Libyan Ammon had been known to the Greeks as an oracle god for over a century, with a rank equal to Zeus. According to Greek legend—for contemporaries it was history—the heroes Perseus and Heracles had once visited the sanctuary of Ammon. What a deep and lasting impression it must have made on the mind of the young king when the prophet of the god solemnly hailed him as the son of Ammon![41] Alexander maintained absolute silence on what had transpired in the holy of holies of the temple, which he alone had entered. In consequence all conjectures on this subject, both ancient and modern, are built on sand.[42] But the certainty of his divine paternity must have penetrated into the soul of the king like a flash of lightning. What he had felt and hoped, this the highly famous oracle had emphatically confirmed. Was it any wonder that after this he began to feel himself the executor of a higher mission? The echo throughout the Greek world was great and enduring. Messengers soon arrived from Ionia asserting that the oracle of Branchidae at Didyma, as well as the Sibyl of Erythrae, had declared Alexander to be the son of Zeus.

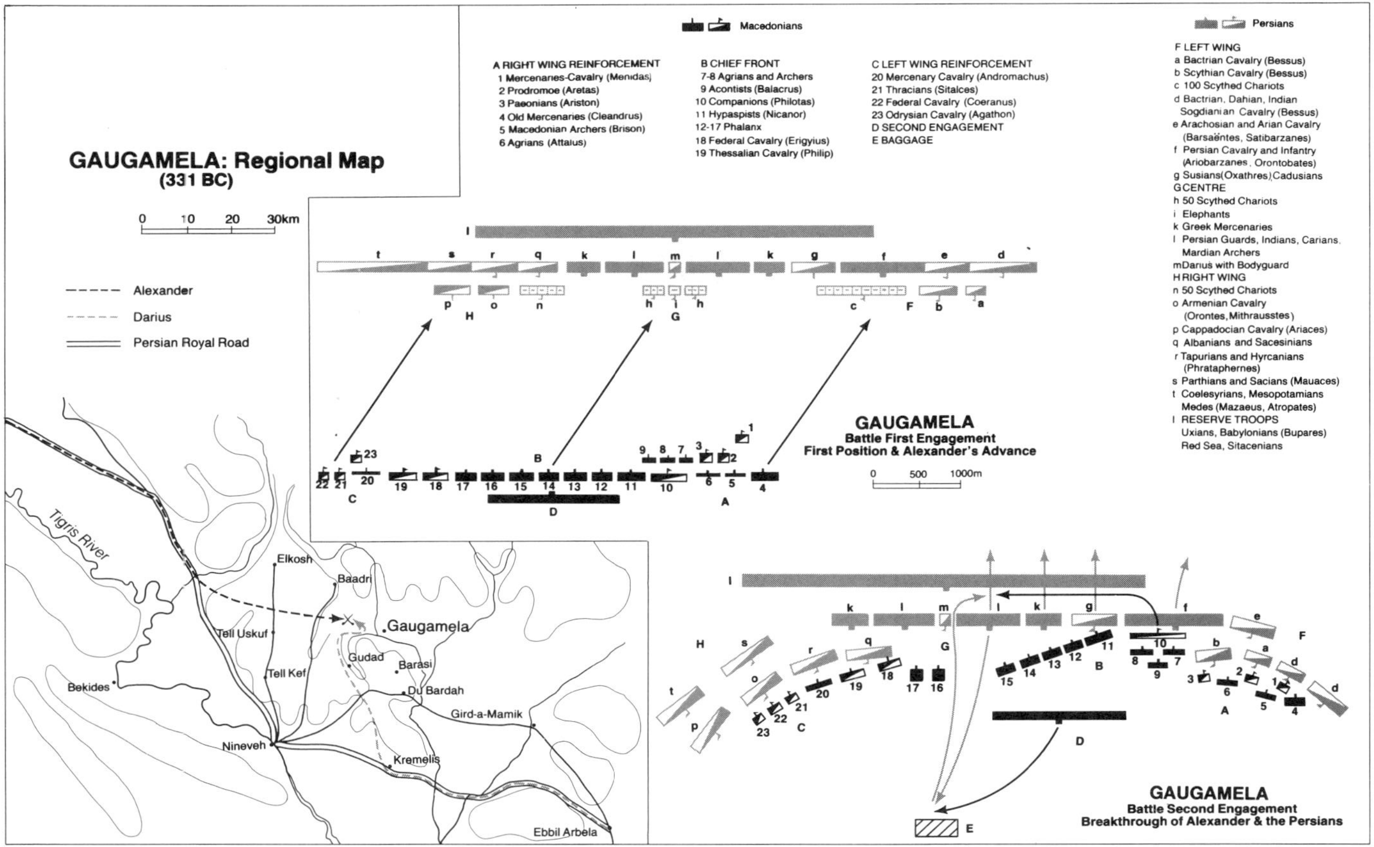

GAUGAMELA: Regional Map
(331 BC)
0 10 20 30km
Alexander
Darius
Persian Royal Road
Tigris River
Elkosh
Baadri
Gaugamela
Tell Uskuf
Tell Kef
Gudad
Barasi
Du Bardah
Bekides
Gird-a-Mamik
Nineveh
Kremelis
Ebbil Arbela
Macedonians
A RIGHT WING REINFORCEMENT
1 Mercenaries-Cavalry (Menidas)
2 Prodromoe (Aretas)
3 Paeonians (Ariston)
4 Old Mercenaries (Cleandrus)
5 Macedonian Archers (Brison)
6 Agrians (Attalus)
B CHIEF FRONT
7-8 Agrians and Archers
9 Acontists (Balacrus)
10 Companions (Philotas)
11 Hypaspists (Nicanor)
12-17 Phalanx
18 Federal Cavalry (Erigyius)
19 Thessalian Cavalry (Philip)
C LEFT WING REINFORCEMENT
20 Mercenary Cavalry (Andromachus)
21 Thracians (Sitalces)
22 Federal Cavalry (Coeranus)
23 Odrysian Cavalry (Agathon)
D SECOND ENGAGEMENT
E BAGGAGE
Persians
F LEFT WING
a Bactrian Cavalry (Bessus)
b Scythian Cavalry (Bessus)
c 100 Scythed Chariots
d Bactrian, Dahian, Indian Sogdianian Cavalry (Bessus)
e Arachosian and Arian Cavalry (Barsaëntes, Satibarzanes)
f Persian Cavalry and Infantry (Ariobarzanes, Orontobates)
g Susians(Oxathres),Cadusians
G CENTRE
h 50 Scythed Chariots
i Elephants
k Greek Mercenaries
l Persian Guards, Indians, Carians, Mardian Archers
m Darius with Bodyguard
H RIGHT WING
n 50 Scythed Chariots
o Armenian Cavalry (Orontes, Mithrausstes)
p Cappadocian Cavalry (Ariaces)
q Albanians and Sacesinians
r Tapurians and Hyrcanians (Phrataphernes)
s Parthians and Sacians (Mauaces)
t Coelesyrians, Mesopotamians Medes (Mazaeus, Atropates)
l RESERVE TROOPS
Uxians, Babylonians (Bupares)
Red Sea, Sitacenians
GAUGAMELA
Battle First Engagement
First Position & Alexander's Advance
0 500 1000m
GAUGAMELA
Battle Second Engagement
Breakthrough of Alexander & the Persians

While en route to the Oasis of Siwah Alexander accepted the submission of the Cyrenaeans. The administration of Egypt was in large measure deliberately decentralised. The chief officials of the general administration of the country, Doloapsis and Petisis[43]—the former name is possibly Persian, the latter typically Egyptian—were increased in number by the appointment of two Macedonian military commanders (*strategoi*), undoubtedly one for Upper and the other for Lower Egypt. The eastern and western frontier commands were detached from the general administration. The western ("Libya") was placed under Appollonius. The eastern ("Arabia") fell to the Greek Cleomenes of Naucratis, who was at the same time invested with the superintendence of finance for the entire land of the Nile.[44]

Alexander gave the last Achaemenid almost a year and a half to mobilise the vast resources of the East. In the spring of 331 B.C. the Macedonian departed from Egypt and, after his march through Syria, across the Euphrates and the Tigris, entered Arbeletis, once the central district of the Assyrian empire. East of the Euphrates a new world opened up to the king and his forces.[45] In Mesopotamia Asia actually begins, with its great fluctuations in temperature and catastrophes of nature. Vast new regions stretched before the Macedonians, with dimensions beyond the comprehension of European thinking.

At Gaugamela (Tell Gomel, north of Jebel Maqlub and about twenty-one miles north of Mosul) the future of Asia was decided, on 1 October 331 B.C.[46] In this battle Alexander employed new tactics to ensure himself against possible outflanking, which he feared from the numerical superiority of the Persians.[47] In the first line he deployed special detachments in hook formation on both wings. In case of emergency they were to swing back, and, after establishing strong connections with the second line—this too an innovation by Alexander—to form into squares. Despite this the Persian right wing under Mazaeus still scored advantages, and it even advanced as far as the Macedonian camp. Decisive again, however, was the behaviour of Darius. Instead of holding out against the charge of the Macedonian cavalry the Achaemenid turned in flight and escaped over the Kurdish mountains into Media. After this victorious battle, Alexander assumed the title "King of Asia."[48]

The next goals of the victor were the great capitals of the Achaemenids, Babylon, Susa and Persepolis. Without exception and without battle they fell into his hands. In Babylon the Macedonian offered sacrifice to Bel-Marduk and commanded the restoration of the temple of Marduk, which had been destroyed by Xerxes. It remains a matter of dispute whether he renewed the special monarchy of Babylonia.[49] Alexander decentralised the administration of the Babylonian satrapy, as he had done before in Egypt. In addition to the Persian satrap Mazaeus, who had gone over to Alexander, he appointed a Macedonian military commander and a Macedonian official as director of finance and taxes.

In Susa the central treasury of the Achaemenid empire, with its vast sums of precious metal in coin and in bullion, fell into the hands of the king. This metal was immediately put into circulation and thus placed Alexander's empire on a new foundation. After the king had broken the tenacious resistance of the wild Uxii and opened the "Persian Gates" (at Tang-i-Rashkan), which had been courageously defended by Ariobarzanes, the satrap of Persis, the king entered Persepolis (the actual name was *Parsa, Persai*).[50] Persepolis was the symbol of the world-embracing Achaemenid empire. Here the palaces and the audience halls of the Achaemenid kings, with their forests of towering columns and with magnificent reliefs and extolling inscriptions,[51] proclaimed the power and greatness of the Persian empire. It was nonetheless Alexander who gave the command to hurl the first torch into the royal palace of the Achaemenidae. This was a symbolic act—the campaign of revenge undertaken by Alexander and his confederate Hellenes thus came to an end. The sacrilege of Xerxes against the Greek temples had been avenged.[52] The burning of Persepolis, a signal to the peoples of the Persian empire and to the Greeks, was the last panhellenic act of the Macedonian king and *hegemon* of Hellas. Long before this he had set his aims higher. He regarded himself as successor to the Achaemenidae and as sovereign of a world-embracing empire uniting Macedonians, Greeks and Persians into a single commonwealth. He took as his models the great founders of the Achaemenid empire, and it was no accident that Alexander had the tomb of the elder Cyrus in Pasargadae rebuilt.

THE CONQUEST OF EAST IRAN AND NORTH-WEST INDIA (330-325 B.C.)

If reducing the royal fortress in Persepolis to ashes formed the symbolic conclusion to the panhellenic war of revenge, then Alexander's official discharge of the Greek contingents in Ecbatana in spring 330 B.C. was the final step. Although the majority of individual Hellenes remained under the banners, henceforth they served as mercenaries, while the king still continued to be the *hegemon* of the Panhellenic Alliance. Alexander now strained every nerve in an effort to overtake the fleeing Darius, but arrived too late in Ecbatana. At Hecatompylus, beyond the Caspian Gates, Darius fell into Alexander's hands—but as a corpse. Bessus, the satrap of Bactria, after conducting the Great King as a prisoner in his company, had him put to death while Alexander was approaching.

The death of Darius, the last Achaemenid, was one of the crucial turning points in the life of Alexander.[53] The Macedonian now regarded himself as the legitimate successor to Darius,[54] and the next and most important aspect of his plans was to avenge the death of the Great King. Alexander himself became more and more the absolute ruler. The adoption of some Persian royal vestments as well as the introduction of Achaemenid court ceremonies—initially only for the Persians and Orientals—reflect the gradual transformation of the man and ruler.[55]

For three full years Alexander engaged in battles in the East Iranian regions of the Achaemenid empire. These were his three most difficult

MAP VII

Alexander's Empire

S C Y T H I A N S
G E T A E
Danube
Tribalii
ILLYRIANS
Dardanians
Nicopolis
Istius
Tyras
Olbia
Tanais
SARMATIANS
Panticapaeum
Theodosia
Heracleia
Black Sea
Odessus
Apollonia
T H R A C E
Philippopolis
Epidamnus
Paeonians
Pelion
MACEDONIA
Amphipolis
Abdera
Odrysi
Pella
Pelinna
Crannon
Maroneia
Sestos
Perinthus
Byzantium
Bithynia
Sesamus
Sinope
PAPHLAGONIA
Heracleia
Amisus
Themiscyra
Pityus
Caucasus
Phasis
COLCHIANS
Trapezus
Gaziora
EPIRUS
HELLAS
Corinth
Thebes
Athens
Sparta
Lemnos
Lesbos
Mytilene
Chios
Elaea
Ilium
Granicus
Zelea
PHRYGIAN HELLESPONT
MYSIA
Pergamum
Gordium
Ancyra
Sardis
IONIA
Ephesus
Samos
Miletus
LYDIA
P H R Y G I A
Celaenae
Sagalassus
PISIDIA
CARIA
Halicarnassus
Rhodes
LYCIA
Xanthus
PAMPHYLIA
Side
Taurus
CILICIA
Soli
Tarsus
Issus
Halys
CAPPADOCIA
Mazaca
Tyana
Melite
Euphrates
Saspirians
Armavira
Sacesinians
Cyrus
CASPI
ARMENIA
Lake Van
Araxes
Amida
Lake Urmia
Cydonia
Cnossus
CRETE
Carpathos
Mediterranean Sea
Cyrene
CYPRUS
Salamis
Aradus
Myriandrus
Chalybon
Nicephorium
Thapsacus
331
MESOPOTAMIA
Nisibis
Gaugamela
Arbela
Tigris
Emesa
Palmyra
ARABIANS
Euphrates
Sidon
Tyre
Damascus
SYRIA
Samaria
Jerusalem
Gaza
Opis
Babylon
331,323
BABYLONIA
324
Bagistana
Celonae
Orchoe
Alexandr
Paraetonium
Alexandria
Pelusium
Ammonium
Memphis
Petra
Aelana
NABATIANS
CEDRAEANS
Dumaetha
E G Y P T
Nile
ARABIANS
Madiana
MADIANITIANS
A R A B I A
Chemmis
Thebes
Syene
Hauara
Hiera Sycaminus
Route of Alexander the Great
Route of Xerxes
Voyage of Nearchus
Empire of Alexander the Great
States subject to Alexander

States not subject to Alexander

Modern place-names in brackets

years. Under the leadership of the Bactrian satrap Bessus, who presented himself as successor to the Achaemenidae, and later under Spitamenes of Bactria, the strong tribes of East Iran put up a heroic resistance to the Macedonian conqueror. The fierceness of the fighting was accentuated by the religious fanaticism of the Iranians. The years from 330 to 327 B.C. were marked not by pitched battles but by bitter guerrilla warfare. After 330/29 B.C. new fighting tactics forced Alexander to carry out a gradual reorganisation of the military system. Through the formation of smaller mixed tactical units of great manoeuvrability he sought to meet the demands which the topography and the tactics of the fanatic enemy made on him. And the enlistment of Iranian troops altered the composition of Alexander's army.[56]

In forced marches in 330 B.C., Alexander advanced eastwards along the Royal Road. His destination was Bactria, the native district of Bessus. In order to secure the military road he founded the cities of Alexandria in Areia (Herât) and Alexandria in Arachosia (Chandahar).[57] Instead of pushing into Bactria over the Margas (Murghab) from the west, Alexander struck deep to the south as far as the Hilmend (Halmund). In the spring of 329 B.C. he mastered the snow-covered Hindu Kush (Paropamisus)—a feat far surpassing Hannibal's much more famous crossing of the Alps. Bessus fled northwards to Sogdiana. Deserted by his followers, he fell into the hands of Ptolemy, one of Alexander's generals. Alexander had Bessus punished in the same repulsively cruel manner as the great Darius in Assyrian fashion had at one time eliminated the "lying kings": his nose and ears were cut off and then he was executed in Ecbatana (probably crucified). In his pursuit of the dangerous Spitamenes of Bactria Alexander set foot in the remotest region of the Achaemenid empire. Here in the north-east, via Maracanda (Samarcand) in Turkestan, he reached the Jaxartes (Syr-darya) and even advanced beyond the river. At the Jaxartes he founded the city of Alexandria Eschate (Chodjend). The winter of 329/8 B.C. was spent in Bactra (Zariaspa). In the following year too (328 B.C.) fighting continued in Bactria and Sogdiana, until Spitamenes, after many vicissitudes, was killed by the Scythians (Massagetae). With Spitamenes' death the spirit went out of Iranian resistance and Macedonian sovereignty was consolidated in East Iran (328/7 B.C.).

Of great political importance was Alexander's marriage to Roxane, the daughter of Oxyartes. It was a gesture of reconciliation towards the valiant people of Iran. The marriage—Arrian explains it expressly in terms of Alexander's disposition[58]—was sealed by the mutual eating of a loaf in accordance with Iranian ritual (327 B.C.), a form still preserved in Turkestan today. The close ties between the king and the Iranians naturally were not without repercussions on Alexander's relationship to the Macedonians. The Macedonian monarchy and the Asiatic empire were two antithetical systems of government, which Alexander never succeeded in harmoniously fusing during his lifetime. In consequence the fusion policy of the king, however seriously it may have been intended, remained incomplete in all spheres: the vigour of the Macedonian people proved to be stronger and more enduring than all artificial planning.

Alexander's attitude to the Macedonians, especially the old Macedonian element, was glaringly illuminated by three events—the "catastrophes" which claimed Philotas, Parmenion and Cleitus as their victims.[59] All three men had rendered the greatest service to the king. Cleitus had saved his life at the Granicus and Parmenion had repeatedly stood by the king as his experienced advisor and general. He was regarded as the representative of the old Macedonian Philippic tradition. His son Philotas, overbearing and personally not very congenial though he was, had nevertheless admirably distinguished himself as commander of the companion cavalry.

Alexander executed Philotas in the autumn of 330 B.C. at Prophthasia (in Drangiana) because he had failed to disclose his knowledge of a conspiracy against Alexander's life. The military assembly declared him guilty, undoubtedly because the king had wished it so. The death sentence can scarcely be designated as anything other than an act of "high-handed royal justice" (F. Granier). The order, given by the king, to kill Parmenion, the father of Philotas, gives us a terrifying glance into the daemonic nature of Alexander. The order, issued from a bad conscience, was conveyed in greatest haste by racing camels to the officers in Ecbatana charged with the execution of the deed. It was the darkest hour in the life of Alexander. The murder of Cleitus "the Black" (in Maracanda in 328 B.C.) was an impulsive decision under the influence of the strong Turkestanian wine. Alexander's deep remorse after the deed shows clearer than anything else that political motives were remote, even though Cleitus may have provoked him by very incautious remarks about the preference shown the Barbarians over the Macedonians.

The extent of the internal tensions in Alexander's court clearly shows in the attitude of the court historiographer Callisthenes on the subject of prostration before the king—*proskynesis*.[60] While the Greek, a nephew and disciple of Aristotle, went to extremes in his history, written while he accompanied the king on his Asiatic conquest, in an effort to glorify Alexander and extol him as the panhellenic champion, he refused to follow him in the *proskynesis*.[61] Alexander never forgave him. When he became involved in the so-called Pages' conspiracy in 327 B.C. he was executed at the command of the king. This precipitated the hostility of the Aristotelian school and the growing estrangement of his tutor Aristotle.[62]

In contrast to the fighting in North-East Iran, Alexander's Indian expedition can scarcely be justified on military grounds. The plan for this conquest sprang much more from the romantic nature of the young king. He wanted to reach the eastern frontier of the inhabited world, the shores of Ocean, thought to be in the East, in India.[63] It was the urge for remote regions and infinite expanses, which gave him direction at a decisive moment of his life.[64] That the conquest of India developed into a regular voyage of exploration was an accident, and not a major aspect of the campaign (U. Wilcken).

As early as 328/7 B.C. Alexander began negotiating from Sogdiana with the Indian rajah Taxiles, the ruler of Taxila (in the vicinity of Rawal

Pindi) in the Punjab. In the summer of 327 B.C. the king, with an army composed of members from all Iranian tribes and from the Macedonian core troops, and a vast baggage train, crossed the Hindu Kush (Paropamisus)—this time southwards. After heavy fighting in the area of the present day north-west frontier province of Pakistan, he broke into the valley of the great Indian rivers by storming the Aornos massif (Pir-sar).[65] Here in the wonderland of India Alexander and his Macedonians found a civilisation completely foreign and bizarre to them, a foreign religion and a foreign race. The ties of the Western world with India had long since been broken off and no bridge led from the religion of the Greeks and Macedonians to Brahmanism and Buddhism.

At the Hydaspes (Jhelam) Alexander fought the last major battle of his life, against the Indian king Porus (c. May/June 326 B.C.).[66] Once more the ingenious commander brilliantly solved an unusually difficult tactical problem. Confronted by a formidable foe who had at his command more than 200 elephants and a large number of chariots, Alexander forced his way across the river by deception and immediately proceeded—from advancing formation—to attack formation against the Indians. After serious losses they were forced to give way. Wounded, Porus was taken prisoner, but he was left in a position of vassal prince by Alexander who admired him for his bravery. To commemorate his victory the Macedonian founded the cities of Nicaea and Bucephala.[67] The further march eastwards took him across the Acesines (Chenab) and the Hydroates (Ravi) as far as the Hyphasis (Beas)—the most easterly point which Alexander reached in his life. Since the departure from Macedonia his troops had in eight and a half years covered a total distance of some 12,000 miles (according to the calculation of Count York von Wartenburg). It was a gigantic feat of marching, surpassing to a considerable degree the achievements of the Napoleonic armies and even those of the infantry in the Second World War. At the Hyphasis, however, the seventy days' tropical rain, the humid climate to which the Europeans were not accustomed and the crippling fear of the Macedonians at being led into endless distances precipitated an unshakeable depression in the army. In the face of it Alexander capitulated—for the first and only time in his life. He abandoned his objective of reaching the Ganges[68] and the Eastern Ocean, and turned back.

After the return march to the Hydaspes (Jhelam), Alexander accelerated the construction of the Indus fleet with which Craterus had been charged. Accompanied by many smaller boats and manned by members of the maritime peoples of Alexander's empire, Greeks, Carians, Cyprians, Phoenicians and Egyptians, an enormous fleet of warships, transports and cargo boats sailed down the Hydaspes in November 326 B.C. under the command of Nearchus. The fleet moved to the Acesines and from the Acesines into the Indus. Strong army divisions (under Hephaestion and Craterus) accompanied the naval expedition. It was the most imposing demonstration of Western power which India had ever seen. After fierce fighting in the region of the Malli—during it, according to his custom, the king daringly exposed himself and incurred a critical wound from an arrow—Alexander reached Pattala in the Indus Delta (Hyderabad) in July 325 B.C. India, that is, the Punjab, lay at his feet. The sacrifices of Alexander at the mouth of the Indus[69] gave symbolic expression to the conclusion of the Indian campaign. By establishing satrapies and confirming native vassal princes the country was incorporated into the framework of Alexander's empire. Naval bases and Alexander-cities placed rule in India on a firm foundation.

Alexander's lively interest in geographical reconnaissance and exploration is shown by the enterprise entrusted to Nearchus and Onesicritus the chief pilot. They were to find a route with the fleet from the Indus Delta to the Persian Gulf, to the mouth of the Euphrates and the Tigris (September 325 B.C.).[70] From Hormuz Nearchus followed the route of Scylax of Caryanda, an expedition made at the time of Darius I. Taking the ship's log-book as a basis, Nearchus gave a concrete and vivid description of the voyage of exploration, which he composed as a special treatise. At the same time he demonstrated in this work a keen eye for foreign plants and animals. Arrian used this account for his *Indike*. While the detachment of land forces under the command of Craterus marched westwards along the northern road through Arachosia, Alexander proceeded, with dreadful privations and many casualties, through the waterless wastes of Gedrosia (Balutchistan).[71] In the vicinity of Hormuz the admiral Nearchus succeeded in re-establishing contact with the king (December 325 B.C.). The meeting between the great land conqueror and the outstanding seaman, whose achievements are worthy of being placed alongside the exploits of the king, practically signified the end of the conquest of Asia. No wonder that new plans now began to ripen in the restless mind of Alexander, plans to conquer the western world! These became reflected in the so-called *memoranda* of Alexander,[72] which the Macedonian military assembly quashed after the early death of the king. After building a gigantic fleet and conducting a large-scale expedition designed to circumnavigate the Arabian Peninsula, Alexander planned to conquer the entire north coast of Africa, cross over to Spain, and incorporate the coastal areas of Gaul and Italy as far as Sicily into his empire. All this signifies Alexander's intention to unite the entire world under his sovereignty.

At the beginning of 324 B.C. Alexander once more entered Pasargadae, the city of the Persian royal tombs. The great circle in his life had closed. More than five years had passed since the king had sojourned in the same place, at that time as "plenipotentiary *strategos*" of the Hellenic Alliance on the point of terminating the "campaign of revenge." Between the two visits there lay an entire world—the fierce battles in East Iran, the conquest of the Punjab, the march through the waterless wastes of Gedrosia. At the time of the first visit, in 330 B.C., Alexander was the happy conqueror stretching out his hand for the diadem of the Achaemenidae. Now he was the master of the world. His empire extended from the Adriatic to the Indian Ocean, from the lower reaches of the Danube and the eternally snow-covered Caucasus to sun-drenched Nubia.

ALEXANDER'S LAST YEARS (324-323 B.C.)

Alexander's prolonged absence in the East had led to unpleasant conditions in the empire. Not only the native satraps but also a number of the Macedonian governors and military commanders had taken liberties which, if not ended, would have meant the breakdown of organised imperial government. Corruption and insubordination, which had once been the hallmark of the late Achaemenid empire, had become widespread in many places. In Pasargadae Baryaxes the Mede was brought before Alexander as prisoner. He had adopted the title "King of the Medes and Persians" and placed the tiara upright on his head, the privilege of the Great King of Persia. Alexander found the tomb of Cyrus the Great destroyed and plundered. In many cases the satraps had adopted a policy of arbitrarily levying mercenaries. This was now expressly forbidden by Alexander. The guilty were punished with severe sentences. In Babylon Harpalus, the corrupt "Imperial Chancellor of the Exchequer," took to flight in order to evade the wrath of the king—with 6000 mercenaries and 5000 talents, in the direction of Greece.[73]

Three events of the spring and summer of 324 B.C. shed a clear light on Alexander's relationship to the peoples of the world empire—the mass wedding at Susa, the demand for divine worship, which the ruler directed towards the Hellenes, and finally his decree for the recall of the exiles in Greece. The Macedonian-Persian wedding at Susa was one of the most important symbols of the fusion of nations in the plans of Alexander. While the king himself married Statira, a daughter of Darius III, and Parysatis, the youngest daughter of Ataxerxes III Ochus, in accordance with Persian custom, no fewer than eighty of his most prominent fellow-soldiers and friends, including Hephaestion, Craterus, Seleucus and Eumenes, and in addition to these, 10,000 members of the Macedonian army, married Persian women.[74] All of them knew the burning desire of the king to fuse together the two nations vital to the subsistence and preservation of the world empire, Macedonians and Persians, and so they voluntarily followed his initiative. At the same time the internal conflict between Alexander and the Macedonians of the old guard who were unable to follow the king's line of thinking became all the more accentuated. Thus the discharge of the veterans in Opis precipitated a regular mutiny. The king, deeply affected, succeeded in subduing it,[75] but the rift between him and the conservative Macedonian circles was by no means healed.

The decree which Alexander issued in 324 B.C. from Susa, to the Greeks of the motherland, commanding the recall of the exiles, was regarded by earlier scholars primarily as a radical infringement of the constitution of the Panhellenic Alliance on the part of the king. The edict, it is argued, reflects the transformation of Alexander from Hellenic commander-in-chief to absolute monarch.[76] But this allows for only the formal side of the issue. In reality this famous decree was most closely connected with the aims which Alexander entertained at that time. His gigantic western plans could only be carried out if he had firm control of

Hellas, through the political exiles waiting to be restored, who would of necessity find themselves closely bound to the king as their benefactor.[77] The king had this manifesto read at Olympia in 324 B.C. by Nicanor, having commissioned him with the task.[78] There were, naturally, many difficulties when it came to implementing the edict. For Athens it involved the restoration of the banished Samians to Samos, an issue which, like many another connected with this edict of Alexander, had not yet been settled at the time of the king's death.

While Alexander was hastening from triumph to triumph in Asia, Macedonian rule in Hellas temporarily sustained a number of severe shocks. The Spartan king Agis III, son of Archidamus III, had taken up relations with the Persians and in 332/1 B.C. created an alliance including almost the whole of the Peloponnesus. Agis was, however, defeated in the summer or autumn of 331 B.C. at Megalopolis by Antipater, the "*strategos* of Europe" and representative of the Macedonian king in the Hellenic Alliance.[79] Sparta was forced to join the Corinthian League,[80] and the Greeks ventured no further disaffection against Macedonian rule during the lifetime of Alexander. To come to terms with the loss of their liberty, however, was completely out of the question for the Greek patriots. The actual feeling in Athens is reflected in the famous "Crown" lawsuit, in which Demosthenes won a tardy victory in 330 B.C. over his rival, the pro-Macedonian Aeschines. Demosthenes' oration *De Corona* was a late justification of his policy and unquestionable patriotism.[80a] When Alexander's disloyal Chancellor of the Exchequer, Harpalus, appeared by ship in Piraeus in 324 B.C., the Athenians could scarcely deny him admission into the city as a private individual. His money was deposited on the Acropolis and from there found its way into the pockets of Attic politicians. A number of Athenians saw themselves seriously compromised in the so-called Harpalus lawsuit.[81] Demosthenes was punished with an enormous fine but chose exile in Troezen rather than imprisonment. Thus from the battle of Megalopolis on (331 B.C.), Hellas was as peaceful as a graveyard. Politics on a large scale had migrated to the theatre of Asia, while in Greece itself the problems of everyday life, especially of a prolonged famine (330-326 B.C.),[82] claimed the energies of the Greeks.

Even after his safe return from India Alexander knew neither rest nor peace. Following a temporary sojourn in Ecbatana—here his best friend Hephaestion died in October 324 B.C.—the king marched on to Babylon. According to his design it was to become the capital of the empire. He was met en route by a large number of envoys, especially from the region of the western Mediterranean, to wit Libyans, and from Italy Lucanians, Bruttians and Tyrrhenians.[83] The conqueror's plans for the West began to appear. In addition, Alexander's uncle and brother-in-law, Alexander king of the Molossians, had been on Italian soil ever since 334 B.C. He had responded to an appeal for help from the Tarentines against the assault of the awakening Italic peoples, namely the Lucanians, Bruttians and Messapians. This brought him into temporary alliance with Rome, but in 331/30 B.C. he fell at Pandosia, the victim of a spear wound from an exiled Tarentine.[84] When the news of his death reached Persia Alexander declared a general mourning throughout the army.

If after the death of Hephaestion Alexander communicated to the Hellenes of the motherland the demand that they honour his friend as a god or a hero in the form of his assistant, this wish included the demand of the king for the divine honour of his own person.[85] The Greeks, despite reluctance, nevertheless acquiesced in the wishes of the world ruler. Heated debates ensued in the Athenian *Ekklesia*, but no one ventured to the point of open rebellion. Hence in 323 B.C., sacred envoys from Greece, crowned with wreaths, appeared before Alexander in Babylon, as before a god.[86]

The *apotheosis*—acceptance as divine—of the living ruler had its roots in Greek thinking, not in the traditions of the ancient Orient. Apart from the short interlude of the divine kingship of a Naramsin and a Sargon of Akkad in the third millennium B.C.—having, however, no connecting link with Alexander—the ancient Orient, including the Achaemenid empire, knew nothing of divine honours paid to a living ruler.[87] The *apotheosis* of the living ruler sprang much more from Greek soil. It was grounded in the genuine Hellenic belief that the mortal who has achieved superhuman exploits is to be placed alongside the divine, and it is of great significance that precisely the last generations before Alexander made many attempts to propagate the idea of the divine human on Hellenic soil. Lysander, Clearchus of Heracleia and Alexander's father, Philip II, all belong to this number. In the *apotheosis* of the living ruler there was more involved than the mere "question of a label" (K. J. Beloch). If Alexander was a god in the eyes of the Hellenes, this would inevitably affect the attitudes of people in general to the deified sovereign. Here religion and politics unite. Alexander, however, stands at the head of a long, momentous development which extends from the Hellenistic monarchs to Julius Caesar, to Roman emperor worship and to the divine right of kings in the Middle Ages.[88]

In Babylon the king made preparations for the great Arabian expedition. It was to form the prelude to his western plans. The object was to circumnavigate South Arabia, from there find a sea route to Egypt and thus establish maritime communications between Babylon and Alexandria. Alexander also followed with keen interest the construction of the Babylonian canal system, and he himself supervised the dike operations at the Pallacottas canal. In the midst of this restless activity sudden death snatched him away. After taking part in a banquet the king was seized by an illness—some suggest endemic malaria, but perhaps a serious case of pneumonia.[89] He died after a ten-day illness, on 10 June 323 B.C., at the age of thirty-three, after a reign of thirteen years.[90] Alexander's life and his achievement no doubt remain, when viewed outwardly, an incomplete picture, although a majestic one which towers far above all previous mortal achievements. What human nature denied him he was granted by posterity—immortality. The figure of the youthful king, snatched away in the prime of life in Babylon, has again and again rekindled the imagination of men. Scipio Africanus Maior, Pompey, Caesar, Trajan, Constantine and Julian—all took him as a model, and the name of Alexander will live as long as European culture endures, which rests not least on his life-work.

ALEXANDER'S ACHIEVEMENT

In its territory and its organisation the empire of Alexander changed steadily during the lifetime of its founder. The empire derived its peculiar tri-partite structure from the juxtaposition of three basically different components—the Macedonian monarchy, the Asiatic empire and the Hellenic Alliance. In Macedonia Alexander was, as successor to Philip, holder of the patriarchal monarchy; in relationship to his "Companions" he was in principle little more than first among equals. In Asia he was, as successor to the Achaemenids, absolute sovereign. In relationship to the Greeks of the motherland he was *hegemon* and "plenipotentiary *strategos*" for the "war of revenge" proclaimed at Corinth. Alexander never attempted to fuse these three elements of his empire together. It was his own person that held the empire together, along with the Macedonian army, which had conquered Asia and kept the freedom-loving Greeks in check. It is the army that, in its racial composition and in its organisation, best reflects Alexander's policy.[91]

When in 334 B.C. the king departed for the struggle against Persia, he left behind in Macedonia, under the command of the imperial viceroy Antipater, no fewer than six of the twelve or thirteen regiments of the *Pezhetairoi*—the heavy infantry—and likewise half the *Hetairoi*—the cavalry—all recruited from the old Macedonian stock. The re-forming and re-fusing process in the field army in Asia was epoch-making. Soon after 330 B.C. this affected the infantry and the cavalry to an equal degree. The ranks of the *Pezhetairoi* were replenished by mercenaries and Asiatics, while the *Hetairoi* cavalry was basically reorganised from 329 B.C. onwards. The discharge of the contingents from the Hellenic Alliance at Ecbatana in 330 B.C. (v.s.p. 212) was more of political than organisational importance. After 326 B.C. 30,000 Iranians were trained in Macedonian fighting tactics. From their ranks a troop was formed under the name of *Epigonoi* ("the Afterborn"), a counterpart to the Macedonian phalanx. In Opis (324 B.C.) the king even conferred on them the honourable title of *Pezhetairoi*—a crushing blow for the Macedonians, who had haughtily looked down on the Asiatics and regarded themselves as the masters of the world.

The internal organisation of the Asiatic empire of Alexander also exhibits evidence of a fusion of Macedonian and Iranian elements, a process which increased progressively. During the early years (until 331 B.C.) Alexander adhered closely to the principle of placing the administration of conquered satrapies exclusively in the hands of Macedonian officers. The few exceptions—such as Ada and Sabictas—prove the rule. At the same time he retained the satrapy as an administrative unit along with the Persian title of satrap. After Gaugamela (October 331 B.C.), however, the picture changes considerably. The appointment of the Persian Mazaeus as satrap of centrally located Babylonia, with the right to strike coins, marked an important precedent. The appointing, moreover, of loyal followers of Darius in Parthia, Tapuria and Bactria shows his continuation of the Iranian element. The revolt of Satibarzanes and of Arsaces in Areia (329 B.C.) prompted the king to fall back on the Macedonians again, and in any case the principle that Macedonian garrisons were to be exclusively under Macedonian commanders was never altered.

There is a view that Alexander divided the empire into a number of large finance districts (headed by "directors of finance"), an unfounded hypothesis held by a number of modern scholars.[92] What may be regarded as certain is that Alexander appointed special officials to guard the important maritime communications on the coasts of Phoenicia and Asia Minor.[93] The appointment, moreover, of Antigonus (Monophthalmus) as satrap of Greater Phrygia with headquarters in Celaenae was primarily military. He held the important land communications between western Asia Minor and the Taurus in his control, communications which had been endangered by Persian advances from Cappadocia.[94] All in all the organisation of the empire shows, as is to be expected, that unconditional priority was given to military considerations—as was later also the case in the organisation of the successors.

When Alexander declared that he had come as liberator of the suppressed peoples in the Achaemenid empire, this was not simply "propaganda." His accommodating attitude towards the Lydians, Carians, Egyptians and Babylonians proves that it was not merely an empty proposition. The deeper he penetrated into the Achaemenid empire, however, the greater became his respect for the achievements of the Persians and their great rulers, Cyrus and Darius I. The greater the territory he conquered became, the less he was able to forego the co-operation of the Persians. In the region of Opis, in the last year of his life, the king prayed to the gods for concord between Macedonians and Persians as a condition for their joint rule.[95] A goal of "unity of mankind," however, as postulated by W. W. Tarn,[96] is a romantic notion, as is the concept of Alexander as founder of the idea of one common human race. Alexander's attitude towards the Persians was in other respects determined by considerations of practical politics. His extensive western plans loomed on the horizon, and racial considerations of any kind were totally absent from the king's mind.[97] Alexander's *memoranda*[98] contained a plan for exchanging people between Asia and Europe. He also intended to expand his fusion process to other peoples in his empire and not restrict it to Macedonians and Persians. In this he wished to achieve, at a somewhat deeper level, what he strove with all his energy to attain in the two leading nations.[99]

The city foundations of the great conqueror inaugurated a new epoch in the history of the Greeks and of the Near Eastern world.[100] They are the outward sign of the beginning of the third Greek colonisation period. It may be that in establishing new Alexander-cities—allegedly more than seventy in number[101] – military considerations were in many cases the motivating factor, providing pacification of the land of the *barbaroi* and securing communications in the rear. But the importance of the colonisation extends far beyond the military sphere. From the very beginning it was not the Macedonian but the Hellenic element which set the pace in the new cities. In many cases the colonists were Greek mercenaries, who for their part were continuously reinforced by immigrants from Europe and Asia Minor. Greek customs, Greek culture and Greek religion found a new home within their walls, as well as a more liberal spirit than in the communities of the restricted conditions of the motherland. Thanks to the keen insight of their founder, a great future lay before many of the new settlements. In addition to Alexandria in Egypt, the Alexander-cities in East Iran – Alexandria in Areia (Herât), in Arachosia and at the Jaxartes (Chodjend) – enjoyed a period of great efflorescence. The effects of the colonisation of the East survived the short life of Alexander by many centuries,[102] and if Hellenism in distant Bactria and India was destined to an incredibly rich Indian Summer in the second century B.C., it was due indirectly to the influence of Alexander.

It was not until the Hellenisation of the East that Greek became the international language. In the East it replaced Aramaic, which had been the official medium of the Achaemenid empire. It was not until the realm of the Achaemenids had been conquered by Alexander that the conditions were created for international commerce – in dimensions and with an intensity such as the ancient world had not hitherto known.[103] In the following era the entire area from the Straits of Gibraltar to the Indus gradually became a single, gigantic economic region. The opening up of the Orient by Alexander has been compared with the discovery of America by Columbus.[104] If anywhere in world history, it is here that the initiative of the individual personality becomes evident, and it was this that gave the world a new aspect. The expedition into the Sudan to investigate the causes of the inundation of the Nile,[105] the voyage of Nearchus and Onesicritus from the Indus Delta to the Hormuz route and from there to the estuaries of the Euphrates and the Tigris, the plan for the circumnavigation of Arabia which had occupied the critically ill king in Babylon, the operations at the canal network in the Land of Two Rivers, the intention to settle the coast of the Persian Gulf – all these enterprises and plans bear witness to an unusual scope in the economic planning of the king. In this respect too he appears as the creative pioneer of a new era.

The material conditions for international commerce were formed by Alexander's creation of a new currency in the empire.[106] With a clear knowledge of the economic results, the king broke with the hoarding policy of the Achaemenids who had heaped up vast amounts of precious metal in bars and ingots in their capitals. Through the mercenaries, chiefly, who were paid with the new money of Alexander, the coins found their way into circulation and placed the economy on a new foundation. The bi-metallic system, the juxtaposition of a gold and silver currency, as in the Persian empire and in Macedonia under Philip II, was dropped. In its place silver served as the foundation of the new imperial coinage. By adopting the Attic standard he eliminated the coinage chaos in Asia and the Greek world. The enormous increase in the circulation of money had positive repercussions on economic life in Greece, and brought a period of prosperity which relieved the general stagnation of earlier decades.[107]

"The empire of Alexander was the first and only world empire known to history, if by world empire we mean an empire that has no second major power existing alongside it" (K. J. Beloch). This statement remains valid even though Alexander did not carry out his western plans. Without Alexander, no Caesar, no Imperium Romanum! Beginning with the successors the model of the Macedonian world ruler has again and again drawn the mighty of this earth into its orbit. The imitation of Alexander has a history of many centuries, extending from Demetrius Poliorcetes to the end of antiquity, to Constantine and Julian, indeed even to modern times (Karl II of Sweden and Napoleon I).

Alexander's most important and momentous achievement was the absolute monarchy,[108] based on divine honours paid to the king in a ruler cult. Alexander was still far removed from the worship of the ruler in an organised imperial cult, characteristic of Hellenism in its full flowering. And yet there was a wide bridge leading from the apotheosising of Alexander in the communities of the Greek motherland to the Hellenistic ruler cult which the second generation of the successors developed fully. That Alexander was prepared to retreat should this prove necessary is shown by his attempt to introduce the prostration to the Macedonians and Greeks[109] in 327 B.C. in Bactra—an attempt which he immediately abandoned when he encountered energetic resistance on the part of the Macedonians and Callisthenes.[110] The *proskynesis* had nothing to do with divine honours paid to the living ruler. Alexander wanted to introduce it because of the deep impression which the Oriental environment had made on the king.

The influence of the strange world of the ancient Orient is perceptible in all areas of Alexander's life. The erecting of an audience tent in Susa on an Achaemenid model, the plan of Alexander to build a tomb for Hephaestion on the model of the Babylonian temple towers (ziggurats) and the project to build a monumental tomb in honour of Philip II to the height of the Cheops Pyramid—all these derived from the influence of ancient oriental cultures. It is true that Greek, especially Sophist, ideas prepared the ground for Alexander's fusion plans, even though clear-headed considerations of practical politics—as the treatment of the *barbaroi* and the fostering of foreign religions—may have been decisive. Yet the deep impression of the oriental environment on the impressionable mind of the young conqueror cannot be denied. In his breast there raged a great struggle—the antithesis between the Orient and the Occident, and after his death it became the principal theme of Hellenistic history. Alexander had already indicated the way in which to overcome this antithesis. "As a creative statesman Alexander was far in advance of his time and demonstrated an originality of thought which has made him for all generations one of the greatest phenomena in world history."[111] Neither the Roman Empire nor the triumphal march of Christianity, whose congregations at the end of antiquity encompassed the vast area from Ireland to India, nor the Byzantine Empire nor Arabic civilisation are conceivable without the life-work of Alexander.

12
THE HELLENISTIC MONARCHIES

THE STRUGGLE FOR ALEXANDER'S EMPIRE—THE FIRST STAGE (323-311 B.C.)

Alexander's death in Babylon (10 June, 323 B.C.) left the empire without a direct heir. It consequently fell to the Macedonian military assembly, that is, to the Macedonians who found themselves in Babylon, the capital of the realm, to decide the fate of the empire.[1] A bitter dispute over the succession between the companions and the infantry of the phalanx was finally settled by the mediation of the astute Greek Eumenes, the former Chief Secretary. In a compromise solution, Arrhidaeus, the feeble-minded half-brother of Alexander, favoured by the phalanx, was to become king under the name of Philip (III), along with the yet unborn child of the Bactrian princess Roxane, should it be a boy. No decision was taken to establish the position of a regular "Imperial Administrator." Perdiccas, as Chiliarch ("Grand Vizier"), was invested with the superintendence of the Asiatic empire. Antipater remained *strategos* of Europe, while Craterus, as "protector of the royal interest," was placed in charge of the imperial forces in Asia, which Philip Arrhidaeus was incapable of leading. Since Craterus, who had proven to be an outstanding general in India and found himself on the return march to the west, was not present in Babylon (he happened to be on his way to Macedonia with the veterans of Alexander's army), Perdiccas became the actual regent of the Asiatic empire of Alexander. He had unlimited control over the vast resources of Asia, and under his leadership, a new division of the satrapies was arranged. Egypt fell to Ptolemy son of Lagus; Paphlagonia and Cappadocia, districts still to be conquered, were promised to Eumenes; Pamphylia, Lycia and Greater Phrygia to Antigonus Monophthalmus (the "One Eyed"); and Hellespontine Phrygia to Leonnatus. On European soil, Lysimachus gained possession of Thrace, nominally under the supervision of Antipater the *strategos* of Europe. In contrast, almost all the satraps of Iranian blood lost their territories. This was the first result of the national Macedonian reaction, which put an end to the fusion policy of Alexander.

The first two decades after the death of the youthful ruler were years of bitter struggle between the idea of the unity of the empire, championed by Perdiccas, then Eumenes and finally and most energetically Antigonus, and the idea of particularistic states, which was most vigorously pursued by the satraps of Egypt and Thrace, Ptolemy and Lysimachus. In this power struggle the kings were merely tools in the hands of ambitious generals. With respect to the women of royal blood the story is very different. In them and not in the men the vitality of the royal house once more comes into focus. Alexander's violent mother Olympias,[2] Eurydice, the wife of Philip III Arrhidaeus (a grand-daughter of Perdiccas III), and Alexander's sister Cleopatra, whom Antigonus caused to be murdered in 309/8 B.C.—all made their own contributions to the vigour of the struggle for power. And the power struggle ultimately destroyed them, like many later female members of the royal Ptolemaic house.

The Greek problem played an important role in the policies of the successors—the *diadochoi*. Whoever controlled Hellas had in his possession the heart and nerve centre of the world. Thus the various rulers repeatedly attempted to renew the Corinthian League of Philip II and Alexander, to establish the hegemony of an external power over the Hellenes, with liberty and autonomy promised to the Greeks.[3] But with continual changes in the power situation the notion of liberty lost more and more of its actual meaning, so that the "liberty of the Hellenes" was just propaganda of diadochian politics.

The transformation of the universal empire into a group of self-interested states went through four different stages. The breaks fall in the years 321, 317/6, 311 and 306/5 B.C., each of which marks an important advance in the divisive idea over that of the unity of the empire. In 321 Perdiccas was murdered; in 317 Philip III Arrhidaeus and Eurydice met their doom; in 317/6 came the death of Eumenes, who up to then had championed the royal interests most decisively and most disinterestedly; in 311 a peace was concluded and practically signified the partitioning of the empire among the various rulers; with the adoption of the royal title in 306, at first by Antigonus and Demetrius, then also by Ptolemy, Lysimachus and Cassander, the idea of the unity of the empire was abandoned. On the battlefield of Ipsus in 301 B.C. it was buried once and for all.

While Asia remained quiet, apart from the revolt of the military colonists[4] which had already broken out previously in Bactria, in Greece Alexander's death precipitated a great deal of unrest. The restoration of ten thousand exiles, as commanded by Alexander, had led to serious tensions. In addition, Athens had not forgotten that there had once been a time when vital decisions of Hellenic policy had been made in the Attic Popular Assembly. One Hypereides, and in particular the Attic *strategos* Leosthenes emerged as the opponent of Macedonia.[5] He organised a large mercenary force, proclaimed the Corinthian League dissolved, and founded a separate Hellenic league under Athenian leadership. Antipater the *strategos* of Europe was no match for the Greek forces, which were strengthened by the Aetolians, who had gone over to the Greek camp.[6] The Greeks shut Antipater and his army up within the stronghold of Lamia (so-called Lamian or Hellenic War).[7] Demosthenes, the hero of the Attic democracy, returned to his native city in triumph. The decisive turn in events occurred in the summer of 322 B.C., at sea. At Amorgos the Athenian fleet was forced to strike the flag before the Macedonian admiral Cleitus. For the Athenians Amorgos signified the loss of maritime supremacy, and with it, the leading position in Greece—and that for all time.[8] When Antipater, reinforced by the arrival of Craterus, ultimately emerged as victor on land at Crannon (in Thessaly), the pro-Macedonians in Athens, led by Phocion and Demades, gained the upper hand over the radicals. Antipater insisted on unconditional surrender. After the capitulation the radical democracy was displaced by a timocracy, in which the exercise of Athenian citizenship was conditional on a census of 2000 drachms. A Macedonian garrison moved into Munichia at Piraeus.[9] Hypereides was executed, and Demosthenes ended his own life in the temple of Poseidon on the island of Calaureia (winter 322 B.C.). A final settlement of the situation in Greece was not achieved, for Antipater and Craterus had to abandon their campaign against the Aetolians, as events in Asia were casting their shadow as far as Greece.

In Asia the departure of Craterus for Europe had given free rein to the ambitions of Perdiccas. With undisputed supreme power over the Asiatic part of the empire Perdiccas planned a marriage alliance with Cleopatra the sister of Alexander, in order to bind himself to the royal dynasty and the dead king, whose name still continued to hold an indescribable fascination for the Macedonians. He set the enterprise in motion when Antigonus the satrap of Greater Phrygia fled to Europe. Soon a large coalition emerged against Perdiccas—a league of almost all the leading successors, with the exception of Eumenes. Perdiccas, forced into a war on two fronts, in Asia Minor and against Egypt, did the worst thing possible in his position. He took the offensive against the land of the Nile, which was superbly fortified by the desert strip on its eastern frontier. The campaign ended in his defeat, and he died in his own tent under the blows of an assassin (321 B.C.). Ptolemy, the victor, did not, however, accept the position of administrator of the empire offered to him, but contented himself with the satrapy of Egypt to which he had already annexed Cyrenaica.[10] It was the most astute decision of his prudent life (K. J. Neumann). In Asia Minor, however, Eumenes, as Perdiccas' general,[11] emerged victorious over Craterus and Antigonus. Craterus, the idol of the Macedonian army, had fallen in battle (321 B.C.).

The reorganisation of the supreme power of the empire in 321 B.C. at Triparadeisus in North Syria brought the aged Antipater as major domo of the kings to the head of the entire empire, eliminating the ruinous juxtaposition of the Asiatic empire to the Macedonian monarchy. The military assembly condemned the Greek Eumenes to death, commissioning his inveterate foe Antigonus to carry out his execution. Antipater's departure from the soil of Asia Minor in the same year, accompanied by both puppet kings, appeared to indicate a decisive shift in the centre of gravity from east to west, from Asia to Europe. In Antipater the empire did indeed have an administrator, but on the other hand no energetic central power, since Asia had been delivered up to the personal ambitions of Antigonus.

Antipater's death (summer 319 B.C.) marked a further step along the road. In appointing the aged veteran Polyperchon to become his successor as "administrator of the empire and *strategos* of Europe"—without the concurrence of the Macedonian military assembly, which alone had the authority to do so—Antipater did not make a fortunate move. In particular Cassander, son of Antipater, opposed the arrangement of his father with the utmost resolution, and in East and West the centrifugal elements moved into the foreground. Cassander, Antigonus, Ptolemy and Lysimachus united against Polyperchon, the inadequate representative of the supreme power. Polyperchon set his hopes on the Greeks of the motherland. With the aid of a decree issued by King Philip Arrhidaeus he once more sought to revive the Corinthian League of Philip and Alexander. To begin with he would proclaim in Hellas a general peace, which the alliances of the various states were to join along with Macedonia.[12]

The naval war, however, brought about a fundamental transformation of the situation. Cleitus, the victor of Amorgos, was, after initial successes, decisively defeated by Antigonus at the Bosporus (autumn 318 B.C.). Athens, where the rule of Polyperchon rested on a weak footing,[13] went over to the side of Cassander (spring 317 B.C.).[14] As caretaker for Cassander, Demetrius of Phalerum seized the reins of power in Athens, and gave the city a ten-year period of a high cultural Indian Summer (317-307 B.C.).[15] When Polyperchon was deposed from his position in 317 B.C. through a decree issued by King Philip Arrhidaeus, but actually instigated by Eurydice,[16] Cassander had attained his goal, the leading position in the empire. At this juncture Alexander's mother, Olympias, returned from Epirus to Macedonia, an event which culminated in a dreadful catastrophe. Philip Arrhidaeus and Eurydice fell victim to her revenge, but Olympias herself was besieged in Pydna by Cassander. She died in the following year (316 B.C.), slain by the swords of the Macedonians.[17] The house of the Argeads focussed on one individual, the seven-year old boy, Alexander (IV), whom Cassander held, together with Roxane, in safe keeping at Amphipolis.[18]

In 318 B.C. Polyperchon had succeeded in winning Eumenes over to his side by appointing the Greek as "Imperial General in Asia" with extensive powers. The heroic tenacity with which Eumenes resisted Antigonus Monophthalmus in the following years commands admiration, considering that the position of Eumenes was void of all legal basis. Eumenes served the Argead dynasty with devoted loyalty. His veneration of the dead king is attested by his order in the military camp to maintain the cult of Alexander. Cut off from Macedonia and the Macedonian resources, Eumenes was ultimately forced back into the highland region of Iran. After an indecisive battle in Paraetacene, victory also eluded him in Gabiene in 317/6 B.C. He was defeated, then handed over by his own demoralised troops to Antigonus, and finally executed for high treason.

The fall of Eumenes meant the end of the dynastic concept in Asia, while the victorious Antigonus adhered to the idea of the empire. The remaining successors now viewed the "One Eyed" as their chief enemy, and never acknowledged his leading position. Seleucus, the satrap of Babylonia, fled to Egypt. Ptolemy, Lysimachus and Cassander formed a new coalition aimed against the ruler in Asia. Antigonus parried this thrust by proclaiming from Tyre in 315 B.C. that he had consummated the takeover as administrator of the empire, using, undoubtedly, a decree of the Macedonian military assembly. At the same time he retained as the basis of his position of power the title "*strategos* of Asia" which he had held since 321 B.C.[19] In Tyre the ambitious Antigonus also proclaimed the "liberty of the Hellenes" and attempted to translate this policy into fact by sending commissioned delegates (*strategoi*) to Greece, to drive out the garrisons of Cassander (315-311 B.C.).[20] The result was a counter declaration of freedom addressed to the Greeks by the Egyptian satrap Ptolemy. As early as this the liberty of the Hellenes began to be used by the successors for propaganda purposes—just as it was later by the Romans.

Although Antigonus had the advantage of the home bases, he did not succeed in exploiting this advantage. In particular, the defeat of his son Demetrius by Ptolemy in the battle of Gaza (312 B.C.) was a serious reverse for the aspiring Antigonus. After this battle the Babylonian satrap Seleucus returned to his old province, where fighting continued until 309/8 B.C. with oscillating results.[21]

With the Peace of 311 B.C., concluded between Antigonus on the one side and Ptolemy, Lysimachus and Cassander on the other (Seleucus was not included in the Peace),[22] the struggle for Alexander's empire saw a temporary conclusion. For Antigonus the result was disappointing. Instead of recognition as "Administrator of the Empire" he was only conceded a kind of superintendent right over Asia. His opponents were confirmed in the possession of their territories, Ptolemy as ruler of Egypt and dependencies, Lysimachus as master of Thrace. Cassander was the only one who found himself in an essentially worsened position. He was to exercise the sovereignty over Macedonia only so long as the young Alexander IV remained a minor. This regulation was the death sentence for the last Argead. In 310/9 B.C. Cassander had him and his mother Roxane put to death.

THE EMERGENCE OF THE HELLENISTIC KINGDOMS (311-301 B.C.)

Although the Peace of 311 B.C. expressly guaranteed the freedom of the Hellenes, nothing whatever changed in the power situation in the Greek motherland. In the following years, the war between Antigonus and Ptolemy which flared up anew in the Aegean and on the south coast of Asia Minor did bring some changes. In these operations Antigonus found a certain degree of support in the Island League, which had been founded by him in 315 B.C.

The peace treaty of 311 B.C. and the obliteration of the Macedonian royal house formed the conditions for the emergence of five large territorial states. The most important was the Asiatic realm of Antigonus

Monophthalmus,[23] derived from the "*strategia* of Asia" created in 321 B.C. It embraced the regions from the Hellespont to the Euphrates, with Celaenae, located at the intersection of an important road network in Greater Phrygia, its initial capital. Later Antigoneia on the Orontes, founded in 306 B.C., became the capital. Until its fall at the battle of Ipsus (301 B.C.) the empire was continuously on the defensive, so that the organisational reform inaugurated by Antigonus was repeatedly interrupted and impeded. The loss of Babylonia (312 B.C.) and the regions between the Tigris and the Indus—conquered by Seleucus in the closing decades of the fourth century—shook the empire. But Antigonus, as lord of Asia Minor and Syria, still controlled the important trade routes from Upper Asia to the Mediterranean, and thereby substantially tapped the revenues from world trade. The state founded by Antigonus was a reflection of Alexander's global empire, both politically and economically overshadowing all other kingdoms of its time.

The vulnerable empire of Antigonus contrasted with the smaller and more compact domain of the Lagid Ptolemy, composed of Egypt, Cyrenaica, South Syria (temporarily) and the island of Cyprus. Cyprus, greatly coveted for its wealth in copper and timber, after 306 B.C. was in the possession of Antigonus, and later of Demetrius (until 295 B.C.). Attempts on the part of Ptolemy to gain a solid foothold on the south coast of Anatolia and above all in Greece were in the long run without important success.[24] Apart from Antigonus, it was Cassander who exerted a decisive influence on Greece. His garrisons were to be found in many regions throughout Hellas and in Epirus (until 307 B.C.). He was especially active in the Peloponnesus, where since 308 B.C. the aged Polyperchon appeared as his deputy (*strategos*). Cassander's confederate Lysimachus held the key to the straits, so important for the subsistence of the Greek motherland. His Thracian empire, extending from the Aegean Sea to the mouth of the Danube, also included the Greek cities on the west coast of the Black Sea. Following in the footsteps of King Philip II, Lysimachus achieved much of an exemplary and enduring character in spreading Greek culture and civilisation in the Balkan countries. His sharp sword maintained a guard against the barbarians surging down from the north.[25]

While the realms of Antigonus, Ptolemy, Cassander and Lysimachus were oriented towards the Mediterranean, the efforts of Seleucus took him in the opposite direction. Beginning with a military campaign from Babylon in 308 B.C. he conquered the entire Iranian East, and halted only at the portals of India. There in western India he confronted the powerful kingdom of the Indian prince Sandrocottus (Chandragupta), founder of the Mauryan dynasty.[26] Founded shortly after Alexander's death, it encompassed the regions of the Indus and the Ganges. Seleucus did not succeed in conquering Sandrocottus; rather, a compromise was reached. The Punjab, Arachosia, Paropamisadae and no doubt also Gedrosia were retained by the Indian ruler, and along with Paropamisadae the important Cabul Valley, the great portal to North-West India. Seleucus settled for 500 war elephants and probably also for economic concessions.[27]

Antigonus was apparently absorbed in indecisive battles with Seleucus in Babylonia until 309/8 B.C. By 307 B.C. Antigonus had mobilised enough to assume the offensive against Ptolemy and Cassander, the masters of Greece. His first objective was Athens, which had been under the sovereignty of the Macedonian ruler since 317 B.C. When the fleet of Demetrius Poliorcetes forced an entry into Piraeus the Athenians openly sided with the party of the Antigonid. The regent of Athens, Demetrius of Phalerum, had no alternative but to capitulate. He himself, the third great legislator of Athens, went into exile in Thebes. Later he found a new sphere of activity for his unceasingly restless mind in Alexandria as adviser to Ptolemy I in matters of religion and science. In exuberant enthusiasm at having regained their "liberty" the Athenians conferred a number of unusual honours on Antigonus and Demetrius Poliorcetes. Both rulers were celebrated as "Saviour Gods," and gilded statues were erected in their honour and placed alongside the heroes of the Attic democracy, Harmodius and Aristogeiton. The Athenians even went to the length of creating two new tribes (Antigonis and Demetrias)! Although some models could be found for such extravagant honours in similar decrees from other communities, for Athens they were unprecedented.[28] The polis bowed to the will of foreign masters and forfeited the highest good which it possessed, the determining of its own destiny. "One had lost faith in the old creed and paid homage to real power, so long as this power endured and remained agreeable" (M. P. Nilsson).

The second blow of Antigonus struck the Egyptian satrap, Ptolemy. In the great naval battle of Salamis (on Cyprus) Demetrius emerged as decisive victor (306 B.C.).[29] For two decades after this control over the Aegean and the eastern Mediterranean was in the hands of Antigonus and the "sea king" Demetrius. As did Alexander after Gaugamela, Antigonus after the naval victory decorated himself with the royal title and conferred it on his son as co-regent. Antigonus regarded himself as the successor to Alexander and as master of the entire former empire of the Macedonian conqueror, with all other rulers his subordinates. The latter were, however, by no means prepared to acknowledge the superiority of the "One Eyed." After Antigonus' attack on Egypt by sea and by land had proved abortive, Ptolemy I also adopted the royal title (305 B.C.). The other successors—Cassander, Lysimachus, Seleucus—followed suit.[30] Seleucus had, incidentally, already been "king of Babylon" since 309/8 B.C., but this title applied only to his rule over the native inhabitants.[31] The royal title had now become the expression of sovereign rule over a territorial realm, and thus the dismemberment of Alexander's empire into five individual kingdoms was formally acknowledged.

Antigonus continued the struggle against Ptolemy with an attack on the island of Rhodes, which was on friendly terms with the Egyptian ruler (305 B.C.).[32] With the latest siege machines, which included a "helepolis" nine storeys high with catapult cannons, Demetrius rammed the walls of the city for a whole year, but without success. A peace treaty was then concluded in 304 B.C. through the mediation of Greek states. The Rhodians retained unlimited possession of their freedom and autonomy. The feat of surviving the siege marked the beginning of a great rise to power for the city. Within a short time Rhodes became the leading commercial power and the great clearing-house of the eastern Mediterranean.[33]

On Greek soil, developments were much more promising for Antigonus and Demetrius. Here Cassander had indeed made progress, chiefly in central Greece, in Boeotia, but also in Attica in the so-called "Four-Year War" (307-304 B.C.). Demetrius, however, succeeded in forcing him into substantial retreat. The military and political progress of Antigonus' highly-talented son was ultimately crowned by the renewal of the Panhellenic Corinthian League at the Isthmian games of 302 B.C.[34] All Hellenic states (with the exception of Sparta, Messenia and Thessaly) sent their representatives to the constituent session of the new Hellenic Alliance, and elected Antigonus and Demetrius as its protectors. As with the League of Philip and Alexander, this present federation was concluded in perpetuity. The League decree made provision for a general peace in Hellas and obliged the member states to furnish contingents for the federal army which was to conduct the war against Cassander. A garrison of Demetrius moved into Corinth, and remained there for sixty years—until 243 B.C.

The opponents answered this with a new alliance against Antigonus.[35] The plan of the members of the coalition provided for a combined attack by Cassander, Lysimachus, Ptolemy and Seleucus. Although seriously threatened by an offensive thrust of Demetrius against Thessaly, Cassander nevertheless placed a considerable part of his troops at the disposal of Lysimachus for the assault on Asia Minor. Cassander had correctly judged the situation. Demetrius was recalled to Asia Minor by his father.

Antigonus' position was greatly weakened at its most sensitive point, in western Anatolia, when two senior provincial governors, Docimus the governor of Greater and Lesser Phrygia and Phoenix the *strategos* of Lydia, went over to the camp of Lysimachus. With the object of splitting the forces of the great coalition, Antigonus sent a flying corps to Babylonia, to force Seleucus to rush back from Asia Minor to Babylonia.[36] This move on the part of Antigonus had no success. Much more effective, the forces of Lysimachus and Seleucus effected a union in the spring of 301 B.C. in northern Phrygia. Lysimachus, the most competent general of the coalition, had until then kept Antigonus saddled down with delaying tactics, although the latter was superior to him in strength. The decision came in the summer of 301 B.C. at Ipsus,[37] in the vicinity of Synnada. In numbers the armies which faced each other were almost equal. The members of the coalition, slightly weaker in infantry, possessed an indisputable superiority in elephants. The 480 elephants which Seleucus, the *elephantarches*, had put into the field[38] were opposed by only seventy-five of Antigonus. In the battle an essential factor was the conduct of Demetrius, who permitted himself to be lured off the battlefield while pursuing the enemy cavalry. Antigonus fell in battle, eighty years of age, his army routed.

From the booty Lysimachus received Asia Minor as far as the Taurus.

From then on he ruled over a powerful empire on both sides of the straits and controlled communications between Europe and Asia. Seleucus obtained the remainder of Antigonus' realm, in the main only Syria. In Asia Minor Cassander did not receive anything, although it is possible that he was granted a free hand in Greece. Cassander's brother, Pleistarchus, was promised a strip of territory on the south coast of Anatolia (undoubtedly Cilicia).[39] Ptolemy, who had kept in the background during the struggle against Antigonus, was ordered to hand over South Syria to Seleucus. He did not, however, and South Syria (Coele Syria) hereafter was the bone of contention between the Seleucids and the Ptolemies for 150 years.

The battle of Ipsus buried the idea of the single, undivided empire of Alexander, and established the system of Hellenistic states. Although the various states would still experience many changes, the system resting on a balance of power remained. It was the hallmark of Hellenistic history until the Romans plunged into the intricate works and knocked one Hellenistic state after another from the political scene. Ipsus was the victory of a new idea, the concept that a particular territory belongs to the individual who acquires it by force of arms and can guarantee it his protection. Empire, on this view, is no more than the *patrimonium* of the ruler which he bequeathes as private property. The new monarchies rested not on birth and not on legitimacy, but on the practical ability of the ruler to conduct the army and the affairs of state.[40]

The army formed the actual basis of the rule of the successors. Its importance extended far beyond the military-political sphere and embraced many other sectors of the state, above all that of economics. Indeed the wandering military camps which moved back and forth through Asia Minor after the times of Alexander became centres of a newly evolving economic life.[41] There was always a vast abundance of money and slaves in the military camps. It was often material interests that determined the political attitude of the armies. Out of concern for their possessions, as well as anxiety for their wives and children in the baggage,[42] the soldiers often broke faith with their generals. The expenditures for provisioning and billetting enormous armies assumed first place in the budgets of the successors, and the cost of building warships and blockading machines was also great. In view of the concern for maintaining an efficient striking force all other problems in the emerging military monarchies were forced into the background. It is noteworthy that Antigonus, the most important of all, alone attempted to introduce new policies in administration. In particularly vulnerable Asia Minor, in place of the satraps, he appointed *strategoi* as sole provincial governors with all civil and military powers.[43] Lysimachus later followed his example, as did Seleucus after the battle of Curupedion (281 B.C.). In Upper Asia, however, in the Iranian satrapies, there were no changes at all. Only the "General Command of the Upper Satrapies," at first from 323-316 B.C. under Peithon, and from 315-312 B.C. under Nicanor, a *strategos* of Antigonus,[44] presents a beginning in administrative reform, later given new life by the Seleucids.

The beginning of a new era shows in the relationship of the rulers to the poleis within the frontiers of their territories.[45] What they created at that time was, since Philip and Alexander, the "first synthesis of the city state and the territorial state encompassing entire countries, and as such became the model for all time, even though it may still not have been complete."[46] Alexander had initiated this trend by incorporating the Greek cities of Asia Minor into the territory of the empire. He had thereby inaugurated a new epoch in the history of the relationship between city and ruler in developments among the Hellenes. Since the Greek cities as a rule lacked the power to preserve their neutrality and independence in the world-wide conflicts of the successors,[47] the will of the ruler became *de facto* the supreme law for the polis. In the Hellenistic empires the Greek cities were centres of economic and intellectual life. Their value is shown by the large number of cities which were founded by Antigonus, Lysimachus, Cassander and Seleucus. In many cases this policy assumed the form of a *synoikismos*, "the settling together" of a number of neighbouring towns into a larger urban centre.[48] Moreover the older regional city federations which rested on religious foundations, the so-called *Koina*, were roused to new life, above all on the west coast of Asia Minor. Here too the example set by Alexander had evidently provided the decisive stimulus.[49]

The relationship of the new rulers to the native population of the Asiatic region also demanded a fundamental settlement. Alexander's fusion plans had been buried at the time of his death in Babylon, and with them the idea of a great Macedono-Iranian community of "nations" of which Alexander had dreamed. The attitude of the successors towards this problem of nationalities was completely different. Their attitude, in contradistinction to his policy, was conservative, actually even retrogressive. The Macedonians, boasting of their superiority, looked down upon the Asiatic natives as mere subjects to share in all the burdens but not in the privileges of the conquerors. That a ruler such as Seleucus I was particularly accommodating to the Babylonians and even re-established the old separate Babylonian kingdom, sprang solely from reasons of political expediency. The city foundations of Seleucus, of which a large number admittedly belong in the period after Ipsus, testify to a very deliberate Macedonising policy—he actually attempted to create a new Macedonia out of Babylonia and North Syria.[50]

The basic attitude of the Egyptian satrap Ptolemy I was no different. He also drew a marked distinction in the political sphere between Macedonians and Greeks on the one hand and Egyptians on the other, while in religion he made substantial concessions to the Egyptians.[51] This shows the strong attraction which the oriental religions held for the Macedonians and Greeks, a development which extends back to the beginnings of Graeco-Oriental ties and which now received a new and powerful stimulus.

THE CONSOLIDATION OF THE HELLENISTIC TERRITORIAL STATES (301—281 B.C.)

The political situation in the two decades following the battle of Ipsus (301 B.C.) was controlled by a system of states comprised of four empires.

Outside this system, represented by the territorial states of Seleucus, Lysimachus, Ptolemy and by Macedonia, was the restless figure of Demetrius Poliorcetes. His domain was not the land, but the sea, over which he had control with his great fleet. He was the first of the successors who allowed his plans to range westwards, to Italy and Sicily, and in this he was the forerunner of Pyrrhus. Through him and the great Sicilian ruler Agathocles, whose confederate and son-in-law he became, events in the Mediterranean world from Sicily to Phoenicia become merged—for the first time since the days of Dionysius I. There arose the vision of a great Mediterranean empire ruled by Macedonians and Greeks, but within a short time this idea sank into oblivion. In general, the inconstant nature of Demetrius was the animating force in the history of the first fifteen years after Ipsus (301–286 B.C.). At one point the strivings of almost all the kings intersected in the attempt to gain control of the Macedonian monarchy. After the death of the energetic and resolute Cassander (298 B.C.) and after the elimination of his sons, practically all the successors in turn had themselves proclaimed "King of the Macedonians" by the military assembly. Demetrius, Pyrrhus, Lysimachus, Seleucus and Ptolemy Ceraunus all took that title—evidence not only for the great material importance of the country which had been the cradle of all their states, but no less also for the indescribable fascination which the Macedonian kingship held.

The sovereignty of Demetrius after Ipsus (301 B.C.) was based essentially on the coastal cities of Ionia, Caria and Phoenicia. He also succeeded in maintaining his control over Cyprus, the islands of the Aegean and a number of places in Hellas, such as Megara and Corinth. He held these Greek cities even though the Panhellenic League of the year 302 B.C. had dissolved upon the news of the outcome of the battle of Ipsus (a result which Demetrius naturally did not acknowledge). The Athenians even refused to admit Demetrius within the walls of the city. With this gesture Athens once more joined the ranks of sovereign states.

The opposition between Seleucus and Ptolemy contributed essentially to the general situation. During the decisive struggle against Antigonus Monophthalmus Ptolemy had occupied South Syria (Coele Syria), and did not return it even after Ipsus. In order to strengthen his position the Lagid established dynastic relations with Lysimachus and later also with the house of Cassander. The Thracian-Asia Minor ruler, Lysimachus, married (his third marriage) Arsinoe, the daughter of Ptolemy, after separating from his second wife Amastris, a woman of Persian lineage and the princess of Heracleia Pontica. Seleucus for his part attempted to bridge the threatening isolation by a dynastic marriage, becoming espoused to Stratonice, the daughter of the "sea king" Demetrius. The wedding was celebrated with great splendour in Rhossus in North Syria (299/8 B.C.). Pleistarchus became the victim of the alliance between Demetrius and Seleucus. He lost his possessions in southern Asia Minor to Demetrius, without his brother Cassander lifting a finger to help him (299 or 298 B.C.). The Macedonian king, Cassander, whose policy was in general characterised by wise restraint, died in the summer of 298 B.C.[52] This was an exceedingly severe loss for the unfortunate country, which was to find no rest now for two more decades. Despite all the severity which cannot be denied in Cassander's character, no one could gainsay his energy and resolve in attaining the sovereignty over Macedonia. That the city of Thessalonica, the present day Saloniki,[53] founded by him, has flourished for two millennia in itself disproves the accusation of a purely negative activity which Droysen levelled against Cassander.[54] At his death, however, the future of the country was completely uncertain. His eldest son (Philip) died after having ruled for a few months; his turn at the helm was followed by a regency of the widowed queen Thessalonice for the younger sons Antipater and Alexander, the latter of whom married Lysandra, a daughter of Ptolemy.

The alliance concluded in Rhossus between Demetrius and Seleucus soon collapsed. Due to the dominions of Demetrius on the Phoenician coast, the empire of Seleucus was greatly confined and robbed of its most important access to the sea. It would seem that fighting ensued in Syria, but the details cannot be determined.[55] The death of Cassander prompted Demetrius to exert his efforts in a new direction. He resumed the struggle for Greece (296 B.C.). After an initial assault on Athens failed, he blockaded the city by sea and by land in 295 B.C. This time the Athenians resisted to the utmost. The Athenian "tyrant" Lachares[56] had the temple treasures melted down; even the golden robe of Pallas Athena which had survived the Peloponnesian War was not spared. When Ptolemy's attempt to send a naval relieving force miscarried, Athens was forced to capitulate. Lachares escaped to Boeotia (spring 294 B.C.). Demetrius stationed garrisons on the *Mouseion* Hill, and at Munichia and Piraeus; the city became part of his empire.

Demetrius had meanwhile suffered serious territorial losses in Asia. Seleucus had taken possession of Cilicia, Lysimachus of numerous Greek cities in Asia Minor, and Ptolemy of important Cyprus. The most vital naval bases were thereby lost. At this juncture the struggle for the inheritance of Cassander presented Demetrius with the desired opportunity to intervene in the throne disturbances in Macedonia. Antipater and Alexander, the sons of Cassander, had divided the country between them. Alexander called in Demetrius and the Epirote king, Pyrrhus.[57] Demetrius was the more unscrupulous; he had Alexander murdered, whereupon the Macedonian military assembly proclaimed Demetrius king of the Macedonians (294 B.C.).[58]

Demetrius, as master of Macedonia and Thessaly, large parts of central Greece and the Peloponnesus, and as protector of the Island League, was at that time, alongside the Sicilian ruler Agathocles, the most powerful figure in Europe. His resources and the number of his forces very considerably surpassed those of Philip II and Alexander (before his departure for Asia). In the centre of his sphere of power, in Thessaly, in the territory of the city of Pagasae, Demetrius created a new, large capital, the city of Demetrias (south of Volos), founded by a *synoikismos*. The walls of the new capital, 4.2 miles long and 23 feet high, and reinforced by 87 towers, were a splendid masterpiece of the art of Hellenistic fortification.

Demetrius did not understand how to exploit his great advantages, for his great deficiency was political adaptability. Inopportune presumption and insufficient tenacity in adhering to plans were the weaknesses in his character. He was indeed a great general but no statesman. For Macedonia his rule was a disaster, and W. W. Tarn[59] has rightly stated that the country never had a worse king than Demetrius.

With the conquest of Boeotia (292 B.C.) the power of Demetrius reached its climax. The appointment of the historian Hieronymus of Cardia as governor (harmost) of the region reveals the intention of the king to reduce the conquered areas, on the model of the territories in Asia, to the status of "provinces." Upon the news of the defeat of King Lysimachus against the Getae under Dromichaetes, Demetrius turned against the Thracians, but was summoned back by a revolt in Greece. The Boeotians, supported by the aspiring power of the Aetolians and by the Epirotes under Pyrrhus, had revolted. After a prolonged siege Demetrius succeeded in taking Thebes (291 B.C.). The city was, however, treated very mildly—in complete contrast to a former occasion after a revolt against Alexander.

Occupying Corcyra in the Ionian Sea (291 or 290 B.C.), Demetrius moved west. Lanassa, the daughter of Agathocles and wife of Pyrrhus of Epirus, had prompted the expedition. She had separated from Pyrrhus and appears to have concluded a new marriage with Demetrius.[60] An alliance with the Sicilian king Agathocles seemed to open up grandiose perspectives on the western horizon for Demetrius. He despatched to Sicily an envoy of his special confidence, accompanied by the son of Agathocles, to ascertain the nature of conditions in those parts.[61]

The mobilisation of the next few years did not, however, concern the West but the East. The dream of the unification of Alexander's empire still continued to occupy the mind of Demetrius. In the midst of his preparations he was surprised by an attack from his opponents. From east and west, at first Lysimachus, and then Pyrrhus also invaded Macedonia.[62] Defection from the unpopular Demetrius rapidly spread throughout the country. His rule collapsed, and Pyrrhus and Lysimachus divided the land between them (summer 287 B.C.). A Ptolemaic fleet appeared in Greek waters, designed to provoke Athens to defect from Demetrius. Under the leadership of the Athenian Olympiodorus the city was liberated. Only Piraeus was still held by a Macedonian garrison (summer 287 B.C.).[63] On a previous occasion, after the return of Demetrius from Corcyra, the Athenians had, in the most extravagant fashion, extolled the king as the manifestation of Dionysus and Lanassa as Demeter.[64] At the time the king's help had been urgently required against the Aetolians. But now all that had been forgotten.

Demetrius also lost the Phoenician harbour cities of Tyre and Sidon, and the Island League, previously under the protectorate of the Macedonian king, went over to Ptolemy. Despite everything, Demetrius did not abandon the hope of a decisive victory in Asia Minor. The rule of Lysimachus was not very popular here, and the rulers of Bithynia and

Pontic Cappadocia were by no means on friendly terms with Lysimachus. The successes of Demetrius in Asia Minor were none the less of only short duration. When Miletus and Sardis had fallen into his hands, Agathocles, the son of Lysimachus, seized the command in Asia Minor and forced Demetrius back towards the east.[65] Abandoned by his followers, Demetrius fell into the hands of Seleucus (286 B.C.), and died in 283 B.C. in royal confinement, in the vicinity of Apameia on the Orontes. With him disappeared the individual who had been the moving force of the period. He kept the world in suspense for fifteen years after the downfall of the empire of Antigonus Monophthalmus (301 B.C.), moved by a restless mind which did not capitulate in the face of even the greatest difficulties —most often created by himself. But to call Demetrius the "most valiant, the most daring and most ingenious of the Diadochi,"[66] is a verdict that in no way takes into account the weaknesses of his character.

Now tensions in the family of the Hellespontine king, Lysimachus, still prevented the world from finding rest. Lysimachus had forced his rival, Pyrrhus, out of western Macedonia (286 B.C.?). He also conquered Paeonia and extended his sphere of influence through Thessaly deep into Hellas. As administrator of a great empire Lysimachus achieved exemplary results, chiefly in the field of finance.[67] His coins were famous and still struck long after his death in Greek cities, valued for commercial reasons, primarily trade with the Balkan peoples. The Greek cities of his empire found Lysimachus a hard master. Governors (*strategoi*) appointed by him are found in the leagues of Asia Minor, and the wealthy commercial cities like Miletus groaned under the burdens which he imposed upon them.[68] Arsinoe, the daughter of Ptolemy and third wife of Lysimachus, was able to prejudice him against his own son from his first marriage to Nicaea, that is, Agathocles, who had just distinguished himself as an outstanding *strategos* against Demetrius. Lysimachus had him executed (283 B.C.). The followers of Agathocles now took up relations with Seleucus. Defection from Lysimachus spread in Asia Minor. The eunuch Philetaerus, who had been appointed Treasurer in Pergamum, went over to the side of Seleucus. Sardis opened her gates to him. The issue was decided at Curupedion[69] (north of Magnesia at Mount Sipylus), where ninety years later Antiochus III was devastatingly defeated by the Scipios. Seleucus emerged as victor, and Lysimachus fell in battle (February 281 B.C.). Seleucus could not remain inactive at the Hellespont, for the European dominions of Lysimachus required a new master. What is more, Seleucus regarded himself as legitimate "king of the Macedonians,"[70] perhaps on the basis of a proclamation by his army after the victory at Curupedion. At that moment, as Seleucus set foot on European soil, he was snatched away by the murderous dagger of Ptolemy Ceraunus (August/September 281 B.C.). Ptolemy Ceraunus (the "Thunderbolt"), eldest son of Ptolemy I and Eurydice, had, for reasons of his right of succession, been brought to Egypt through the intrigues of Berenice, his step-mother, in favour of Ptolemy (the later Philadelphus). From the court of Lysimachus he had come to Seleucus. Perhaps the latter made promises to Ceraunus concerning his restoration, but did not fulfil them. The army now proclaimed Ptolemy Ceraunus king of the Macedonians. With this gesture the European territories of Lysimachus got a new ruler, while Seleucus annexed Asia Minor as war booty; but here Seleucid rule was as yet by no means consolidated.[71]

Hellenism was spread in Thrace by the Thracian king Seuthes III, a contemporary and determined enemy of Lysimachus. The capital, which Seuthes founded as Seuthopolis, near Kasanlik in the valley between the Balkans and the Sredna-Gora Mountains,[72] was fortified, had a spacious market place and a number of sanctuaries, including a temple of the *Megaloi Theoi* (Cabiri) and Dionysus. Seuthes organised the country on a Hellenistic model, and it was probably he who divided the country into a number of administrative districts, *strategiai*.

The death of Ptolemy I (283 B.C.) preceded that of Lysimachus and Seleucus. As early as 285 B.C. he had appointed Ptolemy the son of Berenice as viceroy. Thus the change of sovereigns in Egypt transpired without friction. The Hellenistic system, however, which had experienced two decades of fighting and disturbances since the battle of Ipsus, had stood the crucial test. The idea of a universal empire, a dream that Seleucus had been the last to entertain, had become a thing of the past. From unsettled states with continuously oscillating frontiers, stable empires had emerged: Egypt, with its dependencies, under the Ptolemies; Asia under the Seleucids; while Macedonia alone, in the wake of the Celtic invasions, had still to wait for a few years to become consolidated. With Ptolemy II and Antiochus I a new generation took over the destinies of the Hellenistic world. The great Alexander, whose example had again and again spurred the successors on in the struggle for the universal empire, they knew only from the accounts related by their fathers. His image grew gradually dimmer. The goal was not the struggle for the empire of Alexander, but maintenance of the separate kingdoms which had been won by the sword. As a result of almost endless wars the requirements of peace-time had not received due attention. The problems of population, the economy, the formation of an efficient bureaucracy, the creation of a monarchical constitution and of an official ruler cult—all this and much more claimed the total energies of the new rulers. Problems which the fathers had had to postpone, the sons attempted to solve by their own methods.

THE WESTERN GREEKS IN THE TIME OF AGATHOCLES AND PYRRHUS

During the decades after the death of Alexander, historical developments in the East and West of the Mediterranean world diverged completely. In the East, Alexander's world empire disintegrated into separate states, a process completed with the battle of Curupedion (281 B.C.). In the West, the rise of Rome to control of central Italy had taken place after decades of heavy fighting with Samnites, Etruscans and Celts. At the same time the Greeks in Sicily were involved in a struggle with the Carthaginians, and the Hellenes of southern Italy with the Italic tribes. From the end of the fifth century B.C. on, the Greeks found themselves driven back to the extreme edge of southern Italy. They managed to hold only very small, narrow strips of territory, in the south of Bruttium: regions between Rhegium and Caulonia, and at the Gulf of Tarentum. Thurii, Croton, Elea and Neapolis had become Hellenic enclaves in Italic territory. The increasing distress of the Greeks brought repeated pleas for help to the motherland. The appearance of the Spartan king Archidamus III (he fell in 338 B.C. at Mandonium while fighting against the Messapians and Lucanians), of Alexander of Epirus, king of the Molossians (murdered in 331/30 B.C. at Pandosia),[73] of Cleonymus, son of the Spartan king (after 303/2 B.C.),[74] and finally of Pyrrhus, king of Epirus, is evidence for the great affliction of the Greeks and their culture in southern Italy at the end of the fourth century B.C. For the Sicilian Greeks, however, as they had found Dionysius I and Timoleon, there once more arose in the outstanding personality of Agathocles a deliverer in the struggle against the Carthaginians.

In Sicily the Peace of 339 B.C. had re-established the former state of affairs. The Halycus River once more was the eastern frontier of Carthaginian territory, which encompassed about one third of the island. Power struggles between the oligarchs and the democratic faction in Syracuse began with the death of Timoleon. During these struggles the oligarchs, who had been banished to Gela, took refuge with the Carthaginians. In these times of general unrest at the end of the thirties, Agathocles began his activities. He was the son of an exile from Rhegium and had, after the battle at the Crimisus, obtained Syracusan citizenship through the aid of Timoleon. Agathocles was a typical mercenary leader. In central Sicily, in Morgantina, he created for himself a sphere of political power which he was able to assert against Syracuse and against the Carthaginians. His military qualities soon made him indispensable to the Syracusans. After he was reconciled with them through Carthaginian mediation, he was at first placed in command of the Syracusan fortifications in Sicily, then, in 317/6 B.C., he gained the *strategia* with plenary powers, the highest position in the state.[75] On this foundation Agathocles established a typical military dictatorship, on the model which Gelon and Dionysius I provided. Within a few years he established the hegemony of Syracuse in the east of Sicily, and in 314/3 B.C. the war against Messana, Acragas and Gela was ended with favourable peace terms for Agathocles.[76] Ultimately, in 312/1 B.C., Messana was also forced to submit to Agathocles.

Fighting with the Greek cities of Sicily formed the prelude to the great struggle with Carthage begun in 311 B.C. by Agathocles. The tyrant well knew that a unification of the Sicilian Greeks under Syracusan hegemony could last only if he succeeded in driving the Carthaginians completely off the island. The initial operations took a course that was not very favourable for the Greeks. Upon being defeated at Acragas, Agathocles was pushed back to Syracuse. Here he made the most daring decision of his life. He took his army right through the middle of the Carthaginian blockading fleet to Africa, had his ships go up in flames at Cape Bon and advanced against Carthage. He defeated the Carthaginian militia, but was not able to take the city. He then concluded an alliance with Ophellas, the ruler of Cyrene, who had attained his independence from Ptolemy I, ceding Africa to Ophellas.[77] It was not long, however, before dissension arose. Ophellas was killed, and his army went over into the service of Agathocles (309 B.C.). Thus the large-scale colonisation expedition of the Cyrenaean ruler, in which thousands of Greeks from the motherland, together with their families, had taken part, ended in failure. Had it succeeded, it would have opened up a new province to Greek culture in North-west Africa.[78] In 307 B.C. events in Sicily summoned Agathocles back from Africa for good,[79] and in the same year the African campaign ended in failure. With the peace of 306 B.C. the Halycus River once more became the frontier between Carthaginian and Syracusan Sicily.[80] This was the reward of the tyrant, who now became the first Sicilian ruler to assume the royal title,[81] following the pattern set by the successors in the East. Close ties bound him with Ptolemy I, whose daughter, Theoxene, he took as his wife.

The peace of 306 B.C. marks the beginning of a new chapter in Agathocles' policy. He now joined the struggle of the Greeks in southern Italy against the Italic tribes. The impetus came from a call for help from Tarentum, threatened by the Lucanians. The earlier expedition of Cleonymus, son of the Spartan king (since 303/2 B.C.), had remained virtually void of any results. After defeating the Lucanians, Agathocles crossed over to the important island of Corcyra in the Ionian Sea, and seized it from the Macedonian king, Cassander (299/8 B.C.). As the dowry of Lanassa, daughter of the Sicilian ruler, Corcyra passed to Pyrrhus in 295 B.C., and later to Demetrius Poliorcetes (v.s.p. 237).

By occupying Croton, Agathocles gained control of an important base for operations in southern Italy. Although he had concluded an alliance with the Peucetians,[82] he found himself at war for decades with the Brettians, and took possession of Hipponium from them in 295 B.C., the same year in which the Romans routed the Samnites, Celts and Etruscans at Sentinum. A clash between Agathocles and the Romans did not ensue, although there may have been relations between them.[83] The ultimate objective of Agathocles was probably the union of the Hellenes of southern Italy and Sicily under his hegemony, in order to use the resources of this federation for renewing the struggle against Carthage. The building of a large fleet and the alliance with the sea king, Poliorcetes, had this aim in view. The realisation of it was, however, prevented by Agathocles' death (289 B.C.). Even before his decease the dispute over the succession had broken out in his house. His younger son Agathocles was murdered by his grandson, Archagathus, so the mortally ailing ruler restored Syracuse her freedom.

Agathocles was indisputably the last truly great figure among the western Hellenes.[84] His energy once more made the western Hellenes a determinative factor in the history of the Mediterranean world—the evening glow before the final sunset. In arriving at a verdict on his political and military achievements we should not allow ourselves to be influenced by the prejudiced attitude of the historian Timaeus, his declared opponent. One should rather consider the assertion of the elder Scipio, who placed him on a level with Dionysius I (Polyb. XV 35, 6). Although he paved the way to personal power by means of harsh cruelty,[85] nevertheless, when he actually exercised his rule, he acted with moderation and showed himself conciliatory towards his enemies. His life and his work are overshadowed by deep tragedy. He came too late—time for the Greeks in the West had run out. Not even the expedition of Pyrrhus, king of Epirus (280-275 B.C.) could any longer alter things.

The Pyrrhic War, the first major military conflict between the West and the world of the Hellenistic East, overcame the division of the Mediterranean world into a western and an eastern half, and laid the foundation for a unified Mediterranean culture of Hellenistic character. For Rome the Pyrrhic War was the decisive milestone along the road to sovereignty over Italy. For the first time in their history the Romans moved out beyond the frontiers of central Italy to intervene in the Greek-inhabited south of the country, and became the protectors of the Hellenes in that region. It was an exceptionally fruitful encounter, one that gave Rome a link with Graeco-Hellenistic culture. For the Hellenistic East too, the intervention of Pyrrhus in southern Italy and Sicily was far more than a mere episode. When Pyrrhus departed from southern Italy after five years of fighting, the plan to establish a great western empire had vanished into thin air against the tenacious resistance of the Romans. The West had maintained its autonomy, and from now on pursued political policies of its own—until Rome, upon overthrowing Carthage, at the end of the third century inaugurated its own eastern policy, forcing the Hellenistic states into subjection.

The conflict between East and West, between Pyrrhus and Rome, was kindled by the Tarentine War. Rome despatched the consul of the year 282 B.C., C. Fabricius, to help the city of Thurii, which was being besieged by the Lucanians. The expedition ended in a complete success. The Lucanians were defeated and Thurii secured by a Roman garrison. The intervention of the Romans, however, led to tension with the important Greek city of Tarentum. A Roman squadron was attacked by the Tarentines and the Roman garrison forced to withdraw from Thurii. While the Romans sought satisfaction through envoys, Tarentum entered into relations with King Pyrrhus, to induce him to undertake an expedition to the West.

The situation in Greece and Macedonia favoured the aspirations of the Tarentines. In Macedonia, Ptolemy Ceraunus had acceded to the throne in 281 B.C. He was, however, confronted by two rivals, Antiochus I, son of Seleucus I, and Antigonus Gonatas, son of Demetrius Poliorcetes. Pyrrhus' prospects for asserting himself against this phalanx of aspirants were remote. Worse, he did not have enough freedom of action in his homeland of Epirus, for the power of the king was greatly limited by the federal assembly.[86] In return for 5000 infantry, 4000 cavalry and 50 elephants, which Ptolemy Ceraunus gave him for a period of two years,[87] Pyrrhus waived the Macedonian throne. He set his hopes on the West, above all on Sicily, where the situation since the death of Agathocles, his

MAP VIII

The Hellenistic States, Greece and the West c. 240 B.C.

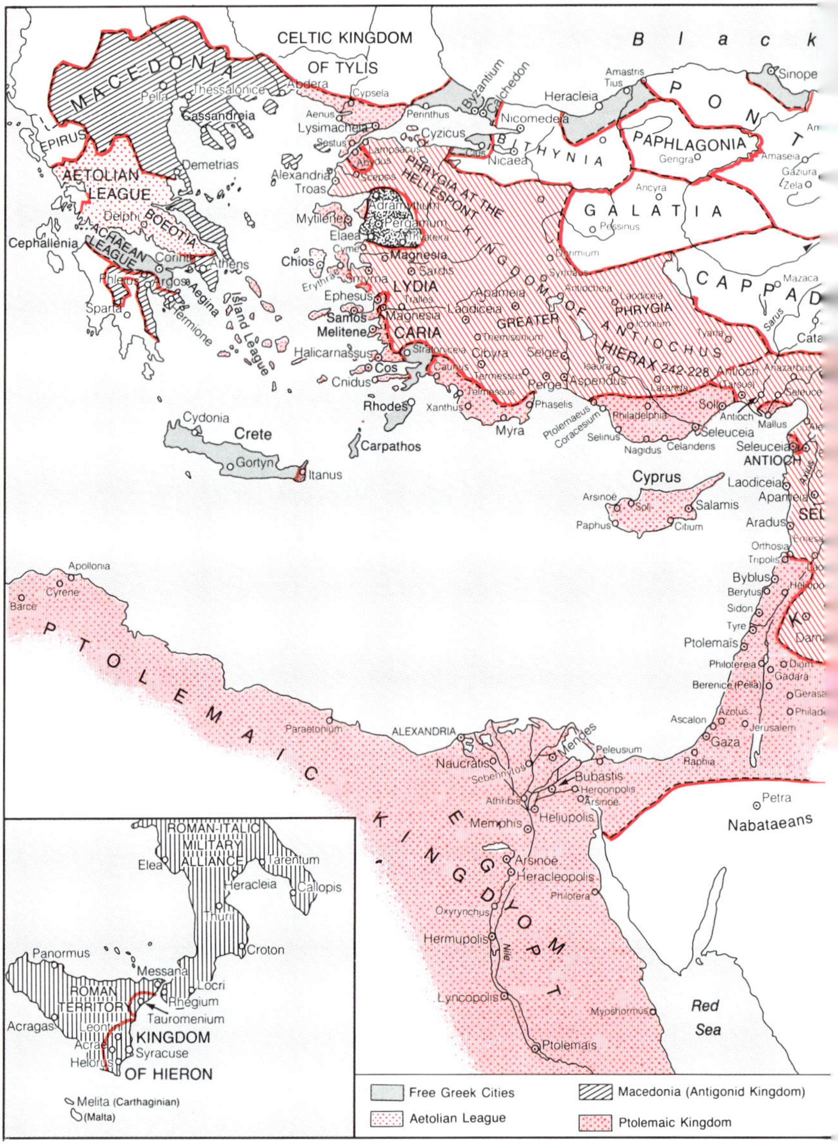
CELTIC KINGDOM
OF TYLIS
B l a c k
MACEDONIA
EPIRUS
AETOLIAN
LEAGUE
BOEOTIA
ACHAEAN LEAGUE
Island League
Pella
Thessalonice
Cassandreia
Abdera
Cypsela
Aenus
Lysimacheia
Sestus
Abydus
Lampsacus
Scepsis
Perinthus
Byzantium
Chalcedon
Cyzicus
Cius
Nicomedeia
Nicaea
Heracleia
Amastris
Tius
Sinope
PONT
PAPHLAGONIA
Gengra
Amaseia
Gaziura
Zela
BITHYNIA
GALATIA
Ancyra
Pessinus
CAPPAD
Mazaca
Sarus
Demetrias
Delphi
Cephallenia
Corinth
Athens
Phleius
Argos
Aegina
Sparta
Hermione
Alexandria
Troas
Mytilene
Elaea
Cyme
Chios
Erythrae
Smyrna
Ephesus
Samos
Melitene
Halicarnassus
Cos
Cnidus
Rhodes
Carpathos
Adramyttium
Pergamum
Thyateira
Magnesia
Sardis
LYDIA
Tralles
Magnesia
CARIA
Stratoniceia
Caunus
Xanthus
Telmessus
PHRYGIA AT THE HELLESPONT
KINGDOM OF ANTIOCHUS HIERAX 242-228
Dorylaeum
Synnada
Apameia
Laodiceia
Antiocheia
Laodiceia
PHRYGIA
Iconium
GREATER
Themisonium
Cibyra
Selge
Termessus
Perge
Aspendus
Isaura
Laranda
Tyana
Anazarbus
Tarsus
Phaselis
Myra
Ptolemaeus
Coracesium
Philadelphia
Selinus
Nagidus
Celanderis
Soli
Antioch
Mallus
Seleuceia
Seleuceia
ANTIOCH
Cydonia
Crete
Gortyn
Itanus
Cyprus
Arsinoe
Soli
Salamis
Paphus
Citium
Laodiceia
Apameia
Aradus
Orthosia
Tripolis
Byblus
Berytus
Sidon
Tyre
Ptolemaïs
Philotereia
Berenice (Pella)
Dium
Gadara
Gerasa
Philadelphia
Ascalon
Azotus
Jerusalem
Gaza
Raphia
Damascus
Apollonia
Cyrene
Barce
PTOLEMAIC KINGDOM
Paraetonium
ALEXANDRIA
Naucratis
Sebennytus
Mendes
Peleusium
Athribis
Bubastis
Heroonpolis
Arsinoe
Heliupolis
Memphis
Arsinoe
Heracleopolis
Philotera
Oxyrynchus
Hermupolis
Nile
Lyncopolis
Ptolemais
Myoshormus
EGYPT
Red
Sea
Petra
Nabataeans
ROMAN-ITALIC
MILITARY
ALLIANCE
Elea
Tarentum
Heracleia
Callipolis
Thurii
Croton
Panormus
Messana
Locri
ROMAN
TERRITORY
Rhegium
Tauromenium
Acragas
Leontini
KINGDOM
OF HIERON
Acrae
Syracuse
Helorus
Melita (Carthaginian)
(Malta)
Free Greek Cities
Macedonia (Antigonid Kingdom)
Aetolian League
Ptolemaic Kingdom

Caspian Sea
Cerasus
Trapezus
ARMENIA
Cyrus
Araxes
Arsamoseia
MEDIA ARTOPATENE
Zadracarha
Hyrcania
PARTHIAN KINGDOM
Europus (Rhagae)
Caspian Gates
Apameia
Samosata
Edessa
Anthemus
Carrhae
Antioch (Nisibis)
Mygdonia
MESOPOTAMIA
Arbela
Tigris
Callinicum
Thapsacus
Euphrates
Palmyra
Dura-Europus
Antioch
Apollonia
Sittace
SELEUCIS
BABYLONIA
Babylon
Apameia
Orchoe (Uruk)
Euphrates
MEDIA
Hydaspes
Ecbatana
Heracleia
Cossaeans
Choaspes
Paraetacene
Gabae
Gabia
SUSIANA
Susa
Eulaeus
Tigris
Uxii
SATRAPY AT THE RED SEA
Alexandria (Mesene)
PERSIS
Persepolis
Persian Gulf
0 50 100 200 300 400 km
Seleucid Kingdom Names of Satrapies (in part uncertain) in large upper case letters (e.g., LYDIA)
Roman-Italic Military Alliance
Pergamene Kingdom
Other States

one time father-in-law, was more confused than ever.[88] Alexander, Pyrrhus' son by Lanassa, was one of Agathocles' heirs. Pyrrhus did not, however, contemplate remaining permanently in the West. On the contrary, if we may trust a late tradition (Zonaras), Pyrrhus had elicited a promise from the Tarentines not to detain him in Italy any longer than would be absolutely necessary.[89] Pyrrhus' personal influence over his troops and his extensive knowledge of warfare and siege tactics made him one of the most significant generals of the Hellenistic period. Hannibal actually regarded him as the greatest general after Alexander! Greek historiographers did not miss the opportunity to capitalise on the welcome material provided by the Pyrrhic War. This became the first event in Italic history to which Graeco-Hellenistic historiography devoted its attention, and although Rome had hitherto been merely a vague concept, it now moved into the foreground of Greek interests.

In the spring of 280 B.C. Pyrrhus crossed the Adriatic with his army of 20,000 mercenaries, 3000 Thessalian cavalry, 2000 archers and 20 war elephants. His advance guard took possession of the citadel of Tarentum. The Hellenes in southern Italy were disunited, and Rhegium and Locri even solicited a Roman garrison. In the first battle, at Heracleia on the Siris (July 280 B.C.), Pyrrhus, leading the decisive thrust with the elephants, with heavy losses retained[90] the upper hand over the Romans under the command of the consul P. Valerius Laevinus. Croton and Locri now went over to Pyrrhus, while in Rhegium, on the other hand, Campanian mercenaries, the so-called Mamertines, seized power, as they had done just a few years before in Sicilian Messana. Thus the straits between Italy and Sicily were controlled by two Campanian mercenary republics. However, the Lucanians, Brettians and the Samnites went over to Pyrrhus, a matter of great importance to him, for their auxiliary troops meant a considerable strengthening of his forces. The allies of central Italy did not, however, defect from Rome, as expected, although Pyrrhus advanced as far as Anagnia (thirty-six miles from Rome). Negotiations between Rome and Cineas, deputy of the king,[91] failed, due to Pyrrhus' stipulations that Rome acknowledge the autonomy of the Samnites, Brettians and Lucanians. The one-time censor Ap. Claudius prompted his compatriots to reject these demands which, had they been accepted, would have nullified the fruits of Rome's resolute Italian policy of almost a hundred years. In the battle of Ausculum (279 B.C.), marked by heavy casualties, Pyrrhus once more emerged as victor,[92] but it was now only with difficulty that he was able to restore the losses in his army. In consequence, fresh negotiations would have offered favourable prospects for reaching an agreement if the Roman connection with the Carthaginians had not brought about a decisive shift in the centre of gravity in favour of Rome. A Roman-Carthaginian treaty was concluded, the third in the series of treaties between Rome and Carthage.[93] Rome received not only assurances of aid from the Carthaginian fleet but also economic donations, *inter alia* silver, which was needed to pay off the allies of southern Italy.[94]

At this juncture Pyrrhus received a call for help from the Syracusans.

Here serious internal conflicts had raged between the tyrant Thoenon and Sosistratus, the ruler of Acragas, and a Carthaginian fleet was blockading the harbour. At Tauromenium Pyrrhus stepped ashore on Sicilian soil (autumn 278 B.C.). The Hellenes of the island looked upon him as the saviour from internal discord and the champion against Carthage. A Congress of Hellenes in Syracuse elected him as "*hegemon* and *basileus*." As "King of Sicily" he became the successor to Agathocles, and Alexander, Pyrrhus' son by Lanassa, was contemplated as successor to the throne.[95]

The first great successes of Pyrrhus appeared to justify the boldest expectations. In a rapid victorious campaign the Epirote advanced through the island. Even the strongholds of Eryx and Heircte (Monte Castellaccio near Palermo)[96] did not hold out against him, and only in Lilybaeum did the Carthaginians succeed in holding their position, though not without difficulty.[97] They were actually prepared to negotiate for peace, provided only the possession of this final base were guaranteed to them. Under pressure from the Greeks, Pyrrhus rejected this offer, which to all intents and purposes would have made him master of the whole of Sicily. In the subsequent period there was a great cooling off in the relations between him and the Hellenes; Greek freedom proved incompatible with the rigid military discipline Pyrrhus demanded of the Hellenes. In Sicily the Greeks defected in ever greater numbers from Pyrrhus, and at the same time the distress of the Greeks in southern Italy demanded his presence beyond the straits. When he left the island (spring 275 B.C.) after two and a half years, the fatal hour had also struck for the Greeks of Sicily. The Hellenes had proven that not even a great national idea could overcome their internal quarrels. The party struggles in Sicily after the death of Agathocles (289 B.C.), lasting for years, did not pass without leaving their mark on the Greeks.

In southern Italy the Romans had meanwhile laid hands on Croton and Locri, and forced the Samnites and Lucanians under their sovereignty again. In the struggle between Rome and Pyrrhus even the last encounter at Maleventum (later called Beneventum)[98] did not decide the issue (275 B.C.), but Pyrrhus' material resources were exhausted, so that he was forced to abandon his Italic positions. In 275 B.C. he left Tarentum by ship, with 8000 infantry and 500 cavalry, to return to Epirus. He left his son Helenus and a garrison behind on the acropolis.[99]

It would appear that it was primarily the prospects for the Macedonian throne that induced him to give up his Italic expedition, but the anticipated successes on the other side of the Adriatic were only ephemeral. He did indeed succeed in driving Antigonus Gonatas out of Macedonia for a short time (274 B.C.), but the plundering of the royal tombs in Aegae alienated the sympathies of the Macedonians. What he had gained he soon lost again. In 272 B.C. Pyrrhus, before whom Rome and Carthage had trembled, met his death in a street fight in Argos.

Pyrrhus' withdrawal from Italy left the Hellenes of southern Italy at the mercy of the Romans. Tarentum fell in 272 B.C., after the Epirote garrison had left the city. From about 270 B.C. onwards the Locrians struck the so-called *pistis* coins which, with the wreathing of Rome by *Pistis*—trust—alluded to the loyalty between Rome and Locri.[100] The Locrians, like most of the Greek communities in southern Italy, also became naval allies of the Romans. In 270 B.C. Rhegium, the last city to do so, fell into the hands of the Romans.

Through contacts between the Greeks and Romans in southern Italy the doors had been opened wide to the fruitful encounter between the Greek and Roman spirit. What the Greeks lost in political power by being deprived of their autonomy, this they regained twofold in the cultural sphere. It is no accident that the figure of the Greek Livius Andronicus from Tarentum stands at the cradle of Latin literature. Rome knew only too well what it had gained in the Hellenes. By careful and graduated treaties, as Roman custom and political practice dictated, Rome determined the positions of the Greek cities from case to case. In the First Punic War the chief burden in the building of the Roman fleet, with which Rome forced the proud, sea-ruling Carthage to her knees, devolved upon the shoulders of the Hellenes.

The Greeks of eastern Sicily were, however, still to have a second political flowering. In the person of Hieron II, who in 275/4 B.C. carried through a coup d'état and established a Syracusan monarchy,[101] a really able leader once more emerged for the Hellenes of the island. Hieron skilfully navigated Syracuse through the great Roman-Carthaginian conflict of the first Punic War. Only after his death (215 or 214 B.C.), and after the capture of Syracuse by Marcellus (212 B.C.), did the Romans take over the last remnants of territory in Sicily.

The end of Greek history in the West saw the incorporation of the Hellenic polis into the territorial state. The Greeks of the West, in Sicily and southern Italy, incapable of asserting their political autonomy in the power struggle between the major states, became cultural standard-bearers of the first order and the leaven in a new civilisation which emerged on the ruins of an old world, under the powerful protection of Roman arms. The Hellenes did not come empty-handed. The century-old close concentration of political and cultural life within the limits of the Greek poleis still fulfilled a great mission after the loss of their political freedom. The marriage of the Greek spirit with Roman virtues created the foundations of that civilisation upon which the Western culture of our own day essentially rests.

THE BALANCE OF POWER TO THE END OF THE FIRST SYRIAN WAR (280-271 B.C.)

With a new generation of rulers, at the close of the eighties, of Ptolemy II in Egypt and Antiochus I in the Seleucid empire, a new spirit made its entry in the Hellenistic world. It was the idea of the balance of power, which determined the character of Hellenistic history for a period of eighty years. Three major powers, Ptolemaic Egypt, the Seleucid empire in western Asia and Antigonid Macedonia, controlled the history of the eastern Mediterranean during this period. The Hellenistic powers neither took note of nor influenced developments in the West—an act of neglect that bitterly avenged itself. The expedition of Pyrrhus to Italy and Sicily remained an episode, and the friendly footing on which the Ptolemaic empire stood with both sides in the First Punic War was chiefly determined by economic motives. Otherwise, however, the new rulers such as Ptolemy II, Antiochus I and Antigonus Gonatas, son of Demetrius Poliorcetes, showed great vigour. All three kings were of the same striking personalities as their fathers and their achievements as statesmen were no less noteworthy.

The collapse of Lysimachus' Hellespontine kingdom had bad consequences for the Hellenistic world. Apart from splitting a large, closely interwoven economic region, whose Asia Minor and European sections had complemented each other most successfully with their raw materials and their factories, the battle of Curupedion (281 B.C.) left a vacuum in the Balkans. Into this vacuum poured the Celts. During those years Celtic tribes were migrating towards the south. There is evidence of them in the region of the Lower Danube as early as the time of Alexander. The Celts did not restrict themselves to plundering expeditions, as their fellow tribesmen had once done during their advance against Rome (the battle at the Allia, 387 B.C.), but migrated with wives and children southwards in search of a new homeland. In military terms the Celtic hordes were far inferior to the highly trained Hellenistic armies. Their weapons were primitive and their art of war was in its infancy. Their great successes in the Hellenistic world could only have been gained under the special circumstances of the times. For the Celts appeared at a moment when the new states in the Hellenistic system were still in the throes of their birth pains.

The first thrust of the Celts struck Macedonia. King Ptolemy Ceraunus fell in battle and the rural districts were fearfully devastated (279 B.C.). With the collapse of Macedonia the heart of Hellas lay open. In the face of the fearful terror from the north the tribes of central Greece which were immediately most threatened, Aetolians, Phocians and Boeotians, united, but, circumvented by the Celts under Brennus, they had to give up their position at Thermopylae. After the Celts advanced as far as Delphi (the sanctuary was spared),[102] the lateness of the season forced them to turn back. On the Greek side it was primarily the Petalians who had distinguished themselves in the fighting, and the retreat of the Celts marks the beginning of Aetolian supremacy in Delphi. This tribe, hitherto so far behind general developments in Greece, now moved into the forefront among the Greek states.

Summoned by Nicomedes I of Bithynia and Mithradates II of Pontus, the Celts crossed the Hellespont in 278 B.C.[103] In Asia Minor they soon became the terror of the land, chiefly of the wealthy Greek cities. Antiochus I ultimately conquered them in the famous "elephant battle" (275/4? B.C.) and settled them according to tribes (Trocmi, Tectosages and Tolistoagii) in the north of Greater Phrygia, probably under compulsion.[104] Nevertheless, even then they did not remain quiet but repeatedly ravaged the surrounding districts.

For Macedonia the death of Ptolemy Ceraunus (279 B.C.) marked the beginning of an anarchy of a number of years. Both the successors of Ptolemy, his brother Meleager and Antipater (with the nickname Etesias), a nephew of Cassander, had proved completely incapable of solving the difficult problems facing the monarchy. The Macedonian military assembly, therefore, gave up the idea of electing a new king and instead appointed a Macedonian aristocrat by the name of Sosthenes as *strategos*, that is, as "royal commander-in-chief."[105] A number of pretenders, however, including Antigonus Gonatas, son of Demetrius Poliorcetes, continued to press their claims to the Macedonian throne. The death of the *strategos* Sosthenes (278 or at the latest 277 B.C.) and above all, a significant victory of Antigonus Gonatas over the Celtic hordes at Lysimacheia (277 B.C.), strengthened the position of the Antigonids, whose rule had hitherto rested solely on a few Greek possessions and bases in Thrace. With the conquest of Cassandreia and the victory over his rival "Etesias" Antigonus Gonatas was recognised as king in Macedonia (276 B.C.). That finally consolidated Macedonia, under the son of Demetrius Poliorcetes.

In the Celtic kingdom of Tylis, however,[106] which had emerged on the soil of the old Thracian kingdom of Lysimachus, Macedonia had a dangerous neighbour. Above all, the Greek cities on the Thracian coast of the Aegean found themselves exposed to the plundering expeditions of the Celts, and had to protect themselves by paying regular tribute. The presence of this wild, foreign people ultimately drove home to the Greeks and Macedonians that they should forget their quarrels and unite against the common foe.

There is no doubt whatever that the resurgence of Macedonia under the rule of Antigonus Gonatas, nephew of Antigonus Monophthalmus and Antipater, was the most astonishing phenomenon in Hellenistic history during the decade after Curupedion (281 B.C.). It was not so much circumstance as personality that proved to be decisive. In his youth Antigonus Gonatas, one of the most highly cultured monarchs of the Hellenistic period,[107] had sat at the feet of Zenon of Citium, the founder of the Stoa in Athens. His personal inclinations predisposed him towards the philosophical teachings of the Stoa, and his ideal was to realise in politics the demands of Stoic philosophy. At the time Macedonia was still the centre of the Hellenistic world. With continuing inexhaustible resources in manpower it placed incomparable reserves at the disposal of the Hellenistic armies. In addition, Macedonian military tradition since the time of Philip II and Alexander could look back on victories equalled by no other people in the world at that time. In the days of their fathers and grandfathers the Macedonian phalanxes had reduced the Achaemenid empire to ruins, and even now Antigonus Gonatas had for the first time defeated the fearful Celts in the open field (277 B.C.). Antigonus also succeeded, in fluctuating battles, in repulsing the threat of Pyrrhus,[108] and when that perpetual instigator of unrest met his death in 272 B.C., the Macedonian king was also rid of the last and most dangerous rival to the Macedonian throne. Outside Macedonia, the rule of Antigonus rested on Thessaly and on extensive regions of eastern and southern Greece. Under the protection of Macedonian arms a great many tyrants held sway, chiefly in the Peloponnesus. Their survival was bound up with Macedonian rule in Greece, for better or for worse. Strong Macedonian garrisons were stationed in Corinth, in Chalcis on Euboea and in Thessalian Demetrias, the three "fetters" of Hellas. Although the Ptolemies had once been the indisputable masters of the Aegean, that is, since the rule of Demetrius Poliorcetes had collapsed (286 B.C.), the Macedonians now set about to contest their naval supremacy.

The political situation in the other two major Hellenistic states, the Seleucid and Ptolemaic monarchies, was, in the first decades of the third century, determined by the deepseated conflict over the "Syrian question." For more than 150 years the struggle for South Syria (so-called Coele Syria) took the energies of both powers. No matter how often the conflict was terminated by peace, it always broke out afresh. Ever since Ptolemy I had taken possession of the region during the decisive battle of the coalition against Antigonus Monophthalmus (301 B.C.) it remained the bone of contention with the Seleucids. The Ptolemies were economically as well as politically dependent on South Syria. Apart from Cyprus and certain coastal regions in southern Anatolia, it was the only country from which Egypt could import the timber required for shipbuilding (the "cedars of Lebanon"). It is therefore no accident that the Pharaohs of the New Kingdom, Thutmosis III and his successors, from 1500 B.C. onwards again and again turned to Syria. Possession of the Syrian coast provided the fleets of the great maritime cities like Tyre, Sidon and Berytus. For example, the naval supremacy of Demetrius Poliorcetes rested on Phoenician ships, until his far-flung maritime empire collapsed in 286 B.C.

The conflict between the two monarchies brought two wars during the seventies. Fighting broke out as early as 280-279 B.C. between Ptolemy II and Antiochus I.[109] The numerical strength facing the Seleucid was great. Opposing him were, apart from Ptolemy II and Antigonus Gonatas, the current pretender to the throne, also the cities on the Propontis and Pontus, united in the so-called Northern League—above all Heracleia, with its powerful navy, and Byzantium—as well as Bithynia and Pontic Cappadocia under Mithradates II.[110] Little is known about the details of these events.[111]

Antiochus I, between 277 and 275 B.C., was tied down in wars against the Celts who had penetrated into Asia Minor. Then in 274 B.C. the so-called First Syrian War broke out. Neither party, however, won a decisive victory, although Ptolemy II succeeded in retaining the Syrian and Phoenician possessions (with the exception of Marathus). The great importance of Ptolemaic sea power was shown by a naval expedition to the Pontus,[112] where Ptolemy II was on friendly terms with Heracleia. The defection of Magas, viceroy of Cyrenaica and a stepson of Ptolemy I,[113] admittedly meant a definite weakening of Egypt's position. Through his marriage (about 275 B.C.?) contracted with Apame, daughter of Antiochus

45. Epidaurus. Theatre.

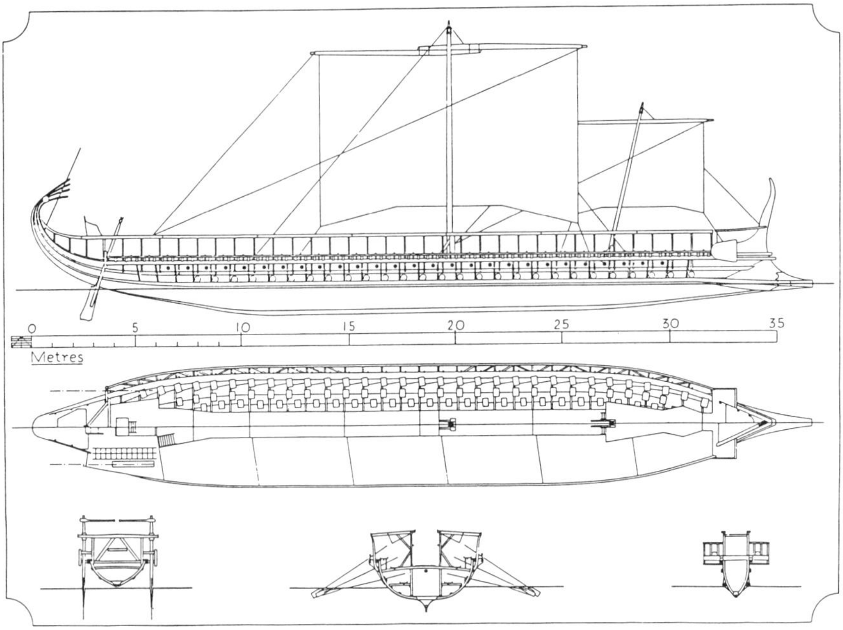

46. Reconstruction drawing of the Greek trireme.

47. Thucydides.
Holkham Hall, Norfolk.

48. Alcibiades (?). Ny Carlsberg Glyptotek, Copenhagen.

49. Xenophon. Archaeological Museum, Alexandria.

50. Miletus. Ancient Palaestra.

51. Philip II of Macedonia. Ny Carlsberg Glyptotek, Copenhagen.

52. Demosthenes. Ny Carlsberg Glyptotek, Copenhagen.

53. Pella. The royal palace. View towards the north.

54. Alexander the Great. Anza herm. Louvre, Paris.

55. Plutarch (?). Archaeological Museum, Delphi.

56. Cos. Sanctuary of Asclepius.

57. Ephesus. View towards the north-east. Agora and theatre (foreground) and site of the Temple of Artemis and the Christian site (background).

58. Didyma. Capital (head of Medusa) from the Temple of Apollo.

59. Pergamum. Site of the Great Altar of Zeus.

60. Detail from the frieze of the Great Altar of Zeus at Pergamum. Staatliche Museen, Berlin.

61. Modern-day ploughing in Asia Minor.

62. Xanthus and the Xanthus River, Lycia. View towards the south.

63. The fertile plain of Cilicia, Asia Minor. View towards the east.

64. Tyre. Late sarcophagus.

I, Magas gained the Seleucid support necessary to assert his independence of Ptolemy II.[114] The latter was finally obliged to recognise him as king of Cyrenaica, with a formal supremacy of Ptolemy II that was only theoretical.

Ptolemy marked the ending of the First Syrian War with great victory celebrations in Alexandria (271/70 B.C.).[115] Callixeinus has left us a vivid description of the procession (preserved in Athenaeus V 196 ff., even though only a small excerpt), the special Dionysus *pompe*. The *pompe* was a vast procession, a parade of the triumphant Ptolemaic army and an impressive display of the power of the empire, power unlike anything the world had seen before. On the occasion of these celebrations the court poet Theocritus composed a hymn in praise of the ruling monarch, Ptolemy II, and his sister-wife Arsinoe, and of the royal couple's parents, under the name of "Divine Saviours."[116] In other respects too Ptolemy II made every attempt to show the outside world the dominating political and economic power of his empire. In the West the threads of his diplomacy extended as far as Rome and Carthage,[117] and in the East as far as India, where he asserted himself alongside the Seleucids. Ptolemy II showed a very shrewd understanding of the political value of the favoured central location and strong economic position of Egypt.

Arsinoe, the second wife of Ptolemy II, played an outstanding rôle in the politics of the day. At first she had been the wife of Lysimachus and then of Ptolemy Ceraunus. Upon returning to Alexandria she manipulated her blood brother into divorcing his wife (Arsinoe I, daughter of Lysimachus) and into taking herself as his bride. For the Greeks, consanguineous marriage was incest of the worst kind, although Egyptian thinking allowed marriage between brother and sister. It is likely that the example of the Achaemenids played an important rôle in this.[118] Until her death (270 B.C.) Arsinoe exerted a decisive influence over her considerably younger brother.[119] She was the first of the great women in the history of the Ptolemaic empire, a forerunner of the great Cleopatra.

FROM THE CHREMONIDEIAN WAR TO THE DEATH OF ANTIGONUS GONATAS (271-239 B.C.)

In the Aegean, Ptolemaic sea power rested on the protectorate of the so-called Island League.[120] Here the keenest rival of the Ptolemies was not the Seleucid empire but newly revived Macedonia under King Antigonus Gonatas. Nothing was more dangerous to the position of the Ptolemaic kingdom than Macedonian sovereignty in the Aegean, which would have meant the re-emergence of the sea power of Demetrius Poliorcetes. If the Macedonian fleet controlled the Aegean and the straits, then Greece would, in terms of the grain supply from southern Russia, be at the mercy of the Macedonians. The Macedonians, indeed, already controlled large areas of Greece through the garrisons and tyrants installed by Antigonus. In consequence, Ptolemy II (Philadelphus) had to stake everything on precipitating the Greeks into war against the Macedonians to topple the predominant position of Antigonus Gonatas. Thus after a triple alliance was concluded by Ptolemy II, King Areus of Sparta, and Athens, on Ptolemaic initiative, a war ensued against Antigonus—the so-called Chremonideian War (267-261 B.C.?).[121] Ptolemy II, however, failed to provide his Greek allies with the necessary aid. It is true that his fleet, under the admiral Patroclus, blockaded the Saronic Gulf and inflicted a certain amount of damage on Antigonus.[122] Ptolemy II also put up more forts in Attica,[123] but despite this the Macedonian army soon proved superior. The Spartan king, Areus, fell in battle at Corinth (265 B.C.); Athens was encircled and forced to capitulate (263/2 B.C.). Piraeus and the hill of the *Mouseion* were secured by Macedonian garrisons, the Attic authorities were forced to abdicate, the city itself received a Macedonian governor and the Macedonian king reserved the right to appoint a number of leading Attic officials, especially the *strategoi*.[124] Not too long after, in 256/5 (or 255/4 B.C.), the conditions were lightened to some extent.[125] Nevertheless Athens, which with Alexandria provided the cultural focus of the ancient world, saw itself reduced politically for a period of thirty-five years (until 229 B.C.) to the level of a Macedonian provincial town. This was a decisive victory of the Hellenistic monarchy over the old Greek polis, a victory such as the Romans in the West won over the Greek cities in southern Italy at almost the same time.

The Second Syrian War (260-253 B.C.) followed almost on the heels of the Chremonideian War. This time Ptolemy II faced the coalition of the Seleucid empire under Antiochus II (261-246 B.C.) and Macedonia under Antigonus Gonatas. Of the two, Macedonia was the more dangerous opponent. Antigonus had staked everything on strengthening his naval position by building a large fleet, an event which has a striking parallel in the West with the building of the Roman fleet in 261 B.C. Ptolemy suffered extensive territorial losses overseas, primarily in Ionia, Pamphylia and Cilicia, but the shrewd diplomat that he was, he split the enemy coalition and concluded a separate peace with Antigonus Gonatas in 255 B.C.[126] Then in the course of the year 253 B.C. he concluded a peace with the Seleucid empire. A year later Antiochus II married Berenice, daughter of Ptolemy II, after he had divorced his first wife Laodice. This Ptolemaic marriage became the cause of a further dangerous war, the so-called Laodice War.[127]

The fresh conflict between the Seleucid and Ptolemaic empires was precipitated by the death of Antiochus II (summer 246 B.C.) and the consequences connected with it. In his will, Antiochus II had designated Seleucus II, the eldest son of his first wife Laodice, as his successor. This brushed aside the recognised hereditary right of the princeling, the younger son of his second wife, the Ptolemaic princess Berenice. Berenice, who was sojourning in Antioch on the Orontes, resolved to defend the hereditary right of her son by resorting to arms. She found a ready ally in her brother Ptolemy III, who in 246 B.C. had acceded to the Lagid throne as successor to Ptolemy II. At precisely that moment Egypt's position was extraordinarily strengthened by the annexation of Cyrenaica. The connection between the Cyrenaean heiress Berenice, daughter of Magas, and the

Egyptian crown prince, the later Ptolemy III, had reunited Cyrenaica with Egypt just before the latter's accession.

Through the activity of Laodice's followers in Antioch, however, events took a different course from what was anticipated at the court of the Seleucid queen Berenice and in Alexandria. The contradictory statements in the sources make it impossible to reconstruct with certainty the events in Antioch, although it is clear that Berenice's young son and the queen herself met death at the hands of a murderer. In the famous "Bulletin," preserved in Papyrus Gurob, the Ptolemaic king has himself described his impressions on his magnificent entry into Antioch.[128] This piece of writing, a document of unusual historical value, was from the outset designed for publication, for it gives the official Ptolemaic version.[129] No lasting results came from the conquering expedition of Ptolemy III in Western Asia. Although Egyptian propaganda (cf. above all the temple inscription of Esne)[130] painted Ptolemy III as a great military prince of the type of the ancient Pharaohs—according to the inscription of Adulis Ptolemy even crossed the Euphrates—the conquests in Western Asia evaporated immediately (spring 245 B.C.).[131] Since the Egyptian forces were inadequate to supply enough occupation troops, Ptolemy did not succeed in controlling the regions of the East for long, particularly because he was not certain of the loyalty of the Seleucid governors. In the peace of 241 B.C. Ptolemy III lost most of his conquests in North Syria, keeping only the important maritime city Seleuceia in Pieria, and a number of Thracian coastal places which were of great importance as naval bases in the Aegean.[132]

The Laodice War precipitated the Seleucid empire into a serious crisis in both internal and foreign affairs. In both East and West of the empire separatist forces erupted, and it almost appeared as if the days of the empire were numbered, after a history of little more than fifty years. In 260 B.C. the so-called empire of Greater Cappadocia emerged in Asia Minor under the Persian Ariarathes,[133] the Iranian element for the first time prevailing over the Macedonians. The rise of this new empire was favoured by the existence of two states in Asia Minor which were hostile to the Seleucids from the very beginning: Bithynia and Pontus. Under its rulers Nicomedes I (280 to about 255 B.C.) and Ziaëlis (255-235 B.C.) Bithynia became a coveted trade partner of the Hellenistic states and poleis on account of its wealth in forests. Despite the fact that it extended over only a small area of the Anatolian hinterland from Cyzicus to Chalcedon, Bithynia was able to assert itself against the Seleucids,[134] just as Pontus, which, studded with a great many temple territories, occupied an important key position as a thoroughfare from Anatolia to Armenia. In Pontus an Iranian princely house, in which the name Mithradates often recurs, ruled over a population composed of the most varied elements (Anatolians, Iranians and Greeks).[135] In addition, the position of the Seleucid empire was decisively weakened by two other factors in Asia Minor—the restless Celts, or the Galatians as they are now called, in northern Greater Phrygia, and by dynastic power struggles in the Seleucid house itself. Supported by his mother Laodice, Antiochus Hierax, younger brother of King Seleucus II, took advantage of the serious situation in the empire and carved out for himself in Asia Minor a kingdom which he ruled, nominally as viceroy with his elder brother, but in fact almost as an independent realm.[136] The Asia Minor dominions were practically severed from the rest of the empire until 228/7 B.C., when Antiochus Hierax fell in Thrace. The Seleucid empire had been completely eliminated as a power factor in the West.

Still bleaker is the picture of the empire in the Iranian east. As in Greater Cappadocia, so here the opposition of the Iranian national element also became active. The Seleucids, with their one-sided preferential treatment of Macedonians, never really succeeded in winning the Iranians over. In addition, satraps, who had been installed by the Seleucids but could not be held in check, were striving towards independence. The details of these events remain shrouded in darkness. It has been established, however, that Diodotus, satrap of Bactria, gradually emancipated himself from the empire, as his striking of coins shows.[137] By obtaining the support of the unusually large number of Greek and Macedonian military colonies in Bactria, he laid the foundations for the later development of the power of colonial Hellenism in Bactria under Euthydemus and Demetrius. In the satrapy of Parthia developments took a different course. Here the Seleucid satrap Andragoras made himself independent, but an invasion of an Iranian equestrian tribe, the Dahaean Parnians, from the great centre of disturbance east of the Caspian Sea, swept away the rule of the Macedonians in Parthia and Hyrcania. Here, on ancient Iranian soil, there emerged under the founder of the kingdom, Arshak (Greek Arsaces), an Iranian state with a feudal organisation like that of the Achaemenid empire.[138] The Parthians—so called after the name of the region—did not reject the Greek culture of the settlements in these remote regions, but in the structure of their political system they consciously pursued a national Iranian policy. They were in no way prepared to come to terms with the Seleucids. In the later Babylonian documents the Parthian era is reckoned from the first of Nisan 247 B.C.,[139] but this is obviously a later fiction which attempts to date the beginning of Parthian independence as far back as possible. The founding of the Parthian state may not have taken place until the beginning of the thirties of the third century.

The rise of the Iranian Parthians saw the appearance of a third power on the political map of the East, alongside the emergent Graeco-Bactrian kingdom of Diodotus and the Seleucid empire ruled predominantly by Macedonians. In the following centuries the Parthians grew tremendously and developed into an equal opponent of the Seleucids, and later even of the Romans. This Parthian kingdom had a history of 500 years, a period exactly double that of the Seleucid empire.

In Greece a completely new situation arose during the fifties. Although the Macedonian rule of Antigonus Gonatas in Hellas appeared to be securely anchored at the end of the Chremonideian War, cracks soon manifested themselves in the proud Macedonian power-house in Greece. The crisis was precipitated by the efforts towards independence by the Macedonian viceroy in Greece, Alexander (son of Craterus), and by the steadily increasing importance of the Greek political leagues in the third century B.C. The Aetolians—mentioned for the first time in an inscription on an Athenian stele from the year 367/6 B.C.[140]—relying on a treaty with the Acarnanians,[141] expanded their power in central Greece. In particular they occupied a dominating position in Delphi, but also could assert themselves on the seas. As pirates they were feared far and wide, and numerous treaties of asylum concluded between the Aetolians and Greek cities attest the wide radius of their operations in Greek waters.[142] The Achaean League (established in 280 B.C.) activated the energies of the northern Peloponnesus, which had for so long been unexploited. In Aratus of Sicyon, who had liberated his native city from tyranny in 251 B.C., the Achaeans possessed an outstanding statesman and a shrewd diplomat. As a *strategos* of many years' experience he determined the fortunes of the League after 245 B.C.[143] The confederations gave the political energies of the Hellenes of the motherland a new form of expression and a new field of activity. It is no wonder that the Leagues inevitably came into conflict with Macedonia, the power in Hellas which more than any other called Greek freedom into question.

When Alexander, the viceroy of Antigonus Gonatas in Greece, defected in 253 or 252 B.C. (?),[144] Antigonus lost Euboea and Corinth. The latter was the cornerstone of Macedonian rule in Hellas. But a combined action was not as yet undertaken by the two major Greek political leagues against the foreign domination of Macedonia. On the contrary, the attack of the Aetolians encroached upon the Peloponnesus, which led to bitter hostility. In capturing Acrocorinth in 243 B.C. (by an assault in peacetime) Aratus scored an important success. He forced the garrison of Antigonus, which had returned in 244 B.C., to withdraw.[145] The union of the entire Peloponnesus under Achaean leadership now seemed only a question of time. The Achaeans found support in King Ptolemy III Euergetes, and in 243 B.C. conferred on him the honorary command of the League forces on sea and land.[146] In return, he paid subsidies to the Achaeans. The Achaeans also concluded an alliance with Sparta even though the latter had been shaken by a serious internal crisis at the end of the forties. In Sparta, the accumulation of property in the hands of a few individuals had brought about such a fundamental change in the structure of the state that not even a shadow of the former ideal of equality remained. A reform had long been overdue. The method, however, by which it was carried out, and the fact that it was bound up with distinctly political objectives of King Agis IV, precipitated resistance on the part of those who were opposed to the reform and culminated in a catastrophe. Agis himself was killed and many of his followers were banished (241 B.C.).[147]

When Antigonus Gonatas died in 239 B.C., after almost forty years of fluctuating rule, a whole era came to an end. The Hellenistic political system, born at the battle of Curupedion (281 B.C.), had withstood many tests. The Ptolemies had maintained, indeed had even partly extended their possessions; the Seleucid kingdom had suffered considerable territorial losses in both East and West; and Macedonian rule in Greece was shaken by the loss of Corinth and additional regions in the Peloponnesus. Without a doubt the most powerful ruler in the Hellenistic world at the time was Ptolemy III Euergetes—despite the long-range failure of his eastern campaign. The supremacy of the Ptolemies in the Hellenistic political system rested on the army, a strong fleet, extensive diplomatic and trade connections, and the rich natural resources of the land of the Nile. The land was exploited as fully as possible by the patient labour of the *fellaheen*—peasants—and the untiring zeal of the Greek officials, a programme that no other major Hellenistic state could match.

In general, the forty-two years from the battle of Curupedion to the death of Antigonus Gonatas (281-239 B.C.) mark the indisputable zenith of Hellenistic history. The development of political power in the major Hellenistic states accompanied a cultural efflorescence, above all in poetry and the mathematical sciences, which has no counterpart in the entire history of antiquity.[148] Thus the power of the Hellenistic states in the East appeared to be securely established. In the West, however, a fundamental change had come about. In the First Punic War (264-241 B.C.) Sicily fell as a prize to the Romans. The sun had forever set on the political independence of the Greek communities there. Syracuse was at first still an exception. Her ruler, King Hieron II, secured a final Indian Summer (until 212 B.C.) for the Greeks in east Sicily by his astuteness in coming to terms at first with the Carthaginians and then with the victorious Romans. The Roman conquest of the remainder of Sicily ended with the establishment of the Province of Sicily (227 B.C.). As the will of the Hellenistic kings constituted the supreme law in the poleis of the East, so the word of the Roman praetor, the representative of the *populus Romanus*, henceforth ruled in Acragas, Camarina and Messana. The life-span of the Greek autonomous polis had expired, its functions in the realm of foreign affairs taken over in the East by the major Hellenistic powers and in the West by the Romans. In only a few instances were the poleis still to play an important rôle among the major states. These were primarily the powerful city-republics on the Black Sea—Sinope, Heracleia, Byzantium, Chalcedon, Cyzicus and the maritime power Rhodes. The last named, along with Ptolemaic Alexandria, assumed great importance as the clearing house of Hellenistic trade.[149] The Hellenic poleis, however, whether independent or not, maintained their great significance as centres of cultural and intellectual life and made definitive contributions to the development of Hellenistic world culture. Thus the Greeks of Sicily and southern Italy, and also a free Greek city like Massalia, fulfilled a mission of greatest importance in the history of civilisation, for their influence passed through Rome to western Europe.

FROM THE DEATH OF ANTIGONUS GONATAS TO THE BATTLE OF SELLASIA (239-222 B.C.)

The years from the death of Antigonus Gonatas (239 B.C.) to the declaration of war against King Philip V of Macedonia (200 B.C.) were decisive for the fate of the Hellenistic world. For the first time since the death of Pyrrhus direct contact between the East and West of the Mediterranean world was re-established. Rome's intervention beyond the Adriatic in Illyria in 229 B.C. is the first indication of a new easterly orientation of the hegemonial power of Italy. The want of political union in the Hellenistic world prevented effective reaction on the part of the East, so Macedonia remained alone in her struggle, and the Roman victory in the Hannibalic War (218-201 B.C.) ultimately also decided the fate of the East.

During this period, the Hellenistic world divided into two spheres which overlapped each other only on the periphery. The western sphere included Macedonia (under Demetrius II, 239-229 B.C., Antigonus Doson, 229-222/1 B.C., Philip V, 222/1-179 B.C.) and the Greek motherland. Political circumstances oriented Hellas and Macedonia more towards the west than the east. For Macedonia the control of the Adriatic was at stake, and the foothold gained by the Romans in Illyria in 228 B.C. was a serious threat to her position. The Ptolemaic and Seleucid kingdoms, which formed the eastern sphere, were so occupied with internal problems that they could not bring any strong influence to bear upon the situation either in the Aegean or in Hellas. The era also saw the rise of medium states, such as Rhodes and Pergamum, who stepped into the gap left by the elimination of the Ptolemies from the Aegean and the decline of Seleucid power in Asia Minor. Pergamum emerged early, during the war between Lysimachus and Seleucus I. At that time the treasurer at Pergamum, Philetaerus, son of a Macedonian and a woman of Paphlagonia, had joined the side of Seleucus.[150] In 263 B.C. he handed the control of the citadel and the city of Pergamum, as well as a small piece of territory,[151] over to his nephew, Eumenes I, who was followed by his nephew, Attalus (I) (241-197 B.C.). Attalus refused to pay the tribute hitherto rendered to the Galatians, and inflicted shattering defeats on them in two engagements (c. 230 B.C.).[152] He then took the royal title to place himself on a level with the kings of Bithynia, Pontus and Cappadocia, as well as the Seleucids in Asia. When Attalus drove the Seleucid Antiochus Hierax out of Anatolia, he temporarily even ruled over all Seleucid Asia Minor from the Aegean to the Taurus mountains (approximately 228-223 B.C.). Pergamum, like the frontier states of northern Anatolia, was forced into opposition against the Seleucids. The Attalids consequently had to be on the alert for allies, and it is no coincidence that Pergamum later became the jumping off point of Rome's intervention in Asia Minor.

In the second half of the third century the Seleucids were involved in a war of attrition on two fronts, in East and West, exhausting the energies of the country. Seleucus II, nicknamed "Callinicus" (246-225 B.C.), was decisively defeated by his younger brother Antiochus Hierax in Anatolia, and then by the Galatians at Ancyra (239 B.C.?).[153] Foreign powers sought to profit from the weaknesses of Seleucid rule in Asia Minor. Thus Antigonus Doson as viceroy of Macedonia made a number of territorial acquisitions in a naval expedition to Caria (227 B.C.).[154] Even more unfortunate than Seleucus II was his son Seleucus III Soter (255-223 B.C.). He made extensive military preparations for a war against Attalus I of Pergamum, but just as he was about to march, he was murdered by one of his officers and the Galatian Apaturius. His nephew Achaeus, however, with great strategic skill soon regained almost the entire former Seleucid territory of Asia Minor and completely undid the great expansion of the Pergamene state under Attalus I.

A new era in Seleucid rule began in 223 B.C. when Antiochus III, a younger brother of Seleucus III and only eighteen years of age, acceded to the throne. Supported by shrewd advisors, in particular by the Carian Hermeias, the young king tried to recreate the greatness of the kingdom under Seleucus I and Antiochus I. His unusual energy once more secured for the kingdom a generation of outward splendour and an inner rebirth.[155]

A strong Seleucid kingdom depended on the regions of South Syria, above all the large maritime cities of Phoenicia. Antiochus, therefore, planned a Syrian campaign, which was, however, postponed for a while because of a dangerous revolt in the so-called Upper Satrapies (222 B.C.) by the governor of the eastern regions, Molon, and his brother, Alexander, governor of Persis. Molon even adopted the royal title, and after taking Seleuceia on the Tigris, advanced with his troops deep into the interior towards Babylonia. He ruled the area from the Lower Euphrates to deep within the interior, in the direction of Iran. Molon had coins struck in Seleuceia on the Tigris, in Babylon, Susa, Persepolis and Ecbatana. Not until King Antiochus III personally intervened did the picture change. Molon was driven out of Babylonia and after being defeated in battle took his own life (220 B.C.).[156]

Now it was possible to resume the operations which had begun in Syria and not even the defection of Achaeus, viceroy of Asia Minor, held Antiochus III back. The struggle for Syria (the so-called Fourth Syrian War) between Antiochus III and Ptolemy IV Philopator, who had succeeded his father Ptolemy III Euergetes to the throne in 221 B.C.,[157] was also a struggle for supremacy over the eastern Mediterranean, over which the powerful Ptolemaic fleet still had control. At the same time Rome and Carthage armed themselves in the West for the decisive second battle for supremacy over the western Mediterranean. In the same year that Hannibal began the siege of Saguntum (219 B.C.), Antiochus took possession of the important maritime city of Seleuceia in Pieria, a Ptolemaic enclave in northern Syria. Tyre and Ptolemaïs (Akko) also fell into his hands. All the successes of the Seleucid were, however, nullified by his defeat at Raphia (217 B.C.).[158] On the Ptolemaic side, large contingents of native Egyptians for the first time fought and proved themselves well in battle. The victory of Ptolemy IV at Raphia made the Egyptian natives aware of their importance—even indispensability—to the Ptolemaic régime. In the peace which followed Raphia, Antiochus retained the important city of Seleuceia in Pieria, but South Syria remained lost to him (217 B.C.).

With the conclusion of peace, Antiochus III gained a free hand for action in Asia Minor against the rebellious Achaeus. The rebel rule rapidly collapsed and Achaeus himself was executed in the barbaric fashion prescribed by Achaemenid penal law, adopted from the Assyrians (213 B.C.).[159] An expedition into the eastern satrapies followed closely on the heels of the liberation of the west. The famous "Anabasis" of Antiochus began in 212 B.C.[160] It took him through the whole of Upper Asia as far as India. The Graeco-Bactrian ruler Euthydemus was allowed to keep his kingdom and his royal title, but like the Indian king Sophagasenus and the Parthian Arsaces II, he had to acknowledge the supremacy of the Seleucid. As Sandrocottus had once furnished Seleucus I with war elephants, so Sophagasenus furnished them for the army of Antiochus. Between 212 and 205 B.C., the Seleucid[161] established a great system of dependent vassal states in the East, although the accomplishment lasted only as long as Antiochus' power remained intact. The "Anabasis," which is in a certain way reminiscent of Alexander's campaign, won Antiochus unlimited admiration from the entire Graeco-Hellenistic world. He now assumed the Achaemenid title of "Great King" which, with a play on Alexander the Great, was recoined into "Antiochus the Great."[162] His imposing successes coincided chronologically with the decisive struggle between Rome and Carthage in the western Mediterranean. Macedonia also became involved, in the so-called First Macedonian War (215-205 B.C.), by reason of its alliance with Hannibal. The success of the Seleucid kingdom in foreign affairs was, however, made possible primarily by the complete passivity of the Ptolemaic kingdom.

While the Seleucid kingdom in the east experienced a resurgence under Antiochus III, Greece suffered almost uninterrupted fighting between the Aetolian League and the Achaean League. The political antagonism of these two sealed the political decline of Hellas. Her Greek possessions repeatedly drew Macedonia into the internal conflicts of the Greeks. The war of Demetrius II of Macedonia against the Aetolians and Achaeans did not bring any decision (from 239/8 B.C. onwards).[163] Both major Greek Leagues reached the zenith of their power in the period immediately after the death of Demetrius II (229 B.C.). At that time the territory of the Aetolians extended directly across central Greece from the Ionian to the Aegean Sea. It included Thessaly and Achaea Phthiotis, as well as Boeotia, Ambracia and Amphilochia.[164] The Aetolians had naval bases on both seas and no coastal region was safe from their ships. No less impressive was the territory of the Achaeans. In addition to Achaea itself, it included the large Peloponnesian communities of Corinth, Sicyon, Argos, Megalopolis and part of Arcadia, predominantly regions which Macedonia had at one time ruled. When the Macedonian garrison withdrew from Athens in 229 B.C.—the money for the outstanding pay of the garrison troops came chiefly from foreign gifts—the city regained the independence which it had lost in the Chremonideian War.[165] Nothing survived of Macedonian rule in Greece except the stronghold of Demetrias, the island of Euboea and certain of the Cyclades. A new epoch in the history of Greece appeared to be dawning.

The inheritance which Antigonus Doson had taken over in 229 B.C.[166] as administrator of the kingdom and guardian for his young relation Philip was an extraordinary burden. It was first necessary to pacify the northern frontier of Macedonia—here the Dardanians had invaded—so Antigonus Doson was forced to remain passive in the face of Roman intervention in Illyria against the pirate states of that region, the natural sphere of Macedonian influence.[167] Despite this Macedonia experienced a gradual revival under Antigonus Doson, made possible by major shifts in power in Greece, especially in the Peloponnesus. Here a bitter struggle for supremacy had been raging between the Achaean League and Sparta since 229 B.C. In Sparta King Cleomenes III, following the model of Agis, attacked the problem of the redistribution of estates and land, seeking a loyal following among the *Perioikoi*. The fact of the matter was that in Sparta fundamental social reform could scarcely be put off any longer. The Spartans had suffered heavy losses of fertile districts, losing Messenia in the days of Epameinondas, and Cynuria through Philip II, and the number of full-blooded Spartan citizens had dropped drastically from 8000 in 479 B.C. to only 700 in the middle of the third century. Only a hundred of these were still landholders and in a position to exercise their political rights. All this had so accentuated the tensions between the rich and the poor that only a thorough-going reform held out any prospect of solving the difficulties.

Cleomenes was aware that he would encounter the most vigorous opposition to his plans for reform from the ephors, so there was no other alternative but to overthrow the government. In 227 B.C. he had all but one of the ephors killed, declared the ephorate abolished, since no provision was made for it in the Lycurgan constitution, and drove eighty of the most eminent Spartan estate owners into exile. The re-establishing of the ancient Lycurgan constitution and the old Spartan military life ultimately served to improve the military striking power of the state. Cleomenes' political programme in internal affairs was essential for an activation of Spartan policy abroad, aimed at Spartan hegemony over the Peloponnesus.[168]

In order to counter Sparta's rise, Aratus, the leading statesman of the Achaean League, reversed his own foreign policy. Corinth, occupied at the time by Cleomenes, was handed back to the Macedonians, and in return Aratus, as plenipotentiary *strategos*, concluded a treaty with Antigonus Doson (225/4 B.C.).[169] The Macedonian king was not slow to exploit the advantage of the moment. He gathered the Achaeans, Thessalians, Epirotes, Acarnanians, Boeotians, Phocians, Locrians and the island of Euboea into a large, general defensive-offensive alliance under Macedonian hegemony (224 B.C.).[170] It was probably modelled on the Corinthian League of Philip II of the year 338/7 B.C. The members were not, however, as in the earlier alliance, primarily individual poleis, but political leagues, much more independent in their relation to the alliance than was formerly the case with the many small "city-states." The Macedonian king was the president of the alliance, and in time of war commander-in-chief of the federal army. The rôle of the congress of the alliance was to decide questions of war and peace, and it was also to determine the contingents which the various members were to furnish to the federal army. Thus for the third time in Greek history Macedonian initiative created a large national federal organisation.

Antigonus Doson soon scored significant successes in the war against Cleomenes III. Tegea, Orchomenus and Mantineia fell into his hands (223 B.C.). Mantineia, whose population was sold into slavery, received Achaean colonists. Even though it enjoyed a revival under the name Antigoneia, the selling of the entire population into slavery evoked shock and horror throughout the whole of Greece.[171] The battle of Sellasia (summer 222 B.C.) decided the struggle for supremacy in the Peloponnesus.[172] The Spartans under Cleomenes were defeated by the Macedonians and their allies and King Antigonus marched into Sparta as victor, the first time in many centuries of its history that a victorious enemy had done so. Cleomenes fled to Egypt; at home his reforms were abolished and the monarchy left vacant; Sparta became a member of the Panhellenic Symmachy.[173] Otherwise the Spartans had suffered devastating losses at Sellasia.

THE FIRST ROMAN INTERVENTIONS (222-201 B.C.)

Sellasia marks the last peak in Macedonian history. Within a few months (222/1 B.C.) King Antigonus Doson died, after a campaign against the Illyrians. His successor, the young prince Philip, at first exercised his rule under the guardianship of the regency council appointed by Antigonus. Polybius has depicted the personality of Philip in an extremely paradoxical manner, and many features of his rule and personality still remain inexplicable today.[174] That the young ruler possessed a keen eye for political realities is proven by the documents, particularly his letters to Larisa in Thessaly, in which he recommends the Roman practice of extending the number of citizens.[175] His political acumen shows in the treaty he concluded in 215 B.C. with the Carthaginians, Rome's enemies. It would appear that Philip lacked the necessary energy to translate his knowledge into fact, and as a result he came to grief.

In 220 B.C. the so-called Allied War split Hellas into two camps.[176] The Macedonians and their numerous Hellenic allies, including the Achaeans, were ranged against the Aetolians, who for their part found allies in the Spartans. Even Crete, which up to then had steered an independent course outside the mainstream of political events, was drawn into the struggle.[177] There were no large-scale military operations, but the war brought acts of destruction and plundering. The Aetolians in barbarian fashion devastated Macedonian Dium at Mount Olympus, while King Philip, after the capture of Thermum, gave as good as he received. On the whole, however, the Hellenic Symmachy established by Antigonus Doson had stood the crucial test. In 217 B.C. the Peace Treaty of Naupactus was concluded, through the mediation of Rhodes, Chios and King Ptolemy IV Philopator.[178] It was the last treaty concluded solely among Greeks; in all later treaties the Romans played a leading rôle. The speech of the Aetolian statesman Agelaus in Naupactus, recorded by Polybius (Polyb. V 104. 10 ff.), reads like a prophecy: "For if you wait until these clouds now looming in the west shall once have discharged themselves over Greece, then I very much fear lest we may find these truces and wars and games at which we are now playing so rudely interrupted that we shall be fain to pray the gods still to give us the power of fighting with each other and making peace when we will—in a word, the power to decide our differences for ourselves."[179]

In truth, the event which decided the fate of the Greeks had already occurred twelve years before—the Roman intervention in Illyria against Queen Teuta. The plundering of Italic merchants at Phoenice in Epirus prompted the Romans to send out an embassy in 230 B.C. to demand reparations. When Teuta answered this move with new provocations, Rome took resolute action by despatching both consuls, charged with active intervention in Illyria (229 B.C.).[180] This was a step which would inevitably entangle the Romans in the political disturbances of the Balkan peninsula.[181] When the Illyrian dynast Demetrius of Pharos joined them the Romans succeeded in gaining a foothold not only on Corcyra and Issa but also in Apollonia and Dyrrhachium (Durazzo). The Atintanians and the Parthinians also joined the side of Rome. The peace concluded between Rome and Teuta in 228 B.C. established a Roman protectorate over these cities and peoples. They became *dediticii*: without receiving Roman garrisons or being under obligation to pay tribute to Rome, but they were required to provide troops and ships.[182] The intervention of the Romans, which finally put a stop to piracy, was enthusiastically welcomed by the majority of Greeks. Aetolians as well as Achaeans officially expressed thanks to the Romans, and when in 228 B.C. Roman envoys for the first time appeared in Greece at Corinth and Athens, which had just been liberated from Macedonian rule, they were received with enthusiastic celebrations. By being admitted to the Isthmian games the Romans were, so to speak, acknowledged as fellow tribesmen of the Greeks.

The second Roman intervention in Illyria occurred at an extraordinarily favourable moment for Rome. Under the influence of the rise of Macedonia under Antigonus Doson the Roman vassal Demetrius of Pharos had defected from Rome to the Macedonian, and with his swift Illyrian ships had inflicted serious damage on Italic and Greek trade in the Adriatic. Although Rome was facing the decisive struggle with the Carthaginians, nevertheless a strong expeditionary force was sent across the Adriatic under the command of the two consuls L. Aemilius Paullus and M. Livius Salinator. After capturing the base of Dimale and the island of Pharos they drove out Demetrius within a few weeks (219 B.C.).[183]

From the time that Rome gained a solid foothold in Greece, her power was a virtual nightmare for Macedonia. Fear of Rome led Philip V into the Carthaginian camp (with the conclusion of a treaty between Philip and Hannibal in 215 B.C.).[184] The ten-year First Macedonian War (215-205)[185] brought no distinction to Macedonia, for the Carthaginians and Macedonians could not bring their operations into harmony with each other. Roman diplomacy in Hellas had a happier issue. By skilfully exploiting Greek internal tensions the Romans turned the Aetolians into a strong enemy of the Macedonians (212 B.C.).[186] The treaty between Rome and the Aetolians survives in part on a large fragment of an inscription found at Thyrrheum. This document corrects the literary tradition (primarily Polybius, but also Livy, XXVI 24) in crucial places.[187] In other respects this treaty, which was incidentally not ratified in Rome until two years later, shows the accommodating attitude that the Romans adopted towards the Aetolians at that time.

It was not long before a number of Peloponnesian states (including Elis, Messenia, Sparta) and foreign powers like Attalus I of Pergamum joined the anti-Macedonian alliance. The Romans took part in the fighting with at least a naval contingent. Philip was compelled to disperse his forces, and had to fight on many fronts—in Illyria, on the northern frontier of Macedonia and in the Peloponnesus. Nevertheless, he held his own, showing his strategic capabilities as well as the unshakeable position of Macedonia and the Hellenic Symmachy under his leadership. The Aetolians were ultimately so weakened that in 206 B.C., without taking the Romans into account, they concluded a separate treaty with Philip, at the price of considerable territorial losses.[188] The Romans were not interested in an immediate, decisive conflict with Philip, for this would have put an increased burden on their own prosecution of the war against Carthage. Thus in 205 B.C. they concluded the Peace of Phoenice (in Epirus) with Philip. The Macedonian king retained Atintania but had to give up the region of the Parthinians as well as some occupied bases in Illyria (Dimale, Bargullum *et al.*). King Prusias of Bithynia, the Achaeans, Boeotians, Thessalians, Acarnanians and Epirotes were included as allies in the Peace on the side of Philip, while King Attalus I of Pergamum and the Illyrian prince Pleuratus were on the side of the Romans. The question whether the Peace of Phoenice was a general peace, the last in Greek history, is still open.[189]

The Peace of Phoenice was followed by a fundamental reorientation of Macedonian policy. Even in the middle of the war, in 208 B.C., King Philip had begun building a large navy at Cassandreia, and now that the danger from the West appeared to have been eliminated, he believed himself to be in a position to move towards the East, the Aegean. Here Rhodes and Pergamum had filled the vacuum left by the decline of Egyptian power during the last quarter of the third century. These states became the next opponents of the Macedonians. In order to divert the attention of Rhodes Philip V intervened in the so-called Cretan War (215/

4 B.C.)[190] and energetically proceeded with the building of his fleet. At Philip's command the Aetolian, Dicaearchus, carried out a formidable plundering expedition in the Aegean.[191] Wherever he landed he erected altars to *Asebeia* and *Paranomia*—Blasphemy and Illegality—to such a degree had Greek religion disintegrated.

In Egypt Josibius, the chief advisor to the king, had conducted a resolute and wholly successful foreign policy which contributed greatly to consolidating the position of the Ptolemaic kingdom. The battle of Raphia (217 B.C.) was the last major success, and the only one of Ptolemy IV Philopator (221-204 B.C.?) A long chain of revolts by the native Egyptians began immediately after Raphia, and never abated. It was particularly the south of the country, the Thebaid, that was affected. Thus from 206 until 185 B.C. southern Egypt was ruled by two Nubian kings,[192] and the Ptolemies thus lost the rich material resources of Nubia and Somaliland. As a result of the Second Punic War the chief export markets of Ptolemaic western trade, Italy, Sicily and Carthage, were closed to the Egyptian economy. The financial difficulties of Egypt are shown by the adoption of copper currency in approximately 210 B.C., prompted by the scarcity of silver. Its standardisation (in ratio of 1:60 to silver) succeeded in eliminating the spectre of inflation.[193]

The death of Ptolemy IV Philopator (autumn 204 B.C.?) created a new situation in Egypt. The all-powerful favourite of the king, Sosibius, at first kept his death a secret.[194] Difficulties were justifiably anticipated in foreign policy, for his successor, Ptolemy V Epiphanes, was still a child and incapable of ruling. Antiochus III and Philip V in fact agreed, in a secret treaty, upon a formal partitioning of the Ptolemaic kingdom (winter 203/2 B.C.).[195] The Seleucid was to receive the lion's share, Cyprus, the Ptolemaic dominions in Cilicia and Lycia as well as South Syria, while Philip V had to be satisfied with the Ptolemaic Cyclades and the Thracian coast. None of the parties concerned suspected that this "plunder-treaty" would generate the decisive conflict between Rome and the Hellenistic world and inaugurate a new epoch in world history.

13
HELLENISTIC CIVILISATION

THE STRUCTURE OF THE HELLENISTIC STATES IN THE THIRD CENTURY B.C.

The Hellenistic states within Alexander's empire in Asia and Egypt owed their origins to conquest. They were "territory won by the sword" of their founders, and were bequeathed as private property within the new dynasties. In Macedonia the situation was different. Here the old military and national monarchy, which was at the same time both hereditary and patriarchal, continued up to Philip V (222/1-179 B.C.). Common to the Hellenistic states (again with the exception of Macedonia) is the absence of an ethnic character – they were states composed of various ethnic groups. Thus in the Seleucid and Ptolemaic kingdoms a numerical minority of foreigners, Macedonians and Greeks, ruled over the broad mass of the native population. The foreigners owed their positions and their social status exclusively to the favour of the king, and their rise and fall was inextricably linked with his person and his dynasty. The Macedonian officers and officials proudly appended the term "Macedonian" to their names; even the king adhered to this custom. When Alexander conquered the Achaemenid empire he created the territorial state within the frontiers of the Greek world. All inhabitants of his empire, conquerors or conquered, were subjects of the king, although in a manifoldly graduated form.

The hallmark of the Hellenistic states was their territorial magnitude. It confronted the new masters of the conquered areas with completely novel problems of organisation, which were brilliantly solved by the Macedonians and Greeks. It is no accident that the period of the successors and the generation after produced an abundance of outstanding personalities. What the narrow limits of the homeland denied them, the Macedonians and Greeks found in the vast regions of Asia and Egypt – an unlimited field for political and economic planning. In addition, a large element in the population demonstrated the greatest competence in the wielding of power. At the time of the death of its founder (281 B.C.) the kingdom of Seleucus incorporated approximately 1.4 million square miles; if the very thinly populated regions of the Iranian highlands and the vast expanse of the unpopulated Persian Desert be subtracted, there would remain 207,000 sq. miles – in Asia Minor, northern Syria and Mesopotamia, to a large extent culturally developed regions. The territory of Ptolemy I was smaller. Together with his foreign dominions, Cyrenaica, Cyprus, South Syria, parts of the Anatolian coast, islands of the Aegean and the possessions in Thrace, the area may be estimated at approximately 40,000 square miles, and the Antigonid kingdom in Macedonia and Hellas was only about 28,000 square miles. All other Hellenistic states were even smaller. The Pergamene state of the first Attalids (before the ephemeral conquest of Seleucid Asia Minor by Attalus I) was a magnified polis, similar to Syracuse under Hieron II. After the peace treaty with Rome the territory of the latter amounted to only 4,300 square miles.[1] It is difficult to estimate the respective sizes in population. In the first century B.C. Egypt (Alexandria excepted) allegedly had 7 million inhabitants.[2] Sources upon which to base any estimates for the remaining states are lacking, and it is preferable not to attempt to give any specific figures.[3]

In their form and in their institutions the Hellenistic states had certain similarities, as the ruler cult, the imperial organisation and the regulation of defence. But diversity of population and traditions in many individual cases constituted major differences, so that only in a restricted sense is it possible to speak of a "unity within a multiplicity."[4]

Alexander's conquest of the Achaemenid empire established the foundations of Hellenistic monarchy, and with this, of Western monarchy as well.[5] Although Alexander's monarchy may appear to be the realisation of certain cosmopolitan tendencies in the Greek philosophy of the fourth century B.C., primarily of Cynicism, in essence it was infinitely removed from the Greek ideal of rule by the surpassing individual. It was the encounter and fusion of the Macedonian military monarchy with the great monarchy of the Achaemenids and with the traditions of the ancient Babylonians and Assyrians (as absorbed by the Persians) which decisively determined the character of Alexander's monarchy. In the land of the Nile Alexander was the successor to the Pharaohs, in Babylon he acknowledged his reverence to the imperial god Marduk, while to the Persians he wished to appear as the legitimate successor to the Achaemenids. Thus all ancient world empires found something of themselves in this new universal monarchy.

What was denied Alexander, the founding of a dynasty, his marshals Seleucus and Ptolemy achieved. They lacked the most important element, legitimacy, and so used mythology to connect themselves with Zeus, Apollo, Heracles or Alexander,[6] in order to overcome this deficiency. It was, however, primarily the Hellenistic philosophy of the Cynics and the Stoics that legitimised the new system of rule. Taking as their point of departure the Greek idea of the special rights of the outstanding individual, the philosophers justified the monarchical rule of the successors on the basis of their great capabilities, which as military leaders and statesmen they had demonstrated to the world.[7] In addition, the monarchical idea in large measure corresponded with the Stoic world view: as Zeus ruled in heaven, so should the king in his likeness rule on earth. It is no accident that a number of Stoic philosophers in the third century B.C. were present at the Hellenistic courts, not only as friends and advisers to Antigonus Gonatas but also to the Spartan king Cleomenes III. To his subjects the king became the inspired law.[8] The Stoics tried to show that the monarchy fitted the rational principle in cosmic events. Transcending all the barriers of birth, race and social position, philosophy created a picture of the ideal state on earth—which found expression in the Stoic symbol of shepherd and flock. It was the patriarchal element which gave the unlimited Hellenistic monarchy its moral justification.

The most important external mark of Hellenistic royal dignity was the diadem, the wreath, which Alexander, on the model of the Achaemenids, was the first to wear. From the Hellenistic courts the diadem made its way to the Thracians, the Scythians and Sarmatians of southern Russia, and indeed as far as India.[9] It was even worn at times by women, of whom the energetic Arsinoe II was undoubtedly the first. On the other hand, neither the first Antigonids nor Agathocles of Syracuse nor the kings of Cyprus and Sparta adopted it. Philip V, whose rule signifies the radical switch to absolutism, was the first in Macedonia to adorn himself with the diadem, as he was also the first of the Antigonids to have his image stamped on coins, long after the successors and other Hellenistic kings had done so. Other symbols of the dignity of the Hellenistic rulers were the signet-ring (at the Hellenistic courts there was also the office of Chief Guardian of the Seal),[10] and, as the sign of the perpetuity of the royal dignity, the sacred fire which burned beside the throne. This feature was also inherited from the Achaemenid period, and the Hellenistic monarchs passed it on to the Roman emperors.[11] Another monarchical usage was the common practice of reckoning according to the regnal years of the king in the Ptolemaic, Antigonid and Attalid kingdoms,[12] a custom adopted by Augustus in counting the years of his tribunician power.

Genuinely Hellenistic is the singular form which the co-regency assumed. After Antigonus Monophthalmus in 306/5 B.C. appointed his son Demetrius co-regent with the title "King," co-regency became very common, chiefly in the Seleucid and Ptolemaic houses (Seleucus I and Antiochus I from 294/3 B.C. and Ptolemy after 285 B.C. are the first examples).[13] Its function was clearly to secure the transition of power to the successor. In the case of the Seleucids the co-regent was on occasion (for instance, Antiochus I as crown prince) "General Governor of the Upper Satrapies," the regions beyond the Euphrates, with the official capital in Seleuceia on the Tigris. Under the later Ptolemies the co-regency was upgraded to the so-called "full co-regency" of two or more rulers, with the first instance that of Ptolemy VI and Ptolemy VIII. The participation of women in the government was an innovation. In this the line may be traced from Arsinoe II to the Ptolemaic queen Cleopatra I, then to Cleopatra II and Cleopatra III, and ultimately to the last Cleopatra. Alongside them the male members of the Lagid throne were nothing more than ciphers. The practice of consanguineous marriage in the ruling houses, often attested for the Hellenistic period, was adopted from Achaemenid custom.[14] In the background of this practice there may have figured the intention to exclude from the very outset hereditary claims on the part of foreign dynasties. In the Hellenistic period, moreover, a kind of "society of kings" soon emerged,[15] and marriages based on equality of birth were the rule (the case of Antiochus III is a noteworthy exception).

At the Hellenistic courts in Alexandria, Antioch and Pella, Macedonian tradition continued in the institution of the Body Guard and the Page Corps. The terms "Relatives" of the King and "Friends," taken over in part from the Achaemenids and partly from Pharaonic Egypt, gradually became, in the form of a number of gradations, nothing more than empty court titles, a phenomenon which may be observed primarily in developments in Ptolemaic Egypt during the second century.[16]

Common to all the Hellenistic monarchies except Macedonia we find the ruler cult. The Hellenistic royal cult is the most conspicuous expression of the absolute form of government, the very foundation of the monarchy, and all subjects, regardless of class, religion or birth, participated in it. Its roots extend back beyond the Hellenistic period (v.s.p. 157 f.) above all to Alexander's demand for divine honours from the Greeks in 324 B.C.

In Egypt there was a clear distinction between the Egyptian and the Hellenistic ruler cult.[17] In the Egyptian royal cult, obligatory only for the old native population, the *fellaheen*, the Ptolemies, like Alexander the Great, Philip Arrhidaeus and Alexander IV before them, were naturally accepted as successors to the Pharaohs. As such they—as at one time the Persian kings—bore the ancient Egyptian titles, especially the epithet "Son of Re." After the Ptolemies the Roman emperors from Augustus to Diocletian found entry into this cult, an example of how deeply rooted this tradition had become by practice over the millennia in this conservative land.

The actual Hellenistic ruler cult was not created until the second generation, in the Ptolemaic as well as in the Seleucid empire. In Egypt it was a creation of the astute Ptolemy II (later, in the second century B.C., called Philadelphus). This born statesman had his father, Ptolemy I, consecrated as "Saviour God" after his death in 283 B.C. To this cult was added that of his wife, Berenice I, after her death. Later Arsinoe II, the sister-wife of Ptolemy II, was deified after her death (9 July 270 B.C.) under the cult name of "Brother-Loving Goddess." The notion of exalting the dead into gods stems from the world of Greek ideas, and expands to making heroes of humans who possessed exceptional qualities—for instance, founders of cities and lawgivers. The Hellenistic royal cult applied equally to all subjects of the Ptolemies: Macedonians, Greeks, Egyptians or any other members of the kingdom.

Ptolemy II, however, went even a step further. He inaugurated the cult of his own person and of his sister-wife, Arsinoe II, under the name "Divine Consanguineous Couple," and thereby commanded the veneration of the living ruler.[18] This was a measure of tremendous significance, for it exalted the king above all his subjects during his lifetime by the apotheosis which he himself commanded. Kingship had moved into a higher realm, and the foundations of absolute rule "by the grace of God" had been laid.[19] Subsequent Ptolemies adhered to the apotheosis of the living ruler. After taking the throne they adopted a cult title under which they and their wives enjoyed such divine honours as "Beneficent Gods," "Father-Loving Gods," "Epiphany Gods," and so forth.[20]

Uniquely Ptolemaic, finally, was the cult of Alexander the Great, created by Ptolemy I at least as early as 311 B.C. This was an imperial cult,[21] in which not only members of the most prominent Macedonian families appeared as priests, but on occasion even the Ptolemaic kings themselves. Alexander became the imperial god of the Ptolemaic kingdom and patron of the Ptolemaic dynasty, an attempt to link the dynasty genealogically with him. Under the name "Alexander"—he is never called "God"—he appears to have been placed on the same level as the Olympian gods. In Alexandria there was a difference between the official cult and the city cult of the city's founder – Alexander. The latter may even have been created during the lifetime of the great Macedonian.[22]

Little is known about the official cult of the Seleucids.[23] It seems likely that Antiochus I introduced it after the death of his father, Seleucus I. He elevated him to the level of a god as Zeus Nicator, and dedicated a temple to him. Antiochus I may perhaps also have created the imperial cult of the living ruler, organised according to satrapies, and expanded at the beginning of the second century by Antiochus III.

Alongside the imperial cult demanded by the king was the cult of the Seleucids, observed by the Greek communities of the empire on a voluntary basis and very diversely organised by the individual poleis.[24]

The Hellenistic ruler cult served well to unify the ethnically diverse empires of the Seleucids and the Ptolemies. In many instances it was also adopted by the small Hellenistic states. Even today an inscription from Nemrud Dagh testifies to the organisation of the ruler cult in the small state of the Commagenean prince Antiochus I (first century B.C.), in which Iranian and Greek elements are combined.[25] There is scarcely a phenomenon of greater importance for the cultural development of the ancient world. The imperial cult stands at the very heart of the spiritual struggle between the Roman state and Christianity, as may be seen in, for instance, the correspondence between the Younger Pliny and Trajan, (Plin., *ep*. X 96), or in Decius' persecution of the Christians in the middle of the third century A.D.

In all three major Hellenistic states the Macedonian military assembly remained, as a residue from the time of the elective monarchy in Macedonia, which existed before the hereditary monarchy. After the era of Alexander the Great—during his Asian campaign it acted often—it survived in the major Hellenistic kingdoms until the end of political Hellenism.[26] The Macedonian military assembly still had the important powers of formal confirmation of the new king, of appointing a guardian in case of minority, of ratifying royal testaments and, finally, passing judgment in cases of high treason. Even after the period of the successors, under the Antigonids, Seleucids and Ptolemies, the military assembly still decided issues of great political significance. Later, however, only the garrisons in Alexandria and Antioch enjoyed the rights of the military assembly. In the course of time the population of the capitals also acquired certain rights, and often in highly tumultuous scenes enforced its wishes. The cause for degeneration which led to the power of a "praetorian" regiment in Alexandria does not lie in the nature of the old Macedonian military assembly, but rather in the decline of "Macedonianism," which in a foreign environment lost its link with its national fountainhead.

The individual Hellenistic states were very different in their ethnic structure, the specific traditions of the countries and the distinctive developments in the individual kingdoms. In the Seleucid empire the Persian inheritance shows particularly clearly. In its territory, stretching in 281 B.C. from the Hindu Kush to the Aegean and from the Caucasus to the Persian Gulf, dwelt an almost unlimited number of races and nationalities —Iranians (Persians, Medes, Bactrians, Parthians *et al.*), Semites (Babylonians, Syrians, Phoenicians and Jews), Anatolians, Macedonians and Greeks. As in the organisation of the Persian empire, there were three categories among the subjects of the king: the dynasts, the poleis and the *ethnoi*. The dynasts, great landlords in Asia Minor and in Iran, acknowledged Seleucid sovereignty, but were in fact all but independent, although under obligation to supply troops and to pay tribute. As well as secular, there were religious dynasties, extensive temple territories of Asia Minor and North Syria, whose lords, the high priests, commanded large numbers of followers and slaves. The Greek poleis too stood outside the Seleucid territorial administration, with only the *ethnoi* and their territory, called "the region," subject to the immediate supervision of the king's governors. The division of the empire into satrapies, hyparchies and toparchies was in part a legacy from the time of Alexander, and beyond this undoubtedly from the Persian empire.[27] On the whole the empire at the height of its power in 281 B.C. may have counted twenty-five to thirty satrapies. Although the total territory continually decreased in the following decades, the number of satrapies increased, particularly in the empire's central region, in Syria and Mesopotamia. In Asia Minor as well the large administrative units were split up—a development which was given further impetus chiefly by Antiochus III.

THE SELEUCID KINGDOM

The Seleucid system refined the coarse satrapy-administration of the Persians in many points.[27] While restless Asia Minor, exposed to constant threats from the Galatians and foreign enemies, was under the administration of military governors (*strategoi*), imitating the practice of Antigonus Monophthalmus and Lysimachus, the satrapies in the centre and Iranian east of the empire remained in the hands of satraps. The satraps had plenary judicial and financial powers, and ruled the provinces placed under their command like miniature kings. The satraps of Macedonian origin had, in addition, command over the entire military forces of their territory, whereas Macedonian officers were regularly appointed as military commanders alongside the native satraps (thus Babylonia, Cappadocia and Cilicia). In the East as in the West the first Seleucids created two large governments of a general character, with Seleuceia on the Tigris and Sardis as capitals. The chief supervision of the Upper Satrapies, more precisely the region east of the Euphrates, was from 294 or 293 B.C. on under the control of the crown prince Antiochus, the later Antiochus I.

An inscription,[28] recently discovered in Nihavend (Iran), names a certain Menedemus as "General Governor of the Upper Satrapies," from the later years of Antiochus III. Still in 149 B.C. a man by the name of Cleomedes filled this office.[28a] In Asia Minor a similar supreme command appears from the first decade of Seleucid rule and under Seleucus II Sardis even became the capital of the co-regent Antiochus Hierax (241-228 B.C.), while under Antiochus III, Achaeus, the brother-in-law of the king, had himself crowned as General Governor of the West (221-213 B.C.).

Antiochus III carried out a thorough reorganisation of the ageing Seleucid empire.[29] He introduced the system of *strategoi* which prevailed in Asia Minor, and thereby achieved a considerable increase in the military capacity of the satrapies. Alongside the *strategos*, as military and civil commander of the satrapy, stood the "Finance Minister" as head of the administration of finance, which was centralised in the *dioiketes*. The Iranian satrapies, which Antiochus III had reconquered for the empire, remained bound to the body of the empire as vassal states (under kings or satraps with a large measure of independence).

Outside this administrative structure were the large Greek poleis in western Asia Minor. The Seleucids did not pursue a unified policy towards them, but regulated the relationship of the communities to the empire from case to case.[30] The attitude of the Seleucids, however, was essentially more liberal than that of the Thracian king Lysimachus, who burdened the Ionian cities with heavy tribute and placed them under the direct supervision of a royal *strategos*. But the Seleucid kings did not succeed in uniting the Greek cities organically with the main body of their empire. In general the freedom and the autonomy of the poleis were respected, so long as they remained loyal to the Seleucids in time of need. Formally, the relationship of the polis to the ruler rested on a treaty, but the king had no difficulty in ordering the internal affairs of the cities, for a Seleucid party existed in most of them and in many there was a Seleucid garrison. Polybius (XXI 41, 2) rightly pointed out that the tribute payments, the garrisons and the receiving of royal commands were characteristic of the position of the Greek cities in Asia Minor.[31] Otherwise the poleis, Greek as well as the large coastal cities of Phoenicia, often took advantage of the critical state of affairs in the Seleucid empire, and in the latter part of the second century B.C. there scarcely remained a single important Phoenician community which had not succeeded in gaining complete independence.[32]

Despite the organisational difficulties, the Seleucids undoubtedly valued the cultural significance of the Hellenic poleis. It is no accident that Seleucus I and his son Antiochus I created support for their rule by founding many urban settlements in the vast regions of the East. A large number of new settlements founded by Seleucus I exhibit Macedonian names.[33] Among the new cities, Seleuceia on the Tigris, newly founded as a "defensive Babylon," the new imperial capital Antioch on the Orontes and the coastal city Seleuceia in Pieria, rank as far the greatest in importance. Some of the old oriental city-states received new settlers and new names—thus Nisibis (Antioch), Carchemish (Europus), Thapsacus (Amphipolis), and Dura-Europus (Salihiyeh) on the Middle Euphrates, which has recently become so famous through the French-American excavations.[34] The great economic opportunities lured many Greek merchants, craftsmen and artists to the Near East. Seleuceia on the Tigris, situated at the crossroads of trade between India and the Phoenician coast as well as of the transit-trade from the north to the Persian Gulf, is alleged to have had 600,000 inhabitants, and the imperial capital Antioch followed very closely. Many of the new foundations may have had a Macedonian model. That is, they did not enjoy complete freedom and autonomy (the very bedrock of existence for the Greek poleis), and were under the administration of royal functionaries. In addition to the cities, there were a considerable number of *katoikiai*, "settlements,"[35] in particular for that element of the population which provided recruits for the Seleucid army. This type of colony prevailed in inner Anatolia, Iran, Media, Persia and Bactria, and the large number of *katoikiai* in the east was the most important condition for the large-scale expansion of Bactrian Hellenism in the first half of the second century B.C.

The army of the Seleucids[36] was composed of the standing forces (chiefly mercenaries) and of reserves. In time of peace the mercenaries served as garrisons in the imperial fortresses (Sardis, Antioch on the Orontes, Apameia, Babylon, Susa *et al.*), whereas the reserves lived in the *katoikiai* until the mobilisation order of the king called them to active duty. The size of the forces was considerable. The army of Antiochus III at Raphia (217 B.C.) numbered 70,000, and just as many faced the Scipios in the field at Magnesia (190 B.C.), about three times the size of the army of the Antigonids. As in the case of the Persian army, the forces of the Seleucids included the most varied elements. The army was a true image of the Seleucid state, composed of many races and nationalities. In addition to mercenaries from the whole of the Greek world,[37] the core of the army was formed by the class of natives designated as "Macedonians," the so-called phalanx. Each division and its subordinate brigades (*chiliarchiai*, and *hipparchiai* in the cavalry) appear to have been appointed to a special region or "Canton," from which the unit, in time of mobilisation, was supplemented. This was a continuation of the old system of organising the Macedonian army according to districts (v.s.p. 187). The Asiatic peoples of the empire furnished the greatest number of contingents to the army. Besides Dahaeans, Cadusians, Carmanians, Medes and Persians, the warlike inhabitants of Anatolia, in particular the Mysians, Pisidians *et al.*, served in the military, more and more as the Macedonian element fused with the natives. The threads of the whole military administration were all held by the "State Secretary for Military Affairs." Only a fleet was lacking, for the Seleucids never possessed a navy of any importance.

The cost of maintaining the army, the court of the king, and the general administration of the empire was defrayed by taxes.[38] All subjects in the empire, the dynasts, poleis and the various peoples, paid a "contribution" (*phoros*), made partly in kind (thus above all in Upper Asia), and partly in coin. In addition to the *phoros* there was a *dekate*, a "tenth,"[39] and various categories of other taxes, which also included the so-called "crown monies."

The last were payments demanded on unusual occasions, and later often assumed the character of legalised extortion. Important among the taxes on consumer goods was the salt tax. The king derived by far the greatest proportion of his revenues from the royal domains. Hosts of serfs and slaves tilled the royal fields, for which there is evidence above all in western Asia Minor. The Seleucids rewarded the services of their leading personalities and their favourites with generous gifts of land. The territories given away came from the "royal land," and were added to the district of neighbouring poleis.

Whether or not the first Seleucids were consciously champions of a Macedonising or Hellenising policy, the work of Seleucus I and Antiochus I was of epoch-making importance. In the newly founded urban centres Greek culture struck firm roots with the new colonists from Macedonia and Hellas, and even in such remote provinces as Media Atropatene and Armenia Minor the Greek language succeeded in asserting itself over Aramaic. The close contact with Greek people, Greek religion and the Greek way of life left its imprint on the inhabitants of Asia Minor. The adoption of Greek names by Babylonians[40] and the Greek formula in manumission documents from the temple of Nanaea in Susa in the second century B.C.[41] show this clearly. In social life the arrival of the Greeks in Asia made for a complete reversal of earlier conditions. Alongside the Iranian landlords and the Phoenician merchants an extensive upper class of Greeks, favoured by the Seleucid rulers, soon found itself in possession of considerable resources and exerted great economic and political influence. There was, however, a numerical disproportion between the Asiatics and the Greeks. Only by continually drawing fresh recruits of Greeks and Macedonians into the vast regions of Asia Minor could the work of the first Seleucids acquire a lasting character. Another danger was the influence which the old oriental religions exerted on the Greeks. Anatolian, Syrian, Phoenician and Arabian gods became a powerful factor in the life of the Hellenes in Asia—evidence for the important influence of oriental culture on the minds and emotions of the Greeks in the new homeland.

The Iranian upper classes played a rôle of considerable importance in the Seleucid empire. A good number of Iranians held important offices in the imperial administration,[42] but their rôle must not be exaggerated any more than that of the native Egyptians in the Ptolemaic kingdom of the third century B.C. It was the Iranians, specifically the Parthians, who launched the first blow against Seleucid rule, shortly after the middle of the third century. The splitting away of Bactria with its many Greek *katoikiai* was also a decisive factor in weakening the position of Hellenism in Asia, even though the Bactrian rulers succeeded in conquering North-West India in the first half of the second century. The fact is that Bactrian Hellenism was oriented towards the east, and its resources were not available to the Seleucids. With the founding of the Parthian kingdom the prelude to the decisive struggle between Hellenism and the native forces of Asia had begun. The actual conflict was the hallmark of the history of Western Asia in the second century B.C. Not until Pompey in 63 B.C. made the Euphrates the frontier between the Romans and Parthians did the Greeks—under Roman rule—find the support which they so urgently needed.

EGYPT UNDER THE PTOLEMIES

The second major Hellenistic state, the Ptolemaic kingdom, was the most compact political organism that Hellenism ever produced. Protected to the east and west by deserts which were difficult to cross, Egypt in the period of the successors frustrated the invasions of Perdiccas and Antigonus. Thus it gained time to consolidate its internal and foreign policy under the astute leadership of Ptolemy I. Under Ptolemy II it reached the height of its power, and it maintained its leading rôle in the Hellenistic world under Ptolemy III Euergetes (246-221 B.C.). It was only at the end of the third century, under Ptolemy IV Philopator, that clear signs of decline become evident. Its foreign dominions—chiefly Cyrenaica, Cyprus and South Syria, as well as the bases on the coasts of southern Anatolia and Thrace, and on the islands of the Aegean—gave the Ptolemaic kingdom the character of a maritime empire around the eastern basin of the Mediterranean. In contrast to the Seleucid empire the Ptolemaic state enjoyed the advantage of external and internal uniformity. While the Seleucids had to cope with a large number of peoples, the Ptolemies ruled over only the Macedonian-Greek upper classes and the Egyptian *fellaheen*, who for thousands of years had been accustomed to patient work in the service of the Pharaohs. Although the enormous scope of the work of the first Seleucids may be impressive, the skill of the Ptolemies in extracting the very utmost from the rich natural resources of the country and from its labour force is without parallel in the whole of Hellenism.

In Ptolemaic Egypt the traditions of the Pharaonic kingdom remained alive, above all in the administration, in the organisation of the priesthood and the temples, and not least in the ingenious system of obligatory work. The first two Ptolemies certainly did not take over in total the Pharaonic institutions,[43] but rather introduced Greek bureaucracy as a completely new element into the administration of the country. The experiment was a complete success. From earliest times Egypt had been the land of "scribes," and it scarcely made any difference to the *fellaheen* whether the administrative language was Aramaic or Greek, since they did not understand either. The uniformity of the administration made it inexpedient to found many Greek poleis. Only with the city of Ptolemaïs in Upper Egypt did Ptolemy I create a new administrative centre for the Thebaid.[44] With the hosts of Greeks and Macedonians Hellenic culture also struck firm roots in the countryside. In the district centres Greek *gymnasia*, Greek education and Greek culture found a home in the entire Nile Valley, as far as the borders of Nubia, and even in an obscure place like Omboi.[45]

In contrast to the federative structure of the Seleucid empire, the Ptolemaic kingdom was highly centralised. At the head of the imperial administration was the king, who, if he took his office seriously, as did the first two Ptolemies, had a gigantic schedule to execute. Every subject had a right to approach the monarch with a direct petition, which was read by the king personally or by one of his secretarial staff, and then referred to the responsible administrative officials for action. The actual administrator of the empire, which the king regarded as his private property, was the *dioiketes*. The Zenon Papyri have revealed one *dioiketes* to us in the person of the wealthy Greek, Apollonius, under Ptolemy II.

As in Pharaonic times, the country was divided into nomes, whose number (c. 40) was subject to change.[46] The administration of the nome was initially shared by three officials. One was the *strategos*, who in the course of the third century rose from the position of commander of the garrison troops to all-powerful chief of the entire nome administration.[47] Second, an *oikonomos* acted as director of finance. Third was the *nomarchos*, whose powers, great during the Pharaonic and Achaemenid periods, were restricted by the first Ptolemies to supervising the cultivation of land. Alongside these there were the *antigrapheus* (as colleague of the *oikonomikos*) and the "Royal Scribe," each with a whole army of subordinate officials. The "nomes" were subdivided into *toparchiai* and the latter into villages—the smallest units of the Egyptian administration, each with its officials, *toparchoi, topogrammateis, komarchoi* and *komogrammateis*. The nomes of the south, beginning with Lycopolis (Assiût), had apparently been united into a large general government under a "strategos of the Thebaid" since the end of the third century.[48] After the disturbances caused by the great native revolts, an *epistrategos*, that is, a military commander, over the whole of Egypt, with the exception of Alexandria, appears in the seventies of the second century.[49] The foreign possessions—Cyrenaica, Cyprus and South Syria (designated officially as "Syria and Phoenicia")—were governed in the name of the king by *strategoi* who possessed full military, civil and financial powers as quasi-viceroys.[50] The governorship of Cyrene and Cyprus was from time to time held by a member of the royal family. Thus Menelaus, the brother of Ptolemy I, was *strategos* of Cyprus, while Magas, the stepson of the monarch, was viceroy of Cyrene. In later centuries problems about the rights of the younger son on occasion grew out of the governorships, and at times the empire was even divided among several rulers. On the whole the administration of Egypt was a rigorous bureaucracy but it should not be regarded as complicated, although especially in Egypt, a clear distinction between the powers of the various officials in the nome-administration may have been lacking—surely a legacy from Pharaonic times.

The administration of justice in Egypt was centralised in the two Alexandrian law courts, the court of the *chrematistai* (for Macedonians and Greeks) and the court of the *laokritai* (for the natives). In other respects, however, the nome *strategos* assumed more and more powers of jurisdiction as his office grew older.[51] In the foreign dominions the provincial governors were probably at the same time the highest authorities in legal matters.

Besides the rich material resources of the empire, the rule of the Ptolemies rested on the army.[52] It was composed of Macedonians and mercenaries—Greeks and non-Greeks like Thracians, Galatians, Mysians, Phrygians, and Persians. There was a strong garrison in Alexandria and the frontier fortresses, especially Pelusium and Elephantine. In the history of the second century B.C. the troops stationed on Cyprus played a decisive rôle.[53] In order to bring the mercenaries, composed of the most varied nationalities, closer to the country and the ruler, the first Ptolemies settled many soldiers in the countryside, especially in the Fayûm. On their own property, as so-called cleruchs (later called *katoikoi*), the professional soldiers performed exemplary services for the improvement of the country and notably justified the confidence which the king placed in them.[54] In contrast to Seleucid practice, the mercenaries were not settled in groups according to their military divisions but in a variegated amalgam, wherever there happened to be a free piece of land. The various nationalities were organised in the form of *politeumata*—similarly to the Jews in the capital of Alexandria. These, however, soon lost their national significance and became "pseudo-ethnic" societies, like the "Persians of the new generation."[55] Ptolemy IV Philopator was the first to enlist the natives in the army.[56] In Egypt, as in the Seleucid empire, the number of Macedonians greatly declined in the second half of the third century, and mercenaries cost much money. The Egyptians soon became aware that they were indispensable, and there was no end to the native revolts from the turn of the third century.

The fleet, the actual power instrument of the Ptolemies in major politics, was in part furnished by the large maritime cities of the empire, Greek as well as Phoenician. Philocles, the king of Sidon, was one of the most important admirals of Ptolemy II.[57] Following Athenian practice of an earlier time, the Ptolemies made use of the *trierarchia*—placing the burdens of building and equipping warships on the shoulders of the wealthiest citizens—as Alexander once had the Indus fleet built by his *trierarchoi*.[58] The core of naval power was probably formed by the king's fleet, in which many Egyptians served as oarsmen. Leading the marine administration in the second century was a special "Secretary of State for Naval Affairs," a counterpart to the "Secretary of State for War."[59]

As official successors to the Egyptian Pharaohs, the Ptolemies were the protectors of the powerful Egyptian priesthood, which looked back upon a very ancient tradition. Indeed, under the Ramessids it had actually formed a state within a state. In contrast to the partially hostile Achaemenids, especially Cambyses, the Ptolemies were determined to keep the Egyptian "Church" under strict economic control but at the same time allow it complete freedom in matters of religion and cults. The Ptolemies accordingly refrained from interfering in the internal organisation of the native clergy. Still, they maintained their supreme right of possession over the land ceded to the temples for their use.[60] The Ptolemies appointed a royal official to supervise the duties of the temples to the crown. On the whole the rulers made sure that the temples produced more for them than they cost to maintain. The first Ptolemies were also very parsimonious in granting the right of asylum to temples. It was not until later generations that the Ptolemies adopted a more generous policy, so that the temples became places of refuge for the natives who fled thither in order to escape *corvée* work, oppressive taxation and the clutches of officials.[61]

The Ptolemaic kings were undoubtedly the wealthiest rulers of the Hellenistic world, with revenue chiefly from land, business and trade. As successors to the Pharaohs the Ptolemies held large districts of land as their personal property.[62] These were cultivated by "royal farmers," free tenants under the supervision of royal officials. The royal farmers had to pay a certain annual rent to the ruler, and, in addition, a large number of other dues, some in kind, some in coin. They were closely supervised in the sowing, threshing and delivery of the grain. Besides the "royal land" there was also the "released land," whose produce was subject to release by the royal administration. Over and above these there were four additional categories: "temple land," "cleruchic land," "feudal land," which was found mostly in the hands of great dignitaries of the king, and "private land." All categories furnished the king with extensive revenues, which were collected by means of an ingenious system of tax payment.[63] The amount of the harvests depended each year on the inundation of the grainland by the Nile. Everything therefore depended on keeping the canal system in good repair, for this guaranteed an even inundation of the fields. Many Greek experts and an army of conscripted Egyptians were continuously occupied with work on dams and dikes. The Ptolemies had at their disposal huge supplies of grain, which were transported from the countryside via the Nile to the royal granaries in Alexandria. Grain was the most important item in Ptolemaic foreign trade and often also played a decisive rôle in foreign politics.

The actual backbone of the Ptolemaic political system, however, was the economy. In its most important aspects it was a monopoly economy.[64] The cultivation of olives and the production of oil, weaving, fulling, brewing, mining, banking, manufacturing of papyrus and many other branches of the economy were under the monopoly of the king. The most rigorously managed was the oil monopoly. It was a production and selling monopoly, production taking place exclusively in the royal factories. The revenues to the king from the economy and from export and import tariffs were enormous. Through these the Ptolemies achieved an active trade balance, which was greatly needed, since expenditures on the fleet, the army and the maintenance of the court in Alexandria absorbed vast sums. The entire world of the time was dependent on Ptolemaic manufactured products. Linen, glassware, ivory work, incense and cosmetics made their way to the frontiers of the inhabited world. Ptolemaic products are found in, among other places, China, India, Central and North Africa, northern and western Europe, and in the steppes of southern Russia. Cicero (*Pro Rab. Post.* 40) mentions papyrus, linen and glass as Egyptian freight bound for Puteoli in Italy in the first century B.C. Alexandria was, moreover, the great port of transshipment for the southern and eastern trade of the Ptolemaic empire with India and East Africa. Ptolemy II repaired the old canal from the Nile through the Bitter Lakes to the Red Sea (at modern Suez), and conquered Arabia (the district of Taema), to establish direct communications between Egypt and Arabian caravan trade.[65] Direct maritime traffic with India, however, did not begin until the end of the second century (117 or 116 B.C.), after the discovery of the regularity of the direction of the monsoon winds opened the direct searoute to India.[66] Before this the island of Socotra and Arabia Eudaemon (South Yemen) were the ports of reshipment for trade between Egypt and India.

In modern scholarship, there has been a tendency to draw a parallel between the Ptolemaic state economy and the mercantilism of modern enlightened despotism.[67] It is true that for the Ptolemies, just as for the mercantilists, the procuring of money was the central problem of the economy. But on closer consideration there are fundamental differences. Modern mercantilism, for instance, begins with the concept of the nation state, whereas Ptolemaic Egypt was anything other than an ancient nation state. As in the Seleucid empire, so in the land of the Nile, a Macedonian dynasty ruled, which as the object of its economic policy exploited the entire country and its enormous labour force. All revenues were for the king's advantage; his appointees and officials alone attained the enjoyment of privileges. As in Pharaonic times, the natives were the burden bearers. The king could not do without their services (*leitourgiai*) for grain transport, for labour in the mines and stone quarries, and in the great buildings and general improvements. Thus Ptolemaic Egypt is the classical ancient example of an economy directed from above, and the great economic and political success, especially of the first three Ptolemies, appeared to justify the system. It was not until the second, and finally in the first century, that the negative aspects became dominant, until the Ptolemaic kingdom, as the last of the Hellenistic empires, fell victim to the Roman policy of annexation. Of the foreigners, Macedonians and Greeks, probably only the confidants of the king, such as the *dioiketes* Apollonius under Ptolemy II, acquired large fortunes, but the Hellenes in the Greek cities of Alexandria, Naucratis and Ptolemaïs were probably also relatively prosperous. Moreover, the steady stream of immigrants pouring into the Egyptian countryside throughout the entire third century indicates that the opportunities for employment and a livelihood must have been considerably better than in the Greek motherland. On Egyptian soil, in the service of the Macedonian dynasty of the Ptolemies, the immigrated Greeks, intellectuals, artisans, merchants, farmers and soldiers, embody the distinct type of specialist, the *homo oeconomicus* or the *homo technicus*.[68] The skill of the Greeks in Egypt shifted from the political sphere to the rational and technical in administration and economy, and their accomplishment in Egypt in politics and economics lasted far into the time of the Roman Empire.[69]

MACEDONIA AND GREECE

The third of the major Hellenistic states, the kingdom of the Antigonids in Macedonia and Greece, was the smallest in size and in population, but thanks to the uniformity of its population it possessed distinct advantages over the other two. Macedonia was a state predominantly feudal in character.[70] The king was also the largest property owner, and he derived extensive revenues from the domains, forests and mines. The actual backbone of the state, however, was not the magnates and the Macedonian aristocracy but the many smaller landowners, who in war, as in the time of King Philip, stood their ground in the phalanx. Close political and economic relations existed between Macedonia and Greece, and Macedonian coins spread widely throughout Hellas. Of the Macedonian harbours, Thessalonica developed into a top-ranking centre of commerce, with particularly close connections with Delos and Rhodes. Of great importance was Demetrias-Pagasae, the stronghold created in Thessaly by Demetrius Poliorcetes. The variegated character of its inhabitants is clearly reflected in the inscriptions on Pagasaean funeral *stelae*.[71]

The Greeks, however, at all times regarded the rule of the tribally related Macedonians as bondage, so that the conflict between Macedonians and Greeks became a decisive factor in third century politics. The Macedonians for their part did not succeed in adjusting themselves to the mentality of the Greeks, so a Macedonian-Greek empire never took shape on European soil.

King Antigonus Gonatas (276-239 B.C.) depended on the loyalty of the Macedonians to the Antigonid ruling house, which carried on the tradition of the Argeads. The strongest pillar of the state was the Macedonian conscript army, in which the traditions of Philip II and of Alexander were zealously cultivated. Many mercenaries served the later Antigonids, above all Philip V, who in general brought about the decisive change from the patriarchal republic to the genuine Hellenistic state. In time of peace the mercenaries acted primarily as garrison troops in Greece. In its form the Antigonid realm[72] was highly dualistic. In addition to the principal country of Macedonia and Thessaly there were the foreign dominions. At the head of these were the Greek regions (of which Corinth formed the centre), and after them came the countries neighbouring on Macedonia, such as Paeonia. Macedonia (and apparently also Thessaly) had a number of "districts," whose administration was centralised in an urban centre under a royal "District Commissioner." The division, however, evidently applied only to Lower Macedonia. Sparsely urbanised Upper Macedonia retained the rural organisation in vogue since Philip II. Here the old established aristocracy furnished the general administration of districts such as Orestis, Eordaea, Tymphaea, Elimeia and so forth, and provided commanders of the army units, which were recruited from the individual regions. There was no urban autonomy in Macedonia. The poleis were incorporated into the general organisation of the rural districts as centres of administration, their separate life restricted within narrow limits. The Macedonian model survived, moreover, not only in the newly-founded cities of Seleucid Asia but also in Ptolemaic Alexandria and in Attalid Pergamum.[73]

The countries neighbouring on Macedonia were under the direct sovereignty of the king, who ruled them through his deputies—*strategoi*. This applies in particular to the Paeonian borderland, governed by a native prince by the name of Didas in the time of Philip V. It was also true of the coastal region of Thrace, which had been reconquered by Philip V at the end of the third century and annexed to Macedonia, and not least to the Greek districts under Macedonian rule. A Macedonian viceroy resided in Corinth as representative of Antigonus Gonatas;[74] after 280 B.C. it was Craterus, son of Craterus and Phila and a half-brother of the king, and after him Alexander, son of Craterus II, who defected from Antigonus during the fifties. This, and the loss of Corinth to the Achaean League (243 B.C.), dealt Macedonian sovereignty a severe blow. The Macedonian garrisons and tyrannical rulers supported by the Macedonians, above all in the Peloponnesus, were a thorn in the flesh to the Greeks. Not until Antigonus Doson regained control of Corinth in 224 B.C. did the Macedonian "dominate" in Hellas revive. From 221 B.C. the Peloponnesus was under Taurion, a special military commander, who played an important rôle in the so-called Social War (220-217 B.C.).[75] Special governorships, possibly under the General Governor in Corinth, existed in Phocis and among the Dolopes. The Carian districts occupied by Philip V in the years from 201 to 197 B.C. were also governed by one *strategos* and several *epistatai*. From the end of the Chremonideian War until 229 B.C. Athens also was under the direct rule of the Macedonians. While in the initial phase of the Macedonian "dominate," until 225 B.C., the Macedonian governor directed the affairs of the city, and while the Athenian *strategoi* were elected on the recommendation of the Macedonian king, and Piraeus, Munichia and a number of other places in Hellas continued to be secured by Macedonian garrisons, after Athens had been given back her "freedom" treatment became more liberal—as may be seen from the formula used in connection with the offerings "for the *demos* and the king" (who accordingly appears here for the first time in second place).[76]

The greatest weakness in the Macedonian position lay in the fact that the kings did not succeed in fusing the foreign possessions and the central country into an organic whole.[77] There never was such a thing as a "Macedonian empire." The rule of Antigonus Gonatas and his successors in Hellas continued to be founded on coercion and force—until Rome, by the proclamation of T. Quinctius Flamininus at the Isthmian games of 196 B.C., obliterated it. In spite of this Macedonia was, thanks to the uniformity of its population and its national army (the only national army in Hellenism) an important power factor in the Mediterranean world, and it was not until the Macedonian phalanx had been vanquished at Pydna by the Roman *manipuli* (168 B.C.) that a new epoch in world history began—the rule of Rome.

Besides the three major Hellenistic monarchies there were no other important powers in the Greek world during the third century. The state

MAP IX

Hellenistic City Foundations

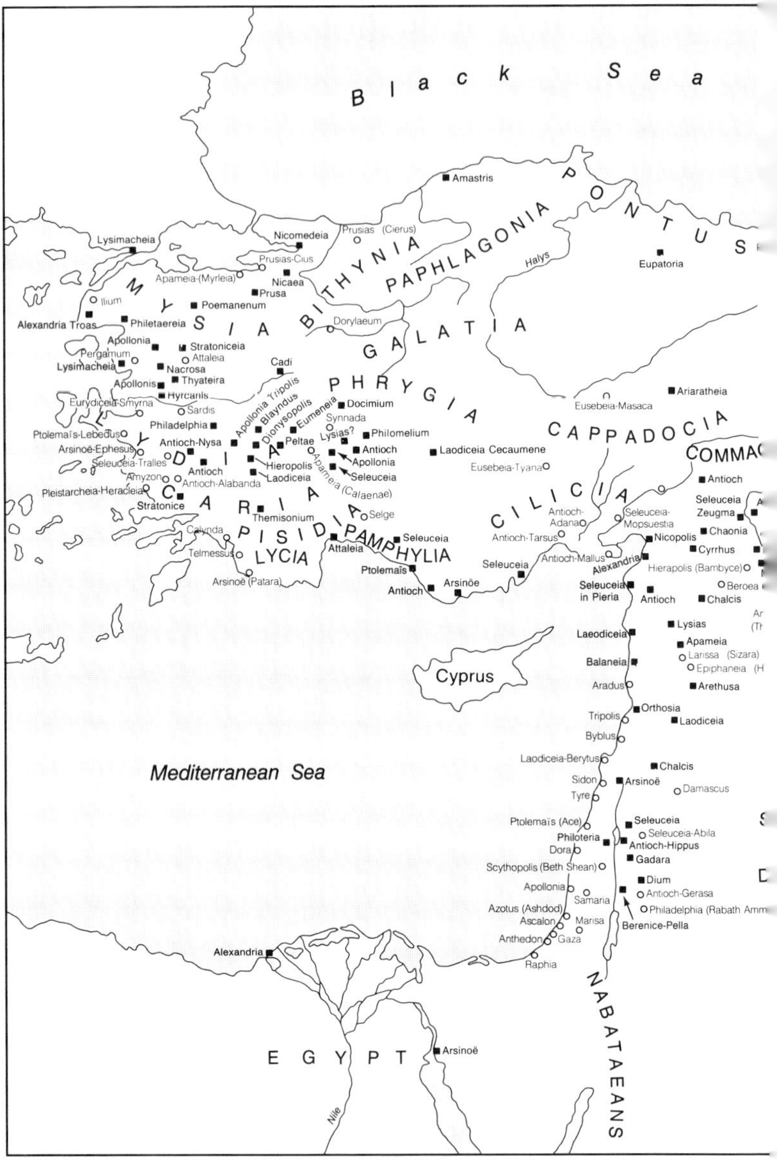

Black Sea
Amastris
PONTUS
PAPHLAGONIA
BITHYNIA
Prusias (Cierus)
Nicomedeia
Prusias-Cius
Lysimacheia
Apameia-(Myrleia)
Nicaea
Prusa
Halys
Eupatoria
MYSIA
Ilium
Poemanenum
Alexandria Troas
Philetaereia
Dorylaeum
GALATIA
Apollonia
Stratoniceia
Pergamum
Attaleia
Lysimacheia
Nacrosa
Cadi
Thyateira
Apollonis
Hyrcanis
PHRYGIA
Eurydiceia-Smyrna
Sardis
Apollonia Tripolis
Blaundus
Dionysopolis
Eumeneia
Docimium
Synnada
Eusebeia-Masaca
Ariaratheia
LYDIA
Philadelphia
Ptolemaïs-Lebedus
Arsinoë-Ephesus
Antioch-Nysa
Peltae
Lysias?
Philomelium
Antioch
Apollonia
Seleuceia
Laodiceia Cecaumene
CAPPADOCIA
COMMAG
Seleuceia-Tralles
Antioch
Hieropolis
Laodiceia
Apameia (Calaenae)
Eusebeia-Tyana
Amyzon
Antioch-Alabanda
Pleistarcheia-Heracleia
CARIA
Stratonice
Themisonium
Selge
CILICIA
Antioch
Seleuceia
Zeugma
Antioch-Adana
Seleuceia-Mopsuestia
Chaonia
Calynda
PISIDIA
PAMPHYLIA
Seleuceia
Antioch-Tarsus
Nicopolis
Cyrrhus
Telmessus
LYCIA
Attaleia
Ptolemaïs
Seleuceia
Antioch-Mallus
Alexandria
Hierapolis (Bambyce)
Arsinoë (Patara)
Antioch
Arsinöe
Seleuceia in Pieria
Antioch
Beroea
Chalcis
Lysias
Laeodiceia
Apameia
Larissa (Sizara)
Epiphaneia
Cyprus
Balaneia
Aradus
Arethusa
Orthosia
Tripolis
Laodiceia
Byblus
Laodiceia-Berytus
Chalcis
Mediterranean Sea
Sidon
Arsinoë
Tyre
Damascus
Ptolemaïs (Ace)
Seleuceia
Philoteria
Seleuceia-Abila
Dora
Antioch-Hippus
Gadara
Scythopolis (Beth Shean)
Dium
Apollonia
Antioch-Gerasa
Samaria
Azotus (Ashdod)
Philadelphia (Rabath Amm
Ascalon
Marisa
Berenice-Pella
Anthedon
Gaza
Alexandria
Raphia
NABATAEANS
EGYPT
Arsinoë
Nile

■ Apollonia = Helenistic New Foundations
o Pergamum = Hellenised Cities
0 100 200 300 400km
Cyrus
Euphrates
Artaxata
Araxes
Caspian Sea
Tigranocerta
Edessa (Orrhöe)
Antioch-Nisibis
(Harran)
MESOPOTAMIA
Demetrias?
Alexandria (Arbela)
Europus (Rhagae)
Apameia
nnae
Nicephorium
Seleuceia
Epiphaneia (Ecbatana)
MEDIA
Laodiceia (Nihavend)
ARAPOTAMIA
Tigris
Apollonia
Chola
ura-Europus
Euphrates
Artemita
Herecleia?
Seleuceia (Opis)
Neapolis
IAN
ERT
Babylon
Apameia?
Seleuceia (Sura)
SUSIANA
BABYLONIA
CHALDAEA
Apameia?
Methone?
Alexandria-Antioch
Persian Gulf

of the Attalids did not become a larger power in Asia Minor until the dictated peace of Apameia (188 B.C.). Of the monarchies in northern and eastern Anatolia, like Bithynia, Cappadocia, Pontus and Armenia, only Pontus, thanks to the outstanding personality of Mithradates Eupator, attained importance in world history.

In Greece in the third century B.C. the era of the polis forever came to an end. If the Greeks were to assert themselves against foreign powers, above all against the Macedonians, the old, inveterate particularism would have to be overcome and replaced by unification. This idea took shape in two large political leagues, the *koinon* of the Aetolians and the league of the Achaeans. There is evidence for the former in 367/6 B.C. and for the latter from 280 B.C. onwards. They played a crucial rôle in determining the fate of central and southern Hellas.[78] It is noteworthy that it was not the old famous poleis which were the bearers of the new federal concept but regions which had hitherto in no way played a leading rôle in Greek history. By creating a federal citizenship, members of the communities belonging to the league obtained an active and passive franchise throughout the entire league. In addition, they had the right to acquire property in other communities of the league and to conclude a legal marriage with a woman from another league town—an extraordinarily important step, which paved the way towards overcoming the narrow limits of the polis.[79] On the other hand, both leagues lacked a genuine hegemony. Neither the Aetolians nor the Achaeans possessed administrative headquarters. The Aetolian Federal Congress met in the sanctuary of Thermum, while the sessions of the Achaeans (*synodoi and synkletoi*)[80] took place in the temple of Zeus Amarius at Aegion, but also, from the end of the third century, in other places. In consequence a centralised power never developed in the leagues. The head of the league, however, was monarchical in form, among the Achaeans at least from 255 B.C. on. The "President" (*strategos*) was responsible for political and military matters. But he, as in the case of the other league officers, the hipparch and the Secretary of State (the Achaeans also had a nauarch for the fleet), was elected annually.

In comparison with the Greek federal states,[81] the old poleis in Hellas were of little importance. The Hellenistic monarchy which King Areus II (309/8-265 B.C.) and later Cleomenes III strove to establish in Sparta remained a pipe-dream. In the battle of Sellasia (222 B.C.) Spartan aspirations were buried once and for all. In the eastern Mediterranean the kingdom of Rhodes asserted its superior economic importance as commercial metropolis, its extensive connections attested by the magnanimous gifts which Rhodes received from all parts of the world after the serious earthquake in 227 (or 226 B.C.).[82] What Rhodes was in the East, this rôle Syracuse played in the West. Under the astute rule of Hieron II it attained a renewed flowering for half a century. Upon acceding to the heritage of Agathocles, Hieron II, after his victory over the Mamertines at the Longanus River, expanded his rule over the city into a "dominate" over eastern Sicily, and succeeded in maintaining his position, despite certain losses in a treaty with Rome (263 B.C.). What Hieron achieved was no Hellenistic state, nor even a Hellenistic monarchy. Certain Hellenistic institutions existed in Syracuse—the diadem, the Crown Council (*synedrion*), composed of the "Friends" of the monarch, and also the famous *Law of Hieron* regulating the collection of the grain tithe, which may be traced back to Ptolemaic models.[83] On the other hand, there is no trace of the Hellenistic ruler cult in Hieron's kingdom, and Hieron's dependence on Rome eliminates any comparison with the plenary sovereigns of the Hellenistic monarchies. Hieron's state in eastern Sicily was in truth the first Roman client state in the Hellenistic period. His treaty with Rome, a formal "treaty of equals," constituted the foundation of the political system and the condition of its existence. Although Hieron had close relations with Alexandria and Rhodes, the vital interests of his state oriented him towards Rome, to whom he rendered himself agreeable by magnanimous gifts of grain.

THE UNIVERSAL SOVEREIGNTY OF THE GREEK MIND

Alexander's victorious campaign marks the beginning of the third and greatest colonisation period of the Hellenes. Untold thousands left the overpopulated Greek motherland and, far from Hellas, found a new home in the vast expanses of Asia and Egypt. Alexander's victories and the founding of monarchies by the successors created the political conditions for the spread of the Hellenes in the new world. Greater security for travelling and the more rapid and easier mastering of great distances are characteristic of the new era, and the experiences of the Greeks are reflected in extensive travel literature. The Greeks brought their language, their way of life and their political institutions with them into their new homeland. As the language of the army and the bureaucracy, Greek became an international medium. Greek documents from the entire expanse of the Hellenistic world exhibit a certain uniformity. Attic jurisprudence became a common foundation for legal intercourse between the Hellenistic monarchies, although developments in the individual states took different courses, due to the influence of the variations in the native legal systems. Everywhere, in Asia as in Egypt, the *Gymnasium* was the centre of the cultural life of the Greeks. Whoever attended this school and the education connected with it passed as a "Hellene," regardless of whether his place of origin was on the Orontes, on the Euphrates or on the Nile. Thus the class of "Those from the *Gymnasium*" was the cultural class in the Hellenistic monarchies.

The Greeks at first adopted a distinctly exclusive attitude and stood aloof from the indigenous foreign population, and the governments of the Hellenistic states supported this attitude with laws and decrees. It is noteworthy that in the entire Zenon correspondence, comprising thousands of letters, not a single Graeco-Egyptian double name appears, an indication that in approximately 250 B.C. in Egypt the immigrants and the natives had not yet found their way to each other. It is not until the end of the third century that, in individual cases, members of the native upper classes rose to the level of the cultural Greeks. They gave expression to this by adopting Greek names in addition to their native names. Besides the gymnasium the Greek theatre found a home everywhere in the new cities, even in Babylon (middle of the second century B.C.). The theatre was accompanied by the stage artists, primarily the societies of Dionysian *technitai*, for whom an extensive new field of activity opened up in the new monarchies and their ruler cult. With the Hellenes the system of Greek guilds also migrated to the East. The number of religious, social and business guilds of the Hellenes in Asia and Egypt was overwhelming.

The technical side of the Greek mind appears in the plans of the innumerable newly founded cities. They were almost without exception drawn up on the Hippodamian plan, with broad, spacious streets intersecting each other at right angles and having a large agora at the centre. New tasks were imposed by the existence of the royal courts in the capitals, in Alexandria and Antioch, and later also in Pergamum. On the model set by Maussollus in Halicarnassus, separate sectors were reserved in the cities for the seat of the royal courts, in which the palaces and temples, military camps and magazines were combined together into larger complexes.

With the rise of the East under Alexander and the successors, Hellas itself shifted from the centre to the periphery of political events. The political decline was followed, although gradually at first, by a decline in the intellectual vitality and originality of the Hellenic motherland, so that Greece fell behind the new cultural and political centres in the East, especially Alexandria. There had never been in the Greek city-state a systematic cultivation of art and science. In former times the representatives of Greek cultural life had often found a home at the courts of the tyrants and in the capitals of the Macedonian kings and the rulers of Sicily. The Macedonian ruling families of the Hellenistic period continued these traditions. It was not in the atmosphere of the free city-states but at the royal courts that Hellenistic art, science and culture reached its greatest flowering. The patronage of letters by the first Ptolemies made Alexandria the home of many poets and scholars from the entire Greek world. Counselled by the philosopher and statesman Demetrius of Phalerum, Ptolemy I created in the *Mouseion* of Alexandria a state research centre on a grand scale, the first in the world. By combining research and teaching it became the model for many similar institutions in antiquity, and not least for the academies and universities in the Middle Ages.

The learned men and poets who were called to the *Mouseion* by the king could devote themselves exclusively to their studies, undisturbed by the cares of everyday life. They formed a cultic guild headed by a priest who was at the same time, as curator appointed by the king, responsible for their material needs. Connected with the *Mouseion* was a vast library consisting of several thousand papyrus rolls, which the poet Callimachus of Cyrene began to catalogue. A stellar observatory, an anatomical institute and a zoo with rare animals, to which Ptolemaic vassal princes such as the sheikh Tubias from the land of the Ammonites contributed, offered an extensive field for specialised researches. Political discussion was not carried on in the *Mouseion*. Here scholars enjoyed the peace and quiet which only the powerful Ptolemaic empire could afford them, and not the Greek poleis which had again and again been exposed to the vicissitudes of Fortune.

The number of scholars and poets who spent a short or long period of time as guests of the Ptolemies in Alexandria is great. At their head stand the poet Callimachus of Cyrene and Theocritus of Syracuse. Callimachus attained international fame through his elegies and epigrams. A fortunate papyrus find has presented us with a number of verses from his *Lock of Berenice*, and with the help of the *Diegeseis*, short summaries of contents, also preserved on a papyrus, we are able to form some idea of the contents and composition of his *Aetia*. Theocritus became known in the Greek world for his bucolic poems, the *Idylls*. Both the *Aetia* and the *Idylls* are learned poetry which grew up in an environment of the highest culture, in the atmosphere of the large city and court surroundings. The rich treasures of the Alexandrian libraries (there was also a library in the *Sarapeum*) created the conditions for the efflorescence of philology, which records such brilliant names as the grammarian Zenodotus, the paedagogus of Ptolemy II, Aristophanes of Byzantium (in the time of Ptolemy III) and Aristarchus (first half of the second century B.C.). Aristarchus, who combined bold textual criticism with penetrating exegesis, became the father of modern philology by his editions of Homer.

The history of Greek culture in the Hellenistic period culminates in the careers of the universal scholar Eratosthenes of Cyrene (c. 285-c. 205 B.C.) and the mathematician Archimedes of Syracuse (c. 280-212 B.C.). Both scholars spent a long period of time in Alexandria. Eratosthenes was the administrator of the library in the *Mouseion* under Ptolemy III Euergetes and tutor of the later Ptolemy IV Philopator. Archimedes spent his years of study in Alexandria and then returned to his native Sicily, to which he remained loyal until his death. Eratosthenes made great advances in theoretical and applied geography, as well as in chronography, which he established as a science in the true sense of the word. In his work *Concerning the Measurement of the Earth*, Eratosthenes' results came close to the facts. Furthermore, the knowledge of his research ultimately reached Christopher Columbus and spurred him on his voyage towards the west. Then, for the whole of Greek history, from the destruction of Troy to the death of Alexander the Great, Eratosthenes attempted to establish fixed points of chronology. Polybius adopted the reckoning by Olympiads, which Eratosthenes employed (he also wrote a separate work entitled *Olympionikai*), and used it as the chronological framework for his universal history of the Mediterranean world.

Under Ptolemy I, Euclid compiled the geometric knowledge of his time in the form of a text book, *The Elements*. The Syracusan genius Archimedes, however, made a decisive advance in the science of mathematics in the Hellenistic period, indeed in the whole of world history. The number of his discoveries in mathematics and physics is legion. He described the ratio of a circle to its diameter (*pi*) more accurately than all his predecessors, and calculated the volume of the sphere at ⅔ of the circumscribed cylinder. Archimedes was the inventor of integral calculus, with the aid of which he determined the area of surfaces and volumes. His work *On Conoids and Spheroids* is concerned with calculating the area of rotating surfaces of the second order. He also discovered the hydrostatic law, by which it was possible to calculate the specific weight of a body (it was tested in determining the gold content in the crown of Hieron II). With the aid of compound pulleys, levers and bolts, which he discovered, Archimedes succeeded in lifting and moving heavy loads, and his catapults and grapnels made significant contributions to the defense of Syracuse against the attacks of the Romans in 213/12 B.C. He was, however, outmatched when M. Claudius Marcellus conquered the city. Only modern mathematics has succeeded in again taking up the achievements of the great Syracusan, for he was in advance of his contemporaries by an entire era. Apollonius of Perge in Pamphylia, younger than Archimedes by approximately a generation, lived in Alexandria and Pergamum. He developed the classic theory of Conic Sections, and introduced into scientific terminology the concepts of ellipse, parabola and hyperbola.

The distinctly rational character of Hellenistic culture is especially evident in the field of technology. As early as the time of Dionysius I of Syracuse and Philip II of Macedonia the art of siegeworks had received a great impetus. Alexander's blockade of Tyre and the achievements of Demetrius, who has gone down in history as "the besieger," brilliantly continued what others had already begun. The art of building fortresses also received close attention. Demetrias-Pagasae in Thessaly and Heracleia on the Latmus in Caria (Pleistarcheia) were two important fortresses of the Hellenistic period whose sites have been uncovered by modern archaeological research. As in all times, technology was enlisted in the service of warfare and destruction. Half of the *Mechanics* by Philo of Byzantium (c. 250 B.C.) is devoted to the art of war. The "king of engineers," however, was Philo's contemporary, Ctesibius, who lived in Alexandria under Ptolemy II. He used compressed air in his inventions, for the first time in the history of technology. But the majority of his inventions—the organ, flame throwers and automatic devices—served only to entertain Alexandrian court society. None the less, he made an epoch-making advance in the field of ancient missile technology. Ctesibius for the first time constructed "torsion catapults," in which the tension was produced by bundles of cords. The torsion catapult soon rendered the earlier so-called bow catapult completely obsolete. Hellenistic technology also showed great achievements in shipbuilding. The luxury vessel of Hieron II, the *Syrakosia*, later called the *Alexandris*, had a capacity of approximately 3300 gross tons. It remained a show-piece, however, devoid of any nautical value. Demetrius Poliorcetes had already built huge ships but they did not prove satisfactory in battle, so that within a short time recourse was again had to the smaller types, such as the trireme, quadrireme and quinquereme.

Under the first Ptolemies Alexandria also became the centre of a world-famous medical school, which even forced the school of Cos into the background. The names of Herophilus (under Ptolemy I) and Erasistratus (under Ptolemy II) actually mark a new era in medical science. Both founded their own school and both worked as anatomists. They even undertook vivisection on human beings, allegedly on criminals whom the king placed at their disposal. Herophilus has gone down in medical history as the discoverer of the nerves, and the first to recognise the brain as the centre of the nervous system. Erasistratus came close to discovering the circulation of the blood, although he missed complete understanding because he thought that the arteries contained not blood but *pneuma*. In surgery, there was no hesitation to perform even difficult operations. Physicians had excellent medical instruments and a highly developed art of making surgical dressings. The use of drugs was widespread, and a whole separate body of literature arose on the subject of animal poisons and the medicines and antidotes to be used against them. The Hellenistic rulers vied with one another to obtain the best doctors for their courts, and the outstanding achievements of the doctors are repeatedly lauded in the honorary decrees of many Hellenistic poleis. Ptolemaic Egypt was apparently the first state in history in which the population had access to state medical care, while the other Hellenistic states appointed special doctors for their armies. Old folk-medicine, however, continued to exist alongside the highly developed medical science of the Hellenistic period. The inscriptions from Epidaurus (c. 300 B.C.) are filled with accounts of miraculous cures, to which the healing god Asclepius pointed the way for the faithful in the temple sleep. The hero Amphiaraus of Oropus also helped many people. A number of inscriptions from Cos, Crete and Asia Minor proclaim the fame of the medical school of Hippocrates. In 219 B.C. the first Greek doctor settled in Rome.

Botany, especially pursued by Aristotle's successor Theophrastus, owed its incentive to Alexander's campaign. This same event also inaugurated a new epoch in geographical exploration. The voyage of Nearchus from the mouth of the Indus to the Euphrates and the expedition of Androsthenes of Thasos to the east coast of Arabia are enterprises to be traced back directly to Alexander's initiative. The Seleucids and Ptolemies continued these explorations. Under Seleucus I, Patrocles, who as governor held a high command in Parthia and Hyrcania, undertook an expedition to the Caspian Sea—unsuccessful, for he did not sail far enough north, and his assumption that the Caspian Sea was a gulf of the northern Oceanus became fixed in the minds of his contemporaries. In the West, the daring Massaliot Pytheas of Gades (Cadiz) in Spain succeeded, in the time of Alexander, in reaching the North-West of Europe, perhaps sailing even as far as the northern tip of Great Britain and the mouth of the Elbe. Pytheas brought back the first accounts of the long summer nights in the North and the ice-covered Polar Sea. His contemporaries refused to believe him, and only modern explorations have vindicated him. The achievement of Pytheas was equalled only by discovery in 117 or 116 B.C. of the direct route from Egypt on the high seas to India, by Eudoxus of Cyzicus and his captain Hippalus on behalf of the Ptolemies. The great universal scholar of the late Hellenistic period, Poseidonius of Apameia (c. 130-50 B.C.), described the voyage in detail in his work *On the Ocean*. The large number of geographical discoveries in the Hellenistic period demonstrate that the old enterprising spirit of the Greeks had in no way come to an end, and could still achieve outstanding feats.

Generally speaking, it was perhaps in the field of Astronomy that the greatest achievements in the Hellenistic period are to be noted—the establishing of the heliocentric solar system. Aristarchus of Samos, pupil of the physicist Straton of Lampsacus, maintained not only that the earth rotated on its axis but also that it revolved around the sun, which for him formed the fixed centre of the universe. (The work of Copernicus took up the researches of the brilliant scholar, for the name of Aristarchus appears in the handwritten drafts.) The revolutionary hypothesis of Aristarchus became known in antiquity but did not prevail, probably because of the extensive influence of Stoicism. The Stoic Cleanthes of Assos even called upon the Hellenes to bring Aristarchus to trial on the charge of impiety! Aristarchus' work was continued in about the middle of the second century B.C. by Hipparchus of Nicomedeia, who created the first scientific stellar catalogue, and also compiled a register of eclipses. His most important achievement, however, was the discovery of the advance of the equinoxes along the ecliptic. In this discovery Hipparchus used the researches and observations of Babylonian astronomers, and it is still probably uncertain whether the Babylonians, especially the astronomer Kidinnu (Kidenas) (c. 314 B.C.), warrant a place of pre-eminence over Aristarchus. Aristarchus took astrology over from the Babylonians, and in this he was an ancient forerunner of such great astronomers and astrologers as Kepler and Tycho Brahe.[84] According to Hipparchus, human destiny was most intricately bound up with the stars, and the human soul was part of the heavens (Pliny, *N.H.* II 95). Poseidonius adopted this view and expanded it into a great cosmological-philosophical system, which had a long-range effect. A regular astrological system was first created in Ptolemaic Egypt. The two principal works go under the name of Nechepso and Petosiris, as well as Hermes Trismegistus—the Egyptian god Thoth. The extensive fusion of the Greeks and the native Egyptians created during the second century B.C. that class of the population which passionately devoted itself to the secret teachings of astrology.

The expression of a new intellectual attitude of the Hellenistic individual towards his environment appears above all in the buildings of the period. Enormous and pompous structures predominate, manifestly under the influence of the structures from the ancient Orient—the Egyptian pyramids and the Babylonian temple towers (ziggurats). Alexander's plan to build a gigantic pyramid in honour of his father, Philip, the enterprise of the architect Deinocrates to create a monument to Alexander out of Mount Athos, so large that in one hand of the statue there would be sufficient room for an entire polis of 10,000 souls—these are examples of the gigantic building projects which can only be compared with the architectural forms of the ancient Orient. The *Sarapeum* of Alexandria, the lighthouse on the island of Pharos, the luxury tent of Ptolemy II Philadelphus, the statue of the sun god Helios on Rhodes (the so-called "Colossus"), the Didymaeum of Miletus, the Great Altar of Pergamum, whose mighty baroque frieze depicting the battle between the giants and the Olympian gods symbolises the struggle of the Attalid rulers against the Galatians—all these (and many more) are genuine Hellenistic structures, which, despite their inner symmetry, lack that feeling of proportion in their dimensions so pre-eminently typical of the works of the classical period. Hellenistic art found an extensive field of activity in the decorating of the new structures and temples. Lysippus and his school attained great achievements in sculpture. The outstanding coin portraits, especially those of the Graeco-Bactrian kings, and the lifelike portraits of Hellenistic queens, such as the head of Berenice II found in Cyrene, attest the high quality of artistic portraiture in the Hellenistic period.[85] In the field of historical paintings the mosaic of the battle of Alexander from Pompeii is excellent evidence for the original by Philoxenus of Eretria (from the successor-period). The wall paintings of Pompeii give something of an idea of Hellenistic painting, although admittedly one-sided, since mythological representations and scenes from daily life predominate. The sacred places of Greece, the sanctuaries of Olympia, Delos and Delphi, and the Acropolis in Athens, were filled with groves of statues. In the remote town of Thermum there were, according to Polybius, some 2000 statues, and M. Fulvius Nobilior, the patronus of Ennius, took no less than 1000 back with him from Ambracia to Italy—a page from the gloomy annals of Roman art plundering in Greece, in which Aemilius Paullus, the victor of Pydna, and Mummius, the destroyer of Corinth, also played a major rôle.

When the development of Hellenistic culture was at the height of its vitality in the third century B.C., it held a strong attraction for the peoples of Asia and Egypt. The historical writings by the Egyptian priest Manetho of Sebennytus (under Ptolemy II) and by the Babylonian priest of Bêl, Berossus (under Antiochus I), bear witness to this. Both Orientals attempted to bring the famous past of their nations before the Hellenic world by writing in Greek. The history of Rome, written, also in Greek, by the senator Q. Fabius Pictor, who spent some time as an envoy at Delphi in 216 B.C., belongs in this category. The military camp of Hannibal held the historians Silenus of Caleacte (in Sicily) and Sosylus of Lacedaemonia, of whose *History* a Würzburg papyrus has provided us a fragment. The Greeks, however, kept entirely aloof from the sources for the history of the ancient Orient, and knowledge of the hieroglyphics and cuneiform writing remained a totally closed book to them. The last Lagid, Cleopatra VII, was the first to learn Egyptian, Aramaic and Parthian. By her time, however, the Orient had long since gripped the souls of the Hellenes. Under Ptolemy I, Hecataeus of Abdera wrote on Egypt and its inhabitants, excerpts of which are preserved in Diodorus (Bk. I), but this work is not, however, real history. It projects philosophical-political ideas, especially the notion of the King Benefactor, into the distant past, so that it resembles an exhortation of the ruler and his subjects more than it does a work of history. Hecataeus was incidentally, in addition to Theophrastus, the first Greek who also concerned himself with the customs of the Jews.

In the third century there was plenty of scope for translators. Ptolemy II Philadelphus allegedly ordered works of the Chaldaeans and Egyptians, and indeed even of the Romans, to be collected and translated into Greek. In Alexandria the Jewish Torah was also translated into Greek, probably in the third century B.C. In the history of civilisation this was an event of the greatest importance, which the so-called *Letter of Aristeas* (from the end of the second century B.C.) embellished with many legendary features. In the West the Romans had the treatise of the Carthaginian Mago on agriculture translated into Latin and Greek. In a later period, at the end of antiquity, the Orientals, and finally the Arabs, translated many Greek writings on philosophy, history and chronology into their native languages and thus often rescued these works for posterity.

The period of Hellenism was a time of religious searching. The connection between the state, the national character and religion for the Greeks of the classical period had begun to dissolve. Many inscriptions still do mention the gods in political treaties and decrees of the Council and *demos*, and the private documents call upon them as witnesses to oaths—but in all this much of what was once living faith had now become mere formality. The educated individual was accustomed to smile at the Olympian gods and the many local deities, or at best shrug his shoulders. A person like the historian Polybius regarded religion as necessary only for the masses. At the same time this "modern" generation was far removed from thoroughgoing atheism—religion had become a convention. Only when violent external upheavals robbed men's souls of equilibrium, as in the invasion of the wild Celtic hordes into Macedonia and Greece, did the excited imagination of the masses believe in manifestations of saving gods—especially when a sanctuary like Delphi was in extraordinary fashion spared from plundering and destruction. In the Hellenistic period Tyche,[86] the goddess of blind chance, became the greatest deity, to whom in this generation of rapid change young and old, rich and poor, masters and slaves alike subjected themselves. But the belief in cruel Tyche certainly could not satisfy those with a deeply religious nature. These people therefore sought refuge in those gods and cults which were heralded by the call of the mysterious—the Mysteries of Demeter and Dionysus who from early times had found a home in Hellas, and the many different Oriental gods with whom the Greeks had become familiar abroad. In Asia Minor, Syria, Mesopotamia and Egypt congregations of the faithful, composed of the most varied nationalities, irrespective of all frontiers of race and social position, met on religious ground, worshipping Isis, or Baal, or Atargatis or Cybele. The strength of Greek cultural awareness often saw in these gods new manifestations of ancient Greek gods, just as the so-called *Interpretatio Graeca* reached a new height in the Hellenistic period. That the gods of the Orient became fully-fledged Greek deities, as a recent one-sided treatment would have us believe,[87] is a great exaggeration. The Isis hymns, for instance, are unquestionably born out of the spirit of Egyptian piety, and yet, despite this, became dispersed throughout the whole of the Greek world.

The gods and goddesses of the Orient did, however, often assume new attributes and new manifestations among the Greeks, and so differed significantly from the original deities. A typical hybrid product of the new Hellenistic religiosity was the imperial god Sarapis, promoted by Ptolemy I while he was still satrap (before 305 B.C.), in consultation with the Egyptian Manetho and the Eumolpid Timotheus of Athens.[88] Originally the Memphite god of the underworld, Osiris-Apis, he excited the interest of the Hellenes as a healing and oracle god, and his close connections with the queen of the gods, Isis (*Isis regina*), who at the same time also set about to gain supremacy over the souls of the Greeks, obtained new widespread esteem for him. From their point of departure at Alexandria, Sarapis and particularly Isis became known to the entire Mediterranean world. Along with the Syrian merchants many gods of the Orient soon also settled in the Greek islands (Delos) and in the Greek harbour cities, such as Athens, Thessalonica and Corinth. The Iranian cults of Mithras and Anahita enjoyed a particularly vigorous life, above all in Anatolia, where there had been a strong Iranian element from time immemorial. Via Asia Minor and Greece the Zoroastrian doctrine of world dispensations also penetrated into the West.

Another Asia Minor deity, the *Magna Mater*—Great Mother—found a home in the West as early as 204 B.C., when the sacred stone fetish of the temple Megalesium at Pergamum was transported to Rome. Greek tradition, however, remains completely mute regarding the success of the Buddhistic or Buddhistic-inspired propaganda of the Indian ruler Asoka of Maurya as related in Indian rock inscriptions, although a Greek-Aramaic inscription in Kandahar in Afghanistan can be regarded as a propaganda inscription of Asoka (he calls himself Piodasses).[89]

What the Hellenes often sought to no avail in religion, the educated among them found in philosophy—a firmly established world view, which enabled them to see even behind the apparently purposeless chance events of human and public life a purposeful world order. Athens, whose political power had, with her defeat at the naval battle of Amorgos (322 B.C.), forever come to an end, became the chief citadel of Greek philosophy. She became a kind of world university, and maintained this lofty position in Greek cultural life until the end of the Hellenistic period, indeed even beyond it, against the competition of Alexandria, Pergamum, Rhodes and later also of Rome.

It was the teachings of the Greek Epicurus of Samos (342/1-271/70 B.C.) and the Phoenician Zenon of Citium (on Cyprus) (336-263 B.C.) that decisively shaped the intellectual countenance of the Hellenistic and, beyond it, of the Roman world. The new schools, the *Kepos* and the *Stoa*, as they were called after the places of their activity in Athens, arose out of nowhere to assert themselves over the firmly established and financially well-endowed older schools, the *Peripatos* and the *Academy*. This success demonstrates their unusually strong appeal among wide circles of the educated classes. Both schools, the Epicurean as a matter of principle and the Stoa at least in its beginnings, assumed an attitude of complete indifference towards the state. The axiom of Epicurus, "live in quiet seclusion," meant that the pupils of the master were, in so far as it was at all possible, to refrain from active participation in public life. "For the Epicurean not the state but the society of like-minded individuals is the actual homeland; in it he finds everything he needs for this life, and this community requires the state only to the extent that every civilised individual needs it to protect his personal existence" (E. Schwartz). By excluding the gods from the world of men Epicurus attempted to liberate the souls of the faithful from fear. By the example of his own life, highly admirable by his unpretentiousness and the patient endurance of pain, he gave a shining example to his followers. His example had such an effect upon his disciples that they revered Epicurus as a saint, while his writings and doctrines soon attained canonical importance. In Lucretius' didactic poem *De rerum natura* the Epicurean world view received its most glorious expression in western literature.

The teachings of the *Stoa* had a far greater effect than those of Epicurus. The *Stoa's* founder, the Phoenician Zenon, until the end a stranger in Athens, disavowed everything that had hitherto given worth and meaning to life for the Greek. Not the polis is the true fatherland, taught Zenon, but the *oikoumene*, the world, in so far as it is at all inhabited. He recognised no difference between free and non-free, between Greek and non-Greek. The object of Stoic ethics was not the good citizen, whose ideal Plato had at one time delineated in his *Republic* and in the *Laws*, but rather the independent, harmonious individual personality. The ideal state which Zenon depicted in his *Politeia*, a deliberate counterpart to Plato's work bearing the same title, negated everything that had been associated with the polis for the Hellenes. Zenon's state required none of the institutions characteristic of the Greek polis, no temples and sanctuaries, no courts and *gymnasia*, which had become the symbols of the Hellenes throughout the entire world. For the Stoa man was not a "political animal," but rather a "social animal," part of the community of all who shared in a particular culture. In contrast to the extreme view held by the founder of the school in his *Politeia*, however, later Stoics, even immediate pupils of Zenon, were active in political life, namely as advisers to Hellenistic monarchs. They frequently also appeared as authors of treatises *On Monarchy*. Persaeus, Cleanthes, Sphaerus and Chrysippus attempted to portray the ruler according to the ideal of the Stoic philosophers, in works like the mediaeval *Fürstenspiegel*. The monarchical trend in the Stoa was altered into a republican notion in the time of the Roman Principate, to which the Stoic opposition under Nero and Domitian bear witness. In the spirit of the Stoa the Macedonian king Antigonus Gonatas, who had at one time sat at the feet of Zenon in Athens, called monarchical rule "glorious bondage"[90]—a sense of duty that prompts the ruler to take upon himself responsibility for the welfare of his subjects. The same spirit animates the writings and deeds of Marcus Aurelius, the pupil of the Stoic philosopher Epictetus, and the statement of Frederick the Great, "I am the first servant of my state," is equally Stoic.

The Stoa held firmly to belief in the existence of the gods, but, in accordance with the spirit of the times, the world of the gods bore a strong pantheistic colouring. The Stoic belief that the world was ruled not by blind chance but by Providence, to which man must submit, offered a stability that popular religion, already in a state of dissolution, could no longer give. It is no accident that the large number of tomb inscriptions from the period of the Roman Republic and the first era of the Principate exhibit a Stoic (and on the other hand frequently also an Epicurean) colouring. The participation of the Oriental, especially the Semitic, spirit in shaping the Stoic system has in recent times generally been greatly overrated. Many of the leading Stoics were indeed Orientals (Zenon and Persaeus came from Citium on Cyprus, Chrysippus from Soli, Antipater from Tarsus and Diogenes from Seleuceia on the Tigris, *et al.*), but no scholars have been able to demonstrate specific Semitic elements in the teachings of the Stoa. The spiritual contacts between the Stoa and Judaeo-Hellenistic literature, and later between the Stoa and Christianity, do not furnish any decisive evidence for the dependence of Stoic teachings on the Orient. They show only a gradual assimilation of goals and ideas, as they find expression in, for instance, the relations of Seneca to Christianity and of Epictetus to the New Testament.

One of the great surprises of late at the excavations in Aï Khanum (at the confluence of the Amu-darya and the Kokea in North-East Afghanistan) was the discovery of an epigram on the philosopher Clearchus of Soli, the pupil of Aristotle. Clearchus was himself present in Bactria at the beginning of the third century B.C. and there had the sayings of the Seven Sages engraved "in the Temenos of Kineas."[90a]

The enduring influence of Graeco-Hellenistic culture is illustrated by its triumph in the West, beginning even in the third century B.C. The Greek Livius Andronicus of Tarentum in 240 B.C., only a year after the long First Punic War, produced a Greek play in Roman dress at the Roman Games. This was done at the behest of the Senate, which in 269 B.C. had struck the first silver coinage[91] (the so-called first Roman-Campanian series on the Hellenistic model). Hannibal too, the great Carthaginian general, was profoundly indebted to Greek culture. His account of his "deeds," in the temple of Lacinian Hera, was written in Punic and in Greek, and his pamphlet to the Rhodians on the crimes of Cn. Manlius Volso was also in Greek (189 B.C.), showing how much he appreciated the political and cultural importance of the Greek language. Hellenism conquered broad circles of Roman intellectuals in the course of the second century B.C. The sojourn of Achaean hostages, including the historian Polybius, in Italy for many years (167-150 B.C.), and the famous Athenian embassy of philosophers in 155 B.C. (Carneades of the Academy, Critolaus the Peripatetic, Diogenes the Stoic) were of unprecedented importance for contact between Greeks and Romans.

MAP X

The Hellenistic States c. 185 B.C.

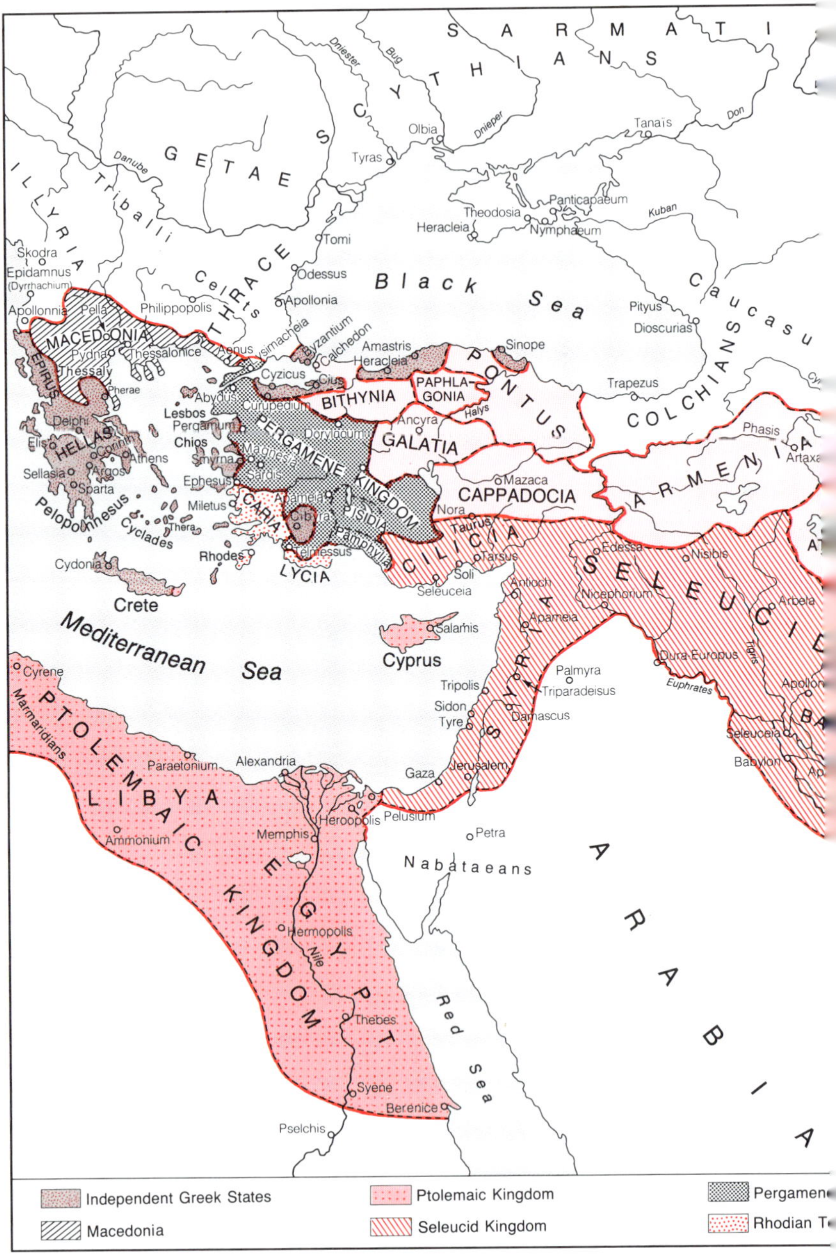
S A R M A T I
S C Y T H I A N S
GETAE
Danube
Dniester
Bug
Dnieper
Don
Kuban
Olbia
Tyras
Tanaïs
Theodosia
Panticapaeum
Nymphaeum
Heracleia
ILLYRIA
Triballi
Celts
THRACE
Skodra
Epidamnus
(Dyrrhachium)
Apollonia
Pella
Philippopolis
Tomi
Odessus
Apollonia
Black Sea
Caucasus
Pityus
Dioscurias
COLCHIANS
Trapezus
Phasis
MACEDONIA
Pydna
Thessalonice
Thessaly
EPIRUS
Pherae
Delphi
HELLAS
Elis
Corinth
Athens
Argos
Sellasia
Sparta
Peloponnesus
Cyclades
Thera
Lysimacheia
Byzantium
Calchedon
Aenus
Cyzicus
Cius
Abydus
Lesbos
Pergamum
Chios
Smyrna
Ephesus
Miletus
Magnesia
Sardis
Curupedium
Dorylaeum
PERGAMENE KINGDOM
CARIA
Apameia
Cibyra
PISIDIA
Pamphylia
Telmessus
LYCIA
Rhodes
Amastris
Heracleia
Sinope
PAPHLAGONIA
PONTUS
BITHYNIA
Halys
Ancyra
GALATIA
Mazaca
CAPPADOCIA
Nora
Taurus
CILICIA
Tarsus
Soli
Seleuceia
ARMENIA
Artaxata
Edessa
Nisibis
Nicephorium
Antioch
Apameia
SELEUCID
Arbela
Tigris
Dura Europus
Euphrates
Apollonia
Seleuceia
Babylon
Palmyra
Triparadeisus
Damascus
SYRIA
Tripolis
Sidon
Tyre
Jerusalem
Gaza
Cydonia
Crete
Mediterranean Sea
Salamis
Cyprus
Cyrene
Marmaridians
PTOLEMAIC KINGDOM
Paraetonium
Alexandria
LIBYA
Ammonium
Heroopolis
Pelusium
Memphis
Petra
Nabataeans
EGYPT
Hermopolis
Nile
Thebes
Syene
Berenice
Pselchis
Red Sea
ARABIA
Independent Greek States
Macedonia
Ptolemaic Kingdom
Seleucid Kingdom
Pergamen
Rhodian T

Other States

Elymaïs and Persis semi-independent vassel states of the Seleucid Kingdom

The supremacy of Greek culture, which in no other century of its more than two thousand years of history produced a similarly large number of outstanding feats, appeared to be established for all time in the third century B.C. From the world-wide supremacy of the Macedonians there emerged a universal sovereignty of Hellenic culture, whose frontiers all but coincided with those of the inhabited world. The oriental world, however, had not been conquered. It continued to exist under the veneer of Hellenic culture, and was ready to awaken to a life of its own. Nor did the Greeks succeed in winning for Hellenism the national elements of the Orient—the Syrians, Babylonians, Iranians and Egyptians—because the numerical disproportion between the ruling Greeks and the subject Orientals was too great. In addition, the great masses of oriental peoples held with unusual tenacity to their own languages and cultures. On the other hand the Greeks and Macedonians did not remain unaffected by the foreign environment, the strange climate and the bizarre world of oriental religions. The judgment of Poseidonius (Livy XXXVIII 17), that the Macedonians in Alexandria, in Seleuceia and in Babylon have degenerated into Syrians, Parthians and Egyptians,[92] does not lack foundation, although it scarcely was true before the second half of the second century B.C. The loss of world-wide sovereignty to the Romans and the beginning of the political reaction of the Orient in the second century B.C. marked the beginning of the decline of Hellenistic culture, which, cut off from its national fountain-head in the Greek motherland, in many places succeeded in asserting itself only with great effort. It was only in the Far East, in India, that it opened up new regions for itself, through the triumphal march of the Bactrian Hellenes.

14
THE HELLENISTIC STATES UNDER ROMAN SUPREMACY

ROME IN CONFLICT WITH PHILIP V OF MACEDONIA

On the basis of the secret treaty concluded with Philip V, in 201 B.C. Antiochus III marched into the Ptolemaic territory of South Syria and brought the region into his possession with the victory of Paneium at the head waters of the Jordan (200 B.C.).[1] His Macedonian confederate was less fortunate. Philip V swiftly conquered a number of cities at the straits, including Lysimacheia (202 B.C.),[2] but the siege of Chios brought him into conflict with the Rhodians, for whom the Macedonian expansion at the Dardanelles was repugnant. Rhodes, Byzantium and Cyzicus united with the Pergamene ruler Attalus I into a coalition against the Macedonian. By sea (the battle of Chios 201 B.C.) they proved themselves a match for Philip V, if not superior. While Philip V was operating in Caria,[3] an embassy from Rhodes and Attalus I appeared before the Senate in Rome (201 B.C.).[4] It seems to have cleverly exploited the Syro-Macedonian treaty of partition, which had meanwhile become public knowledge. At all events the Romans, who had just been victorious over Hannibal at the battle of Zama (202 B.C.), suddenly changed course by holding out the prospects of definite aid to the Rhodians and Attalus I against Philip V. The war could not of course be started by the Romans before 200 B.C.

The decision of the Senate was of world significance. It marks a fundamental turning point in the political situation of the entire Mediterranean. How was it that Rome could arrive at this weighty resolve? That the Romans felt their security to be threatened by the Syro-Macedonian secret treaty[5] is improbable. Antiochus III was involved in a struggle for South Syria, and Macedonia did not constitute any direct danger to

Rome, for in the First Macedonian War it had demonstrated only too clearly its inability to interfere in the developments of the West. Rome had no real cause for war. Rhodes and Athens, who on account of an incident at the Eleusian Mysteries came into conflict with the Acarnanians and Philip V, did not belong to the allies of Rome, and Attalus I, who had fought on the side of the Romans in the First Macedonian War, was not the victim of aggression but the aggressor.

The Roman decision had its roots in the expansionist and imperialist character of Roman policies, which were even further accentuated by the ambitions of leading politicians at Rome. The great victory of P. Cornelius Scipio over the Carthaginians and Hannibal gave the Romans, who had now become the masters of the western Mediterranean, the profound confidence that they could also dictate terms to the East. A thesis of Mommsen, that the general character of Rome's foreign policy was in large measure dictated by the requirements of Roman security, has found great approval among recent scholars,[6] but it is untenable. The Romans hid their imperialism behind phrases about peace and security, which deceived many of their contemporaries. It is impossible to believe that a ruling power comes to world empire because of fear of others, rather than because it actively seeks power.[7] Developments in foreign policy, grounded in the Roman character, were further accelerated by men like M. Valerius Laevinus (in the First Macedonian War), P. Cornelius Scipio and P. Sulpicius Galba, who became the architects of the Roman world empire. Rome's intervention in the destiny of the Hellenistic world gradually broke up the system of Eastern states and in place of the balance of political power established the hegemony of Rome in the East. Even after 201 B.C. there was no doubt such a thing as a Hellenistic policy, a Hellenistic political system, but the centre towards which everything converged from now on lay outside the Hellenistic world. It was Rome who as mistress (*domina Roma*) forced her policy upon the East. The Hellenistic states, which were either isolated (like Macedonia) or greatly impeded by difficulties in economics and population, were no match for the new and heavy burdens dictated by foreign policy.

Rome's immediate aims were to isolate the two confederate rulers, Philip V and Antiochus III, and to destroy Macedonian sovereignty in Greece. A Roman embassy under C. Claudius Nero, P. Sempronius Tuditanus and M. Aemilius Lepidus[8] attempted to stir up sentiment in Hellas against the Macedonians. M. Aemilius Lepidus went to the military camp of Philip V at Abydus (August 200 B.C.) and disclosed to him the demands of Rome. These had been deliberately made so extreme that the king simply could not accept them. The Romans demanded not only that he terminate the war against the Greeks, to wit against the Athenians, and that he return the Macedonian conquests in Asia Minor, but also that the conflict between Philip and Attalus be decided by a neutral court of arbitration. When Philip remained firm,[9] the Romans began the war with the landing of an army under the command of P. Sulpicius Galba in Apollonia (about September 200 B.C.). The Roman envoys had meanwhile tracked down the Seleucid, Antiochus III, and secured his neutrality in the Macedonian War. Alexandria[10] expected that Rome would settle the quarrel over South Syria, but this did not coincide with Roman intentions.

Philip's strategic position was initially not unfavourable. He controlled the internal bases and could restrict himself to defending the fortress of Macedonia, which was difficult of access, while the enemy must adopt an offensive strategy. Greece formed the point of departure for Rome. The Hellenes, however, assumed a remarkable reserve towards the Roman slogans of the "liberation of the Greeks." They adopted a wait-and-see attitude, and did not reckon with a rapid victory for Rome. Operations in the first two years of the war (200 and 199 B.C.) did not bring any decision.[11] The fleets of the allies—the Romans, the Rhodians and Attalus I—united on the Aegean Sea (200 B.C.) and gained the naval supremacy, but even the entry of the Aetolians into the anti-Macedonian coalition (199 B.C.) did not alter the situation. It was not until T. Quinctius Flamininus took over the Macedonian command in May 198 B.C. that Philip encountered an opponent who was his equal. His philhellenism destined Flamininus for the Greek command and soon made him extremely popular in Hellas. Flamininus is the first of a great number of Romans who, with a high regard for Hellenic culture, knew how to use *Realpolitik* at the expense of the Greeks.[12] He forced Philip to abandon his fortified key position on the Aoüs River, at Antigoneia (south of Valonas), and to retreat as far as the defile of Tempe. The entry of the Achaean League into the anti-Macedonian coalition (October 198 B.C.) was a great diplomatic victory for Flamininus. At this juncture Philip asked for negotiations.[13] These took place in Locrian Nicaea, but came to nothing, chiefly because of the excessive demands made by the Greek allies of Flamininus. But Flamininus was the victor. He took possession of the fortified places in Locris, which he had stipulated as the price for his mediation between the Macedonian king and the Roman Senate. Both antagonists now sought a decision on the battlefield. The conflict of arms took place at Cynoscephalae (west of Pherae in Thessaly), in June 197 B.C., a battle which followed from a skirmish.[14] The decision was brought about by the attack of the Roman right wing against the Macedonian phalanx, which in some places was still in marching formation. The elephants employed by the Romans caused confusion and terror in the Macedonian ranks: an inflexible Macedonia had fallen asleep on the laurels of a great past. The Aetolians wanted to prosecute the war against Philip until he was completely annihilated, but Flamininus expedited the conclusion of peace, after having given Philip guarantees for a short truce. Fear of the progress which Antiochus III was making in Asia Minor may have contributed to this. Antiochus had won over many Greek communities in the south and west of Asia Minor, and had secured the friendship of the Rhodians. Smyrna and Lampsacus alone resisted Seleucid demands and turned to Rome for help, whereby Lampsacus availed itself of Massalia's arbitration.[15] In the winter of 197/6 B.C. the Roman peace terms were dictated to Philip. He lost his entire possessions in Hellas and Asia Minor, had to surrender his fleet, was forced to pay an indemnity of 1000 talents and, in a special treaty, pledged himself to Roman military service in time of war.[16] At the Isthmian Games of 196 B.C. T. Quinctius Flamininus proclaimed the freedom of the Hellenes to the tumultuous applause of thousands who had hitherto been under the rule of the Macedonians: Corinthians, Phocians, Locrians, Euboeans, Phthiotic Achaeans, Magnesians, Thessalians and Perrhaebians.[17] For the second time in Greek history a foreign power, this time Rome, had become the guarantor of Hellenic freedom. It was a "Danaid" gift, like the King's Peace guaranteed by Persia almost 200 years earlier (386 B.C.). The Romans, by establishing the principle of freedom in Greece, actually challenged the second major Hellenistic power, the empire of Antiochus III. Ideas do not stop at frontiers, especially when there stands behind them a power that is prepared and able to translate them into reality.

The proclamation of freedom did not have a very happy epilogue. Apart from the fact that Rome left an occupation army in Hellas until 194 B.C., extorted vast contributions from the country and carried off to Italy many thousands of works of art, a kind of panhellenic war emerged from the conflict between the Achaean League and the Spartan tyrant Nabis when the latter refused to hand over Argos. Romans, Achaeans, Thessalians, Macedonians, Pergamenes and Rhodians joined in the Peloponnesian Social War,[18] which ended in the defeat of Nabis. The Roman army, with its commander, thereupon withdrew and left the Greeks to their freedom. Flamininus received extravagant honours. In Gytheum he was celebrated as "Saviour,"[19] gold coins were struck bearing his image and the Greek cities presented him with vast numbers of gold wreaths.

THE DEFEAT OF ANTIOCHUS III

The withdrawal of the Romans from Greece was a serious political and strategical error, for the Seleucid Antiochus III had meanwhile laid hands on the straits and proceeded to rebuild Lysimacheia on the Thracian Chersonese (196 B.C.). In the peace treaty with the Ptolemaic empire (195 B.C.?), which significantly came about without Roman arbitration, the Ptolemaic government renounced its possessions in Syria, Asia and Thrace. The Peace was consolidated by the marriage of the youthful king Ptolemy V Epiphanes to Antiochus' daughter, Cleopatra (I), in the winter of 194/3 B.C.[20] The action of the Seleucid ruler gives the impression of an energetic, resolute policy of expansion, whereby the king secured for his realm indisputable first place among the Hellenistic powers.

In the long run Rome could not idly watch the expansion of Antiochus III. While Rome refused Lampsacus its desired inclusion in the peace treaty with Philip, the Romans, after this peace, issued a categorical order to Antiochus not to attack the cities of Asia Minor. In 195 B.C. Smyrna built a temple in honour of *Domina Roma* as protective patroness. The tension between Rome and the Seleucid was further accentuated by Hannibal. On his flight from Carthage he turned to Syria, and in the summer of 195 B.C. met with Antiochus III in Ephesus.[21]

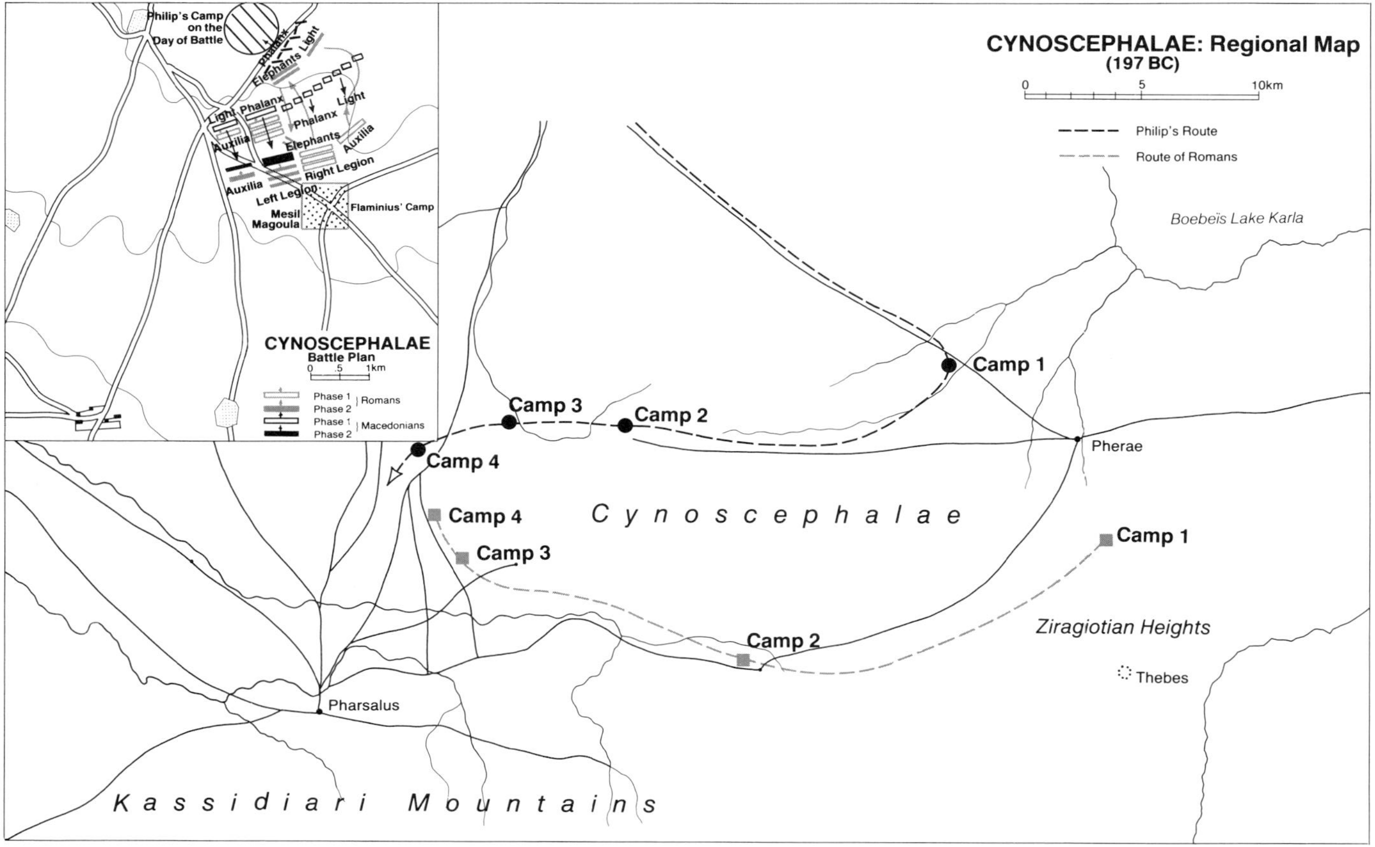

CYNOSCEPHALAE: Regional Map
(197 BC)
0
5
10km
Philip's Route
Route of Romans
Boebeïs Lake Karla
Camp 1
Camp 2
Camp 3
Camp 4
Pherae
Cynoscephalae
Camp 1
Camp 2
Camp 3
Camp 4
Ziragiotian Heights
Thebes
Pharsalus
Kassidiari Mountains
Philip's Camp on the Day of Battle
Phalanx
Elephants
Light
Light
Phalanx
Phalanx
Light
Auxilia
Elephants
Auxilia
Right Legion
Auxilia
Left Legion
Mesil Magoula
Flaminius' Camp
CYNOSCEPHALAE
Battle Plan
0
.5
1km
Phase 1
Phase 2
Romans
Phase 1
Phase 2
Macedonians

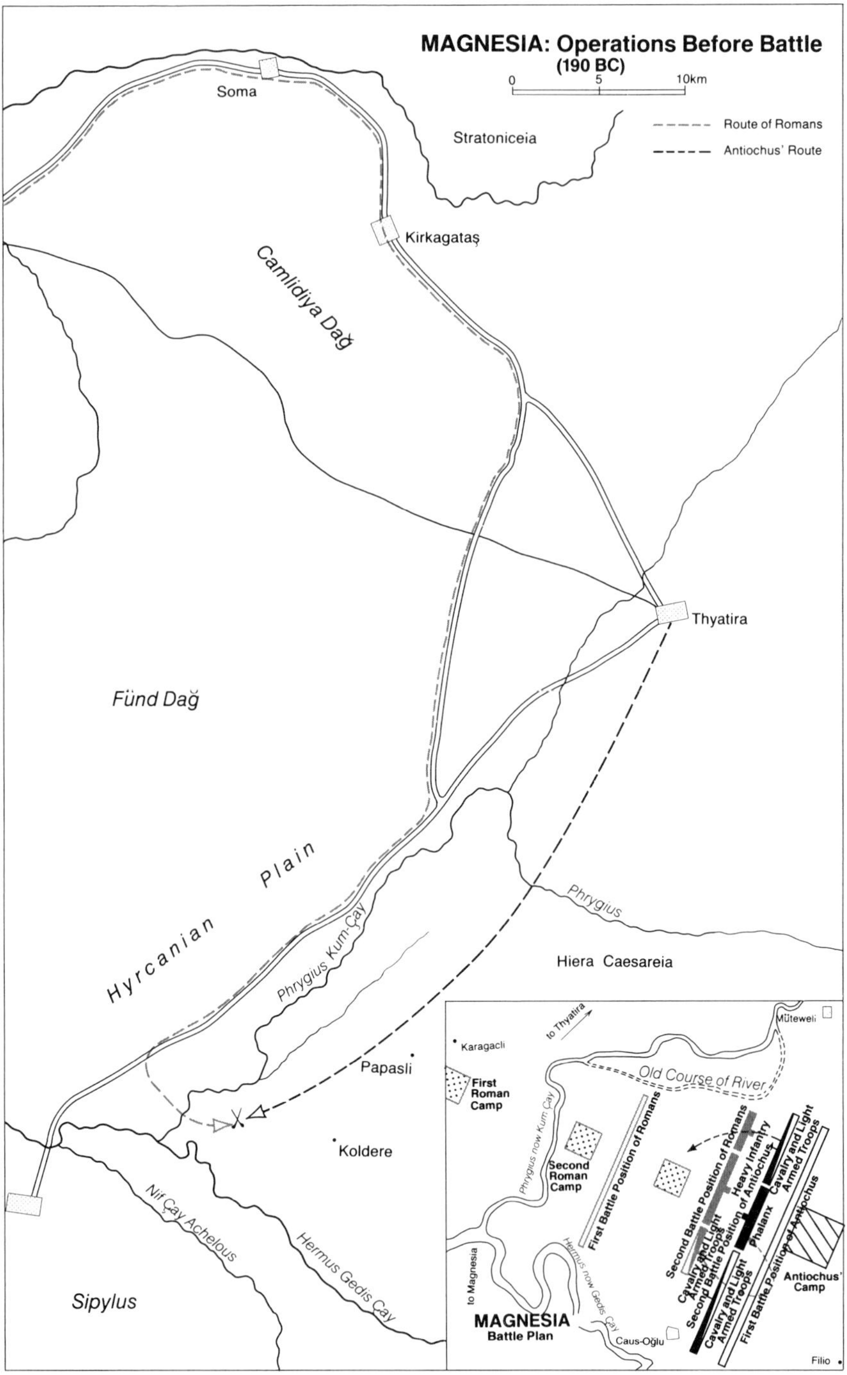
MAGNESIA: Operations Before Battle
(190 BC)
0
5
10km
Route of Romans
Antiochus' Route
Soma
Stratoniceia
Kirkagataş
Camlidiya Dağ
Thyatira
Fünd Dağ
Hyrcanian Plain
Phrygius
Phrygius Kum-Çay
Hiera Caesareia
Papasli
Koldere
Nif Çay Achelous
Hermus Gedis Çay
Sipylus
to Thyatira
Karagacli
Müteweli
Old Course of River
First Roman Camp
Phrygius now Kum Çay
Second Roman Camp
First Battle Position of Romans
Second Battle Position of Romans
Heavy Infantry
Cavalry and Light Armed Troops
Phalanx
Second Battle Position of Antiochus
First Battle Position of Antiochus
Antiochus' Camp
to Magnesia
Hermus now Gedis Çay
MAGNESIA
Battle Plan
Caus-Oğlu
Filio

The Aetolians in Greece caused the war which brought the Romans east again. Greatly disappointed in the reorganisation of Greece, they attempted to form a great coalition against Rome. Nabis of Sparta joined it, but Philip V remained aloof. They thereupon appealed to Antiochus III to protect the freedom of Greece, which was now being threatened and appointed him as *strategos* with plenary powers of the Aetolian League. Antiochus III accepted the Aetolian offer, since the conflict with Rome appeared inevitable to him. The actual execution of the plan, however, left everything to be desired.[22] Antiochus lacked the decisive prerequisites of a material and idealistic character for a really successful prosecution of the war against the world power of Rome. He had nothing to counter the effective Roman propaganda in the Greek world,[23] and his great resources in manpower and material could only be mobilised with difficulty, especially for a war across the Aegean in Greece. Hannibal's bold advice, to carry the offensive against Rome beyond Hellas to southern Italy, would have been a rash move under these circumstances, bringing inevitable ruin in its wake. In addition, Antiochus' efforts were in no way aimed at obtaining world domination. His goal was more modest, but none the less firmly outlined—to re-establish the realm of his ancestor Seleucus I, who had once defeated Lysimachus and had thereby validated the claim of the Seleucids to Thrace.[24]

At the insistence of the Aetolians, Antiochus III allowed himself to be lured into a premature and inadequately prepared campaign to Greece in 192 B.C. It did indeed gain him the strategic initiative but was of little use, since he met with little sympathy in Greece. Even his allies the Aetolians were disappointed in the small number of his troops (10,500). Worse still was the fact that Philip V remained loyal to his treaty with Rome and that the Achaeans on account of their old hatred against the Aetolians went over to the camp of Antiochus' enemies. In the spring of 191 B.C. the Romans replied, landing an army of more than 20,000 troops at Apollonia under the command of the consul M'. Acilius Glabrio. In collaboration with Philip V, whose country served as their strategic base, the Romans sought to cut off the supply lines of the Seleucid through Thrace. The issue was decided at Thermopylae. The Romans circumvented Antiochus' position (the decisive engagement was carried out by a small Roman division under the military tribune M. Porcius Cato), whereupon Antiochus fled to Elateia, and from here to Chalcis on Euboea. From there a ship carried him back to Ephesus (April 191 B.C.). In Greece the war continued against the Aetolians until a military truce for six months was agreed upon in April 190 B.C., in which T. Quinctius Flamininus played a decisive rôle. The chief theatre of the war then shifted to the Aegean, with a bitter struggle for naval supremacy. Defeated in two encounters, at Corycus (c. September 191 B.C.) and at Myonessus (c. September 190 B.C.), Antiochus' fleet left the way clear for the Romans to Asia. Meanwhile, at the end of 191 B.C., the command in Greece had passed to the consul, L. Cornelius Scipio. Marching via the overland route through Macedonia and Thrace, the Roman army reached the Hellespont.

Negotiations initiated by Antiochus with the Romans after the army had crossed the straits came to nothing, since the Romans insisted on the abdication of all Seleucid territory on their side of the Taurus. In consequence weapons had to decide the issue. It was at Magnesia, in the immediate vicinity of Mount Sipylus (near the confluence of the Phrygius and the Hermus), that the decisive battle took place (at the end of 190 or beginning of 189 B.C.). Although Antiochus outnumbered the Romans more than two to one—70,000 of his men faced 30,000 Romans and their allies—his army, composed of the most varied contingents from the realm, was totally defeated.[25] Eumenes II of Pergamum contributed decisively to the Roman victory. In a piercing cavalry thrust he split the Seleucid cavalry squadron and then defeated the left wing of Antiochus' phalanx. Antiochus gave the war up as lost, although Magnesia had decided only the fate of Asia Minor, not of the entire realm. In preliminary negotiations at Sardis[26] Antiochus renounced his European dominions, pledged himself to withdraw from Asia Minor and to pay a high indemnity (15,000 Euboean talents). Although Antiochus was to hand over Hannibal, he allowed him to escape. Cn. Manlius Volso, who in the spring of 189 B.C. took over the command in Asia Minor for L. Cornelius Scipio, moved into Pamphylia with his army, and from there northwards against the Celts in the central regions of Asia Minor.[27] It was a gigantic plundering expedition, which rolled heavily laden through Anatolia. The Galatians were defeated and the three tribes, namely the Tolistobogi (Tolistoagi), Tectosages and Trocmi subjugated, an event which the Greek cities of Asia Minor in particular greeted with great jubilation.

Meanwhile in Rome the Senate, with Eumenes II present, had reached agreement on the reorganisation of Asia Minor. Almost the whole of former Seleucid territory in central and southern Anatolia fell to the Attalid state, while the Rhodians received Caria south of the Maeander and Lycia. Antiochus was forced to surrender his fleet, down to ten ships, as well as his war elephants. He was forbidden to pursue an active policy in the west, and Cape Sarpedonium in Cilicia was henceforth to be the western frontier for his warships. The Romans despatched a ten-man commission to Asia Minor, empowered to settle outstanding questions. Regulating the position of the Greek cities in western Asia Minor more than anything else presented difficulties. While the old autonomous Greek poleis and all those that had supported Rome, and not under obligation to pay tribute to Attalus I, were acknowledged as "free cities," all others passed into the possession of Eumenes II.[28] Of these, Tralles, Ephesus and Telmessus were cited by name in the peace treaty.[29] The "freedom of the Hellenes," which the Romans had so often used in their propaganda against Antiochus, turned out to be an empty slogan when it came to appeasing the Pergamene ruler, the most important Roman ally in Asia Minor. The ratification of the Peace Treaty of Apameia in 188 B.C. by Antiochus III confined the Seleucid empire to Syria, Mesopotamia and the regions of west Iran. It was thrown back far towards the east and cut off from the sources of Hellenism in the west. In Asia Minor itself Pergamum, which had hitherto only been a diminutive state, now rose as the "kingdom of the Attalids" to unanticipated efflorescence. Eumenes II took over the Seleucid organisation in the new territory, which stretched from the Thracian Chersonese to the Taurus.[30] The capital, Pergamum was adorned with splendid structures, above all the Great Altar of Zeus—the monument celebrating the victory over the Galatians, against whom Eumenes still took the field in the following years.[31] The Pergamene *Nikephoria*, a magnificent festival which perhaps was instituted after Magnesia, at any rate before 182/1 B.C.,[32] served to celebrate before all the world the great military victories. The importance of the Attalid kingdom admittedly rested primarily on its good relations with Rome, who had set Eumenes up as custodian of Asia Minor—as some years prior to this it had established the Numidian prince Masinissa over Carthage in Africa. As in Greece, so here too the Romans preferred indirect rule to occupation of the conquered territory. The Romans thereby saved a great amount of energy and money, and left the dependent states to their own devices.

In Greece fighting had broken out afresh in the winter of 190/89 B.C. between the Aetolians and the Macedonians, and in the spring war with Rome flared up once more. The Aetolians had conducted King Amynander back to Athamania and again took possession of the districts of Amphilochia, Aperantia and of the Dolopes. Not until the Romans sent M. Fulvius Nobilior with an army to Greece[33] did the picture change. The result was a protracted siege of Ambracia, the ancient capital of Pyrrhus, which was staunchly defended by an Aetolian garrison. A peace treaty was concluded in the winter of 189 B.C. by which the Aetolians were obliged to Roman military service.[34] Although the Aetolians lost all the territories which had defected from their rule since 192 B.C.—Delphi also regained its freedom, after being an Aetolian protectorate for almost one hundred years—the Aetolian League still remained territorially the largest state in central Greece. The occupation of the islands of Cephallenia and Zacynthus, which now served the Romans as naval bases, brought the pacification of Hellas to a close. The Romans did not pass over the opportunity to drag off a great many works of art to Italy, above all from Ambracia. For the second time the Romans withdrew from the Greek mainland (188 or 187 B.C.).

In Greece the situation was still far from actual peace. In the Peloponnesus the Achaeans were involved in continuous quarrels with Sparta and Messenia. Under the leadership of Philopoemen, the most outstanding *strategos* and statesman Hellas possessed, the Achaean League became the largest power in Greece, although the Romans often supported enemies of the Achaeans in Sparta and Messenia. It was a grave loss for the whole of Greece when Philopoemen, the "last of the Greeks," fell into the hands of the Messenians and was poisoned by them in prison (183 B.C.).[35] Internal upheavals, which continuously received fresh fuel from the great number of exiles and dissatisfied elements, were connected with the struggles for political power.

The Peace of Apameia (188 B.C.) in no way signified the end of the war for Asia Minor. The rapid rise of Pergamum angered its neighbours. Prusias I of Bithynia and Pharnaces of Pontus were enemies of Eumenes II, against whom he had to take the field (the so-called First Bithynian War, 186?-183/2 B.C.),[36] and the wars against Pharnaces, 183-179 B.C.).

The Peace of Apameia, dictated by Rome, broke the power of the Seleucid empire. The severe terms of the treaty, especially the large indemnities, were a heavy burden on the country. Chronic lack of money led to forced loans from temples. Antiochus III was assassinated while plundering a temple of Bêl at Susa in 187 B.C., and his son, Seleucus IV Philopator (187-175 B.C.), alienated himself from the Jewish priestly state while attempting to collect a forced loan there. The king ultimately fell victim to assassination at the hands of his chancellor Heliodorus. While the Seleucids endeavoured to carry out the orders of the Romans, the Bactrian Hellenes experienced the indisputable height of their history. Demetrius, son of Euthydemus, founder of the dynasty, crossed the Hindu Kush with a well-equipped army and advanced through the Punjab as far as the Ganges. The entire north-west of India, far beyond his own frontiers, lay at his feet—as far as Alexander had once been able to penetrate.[37] The institution of the Bactrian military colony[38] proved itself to be an incomparable centre of vitality, even at this late date giving the Hellenes of the East dominion over the wonderland of India (probably shortly after 184 B.C.).

In north-west India the dynasty of Maurya had died out. Pusyamitra, a usurper, appears to have found little sympathy among the Indians, and religious conflicts between the Buddhists and the Brahmans weakened the power of the Indian people to resist, so they became an easy prey of the Hellenic conquerors. The Bactrian Greeks carried Hellenistic forms of administration and Hellenistic culture to India,[39] and the Greek forms survived in the so-called Gandhara art. Even the portrait of Buddha was executed under Greek stimulus. The Indian Hellenes possessed a great organiser in the personality of the Greek king Menander (Milinda). His memory has been preserved in the work *Milindapanha (Questions of Menander)* in Indian writings—a unique circumstance in the history of Indian literature.[40] Developments in Bactria and India had no decisive repercussions on the West, since these regions were practically cut off from the West by the expansion of the Parthians.

In general, political isolation, which the Romans accelerated by diplomatic means, became disastrous for the Hellenistic states. When the Roman war against Antiochus III was impending, the Romans gave the Macedonian ruler Philip V extensive assurances in order to keep him on their side. His expansion, especially at the expense of the Aetolians, was tolerated by the Romans, but at the same time they saw to it that Macedonia did not regain the position as a major power which she had lost at Cynoscephalae (197 B.C.). The proud Macedonian was the only one of all the Hellenistic kings who permitted the Romans to feel that he had not forgotten the humiliation: the sun has not yet set for ever (Livy XXXIX 26, 9), he is alleged to have told the commission from the Senate. It was above all the relationship of Philip V to the Greeks and to Eumenes II which led to uninterrupted political tension. Hosts of complaining Hellenes—Thessalians, Perrhaebians, Acarnanians—appeared in 186/5 B.C. at Rome, where the Senate was only too ready to lend an ear to their grievances. It was an irreparable disaster that the Hellenes at the time failed to recognise or to support the Macedonian people. When Philip died in 179 B.C., after devoting himself to an active Balkan policy during his last years, Macedonia found itself on the way to a renascence, which was of course completely contrary to Roman interests.

THE WAR WITH PERSEUS

Philip's son, Perseus (179-168 B.C.),[41] renewed the treaty of friendship with Rome. His policy attempted to break out of the isolating ring which the Romans had created. A marriage relationship with Prusias II of Bithynia, the marriage of Perseus with a daughter of Seleucus IV (Laodice), closer ties with Rhodes, who had previously been closely connected with Eumenes II, and active Macedonian propaganda in Greece were the characteristics of an energetic policy of the young king, who was being anxiously watched by the Romans. The tension between Macedonia and Rome was accentuated by Eumenes II, who saw himself threatened by a Macedonian-Seleucid-Rhodian alliance. Part of the complaints which he brought against Perseus in 172 B.C. at Rome have been preserved in an inscription on a Delphic stele, which contains the accusations of the Romans against Perseus among the members of the Amphictyony (*Syll.* II³ 643), one of the many examples of inscriptional propaganda in antiquity. In the long run Perseus was no match for Roman diplomacy, not only because he was regarded as the conceptional author of the attempt made on the life of Eumenes II at Delphi on his return from Rome, but also because he had lost the sympathy which he had initially enjoyed among the Greeks. In addition, the Rhodians, with their powerful navy, could not bring themselves to join an anti-Roman coalition. No help could be expected from the Seleucid and Ptolemaic empires, because here the struggle for Coele Syria (the so-called Sixth Syrian War 170?-168 B.C.) was impending. The Romans for their part did not shrink from using reprehensible tactics. The special Roman envoy Q. Marcius Philippus conducted a political conference with Perseus on the Peneius River in the autumn of 172 B.C., its failure assured from the outset, because the Romans wished only to gain time for mobilising. The Senate regarded this perfidious act completely in order.[42]

The war between Rome and Perseus (171-168 B.C.) was of great importance. For the last time in the history of Hellenism a Hellenistic state took the field against the Romans, this time not on account of imperialistic or dynastic aims but to throw off the hated, coercive domination with which the Romans had for thirty years humiliated a hundredfold the monarchy and the state. For a long time the Macedonians had been silent because they could not defend themselves—but now Perseus had done the humanly impossible to prepare his country for this war which would decide the fate and freedom of the Macedonians. As once under Philip V, Macedonia resembled a besieged fortress. The Macedonians had to fight on three fronts: against the Romans, against the Roman satellite Eumenes II in Thrace and against the Dardanians in the north-west. The campaigns of the first two years of the war, for which Perseus had enlisted the population to the last man, brought him little advantage on land. On the seas the Roman fleet, supported by Rhodian and Pergamene contingents, dominated the field. The attempt of Perseus to bring the Aetolians over to the Macedonian camp failed, although a treaty was concluded with the Illyrian Genthius,[43] but did not result in appreciably relieving the situation for Macedonia.

The famous advance of the Romans under the consul Q. Marcius Philippus through Thessaly, over Mount Olympus towards Macedonia,[44] did not decide the issue (169 B.C.). Due to difficulties in procuring provisions the Romans had to withdraw from their positions. Moreover the operations of the Roman fleet against individual coastal towns of the Macedonians did not influence the overall situation. In the spring of 168 B.C. Perseus attempted, through the arbitration of foreign powers, primarily through Rhodes, to send out peace-feelers. The turning point in the war came in this same year, when the command in Macedonia was taken over by L. Aemilius Paullus, both educated and reputedly a Philhellene. In order to force Perseus to abandon his fortified position on the Elpeius River (south-east of Mount Olympus), the Roman commander-in-chief ordered a hazardous circumventing manoeuvre from the west. It was brilliantly carried out by P. Scipio Nasica.[44a] Perseus, whose position had now become untenable, retreated in the direction of Pydna. The decisive battle, south of Pydna, on 22 June 168 B.C.,[45] ended in the total defeat of the Macedonians. The course of the battle entails numerous difficulties which scholars have still not succeeded in solving.[46] The first charge of the tightly-knit Macedonian phalanx appears to have been devastatingly effective. Aemilius Paullus later personally admitted that he had trembled when the charging wall of *sarissai* was advancing against the Romans. Favoured by the topography, however, the flexible maniples of the Romans quickly succeeded in piercing the phalanx, and within an hour the entire battle was decided. Perseus left his Macedonians in the lurch and fled via Pydna to Amphipolis, and from there by ship to the Temple of the Cabiri on Samothrace, where he was taken prisoner by the Romans. The spectacle of a fleeing king, who had discarded all royal insignia in order to remain unrecognised, was a novelty in Macedonia. It is no wonder that one city after another capitulated, and that the followers and friends of the king hastened to declare their submission to Rome.

Even before the battle of Pydna, in the spring of 168 B.C., the Romans had victoriously ended the Illyrian War. The praetor, L. Anicius, had shut Genthius up in Skodra and forced him into unconditional surrender.

The reorganisation of Macedonia was carried out by a Senatorial commission in Amphipolis.[47] The country, like Illyria, was proclaimed

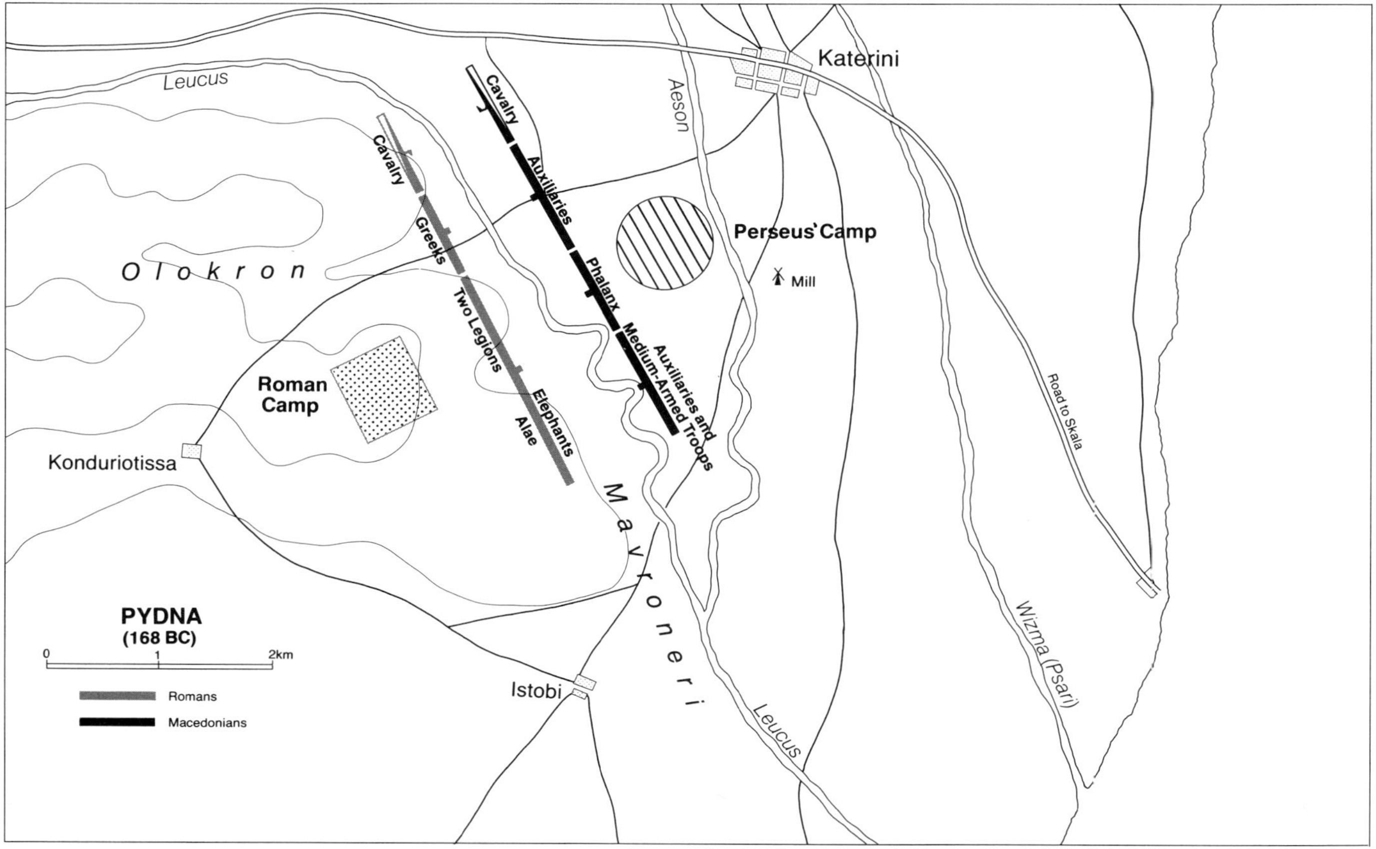
PYDNA
(168 BC)
0
1
2km
Romans
Macedonians
Katerini
Perseus' Camp
Mill
Aeson
Leucus
Road to Skala
Wizma (Psari)
Cavalry
Auxiliaries
Phalanx
Auxiliaries and Medium-Armed Troops
Cavalry
Greeks
Two Legions
Elephants
Alae
Roman Camp
Olokron
Mavroneri
Konduriotissa
Istobi
Leucus

free. The latter was divided into three, Macedonia into four, independent states, with the capitals of Amphipolis, Thessalonica, Pella and Pelagonia (Heracleia Lyncestis). Each of the new states had its own annually elected officers who replaced the royal officials. No commerce was permitted between the individual states, and no intermarriage.[48] Three of the Macedonian zones were permitted to keep militia under arms in order to protect the northern frontier. The economic sanctions weighed heavily upon the country. The Macedonian gold and silver mines had to close down operations,[48a] the cutting of timber for shipbuilding was prohibited and the importing of salt forbidden (for unknown reasons).[49] Some Macedonian possessions in Greece were granted autonomy, while the islands of Lemnos, Imbros and Scyros fell to Athens. In addition Athens, through the clemency of the great Philhellene L. Aemilius Paullus, was presented with Boeotian Haliartus and with Delos. At Delos a free port was established which soon totally ruined Rhodian trade. The friends of Macedonia in Hellas faced severe punishment, above all the Aetolians, Achaeans and Epirotes. Informers flourished, and the Romans took few pains to prove the individual cases. Almost the entire ruling class of the Achaeans, upwards in the thousands, among them the historian Polybius, was deported to Italy. On a punitive expedition in Epirus, under the eyes of the highly cultivated Aemilius Paullus, and on his orders, seventy cities were destroyed and 150,000 free persons sold into slavery.[50] Thus Hellas for the first time experienced Roman disfavour. The unfortunate Macedonian king adorned the triumph of Aemilius Paullus (167 B.C.) and died in 165 B.C.[51] in a Roman prison.

While Rome was engaged in the struggle with Perseus, a new war took place between the Seleucid and Ptolemaic empires. The incompetent guardian-rule on behalf of Ptolemy VI renewed the struggle (in 170 B.C.?) for South Syria, with a declaration of war against Antiochus IV (175-164 B.C.) (the Sixth Syrian War, 170?-168 B.C.).[52] To strike against the well-armed Antiochus, however, was to move against the wrong man. After a decisive victory at Pelusium, Antiochus entered Egypt, and took the entire country, with the exception of the capital Alexandria. He concluded a treaty with the youthful Ptolemy VI Philometor, and had himself crowned in the ancient royal city of Memphis with the double crown of Upper and Lower Egypt. Antiochus attempted to conceal this surprise move from the outside world by pretending that he had merely assumed the guardianship for his nephew Ptolemy. Meanwhile in Alexandria the brother of Philometor, Ptolemy the "Younger" (the later Ptolemy VIII Euergetes II), was proclaimed king. Disturbances in Palestine forced Antiochus to abandon the siege of Alexandria and to return to Syria. He still did not give up his far-reaching plans to weld the Seleucid and Ptolemaic empires together into a large powerblock in the East. A new expedition in the spring of 168 B.C. brought him to the gates of the Egyptian capital, where a joint rule of the two Ptolemies and their sister Cleopatra II had been established.[53] Antiochus now tore away the mask and appeared in Egypt as conqueror.

At this juncture Rome intervened. The progress of the Seleucid had long since been observed with anxiety, for Rome was greatly interested in maintaining a certain balance of power in the East. Immediately after the battle of Pydna the Roman Popillius Laenas appeared in the headquarters of Antiochus at Eleusis, a suburb of Alexandria, and presented the proud Seleucid with the ultimatum of the Senate, namely to terminate the war and withdraw from Egypt forthwith.[54] When the king asked for time to consider the matter, the Roman envoy used his vine stick to draw a circle around the king and declared that before he stepped outside it he had to give a clear answer in terms of yes or no. Antiochus bowed to Roman orders. Thus Rome had, only a few weeks after Pydna, gained a second victory, this time with diplomacy. This sealed the fate of the major Hellenistic states.

The rich commercial city of Rhodes too had to pay dearly for her Macedonian sympathies in the war against Perseus. In Rome the Senate was actually agitating for a war against Rhodes, whereupon M. Porcius Cato in a speech espoused the cause of the Rhodians. The city lost the majority of its mainland possessions in Asia Minor and its protectorate over the Island League. The competition with the free port of Delos, where many Italians settled as merchants and bankers, led to enormous economic losses in Rhodes. The revenue from the harbour dues declined from 1,000,000 to 150,000 drachms.[55] The degradation of Rhodes may have been connected with commercial jealousy on the part of Italic merchant and capitalist circles, as later in the destruction of Carthage and Corinth. The decline in the naval power of Rhodes was followed by an uninterrupted chain of social disturbances and a steady rise in piracy throughout the eastern Mediterranean.

While Roman influence was dominant in Greece, the Greek colonies on the west coast of the Black Sea were engaged in bitter defensive struggles against the advancing tide of Thracians and Getae. An inscription from Istrus (Histria) tells of an urban embassy despatched to a native ruler, bearing the Thracian or Getan name Zalmodegius, on account of the hostages which the city had given him.[56] Similar relations also existed between the city of Olbia at the mouth of the Bug and King Saïtaphernes. The city had to meet certain financial obligations to this ruler, which, in a votive inscription in honour of Protogenes, a citizen of Olbia, are euphemistically called "gifts."[57] The important Greek city of Byzantium on the Bosporus had similar concerns, with its territory repeatedly devastated by Thracian rulers.[58] In addition, the various Greek cities were in many instances at enmity with each other. Thus Mesembria, for instance, carried on a war against neighbouring Apollonia. The conflict revolved around control of the Gulf of Burgas and possession of the salt lagoons in the regions of Anchialus. The citizens of Mesembria had opened the fighting without any declaration of war.[59] In the third century B.C. the vast region between the Don and the Lower Danube was set in motion by migrations among the Thracian-Getan-Sarmatian peoples, and the Greek cities on the north and west coasts of the Pontus were the first to feel the pressure.

THE DECLINE OF THE EASTERN HELLENISTIC STATES AND THE RISE OF PARTHIA

The fall of the Macedonian monarchy at the battle of Pydna (168 B.C.) was the beginning of the end for the Hellenistic states. The Seleucid empire, ultimately restricted to Syria, and the empire of the Ptolemies continued to figure on the political map for more than a century, but at least from the end of the second century they played only a nominal rôle. Roman envoys now repeatedly interfered in the history of the states in the East, with animated and regulative effect. A mission of Scipio Aemilianus, which in 140/39 B.C. took him to Alexandria, Syria, Rhodes and Pergamum,[60] is perhaps the most famous example of Roman surveillance of the Hellenistic East. The Romans contributed not a little towards agitating the centrifugal forces, especially in the Seleucid empire, to weaken this state, and it was completely in Roman interests that the rulers of the Ptolemaic kingdom, Ptolemy Philometor and his younger brother, the later Ptolemy VIII Euergetes, should make war upon each other.

The Roman ultimatum which forced the Seleucid Antiochus IV to withdraw from Egypt must have struck the king like a thunderbolt. His earlier policy was to some degree methodical, but after that unfortunate day the king appeared nervous, overstrained, and bizarre. Blunders increased, and with them, failures.[61] The conflict between the Seleucid and the Jews assumed world historical significance. Hitherto the Jews had not appeared on the political scene, although their peculiar customs, seemingly completely opposed to the open-minded character of Hellenism, were occasionally the subject of ethnographical discussions in Greek literature during the early Hellenistic period (Theophrastus and Hecataeus of Abdera).[62] The conflict between Hellenism and Jewry is most intricately interwoven with the cultural policy of Antiochus Epiphanes, a late attempt to promote the forces of Hellenism to a break-through in the cultural and religious sphere against the Orient, and to establish a new, universal state on Greek foundations. Antiochus IV must have been convinced of the success of his large-scale endeavour, and no wonder, for Greek culture had lost none of its appeal in the Near Eastern world. But the greater the number of Orientals became who showed an openness towards Greek culture and adopted Hellenic ways, the more Greek culture was forced to forfeit in intensity. What was gained in breadth was lost in depth. It is difficult to believe that Antiochus in all seriousness wanted to bring about a systematic fusion of the Greek world with the Oriental.[63] The Greek enthusiasm which he had demonstrated in Athens was genuine and honest. As Antiochus IV later refashioned the ancient city of Babylon into a typical Hellenistic polis with theatre and gymnasium,[64] so Jerusalem, the capital of the Jewish nation, was to become a city along Greek lines. His predecessors had fully respected the exceptional position of the Jewish priestly state which in 200 B.C. had passed under Seleucid rule.[65] Egyptian sympathies, which manifested themselves during the second (?) expedition of Antiochus IV against Ptolemy VI (169 B.C.), forced the king to take decisive action.[66] The high priest Jason, deposed by Antiochus, had succeeded in regaining control of the city (albeit without the citadel).

Before this third (?) expedition against Egypt, in the winter of 169/8 B.C. the king appeared for the second time in Jerusalem and took a forced loan from the Temple treasure with a view to financing the Egyptian war. In Jerusalem there was a relatively large group of Jews who enthusiastically pursued Hellenic ideals. A gymnasium was built in the city, under the high priest Jason, and in it part of the Jewish youth, together with the Hellenes, devoted their time to athletic and cultural pursuits. The devout in the land, the Chasidim, were violently opposed to the declared graecophiles, and rejected any compromise with Hellenism. The conflict reached its climax when Antiochus IV in December 167 B.C. attempted to carry through the Hellenising of Jerusalem by force. The Jaweh cult was abolished and all Jewish rites prohibited. An altar was erected in the Temple to Zeus Olympios, the "Imperial God," and a statue of the reigning sovereign set up beside it, to which the offerings prescribed for the ruler cult were to be brought. The community of Greeks and graecophiles in Jerusalem was established as a special *politeuma* called the *Antiochieneis*.[67] Hellenism had reached its climax.[68]

The resistance of the devout in the land was organised by the family of the Maccabaeans and their followers. Their struggle (from 166 B.C.) was directed against not only the philhellenes among the Jews but at the same time also against part of the propertied citizens in the cities. Religious and socio-revolutionary motives, animosities between urban and rural elements, were interwoven with each other. Exactly three years after the "Abomination of Desolation" had desecrated the temple of Jaweh, Judas Maccabaeus was able to tear down the altar of Zeus and solemnly carry out the dedication of the new Temple (December 164 B.C.). The most important stages in the formation of a separate Jewish state[69]—a circumstance characterised by various reverses coupled with internal and external fighting—were marked by the appointment of the Maccabaean Jonathan to high priest (152 B.C.), and to *strategos* and *meridarches* of Judaea (150 B.C.), through the mediation of Alexander Balas. It was also marked by permitting extensive immunity from tribute, granted to Simon (142 B.C.) by Demetrius II Nicator, and finally by the expelling of the Syrian garrison from the Acropolis in Jerusalem where it had been stationed for twenty-five years. John Hyrcanus, successor of Simon, ultimately, after the fall of the Seleucid Antiochus VII Sidetes in 129 B.C. on his Parthian expedition (v.i.p. 307), succeeded in completely emancipating the state from the Seleucid empire. A few years prior to this (134 B.C.) all previous achievements appeared to have been called into question by the assault of Antiochus VII, who forced the Jews to capitulate after a prolonged siege of Jerusalem.[70] Antiochus Sidetes, however, was no Epiphanes and a coercive Hellenisation of the Jewish nation was as remote from his designs as was its destruction. But by 161 B.C. the Hasmonaeans had turned to Rome,[71] which at that time, as later, was exceedingly well disposed towards the Jews.

The most important phenomenon in the history of Western Asia during the second century B.C., however, is not the rise of the small Hasmonaean state of the Jews but the emergence of the great empire of the Parthians, whose expansion did not stop until it reached the frontiers of India and the banks of the Euphrates. The expansion of the Parthians is connected with the migrations at the beginning of the second century B.C., beginning in the Gobi Desert in central Asia. Moving out from central Asia in about 200 B.C.,[72] the Huns began a series of migrations, first pushing out the Tocharians to the West,[73] these in turn pushed against the Sacaraucae, who moved against Bactria. The Parthians felt the effects of all this.

From the time of Mithradates I (171-138/7 B.C.) the Parthian kingdom was involved in an almost uninterrupted war on two fronts, against East and West.[74] In 150 B.C., or only a few years after, Media, the great bulwark of Seleucid rule in western Iran, was annexed. Allied by treaty with the Sacaraucae who had taken Kashmir from Bactria, Mithradates I conquered almost the whole of east Iran, whereupon he assumed the title "King of Kings" (before 145 B.C.?), on the model once provided by the Achaemenids. In victorious advances towards the west the Parthians conquered Seleuceia on the Tigris (141 B.C.), and then penetrated deep into Mesopotamia. The Seleucids, after the death of Antiochus IV (163 B.C.),[75] were almost continuously debilitated by struggles between pretenders to the throne and by domestic difficulties, and could put up very little resistance to Parthian westward expansion. Demetrius II Nicator was actually taken prisoner by the Parthians (140 B.C.). Not until ten years later, in 130 B.C., was Demetrius' brother, Antiochus VII Sidetes, able to assume a large-scale offensive against the Parthians.[76] His initial successes were considerable. He reconquered Babylonia and Media, and the Greek cities and many Greek vassals welcomed Antiochus as liberator. Since the Seleucid, however, demanded from the Parthian king, Phraates II, not only the return of all lost regions and the restriction of the Parthians to their land of origin but also the payment of tribute, he forced them into strong resistance. Lack of caution on the part of the Seleucid—his forces were taken by surprise in their winter quarters and eventually completely annihilated in a great battle—sealed the destruction of his army and its baggage, along with King Antiochus VII himself. "The defeat of Antiochus Sidetes in 129 B.C. is synonymous with the catastrophe of Hellenism in continental Asia and at the same time with that of the Seleucid empire" (Ed. Meyer). Never again did a Seleucid take the field against the Parthians. The empire of Seleucus I, once so mighty, was now restricted to north Syria and east Cilicia, and was no longer a power factor in Western Asia. In addition, the internal dissolution of the empire rapidly gained momentum. Almost all the large communities, especially the important maritime cities of Phoenicia, gained complete independence when they were granted *asylia* by the Seleucid rulers.[77] The confusion of the kings and of the pretenders to the throne was heightened even further by the fact that the country was entangled with the Ptolemaic kingdom. In particular, the ambitions of Cleopatra Thea and Cleopatra Selene, both of

Ptolemaic lineage, had disastrous consequences. The Seleucid kingdom was in a state of complete decline, exhausted and ravaged, when in 83 B.C. it fell prey to the Armenian king, Tigranes I. The Greeks, who had to a large extent shaped the aspect of Syria, found themselves restricted to the strongly Hellenised poleis. In the rural districts the Orient increasingly regained control over the spirits of the inhabitants. The Orientals, however, be they Jews, Arabs or Iranians, could not evade the influence of Hellenic civilisation. The Hasmonaeans formed their state on the model of Hellenism, the Nabataeans adorned their city of Petra with Hellenistic buildings, and in their state organisation Hellenistic features are unmistakable.[78]

The Parthian kings, however, became the actual protectors of the Greeks and the patrons of Greek culture in the East during the second century B.C. Already the Arsacid, Phriapitius (191 to about 176 B.C.), deliberately adopted the epithet Philhellene, and the coins of Mithradates I exhibit as his epithets Euergetes, Dikaios and Philhellene. This graecophile attitude was not only political propaganda but was determined by political necessity. The powerful state established by Mithradates I in his struggle against East and West urgently required a trained bureaucracy, and this only the Hellenistic Greeks could provide. Besides Aramaic, Greek was the actual language of government, and it is no wonder that documents on parchment brought to light in the somewhat remote Kurdistan are in Greek.[79] Like its predecessor the Seleucid empire, the Parthian kingdom, which finally became consolidated under Mithradates II (c. 123-88 B.C.), had a dual Iranian-Hellenistic aspect. While large general governments under *strategoi* were established at the western frontier, the remainder of the kingdom, with its satraps and half-sovereign vassal kingdoms,[80] was an image of the late Achaemenid empire, or of the Seleucid empire after the conquests of Antiochus III. The Iranian origin of the Parthian kingdom shows above all in its feudal character. Throughout many generations the governorships remained in the hands of the same families, as, for instance, in the case of Monaeses-Manesus in Mesopotamia and Parapotamia. The office of city governors in some cases also actually became hereditary. Evidence for this comes from Dura-Europus, but admittedly not until a later period (first and second century A.D.).[81]

For the Greeks in Bactria and India the period about 130 B.C. marked a decisive turning point. The Indo-European-Mongolian equestrian people, the Tocharians, set out from the regions of the East Sacae, conquered Bactria, and founded a closely-knit state there. This was the first establishment of the equestrian peoples of central Asia on Hellenistic soil. The vivid travel accounts of Tsan K'ien, the Chinese Marco Polo, seem to demonstrate the existence of this state in Bactria as early as 128 B.C. The Hellenes of north-west India were now also forced to submit to the Scythian conquerors, the so-called Sacaraucae, whose expansion at the time embraced the Upper Indus, Arachosia and the regions around Lake Hamun. The expansion of these peoples in east Iran and in north-west India was an enormous reverse for eastern Hellenism, from which it never recovered. Cut off from its fountain-head in the West by the Parthian kingdom, and in hopeless minority compared with the native peoples and the new conquerors, the Greeks of Bactria and India gradually blended into the eastern nations. Recent research by Russian scholars, however, has shown that Graeco-Bactrian civilisation in part survived the "nomadic tide." Greek influence in architecture, in sculpture and in wall painting is traceable even into the third (?) century A.D. (the citadel of Toprak Kala in Chorasmia).[82]

Aï Khanum (at the confluence of the Amu-darya [the ancient Oxus] and the Kokea in Afghanistan) has also been added to the archaeological sites. Here a Greek city was discovered with a theatre and gymnasium.[82a] The kingdoms of Hermaeus and Hippostratus, the last Greek rulers in north-west India, succumbed to the assault of the Scythian conquerors.[83] Hellenistic culture in India, however, survived for centuries the destruction of political Hellenism. Its vitality and originality are attested by imposing vestiges of Hellenistic art which can be traced to the Far East.[84]

In the west too, in Ptolemaic Egypt, the native element was gaining ground over the Greeks in the second century.[85] The rise of Egyptian nationalism was fostered by the unrelenting throne disputes of the Ptolemies. A stream of disputes began after 170 B.C., when the "Younger Ptolemy" (the later Ptolemy VIII Euergetes II) was elevated by the Alexandrians to "counter-regent" against Ptolemy VI Philometor, who was under the guardianship of Antiochus IV. The gradual decline of the Ptolemaic economy was connected with internal disturbances, and with the economy gravely affected, the Ptolemaic kingdom never completely recovered. The devastation of the country by the troops of Antiochus IV Epiphanes, and the revolt of Dionysius Petrosarapis (in the first half of the sixties), forced the administration to take emergency measures. Initially, a high-ranking officer was temporarily appointed as General Governor of the entire Egyptian countryside—Hippalus the *epistrategos* is attested from 185 to 169 B.C.—later, the government tried to reorganise the cultivation of the land, partially lying fallow because of the internal upheavals. In this situation the government resorted to the measure of forced land tenure.[86] In 163 B.C. a regular partitioning of the empire took place for the first time. Ptolemy VI Philometor, who had been exiled by the Alexandrians and then re-instated, received Egypt and Cyprus; his brother had had his eye on the latter but had to be content with Cyrenaica. In order to win Rome over completely to his side the "Younger Ptolemy" in 162/1 B.C. appointed this great power as heir to his kingdom of Cyrenaica, admittedly at first under cover. This is the first testament of a Hellenistic king in favour of the Roman Republic, and was of the greatest importance.[87] It was not until 155 B.C., after an attempt on his life, that the shrewd Ptolemy had a draft of the will made public, on a marble stele in the temple of Apollo at Cyrene. Renewed fighting for the possession of Cyprus was ended by a compromise between the two brothers, Ptolemy Philometor and Ptolemy "the Younger"—but this in no way altered the actual conditions governing their possessions. Cyprus was promised as a nominally independent kingdom to the eldest son of Philometor, Ptolemy Eupator, but he only reigned there for two years (152-150 B.C.), after which the island reverted to the possession of Philometor.[88]

There were complications when Philometor intervened in Syria, where the king appeared initially as the ally of his son-in-law, Alexander Balas, but later was on the side of the young Demetrius II Nicator.[89] Philometor aimed at the annexation of Syria to Egypt, and was in fact proclaimed "King of Asia" by a military assembly and the people of Antioch in 145 B.C.[90] The death of the Egyptian ruler—Philometor died from wounds received in the war against Alexander Balas at the Oenoparas—liberated Syria from its new master and opened the door for renewed struggles among the pretenders to the throne, upheavals which completely ruined the unfortunate country. A usurper by the name of Tryphon rose up (142-138 B.C.), but he was forced into a corner by Antiochus VII, and ended his life by suicide.[90a]

The history of Ptolemaic Egypt in the second half of the second century B.C. is marked by the singular personality of the "Younger Ptolemy." He acceded to the throne in 145 B.C., after the death of his brother Philometor, at the side of his sister, Cleopatra II, and his young nephew, Ptolemy VII Neos Philopator.[91] He later adopted the cult name Euergetes, whereby he sought to link himself with Ptolemy III. As tangible as the human frailties of the highly cultivated Ptolemy VIII Euergetes II may have been—he later also became known as an author of memoirs—equally undeniable, on the other hand, are his qualities as a statesman and politician, which enabled him to cope with unusual foreign and internal difficulties. The actual driving force of his reign (145-116 B.C.) sprang from his two wives. From 142 B.C. onwards Euergetes II lived in double wedlock, with the violent Cleopatra II (his sister, who shrank from nothing), and her daughter, Cleopatra III. Otherwise the reign of Ptolemy VIII was characterised by an almost unbroken chain of dynastic disputes, attempts at insurrection and revolts, indeed by regular "civil wars," which crippled commercial activity throughout the country and often split rulers and subjects into enemy camps.[92] The repeated proclamation of amnesties was characteristic of the king—the first in 145/4 B.C., and another in 118 B.C. In the spring of 131 B.C. a revolt in Alexandria took the king by surprise and forced him to leave the country, and he did not succeed in regaining control of the capital until 127 B.C. His sister, Cleopatra II, had fled to Syria in 129/8 B.C., before the capitulation. In 124 B.C. she returned, whereupon the singular triple-regency of the king and the two queens was re-established.

The direct sea route to India with the aid of the monsoons was discovered immediately before or after the death of Ptolemy VIII Euergetes II, in 117 or 116 B.C. This was a nautical feat of the utmost importance, for which we are indebted to Hippalus and Eudoxus of Cyzicus.[93] The Ptolemaic empire, however, was no longer in a position to take full advantage of this discovery, and the Romans were the first to reap where others had sown.

After the death of Ptolemy VIII (116 B.C.)—his testament was, no doubt on the instigation of Cleopatra II, repudiated by the Alexandrian "pseudo-military assembly"[94]—new throne disputes flared up between Cleopatra III and her sons, Ptolemy IX Soter II and Ptolemy X Alexander I. About 100 B.C., the Ptolemaic kingdom was partitioned into three independent states:[95] Egypt under Ptolemy X Alexander I, Cyprus under Ptolemy IX Soter II and Cyrenaica under Apion, an illegitimate offspring of Ptolemy VIII. At his death in 96 B.C. Apion bequeathed the royal domains in Cyrenaica to the Romans, but it was not, however, until 74 B.C. that the whole of Cyrenaica, together with its cities, was organised into a Roman province.[96] The political decline of the Ptolemaic empire went hand in hand with the rise of the native Egyptian population, at the expense of the Greeks. There arose a broad class of Graeco-Egyptians, natives with Hellenic education who gradually pushed their way to the fore, even to the highest positions in the bureaucracy. Ptolemy VIII did everything to accelerate this process. In 145/4 B.C. he banished the Greek intellectuals, scholars and artists from Alexandria because they had taken sides against him in the civil war.[97] The flowering of Alexandrian science was a thing of the past. Pergamum and Rhodes took up the Alexandrian heritage and passed it on to the western world. The banished Greek intellectuals, however, took to the pen in exile. Due to them the portrait of Ptolemy VIII is totally drawn in unsympathetic lines and the king himself survives in history under the nickname *Physkon* (Potbelly).

THE FIRST PERIOD OF ROMAN RULE IN GREECE AND ASIA MINOR (167-89 B.C.)

The effects of Rome's unscrupulous policy after Pydna were felt most acutely in Macedonia and Greece. As once after Cynoscephalae and Magnesia, so after Pydna Rome contented herself with establishing indirect rule with the aid of devoted partisans. At first Rome did not try to obtain territorial possessions, since she was still too occupied with the reorganisation of the West. In Greece the period from Pydna to the end of the second century was a time of economic decline and social distress. The conflicts between the few rich and the many poor moved increasingly into the foreground, and the Greek capitalists, in league with expatriate Italians, competed in exploiting the economically weaker elements. The increase of cheaper slave labour struck at the very roots of the existence of the free poor. Only very few regions enjoyed better times: thus the acquisition of Delos proved invaluable to Athens. Athenian trade received a new impetus, and Athenian owl-coins found their way into all the world. The defeat of Pydna, together with its consequences, weighed heavily on Macedonia, now torn into four zones. The gold and silver mines, which had been shut down, were in fact permitted to go into operation again in 158 B.C., but this brought very little improvement. Above all, the monarchically inclined Macedonians were not able to adjust themselves to the republican constitutions imposed upon them by the Romans. In 149 B.C. Andriscus, an obscure adventurer from Adramyttium, posing as Philip, son of King Perseus, had himself crowned in Pella, but most of the Macedonians remained aloof.[98] The Romans were at first powerless. The praetor P. Juventius was defeated by the pseudo-Philip and together with a legion was totally annihilated. Through his connections with the Carthaginians the pseudo-Philip posed such a threat to the Romans that a strong land army under the praetor Q. Caecilius Metellus, in co-operation with a fleet, had to corner the adventurer and destroy his forces (148 B.C.). The Romans used the revolt of Andriscus as an occasion to reduce Macedonia to a province (the beginning of the Macedonian era, 148 B.C.),[99] and the Illyrian regions in the west and Epirus were united with it. For juridical purposes the four zones remained intact. A great military road was built, the *Via Egnatia*, beginning at Dyrrhachium, linking the Adriatic coast with the Aegean (Thessalonica and Cypsela on the Hebrus). The Macedonians appear to have come gradually to terms with Roman rule, especially as the new masters of the country took an active part in the cultural life of Macedonia. It is no accident that the place where we meet "the Benefactor Romans" for the first time, so far as Macedonia is concerned, is in a *Gymnasium* inscription from Thessalonica (beginning of the first century B.C.).[100]

Greece fared much worse than Macedonia. Here the Achaean League, whose leadership had fallen into the hands of anti-Roman politicians (Diaeus, Damocritus, Critolaus), succeeded in taking advantage of the general dissension to implement a highly inopportune nationalistic policy.[101] Disputes with Sparta, who was supported by Rome, fired passions to such a pitch that a Roman embassy was insulted in Corinth, and the League declared war on Sparta in the spring of 146 B.C. This of course simultaneously meant war with Rome, who at the time, however, was still in large measure militarily engaged in Spain and North Africa (Carthage). An attempt was made to lure the broad masses with socio-revolutionary measures, such as remission of debts and the emancipation of slaves. Nevertheless a completely abortive strategy on the part of the Achaeans in their defeats at Scarpheia (in Locris) and at the Isthmus (Leucopetra?) rapidly brought about the catastrophe of the League and with it almost all Hellas. At the command of the Senate, the victor L. Mummius had the flourishing commercial city of Corinth thoroughly destroyed—although the allegation of our literary sources that the city was totally destroyed, has not been confirmed by modern excavations.[102] The Achaean League was dissolved and many politically incriminated individuals, who were known as enemies of Rome, were executed and their property confiscated. Thousands of Greek works of art were either senselessly destroyed by the Romans or transported to Italy. The shadow of Hellenic freedom had come to an end. From 145 B.C. Greece was, apart from the states which had remained loyal to Rome, an appendage to the province of Macedonia.[103] The historian Polybius of Megalopolis strove, as much as lay within his power, to alleviate the severe lot of his compatriots through mediation with the Roman victors, and in many instances he did succeed. The peacefulness of a graveyard settled over Hellas. The country lay exhausted, devastated and impoverished by wars, and robbed of many of its best resources. In the subsequent long period of peace, however, lasting

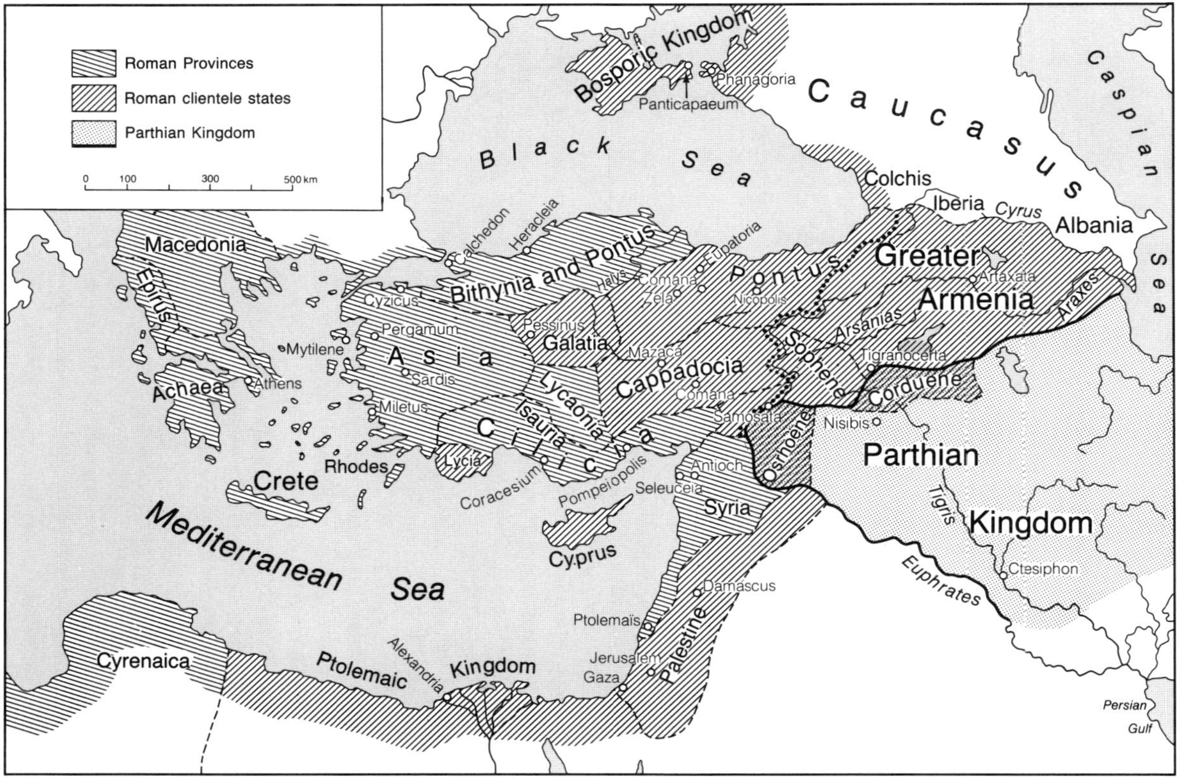

MAP XI Pompey's Reorganisation of Asia Minor (63 B.C.)

for almost sixty years, signs of social unrest again and again became evident,[104] chiefly in the slave revolts (134/3 and between 104 and 100 B.C.), but also in regular class struggles, as, for instance, at Dyme in 115 B.C.[105]

A completely new state of affairs occurred in Asia Minor when the last Attalid, Attalus III (139/8-133 B.C.), bequeathed the Pergamene kingdom (the Greek cities excepted) to the Romans.[106] The king's reasons for doing so – he had a malicious character, and his intensive study of poisonous plants would have sooner predestined him for an apothecary than for a king (E. Kornemann) – are to be sought in the fact that a pretender to the throne had established himself in Synnada and its vicinity, namely Aristonicus, who proclaimed himself as Eumenes on his coins and thereby attempted to establish his legitimacy as the son of Eumenes II.[107] At all events, his testament formed a natural conclusion to the history of the ruling dynasty, which since Attalus I and Eumenes II had been a loyal vassal of the great power of the West.

Rome accepted the inheritance. Western Asia Minor was at the time a wealthy region, as is illustrated, for instance, by the huge temples, in Magnesia on the Maeander (the temple of Artemis *Leukophryene*), the secular buildings in the small town of Priene and other cities, and the rich votive offerings to the Milesian Didymaeum in the second century B.C. Aristonicus (Eumenes) wanted to start afresh:[108] posing as founder of a new state, he called the citizens *Heliopolites*, not, as used to be thought, in reminiscence of Iambulus' "Sun State,"[109] but much more with a view to the sun (*helios*) as protector of justice.[110]

The revolt, which was put down after three years of fighting by the Romans under M. Perperna (consul 130 B.C.) and M'. Aquilius (consul 129 B.C.), ultimately proved abortive, because Aristonicus did not succeed in gaining the sympathies of most cities. Like the capital, Pergamum, they had been declared free by the testament of Attalus, and had no reason to forfeit this favour by a hostile attitude to Rome. Only a narrow strip on the west coast of Asia Minor was organised into a Roman province, with the pretentious name of Asia.[111] The neighbouring Hellenistic rulers who had taken an active part in the overthrow of Aristonicus continued to quarrel for a long time over the other regions. Thus Rome for the first time gained a foothold beyond the Aegean in Asia. Hordes of Roman publicans poured into the country, and even before the law of C. Gracchus in 123 B.C. the province saw itself delivered up to them. Thus the negative side of Roman provincial administration became evident in Asia Minor almost from the very beginning of Roman rule. The Hellenes of Asia Minor showed themselves the more grateful to those members of the Roman nobility who, like the proconsul Mucius Scaevola (94 B.C.) and his *legatus* Rutilius Rufus, had kept their hands untainted and opposed the extortionary activities of the publicans.[112] Rome, having moved much closer to the East, was from then on most intricately involved in the fate of Asia Minor.

THE GREEKS IN THE TIME OF MITHRADATES. THE REORGANISATION OF THE NEAR EAST BY POMPEY. THE END OF THE PTOLEMAIC KINGDOM (88-30 B.C.)

The Greek world during the sixty years before the battle of Actium (31 B.C.) shows clearly the effects of the presence of the Romans—equally in East and West, from Greece, Asia Minor, Syria, and Egypt to Sicily, Magna Graecia and Massalia. The Greeks were eliminated from the scene as an active factor in political life. Greek history became more or less part of Roman provincial history. Even the last independent Hellenistic states, chiefly the Ptolemaic kingdom, owed their existence entirely to the good will of Rome and its leading men. The almost uninterrupted wars of the period—the wars of Mithradates against Rome in Asia Minor and Greece (89-85; 83-81; 74-67 B.C.), the Roman civil wars, at first between Caesar and Pompey (49-48 B.C.) and then Octavian and Antony against the assassins of Caesar (42 B.C.), and then finally between Octavian and Antony (32-30 B.C.)—were in large measure fought on Greek soil. Hellas and Asia Minor were again and again most severely affected, their prosperity destroyed for decades. What the torch of war left intact became the booty of organised plundering by the Roman governors and their patrons, the publicans, who were to be found wherever Roman rule had become consolidated. Cicero's speeches are full of bitter accusations against Roman governors and officials, even though certain details may be exaggerated for the sake of rhetorical effect.

It is not that Roman rule had only a negative side, but the constructive activity of the Romans had to give way to the hard facts of military necessity during the war years. The reorganisation of the Near East by Pompey (64/3 B.C.) was an achievement of the very highest order, worthy of the ambitious Roman general's model, Alexander the Great. For centuries it determined the aspect of the Near East. And ideological forces which the dying political Hellenism of the first century B.C. radiated on the Romans were powerful and enduring. Caesar was under the spell of the idea of Hellenistic monarchy, no less than his rival Antony, who dreamed of a universal empire at the side of the Egyptian queen Cleopatra until the battle of Actium destroyed the vision. Hellenistic institutions and, in part, the spirit of Hellenistic kingship, survived in the *imperium* of the Roman Empire and on into the Byzantine Empire, and from there into the world of the Christian West.

Mithradates VI Eupator (he ruled from 121/0 to 63 B.C.), the creator of the Black Sea kingdom and the most formidable enemy to appear on the scene against the Romans in the first century B.C., came from an Iranian princely family which had been resident in Pontus since Achaemenid times. The kingdom which he established was, like his court, Hellenistic, although with a strong Iranian admixture, somewhat like the contemporary Parthian kingdom. Unlike Parthia, however, the kingdom of Mithradates was not born out of a nationalistic reaction against the Hellenes. Mithradates appeared in the Chersonese (Crimea) as the protector of the colonial Hellenes against the barbarians surging down from the north and east—Scythians, Sarmatians and Roxolanians. When it came to reorganising the country after expelling the Romans from Asia Minor in 88 B.C., Mithradates availed himself extensively of the services of the Greeks. It is no accident that he made Pergamum, the chief fortress of Hellenism in Asia Minor, his capital. He was liberal with gifts for Greek temples and Greek guilds and he surrounded himself with hosts of Greek writers and artists. Without the Greeks in his army and in his fleet he could never have conducted the war across the Aegean into Hellas, for only the Greeks were sufficiently familiar with modern warfare. A certain element among the Greeks of Asia Minor had from the very outset rejected Mithradates' overtures – Magnesia on the Sipylus, Tabae,[113] Stratoniceia and above all Rhodes, whom he attempted, in vain, to coerce by a siege, closed their gates to him. But the hatred of the Roman extortionary system, not only in the province of Asia but also in Hellas, led many Greeks enthusiastically to join the side of the Pontic king, the "Saviour of Asia," the "new Dionysus." Forty years of rule in western Asia Minor had engendered bitter hatred against Rome, and in 88 B.C. it vented itself in the massacre of eighty thousand Italics. Men, women and children fell victim to a pogrom which had been ordered by Mithradates, such as could only have been conceived in the brain of an Asiatic barbarian.

The fact that Athens, under the philosopher Athenion,[114] went over to the camp of the Pontic king was most significant, not only in material terms but even more so from an ideological point of view. Only now could Mithradates rightfully regard himself as the protector and champion against the Romans of all Hellenes between the Adriatic and the Taurus. Only now was his struggle rendered legitimate as a national Hellenic enterprise. Mithradates, however, poorly repaid the confidence which the Greeks had placed in him. His general, Archelaus, defeated by Sulla at Chaeroneia and at Orchomenus (86 B.C.), had to withdraw from Greece, and even in Asia Minor defection from Mithradates gained ground.[115] By establishing many tyrannies in the cities of Asia Minor and by deporting the population of entire regions – thus the Chians were to be transplanted to Colchis[116] – he disseminated terror and horror among the oscillating Greeks. It was above all the Greek upper classes who saw their very existence threatened in the extreme by a number of revolutionary social measures implemented by the Pontic king, the emancipation of a great many slaves and the ordered remission of debts.[117] They also feared, and rightly so, that they would lose what the greed of the Roman *publicani* had left behind.

The Hellenes had to pay a heavy price for Sulla's victories. On 1 March 86 B.C. Athens was stormed and plundered, and Piraeus, on Sulla's express orders, set ablaze. It was the greatest catastrophe in the pages of Athenian history since the Persian conflagration. The sanctuaries at Olympia, Delphi and Epidaurus were bled by huge forced loans, and one of the first measures of Sulla in Asia Minor was the order to collect within a single year the total revenue of five regular tax years.[118] Sulla, cut off from the resources of Italy, needed money, and besides this had to satisfy his troops. There was a brighter side, however, to the dismal picture. Thasos, which had remained loyal to the Romans against Mithradates, was generously rewarded. Not only did it receive back Peraea, but Sciathos and Peparathos were also added to the community. This certainly took place in the years after the Treaty of Dardanus (85 B.C.) had been concluded between Sulla and Mithradates. Later, new naval recruitments were repeatedly required to combat the pirates, the allies of Mithradates, and the Romans put this responsibility upon the shoulders of the Greek maritime cities. Inscriptions from Gytheum and Epidaurus illustrate the circumstances of the expedition of M. Antony, father of the triumvir, in 74 B.C. against the pirates. The vast financial burdens imposed on these cities brought them to the brink of ruin.[119] The large Hellenic commercial republics on the Pontus – Cyzicus, Heracleia, Sinope and Amisus – fared even worse, for they were most severely affected by the so-called Third Mithradatic War.

It was not until the peace between the end of the Third Mithradatic War and the beginning of the Civil Wars, lasting almost twenty years (between 76 and 49 B.C.), that the Greeks of Asia Minor had a period of recovery and new prosperity. With the return of the Roman businessmen a great amount of Italic capital flowed back into Asia Minor, with which the rich agrarian and industrial resources of western Anatolia could be retapped and reorganised. An impressive picture of the province of Asia in the years 60/59 B.C., during the governorship of Q. Cicero, appears in a letter by his brother, the famous orator. New life blossomed from the ruins of demolished cities, there was complete security throughout the land, and the administration of Greek public affairs was in the hands of pro-Roman oligarchs, designated as *optimates* by Cicero.[120] The reorganisation of the Greek East by Pompey comes at the beginning of this time of peace.[121] By uniting the Pontic coastal region with Bithynia – this region had fallen as a legacy to Rome in 74 B.C. by the testament of Nicomedes IV – and by decisively promoting the urbanisation of the Pontic area, Pompey finally opened up the regions of northern Asia Minor to Greek culture and to Greek economic activity.[122] Through the measures taken by the Roman general, Hellenism, in the form of Hellenistic culture, scored a complete victory over "Iranism," Iranian life and religion still indigenous in the Pontic interior on the large estates of the Iranian squires.

In 67 B.C., following the war against the pirates, Pompey had reorganised the province of Cilicia.[123] It now consisted of the eastern parts of Greater Phrygia, Pisidia, Lycaonia and Cilicia proper, which, with its innumerable bays, had previously been the chief seat of the pirates. After the confiscation of Cyprus in 58 B.C. this island was also placed under the governor of Cilicia. Pompey founded a number of new cities in Cilicia – no less than thirty-nine claimed in Anatolia and Syria, competing with the seventy cities of Alexander and the many cities founded by Seleucus I and Antiochus I. A great many Greek communities, including Sinope and Amisus on the Pontus, were confirmed in their self-government, but only a few, as free and immune states, came to enjoy complete exemption from taxes.

Pompey appointed a large number of secular and religious rulers over the rest of central and eastern Asia Minor. The most important of these principalities, whose existence depended on Rome's goodwill, were East Pontus under the Galatian Deiotarus, Paphlagonia under Attalus and Pylaemenes, the dominion of the Cilician petty ruler Tarcondimotus in Hierapolis-Castabala, and above all Cappadocia under Ariobarzanes, as well as Commagene under Antiochus I. The two latter were confirmed in the possession of their regions by Pompey. In eastern Anatolia too Hellenisation was already in an advanced stage. Cappadocia and Commagene emerged from old Seleucid provinces and preserved in their organisation—*strategiai* are attested in both[124]—the common heritage. The king, Ariarthes V Eusebes Philopator (163-130 B.C.), relying on his extensive connections with the Greek world, especially Athens and Delos, had greatly promoted Hellenisation in Cappadocia in the middle of the second century. The new capital, Mazaca-Eusebeia, which had replaced the forgotten Ariaratheia, was governed by the laws of Charondas.[125] A *Gymnasium* is attested in Tyana for the second century B.C.[126] Greek culture also found entry into Galatia. The extensive burial site of the family of the ruler Deiotarus, discovered in 1933, testifies to Hellenic influence in the architecture, the funerary gifts and the use of Greek in the inscription.[127] The knowledge of Greek was generally widespread in central and eastern Asia Minor. Attic *Koine* had long since displaced Aramaic as the language of government and commerce. The splendid "Asianist" sentences in the famous inscription of the ruler Antiochus I of Commagene, from Nemrud Dagh,[128] exemplify the marriage of Eastern thought with Greek modes of expression.

Pompey's reorganisation also marks a new epoch in Syria. This unfortunate land had for decades been the object of perpetual fighting among pretenders to the throne. Foreign powers like the Ptolemies and the Arsacids also interfered in these, until Syria and eastern Cilicia fell to the Armenian king, Tigranes I, in 83 B.C. The rule of Tigranes secured a period of internal tranquillity for the country until 69 B.C. In 63 B.C. Pompey put an end to the monarchy of the last Seleucid, Philip II, who called himself Philoromaios,[129] and who had gained the crown through the goodwill of an Arab sheikh. Pompey created a new province of Syria out of the region of northern Syria, ranging from Mount Amanus to Mount Carmel. A Roman governor and his staff moved into the old Seleucid capital of Seleuceia on the Orontes. The eastern frontier of the new province was camouflaged by a veil of vassal states. The Jewish state lost considerable territory in northern Palestine and on the coast, for at its expense, Pompey favoured the emancipation of Hellenic poleis, in which he rightly saw the strongest pillar of Roman rule in Syria. But the country was still disturbed by wars with the Jews and the Nabataeans, the great Parthian War of M. Licinius Crassus which ended in the Roman defeat at Carrhae (53 B.C.), assaults of Parthian cavalry armies, and by the confusion of the Roman civil wars. The riches[129] of Syria vanished. Caravan trade through Syria to the great harbour cities of Phoenicia, which had at one time brought so much revenue, sought new routes. The Nabataeans channelled it to Egypt, and thereby gained what Syria lost. In the first century B.C. Hellenisation of Syria had undoubtedly long since passed its climax, although Hellenism survived in the governmental forms of the country and in a lively and predominantly Greek cultural life in the cities. Moreover, the contacts which the Jewish religion made with Hellenism established in Judaea the basis on which Christianity was later able to develop.

The Romans on the whole successfully performed their duty in northern Greece, in the Balkan Peninsula, by protecting Greek culture from the assaults of the northern barbarians.[130] The armies of C. Scribonius Curio (75-73 B.C.) and of M. Terentius Varro Lucullus (72-70 B.C.) for the first time advanced in the footsteps of Philip and Alexander as far as the Lower Danube. The west Pontic Greek cities, from Apollonia to Istrus at the mouth of the Danube, which up to then had belonged to the sphere of Mithradates VI Eupator, were annexed to the Roman *imperium*, possibly as allied states.[131] At the same time, the brother of the Roman general, the famous L. Licinius Lucullus, conquered the cities situated on the south coast of the Pontus (72-70 B.C.) – Heracleia Pontica, Tios, Amastris, Sinope and Amisus – cities which had remained loyal to Mithradates. With the defeat of C. Antonius Hybrida against the Bastarnae at Istrus (61 B.C.), however, the Romans lost the conquests on the western Pontus. Macedonia experienced evil times.[132] The Greek cities on the western Pontus, including Olbia, came within the orbit of the expansion of the Dacian kingdom under Byrebista and were in part forcibly annexed by the Dacian king.[133]

With the beginning of the Civil War between Caesar and Pompey (49 B.C.) new storm-clouds gathered over Hellas. Both parties attempted to extort vast contributions from the country. The Greeks of the motherland and of Asia Minor in particular contributed the largest number of ships to Pompey's fleet. So far as the Greeks were concerned, the conflicts between the Roman party leaders were of no particular interest whatsoever. For the moment they submitted to the command of the stronger of the two – or attempted, mostly with insufficient means, to put up a resistance. The victor thereupon had a reason to punish them for their "defection." After the end of the war Caesar generously granted valuable privileges to many Greek communities. Cyzicus, Miletus, Pergamum[134] and Athens belonged to the preferred cities, and remote Chersonesus in Crimea despatched an embassy to Rome in 47 B.C.,[135] probably to obtain recognition as a free city. It was politics, and not philhellenic considerations, that determined Caesar's attitude towards the Greeks. His plans for the Parthian and Dacian wars loomed on the horizon. Thus Corinth, which had been destroyed by Roman brutality, owed to Caesar its restoration as a great thoroughfare from west to east (*Laus Julia Corinthiensis*). Caesar's death and the struggles kindled at his pyre brought in their wake harsh times for the Greeks in the East, especially in Asia Minor. Caesar's assassins, Brutus and Cassius, who appeared empty-handed in the Orient, showed themselves no dilettantes at extortion. Those who opposed them, like Rhodes, Xanthus and Patara, came to feel the mailed fist of Rome. Nor did the battle of Philippi (42 B.C.) end the years of suffering for the Greeks. The treatment accorded to the various communities by the victorious Antony was governed by the attitude which they had adopted in the preceding conflict between the Roman generals. Those who had sided with Caesar's assassins had now to pay the price for it. Antony's confederates, on the other hand, were granted certain privileges. Cos, for example, famous on account of its sanctuary of Asclepius, received, in the person of the linguist (*grammaticus*) Nicias—similarly as at the same time communities like Tarsus and Amisus—a tyrant whose popular rule of approximately eight years (41/40-c. 33 B.C.) once more signified a period of vigorous efflorescence for the city.[136] For the rest, however, the chronic financial straits of Antony, the uncrowned king of the Orient, and the Parthian invasion under Q. Labienus and Pacorus (41/40-38 B.C.), brought renewed calamity to Syria and Asia Minor.[137] Moreover, when Antony in 33 B.C. began mobilising in the Orient against Octavian, it was once more the Hellenes who, together with the client rulers of the East, had to bear the main burdens of the war, a war which interested them just as little as had the preceding conflicts since the beginning of the Civil War between Caesar and Pompey. Plutarch (*Vita of Antony* 68) related from family reminiscences that the inhabitants of Boeotian Chaeroneia, among them Plutarch's great-grandfather, Nicarchus, were on the point of hauling grain from the city down to the harbour of Anticyra, when news came of Antony's defeat at Actium, and thereby ended their compulsory service. Not only the citizens of Chaeroneia but all Hellas and the Orient breathed a sigh of relief and gathered fresh hope for peace and prosperity.

In the maelstrom of the Civil Wars even the last independent Greek city of the West, Massalia, lost its freedom (49 B.C.). As in Sicily, so in the Rhône Valley of southern France, Greek civilisation survived—until the end of antiquity.

The Battle of Actium also decided the fate of the last major Hellenistic state, the Ptolemaic kingdom. From the days of Ptolemy VI the empire was little more than a Roman client state, even though indisputably the largest and most important that Rome controlled in the Hellenistic East. Since then no Ptolemaic ruler had ventured to pursue a policy contrary to the will of the great power of the West. In all matters of conduct eyes were kept focussed on Rome, which gave teeth to its will by specific orders to the Ptolemaic kings. In conjunction, therewith, the Senate kept itself up to date on all important developments in the country by sending out official and unofficial embassies.[138]

The year 88 B.C., in which Mithradates VI established his rule over Asia Minor, also became a year of destiny for Egypt. The Alexandrians banished King Ptolemy X Alexander I, who in 101 B.C. had paved the way to sole rule by murdering his mother.[139] The king lost his life in a naval battle on the Lycian coast and his death once more opened the way to the throne in Alexandria for his brother Ptolemy IX Soter II, who since 107 B.C. had been king of Cyprus. Rome, fully occupied by Mithradates, in no way resisted the unification of Egypt and Cyprus. The danger which the empire of Ptolemy IX constituted for Rome was even less ominous, since a serious native revolt had broken out in the Thebaid in 88 B.C.[140]

It required years to put down. After the death of Ptolemy IX Soter II in 80 B.C. renewed confusion ensued. Sulla was to blame, for he forced Ptolemy XI Alexander II, the son of Alexander I, as co-regent and husband upon Berenice the daughter of Soter II. The forced marriage ended in murder and homicide. Berenice fell victim to her husband, and thereupon Alexander II was killed by the exasperated population of Alexandria, after a reign of only nineteen days (80 B.C.). Ptolemy XII Neus Dionysus, nicknamed *Auletes* (Flute-Player), and son of Ptolemy IX, acceded to the Lagid throne.[141] His brother, who has gone down in history under the dynastic name of Ptolemy, became king of Cyprus. The testament of Alexander II, which authorised Rome to take control of Egypt and Cyprus at any time, hung over the head of Neus Dionysus like a Damocles sword.[142] He had to wait no less than two decades for official recognition as king of Egypt by the protective *imperium* of Rome.

Egypt itself, however, became an increasingly important piece on the chessboard of internal politics at Rome. The Senate in 58 B.C. presided over the liquidation of the Cyprian monarchy.[143] The last Ptolemaic ruler of the island, the younger brother of Neus Dionysus, preferred death to a life under the goodwill of Rome. As early as 65 B.C. Crassus wanted to confiscate Egypt, a design which was thwarted by his opponents in Rome. Later Pompey took a hand. With his consent, the governor of Syria, A. Gabinius, in 55 B.C. conducted the banished Ptolemy XII back to Alexandria. From now on Rome held the trump card in Egypt. A Roman garrison was stationed in the country and Gabinius imposed a Roman knight in the official capacity of *dioiketes* upon the mock-king, so that the finances of the country were under Roman control. The country was not annexed by Rome, but only because of rivalry among eminent Romans. When Pompey, after having been defeated at Pharsalus (48 B.C.), landed in Egypt, he was murdered, at the command of Ptolemy XIII, son of Neus Dionysus (51-48 B.C.).

Because of the energy of Cleopatra, sister of Ptolemy XIII, the Ptolemaic state once more played a significant rôle in world history. Cleopatra's connections with Caesar gave the Romans dominion over Ptolemaic Egypt, which was still rich in resources. For Caesar the country was worth his undertaking the Alexandrine War (48/47 B.C.),[144] even though in itself this struggle was not in the interests of the Roman people. The Ides of March in 44 B.C. destroyed Caesar's plans and Cleopatra's hopes of becoming the rulers of a universal empire, in which Egypt was to be united with the West.[145] The grand notion appeared on the verge of realisation again when Cleopatra succeeded in conquering the heart of the triumvir M. Antony. He had summoned her to Tarsus to give an account there of her conduct in the Civil War between the Caesarians and Brutus and Cassius, since she had supported the latter (41 B.C.).[146]

Thanks to Cleopatra's diplomacy Egypt for a decade enjoyed a central position in the contest of rivalling powers, which threatened to split the world into an eastern and into a western half. Internal conditions in the ancient land of the Nile in no way corresponded to the splendid outer façade. Due to continuous maladministration the countryside had completely declined, and in addition there were years of drought and famine. Moreover, the bureaucracy was corrupt, the central government incompetent, and the working population unruly. Still, the queen was not unpopular among the native Egyptians.[147] She presented herself as the successor of the female members in the Pharaonic line, even learned to speak Egyptian (in addition to many other languages), and her apothcosis as New Isis was aimed equally at the Hellenes as at the Egyptians. Once more, and for the last time, the large-scale plans of Ptolemy II Philadelphus were taken up in Egypt, with the knowledge and approval of Antony. As a "territorial gift of the bridegroom to the bride" the Roman presented Cleopatra with the kingdom of Chalcis in the Lebanon (37/36 B.C.), the Phoenician coast from Eleutherus to Sidon, and the island of Cyprus and parts of Cilicia.[148] The gift precipitated justified ill feeling in Rome towards the triumvir, whose generosity was at the expense of the Roman people.

An indisputable climax in Cleopatra's life was marked by the gymnasium scene in Alexandria.[149] Here in 34 B.C. the triumvir proclaimed the Lagid as "Queen of Queens," and her son by Caesar, whom the Alexandrians called Caesarion, as "King of Kings," while the mutual children of Antony and Cleopatra received subordinate kingdoms: the boy Alexander Helios[150] was given the regions of East Iran, his brother, Ptolemy Philadelphus, Syria and Cilicia, while Cleopatra Selene received Cyrenaica and Libya. A new era appeared to be dawning, in which the Ptolemies were to rule the East under the patronage of Antony! In this circumstance titles had to compensate for what the abortive Parthian expedition of 36 B.C. had denied the Roman—the establishing of a universal Hellenistic-Iranian empire on the model of Alexander the Great.

Cleopatra's liaison with Antony in the approaching decisive war in world history between West and East gave to Octavian the propaganda weapon to claim that the war against Antony was a national war of the Romans against Cleopatra. Thus the first war between Rome and Egypt came at the end of the history of the Ptolemaic kingdom. The defeat of Antony at Actium (2 Sept. 31 B.C.) also sealed the fate of Cleopatra and the fate of her empire. Nevertheless the last female member of the Ptolemaic dynasty did not go down ingloriously. After Antony's end had come she chose death on her own volition, and indeed the most sacred death possible, by the fangs of a viper, which, according to Egyptian religion, vouchsafed immortality[151] (30 B.C.). Roman rule in Egypt began a new period, which found its expression in the creation of a new era by Octavian.[152]

15
THE GREEKS IN THE ROMAN EMPIRE

INTRODUCTION

With the capture of Alexandria by Octavian on 1 August 30 B.C. the destiny of political Hellenism was fulfilled. The Hellenistic monarchy, which now survived only in certain orientalised and Iranised states of the East, was replaced by the one Roman Empire—a fundamental change, which ordered the eastern Mediterranean according to the will of Rome even more than before.

Greek culture during the Roman Empire assumed a two-fold character to an even greater degree than in the Hellenistic period. It is the history of the Greek people living in peace, under the protection of the Roman legions, for almost 200 years, and it is the history of the Greek mind, which struck firm and permanent roots in the provinces of the *Imperium Romanum*. Admittedly what the Hellenes on the one hand gained in the West, Greek culture lost again in the East. The awakening of the world of the Orient and the rise of "Iranism" in the Parthian empire, and above all in the Neo-Persian empire of the Sassanids (after 224 A.D.), inflicted severe reverses on Greek culture, from which it was never able to recover in the East.

The actual core of the region encompassed by Greek culture was no longer old Hellas, which because of the altered world situation had long since shifted to the periphery, but western Asia Minor, particularly the large cities on the west coast. Under the patronage of the philhellenic Roman emperors this area once more enjoyed a great cultural and material flowering, especially in the second century A.D. Even more, Greek culture became a world culture through the philhellenism of Hadrian and the Antonines, and in the *Imperium Romanum* this world culture embraced the learned of all countries alike. Only the revolution of the third century A.D. and the reaction of "Romanism" under the Dalmatian Diocletian brought the rising development of Greek culture to a precipitous end.

The Greek national character, however, survived, with only slight changes in its composition, until the sixth century A.D. The distinct cultural awareness of the Greek upper classes prevented a thoroughgoing fusion of the Hellenes with the other nations within the Roman Empire. Roman influence in the predominantly Greek inhabited regions was slight[1]—strongest in Macedonia, where the advance of Latin at the expense of Greek is unmistakable evidence of progressive Romanisation. For the rest the Roman emperors fully acknowledged the special position of the Hellenes in the empire, and a Greek translation usually accompanied the decrees of the emperors and the edicts of the magistrates in the Greek-speaking East. On the other hand the Greeks only gradually took part in the imperial administration. The rise of Greek freedmen to the highest positions in the imperial cabinet is characteristic of the governments of the emperors Claudius and Nero, but not until the second and above all the third century did the Greeks in large numbers gain entry into the class of higher imperial offices.

The history of the Greeks in the Roman Empire is the history of a people without its own national state, without a political centre and without political or military power. The importance of Greek history between Augustus and Justinian rests simply and solely on the distinct superiority of Greek culture, whereby the heritage of an incomparably great past was cultivated and handed down. The chasm between past and present was naturally not without its repercussions on the Greek people and the Greek national character. The loss of all political responsibility, exclusive restriction to communal affairs, the dependence of the Greeks on the injunctions of the Roman governors and the failure to observe moderation in bestowing honours on Romans—all these to a considerable degree accented the negative side of the Hellenic character, especially the proclivity towards adulation. Still over against these unpleasant features, the positive aspects must not be overlooked. Especially worthy of the highest recognition is the Greek participation in the service of the common weal, in which the Hellenes of the imperial era were surpassed by no other people.

Events of importance within the context of world history are reflected in the gradual shift in Hellenism's centre of gravity from the Greek motherland to the west coast of Asia Minor, and from there to the straits of the Bosporus. Constantinople, founded on the site of ancient Byzantium by Constantine I as the new capital of the Roman Empire, documents this phenomenon to all the world. The Hellenism of the "Rhomaeans," which emerged from the Greek and Graecised people of the Balkans and Anatolia, once more attained, in the Byzantine state, an importance of world dimension.

THE GREEK WORLD FROM AUGUSTUS TO DOMITIAN

Octavian's victory over Antony at Actium (2 September 31 B.C.) brought to an end almost twenty years of suffering for the Greeks of the motherland, Asia Minor and the East. The severe effects from almost two decades of continual fighting in the Civil Wars were felt above all in Greece, where the decisive battles of Pharsalus, Philippi and Actium had been fought. Thus Strabo's pessimistic description of Greece, although perhaps exaggerated in certain details, on the whole doubtless does justice to the conditions of the country. New activity concentrated itself in three centres. One was Nicopolis, which Octavian founded to commemorate the naval victory at Actium, by forcing the Acarnanians and Aetolians to furnish large contingents of population. Another new centre was the Caesarian colony of Corinth (*Laus Julia Corinthiensis*) lying at the intersection of the east-west routes, and the third was in commercially active Patrae. In contrast to these flourishing cities the old cultural centres of Hellas receded further and further into the background.

Athens lived on the fame of her great past, and her relationship with Augustus was cool. His sojourns in the city were short, for he had not forgotten the enthusiastic partisanship of the Athenians for M. Antonius. Athens did everything to conciliate him, building a temple on the Acropolis to Augustus and Roma,[2] the first since the Erechtheum. And the Athenians presumably were also proud that the princeps, as Sulla at one time and in subsequent periods most emperors down to the time of Commodus, allowed himself to be initiated into the Eleusian Mysteries.[3] It is improbable that an official reconciliation came about between Athens and Augustus, as has been assumed for the year 19 B.C.[4] Sparta was more fortunate than Athens. Eurycles,[5] her ruler, was almost the only Greek to fight on the side of Octavian, and he was handsomely rewarded. Octavian gave him the island of Cythera as personal property. The League of free Laconians, however, comprising a total of twenty-four Laconian and Messenian cities, remained independent of Sparta.[6] C. Julius Eurycles—as he styled himself after receiving Roman citizenship—had to go into exile while Augustus was still alive. His successors, however, ruled intermittently over Sparta until the time of Nero. Under Eurycles and his successors the old Lycurgan constitution nominally survived, with the ephors, the *Apella*, the *Gerousia* and indeed even the *syssitia* and the old Spartan education of her youth, the *agoge*. Otherwise a certain degree of prosperity continued in Sparta until the third century A.D. The same was true of Argos. Of the sacred places in Greece, Delphi suffered greatly (Strabo[7] calls it a "miserable sanctuary"). Augustus, however, reorganised the Delphic *Amphictyony*,[8] but in only half measures, since a great many districts were excluded from the union. Not until Hadrian appeared on the scene was the situation transformed. Olympia, on the other hand, soon recovered.[9] The reviving of athletic contests in the Roman Empire and the favours by members of the family of the first Roman princeps contributed essentially to this. Augustus felt himself bound particularly close to Thessaly, shown by his preferential treatment of the Thessalian *koinon* in the Delphic Amphictyony. Along with Nicopolis and Macedonia it possessed six votes. Further evidence is the fact that in 27/6 B.C. Augustus held the office of the Thessalian president (*strategos*).[9a]

From 27 B.C. onwards Greece was administratively organised as a separate province (senatorial) under the name of Achaea, which also included, *inter alia*, parts of Epirus, the Ionian islands and the Cyclades. The representative of the imperial administration was a proconsul of praetorian rank,[10] residing in Corinth. There were no garrison troops.

Asia Minor more than the exhausted and ruined Greek motherland showed the beneficial influence of Augustus' government. The policy of the urbanisation of the empire, introduced by Caesar's establishing of colonies,[11] was continued with great success by his adoptive son and heir. Many new urban communities emerged, above all in inner Anatolia, under the rule of the Julio-Claudian house. With these Greek culture and Greek civilisation spread into those regions of Anatolia which in the first and second centuries A.D. had felt little or no effects, marking a climax in the Hellenisation of Asia Minor. The indigenous people, only slightly affected by the Hellenising development, continued to live in the rural districts, although the native idioms were forced into the background by the Greek language and did not revive until the very late period of the empire. The blessings of the peace ushered in by Augustus were advantageous above all to the Greek cities on the west coast—Ephesus, Pergamum and Smyrna. Ephesus, in its ancient venerable temple of Artemis, possessed an attraction of the very first order, while Pergamum was proclaimed the official capital of the Roman province of Asia, and Smyrna was the metropolis of Hellenic cultural life in the second century A.D. Caligula divided the province of Asia into a total of thirteen dioceses,[12] a number which in the following period became subject to certain changes. Under Roman encouragement the secular guilds enjoyed a new renaissance. At their head was the "League of the Hellenes in Asia,"[13] and alongside it the alliance composed of the Ilian, Ionian and Carian Poleis League. There can be no question of any noteworthy opposition to Roman rule. As in Hellas, so in Asia Minor the Romans relied on the propertied classes, entrusting the entire local and civic government to the Greek notables. Although Rome was not petty in granting citizenship to Greeks (Antonius was exemplary in this),[14] a conscious Romanisation of the country was not pursued. The conflicts between the Italic and Hellenic national elements and their cultures could not be eliminated simply by a stroke of the pen, and in other respects the Greek who received Roman citizenship remained, as before, a citizen of his native city. Like the motherland, so the province of Asia, composed of Mysia, Ionia, Lydia, Caria, Phrygia and the islands on the west coast of Asia Minor, was from 27 B.C. a senatorial province governed by a proconsul of consular rank.

The edicts of Augustus (and the so-called *senatus consultum Calvisianum*) from 7/6 B.C. and 5/4 B.C.,[15] discovered in the agora of Cyrene, have thrown a great deal of light on the position of the Hellenes in Cyrenaica and their relationship to the Romans.[16] Augustus repressed Roman influence in the provincial law courts and commanded the Greeks to take an active part in them. The term Hellenes in the Cyrenaic documents of Augustus evidently embraces all those who had participated in Greek education, that is, those citizens who had passed through the *Gymna-*

sium and the institution of *ephebeia*, without regard, it would seem, to their constitutional affiliation with one of the Greek cities in Cyrenaica or with one of the other Greek communities outside the province.[17] A goodly Libyan element had probably penetrated the Hellenes of Cyrenaica, beginning with Greek colonisation and continuing especially in the Hellenistic period.

Rome continued to maintain the fiction of an alliance with the Cyrenaic communities although such a league relationship had long since ceased to have any practical significance. The Cyrenaic Greeks did not participate in the animated cultural life of the Hellenic world of the first era of the Principate, although Cyrene was as much a member of the *Panhellenion* as other Greek communities of Africa and Asia Minor, and despatched two *synedroi*.[18] Later, at the turn of the fourth century A.D., Cyrene produced an outstanding intellectual in Synesius, the Neoplatonist and later bishop (born c. 370 A.D.). In economic terms too the country was, during the imperial era, far from what it had once been. The cultivation of silphium, the source of its wealth, had undergone an inexplicable regression, although there is still evidence for it in the time of Synesius.[19] In later decades the Romanisation of the country made rapid strides.[20] At the beginning of the third century A.D. approximately half the population was composed of Roman citizens,[21] of whom the great majority were immigrants from Italy and the western provinces of the Empire. In addition to that part of the population included in the term "Hellenes," there were important Jewish communities in the cities of the Pentapolis, which, as in Ptolemaic Egypt, were organised on the lines of *politeumata*. For the rest, however, the old institutions of the poleis continued. The priest of Apollo[22] continued to be eponymous magistrate in Cyrene, and the highest officials in the polis were still, as in bygone centuries, the *strategoi*.

By way of Cyrenaica, but also through the immediate influence of the Greek motherland, Hellenic culture struck deep and permanent roots in western North Africa, in the Roman province[23] and in the Roman client state of Mauretania.[24] During the early empire Greek was understood by all educated individuals from Tripoli to Tangiers. Juba II, ruler of Mauretania (25 B.C. to 23 A.D.), himself an unusually prodigious, if not very original, writer (Felix Jacoby called him the "royal compiler"), spread Greek culture in his country, and at a late hour opened up a new and important province to Greek world culture.[25]

The lapidary statement of Augustus in his *Res gestae* (27) does not explain clearly the position of Egypt in the Roman Empire. In accordance with the will of the first princeps the ancient land of the Pharaohs occupied a special position. It was not a province but a domain of the emperor, whose government he placed in the hands of a Prefect of Alexandria and Egypt.[26] Members of the senatorial class and the knights were not allowed to set foot in the country without permission from the emperor.

The beginning of Roman rule in Egypt marked an important turning point in all phases of life.[27] The Roman emperors even more than the Ptolemies were interested in fiscal affairs and in the economy of the country, for Egyptian grain was invaluable for the sustenance of Rome. In contrast to the rule of the Ptolemies, whose economic policy, despite all visible and invisible weakness, had in the last instance redounded, at least in some measure, to the benefit of the country, Roman policy was one-sided, aimed at exploiting the rich resources of Egypt in the interests of the Empire.[28] The Romans had nothing superior to replace the Ptolemaic hierarchy of officials, and took the system over almost intact. One of the few innovations was the appointing of three *epistrategiai*, joining the nomes of Upper Egypt, Middle Egypt (the so-called Heptanomia) and the Delta into larger districts under Roman administration,[29] but within the individual nomes the old administrative system continued unaltered.[30] From the very outset the Roman administration strove to eliminate many of the abuses which had prevailed under the last Ptolemies. Canals and dikes were rebuilt, and as early as Augustus the yields from the agricultural districts rose to a noteworthy degree. Business and trade too, especially trade with India, enjoyed a new flowering.[31]

In the ethnic sphere Roman rule accentuated the existing conflicts even more. The elimination of the important privileges of the all powerful Egyptian priesthood by Augustus exacerbated the internal tensions. In the capital of Alexandria too there were great internal conflicts, for the most part between the citizens and those who had no share in the franchise, primarily the large number of Alexandrian Jews.[32]

The standard-bearers of Hellenic culture in Egypt came from a politically privileged class, whose members proudly designated themselves as "those of the *Gymnasium*." This class provided the municipal officials, on whose shoulders devolved the burdens, above all the *leitourgiai*.[33] In Alexandria the *Gymnasiarches* (official in charge of the *Gymnasium*) rose to become the most important magistrate under the Romans. In the cosmopolitan metropolis, as in the suburbs of the nomes in the rural districts, the *Gymnasium* still continued to be the centre of Greek cultural and social life. But in the villages the *Gymnasia* came to an end about the time of the birth of Christ[34]—doubtless in accordance with the will of the Roman government, which wanted to concentrate Greek cultural life in the larger centres of the country in order to be able to supervise it better. This made the conflict between city and country noticeably more acute, so that in the rural districts the indigenous Egyptian element soon dominated affairs almost uncontested. In order to maintain the distance between themselves and the natives the Hellenes in the Fayûm, at one time the centre of Ptolemaic cleruch settlements, united to form a closed society of fixed number—the "6475 Hellenes in Arsinoïtes."[35] Moreover, about 37 A.D. the citizen-body of Alexandria also formed a set number—180,000.[36] As under the Ptolemies, so also under Roman rule the Greeks in Egypt lacked scope for political activity, and in the long run this was nothing less than disastrous, although the animated cultural life which still continued to pulsate in the country was a kind of substitute for politics. The discovery of innumerable literary papyri in the countryside[37] shows the interest of broad sectors of the population in the sources of Greek education, whose foundation continued to be centred in the *Gym-*

nasia.[38] In Alexandria the *Mouseion* continued, under the patronage of the Roman emperor. Of its learned members in the time of Augustus one Didymus was particularly important. His industry and breadth of reading were colossal, and his commentaries on almost all the Greek poets and on the speeches of Demosthenes are the worthy end of a great period in Alexandrian scholarship. The seed which had been scattered abroad in the *Mouseion* fell on good ground. Here there arose, towards the end of the second century A.D., the school of the Christian apologists Pantaenus, Clement and Origen,[39] which enlisted Greek scholarship in the service of the Christian cause.

While the governments of Augustus and Tiberius exhibit a distinct bias in favour of Rome (in contrast to the Hellenistic aspirations of Caesar and his follower M. Antonius), the distinguishing feature in the principates of Gaius (Caligula, 37-41 A.D.), Claudius (41-54 A.D.) and Nero (54-68 A.D.) is the advance of Hellenism, which now for the first time also inundated the nerve centre of the imperial government. The Hellenistic divine emperorship of Gaius, the cabinet government of Claudius, patterned on Hellenistic models, the rise of the imperial women to the point of the co-regency of Nero's mother Agrippina, and the *graecomania* of the last emperors of the Julio-Claudian house—all this testifies to the rebirth at the Roman imperial court of Greek, specifically Hellenistic, ideas and models in constitutional affairs.[40]

The exaggeration of the autocratic régime by the successors of Tiberius inevitably brought reactionary forces into play. Open opposition arose not only among the Roman senators, but primarily in the Hellenistic East. The champions of the resistance were the intellectuals, the philosophers and the educated circles among the Hellenes. The attitude of the Roman emperors was just as incompatible with their lofty feeling of self-esteem as with the idea of *libertas*, which the Roman senatorial opposition had adopted as its slogan. The bitter Greek opposition, appearing for the first time under Gaius (Caligula), appears foremost in the papyri designated by Adolf Bauer as *Acts of Pagan Martyrs*.[41] In the garb of official records these documents describe lawsuits before the Roman princeps, in which the leaders of the Alexandrian Greeks had to account for their hostile attitude towards the Alexandrian Jews and for the anti-Semitic disturbances in the metropolis on the Nile. The *Acts* are not authentic, but they do appear to utilise records from genuine cases. On the whole they are a product of ancient propaganda.[42] It would seem that recourse was had again and again to these "Acts" whenever disturbances arose between Greeks and Jews in Alexandria, until the beginning of the third century A.D.[43] The candour which the Alexandrian citizens permit themselves in the presence of the all powerful princeps by hurling the most unpalatable truths in his face is nothing less than astonishing. What one had long since ceased to enjoy under the rule of the Roman emperors and what the Ptolemaic kings had not permitted in Alexandria, namely the free political speech of the classical Greek polis, here once more celebrated a tardy triumph in the *Acts of the Martyrs*—though perhaps only on papyrus.

That Alexandria became the stronghold of Hellenic opposition to

Roman rule is due above all to the Romans' degrading the political classes in the one time so powerful metropolis. It was no accident that the population of Alexandria, for centuries accustomed to housing kings within its walls, tempestuously celebrated the "crown prince" Germanicus on the occasion of his unexpected excursion to Egypt.[44] The Alexandrians fought with particular obstinacy on behalf of their "Council"—the symbol of self-government in the Hellenic polis, which apparently Octavian abolished.[45] All the representations which the Alexandrians made came to nothing. Even Claudius treated the request of the Alexandrian deputation in dilatory fashion,[46] and Septimius Severus was the first to grant the citizens of the old capital a "Council" again, in 199/200 A.D.

Like Alexandria, so the old Seleucid city of Antioch on the Orontes must have taken Roman snubs bitterly. The lot of the north Syrian metropolis was so much the happier when in the years 17-19 A.D. Germanicus, as General Governor of the East with increased plenary powers, ruled the Orient from his headquarters in Antioch. An accelerated building programme dates from this period, and was continued by the bizarre Gaius (Caligula), son of Germanicus.[47]

While Tiberius and Claudius attempted by every possible means to promote the prosperity of the Empire by a distinctly patriarchal régime, including the Greek East,[48] under Nero the situation was different—despite the intense enthusiasm of the princeps for Greece. During his reign a grave economic depression occurred in Egypt, and also affected the other provinces.[49] Nero's philhellenism is reflected in the famous declaration of freedom for Greece, that is, the province of Achaea, on 28 November 67 A.D.[50] In connection with this event the Peloponnesus was renamed "Nero's Island." Extensive material concessions for the Greeks of the motherland accompanied this declaration of freedom; in particular all districts of Hellas were exempted from the oppressive taxes obligatory to Rome. For the rest Nero took as his model the declaration of freedom by T. Quinctius Flamininus at the celebration of the Isthmian games in 196 B.C. To such a degree did Nero carry his imitation that the Greeks were compelled to repeat the celebration of the Isthmian games in the winter of 67 A.D.! As a reciprocal gesture for the "unexpected gift"[51] of freedom the Greeks expressed their thanksgiving to this strange philhellene with extravagant honours, among other things an altar erected to the emperor as "Zeus Liberator."[52]

Vespasian's elevation to emperor (69 A.D.) was to all appearances strongly favoured and jubilantly welcomed by the inhabitants of the old eastern metropolises of Antioch and Alexandria.[53] The dream, however, that a political renaissance would ensue for the Greeks of the East ended in bitter disappointment. The very opposite occurred. Although the emperors of the Julio-Claudian house had maintained a largely friendly policy towards the Greeks, this tendency was abruptly reversed under the rule of the Flavians. Concern for the West of the Empire stood in the forefront of the policy of the Flavian emperors, who did much to Romanise it. After the *graecomania* of Nero the Hellenes must have felt this fundamental change in imperial policy with particular acuteness—little wonder that later it was in the East that impostors masked as a *Nero redivivus* drew large crowds. Already in the first years of Vespasian (69-79 A.D.) regular riots occurred in the Greek half of the Empire, including Alexandria.[54] Although they were easily suppressed, they none the less had serious consequences for those who had taken part in them. Under the first Flavian, Greece (the former province of Achaea), Lycia, Rhodes, Byzantium and Samos lost their "freedom" and exemption from taxes and were placed under the direct jurisdiction of the governor.[55] From the fact that the rebels included important trade and commercial cities it may be supposed that the disturbances were sparked by social problems, for the conflict between the unpropertied proletariat and the class rule of the well-to-do upper strata, supported by Rome, was very characteristic of this time. The Roman government easily dealt with the internal disturbances in the Greek East. Far more dangerous, however, was the opposition by some of the Greek intellectuals, especially the philosophers, to what they regarded as a Principate that had degenerated into a regular *tyrannis*. Even Vespasian knew no other way to cope with the situation than to drive the hostile philosophers—with the sole exception of Musonius Rufus —out of Rome and probably also out of the whole of Italy, in 74 A.D., in order to put an end to the growing opposition.[56] It would seem that the opposition was incited chiefly by the Cynic philosophers from the Greek regions of the Empire.[57]

All this, however, was only a prelude. The real drama began under the reign of Domitian (81-96 A.D.), the "lord and god," the only one of the Flavians who made no pretence of any philhellenism. The life of the Greek Dion of Prusa (c. 40-120 A.D.) testifies to the growing opposition of the philosophers and educated circles to Domitian's autocratic tendencies.[58] The celebrated philosopher and orator, who had been on friendly terms with Vespasian, was banished by Domitian, perhaps in connection with the ruin of Flavius Sabinus. He was forced to avoid Rome and Italy, and not permitted to return to his homeland of Bithynia. Disguised and under a pseudonym, the pampered Greek travelled about the north-east of the empire as a Cynic beggar-philosopher. He visited, among other places, the Greek city of Olbia on the Bug[59] and the Roman permanent quarters at Viminacium in Moesia. For fourteen years Dion lived under cover and everywhere incited hatred of the suppressor, Domitian. In spite of material privation and although forced to adjust to a life of working with his own hands, he was not diverted from his initial resolve. The effect of unyielding personalities such as Dion in the period of Domitian can scarcely be overestimated. With admirable adaptability the Greek mind had here embarked on a high political mission and, in the face of all material obstacles, carried it to conclusion. The effects would doubtless not have been so profound had there not existed at just that time in the Greek East opposition among broad sectors of the population to the rule of the Roman emperors and their governors. That the portrait of Domitian is drawn in such dark colours by later tradition is due above all to the opposition of the Greek philosophers. The men of the word and of the pen avenged themselves on their suppressor, just as at one time those who had been banished from Alexandria took revenge on Ptolemy VIII Euergetes II (v.s.p. 311).

In spite of hostility towards the philosophers, the rule of the Flavians, especially of Vespasian, was a milestone in the history of ancient education, and of Greek culture in general. On 27 December 74 A.D. Vespasian granted orators, grammarians and physicians important privileges—exemption from the oppressive obligations of billetting troops, freedom from taxes, protection from illegal arrest and, finally, the right to form guilds on the basis of cult gatherings. Vespasian's edict, of which a copy designed for the Greek East was found on a stone at Pergamum,[60] has been termed the "charter of ancient universities" (R. Herzog). On the subject of the philosophers the decree is silent, and understandably so, since their opposition had brought them into disfavour. This privileged position granted to learned circles by the emperor may have been modelled on the organisation of the Alexandrian *Mouseion*, with which Vespasian became acquainted during his stay in the Egyptian capital in 69 A.D. It is of special interest that the category of physicians, the so-called *iatroleiptai* ("nature-cure-gymnastic physicians"), was placed on the same level as the others, which can best be explained on the basis of existing conditions in Alexandria. The Pergamene stone contains, beneath the edict of Vespasian, a decree by Domitian (in Latin) from 93/4 A.D., expressly prohibiting the instruction of slaves in the sciences.

FROM TRAJAN AND HADRIAN TO MARCUS AURELIUS

The privileges granted by the Roman emperors benefited the Greek East in particular. A new and happier era began there with the reigns of Trajan (98-117 A.D.) and Hadrian (117-138 A.D.). Under Hadrian in particular the sunshine of imperial favour shed its full rays on the Greek motherland, so rich in classical reminiscences. The Hellenes enjoyed a cultural and economic renascence to which there is nothing even remotely comparable in the entire imperial era. The wars of Trajan against the Dacians and Parthians created the conditions for this, as they opened up new frontiers for imperial trade and commerce and placed the life of the inhabitants of the Empire on new foundations. Along with the Italic businessmen, hordes of Greek mercenaries poured into the newly opened-up regions in the North and East, into the Carpathian basin, into Mesopotamia, Armenia and into Nabataea, the last having been transformed into a Roman province in 106 A.D. Economic prosperity greater than at any time since Alexander the Great lasted for almost two full generations, until the outbreak of the great plague during the reign of Marcus Aurelius. An especially significant share in the sudden rise in economic progress came to the Greek cities of western Asia Minor, chiefly Ephesus, Smyrna and Pergamum. The Bithynian communities of Nicomedeia, Nicaea and Prusa, extremely favourably situated for east-west trade, as well as the cities on the west Pontus, and finally the great commercial metropolises of ancient Syria

—Antioch, Laodiceia *ad mare*, Berytus, the caravan city of Palmyra, Nabataean Petra and many others—all these also prospered. The steadily increasing process of urbanisation beginning in the days of Trajan kept pace with developments, with the extension of the empire to the north and east, and took effect primarily in the hitherto largely unurbanised regions of Thrace, Moesia and central Anatolia, and partly also in Syria. As Alexander of Macedonia had once opened up vast new frontiers for Greek culture by his conquest of the Persian empire and by his city foundations, so the work of Trajan and Hadrian marks a significant advance in Hellenisation, the greatest since the days of Pompey.

The harnessing of the military and economic resources of the empire under Trajan was to a large extent implemented at the expense of the prosperity of the upper ten thousand. The propertied individuals from the districts and cities in question groaned under the construction of roads necessary for the movement of military forces, under the incessant burden of billetting troops, and under the food supply requisitioned for the army. Again and again the well-to-do citizens had to step into the breach on behalf of their native communities in order to advance the necessary money, or even to produce it from their own pockets, as inscriptions from Macedonia (Beroea), Bithynia, Lycia and Galatia demonstrate. That the imperial government, on the other hand, seriously attempted to improve the lot of these regions as much as possible is shown by the mission of the Younger Pliny to Bithynia, who here developed a highly beneficial programme completely in the spirit of Trajan (110-112 or 111-113 A.D.).[61] The spirit which permeated the work of this imperial legate is still vividly preserved for us today in the magnificent letters of the Younger Pliny to Maximus, the friend of the philosopher Epictetus, whom Trajan had despatched to the province of Achaea as *corrector ad ordinandum statum civitatum liberarum*[62] (Plin., *ep*. VIII 24). The letter is an illuminating document of ancient humanitarianism, filled with genuine and deep respect for the great and imperishable achievements of classical Greek culture.[63]

With Hadrian's accession (117 A.D.) the empire once more adopted a defensive policy. Hadrian ended the great Parthian War and suppressed the last resistance of the rebellious Jews in the eastern provinces. His all but uninterrupted journeys made it possible for him to gain a particularly close relationship to the provinces of the empire, but special love and devotion, however, were directed towards the Greeks. Hadrian was the first genuine philhellene on the throne of the Caesars, and at the same time also the greatest, in whose footsteps Gallienus followed in the third and Julianus in the fourth century. Under Hadrian the Greeks became not simply one but *the* educative force in the Roman Empire—a late but complete triumph of the Hellenes over their Roman victors.

The emperor's example was of decisive importance. For Athens the reign of Hadrian marked the beginning of a new flowering.[64] On three occasions the emperor sojourned within the walls of the city (124/5, 128/9, 131/2 A.D.). His first stay marks the beginning of a new era in Athens, beginning in 124 A.D. By developing the spacious Hadrianopolis in the south-east the emperor became the second founder of the city, a new Theseus. Imperial favour bestowed on no other city so many buildings as on Athens. Hadrian completed the Olympieum (on which the Seleucid Antiochus IV Epiphanes had last built), he built the temple of Hera, the Pantheon, the Stoa, with a library, a gymnasium, an aqueduct, a new Pompeium and, finally, the Panhellenium, a temple to Zeus Panhellenius.[65] In accordance with the design of Hadrian, Athens was once more to become the centre of all Hellenes. This idea in particular lay behind the founding of a league of all cities of the Greek tongue, under the aegis of Athens. The alliance, whose representatives met annually at Athens, was headed by an "Archon of the Panhellenes," who at the same time often held the office of Priest of Hadrian Panhellenius.[66] The *Panhellenia*, the quinquennial games, were to keep alive the panhellenic idea and to immortalise Hadrian's creation. Under Hadrian, and probably on his initiative, the Eleusian Mysteries became a panhellenic institution. All cities belonging to the panhellenic League paid tithes to Demeter and Core, so that a new economic foundation was established for the Eleusian cult.[67] As for the Greeks of Asia Minor, they too did not wish to be passed over. In inscriptions from Ephesus, Miletus and Teos, Hadrian bears the epithet "Panionius." By honouring the emperor in this manner the Ionian communities proclaimed that they still regarded themselves as a particularly illustrious group within the panhellenic community.[68]

For the Greeks of the entire world this union under Athenian hegemony was a great step forward towards Hellenic "cultural autonomy." For the first time since the Greeks had come under Roman rule the Hellenes attained the official recognition of the emperor, if only in the sphere of education and culture. Under the personal protection of Hadrian, they enjoyed a privileged position. The refusal to invest the *Panhellenion* with political rights demonstrates Hadrian's political farsightedness. The undesirable consequences of Nero's declaration of freedom were not yet forgotten. The great respect which the emperor had for Greek education is also shown by his holding firmly to the superiority of the Alexandrian *Mouseion* over all other similar institutions throughout the empire, even when in 135 A.D. he founded, on a Greek model, the *Athenaeum* in Rome. The centres of flourishing Hellenic culture in Asia Minor during the second century A.D. were the *Mouseia* of Ephesus and Smyrna.[69] Here eminent grammarians, orators and physicians carried out their educational activities with many students from the entire Greek world.

In urbanising the empire Hadrian energetically followed in the footsteps of his immediate predecessor. His most famous city foundation is the Greek city of Antinoöpolis in Egypt, built in 130 A.D. on the east bank of the Nile across from Hermopolis[70]—in memory of the emperor's favourite, Antinous, who had drowned in the Nile. The new Greek city received its laws from Naucratis and its Greek citizens from Ptolemaïs in Upper Egypt and from the Fayûm. Officially the citizens called themselves *Antinoeis Neoi Hellenes*. They enjoyed the privilege of marriage with the indigenous Egyptians, evidence that the mixing of the Hellenes with the natives of the country had already embraced broad sectors of the population. In Asia Minor, Hadrianutherae and Stratonicea Hadrianopolis, in addition to other cities, trace their foundations back to the emperor. In Thrace the old Adrianople still exists today (under the Turkish name Edirne).

After Trajan's severe wars Hadrian's reign brought a noticeable economic recovery for the entire empire, and foremost for the East, especially benefiting the broad masses who constituted the economically weaker element. The protection of the lower classes from encroachment by their superiors was the noblest axiom of the adoptive Principate, a principle reflected in the edicts of Hadrian as much as in contemporary literature. The *Euboikos* of the astute and widely travelled philosopher Dion of Prusa, an oration of the time of Trajan,[71] is one of the most valuable sources for internal conditions in Greece during the period, although the contours in it are at times drawn somewhat more sharply than the real situation. The depopulation of the country, resulting in a great deficiency in the labour force throughout the rural districts so that large tracts of arable land lay fallow, was due to the altered international situation, with the result that the diminutive country of Hellas had lost all significance. Anyone who wanted to make a success of things went abroad, to Rome or to the Orient, where the sword of Trajan opened up new horizons for commercial activity. That economic and social conditions in Greece were, notwithstanding, far from a serious crisis is shown by, *inter alia*, the delineation, unsurpassed of its kind, of the typical hunting family by the same Dion. It is a literary idyll which magnificently portrays the bright side of Hellenic life, the moderation, the diligence and the distinct spirit of family ties among the simple classes. At the same time that Dion was composing his orations there lived in tiny Boeotian Chaeroneia the highly cultivated Plutarch (46-123 A.D.). He moved within a narrow circle of friends but his life was the symbol of the power of the Hellenic mind, which bore witness to the great past without forgetting the claims of the present.

The principles of Hadrian's social policy found their application in his famous decrees on behalf of the Athenians: the prohibition of unrestricted export of oil and intermediate trade in fish, which was such an exceptionally important item in the diet of the great masses of the poor population.[72] The parcelling out of the large Attic estate belonging to the extraordinarily wealthy Hipparchus, who perished under Domitian, followed along identical lines. The same policy appears in similar measures taken by Hadrian in Egypt, Spain and elsewhere.[73]

The indisputable climax in Greek cultural life during the entire period of the Roman Empire is the era of the Antonines (138-180 A.D.). In Herodes Atticus[74] (his full name was Vibullius Hipparchus Tiberius Claudius Atticus Herodes) of Athens (101-177 A.D.) and in his great pupil Aelius Aristides (117-189 A.D.),[75] a native of Hadrianutherae in Mysia, Greek rhetoric produced two names of international fame. The pompous orations of the Neosophist school combine the pride of the great Hellenic past with an artistically masterful technique picked up from Isocrates and Demosthenes, and a formal proficiency acquired by hard work, which carried the educated of the day to heights of unrestrained enthusiasm. Although the number of those educated to an understanding of the rhetorical works of art was certainly not all that great, it was on these and their applause and their approbation that everything depended. They included not only the aristocracy of the poleis in Hellas, in Asia Minor, Syria and Egypt, but also many Hellene enthusiasts among the Romans, with the emperors themselves heading the lists. Herodes Atticus was, in fact, the tutor of the princes Marcus and Lucius.

The Greeks also played the leading rôle in the field of historiography. The important Flavius Arrianus, a native of Bithynian Nicomedeia (95-175 A.D.), was active in the time of Hadrian and the Antonines. He was an outstanding expert in the field of administration and in warfare (under Hadrian he held the position of a *legatus pro praetore* of Cappadocia, and in that rôle warded off an assault by the Alans—an event which he described in his *Expedition Against the Alans*). And his *Anabasis of Alexander* is nothing less than the model of an outstanding critical work of history, despite all the enthusiasm for the king (v.s.p. 514). The lively interest in the great past of the Greek motherland is revealed in the *Tour of Hellas* from the pen of Pausanias, written in approximately 150 A.D. Far less profound than Arrian's history of Alexander is the History of Rome by the Greek Appian of Alexandria, which appeared about 160 A.D. The Parthian War of Marcus Aurelius and of Lucius Verus produced a large number of contemporary historical works, but these, with their not very happy mixture of archaisms and rhetoric, elicited the ridicule of Lucian of Samosata.[76]

The promotion of Greek culture by the supreme authority in the second century A.D. was thankfully acknowledged by the Greeks. After the throne was occupied by a distinct philhellene, in the person of Hadrian, and by Marcus Aurelius, pupil of Epictetus and a philosopher, the opposition of long standing by the philosophers to the rule of the emperors was muted. The image of the imperial tyrant began to change into that of the guide and leader of the state, as the oration in praise of Rome by Aelius Aristides from 144 A.D. shows. We are indebted to Michael Rostovtzeff for pointing out that this oration of the celebrated Greek from Asia Minor is an outstanding historical source for conditions in the Roman Empire.[77] In this oration the Empire appears as a federation of city-states. Aristides thankfully refers to the great achievements of the Romans, who welded the entire civilised world together. The world has, as it were, become a single "city-state." It is being governed by the best elements, namely by the Romans and the Greek aristocracy. Thanks to the keen edge of its sword, however, the rule of Rome secured for the world its most priceless possession—peace—upon which rests the prosperity of the empire, and above all the great flowering of the Hellenic communities.

The era of the adoptive emperors, foremost the Antonine period, furnishes infinite evidence of private beneficence, to which an unlimited

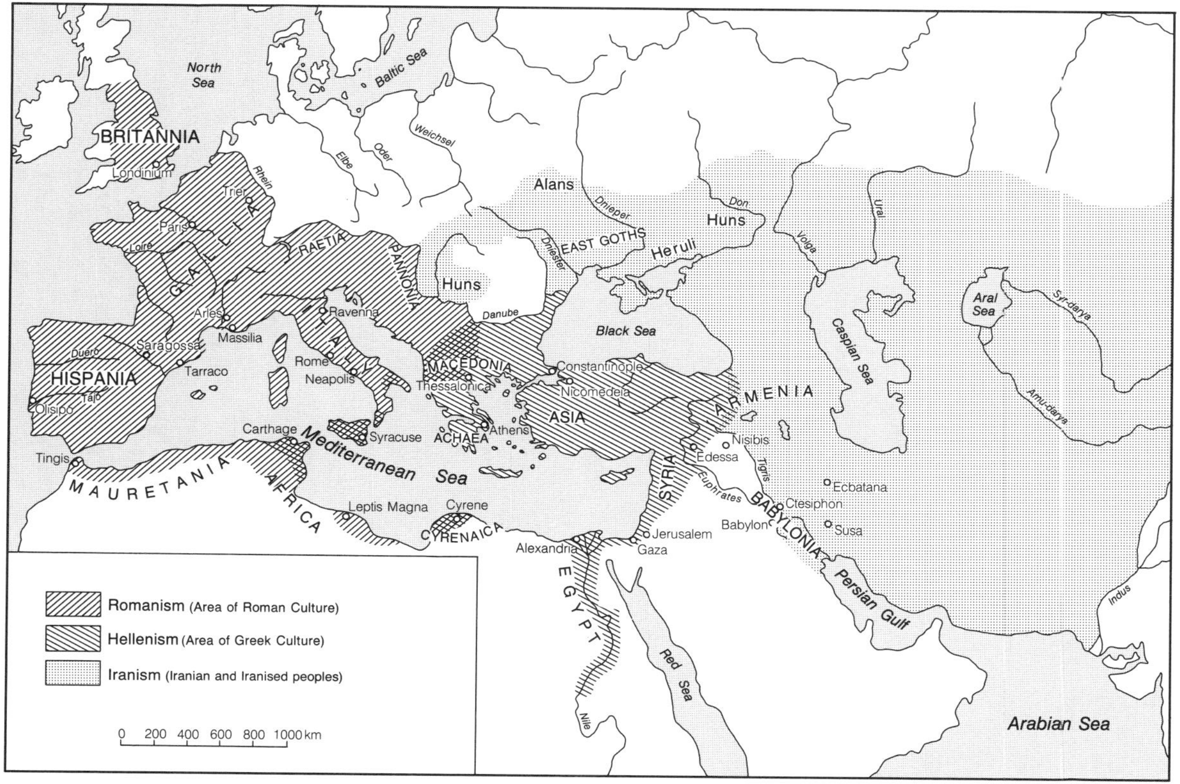

MAP XII Romanism, Hellenism and Iranism c. 400 A.D.

number of honorary inscriptions from the entire Greek world bear witness.[78] At no other time was the Greek aristocracy so conscious of its responsibility to the general public, a duty which sprang from their wealth. The emperors were themselves in the lead, providing the best examples. Thus Antoninus Pius bestowed his help on the Rhodians when, after the earthquake of 155 A.D., they began the work of reconstruction.[79] At the head of the private benefactors there stands the famous orator Herodes Atticus, who used his carefully preserved fortune with positively royal munificence. The panhellenic outlook of Herodes is characteristic of the spirit of the times. In addition to Athens, where he erected the Stadium named after him, and the Odeon, his foundations are also to be found in Alexandria, in the Troad, in Corinth, Delphi and in Olympia.[80] For the rest, almost every Greek city had its benefactor. In Prusa the grandfather of Dion Chrysostom had in fact actually brought himself to ruin in the first century A.D. by extravagant expenditures for the general public. The munificence of the Vedii, the Sophist Flavius Damianus[81] and C. Vibius Salutaris, adorned Ephesus with magnificent buildings, and the tiny Lycian nest of Rhodiapolis possessed the extremely wealthy Opramoas.[82]

Where there is much brightness, there is also much darkness. All the outward splendour with which the leading Greek cities surrounded themselves in the second century A.D. could not conceal the fact that the inner tensions within their walls had become greater than ever before.[83] It was the unresolved social question which menacingly raised its head. The rift cut right through the middle of the population of the Greek poleis. A large number of poor and poverty-stricken on the one side confronted a small number of propertied individuals on the other. The former had no share in the lofty flights of the Greek mind. For them the magnificent buildings meant no alleviation from the toils of every day life. What the masses longed for was bread and games. Among these circles concern for the common weal had completely vanished; life had become a question of bread and the belly. Every crop failure and every shortage and increase in the price of grain inevitably led to riots, in which the multitudes frequently attacked the wealthy. The title "Nourisher of the City" had become one of the most important honorary municipal titles.[84]

It was actually disastrous for the development of the cities in the Empire, above all in the Greek East, that an aggravation of the social tensions was connected with an increase in the system of *leitourgiai*—public services which in the course of the second century A.D. had, beginning in Egypt, embarked on a devastatingly triumphal march through the entire empire, especially through those regions with Greek urban culture.[85] The idea that the rich were obliged to render special services to the general public according to their wealth had of course always belonged to the principles of the Greek city-state. What was found extremely oppressive during the imperial era was not the system of *leitourgiai* in the poleis, but much more the general compulsory services such as the supplying of servants and animals in the travels of the emperors and the higher officials. Also burdensome were the collective and later the personal liability for getting up the taxes which the communities had to pay the empire, the obligation to take fallow land under coercive tenure, and various other duties. This compulsory system, from which there was no escape for the propertied citizens, beginning in the second century A.D., gradually ruined the upper classes of the Greeks in the East. What did it avail if one or another by imperial favour succeeded in evading these compulsory services, such as the orator Aelius Aristides?—the burdens which were imposed on the others were consequently all the greater. In the last instance it was the incompetence of the Roman government that promoted this development, a development which in the third century A.D. contributed decisively to the decline of the ancient social order and ancient civilization.

Even more disastrous than the gradual extension of the compulsory state throughout the whole of the Roman Empire was another cancerous sore in the Greek regions of the Empire—the lack of all political responsibility. It is of course true that the inhabitants of the Hellenistic settlements in Syria and in Egypt—with the noteworthy exception of Alexandria—had on the whole become accustomed to this state of affairs since the times of Alexander's successors. For the Greeks in Hellas and in western Asia Minor the situation was different. The Romans had replaced autonomy and freedom with the substitute of municipal self-government, and that a self-government which was subject to many interventions by the Roman administration, by the emperor, the governor and by individual deputies.[86] That the great emperor Trajan, the Dacian victor, regarded it as expedient to prohibit the city of Nicomedeia in Bithynia from establishing a fire brigade, out of fear that it might become the germ cell of a political club,[87] speaks volumes.

Thus the Greeks, a people with a great and unique political past, were forced to circumscribe their energies and ideas within the sphere of purely municipal affairs. They gradually lost faith in themselves and in their important political capabilities. Only the unusual flexibility of the Hellenic mind prevented the complete collapse of public life in the poleis.

It was into this world of increasing governmental encroachment, of political and religious vacuum that Christianity made its entry.[88] Christian doctrine, by appealing not to the righteous but to the sinner, to those who labour and are heavy laden, and above all by its belief in a personal God and by the message of salvation through Jesus Christ, set itself in antithesis to all other religions, even to the gods of the Greek polis. It is true that at the end of the second century Christianity was still far from triumphant, but many a martyr had demonstrated its inner stability of faith and organisation.[89] Christianity actually encountered bitter opposition in broad circles of the educated Greeks and Romans. The *True Doctrine*, by the Academic, Celsus, published about 180 A.D., is evidence of this. It accuses the Christians, a "new race of mankind without a fatherland," of complete political indifference, which must in fact have filled every genuine patriot with deep apprehension.[90] And yet the rise and spread of Christianity, whose congregations towards the end of the second century were to be found in the vast region from Palestine to Spain and North Africa, is explicable only in terms of the marriage of Christian ideas with the spirit of Hellenism. By employing the Greek language, the Christian mission succeeded in striking firm roots in the countries of the East, in so far as they were inhabited by Greeks or where Greek was at all events the language of the educated. This was particularly true also in the Jewish communities of the Hellenised *diaspora*, where Greek was also the language of worship. It was principally the west coast of Asia Minor, but also the cities of central Anatolia, the great centres of traffic in Hellas and Macedonia, and in addition the cities of Syria, Mesopotamia and Egypt, and above all Upper Egypt, that became the home of the new doctrine.

The kinship of Christian thought with the ideas of individual Hellenistic *philosophemata*, philosophies, especially the Stoic and Cynic idea of one society embracing the entire human race, greatly furthered the spread of Christianity in the countries of the Greek tongue and Greek culture. With the Christian missionaries, at first the apostle to the Gentiles, Paul of Tarsus, a Hellenised Jew, the Greek language migrated from the east into the west, to Rome, to Gaul and to North Africa, and here strengthened Hellenism in the face of Roman culture at a time when the latter was making vigorous strides in politics, government, warfare and law.[91] When towards the end of the second century Christianity for the first time emerged also in the literary sphere, it did so in Greek attire, and so it continued for a long time, until the great ecclesiastical prince, Ambrosius of Milan, at the end of the fourth century assisted national Roman reaction in Italy and the West in a complete triumph over Hellenism.

FROM MARCUS AURELIUS TO THE END OF THE THIRD CENTURY A.D.

Under the rule of Marcus Aurelius (161-180 A.D.) the Roman Empire entered a period of internal and external crisis extending over more than one hundred years. Barbarian invasions, internal upheavals, struggles of pretenders to the throne and economic distress are the outward characteristics of a period in which old Roman culture came to grief. Weighing particularly heavily upon the empire and its inhabitants were the constant wars in the East, at first against the Parthians and then (from 224 A.D.) against the Neo-Persians under the Sassanids, who linked themselves with the ancient world-embracing empire of the Achaemenids and no longer acknowledged the supremacy of the Romans. In the third century A.D., finally, the great cultural conflict between "Hellenism" and "Iranism" began, determining the cultural aspect of fading antiquity until the coming of the Arabs.

In this epoch, from about 235 A.D. to the accession of Diocletian (284 A.D.), Greek culture undoubtedly suffered the severest reverses and losses in its entire history. The recurrence of devastating plagues and famines considerably reduced the population, above all in Greece itself, but also in Asia Minor. The classes among the Hellenes who formed the standard-bearers of culture were brought to the brink of ruin, while in many places cultural life was extinguished by the terrors of barbarian affliction and the cares of everyday life. In Athens the *epheboi* lists end in 266/7 A.D.: confronted with the distress precipitated by the encircling Heruli, there were more important things to do than to immortalise the names of *epheboi* in stone. In general, nothing shows so forcibly the increasing crisis of living conditions as the extraordinarily marked decline in the number of inscriptional recordings throughout the Greek-speaking (but also the Latin) regions of the empire – a phenomenon which becomes clearly perceptible about the middle of the third century. By contrast the Greek papyri from the sands of the Egyptian desert speak the more audibly. In addition to the inscriptions from Asia Minor, they are the most important documents for the period of the radical change in economics and culture in the third century.

What the Roman state lost, the Christian Church gained. In the third century it far outstripped all its oriental kindred religions. By imitating the worldly model, in this period despite the severest persecutions it decisively furthered the formation and development of its organisation – progressively from east to west. While the Roman state was systematically strangling the initiative of all its inhabitants, the Church, in establishing its organisation, built upon the individual congregations and gradually embraced the entire empire, principally with the active help of the Greek-speaking population of the empire. The measure of devotion, of voluntary sacrificial courage and adaptability which the Greeks exhibited in this arduous mission, is difficult to overestimate. This positive achievement warrants the unrestricted admiration of posterity to the same degree as, for instance, the establishing of a Greek administration in the regions of the East by Alexander and the successors.[92]

The sufferings of the Greek territories in the East began under the reign of Marcus Aurelius. As the Parthian campaign of Lucius Verus was being immortalised at Ephesus in a monumental frieze modelled on the Gigantomachy on the Great Altar of Pergamum,[93] a plague from the East had already claimed many victims. All medical skill proved of no avail: characteristic is the flight of the eminent Greek physician Galenus from Rome in 166 A.D. For the first time barbarians, such as the Costobocians (probably a tribe related to the Dacians), in daring expeditions by sea plundered the coasts and hinterland of Hellas.[94] In Elateia the Hellenes opposed them in valiantly-fought battles. The temple of Eleusis, however, went up in flames, an event which found a vivid echo in the *Eleusinios* by the Sophist Aelius Aristides (170 A.D.). Bastrians for the first time threatened the west coast of Asia Minor.[95] These were the forerunners of the great barbarian invasions which began in the middle of the third century. The revolt of the Syrian legate Avidius Cassius, who, on the erroneous news of the death of Marcus Aurelius, attempted to seize the throne in 175 A.D., for the first time revealed the contours of a separate empire, admittedly only ephemeral, but encompassing the entire Hellenised East and also including Egypt.

Marcus Aurelius' unworthy son Commodus (180-192 A.D.) brought much the same state of affairs which had existed under Domitian. The eccentric, violent rule of the autocrat once more re-awakened the clandestine, but soon also the open, opposition of the educated classes, primarily the philosophers. Disturbances broke out in the empire, as, for instance, in Egypt and in Alexandria, disturbances perhaps connected with the persecution of the followers of Avidius Cassius. The *Acts of Pagan Martyrs* tell of the prosecutions of Greek citizens from Alexandria before the tribunal of the princeps.[96] Commodus was the first emperor to throw open the flood gates to the assailing tide of oriental deities from the East: the Magna Mater, Sarapis, Syrian Baal, Jupiter Dolichenus, Mithras and Cappadocian Ma-Bellona – all enjoyed the special favour of the bizarre emperor. In the exaggerated cult of Heracles, the ideal of the Cynic-Stoic philosophers, he no doubt carried the traditions of the enlightened monarchy of the Antonines further, but his identifying himself with Heracles was an affront to the educated circles. Commodus marks the beginning of the anti-aristocratic tendency in the policy of the Roman emperors, which alienated the noble classes, principally those of the East, the very classes which had hitherto been the staunchest pillars of Roman rule in the Orient and in Greece. In spite of everything, the Greek cities naturally continued to confer the customary honours on the emperors. Thus Commodus held the archonship in Athens,[97] and the empress Crispina the eponymous priesthood in Byzantium,[98] an honour which had once been conferred on Domitian.

The lot of the propertied classes, the cultural standard-bearers, and in particular of the well-to-do Greek citizens, was not easy under the reign of Septimius Severus (193-211 A.D.), who came from Leptis Magna. The emperor required money for his wars and his soldiers, and he took it wherever it was to be found. When rich Nicopolis ad Istrum presented him with 70,000 denarii, the emperor accepted it without ceremony.[99] In the Hellenistic East, the military and economic centre of gravity of the empire shifted increasingly in the direction of the Euphrates frontier. The ancient land between the Mediterranean and the Euphrates became the special concern of the emperor and his wife, the Syrian Julia Domna. A merciless chastisement, however, descended upon those cities which, under the force of circumstances, had joined Severus' opponent Pescennius Niger. Flowering Antioch was for a time degraded to a village of her rival Laodiceia, and division of the province of Syria into Coele Syria and Phoenice eliminated her superior position.

On European soil mighty Byzantium, whose capture cost the emperor a long siege, was likewise robbed of privileges (end of 195 A.D.). Other Greek cities escaped in trepidation; they now had nothing more pressing to do than boastfully emphasise in inscriptions their "kinship" with the imperial house.[100] For unknown reasons Athens also came to experience the disfavour of the emperor. She lost the final vestiges of self-government;[101] and from the era of Septimius Severus onwards imperial deputies dwelt almost regularly within the walls of Athens.[102] The fact that the emperor later altered his attitude towards Athens may be traced to the intercession of the Sophist Antipater of Hierapolis (Syria), who enjoyed the emperor's greatest respect and for a time held the office of

Chief of the Greek Chancellery. The cultured empress, Julia Domna, patroness of the most famous of the *Philostratoi*, was honoured in Athens by being included in the cult of Athena Polias.[103]

The development of the municipal system of *leitourgia* into a compulsory institution based on personal liability, resulted, together with the other adversities of the time, in a violent social revolution. This change came about, it would seem, in the time of Septimius Severus and his first successors.[104] This disastrous development, which at the same time decisively affected the life of the private individual, marks the end of the Hellenic city-state based on the principle of voluntary achievement. The curve of private foundations, which drops suddenly in the third century A.D., shows how acutely the Greek well-to-do classes became affected by this circumstance. Documents from the Egyptian countryside from the middle and end of this calamitous century attest the positively desperate attempts by the propertied Hellenic citizenry to extricate themselves from the strangling noose of innumerable personal services: renunciation of property, flight and open opposition were the order of the day, and it was customary to put to the oracle the pertinent question whether or not one would be reduced to beggary by compulsory acceptance of municipal offices.[105] In his effort to expand the circle of those capable of *leitourgiai* Septimius Severus in individual instances allowed the inhabitants of "attributed" land to be enlisted in the services of the poleis. The increasing municipalisation of the Egyptian metropoleis, the nome suburbs, served the same purpose. The ever increasing inflation since the days of Marcus Aurelius further compounded economic problems.

Under the son and successor of Septimius Severus, M. Aurelius Antoninus (Caracalla) (211-217 A.D.), the situation became even worse. The emperor constantly found himself short of money. The granting of Roman citizenship to all inhabitants of the Empire, with the sole exception of the *dediticii* (a group not as yet clearly defined), has to be seen primarily from a fiscal standpoint: it was to provide the emperor with enormous revenues, for instance, from death duty. As a matter of fact the *Constitutio Antoniniana*, as the grant is called, marked the beginning of a great levelling process, in the course of which the lower classes in the provinces gained considerably more than did the propertied citizens in the urban centres of the Empire. The latter, such as the Greek aristocracy of the East, in many instances already had Roman citizenship.[106] The disturbances which broke out in Alexandria in 215 A.D. and which were put down with inhuman severity by Caracalla revealed the real mood of the Greek population throughout the Empire. As one time under Ptolemy VIII, so on this occasion too the leading figures among the Greek citizenry bore the brunt, in particular the Ephebes.[107] The emperor withdrew the pay of the scholars in the *Mouseion* and thereby completely stifled scholarly activity in the Alexandrian *Academy*.[108]

Despite the hostility towards education in some circles, the vitality of the Hellenic mind had by no means come to an end in the third century. Characteristic of this period, peripheral areas, above all Syria, move into the foreground, especially in the Greek schools, as shown by the finds of numerous literary papyri from this period.[109] The work of the Sophist Philostratus on Gymnastics is, in addition to documentary inscriptions,[110] proof that the old ideals of Greek education and the Greek way of life still continued to find a lively response among broad sectors of the population.

Under the sabre rule of the Thracian barbarian Maximinus (225-238 A.D.) the plight of the cities in East and West reached its peak. Since the emperor had, by means of large donatives, to do everything possible to keep up morale in the army, upon which his very rule depended, there was no longer any end to his confiscations. Nor did the emperor stop at the property of the wealthy but even seized municipal funds. Neither the theatre monies nor public endowments, neither votive offerings nor the statues of the gods were safe from the grasp of his agents.[111] What was flushed out in the form of precious metals found its way into the melting furnaces. It has been rightly said[112] that the wealth which had been amassed over centuries by the propertied classes was destroyed at a stroke. There can be no doubt about it: the ruthless policy of the emperor and his like-minded followers dealt a terrible blow to the solidarity of the upper classes. A wide-meshed spy network, organised and promoted by the state, went hand in hand with the extortions.[113] Whoever valued his life and his freedom kept quiet about the injustice everywhere throughout the land. The general state of insecurity had disruptive effects on business life. The empire could no longer pay for the expensive imports of luxury goods, and in consequence trade between Egypt and India, which had undergone vigorous development in the first two centuries of the empire, came to a standstill.[114] In many Hellenistic cities, such as outlying Panticapaeum on the Cimmerian Bosporus (Kertch), there were clear signs of increasing impoverishment.[115]

The coins provide an essential corrective to the gloomy and depressing picture arising out of the inscriptions and papyri.[116] They show that the Hellenisation process in Asia Minor did not come to a standstill even in the third century – in spite of all the contemporary difficulties. Then for the first time districts such as east Pontus, Isauria and the highlands of Lycaonia were affected by it. The fact that coin strikings by Ephesus, Tarsus and Nicaea (in Bithynia) show a great increase in the third century is explicable on economic grounds. The great economic flowering of the Antonine period appears in many cases not to have come to proper fruition until the following century. In addition, the debasement of the imperial silver currency resulted in a substantial revaluation of the urban copper strikings in Asia Minor. In fact, the municipal copper coins in part assumed the character of an imperial currency. The increase in the number of *homonoia* strikings of the Asia Minor communities in the second half of the third century is no less important. The strikings are proof that business life in Anatolia continued, despite distress and war, to maintain a strong momentum.

The invasions of the Goths into the Greek-inhabited districts of the Balkan peninsula and the north and west coasts of Anatolia began in the middle of the third century.[117] Although these plundering raids were at first restricted to the Greek outposts on the northern shores of the Black Sea and along the Lower Danube, after the serious defeat of the Romans and the death of the emperor Decius in the battle of Abrittus in the Dobrudja (251 A.D.) the situation changed fundamentally. From then on no place was safe from the daring incursions of the northern tribes. In 253 A.D. the ships of the Goths, the Burgundians, Carpi and Borani (the last probably a Sarmatian tribe) appeared for the first time in the waters of Asia Minor. Similar expeditions repeated themselves year after year. In 256 A.D. the flourishing communities of Bithynia, Nicomedeia, Nicaea and Prusa were particularly severely affected.[118] This was followed six years later by a great plundering incursion of the Goths into Ionia, Troas, Lydia and Phrygia.[119] In 267 A.D. hordes of plundering and scorching Heruli penetrated deep into the Peloponnesus, took Athens, and ravaged Corinth, Sparta and Argos. Herennius Dexippus went out against them with a small force of 2000 Athenians – that was all the city could throw into the field – and defeated one of their armies.[120] It was no wonder that in these turbulent times the cities of the empire, and especially of the East, protected themselves by strong walls, and that some in fact became actual fortresses. In 263 A.D. construction on the city wall took place in Miletus. Nicaea worked on hers in the years 261-269 A.D. The coins of Thracian and Moesian Greek cities like Trajanopolis, Marcianopolis and Bizye are adorned with mighty gates which were built in these times.[121]

In the turbulent sixties of the third century a remarkable renaissance of Greek culture took place. It is marked by two names – Plotinus (204-270 A.D.) and the Emperor Gallienus (sole ruler from 260 to 268 A.D.).[122] Both men were profoundly influenced by the Eleusian Mysteries, which enjoyed a period of great flowering.[123] The emperor went so far as to have his image in the person of Demeter struck on coins with the legend Galliena Augusta.[124] The not entirely unheard of practise in the Hellenistic period of equating a ruler with a female deity was now, however, no longer understood. Under Gallienus many Greeks filled top posts in the imperial administration. The Empress Salonina, a Greek from Bithynia, took an avid part in the philhellenic efforts of the emperor. Under the patronage of the emperor the Neoplatonist Plotinus created in Rome a philosophical system, the last of expiring antiquity.[125] The influence of Neoplatonism extends far beyond the frontiers of antiquity, deep into the cultural history of the West. With Neoplatonism, which gathered up all that was still of worth in ancient thought and ordered it into an imposing system, Greek philosophy bade farewell to the world. The lofty plans of the Neoplatonic circle – Plotinus wanted to provide a centre for the community of his pupils in a ruined city of Campania – were destroyed by the sudden death of the Greek enthusiast Gallienus (268 A.D.). In the persecution of Aurelian the hosts of Plotinus' pupils were scattered to the four winds.

Many found a new homeland in Syria, under the patronage of Zenobia, for many Syrians were members of the Neoplatonic circle: the pupil and biographer of Plotinus, Porphyry of Tyre,[126] the famous philosopher Cassius Longinus,[127] the Sophist Callinicus who wrote, *inter alia*, a History of Alexandria which he dedicated to the new Cleopatra – Zenobia.[128] With their positive attitude towards the state[129] the Neoplatonists took up links with Plato. Cassius Longinus was political advisor to Zenobia. At the command of the emperor Aurelianus he was executed, on the grounds of being chiefly responsible for the revolt of the caravan city from Rome.

When Plotinus was gathering his pupils around him the universal sovereignty of the Greek mind in East and West had already been undermined. In Rome the learned Hippolytus († 236 A.D.) was the last Christian bishop to avail himself of Greek in his writings. In the East Bardesanes had already, about the turn of the century, elevated Syriac, the language of his homeland, to the rank of a literary medium. The moving of Syriac into the foreground is reflected in, *inter alia*, the fact that in about 260 A.D., in the capital of the bishopric of Persis, in Rev-Ardashir (north of the Persian Gulf), two churches were built, one of which was to serve the Greek-speaking congregation, the other the Christians who understood Syriac.[130] While the Synagogue built c. 245 A.D. in Dura-Europus (on the Middle Euphrates) shows in its decoration clear influence of Hellenism[131] (in an older Synagogue found under its foundations, on the other hand, the prohibition of pictorial representations was strictly observed), at the end of the century-long conflict between Hellenism and the Orient, within the context of Judaism, the Babylonian Talmud triumphed over the Hellenistic Septuagint – a consequence of world wide importance, for it determined the spiritual character of Jewry for all time.

With the raising of the Dalmatian Diocletian to the throne as emperor (284 A.D.), the fifty-year permanent revolution in the Roman Empire came to an end. Instead of attempting to reconstruct the Empire from below, on the base of the local communities, Diocletian created an imperial bureaucracy to supervise the cities of the Empire.[132] Diocletian's reorganisation is the result of a thousand-year development: the polis ceased to exist as an autonomous, self-governing entity. The idea that the Roman Empire was a league of innumerable cities of the Mediterranean world, an idea for which the learned of the Antonine period had shown great enthusiasm, was thereby carried to the grave. It is no accident that towards the end of the eventful third century the countless numbers of local mints in the Greek East, Asia Minor, Syria and even in Alexandria had to close down: the levelling process which embraced the whole empire no longer halted before the gates of the cities.

We come to the end of the Greek polis, which as no other political institution formed and influenced the political life and thinking of the West. But the Greeks, despite all catastrophes, survived the demise of the polis by centuries, just as did the Greek spirit, which found a new home in the bosom of the Christian Church.

PROSPECT: FROM CONSTANTINE TO JUSTINIAN

In the history of the Roman Empire and late Greek culture, the reign of Constantine I forms a break. The agreements reached at Milan in 313 A.D. between Constantine and Licinius to place Christianity on an equal footing with the other religions, and besides this to build Constantinople on the

Bosporus, mark the beginning of a new era. Constantine laid the foundations of the later Byzantine Empire, which was based on Roman political ideas, on the Greek people and on Greek culture. Once more, thanks to Constantine, the political and cultural primacy shifted from the West to the East.

The altered international situation resulted in a notable economic stimulus in the regions of the Propontis, especially in the cities of Bithynia. The central region of the later Byzantine Empire lies at the straits. The other Greek-speaking regions, Hellas (Achaea), Macedonia, as well as central and east Anatolia, gradually receded into the background during the fourth century. A very characteristic feature of developments in Syria and Egypt was the growing opposition on the part of the native peoples to Hellenistic world culture. When the language of the natives, Syriac and Coptic, became a literary medium through ecclesiastical literature, the sole dominion enjoyed by Greek was seriously shaken, indeed actually displaced. This was a circumstance of immense import. It laid the groundwork for the change in civilisation which the Arab conquest completed. The native vernaculars continued into the sixth century in certain regions of Asia Minor, as in Isauria, Lycaonia, Cappadocia, Phrygia and even in Bithynia. Only the intensive Christian mission, which adopted mass baptising of the heathen, let them gradually die out.[133]

The Hellenes and their culture were an affair of the cities—and large cities in particular—to an even greater degree during the post-Constantine epoch than they had been in the time of the Principate. Among these cities the ancient metropolises of Antioch[134] and Alexandria appeared as leaders, alongside newly founded Constantinople, which was adorned with many works of art plundered from the entire Greek world. The period of the free Hellenic polis had forever come to an end. Political responsibility on the part of citizens had become a thing of the past, and the economic misery and autocratic régime of the imperial officials had shackled the individualism of the cities and completely stifled the initiative of their inhabitants.

It was but little help that a ruler like Julian sought to reduce the burdens and bring about a revival of the urban communities. The problems lay in the imperial bureaucracy. It was extensively corrupt, and the moving complaints by the Syrian Libanius concerning the affliction of the burdened class and the corruptible and extortionary officials were only too well founded.[135] A decree by Valens from 370/1 A.D. concerning municipal land throws a glaring light on conditions in the one time so flourishing Ionian communities.[136] After the poleis had been deprived of the lands belonging to them,[137] these communities were faced with financial ruin, for the financial power of the cities had from time immemorial rested in large measure on the revenues obtained from leasing the urban land. Valens, following the model of Julian, attempted to rectify the damage to a certain degree by transferring at least part (⅓) of the revenues from the former municipal land to the Ionian cities—notably for restoring the city walls and other public buildings which had been destroyed by the earthquakes of 358 and 365 A.D.

The inner transformation of the Greeks in the fourth century A.D. was no less momentous. The appearance of a great many new names in the leading families shows that the old generations had in many cases died out or been reduced to poverty. With the ruin of the old Hellenic aristocracy the old Hellenic tradition also died. The attempt of Julian (361-363 A.D.) to revive the ancient gods of the Hellenes was an anachronism. Hellenic religion had long since been divested of its actual content. What Julian regarded as Hellenic, was a hotch potch of philosophical, above all Neoplatonic, idcas, oriental religion and contemporary widespread superstitions. There is no doubt about it. Greek religion died a natural death in the fourth century and did not survive the end of the Greek polis.

The break between the old and the new era becomes evident in all spheres of Hellenic life in the fourth century A.D. The *ephebeia*, which, prompted by the increasing prosperity of the Greek communities, had vigorously blossomed again in the second century AD, now died out. An Egyptian papyrus from 323 A.D. mentions a last contest of the *epheboi* in Oxyrhynchus. Already the sons of Constantine had in many instances made the practice of heathen cults liable to punishment. Theodosius I drew the line under this development when on 8 November 383 A.D. he outlawed the cults of the heathen gods together with their sacrifices throughout the entire empire. The last Olympian games were celebrated in 393 A.D. – long after the games had become the playground for professional athletes of the entire world. The participation of the Greeks in the panhellenic festival had also virtually vanished – primarily Egyptians, Lycians, Lydians and even Phoenicians appear in the victor lists, and the Olympic victor of the 291st Olympiad (385 A.D.), the last whom we know by name, was an Armenian prince, Varzdates.[137a]

The final flowering of Greek rhetoric in antiquity also took place in the fourth century. From the large number of important orators the Hellenised Syrian, Libanius of Antioch (314-c. 393 A.D.), and the Paphlagonian Themistius (c. 317-388 A.D.) far surpass all others. Their influence extends far beyond the literary sphere. Libanius[138] was on close friendly terms with Julian, and his vast correspondence spanned the entire Greek-speaking world. In him we once more find embodied, at a late date, the creative power of Hellenic education, which he proudly emphasised – even over against all that was Roman. Athens, Nicaea, Nicomedeia, Constantinople and Antioch constitute the stations of his career, poor in great adventures, but for that all the richer in inner values – a life which was bathed in radiance by the esteem of his contemporaries and pupils, such men as J. Chrysostom, Basil the Great, Gregory of Nazianzen and the historian Ammianus Marcellinus. How far his influence extends is demonstrated by the homelands of his pupils, Thrace, and western Asia Minor equally represented with Arabia, Egypt and Armenia. Hellenic education had become the salt of the whole earth.

In contrast to the educated Syrian, his contemporary, Themistius[139] was throughout his entire career immersed in the busy life of politics at the court of Constantinople. He succeeded in winning the favour of all the emperors from Constantius II to Theodosius I, and the latter even entrusted him with the education of the prince, Arcadius. The orations of Themistius are not only of literary but also of great political significance. His speech, for instance, *De clementia*, delivered in 350 A.D. in Ancyra before the emperor Constantius II, and the oration congratulating the same emperor (*Or.* 4), reflect the image of the ancient ruler. They have, of course, many conventional features taken from literature of earlier periods, but also show very characteristically new expressions, which only recent scholars have correctly evaluated.[140] Moreover both individuals, Libanius and Themistius, regarded themselves as philosophers. In particular Themistius, who appeared as an interpreter of Aristotle's writings, attempted to use philosophical norms as guiding principles in political life. His position as city prefect of Constantinople (383-384 A.D.) presented him with the opportunity for this. He was not denied the admiration of his contemporaries. Gregory of Nazianzen calls him the "king of rhetoric,"[141] and the Delphic Oracle, before becoming silent for ever, acknowledged him as the wisest of all Greeks, an honour which it had at one time bestowed upon Socrates. Both orators were adherents of the old religion, and in this respect their gaze was also directed backwards. How deeply "Hellenism," namely Greek education, was anchored in Asia Minor Christianity may be seen in the famous speech of the Cappadocian Basil the Great (330-379 A.D.), his *Admonition to youth*, showing how it was possible to profit from Greek (that is, heathen) literature.[142] This is a work saturated with a genuinely humanistic spirit, which assumed permanent importance for appraising the moral strength of the Hellenes.

In the fourth century A.D. a profound transformation of the Greek spirit and the Greek personality began to gain momentum. A new period in world history was dawning. In those days when the Church was gaining more and more ground Hellenic poets became theologians, men in public life became bishops and patriarchs, and philosophers became monks. Whoever wanted to make a success of things had now to enter upon an ecclesiastical career. Honour, fame and power, which the imperial bureaucratic state could now confer on only a select few (on the Greek urban communities not at all), in this era beckoned everyone whose talents qualified him for the higher spiritual career. Besides the great political decisions, it was the ecumenical Councils of Nicaea (325 A.D.), Serdica (342? A.D.), Constantinople (381 A.D.), Ephesus (431 A.D.) and Chalcedon (451 A.D.) that pointed the way for developments in the Greek East. At these councils the issues were not only a struggle for the true faith but also a struggle for power. From the very outset the designs of ambitious Church leaders, especially claims for the primacy by the Eastern metropolises of Alexandria and Antioch, were intimately bound up with questions of doctrine. The contest for supreme power, over which one had once fought for political aims, now shifted to the sphere of faith and Church dogma. Men like the great Alexandrian bishop Athanasius († 373 A.D.) and the patriarch Cyrillus († 444 A.D.) personify the new type of disputatious Greek theologian. Their activity was of world-wide significance. Cyrillus of Alexandria, by succeeding at the Council of Ephesus (431

A.D.) in securing the condemnation of the Syrian Nestorius, the dyophysite patriarch of Constantinople, rose to uncrowned ruler over the souls of the entire Hellenic East, if only for a short time. The opposition between dyophysite Constantinople and monophysite-oriented Egypt and Syria was of the greatest political importance. It severed the eastern regions from the sphere of ancient culture and helped the national separatism of the native inhabitants in the ancient cultural lands to ultimate breakthrough.

The growing force of national awareness, promoted primarily by monasticism in Eastern countries, entailed severe reverses for the Hellenes, especially for Greek education. As early as the fourth century A.D. the monks frequently led the Alexandrian population in hostile riots against the scholars of the *Mouseion*. In 391 A.D. the fanatic multitudes destroyed the *Sarapeum* and the cult image of Sarapis.[143] Still, the *Mouseion* and the *Academy* connected with it, stood until the fifth century. Works of Greek literature were still read in Egyptian country towns in the time of Justinian. Papyrus finds from Aphrodito in the Thebaïd introduce us to the educated Egyptian Dioscorus (end of the sixth century), who not only knew how to compose moderately good Greek poetry but was also astonishingly well read in rare branches of Greek literature. His readings included the *Anacreontea* and Nonnus, as well as Menander and even Eupolis.[144] Dioscorus is admittedly an exception, for since the beginning of the sixth century the sun was setting on Greek culture in the countryside. Even bishops no longer mastered the language of the educated, and the defective Greek in which liturgical texts, hymns, prayers and incantations are written makes it doubtful whether the writers at all still understood what they were writing. Whatever was still viable in Greek science in Alexandria, the Arabs took over after their conquest of Egypt (639 A.D.) and transferred to Damascus and Baghdad. From here the Greek legacy reached the West via Spain.[145] A whole host of Greek administrative terms in Arab Egypt[146] leaves no doubt that the Arabs were also docile pupils of the Greeks in the sphere of administration.

At the beginning of the seventh century the sun also set on Greek cultural life in Syria. Here the Greek-inhabited cities had always been nothing more than oases in a country whose population was predominantly composed of Orientals. By the third century Arabic tribes had infiltrated into the country from abroad. Serious military exigencies in the Justinian period, to which the cities of Antioch and Beroea (Aleppo) fell victim, and the maladministration of imperial officials, had abused the country to such a degree that the Arabs were actually welcomed as liberators in 636 A.D.

In Greece the Justinian era forms the decisive break. In 529 A.D. Justinian prohibited instruction under heathen teachers, deprived the professors of the old religion of their income, and confiscated the endowed wealth belonging to the University of Athens. With this gesture he drew the line under the history of education for an entire millennium. The first great Slavic invasions into Hellas occur in the Justinian period. As erroneous as it would be to speak of a rapid, extensive "Slavonisation" of Greece, still the addition of a new ethnic element, which had never entered into full participation in old Hellenic culture, was of great significance.

Constantinople, the mighty fortress on the Bosporus, continued to be the standard-bearer of the continuity in Hellenic education. Her university,[147] the *Capitolium*, continued the tradition of the learned *Academy* in Alexandria and the University of Athens. From the lecture rooms of the University, however, Hellenism migrated to the studies of the great philologists, namely the patriarchs Photius, Arethas, the emperor Constantius Porphyrogennetus and the archbishop Eustathius. It is principally due to their diligence and their fervour that at least a part of Greek literature was rescued and preserved for the Western world. Byzantium collected, reformed and further developed whatever was still viable in Hellenic culture. The idea of Greek education was kept alive in the history of the Byzantine Empire, and with it the great example of the Hellenic past.

Sources and Notes

INTRODUCTION
MODERN RESEARCH IN THE FIELD OF GREEK HISTORY

Critical scholarship in the realm of Greek antiquity in our day looks back on a history of only a few generations: it begins in the nineteenth century. Its origin is inseparably connected with the work of Barthold Georg Niebuhr (1776-1831), the founder of modern critical historiography.

Knowledge of Hellenic history and civilisation in the West, however, is much older; it is as old as our knowledge of the ancient authors. From the learned men of the Roman empire the line can be traced to Byzantium, and from there down into the West. With the initial printing of most Greek historical texts in the Renaissance, the West at the same time became interested in the history and antiquities of the Hellenic people.[1] In the second half of the sixteenth century the first major studies in history and culture began to appear.

The characteristic feature of these studies is the compilation and exhaustive amassing of material on history and constitutions. This applies not only to the work of the learned Carolus Sigonius of Modena titled *De republica Atheniensium*, which appeared in 1564—the first modern Attic history, written 325 years before the discovery of Aristotle's *Constitution of Athens*; it applies equally to the studies of the Dutchman Joannes Meursius (1579-1639) and the Frisian Ubbo Emmius, the first Rector of the University of Groningen (1547-1625). While Meursius published monographs on Attic institutions,[2] Emmius wrote on Greek constitutions,[3] and thereby became the founder of research into the subject of Greek jurisprudence. Much more important than these Baroque collections of material is the feat of the Englishman Richard Bentley (1622-1742), who brilliantly proved that the letters of Phalaris, of Themistocles and the Socratics are spurious:[4] This is the first exploit of an eminently critical mind, based on a comprehensive knowledge of Greek antiquity, an achievement which had the effect of a purgative shower.

A new epoch in sçholarship, however, did not begin with Bentley, but with Johann Joachim Winckelmann (1717-68); his *Geschichte der Kunst im Alternum* (1764) exerted the most enduring influence on Lessing. Together with Herder's *Ideen zur Philosophie der Geschichte der Menschheit* (1784-91), it inaugurated a new epoch in the scholarship of antiquity. By showing how the flowering of Greek art issued from the congenial conditions of Greek national life, and by differentiating between the various chronological styles which developed from each other (Rudolf Pfeiffer), Winckelmann, the founder of the study of ancient art, also laid the foundations for a historical consideration of the Greeks as such. In this, Winckelmann was following what Scaliger, the great French scholar, had perceived in connection with the age of poetry. It is in other respects a particular coincidence that the stimulus towards a new approach to the Greeks came not from philology but from art, philosophy and poetry. Thus ideas became disseminated among the widest circles, and what had at one time remained buried in the folios of scholars now became known at large. Although the idealising picture of Greece found in German classicism may indeed often contradict the historical facts, it nevertheless ultimately prepared the ground for a new, personal mode of viewing the Greeks and gave Western culture imperishable values, evidence for the marriage of the Greek with the German spirit.[5] A particularly great cultural mission was fulfilled among the German people by the venerable Johann Heinrich Voss' translation of the *Odyssey*, which appeared for the first time in 1781. Along with the *Prolegomena ad Homerum sive de operum Homericorum prisca et genuina forma* (1795) by Friedrich August Wolf, it is, in terms of its enduring influence, perhaps the most important late-eighteenth century work on one aspect of classical antiquity. It is an injustice when certain modern scholars attempt to belittle the merits of Wolf, one time Professor at the University of Halle, in favour of his predecessors, chiefly Abbé d'Aubignac, from the time of Louis XIV. Posterity is not able to deny him the credit for having grasped and formulated the Homeric question in its entire ramifications.

It is the spirit of the founder of modern critical, historical research, Barthold Georg Niebuhr (1776-1831), that also breathed new life into scholarly investigation of the Greeks, regarding them as an historical phenomenon. The young August Böckh (1785-1867) dedicated his *Staatshaushaltung der Athener* (1817) to the "brilliant and eminent authority on antiquity, Barthold Georg Niebuhr."[6] This was the first attempt to investigate the real foundations of the Athenian state by using the epigraphical material—a healthy reaction to the idealising glorification of everything Greek by Classicism. Ulrich von Wilamowitz rightly credited Böckh with success in solving the difficult problem of "comprehending life as it reveals itself in the sum of its separate manifestations, of describing a machine in operation—a machine whose construction he did not understand and which his description was first to disclose." Ten years later, after the Preussische Akademie der Wissenschaften had, on the initiative of B. G. Niebuhr, decided to create a Thesaurus of all ancient inscriptions, there appeared in 1825 the first fasicle of Volume I of the *Corpus Inscriptionum Graecarum*, the whole of Volume I in 1828, but with Volume II not following until 1843. Böckh was responsible for the editing of this epigraphical work.[7] Despite the imperfections of the *Corpus Inscriptionum Graecarum*,[8] the great forward step which it made must not be overlooked. Not until the large number of inscriptions from the entire Greek world had thus been made available was it possible, gradually, to overcome the one-sided study of the Greeks based exclusively on literary sources, and to replace an idealising picture of the Hellenes by a genuinely historical view. Much less known, and yet of very great importance, were Böckh's researches in the field of ancient metrology. K. J. Neumann called his *Metrologische Untersuchungen über Gewichte, Münzfüsse und Masse des Altertums in ihrem Zusammenhange* (1838) a fundamental and pioneering work. Böckh was also the first to succeed in elucidating the threads which linked Greece with the Orient, and this in a field which more than any other calls for precise research. Thus he was also the first to free Greek civilisation from the isolation into which idealising scholarship had sought to force it, an approach that had in no way done justice to the Hellenic character, marked as it was by its openness to the world.

Karl Otfried Müller (1797-1840), a pupil of August Böckh and who during his lifetime regarded himself as a philologist, aspired far beyond his master.[9] His *Aegineticorum liber*, which appeared in the same year as Böckh's *Staatshaushaltung der Athener* (1817), was the first in a series of historical monographs which he combined together under the title *Geschichte hellenischer Stämme und Städte* (*Teil I: Orchomenos und die Minyer, Breslau 1820; Teil II: Die Dorier*, 1824, in the second edition, prepared by F. W. Schneidewin, 2 vols., Breslau 1844). Niebuhr's critical spirit was also active in K. O. Müller, but the analyses of the latter remained, without exception, anchored in the realm of the subjective. Thus his explanation of the Dorian tribal character failed to coincide with the historical facts—despite Müller's firm belief that with his interpretation of cults and customs, which he often erroneously regarded as peculiarly Dorian, he had created a sound basis for his new ideas. As a reaction to the uncritical glorification of Attic democracy, especially in English works of history (*v. infra*), it is scarcely to be denied that the "Philolaconianism" of the highly-gifted Göttingen Professor is in a certain measure justified. It is therefore no accident that K. O. Müller's predilection for "Dorianism'—or what he considered it to be—has found enthusiastic emulation in our day.

K. O. Müller's early death (1840) stopped him from penning a Greek history. Thus the works of English scholars shaped and decisively moulded the historical picture of the Greeks until well into the nineteenth century. There were the party-bound work of the Scotsman and royal historiographer John Gillies (*History of Ancient Greece, Its Colonies and Conquests*, 2 vols [1786] who wrote as a Whig, and its counterpart, the *History of Greece* by William Mitford (London 1784-1810), a Tory adherent. In addition to these there is the later, and scholarly much superior, *History of Greece* by Cannop Thirlwall (8 vols., London [1835-38]), and finally the *History of Greece* by George Grote (London 1846-56) in twelve volumes. Thirlwall, the friend of Grote in his youth, had made no secret of his sympathies with Attic democracy, and Grote's Greek history is "in places more a passionate defence of the Athenian *demos* than an impartial work of history."[10] None the less Grote's History, greatly admired even outside England, marked a very important advance in historiography. As a dispassionate critic, a capacity in which Niebuhr had already highly esteemed him, the parliamentarian and "financial magnate of Lombard Street"[11] had formed an independent judgment on the value of ancient tradition. He regarded K. O. Müller's studies in mythology as valueless, although this did not prevent him from beginning his account of prehistoric Hellas with a discussion of Greek mythology that was too broadly based. In other respects he put forward some stimulating ideas of his own on the nature and origin of the Greek legendary world—for instance, his comparison of Pherecydes and Hellanicus with Saxo Grammaticus and Snorri Sturluson.

It is no accident that the sons of free England, schooled in a parliamentary tradition of many centuries, devoted themselves to the study of Greek political life with particular understanding. In the opposition between the Athenian democrats and oligarchs the English saw reflected the struggle between the Liberal Whigs and the Conservative Tories, and it was in consequence of the one-sided radical party view that the Athenian democrats were, in the eyes of the Liberal Grote, always right. But despite party-bound loyalties, in the works of Thirlwall and Grote, and in the latter to an incomparably greater degree than in the former, the history of ancient Greece—of increasing interest to the educated classes throughout the world because of the struggle for freedom being waged by the modern Greeks—for the first time attained a historico-political reality, as the older Roman history had previously done through the researches of the statesman and historian B. G. Niebuhr. The "picture of a Hellas of handsome and noble men and youths pursuing the cult of beauty and entertaining visions of the beautiful life" and "romantic paintings of solid Dorian wisdom and virtue"—these were now displaced by the "cruel reality of the most passionate political struggle" (U. v. Wilamowitz).

Friedrich Kortüm's *Geschichte Griechenlands von der Urzeit bis zum Untergang des Achäischen Bundes* (3 vols., Heidelberg [1854]) with full justification took issue with a one-sided glorification of Athenian democracy, even though its bizarre presentation denied it a more profound influence. On the other hand, the *Griechische Geschichte* of Ernst Curtius (3 vols., Berlin, Weidmann, 1857-67, ^{6}1887-89) was accepted with nothing less than enthusiasm in the widest circles of the educated classes. Its success is to be compared with no less a work than the *Römische Geschichte* of Theodor Mommsen, the well known work which appeared in the same series. Of the critical spirit blowing from across the Channel Curtius had scarcely felt a breath. An almost rapturous veneration emanates from the pages of the work, and over the brilliant sentences there hovers the melancholy mood of the decline of old Hellenic beauty and greatness, a mood which is accentuated even further by the fact that it gave expression to what this scholar, so sensitive to everything beautiful and noble, experienced while visiting the ruins of Greece itself.[12] Politics and economics were not Curtius' strong points, not surprisingly so, since his importance as a scholar lies in the field of historical geography; his actual masterpiece is his work on the Peloponnesus (2 vols., Gotha 1851-

52). Posterity owes to him the impetus to the excavations of the German Reich in Olympia (1875-81),[13] which inaugurated a new era in archaeological research.

Grote had brought his Greek History down to approximately 300 B.C., thus failing completely to take note of the discovery of Hellenism in the brilliant work of the young Pommeranian vicar's son Johann Gustav Droysen (1808-84), the first volume of which had appeared in 1833.[14] And yet Droysen's discovery marked a decisive turning point, though its full significance did not become completely evident until decades later. For the first time a young scholar attempted to define the universal importance of Alexander of Macedonia, and on the basis of a critical penetration of the period of the *Diadochoi* and the *Epigonoi* after Alexander, to form a bridge from Classical Greece to the *Imperium Romanum*. From now on the battle of Chaeroneia (338 B.C.) was no longer the end of Greek history, it was rather a new beginning: Alexander's conquest of Asia marked the beginning of a new era—of universal Hellenism, in which Greek culture, though in new forms, opened up the entire contemporary world.

The systematic excavations[15] beginning in the seventies of the last century brought a new picture of the ancient world, not least of the ancient Greeks. Although Grote had still drawn a sharp line between "legendary Greece" and "historical Greece" (he began the latter with the first Olympiad [776 B.C.]), and Ernst Curtius had bridged the early period of Greece by means of problematic reconstructions of events, the time had now come for establishing a new, comprehensive picture. Only a conscientious appraisal of the archaeological evidence could do this, with the aid of innumerable and, in large measure, still disconnected, minute stones of a mosaic. The pioneering excavations of the brilliant outsider Heinrich Schliemann (1822-90) in Troy, Mycenae, Tiryns and Orchomenus[16] by no means opened up the world of Homer, as the happy discoverer imagined. They did much more, lifting the veil from a hitherto completely unknown epoch in Greek history—the world of the second millennium B.C. Besides this the fabulous discoveries made in the Cretan excavations (the English under Sir Arthur Evans starting in 1900 at Cnossus, the Italians at Hagia Triada and Phaestus, the Americans, French and other countries), in turn also opened up completely new historical perspectives, whose scope and magnitude scholars up to that time could never have imagined.

The *Griechische Geschichte* of Adolf Holm (1830-1900), who taught at the Universities of Palermo and Naples for many years, remained as good as untouched by the emergent scholarly revolution beginning at the end of the last century. In the glorification of Attic democracy Holm himself even outdid an Ernst Curtius. Otherwise, however, Holm, who like Curtius was a son of the free imperial city of Lübeck, has earned the credit for having emphasised the significance of the Greek *polis* also in the post-Classical period. His work (*Griechische Geschichte*, 4 vols., Berlin 1886-94), which is unfortunately not free of moralising judgments, did not attain major influence – in complete contrast to his studies in Sicilian history and geography,[17] which even today may be cited to his honour alongside recent works.

It must be regarded as a particularly happy coincidence that in the eighties there was a scholar available in Eduard Meyer (1855-1930) of Hamburg, who, on the basis of his universal knowledge of antiquity, was able to absorb the results of archaeological researches which were coming in, to assess these critically, and to mould them together with the knowledge acquired from the literary and epigraphical sources into a new, comprehensive picture of the ancient world.[18] It is indeed true that there had already been scholars prior to this who had argued for the idea of a universal history of antiquity,[19] such as the Tübingen historian Alfred von Gutschmid (1831-87), who was far in advance of his time, and a man like Max Duncker (1811-86), whose particular field was admittedly modern history, and who had actually ventured on the grand concept of a *Geschichte des Altertums*, which in 9 volumes he brought down as far as Pericles.[20] But Duncker did not possess a knowledge of the Near Eastern languages, and so he was forced, as regards the history of the ancient Orient, to work from second-hand evidence. By way of contrast, Eduard Meyer not only had command of the necessary philological tools for the history of the ancient Orient, but also possessed an extraordinarily broad historical perspective and a penetratingly critical mind, which at no time ever contented itself with the *fable convenue*. Particularly stimulating in his *Geschichte des Altertums* (5 vols., Stuttgart 1884-1902) were the brilliant sections on the history of civilisation, which are probably surpassed only by Gibbon's *History of the Decline of the Roman Empire* (1776-88) and by Mommsen's *Römische Geschichte*. In Volumes II-V Meyer delineated Greek history within the framework of a broad history of the ancient world down to Philip II of Macedonia. The new archaeological finds, primarily those on Crete, forced him to begin the work afresh already only half a decade after Volume V had appeared. At the time of his death in 1930 he had in his revision proceeded as far as Tiglathpilesar III († 727 B.C.), in Vol. II, on the history of the Near East. The work remained a majestic torso.

Only now has it become possible for us to measure the full significance of the *Geschichte des Altertums* by Eduard Meyer. This work fully liberated the history of the Greeks from the unhistorical isolation of classicism, and thanks to Meyer, we are now in a position to appraise impartially the imperishable achievements of the most talented of all the peoples of the ancient world. It is not the size of the territory and the number of the population but the individual achievement of a people and its culturally leading class which determines the course of its history, and especially the destiny of mankind and the working of the human spirit. This has become evident in the example of the Greeks against the background of this general history of antiquity. Beloch was not so wrong when he maintained[21] that it lay within the nature of things that a history of antiquity could in essence be nothing other than a Greek history, and that everything else had, from the point of view of universal history, no other value but to elucidate the rise and fall of Greek culture.

Volume II of Meyer's *Geschichte des Altertums*, which was devoted to the beginnings of Greek civilisation, appeared in 1893. In the same year Karl Julius Beloch (1854-1929)[22] began the publication of his *Griechische Geschichte*. The third and final volume (published 1904) ended with the Peace of Naupactus (217 B.C.), that is to say, with the last peace concluded solely between Greeks before the intervention of the great power of the West—the Romans. Based on an admirable knowledge of the sources, with original interpretations, and with the most penetratingly critical mind, Beloch's *Griechische Geschichte* no doubt constitutes the most important scholarly achievement in this field to date. Besides this, it is an indispensable tool in research primarily since it is available in the greatly revised second edition in 4 volumes (1912-27),[23] each of which is broken down into a narrative and an investigative half volume. But where there is much light, there is also much darkness. Even Beloch's achievement had its limitations. In particular, his excessive confidence in his own hypotheses, not seldom in direct contradiction to all the evidence, and above all, his collectivistic historical interpretation, gave the critics considerable opportunities for attacking him. Even though his reaction to the hero worship of a J. G. Droysen, H. v. Treitschke and an U. v. Wilamowitz, among others, may be justified, in many instances Beloch went too far. He was, for instance, negative, indeed paradoxical, in his interpretation of Pericles and Alexander[24] and cut their lives into two parts in the third and fourth volume of the second edition of his work. Most vigorously attacked in his method is his extremely deterministic interpretation, which relates the actions of a person exclusively to the force of circumstances and thus banishes freedom of the will from the realm of history. It is fortunate that in the actual execution of the work Beloch did not remain faithful to the credo of his philosophy of history as laid down in the introduction to the first volume. Otherwise his work would have exhausted itself in the recording of "causalities." And the fact that Beloch regarded success in politics as the sole criterion could only bring further doubt.

In addition to Beloch and Eduard Meyer, among German works the broadly based *Griechische Geschichte* of Georg Busolt (Vol. I, Gotha 1885; II, 1888; Vols. I-III, ²1893-1904) may also be given honourable mention. This work, the product of untiring energy, is a completely indispensable source for the historian of today and tomorrow because it makes accessible all the literary and epigraphical sources available at the time. It is admittedly not a work of the highest rank, and beyond the conscientious discussion of the views of his predecessors, one all too often misses in Busolt a definite viewpoint of his own. Busolt's *Griechische Geschichte* ends with the year 404 B.C., without having reached the desired goal of Chaeroneia (338 B.C.). On the other hand, however, in his *Griechische Staatskunde* (2 vols., Munich 1920 and 1926; Volume II posthumously published by H. Swoboda), Busolt produced a further, actually indispensable tool for research. It is used even by those who have advanced beyond Busolt to an inclusive study of the Greek state, taking into account economic and social factors.

In the eighties of the last century Ulrich Wilcken (1862-1944) published his first studies in Papyrology. From then on, for almost 60 years, they kept pace with the ever increasing finds from the sands of the Egyptian desert.[25] Scholars from all civilised nations took part in bringing in the harvest of literary papyri and documents. Among the British were Sir Frederic Kenyon, who in 1891 produced the *editio princeps* of Aristotle's *Constitution of Athens*; the two 'Oxford Dioscouri' B. P. Grenfell and A. S. Hunt, and H. I. Bell. The French contributed P. Jouguet, J. Lesquier, P. Collart; the Italians gave us G. Vitelli and Medea Norsa; the Germans added W. Schubart, P. Viereck, F. Preisigke and F. Bilabel; the Belgians were M. Hombert and Claire Préaux. There were untold others. The majority of the new finds cast light on the administrative and economic history of Ptolemaic and Roman Egypt. Thanks not least to the papyrus finds, suspect Hellenism gradually moved into the centre of scholarly research, which for decades had remained as good as unnoticed, despite the brilliant work of the young J. G. Droysen. A number of works illustrate the strong interest in Hellenism since the close of the nineteenth century, and not only in Germany: Benedictus Niese's *Geschichte der griechischen und makedonischen Staaten seit der Schlacht bei Chaironeia* (3 vols., Gotha [1893-1903], which discusses the political history of Hellenism down to about 120 B.C. (a work which K. J. Neumann called a "Hellenistic Tillemont" on account of its reliability); Julius Kaerst's *Geschichte des hellenistischen Zeitalters* (2 vols., Leipzig-Berlin 1901-09, later published under the title *Geschichte des Hellenismus*—Vol. I^3 1927; Vol. II^2 1926), whose strength lies in the outstanding discussion of the cultural basis and leading ideas of Hellenism,[26] but also a work like *Hellenistische Dichtung in der Zeit des Kallimachos* (2 vols., Berlin 1924) by U. v. Wilamowitz; and Paul Wendland's *Hellenistisch-römische Kultur in ihren Beziehungen zu Judentum und Christentum* (second and third edition, Tübingen 1912). This interest was heightened even further by the recent excavations in Greece (Delphi, Delos, Athens, Epidaurus *et al.*), in Asia Minor (Pergamum, Priene, Magnesia on the Maeander, Sardis, Ephesus, Aphrodisias *et al.*), in Syria and Mesopotamia (Dura-Europus on the Middle Euphrates, Seleuceia on the Tigris, Uruk-Orchoë, Babylon), in Egypt (Philadelphia, Caranis, *et al.*), and in Cyrene. Moreover the progress made in the Greek epigraphical work of the Preussische Akademie der Wissenschaften, the *Inscriptiones Graecae* (since 1873),[27] furnished a vast amount of material, especially for the Hellenistic period, which in part still awaits historical evaluation. No one, however, has attained greater merit in the epigraphical work of the Berlin Academy than Ulrich von Wilamowitz-Moellendorff (1848-1931). Through his universal conception of classical philology and the development of it into a separate discipline of classical antiquities, von Wilamowitz was the first person who actually overcame classicism and paved the way for a universal, genuinely historical mode of viewing the Greeks: monuments of literary creativity and documents on stone and on papyri, state and society, religion and mythology, law and science—all this the tremendous extent of his indefatigably creative mind encompassed until into the ninth decade of his life. In the depth and breadth of his influence[28] the life-work of this great philologist can be compared only with that of Theodor Mommsen.

The *Griechische Kulturgeschichte* of the great Basle historian Jacob Burckhardt (1818-97) is far from being bound to any specific field of research. To do actual justice to this work seems all the more difficult, since the posthumous publication (4 vols., edited by Jacob Oeri, Berlin and Stuttgart 1898-1902) rests on outdated notes from Burckhardt's lectures, which were, moreover, drafted without knowledge of critical research and the results thereof. But the unusual scope and depth of a mind schooled in world history is imprinted on the work. The idea of the Greek *polis* as a coercive institution, a *città dolente*, to which all the creative energies of the Hellenic individual had to bow, is simply an ingenious conception which finds no counterpart in modern historiography. Although it does not accord with the historical facts, still, as a "fading picture of the *polis* concentrating all the gloomy features from a development over centuries into a uniform, pessimistic general portrait" (Robert von Pöhlmann), it should also have claimed the attention of professional historians and philologists, who, however, almost without exception passed by this work either with a shrug of the shoulders or with unconcealed antipathy.[29] It was incidentally Benjamin Constant who in his work *De la liberté des Anciens* (1819) had argued that the Greeks had sacrificed the freedom of the individual to the all powerful state, an idea which influenced not only Hegel but also Fustel de Coulanges and through him Burckhardt as well.

An attempt has been made from various angles in more recent German scholarship, since the end of the First World War, to advance towards a new interpretation of the ancient Greeks: "to free historical phenomena from distortions produced by modern thinking, in most cases unconsciously, but for that with all the more unshakeable self-confidence" (H. Berve). Knowledge for its own sake did not satisfy this generation: it wanted to make the spiritual content of antiquity its own and use it to construct a new view of life and a new ideal of the individual. The resultant conflict became evident in the dispute over the economic forms of antiquity which took place at the close of the last century between the Leipzig national economist Karl Bücher on the one hand and the historians Eduard Meyer and Julius Beloch on the other. The conflict revived again in the twenties and thirties of this century in the controversy between Johannes Hasebroek and his opponents (Erich Ziebarth and W. Schwahn, among others). This new reflection on the special conditions under which the history of the Greek people ran its course no doubt proved very useful for scholarly understanding, and it is precisely for this reason that the merits of a work like the *Griechische Geschichte* by Helmut

Berve (2 vols., in *Geschichte der führenden Völker*, IV and V, Freiburg i. Br. 1931 and 1933; ²1951 and 1952) are indisputable. This work, a penetrating, comprehensive interpretation, attempts above all to do justice to the ethnic character of the Greek tribes, in which "Dorianism," as embodied in Sparta, is delineated with particular sympathy. In accordance with the character of the series in which this work appeared, it does not provide a compilation of the sources, so that it comes into consideration more for a comprehensive view than for specific research. With his *Alexanderreich auf prosopographischer Grundlage* (2 vols., Munich 1926) and his *Tyrannis bei den Griechen* (2 vols., Munich 1967), Berve has provided scholars with two further, indispensable works.

The publication of *Fragmente der griechischen Historiker* by Felix Jacoby (1876-1959) must be regarded as one of the most important achievements in modern critical research; after more than 50 years of work it has now been almost completed.[30] This edition combines the advantages of an outstanding philological competence with a profound knowledge of history, to which the commentary above all bears witness at every point. We are indebted to Eduard Schwartz (1858-1940) for a great many researches, including very basic studies in Greek history, but primarily on the Greek historians. These are to be found in the first volumes of the *Realencyclopädie* of Pauly-Wissowa,[31] while a number of his articles are combined together in the second volume of his *Gesammelte Schriften* (Berlin 1956). We should not overlook, finally, the profound influence which has been exerted by the writings of Werner Jaeger, above all by his *Aristoteles* (1923),[32] and even more by his *Paideia* (3 vols., 1934-47).

From the great number of ancient historians in Germany who have distinguished themselves through their researches in Greek history the following may be cited: V. Ehrenberg, U. Kahrstedt (†1962), and Walter Otto (†1941). Of these scholars Kahrstedt carried out brilliant investigations in the realm of Greek constitutional law, even though these did not always have fortunate results, while Walter Otto was the undisputed master in Hellenistic history, above all in the Ptolemaic field.[33] The achievements of Victor Ehrenberg lie primarily in the history of culture and civilisation. From the large number of his works published in recent years we may cite here the sociological study, *The People of Aristophanes* (1943; ²1951); *Sophocles and Pericles* (1954; German 1956) and *Der Staat der Griechen* (2 vols., Zurich and Stuttgart 1965; in English *The Greek State*, 1959; ²1969; ³1972).[34] In addition to the historians there are the epigraphists: Friedrich Frhr. Hiller von Gaertringen (1864-1947), for many years the soul of the *Inscriptiones Graecae*, and Johannes Kirchner (1859-1940), to whom we are indebted not only for an Attic Prosopography but also for a model edition of the Attic inscriptions from the post-Euclidian period.

Since the end of the nineteenth century the contributions of English and French scholars have grown steadily. This is due chiefly to the influence of Grote, whose *History of Greece* must be regarded as the leading work until the publication of the histories by Eduard Meyer and

Julius Beloch. Moreover the book written by the Frenchman Fustel de Coulanges, *La cité antique* (Paris [1864]) is indeed one-sided, but nevertheless a highly original achievement.[35] Of great importance were the excavations by the École française d'Athènes at Delphi and on Delos, with their rich yields in monuments and inscriptions. Among French scholars it is primarily Maurice Holleaux (1861-1932) and Pierre Roussel (1881-1945) who have gained an extensive reputation in the field of Greek history. Scholars are especially indebted to the elegant pen of Holleaux for a series of articles and monographs on Hellenistic political history, investigations which are without exception historical "show-case pieces" of the highest quality.[36] From the older generation may here be cited E. Cavaignac and P. Cloche (1881-1961), and from the younger A. Aymard (1900-1964), G. Daux and R. Flacelière. Scholars are indebted to Louis Robert for innumerable and without exception brilliant investigations in the field of Greek epigraphy, which have also yielded results of particular value to the historian. Robert in addition has also achieved surprising new results through his excavations of the oracular sanctuary of Claros near Colophon, the final publication of which the scholarly world is looking forward to with great anticipation.[37] And, finally, in the *Histoire grecque* of Gustave Glotz,[38] which was published within the frame of the *Histoire générale*—of which he was editor—(Paris 1925 ff.),[39] French scholarship possesses a narrative work of the very highest standard. The sections on the history of civilisation, with their great attention to detail, deserve special recognition.

Characteristic of British scholarship is the monumental *Cambridge Ancient History* (12 vols. [1924-1939]), edited by J. B. Bury, S. A. Cook, F. E. Adcock and M. P. Charlesworth. Within the compass of this collective work Greek history receives its due rights. W. W. Tarn (1869-1957) was also among the collaborators, who, along with E. Bevan and the Irishman J. P. Mahaffy, worked primarily in the field of Hellenistic history. Since the beginning of this century Tarn has published a whole series of brilliant studies, of which special attention may here be drawn only to the monographs *Antigonos Gonatas* (1913), *Hellenistic Civilisation* (1927, [3]1952); *The Greeks in Bactria and India* (1938, [2]1951) and the important work *Alexander the Great* (2 vols., 1948).[40] Of great value are the historical commentaries on Thucydides (by A. W. Gomme) and on Polybius (by F. W. Walbank).[41] In general, research in Greek history has received a significant impetus in Great Britain during the last few decades. Alongside the established scholars (M. N. Tod, H. T. Wade-Gery, H. D. Westlake),[41a] the younger generation has now also moved into the foreground (D. M. Lewis, R. Sealey and many others). We are indebted to N. G. L. Hammond for a generally conservative Greek history of recent date.[42] In it the fifth century above all is treated in great detail.

In the United States of America too the study of Greek history, especially the Hellenistic period and, in addition to this, the economic history of the ancient world, has been ardently pursued since the end of the First World War—thanks not least to the initiative of the Russian scholar Michael I. Rostowzew (Rostovtzeff) (1870-1952),[43] who from 1920 onwards worked in Madison, and later at Yale University in New Haven. His great *Social and Economic History of the Hellenistic World* (3 vols., Oxford 1941) will determine the course of research for many years to come. The excavations of the Hellenistic settlement of Dura-Europus (on the Middle Euphrates) are an honourable page in the annals of American scholarship. They have provided new information primarily for the Parthian and Roman period. No less important in their results have been the excavations in the Athenian Agora, regular accounts of which are given in the journal *Hesperia* (1932 ff.). From the large number of contemporary American scholars who have gained distinction through their researches in the field of Greek history the names of only the following historians may here be cited: W. S. Ferguson († 1954),[44] T. Frank († 1938), J. A. O. Larsen, C. B. Welles († 1969) and the late W. L. Westermann. Under the direction of B. D. Meritt, American scholars have published a great number of epigraphical studies, primarily on Attic inscriptions, which include the great edition *The Athenian Tribute Lists*, I-IV (Princeton 1939-1953). In addition to Meritt valuable work has been done in the field of Greek epigraphy also by S. Dow, C. F. Edson, Jr., J. H. Oliver and A. E. Raubitschek. We are indebted to the British scholar A. D. Nock, who worked at Harvard University, for pioneering studies in the religion of the ancient world,[45] and to the Russian scholar E. Bickerman, who taught at Columbia University, for brilliant works in history and constitutional law.

In Italian research in the field of antiquities the initiative of the headstrong German Julius Beloch has been reproduced in a whole generation of reputable scholars. Beloch's oldest pupil, Gaetano De Sanctis (1870-1957), has—after his important *Storia dei Romani* (Turin 1907 ff.)—also presented us with a Greek history that begins with the historical period and goes down to the end of the Peloponnesian War (2 vols., Florence 1939),[46] and in particular affords a wide scope to the discussion of the history of civilisation. In addition to De Sanctis, scholars like E. Breccia, G. Cardinali and L. Pareti, among others, have also produced studies in Greek history—the two former, special investigations in the Hellenistic period.[47] In the present day S. Accame, S. Mazzarino, A. Momigliano and P. Treves have also done valuable work in the field of Greek history. Moreover the younger generation (among others, P. Meloni and F. Sartori) has successfully engaged in research. Of the Italian excavations, primarily the investigations on Crete, in Cyrene, on Rhodes and the epoch-making excavations of Paolo Orsi (1859-1935) in Sicily and southern Italy deserve special recognition.[48] In our own day the investigations in Sicily have been continued primarily under the direction of D. Adamesteanou, P. Griffo and P. Orlandini. Great and lasting credit goes to L. Bernabò Brea for shedding light on the early history of Sicily and the Lipari islands.[49]

With regard to other countries the Swedes indisputably take the lead, thanks not least to such a universal scholar as Martin P. Nilsson (1874-

1967), whose monumental *Geschichte der griechischen Religion* (in the *Handbuch der Altertumswissenschaft* series) is an unrivalled standard work (2 vols., 1941 and 1950; I, ^{3}1967, II, ^{2}1961). Nilsson's researches encompassed the entire range of classical antiquity, from the early period of Greece until late antiquity—with the centre of gravity in Greek history. Moreover the achievements of Swedish excavators on Greek sites deserve admiration, above all in Midea and Asine in the Argolid, but also on Cyprus and recently in Labranda (Caria) under the direction of A. W. Persson († 1951) and E. Gjerstad, among others.[50] The Austrians have also maintained their tradition in the field of archaeological and epigraphical research with special achievements. Among them Adolf Wilhelm (1864-1950)[51] indisputably takes the lead. His phenomenal knowledge of Greek inscriptions is reflected in a great number of works, a study which is essential for every historian. The *Österreichische Archeologische Institut* has conducted fruitful excavations at Ephesus (among others, O. Benndorf, J. Keil and F. Miltner): the *Tituli Asiae Minoris* (I-III, 1, 1901-1944) are an undertaking of the *Österreichische Akademie der Wissenschaften.* Fritz Schachermeyr, who has worked chiefly in the field of early Greek history, descends from the historical school of Adolf Bauer. His studies in prehistory are characterised by the mastery of vast material, by new ideas and a great propensity towards establishing interconnections. Schachermeyr has also written a *Griechische Geschichte mit besonderer Berücksichtigung der geistesgeschichtlichen und kulturmorphologischen Zusammenhänge* (Stuttgart 1960, ^{2}1968), which, however, belongs more in the realm of the philosophy of history and a biologically oriented view of history; in addition, a new, greatly expanded edition of his *Alexander der Grosse*, Vienna 1973, and his *Forschungen und Betrachtungen zur griechischen und römischen Geschichte*, Vienna 1974.

1. See G. Voigt, *Die Wiederbelebung des klassischen Altertums*, ^{3}1893; A. M. Woodward, "Greek History at the Renaissance," *JHS* 63, 1943, 1 ff.
2. *De archontibus Atheniensium*, 1622; *Areopagus*, 1624; *Solo*, 1632; *Regnum Atticum sive de regibus Atheniensium*, 1633, listed (with the studies of others) in *Thesaurus antiquitatum Graecarum* of J. Gronovius (13 vols. Fol., Leiden 1697-1702).
3. *Vetus Graecia illustrata studio et opera Ubbonis Emmii Frisii*, edited by his son, Lugdunum Batavorum 1626; cf. *Graecorum respublicae ab Ubbone Emmio descriptae*, Lugdunum Batavorum 1632.
4. *Dissertation on the Epistles of Phalaris, Themistocles, Socrates, Euripides and Others, and the Fables of Aesopus*, London 1697; *A Dissertation Upon the Epistles of Phalaris With an Answer to the Objection of the Hon. Chr. Boyle*, 1699 (also in Bentley's *Opuscula philologica*, Leipzig 1781).
5. W. Rehm, *Griechentum und Goethezeit. Geschichte eines Glaubens* (Das Erbe der Alten II 26), Leipzig 1936 [^{3}1952].
6. The first edition appeared in 2 vols., Berlin 1817, the third vol. in 1840, containing the documents on the maritime affairs of the Attic state. A second edition appeared in 1851, a third, in 2 vols., by M. Fränkel, Berlin 1886; it had the undeniable misfortune of being published four years before the discovery of Aristotle's *Constitution of Athens* in 1890.
7. Vol. III of *CIG* appeared in 1853; it was edited by J. Franz; Vol. IV in 1856 and 1859, edited by E. Curtius and Ad. Kirchhoff. The Indices were drawn up by H. Röhl in 1877. On the history of *CIG*: A.v. Harnack, *Gesch. d. Preuss. Ak. d. Wiss. zu Berlin* I 2, 1900, 668 ff.

8. It was especially unfortunate that Böckh and his collaborators had in many instances to depend on inaccurate copies of the epigraphical documents. It was Theodor Mommsen who first affirmed that the original of each individual inscription must be examined, and himself carried this out in regard to *CIL*. It was then laid down as a principle also for *Inscriptiones Graecae* (1873 ff.), the successor of *CIG*.

9. On his personality: O. and E. Kern, *C. O. Müller, Lebensbild in Briefen an seine Eltern mit dem Tagebuch seiner italienisch-griechischen Reise*, Berlin 1908; *Carl Otfried Müller, Briefe aus einem Gelehrtenleben 1797 bis 1840*, 2 vols., ed. S. Reiter, Berlin 1950.

10. A. Meder, *Der athenische Demos zur Zeit des Peloponnesischen Krieges im Lichte zeitgenössischer Quellen*, Diss. Munich 1938, VIII.

11. Harriet Grote, *George Grote. The Personal Life of George Grote*, London 1873; cf. the remarks by K. J. Neumann, *Entwicklung u. Aufgabe d. Alt. Gesch.*, Strassburg 1910, 49 f.; also instructive are the statements of R.v. Pöhlmann, "Zur Beurteilung Georg Grotes u. seiner Griech. Gesch.," in *Aus Altertum und Gegenwart* I², 1911, 228 ff.; and a short summary in *GG* ⁵1914, 5; also A. Momigliano, *George Grote and the Study of Greek History*, London 1952 (Inaugural Lecture at University College, London, 19th February 1952) = *Contributo alla storia degli studi classici*, Rome 1955, 213-231.

12. See U.v. Wilamowitz, *Arist.* I, 377, who ascribes the history of Curtius to an Isocratean-oriented style determined to "praise what is noble and censure what is base." On his personality see the book by F. Curtius, *Ernst Curtius. Ein Lebensbild in Briefen*, Berlin 1903, an unusually gripping portrait that places the public personality of the scholar and his importance for the cultural life of the nation in its proper light.

13. Cf. the five-volume work *Olympia. Die Ergebnisse der von dem Deutschen Reich veranstalteten Ausgrabung*, ed. E. Curtius and Fr. Adler, Berlin 1890-97. The German excavations were resumed in 1936, and again in 1952, after an interval brought about by the War: they produced a great many new finds; cf. *Berichte über die Ausgrabungen in Olympia*, 1967, to date 8 vols., published by the Deutsche Archäologische Institut, as well as *Olympische Forschungen*, to date 6 vols.

14. J. G. Droysen, *Gesch. Alexanders d. Gr.*, Berlin 1833; reprinted, with an Introduction by H. Berve, Leipzig, Kröner, 1931; ²1939; *Geschichte des Hellenismus* I: *Gesch. der Nachfolger Alexanders*, Hamburg 1836; II: *Gesch. der Bildung des hellenistischen Staatensystems*, 1843. The second edition was published under the title *Gesch. des Hellenismus*: I. *Alexander*; II. *Diadochen*; III. *Epigonen*, 3 vols., Gotha 1877-78.

15. A. Michaelis, *Die archäologischen Entdeckungen des 19. Jahrh.*, Leipzig ²1908.

16. On Heinrich Schliemann see his characteristic *Selbstbiographie* Leipzig ⁷1949; also *Briefe von Heinrich Schliemann*, ed. Ernst Meyer, Berlin and Leipzig 1936; and the lecture by Ernst Meyer, in *Bericht über den VI. Intern. Kongress f. Archäologie in Berlin 1939* (published 1940), 189 ff. On Schliemann's archaeological enterprises see C. Schuchhardt, *Schliemann's Excavations: An Archaeological and Historical Study*, London and New York 1891; and Ernst Meyer, *Heinrich Schliemann, Kaufmann und Forscher*, Göttingen 1969.

17. See the English translation "The History of Greece from its Commencement to the Close of the Independence of the Greek Nation," 4 vols., New York 1894-98, and in particular, A. Holm, *Gesch. Siziliens im Altertum*, 3 vols., Leipzig 1870-1898.

18. On Eduard Meyer see H. Marohl, *Ed. Meyer, Bibliographie* (with a copy of the *Gedächtnisrede* delivered by U. Wilcken), Stuttgart 1941; also W. Otto, "Ed. Meyer und sein Werk," *ZDMG* NF 10, 1932, 1 ff.

19. Cf. his *Kleine Schriften* (5 vols., ed. Fr. Rühl, Leipzig 1889-94), and the not as yet out of date *Geschichte Irans und seiner Nachbarländer von Alexander d. Gr. bis zum Untergang der Arsaciden*, Tübingen 1888 (ed. Th. Nöldeke).

20. M. Duncker, *Gesch. d. Altertums*, Vols. III and IV: *Die Griechen*, Leipzig ⁵1878-80; Vols. V-IX, 1881-86. On the design of the work see K. J. Neumann, *Entwicklung und Aufgabe d. Alten Geschichte*, 1910, 73 ff.

21. Beloch, *GG* I² 2, 16 ff.

22. On his personality see his *Autobiographie: Die Geschichtswissenschaft der Gegenwart*, 1926, 1 ff.; cf. the necrology by Fr. Oertel, *Gn.* 5, 1929, 461 ff.; and the characteristic remarks by O. Th. Schulz, *Burs. Jb.* 254, 1936, 62 ff. (obituary notice on J. Kromayer). Important is A. Momigliano, in *Dizionario biografico degli Italiani*, VIII, Rome 1966, 3-16.

23. The second edition (Strassburg-Berlin 1912-17) of Beloch's *GG* will be cited throughout.

24. Cf. the pertinent remarks by J. Kromayer, *HZ* 100, 1908, 11 ff.

25. U. Wilcken has, in addition to a great number of studies on specific questions of history, also written a widely read *Griechische Geschichte im Rahmen der Altertumsgeschichte*, Munich 1924; [9]1962, ed. G. Klaffenbach.

26. Cf. the review by M. L. Strack, *GGA*, 1903, 856 ff.; also H. Bengtson, *HZ* 185, 1958, 88 ff. = *KS*, 267 ff.

27. See the survey on the position of the epigraphical work *Inscriptiones Graecae* in G. Klaffenbach, *Griechische Epigraphik*, Göttingen [2]1966, 21 ff.

28. Cf. in particular his work "Staat und Gesellschaft der Griechen," in P. Hinneberg, *Kultur und Gegenwart* II 4, 1, Leipzig and Berlin [2]1923; and his *Der Glaube der Hellenen*, 2 vols., Berlin 1931 and 1932. The collection, *Kleine Schriften*, Berlin 1935 ff., was begun.

29. See, however, Heinrich Gelzer, *Ausgewählte Kl. Schr.* 295 ff.; Pöhlmann, *GG* 10 ff.; and Rud. Stadlemann, in *Ant.* 7, 1931, 49 ff.; Carl Neumann, *Jacob Burckhardt*, 1927; and *Jacob Burckhardt, Briefe, vollständige u. Kritische Ausgabe in 10 Bände mit Benutzung des Nachlasses*, by M. Burckhardt, Stuttgart 1975. The *Griechische Kulturgeschichte* is now available in the "Gesamtausgabe," Vols. VIII-XI, with an Introduction by F. Stähelin (cf. the English translation, *History of Greek Culture*, by P. Hilty, New York 1963).

30. The first volume was published in 1923 in Berlin, and the last volume to date, nos. 709-856, in 1958 in Leiden. The only thing still lacking is the extremely important commentary on the Ethnographers.

31. Newly published under the title *Griechische Geschichtschreiber*, Leipzig 1957.

32. English translation, *Aristotle*, Oxford [2]1962.

33. Bibliography of publications in *Burs. Jb.* 284, 1943, 42 ff. (= *KS*, 599) by H. Bengtson.

34. In addition also the book *From Solon to Socrates*, London 1968 [[2]1973], and *Man, State and Deity. Essays in Ancient History*, London 1974.

35. Fustel de Coulanges championed the idea that religion moulded and held together the family, the clan and the state.

36. Cf. above all, *Rome, la Grèce, et les monarchies hellénistiques*, Paris 1921; also his collected articles which are published by Louis Robert under the title *Etudes d'épigraphie et d'histoire grecques* (to date 5 vols., Paris 1938-1957). Cf. M. Roques, *Notice sur la vie et les travaux de M. Maurice Holleaux* (Inst. de France 1943,1).

37. Of the studies by Louis Robert which have been published in book form the following may be cited: *Villes d'Asie Mineure*, Paris 1935; [2]1962; *Etudes des anatoliennes*, Paris 1937; Amsterdam [[2]1970]. *Etudes épigraphiques et philologiques*, Paris 1938; *Les gladiateurs dans l'Orient grec*, Paris 1940; *Documents de l'Asie Mineure méridionale*, Geneva 1966; *Monnaies antiques en Troade*, Geneva and Paris 1966. *Opera minora selecta. Epigraphie et antiquités grecques*, 4 vols. Amsterdam 1969-1974; in addition the series *Hellenica*, Limoges and Paris 1940 ff., to date 13 vols. On the excavations at Claros see, for instance, L. Robert, *Les fouilles de Claros* (Conférence donnée à l'Université d'Ankara le 26 octobre 1953), Limoges 1953; moreover, *Annuaire du Collège de France* 57, 1957, 365 ff.; *ibid.*, 58, 1958, 404 ff.

38. The posthumously published Vol. IV 1 of Glotz's *HG* edited by R. Cohen and P. Roussel (1938; [2]1945) goes down to the Successor period.

39. Additional important writings by G. Glotz are *La civilisation égéenne*, Paris 1923; [2]1952; and *La cité grecque*, 1928 (English translation, *The Greek City*, London 1929).

40. See the obituary notice on W. W. Tarn by F. E. Adcock, *Pr. Br. Ac.* 44, 1959, 253-262.

41. A. W. Gomme, *A Historical Commentary on Thucydides*, Vols. I-III, Oxford 1945-1956, (Bks I-V 24); Vol. IV, by A. W. Gomme, A. Andrewes, K. J. Dover (Bks. V 25-VII), Oxford 1970; F. W. Walbank, *A Historical Commentary on Polybius*, I, Oxford 1957 (Bks. I-VI); II, Oxford 1967 (Bks. VII-XVIII).

41a. Westlake, *Essays.*

42. N. G. L. Hammond, *A History of Greece to 322 B.C.*, Oxford 1959; [2]1967.

43. A bibliography of his writings is given by C. B. Welles, *H.* 5, 1956, 358 ff. (444 Items).

44. See in particular his *Hellenistic Athens*, London 1911; also the studies on Attic finance during the fifth and fourth centuries B.C., combined together under the title *The Treasurers of Athena*, Cambridge, Mass., 1932; and his investigations on the chronology of Hellenistic Athens. A bibliography of Ferguson's works is given in *HSCP* 51, 1940, 1 ff., with additional information in *Gn.* 27, 1955, 61.

45. A. D. Nock, *Essays on Religion and the Ancient World*. Selected and Edited, with an Introduction and Bibliography of Nock's Writings and Index, by Z. Stewart, Oxford 1972.

46. G. De Sanctis, *Storia dei Greci dalle origini alla fine del secolo V*, 2 vols., Florence 1939 [[6]1961]; cf. the reviews by W. Otto, *HZ* 163, 1941, 305 ff.; and U. Kahrstedt, *Gn.* 16, 1940, 241 ff.

47. E. Breccia, *Il diritto dinastico nelle monarchie dei successori d'Alessandro Magno*, 1903; G. Cardinali, *Il regno de Pergamo*, 1906, both published in *Studi di Storia antica, pubblicati da G. Beloch*. A summary of Italian research in Greek history from 1913 to 1933 may be found above all in A. Momigliano, *Contributo alla storia degli studi classici*, Rome 1955, 299-326.

48. Cf. the bibliography in Paolo Orsi, Rome 1935, 353 ff.; the most important publications are also found in J. Dunbabin, *West.*, 488 f.

49. L. Bernabò Brea, *Sicily Before the Greeks*, London 1957 (Italian: *La Sicilia prima dei Greci*, Milan [2]1960).

50. A. Westholm, "Swedish Excavations in the Mediterranean Countries," *Le Nord* 7, 1944, 67 ff.

51. Of the innumerable studies by Adolf Wilhelm the following may be cited here: *Urkunden dramatischer Aufführungen in Athen* (Sonderschr. d. Österr. Arch. Inst. VI, Vienna 1906); *Beiträge z. griech. Inschriftenkunde, ibid.*, 1909; *Beiträge z. griech. Inschriftenkunde,* 6 Hefte, in SB.W., 1911-1932; *Attische Urkunden* 5 Hefte, *ibid.*, 1911-1942; in addition, there are a great many articles in *Anz. W*, in *Osterr. Jahreshefte*, and in many other periodicals. See now *Akademieschriften zur griechischen Inschriftenkunde (1895-1951)*, 3 vols, Leipzig 1974. Obituary notice, with a bibliography of his works, by J. Keil, *Almanach d. Österr. Akad.*, 101. Jahrg., 1951, 307 ff.

1 THE EARLY AGES OF GREECE

THE SOURCES

Early Greek culture is virtually devoid of any writing. This is in no way altered by the fact that the Cretan script (Linear A) was used on the mainland (cf. G. Klaffenbach, *Forschungen und Fortschritte*, 1948, 193 ff.). From here it was carried by emigrant Greeks (Arcadians) to Cyprus. We also know that the tablets in the so-called Linear B script have been found in various places in Greece, in the so-called "Palace of Nestor" in Ano Englianos on the west coast of Messenia, as well as in Mycenae. In addition there are a number of inscriptions, known for some time now, in Linear B on vases from Thebes, Orchomenus, Tiryns, Mycenae and Eleusis (A. Rehm, *Hdb. Arch.* I, 1939, 191). The tablets from Ano Englianos became famous after two English scholars, Michael Ventris and John Chadwick, published their view that the language of the Linear B script was a Greek idiom, more precisely, an old Achaean dialect: "Evidence for Greek Dialect in the Mycenaean Archives," *JHS* 73, 1953, 84 ff.; *Documents in Mycenaean Greek*, Cambridge 1956 [[2]1973], cf. L. R. Palmer, *Gn.* 48, 1976, 433 ff. The publication of this discovery came like a bombshell. Many, including even critical, scholars declared that they were convinced of its validity, and it was only too natural that the—factually, incidentally, very meagre—results of the decipherment found their way into numerous scholarly and popular works. The discovery of the English scholars was placed on a level with Grotefend's decipherment of the cuneiform script. The results of the decipherment may be found in, *inter alia*, the brief but very learned account by A. Lesky, *Anz. W*, 1954, 6, printed in *Gym.* 62, 1955, 1 ff., cf. also J. Chadwick, *The Decipherment of Linear B*, Cambridge 1958 [[2]1967].

The first detailed and documented challenge of the results of Ventris and Chadwick came from A. J. Beattie, *JHS* 76, 1956, 1 ff., and then from E. Grumach, *OLZ*, 1957, 293 ff. (earlier critical views, especially those of N. Platon and J. Sundwall, may be found cited in Grumach, 293 n.1), who was joined by Beattie, *Mitteilungen des Instituts für Orientforschung* (Berlin) 6, 1958, 33-104. These objections (in addition especially also E. Grumach, *Gn.* 32, 1960, 681 ff.) are so serious that they can no longer be ignored, not even by the most resolute supporters of Ventris and Chadwick. Characteristic of the state of scholarship at the time was, for instance, the *Festschrift für Joh. Sundwall zu seinem 80. Geburtstag*, which appeared under the title *Minoica*, Berlin 1958. It contained contributions by those who supported and by those who contested Ventris' decipherment, mingled together in colourful fashion. Otherwise to date there has been no essential change in the situation.

Doubts pertaining to details of the decipherment of Linear B by Ventris and his collaborators concerned the following principal points (cf. in addition to Grumach, *OLZ*, 1957, 293 ff., also W. Eilers, *Forsch. und Fortschr.* 31, 1957, 326-332): (1) the completely inappropriate liberty in notating the sounds; (2) the suppression of Greek inflexional endings; (3) the phonetic repetition of the ideograms, for which there are no known parallels—at least not from the languages of the ancient Orient; (4) the unsatisfactory separation of ideograms and syllabic symbols (Linear B is not a purely syllabic script but a combination of ideograms and syllabic symbols). In addition, finally, there is still the fact that Ventris never offered an explanation as to how he at the time arrived at his syllabic grid —this too a unique peculiarity in the decipherment of lost scripts and languages. Cf. now, nevertheless, J. Chadwick, *The Decipherment of Linear B*, ²1967, 40 ff. See also W. Merlingen, "Linear B (und A)," *Anz. Alt.* 24, 1971, 1 ff; F. Schachermeyr, "Mykene und Linear B-Schrift im Rahmen der Altertumsforschung," *Saec.* 22, 1971, 114-122; S. Hiller and O. Panagl, "Linear B. Fortschritte und Forschungsstand. Ein Forschungsbericht," *Saec.* 22, 1971, 123-194. Add to this J. Chadwick, "The Linear B. Tablets as Historical Documents," *CAH* ³II,1, 1973, 609-626 (with bibliography).

It is not to be denied that the decipherment of Linear B has been readily accepted by many scholars. I too am prepared to accept that this script possibly conceals a Greek idiom—as for the decipherment by Ventris and Chadwick, however, I do not think that it is valid. One need, for instance, only read the article by M. Lejeune in *H.* 8, 1959, 129 ff., on alleged names of slaves, to see how little Greek this investigation has yielded. One may also note how little progress has been made in most recent years!

The Greeks themselves no longer possessed any historical information from their primitive times, although their mythology and heroic legends have preserved reflections of historical reminiscences. It is therefore no accident that Greek heroic legends coincide with the centres of early Greek culture in the Argolid and in Boeotia. It is primarily M. P. Nilsson ("Der Mykenische Ursprung der griechischen Mythologie," *Antidoron, Festschrift für Jacob Wackernagel*, 1923, 137 ff., and *The Mycenaean Origin of Greek Mythology* Berkeley 1932 [ed. 2, London 1972, with a new Introduction and Bibliography by E. Vermeule]) who has rightly stressed that legend reflects a reminiscence of the heroic period of these regions. Homer's *Iliad* too, in which older elements are fused together with later aspects into an indissoluble whole, exhibits a great many features belonging to the Greek heroic age (Nilsson, *Hom.*).

Non-Greek literary sources are sparse. The *Aqaivasa* in the inscription of the Libyan War from the fifth year of the Egyptian Pharaoh Merneptah (c. 1225 B.C.) are no more Greek than the *Danuna* in the inscription of Ramses III (c. 1200-1168 B.C.) at Medinet Habu. (Cf. Mariette, *Karnak*, Paris 1875, Pls. 52-54, lines 1 f.; 13 f.; 48 ff.; Bossert, *Kr.*, 58 f.; W. Hoelscher, *Libyer u. Ägypter* [Ägyptolog. Forsch. 4], Glückstadt 1937, 61 ff., and Nelson, *Medinet Habu* [Univ. of Chicago, Oriental Inst. Publ.], P1.44, cf. Bossert, *Kr.* 51 f.). Perhaps identical with the *Danuna* are the *Dnnjm*, who have become known through inscriptions from Sendjirli (c. 825 B.C.) and through the Phoenician-Hittite bilingual text from Karatepe (Cilicia) from the end of the eighth century B.C. Some scholars, like W. F. Albright (*AJA* 54, 1950, 171-172) regard these *Dnnjm* as originally Greeks who were ruled by the "Dynasty of Mopsos" (*bt M ps*). All this, however, is purely conjectural. (On the inscription from Karatepe see, for instance, H. F. Güterbock, *Eranos* 47, 1949, 93 ff.; P. Meriggi, *Ath.* NS 20, 1951, 25 ff.; further discussion, for instance, in Cassola, *Ion.*, 110 ff., who is much too optimistic, however, in associating *Dnnjm* with the Greeks. Also fanciful is P. Kretschmer, "Die Danaer (Danuna) und die neuen kilikischen Funde," *Anz. W* 86, 1949, 186-202, and R. D. Barnett, *JHS* 73, 1953, 140 ff.). The Greeks—under the name *Iamani*, that is, "Ionians"—are mentioned for the first time in the inscriptions of the Assyrian king Sargon II (722-205 B.C.) (H. Bengtson, *Ph.* 92, 1937, 148 ff. = *KS*, 76 ff.). The Ionians in the Egyptian list of Hittite auxiliary peoples in the battle of Qadesh (1286/5 B.C. according to J. v. Beckerath) belongs just as much in the realm of fantasy as does its alleged appearance in the cuneiform text from Ras Shamra (Ugarit) in northern Syria (thirteenth/twelfth century B.C.). In explaining the *irwnnz* as the Hittite vassal people *Arawanna*, I had, without knowing it, forerunners in H. Winckler, *OLZ*, 1906, 630 ff., and F. W. v. Bissing, *WZKM* 34, 258 f., *inter al.*; cf. *Ph.* 92, 1937, 149 n. 77. (Cf. also H. Bengtson, *Ph.* 92, 1937, 148 [= *KS*, 76].)

In the face of critical research the "pre-Homeric" Greeks discovered by E. Forrer in Hittite cuneiform tablets have evaporated again (v.s.p.17). The Cretan and old Cypriote literary monuments have not as yet been deciphered.

Language is an important source. From the data of place names P. Kretschmer more than seventy years ago drew basic conclusions concerning the early population of Hellas. They still form the basis of present-day scholarship, while the later investigations of Kretschmer are all very hypothetical in character. (cf. P. Kretschmer, *Einleitung in die Geschichte d. grieche. Sprache,* Göttingen 1896; "Sprache" 1927, 60 ff.; cf. Schwyzer, *Gram.* I, 60 ff., and *Glotta* 14, 1925, 300 ff.; 28, 1940, 231 ff.; 30. 1943, 84 ff.) And, finally, research into the Greek dialects furnishes us with building blocks for early Greek history, but in this case it must never be overlooked that the results from dialect studies are to be used only with great caution in forming anthropological conclusions. (Cf. A. Thumb-E. Kiecker's *Hdb. d. griech. Dialekte* I, 1932; on orientation see A. Thumb, "Griechische Dialektforsch. u. Stammesgeschichte," *NJb*, 1905, 385 ff. Further studies are cited by Schwyzer, *Gram.* I, 82 ff.; see also A. Bartonek, "Greek Dialects in the Second Millennium B.C.," *Eirene* 9, 1971, 49 ff.)

It is the monuments, however, that form the bulk of our evidence. The systematic excavations in Greece, on the Cyclades, the west coast of Asia Minor, Cyprus, Rhodes and above all on Crete since the beginning of the century have opened up a new world of whose existence earlier generations could not have had any idea at all! The historical assessment of the information, which is growing into gigantic proportions, is partly still in its infancy, but in part it enables us, namely for Crete and Mycenaean culture, to form a historical outline, one that is gaining in colour and depth through new investigations. Now largely out of date is the survey by Fimmen, *Km.*, the same holds true for G. Karo *RE Suppl.* VI, 584 ff., s.v. *Mykenische Kultur.* Still useful for the European connections, though one-sided, is Schuchhardt, *Alt.* A short summary may be found in J. Wiesner, *Vor- und Frühzeit der Mittelmeerländer. I. Das östliche Mittelmeer*, Berlin 1943 (*Sammlung Göschen*), with the most important bibliography, but excluding references. Very copious and thorough is Matz, *Ägäis*, 179 ff.; *idem, Kreta, Mykene, Troia. Die minoische Kunst und die homerische Welt*, Stuttgart ²1956; cf. *idem, Crete and Early Greece. The Prelude to Greek Art*, London 1962. Valuable are F. Schachermeyr's contributions, of which only the more recent can be cited here: *RE* XXII, 1352 ff., s.v. *Prähistorische Kulturen Griechenlands; idem, Griech.*, [both studies contain an extraordinary wealth of material, partly with wide-ranging historical combinations, but to be accepted with caution: cf., for instance, R. W. Hutchinson, *JHS* 77, 1957, 358 ff., and M. S. F. Hood, *Gn.* 29, 1957, 511 ff.]; see further his valuable reviews on research: "Die ägäische Frühzeit," in *Anz. Alt.* 4, 1951, 5 ff.; 6, 1953, 193 ff.; 7, 1954, 151 ff.: 10, 1957, 65 ff.; 19, 1966, 1 ff.; 25, 1972, 129 ff.; further: *AA*, 1962, 105-382 [an extensive review of research and of finds made between 1957 and 1960]; also F. Schachermeyr, H.-G. Buchholz, S. Alexiou, H. Hauptmann, "Forschungsbericht über die Ausgrabungen und Neufunde zur Ägäischen Frühzeit, 1961-1965," *AA*, 1971, 295-419; F. Schachermeyr, "Forschungsbericht über die Ausgrabungen und Neufunde zur Ägäischen Frühzeit, 1961-1965. Die Frühmykenische Zeit (SH I-II bzw. Myk. I-II)," *AA*, 1974, 1-28; also H.-G. Buchholz, "Ägäische Funde and Kultureinflüsse in den Randgebieten des Mittelmeeres. Forschungsbericht über Ausgrabungen und Neufunde, 1960-1970. Mit einem Beitrag von V. Karageorghis." *AA*, 1974, 325-462; F. Schachermeyr, *Die Ägäische Frühzeit* (*Bd. I. Die vormykenische Zeit*), *SB.Ö = Mykenische Studien* Vol. 3, Vienna 1975. An earlier historical survey may be found in A. J. B. Wace, "The History of Greece in the IIIrd and IInd Millenniums B.C.," *H.* 2, 1953, 74 ff. In addition there are the following contributions (historical surveys) in the third edition of *CAH* I and II: *The Stone Age in the Aegean*, ³I, 1, 1970, 557-618 (S. S. Weinberg); *Greece, Crete and the Aegean Islands in the Early Bronze Age*, ³I, 2, 1971, 771-807 (John L. Caskey); *Greece and the Aegean Islands in the Middle Bronze Age* ³II, 1, 1973, 117-140 (J. L. Caskey); *The Rise of Mycenaean Civilization*, ³II, 1, 1973, 627-658 (Frank H. Stubbings); *The Expansion of Mycenaean Civilization*, ³II, 2, 1975, 165-187 (F. H. Stubbings); *The Recession of Mycenaean Civilization*, ³II, 2, 1975, 338-358 (F. H. Stubbings); *idem, Mycenae's Last Century of Greatness* (Meyer Foundation Lecture, 1968), Sydney and London 1969; *The End of Mycenaean Civilization and the Dark Age, CAH* ³II, 2, 1975, 658-677 (V. R. d'A. Desborough and N. G. L. Hammond).

The book by Lord William Taylour, *The Mycenaeans*, New York 1964, may also be mentioned, as well as that of E. Vermeule, *Greece in the Bronze Age*, Chicago and London 1964, and G. E. Mylonas, *Mycenae and the Mycenaean Age*, Princeton, N.J., 1966; cf. further J. Chadwick, Aegean History 1500-1200 B.C., *Studii clasice* 11, 1969, 7 ff.; useful is H.-G. Buchholz and V. Karageorghis, *Prehistoric Greece and Cyprus. An Archaeological Handbook* (translated from the German by F. Garvie), London 1973 (German edition published in 1971); N. S. Scoufopoulos, *Mycenaean Citadels*, Göteborg 1971; C. Renfrew, *The Emergence of Civilization. The Cyclades and the Aegean in the Third Millennium* B.C., London 1972. See also D. Theocharis (ed.) *Neolithic Greece*, Athens 1973, and G. A. Christopoulos and J. C. Bastias (eds.), *Prehistory and Protohistory*, Athens and London 1974. On metal see H.-G. Buchholz, "Der Kupferhandel des zweiten vorchristlichen Jahrtausends im Spiegel der Schriftforschung," in E. Grumach (ed.), *Minoica. Festschrift zum 80. Geburtstag von Johannes Sundwall*, Berlin 1958, 92-115; *idem*, "Keftiubarren und Erzhandel im 2. vorchr. Jahrtausend," *Prähist. Zeitschr.* 37, 1959, 1 ff.; *idem*, "Das Blei in der mykenischen Kultur und in der bronzezeitlichen Metallurgie Zyperns," *JdI* 87, 1972, 213 ff.; and K. Branigan, *Aegean Metalwork of the Early and Middle Bronze Age*, Oxford 1974; also J. D. Muhly, *Copper and Tin. The Distribution of Mineral Resources and the Nature of the Metals Trade in the Bronze Age*, Diss. Yale Univ., 1969.

1. Northern Greece: The prehistory of Macedonia, Epirus and Illyria has scarcely been determined even in regard to its basic featûres: beginnings in W. A. Heurtley, *Prehistoric Macedonia*, Cambridge 1939, cf. now D. Theocharis, *Prehistory of Eastern Macedonia and Thrace*, in *Ancient Greek Cities*, published by Athens Technological Organisation, Athens Centre of Ekistics, 1971-72; important is G. E. Mylonas, *Studies in Honor of Frederick W. Shipley*, St. Louis 1942; *idem*, *AJA* 45, 1941, 566 ff.; see also F. Schachermeyr, *RE* XXII, 1939 ff.; 1447; 1474 f.; D. H. French, "Prehistoric Pottery from Macedonia and Thrace," *Prähistorische Zeitschrift* 42, 1964, 30 ff.; R. J. Rodden, "Excavations at the Early Neolithic Site at Nea Nikomedeia, Greek Macedonia (1961 Season)," *Proc. Prehis. Soc.* 28, 1962, 267 ff.; also G. E. Mylonas, *Excavations at Olynthus* I. *The Neolithic Settlement*, Baltimore, Md., 1929; J. Deshayes, "Dikili Tash and the Origins of Troadic Culture," *Archaeology* 25, 1972, 198 ff.; cf. *idem*, *BCH* 97, 1973, 464 ff.; K. Rhomiopoulou and C. Ridley, "Prehistoric Settlement of Servia," *Athens Annals of Archaeology* 7, 1974, 351 ff. The investigation of Neolithic cultures in Thessaly is much more advanced: C. Tsountas, *Hai Proïstorikai Akropoleis Dimeniou kai Sesklou,* Athens 1908; A. J. B. Wace and M. S. Thompson, *Prehistoric Thessaly*, Cambridge 1912; H. D. Hansen, *Early Civilization in Thessaly* (The Johns Hopkins University, Studies in Archaeology, 15), Baltimore, Md., 1933; K. Grundmann, *AM* 57, 1932, 102 ff.; 59, 1934, 102 ff.; 62, 1937, 56 ff. A new era in the prehistoric archaeology of Thessaly began with the excavations of V. Milojčić: Preliminary reports may be found in *AA*, 1954, 1 ff.; 1955, 182 ff.; *idem*, *H.* 4, 1955, 466 ff. [Otzaki Magoula, Arapi and Gremnos]; *AA*, 1956, 142 ff.;

H. Biesantz, *AA*, 1957, 38 ff. [Gremnos and vicinity]; V. Milojčić, "Ergebnisse der deutschen Ausgrabungen in Thessalien (1953-1958)", *Jahrb. Röm.-Germ. Zentralmus. Mainz* 6, 1959, 1-56. Of the final publications of these excavations which took place between 1953 and 1958, the following have appeared: V. Milojčić, J. Boessneck, M. Hopf, *Die deutschen Ausgrabungen auf der Argissa-Magula in Thessalien* I. *Das präkeramische Neolithikum sowie die Tier- und Pflanzenreste*, Bonn 1962; V. Milojčić and H. Hauptmann, *Die Funde der frühen Diminizeit aus der Arapi-Magula, Thessalien*, Bonn 1969; Johanna Milojčić-von Zumbusch and Vladimir Milojčić, *Die deutschen Ausgrabungen auf der Otzaki-Magula in Thessalien. I. Teil. Das frühe Neolithikum*, Bonn 1971; V. Milojčić and E. Hanschmann, *Die deutschen Ausgrabungen auf der Argissa-Magula in Thessalien*, Vol. 3: *Die frühe und beginnende mittlere Bronzezeit*, Bonn 1976. See further V. Milojčić, "Bericht über die deutschen archäologischen Ausgrabungen in Thessalien 1973," *Athens Annals of Archaeology* 7, 1974, 45 ff. [Pevkakia Magoula]; *idem* and D. Theocharis, *Pagasai und Demetrias* (Beiträge zur ur- und frühgeschichtlichen Archäologie des Mittelmeerraumes, 12), Bonn 1976; J. Milojcić-von Zumbusch, K. Kilian, V. Milojcić, A. von den Driesch, K. Enderle, *Die deutschen Ausgrabungen auf den Magulen bei Larisa in Thessalien 1966*, Bonn 1976; as well as J. Makkay, "Das frühe Neolithikum auf der Otzaki Magula und die Körös-Starcevo-Kultur," *Acta Archaeologica* 26, 1974, 131-154. The excavations of D. R. Theocharis at Sesklo also deserve mention (*Praktika* 32, 1957, 151 ff.; *Ergon*, 1962, 39 ff.; 1963, 27 ff.) [as well as at other sites, namely in Attica and Euboea: *idem*, "Nea Makri. Eine grosse neolithische Siedlung in der Nähe von Marathon," *AM* 71, 1956, 1 ff.; *idem*, "Ek tes Proistorias Euboias kai tes Skyrou," *Arch. Eub. Mel.* 6, 1959, 279 ff.].

2. Central Greece: The site which has been best investigated is Orchomenus in Boeotia: H. Bulle, *Orchomenos* I (Abh. Bay 24, 2), Munich 1907; E. Kunze, *Orchomenos* II and III (Abh. Bay n. f. 5 u. 8), Munich 1931 and 1934; also H. Goldman, *Excavations at Eutresis in Boeotia*, Cambridge, Mass., 1931; cf. J. L. Caskey, "The Earliest Settlements at Eutresis. Supplementary Excavations, 1958," *Hesp*. 29, 1960, 126 ff. On Thebes see S. Symeonoglou, *Kadmeia* I. *Mycenaean Finds at Thebes* (SMA 61), Göteborg 1973. For Euboea in general, see L. H. Sackett, *et. al.*, "Prehistoric Euboea," *BSA* 61, 1966, 33-112. For Lefkandi see M. R. Popham and E. Milburn, "The Late Helladic III C Pottery of Seropolis (Lefkandi). A summary," *BSA* 66, 1971, 333 ff.; L. H. Sackett and M. R. Popham, "Lefkandi. A Euboean Town of the Bronze Age and the Early Iron Age (2100-700 B.C.)," *Archaeology* 25, 1972, 8 ff. The older investigations in Athens and Attica were cited by W. Judeich, *Top*., 113 ff.; the results of more recent finds are published in *Hesp*. (since 1932); particularly impressive is a well, discovered on the Athenian acropolis, from the Mycenaean period: O. Broneer, *Hesp*. 8, 1939, 317 ff. A report of further investigations on the early period of Attica may be found in F. Schachermeyr, *RE* XXII, 1383; 1431; 1456. Important are the excavations of G. E. Mylonas in the necropolis of Eleusis: cf. G. E. Mylonas, "Eleusis in the

Bronze Age," *AJA* 36, 1932, 104-117. On Hagios Kosmas see *idem, Aghios Kosmas. An Early Bronze Age Settlement and Cemetery in Attica*, Princeton, N.J., 1959. For Thorikos see H. F. Mussche *et al., Thorikos* V-VI, Brussels 1968 and 1973. And on the Late Helladic necropolis of Perati see S. Iakovidis, *Perate. To Nekrotapheion*, 3 vols. Athens 1969-70. Basic for the Sub-Mycenaean period is W. Kraiker and K. Kübler, *Kerameikos* I-IV, Berlin 1939-1943. Cf. also C. W. Blegen, "Athens and the Early Age of Greece," in *Studies Ferguson*, 1 ff. See also E. Iakovidis, *He Mykenike Akropolis Ton Athenon*, Athens 1962; and S. A. Immerwahr, *The Athenian Agora* XIII. *The Neolithic and Bronze Ages*, Princeton, N.J., 1971. Also worth consulting is F. H. Stubbings, *Prehistoric Greece*, London 1972; and S. Sinos, *Die vorklassischen Hausformen in der Ägäis*, Mainz 1971.
3. North-West Greece and the West Coast of the Peloponnesus: For a summary see N. Valmin, *Das adriatische Gebiet in Vor- und Frühbronzezeit*, Lund 1939 (based on his study, *The Swedish Messenia Expedition*, Lund 1938); see also E. Kirsten, "Vorgeschichliche Ausgrabungen in Messenien," *Ant.* 15, 1939, 338 ff. On Corcyra see G. Sotiriadis, "Investigations of the Prehistory of Corfu during 1964-1966," *Balkan Studies* 10, 1969, 393 ff. Of epoch-making importance are the excavations of C. W. Blegen at Ano Englianos (Messenia), during which the megaron and the commercial quarters (according to Blegen this is the Palace of Nestor) were found. Cf. the reports in *AJA*: 61, 1957, 129 ff.; 62, 1958, 175 ff.; 63, 1959, 121 ff.; and now the final publications: *The Palace of Nestor in Western Messenia*, Princeton, N. J.: I. *The Buildings and their Contents*, 1966, by C. W. Blegen and M. Rawson; II. *The Frescoes*, 1969, by M. Lang; III. *Acropolis and Lower Town, Tholoi and Grave Circle, Chamber Tombs. Discoveries Outside the Citadel*, 1973, by C. W. Blegen, M. Rawson, Lord W. Taylour, W. P. Donovan. See further, S. Hiller, *Studien zur Geographie des Reiches um Pylos nach den mykenischen und homerischen Texten (Mykenische Studien*, 2*)* SB. W, 278, 5), Vienna 1972; and W.A. McDonald and G. R. Rapp, *The Minnesota Messenia Expedition. Reconstruction of a Bronze Age Environment*, Minneapolis 1972. In addition, Marinatos found Mycenaean chamber tombs in the vicinity of Ano Englianos, including two that were completely undisturbed.
4. Corinth and Environs: Korakou, the forerunner of ancient Corinth, has been excavated by C. W. Blegen, *Koraku*, Boston and New York 1921; cf. S. S. Weinberg, "Remains from Prehistoric Corinth," *Hesp.* 6, 1937, 487 ff. See also C. W. Blegen, *Zygouries. A Prehistoric Settlement in the Valley of Cleonae*, Cambridge, Mass., 1928. Important is L. W. Kosmopoulos, *The Prehistoric Inhabitation of Corinth* I, Munich 1948.
5. The Peloponnesus: The classical field for archaeological investigations in Hellas is the Argolid, where Heinrich Schliemann discovered fantastic treasures in his excavations at Mycenae and Tiryns (H. Schliemann, *Mykenae*, 1878, H. Schliemann and W. Dörpfeld, *Tiryns, der prähistorische Palast*, Leipzig 1886; see the summary by C. Schuchhardt, *Schliemanns Ausgrabugen in Troja, Tiryns, Mycene, Orchomenos, Ithaka im Lichte der heutigen Wissenschaft*, Leipzig ^{2}1891; see also A. J. B. Wace, "Excavations

at Mycenae," *BSA* 24, 1919-20, 1 ff., and E. Meyer, *Heinrich Schliemann, Kaufmann und Forscher*, Göttingen 1969). Of modern investigations the following are important: G. Rodenwaldt, *Der Fries des Megarons von Mykenai*, Halle 1921 [with wide-ranging investigations into the nature of Mycenaean culture]; G. Karo, *Die Schachtgräber von Mykenai*, Munich 1930-33. The latest general work is that by A. J. B. Wace, *Mycenae. An Archaeological History and Guide*, Princeton, N.J., 1949 [with a chapter on Mycenaean civilisation]; cf. also his earlier monograph, *Chamber Tombs at Mycenae*, London 1932, and M. S. F. Hood, "Tholos Tombs of the Aegean," *Antiquity* 34, 1960, 166 ff. Since 1951 new shaft graves have been discovered outside the fortress at Mycenae by J. Papadimitriu: see J. Papadimitriu, *Praktika* 1953 [published 1956], 205 ff., and 1954 [published 1957], 252 ff.; see also G. E. Mylonas, *Grave Circle B of Mycenae* (SMA, 7), Lund 1964; *idem*, *Ho Taphikos Kyklos B ton Mykenon*, 2 vols., Athens 1973. On the discoveries by A. J. B. Wace in the lower city, where, *inter alia*, the house of an oil merchant was found, see *BSA* 48, 1953, 103 ff.; 49, 1954, 241 ff.; 50, 1955, 175 ff.; 51, 1956, 103 ff. On Tiryns: K. Müller, "Die Architektur der Burg und des Palastes," in *Tiryns* III, Augsburg 1930; G. Karo, *RE* VI A, 1453 ff., s.v. *Tiryns*; in addition, *Tiryns* V-VII, ed. U. Jantzen, Mainz 1971-1974; and K. Müller, *Der Kuppelgrab von Tiryns*, Mainz 1975. In the Gulf of Nauplia a Swedish expedition has excavated with great success at Asine, and brought to light, *inter alia*, a palace and a necropolis from the Mycenaean period: O. Frödin and A. W. Persson, *Asine. The Results of the Swedish Expedition, 1922-1930*, Stockholm 1938 (cf. G. Weicker, "Asine, eine mykenisch-frühgriechische Siedlung," *Ant.* 15, 1939, 265 ff.). Also Barbouna: I. and R. Hägg (eds.), *Excavations in the Barbouna Area at Asine*, Uppsala 1973. The tombs at Dendra contained rich treasures: Persson, *Dend.*, cf. G. Karo, *RE Suppl.* VI, 591 ff., and A. W. Persson, in *Bericht über den VI. Intern. Kongr. f. Arch. (Berlin 21-26 Aug. 1939)*, Berlin 1940, 294 ff., as well as *idem*, *Den. New*; also P. Åström, "A Midea et Dendra," *Arch.* 51, 1972, 44 ff. There are also the excavations of the Argive Heraeum (C. W. Blegen, *Prosymna. The Helladic Settlement Preceding the Argive Heraeum*, 2 vols, Cambridge, Mass., 1937); at Deiras (J. Deshayes, *Argos. Les fouilles de la Deiras*, Paris 1966); the investigations at Asea (E. Holmberg, *Excavations at Asea in Arcadia, 1936-38, Preliminary Report*, Göteborg 1939, and *idem*, *The Swedish Excavations at Asea in Arcadia*, Lund and Leipzig 1944 [cf. N. Valmin, *Gn.* 21, 1949, 139 ff.]; see also J. L. Caskey, "The Early Helladic Period in the Argolid," *Hesp.* 29, 1960, 285 ff.; and R. Howell, "A Survey of Eastern Arcadia in Prehistory," *BSA* 65, 1970, 79 ff.); furthermore, the discovery of the Mycenaean settlement at Menelaion (near Sparta) by Wace, Thompson, Droop and Dawkins, *BSA* 15, 1908/09, 109 ff., 16, 1909/10, 1 ff. See also H. Waterhouse and R. Hope Simpson, "Prehistoric Laconia: Parts I and II," *BSA* 55, 1960, 67-107; 56, 1961, 114-175. The excavations by J. L. Caskey at Lerna have yielded important results, from the Early Helladic period onwards: cf. the volumes of *Hesp.*, especially: 26, 1957, 142 ff.; 27, 1958, 125 ff.; 28, 1959, 202 ff.; and, of the final publications, *Lerna. A Preclassical Site in the Argolid*, Princeton, N.J.: I. *The Fauna*, 1969, by N.-J. Gejvall; II. *The People*, 1971, by J. L. Angel. There is now also the important site of Franchthi Cave, with an unbroken stratigraphical sequence beginning with possibly the Middle Palaeolithic and running through to the Late Neolithic: see T. W. Jacobsen, *Hesp.* 38, 1969, 343 ff.; 42, 1973, 45 ff.; 253 ff. Excavations have also been carried out on Cythera: J. N. Coldstream and G. L. Huxley (eds.), *Kythera. Excavations and Studies Conducted by the University of Pennsylvania Museum and the British School at Athens*, London 1972. Also for the Peloponnesus see K. E. Syriopoulos, *He Proistoria tes Peloponnesou*, Athens 1964 [survey of the various sites excavated]; R. Hope Simpson, *A Gazetteer and Atlas of Mycenaean Sites*, London 1965; W. A. McDonald and R. Hope Simpson, "Further Explorations in Southwestern Peloponnese, 1964-1968," *AJA* 73, 1969, 123 ff.; moreover, R. C. S. Felsch, "Neolithische Keramik aus der Höhle von Kephalari," *AM* 86, 1971, 1 ff.

6. The East Greek Islands: Cyprus: On the Neolithic period: P. Dikaios, *Khirokitia. Final Report on the Excavation of a Neolithic Settlement in Cyprus*, Oxford 1953 [the settlement is situated in the south of the island between Larnaka and Limassol]; E. Gjerstad, *Studies in Prehistoric Cyprus*, Uppsala 1926; *idem, The Swedish Cyprus Expedition*, I-III; IV 2, Stockholm 1934-49 (cf. B. Schweitzer, *Gn.* 11, 1935, 449 ff.); IV C and IV D, Lund 1972, by L. Åström and P. Åström. Further, E. Gjerstad, "The Colonisation of Cyprus in Greek Legend," *Opusc. Arch.* 3, 1944, 7 ff.; for the Early Bronze Age: E. and J. Stewart, *Vounos 1937-38*, Lund 1950. For the Middle Bronze Age: P. Åström, *The Middle Cypriote Bronze Age*, Lund 1957. On the Late Bronze Age: L. Åström, *Studies on the Arts and Crafts of the Late Cypriote Bronze Age*, Lund 1967; cf. E. Sjöqvist, *Problems of the Late Cypriote Bronze Age*, Stockholm 1940. New results have ensued from the excavations at Enkomi: see C. F. A. Schaeffer, *Enkomi-Alasia* I. *Nouvelles missions en Chypre 1946-1950*, Paris 1950: *idem, Alasia (Mission archéologique IV)*, Paris 1971; and in particular, P. Dikaios, *Enkomi*, I-III, Mainz 1969-1971 (cf. V. Hankey, *JHS* 95, 1975, 92 ff.). The tomb of an Achaean (?) ruler in Kurion has been found: C. H. McFadden, *AJA* 58, 1954, 131 ff. [c. 1150 B.C.]. Also J. L. Benson, *The Necropolis of Kaloriziki*, (SMA, 36), Göteborg 1973. For surveys see H. W. Catling, *Cyprus in the Neolithic and Chalcolithic Periods, CAH* ³I, 1, 1970, 539-556; *idem, Cyprus in the Middle Bronze Age, CAH* ³II, 1, 1973, 165-175; *idem, Cyprus in the Late Bronze Age, CAH* ³II,2, 1975, 188-216; see also his important monograph: H. W. Catling, *Cypriote Bronzework in the Mycenaean Age*, Oxford 1964. Also worth consulting is H.-G. Buchholz and V. Karageorghis, *Prehistoric Greece and Cyprus*, London 1973; see also V. Karageorghis, *Kition—Mycenaean and Phoenician*, London 1974.

Rhodes: In Ialysus a Mycenaean necropolis was discovered with rock chamber tombs. Lindus is a Mycenaean settlement (C. Blinckenberg and K. F. Kinch, *Lindos* I, Berlin 1931). The more recent finds are cited in the Italian publication *Clara Rhodos*, Rhodes 1928 ff. [10 vols.]. The civilisation on Lesbos in the early period inclines towards Asia Minor: W. Lamb,

Excavations at Thermi in Lesbos, Cambridge 1936. **Lemnos:** D. Mustilli, "La necropoli tirrenica di Efestia," *Ann. Scuola Arch. di Atene 15-16,* 1942. The excavations on Lemnos (Poliochni) were resumed by L. Bernabò Brea: see his summary: L. Bernabò Brea, *Poliochni. città preistorica nell'isola di Lemnos*, Rome 1964. **Samos**: Also important are the excavations by V. Milojčić under the Heraeum of Samos: V. Milojčić, *Samos* I. *Die prähistorische Siedlung unter dem Heraion. Grabung 1953 und 1955,* Bonn 1961.

7. The Cyclades: Apart from Renfrew's book, a comprehensive study on the Cyclades is still lacking. Of earlier, specific investigations, see: Ch. Tsountas, "Kykladika I-II", *Arch. Ephem.*, 1898, 137 ff.; 1899, 173 ff.; K. Stephanos, "Kykladika Naxou," *Praktika*, 1903, 52 ff.; 1904, 57 ff.; 1908, 114 ff.; 1909, 209 ff.; 1910, 270 ff.; 1911, 357 ff.; U. Kahrstedt, "Zur Kykladenkultur," *AM* 38, 1913, 166 ff. Of particular importance is the fortified urban settlement which was excavated at Phylakopi on Melos: T. D. Atkinson *et al., Excavations at Phylakopi on Melos* (Soc. Prom. Hell. Stud., Suppl. Paper no. 4), London 1904. Of more recent excavations, the following may be cited: Ch. Doumas, "Anaskaphai en Naxo," *Arch. Delt.* 17, 1962, 272 ff.; *idem*, "Chronika Kyklades" *Arch Delt.* 18, 1963, 275 ff. The excavations at Saliagos for the first time revealed evidence of Neolithic habitation: J. D. Evans and C. Renfrew, *The Excavations at Saliagos near Antiparos*, London 1968. See also J. S. Belmont and C. Renfrew, "Two Prehistoric Sites on Mykonos," *AJA* 68, 1964, 395 ff. Promising too are excavations on Keos: J. L. Caskey, "Excavations in Keos, 1963," *Hesp*. 33, 1964, 314 ff.; cf. *idem, Hesp*. 35, 1966, 363 ff.; 40, 1971, 357 ff.; 41, 1972, 357 ff.; cf. *idem*, *AJA* 76, 1972, 206 ff. In addition, the following studies may also be cited: Ch. Zervos, *L'art des Cyclades du Dêbut à la Fin de l'Age Bronze, 2500-1100 avant notre Ere,* Paris 1957; Ch. Doumas, *The N. P. Goulandris Collection of Early Cycladic Art*, Athens and New York 1969; *idem*, "Notes on Early Cycladic Architecture," *AA* 87, 1972, 151 ff.; *idem*, "Early Bronze Age Settlement Patterns in the Cyclades," in P. J. Ucko, R. Tringham, G. W. Dimbleby (eds.), *Man, Settlement and Urbanization*, London 1972, 227 ff.; *idem*, "Grave Types and Related Burial Practices During the Cycladic Early Bronze Age," in C. Renfrew (ed.), *The Explanation of Cultural Change. Models in Prehistory*, London 1973; C. Renfrew, "The Development and Chronology of Early Cycladic Figurines," *AJA* 73, 1969, 1-32; K. Majewski, "Cycladic Idols in More Recent Research (1935-1970)," *Archaeologia* 22, 1971, 1-41; also K. Branigan, "Cycladic Figurines and their Derivatives in Crete," *BSA* 66, 1971, 57 ff. On metal see C. Renfrew, "Cycladic Metallurgy and the Aegean Early Bronze Age," *AJA* 71, 1967, 1 ff., and the excellent discussion in his book *The Emergence of Civilisation. The Cyclades and the Aegean in the Third Millennium B.C.*, London 1972, 308 ff., a work which is generally, however, to be treated with some caution (cf. F. Schachermeyr, *Anz. Alt.* 25, 1972, 142 f., and M. S. F. Hood, *JHS* 93, 1973, 251 f.).

8. Western Asia Minor: The excavations which Schliemann inaugurated at Troy (final publication: W. Dörpfeld, *Troja und Ilion*, Athens 1902; cf.

H. Schliemann, *Ilios. The City and Country of the Trojans*, New York 1881) were resumed with great success by the Americans under the direction of C. W. Blegen and his collaborators: they have produced revolutionary results for the chronology of Troy; see now the monumental work on Troy by C. W. Blegen and his collaborators: *Troy. Excavations Conducted by the University of Cincinnati 1932-1938*, I-IV, Princeton and London 1950-1958 (cf. the exhaustive review by K. Bittel, *Gn.* 26, 1954, 433 ff.; 28, 1956, 241 ff.). For a summary on Troy see Blegen, *CAH* [3]I,2, 1971, 411-416 (Troy I-II); *ibid.*, 704-706 (Troy III-IV-V); [3]II,1, 1973, 683-685 (Troy VI); [3]II,2, 1975, 161-164 (Troy VII). On Anatolian-European connections see F. Schachermeyr, "Materialien zur Geschichte der ägäischen Wanderung in Kleinasien," *AM* 41, 1916 [published 1926]; cf. the corrections by Bittel, *KS; idem, Grundzüge der Vor- und Frühgeschichte Kleinasiens*, Tübingen [2]1950. The Mycenaean finds in Asia Minor are cited by G. Karo, *RE* Suppl. VI, 612 f., also by Bittel, *KS*; see also K. Bittel, *Istanbuler Forschungen* 17, 1950, 10 ff. [on the oldest colonisation of the lower Caïcus Plain]. From 1953 to 1959 British archaeologists excavated at Beycesultan (in the valley of the upper Maeander). The results have been published: cf. Seton Lloyd and James Mellaart, *Beycesultan*, 2 vols. (Publications of the British Institute of Archaeology at Ankara), No 6, 1962; No. 8, 1965. The finds extend from the Chalcolithic to the Bronze Age. See also J. Mellaart, "The End of the Early Bronze Age in Anatolia and the Aegean," *AJA* 62, 1958, 9 ff.; D. French, "Late Chalcolithic Pottery in North-West Turkey and the Aegean," *Anatolian Studies* 2, 1961, 99 ff.; *idem, Anatolia and the Aegean in the Third Millennium B.C.* [unpublished Ph.D. Dissertation, University of Cambridge No. 5403, 1965].

9. Crete: Fundamental for the whole of Cretan archaeology is the monumental work of Evans, *Knossos*, (cf. G. Karo, *OLZ*, 1922, 377 ff.). Also important is S. Xanthoudides. *The Vaulted Tombs of Mesara*, Liverpool 1924 (cf. Nilsson, *GGA*, 1925, 270 ff.), and now K. Branigan, *The Tombs of Mesara. A Study of Funerary Architecture and Ritual in Southern Crete, 2800-1700 B.C.*, London 1970 (cf. P. Warren, *JHS* 92, 1972, 238 ff.). The surveys by Karo in *RE* (XI, 1743 ff.) and *RL Vorgesch.* (Vol. VII, 1926, 63 ff., s.v. *Kreta*) are out of date, but still useful for the older finds. Valuable is J. D. S. Pendlebury, *Cr.*, (cf. F. Matz, *Gn.* 16, 1940, 1 ff); [2]1971. See also J. W. Graham, *The Palaces of Crete*, Princeton, N.J., 1962; [2]1969, and S. Hood, *The Minoans. Crete in the Bronze Age*, London 1971. F. Schachermeyr's many studies form the basis of the following works: *Die minoische Kultur des alten Kreta*, Stuttgart 1964; *Ägäis und Orient. Die überseeischen Kulturbeziehungen von Kreta und Mykenai mit Ägypten, der Levante und Kleinasien unter besonderer Berücksichtigung des 2. Jahrtausends* (Öst Akad., Denkschriften, 93), Vienna 1967. See also K. Branigan, *The Foundations of Palatial Crete. A Survey of Crete in the Early Bronze Age*, London 1970 (cf. P. Warren, *JHS* 92, 1972, 238 ff.). For an illustrated work of earlier date see Bossert, *Kr., idem, The Art of Ancient Crete*, London 1937. See also *A Land*

Called Crete. A Symposium in Memory of Harriet Boyd Hawes 1871-1945, Northampton, Mass., 1968 [with contributions by J. W. Graham, L. Shear, Jr., E. T. Vermeule, S. Dow], and A. Zois, *Der Kamares-Stil, Werden und Wesen*, Diss. Tübingen 1968. From specific excavations, only the following are cited here: of the French at Mallia, published in *Etudes crétoises* [26 vols. to date], Paris 1928-80; cf. H. and M. van Effenterre, *Fouilles exécutées à Mallia. Le centre politique* I, *L'Agora 1960-1966*, Paris 1969; cf. also J. C. Poursat, "Les fouilles récentes de Mallia et la civilisation des premières palais crétois," *CRAI*, 1972, 178 ff.; of the Italians at Phaestus and Hagia Triada: L. Pernier, *Il palazzo minoico di Festos*, Rome 1935 and 1951 [2 vols.]; see also, as a survey, *idem* and L. Banti, *Guida degli scavi italiani in Creta*, Rome 1947; and of the Americans at Gournia, Vasiliki and on the islands of Pseira and Mochlos. Important for Cretan research is the journal *Kretika Chronika*, 1947 ff. The whole of the evidence was critically assessed by F. Matz, *Ägäis*, 222 ff.; see also his survey: "Minoan Civilization—Maturity and Zenith," *CAH* ³II,1, 1973, 141-164 (maturity); *ibid.*, 557-581 (zenith). Additional material may also be found in the reviews on research by F. Schachermeyr cited above (370). See, moreover, P. Warren, *Myrtos. An Early Bronze Age Settlement in Crete* (British School of Archaeology at Athens Suppl. 7), London 1972, and N. Platon, *Zakros. The Discovery of a Lost Palace of Ancient Crete*, New York 1971. Furthermore, *Die Kretische-mykenische Glyptik und ihre gegenwärtigen Probleme. Das Corpus der minoischen und mykenischen Siegel. Forschungsbericht der DFG*, ed. F. Matz, Boppard 1974.

10. Thera: The recent dramatic discoveries of Marinatos on Thera (Santorini), the "Aegean Pompeii," have turned out to be "the most magnificent since Schliemann and Evans discovered Mycenaean and Minoan culture" (Schachermeyr). What came to light was an independent branch of Minoan culture, which in some respects, especially the frescoes, rivals the finest Minoan work on Crete. See in particular Sp. Marinatos, *Excavations at Thera* I-VI, Athens 1968-73; also *idem, Life and Art in Prehistoric Thera* (British Academy Reckitt Lecture, 1971), London 1972; *idem*, Die Ausgrabungen auf Thera und ihre Probleme (Mykenische Studien 2, SB. W 287), Vienna 1973; *idem* and M. Hirmer, *Kreta, Thera und das mykenische Hellas*, Munich 1973; Sp. Marinatos, "The 'Libya Fresco' from Thera," *Athens Annals of Archaeology* 7, 1974, 87 ff.; D. Gray, *Seewesen, mit einem Beitrag von Spyridon Marinatos. Das Schiffsfresko von Akrotiri, Thera* (Archaeologia Homerica, I,G), Göttingen 1974; M. S. F. Hood, *Kadmos* 9, 1970, 98 ff., S. A. Immerwahr, in *Studies ... Fritz Schachermeyr*, Berlin 1977, 173 ff. The eruption of the volcano has also moved into the forefront of debate: see, for instance: Sp. Marinatos, *Antiquity* 13, 1939, 425-439 (where the thesis was put forward for the first time); D. Nincovich and B. C. Heeze, *Santorini Tephra* (Colston Papers, 17), 1965, 413-453; Sir Denys Page, *The Santorini Volcano and the Desolation of Minoan Crete* (Society for the Promotion of Hellenic Studies, Suppl. Paper No. 12), London 1969; and in particular,

The Acta of the 1st International Scientific Congress on the Volcano of Thera, published by the Archaeological Service of Greece, Athens 1971. The theory of direct connection between the eruption of the Thera volcano and destruction on Crete, however, has now been seriously challenged, by H. Pichler and W. Schiering, "The Thera eruption and Late Minoan-IB destructions on Crete," *Nature* 267, 1977, 819 ff.

11. Eastern Frontier Regions: Ras Shamra (Ugarit) in Northern Syria, north of Ancient Laodiceia, shows close contacts with the Creto-Mycenaean world; see the reports in the journal *Syria*, since 1926; moreover, C. F. A. Schaeffer, "Die Stellung Ras Schamras-Ugarits zur kretischen und mykenischen Kultur," *JdI* 52, 1937, 139 ff.; *Ugaritica* I-VI, Paris 1939-69; O. Eissfeld, "Die Bedeutung der Funde von Ras Schamra für die Geschichte des Altertums," *HZ* 168, 1943, 457 ff.; see also *CAH* ^{3}I,2, 1971, 417-525: *Syria c. 1550-1400 B.C.* (M. S. Drower). On the excavations in Asia Minor, in so far as they are important for early Greek-Anatolian connections, a survey is given by G. M. A. Hanfmann, "Archaeology in Homeric Asia Minor," *AJA* 52, 1948, 135 ff.; he also makes reference to the excavations at Mersin and Tarsus, the results of which were published in the works of J. Garstang, *Prehistoric Mersin*, Oxford 1953, and H. Goldman, *Excavations at Gözlü Kule, Tarsus*, I-III, Princeton, N.J., 1950-1963. Of great importance are the excavations at Çatal Hüyük (in the Konya Plain) and Hacilar (in south-west Anatolia): see J. Mellaart, *CAH* ^{3}I,1, 1970, 304-326: *Anatolia before 4000 B.C. idem, Çatal Hüyük, A Neolithic Town in Anatolia*, London 1967; *idem, Excavations at Hacilar*, 2 vols., Edinburgh 1970: The sites belong to the Neolithic-Chalcolithic periods: Catal Hüyük to about 6700-5700 B.C., Hacilar to about 7000 [Aceramic]-5000 B.C. *idem*, *CAH* ^{3}I,2, 1971, 363-410: *Anatolia c. 4000-2300 B.C.*; *ibid.*, 681-703: *Anatolia c. 2300-1750 B.C.* The problem of the interdependence of these early cultures (for instance with the Jericho culture) and their radiation towards the west, which is probably viewed too optimistically by F. Schachermeyr (cf. his thesis of the "cultural drift from Western Asia"), still requires detailed investigation. For further surveys see O. R. Gurney, *Anatolia c. 1750-1600 B.C., CAH* ^{3}II,1, 1973, 228-255; *idem, Anatolia c. 1600-1380 B.C., CAH* ^{3}II,1, 1973, 659-682; A. Goetze, *Anatolia from Shuppiluliumash to the Egyptian War of Muwatallish, CAH* ^{3}II,2, 1975, 117-129. Reference may also be made to H.-G. Buchholz, "Bemerkungen zu den bronzezeitlichen Kulturbeziehungen im östlichen Mittelmeer," *Acta Praehistorica et Archaeogica* I, 1970.

12. The Anthropological Evidence: Anthropological research in regard to ancient Greece is only in its infancy, especially since larger complexes of sites are lacking. Significant anthropological evidence for the Late Helladic period has been found only in the Argolid (Asine, Kalkani, Dendra, Prosymna) (C. M. Fürst, *Zur Anthropologie der prähistorischen Griechen in der Argolis* [Lunds Univ. Orskr., N.F. Avd. 2, 26 No 8], 1930). According to Fürst, one must here think in terms of a highly mixed population, with only a slight northern strain. The skeletal finds of the Sub-Mycenaean period (E. Breitinger, in *Kerameikos* I, Berlin 1939, 223 ff.) show a strong eastern strain. E. Fischer has attempted to interpret the gold masks from the shaft graves anthropologically (in G. Karo, *Die Schachtgräber von Mykenai*, 320 ff.). The article by J. L. Angel, "Skeleton Material from Attica," *Hesp.* 14, 1945, 279 ff., contains all the Attic material from the prehistoric period to the end of antiquity; cf. also *idem*, "A Racial Analysis of the Ancient Greeks, an Essay on the Use of Morphological Types," *Am. Journ. Phys. Anthrop.* NS 2, 1944, 329 ff. See also the survey in *CAH* ^{3}I, 1, 1970, 156-172: *The Earliest Populations of Man in Europe, Western Asia and North Africa* (D. R. Hughes and D. R. Brothwell).

THE IMMIGRATION INTO GREECE

The older accounts, including the relevant sections in Beloch and Meyer (*GdA* II 1^2, 221 n. 1), are completely out of date. Due to the lack of narrative accounts it is chiefly the following investigations that come into question: J. B. Haley and C. W. Blegen, "The Coming of the Greeks," *AJA* 32, 1928, 141 ff.; F. Schachermeyr, "Wanderung und Ausbreitung der Indogermanen im Mittelmeergebiet," *Festschrift f. Herman Hirt*, Heidelberg 1936, 229 ff.; K. Schefold, "Archäolog. Zeugnisse der griech. Einwanderung," *NJb.*, 1937, 213 ff.; S. Fuchs, *Die griech. Fundgruppen der frühen Bronzezeit und ihre auswärtigen Beziehungen. Ein Beitrag zur Frage der Indogermanisierung Griechenlands*, Berlin 1937 (a study which requires detailed correction on points of fact: see, for instance, F. Matz, *Gn.* 15, 1939, 65 ff.); F. Schachermeyr, *Klio* 32, 1939, 235 ff.; 339 ff.; H. Krahe and W. Kraiker, *Ant.* 15, 1939, 175 ff.; 195 ff.; W. Kraiker, *Alte Sprachen* 4, 1939, 272 ff.: Otto, *Kulturg.*, 13 ff.; H. Herter, *Die Einwanderung der Griechen* (Kriegsvortrag d. Univ. Bonn, 57), Bonn 1941, 3 ff.; 35 ff.; H. Krahe, "Die Indogermanisierung Griechenlands," *Antike, Alte Sprachen u. deutsche Bildung*, 1943, 2 ff.; 6 ff.; F. Matz, "Griech. Vorgeschichte," in *NBAnt.* 1, 13 ff.; F. Specht, *Die Ausbreitung der Indogermanen* (Preuss. Ak., Vortr. u. Schrift., Heft 20, 1944); *idem*, "Die Herkunft der Griechen und Römer und ihre Sprachen," *Lexis* 3, 1953, 63-64 [he assumes three immigrations: about 2000 the Ionians, about 1700 the Achaeans, about 1100 the Dorians]; M. P. Nilsson, "The Prehistoric Migrations of the Greeks," *Opuscula Atheniensia* 1, Lund 1953, 1-8; A. J. B. Wace, "The Coming of the Greeks," *CW* 47, 1953/54, 152-155; F. Schachermeyr, "Zum Problem der griech. Nationalität," in *Atti e Memorie del I° Congr. int. di Micenologia*, Rome 1967, III 105-120; "The First Arrival of Indo-European Elements in Greece," *Acta of the 2nd International Colloquium on Aegean Prehistory*, edited by the Archaeological Service of Greece, Athens 1972; N. G. L. Hammond, "The Arrival of Greek Speech in the Southern Balkans," in *Studies*, 26 ff.; see also "Prehistory and Protohistory," in *History of the Hellenic People* I, ed. by G. A. Christopoulos and J. C. Bastias, Athens and London 1974; and R. A. Crossland and Ann Birchall (eds.), *Bronze Age Migrations in the Aegean. Archaeological and Linguistic Problems in Greek Prehistory* (Proceedings *of the First Intern. Colloquium on Aegean Prehistory*, Park Ridge, N.J., 1974; cf. further, F. Schachermeyr, "Die grossen Zeitwenden am Beginn und am Ende des Altertums," in *Forschungen und Betrachtungen zur griech. u. röm. Geschichte*, Vienna 1974, 7 ff.

MINOAN CULTURE

For the sources and investigations see above 369 f. and 377 f. Cf. further: Meyer, *GdA* II²1, 162 ff.; Pendlebury, *Cr.*, 277 ff. A survey is given by G. Glotz, *La civilisation égéenne*, Paris 1923 (a new edition, with an Appendix by P. Demargne, 1952); F. Matz, *Ägäis*, 222 ff.; *idem, Crete and Early Greece*. 1962; Chr. Zervos, *L'art de la Crête néolithique et minoenne*, Paris 1956; S. Marinatos and M. Hirmer, *Crete and Mycenae*, 1960, and now *iidem, Kreta und das mykenische Hellas*, 1973; R. Higgins, *Minoan and Mycenaean Art*, London 1967; S. Dow, *The Minoan Thalassocracy* (Proc. of the Mass. Hist. Soc., 79), 1961, 3 ff.; A. Zois, *Der Kamares-Stil, Werden und Wesen*, Diss. Tübingen 1968; P. Warren, *Minoan Stone Vases*, London 1969 (cf. W. Schiering, *Gn.* 45, 1973, 697 ff.); L. E. Palmer, *A New Guide to the Palace of Knossos* (cf. however, P. Warren, *CR* 21, 1971, 114 ff.); see also *Graham, Pal.*; J. W. Shaw, *Minoan Architecture. Materials and Techniques*, Rome 1973, and in particular, Hood, *Mins.* On connections between Crete and Asia see K. Schefold, "Unbekanntes Asien in Alt-Kreta," *WG* 15, 1955, 1-15. On Minoan urbanisation F. Tritsch "Die Stadtbildungen des Altertums und die griechische Polis," *Klio* 22, 1929, 20 ff.

MYCENAEAN CULTURE

Of the works cited above 370 ff., cf., in particular Karo, *Sch.*, *RE Suppl.* VI, 584 ff. s.v. *Mykenische Kultur*; cf. Matz, *Ägäis*, 275 ff.; on Mycenaean pottery: Arne Furumark, *Myc. Pot.* (a standard work: cf. F. Matz, *Gn.* 19, 1943, 225 ff.); also A. D. Lacy, *Greek Pottery in the Bronze Age*, London 1967; G. E. Mylonas, *Grave Circle B of Mycenae*, Lund 1964; E. French, *BSA* 66, 1971, 101 ff.; W. Schiering, *AW* 2, 1971, 3 ff. The results of more recent excavations at Mycenae: see above 373 f. **Bibliography**: M. P. Nilsson, "Das homerische Königtum," *OS* II, 871 ff.; *idem, Hom.*, Chap. VI, 212 ff.; E. Bethe, "Troja, Mykene, Agamemnon und sein Grosskönigtum," *RhM* 80, 1930, 218 ff. (against M. P. Nilsson and Ed. Meyer); Schachermeyr, *H.u.A.*; Schuchardt, *Alt.*, cf. G. L. Huxley, *Achaeans and Hittites*, Oxford 1960, and O. R. Gurney, *The Hittites*, Harmondsworth ²1954, 53 ff.; Schuchhardt, *Alt.*, 230 ff.; 248 ff.; H. J. Kantor, *The Aegean and the Orient in the Second Millennium B.C.*, Bloomington 1947, 33 ff., cf. P. Åström, "The International Archaeological Symposium in Cyprus on the Mycenaeans in the Eastern Mediterranean, Nicosia 27 March-2 April 1972," *Kadmos* 11, 1972, 179-181. See further, the book by F. H. Stubbings cited *infra* 385 n. 69, and his contribution in *CAH* ³II, 1, 1973, 627-658: *The Rise of Mycenaean Civilisation*; R. A. Crossland, *Immigrants from the North, CAH* ³I, 2,

1971, 824-876; S. Dow, "The Greeks in the Bronze Age," in *Rapports du XIe Congr. Intern. des sciences historiques*, Stockholm 1960, 1-34; C. W. Blegen, *The Mycenaean Age. The Trojan War, the Dorian Invasion, and Other Problems* (Lectures in Memory of Louise Taft Semple), Cincinnati 1962 [37 pp.] Original is F. Hampl, "Die Chronologie der Einwanderung der griechischen Stämme und das Problem der Nationalität der Träger der mykenischen Kultur," *MusHelv* 17, 1950, 57-86. According to Hampl, the Mycenaeans came from the *East*, and are therefore not Greeks. Opposed to Hampl, correctly, F. Schachermeyr in *Atti e Memorie del I^o Congr. Int. di Micenologia* III, Rome 1967, 113 ff.; N. G. L. Hammond, "The Origins of some Mycenaean Rulers", in *Studies*, 1 ff. See further, J. Chadwick, "Aegean History 1500-1200 B.C.," *Studii clasice* 11, 1969, 7 ff.; Elizabeth French, "The Development of Mycenaean Terracotta Figurines," *BSA* 66, 1971, 101-187; N. C. Scoufopoulos, *Mycenaean Citadels* (SIMA 22), Göteborg 1971; J. Chadwick, *The Mycenaean World*, London-New York-Melbourne 1976 (based on the Linear B Tablets).

1. On Greek geography see C. Neumann and J. Partsch, *Physikalische Geographie von Griechenland*, Breslau 1885; A. Philippson, *Das Mittelmeergebiet*, Berlin-Leipzig [4]1922; *Das Klima Griechenlands*, Bonn 1948; O. Maull, *Das griechische Mittelmeergebiet*, Breslau 1922; C. Vita-Finzi, *The Mediterranean Valleys. Geological Changes in Historical Time*, Cambridge 1969. On the relationship of the country to its history: V. Ehrenberg, "Griechisches Land und griechischer Staat," *Ant.* 3, 1927, 304 ff.= *Polis und Imperium*, Zurich-Stuttgart 1965, 635 ff.; Berve, *GG* I, 1 ff. The most important bibliography on the geography of the various districts of Greece may be found in the major work by A. Philippson, *Griechische Landschaften* I-IV, Frankfurt a.M. 1950-1959 (the earlier parts Bd. I, 1-II,2 contain valuable supplements by E. Kirsten).

2. See, relevant to this, the study by L. Casson, *Ships and Seamanship in the Ancient World*, Princeton, N.J., 1971 (cf. D. Wachsmuth, *Gn.* 44, 1972, 688 ff.).

3. On the question of the original homeland of the Indo-Europeans see, for instance, F. Ratzel, *HZ* 93, 1 ff. Bibliography is cited by W. Otto, *HZ* 146, 1932, 209 n. 1; Schwyzer, *Gram.* I, 53 (with Addenda 822); W. Hauer, *ARW* 36, 1939, 1 ff. (not sufficiently critical), and F. Specht, *Die Ausbreitung der Indogermanen*, Berlin 1944. It is impossible to go into any detail here. Cf. also Ernst Meyer, *Die Indogermanenfrage*, Marburg 1948, and A. Nehring, *Die Problematik der Indogermanenforschung* (Würzburg, 1954), printed, along with other works, in *Die Urheimat der Indogermanen*, ed. A. Scherer, Darmstadt 1968 (Wege der Forschung, 166).

4. P. Kretschmer, "Sprache" 156 ff.; E. Schwyzer, *Gram.* I, 48, ff.; 55; G. Deeters, *Die Stellung des Griechischen innerhalb der indogermanischen Sprache* (Kriegsvortr. d. Univ. Bonn 56), Bonn 1941.

5. Advocated by the historians E. Curtius and Th. Mommsen, the jurist Leist, and revived by the linguist H. Hirt.

6. See, in place of all others, F. Schachermeyr, *RE* XXII, 1452 f.

7. That no conclusive traces can be proved for an Indo-European settlement of Greece in the Middle Helladic period, has been correctly stressed by Nilsson, *Hom.* 85. Archaeologists and also historians almost without exception now regard Middle Helladic culture as Greek.

8. See the bibliography cited above 369 ff.

9. A much closer contact with Western Asia has been argued by F. Schachermeyr, "Zur Entstehung der ältesten Civilisation in Griechenland," *La Nouvelle Clio*, 1950, 367 ff., and in later studies, for instance: *Griech.* 67 ff. (to be used critically).

10. On the chronology of the Dimini layer v.s.p.31 f.

11. K. Grundmann, *AM* 59, 1934, 123 ff.; F. Schachermeyr, *Mitt. d. Anthropol. Gesellsch. Wien* 83, 1953, 1 ff, (also separately: "Dimini und die Bandkeramik," in *Prähistorische*

Forschungen, publ. Anthropol. Gesellsch. in Wien, 1954, pp. 39; cf. S. Benton, *JHS* 77, 1957, 353), and in later, concise studies, for instance: F. Schachermeyr, *Griech.* 111 ff., 271 n. 81.

12. The Proto-Indo-European theory put forward by P. Kretschmer, *Glotta* 14, 1925, 300 ff., is completely lacking in evidence. The arguments of H. Krahe, *Ant.*, 11 f., are also unconvincing. Even Matz, *Ägäis*, 188 ff., and F. Schachermeyr, for instance in *RE* XXII, 1475 ff., *Griech.* 121 ff., are still too generous in assuming immigrants. The same holds true for the contribution by S. S. Weinberg (v.s.p. 370) on the Neolithic period in the Aegean.

13. K. Bittel, *KS*, 138 ff.

14. The theory advanced by, *inter al.*, such scholars as C. W. Blegen, A. W. Persson and S. Fuchs, to wit, an eastern immigration into Hellas in the Early Helladic period expanded on by P. Kretschmer (v.s.n. 12), rests on very shaky foundations. Matz, Ägäis, 203, has also been correct in contesting the so-called "Cycladic migration."

15. In addition to A. Pott, we are indebted in particular to P. Kretschmer for these all important observations (v.s.p. 369); see besides A. Fick, *Vorgriech. Ortsnamen als Quelle fur die Vorgeschichte Griechenlands*, Göttingen 1905 (in part problematic), the summary by A. Debrunner, "Die Besiedlung des alten Griechenland im Licht der Sprachwissenschaft," *NJb*, 1918, 433 ff., *RL Vorgesch.* IV 2, 1926, 525 ff.; Schwyzer, *Gram.* I, 59 ff. A very concise evaluation of the pre-Greek names from the standpoint of the history of civilisation is given by H. Krahe, *Ant.*, 7 ff.

16. On the geographical distribution of the pre-Greek place names see J. B. Haley, *AJA* 32, 1928, 141 ff., cf. Maps 9 and 10 in Schachermeyer, *Griech.* 246 and 247. To date attempts to connect the pre-Greek population with a specific archaeological stratum (cf. C. W. Blegen, *AJA* 32, 1928, 146 ff.), have not been successful.

17. Ed. Meyer, "Die Pelasger," *Forsch.* I, 1 ff., cf. F. Schachermeyr, *EF*, 253 ff. The evidence may be found in F. Lochner-Hüttenbach, *Die Pelasger* (Arbeiten aus dem Institut für vergleich. Sprachwissenschaft in Graz), Vienna 1960.

18. The "substratum theory" advanced by S. Fuchs, *Die griech. Fundgruppen der frühen Bronzezeit und ihre auswärtigen Beziehungen*, 1937, has rightly found no countenance; cf. F. Schachermeyr, *Klio* 32, 1939, 282.

19. Of more recent studies on the Greek dialects, see, for instance: W. Porzig, "Sprachgeographische Untersuchungen zu den altgriech. Dialekten," *Indogerm. Forsch* 61, 1954, 147-169; more problematic is the work of E. Risch, "Die Gliederung der griech. Dialekte in neuer Sicht," *MusHelv* 11, 1955, 61-76 (including Linear B); cf. A. Bartonek, "Greek Dialects in the Second Millennium B.C.," *Eirene* 9, 1971, 49 ff.

20. The essentially earlier dates formerly accepted by scholars are now obsolete.

21. On the chronology see the more recent studies cited above 394 n. 66.

22. On the Hyksos see H. Stock, *Stud. z. Gesch. und Archäol der 13.-17. Dynastie Ägyptens*, Glückstadt 1942; cf. F.W. v. Bissing, *OLZ*, 1944, 85 ff.; further T. Säve-Söderbergh. *JEA* 37, 1951, 53 ff.; and A. Alt, *Die Herkunft der Hyksos in neuer Sicht* (Abh. S 101,6), 1954 (stimulating, although in part problematic). The same holds true for J. van Seters. *The Hyksos*, New Haven 1966.

23. Götze, *Heth.*, 79 ff., who, however, exaggerates the importance of the Churriti (for instance, 101). On the difficulties involved see M. Mayrhofer, *Die Indo-Arier im alten Vorderasien*, Wiesbaden 1966, and A. Kammenhuber, *Die Arier im Vorderen Orient*, Heidelberg 1968.

24. According to F. Schachermeyr (*HM* III 49), it was the Greeks, in league with Ahmose, who brought about the overthrow of Hyksos rule. But so long as we do not know precisely what is concealed in the term *Haunebut*, such an interpretation will of necessity remain a conjecture.

25. The northern influences are no doubt exaggerated by F. Matz, *Die frühkretischen Siegel*, Berlin-Leipzig 1928; cf. also Matz, *Ägäis*, 229.

26. A map in Schachermeyr *Rasse*, 43, also in E. Kirsten, *Ant.* 14, 1938, 299.

27. P. Kretschmer, "Die ältesten Sprachschichten auf Kreta," *Glotta* 31, 1948, 1 ff., maintained that the Cretans originated in Asia Minor. This theory is, however, not founded on sufficient evidence.

28. On the history of Cretan art cf. now the works by F. Matz, Chr. Zervos, Sp. Marinatos and M. Hirmer (v.s.p. 381), also A. Zois, *Der Kamares-Stil*, Diss. Tübingen 1968.

29. The publication of the cuneiform texts from Mari by French scholars is in progress: *Archives royales de Mari* I-X (copies), XI-XIII (transcripts), Paris 1946 ff.

30. C. F. A. Schaeffer, *JdI* 52, 1937, 139 ff.; *Ugaritica* I, 1939, 53 ff. Cf. P. Demargne, "Crète et Orient au temps d'Hammourabi," *Rev. arch.* 1936, 80 ff.; "Crète, Egypte, Asie. Perspectives d'hier et d'aujourd'hui," *Ann. de Gand* II, 1938, 31 ff.

31. On the Cretan script see the material below n. 40.

32. Evans, *Knossos* I, 415 ff.

33. Meyer, *GdA* II² 1, 43 f. (Chian's name is also found on a basalt lion in Babylonia).

34. See W. Otto, *HZ* 146, 1942, 209; F.W.v. Bissing, *AfO*. 11, 1936/37, 325.

35. Evans, *Knossos* II, 313 ff.; Schachermeyr, *Rasse*, 27 f.; Matz, *Ägäis*, 232.

36. This is the estimate of F. Schachermeyr. Sir Arthur Evans has reckoned the number of inhabitants at more than 80,000 (*Knossos* II, 563 f.).

37. Illustrated in, for instance, Bossert, *Kr.* Abb. 170.

38. Thus Sp. Marinatos, *Kreta und die hethische (sic!) -kleinasiat. Welt im 2. Jahrtausend* (Second Turkish History Congress), Istanbul 1937, but caution is urged in respect of his other theories, especially so far as the assumption of a Cretan colonisation of the coasts of Anatolia is concerned; he is followed by U. Wilcken, *GG*, 37. This catastrophe is dated by Sir Arthur Evans in the time soon after 1570 B.C.; cf. also Matz, *Ägäis*, 242 (with n. 6), and F. Schachermeyr, for instance, *HM* III, 45; 49 [approximately 1600 B.C.].

39. Elaborated on by Schachermeyr, *Rasse*, 34 ff.

40. On Cretan writing see the material in Sir Arthur Evans, *Scripta Minoa* I, Oxford 1909; II, 1952, edited by J. L. Myres; *Knossos* I, 270 ff.; 612 ff.; IV, 666 ff.; F. Chapouthier, *Etud. crét.* 2, 1930; also the numerous studies by J. Sundwall, cited in *Min.* 461 ff. Important, moreover, are the researches of Alice E. Kober, *AJA* 52, 1949, 82 ff., who argues for the inflected character of Minoan Linear B. On the question of the decipherment of Linear B by M. Ventris and his collaborators v.s.p. 367 f. On the script as historical evidence, see John Chadwick, "The Linear Scripts and the Tablets as Historical Documents," *CAH* ³II,1, 1973, 609 ff.

41. The origin of the characters on the Phaestus Disc (*Il palazzo min. di Festos* I, 419 ff.), in which the stamping technique was used, is still unexplained; Meyer, *GdA* II² 1, 217, regarded the writing as a syllabic script using ideographic symbols and conjectured a list bearing the names of warriors. It must be a non-Greek language from the Aegean; cf. G. Ipsen, *Indogerm. Forsch.* 47, 1929, 1 ff.; bibliography is cited by F.W.v. Bissing, *Hdb. Arch.* I, 1939, 157 n. 2, also Alice E. Kober, *AJA* 52, 1949, 87 f.

42. Nilsson, *MMRel.* (cf. B. Schweitzer, *Gn.* 4, 1928, 169 ff.), amplified second edition, Lund 1950; Nilsson, *GrRel* I³, 256 ff.; see also B. Rutkowski, "Minoan Cults and History," *H.* 20, 1971, 1 ff. B. C. Dietrich, *The Origins of Greek Religion*, Berlin 1974 and S. Hood, in *Studies... Fritz Schachermeyr*, Berlin 1977, 158 ff.

43. G. Karo, *RE Suppl.* VI, 613, even thinks that there was probably a distinct cultural regression.

44. A brief survey by R. J. Buck, "The Middle Helladic Period," *Px.* 20, 1966, 193 ff.

45. The term "Mycenaean culture" was coined by A. Furtwängler (Furtwängler-Loeschcke, *Mykenische Vasen*, 1886, XI ff.). In view of the predominant position of Mycenae the term has been aptly chosen. More recent excavations have only underlined this.

46. *Odyssey* III 263.

47. H. Lehmann, *Argolis I. Landeskunde der Ebene von Argos und ihrer Randgebiete*, Athens 1937; an earlier survey of the finds may be found in G. Karo, *RE Suppl.* VI, 604 ff., which should now be supplemented by the reports cited above of F. Schachermeyr and Matz, *Ägäis*, Cf. i.p. 390 n. 10 for the work by P. Ålin.

48. G. Welter, *AA*, 1939, 1 ff.

49. On the protection of foreigners in the ancient Indo-European Age see still W. Schulze, *Kleine Schriften*, Göttingen 1933, 203 ff.; P. Thieme, *Der Fremdling im Rgveda*, Leipzig 1938, 14 ff.; 152 ff.

50. The older shaft graves are dated by finds of objects from the time of Amenophis III and of Tehe in the XVIIIth Dynasty of Egypt.

51. W. Otto, *HZ* 146, 1932, 207 n. 2.

52. E. F. Bruck, *Totenteil und Seelgerät im griech. Recht* (Münch. Beitr. 9), Munich 1926, 6 ff.

53. W. A. Heurtley, *BSA* 25, 1921, 126 ff.; G. Karo, *RL Vorgesch.* IV, 1926, 493 f.; illustrations in Bossert, *Kr.*, Abb. 66 and 67. On the introduction of the war chariot cf. J. Wiesner, *Fahren und Reiten in Alteuropa und im Alten Orient* (AO 38, 2-4). 1939, 44 ff.; and F. Schachermeyr, *Arch. Orientalni* 17, 1949, 705 ff.; *Anthropos* 46, 1951, 705 ff.; the Mycenaean Greeks, he argues, took over the war chariot from the Egyptians, a conjecture which is connected with the rôle of the Greeks in liberating the land of the Nile from the Hyksos, as maintained by F. Schachermeyr (v.s.p. 383 n.24).

54. An older survey of the bibliography may be found in G. Karo, *RE Suppl.* VI, 588 f., also in Matz, *Ägäis* 277 ff.

55. On the date see Matz, *Ägäis*, 280.

56. Schuchhardt, *Alt.*, 68 f., thinks that the vaulted tombs trace their place of origin to ancient western Europe, especially Spain which, in addition to Ireland, possesses many such structures.

57. O. Walter, *AA*, 1940, 208 ff. (based on the researches of A. J. B. Wace).

58. On the lion as escutcheon see A. W. Persson, *Dragma M. P. Nilsson dedicatum*, Lund 1939, 379 ff. Matz, *Ägäis*, 285, thinks in terms of Cretan models (on gems).

59. H. Hoffmann, "Innereuropäische Parallelen zum Plattenring von Mykenai," *Bericht VI. Intern. Archäologenkongress in Berlin 1939* (published 1940), 316 ff.

60. Persson, *Dend.*, 8 ff.; *Dend. New.*

61. G. Rodenwaldt, *Tiryns* II, 1912. Further material in G. Karo, *RE Suppl.* VI, 595 f.; cf. Matz, *Ägäis*, 292 (including bibliography no.2).

62. Steffen, *Karten von Mykene*, 8 ff.; Meyer, *GdA* II[2] 1, 244 f.

63. H. Bulle, *Orchomenos* I, 1907, Taf. 7; further studies are cited by Matz, *Ägäis*, 291 n.1. The view of U. Kahrstedt, *AA*, 1937, 1 ff., that the dikes are at the earliest a project of Epameinondas, does not appear to be substantiated in this general form; on the whole question see S. Lauffer, *Gn.* 24, 1952, 482 ff. [review of P. Guillon, *La Béotie antique*, Paris 1948]. See also E. Kenny, *Liverpool Annals of Art and Archaeology*, 22, 1935, 189 ff.

64. See E. Bethe, *RhM* 80, 1931, 218 ff.; W. Otto, *HZ* 146, 1932, 221.

65. F. Dirlmeier, *Ph.* 90, 1935, 76.

66. The conjecture of Meyer, *GdA* II[2] 1, 267 ff., that the union of Attica extends back to the Mycenaean period, is erroneous (v.i.p. 47). A similar attempt has been made by R. A. Padgug, *GRBS* 13, 1972, 135 ff.

67. Cf. A. Furumark, "The Settlement at Ialysos and Aegean History c. 1550-1400 B.C.," *Opusc. Arch.* 6, 1950, 150 ff. The alleged sovereignty of the Cretans over Athens is rightly contested by G. E. Mylonas, *Studies Ferguson*, 11 ff. Probably too negative is Ch. Starr, *H.* 3, 1954-55, 282 ff.

68. That the blockading of a city in Asia Minor by the Achaeans is depicted on a silver rhyton from the fourth shaft grave (photograph in, for instance, Bossert, *Kr.*, Abb. 77), is in fact maintained by Meyer, *GdA* II[2] 1, 232 f., but correctly contested by W. Otto, *HZ* 146, 1932, 221. A connection with the "Trojan War" would, moreover, be excluded already on chronological grounds (the rhyton dates from the sixteenth century!). According to J. T. Hooker, *AJA* 71, 1967, 269 ff., it is not a blockading scene that is depicted; the treasures found in the Mycenaean shaft graves are not, according to Hooker, to be traced to plundering campaigns but to trade connections.

69. See Furumark, *Myc. Pot.*, and Matz, *Ägäis*, 298 ff.; also H. Kantor, "The *Aegean* and the Near East in the Second Millennium B.C.," *AJA* 32, 1948, 17-103; S. Immerwahr, "Mycenaean Trade and Colonization," *Archaeology* 13, 1960, 4-13; F. H. Stubbings, *Mycenaean Pottery from the Levant,* Cambridge 1951, P. J. Riis, *Sukas* I. *The North-East Sanctuary and the First Settling of the Greeks in Syria and Palestine*, Copenhagen 1970; Gunhild Ploug, *Sukas* II. *The Aegean, Corinth* and *Eastern Greek Pottery and Terracottas*, Copenhagen 1973. C. W. Beck *et al.*, "Analysis and Provenience of Minoan and Mycenaean Amber, III," *GRBS* 11, 1970, 5 ff.; C. W. Beck *et al.*, *GRBS* 13, 1972, 375 ff. On Aegean influences (and especially Cretan) in the early Iron Age of Rome (c. tenth century B.C.) see H. Müller-Karpe, *Vom Anfang Roms*, 1959, 43 ff.

70. A. J. B. Wace and C. W. Blegen, "Pottery as Evidence for Trade and Colonisation in

the Aegean Bronze Age," *Klio* 32, 1939, 131 ff.; H. W. Catling, E. E. Richards, A. E. Blin-Stoyle, "Correlations Between Composition and Provenance of Mycenaean and Minoan Pottery," *BSA* 58, 1963, 94-115.

71. The evidence in *Meyer, GdA* II² 1, 281 n. 4.

72. Corresponding to the term used by Homer for the Greeks who participated in the expedition against Troy.

73. C. F. A. Schaeffer, *Ugaritica* I, 1939, 99, thinks in terms of a "véritable colonisation mycénienne" at the end of the fourteenth and during the thirteenth century in Ugarit (Ras Shamra). But the alleged reference to the "Ionians" (*Iman*) on a Ugaritic cuneiform tablet, as well as the alleged appearance of the name of Nicomedes (*Nqmd*), belong in the realm of fancy; cf. J. Friedrich, *ZDMG* 96, 1942, 470; M. Noth *ZDPV* 65, 1942, 161 ff.; also already *supra* 368 f.

74. *JHS* 59, 1939, 203 ff., also M. P. Nilsson, *Kretika Chronika* 3, 1949, 7 ff.

75. K. Bittel, *Grundzüge der Vor- und Fruhgesch. Kleinasiens*, Tübingen ²1950, 55 ff. (with map illustrating finds); *Istanbuler Forschungen* 17, 1950, 10 ff.; W. Schiering, "Die minoisch-mykenische Siedlung in Milet vor dem Bau der grossen Mauer," *Ist. Mitt.* 25, 1975, 9 ff.; W. Voigtländer, "Die mykenische Stadtmauer in Milet und einzelne Wehranlagen der späten Bronzezeit," *Ist. Mitt.* 25, 1975, 17 ff. Conclusive evidence has only been established for Miletus as a Mycenaean settlement. A much too sure affirmation of the presence of "Achaeans" in Asia Minor is made by Cassola, *Ionia*, 308 ff., et al. See for the opposite view the study by Cook, *infra* 389.

76. A. Götze, *Kleinasien zur Hethiterzeit*, Orient und Antike I, Heidelberg 1924, 26, was the first to draw attention to this allusion.

77. E. Forrer, "Vorhomerische Griechen in den Keilschrifttexten von Boghazköi," *MDOG* 63, 1924, 1 ff.; "Die Griechen in den Boghazköi-Texten," *OLZ* 1924, 113 ff. (cf. also *RL Assyrologie* s.v. *Ahhijava*; opposed to him, in particular, J. Friedrich, *Kleinasiat. Forsch.* I, 1927, 87 ff.; cf. also E. Forrer, *ibid.* I 2, 1929, 252 ff., and F. Sommer, *Die Ahhijava-Urkunden* (Abh. Bay, NF 6), 1932 (cf. A. Götze, *Gn.* 10, 1934, 177 ff.); "Ahhijava-frage und Sprachwissenschaft," *ibid.* NF 9, 1934; "Ahhijava and kein Ende?," *Indogerm. Forsch.* 55, 1937, 169 ff. From the very outset Otto (*Kulturg.* 41 n. 80; *DLZ* 1928, 728 ff., *et al.*) was sceptical of Forrer's theories. Forrer has been supported chiefly by P. Kretschmer, *Glotta* 21, 1933, 213 ff.; 24, 1936, 203 ff.; *PhW* 1925, 516 ff., *et al.* The problem has been discussed in detail by Schachermeyr, *H.u.A.*, Leipzig 1935, 20 ff., who adopts a mediating view. In *Min.* 365 ff., Schachermeyr suggests Mycenae, Rhodes and Cyprus as alternatives for Ahhijawa, against K. Völkl (*La Nouvelle Clio* 3, 1952, 329 ff.), who, along with others, argues for Rhodes. For Cyprus: P. Kretschmer, *Glotta* 23, 1954, 1-54; for Pamphylia: F. Cornelius, in *Münchener Studien zur Sprachwissenschaft 6 (Sommer-Festschrift)*, 1955, 33. For North-West Asia Minor: A. Goetze, *KAO*, 183. Rightly very critical, G. Steiner, *Saec.* 15, 1964, 365 ff. Cf. also J. D. Muhly, "Hittites and Achaeans. Ahhijawa *Redomitus*," *H.* 23, 1974, 129 ff.

78. W. Otto, *DLZ*, 1928, 729 ff., was the first to suggest Cilicia; cf. also F. Sommer, *Die Ahhijava-Urkunden*, 1932, 358 ff.; on the other hand, for instance, Schachermeyr, *H.u.A*, 79 ff.

79. H. Bengtson, *Gn.* 18, 1942, 209 f. (= *KS*, 102 f.). Cf., for instance, the name *Ahijababa* in the annals of Assurnasirpal (883 B.C.) as a ruler of Bi-Adini. (cf. also D. Page, *History and the Homeric Iliad*, Berkeley 1959, 3 ff., and E. Vermeule, *Greece in the Bronze Age*, Chicago 1964, 272 n. 3.

80. Following in Forrer's footsteps of late, Cassola, *Ionia*, 331 ff.

81. Nilsson, *MMRel.* 44 ff.; *The Mycenaean Origin of Greek Mythology*, 1932 [²1972]; *idem, Gr. Rel.* I, 26; see already *supra* 368; cf. at the same time R. B. Edwards, *Greek Legends and the Mycenaean Age, with Special Reference to Oriental Elements in the Legend of Kadmos*, Amsterdam 1973.

82. Cf. also the heroic honours conferred on Spartan kings: Xen., *Res publ. Lac.* 15, at the end.

83. A different view is held by Nilsson, *Gr. Rel.* I, 355; cf., however, G. Karo, *Sc.*, 332.

84. Persson, *Dend.*, 68 ff.; Nilsson, *Gr. Rel.* I 375; cf. *Gn.* 15, 1939, 77.

85. J. Wiesner, "Grab u. Jenseits. Untersuch. im ägäischen Raum zur Bronzezeit u. frühen Eisenzeit," *RVV* 26, Berlin 1938, esp. 101 ff.

86. A concise discussion in Nilsson, *Gr. Rel.* I 339 f., cf. also R. V. Nicholls, "Greek Votive Statuettes and Religious Continuity, c. 1200-700 B.C.," in *Auckland Classical Essays Presented to E. M. Blaiklock*, Auckland and Oxford 1970, 1 ff., and W. Burkert, *Greek Religion: Archaic and Classical*, Oxford 1985.

2 MIGRATION AND TRANSITION

On the Egyptian sources see above; the Greek sources on the Dorian Migration, in part very late, are discussed by N. G. L. Hammond, "Prehistoric Epirus and the Dorian Invasion," *BSA* 32, 1931/32, 131 ff.; cf. T. C. Skeat, *The Dorians in Archaeology*, London 1934, 41 ff. (cf. W. Kraiker, *Gn.* 11, 1935, 641 ff., whose judgment, however, is too uncritical). Important is V. Milojčić, "Die dorische Wanderung im Lichte der vorgeschichtl. Funde," *AA*, 1948-49 (published 1950), 12 ff.; he differentiates between three different waves of migration into Greece, connected with great devastations: in the thirteenth century, at the close of the eleventh century and in the ninth-eighth century. Milojčić regards the Early Illyrians (?), the Dorians (with Epirus as their point of departure), and once more the Illyrians as constituting these movements. In view of the current state of scholarship this interpretation must remain a hypothesis for the time being. The observation is certainly correct that the migrations must not be viewed too simply. **Bibliography**: F. Schachermeyr, "Materialien z. Gesch. d. ägäischen Wanderung in Kleinasien," *AM* 41, 1916, 375 ff. (cf. K. Bittel, *KS*, 67 ff.); *EF*, 29 ff.; Götze, *Heth.* 152 ff.; J. Wiesner, *NJb*, 1941, 194 ff.; *Vor- und Frühzeit* I, 1943, 121 ff.; on the Dorian Migration in particular: G. Vitalis, *Die Entwicklung der Sage von der Rückkehr der Herakliden*, Diss. Greifswald 1930; Wilamowitz, *Gl.* I, 68 ff., F. Miltner, *Klio* 27, 1934, 54 ff.; H. E. Stier, *Grundlagen und Sinn der griech. Gesch.*, 1945, 187 ff. (he overestimates the Illyrian element); F. Kiechle, Die Ausprägung der Sage von der Rückkehr der Herakliden, *Helikon* [Messina] 6, 1966, 493-517 [he places too much confidence in Homer as a historical source for specific references of a territorial nature]; cf. the articles in *AJA* 52, 1948, 107 ff., by J. F. Daniel, O. Broneer, H. T. Wade-Gery under the inclusive title "The Dorian Invasion." Interesting, though not completely convincing, is the attempt by Daniel (*op. cit.*, 109) to bring the Trojan War back into history, namely in the period about 1200 B.C.; cf. also W. F. Albright, *AJA* 54, 1950, 173 [Trojan War between 1230 and 1180 B.C.], and A. J. B. Wace, in *Studies Goldman*, 133-134 [the fall of Troy 1209 or 1183]. Very instructive are the articles printed in *JHS* 84, 1964, 1 ff., under the title "The Trojan War," by M. I. Finley, J. L. Caskey, G. S. Kirk, and D. L. Page. Of these writers, Finley is very sceptical, Page, on the other hand, is optimistic. Independent views may be found in A. J. Toynbee, *Some Problems in Greek History*, London 1969, 1 ff.

The archaeological heritage of the Sub-Mycenaean (c. 1150-1000 B.C.) and the subsequent Protogeometric period is much inferior to the rich finds of the Late Helladic. The most important publication is that by W. Kraiker and K. Kübler, *Kerameikos. Ergebnisse der Ausgrabungen* I: *Die Nekropolen des 12. bis 10. Jahrhunderts*, Berlin 1939; IV, 1943; V, 1954: *Die Nekropolen des 10. bis 8. Jhs.*, von K. Kübler. Cf. H. Müller-Karpe,

"Die Metallbeigaben der früheisenzeitlichen Kerameikos-Gräber," *JdI* 77, 1962, 59 ff. Very welcome is V.R.d'A. Desborough, *Protogeometric Pottery*, Oxford 1952, as well as his works *Last M., and GrDA*; cf. also the work by Snodgrass, *DA*. An account of the archaeological finds in western Asia Minor is provided by G.M.A. Hanfmann, *AJA* 52, 1948, 146 ff.; *idem*, "Ionia, Leader or Follower," *HSCP* 61 1953, 1-37. Very instructive is C. Weickert, Die Ausgrabungen beim Athene-Tempel in Milet 1955, *Istanbuler Mitt.* 7, 1957, 56 ff. [he regards a Mycenaean settlement as certain]. The literary tradition of the Greeks (especially Herodotus, I 142-48, as well as Strabo and Pausanias) is restricted to references concerning the Ionian Migration; they were placed in their proper light for the first time by Ed. Meyer, *Ph.* 48, 1889, 268 ff. (cf. *ibid.* 49, 1890, 479 ff.): Ed. Meyer, as compared with Ernst Curtius, showed that the theory of the Ionians having allegedly advanced from Asia Minor to Hellas via the islands is untenable, and that ancient tradition in connection with general considerations points much more in the opposite direction. Ed. Meyer's view has rightly been accepted by scholars; cf. U.v. Wilamowitz, "Über die ionische Wanderung," *SB.B*, 1906, 59 ff.; *idem, "Panionion," ibid.*, 38 ff. (both studies are printed in *Kleine Schriften* V 1, 1937); H. Bolkestein, "Zur Entstehung der ionischen Phylen," *Klio* 13, 1913, 424 ff.; M.O.B. Caspari, "The Ionian Confederacy," *JHS* 35, 1915, 173 ff.; Th. Lenschau, *RE* IX, 1871 ff. s.v. *Iones*; W. Judeich, *RhM* 82, 1933, 305 ff.; A. Momigliano, "Questioni di storia ionica arcaica," *Studi ital. fil. cl.* 10, 1932/33, 259 ff.; H. Bengtson, *Ph.* 92, 1937, 148 ff. The latest work by Th. Lenschau, "Die Gründung Ioniens und der Bund am Panionion," *Klio* 36, 1944, 201 ff., does not constitute any progress. Useful, on the other hand, is C. Roebuck, "The Early Ionian League," *CP* 50, 1955, 26 ff., and Sakellariou, *MG*. On the excavation of Panionion see G. Kleiner, in *Neue deutsche Ausgrabungen im Mittelmeergebiet und im Vorderen Orient*, Berlin 1959, 172 ff. A good concise discussion may be found in J. M. Cook, "Greek Settlement in the Eastern Aegean and Asia Minor," *CAH* ³II, 2, 1975, 773-804. The theory of E. Curtius has been taken up again in the present day by J. Pestalozza, *Archivio Glottologico Italiano* 39, 1954, 27 ff., and in particular by V. Pisani, "Le lingue indoeuropee," in *Grecia e in Italia* (Ist. Lombardo, Rendic. 89), 1956, 14 ff.; cf. also the new version: "Die indoeuropäischen Sprachen in Griechenland und Italien," *Lingua Posnaniensis* 7, 1958, 25 ff., who thinks in terms of an Asia Minor language community with Hittite, Luvian and Ionian.

1. On the movements of the Illyrians see, for instance, H. Krahe, *Ant.*, 5 ff. Krahe views these early Illyrians too much as a national unity.

2. F. Matz, in *NBAnt* I, ed. H. Berve, 32, and other scholars, cf. the evidence in *Hdb. Arch.* II, 1950, 305 n. 2.

3. F. Altheim and E. Trautmann, *Italien und die dorische Wanderung*, Amsterdam 1940, 31.

4. K. Bittel, *KS*, 117 ff.

5. F. Schachermeyr, *Poseidon und die Entstehung des griech. Götterglaubens*, 1950, 194 ff., thinks that Troy VI is Homer's Troy: the legend of the Trojan horse should, he claims, be

referred to the action of Poseidon—a truly elegant solution, but which must unfortunately remain a conjecture.

6. Beloch, *GG* I 2, 76 ff.; U. Kahrstedt, *NJb*, 1919, 71 ff. De Sanctis, *St. Gr.* I, 154 (cf. again U. Kahrstedt, *Gn.* 16, 1940, 242). According to these scholars the Dorians (together with the other Greek tribes) immigrated early in the second millennium B.C.

7. The later literary sources (Tyrt. fr. 8; Pind., *Pyth.* I 65; Herod. I 56; VII 176; IX 26; Thuc. I 12) may be found analysed in the article by Hammond cited at the outset. Homer has no knowledge of the Dorians; they appear only in *Odyssey* XIX 177 as inhabitants of east Crete.

8. W. Schultze, *SB.B*, 1910, 805f. = *Kleine Schriften* 127. Opposed to this, Wilamowitz, *Gl.* I, 70 n. l.

9. K. Müller, *Tiryns* III, Augsburg 1930, 207.

10. See the survey (with map) by P. Ålin, *Das Ende der mykenischen Fundstätten auf dem griech. Festland* (SIMA, 1), Lund 1962; cf. *idem*, "Mycenaean Decline—Some Problems and Thoughts," in *Studies . . . Fritz Schachermeyr*, Berlin 1977, 31 ff.

11. While George Grote concluded that strong Dorian hordes embarked from the Gulf of Malia and by ship reached the southern Peloponnesus, U.v. Wilamowitz, *Staat u. Gesellsch. der Griechen*,[2] 1923, 19, *Gl.* I, 72, and F. Miltner, *Klio* 27, 1934, 58, 63, advocated the view cited above; but opposed to this see already, and correctly, F. Schachermeyr, *EF*, 52. Whether the Dorians advanced across the straits of Rhium or across the Isthmus into the Peloponnesus is a question which has hitherto not been resolved and in all probability cannot be solved.

12. On the names of the Dorian *phylae* see O. Lagercrantz, *Festg. f. Streitberg*, Leipzig 1924, 218 ff.; see further J. Keil, *Mitt. Ver. f. kl. Philologen in Wien*, 1929, 5 ff.; Wilamowitz, *Gl.* I, 69 ff.; H. Krahe, in *WG* 3, 1937, 291 ff.

13. See, for instance, R. Herbig, "Philister and Dorier," *JdI* 55, 1940, 58 ff.

14. Herod. V 76.

15. The fusion process may be seen from the non-Doric names of *phylae* (for instance, in Mycenae and Argos). On vestiges of the Achaean dialect in the Laconian cf. F. Solmsen, "Vordorisches in Lakonien," *RhM* 62, 1907, 329 ff.

16. The end of Mycenaean culture is to be dated to approximately 1150 B.C. or shortly thereafter, in the third quarter of the twelfth century according to Matz, *Ägäis*, 304. The view reiterated by F. Schachermeyr (in, *inter al.*, his public lecture "Das Problem der griech. Nationalität," *Comitato intern. di scienze storiche, 10 Congresso 1955* [*Rome*], *Realazioni*, Vol. VI, 1955, 670), and by J. Wiesner, *AA*, 1939, 316 f.; 333 f.; cf. *AO* 38, 2-4, 1939, 64 ff., that Mycenaean culture was convulsed by an invasion of non-Greek sea peoples and that it was not destroyed until the end of the Mycenaean period, about 1000 B.C., by the Dorians, is admittedly only a hypothesis, which attempts to explain the chronological discrepancy between the attack of the sea peoples, especially in the eastern basin of the Mediterranean (approximately 1200 B.C.) and the Dorian Migration. A long interval must nevertheless be reckoned for the latter and the dating of the Dorian invasion to about 1000 B.C. is certainly much too late. According to V. Milojčić (v.s.p. 388), the sea peoples must, apart from this, be completely left out of the picture for Greece. Z. Rubinsohn, *PP* 30, 1975, 105-131, also separates the fall of Mycenaean culture (cf. also R. J. Buck, "The Mycenaean Time of Troubles," *H.* 18, 1969, 276 ff.) from the Dorian Migration. P. Kretschmer, "Die phrygische Episode in der Gesch. von Hellas," *Miscellanea Academica Berolinensia* II, 1, 1950, 173 ff., advances an ingenious but completely improbable view. The latest attempt to reconstruct the history of this period is that of Desborough, *Last M.* This attempt too is of necessity highly hypothetical, since the archaeological evidence by itself—despite its increasing volume—does not allow compelling historical conclusions. (Cf. also *idem*, *GrDA*, and Snodgrass, *DA*.)

17. A. Erzen, "Das Besiedlungsproblem Pamphiliens im Altertum," *AA* 88, 1973, 388 ff.

18. The Eteocretan inscriptions have been compiled by J. Friedrich, *Kleinasiastische Sprachdenkmäler*, 1932, 147 f.

19. K. Bittel. *MDOG* 70, 1932, 17 f.; 72, 1933, 10 f.; Meyer, *GdA* II[2]1, 586; Götze, *Heth.*, 155.

20. M. C. Astour, *AJA* 69, 1965, 253 ff.

21. Translation after Meyer, *loc. cit.*; cf. also H. Grapow, in Bossert, *Kr.*, 54 no. 5.

22. The *Danuna* too are no Greeks; see 368; for a different view see, for instance, W. F. Albright, *AJA* 54, 1950, 171. Cf. in general F. Schachermeyr, "Die Seevölker im Orient," *Mnêmês Charin. Gedenkschrift P. Kretschmer* II, 1957, 118 ff. An extensive bibliography in Sakellariou, *MG.*, 485 ff.; cf. also P. Gavelli, *Le Proche-Orient, des Origines aux invasions des peuples de la mer*, Paris 1969; R. D. Barnett, "The Sea Peoples," *CAH* ³II, 2, 1975, 359 ff., and A. Nibbi, *The Sea Peoples and Egypt*, Park Ridge, N.J. 1975.

23. O. Eissfeldt, *Philister und Phönizier.* (*AO* 33, 3), Leipzig 1936; *RE* XX, 350 ff. s.v. *Phoiniker* (Phoinikia).

24. Basic is Schachermeyr, *EF* (cf. H. Berve, *Gn.* 7, 1931, 461 ff.); further: J. Wiesner, in *WG* 8, 1942, 193 ff.; *Forsch. und Fortschritte*, 1943, 51 ff.

25. The term "Griechisches Mittelalter" ('the Greek Middle Ages'), which Meyer (following the example of G. Welcker) in his *Geschichte des Altertums* coined for the period following the Dorian Migration (and taken up by, for instance, U. Wilcken, *GG*), derives from comparison with the Middle Ages in Europe. The differences between the two epochs are however much greater than the points of agreement, so that it does not recommend itself as a permanent term; cf. also Beloch, *GG* I 1², 203 n. 1.

26. There is evidence for (terrestrious) iron in the Near East from the third millennium on: see A. W. Persson, *Eisen und Eisenbereitung in ältester Zeit*, Lund 1934; cf. E. Kirsten, *Gn.* 11, 1935, 43 ff., and R. J. Forbes, *Jahrber. Ex Oriente Lux* 9, 1944, 207 ff.

27. Important is H. L. Lorimer, *JHS* 53, 1933, 161 ff.

28. A much too optimistic view on this point is put forward by Cassola, *Ionia*, who considers the Ionians as nothing less than part of the "Achaean empire"; see, opposed to this, for instance, K. Bittel (v.s.p. 386 n. 75). Otherwise, however, Cassola rejects the Ionian colonisation as a historical event, which can in no way be accepted.

29. J. H. Jongkees, "The Date of the Ionian Migration," in *Studia Vollgraff*, Amsterdam 1948, 71 ff., dates the colonisation too late; cf. E. Schefold, *Orient, Hellas und Rom*, 1949, 76 f. The excavations in old Smyrna by E. Akurgal, *JHS* 72, 1952, 104, which have yielded Mycenaean and Protogeometric sherds, also suggest an early settlement. On the Ionian name see J. Chadwick in *Studies... Fritz Schachermeyr*, Berlin 1977, 106 ff.

30. H. Bengtson, *Ph.* 92, 1937, 130; for bibliography the following should be added: H. Volkmann, *PhW*, 1939, 1038 ff. On the Ionian League see Larsen, *Rep. Govt.*, 27 ff.; C. Roebuck, *CP* 50, 1955, 26 ff.; on the excavations, see G. Kleiner *et al., Panionion und Melie*, Berlin 1967.

31. Br. Keil, "Griech. Staatsaltertümer," in Gercke-Norden, *Einl.* III², 515; similarly Wilcken, *GG*, 56; for a different view see Berve, *GG* I², 178 ff.

32. Cf. V. Ehrenberg, "When Did the Polis Rise?," *JHS* 57, 1937, 147 ff., who has arrived at approximately 800 B.C.

33. The fantasies of Bochart Mover (which in recent times have unfortunately been accepted by W. Dörpfeld in his work *Alt-Olympia* 1935), have been refuted by K. J. Beloch, "Die Phöniker am Ägäischen Meere," *RhM* 49, 1894, 111 ff., printed (with certain modifications) in *GG* I 2, 65 ff., although he too undoubtedly was wide of the mark; cf. also Meyer, *GdA* II²2, 61 ff., 113 ff. New aspects on the appearance of the Phoenicians in the West (allegedly already from the tenth century on) may be found in W. F. Albright, "New Light on the Early History of Phoenician Colonisation," *BASOR* no. 83 (Oct. 1941) 14 ff. Figures that are much too low have been advanced by Rhys Carpenter, "Phoenicians in the West," *AJA* 62, 1958, 35 ff. [the founding of Utica and Carthage not until the end of the eighth century]. To be accepted with even greater caution is A. Mentz, *La Nouvelle Clio* 7-9, 1955-57, 5 ff.; the Phoenicians are accordingly thought to have had possession of Cyprus already in the fifteenth century (!). On the Phoenicians in the Homeric epics: Nilsson, *Hom.*, 130 ff.; cf. in general also S. Moscati, "Die Phöniker" (in *Kindlers Kulturgeschichte*), Zurich 1966.

34. *Syria* 15, 1934, 124 ff., cf. Figs. XV and XVI.

35. Shown by Poulsen, *Frühgr.*, who goes too far, however, on points of detail; cf. also G. Karo, "Orient und Hellas in archaischer Zeit," *AM* 45, 1920, 106 ff.

36. B. Hemberg, *Die Kabiren*, Uppsala 1950 (a comprehensive assembling of the evidence); on the name, *ibid.*, 318 ff.

37. Of a different view is, for instance, M. Guarducci, *Geras Antoniou Keramopoullou*, Athens 1953, 342 ff., who argues for Crete, as compared with Margit Falkner, in *Frühgeschichte und Sprachwissenschaft*, ed. W. Brandenstein, Vienna 1948, 110 ff. (for Rhodes).

38. H. Bauer, *Der Ursprung des Alphabets* (AO. 36, 1-2), Leipzig 1937.

39. A survey in A. Rehm, in W. Otto, *Hdb. Arch.* I, 1939, 192 ff. Of earlier works the following may be stressed: M. P. Nilsson, *Die Übernahme des Alphabets durch die Griechen*, 1918 = *OS* II, 1029 ff.; of more recent studies, the article by R. Harder, "Die Meisterung der Schrift durch die Griechen," in *NBAnt.* I, 91 ff. A great amount of material is provided by D. Diringer, *The Alphabet*, 2 vols., London 1948 [^{2}1968]. Valuable, though very concise, Klaffenbach, *Gr. Ep.*, 32 ff.

40. The Greeks called the alphabet "Phoenician letters". (Herod. V 58, cf. the inscription from Teos, *Syll.*^{3} I 38). This is a "trade-mark"; cf. A. Kleingünther, "*Protos heuretes*," Ph. Suppl. 26.1, 1933, 60 ff. Cf. also H. Grassl, "Herodot und die griech. Schrift," *Hermes* 100, 1972, 169 ff.

41. Following the lead of A. Kirchhoff (*Studien z. Gesch. d. griech. Alphabet*) (first printed in Abh. B, 1863; Gütersloh ^{4}1887); additional material in F. Wiedemann, *Klio* 8, 1908, 523 ff.; 9, 1909, 364 f.), scholars distinguish between four principal alphabet groups which, on the basis of the colours used by Kirchhoff in his chart, are designated as: the "green" alphabet, the "dark blue" (Ionian, Isthmus of Corinth), the "light blue" (northern Cyclades, Attica), and the "red" (western Greece, Rhodes). Cf. Klaffenbach, *Gr. Ep.*, 35 ff.

42. On the Hymettus sherds see C. W. Blegen, *AJA* 38, 1934, 10 ff., and A. Rehm, *op. cit.*, 196; on the Corinthian Ostraca see A. N. Stillwell, *AJA* 37, 1933, 605 ff.

43. An important forerunner of Wolf was Abbé d'Aubignac in the time of Louis XIV.

44. In addition to histories of Greek literature (for instance, in Schmid, *GGL* I 1, 129 ff.), a survey of the history of Homeric studies may be found above all in G. Finsler, *Homer in der Neuzeit*, Leipzig and Berlin, 1912 (ed. 3, expanded by E. Tièche, 1924); in E. Drerup, *Homerische Poetik*, I. Band: *Das Homerproblem in der Gegenwart*, Würzburg 1921, 1 ff.; in P. Cauer, *Grundfragen der Homerkritik*, Leipzig ^{3}1921-1923; and in Nilsson, *Hom.* 1 ff.; further references to literature are given in *Fifty Years (and Twelve) of Classical Scholarship* edited by M. Platnauer, Oxford 1968, 31 ff., Revised with Appendices, 38 ff. Fr. A. Wolf regarded Homer as the poet who created the matrix of the *Iliad*, to which other rhapsodists thereafter added new songs, whereas Karl Lachmann in his *Betrachtungen über Homers Ilias* (Abh. Berl. Ak., 1837 and 1841, new ed. M. Haupt, 1847) broke up the poem into a number of independent single poems. More recent studies on the *Iliad* have to some extent again taken up ideas first advanced by G. Hermann, *De interpolationibus Homeri*, 1832, namely the so-called "nucleus theory," which regards the existence of a poem on the wrath of Achilles as the germ cell of the *Iliad*. In addition to the basic researches of U.v. Wilamowitz (*Homerische Untersuchungen*, 1884; *Die Ilias und Homer*, 1916; *Die Heimkehr des Odysseus*, 1927) and of Ed. Schwartz (*Zur Entstehung der Ilias*, 1918; *Die Odyssee*, 1924), we are of late indebted in particular to W. Schadewaldt for new, stimulating ideas; in contrast to the almost generally prevailing analytical interpretation, Schadewaldt has argued with particular cogency for the unitarian point of view and beyond this endeavoured to grasp the personality of Homer and reintroduce him as a historical figure: *Iliasstudien* (Abh. S 43.6), Leipzig 1938; *Von Homers Welt und Werk*, ^{2}1951 (also containing the outstanding article: "Homer und sein Jahrhundert," first published in *NBAnt.* I, 51 ff.). Of late the analytical school has taken up the issue again with important studies; see, for instance: W. Theiler, "Die Dichter der Ilias," *Festschrift für Tièche*, Bern 1947, 125 ff.; R. Merkelbach, *Untersuchungen zur Odyssee* (Zetemata, 2), Munich 1951; P. von der Mühl. *Kritisches Hypomnema zur Ilias*, Basel 1952 (cf. already also *RE* Suppl. VIII, 696 ff. s.v. *Odyssee*); (B. Marzullo. *Il problema omerico*, Florence 1952; G. Jachmann, *Der homerische Schiffskatalog und die Ilias*, Cologne and Opladen 1958. E. Dönt, "Forschungsberichte: Homer. 6. Fortsetzung 1. Teil," in *Anz. Alt.* 25, 1972, 163-182; *idem*, "6 Fortsetzung, 2. Teil," *loc. cit.*, 257-268; A. Heubeck, *Die homerische Frage. Bericht uber die Forschung d. letzten Jahrzehnte* (Erträge der Forschung 27), Darmstadt 1974.

45. Excellently analysed by Nilsson, *Hom.*, 137 ff.; cf. also G. Rodenwaldt, *Epitymbion Tsountas*, 1940, 434 ff. Basic is H. L. Lorimer, *Homer and the Monuments*, London 1950; see also J. T. Hooker, "Homer and Late Minoan Crete," *JHS* 89, 1969, 60 ff., as well as J.

Bouzek, *Homerisches Griechenland im Lichte der archäologischen Quellen*, Prague 1969 (cf., M. Andronikos, *Gn.* 44, 1972, 517 ff.), and the series *Archaeologia Homerica* I ff., 1967 ff.

46. Nilsson, *Hom.,* 137 ff. (with photographs). A Furumark, "Nestor's Cup and the Mycenaean Dove Goblet," *Eranos* 44, 1946, 41 ff., denies any similarity; but he allows too little scope for poetic imagination. Of a different view, Sp. Marinatos, *Festschrift für B. Schweitzer*, 1954, 11 ff., who interprets the cup as a Minoan (?) cult object and the dove as Horus-Falcon.

47. V. Burr, *Neon Katalogos, Untersuch. z. homerischen Schiffskatalog,* Klio-Beiheft 49, Leipzig 1944. But cf. also G. Jachmann, *Der homerische Schiffskatalog und die Ilias*, 1958, 27 ff.

48. Cf., for instance, R. Hampe, *Gym.* 63, 1956, 1 ff.

49. Shown by Poulsen, *Frühgr.*, 172 ff.

50. From the extensive literature on the subject only the following may be cited here: K. Mesiter, *Die homerische Kunstsprache* (Preisschrift der Jablonowskischen Gesellschaft 48), Leipzig 1921; A. Meillet, *Aperçu d'une histoire de la langue grecque*, Paris [3]1930, Ch. 6; J. Wackernagel, *Sprachliche Untersuchungen zu Homer*, 1916; M. Leumann, *Homerische Wörter*, Basel 1950.

51. The predominant view among scholars, substantiated by strong factual evidence, is that the *Iliad* and the *Odyssey* belong to different periods (and to different authors) (the so-called chorisontal point of view). The opposite stance is taken by, *inter al.*, W. Schadewaldt; to date detailed substantiation is lacking.

52. L. Malten, "Aineias," *ARW* 29, 1931, 33 ff.; F. Jacoby, "Homerisches," *Hermes* 68, 1933, 41 ff.; W. Schadewaldt, "Homer und sein Jahrhundert," in *NBAnt.* I, 59 f.

53. Cf. R. Hampe, *Frühe griech. Sagenbilder in Böotien*, Athens 1936; *Die Gleichnisse Homers und die Bildkunst seiner Zeit*, Tübingen 1952; also valuable is K. Schefold, "Archäologisches zum Stil Homers," *MusHelv* 12, 1955, 132 ff.

54. Earlier scholars (*inter al.*, G. Finsler) regarded the Greek kingship of the early period as patriarchal, whereas A. Szabó, "Altmediterranes Königtum und seine Bedeutung für die Anfänge des griechischen Staates," *WG*, 1940, 293 ff., interpreted it as a kingship of office or a limited monarchy. The evidence is, however, insufficient to reach a definite conclusion. Important is M. P. Nilsson, "Das homerische Königtum," *OS* II, 871 ff.; see also F. E. Adcock, *Greek and Macedonian Kingship* (Pr. Br. Ac. 39), London 1953.

55. F. Poulsen, *Die Dipylongräber und die Dipylonvasen*, Leipzig 1905; B. Schweitzer, *AM* 34, 1918, 1-152; cf. also A. Brückner and E. Pernice, "Ein attischer Friedhof," *AM* 18, 1893, 73 ff.

56. E. F. Bruck, *Totenteil und Seelgerät*, 1926, 42: F. Heichelheim, *Wirts, Alt.* I, 262; G. Micknat, *Studien z. Kriegsgefangenschaft und z. Sklaverei in der griech. Gesch.* 1. Teil: *Homer* (Abh. Mainzer Ak., 1954, 11; published 1955).

57. See the survey in Bickerman, Chronology, 27 ff.

58. A different view, it would seem, is held by W. Otto, *HZ* 163, 1941, 312.

59. This applies especially to J. L. Myres, *Who Were the Greeks?*, Berkeley 1930; likewise to W. Kraiker, *Gn.* 11, 1935, 643; and *Kerameikos* I, 1939, 162 ff.; J. Bérard, *Recherches sur la chronologie de l'époque mycénienne*, Paris 1950; A. J. B. Wace, in *Studies Goldman*, 135 f.; G. E. Mylonas, *Ancient Mycenae*, London 1957, *et al.*

60. F. Schachermeyr, *Prähist. Zeitschr.* 34-35, 1949-1950, 17 ff.; *RE* XXII, 1354 ff. s.v. *Prähistorische Kulturen Griechenlands* (partly taken up again in *Die altesten Kulturen Griechenlands*, Stuttgart 1955, 29 ff.); V. Milojčić, *Chronologie der jüngeren Steinzeit Mittel- und Südosteuropas*, 1949, Matz, *Ägäis*, 180; *H.* 1, 1950, 173 ff.: "Zur ägäischen Chronologie der frühen Bronzezeit" (with Table, 193).

61. D. Fimmen, *KM*. A survey in Schachermeyr, *"Rasse,"* 97 ff.

62. A summary in Matz, *Ägäis*, 179 ff.

63. See in particular the publication of the American excavations at Troy: *Troy* I-IV, 1950-58 (cf. K. Bittel, *Gn.* 26, 1954, 433 ff.; 28, 1956, 241 ff., who correctly stresses that this work has yielded less for the absolute than for the relative chronology).

64. See Bengtson, *Einf.* [7]1975, 33; cf. *Anc. Hist.*, 33 f.

65. A. Poebel, *JNES* 1, 1942, 247 ff.; 460 ff.; 2, 1943, 85 ff.; E. F. Weidner, *AfO* 14, 1941-1944, 362 ff. To date it is still impossible to determine with complete certainty the regnal

periods before 1429 B.C., since the regnal periods for two kings are lacking (Assurabi I and Assur-Nadinahhe I): X years must be added to all regnal periods before 1429 B.C. According to Poebel's conjecture, X would indeed practically = 0, while according to W. F. Albright X would = 20.

66. F. Cornelius, "Berossus u. die altorientalische Chronologie," *Klio* 35, 1942, 1 ff.; 7. But cf., on the other hand, Sidney Smith, *Alalakh and Chronology*, London 1940, who argues for 1792-1750 B.C.; he has been followed by M. B. Rowton, *JNES* 17, 1958, 97 ff. In general the so-called middle chronology has in recent years won additional adherents.

67. F. Cornelius, *op. cit.*, 9; but for a different view cf. in particular A. Goetze, lastly in *Journal of Cuneiform Studies* 11, 1957, 53 ff.; 63 ff., who argues for 1651 B.C.; see, on the other hand, however, B. Hroudda, *Vorderasien* I. *Mesopotamien, Iran u. Anatolien* (Hbd. Alt.), Munich 1971, 23.

68. *Acta Orientalia* 17, 1938, 169 ff.

69. "Die Bedeutungslosigkeit des sog. ältesten Datums der Weltgeschichte und einige sich daraus ergebende Folgerungen für die ägyptische Gesch. u. Archäologie," *HZ* 161, 1940, 3 ff.

70. Concise, A. Scharff, *Die Frühkulturen Ägyptens u. Mesopotamiens*, (AO 41), Leipzig 1941. Still lower figures in H. Stock, *Orientalia*, 1949, 479 ff. Reviewed by P. van der Meer, *The Ancient Chronology*, 1947; according to them, the Jamdat-Nasr period and the First Dynasty of Egypt belong in the twenty-eighth century (2800-2700 B.C.).

71. For a date approximately two centuries earlier (2600 B.C.), Matz, *Ägäis*, 180; F. Schachermeyr places the date still earlier (2700 B.C.).

72. The older finds in Fimmen, *KM*, 156 ff.; the Minoan sherds from Harageh, in R. Engelbach, *Harageh*, 1923; and Evans, *Knossos* II, 211 ff.; cf. F. Matz, *H.* 1, 1950, 173-174.

73. Thus Sidney Smith, *AJA* 49, 1945, 1 ff. (on the basis of the date given for Hammurabi *supra* 393 n. 57). Dated somewhat earlier by F. Matz [1900 B.C.] and Schachermeyr [1850 B.C.]

74. H. Stock, *Stud. z. Gesch. u. Archäologie der 13. bis 17. Dynastie Ägyptens* (Ägyptolog. Forsch., 12), Glückstadt 1942; 69, at the time dated Chian "from 1640 on," but today the figure will no doubt have to be lowered by several decades.

75. Fimmen, *KM*, 203 ff.; Bossert, *Kr.*, 304 Abb. 572.

76. Fimmen, *KM*, 161; 174; the Keftiu depicted in Theban tombs from the time of Thutmosis III fall into this period.

77. Meyer, *GdA* II²1, 608 (cf. 585 n.1) places Ramses III in about 1200-1168 (or about 1165) B.C.

78. W. Kraiker, *Kerameikos* I, 1939, 162 ff. In contrast to Kraiker, F. Schachermeyr, *Klio* 36, 1944, 129, dates the Sub-Mycenaean period from 1175 to 1050, whereas C.-G. Styrenius, *Submycenaean Studies*, Lund 1967, 164, argues for the period from 1125-1040/35 B.C.

79. According to V. Desborough, *Protogeometric Pottery*, 1952, 294 f., the Protogeometric style begins (in Attica) about 1025 B.C. with the transition to the Geometric not occurring until about 900-875 B.C.; cf. *idem, GrDA*, 29 ff.

3 THE GREEK COLONISATION (800-500 BC)

THE BEGINNING OF GREEK INDIVIDUALISM

An inclusive narrative study of Greek culture of the archaic period is a desideratum. The earlier histories by Ed. Meyer, K. J. Beloch, G. Glotz, H. Berve and G. De Sanctis, as well as the relevant volumes of *CAH* have rightly devoted extensive space to the emergence and growth of Greek cultural life. Particularly instructive among the specific sketches are: E. Bethe, *Tausend Jahre altgriechischen Lebens*, Munich 1933, 43 ff. (Miletus in the sixth century B.C.), and M. P. Nilsson, *The Age of the Early Greek Tyrants* (Dill Memorial Lecture, the Queen's University, Belfast) 1936. On the subject of the Orient and Greece, see, for instance, H. Thiersch, "Die Kunst der Griechen und der Alte Orient," *Ant.* 9, 1933, 203 ff.; H. E. Stier, "Hellas und Ägypten," *WG* 5, 1939, 438 ff., both, however, not more than sketches. In addition there is also, for instance, H. E. Stier, "Probleme der frühgriechischen Geschichte und Kultur," *H.* 1, 1950, 195 ff., esp. 208 ff. [on Greece and the Orient]. With abundant evidence, but not always critical enough, is R. D. Barnett, "Ancient Oriental Influences on Archaic Greece," in *Studies Goldman*, 212 ff. The following may be cited as particularly outstanding studies on archaic art: G. Rodenwaldt, *Die Bildwerke des Artemistempels von Korkyra* II, 1939; and of Rodenwaldt's earlier studies, "Die Anfänge der Monumentalbaukunst in Stein in Griechenland," *AM* 44, 1919, 175 ff.; and the article by K. Lehmann-Hartleben, "Wesen und Gestalt griechischer Heiligtümer," *Ant.* 7, 1931, 161 ff. On Delphi and the Delphic Oracle see P. Amandry, *La mantique apollinienne à Delphes, essai sur le fonctionnement de l'oracle*, Paris 1950 (cf. H. Berve, *Gn.* 24, 1952, 5 ff.); J. Defradas, *Les thèmes de la propagande delphique*, Paris 1954 (reviewed by H. Berve, *Gn.* 28, 1956, 174 ff.); M. Delcourt, *L'oracle de Delphes*, 1956; R. Crahay, *La littérature oraculaire chez Hérodote*, Liège 1956; M. P. Nilsson, *H.* 7, 1956, 237 ff.; G. Roux, *Orakel und Kultstätten*, Munich 1971; *idem, The Oracle of Delphi*, Amsterdam 1973. On the *Kumarbi* epic and the problems connected with it see H. G. Güterbock, "The Song of Ullikummi," *Journal of Cuneiform Studies* 5, 1951, 135 ff.; 6, 1952, 8 ff. with translation; cf. A. Lesky, *Saec.* 6, 1955, 35 ff.; P. Walcot, *Hesiod and the Near East*, Cardiff 1966. Problematic are most of the studies by F. Dornseiff, *Antike und Alter Orient*, Leipzig 1956; valuable, T. J. Dunbabin, *The Greeks and their Eastern Neighbours, Studies in the Relations Between Greece and the Countries of the Near East in the Eighth and Seventh Centuries B.C.*, London 1957.

THE ORIENT AND THE RISE OF GREEK STATES

SOURCES: Between the Dorian Migration and the period of the tyrants, beginning about 650 B.C., there is a gap in Greek literary tradition of almost half a millennium (Meyer, *Forsch.* I, 185 ff.). Attempts are not lacking in Greek historiography of the fifth century to bridge this gap by mythological and genealogical constructions. Modern scholars, on the other hand, have adopted a different course. To investigate the political, social and economic conditions in early Greece they employ first and foremost the documentary material, the very limited number of archaic inscriptions, the monuments, the historical cult topography, research into legends, and, finally, though with caution, conclusions from historical analogies. Historical information about the Greeks at an early date crystallised around the great personalities of the archaic period, around the Greek tyrants and foreign rulers who, like the Phrygian Midas and the Lydian Gyges, had maintained close connections with Greek cultural circles. In this respect tradition shows distinct legendary features, which have become reflected primarily in the literary form of the short story (B. Erdmannsdörffer, "Das Zeitalter der Novelle in Hellas," *Preuss. Jahrb.* 25, 1870, 121 ff. = *Kl. histor. Schr.* II, ed. H. Lilienfein; basic is W. Aly, *Volksmärchen, Sage und Novelle bei Herodot und seinen Zeitgenossen*, Göttingen 1921).

The chronology of the archaic period is in a particularly unsatisfactory state, especially for the eighth and the first half of the seventh centuries. Not until we have access to synchronisms with the history of the ancient Orient do we find ourselves on a solid footing, that is, practically not before the second half of the seventh century. The records in the form of lists which begin in Greece during the course of the eighth century are of little help for historical questions. Apart from this, their reliability has first of all to be established in each individual case. This applies in particular to the early sections of the Olympian victor lists which begin in 776 B.C. (First Olympiad); the lists for Ol. 1-249 are preserved in Eusebius, *Chron.*, Armenian Version, 98 ff. ed. Karst; cf. L. Moretti, *Olympionikai, i vincitori negli antichi agoni olimpici* (Atti Acc. Lincei, 1957). Supplements for Ol. 75-83 are furnished by a papyrus from Oxyrhynchus (*P. Oxy* II 222); cf. C. Robert, *Hermes* 35, 1900, 141 ff.; H. Diels, *Hermes* 36, 1901, 72 ff. While earlier scholars (A. Körte, *Hermes* 39, 1904, 224 ff.; K. J. Beloch, *GG* I^2 2, 148 ff., cf. *Hermes* 64, 1929, 192 ff., but also still U. Kahrstedt, "Z. Gesch. von Elis u. Olympia," *NGG*, 1927, Heft 3, 173 ff.) reached completely negative conclusions on the trustworthiness of the older sections, lately, however, especially since the investigation by A. Brinkmann, *RhM* 70, 1915, 622 ff., a constructive approach has come about (cf. H. T. Wade-Gery, *CAH* III, 762 ff.). The attempts of later scholars (U. v. Wilamowitz, *Pindaros*, 1922, 483; likewise, Th. Lenschau, *Ph.* 91, 1936, 396 ff.) to deny the penteteric character of the Olympian Games for the early period are not convincing, since they are based on subjective assumptions. Evidence for the early date of such lists may be deduced from the Spartan Ephor lists which began in 754/3 B.C. (F. Jacoby, Apollodors Chronik, *PhU* 16, 1902, 138 ff., but much more sceptical, more recently in his *Att.*, 353 n. 3), and the Athenian Archon lists, which begin in 683/2 B.C., evidently the year in which the archonship was introduced as an annual office (K. J. Beloch, *GG* I^2 2, 156 ff.). Moreover the royal succession in Sparta (the older bibliography in Busolt, *Gr. St.* II, 647 n. 5, cf. in particular P. Poralla, *Prosopogr. d. Lakedaimonier*, Diss. Breslau 1913, 137 ff., also Kroymann, *Paus.* 139 ff.) may in fact, still for the ninth century, rest on a good oral tradition. On the question of chronology in general and calendars in particular see now A. E. Samuel, *Greek and Roman Chronology. Calendars and Years in Classical Antiquity* (Hdb. Alt.), Munich 1972.

The earliest historical information on Spartan history is furnished by Tyrtaeus (second half of the seventh century): cf. E. Diehl, *Anth. Lyr.* I^2, 1936, 6 ff. Important is the fragment of a Berlin papyrus (first published by U.v. Wilamowitz, SB.B, 1918, 728 ff.; cf. A. Gercke, *Hermes* 56, 1921, 346 ff.), which attests the existence of the Dorian phylae for the time of Tyrtaeus (Diehl fr. 1). The attempt often made to prove larger interpolations in the Tyrtaean elegies has thus far not been successful (F. Schachermeyr, *RhM* 81, 1932, 129 ff. = *Forschungen und Betrachtungen zur griech. u. röm. Geschichte*, Vienna 1974, 45 ff., goes too far).

The later secondary literary material is not very productive. (On the beginning of Greek historiography, see C. G. Starr, *The Awakening of the Greek Historical Spirit*, New York, 1968.) Hecataeus of Miletus (c. 500 B.C.) drew up a firm chronological system for Greek legendary history, and attempted to put order into the quasi-history through his reckoning by generations (each 40 years) (the fragments in F. Jacoby, *FgrHist.* no. 1; cf. Meyer, *Forsch.* I, 154 ff.; F. Jacoby, *RE* VII, 2742 f.; on reckoning by generations see D. W. Prakken, *Studies in Greek Genealogical Chronology*, Lancaster 1943). His rationalism (examples in F. Jacoby, *RE* VII, 2739, see further, M. Momigliano, *Atene e Roma* NS 12, 1931, 133 ff.; G. De Sanctis, *RF* NS 11, 1933, 1 ff.) is still far removed from critical history. Hecataeus "entertained the naïve belief that on the strength of his own reason he could establish the truth." While Hecataeus (that Herodotus used him was shown by H. Diels, *Hermes* 22, 1887, 411 ff.; sceptical, K.v. Fritz, *Die griech. Geschichtsschreibung* I, 1967, 409 ff.) remained in the realm of legendary history, Hellanicus of Mytilene, a contemporary of Thucydides, undertook to write a history of Greece from the earliest times. Besides composing mythographical works and specific studies on the great families and important events of the heroic period, he also wrote ethnographies on foreign peoples and on the Greeks, and in addition, three separate studies: *Attic Chronology* (*Atthis* cf. F. Jacoby, *FgrHist.* no. 4., 38 ff., and in particular, *idem, Att.* [basic] from King Cecrops to his own time); the *Carneian Victors*, a festal chronology of the Carneia celebrated in honour of Apollo at Sparta, practically a "history of the music of Hellas" (F. Jacoby); and the *Priestesses of Hera*, a title which conceals an inclusive Greek chronology, with the list of the Argive priestesses of Hera forming the chronological frame. Thanks to the diligence of Hellanicus, with which his historical critique admittedly did not keep pace, his writings have become a mine of historical-antiquarian evidence, chiefly for the heroic period. Thucydides gives an extensive survey of early Greek history (for a detailed discussion see *infra* 465 ff.) in the "Archaeologia" of his *History* (I 1 ff.). The first universal history of the Greek world was written by Ephorus of Cyme in the time of Alexander (Jacoby, *FgrHist.* no. 70; cf. E. Schwartz, *RE* VI, 1 ff.; G. L. Barber, *The Historian Ephorus*, Cambridge 1935); for the older period it is a hotch-potch of history and rationalistic mythological interpretations. Of the other Greek local chronicles, predominantly from the fifth century B.C., next to nothing is extant (R. Laqueur, *RE* XIII, 1083 ff.). From the Hellenistic period, finally, the following may be cited: the works of Myron of Priene (third century B.C.) in prose; and the heroic epic by Rhianus of Bene on Crete (from the same century)! Of these two the Prienian described the First Messenian War, while the Cretan wrote an account of the Second Messenian War [according to F. Kiechle (see *infra*) and others, much more the Third Messenian War]. The periegetes Pausanias used them as the basis of his narratives. They do not possess any independent historical value. Cf. the studies by J. Kroymann, "Sparta u. Messenien," *NPhU* 11, 1937; Ed. Schwartz, "Die messenische Gesch. bei Pausanias," *Ph.* 92, 1937, 19 ff.; Jacoby, *FgrHist.* III no. 265, Commentary (against Kroymann); and, again, Kroymann, *Paus.*; Kiechle, *Messen.*; H. T. Wade-Gery, in *Studies Ehrenberg*, 289 ff., who dates the war recounted by Rhianus to about 600 B.C.

Especially important among modern excavations are the investigations at the sanctuary of Artemis Orthia in Sparta (cf. R. M. Dawkins, *The Sanctuary of Artemis Orthia*, London 1929); at Olympia (cf. W. Dörpfeld, *Alt-Olympia*, Berlin 1935, and the subsequent reports of the Deutsches Archäologische Institut on the excavations resumed in 1936, which are cited above 364 n. 13); at Perachora near Corinth (H. Payne, *Perachora. The Sanctuaries of Hera Akraia and Limenia*, Oxford 1940); at Halae (H. Goldman, *Hesp.* 9, 1940, 381 ff.; 11, 1942, 365 ff.); further excavations in the Cerameicus in Athens (K. Kübler, *Kerameikos* VI. *Die Nekropole des späten 8. bis frühen 6. Jahrhunderts*, Berlin 1970; *idem*, VII.I. *Die Nekropole von der Mitte des 6. bis Ende des 5. Jh.*, Berlin 1974); as well as those by K. Schefold, *Larisa am Hermos* I-III, 1940-42, which have uncovered a settlement from 700-500 B.C. Al Mina, at the mouth of the Orontes, has yielded important archaic finds.

BIBLIOGRAPHY: It is primarily due to the nature of our sources that research on the subject of archaic Sparta and Athens has enjoyed a predominant place in scholarly discussion. Since a survey of the bibliography on Sparta will be given elsewhere (415 f.), it must suffice at this point to refer to the concise articles in *RE* III A, 1165 ff. s.v. *Sparta* (by Bölte, Ehrenberg, Ziehen and Lippold), and to den Boer, *Lac.* For the older history of Attica see Wilamowitz, *Arist.*; De Sanctis, *Att.* (with bold theories); A. Ledl, *Studien zur älteren athenischen Verfassungsgeschichte*, Heidelberg 1914; E. Kornemann, "Athen und Attika," in *Staaten, Völker, Männer*, Leipzig 1934, 30 ff. (on the basis of investigations by S. Soldes, *Die ausserstädtischen Kulte und die Einigung Attikas*, Lund 1931); very penetrating, but partly based on subjective assumptions: Hignett, *Const.*

(cf., for instance, A. Momigliano, *RstI* 65, 1953, 263-67; H. Berve, *Gn.* 27, 1955, 225-32).

Contributions to the older history of the Peloponnesus: L. Heidemann, *Die territoriale Entwicklung Lakedaimons und Messeniens bis auf Alexander* (Sieglins Quellen u. Forsch. z. Alt. Gesch. u. Geogr., Heft 11), 1905; O. Viedebantt, "Forsch. z. altpeloponn. Gesch.," *Ph.* 81, 1926, 208 ff.; U. Kahrstedt, "Z. Gesch. von Elis und Olympia," *NGG*, 1927, Heft 3, 173 ff.; Th. Lenschau, *Ph.* 91, 1936, 278 ff.; 385 ff.; *RE* XIX 1939 ff. s.v. *Pheidon* no. 3; Callmer, *Ark.* Other regions of the motherland: Corinth: T. J. Dunbabin, *JHS* 68, 1948, 89 ff.; E. Will, *Korinthiaka. Recherches sur l'histoire et la civilisation de Corinthe des origines aux guerre médiques*, Paris 1955 (copiously documented, but at times not critical enough on historical questions; moreover his treatment of chronological problems is not satisfactory when dealing with central issues). Thebes and Boeotia: F. Schober, *RE* VA, 1456 ff. Thessaly: Fr. Frhr. Hiller v. Gaertringen, *RE* VI A, 111 ff. (contains nothing on the period in question). Ionia: R. M. Cook, *JHS* 66, 1946, 67 ff.

THE EXPANSION OF THE GREEKS IN THE MEDITERRANEAN WORLD

SOURCES AND BIBLIOGRAPHY: The beginning of the second Greek colonisation falls in a period from which no direct historical information is extant. Apart from a large number of aetiological and mythological legends which are reflected in the different foundation accounts (an example of modern critique is: U.v. Wilamowitz, "Die Herkunft der Maneten am Maeander," *Hermes* 30, 1895, 177 ff. = *Kl. Schr.* V 1, 1937, 78 ff.), there are a great many oracles which the Delphic god is alleged to have given the *oikistai*. As incontestable as the connections between the Delphic oracle and the colonisation may be, they are certain for the period beginning about 700 B.C. There can be no question of an official leadership of the colonisation by the Delphic priesthood (as assumed by Ernst Curtius, *GG* I[6], 475 ff.); cf. already R.v. Pöhlmann, *GG*, 55, esp. n. 3; H. W. Parke, *A History of the Delphic Oracle*, Oxford 1939, 47 ff. [a new edition of the book is the first volume of Parke-Wormell, *Or.*]; and Nilsson, *Gr. Rel.* I[3], 637 ff.; also W. G. Forrest, *H.* 6, 1957, 160 ff. From the sixth century onwards, however, Delphi's influence is evident in the coins: see L. Piccirilli, *Ann, Scuola Norm. Sup. di Pisa, Cl. di Lettere e Filosofia, ser.* III, vol. II,1, 1972, 46 ff. A large number of the oracles (cf. the collection by Parke-Wormell, *Or.*, Vol. II, Oxford 1956 (cf. H. Berve, *Gn.* 30, 1958, 417 ff.]) must be regarded as unhistorical (Meyer, *GdA* II, 442 f.). A separate problem is posed by the dates given for the founding of the colonies. Earlier critical research (for instance, G. Busolt, *RhM* 40, 1885, 466 ff.; K. J. Beloch, *GG*[2] I 2, 218 ff.) regarded them as the result of later conclusions and therefore denied that they had any historical value whatever (cf. also L. Pareti, "La cronologia delle prime colonie greche in Silicia. Contributi alla scienze della 'antichita' I," *Studi siciliani ed italioti* 1914, 310-30). A more accurate interpretation of the archaeological finds in southern Italy and Sicily, however, has shown that the dates of Thucydides (v. *infra*), and those of Eratosthenes, which in general coincide with the former, are essentially reliable: B. Schweitzer, "Untersuchungen z. Chronologie u. Gesch. der geometr. Stile in Griechenland II," *AM* 43, 1918, 8 ff.: the foundation dates of the Greek colonies in Sicily and southern Italy and their significance for vase chronology; A. W. Byvanck, "Untersuch. z. Chronologie der Funde in Italien aus dem 8. u. 7. vorchristl. Jahrh.," *Mn.* 1936/37, 181 ff. According to Byvanck, there is on average a space of only 25 years between the oldest finds and the dates given for the foundations, a space which is confirmed by parallels in other periods (for instance, the time difference between the founding date and the initial finds from Alexandria). A more recent thorough and comprehensive study of the chronological problems may be found in Dunbabin, *West.*, 435 ff. (with additional bibliography, 435). He also argues that the archaeological data essentially confirm the founding dates of Thucydides (460). The dates of A. Åkerström *Der geometr. Stil in Italien*, Lund 1943, later by half a century, have rightly been contested by Dunbabin (466 ff.). There is a series of specific investigations by R. van Compernolle: *Bull. Inst. histor. belge de Rome* 27, 1952; 317-56 (the foundation of Selinus); *ibid.*, 28, 1953, 165-200 (Selinus and Syracuse); 29, 1955, 215-40 (Syracuse, Megara Hyblaea and Selinus); *AC* 25, 1956, 100-105 [on K. J. Dover, "La colonissazione della Sicilia in Tucidide," *Maia* 6, 1953, 1-20]. In addition, finally, also the book *Etude de chronologie et d'historiographie siciliotes*, Brussels and Rome 1959, whose conclusions at the same time, however, are problematic (against reckoning a generation at 35 years, thus van Compernolle; see, for instance: A. Graf Schenk von Stauffenberg, *Trinakria* [Munich, 1963] 307 n. 14; 351 ff.). See further, G. Vallet and F. Villard, *BCH* 76, 1952, 289 ff. [according to whom Megara Hyblaea was founded before Syracuse, c. 750, Syracuse 733 B.C.]. F. Miltner, "Die erste milesische Kolonisation im Südpontos," *Studies Buckler*, 191 ff., has, as compared with the critique of Beloch, *GG* I² 2, 231 ff., argued for the reliability of the foundation dates which Eusebius gives for the colonies on the Black Sea and in the Propontis (the first settlement of Trapezus and Cyzicus: Olymp. 6.1 = 756/5 B.C.).

From the secondary sources (cf. the survey in G. Busolt, *GG* I², 364 ff.), the following may be cited: the non-extant history of Italy and Sicily by Antiochus of Syracuse, more or less a contemporary of Herodotus, which Thucydides used as the basis for his outline of the early history of Sicily in Bk. VI 2-5; cf. De Sanctis, *St. Sic.*, 9 ff.; and F. W. Walbank, *Kokalos* 14-15, 1968-69, 480-81 (in the context of a survey of the historians of Greek Sicily); Book IV of the *Greek History* of Ephorus, also lost; the *History of the West* from the pen of Timaeus of Tauromenium († c. 250 B.C.); cf. J. Geffcken, "Timaios' Geographie des Westens," *PhU* 13, 1892 (unfortunately only for the prehistoric period); De Sanctis, *St. Sic.*,

1958, 43 ff.; A. Momigliano, *RstI* 71, 1959, 529-556 (with bibliography); the geographical didactic poem of the so-called Pseudo-Scymnus of Chios (c. 100 B.C.; cf. Fr. Gisinger, *RE* III A, 672 ff.; U. Hoefer, *RhM* 82, 1933, 67 ff.; M. Rostovtzeff, *SEHHW*, 1530).

The investigation of the archaeological evidence, especially from the West, has made important progress in the last decades. Important for the early period of Sicily is L. Bernabò Brea, *Sicily Before the Greeks*, Oxford 1957. Of interest too is the article by Brea on Sicilian ethnology at the time of the Greek colonisation: *Kokalos* 10-11, 1964-1965, 7 ff.; on the influence of Phoenician civilisation: *ibid.*, 12 ff. See also P. Orlandini, "Arte indigena e colonizzazione greca in Sicilia," *ibid.*, 539 ff. References on the Greek finds at Cumae, Syracuse (Nekropole del Fusco), Megara Hyblaea, Gela, Selinus, etc. may be found in Byvanck's study cited above. Also useful is the somewhat diffuse book by J. Bérard, *La colonisation grecque d'Italie méridionale et de la Sicile dans l'antiquité: historie et légende* (Bibl. des Ecoles franç. d'Athènes et de Rome, 150), Paris 1941 (new edition 1957) (with supplement: "Bibliographie topographique des principales cités grecques de l'Italie méridionale et de la Sicile etc."). More expansive in time, but never completed, due to the author's death, is J. Bérard, *L'expansion et la colonisation grecques jusqu'aux guerres médiques*, Paris 1960. All the evidence for the West is assembled in the study by T. J. Dunbabin cited above; see further, *idem, Contributions to the Bibliography of the Greek Cities in Sicily and South Italy* (Papers of the British School at Rome 18), 1950, 104-16. With regard to the Greek colonies on the Adriatic: A. Gitti, *PP* 77, 1952, 161-92; R. Van Compernolle, *AC* 22, 1953, 50 ff. [on the foundation date of Apollonia in Illyria]. The archaeological finds in the colonies of the Propontis are cautiously assessed by E. G. Minns, *Scythians and Greeks*, 1913; and by M. Rostovtzeff, *Iranians and Greeks in South Russia*, 1922; *idem, Skythien und der Bosporus* I, 1931; and by Ebert, *Südr.* A new survey of the Russian excavations in, for instance, Tyras, Eupatoria, in the Taman peninsula and elsewhere would be very desirable. Some information is provided by Ch. Danov, *Rev. hist.*, 1959, 281 ff. A more recent bibliography in: E. Belin de Ballu, *L'histoire des colonies grecques du littoral nord de la Mer Noire: bibliographie annotée des ouvrages et articles publiés en UdSSR. de 1940 à 1962*, Leiden 1965. An important monograph: M. F. Lambrino, *Les vases archaïques d'Histria,* Bucarest 1938, cf. A. Greifenhagen, *PhW*, 1940, 83 ff.; cf. also E. G. Condurachi, *Problèmes économiques et sociaux d'Histria à la lumière des dernières recherches, Nouv. ét d'histoire*. Bucarest 1955, 71-84. On the Greeks in Spain: P. Bosch-Gimpera "Les Grecs et les Ibères," in *Le rayonnement des civilisations grecque et romaine sur les cultures périphériques (Huitième Congrés intern. d'Archéol. classique, Paris 1963)*, published 1965, 111-118.

BIBLIOGRAPHY: A comprehensive study of the second Greek colonisation is a desideratum in modern scholarship. For the basic aspects the following may be compared: Aubrey Gwynn, "The Character of Greek Colonisation," *JHS* 38, 1918, 88 ff.; H. J. Schultze, "Zur Geographie der altgriechischen Kolonisation," *Petermanns Mitteil.*, 1941, 7-12 (who regards the striving for new land as the actual motive for the colonisation); A. J. Graham, "Patterns in Early Greek Colonisation," *JHS* 91, 1971, 35-47. Instructive is J. Boardman, *The Greeks Overseas*, Baltimore, Md., 1964 [²1973], especially for the archaeological finds. More recent work is also cited by E. Will, *Rev. hist.* 251, 1974, 153-157. Especially important for the antecedents are the studies by A. Blakeway, *BSA* 33, 1932/33, 170 ff.; *JRS* 25, 1935, 129 ff.; they have shown that there was a longer period of Greek trade with Italy and Sicily from the beginning of the ninth century B.C.; cf. also E. Wikén, *Die Kunde der Hellenen von dem Lande und den Völkern der Appeninhalbinsel bis 300 v. Chr.*, Lund 1937, 25 f. Objections to Blakeway, especially to the figures of his chronology being allegedly too high, are voiced by E. H. Dohan, *Italic Tomb Groups*, Philadelphia 1942; cf. already F. Heichelheim, *Trans. Intern. Num. Congr.* 1936 (published 1938), 68 ff.; the last word has not yet been spoken on the subject. See further: G. Vallet, "Megara Hyblaea," *Kokalos* 14-15, 1968-1969, 468 ff.; R. Chevallier, "Problèmes agraires en Grand-Grèce," *REG* 82, 1969, 541 ff.

MONOGRAPHS: Fr. Bilabel, *Die ionische Kolonisation*, Ph. Suppl. XIV 1, 1920; G. A. Short, "The Siting of Greek Colonies on the Black Sea Coasts of Bulgaria and Rumania," *Ann. Arch. and Anthrop.* 24, 1937, 141 ff.; V. Besevliev, "La colonisation grecque dans le basin nord de la mer Egée dans l'antiquité" (Bulgarian, with a German Table of Contents), *Belomorski Pregled*, I, 1942, 157-78. On the Megarian colonisation: Hanell *Meg.* 113 ff. On the colonisation of Sicily and Southern Italy: J. Beloch, *Campanien*, Breslau 1890; moreover, the book by Biago Pace, *Arte e civiltá della Sicilia antica*, Vols. I-III, 1935-45. Very instructive is V. M. Scramuzza, "Greek and English Colonisation," *AHR* 44, 1939, 303 ff. (with interesting parallels). On the Greeks in Southern Italy: *Atti del Convegno di Studi sulla Magna Grecia*, Tarentum 1961 ff. (to date, 11 vols.). Recent research has centred in particular on the question of the cohabitation of the Greek and native populations, above all in Sicily, and this thanks to the excavations by D. Adamesteanu, P. Griffo and P. Orlandini in Gela, Himera and other sites. See, for instance, P. Griffo, *Kokalos* 10-11, 1964-1965, 135 ff. [an extended report on recent excavations in Sicily]. See also *Himera I. Campagna di scavo 1964-1965, a cura di* A. Adriani, Ist. di Archeol. Univ. de Palermo, Rome 1970; D. Adamesteanu, "Greci ed indigeni nell'agro di Heraclea (Policoro)," *RALinc.* 26, 1971, 643 ff. Instructive too is E. Manni, "La Sicile à la veille de la colonisation grecque," *REA* 71, 1969, 5-22 [with a selective bibliography]. Further, C. Roebuck, *Ionian trade and Colonisation*, New York 1959; E. Blumenthal, *Die altgriech. Siedlungskolonisation im Mittelmeerraum*, Tübingen 1963. Also worth consulting, in general, is J. Boardman, *The Greeks Overseas*, Baltimore 1964 [²1973]; and M. I. Finley, *Ancient Sicily to the Arab Conquest*, London 1968. Of interest too is L. Braccesi, *Grecità adriatica. Un capitolo della colonizzazione greca in occidente*, Bologna 1971.

1. Certain items are discussed by H. Volkmann, "Zur Theokratie im alten Griechenland," *Würzb. Jahrb.* 3, 1948, 58 ff.

2. On the Phrygians and their history see G. u. A. Körte, "Gordion. Ergebnisse der Ausgrabung im Jahre 1900," *JdI Reg.* Vol. 5, 1904, 1 ff.; A. Goetze, *KAO*, 201 ff.; Bittel, *KS* 67 ff.; J. Friedrich, *RE* XX, 882 ff. s.v. *Phrygia.* Regular reports on recent excavations in Gordium are carried by *AJA*.

3. J. Keil, in *Anatolian Studies Presented to Sir William M. Ramsay*, 1923, 265.

4. H. Winckler, *Altoriental. Forsch.* 2. Reihe, Leipzig 1901, 131 ff.; S. Eitrem, *RE* XV, 1538 f. s.v. *Midas* no. 3.

5. H. Gelzer, "Das Zeitalter des Gyges," *RhM* 30, 1875, 230 ff.; C. F. Lehmann-Haupt, *RE* VII, 1956 ff. s.v. *Gyges* no. 2; H. Kaletsch, "Zur lydischen Chronologie," *H.* 7, 1958, 1-47.

6. A recent history of the Lydian kingdom based on sound scholarship does not exist. Out of date are, *inter al.*, R. Schubert, *Gesch. der Könige von Lydien,* 1884, and G. Radet, *La Lydie et le monde grec au temps des Mermnades*, Paris 1893. A short survey is given by J. Keil, *RE* XIII, 2161 ff. s.v. *Lydia*; cf. also A. Goetze, *KAO*, 206 ff.

7. A. Erzen, *Kilikien bis zum Ende der Perserherrschaft*, Diss. Leipzig 1940, 76 ff., also H. Bengtson, *Gn.* 18, 1942, 212 (= *KS*, 105).

8. On the Cimmerians, the *Gimirruia* of the cuneiform inscriptions, see C. F. Lehmann-Haupt, *RE* XI, 397 ff.; J. Lewy, *MVAG* 29, 2, 1925; and *RLVorgesch.* VI, 1926, 347 ff.; V. Cozzoli, *I. Cimmeri*, Rome 1968.

9. Diehl, *Anth. Lyr.* I^2, 3 ff.

10. Mimnerm. fr. 13 f.; Herod. I 16 ff.; Theogn. 1104; Strabo XIV 646; cf. Beloch, *GG* I 1^2, 344 f.

11. W.v. Soden, *Der Aufstieg des Assyrerreiches als geschichtliches Problem* (AO 37, 1-2), Leipzig 1937.

12. A. Alt, *ZDPV* 67, 1945, 138 ff.

13. Berossus in Alexander Polyhistor and Abydenus (Berossus fr. 43a and 44, Schnabel); cf. A. Momigliano, "Su una battaglia tra Assiri e Greci," *Ath.* NS 12, 1934, 412 ff.; H. Bengtson, *Ph.* 92, 1937, 148 ff (= *KS*, 77 ff.); A. Erzen, *Kilikien bis zum Ende der Perserherrschaft*, Diss. Leipzig 1940, 64 ff.

14. E. F. Weidner, *AfO* 7, 1931/32, 1 ff.

15. Meyer, *GdA* II^{2}2, 36 ff.

16. According to F. K. Kienitz, *Die polit. Gesch. Ägyptens vom 7. bis zum 4. Jahrh. vor der Zeitwende*, 1953, 12, the Assyrians withdrew from the country without a battle.

17. Strabo XVII 801.

18. The early date (and not the late, namely under Amasis) has correctly been advanced by: H. Prinz, *Funde aus Naukratis* (Klio-Beih. 7), Leipzig 1908, 4; F. Bilabel, *Die ionische Kolonisation* (Ph. Suppl. = Bd. 14, 1), 1920, 58 f.; Beloch, *GG* I^2 2, 236; H. Kees, *RE* XVI, 1956 ff. s.v. *Naukratis*; W. Schubart, *Die Griechen in Ägypten* (Beihefte z. Alt. Orient 10), 1927, 5 ff.; R. M. Cook, "Amasis and the Greeks in Egypt," *JHS* 57, 1937, 227 ff., dates the founding of the city to about 615/10 B.C. The reference in Herodotus II 178 appears to be an allusion to a reform of the settlement under Amasis. C. Roebuck, *CP* 44, 1951, 212 ff., dates the beginnings of the city in the time of Psammetichus I. Additional bibliography in F. K. Kienitz, *Die polit. Gesch. Ägyptens*, 1953, 46 n. 1. On the archaeological evidence, see J. Boardman, *The Greeks Overseas*, Baltimore 1964.

19. Herod. II 158; IV 42. Cf. *supra* 79.

20. A. v. Premerstein, *Mitt. aus der Papyrussammlung der Giessener Univ. Bibl.* V: *Alexandrinische Geronten vor Kaiser Gaius*, 1939, 40 ff.

21. C. J. Gadd, *The Fall of Nineveh*, London 1923; cf. Br. Meissner, *DLZ*, 1924, 136 ff. New text in D. J. Wiseman, *Chronicles of the Chaldaean Kings (626-556 B.C.) in the British Museum*, London 1956, 54 ff.; cf. H. Bengtson, *H.* 6, 1957, 499 f. (= *KS*, 70 f.).

22. For a beginning towards a more positive evaluation of the Assyrians see W. Otto, *HZ* 146, 1932, 236 f.

23. F. Stähelin, *Schweizer Beitr. z. allg. Gesch.* I, 1943, 29.

24. Phocyl. fr. 4 Diehl.

25. Cf. Otto, *Kulturg.*, 90. The term for the classical Greek state, to wit a "city-state," is admittedly misleading; it has therefore been correctly contested by, *inter al.*, U. v. Wilamo-

witz and K. J. Beloch. If one does not wish to use the term "polis," adopted by J. Burckhardt, then the term "community-state" will still be the most appropriate.

26. V. Ehrenberg, "When Did the Polis Rise?," *JHS* 57, 1937, 147 ff. Cf. also the earlier bibliography in Busolt, *Gr. St.* I, 153 ff.; see also *Zur griech. Staatskunde*, ed. F. Gschnitzer, Wege der Forschung 96, 1969, 271 ff.; cf. *idem*, "Stadt und Stamm bei Homer," *Ch.* 1, 1971, 1 ff. The earliest documentary evidence for the *polis* comes from the archaic inscriptions of Drerus (Crete); see P. Demargne and H. van Effenterre, *BCH* 61, 1937, 333 ff. no. 1; cf. V. Ehrenberg, *CQ* 37, 1943, 14 ff.; F. Jacoby, *CQ* 38, 1944, 15 f.; H. Van Effenterre, *BCH* 70, 1946, 590 no. 2 (from the period c. 600 B.C.), and Meiggs-Lewis, no. 2.

27. V. Ehrenberg, *Gn.* 5, 1929, 4 (in his review of Glotz, *La cité Gr.*).

28. In the *Iliad* (II 649) Crete is called "one-hundred-citied;" cf. E. Kirsten, *Das dorische Kreta*, Würzburg 1942, 92.

29. These figures according to K. J. Beloch, *Die Bevölkerung der griech.-rom. Welt*, Leipzig 1886; cf. Busolt, *Gr. St.* I, 163 ff.

30. Whether for centuries, as later sources state (Pausanias III 2. 6 ff. and Schol. Pind., *Isthm.* VII 14), is questionable.

31. V. Ehrenberg, *Hermes* 59, 1924, 45.

32. On the *helioteia* (the term has not been fully explained) cf. T. Meier, *Sp. St.* 30 ff., and Lotze, *Met.* 26 ff. The view held by Kahrstedt, *Stsr.* I, 11, that the *helioteia* arose through the confiscation of land leased to peasants, has correctly found no countenance; cf. also the discussion by A. Toynbee, "The Origins and Status of the Helots," in *Pr.*, 195 ff.

33. B. Niese, *Hermes* 26, 1891, 1 ff.; Kiechle, *Messen.*

34. Whereas the Olympian victor lists attest a clear preponderance of Messenians until 736 B.C., the Spartans dominate from 720 B.C. on; cf. E. Brinkmann, *RhM* 70, 1915, 632; cf. also V. Ehrenberg, *RE* III A, 1378, Callmer, *Ark.*, 55 ff., and Kiechle, *Messen.*, 10 ff. The lowering of the date of the First Messenian War down to about 670-650 B.C. and the Second to approximately 600 B.C. by Th. Lenschau, *Ph.* 91, 1936, 289 ff., 410 ff., rests on presuppositions which are too uncertain to grant probability to the hypothesis.

35. Tyrtaeus frs. 4 and 5 (Diehl), cf. Kiechle, *Messen.*, 61 ff., 65 f.; the Spartans had, accordingly, not conquered the whole of Messenia in the First War but only part of it, in particular the plain of Stenyclarus.

36. The attempt by B. Niese, "Eleier und Pisaten," in *Genethl. f. C. Robert*, Halle 1910, 26 ff., to explain these events as a reflection of circumstances from the fourth century is not convincing.

37. Aristotle, *Pol.* V 6.2; Pausan. IV 18.2.

38. Fr. Frhr. Hiller von Gaertringen and H. Lattermann, *Hira und Adania* (71. Berl. Winckelmannsprogr.), 1911, where the war of Aristomenes is, however, linked with the obscure Helot revolt of 490 B.C.; a similar view has recently been advanced by Kiechle, *Messen.*, 82 ff., 106 ff.; but for a different position see, for instance, Jacoby, *FgrHist.* no. 295, F 38-46, Commentary, 112 ff.

39. On Pheidon see Meyer, *GdA* II, 544 ff. (= III², 502 f); Beloch, *GG* I²1, 332 f.; H. T. Wade-Gery, *CAH* III, 761 f.; further bibliography in Callmer, *Ark.*, 66 n. 134; den Boer, *Lac.*, 55 n. 1; cf. also G. Zörner, *Kypselos und Pheidon von Argos. Untersuchungen zur frühen griechischen Tyrannis*, Diss. Marburg a.d.L. 1971; also H. Chantraine, *JNG* 8, 1957, 70 ff.; Z. Rubinsohn, "Pheidon of Argos, Military Reformer or Capitalist?," *RIL* 105, 1971, 636 ff.

40. Cf. Th. Lenschau, *RE* XIX, 1943 f., also W. Schwabacher, *ibid.*, 1946 ff. s.v. *Pheidonischer Munzfuss*; cf. R. M. Cook, *H.* 7, 1958, 257 ff.

41. Thus by Gruppe, Vollgraff (*NJb*, 1910, 305 ff.), Th. Lenschau (*Ph.* 91, 1936, 386 ff.).

42. The defeat of the Spartans at Hysiae, dated by Pausanias II 24.7 to 669/8 B.C., apparently belongs in this context, but it is impossible to place any confidence in the chronology.

43. As opposed to the doubts expressed by Busolt, *GG* I², 595, concerning the battles at the end of the eighth century, see F. Bölte, in Ziehen, *RE* III A, 1510. The conquest of Thyreatis: Herod I 82, cf. V. Ehrenberg, *RE* XVIII, 1871 f. s.v. *Othryadas*. On the site of the decisive battle (Parparus): F. Bölte, *RhM* 78, 1929, 130 ff., cf. L. Moretti, *RF* NS 24, 1946, 204 ff.

44. Fighting between Sparta and Tegea: Herod. I 65 and 67; cf. L. Moretti, "Sparta alla

metà del VI secolo," *RF* NS 24, 1946, 87 ff. (La guerra contro Tegea). The treaty: Aristotle fr. 592 (cf. F. Jacoby, *CQ* 38, 1944, 15); the late dating to 468 B.C. (Hiller von Gaertringen, *IG* V 2, 3; Busolt, *Gr. St.* II, 1320 n. 3; H. Berve, *HVSchr.* 25, 1929, 13 n. 2); to 464 B.C. or a little later (L. Moretti, *op. cit.*, 101 ff.); or to about 450 B.C. (Busolt *Gr. St.* II, 1399); is erroneous; correct, *inter al.*, are Highby, *ED*, 72 ff, and Callmer, *Ark.* 76. Cf. also M. Caltabiano, "Documenti numismatici a storia del koinon arcade dalle origini al sec. V. a.c.," *Helikon* 9-10, 1969-70, 423 ff.

45. L. Ziehen, "Das spartanische Bevölkerungsproblem," *Hermes* 68, 1933, 218 ff.; T. Meier, *Das Wesen der spartanischen Staatsordnung*, 1939, 6 ff.

46. Cf. the strange prohibition of *conubium* between Pellene and Hagnus in the historical period, Plut., *Theseus* 13.3; cf. F. Erdmann, *Die Ehe im alten Griechenland* (Münch-Beitr. 20), 1943, 139 n. 14; 178.

47. Thus also M. Cary, *CAH* III, 577 ff. Cf. A. Alföldy, "Der Attische Synoikismos und die Entstehung des athenischen Adels," *Rev. belge. de Phil. et d'Hist.* 47, 1969, 5 ff., who argues that the Attic noble families were resettled in Athens and in the interior of Attica.

48. Ernst Kornemann, "Athen und Attika," in *Staaten, Völker, Männer*, 1934, 47. For a different view cf. R. A. Padgug, "Eleusis and the Union of Attika," *GRBS* 13, 1972, 135 ff., who attempts to argue, though not convincingly, for the union of Attica, along with Eleusis, in the Late Mycenaean period.

49. Dittenberger-Purgold, *Inschriften von Olympia* nos. 1 ff; cf. Busolt, *Gr. St.* I, 32 n. 2; 147 f. On the dating of the inscription see the partially problematic conclusions of U. Kahrstedt, "Zur Gesch. von Elis und Olympia," *NGG*, 1927, Heft 3.

50. On the older history of Thessaly see Fr. Frhr. Hiller von Gaertringen, *Das Königtum bei den Thessalern, Aus der Anomia*, Berlin 1890, 1 ff.; cf. *RE* VI A, 112 ff., who incorrectly denies the existence of a Thessalian united state in the period before 500 B.C.; cf. Beloch, *GG* I 1^2, 335 ff.; I 2, 197 ff., also G. Kip, *Thessalische Studien*, Diss. Halle 1910, and M. Sordi, *La lega tessala fino ad Alessandro Magno*, Rome 1958.

51. F. Gschnitzer, *Anz. Alt.* 7, 1954, 191 f. The first certain evidence is the bronze figure from Thetonium (c. 450 B.C.), *IG* IX 2, 257; cf. M. Sordi, *RF* NS 36, 1958, 59-65.

52. Geyer, *Mak.*, 40.

53. Underestimated by H. E. Stier, *Grundlagen und Sinn der griech. Geschichte*, Stuttgart 1945, 88 ff., who incorrectly sees in the original term Hellenes a concept of importance only in regard to the history of civilisation. Cf. as against this, H. Bengtson, "Hellenen und Barbaren. Gedanken zum Problem des Griechischen Nationalbewusstseins," in *Unser Geschichtsbild*, ed. K. Rüdinger, Munich 1954, 25 ff. (= *KS*, 158 ff.); H. Schaefer, "Das Problem der griechischen Nationalität," *Relazioni X Congr. Int. di Scienze stor.*, Rome 1955, VI, 679 ff.

54. Beloch, *GG* I 1^2, 332; cf. Thuc. I 3.

55. Archil., fr. 52; in Hesiod *Works and Days* 528 there appears the term "Panhellenes." In Hesiod's Catalogues (fr. 7 Rzach) Hellen is the eponymous hero of the Greeks.

56. Herod. II 178, cf. G. Plaumann, *RE* VIII, 175 ff. s.v. no. 4 (*Hellenion*).

57. Cf. Nilsson, *Gr.Rel.* I, 645; H. Bengtson, *Einf.* ^{7}1975, 26 f.; cf. *Anc. Hist.* 26 f.; A. E. Samuel, *Greek and Roman Chronology. Calendars and Years in Classical Antiquity* (Hdb. Alt.), Munich 1972, 33 ff. [later date].

58. The early history of the Delphic Amphictyony (cf. H. Bürgel, *Die pylaeisch-delphische Amphiktyonie*, Munich 1877; a useful recent study does not exist) is shrouded in darkness. Certain is that the so-called First Sacred War (c. 590 B.C.), which ended in the destruction of Crisa, was of crucial importance for the development of the Amphictyony. On the First Sacred War see J. Jannoray, "Krisa, kirrha et la première guerre sacrée," *BCH* 61, 1937, 33 ff.; M. Sordi, *RF* NS 31, 1953, 320 ff.; G. Forrest, *BCH* 80, 1956, 33 ff.; new views in P. Guillon, *Etudes béotiennes. Le Bouclier d'Heracles et l'histoire de la Grèce centrale dans la période de la première guerre sacrée*, Aix-en-Provence 1963.

59. Aeschines II 115; III 109 f., cf. Ehrenberg, *State*, 110; J. A. O. Larsen, "Federation for Peace in Ancient Greece," *CP* 39, 1944, 145ff.; G. Daux, *Studies D.M. Robinson* II, 1953, 775 ff.; exaggerated is Hampl, *Staatsv.* 5 f.

60. An up to date comprehensive work on the history of Olympia and the Olympian games is lacking; it is an urgent desideratum. Of earlier works, though to a large degree out

of date, may be cited, for instance: A. H. Gardiner, *Olympia*, 1926; F. Mezö, *Geschichte der Olympischen Spiele*, Munich 1930 (not sufficiently critical); L. Ziehen and J. Wiesner, *RE* XVII, 2520 ff.; XVIII, 1 ff. s.v. *Olympia*; J. Jüthner, "Herkunft und Grundlagen der griechischen Nationalspiele," *Ant.* 15, 1939, 231 ff.; K. Meull, "Der Ursprung der Olympischen Spiele," *Ant.* 17, 1941, 189 ff.; also the archaeological literature cited above 364 n. 13, and the book by L. Drees, *Olympia, Götter, Künstler und Athleten*, Stuttgart, 1967 (illustrated), as well as H. Bengtson, *Die Olympischen Spiele in der Antike*, Zurich and Stuttgart ^{2}1972.

61. Aristotle saw a bronze discus at Olympia on which the *ekecheiria* and the names of the Elean king Iphitus and of Lycurgus were inscribed: Arist. fr. 533; cf. Pausan. 20.1. Even if the discus may have been genuine, it is by no means proven that this Lycurgus had to be the Spartan lawgiver; different views are admittedly held by B. Niese ("Herodotstudien," *Hermes* 42, 1907, 448) and C.F. Lehmann-Haupt, *GG*^{2}, in Gercke-Norden, *Einl.* 108. Weighty objections were already raised by V. Costanzi, Licurgo, *RF* 38, 1910, 38 ff.; important is Jacoby, *Att.*, 363.

62. See the remarks above 399 f. on the alleged influence of the Delphic oracle.

63. On the position of the colony in regard to the mother-city see in particular J. Seibert, *Metropolis und Apoikie*, Diss. Würzburg 1963, and A. J. Graham, *Colony and Mother City in Ancient Greece*, Manchester 1964. Further material in the *Atti del III Convegno di Studi sulla Magna Grecia* (cited *infra* 402); cf. also R. Werner, "Probleme der Rechtsbeziehungen zwischen Metropolis und Apoikie," *Ch.* 1, 1971, 19 ff.

64. Cf. H. Bolkestein, *Klio* 13, 1913, 432 ff.; Meyer, *GdA* III^{2}, 388 ff.

65. R. Tolles, *Untersuch z. Kindesaussetzung bei den Griechen*, Diss. Breslau 1941; P. Roussel, "L'exposition des enfants à Sparte," *REA* 45, 1943, 5 ff.

66. A. Blakeway, "Prolegomena to the Study of Greek Commerce with Sicily, Italy and France in the VIIIth and VIIth Century," *BSA* 33, 1932/33, 170 ff.; "Demaratus," *JRS* 25, 1935, 129 ff.; R. L. Beaumont, *JHS* 56, 1936, 159 ff. On Greek trade with Etruria see also G. Karo, "Etruskisches in Griechenland," *Arch. Eph.*, 1937, 316 ff.

67. W. Schadewaldt, in *NBAnt.*, I, 70 ff.

68. Beloch, *GG* I^{2} 2, 225 ff., esp. 229.

69. B. Schweitzer, *AM* 43, 1918, 27 f.

70. C. L. Woolley, "Excavations at Al Mina, Sueidia," *JHS* 58, 1938, 1 ff.; 133 ff.; M. Robertson, "The Excavations at Al Mina Sueidia," *JHS* 60, 1940, 2 ff.; S. Smith, "The Greek Trade at Al-Mina," *Ant. Journ.*, 1942, 87 ff. See also J. Boardman, *The Greeks Overseas*, Baltimore 1964, 61-79.

71. E. Forrer, *Bericht VI. Int. Kongr. f. Arch.*, Berlin 1939 (published 1940), 360 ff.; P. J. Riis, *Sukas* I. *The North-East Sanctuary and the First Settling of Greeks in Syria and Palestine*, Copenhagen 1970.

72. According to Strabo V 243, Cumae was the oldest Greek colony in Italy; cf. A. Blakeway, *JRS* 25, 1935, 129 ff.

73. Cf. Strabo V 247; Livy VIII 22; cf. Dunbabin, *West.*, 6; A. Lipinsky, "Ausgrabungen in Pithekussai," *AW* 3, 1972, 144 f. On the discovery of Nestor's cup (so-called) in Pithecussae (Ischia) from the eighth century B.C. see G. Buchner and C. F. Russo, *RALinc.* VIII, 10, 1955, 216 ff.; cf. J. and L. Robert, *Bull. épigr.*, 1956, no. 365; K. Rüter and K. Matthiessen, *ZPE* 2, 1968, 231 ff.; and Meiggs-Lewis, no. 1, with additional bibliography; as well as K. Alpers, "Eine Beobachtung zum Nestorbecher von Pithekussai," *Glotta* 67, 1969, 170 ff.; cf. also the bibliographical material in *Antike Welt, Zeitschr. für Archäologie und Kunstgeschichte* 7, 1976, 31. On the foreign trade between Pithecussae, Egypt and Syria see *JHS*, 1958, Suppl. 40 f.

74. Thus F. Altheim, "Griech. Götter in alten Rom," *RVV* 22, 1930; *idem, Römische Religionsgeschichte* I, 1931, 84.

75. R. van Compernolle, *Bull. Inst. hist. belge de Rome* 26, 1950-51, 163 ff. (on the founding of Naxos).

76. Contested by Dunbabin, *West.*, 14.

77. L. Wickert, *RE* IV A, 1478 ff. (with the most important older bibliography).

78. On the chronology of the Lelantine War (end of the eighth to the middle of the

seventh century) see, for instance, F. Geyer, *RE Suppl.* IV, 433 f. s.v. *Euboia*; M. Cary, *CAH* III, 622 f. The dating by Beloch (*GG* I²1, 338) to about 570 B.C., which is based on the article by V. Costanzi, *AR*, 1902, 769 ff., is untenable.

79. W. Ehlers, *Die Gründung von Zankle in den Aiotien des Kallimachos*, Diss. Berlin 1933; Vallet, *Rhêgion.*

80. Others, such as U. Kahrstedt, *Würzb. Jahrb.* 2, 1947, 16 ff., and J. Bovio-Marconi, *Ampurias* 12, 1950, 79 ff., regard the Elymians as Sicanians; cf. R. van Compernolle, *Phoibos* 5, 1950-1951, 213 ff.

81. Thus Mazzarino, *Fr.00*, 271 *et al*; H. Treidler, *H.* 8, 1959, 257 ff.; Graf Stauffenberg, *H.* 9, 1960, 212 ff.

82. P. Wuilleumier, *Tarente des origines à la conquête romaine*, Paris 1939. The view put forward by Ciaceri, *St.MGr.* I², 85 ff., that Tarentum was the oldest Greek colony of all in the West, is unfounded. The evidence in Dunbabin, *West.*, 29 ff.; 146 ff.

83. Strabo VI 263; cf. Meyer, *GdA* III², 448 Dunbabin, *West.*, 365.

84. F. Koldewey-O. Puchstein, *Griechische Tempel in Unteritalien u. Sizilien*, 1891; F. Krauss, Paestum, 1941. Among the recent finds, a silver discus from the temple of Hera with an archaic Greek inscription may be mentioned: *AA*, 1956, 439; 443 Abb. 154.

85. P. Zancani-Montuoro and U. Zanotti-Bianco, *Heraion alla foce del Sele* I-II, Rome 1951 and 1953. Additional finds of metopes: *JHS*, 1958, Suppl. 36.

86. Ciaceri, *St.MGr.* II², 168 ff.; opposed to him: J. Vogt, *Gn.* 8, 1932, 529 ff.

87. Basic is G. Rohlfs, *Scavi linguistici nella Magna Grecia*, Halle-Rome 1933; cf. the studies in SB.B, 1944/46, 5: *Griech. Sprachgeist in Süditalien; Historische Grammatik der unteritalienischen Gräzitat, ibid.*, 1949, 4 (published 1950) (with map, 32).

88. Thus Beloch, *GG* I²1, 236. For a different view, however, see R. Canturella, *Rassegna Pugliese* 3, 1968, 3-15.

89. Beloch, *GG* I²1, 234 n. 4; A. Debrunner, *RLVorgesch.* IV 2, 1926, 509; Wilamowitz *Gl.* I, 51 n. 1; J. Bérard, *REA* 54, 1952, 5 ff.

90. The voyage of Colaeus: Herod. IV 152; cf. R. Hennig, *Terrae incognitae* I, 1936, 41 ff. (uncritical); and F. Heichelheim, *Wirts. Alt.* I, 247 f.; II, 1010. On Tartessus see the studies of A. Schulten (not always sufficiently critical on points of detail), especially *Tartessos*, Hamburg 1922, ²1950; cf. P. Bosch-Gimpera, *Klio* 22, 1929, 357 ff.; J.-P. Morel, *BCH* 99, 1975, 889 ff.

91. M. Clerc, "Les premières colonisations phocéenes dans la Méditerranée occidentale," *REA* 7, 1905, 29 ff.; P. Bosch-Gimpera, "The Phokaians in the Far West," *CQ* 38, 1944, 53 ff. (with a list of the Greek finds in Spain, 59); A. Garcia Y Bellido, *Ampurias* 2, 1940, 55 ff.; Los hallazagos griegos de España, Madrid 1936. E. Lepore, *PP* 25, 1970, 19-54; more recent material in J.-P. More, *BCH* 99, 1975, 853 ff.

92. M. Clerc, *Histoire de Massalia*, Marseille 1927; H. G. Wackernagel, *RE* XIV, 2130 ff.; F. Benoit, *AJA* 53, 1949, 237 ff.; "Relation de Marseille grecque avec le monde occidental," *Rev. étud. ligures* 22, 1956, 5 ff., cf. further J. J. Hatt," Notices sur le commerce grec dans la domaine celtique," *Rev. arch. de l'Est* 6, 1955, 146 ff. The discovery of a large Greek bronze krater in a tomb at Vix (north of Chatillon-sur-Seine) from the end of the sixth century made news: cf. J. Joffroy," La tombe de Vix," *Mon. Piot* 48, 1954.

93. W.v. Wartburg, "Die griech. Kolonisation in Südgallien und ihre sprachlichen Zeugen im Westromanischen," *Zeitschr. f. roman. Phil.* 68, 1952, 1-48 [also separately]. On the Greeks and Greek culture in southern Gaul see (in addition to the works cited in the previous footnote) in particular: P. Jacobsthal and Neuffer, *Préhistoire* 2, 1933, 1-64, moreover the reports in the Journals *Gallia* and *Revue des Etudes anciennes*. Important are the excavations at Ensérune (J. Jannoray, *Ensérune*, Paris 1955), Glanum, St. Blaise, Olbia and Marseille.

94. On the Greeks in Spain see Rhys Carpenter, *The Greeks in Spain*, New York/London 1925; A. Schulten, *RhM* 85, 1936, 289 ff.; A. Garcia Y Bellido, *Hispania Graeca*, Barcelona 1948; *idem* and Martin Almagro, in *Historia d'España* I, 1952, edited by R. Menendez Pidal. Important are the excavations in Ampurias (Emporiae), on which reports are published in the same Journal; cf. further in particular M. Almagro, *Ampurias. Guide de Fouilles et du musée*, Barcelona 1967.

95. Pliny, *n.h.* V 112, cf. F. Bilabel, *Die ionische Kolonisation*, Ph. Suppl. XIV 1, Leipzig 1920, 13 ff.

96. F. Miltner, Die erste milesische Kolonisation im Südpontus, *Studies Buckler*, 191 ff. Cf., on the other hand, K. Hanell, *Megarische Studien*, Lund 1934, 133 n. 3.

97. On the Scythians and their civilisation see the works cited above 401 by E. H. Minns, M. Ebert and M. Rostovtzeff; moreover P. Kretschmer, *RE* II A, 923 ff. s.v. *Scythae*; Christensen, *Die Iranier*, in Hdb. Alt., 1933, 242 ff.; M. Gibellino-Krasceninnicowa, *Gli Sciti, Studio storico-archeologico*, Rome 1942. A survey is given by M. Rostovtzeff, "South Russia in the Prehistoric and Classical Period," *AHR* 26, 1921, 203 ff.

98. See Ebert, *Süd.*, 218 ff. Cf. in general E. v. Stern, "Die griechische Kolonisation am Nordgestade des Schwarzen Meeres im Lichte archäolog. Forsch.," *Klio* 9, 1909, 139 ff.; "Die politische und soziale Struktur der Griechenkolonien am Nordufer des Schwarzmeergebietes," *Hermes* 50, 1915, 161 ff. Of interest is a letter written on lead, published by Y. G. Vinogradov, "A Greek Letter from Berezan," *Vestn. Dreon. Ist.*, 1971, 74-100, from the sixth or the beginning of the fifth century; cf. J. Chadwick, "The Berezan Letter," *Proceed. Cambr. Phil. Soc.* 199, 1973, 35-37; A. P. Miller, *ZPE* 17, 1975, 157 ff.; R. Merkelbach, *ZPE* 17, 1975, 161 ff.

99. The older literature on Olbia may be found in the works by Minns, Ebert and Rostovtzeff, and reports on more recent excavations are given by E. Diehl, *Gn.* 8, 1932, 545 ff.; cf. *RE* XVII, 2405 ff. s.v. *Olbia*, no. 4; moreover, the report by E. H. Minns, "Thirty Years of Work at Olbia," *JHS* 65, 1945, 109 ff. (based on the study by S. A. Zebelev, *Olbia*, Kiev 1940; see also E. Belin de Ballu, *Olbia. cité antique du littoral de la mer noire*, Leiden 1972.

100. For a concise discussion see E. Diehl, *RE* VII A, 1850 ff. s.v. no. 2.

101. A survey in H. G. Gundel, "Die Krim im Altertum," *Gym.* 53, 1942/43, 117 ff. (with bibliography).

102. T. G. Noonan, "The Origins of the Colony of Panticapaeum," *AJA* 77, 1973, 77 ff.

103. H. Merle, *Die Gesch. der Städte Byzantion und Kalchedon*, Diss. Kiel 1916; Hanell, *Meg.*, 122 ff.

104. Thus Hanell, *Meg.*, 135.

105. On Thasos cf. the important publication by J. Pouilloux, *Recherches sur l'histoire et les cultes de Thasos* I-II (Vol. II in collaboration with C. Dunant), Paris 1954 and 1958, with a large number of valuable inscriptions, in particular from the Classical, Hellenistic and Roman periods.

106. Cf. the Archilochus inscription from Paros, *IG* XII Suppl. 213 IV 22, cf. O. Rubensohn, *RE* XVIII, 4, 1806, ff.

107. Cf. the inscription *IG* XII Suppl. 412; cf. O. Rubensohn, *RE* XVIII, 4, 1813.

108. A different view is taken by U. Kahrstedt, along with American scholars; the name Chalcidice is, accordingly, derived from a local tribe; cf. E. Harrison, "Chalkidike," *CQ* 6, 1912, 93 ff. Of still another opinion is D. W. Bradeen, "The Chalcidians in Thrace," *AJP* 73, 1952, 356-380.

109. On Naucratis v.s.p. 49.

110. L. Malten's conjecture, based on conclusions drawn from mythical history (*Kyrene*, 1911), that the Greek settlement goes back to the second millennium B.C., has not been confirmed by excavations: the earliest monuments stem from the second half of the seventh century (R. Horn, *Ant.* 19, 1943, 169). Basic in its day for the history of Cyrene was J. P. Thrige, *Res Cyrenensium a primordiis inde civitatis etc.*, Hafniae 1828 (*iterum imprim. cur. S. Ferri*, Verbania 1940); a more up to date study does not exist; a survey (with the most important bibliography) is provided by R. Horn, *op cit.*, 163 ff. Indispensable is F. Chamoux, *Cyrène sous la monarchie des Battiades*, Paris 1953; cf. also H. Schaefer, "Die verfassungsgeschichtl. Entwicklung Kyrenes im 1. Jh. nach seiner Begründung," *RhM* 95, 1952, 135-170. Of interest is the "Oath of the Founders," which is not, however, authentic: *SEG* IX 3, cf. F. Chamoux, *op. cit.*, 105 ff., and in particular, J. Seibert, *Metropolis und Apoikie*, Diss. Würzburg 1963, 6 ff.; and now Meiggs-Lewis, no. 5, with additional bibliography.

111. Cf. *Iliad* II 867; see A. Eichhorn, *Barbaros quid significaverit*, Diss. Leipzig 1904; U. Wilcken, "Hellenen und Barbaren," *NJb* 17, 1906, 457 ff.; J. Jüthner, "Hellenen und

Barbaren. Aus der Gesch. der griech. Nationalbewusstseins," *Das Erbe der Alten* 8, 1923; cf. W. Otto, *PhW*, 1926, 39 ff.; H. E Stier, *Grundlagen und Sinn der griech. Gesch.*, 1945, esp. 80 ff.

112. E. F. Weidner, *Mél. Dussaud* II, 1939, 123 ff. The texts stem from 595/4-570/64 B.C.

113. *Syll.* I³1 = Meiggs-Lewis no. 7. A new edition was also published by A. Bernand-O. Masson, *REG* 70, 1957, 1 ff. On the dating: G. Lefebvre, "Potasimpto," *Bull. Soc. Arch. Alex.* no. 21, 1923, 48 ff.; on the family see S. Pernigotti, *Studi class. e. orientali* 17, 1968, 251-264.

114. Cf. Ebert, *Südr.*, 296.

115. Ed. Meyer placed trade-political considerations in the foreground as the motivating factor behind the colonial foundations, whereas other scholars (K. J. Beloch, A. Gwynn, J. Hasebroek, H. Berve, G. De Sanctis and F. Heichelheim) regarded the Greek settlements primarily as agricultural colonies. In addition to, *inter al.*, U. Wilcken and Th. Lenschau, it was in particular Otto, *Kulturg.* 84, who adopted a mediating view.

116. K. Lehmann-Hartleben, *Die antiken Hafenanlagen des Mittelmeeres*, Klio Beih. 14, Leipzig 1923.

117. Fr. Heichelheim, "Die Ausbreitung der Münzgeldwirtschaft und der Wirtschaftsstil im archaischen Griechenland," *SJ* 55, 1931, 229 ff.; "Welthistor. Gesichtspunkte zu den vormittelalterlichen Wirtschaftsepochen," *SJ* 56, 1933, 154 ff.; *Wirts. Alt.* I, 1938, 294 ff.

118. B. L. Bailey, "The Export of Attic Black-Figure Ware," *JHS* 60, 1940, 60 ff.

4 POLITICS AND SOCIETY IN THE COLONISATION PERIOD

SOURCES AND BIBLIOGRAPHY: The internal development of the Greek people in the archaic period can be reconstructed only in broad outline. We know so little about this period because of the nature of the tradition. Our primary sources are unusually sparse, and consist of a number of fragments from the lyric poets, a few scattered archaic inscriptions, of which only few go back beyond the beginning of the sixth century, and coins and monuments, whose interpretation is to a large degree disputed. In addition the geographical distribution of the provenance of our sources is unusually disproportionate. Thanks to our secondary sources (v. *infra*), Sparta and Athens completely occupy the foreground, while the tradition of the older Greek *tyrannis*, endowed with anecdotal features, only throws a meagre light on the internal conditions of other communities in Greece, Ionia and the West. The violent upheavals of the time in the cultural and economic spheres, especially the conflicts between the powerful aristocracy and the emergent *tyrannis*, the rise of the hoplite politeia and the ascent of the citizenry are discernible in the transmission only in outline: it is not the individual documents but only the sum of the parts that gives us a picture which is probably correct in outline for the archaic period.

As a peasant counterpart to the aristocratic ethics of the Homeric poems, the *Works and Days* of the Boeotian bard, Hesiod of Ascra (probably c. 700 B.C.), constitute a source of the greatest value. Hesiod is in fact the first individual in Greek history who gives us an account of his own fortunes in that age; toil and piety make up his motto, and combined with extolling the hard work of the farmer there are a great many precepts in the form of a "peasant calendar," narrating the afflictions and miseries of peasant life; cf. Ed. Meyer, "Hesiods Erga und das Gedicht von den fünf Menschengeschlechtern," *Genethliakon f. C. Robert*, Halle 1910, 157 ff. = *Kleine Schriften* II, 1924, 15 ff.; also W. Jaeger's characterisation in *Paid.* I 57 ff.; the earlier bibliography is cited by W. Schmid, *GGL* I 1, 246 ff.; cf. also *Hésiode et son influence* (Fondation Hardt, Entretiens 7), published Paris 1962, especially the contribution by W. J. Verdenius; also H. Diller, *Die dichterische Form von Hesiods Erga* (Akad. Mainz 1962, no. 2). Important observations on points of detail may be found in M. P. Nilsson, "Das frühe Griechenland, von innen gesehen," *H.* 3, 1954-55, 257 ff., esp. 266 ff.

A true representative of the restless colonisation period, however, is Archilochus, whose father was a citizen of Paros and his mother a slave (middle of the seventh century); he took part in the colonisation of Thasos. The fragments of his works are to be found in E. Diehl, *Anth. Lyr.* I² 3, 1936, 3 ff.; M. L. West (ed.), *IEG* (OCT) 1, 1971; J. Ebert-W.

Luppe, "Zum neuen Archilochos-Papyrus," *ZPE* 16, 1975, 223 ff. Archilochus' fr. 74, mentioning a total solar eclipse, can only be that of 6 Apr. 648 B.C. E. Löwy's equation with the eclipse of 19 May 557 B.C., *Anz. W*, 1933, 32 ff., seems to me impossible. So too impossible would be the eclipse of 14 Mar. 711 B.C., as A. Blakeway, "Greek Life and Poetry," *Studies for Gilbert Murray*, 34 ff. Cf. F. Jacoby, *CQ* 35, 1941, 97 ff. Nor does the question seem to be decided by the discovery of the grave of Glaucus (fr. 68 Diehl) on Thasos, from the end of the 7th century: J. Pouilloux, BCH 79, 1955, 75-80. A new find of inscriptions, edited by N. M. Kontoleon, *Arch. Eph.* 1952 [published 1954], 32-95; cf. W. Peek, *Ph.* 99 1955, 4 ff., and in particular J. and L. Robert, *REG*, *Bull. épigr.*, 1955, no. 178, has brought to light new fragments of his poems (30 preserved half lines), and in addition to this the account of a poetic dedication from the pen of Mnesiepes on the monument of Archilochus in Paros from the Hellenistic period. Besides this there are a number of other fragments in *P. Oxy.* XXII, which are unfortunately very mutilated. Cf. the lectures and discussions of Fondation Hardt in the volume *Archiloque* (Entretiens, 10), Vandoeuvres-Genève, 1964 (with contributions by Pouilloux, Kontoleon, Page *et al.*). Younger by almost two generations is Alcaeus of Lesbos (c. 600 B.C.). His poems shed light on the internal struggles between the aristocracy and the tyrants, between a Melanchrus and Myrsilus and the *aisymnetes* Pittacus (the fragments in E. Diehl, *Anth. Lyr.* I^2 4, 86 ff.); the banishment of Alcaeus is recounted by a recently discovered papyrus, *P. Oxy.* XVIII, no. 2165; cf. L. Deubner, *Zu den neuen Bruchstücken des Alkaios*, Abh. B, 1943, no. 7; and S. Mazzarino, "Per la storia di Lesbo nel VI° secolo a.C.," *Ath.* NS 21, 1943, 38 ff. (with the incorrect chronology of Beloch, according to which Alcaeus is located in the middle of the sixth century; cf. *infra* 420 n. 72); also K. Latte, *MusHelv* 4, 1947, 141 ff.; *et. al.* The contemporary of Alcaeus, Solon of Athens, was the first individual to employ his impressive elegies in the political education of his fellow citizens. Solon's poems are the only reliable source for the conditions and the implementing of his reforms in Athens (cf. E. Diehl, *Anth. Lyr.*^{3}, Fasc. 1, 1949, 20 ff.); on the elegy *Our Polis*, the so-called *Eunomia*, the essence of the Solonian elegies, see in particular W. Jaeger, SB.B, 1926, 69 ff.; *Paid.* I, 136 ff.; V. Ehrenberg, *Charisteria f. A. Rzach*, 1930, 22 ff., = *Aspects of the Ancient World*, Oxford 1946, 70 ff.

Both in age and importance the highly controversial Great Rhetra stands at the head of our documents on Greek constitutional life. According to Plutarch (*Lycur.* 6), it is a response of the Delphic god, commanding the Spartan lawgiver Lycurgus to establish phylae and obae, to form a *Gerousia* consisting of 30 members, including the two kings, and to convene periodic assemblies of the people in which the *Damos* was to be granted the final decision (the concluding sentence of the Great Rhetra, which is corrupt in the text, has been restored by M. Treu, *Hermes* 76, 1941, 22 ff.; cf. also H. T. Wade-Gery, *CQ* 38, 1943, 64). The objections which have been voiced against the authenticity of the

Great Rhetra (see in particular Meyer, *Forsch.* I, 227 ff.; cf. also the remarks in Busolt, *Gr. St.* I, 44 n.1) are not convincing; the distichs of Tyrtaeus as transmitted by Plutarch (*loc. cit.*), which assume the existence of the Great Rhetra as early as the seventh century, decisively support its authenticity. The opposite view, that the Great Rhetra developed from the verses of Tyrtaeus (Diehl, *Anth. Lyr.*[3], 1949, 1, 8 f. no. 3 a and b), held by T. Meier, *Sp. St.*, 89, is correctly rejected by H. Berve, *Gn.* 17, 1941, 4 f. It will have to be placed in the early seventh or still at the close of the eighth century. A much earlier date (the latter part of the ninth century) is preferred by N. G. L. Hammond, "The Lycurgean Reform at Sparta," *JHS* 70, 1950, 42-64 = "The Creation of Classical Sparta," in *Studies*, 47-103. For the authentic character of the Great Rhetra: Toepffer, "Die Gesetzgebung des Lykurgos," in *B.gr.Alt.*, 347 ff. (at the same time for the historicity of Lycurgus; likewise N. G. L. Hammond, *op. cit.*); Busolt, *Gr. St.* I, 44 ff.; Ehrenberg, *Neugr.*, 17 ff. (with the emendation, *Epitymbion f. Swoboda*, Reichenberg 1927, 19ff.); H. Berve, *Gn.* 1, 1925, 306 ff.; *idem*, "Sparta," *HVSchr.* 25, 1929, 3 ff.; *Gn.* 17, 1941, 4 ff.; Hasebroek, *Gr. Wirt.-Gesch.* I, 205 ff. The more recent study by H. T. Wade-Gery, "The Spartan Rhetra in Plut., *Lyc.* 6,"*CQ* 37, 1943, 62 ff.; 38, 1944, 1 ff.; 115 ff. = *Essays*, 37 ff., attempts to explain the Rhetra as a decree of the popular assembly at Sparta from the end of the seventh century. This ingenious study, however, in many ways gives the impression of a *petitio principii.* New theories in A. G. Tsopanakis *La rhètre de Lycurge* (Hel. 6), Saloniki 1954 (with another attempt to restore the text of the concluding sentence; disagreeing, however, see, for instance, B. R. Flacelière, *REA* 57, 1955, 372 n. 1; H. Berve, *Gn.* 29, 1957, 12 n. 2); equally unconvincing is H. Rudolph, *Festschr für Bruno Snell*, 1956, 61 ff. A. H. M. Jones, in *Studies Ehrenberg*, 165-175, attempts to link the Great Rhetra with the founding of the Carneia, namely 676-673 B.C.; cf. also Toynbee, *Pr.* 269 ff.; Meiggs-Lewis, no. 8; authenticity of the "Little" Rhetra (cf. Plut. *Lycur.* 13, the other references assembled by C. Trieber, *Forsch. z. spartan. Verfassungsgesch.*, 1871 39 n. 4) is disputed (negative, *inter al.*, Meyer, *Forsch* I, 268 f.; E. Kessler, *Plutarchs Leben des Lykurgos*, 1910, 55 ff.; positive, Ehrenberg, *Neugr.* 33 ff.; rightly with reservations, H. Berve, *Gn.* 1, 1925, 310) and K. Bringmann, "Die Grosse Rhetra und die Entstehung des spartanischen Kosmos," *H.* 24, 1975, 513-538.

Particularly important historically as inscriptional documents are: the Stele of Sigeum (*Syll.* I[3] 2)—the oldest document of Attic rule at the Hellespont—(from the middle, perhaps even from the beginning, of the sixth century B.C.; cf. A. Brouwers, *REG* 41, 1928, 107 ff.; 42, 1929, 1 ff.; H. Bengtson, SB.M, 1939, L 21 ff.; M. Guarducci, *Annuario* III-IV, 1941/42, 135 ff.); the Law of Chios—a counterpart to the Solonian *kyrbeis* (v. *supra* 74)—which mentions a civic council, from approximately 575-550 B.C., attesting a strong democratic colouring in the Chian political system (U.v. Wilamowitz, *Nordionische Steine*, Abh.B, 1909; cf. Tod I, no. 1; on the chronology see L. H. Jeffery, BSA 51, 1956, 157 ff.); the Hundred

Year Alliance (Rhetra) of the Eleans with the Heraeans, Bengtson, *Staatsv.* II, no. 110, also from the sixth century (middle?); and, finally, the Honorary Decree of Cyzicus (*Syll.* I³ 4; *SEG* I 445); and the granting of citizenship to Deucalium by the Elean community of Chaladrium (Cauer-Schwyzer, *Dialect. Graec. exempla*, 1923, no. 415); of the arbitration treaties, published by L. Piccirilli, *Gli arbitrati interstatali greci*, I, Pisa 1973, nos. 1 ff.

The coins constitute an important source, especially for economic developments (the most important are to be found in Head, *HN*, ²1911; cf., as a supplement to this, the Catalogues of the British Museum: R. S. Poole (ed.), *A Catalogue of Greek Coins in the British Museum*, 29 vols., Bologna 1963-1965; for Athens the study by H. Seltman, *Athens, its History and its Coinage Before the Persian Invasion*, 1924; cf., for instance, K. Regling, *PhW*, 1925, 219 ff.). The issuing of coins in the Greek world begins in the seventh century, at first in Ionia, then in the various communities of the motherland (Aegina, Corinth, Athens); the fully developed money economy, however, does not emerge until the latter part of the sixth century (F. Heichelheim, "Die Ausbreitung der Münzgeldwirtschaft und der Wirtschaftsstil im archaischen Griechenland," *SJ* 55, 1931, 229 ff.; see now, however, M. Price and N. Waggoner, *Archaic Greek Coinage. The Asiyut Hoard*, London 1975). Extremely important is the inscription from Perachora near Corinth, published by H. T. Wade-Gery, in H. Payne, *Perachora* I, 1940, 256 ff.; it contains an account of the dedication of a "drachm" of oboloi to Hera; they take the form of iron spits, "pre-coinage money;" differently, J. G. Milne *CR* 58, 1944, 18-19, who argues that it is an Aeginetan half stater; cf. also R. M. Cook, *H.* 7, 1958, 258. According to Wade-Gery, the inscription falls in the first half of the seventh century; according to Cook (and L. H. Jeffery), it is not older than 600 B.C. S. Grunauer-von Hoerschelmann, "Zwei Schatzfunde archaischer Statere von Aigina," *Ch.* 5, 1975, 13 ff.

Of particular importance for economic history are the statistics on coin hoards (S. P. Noe, *A Bibliography of Greek Coin Hoards*. Numismatic Notes and Monographs 25, New York 1925, [1943], and in particular now, M. Thompson, O. Mørkholm, C. M. Kraay, *An Inventory of Greek Coin Hoards* [The American Numismatic Society], New York 1973) which shed light on the regional distribution of local issues. The same applies to the pottery finds, to which recent scholars have devoted themselves in an attempt to assess their significance in terms of economic history. The evidence is given by E. Pfuhl, *Malerei und Zeichnung der Griechen* I, 1923; cf., as a monograph, A. Greifenhagen, *Eine attische schwarzfigurige Vasengattung u. die Darstellung des Komos im 6. Jahrh.*, Diss. Könisberg 1929. On the assessment of the evidence cf. R. Hackl, "Merkantile Inschriften auf attischen Vasen," *Münchener arch. Stud., dem Andenken Ad. Furtwänglers gewidmet*, 1909, esp. 92 ff.; F. Heichelheim, *op. cit.*, 246 ff.; *Wirts. Alt.*; and, in addition, the works cited above 406 n. 66 by Blakeway and Beaumont, as well as the study by Bailey (409 n. 118).

A survey of the secondary sources is best given from the standpoint of the different subjects. For the older *tyrannis* the following in particular (in addition to the Lyric poets cited above) come into question: Herodotus, Ephorus (whose negative attitude is the one that prevails among later writers), Aristotle (*Polit.* IV-VI), Ps.-Heracleides Ponticus, Nicolaus of Damascus, Diogenes Laertius. The study of H. G. Plass, *Die Tyrannis*, ²1859, has been rendered obsolete and is replaced by the two-volume work of Berve, *Tyr.* Of more recent finds the following may be cited: *P. Oxy.* XI no. 1365: an account of the rise of *tyrannis* in Sicyon (published by Bilabel, *P. Kleinform* no. 2; Jacoby, *FgrHist.* no. 105, 2); also the *Diegeseis* of Callimachus, ed. M. Norsa and G. Vitelli, 1934, Col. IV 36 (an episode from the Ephesian *tyrannis* of Pindar and Pericles), cf. J. Stroux, *Ph.* 89, 1934, 310 ff., and Rud. Pfeiffer, *Callimachus* I, 1949, 106 f. On Peisistratus, the Peisistratidae and others see *infra* 424 f.

The internal development of the Spartan state has been the subject of repeated discussions, in particular on the crisis of the fourth century B.C. (cf. W. Jaeger, *Paid.* I, 77 ff.). The pamphlet of the Spartan king Pausanias (II) is directed against the Spartan constitution and against Lycurgus, about 395 B.C.; cf. Meyer, *Forsch.* I, 233 ff.; *idem, Hermes* 42, 1907, 134 ff.; cf. also the emendation by Ehrenberg, *Neugr.*, 14; H. T. Wade-Gery, *CQ* 38, 1944, 5; H. Schaefer, *RE* XVIII 4, 2583 f. s.v. *Pausanias* no. 26. An idealising tendency is shown by Xenophon's *Constitution of the Lacedaemonians* (see F. Ollier, *Le mirage spartiate*, 2 vols., Paris 1935 and 1943). Only a few fragments have been preserved from the large number of later writings, namely the *Constitution of the Spartans* by Dicaearchus of Messana (Müller, *FHG* II 241); the monograph by Sosibius of Laconia (third century B.C.), on the Spartan cults (*FgrHist.* no. 595; cf. Tresp, *RVV* XV 1, 1914, 130 ff.); the works by Sphaerus of Borysthenes, the advisor of King Cleomenes III (*About the Laconian Constitution, About Lycurgus and Socrates*; cf. Hobein, *RE* III A, 1691). Important is Plutarch's biography of Lycurgus (on the sources [Hermippus of Smyrna, about 200 B.C.] see E. Kessler, "Plutarchs Leben des Lyk.," in *Quellen u. Forsch. z. alt. Gesch. u. Geogr.*, hrsg. von W. Sieglin, Heft. 23, 1919, 105 ff.). Besides these the *Constitution of the Lacedaemonians* of Aristotle (fr. 532 ff. Rose) in particular forms the basis of the *Vita.* A detailed survey on all this may be found in G. Busolt, *GG* I², 511 ff. Extensive evidence and more recent bibliography in E. N. Tigerstedt, *The Legend of Sparta in Classical Antiquity*, 2 vols., Stockholm 1965 and 1974.

The constitutional history of Athens has been placed on a new footing by the discovery of Aristotle's *Constitution of Athens* on a London papyrus (1890) (*Editio princeps* by F. G. Kenyon, London 1891; *editio minor* of Teubneriana, 1928, by H. Oppermann, with bibliography); cf. U.v. Wilamowitz-Moellendorff. *Arist.*; De Sanctis, *Att.* and, opposed to him, in part, Ledl, *Verf.* This work clearly exhibits the outstanding qualities of its systematic author; Aristotle was not a historian. On his sources (for the history of the constitution, above all the *Atthis* of

Androtion), see G. Busolt, *Gr. St.* I, 90 ff. On the final redaction of the *Constitution of Athens* see H. Hommel, *Festschrift für Fr. Zucker*, 1954, 195 ff. (according to Hommel, not until after the death of Aristotle). On the date see J. J. Keaney, *H.* 19, 1970, 326 ff.; see also F. Ghinatti, *I gruppi politici Ateniesi fino alle guerra Persiane*, Rome 1970. On the diffuse atthidographical works from Hellanicus of Lesbos to Philochorus (he wrote at the time of the Chremonideian War, 267-262/1 B.C.) cf. G. Busolt, *GG* II², 6 ff.; and *FgrHist.* III B, by F. Jacoby; also *idem*, *Att.*; and the book, controversial, however, in regard to its results, by Hignett, *Const.* (cf. *supra* 398 f.). The radical scepticism of E. Ruschenbusch, *H.* 7, 1958, 398 ff., cf. especially 424, also goes much too far. In antiquity there was extensive secondary literature on the life and work of the Athenian lawgiver Solon. Almost next to nothing, however, is extant from the exegetical writings on the Solonian laws (cf. Sondhaus, *De Solonis legibus*, Diss. Jena 1909) by Aristotle, Theophrastus, Demetrius of Phalerum, Didymus, but we do possess Plutarch's "Life of Solon," which is based on, besides others, Hermippus of Smyrna; cf. G. Busolt, *GG* II², 1895, 58 f.; P. von der Mühll, "Antiker Historismus in Plutarchs Biogr. des Solon," *Klio* 35, 1942, 89 ff. (in its final conclusions erroneous; cf. the remarks above 421 n. 76); A. E. Samuel, "Plutarch's Account of Solon's Reforms," *GRBS* 4, 1963, 231-236. The book by A. Maseracchia (*infra* 420 n. 70) includes a detailed discussion on the tradition concerning Solon. Indispensable is Ruschenbusch, *SN.* See also P. Oliva, "Solon im Wandel der Jahrhunderte," *Eirene* 11, 1973, 31 ff.

MODERN RESEARCH: On the older Greek *tyrannis* (cf. also *supra* 414): J. Burckhardt, *Griech. Kulturgesch.* I, 1898, 169 ff.; (cf. the English translation, *History of Greek Culture*, New York 1963, 56 ff.): H. Swoboda, "Zur Beurteilung der griech. Tyrannis," *Klio* 12, 1912, 345 ff.; *idem*, in C. F. Hermann, *Staatsaltertümer* I 3, ⁶1913, 75 ff.; Ure, *Or.* (special emphasis on the economic basis of Greek *tyrannis*, creditable but modernising); Nilsson, *Gr. Tyr.*; *De grekiska tyrannerna*, Stockholm 1942; *Gr. Rel.* I, 719 ff.; Friedel, *Tmord*; A. Andrewes, *The Greek Tyrants*, London 1956 (sketchy); also, in particular, the recent work by H. Berve (v. *supra*). Cf. also *idem*, "Wesenszüge der griech. Tyrannis," *HZ* 177, 1954, 1-20 (with a one-sided emphasis on the personal political power of the older tyrants); and H. W. Pleket, "The Archaic Tyrannis," *Talanta* 1, 1969, 19 ff.; C. Mossé, *La tyrannie dans la Grèce antique*, Paris 1969; also relevant is J. K. Davies, *Athenian Propertied Families, 600-300 B.C.*, Oxford 1971. The study by R. Drews, "The First Tyrants in Greece," *H.* 21, 1972, 129 ff., is not entirely convincing.

Scholarly research on the subject of archaic Sparta (a survey is given by K. J. Newmann, *HZ* 96, 1906, 2 f.; a more recent bibliography by T. Meier, *Das Wesen der spartanischen Staatsordnung*, Klio-Beih. 42, 1939, V f.) begins with the ingenious but one-sided work of Carl Otfried Müller, "Die Dorier" (in his *Geschichte der hellenischen Stämme und Städte*, Bd. II and III), 2nd ed. F. W. Schneidewin, 1844. Research was taken a step further by the investigation of the Lycurgus legend by U. v. Wilamowitz, "Lykurgos," *PhU* 7, 1884, 267 ff.; and by Ed. Meyer, "Die Entwicklung der Überlieferung über die lykurgische Verfassung," *RhM* 41, 1886, 560 ff.; 42, 1887, 81 ff. = *Forsch.* I, 211 ff.; cf. further, M. P. Nilsson, "Die Grundlagen des spartanischen Lebens," *Klio* 12, 1912, 308 ff.; L. Pareti, *Storia di Sparta arcaica* I, Florence 1917. In our day work on the problems of Spartan constitutional history has been done primarily by U. Kahrstedt, V. Ehrenberg, H. Berve, F. Hampl, H. T. Wade-Gery and W. den Boer. The following works in particular may be mentioned: Kahrstedt, *Stsr.* I (juridical); V. Ehrenberg, "Spartiaten und Lakedaimonier," *Hermes* 59, 1924, 23 ff.; Neugr., 7 ff.; "Der Gesetzgeber von Sparta" (*Epitymb. f. Swoboda*, Reichenberg 1927), 191 ff.; "Der Damos im archaischen Sparta," *Hermes* 68, 1933, 288 ff.; *RE* III A, 1265 ff., s.v. *Sparta* (in collaboration with Bölte, Ziehen and Lippold); *RE* XVII, 1693 ff. s.v. *Obai*; H. Berve, *Gn.* 1, 1925, 305 ff. (review of V. Ehrenberg, *Neugr.*); "Sparta," *HVSchr.* 25, 1929, 1 ff.; "Sparta" (in Meyer's *Kleine Handbücher* 7), 1937; ²1944 (with extremely positive assessment); *Gn.* 17, 1941, 1 ff. (a review of recent studies on Sparta, including P. Roussel, *Sparte*, Paris 1939; T. Meier, *Sp. St.*); F. Hampl, "Die lakedämonischen Periöken," *Hermes* 72, 1937, 1 ff.; H. T. Wade-Gery, *CAH* III, 558 ff.; *CQ* 37, 1943, 62 ff.; 38, 1944, 1 ff.; 115 ff. = *Essays*, 37-85; den Boer, *Lac.* (cf. H. Berve, *Gn.* 29, 1957, 7 ff.). (The study by W. Norvin, "Z. Gesch. der spart. Eunomie," *Class. et Mediaev.* 2, 1939, 247 ff.; 3, 1940, 47 ff., was unfortunately written without taking the results of recent scholarship into account.) Very valuable is F. Kiechle, *Lakonien und Sparta*, Munich 1963. Original, although not always convincing, is also G. L. Huxley, *Early Sparta*, London 1962 [reprint, Shannon 1970] (critical of it, F. Kiechle, *Gn.* 35, 1963, 368 ff.). Specific studies in M. A. Levi, "Quarto studi spartani," *Instituto Lombardo, Rendiconti, Cl. di Lettere*, Vol. 96, 1962, 479-499; 500-512; 513-522; 523-528 (on Dorians and Heraclidae; Phylae and Obae; on the Diarchy and on the Helots). A critical survey: C. G. Starr, "The Credibility of Early Spartan History," *H.* 14, 1965, 257-272. See also C. M. Stibbe, *Sparta. Geschiedenis en cultuur der Spartanen van praehistorie tot persische oorlogen*, Buusum 1969; P. Oliva, *Sparta and her Social Problems*, Amsterdam 1971. Some highly independent views may also be found in Toynbee, *Pr.* (cf. H. Berve, *Gn.* 48, 1976, 156 ff.). Cf. also N. G. L. Hammond, "The Creation of Classical Sparta," in *Studies*, 47 ff.

1. Cahn, Knid. (cf. E. Schönert-Geis, *Gn.* 44, 1972, 270 ff.).

2. W. L. Westermann, *RE Suppl.* VI, 899 ff. s.v. *Sklaverei; idem, The Slave Systems of Greek and Roman Antiquity*, Philadelphia 1955 [a revision of the article in *RE*]; cf. however, R. E. Smith, *JHS* 77, 1957, 338 f. In our day the study of slavery in antiquity has entered a new phase through the researches of the *Mainzer Akademie* (under the direction of J. Vogt). The researches of Russian historians such as A. Lengman may also be mentioned here, as well as the studies by M. I. Finley and others. See, for instance, J. Vogt, *Ancient Slavery and the Ideal of Humanity*, Cambridge, Mass., 1975, 170 ff.; also G. Wickert, *Gn.* 39, 1967, 487 ff. (review of Lengman); N. Brockmeyer, *Bibliographie zur antiken Sklaverei*, Bochum 1971; E. Will, *Rev. hist.* 251, 1974, 160-162; K.-W. Welwei, *Unfreie im antiken Kriegsdienst* (Forschungen zur antiken Sklaverei, 5), Wiesbaden 1975.

3. For its development in Athens see, in addition to the data in the mythical king lists (cf. in general E. Schwartz, "Die Königslisten des Eratosthenes und Kastor," *Abh. Gött.* 40, 1894/95; F. Jacoby, *Klio* 2, 1902, 406 ff.), in particular the not entirely unequivocal statements in Aristotle, *Const. Ath.* 3. Everything which lies before the dating of the Attic eponymous archon of 683/2 B.C. is shrouded in darkness. From the extensive literature on this subject the following may be cited: J. Toepffer, "Die Liste der athen. Könige," *Hermes* 31, 1896, 105 ff. (printed as *B.gr.Alt.*, 275 ff.); O. Seeck, "Quellenstudien zu des Aristoteles Verfassungsgesch. Athens," *Klio* 4, 1904, 292 ff.; De Sanctis, *Att.*, 77 ff.; Ledl, Verf., 218 ff.; E. Kjellberg, *Zur Entwicklung d. att. Theseussage*, Strena Philol. Upsal., 1922, 40 ff.; W. Otto, SB.M, 1923, Schlussh., 16; Busolt *Gr.St.* II, 784 ff.; 1584; also H. Herter, *RE Suppl.* XIII, 1045 ff. s.v. *Theseus* (also separately). On the archon lists: T. J. Cadoux, *JHS* 68, 1948, 70 ff.; and, in particular, Meiggs-Lewis, no. 6, with bibliography.

4. J. Hasebroek, *Gr. Wirt.-Ges.* I, 73 f.

5. Cf. the term *geomoroi* for the ruling nobility of Samos and Syracuse.

6. The results of the study by W. Helbig, "Les *hippeis* athéniens," *Mém. de l'Acad. des Inscr.* 37, 1902, 157 ff., according to which the Hippeis would have been "mounted hoplites," do not stand up to verification, despite the concurrence of reputable scholars like, *inter. al.*, Meyer, *GdA* II, 565. Objections already in E. Lammert, *RE* VIII, 1696 s.v. *Hippeis et al.* Basic now is A. Alföldi, "Die Herrschaft der Reiterei in Griechenland und Rom nach dem Sturz der Könige," in *Gestalt und Geschichte, Festschrift K. Schefold (4. Beiheft zu 'Antike Kunst')*, 1967, 13 ff. Alföldi argues for warfare by the horse in the early period, namely with *two* horses, which the owner was in the habit of exchanging.

7. On the Lelantine War v.s.p. 53.

8. P. Guirard, *La propriété foncière* 407 ff.; Busolt, *Gr. St.* I, 135 ff.; J. Hasebroek, *Gr. Wirt.-Ges.* I, 74.

9. Plut., *Quaest. Graec.* 1 p. 291 e; a different explanation of the name is given by K. Latte, *Gn.* 7, 1931, 116 n. 1.

10. Cf. Meiggs-Lewis no. 9, for one of the earliest extant agonistic dedications.

11. We still meet the *Chilioi* in the fifth century among the Opuntian Locrians, in the West in Croton, Locri and Rhegium, moreover, in the East in Cyme and Colophon, and the "hundred clans" among the Locrians at the beginning of the seventh century (the evidence in Busolt, *Gr. St.* I, 354 ff.).

12. Aristotle, *Pol.* II 3.9.

13. Hesiod, *Works and Days* 39; 221; 264; cf. R. J. Bonner and G. Smith, "Administration of Justice in Boeotia," *CP* 40, 1945, 1 ff.

14. Hasebroek, *Gr. Wirt.-Ges.* I, 109 f.; cf. also above 50 f.

15. See W. Helbig, *Über die Entstehungszeit der geschlossenen Phalanx*, SB.M, 1911, 12. Abh.; and above all the more recent studies by M. P. Nilsson, "Die Hoplitentaktik und das Staatswesen," *Klio* 22, 1929, 240 ff.; *idem*, "The Introduction of the Hoplite Tactics at Rome," *JRS* 19, 1929, 1 ff.; Kromayer-Veith, *Heerw.*, 1929, 22 and 28. The hoplite phalanx is depicted on the Chigi Vase, on the Macmillan Lekythos and on the Aryballos from Rhodes now in Berlin; the last of these is dated by K. F. Johansen, *Les vases sicyoniennes*, 184 (Pls. XXXI and XXXII), in the first half of the seventh century. Cf. also H. L. Lorimer, "The Hoplite Phalanx with Special Reference to the Poems of Archilochos and Tyrtaios" *BSA* 42, 1947, 76 ff. See also R. Sealey, "Probouleusis and the Sovereign Assembly," *CSCA* 2, 1969, 247 ff.

16. Cf. M. P. Nilsson, *JRS* 19, 1929, 2.

17. The elevation of the most wealthy Hippeis to "Five Hundred Bushellers" is secondary, but at the same time doubtless pre-Solonian. On the reforms of Solon see in detail *supra* 70 ff.

18. In explanation of the term *zeugites* see C. Cichorius, "Zu den Namen der attischen Steuerklassen," *Griech. Studien, H. Lipsius dargebracht*, Leipzig 1894, 135 ff., with reference to Plut., *Pelop.* 23 (*Zygon* = a member of the phalanx). The *Zeugites* is the hoplite in rank and file, not the teamster (Pollux VIII 132 is incorrect on this point).

19. The evidence is cited by Meyer, *GdA* II, 566 ff., esp. 568 ff.; see also F. Kohler and E. Ziebarth, *Das Recht von Gortyn*, 1912, 88 ff.; M. Guarducci, *Inscr. Creticae* IV, 1950, no. 72; R. F. Willetts, *Kadmos-Suppl.* I, Berlin 1967. M. Mühl, "Die Gesetze des Zaleukos und

Charondas," *Klio* 22, 1929, 105 ff., 432 ff., who on points of detail admittedly goes much too far in assuming influence from the Near East. The same criticism also applies to the study by M. Mühl, *Untersuchungen z. altoriental. u. althellenischen Gesetzgebung*, Klio-Beiheft 29, Leipzig 1933; cf. the review by M. San Nicolò, *ZSS Röm.* 54, 1934, 429 ff., and E. Seidl, *OLZ*, 1934, 484 f. Important is F. E. Adcock, "Literary Tradition and Early Greek Codemakers," *Camb. Hist. Journ.* 2, 1927, 95 ff., who distinguishes between an older and a later (from about 300 B.C. on) tradition. On the Lawgivers of Magna Graecia see W. Jaeger, *SB.B*, 1928, XXV 30 n. 3.

20. Beloch, *GG* I² 1, 350; I² 2, 257 ff.; G. De Sanctis, *St. Gr.* I, 467; A. Aymard, in *Peuples et Civilisations* I, 1950, 477.

21. Cf. E. Ruschenbusch, *Untersuchungen z. Gesch. d. athenischen Strafrechts* (Gräzistische Abh., 4), Cologne and Graz, 1968, A. R. W. Harrison, *The Law of Athens*, Vol. II, Oxford 1971. (cf. P.J. Rhodes, *CR* 84, 1970, 358 f.). The severity of Dracon's laws is delineated by Plutarch, *Sol.* 17.

22. Aristotle, *Pol.* II 6.16; Plut., *Lycur.* 13.

23. According to *inter al.*, W. Brandenstein, *tyrannos* is to be connected with the Etruscan *turan* ("Master," "Mistress"). Cf. the bibliography in Heichelheim, *Wirts. Alt.* II, 1025, and Mazzarino, *Fr. 00*, 1947, 381 ff.

24. The evidence may be found in Busolt, *GG* I², 625 ff., and Meyer, *GdA* II, 620 ff. = III², 573 ff.

25. A survey in Beloch, *GG*, I 1², 355 ff., cf., otherwise, the literature cited above 414, in particular the study by Berve, *Tyr.*

26. F. Schachermeyr, *RE* VI A, 567 f. s.v. *Thrasybulos* no. 1.

27. F. Schachermeyr, *RE* XX, s.v. *Pittakos*, and the studies by L. Deubner and S. Mazzarino (v.s.p. 411); cf. Berve, *Tyr.* I, 92, ff.

28. A. Momigliano, "La genealogia degli Ortagoridi," *AR* NS 10, 1929, 145 ff.; a concise discussion may be found in F. Schachermeyr, *RE* XVIII, 1430 ff. s.v. *Orthagoriden*; moreover, N. G. L. Hammond, "The Family of Orthagoras," *CQ* NS 6, 1956, 45-53; D. M. Leahy, "The Dating of the Orthagorid Dynasty," *H.* 17, 1968, 1 ff. (656/5-556/5 B.C.); M. White, "The Dates of the Orthagorids," *Px.* 12, 1958, 2 ff.; S. I. Oost, "Two Notes on the Orthagorids of Sicyon," *CP* 69, 1974, 118 ff.; see also K. Kinzl, in the *Kleine Pauly*, s.v. *Orthagoras* no. 2.

29. In Sicyon Cleisthenes carried out a reform of the *phylae* which sprang from an anti-Dorian reaction; cf. Herod. V 68; cf. A. Gitti, "Clistene di Sicione e le sue riforme," *RALinc.* 326, Ser. 6 Vol. II, 1929.

30. Herod. VI 126-131 (with a pro-Alcmeonid bias).

31. J. Miller, *RE* XII, 119 ff. s.v. *Kypselos* no. 2; D. E. Wormell, *Hermathena* 66, 1945, 1 ff.; E. Will, *Korinthiaka*, 1956, 472 ff.; Berve, *Tyr.* I, 15 ff.; S. I. Oost, "Cypselus the Bacchiad," *CP* 67, 1972, 10 ff.; cf. G. Zörner, *Kypselos und Pheidon von Argos. Untersuchungen z. frühen griechischen Tyrannis*, Diss. Marburg a.d.L. 1971.

32. F. Schachermeyr, *RE* XIX, 704 ff. s.v. *Periandros* no. 1; Berve, *Tyr.* I, 19ff. The *diolkos* rediscovered at the Isthmus of Corinth by N. M. Verdelis, *AM* 71, 1956, 51 ff., 73, 1958, 140 ff., however, is scarcely to be connected with Periander. Cf. L. Labarbe, *AC* 40, 1971, 471-504.

33. A. Newhall, "The Corinthian Kerameikos," *AJA* 35, 1931, 1 ff., cf. A. Newhall Stillwell, "The Potters Quarter," in *Corinth* XV, 1, Princeton 1948; cf. Nilsson, *Gr. Tyr.*, 14 ff.; H. Payne, *Perachora* I. *The Sanctuaries of Hera Akraia and Limenia*, Oxford 1940.

34. Thus, however, Ure, *Or.*

35. This is incorrectly regarded as unhistorical by Busolt, *GG* I², 646 f. n. 2; see, on the other hand, for instance, F. Schachermeyr, *RE* XIX, 715.

36. *Korkyra* II. *Die Bildwerke des Artemistempels von Korkyra*, by G. Rodenwaldt, Berlin 1939, esp. 169 ff. On the history of Corcyra see G. P. Karydis, *Historia tes nesou Korkyras mechri tou 229 p. Ch.*, Diss. Leipzig 1936.

37. S. I. Oost, "The Megara of Theagenes and Theognis," *CP* 68, 1973, 186 ff.

38. Balogh, *Ref.*

39. Th. Lenschau, *RE* XIX, 1649 ff. s.v. *Phalaris*; cf. E. de Miro, "Agrigento arcaica e la politica di Falaride," *PP* 11, 1956, 263-273; Berve, *Tyr.* I, 129 ff. (regards the bull of Phalaris as unhistorical; see Pind., *Pyth.* I 95); cf. J. de Waele, *Acragas Graeca*, 1971, 103 ff.

40. V.s.p. 363 n. 4.
41. Thus by Ehrenberg, *Neugr.*, 46 ff.; see, on the other hand, H. Berve, *Gn.* 1, 1925, 311.
42. Theories may be found in, for instance, R. v. Pöhlmann, *GG*, 37 f.; see also A. Momigliano, *AR* 13, 1932, 1 ff.; L. Pareti, *ibid.*, 16 ff.; Th. Lenschau, *RhM* 88, 1939, 123 ff.
43. Cf., for instance, the Molossian double monarchy in which both rulers, however, belong to the same royal house.
44. Bengtson, *Strat.* II, 386 n. 2.
45. V.s.p. 412.
46. Thus den Boer, *Lac.*, 179 ff.; concurring, H. Berve, *Gn.* 29, 1957, 12 f.
47. Perhaps the epithet is connected with the *phyle* of the Hylleis. Cf. Ziehen, *RE* III A, 1489. A. v. Blumenthal, *Hermes* 77, 1942, 212, refers to a gloss of Hesychius; cf. Wade-Gery, *Essays*, 80.
48. S. Luria, *Klio* 21, 1927, 413 ff.; *PhW*, 1926, 701 f.; cf. H. Berve, *HVSchr.* 25, 1929, 7; *GG* I², 1951, 72; now (on the basis of den Boer, *Lac.*, 210 f.) of a different opinion: *Gn.* 29, 1957, 14; the observing of the heavens was, accordingly, first achieved bý the ephor Asteropus (c. 650 B.C.).
49. A different view by St. Witkowski, "Der Ursprung des Ephorats" (*La Pologne au VIIe congres intern. de sciences hist.*), Warsaw 1953, Vol. I, 19 ff.; cf. *idem*, "Die spartanische Heeresgliederung und der Ursprung des Ephorats," *Eos*, 35, 1934/35, 73 ff.; the ephors, whose office extends back into the earliest period of the state, were accordingly from the beginning "overseers of civic discipline," a view which cannot be made to coincide with the evidence.
50. As is the view of some scholars (*inter al.*, Busolt-Swoboda, Wade-Gery, Berve, Hasebroek).
51. B. Niese, "Neue Beitr. z. Gesch. und Landeskunde Lakedämons: Die lakedämonischen Periöken," *NGG, phil.-hist. Kl.*, 1906, 101 ff.; cf. the critique by Meier, *Sp. St.*, 24 f.
52. See F. Hampl, *Hermes* 72, 1937, 1 ff.
53. On the Helots (and the Penestae) see W. L. Westermann, "Between Slavery and Freedom," *AHR*, 50, 1945, 213 ff.; and Lotze, *Met.*, 26 ff.
54. Strabo VIII 365; cf. Lotze, *Met.*, 41 f.
55. Tyrt. fr. 5.
56. That the primitive forms of Spartan community life were neither a Laconian nor a Dorian peculiarity has long since been recognised by scholars (M. P. Nilsson, *Klio* 12, 1912, 308 ff.; S. Luria, "Ein milesischer Männerbund im Lichte ethnologischer Parallelen," *Ph.* 83, 1927, 113 ff.). Cf. Pausanias III 10.8; cf. Ziehen, *RE* III A, 1457 ff. s.v. *Sparta* (with the earlier bibliography); P. Wolters, "Der amykläische Thron bei Kallisthenes," *Ph.* 86, 1931, 419 ff.
57. F. Bölte, "Zu lakonischen Festen," *RhM* 78, 1929, 124 ff.
58. M. J. Mellink, *Hyakinthos*, Utrecht 1943.
59. In Alcman's *Partheneion*, fr. 1 (Diehl), the Spartan maidens wear purple garments and Lydian mitres.
60. M. P. Nilsson, "Die Hoplitentaktik und das Staatswesen," *Klio* 22, 1929, 240 ff.
61. Aristotle, *Pol.* 1271a 34.
62. The expression appears only in Xen., *Hell.* III 3.6; cf. O. Schulthess, *RE* VIII, 2256 f. s.v. *Homoioi*.
63. M. P. Nilsson, "Die Grundlagen des spartanischen Lebens," *Klio* 12, 1912, 308 ff.; cf. also H. Berve, *Sparta*, ²1944, 42 ff. (idealising).
64. According to a Strabo gloss (cf. A. Diller, *AJP* 62, 1942, 499 ff.), the *Eiren* was 20 years old (not 14), which, however, leads to serious factual difficulties; cf., for instance, H. I. Marrou, *REA* 48, 1946, 216 ff.; den Boer, *Lac.*, 248 ff. A solution does not as yet appear to have been found.
65. J. Toepffer, *Attische Genealogie*, Berlin 1889.
66. It can now be regarded as certain that the *Hektemoroi* had to hand over 1/6, not 5/6, of their produce (cf. Plut., *Sol.* 13, as against Arist., *Const. Ath.* 2); cf. the remarks and the older bibliography in Busolt, *Gr. St.* II, 779 ff.; K. v. Fritz, "The Meaning of *hektemoros*," *AJP* 61, 1940, 54 ff.; 64, 1943, 24 ff. The view that they were serfs bound to the soil was held in particular by H. Swoboda, "Beitr. z. griech. Rechtsgesch.," *ZSS Röm.* 26, 1905, 254 ff. That they were not tenants was demonstrated in a very ingenious study by

Woodhouse, *Solon*. His own hypothesis about the economic basis of the *Hektemoroi* (similarly F. E. Adcock, *CAH* IV, 34), however, lacks adequate evidence in the sources.

67. There is not sufficient basis to move Cylon's *coup d'état* down into the post-Solonian era (thus, for instance, O. Seeck, *Klio* 4, 1904, 318 ff.; Beloch, *GG* I 2, 302 ff.; De Sanctis, *Att.*, 274 ff.; Cornelius, *Tyr.*, 36 ff.); the earlier date is also supported by, *inter al.*, Plutarch, *Sol.* 12 and 19; cf. Ledl, *Verf.*, 77 ff.; F. E. Adcock, *CAH* IV, 661 f.; Friedel, *Tmord.*, 12; Jacoby, *Att.*, 366 n. 77. Critical towards the tradition is M. Lang, *CP* 62, 1967, 243-249.

68. See E. Ruschenbusch, "*Phonos.* Zum Recht Drakons und seiner Bedeutung für das Werden des athenischen Staates," *H.* 9, 1960, 129-154; R. S. Stroud, *Drakon's Law on Homicide*, Berkeley and Los Angeles 1968 (cf. E. Ruschenbusch, *Gn.* 46, 1974, 815 ff.).

69. A summary in Busolt, *Gr. St.* I, 52 ff. Important are: Meyer, *Forsch.* I, 236 ff.; and U. Wilcken, "Zur drakontischen Verfassung," *Apophoreton, der 47. Philologenversammlung überreicht von der Graeca Halensis*, Berlin 1903, 85 ff. Among more recent studies cf. A. Fuks, *The Ancestral Constitution*, 1953, 84 ff. (with bibliography, *ibid.*, 98); also the work by H. Hommel (v.s.p. 415) on the final redaction of the *Constitution of Athens*, and E. Ruschenbusch, *H.* 7, 1958, 421 f.; the Draconian constitution, according to this view, originated in the period between 328 and 322 B.C. According to K. v. Fritz, *CP* 49, 1954, 73-93, the Draconian constitution was no interpolation; much more does it constitute a description of the constitution from the pre-Solonian era. Even more positive is F. P. Rizzo S. J., "La constituzione di Draconte nel c. 4 dell'*Ath. Pol.* di Aristotele," *Memorie dell'Ist. Lomb., Cl. di Lett.*, vol. 27, 4, 1963, 271-308, who regards the Draconian constitution as old and authentic. Still, major problems remain connected with a critique of the sources.

70. The most important earlier studies are cited by W. Aly, *RE* III A, 946 ff. s.v. *Solon* no. 1; from these the following may here be mentioned: B. Niese, "Zur Gesch. Solons," in *Histor. Untersuch. für A. Schäfer*, 1882, 1 ff.; *HZ* 69, 1892, 55 ff.; Ch. Gilliard, *Quelques réformes de Solon*, Lausanne 1907; I. M. Linforth, *Solon the Athenian*, Univ. of Calif. Publ. in Class. Phil. 6, Berkeley 1919; Kathleen Freeman, *The Work and Life of Solon*, Cardiff and London 1926; Woodhouse, *Solon*. More recent general works: A. Masaracchia, *Solone*, Florence 1958 (cf. J. H. Oliver, *AJP* 82, 1961, 89-94); G. Ferrara, *La politica di Solone*, Naples 1964. Further the specialised studies: A. French, "The Economic Background to Solon's Reforms," *CQ* NS 6 1956, 11-25; *idem*, "Solon and the Megarian Question," *JHS* 77, 1957, 238 ff.; opposed to him: K. H. Waters, "Solon's Price Equalisation'," *JHS* 80, 1960, 181 ff. Conservative, as always, N. G. L. Hammond, "Land Tenure in Attica and Solon's Seisachtheia," *JHS* 81, 1961, 76 ff. (= "Land and Society in the Athens of Solon," in *Studies*, 104 ff.). F. Cassola, *PP* 1964, 26-28, concludes that Solon restored the state land and temple land which the great landowners had allegedly occupied illegally, and thereby inaugurated a new era in the history of Athenian agriculture. See also P. Oliva, *Solon*, Prague 1971; *idem*, "Solon und seine Seisachtheia," *Ziva Antika* 21, 1971, 103 ff.

71. Cf. Plut., *Sol.* 22.

72. Cf. Alcaeus fr. 49. Complete sources in Busolt, *GG* II², 249 ff.; see also Meyer, *GdA* II, 643 ff., cf. H. Bengtson, SB.M, 1939, H. 1, 20 f. This war is to be distinguished from the later war under Peisistratus (Herod. V 94); cf. J. Toepffer, "Quaestiones Pisistrateae," published as *B. Gr. Alt.*, 234 ff. The dating of Alcaeus and Sappho down to the middle of the sixth century by Beloch (lastly *GG* I 2, 314 ff., 363) has been disproved by papyrus finds: cf. *P. Oxy.* XXI 2295 fr. 28, see M. Treu, *Alkaios*, Munich, Heimeran, 1952, 124 f.

73. A later inscription has provided new information on the relationship of Salamis to Athens after its annexation: W. S. Ferguson, "The Salaminioi of Heptaphylai and Sunion," *Hesp.* 7, 1938, 1 ff.; M. P. Nilsson, "The New Inscription of the Salaminioi," *AJP* 59, 1938, 385 ff.; *idem*, *Gr. Rel.* I, 712 f.; M. Guarducci, *RF* NS 26, 1948, 223 ff.

74. Berve, *GG* I², 171; see, on the other hand, W. Aly, *RE* III A, 974; J. Hasebroek, *Gr. Wirt.-Ges.* I, 55 ff.; H. Hommel, *RE* XVI, 1938 ff. s.v. *Naukraria*; the older bibliography may be found in Busolt, *Gr. St.*, see Index s.v. See also B. Jordan, "Herodotos 5.71.2 and the Naukraroi of Athens," *CSCA* 3, 1970, 153 ff.

75. Solon fr. 3; cf. W. Jaeger, *Solons Eunomie*, SB.B, 1926, 69 ff.; *idem*. Paid. I, 1936, 189 ff. Additional bibliography is cited by E. Diehl, *Anth. Lyr.* I², 30.

76. The date 594/3 B.C. is given by Diogenes Laert. I 62 (=Sosicrates), while the *textus receptus* is represented by Aristotle, *Const. Ath.* 14.1, pointing to 592/1 B.C. (cf. Busolt, *GG*

II², 258 n. 3). Beloch, *GG* I²1, 364, also regards this date as possible, whereas elsewhere (I 2, 165) he accepts the possibility of Solon having perhaps remained in office for several years (which is moreover contradicted by Aristotle, *Const. Ath.* 13.1). According to P. von der Mühll, "Antiker Historismus in Plutarchs Biographie des Solon," *Klio* 35, 1942, 96 ff., Hermippus permitted "Solon's activity to increase step by step and finally to culminate in his legislation." Another solution is proposed by N. G. L. Hammond, *JHS* 60, 1940, 41 ff. (= *Studies*, 1973, 195 ff.) (the archonship 594/3 B.C., and the *nomothesis* 592/1 B.C.). But most probable still is the suggestion of A. Bauer, *Lit. u. hist. Forsch. zu Arist. Ath. Pol.* Munich 1891, 45 f., to explain Aristotle's text [*deutero etei* derived from *d'etei*], whereby we likewise arrive back in 594/3 B.C.; cf. Busolt *Gr. St.* II, 829 n. 4; also F. Jacoby, *Att.*, 346 n. 22. See further M. F. McGregor, "Solon's Archonship. The Epigraphic Evidence," in J. A. S. Evans (ed.), *Polis and Imperium. Studies in Honour of Edward Togo Salmon*, Toronto 1974, 31 ff. Hignett, *Const.*, 316 ff., 321, moves Solon's legislation to the period shortly before 570 B.C., a view which is indeed original but not probable.

77. Cf. Meyer, *GdA*, II, 647 ff.; R.v. Pöhlmann, *GG*, 84 ff.; Busolt, *Gr. St.* II, 828 ff.; Berve, *GG* 1², 172 ff. (cf. W. Otto, SB.M, 1923, Schlussh., 16 f.; 1924, 8 f.); Schaefer, *Staatsf.*, 109 ff.; Heichelheim, *Wirts. Alt.* I, 283 ff.; further, the works cited above 414 f.

78. H. T. Wade-Gery, *Mélanges G. Glotz* II, 1932, 877 f.; Woodhouse, *Solon*, 98 ff.; J. V. A. Fine, *Horoi. Studies in Mortgage, Real Security and Land Tenure in Ancient Athens* (Hesp. Suppl. 9), 1951, 179 ff.; E. Ruschenbusch, "Über das Bodenrecht im archaischen Athen," *H.* 21, 1972 53 ff.

79. Aristotle, *Pol.* II 7 p. 1266b. 17. That the law had retroactive force (thus H. Swoboda. *ZSS Röm.* 26, 1905, 278), has not been transmitted, and is, furthermore, improbable.

80. Principal sources: Aristotle, *Const. Ath.* 10; Plut., *Sol.* 15 (=Androtion); the bibliography on the subject may be found in W. Aly, *RE* III A, 976 ff., cf. also O. Viedebantt, *Forsch. z. Metrologie d. Alt.* (Abh. 34), 1917, 45 ff.; W. Otto, *SB.M*, 1924, Schlussh. 8 f. (without the evidence); J. G. Milne, "The Economic Policy of Solon," *Hesp.* 14, 1945, 230 ff.; H. A. Cahn, "Zur frühattischen Münzprägung," *MusHelv* 3, 1946, 133 ff., whose interpretation of Aristotle's chapter on metrology merits special attention just as much as does the article by K. Kraft, *JNG* 10, 1959-1960, 21 ff.; cf. *idem*, "Zur solonischen Gewichts- und Münzproblem," *ibid.*, 19, 1969, 7-24; Kraft's thesis is rejected by M. A. Crawford, "Solon's Alleged Reform of Weights and Measures," *Eirene* 10, 1972, 5 ff., but without exhaustive argument. Cf. also Th. Fischer, "Zu Solons Mass-, Gewichts- und Münzreform. Ein Diskussionsbeitrag," *Ch* 3, 1973, 1 ff. On this question it is for the time being impossible to move beyond hypothetical views. The explanation given by De Sanctis, *Att.*, 222 ff. (followed by, *inter al.*, Beloch, *GG* I² 2, 337 ff.) has had its foundations cut from under it by the simple and equally obvious conjecture of Th. Reinach on Plut., *Sol.* 15: *Hermes* 63, 1928, 238 ff.

81. According to Cahn (see preceding footnote), Solon introduced the tetradrachm with the owl, which has previously been attributed to Peisistratus, a decisive advance in coinage. This attractive theory is however lacking in certainty.

82. U. Köhler, *AM* 10, 1885, 151 ff.

83. According to Aristotle, *Const. Ath.* 7.3, the class of *Pentekosiomedimnoi* existed prior to this, which is in fact probable. Of interest on the *Pentekosiomedimnoi* is the study by W. E. Thompson, "The Regional Distribution of the Pentekosiomedimnoi," *Klio* 52, 1970, 437 ff.

84. O. Schulthess, *Das attische Volksgericht*, 1922, and H. Hommel, *Heliaia. Untersuch. z. Verfassung u. Prozessordnung des ath. Volksgerichts, insbesondere zum Schlussteil der Ath. Pol. des Aristotles*, Ph. Suppl. XIX 2, 1927; cf. V. Ehrenberg, *Gn.* 3, 1927, 682 ff. That the *Thetes* did not receive citizenship until the time of Cleisthenes has been argued by W. Otto, *Aristoteles und Alt-Athen*, SB.Bay, 1923, Schlussh., 16 f.; cf. Schaefer, *Staatsf.*, 113. As opposed to this, however, see, *inter al.*, Plut., *Sol.* 18.

85. U. Wilcken, *Hermes* 63, 1928, 236 ff., on the basis of a slight emendation to Plut., *Sol.* 23.3; concurring, for instance, F. Heichelheim, *Wirts. Alt.* I, 255. Busolt *Gr. St.* II, 837, argues for Cleisthenes. The decisive note in Pollux VIII 130 unfortunately cannot be chronologically established; see also Hasebroek, *Gr. Wirt. Ges.* I, 290 f.; J. H. Thiel, *Mn.* 4a, ser. 3. 1950, 1 ff.

86. Synopsis in E. Ruschenbusch, *SN*.
87. Cf. the Alexandrian *dikaiomata*, published by *Graeca Halensis*, 1913, 64 ff.
88. K. Latte, "Die Entstehung der Popular-Klage," *Hermes* 66, 1931, 30 ff.
89. Incorrectly explained by J. Hasebroek, *Gr. Wirt. Ges.* 138 and 152.
90. Incorrectly by De Sanctis, *Att.*, 229 ff.
91. Aristotle, *Const. Ath.* 8; cf. F. E. Adcock, *CAH* IV, 51; V. Ehrenberg, *RE* XIII, 1468 f. s.v. *Losung* (with the older bibliography).
92. F. Stähelin, *Hermes* 68, 1933, 343 ff. (with reference to Plut., *Sol.* 19); U. Kahrstedt, *Klio* 33, 1940, 1 ff.
93. Plut., *Sol.* 19; cf. Balogh, *Ref.*, 7 ff.; 90 n. 17.
94. On the question of the *Axones* and *Kyrbeis* see L. B. Holland, *AJA* 45, 1941, 346 ff.; S. Dow, *Proceed. Mass. Hist. Society* 71, 1953-1957 (published 1959), 24 ff.; on the Stoa Basileios see now Leslie T. Shear, Jr., *Hesp.* 40, 1971, 243 ff.
95. Wilamowitz, *Arist.* II, 66. In contrast, and correctly, Meyer, *GdA* II, 648f., and Pöhlmann, *GG*[5], 85, hold a much more positive view.
96. Aristotle, *Const. Ath.* 13.2. Cf. Meyer, *Forsch.* II, 537 ff.; Ehrenberg, *Neugr.*, 76; 130. (Beloch, *GG* I[2] 1, 368 n. 1, is a regression.) The suggestion of L. Gernet, *Rph.* 61, 1940, 54 ff., to eliminate the decisive sentence in the *Const. Ath.* as an interpolation by Aristotle, is not very convincing. F. E. Adcock, *CAH* IV, 60, and Th. Lenschau, *Burs. Jb.* 279, 1942, 167, have suggested different solutions.
97. Complete bibliography in Busolt *Gr. St.* II, 860 f.; on the names: H. Hommel, *Klio* 33, 1940, 186 f. New views were proposed by Cornelius, *Tyr. Ath.* 15 ff.; cf. also *idem*, "Die Partei des Peisistratos," *RhM* 79, 1930, 345 ff. (according to Cornelius, the city Plebs); G. Ferrara, "Solone e i capi del popolo," *PP* 1954, 334 ff.
98. On the name see Herod. I 59; Aristotle, *Const. Ath.* 13.4; Schol. Aristoph., *Vespae* 1223; Plut., *Sol.* 29.1. Bibliography in F. Schachermeyr, *RE* XIX, 161 s.v. *Peisistratos*. R. J. Hopper, *BSA* 56, 1961, 189 ff. The modernising interpretation of Ure (*Or.* 35 ff.; concurring, in part, S. Lauffer, *Die Bergwerkssklaven von Laureion* I, 1956, 13 n. 1), that these were the "miners' of Laurium, is scarcely correct.
99. Meiggs-Lewis, no. 8; cf. J. H. Oliver, *AJP* 80, 1959, 296-301.

5 THE GROWTH OF POWER

SOURCES: A running narrative of the events of Greek history in the second half of the sixth century never existed. It is a series of scattered references in Herodotus, Thucydides and Aristotle's *Constitution of Athens*, and for social conditions primarily the poems of Theognis (E. Diehl, *Anth. Lyr.* I² 2, 1 ff.) which allow us to form a reliable picture, at least in outline. Most amply attested is still the tradition concerning the *tyrannis* of Peisistratus and his sons (well analysed by F. Schachermeyr, *RE* XIX, 156 ff.; cf. Jacoby, *Att.*, 152 ff.; 331 ff., who correctly emphasises that Herodotus was the first to put in writing the tradition concerning the *tyrannis* of the Peisistratidae). Supplementary evidence is furnished by the poets (Pindar, Bacchylides: cf. Wm. Calder and J. Stern, eds., *Pindar and Bacchylides,* Wege der Forschung, Darmstadt 1970). Of the inscriptions the following deserve mention: a dedication by Aeaces of Samos, probably the father of Polycrates: Meiggs-Lewis, no. 16 (about 540 B.C.); the fragment of an Archon list (?) with the names of Hippias, Cleisthenes, Miltiades, published by B. D. Meritt, *Hesp.* 8, 1939, 59 ff., cf. *SEG* X 352; cf. also Meiggs-Lewis no. 6; (Miltiades archon, 524/3 B.C. according to Dionysius of Halicarnassus, *Ant. Rom.* VII 3); and the much-disputed "Salamis inscription," a decree of the Athenian popular assembly concerning the island of Salamis from the period immediately after the Cleisthenic reforms; cf. Ad. Wilhelm, *Att. Urk.* 4, 1939, 5 ff.; cf Meiggs-Lewis, no. 14; in addition the emendation attempted by H. T. Wade-Gery, *CQ* 40, 1946, 101 ff.; cf. *SEG* X 1; and the inscription containing public imprecations at Teos, Meiggs-Lewis, no. 30. From the large number of monuments the structures of Peisistratus and Polycrates tower far above the others; the Athenian tyrant began with construction on the gigantic temple of Zeus, the Olympieum, which was taken up again at a later date by Antiochus IV Epiphanes and Hadrian. In addition Peisistratus built the nine-conduit aqueduct (*Enneakrounos*); the Telesterium of Eleusis (F. Noack, *Eleusis*, Berlin and Leipzig 1927) also stems from the period of the tyrants. On no less grand a scale was the construction of the Heraeum, as well as the Aqueduct of Samos by Polycrates; on the Heraeum see E. Buschor, *AM* 55, 1930, 1 ff.; E. Buschor and H. Schleif, *AM* 58, 1939, 146 ff.; further information in, for instance, *Neue deutsche Ausgrabungen im Mittelmeergebiet und im Vorderen Orient*, Berlin 1959, 197 ff. (E. Buschor). For Athens see K. Kübler, *Kerameikos* VII.1. *Die Nekropole von der Mitte des 6. bis Ende des 5.Jh.*, Berlin 1974.

The evidence for fighting between the Hellenes in the West and the Carthaginians and Etruscans became reflected in local chronicles, but also in later works of history like that of Antiochus of Syracuse (a contemporary of Herodotus). Due to the loss of these works there is almost a complete vacuum, which is only scantily filled by references in

Herodotus and fragments of the great History of the West from the pen of Timaeus of Tauromenium († c. 250 B.C.).

Particularly important for the organisation of the Achaemenid empire under Darius I are the contemporary inscriptions, above all the trilingual inscription of King Darius I, at Behistun (F. H. Weissbach, *Die Keilinschriften der Achämeniden*, Leipzig 1911; Herzfeld, *Altp.*; R. G. Kent, *Old Persian*, New Haven ²1953; cf. also W. Hinz, "Die Behistun-Inschrift des Darius in ihrer ursprünglichen Fassung," *Archäologische Mitteilungen aus Iran* NF 7, 1974, 121-134). In addition the account of Herodotus on the reorganisation of the empire by Darius (III 89 ff.) is particularly important.

BIBLIOGRAPHY: On the history of the older Achaemenid empire: Meyer, *GdA* III, 3 ff. = IV² 1, 3 ff. (basic, but partly out of date through recent research); J. V. Prášek, *Gesch. der Meder und Perser bis zur makedonischen Eroberung* I and II, Gotha 1906-10) (because of the great amount of evidence amassed in this work it is not completely superfluous even today); A. Christensen, *Die Iranier, im Rahmen der "Kulturgeschichte des Alten Orients"* I. *Kleinasien* (in Hdb. Alt.), 1933, 252 ff.; O. Leuze, *Die Satrapieneinteilung in Syrien und im Zweistromlande*, Halle 1935 (Schriften der Königsberger Gelehrt. Ges., Geisteswiss. Kl. 11,4) (cf. the review by H. Bengtson, *Gn.* 13, 1937, 113 ff. = *KS*, 83 ff.); Schaeder, *PW*; P. J. Junge, "Satrapie und Natio I. Reichsverwaltung und Reichspolitik im Staate Dareios' I.," *Klio* 34, 1941, 1 ff.; *idem, Dar.* (with good bibliography); Olmstead, *HPE* (printed posthumously from the author's unpublished papers; a good survey, but the results of recent research are not uniformly taken into account); H. S. Nyberg, in *HM* III, 1954, 56 ff. Worth reading is the outline by G. Walser, "Griechen am Hofe des Grosskönigs," *Festgabe H. von Greyerz*, Bern 1967, 189-202; cf. also E. Herzfeld, *The Persian Empire. Studies in Geography and Ethnography of the Ancient Near East*, Edited from the Posthumous Papers by G. Walser, Wiesbaden 1968; "Persia e il mondo greco-romano," *Atti del convegno, Roma 11-14, 4, 1965,* published Rome, Accademia dei Lincei, 1966. In great detail is Burn, *Pers.* (cf. D. M. Lewis, *JHS* 84, 1964, 204 f.). See also J. Harmatta, "The Rise of the Old Persian Empire. Cyrus the Great," *Acta Antiqua* 19, 1971, 3 ff.; R. Schmitt, "Die achämenidische Satrapie Tayhiy Drayahaya," H. 21, 1972, 522 ff.; also *Beiträge zur Achämenidengeschichte*, hrsg. von G. Walser (H.-Einzelschr. 18), Wiesbaden 1972 (cf. J. Seibert, *Gn.* 47, 1975, 421 f.).

On the history of Peisistratus and the Peisistratidae: F. E. Adcock, *CAH* IV, 59 ff.; Cornelius, *Tyr. Ath.*; F. Schachermeyr, *RE* XIX, 156 ff. s.v. *Peisistratos* no. 3; Friedel, *Tmord*; Berve, *Tyr.* I, 47 ff.; E. Kluwe, "Bermerkungen zu den Diskussionen der drei 'Parteien' zur Zeit der Machtergreifung des Peisistratos," *Klio* 54, 1972, 101 ff.; J. S. Ruebel, "The Tyrannies of Peisistratos," *GRBS* 14, 1973, 125 ff., attempts a new analysis of the chronology; K. Kinzl, "Philochoros FgrHist. 328 F 115 and Ephoros," *Hermes* 102, 1974, 179 ff. On the coinage reform of Hippias see [Arist.] *Oecon.* II 1347a. 8; cf. G. Nenci, "La riforma monetaria di Ippia e l'adozione di un nuovo modulo monetario," in *Critica Storica*, Messina-Florence 1964, 1-4; see also G. D. Rocchi, "Motivi economici pressioni sociali nelle origini dell'espansionismo ateniese," *RIL* 105, 1971, 523 ff. **On Cleisthenes.** V. Ehrenberg, *Neugr.* 57 ff.; cf. H. Berve, *Gn.* 1, 1925, 312 ff.; E. M. Walker, *CAH* IV, 137 ff.; D. M. Lewis, "Cleisthenes and Attica," *H.* 12, 1963, 22 ff.; C. W. J. Eliot, *Coastal Demes of Attica. A Study of the Policy of Kleisthenes*, Toronto 1962 (cf. D. M. Lewis, *Gn.* 35, 1963, 723-725); W. E. Thompson, "The Deme in Kleisthenes' Reforms," *Symbolae Osloenses* 46, 1971, 72-79; and the ingenious book by P. Lévêque et P. Vidal-Naquet, *Clisthene l'Athenien*, Paris 1964; especially interesting is Chap. 6: "Clisthène pythagoricien?" See also M. Ostwald, *Nomos and the Beginnings of Athenian Democracy*, Oxford 1969; F. Ghinatti, *I gruppi politici ateniesi fino alle guerre persiane* (Univ. di Padova, Pubb. dell'Ist. di Storia Antica, 8), Rome 1970; B. Borecky, "Die politische Isonomie," *Eirene* 9, 1971, 5 ff.; Cl. Mossé, *Histoire d'une dêmocratie: Athènes. Des origines à la conquête macedonienne*, Paris 1971, 25 ff.; F. Gall, "Aspetti della politica interna ad estera degli Alcmeonide," *QUUC* 11, 1971, 65 ff.; P. J. Rhodes, *The Athenian Boule*, Oxford 1972, 209 ff.; V. M. Strogeckij, "Cleisthenes and the Alcmeonids," *VDI*, 1972, No. 120, 99 ff. [Russian, with Eng. summary]; Will, *MGr.* I, 63 ff.; M. Nardi, *Demos e kratos. La fondazione della democrazia ateniese*, Pisa 1972; particularly important is J. Martin, "Von Kleisthenes zu Ephialtes. Zur Entstehung der athenischen Demokratie," *Ch.* 4, 1974, 5 ff.; See also J. S. Traill, *The Political Organisation of Attica* (Hesp. Suppl. XIV), Princeton, N.J., 1975 and K. H. Kinzl, "Athens: Between Tyranny and Democracy", in *Studies . . . Fritz Schachermeyr*, Berlin 1977, 199 ff. On the citizenship policy see K.-W. Welwei, *Gym.* 74, 1967, 423-437. **On the history of Polycrates**. F. Bilabel, "Polykrates von Samos und Amasis von Ägypten," *Neue Heidelb. Jahrb.*, 1934, 129 ff. (with unproven theories); H. W. Parke, Polycrates and Delos, *CQ* 40, 1946, 105 ff. (on Suda s.v. *Pythia kai Delia*). New theories in J. P. Barron, *CQ* 58, 1964, 210; *idem, The Silver Coins of Samos*, London 1966, who concludes that there were two tyrants of the same name.

1. Croesus' alliance with the Spartans (Herod. I 69 *et al.*) is regarded as unhistorical by F. Jacoby, *RE Suppl.* II, 383 s.v. *Herodotos*. Also L. Moretti, *RF* NS 24, 1946, 213 ff., more recently advanced powerful arguments against the historicity of the alliance.

2. Sources: Herod. I 46-56; 71-91; Ctesias, *Persica* 4; Ephorus fr. 58; Nicolaus of Damascus fr. 68; Polyaenus VII 6; Justin I 7. According to Eusebius (Armenian transl.), the end of the Lydian kingdom falls in Olympiad 58.3, i.e., 546/5 B.C. The Nabonid-Cyrus Chronicle seems to point towards 547 B.C.; in this instance, however, the crucial place in the text is corrupt (cf. C. F. Lehmann-Haupt, *Klio* 2, 1902, 344; S. Smith, *Babylonian Historical Texts*, London 1924, 98 ff.). The difficulty stems from the fact that according to this Chronicle the king was killed (the lexicographic way out, recommended by F. Cornelius, *Gym.* 64, 1957, 346 f., does not strike me as convincing). It is here, as so often, a question of two different traditions. The attempt by F. W. König, *AfO* 7, 1931, 178 ff., to show that Sardis did not fall until after Babylon, namely after 539 B.C., is based on erroneous presuppositions; see H. Bengtson, *Gn.* 13, 1937, 117 n. 5 (= *KS*, 87, n. 17). The attempt by Mazzarino, *Fr. 00*, 163 ff., to reduce the entire chronology of Croesus by four years, namely from 560-546 to 556-541 B.C., has not been successful. Cf. against him also

H. Kaletsch, *H.* 7, 1958, 45 ff., whose dating I accept. The alleged burning of Croesus on the pyre (Bacchy. III 23 ff.; cf. Furtwängler-Reichhold, *Gr. Vasenmalerei*, Taf 113; according to Herod. I 85 ff., Croesus was wafted away by Apollo) is a legend; more recent attempts to explain the incident may be found in F. H. Welsbach, *RE Suppl.* V, 462 ff.; J. van Ooteghem, *Le Musée belge* 32, 1928, 49 ff.; accepting the legend, on the other hand, L. Moretti, *RF* NS 24, 1946, 219 ff.

3. K. Galling, *ZDPV* 70, 1954, 10 f.

4. See Th. Lenschau, *Klio* 13, 1913, 180 ff.; *RE* IX, 1883 ff. s.v. *Iones*. It is nevertheless (against Lenschau's view) impossible to prove, and also improbable, that the Persians deliberately favoured the Phoenicians over the Ionians. The view advanced by H. Berve, *NJb*, 1927, 513 ff., *GG* I, 1931, 216; *Gn.* 12, 1936, 183, that the Ionians at times found the Persian foreign domination indeed cramping but not intolerable as such, is based on the construction of an antithesis between the Ionians and the rest of the Hellenes; but in view of all that we know from Herodotus such a state of affairs is improbable.

5. See P. J. Junge, *Saka-Studien*, Klio-Beih. 41, 1939, cf. A. Hermann, *Gn.* 17, 1941, 316 ff; see also F. Altheim, "Neues über Kyros den Grossen—sein letztes Jahrzehnt," *Festschrift z. Gründung d. iranischen Kaiserr.*, Cologne 1971, 11 ff.

6. A summary in Junge, *Dar.* 43 ff. Darius came to power at the end of September 522 B.C. and the revolts were put down at the end of November 521 B.C.; cf., for instance, W. Hinz, "Das erste Jahr des Grosskönigs Dareios," *ZDMG* 92, 1938, 136 ff.

7. On the character of Persis see W. Hinz, *RE Suppl.* XII, 1022 ff. s.v. *Persis.*

8. R. Hartmann, *OLZ*, 1937, 145 ff.; Herzfeld, *Altp. I.*, 27 ff.; also A. Christensen, *Essai sur la démonologie iranienne*, 1941, 39 ff.

9. See, for instance, E. Benveniste, *Les mages dans l'ancien Iran*, 1938, also H. H. Schaeder, *OLZ*, 1940, 379 ff. On the problem of the date of Zoroaster see the studies by A. Christensen, *Die Iranier*, 1933, 213 ff., and P. J. Junge, *Dareios* I., 1944, 165 n. 2. On E. Herzfeld, *Zoroaster and his World*, Princeton 1947, see A. D. Nock, "The Problem of Zoroaster," *AJA* 53, 1949, 272 ff. (= Essays on Religion and the Ancient World II, Oxford 1972, 682 ff.); J. Duchesne-Guillemin, "La Religion des Achémenides," in *Beitr. zur Achämenidengesch.*, ed. G. Walser, (H.-Einzelschr., 18), Wiesbaden 1972, 59 ff.

10. H. H. Schaeder, *Iranische Beiträge* (Schrift d. Königsb. Gel. Ges., Geisteswiss. K1.6, 1929/30, Heft 5) 199 ff.

11. G. G. Cameron, *Persepolis Treasury Tablets*, Chicago 1948 (cf. F. Altheim, *Gn.* 23, 1951, 187 ff.); M. Mayrhofer, *Anz. W* 109, 1972, 192-201: N. Hinz, *ZA* 61, 1972, 262-311.

12. P. J. Junge, "Hazarapatis. Zur Stellung des Chiliarchen der kgl. Leibgarde im Achämenidenstaat," *Klio* 33, 1940, 13 ff.

13. Cf. A. Alt, *ZDPV* 67, 1945, 147 ff. (on Assyrian royal roads in Palestine and Syria).

14. On the buildings see, for instance, E. F. Schmidt, *Persepolis* I-II, Chicago 1953 and 1957 (cf. W. Eilers, "Die Ausgrabungen in Persepolis," *ZAss.* NF 19, 1959, 248 ff.); W. Eilers and E. Hauser, *Persepolis* III. *The Royal Tombs*, Chicago 1970; and C. Nylander, *Ionians in Pasargadae* (Studies in Old Persian Architecture), Uppsala 1970 (cf. H. v. Gall, *Gn.* 45, 1973, 701 ff.). H. H. von der Osten, *Die Welt der Perser*, Stuttgart 1957; G. Walser, *Die Völkerschaften auf den Reliefs von Persepolis*, Berlin 1966.

15. F. W. König, "Der Burgbau zu Susa nach dem Bauberichte des Königs Dareios I.," *MVAG* 35, 1, 1930; Herzfeld, *Altp. I.*, 13 ff.

16. Herod. IV 44; the fragments of Scylax in Müller, *GGM* I, praefatio p. XXXIII ff.; 15 ff., cf. F. Gisinger, *RE* III A, 619 ff. s.v. *Skylax* no. 2; H. Schiwek, *Bonner Jahrbücher* 162, 1962, 8 ff.

17. On the Achaemenid claim to universal sovereignty see Schaeder, *PW*, 5 ff.

18. On the origin and organisation of the Peloponnesian League cf. G. Busolt, *Die Lakedämonier und ihre Bundesgenossen* I, 1878; Kahrstedt, *Stsr.* I; Busolt, *Gr. St.* I 1320 ff., on the other hand, Schaefer, *Staats.* 202 ff. (but cf. the correction by Highby, *ED*, 66 ff.); Triepel, *Heg.*, 365 ff., and the studies by J. A. O. Larsen, *CP* 27, 1932, 136 ff.; 28, 1933, 257 ff.; 29, 1934, 1 ff., who is incorrect, however, in dating the origin of the League as late as the period after 506 B.C.; see lastly *CP* 39, 1944, 149. He is followed by K. Wickert, *Der peloponnesische Bund von seiner Entstehung bis zum Ende des archidamischen Kriegs*, Diss. Erlangen-Nürnberg 1961.

19. Theocr., *Id.* XVI 34 ff., with the Schol., cf. U. v. Wilamowitz, *Sappho und Simonides*, 1913, 159 ff.; H. Swoboda, *RE* III A, 567 ff., s. v. *Skopadai*.

20. Herod. I 59 (cf. Aristotle, *Const. Ath.* 14.1); on the date (probably about 565 B.C.) see F. Schachermeyr, *RE* XIX, 160 f.

21. On the proposal of Aristion: Aristotle, *Const. Ath.* 14.1.

22. Like the chronology, the external history of the Peisistratid *tyrannis*, is, on points of detail, obscure; cf. the concise discussion by F. Schachermeyr, *RE* XIX, 164 ff.; T. R. Glover, *The Exile of Peisistratus*, Proceed, of the Cambr. Phil. Soc., 1940 (published 1941); Jacoby, *Att.*, 188 ff., 194; and F. Heidbüchel, *Ph.* 101, 1957, 70 ff., who has shown that all chronological estimates are without foundation and therefore untenable. See now P. J. Rhodes, "Pisistratid Chronology Again," *Px.* 30, 1976, 219 ff. In the transmission it is primarily anecdotal features which have survived. Nevertheless, that Peisistratus was *twice* banished, as related by the principal sources (Herodotus and Aristotle), is not in itself incredible. This view has been supported by, *inter al.*, the following scholars: Busolt, *GG* II^2, 317 ff.; F. E. Adcock, *CAH* IV, 61 ff.; Cornelius, *Ath.*, 8 ff.; Berve, *GG* I^2, 201, and, in great detail, F. Schachermeyr, *RE* XIX, 161 ff.; also J. G. F. Hind, "The 'Tyrannis' and the Exiles of Pisistratus," *CQ* 24, 1974, 1 ff. [unconvincing]. The following have argued for a single banishment, which Polyaenus I 21.1 seems to suggest: Beloch, *GG* I^2 2, 288 ff. (on the basis of the study by M. Herschensohn, *Philol. Obozr.* 10, 1896, Moscow [in Russian]); De Sanctis, *Att.*, 276 ff.; W. Otto, SB.M, 1924, Schulussh. 9, U. Wilcken *GG*, 95 n. 266.

23. H. Berve, "Das Athen des Peisistratos," *Bericht über den VI. Intern. Kongr. f. Archäologie*, 1939 (published 1940), 431 ff., who goes too far, however, in stressing the negative side. See now *idem*, Tyr. I, 47 ff.

24. Aristotle, *Const. Ath.* 16; Ael., *VH* IX 25; cf. R. v. Pöhlmann, *GG*, 90.

25. R. Bonner, "Administration of Justice under Peisistratus," *CP* 19, 1924, 359 ff.

26. F. Heichelheim, *SJ.*, 55, 1931, 229 ff., esp. 240 ff.; *Wirts. Alt.* I, 294 ff.

27. F. Heichelheim, *Wirts. Alt.* I, 241.

28. B. L. Bailey, *JHS* 60, 1940, 67, Map 4.

29. M. Guarducci, *Archeologia Class.* 4, 1952, 241 ff.

30. Cf. Berve, *Milt.*, 7 ff.; against him: Bengtson, *Einz.*, 7 ff.; V. Ehrenberg, *Zur alteren athenischen Kolonisation*, Eunomia I, Prague, 1939, 11 ff.; *AW*, 116 ff.; S. Mazzarino, "La politica coloniale ateniese sotto i Pisistratidi," *Rend. R. Ist. Lombardo*, Ser. 3, 72, 1939, 285 ff.; N. G. L. Hammond, "The Philaids and the Chersonesos," *CQ* NS 6, 1956, 113-129; H. T. Wade-Gery, "Miltiades," *JHS* 71, 1951, 212 ff. = *Essays*, 155 ff.; K. Kinzl, *Miltiades-Forschungen*, Vienna 1968; F. Prontera, *PP* 27, 1972, 111-123.

31. F. Schachermeyr, *RE* XIX, 180 ff.

32. Cheilon and Anaxandridas are mentioned as tyrant "slayers" in *P. Rylands* I 18 (= Jacoby, *FgrHist.* no. 105.1).

33. The ancients had already concerned themselves with the problem of the succession to Peisistratus; cf. Thuc. I 20; VI 54. The question must not be considered from the constitutional point of view; in consequence the altercation between K. J. Beloch and E. v. Stern is superfluous: Beloch, *GG* I^2 2, 294 ff.; E. v. Stern, *Hermes* 52, 1917, 354 ff. ; K. J. Beloch, *Hermes* 55, 1920, 311 ff., also *GG* I^2 2, Nachtr., 1926, 14; cf. also J. J. E. Hondius, *Hermes* 57, 1922, 475 ff.; W. Otto, SB.M, 1924 Schlussh. 9 (Hipparchus "co-regent"). See also D. Loenen, "The Pisistratids, a Shared Rule," *Mn.* 1948, 91 ff.; Jacoby, *Att.*, 337 n. 43. Correctly Cornelius, *Tyr. Ath.*, 79. See further, M. E. White, "Hippias and the Athenian Archon List," in J. A. S. Evans (ed.), *Polis and Imperium. Studies in Honour of Edward Togo Salmon*, Toronto 1974, 81 ff. Aristotle, *Const. Ath.*, 16.7 and 18, also supports the succession of *both* sons, namely a type of 'combined rule'.

34. The evidence in H. Friedel, *Würzb. Studien* XI, 1937, 27 ff., who errs, however, along with others, in ascribing a highly political character to the deed from the very outset. Already in antiquity Thucydides (VI 54) held a more correct view. See now too, for instance, A. Momigliano, "L'excursus di Tucidide in VI 54-59," *Studi di storiografia antica in memoria di Leonardo Ferrero*, Turin 1971, 31 ff.

34a. For a different view, see H. Castritius, *Ch.* 2, 1972, 1 ff.

35. The sources in Meyer, *GdA* II, 779; 793; cf. D. L. Page, *Aegypten* 31, 1951, 158 ff. (on Ibycus fr. 3), and E. Condurachi, "La réforme monétaire de Polycrate," *Ath.* NS 36, 1958,

238 ff. The study by M. White, "The Duration of the Samian Tyranny," *JHS* 74, 1954, 36 ff., is hypothetical. Cf. also B. M. Mitchell, "Herodotus and Samos," *JHS* 95, 1975, 199 f. On the seizure of power see L. Labarbe, *Ancient Society* 5, 1974, 21-41.

36. Athen. VII 540 c/d.

37. Cf. the article by F. Bilabel cited above 425.

38. Sources: Herod. IV 1; 83-144; Ctesias fr. 29, 16 (both highly romantic); better: Strabo VII 305 (the inscription from Behistun 74 is not to be connected with this Scythian expedition, cf. F. H. Weissbach, *ZAss.* 46, 53 ff.); cf. Junge, *Dar.*, 187 n. 11 f.

39. Ed. Meyer, "König Darius I." (in *Meister der Politik*, ed. E. Marcks and K. A. v. Müller, Bd. I, 1923) 25, thinks that the king regarded the Jaxartes as identical with the Don.

40. The historicity of the "bridge counsel" has been supported lastly by H. Bengtson, SB.M, 1939, H. 1, 28 f.

41. The view of R. Grousset, *L'empire des steppes*, 1939, 39, that Darius planned "la persisation de l'Iran extérieur, l'unité paniranienne," is just as much to be rejected as the point of view advanced by E. Täubler, "Iran und die Alte Welt," in *Tyche*, 1926, 97 ff., that an expedition from the mouth of the Danube to Tianshan (!) hovered before the mind of Darius; see, against this, and correctly, Schaeder, *PW*, 38 n. 25. Indemonstrable is the conjecture of M. Rostovtzeff, *Gesch. d. Alt. Welt.* [translated by H. H. Schaeder] I, 1941, 278, that the king wanted to prevent the Scythians from advancing towards the west and to exclude them as rivals in his policy against Greece. M. A. Levi, "La spedizione scitica di Dario," *RF* 61, 1933, 58 ff., has suggested predominantly economic motives in this enterprise (a view revived by J. M. Balcer, *HSCP* 76, 1972, 99 ff.), in particular the inclusion of the entire Black Sea region into the Persian sphere of power. De Sanctis, *St. Gr.* II, 9, ascribes a limited aim to the Scythian expedition. For a further view see H. Castritius, "Die Okkupation Thrakiens durch die Perser und der Sturz des athenischen Tyrannen," *Ch.* 3, 1972, 1 ff.

42. Herod. III 138.

43. Herod. III 133 ff.; Athen. XII 522 B.

44. Cf. the studies of Meltzer-Kahrstedt, *Gesch. d. Karthager*, 3 vols., 1879-1913; St. Gsell, *Histoire de l'Afrique du Nord*, [2]1920 ff.; Oehler and Lenschau, RE X, 2150 ff. s.v. *Karthago*; also the work by J. Vogt, *Rom und Karthago*, Leipzig 1943.

45. U. Cozzoli, "Aristodemo Malaco," in *Miscellanea greca e romana. Studi pubbl. dall' Istituto ital. per la storia antica*, Rome 1965, 3-29; cf. also K.-W. Welwei, *Talanta* 3, 1971, 44 ff.

46. Dunbabin, *West.*, 362 ff.; F. Sartori, *WG* 21, 1961, 195 ff. The site of Sybaris has now been identified: see F. Rainy, "The Location of Archaic Greek Sybaris," *AJA* 73, 1969, 261 ff. [at the mouth of the Crathis]; cf. also P. G. Guzzo, *PP* 28, 1973, 278-314. A valuable document is the treaty between Sybaris and the Serdaeans found at Olympia; see Bengtson, *Staatsv.* II, no. 120, and Meiggs-Lewis, no. 10 (before 510 B.C.).

47. See the shield inscription, published in the third *Olympia-Bericht* (excavations of the years 1938/39) by E. Kunze, in which the Hipponians, the Medmaeans and the (Epizephyrian) Locrians appear as allies against the Crotonians (second half of the sixth century).

48. K.v. Fritz, *Pythagorean Politics in Southern Italy. An Analysis of the Sources*, New York 1940, esp. 94 ff.; E. L. Minar, *Early Pythagorean Politics in Practise and Theory*, Baltimore 1942 (cf. A. Cameron, *CP* 39, 1944, 127 ff.); Dunbabin, *West.*, 360 ff.

49. If the fragment published by B. D. Meritt, *Hesp.* 8, 1939, 59 ff. (cf. *SEG* X 352), is an archon list, then Cleisthenes would have been archon in 525/4 B.C., that is, he would initially have remained in the country under the two sons of Peisistratus. But he could naturally have left Athens later.

50. Sources: Herod. V 66; 69 ff.; Aristotle, *Const. Ath.* 20 f., cf. the results of investigations on the subject of the demes in Attica; A. Milchhöfer, *Untersuch. über die Demenordnung des Kleisthenes*, Abh. B. 1892, Appendix; R. Loeper, "Die Trittyen und Demen Attikas," *AM* 17, 1892, 319 ff.; A. Milchhöfer, *AM* 18, 1893, 277 ff.; H. Hommel, *RE* VII A, 330 ff. s.v. *Trittyes; idem*, "Die 30 Trittyen des Kleisthenes," *Klio* 33, 1940, 181 ff.; E. Kirsten, in A. Philippson, *Griech. Landschaften* I, 3, 1952, 1001 ff.; "Der gegenwärtige Stand der attischen Demenforschung," *Atti III Congr. internaz. di Epigrafia greca e latina* [Rome 1957] (published 1959), 155-171; also the studies by D.M. Lewis and Eliot cited above 425; cf. also W. E. Thompson, "The Deme in Kleisthenes' Reforms," *Symbolae Osloenses* 46,

1971, 72 ff. (the deme is not to be identified with a land mass but with the village); P. J. Bicknell, *Studies in Athenian Politics and Genealogy* (H.-Einzelschr. 19), Wiesbaden 1972, 1 ff. On the date of the reforms: F. Schachermeyr, "Zur Chronologie der kleisthenischen Reformen," *Klio* 25, 1932, 334 ff. = *GRG*, 59 ff. (cf. T. J. Cadoux, *JHS* 68, 1948, 115 n.). Cf. in general H. T. Wade-Gery, "The Laws of Kleisthenes," *CQ* 27, 1933, 17 ff. = *Essays*, 135-154. The attempt by Beloch, *GG* I 2, 328 ff., to shift the organisation of the *phylae* back into the time of Peisistratus, is, despite the concurrence of U. Kahrstedt, *RE* XI, 620 f. s.v. *Kleisthenes* no. 2, untenable; cf. Ehrenberg, *Neugr.*, 128.

51. A map in E. Kirsten, *Atti III Congr. internaz. di Epigrafia greca e latina* [published 1959] 172.

52. Cf. the concise discussion by A. Aymard, in *Peuples et Civilisations* I, 1950, 532 ff. Important more recent studies: H. T. Wade-Gery, "Demotionidai," *CQ* 25, 1931, 129 ff. = *Essays*, 116-134; A. R. Costello, "Notes on the Attic *gene*," *JHS* 58, 1938, 171 ff.; W. S. Ferguson, "The Attic Orgeones," *Harv. Theol. Rev.* 37, 1944, 61 ff.; *Hesp. Suppl.* 8, 1949, 130 ff. (on the pseudo-gentilitial societies).

53. The assumption by H. Hommel, *RE* VII A, 335 ff., that the old pre-Cleisthenic trittyes are found again in the list of the 12 Attic states of Philochorus fr. 94, can scarcely be maintained in view of the inscription published by J. Oliver, *Hesp.* 4, 1935, 5 ff.; cf. Jacoby, *FgrHist.*, Commentary on no. 328, 94. On the *new* trittyes: D. W. Bradeen, *TAPA* 85, 1955, 22-30.

54. In private usage, however, especially among the nobility, naming after the father continued and in many cases was the sole designation. At the end of the fifth century *patronymikon* and *demotikon* became obligatory.

55. Aristotle, *Const. Ath.* 22.2; cf. Berve, *Milt.*, 85 ff.; N. G. L. Hammond, "Strategia and Hegemonia in Fifth-Century Athens," *CQ* 19, 1969, 111 ff. = "Problems of Command in Fifth-Century History," in *Studies*, 346 ff.; also Fornara, *Gen.* 1 ff.

56. P. J. Rhodes, *The Athenian Boule*, Oxford 1972.

57. B. Keil, "Das System des kleisthenischen Staatskalenders," *Hermes* 29, 1894, 321 f.; cf. the bibliography in Busolt, *Gr. St.* II, 883 n. 1; B. D. Meritt, *The Athenian Calendar in the Vth Century*, 1928, 124; E. Bickerman, *Chronology*, 1968, 20.

58. H. A. Thompson, "*The Tholos of Athens and its Predecessors*, Hesp., Suppl. 4, 1940.

59. Aristotle, *Const. Ath.* 22.1. Androtion fr. 6 surely in all probability refers not to the establishment but to the employment of ostracism. Its initial usage in 487 B.C. (or shortly thereafter) is maintained by De Sanctis, *Att.*, 370 and by Beloch, *GG* I^2 2, 332; also by more recent scholars, for instance: H. Schaefer, in *Synopsis. Festschr. für Alfried Weber*, 1948, 491 ff.; A. E. Raubitschek, *AJA* 55, 1951, 221 ff.; R. Werner, *Ath.* NS 36, 1958, 48 ff. For a different view see Jacoby, *FgrHist.* 324, 6, Commentary, who prefers the years shortly after 508/7 B.C. See now also G. R. Stanton, "The Introduction of Ostracism and Alcmeonid Propaganda," *JHS* 90, 1970, 180 ff.; E. Vanderpool, *Ostracism at Athens* (Lectures in Memory of Louise Taft Semple [second series]), Cincinnati 1973; K. Meister, "Zum Zeitpunkt der Einführung des Ostrakismos," *Ch.* 1, 1971, 85 ff.; and, in particular, R. Thomsen, *The Origin of Ostracism* (Humanitas 4), Copenhagen 1972 (date similar to that of Jacoby). The earlier bibliography may be found in Busolt, *Gr. St.* II, 884 ff.; cf. J. Carcopino, *L'ostracisme athénien*, Paris [2]1934; O. W. Reinmuth, *RE* XVIII, 1674 ff. (bibliography, 1685); A. Calderini, *L'ostracismo*, Como 1945. Extremely valuable is H. Bloch, *Gn.* 31, 1959, 492 f.

60. Herod. V 73; cf. Bengtson, *Einz.*, 49 f.; F. Schachermeyr, "Athen als Stadt des Grosskönigs," *Grazer Beiträge* 1, 1973, 211 ff.

61. Cf. Meiggs-Lewis, no. 15.

6 THE PERSIAN WARS

SOURCES AND BIBLIOGRAPHY: In amount and scope the monumental evidence from the Persian era is very limited. From excavations in Greece the following in particular may be cited: the investigations by G. Sotiriadis on the battlefield of Marathon (*Anaskaphai Marathonos*, 1932; "The Campaign of Marathon. According to a Recent Critic," *Prakt. Akad. Athen.* 7, 1933, 377 ff.; *Marathonica* I-III, *op. cit.*, 9, 1934, 14 ff.; 261 ff.; 330 ff.; also a series of articles in *Prakt. Arch. Hetaireias*, 88-91, 1933-36); of late K. P. Kontorlis, *The Battle of Marathon and Recent Archaeological Discoveries*, [2]1973 [discovery of the burial mound of the Plataeans at Vrana]; and the investigations of Sp. Marinatos at Thermopylae (Report in the *VI. Intern. Kongr. f. Arch.*, Berlin 1939 [published 1940], 333 ff.). The portraits, the hermae of Attic *strategoi*, for instance, are still highly standardised and idealised, with one noteworthy exception, the herm of Themistocles found in Ostia (cf. B. Schweitzer, *Studien z. Entstehung des Porträts bei den Griechen*. SB.S 91,4, 1939; *idem, An.* 17, 1941, 77 ff.; on the other hand, L. Curtius, *RM* 57, 1942, 78 ff.). The painting of the battle of Marathon by Polygnotus in the Stoa Poecile of Athens, described by Pausanias (I 15.3), saw an attempted reconstruction at the hands of C. Robert, *18. Hallisches Winckelmannsprogr.*, 1895 (cf. the bibliography cited in Judeich, *Top.*, 337 n. 4.); see also E. B. Harrison, *AJA* 76, 1972, 353 ff. All other monuments are surpassed in importance by the so-called "serpent column," the votive offering of the Greeks which was set up in Delphi after Plataea (479 B.C.), bearing the names of the 31 allied Greek states, now in the At Meydani in Istanbul (the inscription in Bengtson, *Staatsv.* II, no. 130, with additional bibliography; cf. also Meiggs-Lewis, no. 27 = *GHD 5th C* p. 7). The explanation advanced in *ATL III*, 1950, 95 ff., should not be accepted uncritically. Still to be mentioned is the inscribed helmet dedicated by the Athenians in Olympia, which E. Kunze, *Festschr. für Carl Weickert*, Berlin 1955, 7 ff., connects with the conquest of Lemmos by Miltiades at the beginning of the fifth century (cf. Bengtson, *Einz.*, 37 ff.).

Of Greek inscriptions the following are particularly important historically: the epigram dedicated to the Athenian polemarch, Callimachus, who fell at Marathon (*IG* I^2 609; cf. A. Wilhelm, *Anz. W*, 1934, 111 ff.; R. Hampe, *Ant.* 15, 1939, 168 ff.; A. E. Raubitschek, *AJA* 44, 1940, 53 ff.; F. Jacoby, *Hesp.* 14, 1945, 158 n. 8; B. B. Shefton, *BSA* 45, 1950, 140 ff.; Ed. Fraenkel, *Eranos* 49, 1951, 63 f.); also the Persian epigrams from the Athenian Agora (Fr. Frhr. Hiller v. Gaertringen, *Hermes* 69, 1934, 204 ff.; cf. the remaining bibliography in J. Kirchner, *Imagines Inscriptionum Atticarum*, [2]1948, 13 no. 19; also F. Jacoby, "Some Athenian Epigrams from the Persian Wars," *Hesp.* 14, 1945, 161 ff.). New readings by W. Peek, *Hermes* 88, 1960, 494 ff., cf. also B. D. Meritt, *AJP* 83, 1962, 294 ff. The more important older inscriptional evidence has been assembled by Dittenberger and M. N. Tod, and now also by R. Meiggs and D. M. Lewis: the following deserve emphasis: the votive inscription of Histiaeus of Miletus (*Syll.* I^3 3 f. = Tod I^2 no. 9); the dedications of the Sicilian tyrant Gelon in Olympia and Delphi (*Syll.* I^3 33-34 = Meiggs-Lewis no. 28) from 488 or 480 B.C.; as well as those by Hieron of Syracuse in Olympia (*Syll.* I^3 35 = Meiggs-Lewis no. 29 = *GHD 5th C* p. 91). The letter of Darius I to the Satrap Gadatas (found in Magnesia on the Maeander) is informative for assessing the Persian administration of Ionia (*Syll.* I^3 22 = Tod no. 10; cf. F. Lochner-Hüttenbach, in W. Brandenstein and M. Mayrhofer, *Handbuch des Altpersischen*, Wiesbaden 1964, 91 ff.).

The Persian Wars form an important epoch in the cultural life of the Greek people. Although the extant primary historiographical sources are very sparse, it must above all be borne in mind that contemporary historical records were almost totally lacking. It was not until a generation after Salamis and Plataea that Herodotus began to assemble the traditions connected with the Persian Wars, and not until the Peloponnesian War cast its shadow across Greece did he conclude his entire history.

Simonides of Ceos († 468 B.C.) celebrated almost all the important events of the Persian era in his epigrams, but what has been handed down under his name includes a great deal that is spurious (U.v. Wilamowitz, *Sappho und Simonides*, Berlin 1913; J. Geffcken, *RE* III A, 186 ff. s.v. no. 2). The Greek struggle for freedom found only a faint echo in the Odes of Pindar. Of the tragedians Phrynichus produced the *Sack of Miletus* on the stage; his *Phoenissae*, produced in 476, for which Themistocles was probably the *choregos*, also dealt with historical events. With the *Persae* in 472, Aeschylus once more brought the great national theme on the stage; the speech by the herald evidently reflects the impression which the battle of Salamis had made on Aeschylus himself. Valuable, although predominantly philological, is the study by W. Kierdorf, *Erlebnis und Darstellung der Perserkriege. Studien zu Simonides, Pindar, Aischylos und den attischen Rednern*, Göttingen 1966.

Of the older historians Hecataeus of Miletus—Herodotus recounts his activity at the time of the Ionian Revolt (V 36; 124 ff.)—was not a source for the Persian Wars. The *Persika* by Dionysius of Miletus are, like the personality and lifetime of its author, too intangible; their special importance as a source of Herodotus has been contested in particular by C. F. Lehmann-Haupt (*GG*, in Gercke-Norden, *Einl.* III^2, 79 f.; *idem, Klio* 18, 1923, 72 f.; etc.); of late M. Moggi, *Ann. Scuola Norm. Sup. di Pisa, Cl. di Lettere e Filosofia, ser.* III, *vol.* II, 2, 1973, 433-468; as compared with him, the hypothetical aspects are rightly emphasised by F. Jacoby, *RE Suppl.* II, 405, s.v. *Herodotos.*

SECONDARY SOURCES: By far the most important, in many instances the only source at all for the Persian Wars, are the *Logoi* of Herodotus, especially Books V-IX, a "work which indeed towers far above the local Chronicles of the horographers, since it discusses contemporary history as Panhellenic history in terms of a great uniform point of view, and at the same time draws the entire known world within its scope" (R. Pöhlmann).

Born shortly before the second Persian War in Doric Halicarnassus during the reign of the Carian princess Artemisia, into a family whose male line contained Carian names (on the lineage of Herodotus see A. Körte, *Hermes* 59, 1924, 119 ff.), Herodotus, after a temporary stay on Samos (E. E. Cole, *The Samos of Herodotus*, Diss. Yale, New Haven 1912), came to Athens, in any case before 445/4 B.C. In the Periclean circle he gained for himself a close relationship to Attic culture, and it was his enthusiasm for Periclean Athens that prompted him to turn his pen to history (a different view is held by H. Strasburger, *H.* 4, 1955, 1 ff.; see, however, for instance, F. D. Harvey, *H.* 15, 1966, 254 f.). His sojourn in Athens was preceded by extensive travels. Soon after the battle of Papremis (460) Herodotus spent about four months in Egypt (C. Sourdille, *La durée et l'étendue du voyage d'Hérodote en Egypte*, Thèse, Paris 1910; J. Vogt, "Herodot in Ägypten," *Genethliakon f. W. Schmid,* Tübinger Beitr. 5, 1929, 97 ff.; also separately). From Egypt he journeyed to Phoenicia and Mesopotamia. The sojourn of Herodotus in Scythia, where the city of Olbia formed his headquarters, evidently took place before this journey (K.v. Fritz, "Herodotus and the Growth of Greek Historiography," *TAPA* 67, 1936, 315 ff.). Although the details of the Herodotean travels may be disputed, there are nevertheless no grounds for lowering them to the decade from 440 to 430 B.C. (thus, however, Meyer, *Forsch.* I, 155 f.; G. De Sanctis, *Encicl. Ital.* XIV 258 ff. s.v. *Erodoto*; holding a view opposed to this are, *inter al.*, C. F. Lehmann-Haupt, *GG*, in Gercke-Norden *Einl.* III[2], 81; Ph.-E. Legrand, *Hérodote, Introduction*, 1932, 24 ff.). It is certain that Herodotus went to Thurii in southern Italy, and in honour of his new homeland designated himself as "Thurian" in his *Logoi* (F. Jacoby, *RE Suppl.* II, 205 ff.). Whether he set foot in Athens again, after this, is uncertain. His death occurred between 430 and 424 B.C., not as late as 414 B.C. as argued by C. W. Fornara, *JHS* 91, 1971, 25-34.

The genesis of the *Histories* of Herodotus eludes the modern student just as much as the inner development of the native of Halicarnassus does. It is not improbable that the work grew from a large number of *Logoi* which Herodotus delivered in public—by subordinating them to the basic idea of the world-shaking conflict between Hellenes and Barbarians, and thus fusing them together into an inner unity. His *Histories* close with the capture of Sestos by the Greeks in the autumn of 479. Whether the work was completed or not is difficult to judge (that it was, has been powerfully argued by Fr. Egermann, *NJb* 1, 1938, 250 ff.; that it was not, by, *inter al.*, F. Jacoby, *RE Suppl*, II, 372 ff.; Pohlenz, *Hdt.*, 163 ff.). The absence of the Assyrian *Logoi* announced in I 184 (cf. I 106) is no convincing proof that the work remained uncompleted. On the question of composition the following studies in particular deserve mention: H. R. Immerwahr, *Form and Thought in Herodotus* (APA Philological Monographs 23), Cleveland 1966; J. Cobet, *Herodotus Exkurse und die Frage der Einheit seines Werkes* (H.-Einzelschr., 17), Wiesbaden 1971 (cf. R. Drews, *Gn.* 47, 1975, 329 ff.); C. W. Fornara, *Herodotus. An Interpretative*

Essay, Oxford 1971; M. E. White, "Herodotus' Starting Point," *Px*. 23, 1969, 39 ff.

In writing his account of the Persian Wars Herodotus did not use literary sources which he had assimilated (cf., however, the provocative, but not convincing, study by D. Fehling, *Die Quellenangaben bei Herodot* [Untersuchungen zur antiken Literatur und Geschichte, 9], Berlin 1971 [cf. J. Cobet, *Gnomon* 46, 1974, 737 ff.]). The "literary fixed memoirs" by Dicaeus of Athens (VIII 65) (cf. P. Trautwein, *Hermes* 25, 1890, 527 ff.; D. Mülder, *Klio* 13, 1913, 39 ff.) are an invention (cf. F. Jacoby, *RE Suppl.* II, 404). That Herodotus in one instance expressly mentions his authority (Thersander of Orchomenus, for circumstances preceding the battle of Plataea, IX 16), is an exception. The "Thurian" kept essentially to the stories circulating among the *demos*; he reproduced what had become more or less fixed tradition through oral transmission. From the various groups of traditions it is possible to distinguish with certainty an Attic, a Spartan, a Delphic and a Persian tradition (on the last see the admittedly decidedly hypothetical discussion by J. Wells, "The Persian Friends of Herodotus," *JHS* 27, 1907, 37 ff.; *idem, Studies in Herodotus, ibid.*, 95 ff.).

Herodotus' *Histories* are, depending on his attitude towards the tradition before him and his personal relationship to his contemporaries, full of both sympathy and antipathy; they are written "with anger and zeal": Herodotus sides with the Alcmeonidae (cf. VI 121-31: the dream of Agariste the mother of Pericles, in which the lion is not, however, to be interpreted as a bad omen—thus Fr. Focke, *Herodot als Historiker,* Tübinger Beitr. 1, 1927, 26 ff.; see rather, H. Bengtson, SB.B, 1939, H. 1, 51 n. 2.; cf., on the other hand, H. Strasburger, *H.* 4, 1955, 15 ff.); he is hostile to Themistocles, hostile to Miltiades (cf. on his delineation of the Paros expedition: H. Bengtson, *op. cit.*, 53 ff., and in particular, K. Kinzl, "Miltiades' Paros-expedition in der Geschichtsschreibung," *Hermes* 104, 1976, 280 ff.). Herodotus felt himself closely identified with the Delphic Oracle, of whose infallibility he was wholly convinced. In Herodotus, belief in prophecy and the marvellous existed alongside the rational. That Herodotus deliberately falsified tradition in certain instances because of preconceived ideas is not true, even though Greek local patriotism may at times have maintained this (cf. Plutarch's *De malignitate Herodoti*; see Ph.-E. Legrand, *Mélanges G. Glotz* II, 1932, 535 ff. and H. Homeyer, *Klio* 49, 1967, 181 ff.).

It is the unrivalled art of depicting the protagonists in short brilliant strokes, in the animated description, in the rich variegation of details, and above all in portraying landscape and people that the actual qualities of his work lie. Whoever expects more from him, especially precise figures, deeper insights into the interconnections between events and into the motives of the leading statesmen and generals, will admittedly be disappointed. None the less it would be in place to ask to what extent personal motives, which are placed in the foreground by Herodotus, do not in one instance or another coincide with or approximate the truth (cf. also W. Marg, *Hermes* 81, 1953, 196 ff.). Be that as it may, it remains the indisputable merit of Herodotus that within a broad perspective he embarked on a theme of national importance for all Hellas and artistically carried the composition of it through to its sequel. His brilliant excursive technique lends to the *Histories* a significance which far exceeds their value as a historical source: Herodotus is not only the first genuine historian, he is also the first storyteller of the West. On the most important recent editions and aids see Bengtson, *Einf.*, 101 f. (cf. Eng. trans. [by R. I. Frank and F. D. Gilliard] *Anc. Hist.*, 103); from the extensive bibliography on Herodotus and his *Histories* the following may be cited: F. C. Dahlmann, *Forschungen auf dem Gebiet der Gesch.* II 1, 1824; A. Hauvette, *Hérodote historien des guerres médiques*, Paris 1894; F. Jacoby, *RE Suppl.* II, 205 ff. (basic); Pohlenz, *Hdt.*, Fr. Egermann, "Das Geschichtswerk des Herodot," *Neue Jahrb.* 1, 1938, 191 ff.; 239 ff.; E. Powell, *The History of Herodotus*, Cambridge 1939; J. L. Myres, *Herodotus, Father of History*, Oxford 1953; W. W. How and J. Wells, *A Commentary on Herodotus*, 2 vols., Oxford 1912, reprint 1928 (with corrections). Indispensable is K. von Fritz, *Die griechische Geschichtsschreibung* I, 1967, Kapitel V: "Herodot." Interesting is the little study by C. G. Starr, "The Awakening of the Greek Historical Spirit and Early Greek Coinage," *Num. Chron.* 1966, 1-7 (especially on the coin images and symbols of the fifth century B.C.). Ingenious, but at bottom incorrect, was the attempt of E. Howald to explain the historian as a representative of a satiated Ionian businessman's culture, his *Histories* as the product of a "buffer state mentality," as a singularly great show-piece, so to speak, and the struggle between the Hellenes and Barbarians as "stories within a story": "Ionische Geschichtsschreibung," *Hermes* 58, 1923, 113 ff. (and *Vom Geist antiker Geschichtsschreibung*, Munich 1944, 11 ff.). In regard to the personality of Herodotus, Meyer, *Forsch.* II, 196 ff., has stated much that is correct and pertinent (cf. *GdA* III[1] 242 ff.). On the "sources" cf. H. Diels, *Hermes* 22, 1887, 411 ff. (on Hecataeus and Herodotus); F. Jacoby, *RE Suppl.* II, 392 ff.; on the position of Herodotus in ethnographical literature, K. Trüdinger, *Studien z. Gesch. d. griech.-röm. Ethnographie*, 1918, 14 ff.; on his relationship to national traditions, W. Aly, *Volksmärchen, Sage and Novelle bei Herodot und seinen Zeitgenossen*, Göttingen 1921. On Herodotus' trustworthiness see also T. Säve-Söderbergh, "Zu den äthiopischen Episoden bei Herodot," *Eranos* 44, 1946, 68 ff., who rightly emphasises his dependence on Greek tradition; see further, E. Lüddeckens, "Herodot u. Ägypten," *ZDMG* 104, 1954, 330 ff.; on the chronology of Herodotus: H. Strasburger, *H.* 5, 1956, 129-161; cf. K. v. Fritz, *Die griech. Geschichtsschreibung* I, 1967, 364 ff. New views have been advanced by K. Reinhardt, "Herodots Persergeschichten," in *Geistige Überlieferung. Ein Jahrbuch*, Berlin 1940, 138 ff. Cf. also K. Latte, "Die Anfänge der griechischen Geschichtsschreibung," *Fondation Hardt, Entretiens* IV (*2-8 August, 1956*) 3 ff. [published 1959]. Still valuable is Schmid, *GGL* I[2], 550 ff.; see also P. MacKendrick, "Herodotus 1963-

1969," *CW* 63, 1969, 37 ff.; and W. den Boer, "Herodotus in het moderne en der zock," *Tijdschrift Geschiedenis* 83, 1970, 499 ff.; on the text of Herodotus see A.H.R.E. Paap, *De Herodoti reliquiis in papyris et membranis Aegyptiis servatis*, Leiden 1948. To be taken into account for what follows: G. Gottlieb, *Das Verhaltnis der ausserherodoteischen Überlieferung zu Herodot*, Diss. Frankfurt a.M., published Bonn 1963.

It is not in the last analysis due to the influence of the Herodotean *Histories* that at the end of the fifth century the writing of local Chronicles enjoyed such a high degree of flowering (F. Jacoby, *Klio* 9, 1909, 110 ff.). But from the diffuse writings in this field (cf. for a general discussion R. Laqueur, *RE* XIII, 1083 ff.), next to nothing is extant. Thus, for instance, we have only a single large fragment from the *Annals of Lampsacus* by Charon of Lampsacus (about 400 B.C.; cf. F. Jacoby, *Studi ital. di fil. cl.*, NS 15, 1938, 207 ff. = *Abh. z. griech Geschichtsschreibung*, 1956, 178 ff.) (Jacoby, *FgrHist* III no. 262, 1); the *Persika* by Charon, which should not however be regarded as part of the *Annals* (but thus again—following, *inter al.*, Ed. Schwartz—K.v. Fritz, *AJP* 63, 1942, 113 ff.), are practically completely beyond reach. For the outward form of such records by local chroniclers the *Temple Chronicle* of Lindus (on Rhodes), stemming from the early years of the first century B.C., may be called to mind (C. Blinkenberg, *La chronique du temple lindien*, Copenhagen 1912; *Die lindische Tempelchronik, Kl. Texte* no. 131, Bonn 1915; *Lindos* II, 1941, 149 ff.).

In many instances polemically hostile to Herodotus, but drawing heavily on his *Logoi*, Ctesias of Cnidus wrote his *Persika* (from the legendary king Ninus to 398/7 B.C.) in the early years of the fourth century. Ctesias, the private physician of Queen Parysatis, mother of Cyrus the Younger, had lived for 17 (?) years at the court of the Great King, Artaxerxes II Mnemon. Despite his intimate knowledge of Persian court life, his account is on the whole disappointing for the historian; it is romantic in many places, saturated with court gossip, prejudiced in favour of the Lacedaemonians and not free of gross chronological errors. "Herodotus, who was in Babylon for only a few months and perhaps never even saw the real Persia, but for all that made critical use of his scholarly predecessors and passed up no opportunity to acquire information by interrogation, gives a longer and better account of the land and its history than the royal private physician, who had come to know all Persian capitals and could have had access to the best sources if—indeed if that had interested him at all when he was in Persia" (F. Jacoby, *RE* XI, 2046 s.v. *Ktesias*). On the other hand, however, it must not be overlooked that the romantic delineation of Persian court life possesses, as a background description, considerable importance for the history of civilisation. The fragments of Ctesias have been collected by Jacoby, *FgrHist*. no. 688. A surprise was the discovery of a papyrus (*P. Oxy.* XXII, 2330) which has shown that Ctesias used the Attic dialect; for an assessment: F. Jacoby, *RE* XI, 2032 ff. (excellent). Of later writers Diodorus, Pompeius Trogus, Nicolaus of Damascus and Plutarch (*Vita* of

Artoxerxes) used the *Persika* of Ctesias. In the separate work *Concerning the Revenues of Asia* (cf. Athen. II 68 a, X 442 b)—or was it an excursus in the *Persika*?—there appear to have been interesting references to the products of the countries within the Achaemenid empire. Cf. on this question and on Persian tribute in general F. Altheim and R. Stiehl, *Die aramäische Sprache unter den Achaimeniden* I, 1963, 109 ff. F. W. König, *Die Persika des Ktesias von Knidos*, Archiv. f. Orientforsch., Beiheft 18, Graz 1972. A follower of Ctesias is Dinon of Colophon, the father of Cleitarchus, the historian of Alexander (v. *infra* 513); in polemical tone he greatly revised the *Persika* of his predecessor and brought the narrative down at least as far as 343/2 B.C.

For the account which Ephorus of Cyme (he wrote in the time of Alexander) gave of the Persian Wars in his *Universal History* he used, in addition to Herodotus, almost the total existing historiographical material; his account forms the basis of Diodorus XI ff. On Ephorus and his *History* see Ed. Schwartz, *RE* VI, 1 ff.; Jacoby, *FgrHist.* no. 70, Commentary (cf. E. Cavaignac, *Mél. G. Glotz* I, 1932, 143 ff.); G. L. Barber, *The Historian Ephorus*, Cambridge 1935. The arrangement of the work has been clarified by R. Laqueur, *Hermes* 46, 1911, 321 ff. Valuable is G. Schepens, "Ephore sur la valeur de l'autopsie," *Ancient Society* 1, 1970, 163-82.

Of the voluminous world history (*Historiae Philippicae*) by the romanticising Celt (Vocontian) Pompeius Trogus (from the period of Augustus), only the Summaries, actually "Prefaces" (*Prologi*), and the much abused excerpt of M. Junianus Justinus (third century A.D.?) are extant; Just. II 9-14 comes into question for the Persian Wars. On the sources: A. Enmann, *Untersuch. über die Quellen des Pompeius Trogus für die griech. u. sizil. Gesch.*, Dorpat 1880; A.v. Gutschmid, *Kl. Schriften*, V, 1894, 19 ff.; G. Forni, *Valore storico e fonti di Pompeo Trogo*. I. *Per le guerre greco-persiane*, Urbino 1958.

The *Strategemata* of Polyaenus (from the time of the emperors Marcus Aurelius and Lucius Verus) do not constitute an essential enrichment of our sources (on the sources see J. Melber, *Fleckeisens Jbb., Suppl.-Bd.* XIV, 1885, 417 ff.; a higher estimation of this literary form has admittedly been championed by F. Lammert, *RE* IV A, 174 ff., as against the deprecatory judgment of Köchly and Kromayer); the same applies to the speeches *On Behalf of the Four* (Miltiades, Cimon, Themistocles and Pericles), and the *Panathenaikos* of the celebrated Sophist Aelius Aristeides (117-189 A.D.; cf. on him *infra* 593 f.). On the sources of the speeches: A. Haas, *Quibus fontibus Ael. Arists. in componenda diss* ..., Diss. Greifswald 1884; and J. H. Oliver, *The Civilising Power. A Study of the Panathenaic Discourse of Aelius Aristides*, Philadelphia 1968.

From the ancient biographical literature the following come into question for the history of the Persian Wars: the *Vitae* of Miltiades, Aristeides and Themistocles by Cornelius Nepos, a contemporary of Cicero, and the biographies of the last two by Plutarch of Chaeroneia (c. 46-123 A.D.). Despite many investigations (basic for Plutarch's use of his sources was Meyer's treatise on the biography of Cimon, *Forsch.* II, 1 ff.), the problem concerning the sources has seen no essential progress (cf. however, C. Theander, *Plutarch und die Geschichte,* Årsberättelse Lund, 1950-51, I), since there is too much of an uncertainty factor caused by the absence of the large number of Hellenistic intermediary sources. On Plutarch's *Vita* of Themistocles see A. Bauer, *Plutarchs Themistokles, für Quellenkrit. Übungen kommentiert u. herausgegeben*, Leipzig 1844 (2nd ed. agumented and revised, by F. J. Frost, 1967); cf. M. Mohr, *Die Quellen des plutarchischen u. nepotischen Themistokles sowie die entspr. Abschnitte des Diodor u. Justin*, Berlin 1879; further, B. Perrin, *Plutarchus' Themistocles and Aristides*, New York-London 1901: *Vie de Thémistocle*, ed., introduc. and comm. by R. Flacelière, Paris 1972.

Specific Studies on the History of the Persian Wars (for details see in the following sections): Grundy, *PW*; C. Hignett, *Inv.*; Burn, *Pers.;* On the general character of the period: H. Berve, "Fürstliche Herren zur Zeit der Perserkriege," *Ant.* 12, 1936, 1 ff.; *Milt.*; on both see Bengtson, *Einz.*; further, M. F. McGregor, "The Pro-Persian Party at Athens from 510 to 480 B.C.," in *Studies Ferguson*, 71 ff. (thinks in terms too firmly established and of political groups that are too cringing; this suggestive study is unfortunately written without cognizance of the relevant recent research). See rather, F. Schachermeyr, *Die Sieger der Perserkriege* (Persönlichkeit u. Geschichte 82), Göttingen 1974, and in particular, on the whole period, *idem, Die frühe Klassik der Griechen*, Stuttgart-Berlin-Cologne 1966. G. Nenci, *Introduzione alle guerre persiane*, Pisa 1958, deals especially with the so-called "guilt question" and the relations between Persia and Greece up to 490 B.C. For Sparta: J. Wolski, "Les changements intérieures à Sparte à la veille des guerres médiques," *REA* 69, 1967, 31-49. A. T. Olmstead, "Persia and the Greek Problem," *CP* 34, 1939, 305 ff., looks at the history of the Persian Wars from the Persian point of view, but this article does not do justice to the historical significance of this crisis in world history, since Olmstead minimises the events too much in terms of Persian "frontier policy"; cf. *idem, HPE* (cf. *supra* 424 f.). See also the discussion by Will, *MGr.* I, 14 ff., 83 ff. A more recent survey of the bibliography is given by G. Walser, *Schweiz. Beitr. z. allg. Gesch.* 17, 1959, 219 ff.

THE IONIAN REVOLT

SOURCES: Herodotus V 28 ff.; VI 1-33 (unfriendly towards the Ionians, cf. M. Lang, *H.* 17, 1968, 24 ff.); Charon of Lampsacus fr. 10 (= Plut., *De malignitate Herodoti* 24 p 861 a-d); the coins of the Ionian Revolt: P. Gardner, "The Coinage of the Ionian Revolt," *JHS* 31, 1911, 151 ff.; 33, 1913, 105; *A History of Ancient Coinage 700-300 B.C.*, Oxford 1918, 91 ff.; G. Nenci, *Studi in onore di A. Fanfani*, Milan 1962, 71-83. (Miletus, Chios, Samos, Clazomenae, Cyme, Priene and perhaps also Lampsacus, Dardanus and Abydus, among others, took part in the

Ionian "Coinage Union.") On the chronology of the revolt see Ed. Meyer, *GdA* III[1], 1900, 300 n.; cf. Bengtson, *Einz.*, 40 n. 4.

HELLAS AND PERSIA UP TO THE BATTLE OF MARATHON

PRINCIPAL SOURCES: Herodotus VI 19; 76 ff.; 92; VII 148 f. (Sparta and Argos); Herodotus VI 94 ff.; Ctesias fr. 13; Cor. Nep., *Milt.* 4-6 (cf. W. W. How, *JHS* 39, 1919, 48 ff.); Justin II 9, as well as the painting of the battle of Marathon in the Stoa Poecile, see above 430 (the expedition of Datis and Artaphernes, the battle of Marathon). Valuable is J. Labarbe, *La Loi navale de Thémistocle*, Paris 1957 (cf. S. Lauffer, *H.* 8, 1959, 381-84), and K. H. Kinzl, *Studies... Fritz Schachermeyr*, Berlin 1977, 210 ff. Important for Peloponnesian history in the fifth century is R. T. Williams, *The Confederate Coinage of the Arcadians in the Fifth Century*, New York 1965 (cf. W. Schwabacher, *Gn.* 40, 1968, 92 ff.). According to Williams, an Arcadian League came into being in 491/90 B.C. on the initiative of the Spartan king Cleomenes. In general, for the entire era, see F. Schachermeyr, *Die frühe Klassik der Griechen*, 1966.

THE BUILDING OF THEMISTOCLES' FLEET AND PERSIAN MOBILISATION

SOURCES: The Paros expedition of Miltiades: Herodotus VI 132 ff. (hostile towards Miltiades); Ephorus fr. 63; Cor. Nep., *Milt.* 7. See now K. H. Kinzl, "Miltiades' Parosexpedition in der Geschichtsschreibung," *Hermes* 104, 1976, 280 ff. The conflict between Athens and Aegina: Herodotus VI 85 ff., cf. V 82 ff. (the Aeginetan version); Pausanias I 29.7. The building of Themistocles' fleet: Herodotus VII 144; Aristotle, *Const. Ath.* 22.7; Cor. Nep., *Them.* 2; Polyaenus I 30.6; cf. in particular the work cited above, this page, by J. Labarbe. Persian mobilisation: Herodotus VII 5 ff.

XERXES' CAMPAIGN AGAINST GREECE

SOURCES: (on the monumental and epigraphical evidence see above p. 430 f.): Of the contemporary sources the *Persae* of Aeschylus take paramount place with the famous messenger's speech from the battle of Salamis; in addition there are a number of epigrams which are for the most part attributed to Simonides. Of the later sources the account of the Persian Wars by Herodotus towers far above the others: Bks. VII and VIII (see the commentary by R. W. Macan, Herodotus VII-IX, London 1908 and W. W. How and J. Wells, A Commentary on Herodotus, Vol. II, Oxford 1928): all other sources are dependent on him: the epic of Choerilus of Samos (Kinkel, *Epic. Graec. frag.* I 265 ff.) from the time of the Peloponnesian War; the *Histories* of Ephorus (excerpts in Diodorus XI); and in part also the *Lives* of Themistocles and of Aristeides by Plutarch. A scene from the battle at Artemisium is described by the

Würzburger Sosylus Papyrus, which represents an independent tradition (Bilabel *P. Kleinform* no. 10; cf. *infra* 444 n. 75).

As for the Themistocles inscription from Troezen, this is a forgery of the fourth century B.C. which in its present version was inscribed in the third century B.C. The inscription was published by M. H. Jameson, *Hesp*. 29, 1960, 198 ff.; cf. *H.* 12, 1963, 385 ff. It contains an Attic decree, proposed by Themistocles, for the evacuation of Athens in the face of the Persians, still prior to the battles of Thermopylae and Artemisium. Themistocles, so the text runs, made a further proposal, to divide the fleet: 100 triremes were to be sent to Artemisium, 100 others despatched to defend the coasts of Attica. The factors which weigh against the authenticity of this document have been advanced, essentially correct, by C. Habicht, *Hermes* 89, 1961, 1 ff. See further, P. Amandry, *Bull. Fac. des Lettres de Strasbourg*, 1961, 413-435, with the remarks of J. and L. Robert, *REG* 75, 1962, "Bull. épigr." no. 137. The opposite view, adopted by, *inter alia*, H. Berve, *SB.M*, 1961, H. 3, leads to factual difficulties; neither Berve nor other scholars (M. Treu, *H.* 12, 1963, 47 ff.; F. Schachermeyr, *Öst. Jh.*, 46, 1961-63, 158 ff. = *GRG*, 120 ff.) have succeeded in bringing the contents of the inscription into harmony with Herodotus. As for myself, I regarded the inscription from the outset as suspect—see the Addenda to the second edition of my *GG*, 1960, 549. This inscription should be left aside when delineating the relevant events. In the meantime the discussion goes on endlessly. For the recent bibliography see, for instance, F. Sartori, *RF* 95, 1967, 108; also the reports on inscriptions by J. and L. Robert, *REG* 1963 ff.; and Meiggs-Lewis, no. 23 (with bibliography); further, H. B. Mattingly, *Ph.* 119, 1975, 51 ff.

In 1967 a Xerxes inscription was found at Persepolis, bearing an account of the Great King but which lacks any personal touch, see M. Mayrhofer, *Almanach der Wiener Akademie* 119, 1969, 158-170.

Bibliography: Grundy, *PW;* Obst, Xerx.; Köster, *Seewesens* 54 ff. (particularly valuable); Burn, *Pers.*; Hignett, *Inv.* Both Burn and Hignett, by the way, regard the above-cited Themistocles inscription as not authentic (Burn, 364 ff.; Hignett, 458 ff.). On the Persian naval commanders see H. Hauben, *Ancient Society* 4, 1973, 23-37. Also M. Mayrhofer, *Xerxes. König der Könige. Vortrag*, Vienna 1970; G. Roux, "Hérodote, Diodore, Plutarque racontant la bataille de Salamine," *BCH* 98, 1974, 59 ff.

THE GREEK VICTORIES AT MYCALE AND PLATAEA

SOURCES: Herodotus VII 124—IX 122; therefrom Ephorus in Diodorus XI 27 ff.; a few details are furnished by Plutarch, *Arist.* 11 ff. The oath of the Athenians before the battle of Plataea (Tod, II, no. 204) is unhistorical (differently, but not convincing, A. E. Raubitschek, *TAPA* 91, 1960, 178 ff.); see above all L. Robert, *Etud. épigr. et phil.*, 1938, 307 ff.; D. W. Prakken, *AJP* 61, 1940, 62 ff.; also G. Daux, *Rev. arch.*, 1941, I 176 ff.; *Studies Robinson* II, 1953, 775 ff.; E. Benveniste, *Rev. Hist. des* *rél.* 134, 1947/48, 90 ff.; and in particular, P. Siewert, *Der Eid von Plataiai* (Vestigia 16), Munich 1972 (cf. K. Kinzl, *Gym.* 81, 1974, 313 ff.; cf. also A. Dreizehnter, *Gn.* 47, 1975, 379 ff.).

THE WESTERN GREEKS FROM 500-480 B.C.

SOURCES: Herodotus VI 22-24; VII 153-167; Thucydides VI 4-5; Diodorus XI 20-26; 38 (predominantly from Timaeus; see A. Scherr, *Diodors XI. Buch. Kompositions- u. Quellenstudien*, Diss. Tübingen 1933; and R. Laqueur, *RE* VI A, 1076 ff. s.v. *Timaios* no. 3); in addition the coins: cf. E. Boehringer, *Die Münzen von Syrakus*, 1929 (cf. K. Regling, *Gn.* 6, 1930, 629 ff.; H. A. Cahn, *Die Münzen der sizilischen Stadt Naxos*, Basle 1944; G. K. Jenkins, *The Coinage of Gela*, Vols. I-II, Berlin 1970. A number of numismatic questions are discussed by K. Christ, *H.* 3, 1954-55, 385 ff. (cf. the bibliographical survey, *Jb. für Numism. u. Geldgesch.* 5-6, 1954-55, 181 ff., with a graphic survey of the period of striking coins for the individual communities of Sicily, 226-228); and by H. Chantraine, "Syrakus und Leontinoi," *Jb. f. Numism. u. Geldgesch.* 8, 1957, 7 ff. (Aenesidemus, tyrant of Leontini, under Gelon).

BIBLIOGRAPHY: A Holm, *Gesch. Siziliens im Altertum* I, 1870; O. Meltzer, Gesch. der Karthager I, 1879; E. Pais, *Storia della Sicilia e della Magna Grecia* I, Turin-Palermo 1894; E. A. Freeman, *The History of Sicily from the Earliest Times* (4 vols.), Oxford 1891-1894. W. Hüttl, *Verfassungsgesch. von Syrakus. Quellen u. Forsch. auf dem Gebiet der Gesch.*, 8, Prague 1929; L. Wickert, *RE* IV A, 1483 ff. s.v. *Syrakusai*; *Rom und Karthago*, ed. J. Vogt, Leipzig 1943 (especially the contributions by F. Miltner and F. Taeger); concise: Dunbabin, *West.*, 376 ff. (Chaps. XIII and XIV); H. Berve, "Zur Herrscherstellung der Deinomeniden," in *Studies Presented to D. M. Robinson* II, 1953, 537 ff.; Vallet, *Rhég.* Also M. I. Finley, *Ancient Sicily to the Arab Conquest*, London 1968; and the relevant sections in *idem* (ed.), *Problèmes de la terre en Grèce ancienne*, Paris 1973. On the chronology: Beloch, *GG* II 2, 162 ff.; ingenious but not convincing: L. Pareti, "Due ricerche di cronologia greca," in *Entaphia in memoria de E. Pozzi*, Turin 1913 (published as *Studi siciliani ed italiotici*, Florence 1914); cf. the critique by Dunbabin, *West.*, 432 ff.

1. Berve, *GG* I², 225; Beloch, *GG* II 1, 8, with n. 2, gives a more correct appraisal of the Ionians.
2. H. Prinz, *Funde aus Naukratis*, Klio-Beih. 7, 1908, 81.
3. It was above all Th. Lenschau, *Klio* 13, 1913, 180 ff.; *RE* X, 1883 ff. s.v. *Iones*, who drew attention to the economic causes of the Ionian revolt. But, compared with these, the political causes, which were in fact the crucial factors, must not be forgotten.
4. Herod. V 28-34.
5. Cf. Beloch, *GG* II 1, 7 n. 4, who has correctly perceived the essential points. More recent attempts to portray Aristagoras as a far-sighted statesman (for instance, G. De Sanctis, "Aristagora di Mileto," in *Problemi di Storia antica*, Bari 1932, 63 ff.) range wide of the mark. Essentially correct is J. A. S. Evans, "Histiaeus and Aristagoras. Notes on the Ionian Revolt," *AJP* 84, 1963, 113-128.
6. Herod. V 36.
7. J. A. O. Larsen, "Sparta and the Ionian Revolt," *CP* 37, 1932, 136 ff.

8. H. Bengtson, *Einz.*, 41 and 49. Lemnos had been won by Miltiades in 499 or 498. For a somewhat later date (496) N. G. L. Hammond, *CQ* NS 6, 1956, 129, and J. A. S. Evans, *CP* 58, 1963, 168-170. For an earlier date (late 520's), see K. Kinzl, *Miltiades-Forschungen*, 1968, 56 ff.

9. According to Plutarch, *De Herod. malign.* 24 p. 861 b, the expedition was the answer of the Greeks to the Persian blockade of Miletus, a statement which is accepted by M. Cary, *CAH* IV, 221, but rejected by Beloch, *GG* II^2 1, 10 n. 3. But this motive is in fact improbable, for the blockade did not take place until later, provided one does not wish to follow C. F. Lehmann-Haupt, *GG*, in Gercke-Norden, 1914, 27, in assuming a "first" blockade of Miletus.

10. Herod. V 102. That the defeat is not mentioned by Charon of Lampsacus does not weigh against its historicity; cf. Meyer, *GdA* IV^2 1, 285 n. 1; but for a different view see Beloch, *GG* II 1, 11 n. 1. A. E. Raubitschek, *AJA* 44, 1940, 58 f., has connected the fragment of an inscription (*SEG* X 403) found during the American excavations in the Athenian Agora, published by J. H. Oliver, *Hesp.* 4, 1955, 53 no. 15, with the Athenians who fell in the encounter at Ephesus; but this is by no means certain.

11. The appraisal of Histiaeus by St. Heinlein, *Klio* 9, 1909, 341 ff., is much too favourable; see, against this, and correctly, H. Swoboda, *RE* VIII, 2047 ff. s.v. no. 1 (with complete documentation). See also A. Sacconi, "Istieo ed Erodoto per la storia della tiranide a Mileto," *RAAN* 44, 1969, 173 ff.

12. J. Myres, "The Battle of Lade, 494 B.C.," *Greece and Rome* 1, 1954, 50-55.

13. To date remains of archaic Greater Miletus have not been found; cf. A. v. Gerckan, "Zur Lage des archaischen Milet," *Bericht VI. Internat. Archäologenkongr. in Berlin*, 1939 (published 1940) 323 ff.; of a different view G. Kleiner, *Alt-Milet*, Frankfurt 1966; the old city had, accordingly, been built on the same site as the later one.

14. The correct version in Herod. VI 19; later tradition falsely attributed the destruction of the sanctuary to Xerxes; cf. Meyer, *GdA* III^1 309.

15. *Syll.* I^3 no. 3g; cf. Tarn, *Alex.* II, 1948, 273 n. 2.

16. Herod. VI 42 f.; cf. Beloch, *GG* II 1, 18 n. 1.

17. According to Diodorus X 25 (= Ephorus), Hecataeus is alleged to have appealed to the satrap Artaphernes in Sardis for a mild treatment of the Ionians, but this is a tradition whose trustworthiness is open to doubt.

18. Sources: Herod. VI 43 ff.; Charon of Lampsacus fr. 3; on the rôle of Mardonius cf. Junge, *Dar.*, 116 ff.

19. This was first maintained by H. Welzhofer, *Fleckeisens Jbb. f. kl. Phil.* 143, 1891, 145 ff.; and 145, 1892, 145 ff.; cf. Beloch, *GG* II 2, 84 ff.

20. Busolt, *GG* II^2, 569 f.; Meyer, *GdA* IV^2, 1, 304 n. 1; likewise, H. U. Instinsky, *Hermes* 84, 1956, 477 ff.

21. On the political situation in Athens from 500 to 490 B.C. see in particular De Sanctis, *Att.*, 361; *RF* 52, 1924, 289 ff.; E. M. Walker, *CAH* IV, 167 ff.; J. A. R. Munro, *ibid.*, 230 ff.; P. Cloché, *REA* 30, 1928, 271 ff.; Ehrenberg, *OW*, 107 ff.; M. F. McGregor Studies... Ferguson, 71 ff.; A. W. Gomme, *AJP* 65, 1944, 321 ff.

22. On him cf. F. Schachermeyr, *RE* XIX, 155 s.v. *Peisistratiden*.

23. On the beginnings of Themistocles see Ehrenberg, *OW*, 114 ff., 223 f., and A. W. Gomme, *op. cit.*, whose conclusion, however, that Themistocles did not rise to power until the eighties, is not very convincing. Themistocles was under no circumstances a *homo novus*, as Herodotus (VII 143) designates him still in 480 B.C. Cf. also J. H. Schreiner, "Thucydides I. 93 and Themistocles During the 490's," *Symbolae Osloenses* 44, 1969, 23 ff.

24. On the powers of Themistocles as archon see H. T. Wade-Gery, *BSA* 37, 1940, 263 ff. = *Essays*, 171 ff. On the date see R. J. Lenardon, *H.* 5, 1956, 401 ff. (C. W. Fornara, *H* 20, 1971, 534 ff.: he contests the archonship; cf., however, D. M. Lewis, *H.* 22, 1973, 757 f., and W. W. Dickie, *H.* 22, 1973, 758 f.); A. A. Mosshammer, *Hermes* 103, 1975, 222 ff.

25. The view held by some scholars (*inter al.*, U. v. Wilamowitz, K. J. Beloch, G. De Sanctis), that after the overthrow of the *tyrannis* the Athenians became members of the Peloponnesian *Symmachia*, is unfounded.

26. For the sources v.s.p. 438; cf. also Meyer, *GdA* III^1 321; G. De Sanctis, "Argo e i Gimneti," in *Scritti minori*, Rome 1966, 249 f.; Beloch, *GG* II 1, 14 n. 1. That the war began about 500 B.C., as maintained by Th. Lenschau, *RE* XI, 696 f.; 700, *et al.*, and by J. Wells,

lastly in *Studies in Herodotus*, 1923, 74 ff.; is to be rejected. It is nevertheless possible that the rescuing of the city of Argos by the poetess Telesilla, the "Jeanne d'Argos," belongs in this war and is therefore a historical event; cf. R. Herzog, *Ph.* 71, 1912, 1 ff.; SB.M, 1942, H. 12 (Schlussh.) 20 f.; S. Luria, "Frauenpatriotismus und Sklavenemanzipation in Argos," *Klio* 26, 1933, 211 ff; of a different view is Beloch, *GG* II 1, 14 n. 3 (aetiological legend), and M. E. Colonna, *Ann. della facoltà di lettere e filosofia dell'Univ. di Napoli* 5, 1955, 67 ff. (local legend); F. R. Willetts, *Hermes* 87, 1959, 495 ff. On Argive policy from 494 to 465 see W. G. Forrest, "Themistokles and Argos," *CQ* 54, 1960, 221 ff. (especially also on the years after 470). M. Wörrle, *Untersuchungen zur Verfassungsgesch. von Argos im 5. Jahrh. v. Chr.*, Diss. Erlangen-Nürnberg 1964, also makes some contributions.

27. Herod. VI 83; Aristotle, *Pol.* V 2.8; cf. D. Lotze, *Ch.* 1, 1971, 95 ff.

28. Conjectures in S. Luria, *PhW*, 1928, 27 ff. (ritual suicide of a 'temporary king'); A. Giusti, *AR* 10, 1929, 54 ff. (Cleomenes an epileptic); see also Th. Lenschau, *Klio* 31, 1938, 412 ff.

29. H. D. Westlake, "The Medism of Thessaly," *JHS* 56, 1936, 12 ff.

30. Thus already Beloch, *GG* II 2, 86; G. De Sanctis, *RF* NS 8, 1930, 292 ff.; H. Bengtson, SB.Bay, 1939, 1, 47 f.; cf. a different view, for instance, E. M. Walker, *CAH* IV, 259. Meyer, *GdA* IV I² 299 f., dates this event before the expedition of Mardonius, namely in the spring of 492 B.C.; but such a dating is not to be sanctioned.

31. In Pindar's sixth *Paean* the Saronic Sea is called the "Dorian"; cf. U. v. Wilamowitz, SB.B, 1908, 345 ff. On relations between Athens and Aegina see also D. Hegyi, *Acta Antiqua*, 17, 1969, 171 ff.;

32. Meyer, *GdA* IV 1², 306. The numbers of Delbrück, *Krieg.*, 46 ff., of 4000-6000, are too low. Justin's testimony (II 9), 600,000, is worthless.

33. Herod. VI 97; 118; *IG* XI 161 B 96.

34. It is difficult to judge whether the reason given by Herodotus (VI 106), that the Spartans were not permitted to take the field before the full moon, is correct (concurring, Berve, *Milt.*, 74 f.). Pöhlmann, *GG*, 120 n. 2, regards this version as a "spiteful Athenian invention," which is, however, scarcely correct. The Helot revolt related by Plato (*Laws* III 692 D; 698 E) is probably nothing more than a Spartan legend (thus also Jacoby, *FgrHist.* III, Commentary 114 ff.; 169 ff.); of a different view Fr. Frhr. Hiller v. Gaertringen and H. Lattermann, "Hira und Andania," *71. Winckelmannsprogr.*, Berlin 1911, 11, and Kiechle, *Messen.* A detailed study by H. Popp, *Die Einwirkung von Vorzeichen, Opfern und Festen auf die Kriegführung der Griechen im 5. und 4. Jahrh. v. Chr.*, Diss. Erlangen 1957, 75 ff.

35. Cf. W. Judeich, *Top.*, 120 ff. and O. Walter, *Anz. W*, 1949, no, XXII; of a different view U.v. Wilamowitz, *Aus Kydathen*, 1880, 97, and W. Dörpfeld, *Festschr. für Walter Judeich*, 1929, 1 ff.; likewise E. Kirsten, in A. Philippson, *Die griech. Landschaften* I, 3, 1952, 912.

36. The *psephisma* in Cephisodotus, in Aristotle, *Rhet.* III 1411a, cf. Demosth. XIX 303; Plut., *Quaest. conviv.* 628; cf. A. Garzetti, *Aevum* 27, 1953, 18 ff.

37. Against the view of J. A. R. Munro, *CAH* IV, 238, that the intention was to rush to Eretria's aid (which had already fallen several days before), see, correctly, Berve, *Milt.*, 76 n. 1.

38. Not in the Vrana Valley, as is assumed by H. Delbrück and K. J. Beloch.

39. Among older works, cited in Busolt, *GG* II², 560, the following may be stressed: Delbrück, *Pkr.*, 52 ff.; of more recent studies: J. Kromayer, *Drei Schlachten aus dem griech.-römischen Altertum* (Abh. S, 34,5), 1921; *Schl.* IV, 5 ff., 581 ff. (with copious bibliography); Meyer, *GdA* IV 1², 311 ff. n.; a number of further studies are cited by De Sanctis, *St. Gr.* II, 45 ff., and R. Cohen, *La Grèce et l'hellénisation du monde ant.*, ³1948, 173. Against Kromayer's interpretation see in particular H. Delbrück, "Marathon und die persische Taktik," *Klio* 17, 1921, 221 ff.; C. F. Lehmann-Haupt, "Herodotus and the Battle of Marathon," *A Miscellany Presented to J. M. MacKay*, Liverpool 1914, 97 ff.; "Herodots Arbeitsweise und die Schlacht bei Marathon," *Klio* 19, 1923, 65 ff., 309 ff. (with unverified presuppositions). Numerous theories in J. A. R. Munro, *CAH* IV, 235 ff., and in F. Schachermeyr, *HZ* 172, 1951, 1 ff. = *GRG*, 85 ff. Generally conservative is W. K. Pritchett, *Marathon*, Berkeley and Los Angeles 1960, who follows Herodotus on the battle plan; he also regards the Suda gloss cited in n. 40 as reliable; cf. *idem, Top.* I, 83 ff.; cf. N. G. L.

Hammond, "The Campaign and the Battle of Marathon," *JHS* 88, 1968, 13 ff. = *Studies*, 170 ff.; cf. A. R. Burn, *JHS* 89, 1969, 118 f., and Hammond, *Studies*, 245 ff.; A. R. Burn, *Studies . . . Fritz Schachermeyr*, Berlin 1977, 89 ff.; P. J. Bicknell, "The Command Structure and the Generals of the Marathon Campaign," *AC* 39, 1970, 427 ff.

40. As scholars were inclined to conclude from the phrase of the *Suda Lexicon, choris hippeis*; see E. Curtius, *GGA*, 1859, III 2013 ff. (cf., against him, O. Crusius, *RhM* 40, 1885, 316 ff.); cf. also F. Schachermeyr, *HZ* 160, 1939, 113 ff.; 172, 1951, 21 ff., and Hammond, *HG*, 215.

41. Correctly emphasised by, *inter al.*, Meyer, *GdA* IV 1^2, 313 n.; De Sanctis, *St. Gr.* II, 21; U. Wilcken, GG^5, 112.

42. That battle deliberations took place (A. E. Raubitschek, *AJA* 44, 1940, 58), has not been transmitted and is hardly probable.

43. The attempt by J. A. R. Munro, *CAH* IV, 233, to shift the battle back to 491 B.C., has rightly found no countenance.

44. Correctly stressed by H. Berve, *Milt.*, 79 ff. Cf. Meiggs-Lewis no. 18; and E. B. Harrison, *GRBS* 12, 1971, 5 ff.

45. Cf. Berve, *Milt.*, 92 ff. (cf. also already Schaefer, *Staats.*, 200 n. 1), whose view, that it was a private undertaking by Miltiades (thus also Prestel, *Antidem.*, 20 f.), is contested by Bengtson, *Einz.*, 50 ff.; of the same opinion O. Rubensohn, *RE* XVIII 4, 1813 ff. On the other hand, the Herodotean tradition is followed by Ehrenberg, *AW*, 137 ff.; cf. P. J. Bicknell, "The Date of Miltiades' Expedition," *AC* 41, 1972, 225 ff., and K. H. Kinzl, Miltiades' Parosexpedition in der Geschichtsschreibung, *Hermes* 104, 1976, 280 ff.

46. The documentary evidence may be found in O. W. Reinmuth, *RE* XVIII 1, 1680 s.v. *Ostrakismos*; a more recent compilation of the evidence in E. Vanderpool, *Hesp. Suppl.* 8, 1949, 394 ff. (a new ostracon of Xanthippus: A. E. Raubitschek, *AJA* 51, 1947, 257 ff.; O. Broneer, *AJA* 52, 1948, 341 ff.). E. Schweigert, *AJA* 53, 1949, 266 f.; A. Wilhelm, SB, W, 1949, 237 ff.; additional evidence in H. A. Thompson, *Hesp.* 23, 1954, 31-57. From the ostracism of 486 B.C. there are 2200 ostraca bearing the name of Megacles, about 1000 with the name of Themistocles, and a number with that of Mnesiphilus: cf. F. J. Frost, *H.* 20, 1971, 23.

47. The only source: Aristotle, *Const. Ath.* 22.5; cf. Beloch, *GG* II 1, 28 n. 1; Meyer, *GdA* IV 1^2, 321 ff.; V. Ehrenberg, *RE* XIII, 1470 ff., 1475 s.v. *Losung*; R. J. Buck, *CP* 60, 1965, 96 ff.; Fornara, *Gen.*, 11 ff.; cf. M. Pierart, "A propos de l'élection des stratèges Athéniens," *BCH* 98, 1974, 125 ff.

48. Beloch, *AP*, 280 ff.; *GG* II 1, 28 n. 1; Meyer, *GdA* IV 1^2, 326; Wilcken, GG^5, 114; Fornara, *Gen.* 28 ff.;

49. For the sources v.s.p. 438; cf. in particular Wilamowitz, *Arist.* II, 1893. 280 ff.; Beloch, *GG* II, 1, 25 n. 3; A. Andrewes, "Athens and Aegina, 510-480 B.C.," *BSA* 37. 1936-37, 1-7; important is the oracle recorded in Herod. V 89; E. M. Walker, *CAH*, 254 ff.; D. M. Leahy, *CP* 49, 1954, 232 ff., esp. 238 ff.; (Athens becoming a member of the Peloponnesian League between 493 and 491 B.C.); and N. G. L. Hammond, *H.* 4, 1955, 406 ff. (with new suggestions on the chronology: three conflicts took place: 505; 491-90; 483/2 B.C.). Similarly L. H. Jeffery, *AJP* 83, 1962, 44 ff. On the importance of Aegina see H. Winterscheidt, *Aigina. Eine Untersuchung über seine Gesellschaft und Wirtschaft*, Diss. Cologne (published Würzburg 1938); G. Welter, *Ägina*, Berlin 1938 (on both see E. Kirsten, *Gn.* 18, 1942, 289 ff.); Amit, *GSP*, 9 ff.

50. See G. B. Grundy, *Thucydides and the History of his Age*, 1941, 125 ff., who, however, places the economic motives too much in the foreground.

51. Herod. VII 144; Aristotle, *Const. Ath.* 22.7. On points of detail see A. Momigliano, *Ath.* NS 10, 1932, 247 ff.; Ehrenberg, *OW*, 225 (note to p. 126); also the work by J. Labarbe (v.s.p. 438).

52. Meyer, *GdA* 1^2, 338.

53. The programme originally envisaged the construction of 200 triremes but these were not all completed. This may explain the discrepancy between the figures given in Herod. VII 144 (200) and those in Polyaenus I 30.6, as well as those in Nepos, *Them.* 2 = Plut., *Them.* 4 (100 triremes).

54. The statement by U. Kahrstedt, *RE* V A, 1689, that Themistocles "took the tremen-

dous step to create warships as state property, doubtless the first instance of its kind in history, and at the time a completely novel idea," is refuted by Herod. VI 46 (building of warships by the Thasians); see H. Bengtson, *H.* 2, 1953/54, 485 f. = *KS*, 149-150.

55. On the Egyptian revolt see Herod. VII 1; 4; 7; on the measures of Xerxes: Herod. VII 7; on the date: C. F. Lehmann-Haupt. in Obst. *Xerx.*, VIII.

56. On the Babylonian pretenders of 484 and 482 see F. M. Th. de Liagre Böhl, *Bibliotheca Orientalis*, 1962, 110 ff.

57. Two Babylonian revolts are also assumed by Meyer, *GdA* IV 1^2, 123 n.1. Connected with the suppression of the Babylonian revolts is the so-called *Daiwa* inscription of Xerxes, published in Herzfeld, *Altp. I.*, no. 8 (cf. in particular, R. Hartmann, *OLZ*, 1938, 158 ff.); but at the crucial point the interpretation is not as yet certain.

58. E. Struck, "Der Xerxeskanal am Athos," *NJb*, 1907, II, 115 ff.; Obst, Xerx., 45 f.

59. Ephor. fr. 186; Diod. XI 1; 20; (the silence of Herodotus is not a decisive counter argument); concurring, *inter al.*, Busolt, *GG* II^2 788; and Meyer, *GdA* IV 1^2, 355 n. (other scholars are cited in Obst, *Xerx.*, 41 f.); opposed, *inter al.*, Ed. Schwartz, K. J. Beloch, U. Wilcken, H. Berve. Cf. also K. Meister, "Das persisch-karthagische Bündnis von 481 v. Chr.," *H.* 19, 1970, 607 ff.

60. Herod. VII 6; cf. H. Diels, SB.B, 1891, 396 ff.; Bengtson, *Einz.*, 26 n. 3.

61. *Laterculi Alexandrini*, ed. H. Diels, SB.B, 1904. For the route after the bridges, see D. Müller, "Von Doriskos nach Therme. Der Weg des Xerxes-Heeres durch Thrakien und Ostmakedonien," *Ch.* 5, 1975, 1 ff.

62. Of a pioneer character were the researches of Delbrück, *Pkr.*, 137 ff. (45,000-55,000 combatants). In *Krieg.* I^3, Delbrück only assumes 20,000, a figure which is much too low.

63. E.v. Fischer, *Klio* 25, 1931, 289 ff.

64. Sir Frederick Maurice, *JHS* 50, 1930, 210 ff.

65. A Köster, *Seewesens*, 97 ff. On the other hand, W. W. Tarn, *JHS* 28, 1908, 202 ff., and Beloch, *GG* II 2, 69 ff., think only in terms of about 500-600 units.

66. Herod. VII 140 and 141. A defense of the Delphic oracle in H. Berve, *Gestaltende Kräfte der Antike*, ^{2}1966, 21 ff.

67. According to P. Treves, "Herodotus, Gelon, and Pericles," *CP* 36, 1941, 321 ff., the Greeks never sent an embassy to Gelon, a view which J. A. O. Larsen, *CP* 39, 1944, 151, rightly opposes.

68. Pind. fr. 109; cf. Polyb. IV 31.

69. Cf. Herod. VII 132; 145; 148; 172; Plut., *Them.* 6; on the recalling of the exiles: Aristotle, *Const. Ath.* 22.8; Plut., *Arist.* 8.

70. Herod. VII 132; cf. U.v. Wilamowitz, SB.B, 1927, no. XIX, 164; H. W. Parke, *Hermathena* 72, 1948, 82 ff.

71. Schaefer, *Staatsf.*, 67, incorrectly regards the character of the unification as "nonpolitical." On the "*Symmachia* see E. Bickermann, *Mélanges F. de Visscher* III, 1950, 99 ff.

72. Themistocles must doubtless have been an Attic *strategos*; whether he somehow possessed plenipotentiary powers is, in spite of F. Miltner, *Klio* 31, 1938, 222 n. 2 (on the basis of Plut., *Arist.* 8), doubtful.

73. Herod. VII 172 f. Incorrectly held in doubt by G. De Sanctis, *RF* NS 8, 1930, 339 ff.

74. Beloch, *GG* II 1, 43, completely arbitrarily increased the number to 10,000 hoplites, at whose side he placed an equal number of light-armed troops! The statement of Ephorus (in Diod. XI 4), that Leonidas was convinced of his death from the outset, is unhistorical. The oracle in Herodotus (VII 220) turns out to be a *vaticinium ex eventu*.

75. The sources for both battles: Herod VII 201 ff., VIII 1 ff. (cf. Pritchett, *Top.* II, 12 ff.); Diod. XI 4 ff. (Ephorus); see also the previous note. To be connected with the battle of Artemisium is a fragment of the Hannibal historian Sosylus, preserved on a papyrus in the Würzburg collection and published by U. Wilcken, *Hermes* 41, 1906, 103 ff.; also in Bilabel, ***P. Kleinform***, 29 ff. no. 10; and Jacoby, *FgrHist.* no. 176. The account has been incorrectly connected with the Ionian revolt by F. Rühl, *RhM* 61, 1906, 352 ff.; F. Bilabel, *op. cit.*; Jacoby, *op. cit.*; while J. A. R. Munro, *CAH* IV, 289, even thinks in terms of a naval battle in the West, at Iberian Artemisium. The fact that the Sosylus papyrus does not coincide with Herodotus is no conclusive counter-argument (cf. Köster, *Seewesens*, 81 ff., 92 ff.); see also

H. Bengtson, *H.* 3, 1953-1954, 301 ff. (= *KS*, 141 ff.) (as compared with P. Bosch-Gimpera, S. Mazzarino, *et al.*).

76. On the battle of Thermopylae see L. and F. Harmening, in Kromayer, *Schl.* IV, 21 ff., moreover S. Marinatos (v.s.p. 430), and Ernst Meyer, *AM* 71, 1956, 101 ff.; further the detailed study by A. Daskalakis, *Problèmes historiques autour de la bataille des Thermopyles.* Paris 1962. In this study one misses the work by A. Köster (see previous note), who has clearly shown the connection between the battles at Thermopylae and Artemisium. Critical of Daskalakis is G. B. Philipp, *Gym.* 75, 1968, 1-45; his own views, however, are not very convincing; they too betray a failure to understand the tactical course of the battle. Herodotus' account has been confirmed by archaeological excavations. On the date see J. Labarbe, *BCH* 78, 1954, 1-21; according to him the battle took place from 1-3 August 480. Sirius is the star mentioned in Polyaenus I 32.2. The presuppositions of his argument, however, are by no means certain. See also J. A. S. Evans, *H.* 18, 1969, 389 ff., and R. Hope Simpson, *Px.* 26, 1972, 1 ff., who hold that the rôle of the fleet was subordinate to that of the army. See also Pritchett, *Top.* I, 71 ff.; II, 12 ff.

77. Theories spun out in great detail by J. A. R. Munro, *CAH* IV, 295 ff.; cf. W. K. Pritchett, *AJA* 62, 1958, 203 ff., and A. R. Burn, in *Studies... Fritz Schachermeyr*, Berlin 1977, 98 ff.

78. The epigram transmitted under the name of Simonides (Herod. VII 228, cf. R. Heinze, *NJb* 35, 1915, 6), signifies unqualified obedience. As opposed to the attempts of F. Rühl (for instance, *Jbb. f. Philologie* 127, 1883, 746 ff.) and (Beloch, *GG* II 2, 91 ff.), Meyer (*GdA* IV 1^2, 361) and, in a detailed study, F. Miltner (Pro Leonida, *Klio* 28, 1935, 228 ff.) have set the tactical importance of Leonidas' feat in its proper light. Otherwise the Spartan king only performed his duty, as the political system demanded of each citizen as a matter of course.

79. Cf. the view in Pind. fr. 77 (in Plut., *Them.* 8 and *De gloria Athen.* 7); Sim. fr. 1-3; Aristoph., *Lysis*, 1250 ff.

80. That the Persians undertook a plundering expedition against Delphi but that the gods spared the sanctuary, is a legend, although told in good faith by Herodotus (VIII 35 ff.); cf. P. Roussel, "Hérodote et l'expédition des Perses contre Delphes," *REA* 29, 1927, 337 ff.

81. The Acropolis was fortified by a makeshift palisade (cf. O. Walter, *Anz. W*, 1952, no. VII, 97 ff.); that was the "wooden wall" behind which the Athenians on the injunction of the Delphic oracle (Herod, VII 141) were to defend themselves, and not the fleet as Themistocles interpreted the response (W. Schaller, *Themistokles und das Orakel von der hölzernen Mauer,* Gym.-Progr. Freiberg/Sa., 1930). According to Schaller and according to J. Labarbe, *La loi navale de Thémistocle*, 1957, 109 ff., Themistocles inspired the oracle.

82. Aeschylus (*Persae* 339) states that there were 310 ships, Herodotus (VIII 48; 82) a total of 378; Thucydides (I 74) maintains that of the 400 vessels, the Athenians supplied somewhat less than two thirds, which is an exaggeration. The Persian navy had meanwhile lost a considerable number of its 1207 ships, but was still much greater than that of the Greeks (incorrect is Aesch., *Persae* 341 ff.).

83. The authenticity of the message of Themistocles is contested by, *inter al.*, A. Gercke, *NJb* 31, 1913, 617 ff., and Beloch, *GG* II 2, 119, but accepted by, *inter al.*, Wilcken, *GG*, 116, and F. Miltner, *Klio* 31, 1938, 242 n. 2, also by Köster, *Seewesens*, 110, n. 1.

84. The sources for the battle of Salamis: Aesch., *Persae* 249 ff. (the so-called messenger's speech); Herod. VIII 75 ff.; Diod. XI 17-19 (Ephorus): Ctesias fr. 13; Plut., *Them.* 24 f., *Arist.* 9; the epitaph of the Corinthians who died at Salamis, Meiggs-Lewis, no. 24. Of older studies (cited up to 1895 in Busolt, *GG* II^2 700 n.l), the following may be stressed: N. Wecklein, *Themistokles und die Seeschlacht bei Salamis*, SB.M, 1892, 2 ff.; A. Bauer, "Die Seeschlacht bei Salamis," *Öst. Jhh.* 4, 1901, 90 ff.; H Raase, *Ein Beitr. z. Darstellung der Schlacht bei Salamis*, Rostock 1904. These are all rendered out of date by the discussion of W. Keil, in J. Kromayer, *Schl.* IV, 64 ff. Since Keil's contribution the following important studies have also appeared: A. Wilhelm, *Zur Topographie der Schlacht bei Salamis*, SB.W, 211, 1929; F. Miltner, "Der taktische Aufbau der Schlacht bei Salamis," *Öst Jhh.* 26, 1930, 115 ff. (basic); C. Mackenzie, *Marathon and Salamis*, London 1934; Ph. E. Legrand, "A propos de l'énigme de Salamine," *REA* 38, 1936, 55 ff.; J. Keil, *Hermes* 73, 1938, 329 ff.; A. Masaracchia, "La battaglia di

Salamina in Erodoto," *Helikon* 9-10, 1969-70, 68 ff. G. Roux, "Eschyle, Hérodote, Diodore, Plutarque racontent la bataille de Salamine," *BCH* 98, 1974, 51-94. The view held by H. Delbrück and G. Zinn, *Die Schlacht bei Salamis*, Diss. Berlin 1914, that the battle took place within the bay of Eleusis, has not proven correct; likewise the energetic arguments of K. J. Beloch for the Psyttaleia-Hagios Georghios hypothesis (for instance, *Klio* 8, 1908, 477 ff; 11, 1911, 431 ff.; 13, 1913, 128 ff.; *GG* II 2, 106 ff.) did not prove successful. He is, however, followed by N. G. L. Hammond, *JHS* 76, 1956, 32-56 with supplement *JHS* 77, 1957, 311 = *Studies*, 251 ff. See also P. H. Wallace, "Psyttaleia and the Trophies of the Battle of Salamis," *AJA* 73, 1969, 293 ff. Valuable is E. Meyer, *RE Suppl.* XIV, 566 ff., s.v. *Psyttaleia*.

85. Cf. Diod. XI 17, also Herod. VIII 76; Aesch., *Persae* 368, a statement which Meyer, GdA IV² 1, 368 f., and F. Miltner (see previous note), correctly regard as historical, whereas it is rejected by W. Keil, in Kromayer, *Schl.* IV, 73 ff. W. Marg, *Hermes* 60, 1962, 116 ff., is a regression; cf. H. Bengtson, *Ch*, 1, 1971, 89 ff. (= *KS*, 135 ff.)

86. This is revealed both by Herodotus (VIII 86) and by Diodorus (XI 8.4).

87. Cf. A. Köster, *Seewesens*, 97 ff.

88. The attempt by G. Guratzsch, *Klio* 19, 1925, 62 ff., to extol the merits of the Spartan king Eurybiades as against Themistocles was a failure.

89. Beloch, *GG* II 1, 51, is completely incorrect in minimising the achievements of the Greeks; Xerxes allegedly achieved "great things" in the campaign of 480 B.C., and the few hundred ships which he lost were scarcely missed.

90. Herod, VIII 108 ff. (the details are not historical).

91. Herod. VIII 110; cf. Thuc. I 137.4; Plut., *Them.* 16. Rejected by, *inter al.*, N. Wecklein, *Die Tradition der Perserkriege*, 297, and A. Bauer, *Themistokles*, 21; 49; Beloch, *GG* II 2, 148, also contests it. On the other hand, the message is regarded as authentic by M. Duncker, *Abh. aus der griech. Gesch.*, 1887, 59, and Busolt, *GG* II², 710.

92. Herod. VIII 126; 129.

93. On the Babylonian revolt see Herod. I 183; Strabo XVI 738; Arr. VII 17; see in general above 97 f.

94. Mardonius even held out to the Athenians the prospect of the extension of Attic territory, and in addition to this their autonomy and the restoration of the temples which had been destroyed: Herod. VIII 140. On the mission of the Macedonian king see Geyer, *Mak.* 43 f.

95. On this and the following see Herod. IX 1-13. On the devastation of Attica cf. still Aesch., *Persae* 810 ff., cf. P. Perdrizet, "Le témoigne d'Eschyle sur le sac d'Athènes par les Perses," *REG* 34, 1921, 57 ff., also Judeich, *Top.*, 70.

96. The military strength is based on the estimates of Meyer, *GdA* IV² 1, 384 f. The figures of Herodotus (IX 28 ff.) are worthless; for a critique see K. J. Beloch, "Das griechische Heer bei Platää," *Jb. f. kl. Phil.* 137, 1888, 324 ff. (cf. *GG* II 2, 74 ff.): at the most 25,000 hoplites and as many light-armed troops. H. Delbrück, who numbers both armies at 20,000 respectively, exaggerates in the negative direction and, as he is wont, reduces the numbers too greatly, in particular of the Persian army.

97. The sources: Herod. IX 15-85 (according to eye-witness accounts, with a strong pro-Athenian bias); Diod. XI 30 f.; Plut., *Arist.* 11-19. On the topography: G. B. Grundy, *The Topography of the Battle of Plataeae*, London 1894; H. B. Wright, *The Campaign of Plataeae*, Diss. New Haven 1904; A. Boucher, "La bataille de Platée d'après Hérodote," *Rev. arch.*, 1915, II 257 ff. (with a negative view of the achievement of Pausanias); basic now is: E. Ufer, in Kromayer, *Schl.* IV, 107 ff., cf. E. Kirsten, "Athener und Spartaner in der Schlacht bei Plataiai," *RhM* 86, 1937, 50 ff. (with important new conclusions). New theories in A. Mele, *Annali della facoltà die lettere e filosopfia dell'Università di Napoli* 5, 1955, 5 ff., W. K. Pritchett, *AJA* 61, 1957, 9-28; *Top.* I, 103 ff.; A. E. Wardman, *H.* 8, 1959, 49 ff., and A. R. Burn, *Studies . . . Fritz Schachermeyr*, Berlin 1977, 93 ff.

98. Cf. Herod. IX 56, cf. E. Kirsten, *op. cit.*, 61 ff.

99. Cf. Herod. IX 64, also Aesch., *Persae* 816 f. (prophecy of Darius).

100. Honours of the Plataeans: Thuc. II 71; 74; III 58; 68.

101. Sources for the battle of Mycale: Herod. VIII 131 ff.; IX 90 ff.; Ephor. in Diod. XI 34 ff., whose statement, that the battle of Mycale took place on the same day as the battle

of Plataea, does not warrant countenance; this is one of the popular unhistorical synchronisms, of which there is no lack in Greek history. Cf. below n. 114. On the topography: T. Wiegand, *Priene*, Berlin 1904, Chap. I.

102. The Greek fleet numbered 110 ships, whereas the land forces cannot have been more than 4000-5000. The chief contingent of the Persians, to wit the Phoenicians, had already been discharged and sent home. The figures put forward by Herodotus and Diodorus are greatly exaggerated.

103. Herod. IX 99; 104; 107. The Milesians, it is alleged, especially distinguished themselves.

104. Thuc. I 89.2; cf. F. Leo, *Verhandlungen der 32. Philologen-Versammlung*, Wiesbaden 1877, 60 ff.; Highby, *ED*, 40 ff.

105. Plut., *Them.* 20.3; cf. H. Bengtson, *Eranos* 49, 1951, 85-92 (= *KS*, 151 ff.); R. Flacelière, *REA* 55, 1953, 19 ff.

106. The date according to Diod. XI 48.2; cf. Beloch, *GG* II 2, 190 ff., and F. R. Wüst, *Symbolae Osloenses* 30, 1953, 64 ff. [477/6 B.C.]. For 471 B.C.: M. Sordi, *Rend. Ist. Lomb., Sciense e lett., ser. lett.* 86, 1953, 310 ff.; for still a different view see Meyer, *GdA* IV^2 1, 489: 469 B.C., but this is a date which is just as improbable as 471 B.C. The sources: Herod. VI 71; Plut., *De Herod. malign.* 21.2 p. 859 D; Paus. III 7.9; cf. F. Heichelheim, *Z. f. Num.*, 1930, 16 ff.

107. Herod. VI 72 is, as a typical *legomenon,* devoid of historical value (differently Meyer, *GdA* IV^2 1, 490).

108. Plut., *Arist.* 21; R. v. Pöhlmann, *GG*, 133 n. 3, and Meyer, *GdA* IV^2 1, 391 n.l, have contested its authenticity; cf. also already Busolt, *GG* II^2, 741 n. 2, at the end; see, on the other hand, however, J. A. O. Larsen, *CP* 28, 1933, 262 ff.; *HSCP* 51, 1940, 177 ff.; against this, again, I. Calabi, *Ricerche sui rapporti tra le poleis*, Florence 1953, 62 ff., correctly.

109. On Gelon see B. Niese, *RE* VII, 1007 ff. s.v. no. 3, also L. Wickert, *RE* IV A, 1484 f. s.v. *Syrakusai*. According to L. Pareti (v.s.p. 440). Gelon did not come to power in Gela until 485 B.C., a date which is followed by, *inter al.*, R. Hackforth, *CAH* IV, 369 f., and by Vallet, *Rhég.*, 346 ff.

110. M. Scheele, *Str.*, 23 ff.

111. The early history of relations between Dancle and Rhegium are illustrated by an inscription found on a booty shield at Olympia, *Dankleioi Rhegion* (E. Kunze and H. Schleif, *2. Olympia-Bericht* [excavations of the year 1937/38] 69 f.), which belongs in the first years of the fifth century; cf. Vallet, *Rhég.*, 335 n.

112. Thuc. VI 4; Herod. VII 164 is incorrect; erroneous is Beloch, *GG* II 1, 69 n. 2. Cf. in general C. H. Dodd, "The Samians at Zankle-Messana," *JHS* 28, 1908, 56-76; Vallet *Rhég.*, 344 ff.; on the coins: H. E. Gielow, *Die Silberprägung von Dankle-Messana (etwa 525-396 v. Chr.* [extending only down to 490 B.C.]), Diss. Munich 1931 (*Mitt. Bayer. Num. Gesellsch.* 48, 1930, 1-54), and E. S. G. Robinson, "Rhegion, Zankle-Messena and the Samians," *JHS* 66, 1946, 13-20.

113. Correctly emphasised by Dunbabin, *West.*, 422 f. V.s.p. 98.

114. Herod. VII 165-167; Diod. XI 20 ff. (= Timaeus); Polyaenus I 27.2; 28. According to Herodotus (and Aristotle, *Poet.* 23), the battle was simultaneous with the battle of Salamis, according to Diodorus (= Timaeus), with the battle of Thermopylae. These specific statements are of no historical value, rather do they belong to the realm of "synchronistic legend," which R. Henning, *Zeitschr. f. Psychol.*, 1942, 289 ff., has documented with many examples from ancient and modern times.

115. Cf. the inscriptions *Syll.* I^3 34, cf. H. Pomtow, *Die Weihgeschenke der Deinomeniden*, SB.M, 1907, 282 ff.; F. Courby, *Fouilles de Delphes* II, *La terrasse du temple*, fasc. 3, Paris 1927, 349 ff.; Dunbabin, West., 430.

116. Pyth. I 75 ff.

7 FIFTY CRUCIAL YEARS

SOURCES AND BIBLIOGRAPHY: A detailed summary of the sources for the Pentecontaetia may be found in, *inter al.*, Busolt, *GG* III 1, 3 ff.; G. Hill, *Sources for Greek History Between the Persian and the Peloponnesian Wars*, revised edition by R. Meiggs and A. Andrewes, Oxford 1951, and in *CAH* V, 498 ff. Two Athenian monuments from the period of the Pentecontaetia deserve mention: the Themistoclean wall, and the site of Athenian war graves, lying by itself in the outer Cerameicus where it was set up in the form of an honorary cemetery from the time of Cimon; basic on this is A. Brückner, *AM* 35, 1910, 183 ff.; concise, Judeich, *Top.*, 404 ff. (with additional bibliography); K. Kübler, *Kerameikos* VII. *Die Nekropole von der Mitte des 6. bis Ende des 5. Jh.*, Berlin 1974. That the custom of a state burial for the fallen in the Cerameicus probably did not take place until after the defeat of the Athenians at Drabescus in 464 B.C.—and not a decade earlier—has been argued by F. Jacoby, "Patrios Nomos, State Burial in Athens and the Public Cemetery in the Kerameikos," *JHS* 64, 1944 (published 1946), 37 ff. = *Abh. z. griech. Geschichtschreibung*, 1956, 260 ff. The cemetery contained a large number of mass graves with inscriptional casualty lists (*IG* I^2 928 ff.); cf. J. Mälzer, *Verluste u. Verlustlisten im griechischen Altertum bis auf die Zeit Alexanders d. Gr.*, Diss. Jena 1912, 62 ff.; D. W. Bradeen, *The Athenian Agora* XVII. *Inscriptions. The Funerary Monuments*, Princeton, N. J., 1974.

The inscriptional evidence assumes paramount importance for this period which is sparse in literary sources. The Attic documents on stone (for the period to 403/2 B.C.) have been assembled in *IG* I^2, 1924, edited by Fr. Frhr. Hiller von Gaertringen (to a large degree rendered out of date by reason of new discoveries); the supplement urgently required for years has now been published in *SEG* X; it also contains the many recent finds of the Americans in the Athenian Agora, on which reports have been carried by *Hesp.* since 1932; see now also B. D. Meritt and J. S. Traill, *The Athenian Agora* XV. *Inscriptions. The Athenian Councillors,* Princeton, N.J., 1974: Of Chrestomathiae, the following may be mentioned: *Syll.* I^3 nos. 36 ff.; Tod I; Meiggs-Lewis.

The so-called "Tribute Lists of the Attic Maritime League" form a group by themselves. They constitute the calculations of the *hellenotamiai* concerning the amounts paid over to the Treasure of Athena (1/60, a mina per talent), from 454/3 B.C.—the year in which the League Treasury was transferred from Delos to Athens—with lacunae to 406/5 B.C. They are available in *ATL* I-IV. (Cf. also Meiggs-Lewis no. 39.) Of individual documents the following may be singled out: the Attic law governing the standardisation of coinage, weights and measures in the Maritime League, which has been published, together with new fragments from Cos, by M. Segre, "La legge ateniese sull'unificazione della moneta," *Clara Rhodos* 9, 1938, 151 ff.; cf. *IG* XII *Suppl.* 215 (add. no.

480). This law undoubtedly falls in the year 449 B.C. (B. D. Meritt, among others), but later datings have also been attempted (415 B.C.: Th. Reinach, H. Schaefer, *Hermes* 74, 1939, 253 ff.); for the middle of the 20's: E. Erxleben, v. *infra* 455); on the problematic aspects see, for instance, J. Pouilloux, *AC* 22, 1953, 39. It is also printed, with bibliography, in *ATL* II, 1949, 61 ff.

A great deal of light is shed on the internal conflicts in Athens by the many ostraca which, inscribed with the names of Athenian statesmen (Themistocles, Thucydides [son of Melesias], Pericles, *et al.*), attest that ostracism was being implemented; a survey in O. W. Reinmuth, *RE* XVIII 2, 1678 (covering the finds up to 1939; more up to date information is provided by the epigraphical reports in *REG* and *JHS*). Additional ostraca may be found in the third volume of *Kerameikos*, 1941. By 1970 about 6500 ostraca had been found. A large number of ostraca recently discovered in the Cerameicus of Athens (allegedly several thousand) also have not been published. Cf. meanwhile, however, R. Thomsen, *The Origin of Ostracism*, 1972.

From the number of epigrams preserved on inscriptions (cf. Fr. Frhr. Hiller von Gaertringen, *Hist. griech. Epigramme*, 1926), the following may be cited: the epigram concerning those who fell at Eion (Hiller v. Gaertringen, *op. cit.*, no. 34; cf. F. Jacoby, *Hesp.* 14, 1945, 185 ff.); one concerning the battle of Tanagra in 457 B.C. (Tod I^2 no. 27); another concerning the Athenian expedition against Megara in 446 B.C. (*ibid.*, no. 41); and another concerning the Athenians who fell at Coroneia in 447 B.C. (W. Peek, *Hermes* 68, 1933, 353 ff.; C. M. Bowra, *CQ* 32, 1938, 80 ff.; K. Reinhardt, *Hermes* 73, 1938, 234 ff.; A. Cameron, *Harv. Theol. Rev.*, 1940, 97 ff.); a number may also be found in W. Peek, *Griech. Versinschriften* I, 1955; cf. also in general, H. T. Wade-Gery, "Classical Epigrams and Epitaphs," *JHS* 53, 1933, 71 ff. See also P. Friedlaender and H. B. Hoffleit, *Epigrammata*, Berkeley and Los Angeles 1948.

For Hellenic history from the end of the campaign by Xerxes to the beginning of the Peloponnesian War the account by Thucydides in the Introduction of his *History* (Book I 89-138) is basic, although it may not be included among the primary sources (cf. the Commentary by Gomme, *Comm. Thuc.* I; on composition: H. D. Westlake, "Thucydides and the Pentecontaetia," *CQ* 49, 1955, 53-67 = *Essays*, 39-60); on the date of composition (pre-banishment, 424/3 B.C.): F. E. Adcock, *JHS* 71, 1951, 2 ff.). In these chapters Thucydides attempts to show how the power of Athens rose and how in the Pentecontaetia the Spartan-Athenian conflict came about and how it led to the Peloponnesian War. The nature of his sources and the personal attitude of Thucydides determine the one-sidedness of the treatment. Thus a number of important historical events, including the Peace of Callias (449 B.C.) and the Athenian enterprises in the North and West, are not even mentioned (cf. for details, A. W. Gomme, *Comm. Thuc.*, I, 365 ff.). On the other hand, he gives a detailed account of the building of the Themistoclean walls, the founding of the Attic Maritime League and the end of Themistocles and Pausanias.

LITERARY PRIMARY SOURCES: The growing interest in the leading personalities of the time became reflected in memoirs; an idea of their character is given by the fragments of the "Travel Reminiscences" by Ion of Chios (about 490 to approximately 421 B.C.) (the fragments have been collected by A. v. Blumenthal, *Ion von Chios*, Stuttgart 1939; cf. F. Jacoby, "Some Remarks on Ion of Chios," *CQ* 41, 1947, 1 ff.). To be placed in the category of political pamphlets is that by Stesimbrotus of Thasos (published after 430 B.C.), a contemporary of Cimon and Pericles, bearing the title "On Themistocles, Thucydides (i.e. Thucydides son of Melesias) and Pericles" (Jacoby, *FgrHist.* no. 107; cf. Ad. Schmidt, *Das Perikleische Zeitalter*, I 183 ff., II, *passim*, who, however, greatly exaggerates the importance of the pamphlet as a source for later historiography; see for the opposite view, U.v. Wilamowitz, *Hermes* 12, 1877, 361 ff.; Busolt, *GG* III 1, 7 ff.; R. Laqueur, *RE* III A, 2465 ff. s.v.). The work of Stesimbrotus, a document of passionate hatred on the part of the suppressed members of the Maritime League against the leading statesmen of Athens, deserves particular attention as reflecting the mood from the last years of Pericles. F. Schachermeyr, *Stesimbrotos und seine Schrift über die Staatsmänner*, SB.W 247,5, 1965 = *GRG*, 151 ff., has attempted to prove that the pamphlet is non-political in character. The verses of the would-be poet Timocreon of Ialysus (on Rhodes), directed against Themistocles (E. Diehl, *Anthol. lyr.* II 148; a further fragment is recorded in *PSI* XI, no. 1221, 17), sprang from personal hatred. See, on Timocreon, also H. B. Mattingly, in *Studies... Fritz Schachermeyr*, Berlin 1977, 231 ff.

Attic tragedy did not discuss political themes. It is an exception that Aeschylus in his *Eumenides*, performed in 458 B.C., extolled the Areopagus which had been denuded of its political powers by the constitutional reform of Ephialtes. But the politics of the day were the very soil for comedy. The leading statesmen and demagogues became the targets of the comic poets, and in the Pentecontaetia it was especially Pericles. Cratinus in particular took the lead in discussing political issues on the stage, from about 455 B.C., and in doing so did not hesitate to launch attacks against statesmen of his native city (Schmid, *GGL* I 4, 1946, 9 ff.). Comedy must be treated with considerable caution as a historical source (cf. W. Vischer, *Über die Benutzung der alten Komödie als gesch. Quelle*, Basle 1840 = *Kl. Schr.* I, Leipzig 1877, 459 ff.; H. Müller-Strübing, *Aristophanes und die historische Kritik*, Leipzig 1873), although it pertinently reflects the oscillations in public opinion, above all during the Peloponnesian War, to which all extant comedies belong (v.i.p. 464).

LITERARY SECONDARY SOURCES. Of the later historical works, tradition exerted the most enduring influence on the voluminous universal history of the Isocratean Ephorus. Not only does Diodorus (XI 37-XII 28) go back to Ephorus, but the following too rest essentially on him: Pompeius Trogus (in Justin II 15) and the relevant sections in the *Lives* of Themistocles (chaps. 6-9) and Aristeides (2-3.1) from the pen of Cornelius Nepos; a direct fragment from Ephorus came to light in *P. Oxy.* XIII

1610 (Jacoby, *FgrHist.* no. 70, 191), whose contents partly overlap with Diod. XI 56 ff. (According to T. W. Africa, *AJP* 83, 1962, 86 ff., on the other hand, the connection with Ephorus is not certain.) On a far higher level than Ephorus are the *Philippica* of Theopompus of Chios (born c. 380 B.C.), in which the unconcealed antipathy of the aristocrat towards the Attic democracy speaks out from the great excursus on the Attic demagogues (Themistocles, Cimon, Cleon, Hyperbolus) in Book X of the *Philippica* (Jacoby, *FgrHist.* no. 115, 85-100); it must therefore be used with considerable caution as a historical source.

An all but insoluble problem in the study of the sources, finally, is posed by Plutarch's *Lives* of Cimon and Pericles. Recent research (cf. *supra* 436 f.) does not take us essentially beyond Meyer's analysis of Cimon's biography (*Forsch.* II, 1 ff.; cf. Kaerst, *GH* I^3, 525 ff.). A number of good observations on Plutarch may be found in Gomme, *Comm. Thuc.* I, 54 ff.; and in E. Meinhardt, *Perikles bei Plutarch*, Diss. Frankfurt a.M. 1957.

The loss of almost all the atthidographic literature makes for a particularly grave situation; cf. Jacoby, *Att.* A remnant is Aristotle's *Constitution of Athens* (chaps. 23-27), an oligarchically orientated account, giving only a very sketchy outline, and indeed not free of serious errors.

The papyrus finds have not appreciably increased the historiographic evidence. The "Anonymous Argentinensis" (published by Br. Keil, 1901; cf. H. T. Wade-Gery and B. D. Meritt, *Hesp.* 26, 1957, 163 ff.) is no epitome of events of the Pentecontaetia, but an excerpt from a commentary on the oration of Demosthenes against Androtion (U. Wilcken, *Hermes* 42, 1907, 374 ff.), or it consists of chapter headings of this oration (R. Laqueur, *Hermes* 43, 1908, 220 ff.). The Geneva Papyrus on the lawsuit of Pheidias (J. Nicole, *Le procès de Phidias dans les chronique d'Apollodore*, 1910) is also one of the many commentaries on orations in antiquity (see W. Judeich, *Hermes* 60, 1925, 40 ff., with the earlier bibliography).

The chronology of the Pentecontaetia is in very poor state. Gomme, *Comm. Thuc.* I, 389 ff., has cogently argued for the reliability of the few dates proffered by Thucydides (cf. also P. Deane, *Thucydides' Dates 465-431 B.C.*, 1972). Scholars have been very critical—and rightly so—of the chronology of Diodorus, the certainty of which is only apparent (cf. Busolt, *GG* III 1, 15 ff.; and W. Kolbe, "Diodors Wert für die Geschichte der Pentekontaëtie," *Hermes* 72, 1937, 241 ff.; incorrect: Beloch, *GG* II 2, 180 ff.). Partly problematic are the statements in *ATL* III, 175 ff.; 298 ff.; see, on the other hand, N. G. L. Hammond, *H.* 4, 1955, 396 ff.

BIBLIOGRAPHY: In addition to the general histories of Greece (by G. Busolt, K. J. Beloch, G. Glotz, H. Berve, G. De Sanctis, F. Schachermeyr), the *GdA* IV^2 1 by Meyer and Vol. V. of *CAH*, the following may be cited from the great number of specific investigations (a bibliography is given by De Sanctis, *St. Gr.* II, 71 ff.; 140 ff.; *idem, Per.*, 279 ff.; cf. A.

Andrewes, "Modern Work on the History of Athens, 478-403 B.C.," *Didaskalos* 4, 1972, 155 ff.): Beloch, *AP*; U.v. Wilamowitz-Moellendorff, *Arist.* I and II; De Sanctis, *Att.*; A.v. Domaszewski, *Die attische Politik in der Zeit der Pentekontaëtie*, SB. H, 1924/25, Abh. 4 (but see H. Berve, *PhW*, 1926, 856 ff.); F. Taeger, *Ein Beitr. z. Gesch. d. Pentekontaëtie*, Stuttgart 1932; G. Zeilhofer, *Sparta, Delphoi und die Amphiktyonen im 5. Jh. v. Chr.*, Diss. Erlangen 1959 (published 1961), 34 ff.; K. Wickert, *Der peloponnesische Bund von seiner Entstehung bis zum Ende des archidamischen Krieges*, Diss. Erlangen-Nürnberg 1961, 52 ff.; I. Hahn, "Aspekte der spartanischen Aussenpolitik im 5. Jh.," *Acta Antiqua* 17, 1969, 285 ff.; the relevant sections in J. K. Davies, *Athenian Propertied Families, 600-300 B.C.*, Oxford 1971; see also R. Meiggs, *The Athenian Empire*, Oxford 1972 (cf. V. Ehrenberg, *Gn.* 45, 1973, 669 ff.); Will, *MGr.* I. *Le Ve siècle (510-403)*; W. Schuller, *Die Herrschaft der Athener im ersten attischen Seebund*, Berlin New York 1974; and F. Schachermeyr, "Sparta und Athen nach den Perserschlachten," in *GRG*, 139 ff., and especially, *idem, Die frühe Klassik der Griechen*, 1966. On the sources: J. H. Schreiner, *Artistotle and Perikles*, Oslo 1968.

THE FOUNDING OF THE ATTIC MARITIME LEAGUE. THE ERA OF CIMON

SOURCES: Thucydides I 89 ff.; 97 ff.; Diod. XI 39 ff.; 44 ff.; 60 ff.; 70 f.; Plutarch, *Them.* 21; *Arist.* 23-24; *Cimon* 4-14. Of the inscriptions, the Erythrae decree is the most important (cf. H. Bengtson, *Staatsv.* II, no. 134); the dating, however, oscillates between 470 and 450 B.C., and therefore the decree may only be regarded with reservations as being characteristic of internal conditions in the Maritime League (the dating to the year 453/2 B.C. in *ATL* II, 1949, 54 ff., is without guarantee).

BIBLIOGRAPHY: From the large number of modern studies (assembled in Busolt, *Gr. St.* II, 1337 ff., especially 1343 n. 1 and 1360, and in De Sanctis, *Per.*, 280 ff.), the following may be selected as particularly important: U. Köhler, *Urkunden u. Untersuchungen zur Gesch. des delisch-attischen Bundes*, Abh. B, 1869, 150 ff.; A. Kirchhoff, "Der delische Bund im ersten Dezennium seines Bestehens," *Hermes* 11, 1876, 1 ff.; F. Leo, "Die Entstehung des delisch-attischen Bundes," *Verhdl. d. XXXII. Versammlung deutscher Philologen in Wiesbaden*, 1877, 60 ff.; H. Nesselhauf, *Unters. z. Gesch. der delisch-attischen Symmachie*, Klio-Beiheft 30, Leipzig 1933; Highby, *ED* (cf. G. De Sanctis, *RF* NS 15, 1937, 249 ff.); H. Schaefer, "Die attische Symmachie im 2. Jahrzehnt ihres Bestehens," *Hermes* 71, 1936, 129 ff.; W. Kolbe, "Die Anfänge der att. Arché," *Hermes* 73, 1938, 249 ff.; H. Schaefer, "Beitr. zur Geschichte der attischen Symmachie," *Hermes* 74, 1939, 225 ff.; J. A. O. Larsen, "The Constitution and Original Purpose of the Delian League," *HSCP* 51, 1940, 175 ff.; R. Meiggs, "The Growth of the Athenian Imperialism," *JHS* 63, 1943, 21 ff.; *idem*, "A Note on Athenian Imperialism," *CQ* 43, 1949, 9 ff.; *idem, The Athenian Empire*, Oxford 1972, *passim*; H. D. Meyer, "Vorgeschichte u.

Gründung des delisch-attischen Seebundes," *H.* 12, 1963, 405-446; R. Sealey, "The Origin of the Delian League," in *Studies Ehrenberg*, 233-256 (the purpose of the League was to plunder Persian territory); N. G. L. Hammond, "The Origins and Nature of the Athenian Alliance of 478/7 B.C.," *JHS* 87, 1967, 41 ff. = "The Organisation of the Athenian Alliance Against Persia," in *Studies*, 311 ff.; L. S. Amantini, "Sull'aspetto religioso dei rapporti fra Atene e la lege delioattica," *Ist. Lombardo, Rendiconti, Classe di Lettere*, Vol. 107, 1973, 285 ff., who argues that the subjects were treated on an equal footing with the Attic colonies. On Athenian League policy from 480 to 460 B.C. see L. Piccirilli, *Ann. Scuola Norm. Sup. di Pisa, Cl. di Lettere e Filosofia, ser* III, vol. III. 3, 1973, 717-730. D. Lotze, "Selbstbewusstsein und Machtpolitik," *Klio* 52, 1970, 255 ff.; N. Brockmeyer, "Athens maritime Strategie gegenüber dem peloponnesischen Bund von Themistokles bis Perikles," *Altspr. Unterr.* 14, 1, 1971, 37 ff. On the tribute see O. Murray, *H.* 15, 1966, 142-156; in essence hypothetical is A. French, "The Tribute of the Allies," *H.* 21, 1972, 1 ff.; cf. also the relevant sections of D. W. Bradeen and M. F. McGregor, *Studies in Fifth Century Attic Epigraphy* (Cincinnati Classical Studies 4), Norman, Okla., 1973, and *iidem* (eds.), *Phoros. Tribute to Benjamin Dean Meritt*, Locust Valley, New York, 1974. Very worthwhile reading is the survey by F. Kiechle, "Athens Politik nach der Abwehr der Perser," *HZ* 204, 1967, 265-304. On the history of Pausanias: J. Wolski, *Eos* 47, 1954 (published 1956), 75-94; C. W. Fornara, *H.* 15, 1966, 257-271; also the studies cited immediately below.

THE END OF PAUSANIAS AND THEMISTOCLES. THE GREAT HELOT REVOLT. THE CONSUMMATION OF ATTIC DEMOCRACY

SOURCES: Thuc. I 101; 128-138, cf. M. A. Levi, *PP* 23, 1952, 105 ff.; Aristotle, *Const. Ath.* 25; Diod. XI 44 ff.; 54-59; 63-64; Corn. Nep., *Paus.* 3-5; Plut., *Them.* 22-31; *Cimon* 15-17; *Pericles* 9-10; Paus. III 17.7 ff.

BIBLIOGRAPHY: On Pausanias: M. Duncker, "Der Prozess des Pausanias," SB.B, 1883, 1125 ff.; H. Reuther, *Pausanias, Sohn des Kleombrotos* Diss. Münster 1902; C. Lanzani, "Ricerche intorno a Pausania reggente di Sparta," *Riv. di Storia antica* NS 7, 1903, 229 ff.; C. F. Lehmann-Haupt, "Pausanias, Heros Ktistes von Byzanz," *Klio* 17, 1921, 59 ff.; H. Schaefer, *RE* XVIII 4, 2563 ff.; J. Wolski, *Eos* 47, 1954, 75 ff.; A. Lippold, *RhM* 108, 1965, 320 ff. (thinks that Thucydides betrays a hostile attitude towards Pausanias); an alleged portrait of Pausanias: H. P. L'Orange, *Mél. Ch. Picard* II, 1949, 658 ff.; cf. G.M.A. Richter, *Portraits* I, 1965, 99 ff.; on Themistocles: L. Kjellberg, *Zur Themistoklesfrage,* Strena Philologica Upsaliensis, 1922, 229 ff. (on Aristotle's *Const. Ath.* 35. 3 f.); U. Kahrstedt, *RE* V A, 1686 ff. s. v. *Themistokles* no. 1; R. Flacelière, "Sur quelques points obscurs de la vie de Thémistocle," *REA* 55, 1953, 1-28; R. J. Lenardon, "The Chronology of Themistocles' Ostracism and Exile," *H.* 8, 1959, 23-48 (see also *infra* 458 n. 26); W. G. Forrest, "Themistokles and

Argos," *CQ* 54, 1960, 221-241, esp. 226 f.; 241 (on the chronology); G. L. Cawkwell, "The Fall of Themistocles," in *Classical Essays Presented to E. M. Blaiklock*, Auckland 1970, 39 ff.; furthermore, A. J. Podlecki, *The Life of Themistocles. A Critical Survey of the Literary and Archaeological Evidence*, Montreal 1975. See also the bibliography cited in K. Kinzl, *Kleine Pauly* 5, 679 ff. s.v. *Themistokles*. On the Themistocles portrait bust from Ostia see, for instance, F. Miltner, *Öst. Jhh.* 33, 1952, 70 ff.

ATHENS IN THE TIME OF PERICLES

Adolf Schmidt, *Das perikleische Zeitalter* I-II, Jena 1877 and 1879 (out of date; Vol. II dedicated almost entirely to the Stesimbrotus hypothesis, v.s.p. 450 f.); E. Abbot, *Perikles and the Golden Age of Athens*, New York 1891; U. v. Wilamowitz, "Von des attischen Reiches Herrlichkeit," in *Reden u. Vorträge*, Berlin ³1913, 30 ff. (too positive). Further studies on the personality of Pericles: E. Hohl, "Perikles," in *Meister der Politik*, ed. E. Marcks and K. A. v. Müller, Bd. I, 1922, 3 ff.; H. Willrich, *Perikles*, Göttingen 1936; F. Miltner, *RE* XIX, 748 ff. s. v. *Perikles*; H. Berve, *Perikles* (Leipziger Rektoratsrede), 1940; De Sanctis, *Per.* (with good bibliography); and in particular, F. Schachermeyr, *Perikles*, Stuttgart 1970; *idem*, "Das Perikles-Bild bei Thukydides," in *Antike u. Universalgesch.-Festschr. H. E. Stier*, Münster 1972, 464 ff. = *GRG*, 227 ff. C. Weickert, *Studien zur Kunstgesch. des. 5 Jh. v. Chr.* II: *Erga Perikleous*, Abh. Berl. Ak., 1950, 1; cf. G. v. Lücken, *Gn.* 23, 1951, 346-347 (on the relationship of Pericles to art, especially to architecture); C. M. Bowra, *Periclean Athens*, London 1971 (cf. V. Ehrenberg, *Gn.* 44, 1972, 783 ff.); J. Schwarze, *Die Beurteilung des Perikles durch die attische Komödie und ihre historische und historiographische Bedeutung* (Zetemata 51), Munich 1971; also worth consulting is A. Fuks, *The Athenian Commonwealth, Politics, Society, Culture*, Jerusalem 1970; P. Cloché, *Le siècle de Péricles*, Paris 1970; T. B. L. Webster, Athenian culture and Society, London 1973; and H. B. Mattingly, in *Studies . . . Fritz Schachermeyr*, Berlin 1977, 231 ff. On the buildings in Athens see in concise form, Judeich, *Top.*; also J. Travlos, *Pictorial Dictionary of Ancient Athens*, London 1971; H. A. Thompson and R. E. Wycherley, *The Athenian Agora*, XIV. *The Agora of Athens* Princeton, N.J., 1972; on the plastic arts: H. Schrader, *Phidias*, Frankfurt a.M. 1924; A. Hekler, *Die Kunst des Phidias*, 1924; E. Buschor, *Phidias der Mensch*, Munich 1948; on Sophocles: K. Reinhardt, *Sophokles*, Frankfurt a.M. 1933, W. Jaeger, *Paid.* I, 1946, 268 ff.; W. Schadewaldt, *Sophokles u. Athen*, Frankfurt a.M. 1935; V. Ehrenberg, *Sophocles and Pericles*, Oxford 1954; hypothetical, F. Schachermeyr, *Wiener Studien* 79, 1966, 45 ff. = *GRG*, 175 ff.

THE ATTIC MARITIME LEAGUE AND SPARTAN HEGEMONY UP TO THE EVE OF THE PELOPONNESIAN WAR

SOURCES: A sketch is given by Thucydides I 104 ff.; cf. Diod. XI 77 ff. (Ephorus); Plut., *Cimon* 17 ff.; *Per., passim*. The internal development of the Attic Maritime League is illustrated by the inscriptions. From the large number (on the collections v.s.p. 448), only the following may be stressed as particularly important; the proscription decree of Arthmius of Zeleia, from the sixties, restored by H. Swoboda, *Arch.-epigr. Mitt. aus Österreich* 16, 1893, 49 ff.; a more recent bibliography in Balogh, *Ref.*, 95 n. 56; the Erythrae decree, probably from the years between 470 and 460 B.C. (according to L. I. Highby, H. Schaefer, *et al.*): *IG* I^2 10 (in Bengtson, *Staatsv.* II, no. 134; and Meiggs-Lewis, no. 40 = *GHD 5th C* p. 7); the Melian *tyrannis* law: (Meiggs-Lewis, no. 43 = *GHD 5th C* p. 106); cf. also G. Glotz, *CRAI*, 1906, 511 ff.; the Milesian decrees: *IG* I^2 22 (cf. H. Bengtson, *Staatsv.* II, no. 151); D. W. Bradeen and M. F. McGregor, *Studies in Fifth-Century Attic Epigraphy*, Norman, Oklah., 1973, 24 ff.) (this inscription dates from the year 450/49 B.C.); the Attic decree concerning Chalcis: *IG* I^2 39 (446/5 B.C.) (cf. Bengtson, *Staatsv.* II, 1962, no. 155; and Meiggs-Lewis, no. 52); the decree of the Popular Assembly in Athens concerning Brea: *IG* I^2 45 = Meiggs-Lewis, no. 49 = *GHD 5th C* p. 17; the Athenian tribute quota-lists of the second assessment period (449-446 B.C.): Meiggs-Lewis, no. 55; the Athenian treaty with Samos (439-8 B.C.): Meiggs-Lewis, no. 56; the financial decree moved by Koumas (434-3 B.C.): Meiggs-Lewis, no. 58; and finally, the so-called Tribute Lists in *ATL*. From the Doric region one may mention the inscriptions concerning relations between Argos and Tylissus on Crete, probably from the time of the Pentecontaetia: M. Guarducci, *Inscr. Cret.* I, 307 no. 1 and 56 no. 4, cf. Bengtson *Staatsv.* II, no. 147 and 148 (with bibliography).

BIBLIOGRAPHY: In addition to the studies referred to above 452 f., on the development of the Attic Maritime League, the following may be cited: H. Swoboda, "Z. Gesch. d. attisch. Kleruchien," in *Serta Hateliana*, Vienna 1896, 28 ff.; M. Wagner, *Z. Gesch. d. attischen Kleruchien*, Diss. Tübingen 1914; U. Kahrstedt, "Der Umfang des athenischen Kolonialreiches," *NGG*, 1931, 159 ff.; R. Sealey, *Px.* 24, 1970, 13 ff. On the composition of the League, especially on Attic economic policy, see: R. Weil, "Das Münzmonopol Athens im 1. att. Seebunde," *Z. f. Num.* 25, 1906, 25 ff.; *idem*, "Das Münzrecht der *symmachoi* im 1. att. Seebunde," *Z. f. Num.* 28, 1910, 351 ff.; P. Gardner, "Coinage of the Athenian Empire," *JHS* 33, 1913, 147 ff.; Fr. Frhr. Hiller v. Gaertringen and G. Klaffenbach, "Das Münzgesetz des 1. att. Seebundes," *Z. f. Num.* 35, 1925, 217 ff.; M. Segre, "La legge ateniese sull'unificazione della moneta," *Clara Rhodos* 9, 1938, 151 ff. (on the date, 449 B.C., v.s.p. 448); E. S. G. Robinson, "*The Athenian Currency Decree and the Coinages of the Allies*," Hesp. Suppl. 8, 1949, 324 ff.; important is E. Erxleben, "Das Münzgesetz des delisch-attischen Seebundes," *AfP* 19, 1969, 91 ff.; 20, 1970, 66 ff.; 21, 1971, 145 ff.; R. J. Bonner, "The Commercial Policy of imperial Athens," *CP* 18, 1923, 193 ff.; [date: 20's of the fifth century B.C.], Heichelheim, *Wirts. Alt.* I, Chap. 6, *passim*. On law and justice: H. Weber, *Att. Prozessrecht in den att. Seebundsstaaten*, Paderborn 1908; H. G. Robertson, *The Administration of Justice in the Athenian Empire*, Toronto 1924; R. J. Hopper, "Interstate Juridical Agreements in the Athenian Empire,"

JHS 63, 1943, 35 ff. A good bibliography on foreign policy in the time of the Pentecontaetia is provided by De Sanctis, *Per.*, 279 ff.; to be added are: P. Cloché, "La politique extérieure d'Athènes de 462 à 454 av. J.-C.," *AC* 11, 1942, 25 ff.; 213 ff.; "La polit. extér. d'Athènes de 454/3 à 446/5 av. J.-C.," *Les Etud. class.* 14, 1946, 1 ff.; 195 ff. (in part, not more than paraphrasing of the sources); on the Egyptian expedition of the Athenians: H. D. Westlake, *CP* 45, 1950, 204-216 (the account of Thucydides is allegedly in many places incorrect); J. Scharf, *H.* 3, 1954-1955, 308-325 (places the expedition between 462 and 456); S. Accame, *RF* NS 32, 1954, 398-400; cf. NS 30, 1952, 118 (the destruction of the expedition in the summer of 452). The chronology of the Pentecontaetia still presents many problems; of more recent studies, see W. Kolbe, "Diodors Wert für die Gesch. der Pentekontaëtie," *Hermes* 72, 1937, 241 ff.; cf. Gomme, *Comm. Thuc.* I, 389 ff., who, however, with his emendation of Thuc. I 103.12 ("sixth" instead of the transmitted "tenth year," which should much rather be emended, with K. W. Krüger and G. Klaffenbach [cf. *infra* 459 n. 36] to fourth"), errs completely on a fundamental point. On this question see the works cited above 459 n. 36, and, in addition, K. Völkl, *Innsbrucker Beitr. z. Kulturwissenschaft* 3, 2, 1955, 159 ff.; N. G. L. Hammond, *H.* 4, 1955, 396 ff. Completely different, A. E. Raubitschek, *AJA* 70, 1966, 37-41: end of the Egyptian expedition 457/6; Cimon's death 456; Peace of Callias 456/5 B.C. In the last few years no essential progress has been made, at least not in my estimation. For the years 445-431 B.C., see still F. E. Adcock, *CAH* V, 474 ff.

THE WESTERN GREEKS IN THE PENTECONTAETIA: THE AWAKENING OF THE SICELS AND ITALICS

SOURCES: Pindar, *Olymp.* I-VI; XI-XII; *Pyth.* I-III; VI; *Nem.* I; IX; *Isthm.* II and fragments; Bacchy. III-V; Diod. XI 38-92; XII 8-36 (in many instances he follows Timaeus); Supplementary: Aristotle, *Polit.* V 1303a; 1312b; 1313b; *et al.*; in addition, inscriptions: *Syll.* I^3 35; 40; 70; 71; III 1122. The relevant studies are cited above 440; cf. further: R. Hackforth, *CAH* V, 145 ff.; and B. Pace, *Arte e civiltà della Sicilia* 3 vols., 1935-46; A. Graf Schenk von Stauffenberg, "Pindar und Sizilien," *Hist. Jb.* 74, 1955, 12-25 (on Olymp. I-III); H. Wentker, *Sizilien und Athen*, Heidelberg 1956 (not always convincing): see K. Stroheker, *Gn.* 30, 1958, 31 ff.; A. W. Gomme, *JHS* 78, 1958, 156 ff.; D. Adamesteanu, "L'ellenizzazione della Sicilia ed il momento di Ducezio," *Kokalos* 8, 1962, 167 ff.; F. P. Rizzo, *La repubblica Siracusa nel momento di Ducezio*, Palermo 1971. E. Sjöqvist, Sicily and the Greeks. Studies in the Interrelationship Between the Indigenous Populations and the Greek Colonists, Ann Arbour 1973. On conditions in Southern Italy: U. Kahrstedt, "Grossgriechenland im 5. Jahrh.," *Hermes* 53, 1932, 180 ff. (K. v. Fritz, *Pythagorean Policy in Southern Italy*, New York 1940); Dunbabin, *West.*, but he only discusses in detail the period up to 480 B.C.

1. The statement by Theopompus (in Plut., *Them.* 19), that Themistocles bribed the ephors, is a legend.

2. Thuc. I 89 ff.; Diod. XI 39 f.; Plut., *Them.* 19; Corn. Nep., *Them.* 6.5; cf. G. Busolt, "Thukydides und der themistokleische Mauerbau," *Klio* 5, 1905, 255 ff.; Ed. Meyer, "Der Mauerbau des Themistokles," *Hermes* 40, 1905, 561 ff.; F. Noack, "Die Mauern Athens," *AM* 32, 1907, 123 ff.; 473 ff.; for a concise discussion see Judeich, *Top.*, 71 f.; 124 ff.; W. Wrede, *Attische Mauern*, 1933, 10, Abb. 22-23. Beloch, *GG* II 2, 149 ff., and E.v. Stern, *Hermes* 39, 1904, 543 ff., have incorrectly banished Thucydides' account of the hasty construction of the Athenian fortification wall into the realm of legend.

3. The alleged correspondence between Pausanias and Xerxes, King of Persia (Thuc. I 128 f.), accepted by, for instance, Busolt, *GG* III 1, 66, and even by Meyer, GdA IV^2 1, 482 n. 1, and of late also by J. Vogt, in *Satura Festschr. für O. Weinreich,* Baden-Baden 1952, 169 ff., is probably apocryphal (H. Reuther, *Pausanias*, Diss. Münster 1902, 23 ff., who is followed by R.v. Pöhlmann, *GG*, 241 n. 1); Herodotus (V 32) holds a different view from that of Thucydides; he relates the marriage plans of the Spartan king with a daughter of the Persian satrap Megabates of Phrygia. That Pausanias wanted to become a Persian vassal ruler of Greece (Thuc. *loc. cit.*) is a Spartan legend, although it still continues to find countenance (H. Schaefer, *RE* XVIII 4, 2568 ff.).

4. Aristotle, *Const. Ath.* 23.5; Plut., *Arist.* 23; *Cim.* 6. According to Herodotus (IX 106), on the other hand, only the islanders entered the league, a statement which is regarded as correct by E. Bikerman, *Mél F. de Visscher* III, 1950, 114. The claim by Schaefer, *Staatsf.* 69, that the formation of a new league by no means took place, is erroneous; see, to the contrary, Highby, *ED*, 76 ff., and the study by J. A. O. Larsen (see following note).

5. J. A. O. Larsen, *HSCP* 51, 1940, 187 ff., with reference to Aristotle, *Const. Ath.* 23.5; incorrect is Schaefer, *Staatsf.*, 68.

6. Thuc. I 96; V 18; cf. H. Schaefer, *Hermes* 74, 1939, 225 ff. (Incorrectly held in doubt by E. M. Walker, *CAH* V 44 f., and by M. Chambers, *CP* 53, 1958, 26 ff.)

7. The *phoros* of the league members has nothing to do with the Persian tax arrangement; thus, correctly, Schaefer, *Staatsf.*, 232 n. 2 (against Beloch, *GG* II 1, 63 n.1).

8. The assessment intervals are, however, attested only from 454 B.C. on; see H. Nesselhauf, *Untersuch. z. Gesch. d. delisch.-att. Symmachie, Klio-Beih.* 30, Leipzig 1933, 3.

9. According to A. G. Woodhead, *JHS* 79, 1959, 149 ff., the *hellenotamiai* were appointed by the League Assembly until 454 B.C.

10. U. Kahrstedt, "Sparta und Persien in der Pentekontaëtie," *Hermes* 56, 1921, 320 ff.

11. W. Judeich, "Griech. Politik und persische Politik im 5. Jahrh. v. Chr.," *Hermes* 58, 1923, 1 ff.

12. On his personality see W. Vischer, *Kl. Schr.* I, Leipzig 1877, 1 ff.; H. Swoboda, *RE* XI, 438 ff. s.v. no. 2; G. Lombardi, *Cimone.* Rome 1934 (with errors); A.v. Domaszewski, *Die attische Politik in der Zeit der Pentekontaëtie*, SB.H, 1925, 4. Abh., 12; H. Berve, "Fürstliche Herren zur Zeit der Perserkriege," *Ant.* 12, 1936, 21 f.; Prestel, *Antidem.*, 32 ff.

13. Cf. the names of his sons: *Lacedaemonius, Eleius, Thessalus*; they represent a political platform; see W. Judeich, "Politische Namengebung in Athen," *Epitymbion f. H. Swoboda*, Reichenberg 1927, 99 f.; 102.

14. Judeich, *Top.*, 74.

15. On the chronology cf. *P. Oxy.* XIII, 1610 fr. 6 [see n. 17 below]. For a date after 476/5, A. Lippold, *RhM* 108, 1965, 339-341. Justin's dating (IX 1.3), which comes to 472/1 B.C., cannot be correct; see Highby, *ED*, 91 ff., and J. Wolski, *Eos* 47, 1954 (published 1956), 78 ff. H. Schaefer, *RE* XVIII 4, 2572, on the other hand, follows F. Heichelheim, *Z.f. Num.* 40, 1930, 16 ff., whose statements are, however, anything but probable; cf. against this, for instance, Gomme, *Comm. Thuc.* I, 400.

16. A different chronology by J. D. Smart, *JHS* 87, 1967, 136 ff.: conquest of Eion 470/69.

17. Principal sources: Thuc. I 100; Diod. XI 60-62 (= Ephorus, not very reliable; cf. G. De Sanctis, *Scritti minori*, 99 ff.), also *P. Oxy.* XIII, 1610 (printed in Bilabel, *P. Kleinform*, 7 ff. no. 3 [Ephorus] = Jacoby, *FgrHist.* 70 no. 191); Plut., *Cim.* 12 f. (Callisthenes); the remaining sources are enumerated in H. Swoboda, *RE* XI, 445 f. s.v. *Kimon* no. 2; cf. W.

Peek, "Die Kämpfe am Eurymedon," in *Studies Ferguson*, 97 ff.; M. Sordi, "La vittoria dell'Eurimedonte e le due spedizioni di Cimone a Cipro," *RSA* I, 1971, 33 ff.; important are the grave epigram on the fallen of Athens, *Anth. Palat*, VII 258, cf. Pausan. I 29.14, and the victory monument of the Greeks on Samos in honour of the Samian admiral Maeandrius, see U.v. Wilamowitz and G. Klaffenbach, *AM* 51, 1926, 26 ff., also Fr. Frhr. Hiller von Gaertingen, *AM* 51, 1926, 155 f.; E. Buschor, *Ph.* 86, 1931, 424 ff.; W. Peek, in *Studies Ferguson*, 116 ff.; G. Dunst, *AM* 87, 1972, 149 ff.

18. Meiggs-Lewis, no. 31.

19. On the chronology see the summary in H. Swoboda, *RE* XI, 445 s.v. *Kimon* no. 2, and W. Kolbe, *Hermes* 72, 1937, 253 f.; the years 469-466 B.C. are the most probable; the editors of *ATL* III, 175 ff., argue for 469 B.C., with V. Ehrenberg, *HZ* 173, 1952, 545, concurring.

20. Ephorus fr. 191; cf. Diod. XI 60.3-4. The general objections of Gomme, *Comm. Thuc.* I, 289 ff., are not convincing.

21. Plut., *Cim.* 14.

22. Thuc. IV 102; Schol. to Aesch., *de falsa leg.* 31.

23. On the revolt of Thasos see Herod. IX 75; Thuc. I 100 f.; IV 102.2; Isocr. VIII 38; Diod. XI 70.1; XII 68.2; Plut., *Cim.* 14; Corn. Nep., *Cim.* 2.5; Paus. I 29.4 f.; Polyaenus VIII 67; cf. P. Perdrizet, "Skaptésylé," *Klio* 10, 1910, 11 ff. That the Chersonese campaign was in time closely connected with the revolt of Thasos has been shown by *IG* I^2 928 (casualty list of 466/5 B.C.); cf. U. Köhler, "Beiträge zur Gesch. der Pentekontaëtie," *Hermes* 24, 1889, 85 ff., and W. Kolbe, *Hermes* 72, 1937, 247 and 250; additional bibliography in *SEG* X 405.

24. Cenotaph of the fallen Athenians in the state cemetery: Paus. I 29.4; cf. W. Judeich, *Top.*, 406, and F. Jacoby, *JHS* 64, 1944, 37 ff. (published 1946).

25. Herod. IX 35; Isocr., *Archid.* 99. For a later date (469 B.C.) *see. inter al.*, E. M. Walker, *CAH* V, 66 f.; for 466 and 465 B.C. cf. C. Callmer, *Ark.*, 84 ff.; similarly N. G. L. Hammond, *H.* 4, 1955, 380 f. (468/7 and 466 B.C.).

26. In the Chronicle of Eusebius the year 472/1 B.C. is given. According to Cicero (*Laelius* 42), Themistocles was banished 20 years after Coriolanus (*vulg.* 491); but that he was not ostracised as early as 472 B.C. is surely indicated by the performance of Aeschylus' *Persae*. Of a different opinion is R. J. Lenardon, *H.* 8, 1959, 23 ff., who dates the ostracism to about 474/3 B.C., a view which I am not able to accept. In the Athenian Agora a large find of sherds has been made, deriving from the ostracism of Themistocles: cf. *supra* 449.

27. According to Arist., *Pol.* 1301b, Pausanias wanted to abolish the ephorate; cf. V. Costanzi, "Il re Pausania nei Politici d'Aristotele," *AR* 14, 1911, no. 145/46, 30 ff.; 36 ff.; *Se non è vero è ben trovato* (but the individual referred to is Pausanias II: see A. Roobaert, *H.* 21, 1972, 756-758); cf. also G. L. Cawkwell, "The Fall of Themistocles," in *Auckland Classical Essays Presented to E. M. Blaiklock*, Auckland 1970, 49 ff.

28. Thuc. I 128-134.

29. Herod. VI 72; Plut, *De Herod. malign.* 21; cf. R. J. Littman. "A New Date for Leotychidas," *Px.* 23, 1969, 269 ff.

30. See the Craterus fragment in Jacoby, *FgrHist.* 342. 11. On Pronapes, another accuser, see A. E. Raubitschek, *Hesp.* 8, 1939, 158 ff.

30a. L. Piccirilli, *Ann. Scuola Norm. Sup. di Pisa, Cl. di Lettere e Filosofia, ser* III *vol.* III, 2, 1973, 317-355 (Themistocles as *Euergetes* of Corcyra).

31. The later tradition (Plut., *Them.* 27 = Charon of Lampsacus fr. 11; Corn. Nep., *Them.* 9.1 ff.), according to which Themistocles went to Xerxes, is incorrect; cf. L. Bodin, *REG* 28, 1915, 251 ff.: "Phanias d'Erèse. L'arrivée de Thémistocle à la cour de Perse."

32. Coins of Themistocles as lord of Magnesia: Weil, *Corolla Numismatica for B. V. Head*, Oxford 1906, 301 ff.; Head, *HN*, 581; *CAH* Vol. of Plates II 24.

33. An excellent appraisal of Themistocles may be found in Meyer, *GdA* IV^2 1, 493 ff.; by comparison, E. M. Walker, *CAH* V, 65, and H. Berve, *GG* I^2, 275, do not do justice to Themistocles, and still less J. Keil, "Themistokles als Politiker," *Anz. W*, 81. Jahrg., 1944, no. 6, 65 ff. See, to the contrary, H. Bengtson, *The Greeks and the Persians*, 1969, 73 ff.

34. L. Ziehen, "Das spartanische Bevölkerungsproblem," *Hermes* 68, 1933, 218 ff.; cf., correctly, with reservations, Meier, *Sp. St.*, 23 n. 2.

35. The sources: Thuc. I 101/3; Diod. XI 63-64; Plut., *Cim.* 16 f.; Paus. IV 24; Schol. to

Aristoph., *Lysis.* 1138; 1144. Cf. Fr. Frhr. Hiller von Gaertringen and H. Lattermann, *Hira und Andania* (71. Berl. Winckelmannsprogr., 1911.)

36. The alleged ten-year duration of the Messenian revolt is unhistorical. It rests on the fact that Thuc. I 103.1 has been incorrectly interpreted as "in the tenth year," an error which was possibly initiated by the redactor of Thucydides' work (G. Klaffenbach, *H.* 1, 1950, 231 ff.). On this subject there are many recent studies: cf. D. M. Lewis, *H.* 2, 1953-1954, 412 ff.; J. Scharf, *H.* 3, 1954-1955, 153 ff.; N. G. L. Hammond, *H.* 4, 1955, 371 ff.; R. Sealey, *H.* 6, 1957, 368 ff.; R. A. McNeal, *H.* 19, 1970, 306 ff.; for the year 456/5 B.C., lately again D. W. Reece, *JHS* 82, 1962, 111 ff. Instructive, in terms of method, is R. A. McNeal, *H.* 19, 1970, 306 ff.

37. The principal source for the reforms of Ephialtes is Aristotle, *Const. Ath.* 25.2 ff (where the participation of Themistocles is however unhistorical); see further Philoch. fr. 141b; Plut., *Cim.* 15; Diod. XI 77.6. The details of the reforms have been a highly controversial subject among scholars: cf. U.v. Wilamowitz, *Arist.* II, 1893, 186 ff.; Busolt *Gr. St.* II, 894 ff.; Meyer, *GdA* IV²1, 536 ff.; R. Sealey, *CP* 59, 1964, 11-22; and, very critical, E. Ruschenbusch, *H.* 15, 1966, 369 ff.; R. W. Wallace, "Ephialtes and the Areopagus," *GRBS* 15, 1974, 259 ff.; J. R. Cole, "Cimon's Dismissal, Ephialtes' Revolution and the Peloponnesian Wars," *GRBS* 15, 1974, 369 ff. On the chronology: Meyer, *Forsch.* II, 50 ff.; H. Swoboda, *RE* V, 2851 ff. s.v. *Ephialtes* no. 4; *RE* XI, 449 s.v. *Kimon* no. 2.

38. On the beginnings of Pericles see R. Sealey, "The Entry of Pericles into History," *Hermes* 84, 1956, 234-247, arguing that Pericles rose to prominence under the mantle of Cimon; this is not probable.

39. According to Plutarch, *Pericles* 9 (cf. W. Schwahn, *RE* V A, 2233), Pericles also introduced the *theorika*, the "attendance money" paid to the citizens on those days when tragedies were performed, a statement which is however contested by U. Kahrstedt, *NGG*, 1929, 156 ff.; cf. also De Sanctis, *Att.*, 454 n. 5.

40. On the concept of democracy see A. Debrunner, "*Demokratia*," *Festschr für E. Tièche*, 1947, 11-27; on its development in Athens: J. A. O. Larsen, "Cleisthenes and the Development of the Theory of Democracy in Athens," in *Essays in Political Theory Presented to G. H. Sabine*, 1948, 1-16; *idem*, "The Judgment of Antiquity on Democracy," *CP* 49, 1954, 1-14; V. Ehrenberg, "Origins of Democracy," *H.* 1, 1950, 515-548.

41. Prestel, *Antidem.*, 39.

42. See, for instance, De Sanctis, *St. Gr.* II, 138 ff. *idem, Per.*, 1944.

43. Cratinus fr. 300 Kock; cf. Judeich, *Top.*, 155 ff.; Th. Lenschau, *RE* XIX, 88 f. s.v. *Peiraieus.*

44. W. Kolbe, "Die Neugestaltung der Akropolis nach den Perserkriegen," *JdI* 51, 1936, 1 ff.

45. For the accounts of Pheidias' statue see Meiggs-Lewis 54 = *GHD 5th C* p. 18, and those of the Parthenon itself, *Meiggs-Lewis* 59 = *GHD 5th C* p. 18.

46. For the accounts of the Propylaea, Meiggs-Lewis, no. 60.

47. The problem regarding the size of the Athenian population still appears to be insoluble even today; cf. the figures drawn up by Meyer, *Forsch.* II, 149 ff.; also the more recent figures in De Sanctis, *St. Gr.* II, 150 ff., who estimates the total population of the city at 105,000-120,000 souls (of which 35,000 were citizens) and the population of all Attica to 210,000-235,000. Gomme, *Pop., idem, JHS* 79, 1959, 61 ff., has arrived at different figures. For a further discussion of the subject see Ehrenberg, *State*, 30 ff.; 263 (bibliography).

48. F. Heichelheim, *Wirts. Alt.* I, 319.

49. On Aspasia see W. Judeich, *RE* II, 1716 ff.; Meyer, *Forsch.* II, 55 f.; Kornemann, *Fr.*, 63 ff., whose view, that Aspasia exerted a great influence on Euripides, is devoid of evidence; in addition also De Sanctis, *Per.*, 189 ff.; and in general A. W. Gomme, "The Position of Women in Athens in the Vth and IVth Centuries B.C.," in *Essays*, 89 ff. Cf. E. Bloedow, "Aspasia and the 'Mystery' of the Menexenos," *Wiener Studien* NF 9, 1975. 32 ff.

50. Thuc. II 65.9; cf. Jacqueline de Romilly, *REG* 78, 1965, 557-575.

51. Eupolis fr. 94. He himself had still heard Pericles in his youth.

52. A much more positive view is advanced by A. H. M. Jones, "The Economic Basis of the Athenian Democracy," in *Past and Present*, 1952, 13 ff. = *idem, Athenian Democracy*, 1957, 3 ff.

53. The theory put forward by F. Hampl, "Poleis ohne Territorium," *Klio* 32, 1939, 1 ff.,

that even *apoikiai* were established on Attic state land and that these communities therefore did not possess any territory of their own, is contested by Bengtson, *Einz.*, 67. The problem has recently been investigated in a wider context by F. Gschnitzer, *Abhängige Orte im griech. Altertum* (Zetemata, 17), Munich 1958; cf. also C. Habicht, *Gn.* 31, 1959, 704 ff.

54. Cf. J. R. Green and R. K. Sinclair, "Athenians in Eretria," *H.*, 19, 1970, 515 ff.

55. G. Giannelli, "La colonia panellenica di Turî," *Raccolta di scritti in onore di F. Ramorino*, Milan 1927, 515 ff.; H. T. Wade-Gery, *JHS* 52, 1932, 217 ff.; V. Ehrenberg, *AJP* 69, 1948, 149 ff.; S. Accame, RF NS 33, 1955, 164 ff.; F. Castagnoli, "Sull'urbanistica di Thurii," *PP* 26, 1971, 301 ff.; on the form of the name (Thurii and not Thuria) see M. N. Tod, in *Geras A. Keramopoullou*, Athens 1953, 197 ff.

56. For a much earlier date (450 B.C.): *ATL* III, 114 ff., and J. H. Oliver, *H.* 6, 1957, 254 f. On the Bosporus empire see E. H. Minns, *Scythians and Greeks*, Cambridge 1913, 563 ff.; E.v. Stern, *Hermes*, 50, 1915, 179 ff.; M. Rostovtzeff, *CAH* VIII, 561 ff.; R. Werner, *H.* 4, 1955, 412 ff.; V. F. Gajdukevic, *Das bosporanische Reich*, ed. 2, revised and augmented by Dr. G. Janke, Vienna 1974 (cf. B. Nadel, *Gn.* 47, 1975, 567 ff.).

57. Hermippus fr. 63 K = Athen. I p. 27 e.

58. Aristotle, *Const. Ath.* 26.3, also *Pol.* III 1278a 29; Plut., *Per.* 37; Aelian., *Var. Hist.* VI 10; XIII 24; fr. 68; cf. F. Miltner, *RE* XIX, 760 (with earlier bibliography); a divergent view is held by A. W. Gomme, *JHS* 50, 1930, 106 f. = *Essays*, 86 ff., and by H. E. Stier, *Grundlagen und Sinn d. griech. Gesch.*, 1945, 164 f., as well as by J. H. Schreiner, *Aristotle and Pericles*, 1968, 104 ff.

59. Compared with the older studies, now out of date, on the decree of Callias (*IG* I² 91 and 92, *ATL* II 46 with commentary, printed in Tod I² 51) by Ad. Kirchhoff, Ed. Meyer and K. J. Beloch, important progress is marked by the investigations of W. Kolbe, *Das Kalliasdekret*, SB.B, 1927, 319 ff.; *Studien über das Kalliasdekret, op. cit.*, 1929, 273 ff. (printed in *Thukydides im Lichte der Urkunden*, 68 ff.); *Kalliasdekret und Sinking-Fund, op. cit.*, 1933, 154 ff. Among the great number of studies on the subject the following may be stressed: H. T. Wade-Gery, *JHS* 51, 1931, 57 ff.; W. S. Ferguson, *The Treasurers of Athena*, 1932, 153 ff.; A. B. West, *AJA* 38, 1934, 390 ff.; S. Accame, *RF* NS 13, 1935, 468 ff. A detailed bibliography in *ATL* I 208 f.; II 46; moreover, Ad. Whilhelm, *JHS* 68, 1948, 124 ff. (comments on emendations in *ATL*); B. D. Meritt, "The Tribute Quota List of 454-453 B.C.," *Hesp.* 41, 1972, 403 ff. The date of the decree (434/3 B.C.) has been established with certainty by W. Kolbe; cf. also D. W. Bradeen, "The Callias Decrees Again," *GRBS* 12, 1971, 469-483.

60. On Thuc. II 13.3 (and the Scholiast to Aristoph., *Plutus* 1193) see the discussion by A. W. Gomme, *H.* 2, 1953-1954, 1 ff.; against him, B. D. Meritt, *Hesp.* 23, 1954, 185-231, with the reply of A. W. Gomme, *H.* 3, 1954-1955, 333 ff.; on the other hand, cf. H. T. Wade-Gery, *Hesp.* 26, 1957. 163 ff.; see further Gomme, *Comm. Thuc.* II, 26 ff.; J. H. Oliver, *AJP* 79, 1958, 188-190 (on Thuc. II 13.3).

61. For a much more favourable judgment, however, see, for instance, De Sanctis, *St.Gr.* II, 197 f. On the other hand, J. Vogt, "Das Bild des Perikles bei Thukydides," *HZ* 182, 1956, 249 ff., has taken a highly critical view of Pericles, but without devoting any attention to the problems of finance, whereas these are of crucial importance.

62. Herod. III 12 and 15; VII 7; Thuc. I 104; Ctesias fr. 14; Diod. XI 71 and 74 (worthless).

63. Otto, *Kulturg.*, 88 n. 172, has conjectured colonisation designs on the part of Athens.

64. For the chronology Thucydides I 110.1 is decisive: the Egyptian expedition lasted for six years, from the storming of Prosopitis by the Persians in the summer of 454 B.C., reckoning backwards. In many instances more recent studies err on this point.

65. The battle of Oenoe is known only through the monuments mentioned by Pausanias I 15.1 and X 10.4; through the painting in the Stoa Poecile in Athens and through the Argive dedication in Delphi. C. Robert, *Hermes* 25, 1890, 412 ff., *Die Marathonschlacht in der Poikile*, Hallisches Winckelmannsprogr. 1895, placed it in the so-called first Peloponnesian War; cf. F. Koepp, "Das Gemälde der Schlacht bei Oinoë," *RhM* 69, 1914, 160 ff.; Meyer, *GdA* IV² 1, 554 n. 2. The dating of Oenoe concurrently with Oenophyta by Löwy, Beloch and lastly by H. E. Stier, *Eine Grosstat der attischen Geschichte*, Stuttgart 1934, cf. *WG* 2, 1936, 279 ff., is to be rejected; cf. the replies of W. Judeich, *HZ* 152, 1935, 301 ff., and W. Kolbe, *Hermes* 72, 1937, 255 ff. L. H. Jeffery, *BSA* 60, 1965, 41-57, places the battle

in the year 457 and connects it with Tolmides. There is not, however, sufficient evidence to substantiate such a conclusion. Cf. also A. Andrewes, "Could there have been a Battle at Oinoe?," in *The Ancient Historian and his Materials. Essays in Honour of C. E. Stevens on his Seventieth Birthday*, Westmead 1975, 9 ff. (sceptical of Pausanias).

66. See the casualty list in *IG* I² 929 with a total of 186 fallen Athenians in Cyprus, Egypt, Halieis, Aegina and Megara alone from the *phyle* Erechtheïs for the year 459 or 458 B.C.

67. The Athenian decree on Messenians, *IG* I² 37, cf. *SEG* X 9, is dated in 458 B.C. by A. E. Raubitschek.

68. The importance of Spartan intervention in central Hellas has been completely misunderstood by F. Hampl, *Staatsv*. 71 f.; see against this F. R. Wüst, *Klio* 32, 1939, 76 ff. New theories on the size of the forces in D. W. Reece, *JHS* 70, 1950, 75 f.

69. Sources: Thuc. I 107 f.; Herod. IX 35; Diod. XI 79-81 (unreliable); tombs of the fallen Spartan confederates—Cleonaeans and Argives: IG I² 931 f. (new fragments in B. D. Meritt, *Hesp* 14, 1945, 134 ff.; cf. *SEG* X 407); Paus. I 29. 7 f., of Athenian horse: *Anth. Palat*. VII 254; cf. A. Wilhelm, *Öst Jh*. 2, 1899, 221 ff. Spartan votive offerings at Olympia: Tod, I² no. 27; cf. P. Wolters, *Ph*. 84, 1928, 121 ff.

70. On Oenophyta and its consequences: Thuc. I 108; Diod. XI 81-83 (with doublet).

71. According to D. MacDowell, *JHS* 80, 1960, 118-121, Aegina had already been a member of the Attic Maritime League earlier (not of the Peloponnesian League).

71a. Coins attesting a Thessalian league from the period about 470-450 B.C. are discussed by P. R. Franke, *AA* 1970, 85-93.

72. Thuc. I 108.5.

73. The expedition of Diotimus in the West (Schol. Lycophr., *Alex*. 732 f.), which is dated in 455 B.C. by G. De Sanctis, *RF* NS 13, 1935, 71 f., but it probably did not take place until 433/2 B.C.; cf. B. D. Meritt, *Athenian Financial Documents*, Ann Arbor 1932, 69 ff.; and A. E. Raubitschek, *TAPA* 75, 1944, 10 n. 4. The treaty of Athens with Segesta in Sicily is dated to 458/7 B.C. by *idem, ibid*., 10 n. 3, which is evidently correct; cf. Bengtson, *Staatsv*, II, no. 139, and the confirmation by B. D. Meritt, *BCH* 88, 1964, 413-415; cf. Meiggs-Lewis no. 37, but also J. D. Smart, JHS 92, 1972, 128 ff. See also F. J. Brandhofer, *Untersuchungen zur athenischen Westpolitik im Zeitalter des Perikles*, Diss. Munich 1971, and T. E. Wick, *JHS* 95, 1975, 186 ff.

74. Thuc. I 109 f.; Ctesias fr. 14.38; Diod. XI 74; 75; 77; cf. F. Miltner, *RE* XIX, 757. A. E. Parsikov, "On the Chronology of the Athenian Campaign in Egypt" [Russian with English summary], *VDI* 1970, no. 111, 107 ff., has advocated a different date (462-456). The losses given by Ctesias—50 triremes and 6000 men—appear to be approximately correct; cf. J. M. Libourel, *AJP* 92, 1971, 605 ff.

75. Plut., *Per*. 12; Theophr. in Plut., *Arist*. 25 (with incorrect dating). Cf. W. K. Pritchett, H. 18, 1969, 17 ff.

76. Thuc. I 112.1, where the text requires rearrangement; Diod. XI 86.1. The dating of the treaty to 451 B.C. (or 450), based on the *textus receptus*, is, in face of the facts, untenable; Plut., *Cim*. 18, is also no proof for 451/0 B.C. Of a different view is A. E. Raubitschek, *H*. 3, 1954-1955, 379 f.: 458/7 B.C.

77. Thuc. V 14.4, cf. V 28.2.

78. *Anth. Palat*. VII 296. The only useful account is Thuc. I 112; the remaining sources are cited in H. Swoboda, *RE* XI, 451 f. s.v. *Kimon* no. 2; for an analysis see Meyer, *Forsch*. II, 9 ff.; 14 ff.

79. Sources: Herod. VII 151; Diod. XII 4.5; Demosth. XIX 273; Didym. on Demosth. VII 71 ff.; Plut., *Cim*. 13; Paus. I 8.2; Suda s.v. *Kallias*; cf. H. Swoboda, *RE* X, 1617, also A. E. Raubitschek, *Hesp*., 1939, 156.

80. According to H. T. Wade-Gery, *Studies Ferguson*, 150, in 450/49 B.C., according to S. Accame, *RF* NS 33, 1955, 146 ff., in 449/8 B.C. (according to the Attic calendar).

81. This document was accepted by Craterus (first half of the third century B.C.) in his "Collection of Decrees." Theopompus (fr. 154) declared it a forgery on the grounds that it was written in the Ionic dialect (which need not however cause any objection). A number of modern scholars have also contested the authenticity of the treaty: thus M. Duncker, Ed. Schwartz, U.v. Wilamowitz, R.v. Pöhlmann, E. M. Walker (*CAH* V, 88; 470 f.), also R.

Sealey, *H* 3, 1954-1955, 325 ff.; D. Stockton, *H.* 8, 1959, 61 ff.; H. B. Mattingly, *H.* 14, 1965, 273-281; cf. bibliography cited in Bengtson, *Stattsv.* II, no. 152. Basic are Meyer, *Forsch.* II, 71 ff., who errs only in contesting the occurrence of a treaty, and H. T. Wade-Gery, "The Peace of Callias," in *Studies Ferguson*, 121 ff. Also positive is K. Kraft, *Hermes* 92, 1964, 158 ff.; cf. S. K. Eddy, "On the Peace of Callias," *CP* 65, 1970, 8 ff.; and W. E. Thompson, *CP* 66, 1971, 29 f. (Livy XXXIII 20, 1-3, also, incidentally, presupposes the Peace of Callias); challenged, however, again by C. L. Murison, *Px.* 25, 1971, 2 ff., cf. H. B. Mattingly, Ph. 119, 1975, 48 ff. See also C. Schrader, *La paz de Calias; testimonios e interpretacion*, Barcelona 1976.

82. Plut., *Per.* 17 (= Craterus). Cf. M. A. Levi, *PP* 23, 1952, 90 f; exaggerated is K. Dienelt, *Die Friedenspolitik des Perikles*, Vienna 1958; A. E. Raubitschek, *AJA* 70, 1966, 37 ff., also is still too positive. I. Calabi, *Ricerche sui rapporti tra le poleis*, Florence 1953; 77 f., regards the decree as apocryphal, without convincing grounds for doing so. Also as a forgery, from the time of the Peace of Philocrates, R. Seager, "The Congress Decree: Some Doubts and a Hypothesis," *H.* 18, 1969, 129 ff., and A. B. Bosworth (immediately after Chaeroneia), *H.* 20, 1971, 600 ff.

83. The plan is dated to the period between the "Peace of Callias" and the beginning of construction on the Parthenon by, *inter al.*, Busolt, *GG* III 1, 446 n.; Meyer, *GdA* IV² 1, 658 n.1; Nesselhauf, *Symm.*, 31. On the other hand, it is equally possible to date it to the period after the Thirty Years' Peace, as is done by *inter al.*, Pöhlmann, *GG* 153; and by W. Otto, in M. P. Nilsson, *Gr. Rel.* I, 691 n. 1. The congress is dated to the years 450-447 B.C. by H. T. Wade-Gery, *Hesp.* 14, 1945, 222 ff.; to 448 B.C. by Hammond, *HG*, 307.

84. See the so-called *Hellenica Oxyrhynchia*, ed. V. Bartoletti, 1959; cf. primarily Ed. Meyer, *Theopomps Hellenika*, Halle 1909, 81 ff.; 92 ff.; Busolt, *Gr St.* II, 1414 ff., with the bibliography cited 1415 n. 2; also P. Salmon, "L'armée fédérale des Béotiens," *AC* 22, 1953, 347-360; "Les districts béotiens," *REA* 58, 1956, 51-70; Larsen, *Rep. Govt.*, 31 ff.; *idem, Gr. Fed.*, 26 ff. According to Larsen, *CP* 55, 1960, 9-17, not Thebes but *Orchomenus* played the leading rôle in the liberation of Boeotia and in the formation of the Boeotian League. See also R. J. Buck, "The Athenian Domination of Boeotia," *CP* 65, 1970, 200 ff.; and M. Amit, "The Boeotian Confederation During the Pentecontaetia," *Riv. stor. d. Ant.* 1, 1971, 49 ff.

85. Thuc. II 21; Schol. Aristoph., *Clouds* 859; cf. Plut., *Per.* 23.

86. Thuc. I 67; 115; 144; Diod. XII 7 *et al.*; cf. Bengtson, *Staatsv.* II, no. 156.

87. *IG* I² 199 (ATL II 15 no. 9): cf. H. Nesselhauf, *Symm.*, 36 ff.; H. Schaefer, *Hermes* 74, 1939, 246 ff. The division into regions is in fact probably of an earlier date already; see the Craterus fragment in Jacoby, *FgrHist.* 342.1, cf. *ATL* I, 154; 203 f.

88. H. T. Wade-Gery, *BSA* 33, 1935, 112; *Hesp.* 14, 1945, 212 ff.

89. S. Dow, *CP* 37, 1942, 371 ff.; 38, 1943, 20 ff.; opposed to him, again, B. D. Meritt, *CP* 38, 1943, 223 ff.; cf. *ATL* II 13 n. The question does not as yet appear to have been resolved.

90. See the excellent study by E. S. G. Robinson, *Hesp. Suppl.* 8, 1949, 324 ff.

91. Cf. *IG* I² 28.7 (c.450 B.C. cf. *SEG* X 23); 56.14; 72.10 (*SEG* X 88) *et al.*; also the speech of the Mytilenaeans in Thuc. III 10; cf. Ed. Will, "Notes sur les régimes politiques des Samos au Vᵉ siècle," *REA* 71, 1969. 305 ff.

92. B. H. Hill and B. D. Meritt, "An Early Decree Concerning Tribute," *Hesp.* 13, 1944, I ff. (from the year 448/7 B.C.?); cf. *ATL* II 50, D7 = *SEG* X 31.

93. Thuc. I 115 ff.; Duris fr. 65-67; *IG* I² 293 (*SEG* X 221).

94. H. T. Wade-Gery, *JHS* 52, 1932, 205 ff. On the discovery of ostraca see A. Körte, *AM* 47, 1922, 1 ff.; Tod I², p. 93, on 45 = *GHD* 5th C p. 11; F. J. Frost, *H.* 13, 1964, 385 ff.; H. D. Meyer, *H.* 16, 1967, 141 ff.

95. A concise discussion on this in F. E. Adcock, *CAH* V, 477 ff.; F. Miltner, *RE* XIX, 778 f. s.v. *Perikles*: Prestel. *Antidem.*, 60 ff., also fails to go deep enough on this point. The same applies to D. Kienast. *Gym.* 60, 1953. 210 ff. Cf. also the study by F. J. Frost (in the previous note), and, in particular, F. Schachermeyer, *Religionspolitik und Religiösttät bei Perikles*, SB. W 258, 3, Vienna 1968, 75 ff. The Anaxagoras lawsuit took place perhaps already shortly after 450 B.C.; on the Pheidias lawsuit see W. Judeich, *Hermes* 60, 1925, 50 ff.; C. Praschniker, *Epitymbion f. H. Swoboda*, Reichenberg 1927, 210 ff.; B. Schweitzer, *JdI*

55, 1940, 178 ff.; A. W. Byvanck, in *Symbolae van Oven*, Leiden 1946, 82 ff.; O. Lendle, *Hermes* 83, 1955, 284 ff., dates it to 432/1 B.C. Cf. H. Bloch, *Gn.* 31, 1959, 495 ff.

96. The opposition to Pericles is overestimated by J. Vogt, *HZ* 182, 1956, 262 f.

97. U.v. Wilamowitz, SB.B, 1901, 1273 ff., cf. *idem, Pindaros*, 1922, 224 ff.

98. E. Kirsten, *RhM* 90, 1941, 58 ff. Cf. the coins, *CAH* Vol. of Plates II 2 n.

99. Diog. Laert. VIII 63.

100. R. Koldewey and O. Puchstein, *Die griechischen Tempel in Unteritalien und Sizilien*, 1898, 153 ff., Taf. 22 f.; H. Drerup, "Der Tempel des Zeus Olympios in Akragas," *Bericht VI. Int. Kongr. f. Arch.*, 1939 (published 1940), 379 ff.

101. The claim by H. Wentker, *Sizilien und Athen*, Heidelberg 1956, 49 ff., that from 466/5 B.C. on, the aristocratic and not the democratic element was at the helm, is untenable; cf. K. F. Stroheker, *Gn.* 30, 1958, 32 ff.

102. Diod. XI 76; 88 ff.; cf. Freeman-Lupus II, 278 ff.; B. Pace, *Arte e civilità della Sicilia antica* I, 1935, 231 f.

103. In order to prevent a new *tyrannis* the Syracusans established, on the model of Attic ostracism, the *petalismos*, which in the event of conviction was followed by five years in exile; see Diod. XI 86 f.; W. Hüttl, *Verfassungsgesch. von. Syrakus*, 1929, 68 ff.; H. Hommel, *RE* XIX, 1117 ff. s.v. *Petalismos*.

104. Herod. VII 170.

105. Polyb. II 39.

8 THE PELOPONNESIAN WAR

SOURCES AND BIBLIOGRAPHY: It is the inscriptions which enable us to gain immediate insight into Greek, above all Attic, political life; the most important have been collected by *Syll.*³ I nos. 72 ff.; M. N. Tod, I², nos. 60 ff.; Meiggs-Lewis, nos. 65 ff.; cf. also *SEG* X 49 ff. From the great mass (a survey of earlier date on the most important is provided by Busolt, *GG* III 2, 591 ff.; cf. *CAH* V, 507; 511; 513; 515), the following groups deserve to be stressed: 1. The so-called Tribute Lists of the Attic Maritime League, now available in *ATL* I, 148 ff.; II, 28 ff.; III, IV, including the important document of the so-called Cleon assessment of 425/4 B.C. (I 154 ff.; II 40 ff.). 2. The inventory of temple furniture, conducted by the Treasurers of Athena Polias (434/3-407/6 B.C.): *IG* I² 232 ff. (cf. *SEG* X 184 ff.). 3. The calculations of the Treasurers of Athena Polias on payments to *strategoi* and *hellenotamiai* (with important information on the sums allotted to military campaigns): *IG* I² 294 ff. (cf. *SEG* X 222 ff.). 4. The political treaties, collected by Bengtson, *Staatsv.* II [with addenda].

The works of Attic comedy, the orations and pamphlets actually breathe with the spirit of that agitated period. Alongside the highly gifted Eupolis (fell in 411 B.C. at the Dardanelles), it was primarily Aristophanes who enjoyed sovereignty over the Attic stage: the *Acharnians* (425; but according to M. Sordi, *Ath.* 33, 1955, 47 ff., not indeed until 423-422 B.C.); the *Knights* (424); the *Clouds* (423); the *Wasps* (422); the *Peace* (421); the *Birds* (414); *Lysistrata* (411); the *Thesmophoriazusae* (411); the *Frogs* (405)—all these are important contemporary documents which reflect the problems of everyday life, major politics, and the wishes and hopes of the multitudes; for the understanding of these comedies the introductions by J. G. Droysen in his translation of Aristophanes (³1881) are still worth consulting today; copious bibliography is furnished by A. Meder, *Der athenische Demos zur Zeit des Peloponnesischen Krieges im Lichte zeitgenössischer Quellen*, Diss. Munich 1938, 232 ff.; cf. further, V. Ehrenberg, *The People of Aristophanes. A Sociology of Old Attic Comedy*, Oxford ²1951 (a valuable study on cultural aspects). A. W. Gomme, "Aristophanes and Politics," *CR* 52, 1938, 97 ff., is also worth reading; cf. W. G. Forrest, "Aristophanes and the Athenian Empire," in *The Ancient Historian and his Material. Essays in Honour of C. E. Stevens on his Seventieth Birthday*, Westmead, 1975, 17 ff; cf. also the study by F. Sartori, "Riflessi di vita politica ateniese nelle 'Rane' di Aristofane," in *Scritti in onore di Caterina Vasalini*, Verona 1974, 413-441. On Eupolis see K. Plepelits, *Die Fragmente der Demen des Eupolis*, Vienna 1970, and F. Sartori, *Una pagina di storia ateniese in un frammento dei 'Demi' eupolidei*, Rome 1975 (with extensive bibliography).

The anonymous pamphlet, the pseudo-Xenophontic, *Constitution of Athens*, the oldest document in Attic prose, comes from the first years of the War. (On the date of composition—in the first years of the Archidamian War—see K. I. Gelzer, *Die Schrift vom Staate der Athener*, (Hermes-Einzelschr. 3), 1937, 62 ff.; differently, H. U. Istinsky, *Die Abfassungszeit der Schrift vom Staate der Athener*, Diss. Freiburg i. Br. 1931 (published Freiburg i. S. 1933), who places it between 440 and 437 or 432 B.C.; similarly, E. Hohl, *CP* 45, 1950, 26 ff. This early date, however, appears to be untenable; also problematic is the late dating, in the period from 421 to 415, argued by G. Serra, *RALinc.* ser. VIII, vol. XVII, fasc. 5-6, 1962, 285-307; cf. also W. G. Forrest, "The Date of the Pseudo-Xenophontic Athenaion Politeia," *Klio* 52, 1970, 107 ff. (425/4 BC); D. Lotze, "Marginalien zu einer neuen Datierungsvariante für Ps.-Xenophons Athenaion Politeia," *Helikon* 9-10, 1969-70, 701 ff. The pamphlet is a sarcastic critique of the abuses of Attic democracy; edition (with translation) by E. Kalinka, Leipzig and Berlin 1913; by H. Frisch, *The Constitution of the Athenians*, Copenhagen 1942 (with a good bibliography); and a new edition by G. W. Bowersock, "Pseudo-Xenophon" (Xenophontic *Athenaion Politeia*), *HSCP* 71, 1966, 33-55; cf. M. Volkening, *Das Bild des att. Staates in der pseudo-Xenoph. Schrift vom Staate der Athener*, Diss. Münster i. W. 1940; M. Treu, *RE* IX A, 1928-1982.

In the history of ancient rhetoric the names of the triad Antiphon, Andocides and Lysias constitute an initial climax. From the great number of their orations (Busolt, *GG* III 2, 599 ff.), the following may be stressed as historically important: the defense of Antiphon in 411 B.C. who had been condemned to death for participating in the oligarchic revolution (J. Nicole, *L'apologie d'Antiphon ou Logos peri Metastaseos* [= *"changes in the constitution"*] *d'après fragments inédits sur papyrus d'Egypt*, Geneva-Basle 1907; W. S. Ferguson, "The Condemnation of Antiphon," *Mélanges G. Glotz* I, 1932, 349 ff.; the oration (407 B.C.) of Andocides, who was implicated in the *Hermocopidae* lawsuit; as well as his oration *Concerning the Mysteries* (399 B.C.), important for the history of religion (cf. the edition of Andocides by G. Dalmeyda, Paris 1930); and, finally, the orations of Lysias, above all *Against Agoratus* and *Against Nicomachus*; on these cf. Ferckel, *Lysias u. Athen. Der Redner und sein Gaststaat*, Diss. Würzburg 1937 (excellent); see also K. J. Dover, *Lysias and the Corpus Lysiacum* (Sather Classical Lectures, 39), Berkeley and Los Angeles 1968.

The historian of the great war is Thucydides, son of Olorus, from the Attic Deme Halimus; on his mother's side he stemmed from a Thracian ruling family (c. 460 until after 400 B.C.). On his lineage see, on the one hand, Ion I. Russu, *Serta Kazaroviana* I, Sofia 1950, 35 ff. (Thucydides is alleged to have sprung from the simple Thracian populace, but this is not probable); on the other hand, O. Luschnat, *Ph.* 100, 1956, 134 ff., who sticks to his father's name, Olorus. After the loss of Amphipolis in 424 B.C., Thucydides, one of the Thracian *strategoi* in command, went into voluntary exile (cf. H. D. Westlake, "Thucydides and the Fall of Amphipolis," *Hermes* 90, 1962, 276 ff. = *Essays*, 123-137), and did not return to his homeland until after the end of the war. (On his biography see U. v. Wilamowitz, "Die Thukydideslegende," *Hermes* 12, 1877, 326 ff.; R. Schoell, "Zu Thuk.-Biographie," *Hermes* 13, 1878, 433 ff.; E. Schwartz, *Das Geschichtswerk des Thukydides*, Bonn 1919 [^{2}1929], 217 ff.; H. Berve, *Thukydides*, Frankfurt a.M., 1938, 5 ff.). In exile Thucydides became an objective observer, with the greatest acuteness, of the great struggle in world history. He made it his life's aim to realise the plan which he had no doubt conceived at an early date, to immortalise in a work of history the war between the Athenians and the Peloponnesians. The question concerning the origin of Thucydides' *History* was first posed by Franz Wolfgang Ullrich, in his *Beiträge zur Erklärung des Thukydides*, Progr. d. Johanneums zu Hamburg I, 1845, II, 1846. According to Ullrich, Thucydides originally planned to write an account of only the Archidamian War —this is what is meant in I 1.1—and only in the further course of the military conflict did the understanding of the internal unity of the entire war grow on the historian. Apart from a series of other noteworthy arguments (well outlined by J. Geffcken, *Griech. Lit.-Gesch.* I, p. 240 n. 149), the "analytical" approach inaugurated by Ullrich envisaged the strongest element in its position in the so-called second Thucydidean Prooemium (V 26.I), and the ingenious book by E. Schwartz (*Das Geschichtswerk des Thuk.*, Bonn 1919 [^{2}1929]) attempted to support this thesis with new arguments. In other respects, however, there is far from unanimity of opinion on the genesis of the work; W. Schadewaldt, *Die Geschichtsschreibung des Thukydides*, Leipzig 1929, has impressively argued against the attempt of E. Schwartz to date the writing of the Sicilian books in the period before 410 B.C.; cf. also A. Rehm, "Über die sizilischen Bücher des Thukydides," *Ph.* 89, 1934, 133 ff. Both argued for the period after 404. The "unitarian" school, that is, those scholars who, like Meyer (*Forsch.* II, 269 ff.) and H. Patzer (*Das Problem der Geschichtsschreibung des Thuk. und die thukydideische Frage*, Berlin 1937), see only a single plan in the work, namely a conception based on the comprehension of the entire war, has gained much ground in recent years (see. for instance, J. H. Finley Jr., "The Unity of Thucydides' History," in *Studies Ferguson*, 1940, 255 ff., and his book *Thucydides,* 1942); the strong objections which this view faces have not, however, eliminated it. To that extent the explanations by K. Ziegler, "Zur Datierung der sizilischen Büchern des Thukydides," *Gym.* 74, 1967, 327 ff., are very instructive. Ziegler has shown that the history of the Sicilian expedition was at all events written before 409, since it contains no reference to the Carthaginian invasion (see also already *PhW*, 1930, 195-196). Otherwise, the unfinished character of the entire work in its extant form has become increasingly evident, even though there is understandably great difference of opinion on the degree to which the "redactor's" hand is involved (see in particular U. v. Wilamowitz, "Thukydideische Daten," *Hermes* 20, 1885, 477 ff.; 37, 1902, 308 f.; SB.B, 1915, 620 ff.; E.

Schwartz, *op. cit.*, 187 ff.; and, opposed to him, again U. v Wilamowitz, *Hermes* 60, 1925, 297 ff.). The documents inserted into the work constitute a special problem, for which reference should be made to the discretionary and on the whole convincing work by Carl Meyer, *Die Urkunden im Geschichtswerk des Thukydides.* Zweite durchgesehene Auflage (Zetemata 10), Munich 1970 [published posthumously by H. Erbse].

Thucydides is not only the creator of the historical monograph, but is at the same time also the founder of historiography as a science, and this by reason of the fact that he was the first to differentiate between more fundamental causes and external reasons. With some exaggeration, but on the whole not without a semblance of truth, E. Howald called him the "natural scientist" among the historians (*Vom Geist antiker Geschichtsschreibung*, Munich 1944, 81). What Thucydides presents is military history, divided according to summers and winters; in following this plan, account is taken of diplomatic history only in so far as it is necessary for understanding historical connections. Everything else, economic, social and especially cultural features, recedes into the background. A special artistic feature is offered by the carefully composed direct speeches. The only section in which they are completely lacking is Book VIII, unmistakable evidence that death seized the pen from the hand of the historian before the work had been completed (cf. U. v. Wilamowitz, *Hermes* 43, 1908, 578 ff.). It has long been recognised that the speeches could not have been delivered in the form in which we read them today (see, for instance, Meyer, *Forsch.* II, 379 ff.). In the "Chapter on Method" (I 22) Thucydides himself states that he has kept as close as possible to the "general political attitude" and the "general political intention of what was in fact said." According to the design of the historian, this was to be expressed in the inserted speeches, in conjunction with the different views of the various parties, and, accordingly, Thucydides had his speakers express themselves in the most likely words that they would have chosen, in his view, in terms of what the occasion demanded (Fr. Egermann, *DLZ*, 1937, 1471 ff.; 1476; 1503 ff.; and in *NBAnt.* ed. H. Berve, I, 285 ff.; cf. O. Luschnat, *RE Suppl.* XII, 1085 ff.; cf., again, opposed to him F. Egermann, "Thukydides über die Art seiner Reden und Darstellung der Kriegsgeschehnisse," *H.* 21, 1972, 575 ff.; also P. A. Stadter [ed.], *The Speeches in Thucydides. A Collection of Original Studies with a Bibliography*, Chapel Hill, N.C., 1973). This principle led to the circumstance that in Thucydides' *History* speeches are also found in, for instance, such places where the speakers of the party in question were not even present (cf. I 73-78: the speech of the Athenians in Sparta; cf., on the other hand, F. E. Adcock, *JHS* 71, 1951, 2 ff., especially 6, who thinks it possible that Thucydides could have invented this embassy; cf. also *idem, Thucydides and his History*, Cambridge 1963 [reprint, 1973], 31-32). The speeches must therefore be used with the greatest caution for reconstructing the diplomatic negotiations (E. Schwartz, *op. cit.*, 130 ff.). On their typology see G. P. Landmann, *Eine Rede des Thukydides: Die Friedensmahnung des Hermokrates*, Diss. Kiel 1932; K. Oppenheimer, *Zwei attische Epitaphien*, Berlin 1933; Rose Zahn, *Die erste Periklesrede (I 140-144)*, Diss. Kiel 1943 (with remarks by F. Jacoby); O. Luschnat, *Die Feldherrnreden im Geschichtswerk des Thukydides*, Ph. Suppl.-Bd. 34,2 Leipzig 1942. Valuable are the more recent studies by H. Strasburger, "Thukydides und die politische Selbstdarstellung der Athener," *Hermes* 86, 1958, 17 ff. (also on the speeches); *idem*, "Die Entdeckung der polit. Gesch. durch Thukydides," *Saec.* 5, 1954, 395 ff. A number of specific observations may be found in M. A. Levi, *PP* 23, 1952, 81 ff.

That Thucydides endeavoured in his account to do justice to all parties, to the Athenians as well as to the Peloponnesians, is no longer disputed by any competent scholar. (Cf. P. Cloché, "Thucydide et Lacédémone," *Les Etudes Class.* 12, 1943, 81 ff.). The attacks which the ingenious Hermann Müller-Strübing at one time levelled at the trustworthiness of Thucydides (cf. in concise form, F. Rühl, "H. Müller-Strübing als Gelehrter," in *Dr. H. Müller Strübing*, London 1894) are today forgotten. Nevertheless Thucydides did not withhold his own views, as is shown by the exquisite caricature of Cleon, whom the historian regarded as responsible for his own banishment. The earlier bibliography on Thucydides may be found essentially complete in Busolt, *GG* III 2, 616 ff.; later bibliography in De Sanctis, *St. Gr.*, II, 434 ff.; cf. also Bengtson, *Einf.* 102 f. (see Eng. trans. *Anc. Hist.*, 104), also containing references to editions and commentaries. A detailed discussion of the problems connected with Thucydides may be found in K. v. Fritz, *Die griech. Geschichtsschreibung* I, 1967, Chap. VII. A more recent example of the analytical view is the book by Jacqueline de Romilly, *Thucydide et l'impérialisme athénien. La pensée de l'historien et la genèse de l'oeuvre*, Paris ²1951 (Eng. trans. *Thucydides and Athenian Imperialism*, New York 1963); see also K. J. Dover, *Thucydides*, Oxford 1973; J. R. Grant, *Px.* 28, 1974, 81 ff. Very valuable is Gomme, *Comm. Thuc.*, Vols. I-IV. Add to this L. Canfora, *Tucidide continuato* (Proagones 10), Padua 1970 (cf. K. Meister, *Gn.* 47, 1975, 464 ff.); and A. G. Woodhead, *Thucydides on the Nature of Power* (Martin Classical Lectures, 24), Cambridge, Mass., and London 1970 (cf., however, G. L. Cawkwell, *CR* 8, 1972, 186 ff.); C. Schneider, *Information und Absicht bei Thukydides. Untersuchungen z. Motivation d. Handelns* (Hypomnemata 41), Göttingen 1974. For the later influence of Thucydides: H. G. Strebel, *Wertung und Wirkung des thukydideischen Geschichtswerkes in der griech.-röm. Lit.*, Diss. Munich (published Speyer a. Rh.) 1935; L. Edmunds, *Chance and Intelligence in Thucydides*, Cambridge, Mass., 1975.

Thucydides' *History* breaks off in the middle of the account of the year 411 B.C. Of subsequent accounts the *Greek History* by Xenophon of Athens (c. 430-354 B.C.) acquired a fame which it does not entirely deserve, by reason of the fact that it is the only extant account. It encompasses the period from 411 to 362 B.C.; Books I-II 3.10 comprise an account of the end of the Peloponnesian War. As for depth and comprehension of the major issues, the lively account of the aristocrat and philolaconian is greatly inferior to that of Thucydides; for an assessment see in particular A. Banderet, *Untersuch. z. Xenoph. Hell.*, Diss. Berlin 1919; H. R. Breitenbach, *Historiographische Anschauungsformen Xenophons*, Diss. Basle (published Freiburg [Switzerland] 1950); E. Delebecque, *Essai sur la vie de Xenophon*, Paris 1957; basic now is H. R. Breitenbach, *RE* IX A, 1569-2051 (also published separately); cf. also H. Baden, *Untersuchungen zur Einheit Xenophons*, Diss. Hamburg 1966; P. Krafft, "Vier Beispiele des Xenophontischen in Xenophons Hellenika," *RhM* 110, 1967, 103 ff.; also worth reading is H. D. Westlake, *Individuals in Xenophon, Hellenica* (Bull. of the John Rylands Library, vol. 49, no. 1), Manchester 1966; moreover, K. Bringmann, "Xenophons Hellenika und Agesilaos. Zu ihrer Entstehung und Datierung," *Gym.* 78, 1971, 224 ff. The best edition, with notes, is by J. Hatzfeld, *Xênophon Helléniques*, 2 vols., Paris 1936 and 1939 [reprint, 1949 and 1948] (with remarks on the composition of the work in the Introduction).

On Hellanicus see A. Momigliano, "Ellanico e gli storici della guerra del Peloponneso," *Athenaeum* NS 44, 1966, 134 ff. (on granting Attic citizenship to the Plataeans in the Archidamian War and on slaves as fellow-combatants in the battle of Arginusae, v.s.p. 153 f.).

Only a few scattered fragments are extant (Jacoby, *FgrHist.* no. 115 and 64) from the two other histories following Thucydides, namely the *Hellenica* by Theopompus of Chios, extending from 411 to 394 B.C., and the *Hellenica* of Cratippus, probably a late Hellenistic writer (according to A. W. Gomme, *CQ* 48, 1954, 53 ff., he is, rather, a younger contemporary of Thucydides); similarly P. Pédech, *REA* 72, 1970, 31-45, who places him in the fourth century). On the *Hellenica of Oxyrhynchus* see *supra* 182.

Of the later historians Diodorus (XII 30-XIII 107) follows Ephorus, as does Justin (IV 3-V 8). The information in Plutarch's *Lives* of Pericles, Nicias, Alcibiades and Lysander (cf. the edition by J. Smitz, *Plutarchus' Leven van Lysander*, Amsterdam-Paris 1939) ultimately goes back to the standard works of Thucydides, Xenophon, Ephorus and Theopompus, and for events in the West, to Philistus and Timaeus. The *Vitae* of Alcibiades and Lysander by Cornelius Nepos are practically worthless; interesting is *P. Oxy.* 411 (a *Vita* of Alcibiades).

GENERAL BIBLIOGRAPHY: G. B. Grundy, *Thucydides and the History of his Age*, London 1911 (ed. 2, in 2 vols., London 1948); B. W. Henderson, *The Great War Between Athens and Sparta. A Companion to Military History of Thucydides*, London 1927; A. Ferrabino, *L'impero ateniese*, Turin 1927. Much too positive is the judgment of G. E. M. de Ste. Croix, "The Character of the Athenian Empire," *H.* 3, 1954/55, 1-41; see, as opposed to this, D. W. Bradeen, *H.* 9, 1960, 257 ff. Further studies by: H. B. Mattingly, *H.* 12, 1963, 257 ff.; H. W. Pleket, *H.* 12, 70 ff.; T. J. Quinn, *H.* 13, 1964, 257 ff.; Ed. Will, "Le Ve siècle (510-403)," in *Le* *monde grec et l'Orient* 1, 1972, 149 ff. On internal affairs: G. Gilbert, *Beitr. z. inneren Gesch. Athens im Zeitalter des Peloponnes. Krieges*, Leipzig 1877; J. Beloch, *AP*.

EVENTS LEADING UP TO THE PELOPONNESIAN WAR

PRINCIPAL SOURCES: Aristophanes, *Acharn.* 526 ff.; *Peace* 605 ff.; Thucydides I 24-68 (on I 61, the account of the Athenian expedition against Potidaea, see J. A. Alexander, *AJP* 83, 1962, 267 ff.); 119-125; 139; Hellanicus, *FgrHist.* 323a fr. 24 (cf. F. P. Rizzo, *RF* 94, 1966, 271 ff.); Plutarch, *Per.* 30. Documents: *IG* I² 212 (*ATL* II 27 no. 22); 295 (cf. *SEG* X 222); 296 (*SEG* X 223); cf. W. Kolbe, *Thuk.*, 18 ff.; Meiggs-Lewis, no. 61 (expenses of the Athenian squadron sent to Corcyra).

BIBLIOGRAPHY: H. Nissen, Der Ausbruch des Peloponnesischen Krieges, *HZ* 63, 1889, 385 ff.; Meyer, *Forsch.* II, 296 ff.; E. Bethe, "Athen und der Peloponnesische Krieg im Spiegel des Weltkrieges," *NJb.* 39, 1917, 73 ff.; R. J. Bonner, "The Megarian Decrees," *CP* 16, 1921, 238 ff.; P. A. Brunt, *AJP* 72, 1951, 269-282 [the psephisma—before 433 or 432—is allegedly of no significance for the outbreak of the war]; K. Völkl, *RhM* 94, 1951, 330-336, who places it in the summer of 432; cf. G. L. Cawkwell, *REG* 82, 1969, 327 ff.; Ch. Fornara, *YCS* 24, 1975, 213 ff.; H. Brauer, *Die Kriegsschuldfrage in der geschichtl. Überlieferung des Pelop. Krieges*, Diss. Münster i.W. 1933; H. Nesselhauf, "Die diplomat. Verhandlungen vor dem Pelop. Kriege," *Hermes* 69, 1934, 286 ff. On relations between Corinth and Corcyra: R. L. Beaumont, *JHS* 72, 1952, 171-179. On the whole question see also D. Kagan, *The Outbreak of the Peloponnesian War*, Ithaca, N.Y., 1969 (cf. S. K. Eddy, *CP* 68, 1973, 208 ff.); and G. E. M. de Ste. Croix, *The Origins of the Peloponnesian War*, London 1972 (cf. D. Lotze, *Gn.* 48, 1976, 43 ff.); R. Sealey "The Causes of the Peloponnesian War," *CP* 70, 1975, 89-109, who argues that Athens was the guilty party.

For the chronology of events in Potidaea Thuc. II 2.1 is crucial; the attack on Plataea, accordingly, followed "in the sixth month after the battle in Plataia" not "in the sixteenth month" (J. H. Lipsius, F. Jacoby), nor "in the tenth month" (A. W. Gomme). Fighting before the walls of Potidaea, therefore, began in September 432, approximately six months before the Theban assault on Plataea (about March 431 B.C.) (in Thuc. I 125.2 something has evidently disappeared from the text). See W. Kolbe, *Thuk.*, 1 ff. The chronology of the years 432/431 B.C. has also been re-examined by W. E. Thompson, *Hermes* 96, 1968, 216-231. According to Thompson, the battle at the Sybota islands took place in late summer of 433, Potidaea revolted at the beginning of June 432, and the attack on Plataea followed at the beginning of April 431 B.C.

THE ARCHIDAMIAN WAR

SOURCES: Thucydides II 1-V 20; Diod. XII 38-72; Plut., *Per.* 30-38;

Nicias 1-10; the comedies, above all Aristophanes (v.s.p. 464); the Pseudo-Xenophontic *Constitution of Athens*; the most important inscriptions appear in Meiggs-Lewis, nos. 65 ff.; see also *SEG* X 49 ff.; the political treaties are assembled in Bengtson, *Staatsv.* II nos. 166 ff.

BIBLIOGRAPHY: D. Kagan, *The Archidamian War*, Ithaca, N.Y., and London 1974.

THE PEACE OF NICIAS AND THE GREAT SICILIAN EXPEDITION OF ATHENS

PRINCIPAL SOURCES: For the period of the Peace of Nicias: Thuc. V 21 ff.; Diod. XII 75-81; the political treaties appear in Bengtson, *Staatsv.* II, nos. 189 ff.; of the comedies, chiefly the *Birds* of Aristophanes (cf. C. Bursian, SB.M, 1872, 2. Heft, 375 ff.). The Athenian decree on the dedication of the firstfruits of the harvest to the Eleusian deities (*IG* I^2 76; cf. *SEG* X 110) no doubt belongs in the period after 421 B.C., but its precise date is admittedly disputed (cf. Meiggs-Lewis, no. 73 = *GHD 5th C* p. 21. For the Sicilian Expedition: Thuc. VI and VII (cf. A. Rehm, *Ph.* 89, 1934, 133 ff.); Diod. XII 82-XIII 33; Plut., *Alcib.* 17-23; *Nicias* 12-30 (Philistus); *IG* I^2 98 and 99 = Meiggs-Lewis no. 78; cf. *SEG* X 107.

BIBLIOGRAPHY: Meyer, *Forsch* II, 351 ff. (on the period of peace and the unity of the Peloponnesian War); U.v. Wilamowitz, *Das Bündnis zwischen Sparta und Athen*, SB.B, 1919, 934 ff.; G. De Sanctis, "La pace di Nicia," in *Problemi di storia antica*, Bari 1932, 93 ff.; H. D. Westlake, "Thucydides and the Uneasy Peace—a Study in Political Incompetence," *CQ* 21, 1971, 315 ff. On the policy of Nicias after 421 B.C.: H. D. Westlake, *AJP* 61, 1940, 414 ff.; *idem*, *CQ* 21, 1971, 315-325 (emphasises the incompetence of politicians at Argos, Sparta, etc.). On the Sicilian Expedition: B. Lupus, *Die Stadt Syrakus im Altertum*, Strassburg 1887; F. S. Cavallari-A. Holm, *Topographia archaeologia di Siracusa*, Palermo 1883 (with Appendix), Turin 1891; H.-P Drögemüller, *Syrakus. Zur Topographie und Geschichte einer griech. Stadt* (Gym. Beih. 6), Heidelberg 1969; E. A. Freeman, *History of Sicily* III, 1892; E. Odermann, *Der Festungskrieg von Syrakus in den J. 414-413 v. Chr.*, Diss. Leipzig 1927 (cf. G. De Sanctis, *RF* NS 6, 1928, 153 ff. = *Scritti Minori* VI 1, 1972, 398 ff.); A. Momigliano, "Le cause della spedizione di Sicilia," *RF* NS 7, 1929, 371 ff. (the Athenians, resolved to undertake the expedition in order to forestall Sparta—a completely unfounded hypothesis); G. De Sanctis, "I precedenti della grande spedizione ateniese in Sicilia," in *Problemi di storia antica*, Bari 1932, 109 ff.; K. Fabricius, *Das antike Syrakus, eine hist.-arch. Untersuch.*, Klio-Beih. 28, 1932; L. Wickert, *RE* IV A, 1494 ff. s.v. *Syrakusai.* Additional bibliography in *CAH* V, 513/14. On coins illustrating the character of Syracuse at the end of the fifth century see R. Baldus, *Ch.* 2, 1972, 37 ff. On internal affairs in Athens see O. Aurenche, *Les groupes d'Alcibiade, de Léogoras et de Teucros. Remarques sur la vie politique athénienne en 415 av. J.-C.*, Paris 1974.

THE DECELEIAN AND THE IONIAN WAR

PRINCIPAL SOURCES: Aristoph., *Lysistrata, Thesmophoriazusae, Frogs*; Thuc. VIII; Xenoph., *Hell.* I 1-II 2.23; Diod. XIII 34-XIV 3; Corn. Nep., *Alcibiades, Lysander, Thrasybulus;* Plut., *Alcibiades, Lysander;* of the Orators, chiefly Lysias (*Against Eratosthenes; Against Agoratus*); also Aristotle, *Const. Ath.* 29-34. For the events of the years 409 and 407 (the battle of Notium) new fragments from the *Hellenica Oxyrhynchia* have furnished additional information; see Vitt. Bartoletti, *PSI* XIII, 1949, no. 1304; cf. F. Jacoby, *CQ* 44, 1950, 1 f. (with a copy of the newly discovered fragments in the review of P. Maas, 8 ff.), repeated in *Abh. z. griech. Geschichtsschreibung*, 1956, 322 ff. (without the text). Edition by V. Bartoletti, *Hellenika Oxyrhynchia*, Leipzig 1959. I. A. F. Bruce, *A Historical Commentary on the 'Hellenica Oxyrhynchia'*, Cambridge 1967. On the question of authorship v.i.p. 482. A selection of the most important historical inscriptions appears in Meiggs-Lewis, 79 ff.; cf. the survey in *CAH* V, 515. Important for developments on Thasos in 411 is J. Pouilloux, *Recherches sur l'hist. et les cultes de Thasos*, I, Paris 1954, Chap. 4; cf. *idem, AC* 22, 1953, 41-42. S. Accame, *RF* NS 28, 1950, 30 ff., has connected the new Fragment C from the *Hellenica Oxyrhynchia* with the blockade of Thasos by Thrasybulus in 408 B.C. (Xen., *Hell.* I 4.9; Diod. XII 72); but see M. Treu, *Gym.* 59, 1952, 302 ff., especially 311, who would prefer to connect it with Lysander before the city of Byzantium (Xen., *Hell.* II 2.1); similarly, I. A. F. Bruce, *Px.* 18, 1964, 272 ff.

BIBLIOGRAPHY. On events in foreign politics: A. Boerner, *De rebus a Graecis inde ab a. 410 usque ad a. 403 a. Chr. n. gestis quaestiones hist.*, Diss. Göttingen 1894; L. Pareti, "Ricerche sulla potenza marittima degli Spartani," *Mem. R. Acc. delle Scienze di Torino*, Ser. II, Vol. 59, 1909, 71 ff.; P. Cloché, "L'affaire des Arignuses," *Rev. hist.* 130, 1919, 5 ff.; G. De Sanctis, "La battaglia di Notion," *RF* NS 9, 1931, 222 ff.; "Contributi epigrafici allia cronologia della guerra deceleica," *RF* NS 13, 1935, 305 ff.; H. R. Breitenbach, "Die Seeschlacht bei Notion (407/406)," *H.* 20, 1971, 152 ff.; J. A. R. Munro, "The End of the Peloponnesian War," *CQ* 31, 1937, 32 ff.; W. Schwahn, *RE* V A, 2304 ff. s.v. *Theramenes*; H. Schaefer, *RE Suppl.* VII, 1579 ff. s.v. *Tissaphernes*; A. Andrewes, "The Generals in the Hellespont 410-407," *JHS* 73, 1953, 2 ff. (on operations after the naval battle of Cyzicus); Very valuable, too, is D. Lotze, *Lysander und der Peloponnesische* Krieg (Abh S 57, 1), 1964; cf. also Bloedow, *Alc.*, 56 ff.

Of events in internal politics the revolution of the Oligarchs in Athens in 411 B.C. (sources: Thuc, VIII 65-70; [Lysias] *On Behalf of Polystratus* XX; Aristotle, *Const. Ath.* 29-32), the first revolution in world history—on whose course details are known—has elicited a vast amount of research. From the large number of older and of more recent investigations (enumerated in Busolt, *Gr. St.* I, 69 ff.; 78; 630/d/e; II, 1577; cf. also De Sanctis, *St. Gr.* II, 1939, 406 ff.), the following may be cited as particularly important: U.v. Wilamowitz, *Arist.* I, 99 ff.; II, 113 ff.; 356 ff.; U.

Köhler, *Die athen. Oligarchie des J. 411*, SB.B, 1895, 451 ff.; *Der thukydideische Bericht über die oligarchische Umwälzung in Athen im J. 411*, SB.B, 1900, 803 ff.; Meyer, *Forsch.* II, 406 ff. (still basic today); V. Ehrenberg, "Die Urkunden von 411," *Hermes* 57, 1922, 613 ff.; W. S. Ferguson, "The Constitution of Theramenes," *CP* 21, 1926, 72 ff.; U. Wilcken, "Zur oligarchischen Revolution in Athen vom J. 411 v. Chr.," SB.B, 1935, no. III, 34 ff. (cf. F. Taeger, *Gn.* 13, 1937, 347 ff.); G. H. Stevenson, "The Constitution of Theramenes," *JHS* 56, 1936, 48 ff.; Th. Lenschau, "Die Vorgänge in Athen nach dem Sturze der 400," *RhM* 90, 1941, 24 ff.; F. Sartori, *La crisi del 411 a.C. nell'Athenaion Politeia de Aristotele*, Padua 1951; M. Cary, "Notes on the Revolution of the 400 at Athens," *JHS* 72, 1952, 56 ff. (on the documents in Aristotle, *Const. Ath.* 30 and 31); G. Vlastos, *AJP* 73, 1952, 56 ff.; Hignett, *Const.*, 276 ff.; 356 ff.; A. Fuks, *The Ancestral Constitution*, London 1953, esp. 84 ff.; M. Lang. "Revolution of the 400: Chronology and Constitutions," *AJP* 88, 1967, 176-187 (regards Thucydides' account as reconcilable with that of Aristotle); W. J. McCoy, *Theramenes, Thrasybulus and the Athenian Moderates*, Diss. Yale Univ. 1970; M. I. Finley, *The Ancestral Constitution. An Inaugural Lecture*, London 1971; P. J. Rhodes, "The Five Thousand in the Athenian Revolution of 411 B.C.," *JHS* 92, 1972, 115 ff. On the *Hetairiai* (149) see F. Sartori, *Le eterie nella vita politica ateniese del VI e V secolo a.C.*, Rome 1957, 115 ff.

THE CHRONOLOGY OF THE YEARS 410-406: H. Dodwell, *Ann. Thucy. et Xenophont.*, Oxford 1702, put forward the thesis that Xen., *Hell.* I encompassed not only the events from the winter of 411/10 but also the entire military year 410/09. If this were so, the voyage of Thrasyllus to Ionia would fall in the year 409, the return of Alcibiades to Athens in 407, and Notium in 406. The Dodwell hypothesis has been accepted by, *inter al.*, Clinton, Grote, Beloch and Ferguson (*CAH* V, 483 ff.), and of late by D. Lotze (*Lysander und der Peloponnesische Krieg*, 1964, 72 ff.), as well as by Bloedow (*Alc.*, 67 ff.). It is however discredited by, *inter al.*, the fact that its acceptance would leave an inexplicable gap between the summer of 410 (Xen., *Hell.* I 21) and the beginning of winter 409 (I 2.14). For these reasons the view of Haacke, *Diss. chron. de postremis belli Pelop. annis*, Stendal 1822, that Xen., *Hell.* I 1 encompasses only the time from autumn 411 to spring 410, rests on better foundations (cf., *inter al.*, also Busolt, *GG* III 2, 1521 ff. n.; Meyer, *GdA* IV 616 ff.). The events cited above thus move up one year, causing the return of Alcibiades to fall in the year 408 B.C. See also, of late, D. P. Orsi, *Quaderni di Storia* 1, 2, 1975, 127 ff. The thesis of Th. Lenschau, *Ph. Suppl.* VIII, 1900, that the beginning of Xen., *Hellenica* is mutilated and that "the beginning of winter" (Xen., *Hell.* I 1.2) is to be connected, not with the winter of 411/10, but of 410/09, has rightly found no approbation.

1. On the name see L. Elter, "Thukydides u. der Name des Peloponnesischen Krieges," *NJb*, 1915, 77 ff.; and, opposed to him, Br. Keil, *Hermes* 51, 1916, 441 ff. The earliest piece of evidence is an Attic inscription (*psephisma*): *IG* II/III² 1035 (c. 100 B.C.)

2. B. Schmidt, *Korkyraeische Studien*, Leipzig 1890.

3. On the term see E. Bikerman, *REG* 56, 1943, 291 ff.

4. N. G. L. Hammond, "Naval Operations in the South Channel of Corcyra," *JHS* 65, 1945, 26 ff. = "Naval Operations off Corcyra," in *Studies*, 447 ff.; S. Accame, "Tucidide e la questione de Corcira," in *Studi filologici e storici in onore de V. de Flaco*, Naples 1971, 141-164.

5. On the Bottiaeans see F. Hampl, *"Hoi Battaioi,"* *RhM* 84, 1935, 120 ff.; on the Chalcidian state see *idem, Hermes* 70, 1935, 177 ff. (refuted by the inscription in H. Bengtson, *Staatsv.* II, no. 308, 311 n. 6). The older bibliography in Busolt, *Gr. St.* II, 1501 ff.; also F. Schehl, *DLZ*, 1933, 1999 f. As to when and if a unified Chalcidian state was created at all, opinions still differ greatly among modern scholars. See D. M. Robinson-P.A. Clement, *Excavations at Olynthus IX. The Chalcidic Mint*, Baltimore 1938, 112 ff.; Larsen. *Rep. Govt.*, 42 ff., who argues for a Chalcidian federal state with Olynthus as administrative headquarters; see now also *idem, Gr. Fed. S.*, 58 ff.; and M. Zahrnt, *Olynth und die Chalkidier. Untersuchungen zur Staatenbildung auf der chalkidischen Halbinsel im 5. u. 4. Jahrh. v. Chr.*, Munich 1971, 1 ff. (Vestigia 14) (cf. T. Schwertfeger, *Gn.* 46, 1974, 259-263); M. Moggi, *Critica Storica* 11, 1974, 1-11.

6. Thuc. I 139.3.

7. The term "Archidamian War" (appearing for the first time in Lysias fr. IX Thalheim) for this period of the conflict derives from the Spartan king Archidamus († 427 B.C.), who led the Peloponnesian invading forces into Attica.

8. Thuc. II 9; cf. Map 4.

9. Thuc. II 13.6; on the numerical strength of the armies cf. Meyer, *Forsch.* II, 149 ff. (basic); Busolt, *GG* III 2, 858 ff.; 878 ff.; K. J. Beloch, *Klio* 5, 1905, 341 ff.; 6, 1906, 34 ff.; A. W. Gomme, "The Athenian Hoplite Force in 431 B.C.," *CQ* 21, 1927, 142 ff.; *Pop.*; *Comm. Thuc.* II, 34 ff. It is of utmost importance to emphasise that every interpretation which avoids the figures given by Thucydides, as, for instance, that of Gomme, moves on precarious ground and ends up in the realm of pure speculation.

10. *IG* VI, 1= Meiggs-Lewis no. 67; cf. F. E. Adcock, "Alcidas *argyrologos*," *Mél. G. Glotz*, 1932, 1 ff.

11. W. S. Ferguson, "Athenian War Finance," *Proceed. Mass. Hist. Soc.* 64, 1932, 374 ff.

12. L. Chandler, *JHS* 46, 1926, 1 ff.

13. On the strategy of Pericles, who has been most unjustly criticised by Pflugk-Harttung, *Perikles als Feldherr*, Stuttgart 1884, and by Beloch, *AP*, 22 f. (cf. *GG* II 1, 300 n.1), see in particular H. Delbrück, *Die Strategie des Perikles erläutert durch die Strategie Friedrichs d. Gr.*, 1890; earlier bibliography in Pöhlmann, *GG*, 172 n. 4; see in particular Delbrück, *Krieg.* I^3, 300 ff.; H. D. Westlake, "Seaborne Raids in Periclean Strategy," *CQ* 40, 1945, 75 ff. = *Essays*, 84-100; cf. B.X. de Wet, "The So-called Defensive Policy of Pericles," *Acta Classica* 12, 1969, 103 ff. It must indeed be admitted that the *offensive* aspect of his strategy does not assume a very energetic or resolute character in the eyes of the modern scholar, despite Westlake's disagreement. Cf. also G. Cawkwell, "Thucydides' Judgment of Periclean Strategy," *YCS* 24, 1975, 53 ff.

14. According to W. Ebstein, *Die Pest des Thukydides*, Stuttgart 1899, it was a devastating infectious disease and at all events not the oriental Bubonic Plague; other scholars think in terms of tuberculosis: Benno v. Hagen, *Gym.* 49, 1938, 120 ff.; cf. *Die Pest im Altertum*, Jena 1939; and in terms of a combined typhus and smallpox epidemic. More recent studies: D. L. Page, *CQ* 3, 1953, 97 ff. (measles); W. P. MacArthur, *CQ* 4, 1954, 171 ff. (typhoid fever). The same disease also spread as far as Rome at the time, cf. Livy IV 21 for the year 436 B.C.); Livy's chronology is however six years too high. For the effects of the plague on political life: H. N. Couch, "Some Political Implications of the Athenian Plague," *TAPS* 66, 1935, 92 ff.; A. Gervais, "A propos de la peste d'Athènes. Thucydidé et la littérature de l'épidémie," *Bull. de l'Assoc. G. Bud.*, 1972, 395-429. The question concerning the degree to which the Athenian plague was responsible for ravaging the character of the population still requires investigation. Cf. B. G. Niebuhr, *Vortr. über Alte Gesch.* II, 1848, published by M. Niebuhr, 64: "The history of disease is a branch of world history which has not as yet been investigated, but is of such great importance. Whole periods of history are explained by the appearance and disappearance of murderous plagues." See also Bengtson, *Einf.*, 62 f.; cf. *idem, Anc. Hist.*, 62 f.

15. Thuc. II 59-65; Plut., *Per.* 34-35; Diod. XII 45; it was the so-called *apocheirotonia*, cf. H. Swoboda, *Hermes* 28, 1893, 536 ff. (basic); F. Miltner, *RE* XXI, 786 s.v. *Perikles.*

16. Bengtson, *Staatsv.* II, 165.

17. Geyer, *Mak.*, 60.

18. M. P. Nilsson, *Bendis in Athens, From the Collections of the Ny Carlsberg Glyptotek* 3, 1942, 169 ff.; 178; cf. *SEG* X 64; and W. S. Ferguson, *Hesp. Suppl.* 8, 1949, 131 ff.

19. Köster, *Seewesens*, 81 ff.; Th. Lenschau, *RE* XX, 537 ff. s.v. *Phormio* no. 4.

20. V. Ehrenberg, "Perikles and his Colleagues Between 441 and 429 B.C.," *AJP* 66, 1945, 113 ff., has referred to the rôle of Phormio under Pericles. On Damon see K. Meister, *Riv. stor. dell'antichità* (Bologna) 3, 1973, 29-44.

21. On the sources see M. L. Paladini, *H.* 7, 1958, 48-73.

22. Following in the footsteps of George Grote in adopting a much too favourable attitude towards Cleon is U. Kahrstedt, *RE* XI, 714 ff.; cf. M. Lang, "Cleon as the Anti-Pericles," *CP* 67, 1972, 159 ff. Generally correct Meyer, *Forsch.* II, 333 ff.; the earlier bibliography, virtually complete, in Busolt, *GG* III 2, 988 ff. Vigorously opposed to Cleon is a scholar like Pöhlmann, *GG* 180 f.; cf. also W. R. Connor, *The New Politicians of Fifth-Century Athens*, Princeton, N.J., and London, 1971, 119 ff. (cf. J. K. Davies, *Gn.* 47, 1975, 374 ff.).

23. On Nicias see Thuc. V 16; VII 86 (cf. I Bruns, *Das literarische Porträt der Griechen*, 1896, 17 ff.); G. Eincke, *RE* XVII, 323 ff. s.v. *Nikias* no. 5; L. Kirtland, *Nicias, his Family and the Tradition of his Great Wealth*, Diss. Princeton, N.J., 1939.

24. In those days a property tax of 200 talents was for the first time proclaimed and apportioned; Thuc. III 19. Payments for suppressing the revolt of Lesbos: *SEG* X 226.

25. Thus H. Müller-Strübing, *Thuk.-Forschungen*, 1881, 41 ff., struck from the historical record the account of Thucydides concerning the execution of the thousand Mytilinaeans (III 50) as the invention of a "bloodthirsty interpolator" and enemy of Attic democracy. Busolt, *GG* III 2, 1030, thinks it is possible that there may have been a slip of the pen concerning the exact number; the figure of 1000 is accepted by, *inter al.*, G. Mathieu, *Mél. G. Radet*, 1940, 247. On the settlement of Attic cleruchs see *IG* I² 60 = Tod I² 63; cf. *ATL* II 76, D 22.

26. The first Sicilian expedition of the Athenians, it seems, preceded the famous mission of Gorgias of Leontini to Athens; it is placed in the year 428/7 B.C. by B. J. H. Williams, "The Political Mission of Gorgias to Athens in 427 B.C.," *CQ* 25, 1931, 52 ff.; see also H. D. Westlake, "Athenian Aims in Sicily, 427-424 B.C.," *H.* 9, 1960, 385 ff. = *Essays*, 101 ff. Besides Thucydides (III 88-103), a Florentine Papyrus, published by G. Coppola, *RF* NS 8, 1930, 449 ff.; cf. A. Momigliano, *ibid.*, 467 ff.; and S. Mazzarino, *Bull. stor. Catanese* 4, 1939, 5 ff.; cf. *PSI* XII, 1950, no. 1283, discloses information on events in Sicily; to ascribe the Papyrus to Philistus (Coppola and Momigliano) appears to be certain; see, for instance, A. Körte, *AfP* 10, 1932, 67 f., but of a different opinion, R. Laquerur, *RE* XIX, 2417.

27. For the treaties see Meiggs-Lewis, 63 = *GHD 5thC* p. 19 and 64, and E. Ruschenbusch, ZPE 19, 1975, 225 ff.

28. A. E. Raubitschek, "Athens and Halikyai," *TAPA* 75, 1944, 10 ff.; Bengtson, *Staatsv.* II no. 174. But see *SEG* X 68, where the decree is dated about 433/2 B.C. Of an even different view, M. T. M. Piraino, *Kokalos* 6, 1960, 58 ff.: 458/7 B.C.; cf. Meiggs-Lewis no. 37; D. W. Bradeen and M. F. McGregor, *Studies in Fifth-Century Epigraphy*, 1973, 71 ff.

29. The earlier studies on military operations are cited in Busolt, *GG* III 2, 626 n. 2; cf. further U.v. Wilamowitz, *Sphakteria*, SB.B, 1921, 306 ff.; A. W. Gomme, *CQ* 17, 1923, 36 ff.; A. Momigliano, "Pilo," *Ath.* NS 8, 1930, 226 ff.; cf. H. Nesselhauf, *Ant.* 13, 1937, 151 ff.; Pritchett, *Top.* I, 6 ff.; H. D. Westlake, "The Naval Battle at Pylos and its Consequences," *CQ* 24, 1974, 211 ff.

30. The document on the Cleon assessment in *IG* I² 63, also in *ATL* I, 154 ff. n. 9; II, 40 ff.; Meiggs-Lewis 69; from the large number of more recent studies the following may be emphasised: W. Kolbe, *Die Kleonschatzung des J. 425/4 v. Chr.*, SB.B, 1930 (no. XXII) 333 ff.; B. D. Meritt, *Athenian Financial Documents of the Vth Century*, Ann Arbor, 1932; Meritt-West, *Ath.A.* (cf. H. Nesselhauf, *Gn.* 12, 1936, 296 ff.; L. Robert, *Rph.*, 1936, 274 ff.); M. F. McGregor, "Kleon, Nikias and the Trebling of the Tribute," *TAPA* 66, 1935, 146 ff.; G. De Sanctis, "La *taxis phorou* del 425 a. C.," *RF* NS 13, 1935, 52 ff.; 508 ff.; H. T. Wade-Gery and B. D. Meritt, "Pylos and the Assessment of Tribute," *AJP* 57, 1936, 377 ff.;

B. D. Meritt, "The Athenian Assessment Decree," *AJP* 58, 1937, 152 ff.; *idem*, "A Note on Kleon's Assessment," *AJP* 59, 1938, 297 ff.; W. Kolbe, *Thukydides u. die Urkunde IG I² 63* SB.B, 1937, (no XXII) 172 ff.; a number of further works are cited in *ATL* II, 40.

31. The figure 1460, claimed by W. Kolbe (not 960), has been confirmed by the investigations of Meritt-West, *Ath.A*; see H. Nesselhauf, *Gn.* 12, 1936, 301.

32. B. Niese, *RE* III, 815 ff.

33. Geyer, *Mak.*, 64 ff. In 430/29 B.C. Perdiccas II had been involved in a dispute with Methone in Pieria, when Athens sought to come to terms with him: *IG* I² 57 = Tod I² 61; *ATL* II. 48, D 3-6; see also J. W. Cole, "Perdiccas and Athens," *Px.* 28, 1974, 55 ff.

34. Thuc. IV 89-101; Plato, *Symp.* 221a; *Laches* 181b; *IG* VII 1888 (grave stele of the Thespians who fell on the Boeotian side); Delium is situated in the vicinity of Tanagra; see Beloch. *GG* II 1, 335 n. 1; Kromayer-Veith, *Atlas, Griech. Abt.* I, Blatt 3; J. Beck, in Kromayer, *Schl.* IV, 177 ff.; Pritchett, *Top.* II, 24 ff.

35. H. D. Westlake, "Hermocrates the Syracusan," *Bull. John Rylands Library*, Vol. 41.1, 1958 = *Essays*, 174 ff.; F. Grosso, *Kokalos* 12, 1966, 102-143. On the Peace Oration by Hermocrates (Timaeus, *FgrHist.* 566.22 = Ephorus) see H. Fuchs, "Antike Gedanken über Krieg und Frieden," printed from the *Sonntagsblatt der Baseler Nachr.*, no. 27-28 (7 and 14 July, 1946) 28 ff.

36. Thuc. III 115; IV 1: 58-65; Polyb. XII 25 k. 26 (=Timaeus); on the speech of Hermocrates see the Dissertation by Landmann cited above 467 f.

37. Aristoph., *Wasps* 715-718 (performed in 422 B.C.) and Schol. to Philochorus (*FgrHist.* 328) fr. 119; cf. G. Nenci, *RF* 92, 1964, 173-180.

38. P. Cloché, "Les procès des stratèges athéniens," *REA* 27, 1925, 104 ff.

39. Thuc. IV 118 f.; cf. Bengtson, *Staatsv.* II, no. 185. On the question concerning the degree to which Thucydides used documentary evidence see A. Kirchhoff, *Thuk. u. sein Urkundenmaterial*, 1895, 5 ff.; and, opposed to him, Meyer, *Forsch.* II, 285 ff.; of a different view is U.v. Wilamowitz, SB.B. 1915, 607 ff.; cf. C. Meyer (v.s.p. 467).

40. Thuc. IV 50.3; Andocides, *Peace* 29; cf. Bengtson, *Staatsv.* II, no. 183. Basic now is the study by H. T. Wade-Gery, "The Peace of Kallias," in *Studies Ferguson*, 127 ff., whose conclusions are not refuted by D. Stockton, *H.* 8, 1959, 61 ff.; cf. also S. K. Eddy, *CP* 65, 1970, 8 ff.; *idem*, *CP* 68, 1973, 241 ff.

41. According to A. B. West and B. D. Meritt, "Cleon's Amphipolitan Campaign and the Assessment List of 421," *AJA* 29, 1925, 59 ff., 'Cleon's successes can be established on the basis of the tribute lists' (*ATL* I, 152 no. 34; II, 33 f. no. 34), whereas Thucydides has suppressed them; see, on the other hand, correctly, P. Roussel, *Festschr. für G. Kazarow* I, Sofia 1950, 257 ff. B. D. Meritt, "Peace Between Athens and Bottice," *AJA* 29, 1925, 29 ff., incidentally transfers into this period the treaty concluded with the Bottiaean communities (*IG* I² 90 = Tod I² no. 68, cf. *Hesp.* 7, 1938, 80 f. no. 8, see also *SEG* X 89), while Meyer (*GdA* IV², 494 ff.) and Beloch, *GG* II 1, 352 n. 5) argue for 417/6 B.C.

42. Thuc. IV 132; *IG* I² 71 = *SEG* X 86 (beginning of 422 B.C. according to P. H. Davis, *AJA* 30, 1926, 179 ff.); cf. Bengtson, *Staatsv.* II, no. 186.

43. Cf. on operations, J. K. Anderson, *JHS* 85, 1965, 1-4, and Pritchett, *Top.* I, 30 ff.

44. Thuc. V 18; Bengtson, *Staatsv.* II, no. 188 (with commentary); F. E. Adcock, *CAH* V, 250 ff.

45. Of a different opinion G. De Sanctis, "La pace di Nicia," in *Problemi di storia antica*, 1932, 93 ff., seeing in it the work of Attic pacifists, who would have forfeited an irretrievable opportunity to overthrow Sparta once and for all.

46. Thuc. V 23; 25; Diod. XII 75.2; cf. Bengtson, *Staatsv.* II, no. 189.

47. Thuc. V 28; 31.1 and 5; cf. Bengtson, *Staatsv.* II, no. 192; H. D. Westlake, "Corinth and the Argive Coalition," *AJP* 61, 1940, 414 ff.

48. Thuc. V 39.2 f.; cf. Bengtson, *Staatsv.* II, no. 191.

49. On the ancestry of Alcibiades see W. Dittenberger, "Die Familie des Alkibiades," *Hermes* 37, 1902, 1 ff.; E. Vanderpool, *Hesp.* 21, 1952, 1 ff.; W. E. Thompson, *GRBS* 11, 1970, 27 ff.; on his personality, the older works by G. Hertzberg, *Alkibiades, der Staatsmann u. Feldherr*, Halle 1853; Philippi, "Alkibiades, Sokrates, Isokrates," *RhM* 41, 1866, 13 ff.; "Einige Züge aus dem Leben des Alkibiades," *HZ* 57, 1887, 398 ff.; J. Toepfer, *RE* I, 1516

ff. s.v. no. 2; J. Hatzfeld, *Alcibiade. Etude sur l'hist. d'Athènes à la fin du lé siècle*, Paris ²1951 (the best modern critical study); F. Taeger, *Alkibiades*, Munich ²1943 (modern rescue attempt); see now E. Bloedow, *Alc.*

50. *IG* I² 86 = Tod I² 72; Thuc. V 47; Bengtson, *Staatsv* II, no. 193.

51. Thuc. V 70 ff.; Paus. I 29.13; cf. W. J. Woodhouse, *King Agis of Sparta and his Campaign in Arcadia in 418 B.C.*, Oxford 1933; cf. the objections by Th. Lenschau, *PhW*, 1934, 492 ff.; and Gomme, *Essays*, 132 ff. On the political situation see D. Gillis, *Ist. Lombardo, Cl. di Scienze e Lettere, Rendiconti* Vol. 97, 1963, 199-226; on the battle itself see Pritchett, *Top.* II, 37 ff.

52. Even Perdiccas II of Macedonia and the Chalcidians joined the federation; cf. Bengtson, *Staatsv.* II, no. 194.

53. G. De Sanctis and A. Momigliano (see the studies cited above 471), on the other hand, hold the view that the enmity between Alcibiades and Nicias was only outward. In actual fact both co-operated, especially with a view to bringing about the dissolution of the Peloponnesian League both were of one opinion. This view, however, finds no support in our sources (Thucydides).

54. Plut., *Nicias* 11; *Alcib.* 13; that the ostracism belongs in the period immediately after the battle of Mantineia has been established by Beloch, *AP*, 339 f.; *GG* II²1, 350; 351 n. 1, on the basis of Theopompus fr. 96; cf. H. Neumann, "Die Politik Athens nach dem Nikiasfrieden u. die Datierung des Ostrakismos des Hyperbolos," *Klio* 29, 1936, 36 ff., who argues for 418 B.C.; on the other hand, see W. Peek, *Kerameikos* III, 1941, 101 ff. For the year 416: A. G. Woodhead, *Hesp.* 18, 1949, 78 ff., and, of late, Ch. Fuqua, *TAPA* 96, 1965, 165-179. For the year 415: A. E. Raubitschek, *TAPA* 79, 1948, 192 f.; *Px.* 9, 1955, 122 ff. For a detailed general study see F. Camon, *Giornale ital. di fil* 15, 1962, 364 ff.; 16, 1963, 46 ff., 143 ff. An ostracon with the name of Hyperbolus: T. L. Shear, *Hesp.* 8, 1939, 246.

55. Thuc. V 85 ff.; cf. G. Deininger, *Der Melierdialog*, Diss. Erlangen 1939; further bibliography in M. Platnauer, *Fifty Years (and Twelve) of Classical Scholarship*, Oxford 1968, 213; see also W. Liebeschuetz, "The Structure and Function of the Melian Dialogue," *JHS* 88, 1968, 73 ff.; L. Canfora, *Belfagor* (Florence) 4, 1971, 409 ff. (regards the Dialogue as an interpolation). The inscription *IG* I² 97 (without fr. C) is a very mutilated Attic decree on the Melian expedition; cf. Tod I² 76; cf. Thuc. V 84.1. The view put forward by M. Treu, that Melos was in actual fact *not* neutral (*H.* 2, 1953/4, 253 ff., with supplement, *H* 3, 1954/5, 58 f.) has no doubt been refuted by W. Eberhardt, *H.* 8, 1959, 284 ff.; see also E. Buchner, "Die Aristophanes-Scholien und die Frage der Tributpflicht von Melos," *Ch.* 4, 1974. 91 ff.

56. *IG* I² 96 (more complete *SEG* X 104); Bengtson, *Staatsv.* II, 196. Thucydides has not related the actual conclusion of the treaty but only the intention (V 82).

57. The evidence in *IG* I² 294, 40 ff.; cf. C. M. Bowra, *H.* 9, 1960, 68 ff.

58. On the mood in Athens cf. Thuc. VI 24; Plut., *Nicias* 12 f.; *Alcib.* 17.

59. Thuc. VI 8.2 ff.; 25.2 ff.; Diod. XII 84.3; Plut., *Nicias* 12.; *Alcib.* 18; *IG* I² 98 and 99; cf. *SEG* X 107 = Meiggs-Lewis, no. 78.

60. Scheele, *Str.*, 3 ff.

61. Modern scholars (A. Momigliano, *RF* NS 7, 1929, 371 ff.; and in particular S. Mazzarino, *Mem. dell'Acc. delle scienze di Bologna*, 1944/45, 3 ff.: "Pericle e la Sicilia") have drawn attention to the fact that Thucydides in his account isolates the great Sicilian expedition too greatly, that it is to be viewed much more within the context of Periclean western policy. On the other hand, Pericles' western policy is greatly exaggerated by Mazzarino; it never exceeded initial stages (v.s.p. 127).

62. Thuc. VI 27-29; 60-61; Plut., *Alcib.* 18-22; Andocides, *On the Myst.* II ff.; *IG* I² 329; 330 = Meiggs-Lewis no. 79, cf. *SEG* X 241 (on the sale of Alcibiades' confiscated property by the *poletae*, cf. Pollux X 36 = Craterus; a very instructive study on the basis of the inscriptions by W. K. Pritchett, *Hesp.* 22, 1953 225 ff.; 25, 1956, 178 ff.); the earlier bibliography is cited by Busolt, *GG* III 2, 1287 n. 2; cf. De Sanctis, *St. Gr.* II, 309 f. Basic to the chronology is B. D. Meritt, "The Departure of Alcibiades for Sicily," *AJA* 34, 1930, 125 ff. The *Hermae* sacrilege, he suggests, took place on 6 June and the departure of the expedition on 21 June 415 B.C. A. Piganiol, *REG* 50, 1937, 1 ff., has arrived at a different

conclusion (departure about 22 July 415 B.C.); but see, on the other hand, J. Hatzfeld, *Alcibiade*, ²1951, 293 ff.; see also D. MacDowell, *Andocides on the Mysteries*, 1962, cf. J. L. Marr, *CQ* 21, 1971, 327 ff.

63. On Alcibiades' connections with Sparta see G. Daux, "Alcibiade, proxène des Lacédémoniens," *Mélanges Desrousseaux*, 1937, 117 ff.

64. According to B. D. Meritt, "The Battle of the Assinarus," *CP* 27, 1932, 336 ff., the final catastrophe occurred on 8 October 413 B.C. (not already in September).

65. On the end of the great Sicilian expedition: Thuc. VII 72-87; Plut., *Nicias* 25 ff.; Diod. XIII 18 ff.; Polyaenus I 43.2. On the retreat of the Athenians to the Assinarus: Kromayer-Veith, *Atlas, Griech. Abt.*, 4. Lief., Blatt 3, 9, 1926; E. Pais *Italia antica* I, 1932, 217 ff.; M. Margani, *RF* NS 8, 1930, 189 ff.; on the *heorte Asinaria* in Syracuse, cf. Plut., *Nicias* 28.1 f.; on the Treasury at Delphi, Paus. X 11.5 (cf. J. Bousquet, *BCH* 64/65, 1940/41, 128 ff.); on the issues of decadrachms, *inter al.*, C. Seltman, *Greek Coins*, 1933, 127; a different view is admittedly held by J. Liegle, *Euainetus* (101. Winckelmannsprogr.), Berlin 1941, who dates the coins a decade earlier; cf. K. Christ, *H.* 3, 1954-55, 387; thus far the question has not been resolved.

66. On Thucydides' appraisal of Nicias see H. D. Westlake, *CQ* 35, 1941, 58 ff. The attempt of E. Bethe, *NJb* 39, 1917, 83 f., to trace the miscarriage of the Sicilian expedition back to a chain of unfavourable coincidences is not convincing.

67. See H. T. Wade-Gery. "The Peace of Kallias," *Studies Ferguson*, 217 ff.); cf. H. B. Mattingly, *Ph.* 119, 1975. 48 ff. For the sources v.s.p. 476 n. 40.

68. It is uncertain whether the stele of Xanthus refers to the war of the Persians against Amorges (cf. *Gn.* 14, 1938, 116).

69. Thuc. VIII 18; 43; 52; 58; see Bengtson, *Staatsv.* II, nos. 200, 201, 202. Persian subsidy coins are possibly the types discussed by E. S. G. Robinson, *Num. Chron.*, 1948, 48 ff., which bear a satrap portrait on the obverse side and an owl and the legend *BAS* on the reverse side; see also W. Schwabacher, in Charites (*Festchr. f. E. Langlotz*), 1957, 27 ff.

70. Thuc. VII 28.4; cf. K. J. Beloch, *RhM* 39, 1884, 43 ff.

71. F. D. Smith, *Athenian Political Commissions*, Diss. Chicago 1920, 32 ff.

72. D. M. Lewis, *H.* 7, 1958, 392 ff. (on the basis of the new Aramaic Papyri from Elephantine).

73. Thuc. VIII 65.3; 67 f.; Aristotle, *Const. Ath.* 29. On the relationship of the Thucydidean account to the *Const. Ath.* of Aristotle see in particular Meyer, *Forsch.* II, 406 ff., esp. 413 ff.; cf. also C. F. Lehmann-Haupt, *GG*, in Gercke-Norden, *Einl.*, 90. Here, as elsewhere, our decisive authority can only be Thucydides, who admittedly errs in stating that there were only 10 *syngrapheis autokratores* (67.1) (in so far as it is not the result of a simple scribal slip of the pen). Cf. also the study by M. Cary cited above 473.

74. De Sanctis, *St. Gr.* II, 368.

75. Mistaken is U. Köhler, SB.B, 1885, I 460: "Perhaps never again in history did a political revolution come about in such legal forms as the revolution in Athens in the spring of 411."

76. H. Swoboda, "Zur Verfassungsgesch. von Samos," *Festschr. f. O. Benndorf*, Vienna 1899, 250 ff.

77. See E. Bethe, *NJb* 39, 1917, 86 f. The Study by K. Köster, *Die Lebensmittelversorgung der altgriech. Polis* (Neue Deutsche Forsch. 245), Berlin 1939, 27, is unfortunately also inadequate on this question.

78. Thus U. Wilcken, SB.B, 1935, 48 ff., and more recently J. A. O. Larsen, *Rep. Govt.*, 13; 197 n. 30. On the other hand, Meyer, *GdA* IV, 591, Wilamowitz, *Arist.*, II, 116 and 121, and A.v. Mess, *RhM* 66, 1911, 377, *inter al.*, regard this constitution of Aristotle as a utopia; see also P. J. Rhodes, "The Five Thousand in the Athenian Revolution of 411 B.C.," *JHS* 92, 1972, 115 ff.

79. See Bloedow, *Alc.*, 46 ff.

80. A different view is held by De Sanctis, *St. Gr.* II, 382 f.

81. The attitude towards Theramenes varies in the ancient sources just as it does among modern scholars; see, for instance, Pöhlig, "Der Athener Theramenes," *Jbb. f. Kl. Phil. Suppl.* 9, 1877, 227 f.; Wilamowitz, *Arist.*, I, 168; B. Perrin, "The Rehabilitation of Theramenes," *AHR* 9, 1904 649 ff.; Beloch, *GG* II²1, 392 (on the whole a favourable

appraisal); on the other hand, for instance, W. Schwahn, *RE* V A, 2319 f. s.v. *Theramenes*. L. van der Ploeg, *Theramenes en zijn Tijd*, Utrecht 1948, has arrived at a very negative verdict on him.

82. Earlier literature in Busolt, *GG* III 2, 1538 n. 2; cf. H. T. Wade-Gery, "The Charter of the Democracy in 410 B.C., *IG* I² 114," *BSA* 33, 1932/33, 113 ff. (cf. *CQ* 24, 1930, 116 ff.); A. Wilhelm, *Attische Urkunden* IV, SB.W, 217,5, 1939, 48 f.; S. Dow, *Hesp.* 10, 1941, 31 ff.; B. D. Meritt, *Hesp.* 10, 1941, 319 f.; 328 ff.; cf. *SEG* X 119; E. Ruschenbusch, *H.* 5, 1956, 123; cf. Meiggs-Lewis no. 86 (*IG* I² 115).

83. Aristotle, *Const. Ath.* 28.3. Beloch's objection (*GG* II²1, 398 n.1) is not convincing. On his personality see R. Renaud, *Et. class.* 38, 1970, 458-477 (positive); B. Baldwin, *Acta Class*, 17, 1974, 36-47.

84. Cf. Meiggs-Lewis no. 87.

85. Xen., *Hell.* I 3.9.

86. L. Deubner, *Attische Feste*, 1932, 17 ff.

87. Xen., *Hell.*, I 4.8 ff.; cf. Busolt, *GG* III 2, 1564;M. Scheele, *Str.*, 8 f.

88. Cf. W. K. Prentice, "The Character of Lysander," *AJA* 38, 1934, 37 ff.

89. Archelaus the king of Macedonia supplied the Athenians with timber for ship-building; see *IG* I² 105 (= Meiggs-Lewis no. 9 1); cf. B. D. Meritt, "Archelaos and the Decelean War," *Classical Studies Presented to E. Capps*, Princeton, N.J., 1936, 246 ff., whose restoration of the archon's name in line 3 of the inscription is, however, contested by G. De Sanctis, *RF* NS 13, 1935, 205 ff.; cf. *SEG* X 138.

90. P. Cloché, L'affaire des Arginuses," *Rev. hist.* 130, 1919, 5 ff.; J. Hatzfeld, Socrate au procès des Arginuses, *Mél. G. Radet*, 1940, 165 ff.; cf. A. Andrewes, "The Arginousai Trial," *Px.* 28, 1974, 112 ff.; G. Marindakis, *The Lawsuit of the Victors at Arginusae* (in Greek), Athens 1975 [juridical].

91. There is no reason to regard this peace offer by Sparta as apocryphal, as De Sanctis, *St. Gr.* II, 396, is inclined to do.

92. B. D. Meritt, "Athens and Carthage," in *Studies Ferguson*, 247 ff., cf. Bengtson, *Staatsv.* II, no. 208 = Meiggs-Lewis no. 92.

93. Cf. Meiggs-Lewis no. 95.

94. The Athenian *strategos* and statesman Philocles put forward the proposal to cut off the right thumb of all prisoners in order to make them incapable of military serivce; cf. F. Kiechle, *H.* 7, 1958, 141.

95. The decree of the Attic Popular Assembly is extant: *IG* II/III²1 = Meiggs-Lewis no. 94 = *GHD 5th C* p. 41.

96. Theories on the mission of Theramenes and his own plans have been put forward by J. A. R. Munro, "Theramenes Against Lysander," *CQ* 32, 1938, 18 ff. The sources (Xen., *Hell.* II 16-17; Lysias XIII 68 f.; XIII 8 ff.) are now supplemented by a papyrus from Karanis, published by H. C. Youtie and R. Merkelbach, *ZPE* 2, 1968, 161 ff. Theramenes had, according to this source, been invested with plenary powers on his first mission.

97. Xen., *Hell.* II 2.20; Andocides, *On Peace* II; Diod. XIII 107.4; XIV 3.6; Plutarch, *Lys.* 14 (the text of the decree passed by the ephors); Bengtson, *Staatsv.* II, no. 211.

98. According to J. A. R. Munro, "The End of the Peloponnesian War," *CQ* 31, 1937, 32 ff., already in March 404 B.C. peace was concluded, whereas Lysander's arrival fell four weeks later.

9 THE DECLINE OF THE GREEK POLIS

SOURCES AND BIBLIOGRAPHY: No significant evidence from monuments for the period from 404 to 360 B.C. has been preserved. The Conon Wall in Athens (the so-called Piraeus Ring) is attested by inscriptions: *IG* II/III^2 1656 ff.; cf. Tod II 107 = *GHD 4th C* 10; F. G. Maier, *Griechische Mauerbauinschriften* I, Heidelberg 1959, 21 ff. nos. 1-9; see Judeich, *Top.*, 83 ff. In Syracuse Dionysius I continued construction on and strongly fortified the citadel of Euryalus: Mauceri, *Il castello Eurialo nella storie e nell'arte*, 1928. On the fortifications and temples built by the Carian dynast Maussollus in Halicarnassus see Judeich, *KS*, 246 ff., and the archaeological investigations by Ch. Th. Newton, *A History of Discoveries at Halicarnassus, Cnidus and Branchidae*, 1862-63. The famous Maussolleum, the tomb of Mausollus, was not built until the middle of the fifties by Artemisia and perhaps not completed until under the rule of Ada in the time of Alexander (E. Buschor, *Maussollos u. Alexander*, Munich 1950; cf. K. Jeppesen and J. Zable, "The Site of the Mausoleum at Halicarnassos Reexcavated," *AJA* 77, 1973, 336 ff.).

The coins provide a great many details (a survey in, for instance, P. Gardner, *A History of Ancient Coinage, 700-300 B.C.*, Oxford 1918, Chaps. XIV ff.; bibliography in *CAH* VI, 566 f.). The amount of epigraphical evidence is steadily increasing (cf. the selection in *Syll.* I^3 nos. 116-185; very important are the Attic inscriptions in *IG* II/III^2), and indeed one can only keep up with it by means of epigraphical reports, for instance, those by J. and L. Robert, in *REG*, 1938 ff. An excellent selection, with good bibliography, is that of Tod, II.

The fourth century is the period of political pamphlets, which were often published in the form of orations; see P. Wendland, "Beitr. zur athenischen Politik and Publizistik des 4. Jahrh.," *NGG*, 1910, 123 ff., additional studies are discussed by F. R. Wüst, *WG* 4, 1938, 328 ff. The towering personality in Panhellenic journalism is the orator Isocrates of Athens (436-338) B.C. His actual field is the political speech, that is, the pamphlet in the form of an oration. He did not take part in the verbal battles of the popular assembly. The writings of Isocrates again and again revolve around the idea of panhellenism and the notion of an aristocratic democracy, namely rule by the "best" citizens (cf. R.v. Pöhlmann, *Isokr. und das Problem der Demokratie*, SB.M, 1913, H.1). On his attitude to history see C. B. Welles, "Isocrates' View of History," in *The Classical Tradition. Studies in Honor of Harry Caplan*, Ithaca, New York, 1966, 3-25. On his attitude to economics, A. Fuks, "Isocrates and the Social-Economic Situation in Greece," *Ancient Society* 3, 1972, 17 ff. From his "showpieces," the following may be cited: the *Panegyrikos*, published in 380

B.C. (according to Wilamowitz, *Arist.* II, 380 ff. (cf. E. Drerup, "Epikritisches zum Paneg. des Is.," *Ph.* 54, 1895, 636 ff.; Meyer, *GdA* V, 370 ff.; K. Münscher, *RE* IX, 2185 ff.), this is a "piece of propaganda for the Second Attic Maritime League," but see, opposed to this, Jaeger, *Dem.*, 209 n. 31, and in particular, E. Buchner, *Der Panegyrikos des Isokrates* [Historia-Einzelschr. 2], 1958; cf. also E. Skard, *Zwei relig.-polit. Begriffe: Euergetes-Concordia*, 1932, 51 ff.; the *Plataïkos*, directed against the Theban claims to power, from the year 373 B.C. (on the date of composition see A. Momigliano, *Ath.* NS 14, 1936, 27 ff., as opposed to G. Mathieu, *Les idées polit. d'Isocr.*, 1925, 87 ff., who places it in the year 371 B.C.; on the attitude of Isocrates towards Thebes cf. P. Cloché, *Rev. hist.* 193, 1942/43, 277 ff.); and, finally, the *Euagoras*, an encomium on the ruler bearing the same name, an ancient *Fürstenspiegel* (374/3 B.C.) (cf. K. Spyridakis *Euagoras I. von Salamis*, 1935, 5 ff.), a work that is very characteristic of the famous Athenian orator in turning to monarchy. The great period of Isocrates, however, does not come until the fifties, and above all the forties, of the fourth century, when he addressed his pamphlets to the Macedonian king, Philip II (v.i.p. 496 f.).

From the orations transmitted under the name of the logographer Lysias (a short survey in Beloch, *GG* III 2, 14 f., and in Plöbst, *RE* XIII, 2533 ff.), the *Epitaphios*, the speech on the Athenians who fell in the Corinthian War (394 B.C.), has been regarded as authentic again by J. Waltz, Ph. Suppl.-Bd. 29, 4, 1936 (but a different view is taken by P. Treves, *RF* NS 15, 1937, 113 ff.; 278 ff.). On Lysias there is (in addition to the historically as good as useless study by F. Blass, *Die attische Beredsamkeit*,[2] 3 vols., Leipzig 1887 and 1893) the excellent Würzburg Diss. by F. Ferckel, *Lysias u. Athen. Der Redner und sein Gaststaat*, 1937, which should be consulted; cf. also K. J. Dover, *Lysias and the Corpus Lysiacum*, 1968. The lawyer Andocides was the first writer to put forward, in his "Peace Oration" of 392 B.C., the idea of a general peace; on the date see W. Judeich, *Ph.* 81, 1926, 141 ff.

HISTORIOGRAPHY: The *Hellenica* by Xenophon of Athens (v.i.p. 486 f.) betrays a distinct pro-Spartan point of view. Important events such as the founding of the Second Attic Maritime League are not mentioned, and particular injustice is done to Thebes, the great opponent of Sparta (A. Momigliano, "L'egemonia tebana in Senofonte e in Eforo," *Atene e Roma*, 1935, 101 ff.). In regard to the date of composition, not even relative certainty has thus far been achieved by scholars; cf. in particular H. R. Breitenbach, *RE* IX A, 1679 ff. Contiguous with the *Hellenica* is the *Agesilaus* (I. Bruns, *Das literar. Porträt*, 1896, 126 ff.; F. Dümmler, *Kl. Schr.* I, 1901, 271 ff.). A document of greatest importance for the history of civilisation is the *Anabasis of Cyrus*, a glorification of the spirit of Hellenic soldiery and its triumph over the power and greatness of the Persian empire. Xenophon at first published the work under the pseudonym Themistogenes of Syracuse (a different view is held by W. K. Prentice, "Themistogenes of Syracuse, an Error of a Copyist," *AJP* 68,

1947, 73 ff., but the conjecture suggested by him appears too daring); he plagiarised extensively from his predecessors, especially Sophaenetus of Stymphalus. By pushing his own personality into the foreground, the work assumed the character of an apologia. The investigations undertaken hitherto (see the bibliography in *CAH* VI, 567 f.) are without exception hypothetical. The problem of Xenophon's dependence on earlier accounts should be re-examined on the basis of an analysis of Diodorus XIV 19-31 (Ephorus-Sophaenetus). Valuable results on this subject were achieved by W. Otto in the seminar studies on Ancient History at the University of Munich, but these have unfortunately not been published. A more recent study is that of A. Garzetti, *Ath.* NS 33, 1955, 118-136; cf. H. Erbse, *Gym.* 73, 1966, 485-505; and in particular the above cited *RE* article by H. R. Breitenbach. On the *Hellenica* of Theopompus and of Cratippus see above 469. The events of the year 396/5 B.C. are delineated by a papyrus fragment from Oxyrhynchus (published by B. P. Grenfell and A. S. Hunt, *The Oxyrhynchus Papyri* V, no. 842, 110 ff.; by Jacoby, *FgrHist.* no. 66; and by V. Bartoletti, *Hellenica Oxyrhynchia*, Leipzig 1959); in essence it follows Xenophon's account, or consciously corrects it (G. Busolt, "Der neue Historiker und Xenophon," *Hermes* 43, 1908, 255 ff.; K. Münscher, *Xenoph. in der griech.-röm. Lit.*, Leipzig 1920, 31 f.; sceptical is Jacoby, *FgrHist.* no. 66, VI-VII, Commentary). On the basis of the previous evidence it is not possible to solve the question of authorship; the Daïmachus hypothesis of F. Jacoby (and W. Otto) also rests on a weak footing; cf. lastly H. Bloch, "Studies in Historical Literature of the IVth Century B.C.," *Studies Ferguson*, 303 ff., who no doubt rightly argues that it must have been written by some anonymous author of the fourth century. Nor is the question of authorship, incidentally, solved by the new fragments of the *Hellenica Oxyrhynchia* (v.s.p. 472). G. A. Lehmann, *H.* 21, 1972, 385 ff., has attempted to show a link between the *Hellenica Oxyrhynchia* and Isocrates' *Philippos*, but see also H. R. Breitenbach, *RE* Suppl. XIII, 383 ff.

The *Hellenica* by Callisthenes of Olynthus (10 Books; from the Peace of Antalcidas to the beginning of the Third Sacred War, 357/6 B.C.; the fragments in Jacoby, *FgrHist.* no. 124; cf. on Callisthenes, *idem*, *RE* X, 1674 ff.; Alex. Schäfer, *Die Berichte Xenophons, Plutarchs u. Diodoros' über die Besetzung u. Befreiung Thebens*, Diss. Munich 1930; H. D. Westlake, *CQ* 33, 1939, 11 ff.); and the *Hellenica* by the orator Anaximenes of Lampsacus (from prehistoric times to the battle of Mantineia, 362 B.C.) were utilised by Ephorus of Cyme (on him v.s.p. 436 f.) in his *Histories*—a work which in terms of sources is incomparably more valuable for the time of the author himself than for the earlier centuries. The *Histories* of Ephorus form the basis of Books XIV and XV of Diodorus, but are contaminated by other sources; cf. C. A. Volquardsen, *Untersuch. über die Quellen der griech u. sizil. Gesch. bei Diod. XI bis XVI*, Kiel 1868.

Relevant in regard to Persian history are the fragments of Ctesias (v.s.p. 435 f.), and of Dinon (*FgrHist.* no. 690), and of Plutarch's Lives, that of Artaxerxes, as well as the *Vita* of Datames by Cornelius Nepos.

The history of Sicily in the time of Dionysius I and II was recounted in the *History* of Philistus († 357 B.C.) (*FgrHist.* no. 556); Philistus is the source on which the *History of the West* from the pen of Timaeus of Tauromenium is based. See R. Zoepffel, *Untersuchungen zum Geschichtswerk des Philistos von Syrakus*, Diss. Freiburg i. Br. 1965.

The *Vitae* of Cornelius Nepos (Thrasybulus, Cono, Iphicrates, Chabrias, Timotheus, Datames, Agesilaus) contain little that is of any use; more valuable are the biographies of Lysander, Agesilaus, Artoxerxes and Pelopidas by Plutarch. On the *Life* of Lysander reference should be made to the commentary cited below (485 n. 5) by J. Smits; on the *Vita* of Agesilaus, that by I. Bos (*Plutarchs Leven van Agesilaus*, Groningen 1947). The *Vita* of Epameinondas is lost; a short excerpt appears in Paus. VIII 11.5-10; IX 13-15 (cf. L. Peper, *De Plutarchi "Epaminonda,"* Diss. Jena, Weida 1912). The relationship of Plutarch's Lives to the *Hellenica* of Xenophon has been investigated by R. Dippel, *Quae ratio intercedat inter Xenoph. hist. Graec. et Plut. vitas quaeritur*, Diss. Giessen 1898. Finally, reference may also be made to Justin V 11-VI (a scanty excerpt from the *Historiae Philippicae of Pompeius Trogus*).

BIBLIOGRAPHY: G. R. Sievers, *Gesch. Griechenlands vom Ende des Peloponnesischen Krieges bis zur Schlacht bei Mantineia*, 1840; K. J. Beloch, *AP*; E.v. Stern, *Gesch. der spartanischen u. thebanischen Hegemonie vom Königsfrieden bis zur Schlacht bei Mantineia*, Diss. Dorpat 1884; Judeich, *KS*; J. V. Prášek, *Gesch. der Meder und Perser* II, Gotha 1910 (partly out of date); Kaerst, *GH* I^3, 110 ff.; H. W. Parke, *Greek Mercenary Soldiers from the Earliest Times to the Battle of Ipsus*, Oxford 1933, 20 ff.; P. Cloché, *La politique étrangère d'Athènes de 404 à 338 av. J.-C.*, Paris 1934; H. Dombrowski, *Die politischen Prozesse in Athen vom Archonat des Eukleides bis zum Ausgang des Bundesgenossenkrieges*, Diss. Greifswald 1934; O. Huber, *Die wirtschaftlichen Verhältnisse Athens vom Ende des Pelop. Krieges bis zum Königsfrieden*, Diss. Munich 1939; H. E. Stier, *Der Untergang der klassischen Demokratie*, Opladen 1972. A particularly large number of investigations have been undertaken on the central question of the general peace in the fourth century B.C.: F. Taeger, *Der Friede von 362/1. Ein Beitr. z. Gesch. der panhell. Bewegung im 4. Jahrh.* (Tübinger Beitr. 11), Stuttgart 1930 (cf. H. Berve, *Gn.* 9, 1933, 301 ff.); A. Momigliano, "La Koine Eirene dal 386 al 338 a.C.," *RF* NS 12, 1934, 482 ff.; "Per la storia della pubblicistica sulla Koinè Eiréne nel IV secolo av. Cr.," *Annali R. Scuola Norm. Sup. di Pisa*, ser. II 5, 1936, 97 ff.; "La pace del 375 e il Plataico di Isocrate," *Ath.* NS 14, 1936, 3 ff.; G. De Sanctis, "La pace del 362/1," *RF* NS 12, 1934, 145 ff.; Hampl, *Staatsv.* (cf., however, the critical remarks on this work by F. R. Wüst, *Gn.* 14, 1938, 367 ff.; by Ernst Meyer, *ZSS Röm.* 59, 1939, 498 ff.; and J. A. O. Larsen, *CP* 34, 1939, 375 ff.); V. Martin, *MusHelv* 1, 1944, 13 ff. A detailed survey is provided by F. R. Wüst, *WG* 4, 1938, 328 ff. T. T. B. Ryder, *Koine Eirene*, London/Oxford 1965, furnishes little that is new (cf., for instance, J. A. O. Larsen, *Gn.* 38, 1966, 256 ff.). Cf. also J. K. Anderson, *Military Theory and Practice in the Age of Xenophon*, London 1970.

GREECE AFTER THE PELOPONNESIAN WAR

PRINCIPAL SOURCES: Xen., *Hell.* II 3.1-4., 43 (deliberately concise and vague; cf. G. Colin, *Xénophon historien d'après le livre II des Helléniques*, Paris 1933); III 2.2 1 ff. Lysias, *Against Eratosthenes* (XII); *On the Constitution* (XXXIV) (both orations delivered in 403/2 B.C:), *Against Agoratus* (XIII) (from the year 398 B.C.); *Against Hippotherses* (*P. Oxy.* XIII 1606) (from 394 or later) (cf. on this oration Th. Reinach, *REG* 32, 1919, 442 ff.); Isocrates IV 110 ff.; VIII 95 ff; XII 54; 67 f.; 103 f.; Plut., *Lys.* 16 ff. The oration *On the Constitution*, transmitted under the name of the Sophist Herodes Atticus (v.s.p. 337), provides information on Thessaly about 400 B.C. (edition by E. Drerup, in *Studien z. Gesch. u. Kult. des Altertums* II 1, Paderborn 1908). According to K. J. Beloch, the author is a Thessalian Sophist from the period about 400 B.C. (concurring, for instance, Ed. Meyer and R. v. Pöhlmann), a view which is not, however, beyond all doubt (see K. Münscher, *RE* VIII, 951 ff.). H. T. Wade-Gery, *CQ* 39, 1945, 19 ff., attempts, for instance, to prove that Critias is the author of the work and that it was written in 404; different theories in M. Sordi, *RF* NS 33, 1935, 175 ff., who ascribes it to Thrasymachus or one of his pupils, and who dates it in the year 401 or 400 B.C. On Plato's dialogue, the *Meno*, see J. S. Morrison, "Meno of Pharsalus, Polycritas and Ismenias" *CQ* 36, 1942, 54 ff., who dates the situation forming the basis of the dialogue in the beginning of 402.

THE EXPEDITION OF CYRUS THE YOUNGER. THE SPARTAN-PERSIAN WAR IN WESTERN ASIA MINOR

PRINCIPAL SOURCES: a) Xen., *Anab.*; Diod. XIV 19 ff.; Ctesias; b) Xen., *Hell.* III-IV; *Agesilaus* (cf. Ed. Schwartz, *RhM* 44, 1889, 169 ff.); *Hellenica Oxyrhynchia*; Plut., *Agesilaus* and *Artoxerxes*.

BIBLIOGRAPHY: a) On the march of the Ten Thousand: G. Cousin, *Kyros le Jeune en Asie Mineure*, Paris-Nancy 1905; E. v. Hoffmeister, *Durch Armenien, eine Wanderung, und der Zug Xenophons zum Schwarzen Meer*, Leipzig-Berlin 1911; C. F. Lehmann-Haupt, *Armenien einst und jetzt* I, Berlin 1910, 327 ff.; II 2, 1931, 761 ff.; Fr. Segl, *Vom Kentrites bis Trapezus*, Erlangen 1925. b) On the war between the Spartans and Persians: Judeich, *KS*, 38 ff.; Ed. Meyer, *Theopomps Hellenika*, 1909, 3 ff.; L. Pareti, "Le imprese di Tibrone in Asia nel 400-399 e nel 391 av. Cr.," *Entaphia E. Pozzi*, Turin 1913, 48 ff.; H. Lins, *Kritische Betrachtung der Feldzüge des Agesilaos in Kleinasien*, Diss. Halle 1914; W. Kaupert, in Kromayer, *Schl.* IV 2, 261 ff.; E. Zierke, *Agesilaos*, Diss. Frankfurt a.M. 1936; P. Meloni, "Tiribazo," *Ath.* NS 28, 1950, 292-339;

cf. the following articles in *RE*: *Agesilaos* I, 796 ff. s.v. no. 4 (B. Niese); *Kyros* (the Younger), *Suppl.-Bd.* IV, 1166 ff. s.v. no. 7 (F. H. Weissbach); *Pharnabazos*, Bd. XIX, 1842 ff. s.v. no. 2 (Th. Lenschau); Thibron, VI A, 273 ff. no. 1 (V. Ehrenberg); Tissaphernes, *Suppl.-Bd.* VII, 1579 ff. (H. Schaefer).

THE REVOLT OF THE GREEKS AGAINST SPARTA, AND THE KING'S PEACE

PRINCIPAL SOURCES: Xen., *Hell.* III 5-V 1 (for an assessment of Xenophon see P. Cloché, "Les 'Helléniques' de Xenophon [livres III-VII] et Lacédémone," *REA* 46, 1944, 12 ff.); *Agesilaus*; *Hellenica Oxyrhynchia* I-III; X-XIII (cf. on this the detailed discussion by G. De Sanctis, *Atti Accad. Torino* 66, 1931, 157 ff.); Andocides, *On Peace*; Diod. XIV 81-110 (on Diod. XIV 84.3 f. see L. Robert, *Rev. de Phil.*, 1934, 43 ff.); Plut., *Lysander, Agesilaus;* Lysias, *Epitaphius* (on the question of authenticity v.s.p. 481).

BIBLIOGRAPHY: Ed. Meyer, *Theopomps Hellenika*, 1909; Th. Lenschau, "Die Sendung des Timokrates und der Ausbruch des Korinthischen Krieges," *PhW*, 1933, 1325 ff. (cf. Ad. Wilhelm, *Att. Urk.* V, 1942, 101 ff.); P. Treves, "Note sulla guerra corinzia," *RF* NS 15, 1937, 113 ff.; "Introduzione alla storia della guerra corinzia," *Ath.* NS 16, 1938, 65 ff.; 164 ff.; P. Cloché, "Notes sur la politique athénienne au début du IVe siècle et pendant la guerre du Péloponnèse," *REA* 43, 1941, 16 ff. (especially on the mood for peace in Athens); S. Accame, *Ricerche intorno alla guerra corinzia*, Naples 1951 (a valuable critical study); K. L. McKay, "The Oxyrhynchus Historian and the Outbreak of the Corinthian War," *CR* 3, 1953, 6-7. D. Kagan, "The Economic Origins of the Corinthian War," *PP* 16, 1961, 321-341; valuable is S. Perlman, "The Causes and the Outbreak of the Corinthian War," *CQ* 39, 1944, 64-81 (the fear of Sparta in particular was the cause of the war). On Conon: G. Barbieri, *Conone*, Rome 1955 (a thorough piece of scholarship, but containing little that is new); R. Seager, "Thrasybulus, Conon and Athenian Imperialism, 396-386," *JHS* 87, 1967, 95 ff.; moreover the articles in *RE Konon*, XI, 1319 ff. s.v. no. 3 (H. Swoboda); *Tiribazos*, VI A, 1431 ff. (H. Schaefer); *Tithraustes*, VI A, 1522 f. (Graf Stauffenberg). On the chronology: G. Zunkel, *Untersuch. z. griech. Gesch. d. Jahre 395-386 v. Chr.*, Diss. Jena (published Weimar 1911). For the bibliography on the King's Peace v.i.p. 490 n. 45.

SPARTA AND THEBES IN THE STRUGGLE FOR SUPREMACY. THE SECOND ATHENIAN MARITIME LEAGUE

SOURCES: Xen., *Hell.* V 2-VI 4.26; *Agesilaus*; Diod. XV; Corn. Nep., *Vitae* of *Iphicrates, Chabrias, Datames, Epaminondas, Pelopidas, Agesilaus*; Plut., *De genio Socratis* (cf. W. v. Christ, SB. Bay. 1901, Heft 1, 59 ff.); *Pelopidas, Agesilaus*; Paus. IX 13 ff.; Polyaenus VIII 42 ff.; Justin VI.

BIBLIOGRAPHY: In addition to the studies in the survey cited above (483), see in particular: W. Judeich, "Athen und Theben vom Königsfrieden bis zur Schlacht bei Leuktra," *RhM* 76, 1927, 171 ff.; A. Schaefer, *Die Berichte Xenophons, Plutarchs u. Diodors über die Besetzung und Befreiung Thebens* (382, 379 v. Chr.), Diss. Munich 1930; P. Cloché, *La politique étrangère d'Athènes*, 1934, Chaps. 3 and 4; R. Seager, "The King's Peace and the Balance of Power in Greece 386-362 B.C.," *Ath.* 62, 1974, 36 ff.; specifically on the Second Attic Maritime League: G. Busolt, "Der 2. athen. Bund," *Jahrb. f. klass. Phil., Suppl.-Bd.* 7, 1875, 641 ff.; J. Lipsius, *Beitr. z. Gesch. griech. Bundesverfassungen*: I. *Der athenische Seebund*, SB. Sächs. Ges. d. Wiss. phil.-hist. Kl., 1898, no. 4, 146 ff.; F. H. Marshall, *The Second Athenian Confederacy*, Cambridge 1905; H. G. Robertson, "The Administration of Justice in the Second Athenian Confederacy," *CP* 23, 1928, 30 ff.; V. Ehrenberg, "Zum 2. attischen Bund," *Hermes* 64, 1929, 322 ff.; Hampl, *Staatsv.*, 117 ff.; Accame, *Lega*, with new epigraphical readings; cf. also Ad. Wilhelm, *Vier Beschlüsse der Athener*, Abh.B, 1939, no. 22 (published 1940), 3 ff.; as well as H. Volkmann, *PhW*, 1942, 364 ff. (in his review of Accame); Triepel, *Heg.*, 387 ff. For the history of the Maritime League from 374-371: R. Sealey, "IG II^2 1609 and the Transformation of the Second Athenian Sea-League," *Px.* 11, 1957, 95-111; A. G. Woodhead, "Chabrias, Timotheus, and the Aegean Allies, 375-373 B.C.," *Px.* 16, 1962, 258-266; T. Wilson, "Athenian Military Finances, 387/7 to the Peace of 375," *Ath.* 48, 1970, 302 ff.; G. L. Cawkwell, "The Foundation of the Second Athenian Confederacy," *CQ* 23, 1973, 47 ff. Important are the new documents on the legal treaties which Athens concluded with a number of states from about 375 B.C. on (Troezen, Stymphalus, Siphnos, *et al.*): A. G. Woodhead, *Hesp.* 26, 1956, 198 ff. On Spartan policy: T. T. B. Ryder, "Spartan Relations with Persia after the King's Peace: a Strange Story in Diodorus XV 9," *CQ* 13, 1963, 105-109. See also G. L. Cawkwell, "Agesilaus and Sparta," *CQ* 26, 1976, 62-84.

THE ERA OF THE THEBAN HEGEMONY (371-362 BC)

SOURCES: Xen., *Hell.* VI 4.19 ff. (anti-Theban); *Agesilaus*; Diod. XV 57 ff.; Plut., *Ages.* 30 ff.; *Pelop.* (pro-Theban); Paus. VIII 11; IX 14 f.; Just. VI 7 and VII 5; Bilabel, P. Kleinform, no. 14. Inscriptions: Tod, II, nos. 131 ff.

BIBLIOGRAPHY: E.v. Stern, *Gesch. der spartanischen u. thebanischen Hegemonie vom Königsfrieden bis zur Schlacht bei Mantinea*, Dorpat 1884; B. Niese; "Beitr. z. griech. Gesch. der Jahre 370-364 v. Chr.," *Hermes* 34, 1899, 520 ff.; "Chronologische und historische Beiträge z. griech. Gesch. der Jahre 370-364 v. Chr.," *Hermes* 39, 1904, 84 ff.; A. Bauer, "Der zweimalige Angriff des Epameinondas auf Sparta," *HZ* 65, 1890, 240 ff.; Momigliano, *Fil.*, 59 ff.: "L'egemonia tebana;" P. Cloché, *La politique étrangère d'Athènes*, 1934, 94 ff.; in addition the monographs cited above

492 ns. 72 and 73; also J. Wiseman, "Epaminondas and the Theban Invasions," *Klio* 51, 1969, 177 ff.; H. Beister, *Untersuchungen zu der Zeit der thebanischen Hegemonie*, Diss. Bonn 1970 [also on Leuctra] (cf. G. L. Cawkwell, *JHS* 92, 1972, 229); G. S. Shrimpton, "The Theban Supremacy in Fourth Century Literature," *Px.* 25, 1971, 310 ff.

THE EMPIRE OF DIONYSIUS I AND HIS SUCCESSORS IN SICILY. TIMOLEON

MAIN SOURCES: Of the contemporary historians Philistus has been lost; the fragments are in Jacoby, *FgrHist.* no. 556. A valuable contemporary source is furnished by the *Letters of Plato*, especially 3, 7, 8, and 13, which must be regarded as authentic; of these, *ep.* 7 and 8 were written after the death of Dion (354); cf. F. Egermann, *Die platonischen Briefe VII u. VIII*, Berlin Diss. 1928; cf. *Gn.* 9, 1933, 628 ff. (in the review by F. Novotny); and G. Hell, *Hermes* 67, 1932, 295 ff. (on the dating). See in particular G. Pasquali, *Le lettere di Platone*, Florence 1938. In addition, there is Xenophon's *Hieron*; according to J. Hatzfeld ("Note sur la date et l'objet du Hiéron," *REG*, 1946/47, 54 ff.), it is "a work written for a special occasion," drawn up in 358/7 B.C. designed to convey advice to Dion. Cf. also G. J. D. Aalders, *Mn.* 4, 1953, 208 ff., who places it between 360 and 355 B.C.

OTHER SOURCES: Pseudo-Aristotle, *Oeconomica* II; Diod. XIII-XVI; (cf. in detail, F. Sartori, "Su Dionisio il Vecchio nell'opera diodorea," *Critica Storica*, 1966, 3-61; Corn. Nep., *Vita of Dio*; Plut., *Dion* (based chiefly on Timaeus); *Timoleon* (cf. H. D. Westlake, "The Sources of Plutarch's Timoleon," *CQ* 32, 1938, 65 ff.); Polyaenus, *Strategems*; Just. XX f.

On the Coins: Ad. Holm, *Geschichte Siziliens* III, 1898; G. F. Hill, *Coins of Ancient Sicily*, Westminster 1903; W. Giesecke, *Sicilia numismatica*, Leipzig 1923; G. E. Rizzo, *Monete greche della Sicilia*, 1946; K. Christ, *Jb. f. Num. u. Geldgesch.* 5-6, 1954/55, 181 ff.; E. Gàbrici, *Problemi di numismatica greca della Sicilia e Magna Grecia*, 1959.

BIBLIOGRAPHY: In addition to the general histories by Ed. Meyer (*GdA* V), Beloch (*GG* II and III), Glotz (*HG* III, 380 ff.), *CAH* VI (Chap. 5: "Dionysius of Syracuse," by J. B. Bury: Chap. 10: "Sicily, 367 to 330 B.C.," by R. Hackforth), and H. Berve (*GG* II), the following may be cited: A. Holm, *Geschichte Siziliens* II, 1874, 77 ff.; O. Meltzer, *Gesch. der Karthager* I, 1879, 249 ff.; E. A. Freeman, *History of Sicily* III, 1892, 444 ff.; IV, 1894, 61 ff.; E. Païs, *Storia della Sicilia e della Magna Grecia* I, 1894; Ciaceri, *St. MGr.* II, 401 ff.: Basic, among specific studies, in its day, was K. J. Beloch, "L'impero siciliano di Dionisio," *RALinc.*, ser. 3 a, VII, 1880/81, in modified form in Beloch's *GG* III 2, 185 ff. Useful are the articles in *RE* V, 882 ff s. v. *Dionysios I.*; *ibid.*, 904 ff. (*Dionysios* II); 834 ff. (*Dion*), all by B. Niese; *RE* IV A, 1507 ff. s.v. *Syrakusai*, by L. Wickert. Indispensable is K. F. Stroheker, *Dionysios I. Gestalt u. Gesch. des Tyrannen von Syrakus*, Wiesbaden 1958, a study which also marks important advances in understanding the personality of the tyrant. Important now is Berve, *Tyrannis*, I, 222 ff. The book by Renata v. Schelihas, *Dion* (Das Erbe der Alten, 2. Reihe, Heft 25), 1934, is not very fortunate in its conclusions (cf. H. Berve, *Gn.* 13, 1937, 465 ff.; and J. H. Thiel, *Rond het syracusanische experiment* [Meded. Nederl. Ak. Letterk, NR 4, 5, Amsterdam 1941, 135 ff.]); H. D. Westlake, *Durham Univ. Journ.* 38, 1946, 37 ff.; E. D. Frolov, "First Steps and Accession to Power of Dionysius the Elder," *VDI*, 1971, No. 117, 47 ff. [Russian, with English summary]; H. Berve, *Dion* (Abh. Mainzer Ak., Jahrg. 1956, no. 10) (published 1957): a detailed critical study (141 pages); *idem*, "Dion," *HZ* 184, 1957, 1-18; G. A. Lehmann, "Dion und Herakleides," *H.* 19, 1970, 401 ff. J. Sprute, "Dions syrakusanische Politik und die politischen Ideale Platons," *Hermes* 100, 1972, 294 ff. [opposed to Berve and K. v. Fritz, *Platon in Sizilien und das Problem der Philosophenherrscher*, Berlin 1968]. Sprute correctly emphasises Dion's co-operation with the oligarchs. On Timoleon: H. E. Stier, *RE* VI A, 1276 ff. s.v. *Timoleon*; H. D. Westlake, "Timoleon and the Reconstruction of Syracuse," *Cambr. Hist. Journ.* 7, 1942, 73 ff. = *Essays*, 276-312; *idem*, "The Purpose of Timoleon's Mission," *AJP* 70, 1949, 65 ff. = *Essays* 265-275; *idem, Timoleon and his Relations with Tyrants*, Manchester 1952 (cf. H. Berve, *Gn.* 25, 1953, 527 ff.). More recent bibliography may be found in M. Sordi, *Timoleonte*, Palermo 1961 (critical of it, H. Berve, *Gn.* 35, 1963, 378 ff.); cf. also P. Levêque, "De Timoleon à Pyrrhos," *Kokalos* 14-15, 1968/69, 135 ff.; cf. also R. J. A. Talbert, *Timoleon and the Revival of Greek Sicily 344-317 B.C.*, London 1974, and C. M. Kraay, "Timoleon and Corinthian Coinage in Sicily," *Num. Chron.*, 1973, 4 ff. J. H. Kent, "The Victory Monument of Timoleon at Corinth," *Hesp.* 21, 1952, 9-18 (the monument commemorating the victory at the Crimisus); cf. also *Corinth* VIII 1, no. 23; and also D. Musti, *PP* 17, 1962, 450 ff., with new emendations. For additional studies on Timoleon see *Kokalos* 4, 1958 (published 1959). On internal developments see W. Hüttl, *Verfassungsgeschichte von Syrakus*, Prague 1929, 99 ff.

1. Cf. H. W. Parke, "The Development of the Second Spartan Empire (405-371 B.C.)," *JHS* 50, 1930, 37 ff., esp. 50 ff. C. D. Hamilton's thesis (*AJP* 91, 1970, 294 ff.) remains hypothetical.

2. According to Meyer, *GdA* V, 30, 2000 Spartans capable of bearing arms ruled over no less than three to four million souls!

3. H. Cavaignac, "Les décarchies de Lysandre," *Rev. ét. hist.* 25, 1924, 285 ff.; A. Andrewes, "Two Notes on Lysander," *Px.* 25, 1971, 206 ff.

4. Xen., *Hell.* III 3.4 ff.

5. See in particular Duris of Samos in Plutarch, *Lys.* 18; cf. E. Kornemann, *Klio* 1, 1901, 54; Kaerst, *GH* I³, 478 ff.; A. D. Nock, *HSCP* 41, 1930, 60; J. Smits in the commentary on Plutarch, *Leven van Lysander*, 1939, 176 ff. On the other hand, Wilamowitz, *Gl.* II, 263, and F. Taeger, *Hermes* 72, 1937, 358 n. 4, have contested the view that the veneration of Lysander is to be regarded as a preliminary stage to the Hellenistic ruler cult, but incorrectly; important is Nilsson, *Gr. Rel.* II, 139 f.; and Habicht, *Gott.*, 3 ff.; 213 ff.

6. Lysias XII 43 ff.; 76. On the character of the Athenian ephors see Meyer, *GdA* V, 19 n.; incorrect, W. Judeich, *RhM* 74, 1925, 254 ff.

7. O. Blank, *Die Einsetzung der Dreissig zu Athen im J. 404 v. Chr.*, Diss. Freiburg i. Br., Würzburg 1911; O. Armbruster, *Über die Herrschaft der Dreissig zu Athen 404/3 v. Chr.*,

Diss. Freiburg i. Br. 1913; Th. Lenschau, *RE* VI, 2355 ff. (with bibliography): G. A. Lehmann, "Die revolutionäre Machtergreifung der Dreissig und die staatliche Teilung Attikas (404-401/0 v. Chr.)," in *Festschr. H. E. Stier*, Münster 1972, 201 ff.; W. J. McCoy, "Aristotle's *Athenaion Politeia* and the Establishment of the Thirty Tyrants," *YCS*. 24, 1975, 131 ff.

8. P. Cloché, "Les expulsions en Attique avant la prise de Phyle," *REG* 24, 1911, 63 ff.

9. Cf. P. Cloché, *La restauration démocratique à Athènes en 403 av. J.-C.*, Paris 1915 (basic); G. De Sanctis, "Atene e i suoi liberatori," *RF* NS 1, 1923, 287 ff. The decree for the Phyle fighters of 401/0 B.C.: *IG* II/III^2 10, now best in Tod II no. 100 (with bibliography). New fragments: D. Hereward, *BSA* 47, 1952 (published 1953), 102-117. On Phyle see W. Wrede, *AM* 49, 1924, 153 ff.

10. On the chronology see the survey by Th. Lenschau, *RE* VI A, 2357 ff.

11. A. Fuks, *Mnem.* IV 6, 1953, 198-207.

12. The grave of the Spartans who fell in this encounter (Xen., *Hell.* II 4.33) has been found again in the Cerameicus; cf. La Rue van Hook, *AJA* 36, 1932, 290 ff.; S. Accame, "La battaglia presso il Pireo del 403 a. Chr.," *RF* NS 16, 1938, 346 ff.

13. Xen., *Hell.* II 4.38 ff.; Arist., *Const. Ath.* 39-40; cf. Bengtson, *Staatsv.* II, no. 213. J. H. Kühn, "Die Amnestie von 403 v. Chr. im Reflex der 18. Isokrates-Rede, "*Wiener Studien* 80, 1967, 31-73 (with bibliography 33 n. 2).

14. Kourouniotis, *Hellenika* II 5 ff.; Kougeas, *ibid.*, 116 ff.; U. Kahrstedt, "Eine Urkunde der Republik Eleusis," *NGG*, 1932, 77 ff.

15. On the overthrow of Lysander and his sytem see W. Judeich, *KS*, 33 ff.; on the chronology Beloch, *GG* III 1, 16 n. 1. E. R. Smith, "Lysander and the Spartan Empire," *CP* 43, 1948, 145 ff., denies the "overthrow" of Lysander.

16. Xen., *Hell.* III 2.21 ff.; Diod. XIV 17; 34; Paus. III 8.3 ff.; cf. Callmer, *Ark.* 100. For a different chronology (400-398 B.C.) see J. Hatzfeld, *REA* 35, 1933, 395 ff.

17. Cf. M. Rostovtzeff, in *Anatolian Studies Presented to W. M. Ramsay*, 1923, 372 ff., also H. Bengtson, *Gn.* 13, 1937, 113 ff. = *KS*, 83 ff.; *Gn.* 18, 1942, 213 ff. = *KS*, 105 ff.

18. Xen., *Anab.* I 1.6.

19. Isocr. VIII 98; XII 104.

20. Due to the attitude of the Syennesis, Artaxerxes transformed Cilicia from a vassal state into a satrapy; see A. Erzen, *Kilikien bis zum Ende der Perserherrschaft*, Diss Leipzig 1940, 120 ff., cf. H. Bengtson, *Gn.* 18, 1942, 215 = *KS*, 108.

21. The earlier bibliography on Cunaxa may be found in Kromayer, *Schlt.*. IV, 221 ff.; cf. R. Weynand, "Der Aufmarsch der Heere zur Schlacht bei Kunaxa," *NJb*, 1941, 106 ff. On the localisation see F. H. Weissbach, *Altorientalische Studien f. B. Meissner* II, 1929, 241 ff.

22. The Spartan Cheirisophus took over the leadership, a fact which Xenophon astutely suppressed in order to place his own rôle in its proper light.

23. Xen., *Anab.* V 6.15 ff.; VI 4 ff. The account is very instructive for the history of civilisation.

24. A. Höck, *Hermes* 26, 1891, 85 ff.; H. Swoboda, *RE* II A, 2020 ff.

25. Meyer, *GdA* V, 1902, 193 n. (apropos Isocrates, *Euag.* 54 and Justin VI 1), has given an excellent appraisal of the reasons behind the Spartan resolution.

26. The sources—on the one hand, Xen., *Hell.* III 4.21-25; *Agesil.* 1.28 ff., and on the other, *Hell. Oxy.* VI and Diod XIV 80—contradict each other; it is virtually impossible to reach a conclusion in favour of one version over the other; for the *Hell. Oxy.* F. Jacoby, *FgrHist.* no. 66, VI-VII, Comm., but see also the more recent studies cited above 481 f.

27. According to Xen. III 5.3, the Opuntian Locrians, according to *Hell. Oxy.* XIII 2 (and Paus. III 9.9), the Ozolian Locrians.

28. *IG* II/III^2 14, cf. a new fragment, published by E. Schweigert, *Hesp.* 8, 1939, I ff. no. I; Bengtson. *Staatsv.* II, no. 223. The treaty was concluded *in perpetuum*, a fact which is noteworthy in regard to the "King's Peace" (v.s.p. 166).

29. On the battle at the Nemea brook see E. Cavaignac, *REA* 27, 1925, 273 ff.; Kromayer-Veith, *Atlas* I 5 nos. 1 and 2; Pritchett, *Top.* II, 73 ff. On the number of Tegeans at the Nemea brook see J. Roy, *PP* 26, 1971, 439-441. Inscriptional stele of the Athenian Dexilaus who fell: *Syll.* I^3 130 = Tod II no. 105 = *GHD 4th C* 9; cf. also *Syll.* I^3 131 = Tod II no. 104 = *GHD 4th C* 8.

30. On the battle of Coroneia see Pritchett, *Top.* II, 85 ff.

31. On the basis of silver coins (with portrait of Heracles throttling the serpent and legend) from Rhodes, Cnidus, Iasus, Samos, Ephesus and Byzantium, earlier scholars concluded that a special league was founded after the battle of Cnidus in Asia Minor; see, for instance, K. Regling, *Z. f. Num.* 25, 1906, 207 ff.; others, like Meyer, *GdA* V, 308 and 310, and Beloch, *GG* III 1, 95 n. 3, are of a different view, and place the league after the Peace of Antalcidas, in 386 B.C. Noteworthy objections to this theory may be found in Accame, *Dom.*, 119 (cf. also L. Baldwin, *Z. f. Num.* 32, 1915, 11 ff.), who thinks in terms of a non-political coinage union. J. M. Cook (*JHS* 81, 1961, 67-68), on the other hand, argues for a pro-Spartan league from 391 and 390; see, however, G. L. Cawkwell, *JHS* 83, 1963, 152-154 (also already *Num. Chron.* 16, 1956, 69 ff.).

32. See, for instance, *IG* II/III² 1425, 283 ff.; cf. A. Wilhelm, *Attische Urkunden* 5, 1942, 108 f.: bestowing of a golden crown on Conon.

33. Details in H. Swoboda, *RE* XI, 1329 f. s.v. *Konon.*

34. *Syll.* I³ 129, lines 29 ff., cf. 123; 126; 127; cf. H. Swoboda, *RE* XI, 1330.

35. Xen., *Hell.* IV 4.1 ff.; Diod. XIV 86; 91.2, 92.1 Cf. G. T. Griffith, *H.* 1, 1950, 236 ff.; C. D. Hamilton, *H.* 21, 1972, 21 ff.

36. On the chronology see Xen., *Hell.* IV 5.13 ff.; also W. Judeich, *Ph.* 81, 1926, 147 n. 6.

37. Cf. the writings of Xenophon on tactics and the *Tactics* of the Arcadian Aeneias of Stymphalus.

37a. Cf. Y. Garlan, *Recherches de poliorcétique grecque*, Paris 1974.

38. There are in addition also the data of the excerpt from Philochorus, extant in Didymus (H. Diels and W. Schubart, *Didymi de Demosthene commenta*, Leipzig 1904); H. Diels and W. Schubart, in *Berl. Klass. Texte* I, 1904, Col. 7, 19 ff.; cf. also W. Judeich, *Ph.* 81, 1926, 141 ff.; Wilcken, *Ent.*, 4 ff.; "Andocides' negotiations in Sparta [beginning 392 B.C.]". V. Martin, "Sur une interprétation nouvelle de la 'Paix du Roi,' " *MusHelv* 3, 1949, 126 ff., who thinks that the Congress in Sparta *followed* the negotiations in Sardis; although this view is highly ingenious, in my estimation it is not convincing.

39. See Andocides, *Or.* III § 17; cf. also A. Momigliano, *Ann. R. Scuola Norm. Sup. di Pisa*, ser. II 5, 1935, 101; Wilcken, *Ent.*, 7.

40. W. Judeich, *RE* I, 2344 ff. s.v. *Antialcidas*; P. Porallia, *Prosopogr. d. Laked.*, Diss. Breslau 1913, 23. On the form Antialcidas see *IG* V 1.93, 15 and 212.6 (pointed out by G. Klaffenbach).

41. Plato, *Menex.* 17; Didym. VII 20 (= Philochorus). Wilcken, *Ent.*, 11), is no doubt correct in his view that the Athenian protest was not made public in Sardis but only, later, in the *Ekklesia* in Athens.

42. H. Bengtson, *Staatsv.* II, nos. 234, 236.

43. Beloch, *GG* III 1, 150, is incorrect in describing what Thrasybulus achieved as the "Second Attic Maritime League." Conclusive evidence to the contrary is the fact that it was a question of individual treaties and not of an organised league; cf., for instance, Triepel, *Heg.*, 387 n. 165.

44. It is, for instance, incorrect of W. Schmidt, *GGL* I 4, 1946, 373, to deny that the Pluto is based on a concrete historical situation. It is, accordingly, unnecessary to disavow that the ever prevailing wish to become wealthy, forms part of the background.

45. On the negotiations of 387 B.C. in Susa cf. Xen., *Hell.* V 1.25; Diod. XIV 110 (cf. Plut., *Artox.* 22), also the detailed discussion by Wilcken, *Ent.*, 12 ff. On the events leading up to and the conclusion of the King's Peace see in particular the following studies: B. Keil, *Eirene*, Ber. Sächs. Ak. 68, 1916, no. 4; F. Nolte, *Die historisch-politischen Voraussetzungen des Königsfriedens von 386 v. Chr.*, Frankfurter Diss., Bamberg 1923 (excellent); Hampl, *Staatsv.*, esp. 8 ff. (see also the reference above 483); V. Martin, *La vie internat. dans la Grèce des cités*, Paris 1940, 484 ff.; as well as the above cited work by Wilcken; moreover (on the sources): M. A. Levi, *Acme* 8, 1955, 105-111.

46. F. Graefe, "Die Operationen des Antialkidas am Hellespont," *Klio* 28, 1935, 262 ff.; P. Meloni, "Il contributo di Dionisio I alle operazioni di Antalcida del 387 a.C.," *RALinc.* Ser. 8.4, fasc. 3-4, 1949, 190 ff.

47. Cf. F. Nolte, *op. cit.* [n. 45 *supra*] 7 f.

48. The sources in Bengtson, *Staatsv.* II, no. 242, = *GHD 4th* C 15.

49. Xen., *Hell.* V 1.36 (the Spartans as *prostatai* of the King's Peace).

50. An allusion in Xen., *Hell.* V 1.35; Justin VI 6; cf. Wilcken, *Ent.* 18.

51. Incorrect are Hampl, *Staatsv.* 12, and V. Martin, *MusHelv* 6, 1949, 127, in maintaining that the King's Peace as such was a general peace.

52. G. Fougères, *Mantinée et l'Arcadie orientale*, 1898, 130 ff.; 408 ff.; F. Bölte, *RE* XIV, 1322 f. s.v. *Mantinea*; cf. Amit, *GSP*, 121 ff.

53. E. Meyer, *RE* XX, 284 s.v. *Phleius*; Balogh, *Ref.*, 66. On the battle see W. K. Pritchett, *Top.* II, 96 ff.

54. Xen., *Hell.* V 2.25 ff., Diod. XV 20.1 ff.; Isocr. IV 126; XIV 19; Plut., *Pelop.* 5.1 ff.; Corn. Nep., *Pelop.* 1.2.

55. H. Swoboda, *RE* IX, 2136 ff. s.v. *Ismenias* no. 1.

56. W. Judeich, *RhM* 76, 1927, 171 ff.; Accame, *Lega*, 17 ff., esp. 22 ff.

57. The treaty between Athens and Chios: Bengtson, *Staatsv.* II, no. 248 = *GHD 4th C* 17; cf. I. A. F. Bruce, *Px.* 19, 1965, 281 ff.; treaty with Byzantium: Bengtson, *Staatsv.* II, no. 256; additional treaties (with Chalcis on Euboea, Methymna, Corcyra, et al.): Bengtson, *Staatsv.* II, nos. 258; 259; 262; 263 = *GHD 4th C* 20; 23; 25; 26.

58. Referring to all these is the Attic *psephisma* of Aristotle, *IG* II/III² 43 = *Syll.* I² 147 = Tod II 123 = *GHD 4th C* 22; cf. Bengtson, *Staatsv.* II, no. 257, from February/March 377 B.C.; the term "bequest" or "foundation document" of the League is not appropriate in this instance; cf. Hampl; *Staatsv.* 131; A. Wilhelm, *Abh. Preuss. Ak.*, 1939, *phil.-hist. Kl.* no. 22 (published 1940) 7.

59. On the organisation of the League see, in addition to the works cited above 486, in particular Accame, *Lega*, 107 ff.; on the *suntaxeis*, *ibid.*, 132 ff.

60. H. Swoboda, *RE* X, 1730 ff. s.v. *Kallistratos* no. 1; P. Cloché, "La politique de l'Athénien Callistratos," *REA* 25, 1923, 22 ff.; "Isocrate et Callistratos," *Rev. belge de Phil. et d'hist.* 6, 1927, 673 ff.; R. Sealey, *H.* 5, 1956, 178 ff.

61. The constitution of the contemporary Boeotian League is controversial, but there can be no question that Boeotia became a unified state like Olynthus, as is assumed by Meyer, *GdA* V, 390 f.; see H. Swoboda, in Hermann, *Griech. Staatsaltertümer*, 1913, 262 ff.; Busolt, *Gr. St.* II, 1426 ff.; on the other hand, J. H. Thiel, *Mnem.* 54, 1926, 19 ff.; and Triepel, *Heg.* 435, hold a different view.

62. *IG* II/III² 102 = *Syll.* I³ 157 = Tod II 129 = *GHD 4th C* 29; cf. Bengtson, *Staatsv.* II no. 264. On Chabrias and the events of 375 B.C. see A. Wilhelm, "Ein Stützpunkt der Athener im Hellespontos," *Anz. W*, 84. Jahrg., 1947, 190 ff.

63. On Jason see, besides the older study by G. Tropea, "Giasone il tago della Tessaglia," *Riv. di Stor. ant.* 3, 1898, 37 ff., in particular: F. Stähelin, *RE* IX, 771 ff. s.v. no. 3; U. Wilcken, *Hermes* 59, 1924, 123 ff.; H. T. Wade-Gery, *JHS* 44, 1924, 55 ff.; K. Lemmermann, *Iason von Pherai*, Diss. Jena 1927 [typewritten]; H. D. Westlake, *Thessaly in the IVth Century*, London 1935.

64. The oration of Polydamas in Sparta, recorded in Xen., *Hell.* VI 1.4 ff., is one of the most important sources on the designs and plans of Jason, and must in nucleus be regarded as historical; see the study by U. Wilcken cited in n. 63 (too sceptical is B. Niese, *Hermes* 39, 1904, 108 ff.). The speech belongs in 375 B.C. (on the other hand, Beloch, *GG* III 2, 237 ff., and Accame, *Lega*, 92 ff., argue for 371 B.C.).

65. *IG* II/III² 43 = *Syll.*³ I 147 = *GHD 4th* C 22 line 111 (decree of Aristotle); cf. E. Fabricius, *RhM* 46, 1891, 594; cf. F. Stähelin, *RE* IX, 772; J. Hatzfeld, "Iason de Phères a-t-il été allié d'Athènes?" *REA* 36, 1934, 441 ff., who is completely incorrect in denying that Jason's name was in the erasure; see, correctly, on the other hand, Accame, *Lega*, 91, with Illustration II 3; cf. A. G. Woodhead, *AJA* 61, 1957, 367 ff.

66. Philoch. in Didymus, col. VII 62 ff.

67. The sources in: Bengtson, *Staatsv.* II no. 265 = *GHD 4th C* 28; cf. the works cited above 483 f., and A. G. Roos, *Mnem.* 4, 1949, 265 ff.; also in particular S. Lauffer, *H.* 8, 1959, 315 ff. (on the doublet of Diodorus XV 38 = 50); on the chronology: *H.* 8, 1959, 321 n. 18; also G. L. Cawkwell, *H.* 12, 1963, 84 ff.; and J. Buckler, "The Dating of the Peace of 375/4 B.C.," *GRBS* 12, 1971, 353 ff.

68. The source is the pseudo-Demosthenic oration against Timotheus ([Demosthenes] XLIX); see, otherwise, K. Klee, *RE* VI A, 1324 ff.; and G. L. Cawkwell (see previous note) 93 ff.

69. According to Diodorus (XV 46.6), 374/B.C.; according to Pausanias (IX 1.8), 373/2 B.C.; cf. Amit, *GSP*, 61 ff.

70. Hampl, *Staatsv.*, 19 ff.; 104 ff.; the sources in Bengtson, *Staatsv.* II, no. 269 = *GHD 4th* C 32; cf. the work by S. Lauffer cited above n. 67; and T. T. B. Ryder, *CQ* 57, 1963, 237 ff.

71. Xenophon's account (*Hell.* VI 3.18 ff.) is to be preferred to Plutarch (*Ages.* 27 f.); see E. v. Stern, *Xenophons Hellenika und die böotische Geschichtsüberlieferung*, Dorpat 1887, 123 ff.; H. Swoboda, *RE* V, 2680 f. s. v. *Epameinondas* no. 1.

72. On Epameinondas see H. Swoboda, *RE* V, 2674 ff. (excellent); a good characterisation by Meyer, *GdA* V, 410 ff.; 474 f.; M. Fortina, *Epaminonda*, Turin 1958; G. L. Cawkwell, "Epaminondas and Thebes," *CQ* 22, 1972, 254 ff. (also on the lawsuits, 276 ff.).

73. G. M. Bersanetti, *Pelopida*, Pavia 1949.

74. Cf. G. Roloff, *Probleme der griechischen Kriegsgeschichte*, 1907, 200 ff.; E. and F. Lammert, *RE* II A, 455 ff. s.v. *Schlachtordnung*; Kromayer-Veith, *Heerw.*, 93 ff.

75. Kromayer, *Schl.* I, 76 ff., is, on the other hand, of the opinion that the choice of the striking wing depended on the terrain.

76. Sources: Xen., *Hell.* VI 4.1-15 (inadequate, Epameinondas is not even mentioned); Diod. XV 51 ff. (of doubtful value); Plut., *Pelop.* 20 ff.; Paus. IX 13.3-12; Polyaenus II 3.8; *IG* VII 2462 = Tod II no. 130 = *GHD 4th C* 9; [cf. H. Beister, *Ch.* 3, 1973, 65 ff.]; cf. also J. Wolter, in *Antike Schlachtfelder* IV, 290 ff. (containing the earlier bibliography, from which the following may be cited: G. Busolt, "Spartas Heer u. Leuktra," *Hermes* 40, 1905, 387 ff.; Delbrück, *Krieg.* I³ 158 ff.); W. Judeich, *RhM* 76, 1927, 191 ff.; Pritchett, *Top.* I, 49 ff.; P. Pédech, "La date de la bataille de Leuctres (371 av. J.-C.)," *Riv. stor. dell'Ant.* 2, 1972, 1 ff.

77. Polyb. II 39.9 (cf. Strabo VII 384) implies that the Achaeans acted as arbitrators between Thebes and Sparta; see M. Cary, *CQ* 19, 1925, 165 f.

78. For details see Fr. Frhr. Hiller von Gaertringen, *RE* VI A, 124 s.v. *Thessalia*; H. D. Westlake, *Thessaly in the IVth Century*. 1935, 67 ff.

79. The first evidence for the Aetolian League is found in an Attic inscription from 367/6 B.C. (E. Schweigert, *Hesp.* 8, 1939, 5 ff. no. 3 = Tod II no. 137). Cf. M. Sordi, "Le origini del koinon etolico," *Acme* 6, 1953, 419-445.

80. Xen., *Hell.* VI 5.1-3; for an evaluation cf. Hampl, *Staatsv.*, 19 ff.; 106 f.; M. Sordi, *RF* NS 29, 1951, 34-64. The theory put forward by H. Swoboda, *RhM* 49, 1894, 321 ff., that in this instance the Athenians were attempting to expand the Second Maritime League to include large parts of Hellas (with the exception of Sparta), has been disputed by modern scholars (*inter al.*, Glotz, *HG* III, 152 n. 25, Hampl, *Staatsv.*, 20 f. n. 1).

81. See the account in Isocrates, *Archid.* 64 ff.

82. H. Swoboda, *"Skutalismos," Hermes* 53, 1918, 94 ff.; *RE* III A, 692.

83. Xen., *Hell.* VI 5.6; Diod. XV 59.1 (on the date cf. *Marmor Parium* 73). Further sources on the origin and organisation of the Arcadian League: Xen., *Hell.* VII 4, 33 ff.; 38; Paus. VIII 32.1; Harpocration s.v. *murioi en Megalê poleis*, bibliography in Busolt *Gr. St.* II, 1395 ff.; see also S. Dusanic, *Arkadski savez IV veka (The Arcadian League of the Fourth Century)*, Belgrade 1970; J. Roy, "Arcadia and Boeotia in Peloponnesian Affairs, 370-362 B.C.," *H.* 20, 1971, 569 ff.

84. V. Ehrenberg, *RE* III A, 1412 s.v. *Sparta*, is entirely incorrect in viewing the loss of Messenia as a positive gain for Sparta; a similar view already by G. B. Grundy, *JHS* 28, 1908, 95.

85. The wall of circumvallation at Messene is a masterpiece of Greek fortification; it is still partially extant; cf. *CAH*, Volume of Plates II 12 a. Founding of Messene: Paus. IX 14.5; IV 26 f. Cf. H. Braunert and T. Petersen, *Ch.* 2, 1972, 57 ff.; M. Moggi, *Ann. Scuola Norm. Sup. di Pisa, Cl. di Lettere e Filosofia, ser.* III, *vol.* IV, 1, 1974, 71-107. On the history of Messenia see C. A. Roebuck, *A History of Messenia from 369 to 146 B.C.*, Chicago 1941; cf. P. Treves, *JHS* 64, 1944, 102 ff.

86. Described by Pausanias VIII 32.1, and rediscovered by British excavations (*Excavations at Megalopolis 1890-91*, JHS Suppl. I, 1892; see also H. Braunert-T. Petersen, "Megalopolis: Anspruch und Wirklichleit," *Ch.* 2, 1972, 57 ff.

87. Xen., *Hell.* VII 1.1; *Poroi* 5.7; cf. Bengtson, *Staatsv.* II, no. 274.

88. This date according to Beloch, *GG* III^2 2, 238 ff. Of a different view is B. Niese, *Hermes* 39, 1904, 84 ff. (spring 368 B.C.).

89. Diod. XV 72.2; cf. Beloch, *GG* III^2 2, 247 ff., against H. Swoboda, *RhM* 55, 1900, 460 ff.; P. J. Cuff, *Ath.* NS 32, 1954, 259 ff., who, in contrast to Beloch, thinks there were two lawsuits.

90. Geyer, *Mak.*, 127 ff. (also for the following events).

91. A. Wilhelm, *Öst. Jh.* 33, 1941, 35 ff., relates the epigram published by J. Bousquet, *Rev. arch.*, 1939, I, 125 ff., to the first Thessalian expedition of Pelopidas.

92. Cf. G. H. Macurdy, "Queen Eurydice and the Evidence of Women Power in Early Macedonia," *AJP* 48, 1927, 201 ff.; *Hellenistic Queens*, Baltimore 1932, 17 ff. (with erroneous theories).

93. Diod. XV 67.4 and Plut., *Pelop.* 26, have advanced the event; the correct account is given by Aeschines II 26 ff.; see Beloch, *GG* III^2 1, 182; Geyer, *Mak.*, 129. For a different view: A. Aymard, *REA* 56, 1954, 15 ff., who shows preference for Diodorus (369 B.C.).

94. The sources in Bengtson, *Staatsv.* II, no. 282.

95. His fellow envoy Leon charged him with openly betraying the Athenian cause in Susa, no doubt to clear himself; cf. Xen., *Hell.* VII 1.38; Plutarch, *Pelop.* 30, on the other hand, adorns the event with legendary trappings.

96. Judeich, *KS*, 193 ff.; P. Meloni, *Riv. stor. ital.* 63, 1951, 5 ff.

97. For details on the Oropian quarrels see A. Schaefer, *Demosthenes und seine Zeit* I^2 106 ff.

98. In the spring of 367 B.C. Athens concluded a defensive alliance with the much courted Dionysius I (*IG* II/III^2 105 + 523 = Tod II no. 136, cf. Bengtson, *Staatsv.* II, no. 280); prior to this, Attic citizenship and golden crowns had been conferred on him and two of his sons (*IG* II/III^2 103 = Tod II no. 133). At the beginning of 367 B.C. the tragedy of Dionysius, *The Ransom of Hector*, was awarded first prize in Athens. Dionysius, however, died in the same year.

99. Bengtson, *Staatsv.* II, no. 285; cf. Hampl, *Staatsv.*, 61 ff.; and T. T. B. Ryder, "The Supposed Common Peace of 366/5 B.C.," *CQ* 7, 1957, 199-205.

100. E. Schweigert, "The Athenian Cleruchy at Samos," *AJP* 61, 1940, 194 ff.

101. *Syll.* I^3 180. On events in the north see K. Klee, *RE* VI A, 1328 s.v. *Timotheos* no. 3. Important is *Syll.* I^3 174 = *GHD 4th C* 45, an Athenian honorary decree for Pelagonian Menelaus.

102. Cf. Kromayer, *Sch.* II, 116 ff.; Pritchett, *Top.* II, 112 ff.

103. See the Boeotian honorary decree for "Annobal" son of "Asrubal," *Syll.* I^3 179, cf. G. Glotz, "Un Carthaginois à Thèbes en 365 av. J.-C.," *Mélanges N. Jorga*, Paris 1933, 331 ff.; F. Carrata Thomes, *Egemonia beotica e potenza marittima nella politica di Epaminonda*, Turin 1952.

104. Diod. XV 78 f.; cf. R.v. Scala, *Staatsverträge* I, 1898, 160 no. 169.

105. Thus Julis on Ceos, which had apparently joined the Thebans at first, in 363/2 B.C., again concluded a treaty with Athens; cf. *Syll.* I^3 173 = *GHD 4th C* 44; cf. Bengtson, *Staatsv.* II, no. 289; for Athens the alliance with Ceos was particularly valuable because of the availability of red ochre there, important for coating ships; cf. *IG* II/III^2 1128 = Tod II no. 162 = *GHD 4th C* 61 (before 350 B.C.), cf. Bengtson, *Staatsv.* II, no. 320 (with bibliography).

106. *Syll.* I^3 181 = Tod II no. 144 = *GHD 4th C* 46.

107. Xen., *Hell.* VII 5.3.

108. A detailed account of the battle of Mantineia is lacking; the basic aspects are related by Xenophon, *Hell.* VII 5.19 ff.; Diodorus XV 84-87 (=Ephorus), on the other hand, is inadequate. Of more recent studies see Kromayer, *Sch.*. I, 47 ff., and, opposed to him, E Lammert, *NJb* 13, 1904, 112 ff.; cf. the reply by Kromayer, *Wien. Stud.* 27, 1905, 1 ff.; *Schl.* IV, 317 ff.; Pritchett, *Top.* II, 63 ff.

109. F. Taeger, *Der Friede von 362/1. Ein Beitrag zur Gesch. der panhellenischen Bewegung im 4. Jahrh.*, Stuttgart 1930; Hampl, *Staatsv.*, 26 ff.; 107 ff. (with additional bibliography).

110. *Syll.* I³ 182 = Tod II no. 145 = *GHD 4th C* 47 (from Argos); cf. A. Wilhelm, *Öst. Jh.*, 3, 1900, 145 ff., who has correctly referred the inscription to the settlement of 362/1 B.C.; see also G. De Sanctis, "La pace del 362/1," *RF* NS 12, 1934, 145 ff.; and Bengtson, *Staatsv* II, no. 292 = *GHD 4th C* 47. Cf. also J. Hatzfeld, "Agésilaos et Artaxerxès II," *BCH* 70, 1946, 238 ff. (on Xenophon, *Ages.* 8.3, the letter of the Great King to Agesilaus).

111. The inscription *Syll.* I³ 185 (= *IG* II/III² 141), discussed in the posthumously published article of R. P. Austin, *JHS* 64, 1944, 98 ff., too, scarcely proves an active rôle on the part of Athens in the great satrap revolt in the years 362-360 B.C.

112. M. Märker, *Die Kämpfe der Karthager auf Sizilien von 409 bis 405 v. Chr.*, Diss. Leipzig (published Weida 1930); F. Graefe, "Karthagische Seestrategie im Jahre 406 v. Chr.," *Hermes* 52, 1917, 317 ff.

113. Scheele, *Str.*, 38 ff.

114. Diod. XIII 114; cf. Bengtson, *Staatsv.* II, no. 210.

115. Cf. *Syll.* I³ 128 = *GHD 4th C* 11 (from 394/3 B.C.); 159 (369/8 B.C.); 163 = *GHD 4th C* 38 (368/7 B.C.). The conjecture by J. B. Bury, *CAH* VI, 118, that Dionysius bore the title, so to speak, as successor of Ducetius (v.s.p. 131), is not probable. A detailed discussion by K. F. Stroheker, *Dionysios I.*, 1958, 172 ff.

116. Pseudo-Aristotle, *Oeconomica* II 20; cf. J. G. Droysen, *Kl. Schr.* II 306 ff.; B. Niese, *RE* V, 900. W. Hüttl, *Verfassungsgeschichte von Syrakus*, 1929, 102 ff.; K. F. Stroheker, *op. cit.*, 161 ff.

117. Diod. XIV 46.

118. An outstanding account in Diod. XIV 47 ff., esp. 51 ff.; cf. J. B. Bury, *CAH* VI, 121 f.; Kromayer, *Schl.* IV, 325 ff.; J. L. S. Whitaker, *Motya, a Phoenician Colony in Sicily*, London 1921, 75 ff.

119. Diod. XIV 96.3; cf. Bengtson, *Staatsv.* II, no. 233.

120. Diod. XIV 105.4; Strabo VI p. 261.

121. The date of the conclusion of the Peace is not known; Meyer, *GdA* V, 169, places it in 376 B.C., Beloch, *GG* III 2, 377, in 374 B.C. The latter is followed by K. F. Stroheker, *op. cit.*, 232 n. 30.

122. On the war see K. F. Stroheker, *op. cit.*, 145-146; on the conclusion of peace (not until the reign of Dionysius II, namely not before the end of 366 B.C.), *ibid.*, 237 n. 84.

123. On his personality see Meyer, *GdA* V, 170 ff.; Berve, *Tyrannis* I, 213 ff.

124. A much more favourable verdict on him is given by Beloch, *GG* III 1, 130.

10 PHILIP II OF MACEDONIA

PRINCIPAL SOURCES: The American excavations conducted by the Johns Hopkins University of Baltimore on the site of Olynthus, which was destroyed by Philip II in 348 B.C., have shown it to be an excellent example of a Hellenic settlement in the fourth century B.C. The rectangular layout of the city on the Hippodamian plan is clearly discernible, and, *inter al.*, the floors of many villas decorated with mosaics testify to the great wealth of their occupants. Cf. the *Excavations at Olynthus* I-XIV, and in this connection the concise reports by D. M. Robinson, *Ant.* 11, 1935, 274 ff., and *RE* XVIII 1, 325 ff. Of the coins from this period those of Macedonia are particularly informative; their issues and emblems reflect Philip's attempt to place special emphasis on the cultural ties between Macedonia and Greece: A. B. West, The Early Diplomacy of Philip II of Macedon Illustrated by his Coins," *Num. Chron.*, 1923, 109 ff. A wealth of information is furnished by M. L. Strack, *Die antiken Münzen von Thrakien*, Berlin 1912.

The number of inscriptions is increasing. The most important documents, a large number of which stem from Attica and Delphi, are assembled in *Syll.* I^3 175 ff., and Tod, II, nos. 148 ff., as well as Schmitt, *Staatsv.* III, nos. 403 ff. A wealth of inscriptional material may also be found in *IG* X 2. *Inscriptiones Macedoniae*, ed. C. Edson, Berlin 1972. Those which should be stressed are: the treaty between Philip and the Chalcidian League, from the year 356 B.C.: Bengtson, *Staatsv.* II, no. 308 = *GHD 4th C* 58; and the oath of the Hellenes on the occasion of the treaty concluded with Philip in 338/7 B.C. (*Syll.* I^3 260 = *GHD 4th C* 74; cf. U. Wilcken, SB.B, 1929, no. XVIII, 316 ff.; Tod II no. 177; as well as Schmitt, *Staatsv.* III, no. 403). H. Metzger *et al.*, *CRAI*, 1974, 82 ff.

OTHER DOCUMENTS: The documents preserved in the Attic orators pose a special problem which on the whole still remains unresolved. It is necessary to prove the authenticity of the form and content of each of them in turn; cf. J. G. Droysen, "Über die Echtheit der Urkunden in Demosthenes' Rede 'Vom Kranze'," *Kl. Schr.* I, 95 ff. (negative); E. Drerup, "Über die bei den att. Rednern eingelegten Urkunden," *Fleckeisens Jahrb. f. klass. Phil., Suppl.-Bd.* 24, 1898; L. Schläpfter, *Untersuch. zu den Staatsurkunden und Amphiktyonenbeschlüssen der demosthenischen Kranzrede*, Rhetor. Stud. 21, Paderborn 1939 (both too positive); cf. the remarks in Wüst, *Phil.*, 138 n. 1. In regard to method, important is T. Larsen, *Papyri Graecae Haunienses*, Copenhagen 1942, no. 5 (Demosthenes, *De Corona* §§ 217-223), with three documents, only the headings of which are preserved in the literary texts; see also P. Treves, "Les documents apocryphes du Pro corona," *Et. class.* 9, 1940, 138 ff. In assessing the authenticity of these documents the stichometric information, if such occurs, plays an important rôle (cf. in general, W. Schubart, *Das Buch bei den Griechen u. Römern*, ^{2}1921, 72 ff. Of the nine letters by

Isocrates the second is certainly authentic (E. Meyer, *Isokrates' 2. Brief an Philipp u. Demosthenes' 2. Philippika*, SB.B, 1909, 758 ff.); a certain amount of evidence may also be adduced to support the authenticity of the third letter, written after Chaeroneia (v.s.p. 199 f.). A new study of the problem would be welcome. On the letters of Demosthenes see H. Sachsenweger, *De Demosthenis epistulis*, Diss. Leipzig 1935; with additional bibliography in Bengtson, *Strat.* I, 129 n. 1.; cf. E. Bickerman, *Rev. de phil.* NS 11, 1937, 52 ff., as well as J. A. Goldstein, *The Letters of Demosthenes*, New York 1968, who argues that Letters 1-4 are authentic, whereas 5 and 6 are spurious.

An authentic document written in 340 B.C. by Philip II, is preserved in the corpus of the Demosthenic orations (no. XII): see M. Pohlenz, "Philipps Schreiben an Athen," *Hermes* 64, 1929, 41 ff. A. Momigliano, "Due problemi storiografici I. Anassimene e la lettera di Filippo," *Rend. Ist. Lombardo* 65, 1932, 569 ff., is a regression; Momigliano reverts to the view held by P. Wendland, *Anaximenes von Lampsakos*, Berlin 1905, 13 ff., according to which it is alleged that Philip's original letter was recast by Anaximenes; see, opposed to this view, and correctly, Wüst, *Ph.*, 133 ff. Stemming from the spring of 342 B.C. is the letter of Speusippus addressed to King Philip, which has been shown to be authentic by the brilliant analysis of E. Bickermann and J. Sykutris, *Berichte über die Verhandl. Sächs. Ak., phil.-hist. Kl.* 80, 1928, Heft 3; cf. R. Harder, *Ph.* 85, 1930, 225 ff.

The Attic orators provide a large amount of valuable historical information; chief among them are Isocrates, Demosthenes and Aeschines. In so far as the orations deal with legal questions they display a very strong prejudice. In them, exaggerations, distortions and untenable personal accusations are the rule, with the result that they can be used only with the greatest caution in assessing the character of the personalities involved. In the pertinent words of Ivo Bruns, *Das literarische Porträt* 585), "falsehood like an impenetrable veil" lies between our line of vision and the reality of Demosthenes and Aeschines. With the unmistakable design to influence the multitudes in the popular assembly, the orations, especially those of Demosthenes, are excellent examples of mass propaganda in antiquity.

In arriving at a judgment on the speeches and the personalities of the orators the decision must fall in favour of Isocrates, who otherwise deliberately kept aloof from the *Ekklesia*. His orations, written in an incomparably superb style, are in fact political pamphlets—as the *Philippos* (346 B.C.) and the *Panathenikos*, (339 B.C.), both addressed to Philip II. While earlier scholars concluded that Isocratean journalism had exerted a profound influence on the policy of the Macedonian king (R.v. Scala, *Isokr. u. die Geschichtsschreibung*, Verhandl. der 41. Philologenversamml. 1891, Munich 1892, 102 ff.; B.v. Hagen, "Isokr. u. Alexander," *Ph.* 67, 1908, 113 ff.; J. Kessler, *Isokrates u. die panhell. Idee*, Paderborn 1911; Beloch, *GG* III 1^2, 576 f.; K. Münscher, *RE* IX, 2215, *et al.*), this view has been vigorously contested (Wilcken, *Ph.*, SB.B, 1929, no. XVIII;

H. Berve, *Gn.* 13, 1937, 470 ff.). Meanwhile the reaction, which is in itself justified, has certainly gone too far (correctly opposed by H. E. Stier, *Grundlagen u. Sinn der griech. Gesch.*, Stuttgart 1945, 470 f.). The ideas and suggestions put forward by the great orator are of greatest historical interest and not simply as the expression of an important mood of the times. Politics and journalism mutually determine each other, so that it would be completely misleading to use the measure in which his suggestions were actually realised in practice as a criterion in judging the importance of Isocrates as a statesman. In arriving at a judgment on Isocrates see (in addition to the works already cited above) P. Wendland, "Beitr. z. athenischen Politik u. Publizistik des 4. Jahrh.," *NGG*, 1910, 123 ff.; 289 ff. (basic); M. Mühl, *Über die politischen Ideen des Isokr. u. die Geschichtsschreibung* I, Diss. Würzburg 1917; R.v. Pöhlmann, *Isokr. u. das Problem der Demokratie, SB.M*, 1913, 1 (modernising); J. Jüthner, *Hellenen u. Barbaren*, Leipzig 1923, 34 ff.; "Isokr. und die Menschheitsidee," *Wien. Stud.* 47, 1929, 26 ff.; G. Mathieu, *Les idées politiques d'Isocrate*, Paris 1925; P. Treves, "Tre interpretazioni isocratee," *Rend. Ist. Lomb.*, Vol. 66 fasc. 1-5, 1933, 303 ff. (*inter al.*, on the third letter of Isocrates, with erroneous conclusions); G. Schmitz-Kahlmann, *Das Beispiel der Geschichte im politischen Denken des Isokr.*, Ph.-Suppl. 31, 4 Leipzig 1939; W. Steidle, "Redekunst und Bildung bei Isokrates," *Hermes* 80, 1952, 257 ff.; E. Buchner, *Hermes* 82, 1954, 378 ff. (on the attitude of Isocrates and Aristotle towards the barbarians; Buchner attempts, in vain, to explain the contradiction away); S. Perlmann, *H.* 6, 1957, 306 ff. (on the *Philippus* of Isocrates); cf. *idem, H.* 18, 1969, 370 ff. and G. Dobesch, *Der panhellenische Gedanke im 4. Jh. v. Chr. und der 'Philippos' des Isokrates*, Vienna 1968; M. A. Levi, "Postille semantiche isocratee," *Rend. Ist. Lomb.* 91, 1957, 1049 ff.; 92, 1958, 393 ff.; *Isocrate, Sagio critico*, Milan 1959; P. Cloché, *Isocrate et son temps*, Paris 1963; K. Bringmann, *Studien zu den politischen Ideen des Isokrates*, Hypomnemata, Heft 14, Göttingen (no year given) [1965]; also G. Bockisch, "Der Panhellenismus bei Isokrates und Demosthenes," in *Actes de la XIII conférence intern. d'études class. "Eirene," Cluj-Napoca 2-7 octobre 1972*, Amsterdam 1975, 239 ff.

To arrive at a just assessment of Demosthenes (c. 384-322 B.C.), unquestionably the greatest orator of antiquity, is a much more difficult task. The collapse of Attic policy on the battlefield at Chaeroneia (338 B.C.), of which he was the exponent, has become the decisive touchstone much more for his modern than for his ancient critics: accordingly, if he is judged by the success of his policy, Demosthenes appears as a visionary politician without any sensitivity for the possibilities of shrewdly calculated statecraft. Judged in these terms, his reputation as an orator has also suffered in the eyes of modern scholars. as may be seen from K. J. Beloch's assessment of Aeschines, the rival of Demosthenes, in which his positive judgment is exaggerated. In the period of Classicism a different verdict was reached on Demosthenes: the erudite Arnold Schaefer, for instance, in his *Demosthenes und seine Zeit* (3 vols., Leipzig 1856-

58; [²1885-87]), more or less oriented the entire history of the fourth century on the personality of the great hero. Nor was there any difference in the view advanced by F. Blass in his *Attische Beredsamkeit* (III 1 and 2, [²1893 and ²1898]), a work which otherwise is to a large extent admittedly lacking in impartial historical judgment; the same is still the case even in F. Altheim, (*RE* V, 181). It is indisputably to the credit of the historians, above all K. J. Beloch and Ed. Meyer, for having made a wide breach in the wall of the "Demosthenes orthodox school." Together with P. Wendland ("Beitr. z. anthenischen Politik u. Publizistik des 4. Jahrhunderts. Isokrates und Demosthenes," *NGG*, 1910, 289 ff.), they reduced the importance of Demosthenes as a statesman to its correct proportions. In contrast to this the belated rescue attempt by Jaeger, *Dem.*, which depicts the great orator as a Panhellenic statesman, has not succeeded in convincing scholars (cf. A. Körte, *DLZ*, 1940, 224 ff.; H. Berve, *GGA*, 1940, 464 ff.). Posterity will not cease to admire the glowing patriotism of the man, even though it knows that as a politician he often resorted to reprehensible means, such as falsehood. It was the uncontrollable political temperament, the volcanic personality of Demosthenes, which cast its spell over even important statesmen of modern times: P. B. Niebuhr, Lord Brougham, Clemenceau (cf. his book *Démosthène*, Paris 1926). "In the struggle of the Athenians against Philip" Demosthenes sees "the struggle of the *politeia* against the *monarchia*, that is, in his view the free state ruled by law against the arbitrary rule of the individual" (Kaerst, *GH* I³, 222). The struggle for this idea, which he conducted with all the power of his passionate soul, elevates him far above the mass of ordinary demagogues: Demosthenes had a political ideal, and in the struggle for this ideal he came to grief.

That Demosthenes wanted to be regarded as a statesman is shown by, *inter al.*, the fact that his great political orations, beginning with the anti-Philippic speeches from 350/49 B.C. on, were "political pamphlets" in the form of orations; as such they were from the outset earmarked for journalistic distribution (W.v. Hartel, *Demosthenische Studien*, SB. W 87, 1877, 3 ff.; 88, 1878, 365 ff.; Ed Schwartz, *Festschr. f. Th. Mommsen*, Marburg 1893, 40 ff.; K. Hahn, *Demosthenis contiones num re vera in contione habitae sint quaeritur*, Diss. Giessen 1910; *et al.*). Of the orations handed down under his name no. VII is spurious: it is the speech *On the Island of Halonnesus* (342 B.C.), whose author is perhaps Hegesippus of Sunium. No. XI, the reply to Philip's ultimatum in 339 B.C., is also non-Demosthenic; it belongs to the orator Anaximenes of Lampsacus, who, after revising it, inserted it in his *Philippica* (v. *infra*). By contrast, the authenticity of the *Fourth Philippic* (X), from the spring of 341 (A. Körte, *RhM* 60, 1905, 388 ff.) and the *Epitaphios*, from 338 (LX), today seem assured (J. Sykutris, *Hermes* 63, 1928, 241 ff.). For deciding questions of authenticity the law discovered by F. Blass on avoiding abridgement is of importance (F. Vogel, *Hermes* 58, 1923, 87 ff.). On the chronology of the speeches see Ed. Schwartz, "Demosthenes' I. Philippika," *Festschr. f. Th. Mommsen*, Marburg 1893 (for a critique see the study cited below [502] by G. L. Cawkwell); E. Pokorny (in the Dissertation cited below); A. Rehm, *Silvae Monacenses*, 1926, 64 ff. (on the Olynthus orations); F. Focke, *Demosthenesstudien*, Tübinger Beitr. z. Altertumswiss. 5, 1929, 1 ff. (cf. A. Körte, *Gn.* 11, 1935, 342 ff.); H. Erbse, *RhM* 99, 1956, 364-380.

There is an almost unlimited amount of modern literature on Demosthenes (summaries may be found in *CAH* VI, 582 ff., and in Momigliano, *Fil.*, 128 n. 1.; cf. P. Cloché, *Etudes class.*, 1940, 294 ff.; and D. F. Jackson and G. O. Rowe, "Demosthenes 1915-1965," *Lustrum* 14, 1969, 5-109. The following deserve to be stressed: Beloch, *AP.*, 196 ff.; U. Kahrstedt, *Forschungen z. Gesch. des ausgehenden 5. und des 4. Jahrh.*, Berlin 1910 ("Die Politik des Demosthenes," *ibid.*, 1 ff.); cf. P. Wendland, *GGA*, 1912, 617 ff.; and E. Pokorny, *S. gr. G.* (excellent). Partial, but not without interesting parallels, is E. Drerup, *Aus einer alten Advokatenrepublik*, Paderborn 1915; *Demosthenes im Urteile des Altertums*, Würzburg 1923. The following concise studies may also be cited: A. W. Pickard-Cambridge, *Demosthenes and the Last Days of Greek Freedom*, New York and London 1914; P. Treves, *Demostene e la libertà greca*, Bari 1933 (cf. F. Hampl, *Gn.* 10, 1934, 384 ff.); P. Cloché, *Démosthène et la fin de la démocratie athénienne*, Paris 1937 (excellent but very apologetic). Instructive is H. Strohm, Eine Demosthenes-Interpretation, *Gym.* 79, 1962, 326 ff. [on the trustworthiness of the orator]; G. L. Cawkwell, "The Crowning of Demosthenes," *CQ* 19, 1969, 163 ff. In the face of the powerful and genuine pathos of Demosthenic oratory the formal talent of Aeschines recedes into the background. For a judicious recent assessment see G. Ramming, *Die politischen Ziele und Wege des Aischines*, Diss. Erlangen-Nürnberg 1965; cf. also G. Daverio, "Sul ruolo politico di Eschine," *RF* 97, 1969, 375 ff.

The works of the contemporary historians have, so far as their complete contents are concerned, without exception been lost. There are only a few fragments extant from the *Philippica* by the orator Anaximenes of Lampsacus, (P. Wendland, *Anaximenes v. Lampsakos*, Berlin 1905; the fragments are in Jacoby, *FgrHist.* no. 72), and from the 58 Books of the *Philippica* by Theopompus of Chios (Th. Schranz, *Theopomps Philippika*, Diss. Freiburg i.Br. 1912; A. Momigliano, "Teopompo," *RF* NS 9, 1931, 230 ff.; 335 ff.; *Fil.*, 197 n.1.; R. Laqueur, *RE* V A, 2176 ff. s.v. no. 9; K.v. Fritz, *AHR* 46, 1941, 765 ff., who rightly emphasises that Theopompus views personalities and events solely from the idealistic premise of his oligarchic-aristocratic outlook) (cf. Jacoby, *FgrHist.* no. 115). The *Histories* by Ephorus of Cyme (on him v.s.p. 436 f.) end before the blockade of Perinthus by Philip (340 B.C.). The account of the Third Sacred War in this work stems from Demophilus, son of Ephorus. A valuable source for internal developments in Athens are the *Poroi* of Xenophon (J. H. Thiel, *Xenophontos Poroi*, Vienna 1922) (edition with commentary); K.v. der Lieck, *Xenophons Schrift von den Einkünften*, Diss. Cologne 1933; cf. A. Wilhelm, *Wien. Stud.* 52, 1934, 18 ff.

SECONDARY SOURCES: The most important is Diodorus XVI. To what degree details in it are to be traced back to Ephorus, Theopompus,

Callisthenes and to Hellenistic intermediary sources (Diyllus and Duris) (cf. XVI 14), remains controversial. Modern investigations on this subject have reached conclusions which contradict each other (cf. in addition to the bibliography cited in *CAH* VI, 581, in particular, A. Momigliano, *Rend Ist. Lomb.* 65, 1932, 523 ff. (unsatisfactory); N.G.L. Hammond, *CQ* 31, 1937, 79 ff.; and P. Treves, "Per la critica e l'analisi del libro XVI di Diodoro," *Ann. Reale Scuola Norm. Sup. di Pisa, Lett., stor., e fil.*, II 6, 1937, 255 ff.). From the local Histories the following may be mentioned: the *Atthis* of Androtion (extending to 344/3 B.C.?), which incidentally counts as a primary source for the period of Philip II; and the *Atthis* of Philochorus (to the end of the sixties in the third century B.C.); the fragments have been published by F. Jacoby, *FgrHist.* II B nos. 324 and 328. Cf. also L. Pearson, *The Local Histories of Attica* (Philological Monographs Published by APA 11), 1942; and Jacoby, *Att.* Important information is provided by the commentary of the Alexandrian scholar Didymus (Augustan period) on the orations of Demosthenes; it is partly (for the orations IX-XII) preserved on a papyrus (published by H. Diels and W. Schubart, *Didymi de Demosthene commenta*, Leipzig 1904, also in the *Berl. Klass. Texten* [likewise 1904]; also the important study by P. Foucart, *Etude sur Didymos*, Mém. Acad. des Inscr. et Belles-Lettres, 38, 1, 1909, 27 ff.). There are, furthermore, Plutarch's *Vitae* of *Demosthenes, Phocion, Dion, Timoleon*; his *Apophthegmata regum*; and, finally, the excerpt by Justin from the *Historiae Philippicae* of Pompeius Trogus, Books VII-IX. The general treatment of the sources by R. Schubert, *Unters. über die Quellen z. Gesch. Philipps II. von Makedonien*, Königsberg 1904, is not satisfactory.

BIBLIOGRAPHY: In addition to the Histories of Greece by G. Grote, K. J. Beloch, G. Glotz, H. Berve, Vol. 1 of *GH* by Kaerst, and *CAH* VI, the following more recent monographs may be cited: Momigliano, *Fil.* (cf. F. Hampl, *Gn.* 13, 1937, 474 ff.; F. R. Wüst, *WG* 4, 1938, 33 f.); Wüst, *Phil.* (cf. P. Cloché, *REA* 41, 1939, 155 ff.). F. Geyer, *RE* XIX, 2266 ff. s.v. *Philippos* (II.) no. 7. Excellent is P. Cloché, *La politique étrangère d'Athènes de 404 à 338 av. J.-C.*, Paris 1934; also worth reading is the biography of Philip II by V. Chapot, in *Hommes d'Etat*, edited by A. B. Duff and F. Galy, Paris 1936, also P. Cloché, *Un fondateur d'empire. Philippe II roi de Macédoine*, Saint Etienne 1955. A special problem: F. Carrata Thomes, *Cultura greca e unità macedone nella politica di Filippo II*, Turin 1949. The more recent bibliography on Demosthenes is cited above 499.

MACEDONIA BEFORE PHILIP II

PRINCIPAL SOURCES: Thuc. II 99 ff.; [Herodes] *On the Constitution* (edition by E. Drerup, *Stud. z. Gesch. u. Kultur des Alt.* II 1, 1908, from the end of the fifth century B.C. (cf. *supra* 484); additional scattered information in Herodotus (for instance, VIII 136 ff.); Aristotle, *Polit.* V 1311b, *et al.*). The Macedonian King List (discussed in detail by H. Pack,

Hermes 10, 1875, 281 ff.; A.v. Gutschmid, *Kleine Schriften* IV, 1893, 1 ff.; Ed. Schwartz, *Die Königslisten des Eratosthenes u. Kastor*, Abh. Gött. Ges., phil.-hist. Kl., XL, 1895) does not come into question as a historical source; it is a late construction (cf. the survey in Beloch, *GG* III 2, 49 ff.).

BIBLIOGRAPHY: L. Flathe, *Gesch. Makedoniens und der Reiche, welche von makedonischen Königen beherrscht wurden*, Leipzig 1832; O. Abel, *Makedonien vor König Philipp*, Leipzig 1847; V. Costanzi, *Studi di storia macedonica sino a Filippo*, Pisa 1915; F. Geyer, *RE* XIV 1, 638 ff. s.v. *Makedonia* (including the section 681-697, by O. Hoffmann); Geyer, *Mak*.; Glotz, *HG* III, 202 ff.; R. Paribeni, *Macedonia sino ad Alessandro Magno*, Milan 1947 (contains little that is new). On the prehistory of Macedonia: S. Casson, *Macedonia, Thrace, and Illyria*, 1926; and in particular, N.G.L. Hammond, *A History of Macedonia*. Vol. I. *Historical Geography and Prehistory*, Oxford 1972. On coinage: D. Raymond, *Macedonian Royal Coinage to 413 B.C.*, New York 1953; cf. the report by P. R. Franke, *Jahrb. f. Num. u. Geldgesch.* 7, 1956, 105 ff., and the specialised study "Geschichte, Politik u. Münzprägung im früheren Makedonien," *ibid.* 3-4, 1952-53, 99-111.

THE FIRST YEARS OF PHILIP'S REIGN

PRINCIPAL SOURCES: Theopompus frs. 30 ff.; Carystius of Pergamum (second century B.C.) fr. 1 (= Athen. XI 506e-f); Diod. XVI 2.4-4; 8; 14 (cf. Chr. Ehrhardt, *CQ* 17, 1967, 296-301; there can, accordingly, be no question of an intervention by Philip in Thessaly in 357 or 356 B.C.); for a different view, see G. T. Griffith, *CQ* 20, 1970, 68-70); Justin VII 5-6.

GREECE AND MACEDONIA IN THE TIME OF THE THIRD SACRED WAR

PRINCIPAL SOURCES: Diod. XVI 23-40; 56-60; N. G. L. Hammond, "Diodorus' Narrative of the Sacred War," *JHS* 57, 1937, 44 ff. = *Studies*, 486-533, and E. Link, *Untersuchungen zur Symmorienrede des Demosthenes*, Diss. Frankfurt a.M. 1940, 12 ff., have no doubt rightly contested the view that there are two different versions in Diodorus ch. 24 f. and 27 f., on the beginning of the Third Sacred War, as U. Kahrstedt, *Forsch. z. Gesch. d. ausgehenden 5. u. des 4. Jahrh.*, 1910, Pokorny, *St.*, 5 ff.; P. Cloché (v. *infra*), and Beloch, *GG* III 2, 262 ff., concluded, having followed the lead of A. Schaefer (1856) and others; Paus. X 2 f.; Just. VIII 1-5; Aristotle, *Polit.* V 3.4; Duris fr. 2; *Syll.* I³ 237 f. (building calculations from Delphi which supply information on the composition of the Council of *Naopoioi*; cf. Beloch, *GG* III 2, 265; M. Sordi, *BCH* 81, 1957, 38-75: particularly on the beginnings of the *Naopoioi* Council, from 366 B.C. on). On Diodorus see further, P. Treves, "Per la critica e l'analisi del libro XVI di Diodoro," *Annali Scuola Norm. Sup. di Pisa* II 3-4, 1937, 255 ff.

Instructive for the position of the Greek polis is the work of Aeneas

Tacitus, *De obsidione toleranda*, from c. 350 or, at the latest, 340 B.C.; see H. Bengtson, *H.* 11, 1962, 458 ff. = *KS*, 178 ff., also *idem*, *The Greeks and the Persians*, London 1968, 263 ff.

BIBLIOGRAPHY: Momigliano, *Fil.*, 103 ff.; K. Fiehn, *RE* XIX, 2524 f. s.v. *Philomelos* no. 3; W. S. Ferguson, *RE* XVIII, 493 ff. s.v. *Onomarchos* no. 1; F. Schober, *RE* XX, 487 ff. s. v. *Phokis*. On the chronology see further, A. Pintschovius, *Xenophon De vectig. V 9 und die Überlieferung vom Anfang des Phokischen Krieges*, Hadersleben 1900; P. Cloché, *Etude chronologique sur la troisième guerre sacrée*, Paris 1915, cf. *Etud. class.*, 1939, 161 ff.; E. Bourguet, *Fouilles de Delphes* III 5, 1932, 6 ff.; M. Toney, *Die Chronologie des 3. Heil. Krieges und die Jahreseinteilung im XVI. Buche Diodors* (Stud. hist.-phil. Serdicensia 38, 165 ff., Sofia 1938); also Th. Lenschau, *Burs. Jb.* 279, 1942, 190 ff.; M. Sordi, *RF* NS 36, 1958, 134-166 (on the Third Sacred War); N. J. Hackett, *The Third Sacred War*, Diss. Univ. of Cincinnati 1970.

On the Olynthian War: G. L. Cawkwell, "The Defense of Olynthus," *CQ* 12, 1962, 122-140 (against dating the *First Philippic* of Demosthenes in 349 B.C. by Ed. Schwartz; the first half of the oration is allegedly to be dated in 351, the second half in 347/6 B.C.). Further recent attempts at dating (v. also s. 498): R. Sealey, *REG* 68, 1955, 77 ff. (spring 351); J. R. Ellis, *REG* 79, 1966 636 ff. (beginning of 350, at the earliest).

On the date of the Olynthian speeches v.s.p. 498, in particular the more recent studies by R. Sealey, *REG* 68, 1955, 77 ff., and J. R. Ellis, *H.* 16, 1967, 108 ff. (the chronological sequence of the orations, accordingly, is II-I-III).

FROM THE PEACE OF PHILOCRATES TO THE DEATH OF PHILIP II

PRINCIPAL SOURCES: Included in the documentary material there are, in addition to the inscriptions (*Syll.* I³ 221 ff.), the following: the letter of Speusippus to King Philip (cf. E. Bickermann and J. Sykutris, *Ber. Verh. Sächs. Ak. d. Wiss., phil.-hist. Kl.* 80, 1928, Heft 3), from the spring of 342 B.C.; and Philip's letter to Athens (340 B.C.), preserved in the *Corp. Demosth.* no. XII (v.s.p. 496 f.); the second and third letters of Isocrates. From the orations, the following may be mentioned: Demosthenes, *Second Philippic* (VI), from the autumn of 344; *On the Fraudulent Embassy* (XIX), from 343; *On the Chersonese* (VIII), approximately April 341 (a different date, namely the summer of 340, is advocated by S. G. Daitz, *CP* 52, 1957, 145-162); the *Third Philippic* (IX), from June 341 (on the two drafts of the oration see P. Treves, "La composition de la troisième Philippique," *Mél. G. Radet*, 1940, 354 ff.); the *Fourth Philippic* (X), from July of the same year; the *Epitaphios* (LX), from 338; Aeschines, *Against Timarchus* (I), from 346/5; *On the Fraudulent Embassy* (II), from 343; Hegesippus of Sunium (?), *On the Island of Halonnesus*, (no. VII in the *Corpus Demosth.*), from 342; the *Panathenäikos* of Isocrates, from 339 (cf. P. Wendland, *NGG*, 1910, 137 ff.). Valuable from the later speeches of

Demosthenes are: *De Corona*; and the reply of Aeschines, *Against Ctesiphon* (III), both from 330.

The historians: Theop. frs. 171 ff. Jacoby *FgrH* 115; Diod. XVI 69; 71; 74 ff.; 84; Just. VIII 6; IX 1 ff.; Didymus on Demosth. IX-XII; Plut., *Phoc.* 14 ff.; *Demosth.* 16-22; Corn. Nep., *Phoc.* 2. For the sources and bibliography on the Corinthian League v.i.p. 508 n. 110.

BIBLIOGRAPHY: Ed. Meyer, *Isokrates' 2. Brief an Philipp und Demosthenes' 2. Philippika*, SB.B, 1909 758 ff.; U. Wilcken, *Phil.*, 291 ff.; Momigliano, *Fil.*, 127 ff.; Wüst, *Phil.*; F. Geyer, *RE* XIX, 2284 ff. s. v. *Philippos* no. 7; G. L. Cawkwell, "Demosthenes' Policy after the Peace of Philocrates," *CQ* 13, 1963, 120 ff.; 200 ff.; D. Kienast, *Philip II. von Makedonien und das Reich der Achaimeniden*, Munich 1973. On the chronology: P. Cloché, "La Grèce de 346 à 339 av. J.-C.," *BCH* 44, 1920, 106 ff.; Beloch, *GG* III 2, 288 ff.; E. Bickermann, "*Note sur la chronologie de la XXX*[e] *dynastie*" (Mém. de l'Inst. franç. d'arch. orient du Caire, 1934); *Mél. Maspero* I, 377 ff.; P. Cloché, "La Grèce et l'Egypte de 405 à 342/1 a. J.-C.," *Rev. égyptienne* NS I, 1919, 210 ff.; II, 1920, 32 ff. On a recent, unsuccessful, attempt to redate the conquest of Egypt (to 345/4 B.C.) by M. Sordi, *Kokalos* 5, 1959, 107 ff., see G. L. Cawkwell, *CQ* 13, 1963, 136 ff.

1. The one-sided emphasis on this aspect of the *trophe* by scholars like J. Hasebroek, *Staat u. Handel im Alten Griechenland*, 1928, and Hampl, *Staatsv.* and to a certain degree also by Berve, *GG* II, goes much too far.

2. See the characteristic delineation of Isocrates in his *Panathenaïkos* § 259.

3. It has been reckoned that of the 85 years between 431 and 346 B.C. no less than 53 were years of warfare in Greece.

4. Thus, for instance, H. Berve, *Gn.* 9, 1933, 301 ff.; see also G. Dobesch, *Der panhellenische Gedanke im 4. Jh. v. Chr. und der 'Philippos' des Isokrates. Untersuchungen zum korinthischen Bund* I, Vienna 1968.

5. Essential phenomena of this development have been well delineated, although in very brief form, by Altheim, *As.* I. 118 ff.

6. Cf. A. Scharff, in *Hdb. d. Arch.* ed. W. Otto, I, 1939, 632 ff.

7. Characteristic of the Hellenisation of Caria in the fourth century B.C. are the dedications of Carian satraps (Hecatomnus, Idrieus, Ada) in the Greek language in the temple of Sinyri near Mylasa; see L. Robert, *Le sanctuaire de Sinuri près de Mylasa*, 1945, 93 ff.; *Le sanctuaire d'Artémis à Amyzon* (Inst. de France, 1953-56); in addition there are now the results of the Swedish excavations at Labranda, of which only some have been published to date: cf. J. Crampa, *Labraunda. Swedish Excavations*. Vol. II Part 1. *The Greek Inscriptions*, I 1,12 (Period of Olympichus, 240-220 B.C.), Lund 1969; Bengtson, *Lab.*

8. *Acta Apostol.* 6.1: the *Hellenistai* are not orientalised Greeks, as J. G. Droysen thought.

9. On the term Hellenism see the concise discussion by R. Laqueur, *Hellenismus, Giessener Ak. Rede*, 1925, and the article "Hellenismus," in *Die Religion in Geschichte und Gegenwart* (Handwörterbuch f. Theologie u. Religionswissenschaft), 2nd ed., H. Gunkel and L. Zscharnack, II, 1928, 1781 ff.; A. Momigliano, "Genesi storica e fonzione attuale del concetto de ellenismo," in *Contributo alla storia degli stud. classici*, Rome 1955, 165 ff. [first published in 1935]; H. Herter, in *NBA* 1, 1942, 334 ff.

10. To this extent more recent attempts to regard Hellenism as an organic further development of Greek civilisation, which should have led to a fundamental remoulding of the Orient through Greek culture (above all in the realm of religion) (cf., for instance, C.

Schneider, "Die griechische Grundlagen der hellenistischen Religionsgeschichte," *ARW* 36, 1939, 300 ff.), are not entirely without justification. On points of detail, however, they are far wide of the mark.

11. Recent scholars go even further, as C. H. Becker and above all Otto (*Kulturg.*, 93 ff.; *Antike Kulturgesch.*, SB.M, 1940, Heft 6, 18 ff.), who also subsume the entire culture of the *Imperium Romanum* under the concept of Hellenism, a view which does not do justice to the significance of Roman culture as renewed by Augustus; see, for instance, U. Wilcken, *DLZ*, 1925, 1530 ff.

12. Cf. O. Hoffmann, *Die Makedonen*, Göttingen 1906; *RE* XIV, 681 ff. s.v. *Makedonia*. Macedonian is, accordingly, a sister-dialect of Thessalian. A new assembling of the evidence has been made by I. I. Russu, Macedonia," in *Ephemeris Dacoromana, Annuario della Scuola Romana di Roma* VIII, 1938; J. N. Kalléris, *Les anciens Macédoniens. Etude linguistique et historique*, I, Athens 1954.

13. *Einleitung in die Gesch. d. griech. Sprache*, 1896, 283 ff.; Die griech. Sprache, in Gercke-Norden, *Einl.* I 3, 86 ff.

14. Kaerst. *GH* I[3], 154 ff.

15. Cf. C. O. Müller, *Über die Wohnsitze, die Abstammung und die ältere Geschichte des makedonischen Volkes*, Berlin 1825; O. Abel, *Makedonien vor König Philipp*, Leipzig 1847; R. Fick, *KZ* 22, 1874, 193 ff.; *Beitr. z. Kunde d. indogerm. Sprache* 24, 291 ff.; G. N. Hatzidakis, *Zur Abstammung der alten Makedonier*, Athens 1897; Beloch *GG* IV 1 ff.; Geyer, *Mak.* 30 ff. A thorough survey is given by J. N. Kalleris (see n. 12 above, 20 ff.).

16. Herod. V 94.

17. Herod. V 22. On the epithet Philhellene cf. Schol. Thuc. I 57; Schol. Demos., *Olynthos* III 130; Dio Chrysostum II 33; Harpocration s.v. *Alexandros*. J. Papastavru, *Makedonikè politikè kata ton 5on p.Ch. aiòna: Alexandros* I, Thessalonike 1936, provides little that is new.

18. Anaximenes of Lampsacus fr. 4 Jacoby, *FgrHist.* no. 72). The best discussion on the controversy connected with this fragment may be found in A. Momigliano, *Fil.* 8 ff. To think in terms of Alexander II (thus Berve, *Alex.* I, 104; Jacoby, Commentary to *FgrHist.* 72.4), is virtually excluded on factual grounds (see H. Bengtson, in E. Kornemann, *Weltgeschichte des Mittelmeerraumes* I, 1948, 71 n.1). The suggestion by U. Köhler, SB.B, 1893, 493 f., to emend "Alexander" to "Archelaus," does not recommend itself; even less convincing is the conjecture of Kaerst, *GH* I[3], 194, and G. Plaumann, *RE* VIII, 1378 s.v. *Hetairoi*, that Philip II was the instigator of this reform. Completely impossible is the view of Ernst Meyer, *GGA*, 1932, 449 ff., who claims that as late as the beginning of the fourth century B.C. Macedonia did not have an infantry. On the *hetairoi* see Hampl, *KM*, 66 ff. (cf. W. S. Ferguson, *Gn.* 11, 1935, 519 f.).

19. On him see W. Vischer, *Kl. Schr.* I, 1877, 239 ff.; Geyer, *Mak.*, 50 ff.; *RE* XIX, 590 ff. s.v. no. 2.

20. Thuc. II 100.2; cf. U. Köhler, *Makedonien unter König Archelaos*, SB.B, 1893, 490 ff.; Geyer, *Mak.*, 84 ff.

21. Cf. the work of [Herodes] *Peri politeias*, and Ed. Meyer, *Theompomps Hellenika*, 1909, 247 ff. (See also above 484.)

22. Geyer, *Mak.*, 101 ff.; Bengtson, *Strat.* II, 322 f.

23. A. Momigliano, *Fil.*, 25 n. 3, cf. also his study "La leggenda de Carano, re di Macedonia," *AR* 12, 1931, 203 ff.; further, Schmid, *GGL* I 3, 1940, 627.

24. C. Schütt, *Untersuch. z. Gesch. d. alten Illyrier*, Diss. Breslau 1910.

25. On the reign of Amyntas III cf. V. Costanzi, "Le vicende di Aminta III nel primo decennio del suo regno," *Klio* 6, 1906, 297 ff.; A. Rosenberg, "Amyntas der Vater Philipps II.," *Hermes* 51, 1916, 499 ff.; Geyer, *Mak.*, 111 ff.

26. U. Kahrstedt, "Städte in Makedonien," *Hermes* 81, 1953, 85 ff., attempts to revise the picture, but the results remain problematic.

27. F. Granier, *Die makedonische Heeresversammlung* (Münch. Beitr. 13), 1931.

28. Hampl, *KM*.

29. For a critique see in particular A. Momigliano, "Re e popolo in Macedonia," *Ath.* NS 13, 1935, 7 ff.; W. S. Ferguson, *Gn.* 11, 1935, 519; Bengtson, *Strat.* I, 24 n. 2. The reply by Hampl, *Staatsv.*, 136 ff., is not convincing; see F. R. Wüst, *Gn.* 14, 1938, 376 f., and A. Aymard, *"Basileus Makedonōn," Revue Intern. des Droits de l'Ant. IV (Mél. F. de Visscher III)*, Brussels 1950, 61 ff.

30. See also K. Rosen, *King and People in Macedonia. A Study on Their Relations under Philip and Alexander*, Diss. Univ. of South Africa, Pretoria 1970.

31. V.s.p. 173.

32. Carystius fr. 1 (*FHG* IV, 356); cf. the letter of Speusippus to Philip § 12, see E. Bickermann and J. Sykutris, *Ber. Sächs. Ak., phil.-hist. Kl.* 80, 1928, Heft 3, 17; Momigliano, *Fil.*, 36 n. 1.

33. On Ptolemy of Alorus see Geyer, *Mak.*, 132 ff.; on Perdiccas III, *ibid.*, as well as *RE* XIX, 602 ff. s.v. *Perdikkas* no. 3.

34. Formally, Amphipolis remained autonomous, as is shown by *IG* IV^2 1, 94/95.

35. [Aristotle] *Oeconomica* II 1350a; Hypereides III 18; Demosthenes L 48; Lycurgus, *Against Leocrates* 93; cf. F. Geyer, *RE* XIX, 603. It is not advisable to place Callistratus' stay in Macedonia as late as Philip's reign; see Momigliano, *Fil.*, 35 n. 2.

36. According to another tradition (Justin VII 5.6 ff.; *Suda* s.v. *Karanos*; Curtius Rufus VI 11.26), Perdiccas met his end in the persecution of his mother.

37. The sources in Bengtson, *Staatsv.* II, no. 298. Sceptical of the existence of the treaty: Momigliano, *Fil.*, 45 ff. The treaty is rejected by G. E. M. de Ste. Croix, *CQ* 57, 1963, 110-119.

38. At that time Philip built the fortress of Heracleia (Monastir), Steph. Byz. s.v. *Herakleia*; cf. Beloch, *GG* III 1, 528 n. 2.

39. Lyncestis appears to have been planned under Perdiccas III: *IG* II/III^2 110 = Tod II no. 143 = *GHD 4th C*, 45; Geyer, *Mak.*, 81 f.

40. The date is unknown (Justin VII 5.9 f.). Beloch, *GG* III 1, 232, and F. Geyer, *RE* XIX, 2271, place the event in the period about 355 B.C. This must be approximately correct.

41. That the oration belongs in 357 B.C., *before* the outbreak of the so-called Social War, has now been shown by W. Jaeger, "The Date of Isocrates' Areopagiticus and the Athenian Opposition," *Studies Ferguson*, 499 ff., as opposed to Ed. Meyer and F. Miltner, who place the speech *in* the time of the war. On the beginning of the Social War (in the archonship of Cephisodotus, to wit 358/7 B.C.) see E. Schweigert, *Hesp.* 8, 1939, 14 ff.

42. The principal sources on the Social War are Isocrates, *On the Peace* (355 B.C.); Xenophon, *Poroi* (cf. *supra* 499); Diod, XVI 7.3 and 21 f.; Corn. Nep., *Timotheus* 3; Polyaenus III 9.29; cf. the references in Demosthenes and Aeschines; cf. R. Weise, *Der athenische Bundesgenossenkrieg*, Diss. Berlin 1895; Meyer, *GdA* V, 490 ff.; A. W. Pickard-Cambridge, *CAH* VI, 209 ff.; Momigliano, *Fil.*, 92 ff.; R. Sealey, "Athens after the Social War," *JHS* 75, 1955, 74 ff.

43. Bengtson, *Staatsv.* II, no. 313.

44. Beloch, *GG* III 1, 245, greatly exaggerates the importance of Athens after the war. The figure of 349 triremes which Athens had at her disposal in 353/2 B.C. (*IG* II/III^2 1613 line 302) is only relative. The majority of the vessels were not ready to sail and lay in dock.

45. Amphipolis did not become part of the royal dominions, as is maintained by Hampl, *KM*, 22 ff. On Amphipolis cf. J. Papastavru, *Klio-Beih.* 37, 1936.

46. Demosth. I 5; Diod XVI 8.3.

47. The treaty is extant (mentioned by Diod. XVI 8.3-5); cf. the evidence *supra* 495. Noteworthy is the co-operation of the Delphic oracle; cf. A. D. Nock, *Proceedings of the American Philosophical Society* Vol. 85 no. 5 (Sept. 1942) 472.

48. P. Collart, *Philippes, ville de Macédoine*, Paris 1937. The renaming of the place is attested in particular by the coins of the settlement; cf. Head, HN^2, 217 f.

49. According to V. Martin, "La durée d'exploitation des gisements aurifères de Philippes en Macédoine," in *Etudes dediées à la mém. d'André Andréades*. Athens 1940. 17 ff., the treasury would, however, have soon become exhausted, at all events *before* Alexander's accession.

50. On the reorientation of Macedonian coinage policy cf. the concise discussion by Kaerst, *GH* I^3, 210 f. At that time Philip abandoned the Persian standard and reintroduced the Phoenician.

51. The treaty of alliance is preserved in *IG* II/III^2 127 = Bengtson, *Staatsv.* II, no. 309 = *GHD 4th C* 57.

52. Diod. XVI 31.6; on the chronology see N. G. L. Hammond, *JHS* 57, 1937, 58 = *Studies*, 500. On the basis of *IG* II/III^2 130 the siege of Methone by Philip must have been feared already in December 355 B.C.

53. This date is firmly established. Various dates appear in ancient tradition for the

beginning of the war; its ten year duration (until 346 B.C.) is, however, certain from Aeschines (*On the Embassy* 131; *Against Ctesiphon* 148). His account is to be preferred to Diodorus XVI 14.3 and 23.1.

54. Scheele, *Str.*, 10 ff.

55. Cf. N. G. L. Hammond, *JHS* 57, 1937, 62 ff. = *Studies*, 510 ff.

56. Head, *HN*², 339, cf. Ferguson, *RE* XVIII, 497.

57. It is to this campaign that Diod. XVI 14.2 refers; cf. H. Swoboda, *Öst. Jh.* 6, 1903, 202 ff.; Pokorny, *St.*, 46 ff.; a different view by Beloch, *GG* III 1, 228.

58. Judeich, *KS*, 211 f.; Beloch, *GG* III 1, 251; Th. Lenschau, *RE* XVIII 3, 298 f.

59. Demosth. XIX 319; Diod. XVI 35.4-6; 61.2 (inadequate); Paus. X 2.5; Justin VIII 2.1-6.

60. Justin VIII 2.1.

61. Thus, however, Ed. Meyer, *Kleine Schriften* I, 273.

62. This has been correctly emphasised, against A. Schaefer, *Demosthenes und seine Zeit* I², 186 ff., and Beloch, *AP*, 173 ff., above all by E. Schwartz, *Marburger Festschrift für Th. Mommsen*, 1893, 50 ff., and Pokorny, *St.*, 77 ff., cf. also Jaeger, *Dem.*, 58.

63. Demosth. XIV; cf. A. Momigliano, *La Civiltà Moderna* 3, 1931, 715; Jaeger, *Dem.*, 77 ff.; E. Link, *Untersuch, zur Symmorienrede des Demosthenes*, Diss. Frankfurt 1940 (cf. A. Körte, *Gn.* 19, 1943, 34 ff.). In accord with the finance policy of Eubulus at the time, Demosthenes put forward the proposal to increase the number of Athenians liable to *trierarchia* from 1200 to 2000. On the financial straits of Athens see G. E. M. de Ste. Croix, "Demosthenes' *timema* and the Athenian *eisphora*, in the 4th Century," *Class. et Mediaev.* 14, 1953, 30-70.

64. The view put forward by U. Kahrstedt, *Forschungen*, 1910, 1 ff., and "Zur politischen Tendenz der Aristocrateia," *Hermes* 46, 1911, 464 ff., that from the very outset Demosthenes appeared as the standard bearer of a deliberate pro-Persian policy, is completely unfounded. The theory has been advanced, but with strong reservations, by P. Wendland, *GGA*, 1912, 618 ff., and conclusively refuted by Pokorny, *St.* U. Kahrstedt himself incidentally had long since ceased to advocate it unreservedly (cf. the Journal *Sokrates*, 1918, 130).

65. See the oration of Demosthenes, *On Behalf of the Megalopolitans* (XVI); on the date, Momigliano, *Fil.*, 106 n. 1. On the other hand, the verdict on this speech by Jaeger, *Dem.*, 82 ff., is not very convincing.

66. P. Cloché, "Athènes et Kersebleptès de 357/6 à 353/2," *Mél. G. Glotz* I, 1932, 215 ff.

67. The chronology is not certain; the year 351 B.C. is also possible.

68. Diod. XVI 52.9, who does not however date the event until 349/8 B.C.; on the chronology see A. Rehm, *Silvae Monacenses*, 1926, 66 ff.; F. Focke, *Demosthenes-Studien*, 1929, 10 ff.; but for a different view cf. Momigliano, *Fil.*, 113 n.

69. On the conflict between Philip and Olynthus see above all the three Olynthic orations of Demosthenes (delivered in the autumn of 349 or, at the latest, in the spring of 348 B.C.); cf. on these speeches, besides the studies cited above 498 f., also: P. Treves, "Le Olintiache di Demostene," *Nuova Riv. Stor.* 22, 1938, 1 ff.; moreover, Demosth. XXIII 107 ff.; III 7; IX 56; 63 ff.; XIX 263 ff.; also Hypereides fr. 76; Theopompus fr. 127; Diod. XVI 53; Justin VIII 3.10 f.

70. Bengtson, *Staatsv.* II, 323.

71. H. W. Parke, *Proceed. of the Royal Irish Acad.* XLIII, Section C, no. 12, Dublin 1936, places the inscription *IG* II/III² 207 (cf. Bengtson, *Staatsv.* II, no. 324) in 348 B.C. and concludes from it that in April 348 B.C. Athens resolved to despatch an additional large auxiliary expedition under Chares and Phocion to Olynthus. At the time Athens allegedly also took up relations with Orontes the satrap of Mysia (on him see M. Osborne, *It.*, 22, 1973, 515-551) to provision Olynthus. A sceptical interpretation of the inscription by G. L. Cawkwell, *CQ* 56, 1962, 131 f.

72. H. W. Parke, "Athens and Euboea 349-348 B.C.," *JHS* 49, 1929, 246 ff.; Th. Lenschau, *RE* XX, 460 f. s.v. *Phokion* no. 2; P. A. Brunt, "Euboea in the Time of Philip II," *CQ* NS 19, 1969, 245 ff.

73. *Syll.* I³ 332; Appian, *Bell. Civ.* IV 428. A number of arrow-heads and catapult leads found at Olynthus bearing Philip's name stem from the time of the siege.

74. Sources are: the orations of Demosthens and Aeschines on the *De Falsa Legatione*,

and the speech of Aeschines, *Against Ctesiphon*. The details of the evidence must be weighed against each other. The view that the facts are to be found only in Demosthenes (thus A. Schaefer), or only in Aeschines (thus U. Kahrstedt) is erroneous. Cf. the discussion by Pokorny, *St*., 139 ff.; M. M. Markle, "The Strategy of Philip in 346 B.C.," *CQ* NS 24, 1974, 253 ff.

75. The sources in H. Bengtson, *Staatsv.* II no. 329; the proviso is recorded by Demosthenes (XIX 159; 174).

76. Aeschines II 81 ff.; Schol. on Demosth. XIX 156; 334; Isocrates V 21.

77. The most important bibliography on the Peace of Philocrates may be found in Momigliano, *Fil.*, 119 n. 1; see further P. Cloché, *La politique étrangère d'Athènes*, 1934, 224 ff.; Hampl, *Staatsv.*, 56 ff.; 111 ff. (cf. the corrections by Wüst, *Phil.*, 178 ff.). F. R. Wüst has shown that the treaty contained a proviso against piracy and to that extent went beyond the context of ordinary peace treaties.

78. Demosth. XIX 53 ff.; Diod. XVI 59. On the punishment of the Phocians see the proposal of the Dorians at Mount Oeta: Aesch. II 142, also Diod, XVI 60; cf. Momigliano, *Fil.*, 121; Wüst *Phil.*, 17.

79. On the organisation of the Delphic Amphictyony see the details in Wüst *Phil.*, 18 ff.

80. Diod. XVI 60.3; cf. Wüst, *Phil.*, 20 ff.; 177 ff.; for a different view see Hampl, *Staatsv.*, 64 f.; *Klio* 31, 1938, 411 ff.; and G. T. Griffith, *JHS* 59, 1939, 71 ff.

81. Demosth. XIX 128; for an appraisal of the Athenian attitude see Wüst, *Phil.*, 40.

82. Cf. E. Skard, *Zwei religiös.-politische Begriffe: Euergetes-Concordia*, Oslo 1932, 55 ff.; G. Dobesch, *Der panhellenische Gedanke im 4. Jh. v. Chr. und der Philippos des Isokrates*, Vienna 1968.

83. Justin VIII 5.7 ff.; cf. U. Köhler, SB.B, 1891, 485 f.

84. Ed. Meyer, SB.B, 1909, 758 ff.; F. Papazoglu, *H.* 14, 1965, 156 ff.

85. S. Ferri, "I capisaldi della costituzione tessalica.I. Il significato della tetrarchia," *RF* NS 7, 1929, 359 ff.; A. Momigliano, "Tagia e tetrarchia in Tessaglia," *Ath.* NS 10, 1932, 47 ff.; a concise discussion by Wüst, *Phil.*, 99 ff.

86. For 344/3 B.C. (on the basis of Diod. XVI 69.8) Beloch, *GG* III 1, 529 n. 1, and F. Geyer, *RE* XIX, 2284 s.v. *Philippos*; for 342 B.C. Wüst *Phil.*, 101. F. Hampl, *NJb*, 1938, 144 n. 1, argues for a much earlier date (352 B.C.?).

87. Demosth. IX 71; X 31 ff.; XI 5 f., *et al.*

88. [Demosth.] VII 22, cf. XVIII 136; XIX 353. Cf. E. Bickermann and J. Sykutris, *Speusipps Brief an König Philipp*, 1928, 39 ff.

89. Arrian, *Anab.* II 14.2; cf. Wüst, *Phil.*, 89 ff.

90. The Epirote king Arybbas was driven out by Philip, after which he lived for years in Athens; cf. *Syll.* I³ 228 (cf. O. Walter, *Wien. Jh.* 32, 1940, 1 ff.) = Tod II 173 = *GHD 4th C* 71; further P. Treves, "The Meaning of 'consenesco' and King Arybbas of Epirus," *AJP* 63, 1942, 120-153.

91. The final work on establishing the chronology has been done by E. Bickermann (v.s.p. 503); cf. Wüst *Phil.*, 59 ff.

92. On the organisation of Thrace cf. Hampl, *KM*, 40 ff.; for a different view Bengtson, *Strat.* I, 38 ff.; Wüst, *Phil.*, 102 ff. That Thrace became the personal property of the Macedonian king, as Hampl has maintained, is incorrect.

93. At that time Aristotle, the son-in-law of Hermias, came to the Macedonian court in Pella as tutor to the young crown prince Alexander, but his mission was certainly also of a political character; cf. W. Jaeger, *Aristotle*, ²1962, 117 ff.; and A.-H. Chroust, *H.* 21, 1972, 170 ff. On Hermias see D. E. W. Wormell, *YCS* 5, 1935, 57 ff.

94. W. Jaeger, *loc. cit.* F. R. Wüst, *Phil.*, 97.

95. No doubt soon after the conquest of Egypt, probably in 341 B.C.; the sources are cited by U. Kahrstedt, *RE* XV, 694 s.v. *Mentor* no. 6; cf. also Beloch, *GG* III 1, 539 n.1; and the study by Wormell (s.n. 93 *supra*).

96. Members of the League were: Euboea, Megara, Achaea, Acarnania, Corinth, Leucas, Corcyra *et al.*; cf. Demosth. XVIII 237; 244; Aesch. III 95 ff.; 256; *Vitae* X *orat.* 845a. The importance of the League is greatly exaggerated by Jaeger, *Dem.*, 175 f.; as opposed to him cf. Wüst, *Phil.*, 119.

97. The sources in Wüst, *Phil.*, 127 n. 3.

98. [Demosth.] XII 16.

99. Didymus X 45 ff.; further, Demosth. XVIII 139; Justin IX 1; cf. Wüst, *Phil.*, 131.

100. Nicorescu, "La campagne de Philippe en 339," *Dacia* 2, 1925, 22 ff.; A. Momigliano, "Dalla spedizione scitica di Filippo alla spedizione scitica de Dario," *Ath.* NS 11, 1933, 336 ff.

101. The charge was introduced by Aeschines, accusing the Locrians of tilling the sacred district of Cirrha. The sources: Aesch. III 106 ff.; Demosth. XVIII 140 ff. Cf. G. De Sanctis, "Eschine e la guerra contro Amfissa," *Scritti Minori*, 1966, 139 ff. The events are also very thoroughly treated by Wüst, *Phil.*, 146 ff. (the chronology, 153 ff.).

102. G. Glotz, "Philippe et la surprise d'Elatée." *BCH* 33, 1909, 525 ff.

103. Principal accounts: Diod. XVI 85 f.; Polyaenus IV 2.2;7; Frontin. Strat. II 1.9; Justin IX 3.9 ff.; Plut., *Alex.* 9; Paus. IX 10.1. Cf. Kromayer, *Schl.* I, 158 ff., with the corrections of Kromayer, *Wien. Stud.* 27, 1905, 16 ff. (in dispute with E. Lammert); further, Kromayer-Veit, *Atlas* I 5 (based on the researches of G. Sotiriadis, *AM* 28, 1903, 301 ff.; 30, 1905, 113 ff.); G. Roloff, *Probleme aus der griech. Kriegsgesch.*, Berlin 1903, 62 ff. Further studies are cited by Wüst, *Phil.*, 166 n. 2, cf. also N. G. L. Hammond, *Klio* 31, 1938, 186 ff.; E. Braun, *Öst. Jh.* 37, 1948, 81 ff.; W. K. Pritchett, *AJA* 62, 1958, 307 ff.

104. U. Wilcken, *GG*, [5]1943, 176.

105. The Boeotian League continued to exist (cf. Arrian I 7.11), but Thebes lost her leading rôle; incorrect, A. Momigliano, *Fil.*, 159.

106. Wüst, *Phil.*, 166 ff. On the personality of Demades: P. Treves, "Demade," *Ath.* NS 11, 1933, 105 ff.

107. Accepting the authenticity of the letter is, in addition to Ed. Meyer, SB.B, 1909, 766, and P. Wendland, *NGG*, 1910, 177 ff. (against U. v. Wilamowitz and Münscher, cf. also P. Treves, *Rendic. R. Ist. Lombardo* 66, 1936, 308 ff.; "Tre interpretazioni isocratee"), also, and correctly, Wüst, *Phil.*, 171 n. 2.

108. To see only a "gnomic phrase" in Isocrates' statement (thus F. Taeger, "Isokr. u. die Anfänge des hellenistischen Herrscherkultes," *Hermes* 72, 1937, 356), is scarcely correct; as opposed to this, already Wüst, *Phil.*, 172 n. 4. On Philip's importance for the ruler cult in antiquity see Momigliano, *Fil.*, 177 ff. (with copious bibliography, 177 n.1); cf. also F. Taeger, "Zum Kampf gegen den antiken Herrscherkult," *ARW* 32, 1935, 282 ff.; Habicht, *Gott.*, 12 ff.; 138 ff.

109. C. Roebuck, "The Settlements of Philip II with the Greek States in 338 B.C.," *CP* 43, 1948, 73 ff.

110. The sources: Diod. XVI 89; Justin IX 5; *Syll.* I[3] 260 (with the emendations of U. Wilcken, *Phil.*, 316 f.); Cf. also Tod II no. 177 = Schmitt, *Staatsv.* III, nos. 402, 403 (with copious bibliography); cf. G. Dobesch, "Zur Philia im Korinthischen Bund," in *Beiträge zur Alten Gesch. und deren Nachleben. Festschrift f. F. Altheim,* Berlin 1969, 245-250. More recent scholarship begins with the study of U. Wilcken, *Beitr. z. Gesch. des korinthischen Bundes,* SB.M, 1917, 10. Abh. (including the earlier bibliography as well, 3 n. 1); cf. further, *idem, Alexander d. Gr. und der korinthische Bund.* SB.B, 1922, no. XVI 97 ff.; *idem, Phil.*; Berve, *Alex.* I, 228 ff. (with good notation of earlier studies); W. Schwahn, *Heeresmatrikel und Landfriede Philipps von Makedonien*, Klio-Beih. 21, 1930, [very hypothetical, cf. H. Berve, *Gn.* 9, 1933, 309 ff.]; F. Schehl, "Zum korinthischen Bund vom Jahre 338/7 v. Chr.," *Öst. Jh.* 27, 1932, 115 ff.; Hampl, *Staatsv.*, 34 ff.; 89 ff.; 134 ff.; A. Heuss, *Hermes* 73, 1938, 171 ff.; Triepel, *Heg.*, 394 ff. Additional theories are put forward by K. Dienelt, *Ost. Jh.* 43, 1956, Beiblatt, 247-274.

111. Incorrectly denied by F. Hampl and A. Heuss, who are followed by F. R. Wüst, *Gn.* 14, 1938, 371. See, on the other hand, however: U. Wilcken, *GG*, [5]1943, 271 (note to p. 178), with reference to the oath of the Greeks in *Syll.* I[3] 260 = *GHD 4th C* 74 (= Pseudo-Demosth. XVII 10) and Arrian III 24.5; also J. A. O. Larsen, *CP* 34, 1939, 378 (with reference to *Syll.* II[3] 665, 19 f.).

112. H. Belten, "Der Rachegedanke in der griechisch-persischen Auseinandersetzung," *Ch.* 4, 1974, 43 ff.

113. U. Wilcken, SB.M, 1917, 10. Abh., 27 (the title of *hegemon autokrator* is cited from Arrian VII 9.5); cf. Diod. XVI 60.5; 89.3 *et al.* The fact is incorrectly disputed by Scheele, *Str.*, 16 ff. (likewise by Hampl, *Staatsv.*, 135 f.); see, on the other hand, Bengtson, *Strat.* I, 3 ff.

114. In 337 B.C. both Olympias and her son Alexander had withdrawn from Macedonia, since Philip had insulted the proud princess from Epirus (see Kornemann *Fr.*, 77 ff.) by simultaneously elevating Cleopatra the niece of Attalus as his legitimate wife.

115. Tradition emphasises the personal motive (Arist., *Pol.* V 1311b; Diod. XVI 93 f.; Plut., *Alex.* 10; Justin IX 6). Cf. however, Arrian I 25 on the execution of Heromenes and Arrhabaeus of Lyncestis by Alexander; Wilcken, *GSoph.*, 151 ff. It is impossible to adduce *proof* for the guilt of Olympias (cf. H. Willrich, "Wer liess König Philipp von Makedonien ermorden?," *Hermes* 34, 1899, 174 ff.). U. Köhler, *Über das Verhältnis Alexanders d. Gr. zu seinem Vater*, SB.B, 1892, 497 ff., has incorrectly charged Alexander with moral complicity (cf. Justin IX 7.1). The evidence may be found in Berve, *Alex.* II, 308 f. no. 614 (Pausanias), and Momigliano, *Fil.*, 168 n.l. E. Badian, *Px.* 17, 1963, 244 ff. does not produce anything new.

11 ALEXANDER THE GREAT

SOURCES AND BIBLIOGRAPHY: The tradition on Alexander was conflicting even in antiquity. Alongside the panegyric version, which flows into the Alexander legend and ultimately into the Alexander novel, there is a tradition predominantly coloured by Peripatetic and Stoic influence, which deliberately underrates Alexander's exploits by attributing them to *Tyche* rather than to Alexander's *arete* (cf. Plutarch, *De Alex. Magn. fortuna*; see W. Hoffmann, *Das literarische Porträt Alexanders d. Gr.*, (Leipz. Hist. Abh. 8), 1907, 87 ff.; J. Stroux, "Die stoische Beurteiling Alex. d. Gr.," *Ph.* 88, 1933, 222 ff.). The same cleft runs through the portraits. The ideal type of a superhuman Alexander, embodied in the statues of Lysippus (an imperial copy is the so-called Azara Herm), is contrasted, above all in the Alexandrian portraits, by a much softer representation, in which all heroic features are wanting. Cf. Th. Schreiber, *Studien über das Bildnis Alexanders d. Gr.*, Leipzig 1903; C. Bernoulli, *Die erhaltenen Darstellungen Alexanders d. Gr.*, Munich 1905; K. Gebauer, "Alexanderbildnis u. Alexandertypus," *AM* 63/64, 1938/39, 1 ff.; cf. also E. G. Suhr, *Sculptured Portraits of Greek Statesmen with a Special Study of Alexander the Great* (The Johns Hopkins University Studies in Archaeology 13), Baltimore 1931; H. P. L'Orange, *Apotheosis in Ancient Portraiture*, Oslo 1947, 19 ff. (with new conclusions); and M. Bieber, *Alexander the Great in Greek and Roman Art*, Chicago 1964; cf. G. M. A. Richter, *Portraits* III, 1965, 255 f.; also T. Hölscher, *Ideal und Wirklichkeit in den Bildnissen Alexanders d. Gr.* (Abh. d. Heidelb. Ak., phil.-hist. Kl., 1971-2), 1971 (cf. A. Krug, *Gn.* 46, 1974, 691 ff.). For the earlier bibliography see *CAH* VI, 599 f. The coins of Alexander: The work by L. Müller, *Numismatique d'Alexandre le Grand*, Copenhagen 1855, is out of date, although on the whole it has not been replaced. (Many of Müller's conclusions about the places where coins were struck are no longer tenable; see, for instance, W. Schwabacher, *Gn.* 37, 1965, 87.) In addition to the bibliography cited in *CAH* VI, 593 f., reference should be made in particular to the many studies by E. T. Newell (bibliography: *AJP* 68, 1947, 427 ff.), and to the work by G. Kleiner, *Alexanders Reichsmünzen* (Abh. B. 1947, no. 5) (published 1949), as well as to A. R. Bellinger, *Essays on the Coinage of Alexander the Great*, New York 1963 (cf. W. Schwabacher, *Gn.* 37, 1965, 83 ff.).

The documentary evidence on the history of Alexander is relatively limited. The following inscriptions may be cited: *Syll.* I^3 no. 272: Alexander as Stephanephorus of Miletus (334/3 B.C.); no. 277: the dedication of Alexander to Athena Polias of Priene (autumn 334); no. 283: Alexander's decree on the exiles of Chios (probably from 334 B.C.: cf. A. J. Heisserer, *H.* 22, 1973, 191 ff.); cf. F. W. Walbank, *Px.* 16, 1962, 178-180;

OGI 1: Alexander's decree on the autonomy of the Prieneans of Naulochus (cf. D. van Berchem, *MusHelv* 17, 1970, 198-205). The inscription published by G. Zolotas, *Athena* 1908, 159 ff. (with improvements by A. Wilhelm, *Griech. Königsbriefe*, Klio-Beih. 48, 1943, 1 ff.), contains a letter of Alexander to Chios; cf. W. G. Forest, "Alexander's Second Letter to the Chians," *Klio* 51, 1969, 201 ff. A fragmentary letter of the king to Philippi is reported in various places, but has still not been published; cf. J. Coupry, *CRAI*, 1938, 185 f., and Tarn, *Alex.* II, 247 n. 2. An important document is Alexander's edict on the return of the exiles in Greece, as found in Diodorus XVIII 8.4; see E. Bickerman, "La lettre d'Alexandre le Grand aux bannis grecs," *Mél. G. Radet*, 1940, 25 ff. A letter of Aristotle to Alexander (extant in an Arabic version) has moved into the forefront of debate (first published by J. Lippert in 1891): J. Bielawski, "Lettre d'Aristote à Alexandre le Grand en version arabe," *Recznik Orientalistyczny* 28, 1964, 7 ff.; M. Plezia, *Aristotelis epistularum fragmenta cum testamento*, Warsaw 1961; *idem*, "Die Geburtsurkunde des Hellenismus," *Eos* 58, 1969-70, 51 ff.; J. Bielawski and M. Plezia, *La lettre d'Aristote à Alexandre sur la politique envers les cités*, Warsaw 1970 (cf. K. v. Fritz, *Gn.* 44, 1972, 442 ff.); M. Plezia, "De Aristandri vaticinio," *Eos* 59, 1971, 227 ff.; cf. also P. Thillet, "Aristote conseiller politique d'Alexandre vainqueur des Perses?," *REG* 85, 1972, 527 ff., and M. A. Wes, "Quelques remarques à propos d' une 'lettre d'Aristote à Alexandre,'" *Mn.* 25, 1972, 261-295. The letter may well be spurious, although K. v. Fritz regards it as authentic.

A cuneiform inscription on a small tablet contains evidence on the rebuilding of the Temple of Marduk in Babylon at the command of the king: E. Unger, *Babylon, die heilige Stadt*, 1931, 318 no. 56; Bengtson, *Strat.* I, 213 n. 3. There is additional evidence from cuneiform inscriptions: E. Cavaignac, *Rev. d'Assyriol.* 34, 1937, 140; and A. Aymard, *Etudes d'Hist. ancienne*, 1967, 183 n. 1 (*REA* 40, 1938 10 n. 2). Egyptian documents from the time of Alexander: K. Sethe, *Hierogl. Urk. d. griech.-röm. Zeit* II, 1904; a survey in Gauthier, *Le livre des rois d'Egypte* IV, 1916, 119 ff.

The *Ephemerides* which were kept in Alexander's headquarters, and earlier designated as the "Court and Royal Journal," are perceptible only in Arrian, *Anab.* VII 25 f., and in Plutarch, *Alex.* 76; cf. U. Wilcken, "Hypomnematismoi," *Ph.* 53, 1894, 113 ff. J. Kaerst, *RE* V, 2749 ff. s.v. *Ephemerides*; Jacoby, *FgrHist.* no. 117 (with commentary); Berve, *Alex.* I, 50 f.; not very useful is C. A. Robinson, *The Ephemerides of Alexander's Expedition*, Providence 1932. Altheim, *As.* I, 115 ff., on the other hand, has explained the Ephemerides as a diary-like presentation of the life of Alexander by Eumenes and Diodotus, a view which in fact has considerable to recommend it. Very sceptical is A. E. Samuel, *H.* 14, 1965, 1 ff. The *Bematistai Journal* (cf. Strabo XV 723) served as a basis for topographical mapping, in which were recorded the sketches of the "pedometers" on Alexander's staff (Jacoby, *FgrHist.* no. 119). On the *Bematistai* see H. Bengtson, *Symbolae Osloenses* 32, 1956, 35 ff. = *KS*, 208 ff.;

(Philonides, referred to in Tod II no. 188 and in the inscription published by J. Bingen, *BCH* 78, 1954, 407 ff.). In regard to the authenticity of Alexander's correspondence (in the literary sources there are references to 72 letters written by and 43 addressed to him) the views of modern scholars are at variance; very sceptical is J. Kaerst, "Der Briefwechsel Alexanders d. Gr.," *Ph.* 50, 1891, 692 ff.; cf. 56, 1897, 406 ff.; similarly Tarn, *Alex.* II, 196; 300 ff.; and L. Pearson, *H.* 3, 1954-55, 429 ff.; more positive, for instance, E. Pridik, *De Alexandri Magni epistularum commercio*, Diss. Dorpat 1893 (with a collection of the fragments); and Berve, *Alex.* I, 44 n. 2. An attempt has been made by R. Merkelbach, *Aeg.* 27, 1947, 144 ff., to prove the existence of an ancient letter novel on the basis of papyrus finds: cf. *idem, Die Quellen des griech. Alexanderromans* (Zetemata 9), Munich 1954. But it is undoubtedly more probable that the source used here is a romantic presentation of Alexander, from which the letter collections were extracted.

The following contemporary works of history may be cited: Callisthenes' *Deeds of Alexander* (Jacoby, *FgrHist.* no. 124; cf. A. B. Bosworth, *H.* 19, 1970, 407 ff.), from 334 B.C. to at least the battle of Gaugamela; it is highly panegyric; Polybius (XII 17 ff.) severely criticised the battle descriptions by the "civilian" Callisthenes. The work, bearing the same title, by Anaximenes of Lampsacus does not appear to have exerted any influence on the historiographical tradition (A. Körte, Anaximenes v. Lampsakos als Alexanderhistoriker," *RhM* 61, 1906, 476 ff.).

After Alexander's death the following took up the pen: Ephippus of Olynthus (*On the Death of Alexander and Hephaestion*, Jacoby, *FgrHist.* no. 126), wrote in a spirit hostile to Alexander; Marsyas of Pella, the brother of the Diadochian Antigonus Monopthalmus, probably wrote within the context of his *Makedonica* (Jacoby, *FgrHist.* no. 135); Onesicritus of Astypalaea, whose work is a glorification of the king, full of ardour and fire, permeated with the spirit of Cynicism, and was often used by later writers (Jacoby, *FgrHist* no. 134; cf. H. Strasburger, *RE* XVIII, 460 ff.; T. S. Brown, *Onesicritus*, Berkeley 1949); and, finally, Chares of Mytilene, the "master of ceremonies" at Alexander's court (Jacoby, *FgrHist.* no. 125), with many individual features that are unhistorical.

The work of the Lagid, Ptolemy, the founder of the Ptolemaic Dynasty in Egypt, towers far above the historians of Alexander. As one time general adjutant to Alexander, Ptolemy as king (at any rate after 306/5 B.C.) created a genuinely royal portrait of the great monarch, a portrait outstanding for its factualness and love of truth, based predominantly on personal recollections and probably in part also on the *Ephemerides*. Ptolemy's work—the exact title is not known—forms the basis of Arrian's *Anabasis of Alexander*, and through this medium it forms the basis on which the modern picture of Alexander is drawn. On its reconstruction cf. Jacoby, *FgrHist.* no. 138 (with commentary); H. Strasburger, *Ptolemaios und Alexander*, Leipzig 1934; E. Kornemann, *Die Alexandergesch. des Königs Ptolemaios I. von Ägypten*, Leipzig 1935, with underestimation of the Arrian element (see H. Berve, *DLZ*, 1937, 842 ff.; H. Strasburger,

Gn. 13, 1937, 483 ff.; P. Treves, *REA* 39, 1937, 287 ff.; like Strasburger, his critique of Kornemann's book is too negative). Recently a new trend has become evident, in which a more or less critical attitude is adopted towards Ptolemy; see E. Badian, *Gn.* 33, 1961, 660 ff., and C. B. Welles, "The Reliability of Ptolemy as an Historian," in *Miscellanea di Studi Alessandrini in memoria di Augusto Rostagni*, Turin 1963, 101-116, who is opposed by J. Seibert, *Untersuchungen zur Geschichte Ptolemaios' I.*, Munich 1969, 1-26, who is opposed by E. Badian, *Gn.* 46, 1974, 517 f. cf. R. M. Eerrington, Bias in Ptolemy's History of Alexander," *CQ* 19, 1969, 233 ff.; F. Schachermeyr, *Alexander in Babylon*, Vienna 1970, 88-133; 221-224.

Aristobulus of Cassandreia, also a member of Alexander's staff, an engineer of officer rank (cf. on his character L. Pearson, *AJP* 73, 1952, 71 ff., who, on the basis of an inscription published in *Fouilles de Delphes* III, 2, 207, regards him as a Phocian), did not write his *History* (the fragments are in Jacoby, *FgrHist.* no. 139) until the beginning of the third century B.C., and in it used a series of earlier writers (Ephippus, Cleitarchus, Onesicritus *et al.*). The article by Ed. Schwartz, *RE* II, 911 ff., is still basic, while F. Wenger, *Die Alexandergesch. des Aristobul von Kassandreia*, Diss. Würzburg 1914, is not very fortunate in its conclusions; some of the details in the remarks by Tarn, *Alex.* II, cf. the Index. s.v., according to which Aristobulus wrote before Ptolemy (and before Cleitarchus, see *infra*), are untenable; more recent views in P. A. Brunt, *CQ* 24, 1974, 65-70.

The rhetorical and romantic work of Cleitarchus was destined to exert an influence of far-reaching dimensions; it is the starting point of the so-called Alexander vulgate, as reflected in the later *Histories* of Diodorus (Book XVII) (cf. J. R. Hamilton, "Cleitarchus and Diodorus 17," in *Studies... Fritz Schachermeyr*, Berlin 1977, 126 ff.), Curtius Rufus and Justin. Chronologically, Cleitarchus comes before Ptolemy and Aristobulus; he may have written his work about 310 B.C. (Jacoby, *FgrHist.* no. 137; cf. the important article on *Kleitarchos* in *RE* XI, 622 ff.). The attempt by Tarn, *Alex.* II, 5 ff., to move Cleitarchus down into the middle of the third century B.C. does not appear to me to have been successful, despite all its acumen (see, on the other hand, *inter al.*, T. S. Brown "Clitarchus," *AJP* 71, 1950, 134 ff.; H. Strasburger, *Bibl. Orientalis*, 1952, 202 ff., with important remarks on Tarn's thesis concerning the sources; also E. Badian, "The Date of Clitarchus [before 300 B.C.]." *Proceedings of the African Class. Assoc.* 8, 1965, 1 ff.; R. A. Hadley, *H.* 18, 1969, 142 ff.). Georges Radet in particular has argued that extensive consideration should be given to the view that a branch of the ancient Alexander tradition ultimately goes back to Cleitarchus; cf. his *Notes critiques sur l'histoire d'Alexandre* I-VIII, Bordeaux-Paris 1925-33, and his book *Alexandre le Grand*, Paris 1931; cf. the bibliography, *Mél. G. Radet* 1940, XVIII f.

Not very fortunate is the thesis which claims that Diodorus (Bk. XVII) down to the battle of Issus is based on a source which goes back to Greek mercenaries in Persian service; see above all Tarn, *Alex.* II, in many places; opposed to him, *inter al.*, P. A. Brunt, "Persian Accounts of Alexander's Campaigns," *CQ* 56, 1962, 141-155, who rightly takes it as self-evident that a certain amount of Persian information also became assimilated in the sources.

The *Historiae Alexandri Magni* by Q. Curtius Rufus belong in the early Roman Empire; their exact date is disputed; see the remarks in Schanz-Hosius, *Gesch. d. röm. Lit.* II[4], 1935, 598; cf. Tarn, *Alex.* II, 111 ff., who has argued for the time of Augustus. For dating them under Vespasian, J. Stroux, *Ph.* 84, 1929, 233 ff.; H. U. Instinsky, *Hermes* 90, 1963, 371-383; U. Vogel-Weidemann, *AC* 13, 1970, 79 ff.; G. Scheda, *H.* 18, 1969, 380 ff.; H. Grassl. *Ph.* 118, 1974, 160 ff.; J. Rufus Fears, *Hermes* 102, 1974, 623 ff. The view held by F. Altheim, *Lit. u. Gesellsch. im ausgeheden Alt.* I, 1948, 153 ff., that Curtius belongs in the Severan era, is improbable. (This late date, incidentally, derives from Niebuhr, it was taken over by Ranke, *Weltgesch.* III 2, 83). Curtius' work, which is based on a Peripatetic judgment of Alexander, a tradition unfriendly towards him, is only partly extant (the beginning, Books I and II, and parts of Books V, VI and X are missing); it should only be used with caution as a source; a good assessment is given by W. W. Tarn, *Alex.* II, 91 ff.; 129 f.

The *History* of Flavius Arrianus from Nicomedeia in Bithynia is completely different in quality. The hallmark of this Greek—an outstanding administrative official and officer, who governed Cappadocia († c. 175 A.D.) as *legatus Aug. pr. pr.* under Hadrian—is a solid knowledge of history and ethnography, combined with detailed studies in the natural sciences. Arrian is an example of that not altogether infrequent type in antiquity who combines great practical experience with a wealth of theoretical knowledge. In his principal work, the *Anabasis of Alexander*, written in a Xenophontic style, he attempts for the first time to differentiate between information that is vulgar and that which is authentic, namely Ptolemy and Aristobulus (v. *supra*) (edition of his *History* by A. G. Roos, Leipzig 1907). In a separate work, the *Indike*, Arrian gave an account of the voyage undertaken by Nearchus and Onesicritus from the Indus Delta to the Persian Gulf. It is based on the voyage of Nearchus (cf. Jacoby, *FgrHist.* no. 133; H. Berve and W. Capelle, *RE* XVI, 2132 ff.; edition of the *Indike* by A. G. Roos, in the second volume of Arrian, 1928, and by P. Chantraine in the Collection Budé, Paris 1927). Ed. Schwartz, *RE* II, 1230 ff., is still basic in an assessment of Arrian; on the composition date of the *Anabasis* see H. Nissen, *RhM* 43, 1888, 236 ff.; opposed to him, Niese, *Mak.* I, 8 n.1. The study by G. Wirth, *H.* 13, 1964, 209 ff., is not fully mature; see, by comparison, A. B. Bosworth, "Arrian's Literary Development," *CQ* 22, 1972, 163 ff.; cf. G. Schepens, *AncSoc* 2, 1971, 254 ff.

Plutarch's *Life of Alexander* is no work of history, but a biography whose delineation of Alexander's character coincides with the basic elements of the Peripatetic school; see Tarn, *Alex.* II, 296 ff. The hypothesis of J. W. Powell, *JHS* 59, 1939, 229 ff., according to which Plutarch used a "source-book" for his biography, is unsuccessful. At all events, however, a collection of letters by Alexander belongs to the sources (see already above 512). On Plutarch's sources see Inge Rabe, *Quellenkritische Untersuchungen zu Plutarchs Alexanderbiographie*, Diss. Hamburg, 1964. See also J. R. Hamilton, *Plutarch, Alexander. A Commentary*, Oxford 1969. As for Strabo, see P. Pédech, "Strabon historien Alexandre," *Grazer Beiträge* 2, 1974, 129 ff. On the Stoics and Alexander: J. R. Fears, "The Stoic View of the Career and Character of Alexander the Great," *Ph*, 118, 1974, 113 ff.

In the wider sense the Alexander legend, issuing from the *History* of Callisthenes (Mederer, *A. leg.*), belongs to the historical tradition, as does, finally, the *Alexander Romance* of the so-called Pseudo-Callisthenes, which exists in many recensions and in about 35 languages from antiquity (edition of the Latin version by W. Kroll, *Hist. Alex. Magn.* I, *Recensio vetusta*, Berlin 1926). It is the product of semi-learned, semi-popular literary activity (Th. Nöldecke, *Denkschr. Ak. Wien* 38, 1890, 1 ff.; A. Ausfeld, *Der griech. Alexanderroman*, 1907; F. Pfister, "Studien z. Alexanderroman," Würzb. Jahrb. 1, 1946, 29 ff., with a bibliography of earlier studies; A. M. Wolohjian, *The Romance of Alexander the Great by Pseudo-Callisthenes*, London 1970; B. Berg, "An Early Source of the Alexander Romance," *GRBS* 14, 1973, 381 ff. Offshoots of the Alexander Romance are the work of the Arch-Presbyter Leo of Naples (tenth century), and the Alexander Ballad of the priest Lamprecht (twelfth century). Cf. A. Hübner, "Alexander d. Gr. in der deutschen Dichtung des Mittelalters," *Ant.* 9, 1933, 32 ff.; E. Pfister, *Hermes* 76, 1941, 143 ff. (Alexander and the Brahmans); *Alexander d. Gr. in den Offenbarungen der Griechen, Juden, Mohammedaner u. Christen*, Berlin 1956; "Alexander der Grosse. Die Geschichte seines Ruhmes im Lichte seiner Beinamen," *H.* 13, 1964, 37 ff.; and in many other works (U. Wilcken, *GSoph.*, 150 ff. [including evidence on the so-called Metz *Epitome*] 159, provides information on some papyrus fragments containing legendary accounts of Alexander.)

A survey of the literature on Alexander in antiquity: W. Hoffmann, *Das literarische Porträt Alexanders d. Gr. im griech.-röm. Altertum,* Leipz. Hist. Abh. 8, 1907; F. Weber, *Alexander d. Gr. im Urteil der Griechen und Römer bis in die Konstantinische Zeit*, Diss. Giessen (published Borna-Leipzig 1909). A survey of the ancient sources on the life of Alexander: Droysen, "Materialien z. Gesch. Alexanders," in his *GH* I^2, 375 ff.; Beloch, *GG* III 2, 34 ff.; Kaerst, *GH* I^2, 375 ff. (cf. also *idem, Forschungen z. Gesch. Alexanders d. Gr.,* Stuttgart 1887); also *CAH* VI, 352 n.; 590 ff.; Glotz-Cohen, *HG* IV 1^2, 33 f. n.; L. Pearson, *The Lost Histories of Alexander*, New York 1960.

MORE RECENT BIBLIOGRAPHY ON ALEXANDER: While B. G. Niebuhr characterised Alexander as a "big time comedian and plunderer," and saw in him a spirit akin to that of Napoleon, Johann Gustav Droysen in his *Geschichte Alexanders des Grossen* (1833) was the first who undertook to delineate a truly life-like portrait of the great ruler and conqueror, even though it was not free of panegyrical glorification (reprint of the first edition with an Introduction by H. Berve, in Kröners Taschenausgabe, Bd. 87, 1931; ^{3}1942). In Droysen's *GH* I, 1877, the portrait of Alexander is greatly revised, having lost much of the youthful ardour and fire of the first edition. Critical scholars from the end of the nineteenth and the beginning of the twentieth century have adopted a much more reserved attitude towards Alexander, as is reflected in, for instance, Niese, *Mak.* I (1893), and in Beloch, *GG* (III ed. 1, 1904; III/IV ed. 2, 1922 ff.). Beloch also attempted to play down the importance of Alexander by unduly extolling the merits of King Philip and the great assistants of the young ruler (Parmenion and Antipater); see, on the other hand, the very legitimate objection by J. Kromayer, "Alexander d. Gr. und die hellenistische Entwicklung in dem Jahrhundert nach seinem Tode," *HZ* 100, 1908, 11 ff. The First World War then brought about a renaissance in studies on Alexander in Germany, with the lectures of W. Kolbe (Rostock 1916), W. Otto (Marburg 1916), and U.v. Wilamowitz-Moellendorff (1916, printed in *Kleine Schriften* VI, 1937, 181 ff.). But it was not until F. Jacoby published his edition and commentary of the historians on Alexander within the framework of the *FgrHist.* II (1927), and H. Berve his work on Alexander which appeared just prior to that, *Alex.* (1926) (cf. U. Wilcken, *DLZ*, 1927, 359 ff.; F. Oertel, *NJB.*, 1928, 385 ff.), that a new sound footing was established for future research. Building on this foundation, together with a number of excellent studies of his own, Wilcken in *Alex.* (1931) (cf. the English translation, *Alexander the Great* by G. C. Richards, with "preface, an Introduction to Alexander Studies, Notes and Bibliography" by E. N. Borza, New York 1967), has drawn a well-founded portrait of Alexander, whose essential features are determined by the Arrian tradition (cf. the instructive reviews by W. Kolbe, *DLZ*, 1931, 884 ff., and by G. Radet, *Rev. hist.* 173, 1934, 80 ff.). Wilcken's antipode was the Frenchman Georges Radet, whose *Alexandre le Grand*, Paris 1931, is in essential lines imprinted by the tradition of Cleitarchus and Curtius. The same, moreover, holds true for A. Weigall, *Alexander the Great*, 1933. The widely read book by Theodor Birt, *Alexander und das Weltgriechentum*, 1924, is heavily laden with anecdotes; on the other hand, the delineations of Kaerst, in his *GH* I^3, are profound and stimulating in many instances (cf. also his portrait of Alexander in *Meister der Politik*, ed. E. Marcks and K. A. v. Müller, I^2, 1923, 67 ff.); the same holds for H. Berve in his *GG* II, 159 ff. (cf. J. Kromayer, *HZ* 150, 1934, 10 ff.), now II^2, 173 ff.; as it does for Vol. IV of *HG* by Glotz-Cohen ("Alexandre et l'hellénisation du monde antique, $1^{eré}$ partie: Alexandre et le démembrement de son empire," Paris 1938; ^{2}1945); and, finally, Tarn, *Alex.*, of which Vol. I contains an excellent account of the history of Alexander, based on the sections written by Tarn in *CAH* VI, 1927, 352 ff., and the more important Vol. II, with a whole series of ingenious monographs on the sources and various problems connected with the history of Alexander—despite the fact that there are a number of points on which views must be rejected in this the most important achievement in decades in this field. The negative features in the Alexander tradition have been emphasised in particular by F. Schachermeyr, *Alexander der Grosse. Ingenium und Macht*, 1949, on the basis of experiences drawn from the recent past (cf. F. Oertel, *OLZ*, 1957, 93 ff.); see now the second edition, *Alexander der Grosse. Das Problem seiner Persönlichkeit und seines Werkes*, Vienna 1973 (largely revised and expanded) (cf. E. Badian, *Px.* 28, 1974, 369 ff.). F. Hampl, "Alexander der Grosse und die Beurteilung geschichtlicher Persönlichkeiten in der modernen Historiographie," *La Nouvelle Clio* 6, 1954, 91-136 (cf. his little book, *Alexander der Grosse*, Göttingen 1958) is in many instances paradoxical; cf. H. E. Stier, *Roms Aufstieg zur Weltmacht und die griechische Welt*, 1957, 21 n. 20. P. Cloché, *Alexandre le Grand et les essais de fusion entre l'Occident grèco-romain et l'Orient*, Neuchâtel 1953, does not constitute any progress. Well worth reading, on the other hand, is J. F. C. Fuller, *The Generalship of Alexander the Great*, London 1958, even though the principal thesis, that Alexander was primarily concerned with security, can scarcely be made to coincide with the facts. Modern verdicts: C. B. Welles, "Alexander's Historical Achievement," *Greece and Rome* 12, 1965, 216-228; cf. *idem*, *Alexander and the Hellenistic World*, Toronto 1970; H. Bengtson, *The Greeks and the Persians*, 1969, 303 ff.; K. Kraft, *Der 'rationale' Alexander, Bearb. und aus dem Nachlass hrsg. von Helga Gesche*, Kallmünz 1971 (cf. E. Badian, *Gn.* 47, 1975, 45 ff.); see also J. R. Hamilton, *Alexander the Great*, London 1973; and P. Green, *Alexander of Macedon, 356-323 B.C. A Historical Biography*, Harmondsworth ²1974. To be read with caution, R. L. Fox, *Alexander the Great*, London 1974 (cf. the critique by E. Badian, *NYRev* 19 Sept., 1974, 8 f., *JHS* 96, 1976, 229-230). F. Altheim, *Alexander und Asien. Geschichte eines geistigen Erbes*, Tübingen 1953, overlaps with *Weltgeschichte Asiens im griech. Zeitalter*, 2 vols., Halle 1947 and 1948; the thesis that Alexander had the *Avesta* (two million verses!) translated from Aramaic into Greek (*Alexander und Asien*, 86 ff.) does not seem probable to me at all. A survey of the research on Alexander published between 1933 and 1938 is given by H. Bengtson, *WG* 5, 1939, 168 ff. = *KS*, 241-246; cf. further, R. Andreotti, *H.* 1, 1950, 583-600; G. Walser, *Schweizer Beitr. z. allg. Gesch.* 14, 1956, 156-189; E. Badian, "Alexander the Great 1948-1967," *CW* 65, 1971, 37 ff.; 77 ff.; and in particular, J. Seibert, *Alexander der Grosse* (Erträge der Forschung, 10), Darmstadt 1972 (cf. E. Badian, *Gn.* 46, 1974, 517 f.), with addenda by P. Goukowsky, *REG* 87, 1974, 425-428. See also the contributions in *Entretiens sur l'Antiquité classique, 22: Alexandre le Grande, image et réalité, Fondations Hardt*, Vandoeuvres-Genève 1976. On Scientific research, H. Bretzl, *Botan. Forsch. d. Alexanderzuges*, Leipzig 1903.

ALEXANDER IN GREECE

TRADITION ON ALEXANDER'S YOUTH: Aeschines I 166 ff.; Plutarch, *Alex.* 2-10; cf. Kaerst, *GH* I³, 313 ff.; U. Köhler, *Über das Verhältnis Alexanders d. Gr. zu seinem Vater Philipp*, SB.B, 1892, 497 ff. (hostile towards Alexander); Wilcken, *Alex.*, 61 ff.; Tarn, *Alex.* I, 1 ff.; N. G. L. Hammond, "Alexander's Campaign in Illyria," *JHS* 94, 1974, 66 ff.; Will, *MGr* II, *Le IVᵉ siècle et l'époque hellenistique*, 1975, 245 ff. (also for the following sections).

FROM THE HELLESPONT TO PERSEPOLIS

PRINCIPAL SOURCES: Arr., *Anab.* I 11.3-III 18; cf. Diod. XVII 17-72 (on the sources of Diodorus see Tarn, *Alex.* II, 63 ff., whose views, however, require critique; it can be regarded as certain as opposed to Tarn—that Diodorus is in part based on Cleitarchus; cf. J. R. Hamilton, in *Studies... Fritz Schachermeyr*, Berlin 1977, 126 ff.); Curtius Rufus III 1-V 7; Plut., *Alex.* 15-33; Just. XI 6-14; and the documentary material cited above 510 f.

BIBLIOGRAPHY: U. Köhler, *Die Eroberung Kleinasiens durch Alexander d. Gr. u. der Korinth. Bund.* SB.B, 1898, 120 ff.; *idem*, "Reichsverwaltung u. Politik Alexanders d. Gr.," *Klio* 5, 1905, 303 ff.; Th. Lenschau, *De rebus Prienensium*, Leipz. Stud. XI, 1890, 111 ff.; G. Schlotz, "Die militärischen und polit. Folgen der Schlacht am Granikos," *Klio* 15, 1917, 199 ff.; Ehrenberg, *Al. Äg.*, W. Judeich, "Darstellung der Alexanderschlachten," in Kromayer, *Schl.* IV, 345 ff. (Granicus, Issus, Gaugamela); H. Gallet de Santerre, "Alexandre le Grand et Kyme d'Eolide," *BCH* 71/72, 1947-48, 302 ff. (on the endowment of Alcimachus referred to in Pliny *N.H.* 34.14); A. R. Burn, *JHS* 72, 1952, 81 ff. (on the campaigns from 332-330 B.C.); E. Mikrojannakis, "The Diplomatic Contacts between Alexander III and Darius III," in *Ancient Macedonia*, edited by B. Lourdas, Thessaloniki 1970, 68 ff. On the organisation of Asia Minor by Alexander see: A. Baumbach, *Kleinasien und Alexander d. Gr.*, Diss. Jena 1911; P. Julien, *Zur Verwaltung der Satrapien unter Alexander d. Gr.*, Diss. Jena, Weida i. Th. 1914; Berve, *Alex.* I, 253 ff. Additional works are cited in *HG* by Glotz-Cohen, IV², 36, and n.; G. Wirth, "Die Anabasis von Kleinasien 334 v. Chr.," *Ch.* 2, 1972, 91-98 [on Arr. I 17, 7].

THE CONQUEST OF EAST IRAN AND NORTH WEST INDIA

PRINCIPAL SOURCES: Arr., *Anab.* III 19—VII 1; Diod. XVII 73-107; Curt. Ruf. V 7.12-X 1; Plut., *Alex.* 42-69; Just. XI 15—XII 10; also Arrian's *Indike* (edition by Roos, II); and the fragments of Onesicritus (Jacoby, *FgrHist.* no. 134)).

BIBLIOGRAPHY: On the Iranian Campaign; F.v. Schwartz, *Alexanders d. Gr. Feldzüge in Turkestan*, Stuttgart ²1906; J. Marquart, *Untersuch z. Gesch. von Eran* II § 2: *Alexanders Marsch von Persepolis nach Herât*, Phil. Suppl. 10, 1907, 19 ff.; G. Radet, "La dernière campagne d'Alexandre contre Darius," *Mélanges G. Glotz* II, 1932, 765 ff. Further references in Glotz-Cohen, *HG* IV 1², 116 f. n.; see also F. Altheim and R. Stiehl, *Geschichte Mittelasiens im Alterum*, Berlin 1970. On the Indian Campaign: The studies of Sir Aurel Stein are basic: *On Alexander's Track to the Indus*, London 1929 (cf. U. Wilcken, *DLZ*, 1930, 28 ff.); *Geographical Journal* 80, 1932, 32 ff.; *Archaeological Reconnaissances in North-Western India and South Eastern Iran*, London 1937; "On Alexander's Route into Gedrosia: An Archaeological Tour in Las Bela," *Geographical Journal* 102, 1943, 193-227; cf. H Strasburger, *Hermes* 82, 1954, 251-254.

Cf. further, J. McCrindle, *Ancient India, Its Invasion by Alexander the Great*, Westminster ^{2}1896 (reprint, New York 1972); A. E. Anspach, *De Alex. Magn. expeditione Indica*, Diss. Leipzig 1903; V. A. Smith, *Early History of India*, Oxford ^{2}1908; ^{3}1914; E. R. Bevan, *The Cambridge History of India* I, 1922, Chaps. 15 and 16; Wilcken, *G.Soph.*, 150 ff.; L. de la Vallée-Poussin, *L'Inde aux temps des Mauryas*, Paris 1930: B. Breloer, *Alexanders Kampf gegen Poros. Ein Beitrag z. indisch. Gesch.*, Bonner Orientalist. Stud. 3, Stuttgart 1933 (cf., however, W. Otto, *Gn.* 12, 1936, 301 ff.); *idem*, *Alexanders Bund mit Poros. Indien von Dareios bis Sandrokottos*, Leipzig 1941. Additional bibliography may be found in *CAH* VI, 596 f.; and in Glotz-Cohen, *HG* IV 1^{2}, 116 n.

ALEXANDER'S LAST YEARS

PRINCIPAL SOURCES: Arr., *Anab.* VI 29 ff.; Diod. XVII 107-118; Curt. Ruf. X 1-5; Plut., *Alex.* 68 ff.; Just. XII 10 ff. The sources for the history of Greece from 325 to 321 B.C. are given in *CAH* VI, 601 ff.; cf. further, Glotz-Cohen, *HG* IV 1^{2}, 183 ff. n. Important bibliography: A. Aymard, "Un ordre d'Alexandre," *REA* 39, 1937, 5 ff. (on Hyperides against Demosthenes, Col. 18, 13 ff. edition Jensen^{2}); the work by Bikerman cited above 524 n. 78; and now in particular F. Schachermeyr, *Alexander in Babylon und die Reichsordnung nach seinem Tod* (Jb. Wien, Bd. 268-3). Vienna 1970 [on the chronology of the last weeks of Alexander. etc.].

1. Wilamowitz, *Arist.* I, 335 ff.; W. Jaeger, *Aristotle*, ^{2}1962, 117 ff.; Ehrenberg, *Alex.*, 62 ff.

2. Bengtson, *Strat.* I,14 n. 2. According to Tarn, *Alex.* II, 248 f., Alexandropolis was a military colony, a view which in fact has considerable to recommend it. On the localisation see D. Detschew, *Öst Jh.* 41, 1954, 110 ff. (= Svets Vrač).

3. Caranus (Justin XI 2.3), an alleged half-brother of Alexander, who is supposed to have been killed at the time, is to be deleted from history according to Tarn *Alex.* II, 260 ff.

4. B. D. Meritt, *Hesp.* 21, 1952, 355 ff. no. 5; M. Ostwald, *TAPA* 86, 1955, 103 ff.; cf. C. Mossé, "A propos de la loi d'Eucratès sur la tyrannie," *Eirene* 8, 1970, 71 ff. On the situation in Athens see F. W. Mitchel, *Lycourgan Athens: 338-322* (Lectures in Honor of Louise Taft Semple), Cincinnati 1973.

5. Diod. XVII 4.1 f. (cf. U. Wilcken, SB.B, 1922, 99 ff.); Arrian I 1.2, and Diod. XVII 4.9 (cf. Bengtson, *Strat.* I, 3 ff.).

6. M. Graf Yorck von Wartenburg, *Kurze Übersicht über die Feldzüge Alexanders des Grossen*, 1897, 3 ff.; also the bibliography cited by E. Polaschek, *RE* VI A, 2397; as well as W. O. Jacobs, *Milit.-philolog. Untersuch. z. Feldzug Alexanders gegen die Triballer*, Münster i.W., 1928; V. Parvan, "La pénétration hellénique et hellénistique dans la vallée du Danube," *Bull. sect. hist. de l'Acad. Roum.* 10, 1923, 23 ff.; "Getica," *Mém. soc. hist. Acad. Roum.*, 2. série III, Mém. II Bucharest 1926, 43 ff (summary in French, 703 ff.).

7. Arrian I 3.5; cf. Ehrenberg, *Alex.*, 52 ff. The discussion by H. U. Instinsky of the *"pothos"* question ["Mensch und Gott in der Geschichte," in *Beiträge zur geistigen Überlieferung*, Godesberg 1947, 184 ff.], is a regression; see V. Ehrenberg, *JHS* 67, 1947 (published 1949), 62 ff.

8. Documents on donations for the restoration of Thebes in the Diadochian period (316 B.C.). [Dittenberger, *Syll.* I^{3} 337] have been discussed by M. Holleaux, *Et. ép.* I, 1 ff. On the treatment of Thebes see the evidence in F. Schober, *RE* V A, 1481 ff. s.v. *Thebai.*

9. Onesicratus fr. 2 (Jacoby, *FgrHist.* no. 134); cf. Duris fr. 40 (Jacoby, *FgrHist.* no. 76);

cf. A. Andreades, "Les finances de guerre d'Alexandre le Grand," *Annales d'hist. écon. et sociale*, 15 Juillet 1929, 321 ff.

10. Ptolemy fr. 4 and Aristobulus fr. 4; higher figures are given by Callisthenes (Jacoby, *FgrHist.* no. 124) fr. 35 and Anaximenes (no. 72) fr. 29; see also Jacoby, *FgrHist.* no. 72, 29 (Commentary).

11. On the Hellenic contingent see Berve, *Alex.* I, 139 ff.; 159 ff.; U. Kahrstedt, "Das athenische Kontingent zum Alexanderzuge," *Hermes* 71, 1936, 120 ff.

12. The importance of the Hellenic fleet is greatly exaggerated by M. L. Strack, *GGA*, 1903, 872.

13. Diod. XVII 118.1; XVIII 12.1; cf. Bengtson, *Strat.* I, 15 ff.

14. On the personality of Darius see Berve, *Alex.* II, 129. Part of ancient tradition (Diod. XVII 6; Justin X 3.5 f.) is completely incorrect in portraying Darius as a match for Alexander.

15. W. Kolbe, *DLZ*, 1931, 885, as opposed to U. Wilcken, who probably arrives at too positive a conclusion on the late Persian empire.

16. Justin XI 5.10; cf. W. Schmitthenner, *Saec.* 19, 1968, 34 ff.

17. On Alexander at Ilium see in particular the discussions by G. Radet, *Notes critiques*, 1 sér., 1925, 1 ff.; 88 ff; 2 sér., 1933, 119 ff.; 144 ff.; *Alexandre le Grand* 30 ff.; 426. The study by H. U. Instinsky, *Alexander d. Gr. am Hellespont*, Bad Godesberg 1949, is not convincing.

18. The best account is that of Arrian I 13-16 (= Ptolemy); see further Plut., *Alex.* 16 (= Aristobulus); Justin XI 6; Polyaenus IV 3.16; *P. Oxy.* 1798. The claim by Diodorus (XVII 18-21), that Alexander did not open battle immediately upon the advance from Priapus but only at the break of dawn on the following day, is not credible (for a different view see K. Lehmann, *Klio* 11, 1911, 230 ff., and Beloch, *GG* III 1, 625 n. 1). Arrian's account has rightly been followed by J. Keil, *Mitt. Verein Klass. Philologen Wien* I, 1924, 13 ff., A.v. Domaszewski, H. Berve (after initial oscillation), J. Kaerst and U. Wilcken; see also N. T. Nikolitsis, *The Battle of the Granicus*, Stockholm 1974. On the topography see A. Janke, *Auf Alexanders des Grossen Pfaden*, 1904, 136 ff.; a concise discussion by W. Judeich, in Kromayer, *Schl.* IV, 347 ff. (including earlier bibliography).

19. Arrian I 16.7.

20. Arrian I 17.4.

21. A similar idea was, incidentally, advanced already by Isocrates at the end of his pamphlet *Philippos* (§ 154).

22. Cf. the survey on the older bibliography by Bengtson, *Strat.* I, 34 n.1.

23. Basic is the study by E. Bikerman, "Alexandre le Grand et les villes d'Asie," *REG* 47, 1934, 346-374; see further, F. Miltner, *Klio* 26, 1933, 43 ff.; Bengtson, *Strat.* I, 34 ff.; Ehrenberg, *Alex.*, 2 ff.; Th. Lenschau, *Klio* 33, 1940, 215 ff. The objections raised to Bikerman's view by Tarn, *Alex.* II, 199 ff. (cf., 30 ff.), have not succeeded in refuting his thesis as a whole. Cf. also C. Tibiletti, *Ath.* NS 32, 1954, 3 ff. (mediating): similarly E. Badian in *Studies Ehrenberg*, 37-70; see also Schmitt. *Staatsv.* III, no. 405; and G. Wirth. "Die *syntaxeis* von Kleinasien 324 v. Chr.," *Ch.* 2, 1972, 91 ff.

24. For Alexander, *inter al.*: H. Bengtson, *Ph.* 92, 1937, 139; Th. Lenschau, *Klio* 33, 1940, 220 ff.; but see the objection by Tarn, *Alex.* II, 231 f. Further bibliography on this subject may be found in Rostovtzeff, *SEHHW* III, 1348.

25. *Syll*, III^3 1014 line 111 (from Erythrae); cf. the important suggestions by Nilsson, *Gr. Rel.* II, 147; also Habicht, *Gott.*, 19 f.

26. On Ada see Berve, *Alex.* II, no. 20; *Klio* 31, 1938, 136 f.

27. On the history of the Gordian Knot see E. Mederer, *A. leg.*, 1 ff., and above all Tarn, *Alex.* II, 262 ff., whose arguments against the authenticity of the account are to be given much weight. Of a different opinion is Wilcken, *Alex.*, 96, and E. A. Fredricksmeyer, "Alexander, Midas, and the Oracle at Gordium," *CP* 56, 1961, 160-168, who does not, however, enter into controversy with Tarn. A parallel from Irish legend is suggested by P. Frei, *MusHelv* 29, 1972. 110-123.

28. The sources for the battle of Issus: Arrian II 6-11 (predominantly based on Ptolemy); Polyb. XII 17-22 (Callisthenes); Diod. XVII 32-35; 37.1; Strabo XIV 676; Curtius Rufus III 7-11; Plut., *Alex.* 20; Justin XI 9.1-10; Bilabel, *P. Kleinform*, 16 ff. no. 7. The sources are one-sided, namely pro-Macedonian. It is, however, incorrect to view the movement of the

Persian army before the battle as issuing from well-considered strategy (thus, however, K. J. Beloch and W. Judeich). Scholars are not agreed on whether the Mosaic of Alexander from the Casa del Fauno in Pompeii, now in the Museo Nazionale in Naples, depicts the decisive moment in the battle of Issus or Gaugamela; see the discussion by H. Fuhrmann, *Philoxenos von Eretria*, 1931, cf. A. Ippel, *Gn.* 10, 1934 75 ff.; Rostovtzeff, *SEHHW* I, 128. From the extensive bibliography on military history the following studies may here be cited: A. Janke, *Auf Alexanders des Grossen Pfaden*, 1904, 5 ff., cf. the supplement, *Klio* 10, 1910, 137 ff. (valuable, because of topographical observations at the site); Delbrück, *Krieg.* I, 154 ff.; [3]1920, 185 ff.; W. Judeich, in Kromayer, *Schl.* IV, 354 ff. (with *Atlas, Griech. Abt.* Blatt 6, Karte 5-8); J. Keil, "Der Kampf um den Granikosübergang und das strategische Problem der Issosschlacht," *Mitt. Verein Klass. Philologen, Wien* I, 1924, 13 ff.; F. Miltner, "Alexanders Strategie bei Issos," *Öst. Jh.* 28, 1933, 69 ff. (whose view, that Alexander wanted to give Darius the slip and therefore marched along the coast, cannot be correct); see further, Glotz-Cohen, *HG* IV 1[2], 70 ff.; and C. L. Murison, "Darius III and the Battle of Issos," *H.* 21, 1972, 399 ff. The classic discussion of the event is still that of Droysen in *GH* I[2], published separately by H. E. Stier, J. G. Droysen, *Die Schlacht bei Issos*, Kriegsgeschichtliche Bücherei, Bd. 17, Berlin 1936.

29. Arrian, *Anab.* II 14; cf. Kaerst, *GH* I[3], 374 n. 1. On the negotiations between Alexander and Darius, including the later overtures, see G. Radet, "Alexandre en Syrie: Les offerts de paix que lui fit Darius," *Mélanges R. Dussaud* I, 1939, 235 ff.; and E. Mikrojannakis, *Ho diakritikos dialogos kata ten archaiotata, Hai metaxu Alexandrou G kai Dareiou G diplomatikai epaphai*, Athens 1969.

30. C. Clemen, *Lukians Schrift über die syrische Göttin*, AO 37, Leipzig 1938, 28 ff.

31. On the siege of Tyre see principally E. Schramm, in Kromayer-Veith, *Heerw.* IV 3,2, 1928 (reprint, 1963) 218; further, O. Eissfeldt, *RE* VII A, 1893 ff. s.v. *Tyros*; on topography see A. Poidebard, *Un grand port disparu*: Tyr, Bibl. archéol. et histor. 29, 1939.

32. Arrian, *Anab.* II 25; cf. J. Kaerst, *GH* I[3], 376 ff. n. 2; Wilcken, *Alex.* 101 f. Wilcken sees in this second offer by Darius and Alexander's decline of it 'the hour of destiny for the ancient world'.

33. Graf Yorck von Wartenburg, *Kurze Übersicht der Feldzüge Alexanders des Grossen*, 1897, 31 f.

34. The strategical factor is also incorrectly disputed by Ehrenberg, *Al. Äg.*, 10.

35. Proven by F. Pfister, *Eine jüdische Gründungsgeschichte Alexandrias, mit einem Anhang über Alexanders Besuch in Jerusalem*, SB.H, 1914; Tarn, *Alex.* I, 41. Of a different view are G. Radet, F. M. Abel (*Rev. bibl.* 43, 1934, 528 ff.; 44, 1935, 42 ff.) and A. Allgeier, *Biblische Zeitgesch.*, 1937, 257 ff.

36. The only evidence is from Pseudo-Callisthenes I 34.2, but this is confirmed by the fact that in the hieroglyphic inscriptions Alexander bears the traditional titles of the Pharaohs: see Wilcken, *Alex.*, 114: Tarn, *Alex.* II, 347 n. 3.

37. On the founding of Alexandria see A.v. Gerkan, *Griech. Städteanlagen*, 1924, 67 ff.; 78 f.; cf. further, E. Breccia, *Alexandrea ad Aegyptum*, Bergamo 1922; A. Calderini, *Dizionario dei nomi geografici e topografici dell'Egitto greco-romano* I 1, Cairo 1935, s.v.; a more recent account is that of A. Bernand, *Alexandrie la Grande*, Paris 1966; and in particular, P. M. Fraser, *Ptolemaic Alexandria* [3 vols.] I, Oxford 1972, 3 ff. Alexandria was founded on the site of the Egyptian fishing village of Rhacoti (the city is called Rhacoti in the Demotic documents from the Ptolemaic period). On the question whether Greeks had already settled here prior to this see above 43.

38. A temple of Isis was planned by Alexander: Arrian III 1.5; cf. H. Berve, *Klio* 31, 1938, 141; he rightly rejects the proposals of Ehrenberg, *Al. Äg.*, 26 ff., who saw in the founding of the city nothing less than the idea of a fraternisation of Greek with Oriental and Egyptian civilisations. The conclusive arguments against Ehrenberg may be found in U. Wilcken, SB.B, 1928, no. XXX 596 f.

39. Principal sources are: Arrian, *Anab.* III 3-4; Callisthenes fr. 14a (= Strabo XVII 814). The Cleitarchus tradition (so-called Vulgata, cf. E. Mederer, *A. leg.*, 58 ff.) is spurious. From the large number of modern studies (cited by Mederer, *A. leg.*, 37f.) the following are particularly useful: Wilcken, *Alexanders Zug in die Oase Siwa*, SB.B, Berlin, 1928, no. XXX 576 ff.; *Alexanders Zug zum Ammon. Ein Epilog*, SB.B, 1930, no. X, 159 ff.; = *Opuscula* II.

Berliner Akademieschriften zur alten Geschichte und Papyruskunde, I [1883-1931], 1970, 576 ff., 159 ff.; *idem, Zur Entstehung des hellenistischen Königskultes*, SB.B, 1938, no. XXVIII 298 ff. Opposed to Wilcken, see above all H. Berve, *Gn.* 5, 1929, 370 ff.; G. Radet, "La consultation de l'oracle d'Ammon par Alexandre," *Mélanges Bidez* II, 1934, 779 ff.; E. Mederer, *op. cit.*, 37 ff.; mediating, F. Oertel, *RhM* 89, 1940, 66 ff.; in essential agreement with Wilcken: Tarn, *Alex.* II, 347 ff.; No progress is marked by P. Jouguet, "Alexandre à l'oasis d'Ammon et le témoigne de Callisthène," *Bull. Inst. de l'Egypte* 26, 1943/44, 91 ff. A diffuse study by A. Gitti, *Alessandro Magno all'oasi di Siwah. Il problema delle fonti.* Bari 1951, (cf. H. Strasburger, *Gn.* 25, 1953, 217 ff.); F. Taeger, *Charisma* I, 1957, 191 ff. A. B. Bosworth, "Alexander and Ammon," in *Studies... Fritz Schachermeyr*, Berlin 1977, 51-57 [a good expansion on views advanced by Schachermeyr in his *Alexandre der Grosse* 298 ff.]. On the location see G. Steindorff, H. Ricke, H. Aubin, *AZ* 69, 1933, 1 ff.

40. Arrian, *Anab.* III 3.1 f.; shown as Ptolemaic by H. Strasburger, *Ptolemaios und Alexander*, 1934, 29 ff.; the objection by U. Wilcken, SB.B, 1938, no. XXVIII 300 n. 2, is not convincing.

41. F. Oertel, *op. cit.*, 70 ff., has also argued that the proclamation of Alexander as the son of Ammon assumed the form of a greeting (thus U. Wilcken) and not as a response of the oracle.

42. Thus also the conjecture often made on the basis of Plutarch, *Alex.* 27, that Alexander put to the oracle the question whether he were destined to become the ruler of the world (thus Altheim, *As.* I, 203 ff.).

43. Petisis abnegated his position shortly after 332/1 B.C., whereupon Doloaspis was invested with the entire civil government of the country.

44. On the government of Egypt see in particular Ehrenberg, *Al. Äg.*, 42 ff.; Berve, *Alex.* I, 259 f.; J. Vogt, *Klio* 31, 1938, 304 ff.; Bengtson, *Strat.* III, 4 ff.; J. Vogt, *Ch.* 1, 1971, 153 ff., and the rejoinder by J. Seibert, *Ch.* 2, 1972, 99 f.

45. An excellent description by Altheim, *As.* I, 122 f.

46. The principal sources on the battle of Gaugamela: Arrian III 7-15 (the enormous figures he gives for the Persian army are of no value), important for, *inter al.*, the exploited "ordre de bataille" of Darius (Arrian III 11.3 = Aristobulus); cf. Diod. XVII 53-61; Curt. Ruf. IV 9-16 (with a number of valuable details, which have been particularly stressed by Tarn [v. *infra*]; Plut., *Alex* 31-33; Justin XI 12-14. Bibliography: W. Rüstow, *Gesch. d. griech. Kriegswesens*, 1852, 282 ff.; Delbrück, *Krieg.* I, 171 ff.; ³1920, 207 ff.; F. Hackmann, *Die Schlacht bei Gaugamela*, Diss. Halle 1902; W. Judeich, in Kromayer, *Schl.* IV, 372 ff.; Glotz-Cohen, *HG* IV 1² 98 ff.; Tarn, *Alex.* I, 47 ff.; II, 182 ff.; G. T. Griffith, *JHS* 67, 1947 (published 1949), 77 ff.; E. W. Marsden, *The Campaign of Gaugamela*, Liverpool 1964 (with new theories; cf. N. G. L. Hammond, *JHS* 86, 1966, 252-3). On the location: Streck, *RE* VII, 861 ff. s.v. *Gaugamela*; for a different view see Sir Aurel Stein, *Geogr. Journal* 100, 1942, 155 ff., who is followed by Tarn, *Alex.* II, 189.

47. The conjecture by Tarn, that the Persians were probably numerically inferior (*Alex.* II, 188), is an invention.

48. Plut., *Alex.* 34. That Alexander was proclaimed "King of Asia" by the Macedonian military assembly (thus U. Wilcken, SB.B, 1922, no. VI 110 ff.; *Alex.*, 137; F. Granier, *Die maked. Heeresversammlung*, 1931, 31 f.), is scarcely correct; for an opposite view see already W. Kolbe, *DLZ*, 1931, 887; H. Berve, *Klio* 31, 1938, 145; Altheim, *As.* I, 177.

49. The evidence in Altheim, *As.* I, 178.

50. On the name Parsa see J. Wackernagel, *Glotta* 14, 1925, 40 ff.; J. Sturm, *RE* XIX, 1263 f. s.v. *Persepolis*; further, Glotz-Cohen, *HG* IV 1², 107 ff.

51. On the buildings in Persepolis: E. Herzfeld, *Klio* 8, 1908, 1 ff.; Fr. Sarre and. E. Herzfeld, *Iranische Felsreliefs*, 1910; F. Sarre, *Die Kunst des alten Persien*, 1923, 8 ff.; E. Herzfeld, *Archaeological History of Iran*, London 1936; J. Sturm, *RE* XIX, 1265 ff. s.v. *Persepolis*, as well as the monumental study by E. F. Schmidt cited above 426 n. 14; and R. T. Hallock, *Persepolis Fortification Tablets* (Univ. of Chicago Oriental Inst. Publ., 92), Chicago 1969: C. Nylander. *Ionians in Pasargadae*. Studies in Old Persian Architecture, Uppsala 1971.

52. This view is advocated by, *inter al.*, Droysen, *GH* I², 361 f.; T. Nöldeke, *Aufsätze z. persischen Geschichte*, 1888, 83 f.; A. v. Gutschmid, *Geschichte Irans*, 1888, 1; and then by

K. J. Beloch, J. Kaerst, U. Wilcken, W. W. Tarn, *et al.* Other scholars, however, view the burning of the Royal Palace as an emotional gesture of Alexander, thus: Berve, *Alex.* II, 175 s.v. Thaïs; G. Radet, *Notes critiques* II, 1927, 89 ff.; Mederer, *A. leg.*, 69 ff. An impressive counter-argument is advanced by Altheim, *As.* I, 179 ff. On the destruction of Persepolis, E. Bickerman, *CP* 45, 1950, 42; cf. G. Wirth, *H.* 20, 1971, 625 ff.

53. This view is rejected, entirely without justification, by Kaerst, *GH.* I^3, 416, and in particular by W. Kolbe, *DLZ*, 1931, 887.

54. Shortly before the death of Darius Alexander took over his signet-ring, with which he henceforth sealed decrees affecting Asia (Curt. Ruf. VI 6.6).

55. The diadem (around the *kausia*) is attested for Alexander from the death of Darius on (E. Neuffer, *Das Kostüm Alexanders d. Gr.*, Diss. Giessen, 1929, 34 ff.; H. Berve, *Klio* 31, 1938, 148 ff.). Altheim, *As.* I, 194 ff., has rightly emphasised that Alexander was always cautious in introducing any innovations.

56. See lastly Altheim, *As.* I, 190 ff. (including the earlier bibliography).

57. According to Tarn, *Bact.*, 470 ff., it much more = Ghazni. The question remains controversial.

58. Arrian IV 19.5; cf. Berve, *Alex.* II, 346 f. no. 688.

59. The evidence may be found complete in the following studies: Berve, *Alex.* II, no. 802 s.v. Philotas, no. 606 s.v. Parmenion, no. 427 s.v. Kleitos. On Parmenion see further, Tarn, *Alex.* II, 270 ff., and, on the other hand, E. Badian, *TAPA* 91, 1961, 324 ff.

60. Berve, *Alex.* II, no. 408 s.v. Kallisthenes; Tarn, *Alex.* I, 80 ff.; T. S. Brown, "Callisthenes and Alexander," *AJP* 70, 1949, 225 ff.; A. B. Bosworth, "Aristotle and Callisthenes," *H.* 19, 1970, 407 ff.

61. Arrian IV 12.3 ff.; Plut., *Alex.* 54 (= Chares fr. 14) (cf. on this E. J. Bickerman, *PP* 18, 1963, 241 ff.). The controversy which has long surrounded the reference to the "hearth" in Plutarch (*loc. cit.*) is under no circumstances to be resolved by emending the text; "hearth" relates much more to the altar upon which burned the sacred flame, the symbol of the everlasting nature of the rulership which Alexander had taken over from the Achaemenidae; cf. Otto-Bengtson, *Ptol.*, 154 n. 1, and equally also Altheim. *As.* I. 198 f.; for a different view see L. R. Farnell, *JHS* 49, 1929, 79 ff. (Greek cult of the hearth), who is followed by Nilsson, *Gr. Rel.* II. 148 n. 4; cf. also L. Edmunds. "The Religiosity of Alexander," *GRBS* 12. 1971. 363 ff. On the question of the *proskynesis see*, in a different context, *supra* 223.

62. Ehrenberg, *Alex.*, 62 ff.

63. A detailed study on Alexander's conception of the world remains a desideratum.

64. A different view is, however, held by Tarn, lastly *Alex*, I, 85 ff., and by E. Kornemann, *Weltgesch. d. Mittelmeerraumes* I, 1948, 138; Alexander, accordingly, wanted to conquer India because it had belonged to the Persian empire of Darius I.

65. On the location see Sir Aurel Stein, "Alexander the Great, Aornos:" *The Times* (25 and 26 October 1926); *On Alexander's Track to the Indus*, 1927, 417 ff.; 515 ff.

66. Principal sources: Arrian, *Anab.* V 8.4-19.3; Diod. XVII 87-89; Curt. Ruf. VIII 13-14; Plut., *Alex.* 60; Polyaenus IV 3.9; 22; Justin XII 8. The earlier studies, of which that by G. Veith, *Klio* 8, 1908, 131 ff., should be emphasised, have been discussed and assessed by W. Judeich, in Kromayer, *Schl.* IV, 385 ff. From more recent works may be cited the following studies by B. Breloer, which, in part, are admittedly hypothetical: *Alexanders Kampf gegen Poros*, Stuttgart 1933 (cf. W. Otto, *Gn.* 12, 1936, 301 ff.); *Alexanders Bund mit Poros. Indien von Dareios bis Sandrokotos*, Leipzig 1941; on specific questions: Tarn, *Alex.* II, 190 ff., and, with a different view, J. R. Hamilton, *JHS* 76, 1956, 26-31. The location of the battlefield has been a matter of controversy from time immemorial: that it is to be sought at the village of Jhelum (at the crossing of the Peshawar-Lahore road), has been advocated by Breloer; at a point lying further to the south (Jalapur), by Sir Aurel Stein, *Geogr. Journ* 80, 1932, 31 ff., and in *Archaeological Reconnaissances*, 1937; cf. Tarn, *Alex.* II, 197 f.

67. On the location of Bucephala see Tarn, *Alex.* II, 236 ff., who—in contrast to earlier scholars—places it on the east bank of the Hydaspes (Jhelum).

68. That Alexander obtained knowledge about the existence of the Ganges should not be disputed, despite the argument to the contrary by W. W. Tarn, *JHS* 43, 1923, 93 ff.; cf. also *Alex.* II, 275 ff.; cf. further, E. Kornemann, *Die Alexandergeschichte d. Ptolemaios* I., 1935,

80 n. 143 (see, for instance, E. Meyer, *Klio* 21, 1927, 183 ff.; F. Schachermeyr, *Innsbrucker Beitr. z. Kulturwiss.* 3, 2, 1955, 123 ff. The speech of Alexander in Arrian, *Anab.* V 25.3 ff., in which the Ganges is mentioned (V 26.1), must be regarded as essentially authentic (according to Tarn, *Alex.* II, 287 f., the speech is "full of errors"; cf. also E. Kornemann, *op. cit.*, 148 ff., and D. Kienast, *H.* 14, 1965, 180 ff.).

69. V. Ehrenberg, *Festschrift für M. Winternitz*, 1933, 287 ff.

70. On the voyage of Nearchus (topography): E. Mockler, "On the Identification of Places on the Macran Coast," *Journ. of the Asiatic Soc.* 11, 1879, 129 ff.; W. Tomaschek, *Topogr. Erläuterung der Küstenfahrt Nearchs vom Indus bis zum Euphrat,* SB.W, 121, 1890, Abh. 8, 110 ff. (without a map, but which is provided in, for instance, Chantraine's edition of the *Indike*); also valuable is H. Schiwek, *Bonner Jahrbücher* 162, 20 ff. (in great detail). On the researches of Nearchus see the excellent book by Bretzl, cited above 517, as well as W. Capelle, *RE* XVI, 2144 ff. s.v. *Nearchos*; and G. Wirth, "Nearchos der Flottenchef," *Eirene* II, 1969, 615 ff., and E. Badian, "Nearchus the Cretan," *YCS.* 24, 1975, 147 ff.

71. H. Strasburger, *Hermes* 80, 1952, 456 ff.; 82, 1954, 251 ff., according to which Nearchus is to be regarded as the source for Arrian, *Anab.* VI 24-26 and Strabo XV 2.5-7.

72. The *Hypomnemata*: Diod. XVIII 4 (probably = Hieronymus of Cardia); on the last plans cf. also Curt. Ruf. X 1.17-18. Following the lead of B. Niese, *HZ* NF 43, 1897, 1 ff., and Beloch, *GG* IV 1, 63 n. 2, the authenticity of the *Hypomnemata* has been disputed chiefly by W. W. Tarn, in the following penetrating studies: "Alexander's *Hypomnemata* and the 'World-Kingdom'," *JHS* 41, 1921, 1-17; "Alexander's Plans," *JHS* 59, 1939, 124-135; *Alex.* II, 378 ff. Opposed to Tarn, however, see Berve, *Alex.* I, 52; and above all U. Wilcken, *Die letzten Pläne Alexanders d. Gr.*, SB.B, 1937, no. XXIV 192-207, also already SB.B, 1928, no. XXX 593 n. 1; also F. Schachermeyr, *Öst. Jh.* 41, 1954, 118-140=*GRG*, 292-314 (opposed to F. Hampl *et al.*). U. Wilcken has at all events made the meeting between Alexander and Nearchus in December 325 B.C. probable as the earliest point at which the king conceived his western plans. E. Kornemann, "Die letzten Ziele der Politik Alexanders d. Gr.," *Klio* 16, 1920, 209 ff., also regards the *Hypomnemata* as genuine, but rejects the view that Alexander intended to conquer the entire western *oikoumene*; but this conclusion rests on an erroneous interpretation of the relevant sources; see U. Wilcken, *SJ* 45, 1921, 353 n. 2; SB.B, 1937, no. XXIV 194. According to G. Nenci, *Introduzione alle guerre persiane e altri saggi*, Pisa 1958, 215 ff., the actual design of the king was to destroy Carthaginian sovereignty (Diod. XVIII 4.4); E. Badian *HSCP* 72, 1968, 183 ff., interprets the *Hypomnemata* within the context of the Diadochian period.

73. On Harpalus see F. Stähelin, *RE* VII, 2397 ff. s.v. no. 2; Berve, *Alex.* II, no. 143; Glotz-Cohen, *HG* IV 1^2, 170 ff.; E. Badian, *JHS* 81, 1961, 16 ff.

74. Arrian, *Anab.* VII 4.4 ff.; Diod. XVII 107.6; Plut., *Alex.* 70 (cf. Athenaeus XII 538 B ff. = Chares fr. 4, the "programme" of festivities); Justin XII 10.9 f.; cf. Glotz-Cohen, *HG* IV I^2, 171 ff.

75. Alexander's speech in Arrian VII 9 f. is to be regarded as essentially genuine; see E. Kornemann, *Die Alexandergeschichte des Ptolemaios*, 159 ff.; concurring, with certain reservations, Tarn, *Alex.* II, 290 ff. For Cleitarchus as source: F. R. Wüst, *H.* 2, 1953-54, 177 ff., esp. 187 ff.

76. This is the view of many scholars from J. G. Droysen to H. Berve, cf. the survey by E. Bikerman, *Mél. Radet*, 1940, 32 n. 3.

77. It is significant that Alexander's decree only applied to the motherland and not to the Greek cities of Asia Minor, in which conditions were no different.

78. E. Bikerman, *Mél. Radet*, 1940, 25 ff., has clarified the manner in which the decree was made public: it was a proclamation of Alexander which is also referred to by, for instance, a law of Tegea (*Syll.* I^3 no. 306 = Schwyzer, *Dial. Graec, exempla epigr. pot.* [1923] no. 657 = Tod II no. 202, with a translation in Balogh, *Ref.*, 72 ff., cf. *ibid.*, 125 n. 281); cf. also E. Bikerman. *Rev. de phil.* 12, 1938, 299 ff.

79. The sources in Berve, *Alex.* II, no. 15 s.v. Agis. See also E. Badian, *Hermes* 95, 1967, 170 ff.; and E. N. Borza, *CP* 66, 1971, 230 ff.; but also A. B. Bosworth, *Px.* 29, 1975, 27 ff.

80. Berve, *Alex.* I, 245.

80a. Cf. G. L. Cawkwell, *CQ* 19, 1969, 163-189.

81. On the Harpalus affair see A. Körte, "Der harpalische Prozess," *NJb.* 53, 1924, 217

ff.; G. Colin, "Le discours d'Hypéride contre Démosthène sur l'argent d'Harpale," *Ann. de l'Est, Mém.* no. 4, Paris 1934; cf. P. Treves, "Notes sur la chronologie de l'affaire d'Harpale," *REA* 36, 1934, 513 ff. (Important for the chronology is an inscription from Oropus, cf. P. Roussel, *BCH* 54, 1930, 280 f., also G. Mathieu, *Rev. de phil.* 55, 1929, 159 ff.; P. Treves, *RE* XIX, 2489 ff. s.v. *Philokles* no. 4). The older bibliography is copiously cited by Berve, *Alex.* II, 78 ff., with further works quoted in Glotz-Cohen, *HG* IV 1^2, 186 n.

82. *SEG* IX 2; cf. E. Schweigert, *Hesp.* 8, 1939, 30, and Ad. Wilhelm, *Att. Urkunden* V, 1942, 150 ff.; cf. Tod II no. 196.

83. Arrian, *Anab.* VII 15.4 ff. In the "*legetai*"-group there still appear in Arrian the Carthaginians, Ethiopians, Scythians, Celts and Iberians. The Roman embassy, which according to Arrian is mentioned neither by Ptolemy nor by Aristobulus, must certainly be regarded as unhistorical, that is, it was not recorded in the *Ephemerides*. Despite Arrian's scepticism, it has been taken as genuine by, *inter al.*, B. G. Niebuhr, J. G. Droysen, Ed. Meyer, Berve, *Alex.* I, 326, and Mederer, *A. leg.*, 108 ff. For myself, I (just as Tarn, *Alex.* II, 23 f.; 374 ff.) am of a different opinion. A negative view is also adopted by G. Nenci, *Introduzione alle guerre persiane e altri saggi di storia antica*, Pisa 1958, 261 ff.

84. See W. Hoffmann, *Rom und die griechische Welt im 4. Jahrh.* Ph.-Suppl. 27, 1, 1934, 17 ff.

85. Habicht, *Gott.*, 28 ff.; 225 ff.; for a different view see E. J. Bickerman, *Athen.* NS 41, 1963, 70 ff.

86. Arrian, *Anab.* VII 23.2—an unusual piece of evidence, the importance of which should not be minimised, as in the case of R. Andreotti, *Il problema politico d'Alessandro Magno*, 1933, 158 n. 27.

87. The ascribing of divine honours to the living kings of Persia, viz. to their *daemon* (fravishi), has, however, been advocated by L. Ross Taylor in conjunction with the theory of P. Schnabel on the alleged veneration of Alexander's *agathos daimon* (*Klio* 19, 1925. 113 ff.; 20, 1926, 398 f.), *JHS* 47, 1927, 53 ff., *CP* 22, 1927, 162 ff., and lastly in her book. *The Divinity of the Roman Emperor*, Philological Monographs, published by the American Philological Association 1, Middletown 1931, Chap. 1 and App. 2, but in this she is completely incorrect; see, on the other hand, already H. Berve, *Klio* 20, 1926, 179 ff.; *Alex.* I, 339 f. (controversy with P. Schnabel), and above all W. W. Tarn, *JHS* 48, 1928, 206 ff.; A. D. Nock, "*Synnaos theos,*" *HSCP* 41, 1930, 61; *Gn.* 8, 1932, 513 ff., and, again, Tarn, *Alex.* II, 359 ff. It was really not necessary for Altheim, *As.* I, 198 f., to take up Schnabel's theory again; it is also rejected by Nilsson, *Gr. Rel.* II, 148 n. 4. On the *proskynesis*, connected with this question, see *infra* 526 n. 110.

88. Despite the opposite view held by, *inter al.*, D. G. Hogarth, *Hist. Rev.* 2, 1887, 317 ff.; B. Niese, *HZ* 79, 1897, 1 ff.; E. Kornemann, *Klio* 1, 1901, 56, it may be regarded as certain that Alexander demanded the *apotheosis* from the Greeks of the motherland, a view which was already advocated by B. G. Niebuhr, G. Grote, Ed. Meyer (*Kl Schr.* I, 300), and above all by Kaerst (*Mon.*, 38 ff.; lastly in his *GH* I^3, 484 ff.). A survey of the earlier bibliography may be found in E. Kornemann, *Klio* 1, 1901, 56 n. 3, Berve, *Alex.* I, 96 n. 4, and in U. Wilcken, *Kult.*, 302 ff. Cf. further, G. De Sanctis, *RF* NS 18, 1940, 1 ff. That Alexander's demand of the *apotheosis* is to be viewed from a religious point of view has been argued in particular by U. Wilcken, *Kult.*, 304 f., as opposed to Meyer, *Kl. Schr.* I 302; 312 ff. The other view—that the *apotheosis* was from the very beginning to be regarded as a political claim—found an advocate in Tarn. *Alex.* II. 370 ff. The truth of the matter lies somewhere in between.

89. Thus Prof. A. E. Lampé, M.D., in E. Kornemann, *Weltgesch. des Mittelmeerraumes* I, 1948, 150; cf. F. Schachermeyr, *Alexander in Babylon und die Reichsordnung nach seinem Tod*, SB.W, 268, 3, Vienna 1970, 65 ff., who suggests malaria, accompanied by virulent leukemia.

90. A. E. Samuel, *Ptolemaic Chronology*, 1962, 46-47.

91. See W. Rüstow and H. Köchly, *Geschichte d. griech. Kriegswesens von der ältesten Zeit bis auf Pyrrhos*, Aarau 1852, 216 ff.; H. Droysen, *Untersuch. über Alexanders d. Gr. Heerwesen und Kriegführung*. Freiburg i.Br. 1885; Delbrück, *Krieg.* I^3 1920. 167 ff.: Berve, *Alex.* I. 103 ff. (a comprehensive discussion on the organisation of Alexander's army);

Kromayer–Veith, *Heerw.*, 95 ff.; Tarn, *Alex.* II, 135 ff. (as a monograph, *idem, Hellenistic Military and Naval Developments*, Cambridge 1930).

92. A particularly copious version of it by Berve, *Alex.* I, 314 ff. I too advocated this view in *Ph.* 92, 1937, 127, in my article on Philoxenus. Correct, on the other hand, is the counter-argument by O. Leuze, *Die Satrapieneinteilung in Syrien und im Zweistromland*, Halle 1935, 273, and by Tarn, *Alex.* II, 171 ff.

93. Tarn, *Alex.* II, 171 ff.

94. Curt. Ruf. IV 1.34 f. (in this passage Lydia is mistaken for Phrygia).

95. Arrian, *Anab.* VII 11.8-9. See U. Wilcken, *Die letzten Pläne Alexanders d. Gr.*, SB.B, 1937, no. XXIV 198 ff.; H. Berve, "Die Verschmelzungspolitik Alexanders d. Gr.," *Klio* 31, 1938, 161.

96. W. W. Tarn, *Alexander the Great and the Unity of Mankind* (The Raleigh Lecture of History, Proceedings of the British Academy XIX, 1933), in a greatly expanded form: *Alex.* II, 399-449; concurring: C. A. Robinson, Jr., "Alexander the Great and the Barbarians," in *Classical Studies Presented to E. Capps*, Princeton 1936, 298 ff.; of German scholars: W. Kolbe, *Die Weltreichsidee Alexanders d. Gr.*, Frieburg. Wiss. Ges. 25, 1936; cf. the survey by H. Bengtson, in *WG* 5, 1939, 171 f. = *KS*, 245 f. It will not do to trace back to Alexander the train of thought of Eratosthenes (in Strabo I p. 66; Plut., *De fort. Al. Magn.* I 6 p. 329), as has been attempted by W. W. Tarn, *AJP* 60, 1939, 65 ff.; *Alex.* II, 437 ff., and H. E. Stier, *Reallex. f. Antike und Christentum* I 264 s.v. *Alexander*. See, on the other hand, E. Badian, *H.* 7, 1958, 425 ff., esp. 432 ff. Fertile in ideas is the article by R. Andreotti, "Per una critica dell'ideologia di Alessandro Magno," *H.* 5, 1956, 257 ff.; also "Die Weltmonarchie Alexanders d. Gr. in Überlieferung und geschichtlicher Wirklichkeit," *Saec.* 8, 1957, 120 ff. Cf. also P. Merlan, *CP* 45, 1950, 161 ff.; on this view the Sophist Antiphon had already adovcated the idea of the unity of mankind.

97. A different view is argued by H. Berve, *Klio* 31, 1938, 168.

98. V.s.p. 524 n. 72.

99. Diod. XVIII 4.4; cf. Kaerst, *GH* I³, 493; Ed. Meyer, *Blüte u. Niedergang d. Hellenismus in Asien*, 1925, 11 f.; H. Berve, *Klio* 31, 1938, 163 f.

100. Droysen's survey, *GH* III 2, 189 ff., is out of date; cf. Berve, *Alex.* I, 291 ff.; V. Tscherikower, *Die hellenistischen Städtegründungen von Alexander dem Grossen bis auf die Römerzeit*, Phil.-Suppl. XIX 1, 1927, 138 ff. *et al.*; Tarn, *Alex.* II, 232 ff.

101. Tarn, *Alex.* I, 233, is incorrect in regarding the figure given in Plut., *De Alex. fortuna* I 328E, as greatly exaggerated.

102. Of a different view is V. Chapot, "Alexandre fondateur de villes," *Mélanges G. Glotz* I, 1932, 173 ff., who minimises the effects of Alexander's colonisation; for the opposite view see, correctly, Rostovtzeff, *SEHHW* I, 131 ff.; III 1338 (with additional bibliography).

103. U. Wilcken, "Alexander d. Gr. und die hellenistische Wirtschaft," *SJ* 45, 2, 1921, 45 (349) ff.; *Alex.*, 239 ff.; Rostovtzeff, *SEHHW* I, 126 ff. (with bibliography, III, 1337 f.).

104. U. Wilcken, *SJ* 45, 1921, 50 (354); opposed to Wilcken, only partly correct, Rostovtzeff, *SEHHW* I, 127; III, 1338.

105. Incorrectly regarded as unhistorical by Tarn, *Alex.* I, 44 f.

106. On Alexander's coinage policy see U. Wilcken, *SJ* 45, 1921, 56 f. (360 f.); Beloch, *GG* IV 1, 40 ff.; C. Seltman, *Greek Coins*, ²1955, 203 ff.; Rostovtzeff, *SEHHW* I, 134 f.; III, 1338 f.; Tarn, *Alex.* I, 130 ff.

107. See Rostovtzeff, *SEHHW* I, 149 ff. (on the accumulation of wealth under Alexander and the *Diadochoi*); 164 ff. (on the hoards of Alexander coins in Greece). Athenaeus (VI 231e) has given an excellent description of the new economic situation in Greece.

108. Still basic is Ed. Meyer, "Alexander d. Gr. und die absolute Monarchie," *Kl. Schr.* I², 1924, 265 ff.

109. For the Orientals the *proskynesis* was and remained a foregone conclusion.

110. See the evidence in Berve, *Alex.* I, 19; 340; II no. 408 s.v. Kallisthenes; additional bibliography in R. Andreotti, *Il problema politico di Alessandro Magno*, 1933, 142 n. 2; cf. also G. C. Richards, *CR* 48, 1934, 168 ff.; B. Meissner, *Der Kuss im Alten Orient*, SB.B, 1934, no. XXVIII 922 ff.; A. Alföldi, *RM* 49, 1934, 40 ff.; J. P. V. D. Balsdon, *H.* 1, 1950, 371 ff.; F. Taeger, *Charisma* I, 1957, 209 ff.; and the works cited above 525 n. 88.

111. W. Kolbe, *DLZ*, 1931, 895.

12 THE HELLENISTIC MONARCHIES

PRINCIPAL SOURCES AND BIBLIOGRAPHY: The historical tradition of the first century after Alexander's death presents a broad spectrum of ruins. Of the great contemporary works of history, not a single one is extant. Scholars of the last several generations have endeavoured to assess the wealth of epigraphical evidence accruing from the systematic excavations in order to reconstruct the historical events and internal developments in the Hellenistic states; the papyri, too, have yielded a certain amount of new information, especially for the internal history of Ptolemaic Egypt. But as valuable as the documents in fact are, they cannot begin to act even as an approximate substitute for a historiography of actual flesh and blood. The motives of the various protagonists in particular remain in the dark, and due to the absence of a court historiography, not even the rulers themselves attain a proper portrayal in relief. Interesting are the genealogical statements on several Ptolemies preserved, unfortunately, only in a fragmentary state, on a Copenhagen papyrus (*P. Haun.* 6, published by T. Larsen, 1942; see M. Segre, "Una genealogia dei Tolemei e le 'imagines maiorum' dei Romani," *Rend. Pontif. Acc. Rom. Arch.* 19, 1942/43, 269 ff. [not convincing]).

There are three names which determine the tradition from Alexander's death to the end of the third century; two of them are contemporary: Hieronymus of Cardia and Phylarchus, while the lifetime of the third, Polybius of Megalopolis, falls in the second century B.C.

The principal features of the fluctuating developments in the first two decades after the death of Alexander are assured; for this we are indebted to Hieronymus of Cardia (c. 350-260 B.C.), the friend and fellow-combatant of Eumenes, later of Antigonus Monophthalmus and Demetrius Poliorcetes (cf. on Hieronymus Jacoby, *RE* VIII, 1540 ff.; *FgrHist.* no. 154; and the Dissertation by W. Nietzold, *Die Überlieferung der Diadochengesch. bis zur Schlacht bei Ipsos*, Würzburg 1905; as well as R. Engel, "Zum Geschichtsbild des Hieronymos von Kardia," *Ath.* 50, 1972, 120 ff.). Hieronymus' work (the title has not been transmitted), which ends perhaps with the death of Pyrrhus (272 B.C.), forms the basis of Diodorus' sketch (XVIII-XX, to 302 B.C.), as well as the very detailed, but unfortunately extant only in scanty extracts, *Diadochian History* by Arrian, extending down to 321 B.C. (edition of Arrian by A. G. Roos, II, 1928, 253 ff.). Hieronymus is equally important as a source for Plutarch's *Vitae* of Eumenes, Demetrius and Pyrrhus. Hieronymus' *History* deserves the full scope of praise that modern scholars have bestowed upon it: thoroughly grounded knowledge of military matters, strict factualness and an impartial attitude towards the leading protagonists of the time place it alongside the classical narrative of Alexander from the pen of Ptolemy. A more recent characterisation: T. S. Brown, *AHR* 52, 1946-47, 684 ff; cf. R. Engel, "Zum Geschichtsbild des Hieronymos von Kardia," *Ath.* 50, 1972, 120 ff., and K. Rosen, "Political Documents in Hieronymus of Cardia," *Acta Classica* (Capetown) 10, 1968, 41-94.

For the half century from the death of Pyrrhus (272 B.C.) to the time when the *Histories* of Polybius actually begin (220 B.C.), the principal author was Phylarchus of Athens (or of Naucratis). As a writer of history he is much inferior to Hieronymus. It was especially the inclination of Phylarchus towards anecdotes, moralising and tragic description that fundamentally spoiled his work. But it is precisely for this reason that it was widely read, and even Polybius culled from it. In addition, this work was used both by Pompeius Trogus (Justin XXV-XXVIII) and Plutarch (*Agis* and *Cleomenes* (cf. E. Gabba, *Ath.* NS 35, 1957, 3 ff.; 193 ff.), and in part also in the *Vitae* of Aratus and Pyrrhus). More recent studies on the work of Phylarchus: T. W. Africa, *Phylarchus and the Spartan Revolution*, Berkeley and Los Angeles 1961; B. Shimron, "Some Remarks on Phylarchus and Cleomenes III," *RF* 94, 1966, 452-459; and J. Kroymann, *RE* Suppl. VIII, 471 ff.

The work by Polybius of Megalopolis (before 200 to c. 120 B.C.) is completely different in quality. Having grown up as son of the Achaean statesman Lycortas and himself hipparch of the Achaean League in 169 B.C., Polybius was predestined to become a historian. Deported to Italy along with the Achaean hostages in 167 B.C., Polybius gained entry into the house of Aemilius Paullus. He struck a life-long friendship with P. Cornelius Scipio Aemilianus, the son of the victor of Pydna (Polyb. XXXI 23 ff.). On Scipio's staff the Hellene stood amidst the ruins of Carthage (146 B.C.), and in the camp before Numantia (134/3 B.C.). (The latter is disputed by Walbank, *Comm. Polyb.* I, 6.) From an understanding of the universal historical importance associated with the rise of the Roman Empire and from an insight into the fact that the destiny of the entire Mediterranean was interwoven grew Polybius' great design to write a true universal history of the Mediterranean world of his own time; it could only become a history of the emergent world empire of Rome. Thanks to his political insight, his sober sense of the realities of historical life, but above all to his understanding for the achievements of the Romans, Polybius became preeminently successful in his design: in the footsteps of Thucydides he created a work which he confidently hoped would be useful precisely to politicians and statesmen. Thus the former Achaean statesman became the founder of "pragmatic historiography" (for the term see M. Gelzer, *Festschr. für C. Weickert*, Berlin 1955, 87 ff.).

As a preface to the actual narrative, which encompasses the decisive 53 years from 220 to 168 B.C., Polybius wrote an Introduction covering the First Punic War (Bks. I-II). With this Introduction Polybius' work became linked to the *History* of Timaeus, which terminated with 264 B.C. The continuation of the work, covering the period from 167 to 145/4 B.C. (Bks. XXX-XXXIX) no doubt reflects the results of a later plan. Of the 40 Books comprising the total of the *Histories* by Polybius, only Books I-V are extant *in toto*; of these, Books III-V contain a detailed account of events in the 140th Olympiad (220/19-217/16 B.C.). From Books VII-XVI (Book VI, as is well known, contains the famous account of the Roman constitution, so greatly admired by Polybius), that is for the events from 216/5 to 201/0 B.C., only fragments have been preserved—just as for the later books—namely extracts in the Codex Urbinas (for Books I-XVIII); in addition, there are extracts from the entire work by the emperor Constantinus VII Porphyrogennetus (912-959 A.D.). An edition (including the fragments) by Th. Büttner-Wobst, in 4 vols., with an Appendix (reprint, Teubner-Stuttgart, 1962-63); see also the edition in the Collection Budé: Polybe, *Histoires*, livre i, by P. Pédech, 1969; livre ii, by P. Pédech, 1970; livre iii, by J. de Foucault, 1971. A comprehensive commentary and lexicon are in progress: Walbank, *Comm. Polyb.* I (Books I-VI); II (Books VII-XVIII); *Polybios-Lexikon*, compiled by A. Mauersberger, Berlin 1966 (to date only the letters a-k).

The details connected with the genesis of Polybius' *Histories* are obscure. It is doubtful whether the account of conditions relating to the Achaeans (see the Excursus II 37-71) formed the core of the work (M. Gelzer, *Die Achaica im Geschichtswerk des Polybios*, SB.B, 1940, no. 2). To conclude that there were five different versions (thus R. Laqueur, *Polybios*, 1913), is about as improbable as can be (see, correctly, the objections raised by F. Leo, *Gesch. d. röm. Lit.* I, 1913, 318 ff.; Ed. Meyer, SB.B, 1913, 689; K. Lorenz, *Untersuch. z. Geschichtswerk des Polybios*, Stuttgart 1931, 69 ff.; M. Holleaux, "Polybe et le tremblement de terre de Rhodes," *Et. ép.* I, 445 ff.). The unitarian theory, moreover, put forward in particular by H. Erbse, *RhM* 94, 1951, 157 ff., *Ph.* 101, 1957, 269 ff., does not appear convincing to me. See, on the other hand, for instance, W. Theiler, *Hermes* 81, 1953, 216 ff. (for Book VI).

BIBLIOGRAPHY: (the most important earlier studies may be found in K. Ziegler, *RE* XXI, 1440 ff. s.v. *Polybios*; cf. Bengtson, *Einf.*, 104, *Anc. Hist.*, 106) (a survey of publications from 1950-1970 is also provided by D. Musti, in "Aufstieg und Niedergang der römischen Welt," *Festschrift für J. Vogt* I, 2, 1972, 1114-18); cf. F. W. Walbank, *CQ* 25, 1975. 87 ff. P. La Roche, *Charakteristik des Polybios*, Leipzig 1857; R. von Scala, *Die Studien des Polybios* I, 1890 (more not published); O. Cuntz, *Polybios u. sein Werk*, Leipzig 1902; J. B. Bury, *The Ancient Greek Historians*, London 1909, 210 ff.; C. Wunderer, *Polybios. Lebens- und Weltanschauung aus dem 2. vorchristlichen Jahrh.*, Leipzig 1927; W. Siegfried, *Studien zur geschichtlichen Auffassung des Polybios*, Leipzig 1928; E. Ibendorff, *Untersuch. z. darstell. Persönlichkeit des Polybios*, Rostock 1930; T. R. Glover, *CAH* VIII, 1 ff.; E. Howald, *Vom Geist antiker Geschichtsschreibung*, Munich 1944, 87 ff. (aphoristic); P. Pédech, *La méthode historique de Polybe*, Paris 1964 (cf. K.-E. Petzold, *Gn.* 45, 1973, 367 ff.); G. A. Lehmann, *Untersuchungen zur historischen Glaubwürdigkeit des Polybios*, Münster i.W., 1967; K.-E. Petzold, *Studien zur Methode des Polybios und zu ihrer historischen Auswertung*, Munich 1969 (cf. Renate Zoepffel, *Gn.* 45, 1973, 58 ff.; R. M. Errington, *CR* 21, 1971, 383 ff.); J.-A. de Foucault,

Recherches sur la langue et le style de Polybe, Paris 1972. A copious bibliography may otherwise be found in Walbank, *Comm. Polyb.* I, II; also in E. Mioni, "Polybio," Padua 1949. Valuable specialised studies on Polybius have been published by F. W. Walbank; "Polybius, Philinus and the First Punic War," *CQ* 39, 1945, 1 ff. (on the sources of Bk. I); "Polybius and the Roman Constitution," *CQ* 37, 1943, 43 ff. (on Bk. VI and the question of the edition of the work). Of Walbank's more recent studies, cited for the most part in his commentary on Polybius, the following deserve to be stressed: the public lecture: *Speeches in Greek Historians* (The J. L. Myres Memorial Lecture [no year given] Oxford 19 pp.); and *idem*, *Polybios* (Sather Classical Lectures, 42), Berkeley and Los Angeles 1972. See also, along with others, his participation in *Entretiens sur l'antiquité classique*, 20: *Polybe*, Vandoeuvres-Genève 1974. Of some value, especially in regard to Bk. VI, is K. F. Eisen, *Polybiosinterpretationen*, Heidelberg 1966. Problems connected with the sources are treated by V. La Bua, *Filino-Polibio-Sileno-Diodoro. Il problema delle fonti dalla morte di Agatocle alla guerra mercenaria in Africa*, Palermo (no date) (1966). Also important is M. Gelzer, *Über die Arbeitsweise des Polybios*, SB.H, 1956, 3. Also valuable is K. Meister, *Historische Kritik bei Polybios*, Wiesbaden 1975. Essential on the conception of history by Polybius is K.v. Fritz, *The Theory of the Mixed Constitution in Antiquity. A critical Analysis of Polybius' Political Ideas.* New York 1954 (cf. M. Gelzer, *Gn.* 28, 1956, 81 ff.). Although Polybius deserves the greatest esteem, it must not be forgotten that his account is dependent on his sources, which often determine his own views.

Other Histories from the period after Alexander cannot even begin to compare in importance with the Histories of Hieronymus, Phylarchus and Polybius. Neither the work by Diyllus of Athens (he lived from c. 340 to 290 B.C.; his work probably covered the period from 357 to 297 B.C.; cf. Jacoby, *FgrHist.* no. 73; also A. Momigliano, *Rendic. Ist. Lomb.* 65, 1932, 523 ff., who, however, does not advance any distinctively new views), nor that of his compatriot Demochares, the nephew of Demosthenes (he lived from about 350 to before 271/0 B.C.), attain any real portrait in relief (on Demochares see Jacoby, *FgrHist.* no. 75; on his influence cf. still A. Wilhelm, *Abh. Berl. Ak.*, 1941, no. 4; A. Momigliano, *Riv. stor. it.* 71, 1959, 537 f., etc.).

Of a different character is the pupil of Theophrastus, Duris of Samos, whose life falls in the period from about 340 to 270 B.C. His *Histories* (the fragments are in Jacoby, *FgrHist.* no. 76) cover the period from 371 to 281 (?) B.C. In addition to the work of Phylarchus they are a famous example of the "tragic style" in Hellenistic historiography (see P. Scheller, *De hellenist. hist. conscr. arte*, Diss. Leipzig 1911, 68 ff.; F. W. Walbank, *Bull. of the Inst. of Class. Stud. of the Univ. of London*, No. 2, 1955, 4 ff.). The article by Ed. Schwartz, *RE* V, 1853 ff., is still basic.

From among the statesmen of the Diadochian period, Demetrius of Phalerum, the regent of Athens under Cassander, himself took up the pen and wrote a work entitled *Peri Dekaitias*; cf. F. Wehrli, *Demetrios von*

Phaleron (Texts), Basle, 1949. As for Pyrrhus, he composed memoirs, and the memoirs of the Achaean statesman Aratus of Sicyon († 213 B.C.), which terminate with the battle of Sellasia (222 B.C.), form the basis of the biography of Aratus by Plutarch (edition of the *Vita*, with an excellent commentary, by W. P. Theunissen, Nijmegen 1955, and by H. W. Porter, Dublin and Cork 1937), and in part also Book II of Polybius' *Histories* (cf. II 56.2; see E. Bikerman, *REG* 56, 1943, 297 ff.).

The rise of the native-oriental historiography in Greek dress is characteristic of the spread of Hellenistic culture. Thus the Babylonian Priest of Bêl, Berossus (c. 280 B.C.), the Egyptian Manetho of Sebennytus, (under Ptolemy II), as well as Q. Fabius Pictor and Cincius Alimentus used Greek in their histories.

THE DOCUMENTS: The epigraphical documents which are of historical importance may be found in *Syll.*[3] I, and in *OGI* I; the Hellenistic royal correspondence in Asia has been published by Welles, *RC* (cf. A. Wilhelm, *Griech. Königsbriefe*, Klio-Beiheft 48, 1943). The treaties are now available in Schmitt, *Staatsv.* III, nos. 403 ff. Otherwise more recent finds are discussed in the reports carried by *REG* (J. and L. Robert). Of particular importance are the decrees of the Popular Assembly in Samos, published by C. Habicht, *AM* 72, 1957 (published 1959), 154 ff.: nos. 1-48; 87, 1972, 191-218. A good collection of the papyri which are of historical importance may be found in *CAH* VII, 889 ff. (by M. Rostovtzeff); cf. also the copious sources cited in Rostovtzeff's *SEHHW*; also Chr. Habicht, "Literarische u. epigraphische Überlieferung zur Gesch. Alexanders u. seiner ersten Nachfolger," *Akten des VI. internat. Kongr. f. gr. u. lat. Epigraphik* (Vestigia 17), Munich 1972, 367 ff.

For the coinage we possess, in Head, *HN*, a handbook, but one that has long since needed supplementing. More recent bibliography may be found in K. Christ, *Antike Numismatik. Einführung und Bibliographie*, Darmstadt 1967, 36 ff. Indispensable are the catalogues of the great coin collections, especially those of the British Museum in London and of the Bibliothèque Nationale in Paris, and of the *Corpus Numorum* of the *Preussische Akademie der Wissenschaften*, namely the three volumes *Antike Munzen Nordgriechenlands*, 1898-1935, and the volume *Antike Münzen Mysiens*, 1913. As for specific publications, in addition to the older work by J. N. Svoronos, *Ta Nomismata tou Kratous ton Ptolemaion*, 4 vols., Athens 1904-08 (with important comments by K. Regling), reference may be made to the more recent works by E. T. Newell, *The Coinage of the Eastern* (or *Western*) *Seleucid Mints*, New York 1938 (or 1941); and C. Boehringer, *Zur Chronologie mittelhellenistischer Münzserien 220 bis 160 v. Chr.*, Berlin 1972; M. Thompson, O. Mørkholm, C. M. Kraay, *An Inventory of Greek Coin Hoards*, The American Numismatic Society, New York 1973, 171 ff. On iconography see F. Imhoof-Blumer, *Porträtköpfe auf antiken Münzen hellenischer und hellenisierter Völker*, Leipzig 1885.

In addition to depending on the documents on stone and papyrus, the chronology of the third century B.C. rests primarily on the *Chronicle* of the Church Father *Eusebius* († 338 A.D.): edition of the *Chronicle* by A. Schoene, translation from the Armenian version by J. Karst (1911). One source used by Eusebius was the *Chronicle* of the Neoplatonist Porphyry of Tyre (cf. Jacoby, *FgrHist.* no. 260). The chronological dates in cuneiform texts have been collected by A. T. Olmstead, "Cuneiform Texts and Hellenistic Chronology," *CP* 32, 1937, 1 ff. (cf. also R. A. Parker and W. H. Dubberstein, *Babylonian Chronology*, Providence ^{3}1956); and the dates on papyri, in so far as they are connected with the regnal years of the Ptolemies, by T. C. Skeat, *The Reigns of the Ptolemies* (Münch. Beitr. 39), ^{2}1969. (*P. Oxy.* XIX, 2222 unfortunately contains only a short fragmentary list of the regnal years from Ptolemy VII to Ptolemy XIV). Important too is P. W. Pestman, *Chronologie égyptienne d'après les textes démotiques (332 av. J.-C. - 453 ap. J.-C.)*, Leiden 1967. For the Seleucids: A. J. Sachs and D. J. Wiseman, "A Babylonian King List of the Hellenistic Period," *Iraq* 16, 1954, 202 ff.; cf. A. Aymard, *REA* 57, 1955, 102 ff.; H. Bengtson, *H.* 4, 1955, 113-114 = *KS.*, 343 ff. See also now A. E. Samuel, *Greek and Roman Chronology. Calendars and Years in Classical Antiquity* (Hdb. Alt.), Munich 1972, 139 ff. Attic and Delphic chronology has assumed a central place in scholarship during the last decades. On Attic chronology the following major works may be cited: B. D. Meritt, *Hesp.* 7, 1938, 131 ff.; W. B. Dinsmoor, *The Athenian Archon List in the Light of Recent Discoveries*, New York 1939; W. K. Pritchett and B. D. Meritt, *The Chronology of Hellenistic Athens*, Cambridge, Mass., 1940; W. B. Dinsmoor, *Hesp.* 23, 1954, 248 ff. The Delphic chronology has seen considerable progress in recent decades by the investigations of French scholars (P. Roussel, G. Daux, R. Flacelière). The last major work is that of G. Daux, *Chronologie delphique*, Paris 1943 (cf. G. Klaffenbach, *DLZ*, 1947, 17 ff.).

BIBLIOGRAPHY: In addition to the older works by Droysen (*GH* II–III) Niese, (*Mak.* I, II), the following may be cited: Beloch, *GG* IV 1 and 2, extending to 217 B.C.—an outstanding achievement in narrative and critical scholarship; Kaerst, *GH* II^{2}, only to 301 B.C., in which ideas are to some extent exaggerated as compared with the realities of the historical situation; P. Jouguet, *L'impérialisme macédonien et l'hellénisation de l'Orient*, Paris 1926 (^{2}1937: expanded only by Addenda); *CAH* VI, Chap. 15: "The Heritage of Alexander" (by W. W. Tarn); VII, "The Hellenistic Monarchies and the Rise of Rome" (to 217 B.C.); VIII, "Rome and the Mediterranean;" the names of eminent scholars appear in the section on Hellenistic history: W. S. Ferguson, W. W. Tarn, M. Rostovtzeff, M. Cary, T. Frank, M. Holleaux. Also solid is Glotz-Cohen, *HG* IV: "Alexandre et l'hellénisation du monde antique." Iere partie: Alexandre et de démembrement de son empire (to 280 B.C.), Paris ^{2}1945. Shorter accounts (without sources): M. Cary, *A History of the Greek World from 323 to 30 B.C.*, London 1932 (^{2}1972 with a new select bibliography by V. Ehrenberg); C. B. Welles, *Alexander and the Hellenistic World*, Toronto 1970; H. Berve, *GG* II^{2}, Freiburg i.Br. 1952, 216 ff. Furthermore, Ed. Will, *Histoire politique du monde hellénistique (323-30 av. J.-C.)*, I. *De la mort d'Alexandre aux avènements d'Antiochos III et de Philippe V*, Nancy 1966 (with a discussion of specific problems); cf. *idem*, "Le monde hellénistique," in *Le monde grec et l'Orient* II, Paris 1975, 335 ff. and F. Schachermeyr, *Alexander in Babylon und die Reichsordnung nach seinem Tod*, Vienna 1970, as well as Bengtson, *Herrs.* Indispensable for economic and social history is Rostovtzeff, *SEHHW*.

THE STRUGGLE FOR ALEXANDER'S EMPIRE

PRINCIPAL SOURCES: a) Primary Sources: Stress may be placed on the following inscriptions (collected in *Syll.* I³ 310 ff.; *OGI* I 3 ff.; Welles, *RC*, New Haven 1934; Schmitt, *Staatsv.* III): a letter of King Philip Arrhidaeus (*OGI* I 8); the letter of the Diadochian Antigonus Monophthalmus to the people of Scepsis, from the year 311, containing the notice of the peace concluded between Antigonus, Cassander, Lysimachus and Ptolemy (Wells *RC*, no. 1 = Schmitt *Staatsv.* III, no. 428); two letters of Antigonus to Teos on the synoecism with Lebedus (Welles *RC* nos. 3 and 4; cf. A. Wilhelm, *Klio* 28, 1935, 280 ff.); the so-called Epidaurian League Stele, from the year 302 (*IG* IV² 1. 68; Schmitt *Staatsv.* III, no. 446); the so-called Magna Charta of Cyrene (*SEG* IX no. 1), from 322/1, cf. A. Laronde, REG 85, 1972, XIII f.; and, finally, an honorary decree for Demetrius found in Athens (after 304/3 B.C.), published by W. Peek and N. Kyparissis, *AM* 66, 1941, 221 ff., with the corrections of A. Wilhelm *Öst. Jh.* 35, 1943, 157 ff.

b) The works of contemporary historians, especially that by Hieronymus of Cardia (cf. *supra* 527 f.) are as such lost, without exception. A primary source of the highest quality is the so-called *Diadochian Chronicle*, an account of events in Babylonia after Alexander's death, published by S. Smith, *Babylonian Historical Texts*, London 1924, 140 ff.; cf. W. Otto, *SB.Bay.*, 1925, Schlussheft, 9 ff.; G. Furlani and A. Momigliano, *RF* NS 10, 1932, 462 ff.; B. Funk, *In Memoriam E. Unger*, Baden-Baden 1971, 217-240.

Of the later writers, Diodorus (XVIII-XX), as well as the *Diadochian History* of Arrian, which is comprehensive but breaks off in 321 (a new fragment in *PSI* XI, 1950, no. 1284; cf. K. Latte, *Nachr. Gött. Akad., phil.-hist. Kl.*, 1950, 23 ff.; G. Wirth, *Klio* 46, 1965, 283-288) is based principally on Hieronymus of Cardia. Justin's *Epitome* of the *Historiae Philippicae* by Pompeius Trogus is superficial, but none the less contains good material, as do the *Prologi.* The information in Q. Curtius Rufus (X 6 ff.) on events after the death of Alexander must only be used with caution (cf., however, R. M. Errington, *JHS* 90, 1970, 72 ff.). Valuable are Plutarch's *Vitae* of Phocion, Eumenes and Demetrius, which are supplemented only in points of detail by the *Lives* of Phocio and Eumenes by Cornelius Nepos. And, finally, the historical excursus of Pausanias on Diadochian history (cf. M. Segre, *Historia* [Milan] 2, 1928, 217 ff.) should be mentioned; and from chronological works, the so-called *Marmor Parium*; cf. F. Jacoby, *Das Marmor Parium*, 1904, and *FgrHist.* no. 239.

An interesting sidelight is cast on Athenian society by the newly discovered *Dyscolus* of Menander, produced in 317/6 B.C. (?); cf., for instance, W. Schmid, *RhM* 102, 1959, 157 ff.; A. Momigliano, *Riv. stor. it.* 71, 1959, 326, 529-530; S. Perlman, *RF* NS 43, 1965, 271-277.

BIBLIOGRAPHY: Hermann Schaefer, *Der lamische oder hellenische Krieg nach den Quellen dargestellt*, Diss. Giessen 1866; G. De Sanctis, *Contributi alla storia ateniese della guerra lamiaca alla guerra cremonidea* (Studi di Storia antica I), Rome 1893 = *Scritti Minori*, 1966, 249 ff.); F. Granier, *Die makedonische Heeresversammlung* (Münch. Beitr. 13), 1931; Bengtson, *Strat.* (principally on the organisation of Alexander's empire after his death); for the initial phases, cf. F. Schachermeyr, *Alexander in Babylon und die Reichsordnung nach seinem Tode*, 1970. In addition, there are a number of articles in *RE*, dissertations and other studies on individual personalities of the Diadochian era. Stress may be placed on: *Antigonos* (*RE* I, 2406 ff. s.v. no. 3); *Antipatros (RE* I, 2501 ff. s.v. no. 12); *Demetrios* (*RE* IV, 2769 ff. s.v. no. 33); *Eumenes* (*RE* VI, 1083 ff. s.v. no. 4), all by Julius Kaerst; *Kassandros (RE* X, 2293 ff. s.v. no. 2); *Seleukos* (*RE* II A, s.v. 1208 ff. s.v. no. 2), both by F. Stähelin; *Krateros (RE* Suppl. IV, 1038 ff.); *Lysimachos* (*RE* XIV 1 ff.); *Perdikkas* (*RE* XIX 604 ff. s.v. no. 4), all three by F. Geyer; *Ptolemaios I. (RE* XXIII, 1603 ff. s.v. no. 18), by H. Volkmann. In addition the following studies (in order of publication): W. Hünerwadel, *Forsch. z. Gesch. des Königs Lysimachos von Thrakien*, Diss. Zurich 1900; G. B. Possenti, *Il re Lisimaco di Tracia*, Turin-Rome 1901; (the study by Giovanna Saitta, "Lisimaco di Tracia," *Kokalos* 1, 1955, 62 ff., contains little that is new); A. Vezin, *Eumenes von Kardia*, Diss. Tübingen, published Münster i.W. 1907; P. Cloché, "Les dernières années de l'Athénien Phocion," *Rev. hist.* 144, 1923, 161 ff.; 145, 1924, 1 ff., G. Dimitrakos, *Demetrios Poliorketes und Athen*, Diss. Hamburg 1937 (its usefulness is limited); G. Elkeles, *Demetrios der Städtebelagerer*, Diss. Breslau 1941; E. Bayer, *Demetrios Phalereus der Athener* (Tübing. Beitr. z. Altertumswiss. 36), 1942 (reprint, Darmstadt 1969); F. Robert, "La réhabilitation de Phocion et la méthode historique de Plutarque," *CRAI*, 1945, 256 ff.; H. D. Westlake, *Eumenes of Cardia* (Bull. J. Rylands Library 37.1), 1954 = *Essays*, 313-330; P. Briant, *REA* 74, 1972, 32 ff.; 75, 1973, 43 ff., M. Fortina, *Cassandro re di Macedonia*, Turin 1965 (cf. G. Wirth, *Gn.* 38, 1966, 306-308) does not contain anything new; R. M. Errington, "From Babylon to Triparadeisos: 323-320 B.C.," *JHS* 90, 1970, 49 ff.; J. Seibert, *Untersuchungen z. Gesch. Ptolemaios' I.* (Münch. Beitr. 56), 1970; H. Bengtson, *Herrs.*: Ptolemy I, 9 ff.; Seleucus I, 37 ff.; Demetrius Poliorcetes, 63 ff.; P. Briant *Antigone le Borgne* (Ann. L. H. de l'Université de Bescançon, 152) Paris 1973.

THE CONSOLIDATION OF THE HELLENISTIC TERRITORIAL STATES

SOURCES AND BIBLIOGRAPHY: The monumental material to be cited includes the ruins of Demetrias in Thessaly, the city founded by King

Demetrius (F. Stähelin, Ernst Meyer, A. Heidner, *Pagasai und Demetrias*, 1934); and the fortifications of Pleistarcheia, a Diadochian foundation (formerly Heracleia on the Latmus) in Caria (F. Krischen, *Milet* III 2, 49 ff.). The coin portraits are an important source for the iconography of the Diadochians; a survey is given by E. T. Newell, *Royal Greek Portrait Coins*, 1937. On the coinage of Demetrius see E. T. Newell, *The Coinages of Demetrius Poliorcetes*, London 1927.

The running narrative of Diodorus, based principally on Hieronymus of Cardia, breaks off in 302 B.C.; for the period to 280 B.C., only fragents of Book XXI have survived. In addition, there are: Plutarch, *Demetrius* 30-53; *Pyrrhus* 1-12; scattered references in Pausanias (especially I 9-11; 16; 25-26); Justin XVI 1-3; XVII 1-2; Memnon's *City Chronicle of Heracleia on the Pontus* (based on his contemporary, Nymphis of Heracleia), in Jacoby, *FgrHist.* no. 434, with important sidelights on the history of Asia Minor under Lysimachus; a number of *Strategemata* by Polyaenus (for instance, III 7; IV 7; VII 25); and Appian, *Syr.* 59 ff. New information on the *tyrannis* of Lachares in Athens has been furnished by *P. Oxy.* XVII 2082, printed in Jacoby, *FgrHist.* no. 257a; cf. G. De Sanctis, "Lacare," *Scritti Minori*, 1966, 349 ff. (first published in 1928); W. S. Ferguson, "Lachares and Poliorcetes," *CP* 24, 1929, 1 ff.

The epigraphical material has stepped into the breach, the most important of which is assembled in *Syll.* I³ nos. 352 ff.; and in Schmitt, *Staatsv.* III, nos. 451 ff. Important are: the letter of Seleucus I to Miletus (Welles, *RC* no. 5), from the year 288; the letter of Lysimachus to Priene, from the year 286 (?) (Welles, *RC* no. 6); and the alliance between the Aetolians and Boeotians (*Syll.* I³ 366 = *IG* IX 1², 170; cf. Schmitt *Staatsv.* III, no. 463); its date fluctuates between 301 and 281; the most probable date, however, is 291 (see the bibliography in Rostovtzeff, *SEHHW III*, 1316); for 292 (?) Schmitt, *Staatsv.*, no 463 [with extensive bibliography]. It is also difficult to fix the date of the inscription from Aspendus (published by M. Segre, *Aeg.* 14, 1934, 253 ff.). Segre's dating between 301 and 298 is hypothetical (see Rostovtzeff, *SEHHW* III, 1315). And, finally, reference may be made to the grave inscription of an Athenian who probably fell in 287/6 B.C. when Munichia was liberated from Macedonian occupation: N. Kyparissis and W. Peek, *AM* 57, 1932, 146 ff. no. 2.

BIBLIOGRAPHY: In addition to the general histories cited above 532 f.—Beloch, *GG* IV 1, 210 ff.: "Das neue Staatssystem des Ostens," is probably the most important—the following in particular deserve mention: W. W. Tarn, *CAH* VII, Chap. 3: "The New Hellenistic Kingdoms;" P. Roussel, in Glotz-Cohen, *HG* IV 1², 346 ff.: "Démétrios Poliorcète et Lysimaque de Thrace." On Demetrius see G. Dimitrakos, *Demetrios Poliorketes u. Athen*, Diss. Hamburg 1937; G. Elkeles, *Demetrios der Städtebelagerer*, Diss. Breslau 1941; E. Manni, *Demetrio Poliorcete*, Rome 1952 (with an Appendix on chronological problems); on Lysimachus (in addition to the works by Possenti, Hünerwadel, F. Geyer cited above 534): H. Bengtson, *Strat.* I, 209 ff.: "Die Strategen im Reich des Lysimachos." R. A. Hadley, "Royal Propaganda of Seleucus I and Lysimachus," *JHS* 94, 1974, 50 ff.

SPECIALISED STUDIES: P. Treves, "Jeronimo di Cardia e la politica di Demitrio Poliorcete," *RF* NS 10, 1932, 194 ff. On the policy of Demetrius after the battle of Ipsus: Ed. Meyer, *Klio* 5, 1905, 180 ff.; P. Treves, Dopo Ipso, *RF* NS 9, 1931, 73 ff.; 355 ff.; G. De Sanctis, "Atene dopo Ipso e un papiro florentino," *RF* NS 14, 1936, 134 ff.; 253 ff., and also the objections raised by P. Roussel, *Mél. Desrousseaux*, 1937, 429 ff. Further: A. Momigliano, *Riv. stor. ital.* 71, 1959, 534 ff. On the beginnings of Pyrrhus: Lèvêque, *Pyr.* (very detailed). On Ptolemy Ceraunus: Heinen, *Untersuchungen zur Hell.*, 3 ff.

The chronology is very uncertain (see above 531 f.). Important are the lists of Macedonian and Thessalian kings by Porphyry, preserved in the *Chronicle of Eusebius* I (ed. Schoene), 229 f., 241 f., in the Armenian version (ed. Karst) 113 f., 116, 151 ff. It is impossible to attain complete certainty; the most probable system is no doubt that which has been established by W. S. Ferguson, *CP* 19, 1924, 21 ff.

THE WESTERN GREEKS IN THE TIME OF AGATHOCLES AND PYRRHUS

PRINCIPAL SOURCES: Within the framework of his comprehensive History of the West, Timaeus of Tauromenium († c. 250 B.C.) wrote an account of the exploits of Agathocles; it places the negative features in the foreground. Duris of Samos actually dedicated a separate work to the Sicilian ruler Agathocles (Jacoby, *FgrHist.* no. 76 F 16 ff.). Diodorus XIX-XXI is based in part on Duris; cf. A. H. Haake, *De Duride Samio Diodori auctore*, Diss. Bonn 1874; A. F. Roesiger, *De Duride Samio Diodori Siculi et Plutarchi auctore*, Diss. Göttingen 1874; E. Schwartz, *RE* V, 687 s.v. *Diodoros*; 1855 s.v. Duris; T. Orlandi, *PP* 19, 1964, 216 ff.; for a different view see R. Laqueur, *RE* VI A, 1161 ff. s.v. *Timaios*, who attempts to prove that Diodorus used Timaeus. Cf. on the problem of the sources in particular H. Berve, *Die Herrschaft des Agathokles*, SB.M, 1952 no. 5, 4 ff., who correctly opposes Laqueur. It is impossible to determine any certainty on the extent to which Diodorus used Timaeus and Duris. Compared with this, K. Meister, *Die sizilische Gesch. bei Diodor von den Anfängen bis zum Tode des Agathokles. Quellenuntersuchungen zu Buch IV-XXI*, Diss. Munich 1967, has attempted to prove that Diodorus made extensive use of Timaeus. In addition to the sketch by Justin (XXII-XXIII 1 and 2), the views of Polybius concerning Agathocles are valuable, especially IX 23, XII 15 and XV 35.

Accounts of the expedition by Pyrrhus to Italy and Sicily were written by the Greek historians Hieronymus of Cardia, Timaeus and the Epirote Proxenus. The *Memoirs* of Pyrrhus were clearly an important source, whose existence should not be disputed, as is done by F. Jacoby. See on the other hand, V. La Blua, in *Terza Miscellanea greca-romana*, Rome 1971, 1-61. The only extant source in the form of a running narrative is

Plutarch's Life of Pyrrhus (cf. A. B. Nederlof, *Plutarchus Leven van Pyrrhus*, Amsterdam 1940, with a detailed commentary). The Roman accounts based on the annalistic form, must be used with caution (Livy, *epit.* 12-15; Dionysius of Halicarnassus XIX and XX; Appian, *Samn.* 7-12; Cass. Dio IX and X with the *Epitome* of Zonaras VIII 2-6). Diodorus (XXII 6-10) and Justin (XVIII 1-2) have little to offer. On the question of sources B. Niese, "Zur Gesch. des pyrrhischen Krieges," *Hermes* 31, 1896, 481 ff., is still basic; cf. also E. Bickerman, "Apocryphal Correspondence of Pyrrhus," *CP* 42, 1947, 137 ff. (on Dionysius of Halicarnassus XIX 9-10, the correspondence between Pyrrhus and P. Valerius Laevinus). Portrait of Pyrrhus: F. Poulsen, *Ant.* 14, 1938, 137 ff. A survey of the sources is given by Lévêque, *Pyr.*, 15 ff. (in great detail).

Of interest are the bronze tablets (39 in number) found in Locri Epizephyrii, with inscriptions on payments. The editor, A. de Franciscis, takes the "King" to be Pyrrhus (in possession of Locri from 280 to 276 B.C.); see the Journal *Klearchos*, Naples, 1961, 17-41; 1964, 73-95; cf. J. and L. Robert, *REG* 78, 1965, Bull. épigr. no. 494; 79, 1966, no. 508, and now A. de Franciscis, *Stato e società in Locri Epizefiri*, Naples 1972 (cf. E. Meyer, *Gn.* 47, 1975, 665 ff.).

BIBLIOGRAPHY: In addition to the general Histories by A. Holm, *Gesch. Siziliens* II, 1874; E. A. Freeman, *History of Sicily* IV, 1894; Niese, *Mak.* I, 417 ff.; G. De Sanctis, *Storia dei Romani* II, 1907; Ciaceri, *St. MG*; K. J. Beloch, *GG* IV; *Röm. Gesch.*, 1926; S. Gsell, *Hist. ancienne de l'Afrique du Nord* III, 1920; see above all R. Schubert, *Gesch. des Agathokles*, Breslau 1887; H. J. W. Tillyard, *Agathocles*, Cambridge 1908; G. De Sanctis, "Agatocle," in *Scritti Minori*, 1966, 205 ff. (first published in 1909); M. Cary, *CAH* VII, Chap. XIX; M. Müller, *Der Feldzug des Agathokles in Afrika*, Diss. Leipzig 1928; W. Hüttl, *Verfassungsgesch. von Syrakus*, Prague 1929, 128 ff.; L. Wickert, *RE* IV A, 1518 ff. s.v. *Syrakusai*; F. Taeger, in *Rom u. Karthago*, 1943 (ed. J. Vogt), 76 ff.; P. Roussel, in Glotz-Cohen, *HG* IV 1^2, 375 ff.; H. Berve, *Die Herrschaft des Agathokles*, SB.M, 1952, no. 5 (published 1953); G. J. D. Alders, *Tijdschr. voor Geschied.* 68, 1955, 315-366.

A richly documented study on Pyrrhus is available in the work by Lévêque, *Pyr.* G. Nenci, *Pirro. Aspirazioni egemoniche ed equilibrio mediterraneo*, Turin 1953, is aphoristic; see also *idem*, "Il segno regale e la taumaturgia di Pirro," in *Miscellanea di studi alessandrini in memoria di Augusto Rostagni*, Turin 1963, 152-161 (in particular on Plutarch, *Pyrrhus* 3.6). On conditions in Epirus see P. R. Franke, *Alt-Epirus und das Königtum der Molosser*, Diss. Erlangen 1955 (cf. G. Dunst, *DLZ*, 1956, Heft 7-8). Further studies on Pyrrhus: O. Hamburger, *Untersuch. über den pyrrh. Krieg*. Diss. Würzburg 1927; G. N. Cross, *Epirus*, 1932, 115 ff.; F. Sandberger, *Prosopographie zur Gesch. d. Pyrrhos*, Diss. Munich 1970. On the Tarentine War: W. Hoffman, "Der Kampf zwischen Rom und Tarent im Urteil der antiken Überlieferung," *Hermes* 71, 1936, 11 ff.; P. Wuilleumier, *Tarente des origines à la conquête romaine*, Paris 1939, 99 ff. A good survey: F. Sartori, "La Magna Grecia e Roma," *Arch. Stor. per la Calabria e la Lucania* 28, 1959, 137 ff.; cf. also *idem, Problemi di storia costituzionale italiota*, Rome 1953 (with valuable bibliography). Also worth consulting is D. Roussel, *Les Siciliens entre les Romains et les Carthaginois à l'époque de la première guerre punique*, Paris 1970; Bengtson, *Herrs.*, 91 ff. (Pyrrhus).

THE BALANCE OF POWER IN THE HELLENISTIC STATES

SOURCES AND BIBLIOGRAPHY: Due to the fact that the *Histories* of Phylarchus (v.s.p. 527) are almost totally lost, the history of the third century B.C. actually lacks a master key. For isolated events we possess the following primary sources which are of first rate quality: a cuneiform chronicle on events in Babylonia at the time of the First Syrian War (274/3 B.C.), published by Sidney Smith, *Babylonian Historical Texts*, London 1924, 150 ff. (cf. above all C. F. Lehmann-Haupt, in *Epitymbion H. Swoboda dargebracht*, Reichenberg 1927, 142 ff.; W. W. Tarn, *JHS* 46, 1926, 155 ff.; Otto, *Sel.*, 1 ff.; W. W. Tarn, *Hermes* 65, 1930, 446 ff.; W. Otto, *Ph.*, 86, 1931, 400 ff.); the bulletin of Ptolemy III on his Syrian campaign in 246/5 B.C. preserved on a papyrus (U. Wilcken, *Chrestomathie der Papyruskunde* no. 1, cf. Jacoby, *FgrHist.* no. 160; the extensive bibliography has most recently been assembled by M. Holleaux, *Et. ép.* III, 309 n. 7 [the footnote is by the editor, Louis Robert]).

Secondary Sources in the form of a running narrative are also lacking. Justin's *Epitome* of the *Historiae Philippicae* by Pompeius Trogus, Books XXIV-XXIX, is only a slight effusion, superficial, fragmentary and full of errors, but due to the sparseness of other sources it is by no means worthless for the historian. From the *Histories* of Polybius the following come into question: Book I, with the account of the First Punic War, based chiefly on Fabius Pictor and Philinus of Acragas; Book II 37-71, a detailed description of the beginnings of the Achaean League; Books IV and V, a history of the Hellenistic East from 220-216 B.C.; the fragments of Books VII-XVI for the end of the third century B.C. In regard to Rome's relations with the Hellenistic world these fragments are supplemented by passages from the third "Decade" of Livy (Books XXVI ff.), which, as far as events in Hellas and the Orient are concerned, are to be traced back primarily to Polybius (cf. H. Hesselbarth, *Histor.-krit. Untersuch. z. 3. Dek. des Liv.*, 1889; A. Klotz, *RE* XIII, 841 ff.). And, finally, Plutarch's *Vitae* of Aratus, Agis and Cleomenes contain valuable material. A sketch of Seleucid history is to be found in Appian, *Syriake* chs. 52 ff.; cf. E. Gabba, *RALinc.* Vol. 12, 1957, 339-351. Important for the history of civilisation are the *Greek City Portraits* of Heracleides, which at all events belong in the third century B.C. (W. Otto, *GGA*, 1914, 641 n. 2, places them in the period from 261 to 255). Edition (with Commentary) by F. Pfister, *Die Reisebilder des Herakleides*, SB.W 227, 2, 1951.

From the large number of inscriptions (the most important documents are assembled in the collections of W. Dittenberger, in *RC* by C. B. Welles, and in Schmitt, *Staatsv.* III; see on details also the bibliographies in *CAH* VII, and *CAH* VIII), only the most important may be cited here: the inscription, from 267 B.C., found in Denizli, on the Galatian War: (see M. Wörrle," Eire [sic!] neue Inschrift aus der Zeit Antiochos in Denizli," *Türk Ärkeoloji Dergisi* 22,2, 1975, 159-162, cf. *idem*, "Antiochos I., Achaios der Altere und die Galater," *Ch.*, 5, 1975, 59-87); the treaty between Athens and the Aetolian League on legal security (Schmitt, *Staatsv.* III, no. 470); the Attic decree concerning the alliance with Sparta at the beginning of the Chremonideian War (*Syll.* I³ 434/5); the letter of Ptolemy II to Miletus (Welles *RC* no. 14); the inscription from Adulis on the conquests of Ptolemy III in the Third Syrian War (*OGI* I no. 54); the inscription from Canopus, an Egyptian priestly decree from 238 B.C. (*OGI* I no. 56); a Delian inscription of King Antigonus Doson commemorating the battle of Sellasia (*Syll.* I³ no. 518, cf. Holleaux, *Et. ép.* III, 55 f.). See now also J. Crampa, *Labraunda. Swedish Excavations*, Vol. II Part 1. *The Greek Inscriptions*, I 1-12 (Period of Olympichus, 240-220 B.C.), Lund 1969; and Bengtson, *Labr.* Also E. Bernand, *Les inscriptions grecques de Philae I. Epoque ptolémaique*, Paris 1969.

For the history of the Aegean about 242 B.C. the "*Asylia* documents from Cos" are important (published by R. Herzog and G. Klaffenbach, Abh. B, 1952, no. 1; cf. H. Bengtson, *H.* 3, 1954-55, 456 ff. = *KS*, 358 ff.). Of greatest importance, finally, is the treaty of alliance between the Romans and Aetolians from 212 B.C., which G. Klaffenbach discovered on an inscription from Thyrreum: SB.B, 1954, no. 1, also in Schmitt, *Staatsv.* III, no. 536.

Non-Greek inscriptions of historical importance are, *inter al.*, the rock edict issued by Aśoka the ruler of Maurya, on the propaganda of the Buddhist faith in the West (*Corp. Inscr. Ind.* I no. 48); also a second Aśoka inscription (a Greek-Aramaic bilingual) from the region of Candahar (D. Schlumberger, Louis Robert, A. Dupont-Sommer, E. Beneviste, *Journ. Asiatique*, 1950, 1 ff.); and another inscription from the same region (D. Schlumberger, *Acad. des Inscr. et Belles Lettres* 22 May 1964, with valuable contributions by, *inter al.*, L. Robert); as well as the trilingual Pithom decree from the sixth year of Ptolemy IV Philopator, with information on the battle of Raphia, 217 B.C. (H. Gauthier and H. Sottas, *Un décret trilingue en l'honneur de Ptolémée* IV, 1925,; cf. W. Otto, SB.M, 1926, 2. Abh., 18 ff.; *idem, Sel.*, 80 ff.; A. Momigliano, *Aeg.* 10, 1930, 180 ff.; P. Roussel, *REA* 43, 1941, 153 ff.; H. J. Thissen, *Studien zum Raphiadekret.* Meisenheim an der Glan 1966).

The number of monuments discovered during recent generations in systematic excavations is so great that at this point reference to the bibliography in Rostovtzeff's *SEHHW* and to reports in the relevant journals must suffice. Besides Asia Minor, in particular the west coast (Miletus, Ephesus, Priene, Pergamum, Sardis, *et al.*), in Greece itself, Delphi and Delos are the most important. Of interest is the recently discovered fortified camp at Koroni in Attica, which is connected with the Chremonideian War; see E. Vanderpool, J. R. McCredie, A. Steinberg, "Koroni, a Ptolemaic Camp on the East Coast of Attica," *Hesp.* 31,

1962, 26-61; J. R. McCredie, *Fortified Military Camps in Attica* (Hesp. Suppl. 11), Princeton, N.J., 1966. A well oriented survey may be found in Heinen, *Hell.*, 160 ff. Of importance, too, are the coins found in Attica; see J. Varoucha-Christodoulopoulou, *Arch. Ephem.*, 1953-1954 (published 1961), 321-349 (cf. J. and L. Robert, *REG* 75, 1962, no. 128); and "Les témoignages numismatiques sur la guerre chrémonidienne," in *Congresso intern. di Numismatica*, 1961, vol. II: *Atti* (published, Rome 1965), 225-226.

BIBLIOGRAPHY: *CAH* (VII, 850 ff.; VIII, 738 ff.) contains a detailed bibliography on specific investigations and studies; it is supplemented by Rostovtzeff, *SEHHW* III, 1316 ff. From the almost unlimited number of modern works, only the following can here be cited: On the history of the Celtic Invasion into Greece and Asia Minor: F. Stähelin, *Gesch. der kleinasiatischen Galater*, Leipzig ²1907; M. Segre, "La più antica tradizione sull'invasione Gallica in Macedonia e in Grecia (280-279 av. Cr.)," *Historia* [Milan] 1, 1927, 18 ff.; M. Launey, "Un épisode oublié de l'invasion galate en Asie mineure (278/7 av. J. C.)," *REA* 46, 1944, 217 ff. (on *OGI* II 748); P. Moraux, "L'établissement des Galates en Asie Mineure," *Istanbuler Mitt.* 7, 1957, 56 ff. (does not contain much that is new).

On Ptolemaic and Seleucid history of the third century: H. v. Prott, "Das *Enkomion eis ptolemaion* und die Zeitgeschichte," *RhM* 53, 1898, 460 ff.; B. Haussoullier, *Etudes sur l'histoire de Milet et du Didymeion*, Paris 1902; Otto, *Sel.*; W. Otto, "Zu den syrischen Kriegen der Ptolemäer," *Ph.* 86, 1931, 400 ff.; G. Corradi, *Studi ellenistici*, Turin 1929 [a synopsis of earlier specialised studies]; M. Holleaux, *Et. ép.* III (articles on the history of the Ptolemies and the Seleucids); Heinen, *Hell.* [on Ptolemy Ceraunus and the Chremonideian War]; Bengtson, *Herrs.*, 185 ff. [Antiochus III]; the articles in *RE*: U. Wilcken, *RE* I, 2450 ff. s.v. *Antiochos* nos. 21-25; F. Stähelin, *RE* II A, 1235 ff. s.v. *Seleukos* nos. 4 and 5; *idem, RE* XII, 701 ff. s.v. *Laodike* no. 13; and the general works such as: E. Bevan, *The House of Seleucus*, 2 vols., London 1902; A. Bouché-Leclercq, *Histoire des Lagides*, 4 vols., Paris 1903-07; *Histoire des Séleucides*, Paris 1913/14 (2 vols.); the account of Ptolemaic history (L'Egypte ptolémaïque) by P. Jouguet, in *Histoire de la nation égyptienne* III, 1933, by G. Hanotaux; and the *RE* articles on the different Ptolemies: *RE* XXIII, 1645 ff., by H. Volkmann; Bengtson, *Herrs.*, 111 ff. (Ptolemy II and Arsinoe II).

On the history of the Attalids: G. Cardinali, *Il regno di Pergamo*, Rome 1906; A. Ferrabino, "La guerra di Attalo I contro i Galati e Antioco Ierace," *Atti Acc. di Torino* 48, 1912/13, 707 ff.; B. Bar-Kochva, *On the Sources and Chronology of Antiochus' Battle Against the Galatians* (Proceed. of the Cambridge Philological Society 199), 1973, 1 ff. U. Wilcken, *RE* II, 2159 ff. s.v. *Attalos* (I) no. 9; W. Hoffmann, *RE* XIX, 2157 ff. s.v. *Philetairos*; E. V. Hansen, *The Attalids of Pergamon*, Ithaca N.Y. 1947 (a work which is unfortunately not of the very highest quality) (cf. now, the second edition, 1972). R. B. McShane, *The Foreign Policy of the Attalids of Pergamum*, (Illinois Studies in the Social Sciences, 53), 1964, is of no importance. Further bibliography in Rostovtzeff, *SEHHW* III, 1448 ff.

On the history of the Hellenistic East: Tarn, *Bact.* (^{2}1951, with a number of Addenda); cf. H. Bengtson, *HZ* 166, 1942, 336 ff.; and above all Altheim, *As.* (cf. E. Bickerman, *Bibliotheca Orientalis*, 1949, 68 ff.); H. G. Rawlinson, *Bactria. The History of a Forgotten Empire*, New York 1969 [ed. 1, London 1912]. On the history of the Parthian Kingdom: N. C. Debevoise, *A Political History of Parthia*, Chicago 1938 (cf. H. Bengtson, *WG*, 1939, 182 f. = *KS*, 260); E. Bickerman, "Notes on Seleucid and Parthian Chronology," *Berytus* 8, 1944, 73 ff.; in addition the numerous studies by J. Wolski, of which only a few can be cited here: *L'effondrement de la domination des Séleucides en Iran au IIIe siècle av. J.-C.*, Bull. Inst. Acad. Polon., Hist. et Phil., Suppl. 5, Krakau 1947; "L'état parthe des Arsacides," *Palaeologia* (Osaka) 7, 1959, 91-98; "L'historicité d'Arsace Ier," *Historia* 8, 1959, 222-238; "Arsace II et la généalogie des premiers Arsacides," *H.* 11, 1962, 138-145; "Aufbau und Entwicklung des parthischen Staates," in *Neue Beiträge zur Gesch. der Alten Welt*, Bd. I, Berlin, Akademie-Verlag 1964, 379-388; "Les Achéménides et les Arsacides. Contribution à l'histoire de la formation des traditions iraniennes," *Syria* 43, 1966, 65-89; "Der Zusammenbruch der Seleukidenherrschaft im Iran im 3. Jh. v. Chr.," in *Der Hellenismus in Mittelasien*, Darmstadt 1969, 188-254; "Die Iranier und das graekobaktrische Königreich," in *Der Hellenismus in Mittelasien*, Darmstadt 1969, 255-274; "Widerstandsbewegungen gegen die Makedonenherrschaft im Orient," *Klio* 51, 1969, 207-215. Important is E. Bickermann, "The Parthian Ostracon No. 1760 from Nisa," *Bibl. Orient.* 1966, 15 ff. [on the beginnings of the Parthian kingdom]. H. Bengston, *Hist. Jahrb.* 74, 1955, 26 ff. = *KS*, 346 ff. [on some causes of the decline of the Hellenistic world].

On the history of the Antigonids: Tarn, *Antig.*, a work which is still basic today (cf. W. Kolbe, *GGA*, 1916, 433 ff.); W. Fellmann, *Antigonos Gonatas, König der Makedonen, und die griech. Staaten*, Diss. Würzburg 1930 (contains little that is new); C. F. Edson, Jr., "The Antigonids, Heracles and Beroea," *HSCP* 45, 1934, 213 ff. Bengtson, *Herrs.*, 137 ff. (Antigonus Gonatas). On Antigonus Doson: W. Bettingen, *König Antigonos Doson von Makedonien (229-220 v. Chr.)*, Diss. Jena 1912; P. Treves, "Studi su Antigono Dosone," *Ath.* NS 12, 1934, 381 ff.; 13, 1935, 22 ff.; Maria Teresa Piraino, *Antigono Dosone re di Macedonia*, Palermo 1954; K.-W. Welwei, "Das makedonische Herrschaftssystem in Griechenland und die Politik des Antigonos Doson," *RhM* 110, 1967, 306-314; Bengtson, *Labr.* On Demetrius II: P. Treves, "La tradizione politica degli Antigonidi e l'opera di Demetrio II," *RALinc.* 8, 1932, 168 ff. On Philip V: Walbank, *Phil. V* (with excellent bibliography); cf. W. W. Tarn, *JRS* 31, 1941, 172 f.; A. Aymard, *REA* 48, 1946, 107 ff. On Thessaly under Macedonian rule: C. Habicht, "Epigraphische Zeugnisse zur Geschichte Thessaliens unter der makedonischen Herrschaft," *Archaia Makedonia* 1970, 265-279; cf. also IG X 2,1, 1972, and C. Habicht, *Gn.* 46, 1974, 487-

488. The articles in *RE* on Antigonus Gonatas and Antigonus Doson (*RE* I, 2413 ff. s.v. nos. 4 and 5), as well as those on Demetrius II and Demetrius the "Handsome" (*RE* IV, 2792 ff. s.v. nos. 34 and 35), all by Julius Kaerst, have been rendered out of date by more recent studies. Still useful, on the other hand, however, are the articles *Philippos* (*RE* XIX, s.v. no. 10 and *Makedonia* (*RE* XIV, 740 ff.), by F. Geyer. On the Chremonideian War: Heinen, *Hell.*

On the history of Greece in the third century: Ferguson, *Ath.* (cf. W. Otto, *GGA*, 1914, 633 ff.). Flacelière, *Ait.* (cf. G. Klaffenbach, *Klio* 32, 1939, 189 ff.); Feyel, *Pol.*; P. Guillon, *Bases et colonnes de trépieds retrouvées au Ptoion*, and: *Les trépieds du Ptoion*, Paris 1943 [on the works by Feyel and Guillon see A. Aymard, *Rev. hist.* 196, 1946, 287 ff.]; A. G. Roos, *Athene van Alexander den Grooten tot het midden der derde eeuw v. Chr.* (Med. Niederl. Ak. d. Wiss. 8,2), Amsterdam 1945. On the history of the Achaean League: F. W. Walbank, *Aratos of Sicyon*, Cambridge 1933; W. P. Theunissen, *Ar.*, with copious bibliography (XIII ff.); see also H. Chantraine, "Der Beginn der jüngeren achäischen Bundesprägung," *Ch.* 2, 1972, 175 ff. On Crete: H.v. Effenterre, *La Créte et le monde grec de Platon à Polybe*, Paris 1948. On Crete in the Hellenistic period: E. I. Mikrojannakis, *He Krete kata tous Hellenistikous chronous*, Athens, 1967.

Basic for the early connections between Rome and the Hellenistic world is: Holleaux, *Rome*; and, as supplementary, the debate between Holleaux and T. Walek-Czernecki: "La politique rom. en Grèce et dans l'Orient hellénistique au IIIe siècle," *Et. ép.* IV, 26 ff. (a reply to Walek's article in *Rev. phil.* 49, 1925, 28 ff.; 118 ff.); H. H. Schmitt, *Rom und Rhodos* (Münch. Beitr., 40), Munich 1957 (debate with Holleaux, especially in regard to the treaty between Rome and Rhodes from the end of the fourth century).

1. On the regulating of the empire carried out at Babylon, the details of which are highly controversial, see the detailed discussion by Bengtson, *Strat.* I, 63 ff.; on the extensive bibliography, *ibid.*, 11 n. 2; as well as in Glotz-Cohen, *HG* IV 1^2, 258 n. The more recent studies like that of M. J. Fontana, *Atti Acc. Palermo*, ser. 4, vol. 18, 1957/58, parte 2 (published 1960), and that of G. Vitucci, in *Miscell. di Studi in memoria di A. Rostagni*, Turin 1963, 63 ff., do not take us significantly further; still the best is K. Rosen, *Acta Classica* (Capetown) 10, 1968, 95-110, but even here there is much that lacks probability. F. Schachermeyr's interpretations (*Alexander in Babylon und die Reichsordnung nach seinem Tode*) too do not mark any progress.

2. Kornemann, *Fr.*, 77 ff.; cf. also H. Strasburger, *RE* XVIII, 177 ff. s.v. no. 5.

3. M. Britschkoff, *Uber Freiheitserklärungen der Machthaber an Griechenland*, Diss. Berlin [typewritten], 1923; A. Heuss, *Hermes* 73, 1938, 133 ff.

4. Cf. Beloch, *GG* IV 1, 31 f.; 67.

5. Cf. E. Lepore, Leostene e le origini della guerra lamiaca, *PP* 10, 1955, 161 ff.

6. On the coalition of the Greeks see Diod. XVIII 11.1-2; Paus. I 25.4; cf. G. Glotz-Cohen, *HG* IV 1^2, 268 f.; now also Schmitt, *Staatsv.* III, no. 413.

7. Cf. *IG* II/III^2 505; 506; Plut., *Phocion* 23.

8. Cf. Schmitt, *Staatsv.* III, no. 415.

9. On the reforms in Athens see Ferguson, *Ath.*, 22 ff.; Bengtson, *Strat.* I, 51 f., including earlier bibliography.

10. Cf. Diod. XVIII 19-21; Arrian, *Diad.* 16-19; the so-called Magna Charta of Cyrene

(*SEG* IX 1) is to be dated in 322/1 B.C. or not until 312/11 or 308/7 B.C. (On the basis of prosopographical researches by A. Laronde, *REG* 85, 1972, XIII f.)

11. On the plenary powers of Eumenes see Bengtson, *Strat.* I, 171 ff.

12. Diod. XVIII 55 f.; cf. Bengtson, *Strat.* I, 84 ff. On Polyperchon's operations in the Peloponnesus in 318 B.C. see Diod. XVIII 69 ff. and M. Guarducci, "Un decreto di Argo ritrovato a Pallantion," *Ann. Scuola Arch. di Atene* 3-4, 1941-43 (published 1948), 141 ff. Cf. *SEG* XI no. 1084.

13. Phocion had been sentenced to death in 318 B.C. by the Athenians; he, who was elected strategos 25 times in Athens, has been called the "last old man of honour in Athens" (J. Bernays); on Phocion see the work cited above 534 by P. Cloché 36 ff.; cf. Th. Lenschau, *RE* XX, 458 ff., esp. 469 ff.

14. On the date, P. Roussel, *Rev. arch.*, 1941, II 220 ff. On the settlement with Athens see Schmitt, *Staatsv.* III, no. 421.

15. Ferguson, *Ath.*, 38 ff., cf. W. Otto, *GGA*, 1914, 643 f.; on the law issued by Demetrius against luxury in connection with funerals see J. Kirchner, *Ant.* 15, 1939, 93 ff.; S. Dow. "Demetrios of Phaleron and his Lawgiving," *Hesp.* 12, 1943, 144 ff., but cf. also A. Aymard, *REA* 48, 1946, 305 f.

16. Justin XIV 5.1 ff.; cf. Bengtson, *Strat.* I, 87 f.

17. Diod. XIX 35 f., 49-51; Justin XIV 6.1-12; Paus. IX 7.2 (a stoning of Olympias). The Vienna Papyrus (*Mél. G. Glotz* I, 1932, 315 ff.) is *not* related to the death of Olympias; see M. Segre, *RF* NS 11, 1933, 225 f.; H. Fuhrmann, *AfP* 11, 1935, 107 ff. Cf. also Ch. Edson, "The Tomb of Olympias," *Hesp.* 18, 1949, 86 ff. (on an inscription from Makrigialos).

18. Heracles son of Alexander by Barsine was regarded as illegitimate and did not come into question as heir.

19. Diod. XIX 61.3; cf. Bengtson, *Strat.* I, 115 f.

20. See Schmitt, *Staatsv.* III, no. 433.

21. This emerges from the Babylonian Diadochian Chronicle; cf. W. Otto, SB.M, 1925, Schlussheft 12; A. Momigliano, *RF* NS 10, 1932, 478 ff.; A. Neppi-Modona, *Ath.* NS 11, 1933, 3 ff.

22. The opposite view, held by Beloch, *GG* IV 1, 133, IV 2, 618, is untenable; cf. Bengtson, *Strat.* I, 118 f. The most important source is the inscription from Scepsis, in Welles, *RC* no. 1. Cf. R. H. Simpson, *JHS* 74, 1954, 25 ff.; see now also Schmitt, *Staatsv.* III, no. 428.

23. U. Köhler, *Das asiatische Reich des Antigonos*, SB.B, 1898, 824 ff.; Bengtson, *Strat.* I, 197 ff.; 207 ff.

24. On the policy towards Greece by Ptolemy I, cf. G. Moser, *Unters. über die Politik Ptolemaios' I. in Griechenland*, Diss. Leipzig 1914; W. Kolbe, *Hermes* 51, 1916, 530 ff.; Bengtson, *Strat.* I, 142 ff.; also Schmitt, *Staatsv.* III, no. 434.

25. F. Geyer, *RE* XIV, 6 ff.; on the economic importance of Lysimachus' empire see Rostovtzeff, *SEHHW* I, 161; III 1351.

26. On Sandrocottus see above all L. de la Vallée-Poussin, *L'Inde aux temps des Mauryas*, Paris 1930, 49 f.; Tarn, *Bact.*, 46 f., and the Index s.v. Chandragupta; B. Breloer, *Alexanders Bund mit Poros*, 1941, 166 ff.

27. Thus W. W. Tarn, *CAH* VI, 503. On the peace between Seleucus and Sandrocottus see in particular Schmitt, *Staatsv.* III, no. 441; L. Skurzak, *Eos* 54, 1964, 225-229.

28. On the honours conferred on Demetrius in Athens see K. Scott, "The Deification of Demetrius Poliorcetes," *AJP* 49, 1928, 137 ff.; 217 ff.; G. Dimitrakos, *Demetrios Poliorketes und Athen*, Diss. Hamburg 1937, 31 ff.; cf. A. Wilhelm, "Ein Gedicht zu Ehren der Könige Antigonos und Demetrios" (IG II^2 3424), *Arch. Ephem.*, 1937, 203 ff. See the concise discussion by Nilsson, *Gr. Rel.* II, 150 f.; Habicht, *Gott.*, 44 ff.

29. Diod. XX 49 ff.; Plut., *Demet.* 16; Polyaenus IV 7.7; *Marm. Par. ep.* 122. It is disputed whether the *Nike* of Samothrace is a copy of the victory monument to Demetrius; the bibliography on this subject may be found in Glotz Cohen, *HG* IV 1^2, 333 n. 88.

30. Details in Kaerst, *GH* II^2, 68 f., and in Glotz-Cohen, *HG* IV 1^2, 333.

31. Plut., *Demet.* 18. Later Seleucus must, however, have reckoned his reign from 1 October 312 B.C., the beginning of the Macedonian year, after his return to Babylon (August 312 B.C.); the Babylonians, however, did not begin reckoning his regnal years until

the first of Nisan (April 1) 311 B.C., the Babylonian New Year. By reason of the fact that Antiochus I, the successor of Seleucus, continued the reckoning, the Seleucus era became the Seleucid period (with different "epochs"); see E. Bickerman, *Chronology*, 1968, 71; *Berytus* 8, 1944, 73 ff. (with new theories); cf. Bengtson, *Einf.*, 31, cf. *idem*, *Anc.*, *Hist.*, 31.

32. Besides the other sources (in particular Diod. XX 81 ff.; 91 ff.; Plut., *Demet.* 21 f.), there is a papyrus in the Ionian dialect; it has been published by Fr. Frhr. Hiller von Gaertringen, SB.B, 1918, 752 ff. (also in Bilabel, *P. Kleinform*, 1923, no. 8).

33. On the peace and the treaty between Antigonus Monophthalmus and Rhodes see Schmitt, *Staatsv.* III, no. 442.

34. The chief source is the so-called federal stele of Epidaurus, *IG* IV^{2}1, 68 (cf. Plut., *Demet.* 25). Important studies on it: U. Wilcken, SB.B, 1922, 122 ff.; 1927, 277 ff.; 1929, 303 f.; W. W. Tarn. *JHS* 42, 1922, 198 ff.; A. Wilhelm, *Anz. W*, 1922, no. XIII-XIV 52 ff.; M. Cary, *CQ* 17, 1923, 137 ff.; P. Roussel, *Rev. arch.*, 1923, I 117 ff.; F. Schehl, *Öst. Jh.* 27, 1932, 118 f.; J.A.O. Larsen, *CP* 20, 1925, 313 ff.; 21, 1926, 52 ff.; 27, 1932, 395 ff.; Bengtson, *Strat.* I, 154 ff.; Hampl, *Staatsv.*, 113 ff.; bibliography in *IG* IV^{2}1, 68, also in Rostovtzeff, *SEHHW* III, 1315 n. 6, and Balogh, *Ref.*, 107 n. 126 [by F. Heichelheim]. The date (spring 302 B.C.) has been established by Louis Robert in his excellent study, "Adeimantos et la ligue de Corinthe. Sur une inscription de Delphes," *Hel.* 2, 1946, 15 ff. (cf. G. Daux, in *Eis Mnemen G.P. Oikonomou*, Athens 1955, 245 ff.). On the inscription from the Athenian Agora published by W. S. Ferguson, *Hesp.* 17, 1948, 112 ff., see the critical remarks by J. and L. Robert, *REG* 62, 1949, Bull. épigr. no. 51. See now also Schmitt, *Staatsv.* III, no. 446 (with copious bibliography).

35. See Schmitt, *Staatsv.* III, no. 448.

36. W. W. Tarn, *CR* 40, 1926, 13 ff. (on the basis of the cuneiform tablet BM S † 1881 [76-11-17], published by Schaumberger, *Orientalia* NS 2, 1933, 103; *Analecta Orientalia* 6, 1933, 4 ff.; cf. Bengtson, *Strat.* I, 112.

37. On the location see E. Honigmann, *Byzantion* 10, 1935, 647 ff. (Ipsus = Sipsin, 6 miles north of Afyon-Karahissar), cf. L. Robert, *Hel.* 7, 1949, 217.

38. Arguments against the high figures for the elephants in W. W. Tarn, *JHS* 60, 1940, 84 ff.

39. On the empire of Pleistarchus see Plut., *Demet.* 31, cf. Ernst Meyer, *Die Grenzen der hellenistischen Staaten in Kleinasien*, 1925, 28 f.; on the other hand, L. Robert, "La sanctuaire de Sinuri près de Mylasa. Iere partie: Les inscript. grecques." *Mém. Inst. franç. de Stamboul* 7, 1945, no. 44, 55 ff. L. Robert is of the view that Pleistarchus did not obtain Heracleia on the Latmus (Pleistarcheia) and environs (by no means *all* Caria) until he had lost Cilicia to Demetrius. The Peripatetic Diocles of Carystus had connections with Pleistarchus, dedicating one of his works to him; see W. Jaeger, Abh.B, 1938, no. 3, 14.

40. See *Suda s.v. basileia* § 2 (= Chrysippus of Soli). Cf. Kaerst, *Mon.*, 59 ff.; Tarn, *Antig.*, 253 ff.; Rostovtzeff, *SEHHW* III, 1346 f.

41. Rostovtzeff, *SEHHW* I, 144 f.; III 1344 f.

42. Cf. M. Holleaux, *Et. ép.* III, 15 ff.

43. Bengtson, *Strat.* I, 197 ff.

44. See Bengtson, *Strat.* I, 176 ff.

45. A. Heuss, *Stadt und Herrscher des Hellenismus in ihren Staats- und völkerrechtl. Beziehungen*, Klio Beih. 39, 1937, is historically unsatisfactory, and the treatment of the inscriptions is in many instances inadequate; cf. H. Bengtson, *DLZ*, 1939, 561 ff.; further, A. Heuss, "Antigonos Monophthalmos und die griech. Städte," *Hermes* 73, 1938, 133-194 (the explanations require correction). Further bibliography in Rostovtzeff, *SEHHW* III, 1342; 1347; cf. C. Préaux, *Recueil de la Société J. Bodin* 6, 1954, 69 ff.; 7, 1956, 89 ff., and Ehrenberg, *Staat*, 230 ff.; 336 = *State*, 190 ff.; 284 ff.; R. H. Simpson, "Antigonus the One-Eyed and the Greeks," *H.* 8, 1959, 385 ff.

46. J. Kromayer, "Die kulturelle und politische Entwicklung des ausgehenden Griechentums—Stadtrepublik und monarchischer Flächenstaat," *HZ* 150, 1933, 10 ff. (the quotation, 14).

47. Particularly instructive on this point are the Ephesian decrees from the end of the fourth and the beginning of the third centuries B.C., published by J. Keil, *Öst Jh.* 16, 1913,

231 ff. They show Ephesus respectively on the side of Perdiccas, Antipater, Demetrius, Ptolemy and finally Lysimachus!

48. U. Kahrstedt, *RE* IV A, 1440 ff. s.v. *Synoikismos*; V. Tscherikower, *Die hellenist. Städtegründungen*, 1926, 154 ff.; Rostovtzeff, *SEHHW* I, 155; III 1348 f.

49. For the Asia Minor *Koina* under Alexander cf. H. Bengtson, *Ph.* 92, 1937, 139 ff., and Th. Lenschau, *Klio* 33, 1940, 220 ff.; further, in general, E. Kornemann, *RE* Suppl IV, 1918 ff. s.v. *koinon*; on the Island League founded by Antigonus Monophthalmus in 315 B.C., W. König, *Der Bund der Nesioten*, Diss. Halle 1910; A. Guggenmos, *Die Gesch. d. Nesiotenbundes bis zur Mitte des 3. Jahrh v. Chr.*, Diss. Würzburg 1929; cf. the bibliography cited by Rostovtzeff, *SEHHW* III 1348; also I. L. Merker, *H.* 19, 1970, 141 ff.

50. E. Kornemann, "Zur Politik der ersten Nachfolger Alexanders d. Gr.," *Vergangenheit und Gegenwart* 16, 1926, 333 ff.

51. U. Wilcken, *Grundz. d. Papyruskunde*, 1912, 19. The most important new creation in the religious sphere was the god Sarapis, emerging from Osiris-Apis or Osorapis in Memphis as the work of Ptolemy I already at the time when he was satrap; on the problem of Sarapis see the penetrating discussion by U. Wilcken, *UPZ* I, 1922, 7 ff., who has correctly stressed the Egyptian origin of the god (as opposed to C. F. Lehmann-Haupt, who regarded Sarapis as originally a Babylonian deity); see also J. N. Stambaugh, *Sarapis under the Early Ptolemies*, London 1972. Nilsson, *Gr. Rel.* II, 156 f., sees the creation of Sarapis in conjunction with the policy of Ptolemy I towards Greece. New ideas were advanced by C. B. Welles, "The Discovery of Sarapis and the Foundation of Alexandria," *H.* 11, 1962, 271 ff. The Sarapis cult, he suggests, was founded by Alexander, but this is not probable. The spot where the Sarapeum stood was rediscovered by A. Rowe: cf. A. Rowe, *The Discovery of the Famous Temple and Enclosure of Sarapis at Alexandria*, Suppl. to Annales de Service des Antiquités de l'Egypte, Cahier no. 2, 1946; cf. P. Jouguet, "Les dépôts de fondation du temple de Sarapis à Alexandrie," *CRAI*, 1946, 680 ff., and: "Les premiers Ptolémées et l'hellénisation de Sarapis," *Hommages à J. Bidez et F. Cumont, Latomus* 2, 1949, 159 ff. Our sources furnish no evidence for the view advocated by E. Kornemann, "Die Satrapenpolitik des ersten Lagiden," in *Raccolta di scritti in onore di G. Lumbroso*, Milan 1925, 235 ff., that there was a complete reversal of policy under Ptolemy I, namely from a friendly attitude towards the indigenous population to a "rigid Macedonian policy;" cf. P. Jouguet, "La politique intérieure du premier Ptolémée," *Bull. de l'Inst. fr. d'arch. or.* 30, 1931, 513 ff. Highly valuable is W. Swinnen, "Sur la politique religieuse de Ptolémée Ier," in *Bibliothèque des centres d'études superieures spécialisés*, Paris 1973, 115-133, who argues that Ptolemy I attempted to achieve a *modus vivendi* between the Greeks and the native population.

52. Evidence for the date (intercalary month Artemisios) derives from the anonymous Olympiad-Chronicle (the so-called Lachares Papyrus), in Jacoby, *FgrHist.* no. 257a § 3; for the year 298 B.C.: W. S. Ferguson, *CP* 24, 1929, 1 ff.; for 297 B.C.: G. De Sanctis, *Scritti Minori*, 1966, 349 ff. (first published 1928); *RF* NS 14, 1936, 261 ff.; P. Roussel, in Glotz-Cohen, *HG* IV 1^2, 351 ff.

53. On Thessalonica see M. Vickers, *JHS* 92, 1972, 156 ff.

54. Opposed to Droysen, *GH* II 2, 1, 252, see in particular F. Stähelin, *RE* X, 2312.

55. Hieronymus (= Euseb. II 118 f. ed. Schoene) relates, for the year 296 B.C.—the Armenian version of Eusebius (ed. Karst 199) for the year 297 B.C.—a devastation of Samaria by Demetrius; cf. Beloch, *GG* IV 1, 214; also G. Elkeles, *Demetrios der Städtebelagerer*, Diss. Breslau 1941, 37 f.

56. On Lachares see the bibliography cited above n. 52; further, P. Roussel, in Glotz-Cohen, *HG* IV 1^2, 351 ff.

57. Schmitt, *Staatsv.* III, no. 458.

58. On events in Macedonia: Plut., *Demet.* 36 f.; *Pyrrhus* 6 f.; Justin XVI 1; the accounts of Diodorus (XXI 7), Pausanias (IX 7.3), and Eusebius (I 231) are not free of errors. A short survey in F. Geyer, *RE* XIV, 736 f. s.v. *Makedonia*; P. Roussel, Glotz-Cohen, *HG* IV 1^2, 365 f. See also Schmitt, *Staatsv.* III, no. 460.

59. W. W, Tarn, *CAH* VII, 80.

60. Beloch, *GG* IV 1, disputes the historicity of the marriage (cf. Plut., *Pyrrhus* 10.7). But for an opposing view cf., for instance, Lévêque, *Pyr.*, 139 ff.; 677 ff. Demetrius was at the

time married to Phila the daughter of Antipater; but polygamy is otherwise attested for the first generations of the successors. See also J. Seibert, *Histor. Beitr. zu den dynastischen Verbindungen*, 1967, 30.

61. Diod. XXI 15.

62. See C. F. Edson, Jr., "The Antigonids, Heracles and Beroea," *HSCP* 45, 1934, 236 ff.

63. Cf. *Syll.* I[3] 367; 386; 387; Plut., *Demet.* 46; Paus. I 26.1; 29.13; also the inscription referred to above 535, published by Kyparissis and Peek, *AM* 57, 1932, 146 ff. Like the overthrow of Demetrius in Macedonia, the liberation of Athens fell in the year of the archonship of Diocles, that is, probably in 288/7 B.C.; the latest advocate is M. Chambers, *AJP* 75, 1954, 393; other scholars admittedly place Diocles in 286/5 B.C.; cf. for instance, A. Momigliano, *Riv. stor. it.* 71, 1959, 535 f. (including bibliography).

64. On the paean composed in honour of Demetrius (Duris, in Athenaeus VI 253 d) see O. Weinreich, *NJb*, 1926, 646 ff.; K. Scott, AJP 49, 1928, 229 ff.; V. Ehrenberg, *Ant.* 7, 1931, 279 ff.; H. Kleinknecht, *ARW* 34, 1937, 294 ff.

65. W. W. Tarn's theory (*CAH* VII, 88), that Demetrius wanted to establish a new empire in Seleucus' rear, that is, in the Iranian satrapy, as Seleucus had once done under Antigonus, is difficult to substantiate.

66. Berve, *GG* II, 1933, 236 [altered in the second edition, 249]. See, on the other hand, Beloch, *GG* IV 1, 237 f.

67. A. Andreades, "L'administration financière du roi Lysimaque," *Mél. P. Thomas*, Bruges 1930, 6 ff.; on the general administration of the empire: Bengtson, *Strat.* I, 209 ff.

68. A. Rehm, *Milet* III 3 no. 138; cf. A. Andreades, *Viertelj.-Schr. f. Soz. u. Wirtsch.-gesch.* 20, 1928, 296 ff.; cf. Bengtson, *Strat.* I, 211 n. 4.

69. On the location see the funerary inscription of a Bithynian officer, published by G. Mendel, *BCH* 24, 1900, 380; cf. P. Roussel, in Glotz-Cohen, *HG* IV 1[2], 372 n. 86 (with additional bibliography).

70. The cuneiform inscription from Borsippa of the year 268 B.C. (Weissbach, *Keilinschr. d. Achämen.* 132 f. Kol. I f 4.), in which Seleucus is called "King, the Macedonian (sic!), King of Babylon," may not indeed be used as evidence in this instance; see F. Stählin, *RE* II A, 1226; Hampl, *KM*, 19; A. Aymard, *Mél. F. de Visscher* III, 1950, 67.

71. See in particular Heinen, *Hell.*, 3 ff.

72. The city was discovered by Bulgarian archaeologists, in excavations conducted by D. P. Dimitrov. A final report is lacking. See H. Bengtson, *H.* 11, 1962, 18 ff. = *KS*, 377 f.

73. See W. Hoffman, *Rom und die griechische Welt im 4. Jahrh.*, Ph., Suppl. 37,1, 1934.

74. On Cleonymus see P. Meloni, *Giorn. ital. di fil.* [Naples] 3, 1950, 103 ff.

75. *Marm. Par.* [*FgrHist.* no. 239], B. 12; Diod. XIX 6-9; Justin XXII 2.5-12; Polyaenus V 3.8; cf. H. Berve, *Die Herrschaft des Agathokles*, SB.M, 1952, no. 5, 29 ff.

76. Diod. XIX 70 f.; cf. Schmitt, *Staatsv.* III, no. 424.

77. See Schmitt, *Staatsv.* III, no. 432.

78. H. Berve, *RE* XVIII, 632 ff.; V. Ehrenberg, "Ophellas von Kyrene," in *Polis und Imperium*, Stuttgart 1965, 539 ff. (first published in 1938); A. Laronde, *Rev hist.* 245, 1971, 297-306.

79. On the treaty concluded between his army in Africa and the Carthaginians see Schmitt, *Staatsv.* III, no. 436.

80. R. van Compernolle, *Rev. belge de phil. et d'hist.* 32, 1954, no. 2; see now also Schmitt, *Staatsv.* III, no. 437.

81. Cf. Diod. XX 54.1; but cf. Beloch, *GG* IV 2, 252; and already B. Niese, *RE* I, 755 s.v. *Agathokles* no. 15.

82. See Schmitt, *Staatsv.* III, no. 457.

83. Thus Callias, the historian of Agathocles, was one of the first to write about the Romans: *FgrHist.* 564, 5.

84. Cf. Beloch, *GG* IV 1, 208 ff.; M. Cary, *CAH* VII, 636.

85. For instance, Diod. XIX 107.4 f.; XX 71 (on the treatment of Gela and Segesta).

86. On Pyrrhus' position in Epirus see P. R. Franke, *Alt-Epirus und das Königtum der Molosser*, Diss. Erlangen 1955, 55 ff.

87. Justin XVII 2.14; the figures given in this passage cannot be reconciled with those in Plut., *Pyrrhus* 15; on the other hand, there is no reason to regard them as invented.

88. Beloch, *GG* IV 1, 541 ff.; L. Wickert, *RE* IV A, 1523 ff. s.v. *Syrakusai.*

89. Zon. VIII 2; cf. E. Bickerman, *CP* 42, 1947, 145.

90. Cf. *Syll.* I[3] 392, the inscription of the votive offering of Pyrrhus to Zeus of Dodona.

91. A number of modern scholars have, on the initiative of B. Niese, *Hermes* 31, 1895, 465 ff., been incorrect in denying the negotiations after Heracleia (cf., for instance, Beloch, *GG* IV 1, 551 n. 1; E. Kornemann, *Röm. Gesch.* I 160, *et al.*). In contrast to this, W. Judeich, *Klio* 20, 1926, 11 ff., has shown that peace negotiations must be reckoned with on *two* different occasions: in 280 B.C. (after Heracleia), and in 279 B.C. (after Ausculum); cf. also Lévêque, *Pyr.*, 341 ff.; 359 ff.; see also Schmitt, *Staatsv.* III, no. 467.

92. E. T. Salmon, *A Topographical Study of the Battle of Ausculum*, Papers of the British School at Rome XII, 1932, 45 ff.; a further discussion by P. Lévêque, *op. cit.*, 380 ff.

93. The text in Polyb. III 25; the date by Polybius "according to the crossing of Pyrrhus" can only be taken as approximate. The treaty will have been concluded in 279/8 B.C., thus too, K. Meister, *PP* 26, 1971, 196-201. Of a different opinion is G. Nenci, *H.* 7, 1958, 263 ff. Cf. also Schmitt, *Staatsv.* III, no. 466.

94. T. Frank, *CAH* VII, 649.

95. Polyb. VII 4.5; Justin XXIII 3.2: *rex Siciliae sicut Epiri appellatur.* Cf. H. Berve, "Das Königtum des Pyrrhos in Sizilien," *Festschr. f. B. Schweitzer*, 1955, 272 ff.; on the *regnum Italiae* in Justin *op. cit.*, § 3, see H. Bengtson, *WG* 18, 1958, 5 ff. = *KS*, 120 ff.

96. These are the two points from which approximately 30 years later Hamilcar Barca kept the Romans in Sicily so tenaciously on the stretch.

97. J. A. Vartsos, "Osservazioni sulla campagna di Pirro in Sicilia," *Kokalos* 16, 1970, 89 ff.

98. Livy transfers the battle to the *Arusini campi* in Lucania (thus also Beloch, *GG* IV 1, 557 with n.1); it is possible that there were *two* encounters. Another solution (regarding the name Calor as interchangeable for the two rivers, at Beneventum and in Lucania) has been suggested by P. Lévêque, *Pyr.*, 519.

99. Cf. also Schmitt, *Staatsv.* III, no. 475.

100. According to, *inter al.*, Th. Mommsen and A. Piganiol (*Mél. F. de Visscher* IV, 1950, 344 n.15), *pistis* would in this instance = *fides.*

101. A. Graf Schenk von Stauffenberg, *König Hieron II. von Syrakus*, Stuttgart 1933; H. Berve, *Hieron II.* Abh. Bay. [cf. 326. n. 158] NF 47, Munich 1959, whose dating is accepted here. Hieron did not assume the royal title until after the victory over the Mamertines at the Longanus river (269 BC).

102. Cf. *Syll.* I[3] no. 398 (from Cos); incorrect is, for instance, Beloch, *GG* **IV 2, 487 ff.** The original founding of the Delphic *Soteria* by the Amphictyons probably falls in 278 B.C., but the *Soteria* festivals were reorganised in the year of the Attic archon Polyeuctus—in the forties of the third century. Besides the annual *Soteria* festivals celebrated from 278 B.C. on, there appears to have been a penteteric *Soteria* since the archonship of Polyeuctus. The much disputed problem concerning the date of Polyeuctus has now been decided in favour of the view held by P. Roussel; cf. Flacelière, *Ait.*, 138 ff., and G. Klaffenbach, *RE* XXI, 1623 ff. s.v. *Polyeuktos* no. 6. The latest contribution is that of C. Pélékidis, *BCH* 85, 1961, 53-68, which places Polyeuctus in the year 247/6 B.C.

103. See Schmitt, *Staatsv.* III, no. 469.

104. Otto, *Sel.*, 22 ff.; cf. M. Wörrle, *Türk. Arkeoloji Dergisi* 22, 2, 1975, 159-162; *idem, Ch.* 5, 1975, 59-87.

105. Justin XXIV 5.12 ff.; cf. Bengtson, *Strat.* II, 383 ff. The conjecture by Beloch, *GG* IV 1, 565, that Sosthenes intended to establish a republican form of government in Macedonia, is incorrect.

106. Niese, *Mak.* II, 1899, 25.

107. Tarn, *Antig.*; *Hellenistic Civilisation*, [2]1930, 58 ff.; *CAH* VII, 197 ff.

108. V.s.p. 244.

109. The term "Carian War" used by W. W. Tarn for this the first encounter between Ptolemies and Seleucids is not entirely appropriate; in view of the fact that it was linked with the assumption of power by Antiochus I, W. Otto (*Ph.* 86, 1931, 400 n.1) termed it the "Syrian War of Succession." On the Northern League see also Rostovtzeff, *SEHHW* I, 26 f.

110. On the northern league see Rostoftzeff, *SEHHW* I, 26 f.

111. Otto, *Sel.*, 20 f., 27; *Ph.* 86, 1931, 405. On the peace treaty between Antiochus I and Antigonus (not until 278 B.C.) see Bengtson, *Strat.* II, 336 n. 1 (with bibliography).

112. Stephanus, Byz. s.v. *Agkyra*; cf. W. Otto, *Ph.* 86, 1931, 408 ff.

113. F. Chamoux, "Le roi Magas," *Rev. Hist.* 216, 1956, 18 ff.; *BCH* 82, 1958, 571 ff. (epigram from Apollonia near Cyrene); on the marriage see J. Seibert, *Histor. Beitr. zu den dynastischen Verbindungen*, 1967, 51 ff. On the treaty between Magas and the *Koinon* of the Oreis (Western Crete) see Schmitt, *Staatsv.* III, no. 468.

114. The view put forward by C. F. Lehmann-Haupt, *Klio* 3, 1903, 539 ff., 5, 1905, 381, and in *Epitymbion H. Swoboda dargebracht*, Reichenberg 1927, 152 ff., that the First Syrian War assumed international political proportions in which not only Macedonia but also Pyrrhus and Tarentum, and indeed even Rome, were affected by the War, partly as allies of the Seleucid, partly as confederates of Ptolemy II, is a figment of the imagination; see Otto, *Sel.*, 29, also already W. Kolbe, *Hermes* 51, 1916, 536 ff., and Holleaux, *Rome*, 61 n. 3.

115. On the date Otto, *Sel.*, 6 ff.; *Ph.* 86, 1931, 414 f. The date suggested by W. W. Tarn (lastly *JHS* 53, 1933, 59 f.), namely 279/8 B.C. appears to be out of the question. Cf. P. M. Fraser, *BCH* 78, 1954, 57 n. 3. On the *pompe* see in particular F. Caspari, "Studien zu dem Kallixeinosfragment Athenaios V 197c–203b," *Hermes* 68, 1933, 400 ff. Additional bibliography in Rostovtzeff, *SEHHW* III, 1419 n. 205; cf. also the discussion *SEHHW* I, 407 ff.

116. On Theocritus' "Encomium to Ptolemy" (*Id.* XVII) see, besides the basic study by H.v. Prott cited above 540, above all U.v. Wilamowitz-Moellendorff, *Hellenistische Dichtung* II, 1924, 130 ff.; cf. Schmid-Stählin, *GGL*[6] II 118 n. 6; A.v. Blumenthal, *RE* V A, 2002 f.; U. Wilcken, SB.B, 1938, 311 n.5.

117. Rostovtzeff, *SEHHW* I, 394 ff.

118. E. Kornemann, "Die Geschwisterehe im Alterum," *Mitt. Schles. Gesch. f. Volkskunde* 24, 1923, 17 ff.; 25 ff.; for the attempts at a different interpretation see J. Seibert, *Histor. Beitr. zu den dynastischen Verbindungen*, 1967, 81 ff.

119. Significant in this respect is the statement in the Athenian inscription *Syll.* I[3] no. 434/5 line 17 from 267 B.C. On Arsinoe see above all Kornemann, *Fr.*, 110 ff. Arsinoe on coins: W. Koch, "Die ersten Ptolemäerinnen nach ihren Münzen," *Z. f. Num.* 34, 1924, 80 ff.

120. On the Island League see the bibliography cited above 545 n.19.

121. The war is named after the Attic statesman Chremonides, who brought in the crucial proposal in the Popular Assembly: *Syll.* I[3] 434-435; Schmitt, *Staatsv.* III, no. 475; see F. Sartori," Cremonide: un dissidio fra politica e filosofia," in *Miscellanea di studi allessandrini in memoria di Augusto Rostagni*, Turin 1963, 117-151, esp. 144 ff. The chronology of the war is not certain; we do know for a fact, however, that Athens capitulated in the year of the archon Antipater, who is dated in 262/1 B.C. by Heinen, *Hell.*, 182 ff. W. W. Tarn, *JHS* 54, 1934, 26 ff., placed the outbreak of hostilities in 267 B.C.; but cf. Flacelière, *Ait.*, 195 n. 2; Bengtson, *Strat.* II, 351 n. 2; for a detailed discussion of the Chremonideian War, including the chronology, see now in particular, Heinen, *Hell.*, 95 ff.; see also C. B. Welles, "Gallic Mercenaries in the Chremonideian War," *Klio* 52, 1970, 477 ff.

122. It is not certain whether the sea battle of Cos, in which Antigonus Gonatas was victorious, belongs in this war (thus E. Bikerman, *REA* 40, 1938, 369 ff.; A. Momigliano and P. Fraser, *CQ* 44, 1950, 107 f. [262/1 B.C.]; according to W. Otto, *GGA*, 1914, 653, this was the decisive naval battle which brought about the fate of Athens and, accordingly, the end of the war); it is therefore dated by W. W. Tarn, *CAH* VII, 862 f., in 258 B.C., by W. Peremans, *Rev. belge* 12, 1933, 50 ff., 54 ff., in 256 B.C.; cf. *idem*, *AC* 8, 1939, 401 ff.; and A. Wilhelm, Abh. B., 1939, no. 22, 25 f. The older bibliography is cited by Beloch, *GG* IV 2, 518, with additional works in H. Volkmann, *RE* XXIII, 1653; see also Heinen, *Hell.*, 189 ff.

123. Important is the inscription from Rhamnus, published by B. X. Petrakos, *Arch. Deltion* 22, 1967, 38 ff.; cf. Heinen, *Hell.*, 152 ff.

124. Bengtson, *Strat.* II, 372 ff.; J. Pouilloux, *BCH* 70, 1946, 488 ff.; cf. Schmitt, *Staatsv.* III, no. 477.

125. W. Otto, *GGA*, 1914, 651 f.

126. The date is fully established by a Zenon Papyrus in the British Museum, published by H. I. Bell, *Symbolae Osloenses* 5, 1927, 1 ff.; cf. Otto, *Sel.*, 1928, 43 ff.

127. The name may be found in *Inschriften von Priene* 37, 134.

128. According to this bulletin, Berenice, the sister, was still alive.

129. The extensive modern literature on the "Bulletin" of Ptolemy III is cited by Otto,

Sel., 49 n. 4; see further, the studies cited above 538. See the diffuse investigation by A. Pridik, "Berenike, die Schwester des Königs Ptolemaios III. Euergetes," *Act. et Comm. Tartuens* XXXV-XXXVI, 1935, esp. 76 ff., in large measure in controversy with W. Otto, produces few new points of view. A. G. Roos, *Mn.* 51, 1923, 629, and W. W. Tarn, *CAH* VII, 716, are incorrect in denying the authorship of the king.

130. Published by K. Sethe, *Hierogl. Urkunden d. griech.-röm. Zeit*, Heft II 158; cf. Otto, *Sel.*, 54.

131. The ephemeral victories in the east are enumerated in the inscription from Adulis (245 B.C.), *OGI* I no. 54, lines 13 ff. The *Lock of Berenice* by Callimachus, transmitted by Catullus (LXVI) is related to the campaign of Ptolemy III in Asia Minor. A papyrus has furnished us with part of the Greek original: see R. Pfeiffer, *Callimachus* I, 1949, no. 110. W. Otto was the first to take issue with the exaggerated view that Ptolemy III was one of the greatest rulers of the Lagid Dynasty (initially in *Zeitschr. f. Sozialwiss.* 8, 1905, 792 f., and then in *Sel.*, 49 ff., *et al.*; a similar stance is incidentally taken by Beloch); his counter-argument has no doubt admittedly taken him too far in the other direction; see H. Bengtson, *Burs. Jb.* 284, 1944, 29 f. [necrology] = *KS*, 606. On the chronology see *idem*, *H.* 4, 1955, 114.

132. See, besides Ernst Meyer, *Die Grenzen der hellenistischen Staaten in Kleinasien*, 1925, 45, 92 f., and Beloch, *GG* IV 2, 333 ff., also Otto, *Sel.*, 74.

133. Diod. XXXI 19.5; cf. Bengtson, *Strat.* II, 77 (with the earlier bibliography). The numismatist K. Regling is incorrect in placing the founding of the empire before Ipsus: *Z. f. Num.* 42, 1935, 1 f.

134. On Bithynia and Pontus see Rostovtzeff, *SEHHW* I, 566 ff.; G. Vitucci, *Il regno di Bitinia*, Rome 1953; Schmitt, *Staatsv.* III, no. 465.

135. No less than 22 different languages are alleged to have been spoken in Pontus.

136. Justin XXVII 2.6; cf. Bengtson, *Strat.* II, 104 ff. According to E. Bickerman, *Berytus* 8, 1944, 78, who bases his argument on E. T. Newell, *The Coinage of the Western Seleucid Mints*, 1941, 292, the rule of Antiochus Hierax from about 238 to 230 B.C. in western Asia Minor, Lydia, the Troad and Caria can be proven by the coins; Sardis was the capital of the Anatolian realm of Antiochus. Cf. Map 8.

137. On the disaffection of Diodotus (probably not until after 246 B.C.) see, besides the older works cited by Bengtson, *Strat.* II, 54 n. 1, above all Tarn, *Bact.*, 72 ff.; E. Bickerman, *Berytus* 8, 1944, 79.

138. While the tradition on the rise of the Parthian empire was hitherto regarded as inconsistent and legendary by scholars (thus, for instance, Ed. Meyer, *Blüte und Niedergang des Hellenismus in Asien*, 1925, 49 n. 1; Debevoise, *Parth.*, 9 f., and also Bengtson, *Strat.* II, 55), E. Bickerman, *Berytus* 8, 1944, 79 ff., has attempted to establish order out of the chaos. See, on the other hand, J. Wolski, "L'historicité d'Arsace Ier," *H.* 8, 1959, 222 ff.

139. Formerly the spring of 248 B.C. was regarded as a turning point in the Arsacid era (F.X. Kugler, *Sternkunde* II, 444); E. Bickerman (on the basis of Welles, *RC*, no. 75) has attempted to show 1 Nisan 247 B.C. as a turning point: *Berytus* 8, 1944, 80 f.

140. Tod, II, no. 137; cf. *supra* 492 n. 77.

141. *IG* IX 1^2, 3 (= *Syll.* I^3 no. 421). The treaty was probably concluded towards the end of the sixties; G. Klaffenbach, *H.* 4, 1955, 46 ff., esp. 50, places it in 263 or 262 B.C.; cf. now esp. Schmitt, *Staatsv.* III, no. 480.

142. H. Benecke, *Die Seepolitik der Aitoler*, Diss. Hamburg 1934; G. Klaffenbach, SB.B, 1937, 155 ff.; Rostovtzeff, *SEHHW* I, 198 ff.; III 1361 f.

143. On Aratus cf. above all F. W. Walbank, *Aratos of Sicyon*, Cambridge 1933 (with good bibliography), and *idem, JHS* 56, 1936, 64 ff. Concerning the verdict of recent scholars on Aratus see Theunissen, *Ar.*, 306 ff.

144. The date is disputed. For 253 or 252 B.C.: Tarn, *Antig.*, 355; Beloch, *GG* IV 2, 519 ff. On the other hand, W. Kolbe, *GGA*, 1916, 470 ff., W. H. Porter, "Aratus of Sicyon and King Antigonus Gonatas," *Hermathena* 45, 1930, 293-311, and Theunissen, *Ar.*, 144 ff., argue for 249 B.C. Additional bibliography in Theunissen, *Ar.* and Flacelière, *Ait.*, 205 n. 2.

145. On the event see the detailed topographical study by Theunissen, *Ar.*, 184 ff. (with Plates).

146. Plut., *Aratus* 24.

147. On the reforms of Agis see Plut., *Agis*, and above all W. W. Tarn, *CAH* VII, 739

ff.; bibliography, *ibid.*, 885; and in Rostovtzeff, *SEHHW* III, 1367. See further, P. Cloché, "Remarques sur les règnes de Agis IV et Cléomène III," *REG* 56, 1943, 53 ff., and otherwise the studies on Cleomenes cited below 551 n. 168.

148. Cf. the section: "The Universal Sovereignty of the Greek Mind," *infra* 280 ff.

149. On Rhodes see the work by Schmitt cited above 542. Also the bibliography, *infra* 561.

151. On the beginnings of Attalid rule see G. Cardinali, *Il regno de Pergamo*, Turin 1906, 4 ff.; L. Robert, *Villes d'Asie Min.*, 1935, 37; Rostovtzeff, *SEHHW* I, 553 ff.; Bengtson, *Strat.* II, 195 f.; cf. also Schmitt, *Staatsv.* III, no. 481.

152. A. Ferrabino, "La guerra di Attalo I contro i Galati e Antioco Ierace," *Atti Acc., Torino* 48, 1912/13, 707 ff.; E. V. Hansen, "The Great Victory Monument of Attalus I," *AJA* 41, 1937, 52 ff.

153. Trog. *Prol.* 27; Justin XXVII 2.10 f.; XLI 4.7; Plut., *de frat. amore* 18 p. 489; cf. Beloch, *GG* IV 1, 680.

154. Trog. *Prol.* 28. W. Kolbe, *GGA*, 1916, 461 ff., was incorrect in denying the historicity of the Carian expedition; cf., on the other hand, Bengtson, *Strat.* II, 367; E. Bikerman, *REG* 56, 1943, 269 f. Cf. the important reference to an inscription from Labranda by L. Robert, in M. Holleaux, *Et. ép.* IV, 162 n. 1; see now also Bengtson *Labr.*, 19 ff.

155. On Antiochus III down to the time of his conflict with Rome see H. H. Schmitt, *Ant.*

156. On the disaffection of Molon see Polyb. V 41 ff., the coins with the legend *Basileos Molonos* (cf. E. T. Newell, *The Eastern Seleucid Mints*, 1938, 204 ff.), and the liver omen from Uruk from 30 April 221 B.C. (Debevoise, *Parth.*, 13 f.); cf. in detail, Schmitt, *Ant.*, 121 ff.

157. For an assessment of him see C. Préaux, "Polybe et Ptolémée Philopator," *Cd'E* 40, 1965, 364-375, but now, W. Huss, *Untersuchungen zur Aussenpolitik Ptolemaios' IV.* (Münch. Beitr., 69), 1976 (positive); cf. also W. Peremans, "Ptolémée IV et les Egyptiens," in *Le monde grec. Hommages à Claire Préaux*, Brussels 1975, 393 ff.

158. On events in Syria see Polyb. V 79 ff., and the trilingual Pithom stele (cf. the bibliography above 539). On the basis of both sources the rule of Antiochus in South Syria suddenly collapsed after Raphia, and on the evidence in the Pithom stele Ptolemy IV carried out an assault against Seleucid territory, a fact which Polybius, who in this instance follows a pro-Syrian source, does not mention; see Otto, *Sel.*, 80 ff.; 85 ff. and W. Huss (previous note), 74 ff. On the celebrations of the victory in Memphis see, besides the Pithom stele, also the evidence in a Demotic Papyrus from Elephantine, discussed by W. Spiegelberg and W. Otto, *Eine neue Urkunde zu der Siegesfeier des Ptolemaios IV. und die Frage der ägyptischen Priestersynoden.* SB.Bay., 1926, 2. Abh.

159. On Achaeus see Bengtson, *Strat.* II, 106 ff.; Holleaux, *Et.ép.* III, 125 ff.; on his end: B. van Proosdij, *Hermes* 69, 1934, 347 ff.; P. Meloni, L'usurpazione de Acheo sotto Antioco III di Siria, *RALinc.*, Serie 8,4. fasc. 11-12 (Nov.-Dec. 1949) 525 ff.; 8,5 fasc.3-4 (March-April 1950) 161 ff. On coins struck by Achaeus see E. T. Newell, *The Western Seleucid Mints*, 1941, 267 ff. The *Münzkabinett* in Munich contains an exceptionally fine gold coin of King Achaeus; cf. G. Kleiner, *JNG* 5-6, 1954-55, 143 ff.

160. M. Holleaux, *CAH* VIII, 138 ff. (principal sources are the excerpts of Books VIII-XI by Polybius).

161. Bengtson, *Strat.* II, 60 ff.

162. M. Holleaux, *CAH* VIII, 142; *Et. ép.* III, 159 ff.; cf. Bengtson, *Strat.* II, 63 n.1; in general see P. Spranger, "Der Grosse," *Saeculum* 9, 1958, 22 ff.

163. V. Costanzi, "*Demetriakos polemos*," in *Saggi di storia antica e di archeologia, offerti a G. Beloch*, Rome 1910, 59 ff.; W. W. Tarn, *CAH*, VII, 744 ff.; P. Roussel, "Un nouveau document relatif à la guerre démétriaque," *BCH* 54, 1930, 268 ff. (cf., however, B. D. Meritt, *AJA* 37, 1933, 46 f.); S. B. Kougeas, "*Ho Demetriakos polemos kai hai Athenai*," *Hellenika* 3, 1930, 281 ff.; Feyel, *Pol.*, 83 ff.

164. See Flacelière, *Ait.*, Chap. VI: "L'apogée des Aitoliens (245-226)," esp. 256; cf. G. Klaffenbach, *Klio* 32, 1939, 200 ff. R. Flacelière (258) even reaches the conclusion: "Leur puissance devait être considérée alors comme égale, sinon comme supérieure à celle de la Macédoine," cf. J. A. O. Larsen, *CP* 70, 1975, 159 ff. On method see the reservations of G. Daux, Studia antiqua (*Mélanges Salac*), Prague, 1955, 35-39.

165. Ferguson, *Ath.*, 206 f.; W. W. Tarn, *CAH*, VII, 748 f. On the date see Feyel, *Pol.*, 123 n. 3.

166. W. Bettingen, *König Antigonos Doson von Makedonien*, Diss. Jena (published Weida 1912) (the epithet "Doson" probably means "he who will hand over his rule," Bettingen, 15). On the regency of Antigonus (229-227 BC ?) see Bengtson, *Strat.* II, 386 ff.; on his foreign policy see the works cited above 541 f. by P. Treves and M. T. Piraino, who however, place his succession in 230 B.C.; and now also Bengtson, *Labr.*, 19 ff.

167. Cf. in context, *supra* 259 ff.

168. On the reforms of Cleomenes see in particular G. De Sanctis, "Questioni politiche e riforme sociali," *Scritti Minori*, 1966, 371 ff. (first published 1904); G. Kazarow, "Z. Gesch. d. sozialen Revolution in Sparta," *Klio* 7, 1907, 45 ff.; E. v. Stern, "Kleomenes III. und Archidamos," *Hermes* 50, 1915, 554 ff.; Th. Lenschau, *RE* XI, 702 ff. s.v. *Kleomenes* no. 6; E. Bux, "Zwei sozialistische Novellen bei Plutarch," *Klio* 19, 1925, 413 ff.; W. W. Tarn, "The Social Question in the Third Century," in J. B. Bury, E. A. Barber, E. Bevan, W. W. Tarn, *The Hellenistic Age*, Cambridge 1923, 128 ff.; R. v. Pöhlmann, *Gesch. d. sozialen Frage u. des Sozialismus in der ant. Welt*, ed. F. Oertel, 1925, 385 ff.; M. Hadas, "The Social Revolution in Third Century Sparta," *CW* 26, 1932/33, 65 ff.; 73 ff.; M. Daubies, "Cléomène III, les hilots et Sellasie," *H.* 20, 1971, 665 ff. The rôle of the Stoic philosopher and collaborator of Cleomenes, Sphaerus (cf. F. Ollier, *REG* 49, 1936, 536 ff.) is obscure. A *meliambos* by the poet and statesman Cercidas of Megalopolis, preserved in *P. Oxy.* VIII, no. 1082, furnishes many details on the general mood in the Peloponnesus and especially for the striking conflict between rich and poor; cf. J. U. Powell, *Collect. Alexandrina*, 1925, 203 ff., and the bibliography cited by M. Rostovtzeff, *SEHHW* III, 1367; also Nilsson, *Gr. Rel.* II, 193.

169. Cf. Polyb. II 45-51; cf. E. Bikerman, "Notes sur Polybe II: Les négotiations entre Aratos et Antigonos Doson," *REG* 56, 1943, 287 ff.; a different interpretation is attempted by E. S. Gruen, "Aratus and the Achaean Alliance with Macedon," *H.* 21, 1972, 609 ff. On the policy of Antigonus Doson see Bengtson, *Labr.*, 37 ff.

170. In Polyb. II 54 Antigonus is called "hegemon" of all the allies. The confederates are listed in Polyb. IV 9.4; cf. XI 5.4; the bibliography in Bengtson, *Strat.* II, 356 n. 2; cf. Schmitt, *Staatsv.* III, nos. 506; 507.

171. Cf. Plut., *Aratus* 45 (Phylarchus); Polyb. II 58.12; 62.11 ff.; cf. F. Bölte, *RE* XIV, 1328 f. s.v. *Mantinea.*

172. The battle took place in the summer (Polyb. II 65), to wit before the death of Ptolemy III Euergetes; since he died in February 221 B.C. (T. C. Skeat, *The Reigns of the Ptolemies*, [2]1969, 31), only the summer of 222 B.C. comes into question; already correct is B. Niese, *Hermes* 35, 1900, 60 ff.; Beloch, *GG* IV 2, 219 f.; cf. lastly, E. Bikerman, *REG* 56, 1943, 287 n. 2. The question of the date has often been discussed (but not always convincingly); bibliographies in Th., Lenschau, *RE* XI, 708 f.; Holleaux, *Et. ép.* III, 60 n. 2; *ibid.*, 315 n. 4; not cited there is the study by H. Frank, *AfP* 11, 1935, 53 ff. (for 222 B.C.). On the course of the battle of Sellasia see Polyb. II 65-69; Plut., *Cleom.* 28 f.; *Philop.* 6: cf. Kromayer, *Schl.* I, 199 ff.; opposed to him: G. Soteriades, "*To pedion tes en Sellasia maches*," *BCH* 34, 1910, 5 ff.; Kromayer's reply: *BCH* 34, 1910, 508 ff.; counter-reply by Soteriades: "Anti-Sellasia," *BCH* 35, 1911, 87 ff.; 241 ff. Further: U. Kahrstedt, *Hermes* 48, 1913, 286 ff.; G. Roloff, "Probleme aus der griechischen Kriegsgeschichte," *Eberings Histor. Studien* 39, Berlin 1904, 80 ff.; Delbrück, *Krieg.* I[3], 244 ff.; E. Honigmann, *RE* II A, 1317 ff. s.v. *Sellasia*; Holleaux, *Et. ép.* III, 55 ff. (= *Syll* I[3] 518); Pritchett, *Top.* I, 59 ff.; Bengtson, *Labr., idem, Herrs.*, 177 f., 182; Daubies, *H.* 20, 1971, 665 ff.; R. Urban. "Das Heer des Kleomenes bei Sellasia," *Ch.* 3, 1973, 95 ff. The account of Polybius may be regarded as reliable in all essential aspects, but it must be borne in mind that he is to be regarded as not only a scholar but also an artist; see, on the other hand, W. W. Tarn, *CAH* VII, 761.

173. Polyb. IV 9.6; 15.4; 16.5; cf. Beloch, *GG* IV 1, 718 n. 1. On the personality of Cleomenes see H. Bengtson, "Kleomenes III. ein spartanischer König im Exil," in *Geschichte in der Gesellschaft, Festschr, für Karl Bosl zum 65. Geburtstag*, (eds), F. Prinz. F.-J. Schmale. F. Seidt, Stuttgart 1974, 1 ff.; *idem, Herrs.*, 165 ff. On the consequences of the Spartan defeat see B. Shimron, "The Spartan Policy after the Defeat of Cleomenes III," *CQ* 58, 1964, 232-239.

174. F. W. Walbank, "*Philippos tragodoumenos*. A Polybian Experiment," *JHS* 58, 1938, 55 ff.; *idem., Phil. V.*

175. *Syll.* II³ 543, from 219 and 214 B.C.

176. Niese, *Mak.* II, 409 ff.; Beloch, *GG* IV 1, 719 ff.; W. W. Tarn, *CAH* VII, 763 ff.; Flacelière, *Ait.*, 288 ff.; J. Fine, "The Background of the Social War 220-217 B.C.," *AJP* 61, 1940, 129 ff.; Walbank, *Phil. V*, 24 ff. (the best detailed discussion).

177. A. Scrinzi, "La guerra di Lyttos," *Atti Ist. Veneto* 9, 1897/98, 1509 ff.; G. Cardinali, "Creta e le grandi potenze ellenistiche sino alla guerra di Litto," *Riv. stor. ant.* 9, 1904, 69 ff. (background); *idem, La guerra di Litto, RF* 23, 1905, 519 ff.; cf. Schmitt, *Staatsv.* III, no. 511.

178. Schmitt, *Staatsv.* III, no. 520.

179. On the speech of Agelaus see O. Mørkholm, *Clas. et Med.* 28, 1970, 240 ff.; cf. the reply by J. Deininger, *Ch.* 3, 1973, 103 ff.; and the counter-reply by O. Mørkholm, *Ch.* 4, 1974, 127 ff.

180. On the chronology see M. Holleaux, *CAH* VII, 834 n.1; cf. *idem, Et. ép.* IV, 9ff.; Beloch, *GG* IV 1, 664; 2, 262, incorrectly dates the event to 228 B.C.

181. The principal source for the First Illyrian War is Polyb. II 2-12 (cf. N. Vulič, *Acad. Royale Serve, Bull. de l'Acad. des Lettres.* no. I, 1935, 231 ff.). Modern studies and investigations: G. Zippel, *Die römische Herrschaft in Illyrien*, Leipzig 1877, 5 ff.; A. Bauer, "Die Anfänge öster, Geschichte," *Arch.-epigr. Mitt. aus Österr.-Ung* 18, 1895, 129 ff.; C. Schütt, *Untersuch. z. Gesch. d. altén Illyrier*, Diss. Breslau 1910; Holleaux, *Rome*, 97 ff.; Th. Walek, "La politique rom. en Grèce et dans l'Orient hellénist. au IIIe siècle," *Rev. phil.* 49, 1925, 28 ff.; 118 ff.; M. Holleaux, "La politique rom. en Grèce et dans l'Orient hellénist. au IIIe siècle. Réponse à M. Th. Walek," *Et. ép.* IV, 26 ff.; *CAH* VII, 822 ff. (basic, with bibliography 932 f.); P. Treves, "Studi su Antigono Dosone," *Ath.* NS 12, 1934, 384 ff.; 13, 1935, 22 ff.; M. Fluss, *RE* V A, 1140 ff. s.v. *Teuta* (with good map, 1147/48); E. Kirsten, "Die albanische Frage im Altertum," *WG* 8, 1942, 75 ff. Also the studies by A. Gitti, "Contributi alla storia dell'espansione romana in Illiria: Sulla storia degli Ardici dopo la prima guerra romano-illirica," *Bull. del Museo dell'Imp. Rom.* 6, 1935, 11 ff.; "Sulle origini e i caratteri della monarchia di Agrone," *Historia* [Milan] 13, 1935, 183 ff.; "La politica degli re illiri e la Grecia," *Historia* [Milan] 14, 1936, 7 ff. Further: E. Badian, Notes on Roman Policy in Illyria (230-201 B.C.)," *Papers of the British School at Athens* 20, 1952, 72-93; H. Dell, "The Origin and Nature of Illyrian Piracy," *H.* 16, 1967, 344 ff.; K.-E. Petzold, "Rom und Illyria," *H.* 20, 1971, 199 ff.

182. Cf. Schmitt, *Staatsv.* III, no. 500.

183. On the so-called Second Illyrian War cf. Polyb. III 16-19; IV 16.6-9 (probably Fabius Pictor). The other tradition, recounted by Appian, *Illyr.* 7-8; Zonar. VIII 19.3-7; 20.11-13, betrays the influence of the later annalists and is disputable; cf., on the other hand, G. Walser, *H.* 2, 1953/54, 308 ff. Bibliography: In addition to the works cited above n. 181, see further: J. Fine, "Macedon, Illyria and Rome 220-219 B.C.," *JRS* 26, 1936, 24 ff.

184. Polyb. VII 9. Cf. G. Egelhaaf, "Analekten z. Gesch. d. 2. Pun. Krieges. 2. Der Vertrag Hannibals mit Philippos V.," *HZ* 53, 1885, 456 ff.; J. Beloch, "Die 'Herren Karthager,'" *Klio* 1, 1901, 283 f.; Holleaux, *Rome*, 179 ff.; U. Kahrstedt, "Zwei Urkunden aus Polybios. II. Die 'Herren Karthager,'" *NGG*, 1923, 99 ff.; E. Groag, *Hannibal als Politiker*, 1929, 81 ff.; 97; cf. E. Bickerman, *TAPA* 75, 1944, 87 ff.; and R. Dussaud, *CRAI*, 1947, 217 ff.; also E. Bickerman, *AJP* 73, 1952, 1 ff.; A. H. Chroust, *Classica et Mediaevalia*, 15, 1954, 60 ff. Detailed bibliography in *CAH* VIII, 745; cf. Walbank. *Phil. V*, 71 n. 3; see also Schmitt, *Staatsv.* III, no. 528.

185. The principal source is Polyb. VII-XI; Livy XXVI-XXIX; cf. M. Holleaux, *CAH* VIII, 116 n., who furnishes the best discussion, 116 ff. (with extensive bibliography, 730 ff.), cf. Walbank, *Phil. V*, 70 ff.

186. On the date (212 and not 211 B.C.) see M. Holleaux, *CAH* VIII, 124 n. 2; cf. the bibliography cited *ibid.*, 745 f.

187. G. Klaffenbach, *Der römisch-ätolische Bündnisvertrag v. J. 212 v. Chr.*, SB.B, 1954, no. 1; cf. A. H. McDonald, *JRS* 46, 1956, 153 ff.; also *SEG* XVI no. 370; and Schmitt, *Staatsv.* III, no. 536. A defense of Polybius in H. E. Stier, *Roms Aufstieg zur Weltmacht u. die griech. Welt*, 1957, 26 ff.

188. On the Aetolian territorial losses see M. Holleaux, *CAH* VIII, 134 f.; Flacelière, *Ait.*, 306 ff. Bibliography: F. Stähelin, "Pharsalica II. Die Phthiotis und der Friede zwischen Philippos V. und den Ätolern," *Ph.* 77, 1921, 199 ff.; G. Klaffenbach, "Zur Gesch. von Ostlokris," *Klio* 20, 1925, 82 ff. Further bibliography: *CAH* VIII, 745 f.; Walbank, *Phil. V*, 100 n. 1.

189. Livy XXIX 12 (= Polyb., cf. H. Nissen, *Krit. Untersuch über die Quellen des Livius*, 1863, 84); cf. E. Bikerman, "Les préliminaires de la seconde guerre de Macédoine. La paix de Phoiniké," *Rev. phil.* 61, 1935, 59 ff. (basic); cf. Schmitt, *Staatsv.* III, no. 543. If Bikerman's theory in respect of the general peace is correct, then the intervention of the Romans in Greece in 200 B.C. would appear in a new light: as a signatory power, Rome would have been justified in forbidding Philip V to attack the Greeks. Opposed to him, is J. A. O. Larsen, "The Peace of Phoinike and the Outbreak of the Second Macedonian War," *CP* 32, 1937, 16-31. See also Walbank, *Phil. V*, 103, including n. 6; and M. T. Piraino, *RF* NS 33, 1955, 57 ff.

190. R. Herzog, *"Kretikos polemos,"* *Klio* 2, 1902, 316 ff.; G. Cardinali, "Creta nel tramonto dell'Ellenismo," *RF* 35, 1907, 5 ff.; Holleaux, "Remarques sur les décrets des villes de Crète," *Et. ép.* IV, 178 ff.; "Sur la 'Guerre crétoise,'" *Et. ép. IV*, 163 ff.; M. Segre, *"Kretikos polemos,"* *RF* 61, 1933, 365 ff.

191. Holleaux, "L'expédition de Dikaiarchos," *Et. ép.* IV, 124 ff.; cf. W. L. Westermann, *Upon Slavery in Ptolemaic Egypt*, New York, 1929, 22 ff.; H. Benecke, *Die Seepolitik der Aitoler*, Diss. Hamburg 1934, 41 f.

191a. W. Huss, *Untersuchungen zur Aussenpolitik Ptolemaios' IV.*, Munich 1976.

192. C. Préaux, "Esquisse d'une hist. des révolutions égyptiennes sous les Lagides," *Cd'E* 22, 1936, 526 ff.; M. Alliot, *Revue belge de phil. et d'hist.* 79, 1951, 421 ff.

193. Concise: Rostovtzeff, *SEHHW* II, 711 f. (bibliography, *ibid.*, III, 1494 n. 131); A. Segrè, "The Ptolemaic Copper Inflation, ca. 230-140 B.C.," *AJP* 63, 1942, 174 ff.; R. Reckmans, *Cd'E* 24, 1949, 324 ff.

194. F. W. Walbank, "The Accession of Ptolemy Epiphanes," *JEA* 22, 1936, 20 ff. (Aug./Sept. 204 B.C.); cf. C. F. Nims, *JEA* 24, 1938, 73 f.; E. Bikerman, *Cd.'E.* 29, 1940, 124 ff.; cf. T. C. Skeat, *The Reigns of the Ptolemies*, [2]1969, 32; and Schmitt, *Ant.*, 189 ff. The question has still not been finally resolved.

195. Polyb. III 2.8; XV 20; XVI 1.9; Appian, *Mac.* 4; Justin XXX 2.8; Hieronymus, in Daniel. XI 13; cf. Schmitt, *Staatsv.* III, no. 547; Holleaux, *Rome*, 290; *CAH* VII 150; A. H. McDonald-F. W. Walbank, *JRS* 27, 1937, 182; D. Magie, "The 'Agreement' Between Philip V and Antiochus III for the Partition of the Egyptian Empire," *JRS* 29, 1939, 32 ff. (doubting the existence of the secret treaty and seeing in it an invention of the Rhodians; see, opposed to this view, however, H. H. Schmitt, *Rom und Rhodos*, 1957, 62 n. 1); K. E. Petzold, *Die Eröffnung des 2. röm-maked. Krieges*, Berlin 1940, 32 ff.; *Gn.* 25, 1953, 405; and, in detail, Schmitt, *Ant.*, 237 ff.

13 HELLENISTIC CIVILISATION

SOURCES AND BIBLIOGRAPHY: The sources for Hellenistic constitutional law are on the whole the same as for Hellenistic history. In addition to the historians (Polybius, Poseidonius, Livy, Strabo, Josephus, Appian, Porphyry, Justin, *et al.*), it is in particular the inscriptions, papyri, ostraca and coins that come into question. The evidence is scattered over a broad field, is fragmentary and very uneven in quality. It is no wonder that to date no comprehensive work on "Hellenistic Constitutional History" has been written. Shorter discussions (without documentation of the entire sources) are to be found in the general histories by K. J. Beloch (*GG* IV 1, 1925, 328-400: "Die neuen Grosstaaten," "Die Monarchie und ihr Staatsrecht"), by Kaerst (*GH* II², 296-361: "Der hellenistische Staat"), by Berve (*GG* II², 271 ff.: "Die hellenistische Welt"), and the relevant chapters in *CAH* (VII, 1928; VIII, 1930). Useful as surveys are: W. W. Tarn, *Hellenistic Civilisation*, London ³1952, and Ehrenberg, *State*, 254 ff. (with copious bibliography); stimulating is U.v. Wilamowitz-Moellendorff, *Staat und Gesellschaft der Griechen*, ²1923, 142-206: "Die makedonischen Königsreiche"; and also very worthwhile reading are W. Otto's expositions on "Der Staat des Hellenismus," in *Kulturg.*, 96 ff.; further, J. Béranger, "Grandeur et servitude du souverain hellénistique," in *Etudes de Lettres* II, 7, Lausanne 1964, 1-14. Basic for the economic and social history of the Hellenistic Age is Rostovtzeff, *SEHHW*. In scope and in the vast amount of evidence discussed, this standard work also makes an essential contribution to an understanding of the composition of the Hellenistic states in regard to their political character, their population and their organisation. Also worth consulting is H. Braunert, "Hegemoniale Bestrebungen der hellenistischen Grossmächte in Politik und Wirtschaft," *H.* 13, 1964, 80-104; *idem*, "Das Mittelmeer in Politik und Wirtschaft der hellenistischen Zeit," *Veröff. der Schlesw.-Holst. Univ.-Gesellschaft* NF 49, Kiel 1967, 5-33.

From among specialised studies the following may be cited: E. Breccia, *Il diritto dinastico nelle monarchie dei successori d'Alessandro Magno* (Studi di Storia antica, pubbl. da G. Beloch, 4), Rome 1903; J. Seibert, *Historische Beiträge zu den dynastischen Verbindungen in hellenist. Zeit* (H.-Einzelschr. 10), Wiesbaden 1967; W. Otto, "Zum Hofzeremoniell des Hellenismus" (on the eternal flame) in *Epitymbion H. Swoboda dargebracht*, Reichenberg 1927, 194 ff.; F. Granier, *Die makedonische Heeresversammlung* (Münch. Beitr. 13), Munich 1931 (cf. W. S. Ferguson, *Gn.* 11, 1935, 518 ff.); Bengtson, *Strat.* I-III (improved reprints, 1964 and 1967); M. Trindl, *Ehrentitel im Ptolemäerreich*, Diss. Munich 1938 (published 1942 [photocopy]); L. Mooren, *The Aulic Titulature in Ptolemaic Egypt*, Brussels 1975. Important are the more recent studies by A. Aymard: "Le protocol royal grec et son évolution," *REA* 50, 1948, 232 ff.; *"Basileus Makedonon," Rev. Int. des Droits de l'Ant.* 4 *(Mél. F. de*

Visscher, 3), Brussels 1950, 61 ff. On the survival of Hellenistic institutions in the Principate and Dominate the following are basic: A. Alföldi, "Die Ausgestaltung des monarchischen Zeremoniells am röm. Kaiserhofe," *RM* 49, 1934, 1 ff.; "Insignien und Tracht der römischen Kaiser," *RM* 50, 1935, 1 ff. On international law: P. Klose, *Die völkerrechtliche Ordnung der hellenistischen Staatenwelt in der Zeit von 280-168. Ein Beitrag zur Geschichte des Völkerrechts* (Münch. Beitr. 64), Munich 1972.

The Seleucid Empire: In addition to the references in Polybius and the pseudo-Aristotelian *Oeconomica* II (cf. Rostovtzeff, *SEHHW* I, 440 ff.; cf. also Bengtson, *Strat.* II, 50), our information for the third century rests on a number of chance epigraphical finds. The most important inscriptions have been assembled and discussed by W. Dittenberger, *OGI* I nos. 211 ff., and by Welles, *RC*, with some also in Schmitt, *Staatsv.* III, nos. 458 ff. Of finds dating from the second century there are the inscriptions from Susa, published in *SEG* VII nos. 1 ff.; and, finally, reference may be made to the epigraphical reports by J. and L. Robert in *REG*. The cuneiform inscriptions contain little information of historical importance (cf. the survey by M. Rostovtzeff, *CAH* VII, 898 f.; A. Aymard, "Une ville de la Babylonie séleucide d'après les contrats cunéïforms," *REA* 40, 1938, 5 ff. (= *Etudes*, 1967, 178 ff.). A small number of documents is discussed by O. Krückmann, *Babylon. Rechts- und Verwaltungsurkunden aus der Zeit Alexanders u. der Diadochen*, Diss. Berlin 1931; M. Rutten, *Contrats de l'époque séleucide conservés au Musée du Louvre*, Paris 1935; cf. Rostovtzeff, *SEHHW* III, 1423; 1427. The Coins: a good survey appears in J. G. Milne, *Greek Coinage*, 1931, 108 ff.; specific bibliography: R. H. McDowell, *Coins from Seleucia on the Tigris*, 1935, XIII f.; E. T. Newell, *The Coinage of the Eastern* (or *Western*) *Seleucid Mints*, New York 1938 (or 1941); cf. Rostovtzeff, *SEHHW* III, 1429 f. Important is G. Le Rider, *Suse sous les Séleucides et les Parthes. Les trouvailles monétaires et l'histoire de la ville* (Mém. de la mission archéol. en Iran 38), Paris 1965. Cf. also the references above 531.

From the extensive bibliography, which stands in opposite relationship to the sparseness of our sources (see the survey by Rostovtzeff, *CAH* VII, 898 ff.; *SEHHW* III, 1422 ff.; 1489 ff.; 1533 ff.), only the following may be cited here: Bikerman, *Sél.* (a comprehensive and detailed study of kingship, the court, the military system, taxation, administration, coinage and the ruler cult—a notable achievement, despite the objections which must be made on various points); cf. the review by C. B. Welles, *AJA* 43, 1939, 536 f. See in addition: E. Bickerman, "The Seleucids and the Achaemenids," in *La Persia e il mondo greco-romano* Rome 1966, 87-117; D. Musti, "Aspetti dell'organizzazione seleucidica in Asia Minore nel III sec. av. Cr.," *PP* 20, 1965, 153-160; *idem*, "Lo stato degli Seleucidi," *Studi classici e orientali* 15, 1966, 61-200 (a number of critical observations). On the organisation of the Seleucid empire see further: Bengtson, *Strat.* II, 1 ff. On the founding of cities by the Seleucids: Ed. Meyer, *Blüte und Niedergang des Hellenismus in Asien*, Berlin 1925; E. Kornemann, "Zur Politik der ersten Nachfolger Alexanders d. Gr.,"

Vergangenheit und Gegenwart 16, 1926, 333 ff.; V. Tscherikower, *Die hellenistischen Städtegründungen von Alexander d. Gr. bis auf die Römerzeit*, Ph. Suppl. XIX 1, Leipzig 1927; F. Oertel, *RE* XI, 1 ff. s.v. *Katoikoi*; M. Streck, *RE* II A, 1149 ff. s.v. *Seleukeia am Tigris*; Tarn. *Bact.*, 1 ff. On the administration and organisation of the Seleucid Empire see, in addition to the works cited above, in particular: W. L. Westermann, "Land Registers of Western Asia under the Seleucids," *CP* 16, 1921, 12 ff.; 391 f.; Ernst Meyer, *Die Grenzen der hellenistischen Staaten in Kleinasien*, Zurich 1925 (cf. the important addenda and corrigenda by L. Robert, "Hellenistica," *REA* 36, 1934, 522 ff.); U. Kahrstedt, *Syrische Territorien in hellenist. Zeit.* Abh. Gött. Ges. d. Wiss., phil.-hist. Kl., NF 19, 2, 1926 (unfortunately careless in places, cf., for instance, W. Otto, *Sel.*, 30 ff.); E. Honigmann, *RE* IV A, 1549 ff. s.v. *Syria.* Of importance is the inscription from the region of Kermanshah (Iran), discussed by L. Robert, *CRAI* 1967, 281 ff.; it uses the term *Phylake* for a territorial unit (a parallel in Ptolemaic Egypt: Agatharchides, *GGMin* I p. 122,29). On the vice-regency of Asia Minor see L. Robert, *Nouvelles inscriptions de Sardes* I, Paris 1964, 9 ff. (Zeuxis, from the time of Antiochus III). On the Dynasts in Asia Minor: Rostovtzeff, *SEEHW* III, 1425 f. (with the earlier bibliography). On the relationship of the Greek cities to the imperial power see M. Holleaux, "Une inscription de Séleucide-de-Piérie," *Et. ép.* Ill, 199 ff. The study by A. Heuss, *Stadt und Herrscher des Hellenismus in ihren staats -und völkerrechtlichen Beziehungen*, Klio-Beih. 39, 1937, requires detailed correction (cf. the remarks in Bengtson, *Strat.* II, 8; 142 n. 1); the work by A. H. M. Jones, *The Greek City from Alexander to Justinian*, Oxford 1940, is also not satisfactory on this point.

For the Ptolemaic Empire, on the other hand, the papyri, ostraca and inscriptions provide a wealth of information, especially for the time of Ptolemy II and Ptolemy III. In using the papyri, however, it should be noted that by far the greater majority are of "rural" derivation, particularly from the Fayum. Documents of Alexandrian provenance are scarce; the so-called *dikaiomata* (published in *Graeca Halensis*, 1913, cf. L. Wenger, *Krit. Vierteljahresschr. f. Gesetzgeb. u. Rechtswiss.*, 1913, 339 ff.; W. Schubart, "Causa Halensis," *AfP* 12, 1937, 27 ff.) are extracts from Alexandrian laws and ordinances, and form a category entirely by themselves. Basic for an understanding of the Ptolemaic political economy, especially for the management of the oil monopoly, are the so-called *Revenue Laws of Ptolemy Philadelphus*, published by B. P. Grenfell, Oxford 1896; revised version by J. Bingen, *Sammelbuch griech. Urkunden*, Beih. 1, Göttingen 1952—in reality, probably tax laws or a *diagramma* on the leasing of royal revenues. The orders of a *dioiketes* issued to an *oikonomos*, from the end of the third century B.C. (*P. Teb.* III 703), are also of an official character. Of very special importance is the large group of Zenon papyri from the Fayum (the greater majority have been published by C. C. Edgar, *Zenon Papyri, Cat. gén. des ant. égypt. du Musée du Caire* I-IV, Cairo 1925-31; in addition Vol. V, published posthumously, edited by O. Guéraud and P. Jouguet, *op. cit.*,

1940); scattered publications on a smaller scale are cited by C. Préaux, *Les Grecs en Egypte*, 1947, 87 ff. The extensive correspondence carried on by Zenon, the administrator of the *dioiketes* and "landed proprietor" Apollonius, is of inestimable value not only for trade and commerce but also for connections between Egypt and her foreign dominions (Caria and Syria), for provincial administration and for the spirit of the Greek upper class under Ptolemy II; see the concise discussion by M. Rostovtzeff, *A Large Estate in Egypt in the Third Century B.C.*, Madison 1922, and the remarks in his *SEHHW* III, 1400 n. 132a and 134; further, R. Seider, *Beitr. z. ptol. Verwaltungsgesch. Der Nomarch. Der Dioiketes Apollonios*, Heidelberg 1938. See also Anna Świderek, "Zenon fils de agréophon de Caunos et sa famille," in *Symbolae R. Taubenschlag* II, 1957, 133-141; *W 'państwie' Apolloniosa*, Warsaw 1959. Also important are the papyri originating from Magdola and Chorân, which have been published by O. Guéraud, *Enteuxeis*, Cairo 1931/32. These "petitions" are of great importance, not only furnishing information on the organisation of justice but also providing an understanding of social and cultural conditions in Egypt at the end of the third century B.C. Of other groups, the following may also be mentioned: *P. Hibeh* I (= Ancyronpolis in central Egypt), published by Grenfell and Hunt, 1906, and *P. Elephantine* from the south of the country, published by O. Rubensohn, 1907. An important single document, finally, is the *Vienna Papyrus* (P.E.R. Inv. 24552 gr.), published by H. Liebesny, "Ein Erlass des Königs Potlemaios II. Philadelphos über die Deklaration von Vieh und Sklaven in Syrien und in Phönikien," *Aeg.* 16, 1936, 254 ff. (in F. Bilabel, *SB* V 8008) cf. Rostovtzeff, *SEHHW* I, 340 ff.

A survey of the principal sources for the history of Egypt in the third century B.C. is given by Rostovtzeff, *SEHHW* I, 255 ff., and a list of the papyrus editions for the entire Ptolemaic period may be found in *CAH* VII, 889 ff.; cf. the more recent survey by W. Peremans, *AC* 17, 1948, 473 ff.; further, H. Braunert, *Zeitscher, für vergl. Rechtswissenschaft* 60, 1957, 117 ff. and especially C. Préaux, *La place des papyrus dans des sources de l'histoire hellénistique* (Münch Beitr., 66), Munich 1974, 1-26. The entire documentary evidence for Ptolemaic history, in so far as it consists of papyri and ostraca, was assembled and discussed in his day by U. Wilcken, *AfP* 1-15 (in the outstanding *Urkundenreferate*). Critical reports are also carried by *JEA, Aeg., Cd'E* and *REG.* The inscriptions have been collected (in selective form) by Dittenberger, *OGI* I nos. 16 ff. (Adden. Vol. II nos. 724 ff.); *Sammelbuch griechischer Urkunden aus Ägypten*, Berlin 1915 ff., edited by F. Preisigke, later by F. Bilabel (to date 12 vols., 1915-76) also provides inscriptions. And in addition there are the papyri and ostraca in scattered publications. Of very great value are the popular decrees of Samos from the Ptolemaic period, published by Chr. Habicht, *AM* 72, 1957 (published 1959), 209 ff. The Coins: Still not replaced is J. N. Svoronos, *Ta Nomismata tou kratous ton Ptolemaion*, 4 vols., Athens 1904-08 (with important supplementary explanations by K. Regling); and in addition the catalogues of the British Museum (R. S.

Poole, *The Ptolemies of Egypt*, 1883; H. Kyrieleis, "Die Porträtmünzen Ptolemaios' V. und seiner Eltern. Zur Datierung und historischen Interpretation," *JdI* 88, 1973, 213 ff.; E. S. G. Robinson, *Cyrenaica*, 1927).

The bibliography is almost unlimited; surveys appear in M. Rostovtzeff, *CAH* VII, 891 ff.; *SEHHW* III, 1376 ff.; 1493 ff. (Philopator-Philometor); 1541 ff. (Euergetes II-Cleopatra VII); Préaux, *Econ.*, 571 ff. A general survey on the organisation and economy of Ptolemaic Egypt is given by (in addition to the general Histories of A. Bouché-Leclercq, *Hist. des Lagides* III and IV; E. R. Bevan, *A History of Egypt under the Ptolemaic Dynasty*, 1927; P. Jouguet, in Hanotaux, *Hist. de la nat. égypt.* III): U. Wilcken, *Grundzüge und Chrestomathie d. Papyruskunde* I 1, Leipzig 1912; W. Schubart, *Einführung in die Papyruskunde*, Berlin 1918; *Ägypten von Alexander d. Gr. bis auf Mohammed*, Berlin 1922; *Verfassung und Verwaltung des Ptolemäerreiches*, (AO 35,4). 1937; W. Peremans and J. Vergote, *Papyrologisch Handboek*, Louvain 1942 (in Flemish). M. L. Strack, *Die Dynastie der Ptolemäer*, Berlin 1897, is still indispensable. For the chronology of the individual Ptolemies: Skeat, *Reigns*, cf. the reference 532. On the question of population see in particular F. Heichelheim, *Die auswärtige Bevölkerung im Ptolemäerreich*, Klio-Beih. 18, 1925; also the supplements in *AfP* 9, 1930, 47 ff.; 12, 1937, 54 ff.; W. Peremans, "Ptolémée II Philadelphe et les indigènes égyptiens," *Rev. belge de philol. et d'hist.* 12, 1933, 105 ff.; C. Préaux, "Politique de race ou politique royale," *Cd'E* 11, 1936, 111 ff.; W. Peremans, *Vreemdelingen en Egyptenaren en Vroeg-Ptolemaeisch Egypte*, Louvain 1937 (cf. F. Oertel, *ZSS Röm.* 59, 1939, 606 ff.); F. Zucker, in *NBAnt.* ed. H. Berve 1, 1942, 369 ff.; *Gym.* 60, 1953, 8-20; C. Préaux, *Les Grecs en Egypte d'après les archives de Zénon*, Brussels, Coll. Lebèque, 1947; H. Braunert, "*Idia*, Studien zur Bevölkerungsgesch. des ptol. u. röm. Ägypten," *JJP* 9-10, 1955-56, 211-328; *Die Binnenwanderung. Studien zur Sozialgesch. Ägyptens in der Ptolemäer- u. Kaiserzeit*, Bonn 1964; W. Peremans, "Egyptiens et étrangers dans l'Egypte ptolémaïque," in *Fondation Hardt, Entretiens* 7, 1962, 123-166; *idem*, "Über die Zweisprachigkeit im ptolemäischen Ägypten," in *Studien zur Papyrologie und antiken Wirtschaftsgeschichte, Friedrich Oertel gewidmet*, Bonn 1964, 49-60. Also to be noted are the studies by A. Świderek on the native population of Egypt, *JJP* 7-8, 1953-1954, 231-284, and on Greek society in Egypt, based on the documents of the Zenon archive, *JJP* 9-10, 1955-1956, 365-400. See also J. Crawford, *Kerkeosiris, an Egyptian Village in the Ptolemaic Period*, Cambridge 1972. A valuable aid is the *Prosopographia Ptolemaica*, edited by W. Peremans and E. van t'Dack, to date 8 vols., Louvain 1950-1975; also his assessment of the evidence in the articles: W. Peremans, *Ancient Society* 1, 1970, 1-38; 5, 1974, 127-135; 6, 1975, 61-69; *idem*, *Orientalia Lovanensia Periodica* 6-7, 1975-76, 443-453 (on the social classes and national consciousness in Ptolemaic Egypt); as well as *idem*, Ethnics et classes dans l'Egypte ptolemaïque," in *Recherches sur les structures sociales dans l'antiquité classique*, Paris 1970, 213-223.

On jurisprudence and administration: L. Mitteis, *Reichsrecht und Volksrecht in den östlichen Provinzen des röm. Kaiserreiches*, Leipzig 1891 (reprint 1935); F. Zucker, *Beitr. z. Kenntnis der Gerichtsorganisation im ptol. u. röm. Ägypten*, Ph. Suppl. XII 1, 1912; E. Seidl, *Der Eid im ptol. Recht,* Diss. Munich 1929; E. Berneker, *Zur Gesch. der Prozesseinl. im ptol. Recht*, Diss. Munich 1930; *Die Sondergerichtsbarkeit im griechischen Recht Ägyptens*, Munich 1935; H. J. Wolff, "Faktoren der Rechtsbildung im hellenistisch-römischen Ägypten," *ZSS Röm.* 70, 1953, 20 ff.; *Das Justizwesen der Ptolemäer* (Münch. Beitr. 44), Munich 1962; "Organisation der Rechtspflege und Rechtskontrolle der Verwaltung im ptolemäisch-römischen Ägypten bis Diokletian," *Tijdschrift voor Rechtsgeschiedenis* 34, 1966, 1 ff.; R. Taubenschlag, "The Ancient Greek City Laws in Ptolemaic Egypt," *Actes Vème Congr. de Papyr.*, 1938, 471 ff.; *The Law of Greco-Roman Egypt in the Light of the Papyri*, Warsaw ²1955; E. Seidl, *Ptolemäische Rechtsgeschichte* (Ägyptolog. Forschungen 22), Glückstadt 1962. On the administration of Egypt see, in addition to the earlier works cited in M. Rostovtzeff, *CAH* VII, 893 f., and Préaux, *Econ.*, 586, also M.-Th. Lenger, *Corpus des ordonnances des Ptolémées*, Acad. Royale de Belgique, Mémoires, Classe des Lettres 57,2, Brussels 1964; P. Handrock, *Dienstliche Weisungen in den Papyri der Ptolemäerzeit*, jur. Diss. Cologne 1967; M.-Th. Lenger, "Ordres administratifs et *prostagmata* dans l'Egypte ptolémaïque," *Cd'E* 42, 1967, 145 ff.; C. B. Welles, "The Ptolemaic Administration of Egypt," *JJP* 3, 1949, 21 ff.; as well as Bengtson, *Strat.* III (reprint 1967 [with additional references]); cf. also the contributions by H. Bengtson and B.A. van Gronningen, *MusHelv* 10, 1953, 161 ff. or 178 ff.; J. D. Thomas, *The Epistrategos in Ptolemaic and Roman Egypt. Part 1: The Ptolemaic Epistrategos*, Opladen 1975. On topography: E. van t'Dack, *Cd'E* 23, 1948, 147 ff. On the administration of the Thebaid: *idem*, *Aeg.* 29, 1949, 3 ff. On the administration of Cyprus: T. B. Mitford, *Aeg.* 33, 1953, 80 ff. On the administration of Pamphylia: L. Robert, *Documents de l'Asie Mineure méridionale*, Geneva-Paris, 1966 (decree of Termessos, from 281/0 B.C., mentioning a Pamphyliarch and *Dikastai*). On the military system: J. Lesquier, *Les institutions milit. de l'Egypte sous les Lagides*, Paris 1911; F. Zucker, *Doppelinschrift spätptolemäischer Zeit aus der Garnison von Hermopolis Magna*, Abh. B, 1937, no. 6 (with a supplementary article in *Aeg.* 18, 1938, 279 ff.). On the Ptolemaic fleet: U. Wilcken, "Zur Trierarchie im Lagidenreich," in *Raccolta in onore di G. Lumbroso,* Milan 1925, 93 ff. On the Priesthood and its attitude towards the state: W. Otto, *Priester und Tempel im hell. Ägypten* I-II, Leipzig 1905 and 1908 (cf. the review by M. Rostovtzeff, *GGA*, 1909, 603 ff.); W. Spiegelberg and W. Otto, *Eine neue Urkunde zur Siegesfeier des Ptolemaios IV. und die Frage der ägyptischen Priestersynoden*, SB.M, 1926, 2. Abh.; cf. T. Säve-Söderbergh, *Einige ägyptische Denkmäler aus Schweden*, Uppsala 1945, 39 ff.; E. Visser, *Götter und Kulte im ptolem. Alexandrien*, Amsterdam 1938. Of value is J. Ijsewijn, *De sacerdotibus sacerdotisque Alexandri Magni et Lagidarum eponymis*, Brussels 1961. On Asylia: F.v. Woess, *Das Asylwesen Ägyptens in der Ptolemäerzeit und die spätere Entwicklung*, Munich 1923; and the extensive bibliography on the *katochoi* of the Serapeum at Memphis, cited by Rostovtzeff, *SEHHW* III, 1497; cf. Nilsson, *Gr. Rel.* II 190 n. 3. On Ptolemaic Economics: U. Wilcken, *Griech. Ostraka aus*

Ägypten und Nubien I-II, Berlin 1899; M. Rostovtzeff, *Studien z. Gesch. d. röm. Kolonates*, 1. Beiheft z. *AfP*, Leipzig 1910; *idem*, "The Foundations of Social and Economic Life in Egypt in Hellenistic Times," *JEA* 6, 1920, 161 ff.; *A Large Estate in Egypt in the IIIrd Century B.C.*, Madison 1922; U. Wilcken, "Alexander d. Gr. u. die hellenist. Wirtschaft," *SJ* 45, 1921, 349 ff.; F. Heichelheim, *RE* XVI, 158 ff. s.v. *Monopole*; *RE* Suppl. VI, 863 ff. s.v. *Sitos*; *Wirts. Alt.*, 458 ff.; Préaux, *Econ.* (a comprehensive study of Ptolemaic political economy); also her many other specialised studies, mostly in *Cd'E*: for instance: "Sur les communications de l'Ethiopie avec l'Egypte hellénistique," *Cd'E* 27, 1952, 257 ff.; "Sur les origines des monopoles lagides," *Cd'E* 29, 1954, 312 ff.; "Tradition et imagination dans la civilisation hellénistique en Egypte," *Acad. royale de Belgique, Bull. de Classe des Lettres*, 5ème serie, Vol. 44, 1958, 199-217. On trade: U. Wilcken, "Puntfahrten in der Ptolemäerzeit," *ÄZ* 60, 1925, 86 ff.; H. Kortenbeutel, *Der ägypt. Süd- und Osthandel in der Politik der Ptolemäer und römischen* Kaiser, Diss. Berlin 1931; M. Rostovtzeff, "Foreign Commerce in Ptolemaic Egypt," *Journ. of Economic and Business History* 4, 1932, 728 ff; *idem*, "Alexandrien und Rhodos," *Klio* 30, 1937, 70 ff.; and otherwise the relevant chapters in *SEHHW*. On industry: Th. Reil, *Beitr. z. Kenntnis des Gewerbes im hellenist. Ägypten*, Diss. Leipzig 1913 (in great detail). On leitourgia and corvée work: F. Oertel, *Die Liturgie*, Leipzig 1917. On agriculture: M. Schnebel, *Die Landwirtschaft im hellenist. Ägypten* I (Münch. Beitr. 7), Munich 1925 (incomplete). On the Ptolemaic system in general see W. L. Westermann, "The Great Exploitation of Egypt," *Political Science Quarterly* 40, 1925, 517 ff; *idem*, "The Ptolemies and the Welfare of their Subjects," *AHR* 46, 1938, 271 ff.; H. Heinen, "Heer und Gesellschaft im Ptolemäerreich," *Ancient Society* 4, 1973, 91-114.

The more recent material for the Antigonid Kingdom has been assembled by Rostovtzeff, *SEHHW* III, 1470 f.; cf. Bengtson, *Strat.* II, 317 ff. The most important publication of inscriptions is that by C. B. Welles, "New Texts from the Chancery of Philip V of Macedonia," *AJA* 42, 1938, 245 ff.; cf. F. Papazoglou, *Klio* 52, 1970, 305 ff. Of importance for an understanding of the Macedonian army under Philip V are the inscriptions found at Amphipolis: see P. Roussel, "Un réglement militaire de l'époque macédonienne," *Rev. arch.*, 1934, I 39 ff.; M. Feyel, *Rev. arch.*, 1935, II 29 ff.; bibliography in Bengtson, *Strat.* II, 333 n.1; cf. Walbank, *Phil. V*, 289 ff. On Macedonian coins cf., in addition to the standard work by H. Gaebler, *Die antiken Münzen Nordgriechenlands* III (*Makedonia und Paionia*), Berlin 1906 and 1935, also E. Mamroth, *Z. f. Num.* 40, 1930, 277 ff.; 42, 1932-35, 219 ff.; and the report by P. R. Franke, *JNG* 7, 1956, 105 ff.

On the beginnings of the Attalid Kingdom of Pergamum see M. Rostovtzeff, "Notes on the Economic Policy of the Pergamene Kings," in *Anatolian Studies Presented to Sir William Ramsay*, 1923, 359 ff.; *CAH* VIII, 590 ff.; *SEHHW* I, 553 ff.; III, 1448 ff.; Bengtson, *Strat.* II, 195 ff.

The institutions of the Greek Federal Leagues, especially the Aetolian and Achaean Leagues, are known primarily through inscriptions (particularly important is *IG* IX 1², edited by G. Klaffenbach), and literary sources (Polybius, Livy, Plutarch's *Vitae* of Aratus, Philopoemen, *et al.*). Detailed modern studies may be found in *Staatsaltertümer* of the nineteenth century, cited by Ehrenberg, *State*, 257 f. The following specialised studies may be cited here (survey of bibliography in *CAH* VII, 883 ff.): H. Swoboda's work within the framework of K. F. Hermann's *Lehrbuch der griechischen Staatsaltertümer* I 3, Tübingen 1913; G. Busolt and H. Swoboda, *Griech. Staatskunde* II (HdA IV 1,1,2), 1926, 1507 ff.; E. Kornemann, *RE* Suppl IV, 923 ff. s.v. *Koinon*; W. Schwahn, *RE* IV A, 1171 ff. s.v. *Sympoliteia.* Also the following more recent studies may be cited here: For the Aetolian League: Flacelière, *Ait.* (cf. the excellent review by G. Klaffenbach, *Klio* 32, 1939, 189 ff.); F. W. Walbank, *Aratos of Sicyon*, Cambridge 1933; A. Aymard, *Les assemblées de la confédération achaienne*, Bordeaux 1938; *Les premiers rapports de Rome et de la conféd. achaienne (198-189 av. J.-C.)*, Brussels 1938 (on both works see M. Gelzer, *Gn.* 15, 1939, 614 ff.); and, finally, a number of shorter studies by Aymard, enumerated in *WG* 5, 1939, 185 n. 79.; also J. A. O. Larsen, "The Rights of Cities Within the Achaean Confederacy," *CP* 66, 1971, 81 ff. Important for assessing relations between communities (Megara) and the Achaean League are the inscriptions from Pagae (from c. 200 B.C.) (*IG* VII 188 and 189), which have been discussed by L. Robert, *Rev. de phil.* 13, 1939, 97 ff. On the League of the Acarnanians: C. Habicht, *Hermes* 85, 1957, 86 ff. (= *IG* IX 1,2² no. 583). On the Boeotian League: P. Roesch, *Thespies et la Confédération béotienne*, Paris 1965. An excellent general study is J. A. O. Larsen, *Gr. Fed. S.*

Smaller Greek states: Rhodes: H. van Gelder, *Gesch. d. alten Rhodier*, 1900 (partly out of date); Fr. Frhr. Hiller von Gaertringen, *RE* Suppl. V, 772 ff. s.v. *Rhodos*; M. Rostovtzeff, *CAH* VIII, 620 ff.; *SEHHW* III, Index s.v. Rhodes, especially I, 169 ff.; 228 ff.; E. Ziebarth, "Zur Handelsgeschichte der Insel Rhodos," *Mélanges G. Glotz* II, 1932, 911 ff.; and the study cited above 542 by H. H. Schmitt. Sparta in the Hellenistic period: V. Ehrenberg, *RE* III A, 1421 ff.; P. Cloché, "La politique extérieure de Lacédémone depuis la mort d'Agis III jusqu'à celle de Acrotatos, fils d'Areus Ier" [331-262 B.C.], *REA* 47, 1945, 219 ff. (containing little that is new).

The Syracusan Kingdom: W. Hüttl, *Verfassungsgeschichte von Syrakus*, Prague 1929, 128 ff.; also the works cited above 547 n. 101 by Graf Stauffenberg and H. Berve. The *Lex Hieronica*: J. Carcopino, *La loi d'Hiéron et les Romains*, Paris 1919. Cf. also R. R. Holloway. *The Thirteen-Months Coinage of Hieronymos of Syracuse* (Antike Münzen und Geschnittene Steine Bd. III), Berlin 1969, and Bengtson, *KS*. 367 ff.

THE UNIVERSAL SOVEREIGNTY OF THE GREEK MIND

BIBLIOGRAPHY: Among modern works on Hellenistic culture Rostovtzeff's *SEHHW* towers far above the rest. Chapter VIII in particular ("Summary and Epilogue," Vol. II 1026 ff.) contains an outstanding sketch of the most important cultural, economic and social aspects of Hellenism. A great amount of material and the most important modern studies are amassed in the copious footnotes on the chapter (III 1582 ff.). In addition to Rostovtzeff's work, the following may be cited as outstanding achievements within a smaller framework: P. Wendland, *Die hellenistisch-römische Kultur in ihren Beziehungen zu Judentum und Christentum* (Hdb. z. NT I 2), [2-3]1912; Otto, *Kulturg.*, 93 ff.; and *Antike Kulturgeschichte, Betrachtungen zu Ernst Howalds "Kultur der Antike,"* SB.M, 1940, Heft 6 (it should be noted that Otto includes the entire Roman Empire in the term Hellenism); further, W. W. Tarn, *Hellenistic Civilisation*, London [2]1930; [3]1952 (together with G. T. Griffith); Wilcken, *Alex.* (Chapter X: "Prospect"); H. Herter, "Hellenismus und Hellenentum," in *NBAnt.* 1, 1942, 334 ff. In addition, the following, still more recent, studies: M. Hadas, *Hellenistic Culture, Fusion and Diffusion*, New York 1959; [2]1972; C. Schneider, *Kulturgeschichte des Hellenismus* I, Munich 1967 (a wealth of material; the narrative is in part aphoristic); H. Bengtson, *Wesenszüge der hellenistischen Zivilisation* (Meded. Vlaamse Akad. van Wet., XXX,3), Brussels 1968 (lecture) = *KS*, 274 ff.

From the vast number of specialised studies only a small selection can be cited here. Reference will be made above all to such works and studies which, through their bibliography, make further progress in the subject possible.

On the condition of communications in the Hellenistic period: Rostovtzeff, *SEHHW* II, 1032 ff.; III, 1583 ff.; on the *Periploi*: F. Gisinger, *RE* XIX, 841 ff.; also A. Köster, *Das antike Seewesens*, 1923, 187 ff.; and R. Güngerich, *Die Küstenbeschreibung in der griech. Literatur*, Münster i.W. 1950. On the *Koine*: P. Kretschmer, *Die Entstehung der Koine*, SB.W 143, 1900, no. 10; A. Thumb, *Die griechische Sprache im Zeitalter des Hellenismus*, 1901; a concise discussion of more recent date: L. Radermacher, *Koine*, SB. W 224,5, 1947; excellent orientation: E. Schwyzer, *Griech. Grammatik* I, 1939, 116 ff. Also instructive is S. G. Kapsomenos, "Das Griechische in Ägypten," *MusHelv* 10, 1953, 248 ff. On the system of Greek documents: U. Wilcken *Über antike Urkundenlehre* (Münch. Beitr. 19), 1934, 42 ff. On the development of jurisprudence: L. Mitteis, *Reichsrecht u. Volksrecht in den östlichen Provinzen des röm. Kaiserreiches*, 1891 (reprint 1935); P. Koschaker, *Über einige griech. Rechtsurkunden aus den östl. Randgebieten des Hellenismus*, Abh. Sächs. Ak., phil. hist. Kl. 42, 1, 1931; further, above all the works by L. Wenger and the Munich papyrological school, published in Münch. Beitr. Valuable are L. Wenger's "Juristische Literaturberichte," in *AfP* 7 ff.; cf. also *idem, Ludwig Mitteis und sein Werk*, 1923; "Ludwig Mitteis u. die hellenist. Rechtsgeschichte," *Arch. d'Hist. du Droit orient.* I, 1937, 181 ff. The

Greek Gymnasium: F. Zucker, "*Gymnasiarchos Komes*" *Aeg.* 11, 1931, 485 ff.; T. A. Brady, *The Gymnasium in Ptolemaic Egypt*, Univ. of Missouri Studies II, 3, 1936, 9 ff.; Rostovtzeff, *SEHHW* III, 1395, 1588 (bibliography and sources); Nilsson, *Sch.*, especially 83 ff. Double names: Otto, *Kulturg.*, 100 n. 201; Rita Calderini, "Ricerche sul doppionome personale nell'Egitto greco-romano," *Aeg.* 21, 1941, 221 ff.; 22, 1942, 3 ff. (cf. L. Robert, *REG* 59-60, 1946/47, 207). The Dionysian artists: G. Klaffenbach, *Symb. ad histor. colleg. artif. Bacchior.*, Diss. Berlin 1914; concise is F. Poland, *RE* V A, 2473 ff.; cf. L. Robert, *BCH* 59, 1935, 193 ff. The Societies and Guilds: E. Ziebarth, *Das griech. Vereinswesen*, 1896, 101 ff.; F. Poland, *Gesch. d. griech. Vereinswesens*, 1909, 116 ff.; M. San Nicolò, *Aegyptisches Vereinswesen zur Zeit der Ptolemäer und Römer* I, 1913; II 1, 1915; also the references in Rostovtzeff, *SEHHW* III, 1388 f.; 1590 ff.; and in Nilsson, *Gr. Rel.* II, [2]1961, 117 ff. (on the religious societies); especially interesting is the older article by M. L. Strack, "Die Müllerinnung in Alexandrien," *Z. Neutest. Wiss.* 4, 1903, 213 ff.; very important is C. Roberts, T. C. Skeat, A. D. Nock, "The Gild of Zeus Hypsistos," *Harv. Theol. Rev.* 29, 1936, 39 ff. The Greek city complexes in the East: G. Cultrera, "Architettura Ippodamea," *Mem. Acc. Lincei* 17, 1924, 357 ff.; A. v. Gerkan, *Griech. Städteanlagen*, 1924, 62 ff.; K. A. Doxiadis, *Raumordnung im griech. Städebau*, 1937; Fr. Krischen, *Die griech. Stadt, Wiederherstellungen*, 1938; E. Fabricius, *RE* III A, 2001 ff. s.v. *Städtebau (der Griechen*); cf. Rostovtzeff, *SEHHW* III, 1587. Valuable is the work by F. G. Maier, *Griech. Mauerbauinschriften* 2 vols., 1959 and 1961. The *Mouseion* of Alexandria and Alexandrian Philology: R. Pfeiffer, *History of Classical Scholarship*, 1968; P. M. Fraser *PA*, 447 ff.; 495 ff. Hellenistic Poetry: F. Susemihl, *Gesch. d. griech, Lit. in der Alexandrinerzeit*, Leipzig 1891-1892; A. Rostagni, *Poeti alessandrini*, 1916; Schmid-Stählin, *GGL* II I[6], Munich 1920; U. v. Wilamowitz-Moellendorff, *Hellenistische Dichtung*, 1924; A. Körte, *Die hellenistische Dichtung*, 1925; W. W. Tarn, *Hellenistic Civilisation*, [3]1952, 235 ff.; H. Herter, *Burs. Jb.* 225, 1937; Fraser, *PA* I, 305 ff.; 553 ff.; 618 ff.; 674 ff.; 717 ff. On Greek literature in the Seleucid empire: Altheim, *As.* II, 1948, 137 ff. A new edition of Callimachus was published by R. Pfeiffer, Oxford 1949 and 1953. Libraries in the Hellenistic period: Bibliography in M. Rostovtzeff, *SEHHW* III, 1589 f.; C. Wendel, *Gesch. der Bibliotheken im griech.-röm. Altertum*, in Hdb. der Bibliothekswissenschaft III, Leipzig 1940; an excellent specialised study: C. Callmer, in *Opusc. Arch.* 3, 1944, 145 ff. The Exact Sciences: J. L. Heiberg, *Die Gesch. der Mathematik u. Naturwissenschaften* (HdA V 1, 2), 1925 (cf., however, A. Rehm, *DLZ*, 1926, 2275 f.); A. Rehm and K. Vogel, "Exakte Wissenschaften," in Gercke-Norden, *Einl.* II 5, [3]1933, 40 ff. (with excellent bibliography); Fraser, *PA* I, 336 ff. Eratosthenes: basic is Knaack, *RE* VI, 358 ff.; additional bibliography, especially on the question of geodesy, in A. Rehm, in Gercke-Norden II 5, 44; also P. M. Fraser, *Eratosthenes of Cyrene* (*British Academy Lecture on a Mastermind*, 1970), London 1971; and *idem, PA* I, 526 ff. Archimedes: basic is the edition of his works by J. L. Heiberg, Leipzig ²1910-15; cf. F. Hultsch, *RE* II, 507 ff.; F. Arendt, *RE* Suppl. III, 144 ff. Technology: H. Diels, *Antike Technik*, ³1924; A. Rehm, *Exakte Wissenschaften*, 1933, 55 ff.; "Zur Rolle der Technik in der griech-röm. Antike," *Arch. Kult. Gesch.* 28, 1938, 135 ff.; *ibid.*, 138 n. 4 contains a survey of the relevant bibliography. Important for the *poliorketai* is E. Schramm, in J. Kromayer and G. Veith, *Heerw.*, 109 ff.; and E. Pernice, *Literarische Zeugnisse*, in Hdb. d. Arch. I, 1939, 260 ff. (in collaboration with A. Rehm); cf., finally, Rostovtzeff, *SEHHW* III, 1595 f. Hellenistic Shipbuilding: A. Köster, *Das antike Seewesens*, 1923, 158 ff.; 20 ff.; F. Miltner, *RE* Suppl. V, 914 ff. s.v. *Seewesen*; A. W. Persson, "Die hellenist. Schiffsbaukunst u. die Nemischiffe," *Opusc. Arch.* I, 1935, 129 ff.; additional studies are cited in Rostovtzeff, *SEHHW* III, 1584 f. Hellenistic Physicians and Hellenistic Medicine: R. Pohl, *De Graecorum medicis publicis*, Diss. Berlin 1905; J. Oehler, *Epigr. Beitr. z. Gesch. d. Arztestandes*, Progr. Maximiliansgymn., Vienna 1907; M. Wellmann, "Beitr. z. Gesch. d. Medizin im Altertum," *Hermes* 65, 1930, 322 ff.; W. Jaeger, *Diokles von Karystos. Die griechische Medizin u. die Schule des Aristoteles*, 1938. On the Medical School of Cos: R. Herzog, *JdAI* 47, 1932, *AA*, 274 ff.; *Kos. Ergebnisse d. Ausgrabungen* I, 1932; "Die Asklepiosheiligtümer als Heilstätten und Gnadeorte," *Münch. Med. Wochenschr., Jubiläumsjahrg.*, 1933, 1 ff. Epidaurus: R. Herzog, *Die Wunderheilungen von Epidauros*, Ph. Suppl. 22,3, 1931; On Drugs: A Schmidt, *Drogen u. Drogenhandel im Altertum*, 1924; *RE* Suppl. V, 172 ff. Abundant material in Rostovtzeff, *SEHHW*, III, 1597 ff. Geographical Explorations: F. Gisinger, *RE* Suppl. IV 592 ff. s.v. *Geographie*; M. Cary and E. H. Warmington, *The Ancient Explorers*, 1932; E. H. Warmington, *Greek Geography*, London 1934; R. Hennig, *Terrae incognitae* I², Leiden 1944 (needs to be examined critically); J. O. Thomson, *History of Ancient Geography*, Cambridge 1948. The discovery of the direct sea route to India: Otto-Bengtson, *Ptol.*, 194 ff.; also the study cited *infra* 588 n. 94, by J. H. Thiel; also R. Delbrueck, "Südasiatische Seefahrt im Altertum," *Bonner Jahrbücher* 155-156, 1955-1956, 8-58. Mention may be made in particular of Agatharchides of Cnidus, who in the second century B.C. wrote a work on the Red Sea: see D. Woelk, *Agatharchides von Knidos, Über das Rote Meer. Übersetzung und Kommentar*, Diss. Freiburg i. Br., published Bamberg 1966. See also the discussion by Fraser, *PA* I, 520 ff. Still valuable, from earlier works, is H. Berger, *Gesch. d. wiss. Erdkunde d. Griechen*, Leipzig ²1903. Astronomy and Astrology: A brief survey may be found in A. Rehm, *Exakte Wissenschaften*, 1933, 46 ff.; F. Boll, C. Bezold, W. Gundel, *Sternglaube und Sterndeutung. Die Geschichte und das Wesen der Astrologie*, ed. 5 (by H. G. Gundel), Darmstadt 1966; W. Gundel and H. G. Gundel, *Astrologomena. Die astrologische Literatur in der Antike und ihre Geschichte*, Sudhoffs Archiv, 6. Beiheft, Wiesbaden 1966. On Aristarchus: T. L. Heath, *Aristarchus of Samos*, Oxford 1923. On Hipparchus: A. Rehm, *RE* VIII, 1666 ff. On Astrology: In addition to the works cited above see also J. Bidez, "Les écoles chaldéennes sous Alexandre et les Séleucides," *Ann.*

Inst. de Phil. et d'Hist. Or. III, 1935, 41 ff.; M. P. Nilsson, *The Rise of Astrology in the Hellenistic Age* (Meddelande frên Lunds Astronomiska Observatorium, Hist. Notes and Papers 18), Lund 1943; R. P. Festugière, *La révélation d'Hermès Trismégiste.* I-IV, Paris 1944-1954. From the many relevant studies by F. Cumont (enumerated and discussed to 1933 by W. Gundel, *Burs. Jb.* 243, 1934, cf. also the bibliography in *Mélanges F. Cumont*, 1936, VII ff.), the following may be cited: L'Egypte des astrologues, Brussels 1937 (cf., however, L. Robert, *Et. d'épigr. et de philologie*, 1938, 76 ff.; 84 ff.). For an excellent summary see Nilsson, *Gr. Rel.* II, 268 ff. Important for Greek Astronomy in the early part of the second century B.C. is *P. Ryl.* IV 589. The papyrus proves the existence of the 25-year-moon-cycle as early as the year 180 B.C.

Hellenistic Architecture: A. Rumpf, in Gercke-Norden, *Einl.* II 1,3, 65 ff. (with a list of Hellenistic temples and secular buildings of which ruins are extant); Th. Fyfe, *Hellenistic Architecture*, Cambridge 1936; interesting aspects in W. v. Massow, *Führer durch das Pergamonmuseum*, Berlin 1932, 17 ff.; and H. Kähler, *Wandlungen der antiken Form*, Munich 1949. Deinocrates: W. Körte, "Deinokrates u. die barocke Phantasie," *Ant.* 13, 1937, 289 ff. The Temple of Apollo at Didyma: *Didyma* I: *Die Baubeschreibung*, by H. Knackfuss, 1941. The Great Altar of Pergamum: H. Kähler, *Der grosse Fries von Pergamon*, Berlin 1948; *Pergamon* (Bilderhefte ant. Kunst, 9), Berlin 1949. Some information on Hellenistic painting may be found in C. M. Dawson, "Roman-Campanian Mythological Landscape Painting," *YCS* 9, 1944.

Hellenistic Historiography: A modern comprehensive study is lacking. On Manetho: R. Laqueur, *RE* XIV, 1060 ff. s.v.; on Berossus: P. Schnabel, *Berossos u. die babylonisch-hellenistische Literatur*, Leipzig 1923; C. F. Lehmann-Haupt, "Neue Studien zu Berossos," *Klio* 22, 1929, 125 ff.; Fraser, *PA* I, 495 ff.; on Hecataeus of Abdera: F. Jacoby, *RE* VII, 2750 ff. (cf. *FgrHist.* III no. 264); on the orientation of the work: Ed. Schwartz, *RhM* 40, 1885, 223 ff., and, in part opposed to him, F. Jacoby, *RE* VII, 2754 ff.; new views are advanced by C. B. Welles, *JJP* 3, 1949, 40 ff. Hecataeus and the Jews: W. Jaeger, "The First Greek Records of Jewish Religion and Civilisation," *Journal of Religion* 18, 1938, 127 ff., esp. 136 ff. Of value is the document collection *Corpus Papyrorum Judaicarum* I-III, edited by V. A. Tcherikover and A. Fuks, Cambridge, Mass., 1957-1964; and V. Tcherikover, *Hellenistic Civilisation and the Jews*, Philadelphia 1959, as well as M. Hengel, *Judentum und Hellenismus*, Tübingen 1969. The religious attitudes of the Greeks in the Hellenistic period: K. Latte, "Religiöse Strömungen in der Frühzeit des Hellenismus," *Ant.* I, 1925, 146 ff.; F. Pfister, *Burs. Jb.* 229 *Suppl.*, 1930; Wilamowitz-Moellendorff, *Gl.* II, 1932, (ed. G. Klaffenbach); A. D. Nock, *Conversion. The Old and the New in Religion from Alexander the Great to Augustine of Hippo*, Oxford 1933; O. Kern, *Die Religion der Griechen* III, 1938; W. Schubart, *Die religiöse Haltung des frühen Hellenismus* (AO 35, 2), Leipzig 1937 (= *Glaube u. Bildung im Wandel der Zeiten*, Munich 1947, 9 ff.); E. Visser *Götter u. Kulte im ptol. Alexan-*

drien, Amsterdam 1938; H. I. Bell, "Graeco-Egyptian Religion," *MusHelv* 10, 1953, 222 ff.; *Cults and Creeds in Graeco-Roman Egypt*, Liverpool 1953; Fraser, *PA* I, 189 ff. On the Iranian religion of Zoroaster and its Hellenisation: J. Bidez and F. Cumont, *Les Mages hellénisées. Zoroastre, Ostanès et Hystaspe d'après la tradition grecque*, 2 vols., Paris 1938. On religious syncretism: F. Cumont, *Les religions orientales dans le paganisme rom.*, Paris [4]1929; also available in a German translation (with improvements by A. Burckhardt-Brandenberg) under the title *Die orientalischen Religionen im röm, Heidentum*, [3]1930 and [1959]; T. A. Brady, *The Reception of the Egyptian Cults by the Greeks 330-30 B.C.*, 1935. F. W. Frhr. v. Bissing, *Ägyptische Kulturbilder der Ptolemaier- und Römerzeit* (AO 23, 1/2), Leipzig 1937. In denying syncretism, C. Schneider, "Die griech. Grundlagen der hellenist. Religionsgesch.," *ARW* 36, 1939, 300 ff., goes too far, even though it is legitimate and fruitful to raise the question to what extent the phenomena of Hellenistic religious history are to be explained in terms of Greek derivation. A similar approach to Schneider's is that of G. Vandebeek, *De interpretatio Graeca van de Isisfiguur*, Louvain 1946, and D. Müller, *Ägypten und die griech. Isis-Aretalogien*, Abh. Akad. Leipzig 53, 1, 1961. Hellenistic Philosophy: In addition to the large handbooks (Überweg-Prächter, *Philos. d. Alt.*, [12]1928; E. Zeller, *Grundriss d. Gesch. d. griech. Philosophie*, ed. 13, by W. Nestle, 1926), the following are useful for orientation: A. Gercke, *Gesch. d. Philos.*, ed. 4, by E. Hoffmann, in Gercke-Norden, *Einl.* II 6, 1933 (with the most important bibliography), on Hellenism, 72 ff.; and W. Capelle, *Geschichte der Philosophie* IV, in *Sammlung Göschen* Bd. 859, Berlin [2]1954. Indispensable as compilations of the sources are: H. Usener, *Epicurea*, 1887; and H. v. Arnim, *Stoicorum veterum fragmenta*, 4 vols., 1905-24. Outstanding sketches on the founders of the great Hellenistic schools of philosophy may be found in particular in Ed. Schwartz, *Charakterköpfe aus der Antike*, ed. 3, by J. Stroux, 1943 (a survey of the most important bibliography in the Appendix); see also Fraser, *PA* I, 480 ff. On Zenon's *Politeia* (the fragments in H. v. Arnim, *Stoic. Vet. frag.* I nos. 259-71), see O. Rieth, *Grundbegriffe der stoischen Ethik* (Problemata 9), 1933; "Über das Telos der Stoiker," *Hermes* 69, 1934, 13 ff.; E. Elorduy, *Die Sozialphilosophie der Stoa*, Ph. Suppl. 28, 3, 1936; R. Philippson, "Zur Psychologie der Stoa," *RhM* 86, 1937, 140 ff. The standard work on the Stoa is now that by M. Pohlenz, *Die Stoa*, 2 vols., Göttingen 1948 [[2]1955 and 1959]. On the beginnings of Greek philosophy in Rome: R. Harder, "Die Einbürgerung d. Philosophie in Rome," *Ant.* 5, 1929, 291 ff. = *KS*, 1960, 330 ff. On Hellenistic Kingship: see the many works under the title *Peri Basileias* from the Hellenistic period (extensive bibliography in Rostovtzeff, *SEHHW* III, 1343; 1347; 1379; 1594), and the discussions by E. Goodenough, "The Political Philosophy of the Hellenistic Kingship," *YCS* 1, 1928, 55 ff.; E. Skard, *Zwei religiös-politische Begriffe, Euergetes-Concordia*, Oslo 1932; W. Schubart, "Das hellenistische Königsideal nach Inschriften u. Papyri," *AfP* 12, 1937, 1 ff.;

"Das Königsbild des Hellenismus," *Ant.* 13, 1937, 272 ff.; L. Delatte, *Les traités de la royauté d'Ecphante, Diotogène et Sthénidas*, 1942; Fraser, *PA* I, 93 ff.

1. The figures according to Beloch, *GG* IV 1, 328 f.
2. Diod. I 31.6 ff.; cf. Flavius Josephus, *bell. Jud.* II 385; cf. Rostovtzeff, *SEHHW* II, 1135 ff.; III 1604 ff.
3. The figures of Beloch, *Die Bevölkerung der griech.-röm. Welt.* 1886, are based on too uncertain a foundation. The same applies to the estimates by A. Segrè, *Bull. Soc. Arch. Alex.* 29, 1934, 256 ff.
4. Otto, *Kulturg.*, 105.
5. On the intellectual basis of Hellenistic rulership see in particular Kaerst, *Mon.*; *GH* II^2, 296 ff.; E. R. Goodenough, "The Political Philosophy of the Hellenistic Kingship," *YCS* 1, 1928, 55 ff. Further bibliography in Rostovtzeff, *SEHHW* III, 1594; also W. S. Ferguson, *CAH* VII, 7 ff.
6. The Ptolemies and Alexander: W. W. Tarn, *JHS* 53, 1933, 57 ff.; the Seleucids: M. Rostovtzeff, "*Progonoi*," *JHS* 55, 1935, 62; the Antigonids: C. F. Edson Jr., "The Antigonids, Heracles and Beroea," *HSCP* 45, 1934, 213 ff.; cf. also Nilsson, *Gr. Rel.* II, 154.
7. *Suda* s.v. *Basileia*; cf. Kaerst, *Mon.*, 59; also already *supra* 234.
8. Noteworthy are the after-effects of this idea (in conjunction with Justinian's *Novellae* 105, II 4) in the Middle Ages: cf. A. Steinwenter *Anz. W*, 1946, no. XIX 250 ff.
9. Otto, *Kulturg.*, 112 f. (on the investigations of S. Grenz. *Beitr. z. Gesch. d. Diadems in den hellenist. Reichen*, Diss. Greifswald 1921). In detail, H.-W. Ritter, *Diadem und Konigsherrschaft*, Munich 1965.
10. W. Otto, *AfP* 6, 1920, 321 f.; cf. *SEG* I no. 374.
11. W. Otto, *Epitymbion, H. Swoboda dargebracht*, 1927, 194 ff.; also Otto-Bengtson, *Ptol.*, 154.
12. The Seleucids, Parthians and the Pontic rulers, etc., took advantage of the times.
13. For the Ptolemies see M. L. Strack, *Die Dynastie der Ptolemäer*, 1897, 24 f.; for the Seleucids: Bikermann, *Sél.*, 22; Bengtson, *Strat.* II, 83 n. 1. For Macedonia (Demetrius II) along with Antigonus Gonatas: M. Andronikos, *Archaiai epigraphai Beroias*. Saloniki 1950, no. 1.
14. V.s.p. 249.
15. On the further effects cf. F. Dölger, "Die 'Familie der Könige' im Mittelalter," *Hist. Jb.*, 1940, 397 ff. (*Festg. f. R.v. Heckel*).
16. On the subject of titles in the Hellenistic period see M. L. Strack, *RhM* 55, 1900, 161 ff.; A. Momigliano, "Honorati amici," *Ath.* NS 11, 1933, 139 ff.; T. C. Skeat. *Mizraim* 2, 1936, 30 ff.; H. Kortenbeutel, *RE* XX, 95 ff. s.v. *Philos*; extensive bibliography in M. Trindl, *Ehrentitel im Ptolemäerreich*, Diss. Munich 1938 (photocopy, published 1942); further H. Henne, *Mélanges G. Radet*, 1940, 173 ff.; W. Peremans, "Sur la titulature aulique en Egypte au IIe et Ier siècle av. J.-C." in *Symbolae van Oven*. Leiden 1946, 129 ff. [Charts]; K. M. T. Atkinson, *Aeg.* 32, 1952, 204 ff. Important now is L. Mooren, in *Antidorum W. Peremans,* Louvain 1968, 161-180; *idem, The Aulic Titulature in Ptolemaic Egypt*, Brussels 1975 (with inclusive bibliography).
17. Wilcken, *Kult.*, 308. The latest summary is that of Nilsson, *Gr. Rel.* II, 154 ff. J. A. Tondriau has published a series of investigations with abundant evidence; see the study by L. Cerfaux and J. Tondriau, *Un concurrent du christianisme: Le culte des souverains dans la civilisation grécoromaine*, Tournai 1957, in which the earlier bibliography is cited. On the character of the cult see also Habicht, *Gott.*, 185 ff.
18. The question whether Arsinoe II shared in this cult as living or dead has now been decided in favour of the former alternative, on the basis of *P. Hib.* II 199 (fourteenth year of Ptolemy II = 272/1 B.C.). On the cult see also H. Hauben, *Callicrates of Samos. A Contribution to the Study of Ptolemaic Admiralty*, Uitgaven 1970, 33 ff.
19. W. Ensslin, *Gottkaiser und Kaiser von Gottesgnaden*, SB.M, 1943, Heft 6, 17.
20. See the study by J. Ijsewijn cited above 559.

21. In the foreign dominions of the Ptolemies dating was also based on the eponymous priest of Alexander; cf. *P. Cairo Zenon* I 59003 from Birta in the land of the Ammonites.

22. G. Plaumann, *AfP* VI 85, (cf. F. Bilabel, *Sammelbuch* 6611), cf. U. Wilcken, SB.B, 1938, no. XXVIII 306 ff.

23. The most important document is the inscription from Dodurga (printed in Welles, *RC* no. 36/7), from 193 B.C., which has in the meantime found an exact counterpart in the inscription from Nihawend (L. Robert, *Hel.* 7, 1949, 5 ff.). M. Rostovtzeff, "Progonoi," *JHS* 55, 1935, 56 ff.; *idem*, "Le Gad de Doura et Seleucus Nicator," *Mél. syr. offerts à R. Dussaud*, Bibl. arch et hist. 30, 1939, 281 ff.; Bikerman, *Sél.*, 236 ff.; Nilsson, *Gr. Rel.* II, 165 ff.; L. Cerfaux et J. Tondriau, *op. cit.*, 229 ff.; F. Taeger, *Charisma* I, 1957, 309 ff.

24. See, for instance, Habicht, *Gott.*, 82 ff.

25. *OGI* I 383 = Jalabert-Mouterde, *Inscr. grecq. et. lat. de la Syrie* no. 1; for bibliography v.i.p. 590 n. 128. F. Granier, *Die makedonische Heeresversammlung*, (Münch. Beitr. 13), 1931; cf. Otto-Bengtson, *Ptol.*, 58 n. 3 (opposed to Bikerman, *Sél.*, 8 f.); K. Latte, *NGG*, 1934, 64 ff.

26. Meridarchies also existed in East Iran and in the former Ptolemaic dominion of South Syria, with those in the East apparently being an intermediary stage between the large satrapies and the extremely small hyparchies; cf. Bengtson, *Strat.* II, 26 ff. The eparchies, on the other hand, advocated by W. W. Tarn, *Seleucid-Parthian Studies*, Proceedings of the British Academy 16, 1930, 24 ff. (cf. *idem*, *Bact.*, 1 ff.), are an invention; see Bengtson, *Strat.* II, 30 ff.; Altheim, *As.* I, 273 ff.

27. On the organisation of the Seleucid empire see, besides Bikerman, *Sél.*, 133 ff., the concise discussion in Bengtson, *Strat.* II, 1 ff.

28. L. Robert, *Hell.* 7, 1949, 22 ff.; 8, 1950, 73 ff.

28a. Inscription from Behistun, cf. L. Robert, *Gn.* 35, 1963, 76.

29. Cf. H. Bengtson, *Strat.* II, 143 ff.

30. On the relationship between city and ruler in the Seleucid empire see above all W. Kolbe, *Staat und Stadt im Zeitalter des Hellenismus,* Freiburg. Wiss. Ges. Heft 16, Freiburg 1928; E. Bickermann, "Bellum Antiochicum," *Hermes* 67, 1932, 47 ff.; *Sél.*, 133 ff.; *Rev. de phil.* 65, 1939, 335 ff.; P. Zancan, *Il monarcato ellenistico nei suoi elementi federativi*, Padua 1934, 49 ff.; A. Heuss, *Stadt und Herrscher des Hellenismus in ihren staats- und völkerrechtlichen Beziehungen*, Klio-Beih. 39, 1937 [cf. *supra* 544 n. 45]; A. H. M. Jones, *The Greek City from Alexander to Justinian*, Oxford 1940; Bengtson, *Strat.* II, 8 f., 133 f.; Ehrenberg, *Staat*, 336 = *State*, 284 f.

31. Bengtson, *Strat.* II, 134.

32. U. Kahrstedt, *Syrische Territorien in hellenist. Zeit.*, 1926, 73 ff.; Bikerman, *Sél.*, 149 ff.; H. Seyrig, *Syria* 20, 1939. 35 ff.; Rostovtzeff, *SEHHW* II, 843 ff.; III, 1534.

33. In later sources the Seleucid empire appears as nothing less than an *Imperium Macedonicum* (C. Edson, *CP* 53, 1958, 153 ff.). On the city foundations of the Seleucids see E. Kornemann, "Zur Politik der ersten Nachfolger Alexanders d. Gr.," *Vergangenheit und Gegenwart* 16, 1926, 333 ff.; V. Tscherikower, *Die hellenistischen Städtegründungen*, Ph.-Suppl. XIX 1, 1927, 165 ff., *et passim*; Rostovtzeff, *SEHHW* I, 476 ff.; III, 1436 ff. Important is Appian, *Syr.* 57.

34. On Dura-Europus see F. Cumont, *Fouilles de Doura-Europos*, Paris 1926; cf. *The Excavations at Dura-Europos, Preliminary Reports*, 9 vols., as well as *The Final Reports*, to date, 8 parts; finally, M. Rostovtzeff, "The Foundations of Dura-Europos on the Euphrates," *Ann. Inst. Kondakov* 10, 1938, 99 ff.; A. R. Bellinger, "Seleucid Dura: The Evidence of the Coins," *Berytus* 9, 1948, 51 ff.; of great value is: *The Parchments and Papyri*, edited by C. B. Welles, R. O. Fink and J. F. Gilliam, New Haven 1959 (= *Final Reports* V 1); see also A. Perkins, *The Art of Dura-Europos*, Oxford 1973.

35. F. Oertel, *RE* XI, 3 ff. s.v. *Katoikoi*, Bikerman, *Sél.*, 80 ff., and Tarn, *Bact.*, 1 ff., who, however, places too much emphasis on the importance of the *katoikiai* as compared with the poleis; see, on the other hand, Rostovtzeff, *SEHHW* III, 1437 f. n. 268.

36. Bikerman, *Sél.*, 51 ff.; Bengtson, *Strat.* II, 67 ff.

37. G. T. Griffith, *The Mercenaries of the Hellenistic World*, 1935, 142 ff.

38. Bikerman, *Sél.*, 106 ff., M. Rostovtzeff, *SEHHW* I, 464 ff.; 469 ff.

39. Bengtson, *Strat.* II, 137 n.1.

40. See lastly Rostovtzeff, *SEHHW* I, 514; III, 1442.

41. *SEG* VII nos. 15 ff.; cf. L. Robert, *Rph.*, 1936, 137 ff.; and Rostovtzeff, *SEHHW* III, 1428, 1438.

42. H. Bengtson, *WG* 11, 1951, 135 ff. = *KS.* 293 ff.

43. Thus, however, C. B. Welles, "The Ptolemaic Administration in Egypt," *JJP* 3, 1949, 21 ff. (cf. esp. 47 n. 144).

44. G. Plaumann, *Ptolemäis in Oberägypten*, Leipz. Hist. Abh., 1910.

45. U. Wilcken, *AfP* 5, 1913, 410 ff. (inscription from the second half of the second century); cf. in general T. A. Brady, *The Gymnasium in Ptolemaic Egypt*, Univ. of Missouri Studies II 3, 1936, 9 ff.; and Rostovtzeff, *SEHHW* III, 1395 (extensive bibliography); Nilsson, *Sch.*, 85 ff.

46. H. Gauthier, "Les nomes d'Egypte depuis Hérodote à la conquête arab," *Mémoires présentés à l'Inst. de l'Egypte* 25, Cairo 1935; H. Kees, *RE* XVII, 837 ff.

47. On the Ptolemaic administration cf. M. Rostovtzeff, *CAH* VII, 116 ff.; on the nome *strategos*, Bengtson, *Strat.* III.

48. Bengtson, *Strat.* III, 91 ff.

49. Bengtson, *Strat.* III, 121 ff. L. Mooren, *Ancient Society* 4, 1973, 115 ff.; 5, 1974, 137 ff.; J. D. Thomas, *The Epistrategos in Ptolemaic and Roman Egypt. Part 1: The Ptolemaic Epistrategos*, Opladen 1975.

50. Rostovtzeff, *CAH* VII, 126 ff.; Bengtson, *Strat.* III, 136 ff.

51. On jurisprudence see, besides the studies cited in *CAH* VII, 894, above all the recent investigations carried out in the *Münchener Rechtshistorikerschule* by L. Wenger and especially E. Berneker, *Die Sondergerichtsbarkeit im griech. Recht Ägyptens*, 1935; "Die Rolle des Strategen im Verfahren vor den ptol. Kollegialgerichten," *Mél. Maspero* II, 1934, 1 ff.; in addition also the studies by E. Seidl and J. Wolff cited above 559.

52. The work, standard in its day, by J. Lesquier, *Les instit. milit. de l'Egypte sous les Lagides*, Paris 1911, now requires a complete revision. The study by G. T. Griffith, *The Mercenaries of the Hellenistic World*, Cambridge 1935, 108 ff., is not sufficient. Extensive evidence is furnished by *Recherches sur les armées hellénistiques*, by M. Launey, Bibl. Ecol. franç. d'Ath. et de Rome, 169, Paris 1949 and 1950.

53. See Otto-Bengtson, *Ptol.*, Index s.v. Kypern; cf. A. Rehm, *Ph.* 97, 1948, 267 ff.; 369.

54. On the question of the Ptolemaic cleruchy see, besides the older studies by J. Lesquier, *Les instit. milit.*, 1911, 202 ff.; M. Rostovtzeff, *Stud. z. Gesch. d. röm. Kolonats*, 1910. 6 ff.; U. Wilcken, *Grundzüge*, 280 ff., above all the more recent bibliography cited by Rostovtzeff, *SEHHW* III, 1385. The view occasionally put forward, that the cleruchy was of no economic significance, in particular by M. Gelzer on the basis of the important *P. Freib.* 7, and by E. Kiessling, "Streiflichter zur Katökenfrage," *Actes du IVme congr. de pap.*, 1938 213 ff., is too subtle.

55. On the *politeumata* see above all W. Ruppel, *Ph.* 82, 1927, 269 ff.; M. Rostovtzeff, *CAH* VII, 1222; A. Wilhelm, *AfP* 9, 1930, 214 ff.; on the *Persai tes epigones*, F. Zucker, *RE* XIX, 910 ff.; *NBAnt.* I, 1942, 378 ff.; J. F. Oates, *YCS* 18, 1963, 7-127; E. Bresciani, *PP* 27, 1972, 123-128 (for the Demotic).

56. M. Rostovtzeff, *CAH* VII, 118; *SEHHW* I, 414 (cf. Index s.v. machimoi).

57. See also H. Hauben *Callicrates of Samos: A Contribution to the Study of Ptolemaic Admiralty*, 1970, 33 ff.; I. L. Morken, *H.* 19, 1970, 143 ff.; J. Seibert, *H.* 19, 1970, 337 ff.

58. U. Wilcken, "Zur Trierarchie im Lagidenreich," *Racolta Lumbroso*, 1925, 93 ff.

59. Otto-Bengtson, *Ptol.* 185.

60. See, in addition to W. Otto, *Priester und Tempel im hellenist. Ägypten*, in particular: Rostovtzeff, *SEHHW* I, 280 ff.; also the bibliography, *ibid.*, III, 1383 f.

61. On asylia see, besides the work by E. von Woess, cited above 559. Rostovtzeff, *SEHHW* III, 1549 (with more recent bibliography); on fleeing the land: V. Martin. *Les papyrus et l'hist. admin.*, Münch. Beitr. 19, 1934, 144 ff. (chiefly for the Roman period); C. Préaux, *Econ.*, 500 ff.; W. L. Westermann, *AHR* 43, 1938, 276 ff.

62. On the different categories of land cf., lastly, Rostovtzeff, *SEHHW* I, 276 ff.; III, 1381 ff. (with earlier bibliography) On the "released land" see *P. Teb* III 705, and J. Herrmann, *Cd'E* 30, 1955, 95 ff.

63. U. Wilcken, *Ostraka* I, 650 ff.; *Grundzuge*, 179 ff.; Rostovtzeff. *Gesch. der Staatspacht*, 1902; G. McLean Harper, *Aeg.* 14, 1934, 49 ff.; 269 ff.; Rostovtzeff. *SEHHW I*, 327 ff.; III, 1396 f.

64. On Ptolemaic "monopolies" see above all the "Revenue Laws" of Ptolemy II and *P. Teb.* III, 703; cf. U. Wilcken, *SJ* 45, 2, 1921, 395 ff.; F. Heichelheim, *RE* XVI, 158 ff.; Rostovtzeff, *SEHHW* I, 302 ff.; III, 1388 ff.; Préaux, *Econ.*, 430 ff.; A. Andréades, "De l'origine des monopoles ptolémaïques," *Mél. Maspero* II, 1934-37, 289 ff.

65. W. W. Tarn, "Ptolemy II and Arabia," *JEA* 15, 1929, 9 ff.; H. Kortenbeutel, *Der ägypt. Süd.-und Osthandel*, 1931, 16 ff.; Rostovtzeff, *SEHHW* I, 386 ff.; III, 1414.

66. Otto-Bengtson, *Ptol.*, 195 ff.

67. Droysen, *GH* III 1, 1878, 56; cf. in particular U. Wilcken, *SJ* 45, 2, 1921, 65 (369) ff.

68. Rostovtzeff, *SEHHW* I, 421 f.

69. E. Kornemann, "Ägyptische Einflüsse im röm. Kaiserreich," *NJb.*, 1899, I 118 ff.

70. Rostovtzeff, *SEHHW* I, 255 f.

71. F. Stähelin, E. Meyer, A. Heidner, *Pagasai und Demetrias*, 1934, 194 ff.; Rostovtzeff, *SEHHW* III, 1467.

72. See Bengtson, *Strat.* II, 317 ff.

73. Bengtson, *Strat.* II, 399 ff. Cf. in particular the important decree from Laodiceia ad Mare of the year 174 B.C. published by P. Roussel, *Syria* 23, 1942-43, 21 ff. (cf. G. Klaffenbach, *Ph.* 97, 1948, 376 f.), furnishing evidence for the survival of Macedonian institutions in a Seleucid settlement.

74. Bengtson, *Strat.* II, 345 ff.

75. Polybius IV 6.4; cf. Bengtson, *Strat.* II, 357 ff.; J. A. O. Larsen, *CP* 70, 1975, 159 ff.

76. Otto, *GGA*, 1914, 650 ff.; W. Kolbe, *GGA*, 1916, 446 ff.; Bengtson, *Strat.* II, 372 ff.

77. Bengtson, *Strat.* II, 392 ff.

78. H. Swoboda, *Die griech. Bünde und der moderne Bundesstaat* (Rektoratsrede), Prague 1915. Important is Larsen, *Rep. Govt.*

79. On League citizenship see W. Kolbe, *ZSS Röm.* 49, 1929, 129 ff.; W. Schwahn, *Hermes* 66, 1931, 97 ff. The inclusion of *egktesis* and *epigamia* in League citizenship has been incorrectly contested by H. Swoboda, *Zwei Kapitel aus dem griechischen Bundesrecht*, SB.W, 199, 2, 1924. But, in contrast to W. Kolbe, cf. the reservations of K. Latte, *Gn.* 7, 1931, 124 ff.

80. On the sessions of the Achaean League see A. Aymard, *Les assemblées de la conféd. achaienne*, Bordeaux 1938 (cf. M. Gelzer, *Gn.* 15, 1939, 614 ff.); and *idem*, "Le Zeus fédéral achaien Hamarios-Homarios," *Mél. O. Navarre*, 1935, 453-470; further, Larsen, *Rep. Govt.*, 75 ff.; new views on the League assemblies in A. Giovannini, *MusHelv* 26, 1969, 1-17; see, on the other hand, F. W. Walbank, *MusHelv* 27, 1970, 129-143, and J. A. O. Larsen, *CP* 67, 1972, 178-189. On the sessions of the Aetolian League see the bibliography in W. Schwahn, *RE* IV A, 1212 s.v. *Sympoliteia*, in particular Holleaux, *Et. ép.* I, Chps. XIII-XIV; and J. A. O. Larsen, *TAPA* 83, 1952, 1-33.

81. In addition to the Aetolian and Achaean Koina there were, for instance, also the Leagues of the Phocians, Boeotians, Thessalians, Acarnanians, Locrians and the Cretan Koinon (cf. M. Van der Mijnsbrugge, *The Cretan Koinon*, Louvain and New York 1931; H. Van Effenterre, *La Crète et le monde grec de Platon à Polybe*, Paris 1948, 127 ff.; M. Guarducci, *RF* NS 28, 1950, 142 ff.).

82. Polyb. V 88 ff.; cf. Rostovtzeff, *SEHHW* I, 230.

83. H. Bengtson, *Kokalos* 10-11, 1964-65, 319 ff. = *KS*, 367 ff.

84. In contrast to earlier scholars (F. Boll, F. Cumont, *etc.*), Nilsson, *Gr. Rel.* II, 270 ff., thinks that the astrological system obtained its decisive character through Greek science; Babylonia had only laid the foundations.

85. Cf. E. Buschor, *Das hellenistische Bildnis*, Munich 1949.

86. Cf. Nilsson, *Gr. Rel.* II,[2] 200 ff.

87. C. Schneider, "Die griechischen Grundlagen der hellenistischen Religionsgeschichte," *ARW* 36, 1939, 300 ff.

88. V.s.p. 545 n. 51.

89. See the evidence cited above 539.

90. New views in L. Früchtel, *Gym.* 59, 1952, 350-351, and in A. Volkmann, *Ph.* 100, 1956, 52 ff.; *H.* 16, 1967, 155 ff.

90a. L. Robert, *CRAI*, 1968, 416-457. On the excavations see P. Bernard: *Fouilles d'Ai Khanoum* I, *Campagnes 1965, 1966, 1967, 1968*, Paris 1973.

91. But cf., for instance, R. Thomsen, *Early Roman Coinage* I, Copenhagen 1957, 49 ff.; the beginning of silver issues, accordingly, falls already in the time of the Pyrrhic War.
92. Cf. W. Capelle, *MusHelv* 6, 1949, 83 (with bibliography).

14 THE HELLENISTIC STATES UNDER ROMAN SUPREMACY

PRIMARY LITERARY SOURCES: There are only fragments extant from the major contemporary works on the history of later Hellenism, namely the accounts of Polybius, Poseidonius and Strabo. The *Histories* of Polybius (for a detailed discussion on his life and work see above 528 f.) in Books XVIII-XXXIX dealt with the history of the Mediterranean world from 197 to 145/4 B.C. (Book XVII, dealing with events from 200/199 to 198/7, is totally lost). The loss of the work as a whole is the more disconcerting in view of the circumstance that Polybius, as an immediate protagonist himself, experienced the period from 169 to 145/4 B.C., first as statesman and later as an observer in the camp of Scipio Aemilianus. Whoever, like the former Achaean statesman, perceived in the rise of Rome to world dominion an event of natural necessity, could indeed sympathise with the efforts of the Achaean League, but a profounder understanding of the problems inherent in the Hellenistic states must remain barred to him. The successor of Polybius, Poseidonius of Apameia (c. 130 - c. 50 B.C.), the great universal scholar who for many years lived and taught at Rhodes, enjoying great esteem among the Romans, with the 52 Books of his *Histories* (extending from 145/4 B.C. to the time of Sulla, cf. Jacoby, *FgrHist.* 87, and, on the terminus of the work, see the discussion by Jacoby, Commentary, 156; cf. also L. Edelstein and Ilg. Kidd, *Posidonius* Vol. I, *The Fragments*, Cambridge and New York 1972), produced an imposing picture of the time and its mores, drawn in sombre colours, and in which primary consideration was also given in detail to social and ethnographical aspects. In the latter part of the first century B.C. the work of Poseidonius was used by Diodorus (*Bibl. hist.* XXXII-XXXVII) and by Timagenes (cf. Justin XXXVIII f.), while Strabo also culled from it. In his positive verdict on the universal dominion of the Romans, Poseidonius shows himself to be closely in accord with his predecessor Polybius, but in contrast to the Arcadian he was not blind to the negative side of Roman behaviour. The ideas of Poseidonius on the decay and degeneration of the old genuine Roman virtues found an echo above all in Sallust. Important for the views of Poseidonius on the philosophy of history are the remarks by E. Skard, *Zwei religiös-polit. Begriffe: Euergetes-Concordia*, Oslo, 1932, 82 ff. The *Histories* of Strabo of Amaseia (in the Pontus) (he lived from approximately 64 B.C. to about 20 A.D.) are also linked to Polybius, but the terminus is uncertain (27 B.C. ?); cf. on Strabo's *Histories* in particular F. Jacoby, *FgrHist.* no. 91, and E. Honigmann, *RE* IV A 85 ff. s.v. *Strabon*. As in the case of Polybius the actual narrative was preceded by a longer Introduction which went back to Alexander. The work "lacked a distinct character of its own, was banal but useful" (F. Jacoby), and chiefly because it contained references to many authors whom he had used as his sources, including Timagenes, Hypsicrates of Amisus, Poseidonius, the Parthian historian Apollodorus of Artemita, Metrodorus of Scepsis (the historian of Mithradates Eupator), Theophanes of Mytilene (the favourite of Pompey), and so forth; they are in fact quoted by name. The fragments of Strabo's *Histories*, preserved primarily in the *Antiquitates Judaeorum* of Josephus, should now be supplemented by an analysis of the *Geographica*, also from Strabo's pen.

Maccabees I and II also form part of contemporary historiography (the best edition is by H. Rahlf, within the framework of the *Septuaginta*, 1935; and the commentary by F. M. Abel, *Les livres des Maccabées*, Paris 1949); both portray the great Jewish revolt against Antiochus IV Epiphanes: Book II is written within a more limited context, although it does contain a detailed account of previous events (from 180 to 161 B.C.), while Book I, translated from the Hebrew, encompasses the events from about 175 to 135 B.C. Book II is an extract from the work by Jason of Cyrene (otherwise unknown). The Books of the *Maccabees* stem from the end of the second or the beginning of the first century B.C., with Book II actually being the older; for a concise discussion see E. Bickermann, *RE* XIV, 779 ff. s.v. *Makkabäerbücher*. O. Eissfeldt, *Einleitung in das AT*., Tübingen [3]1964, 781 ff. On Bk. II see A. Momigliano, *CP* 70, 1975, 81-88. On the sources: K.-D. Schunk, *Die Quellen des I. u. II. Makkabäerbuches*, Diss. Greifswald, published Halle 1954.

A large number of isolated pieces of information on late Hellenism may be found in the speeches and letters of Cicero, as well as in the *Corpus Caesarianum*. It would be desirable to have a work in which the evidence is compiled, along with a historical Commentary.

SECONDARY HISTORIOGRAPHICAL SOURCES: In *Livy's* work the history of Hellas and the Hellenistic world was taken into account only in so far as it was interconnected with that of Rome. Livy based his narrative of the history of the East in the fourth and fifth "Decade" primarily on the work of Polybius, and in addition also on the annalistic tradition (H. Nissen, *Kritische Untersuchungen über die Quellen der 4. u. 5. Dekade des Livius*, Berlin 1863). The running narrative breaks off with Book XLV, in the year 167 B.C.; for subsequent events we are left with the *Epitomes* of Livy and with the *Periochae*. The trustworthiness of Livy is that of his sources, being particularly good when his account follows Polybius. The delineation of political and diplomatic events which transpired at Rome is often adulterated by the use of sombre annalistic sources, above all Valerius Antias (cf. for an important specific instance: K.-E. Petzold, *Die Eröffnung des 2. röm-maked. Krieges. Untersuchungen zur spätannalistischen Topik des Livius*, Berlin 1940). The *History* by the Celt (Vocontian) Pompeius Trogus also belongs in the period of Augustus, namely the *Historiae Philippicae*, which are preserved only interspersed in Justin. Books XXX-XLII come into question, as well as the corresponding *Prologi* (summaries). The tendency of these works to be unfriendly towards Rome has been disputed (E. Schneider, *De Pomp. Trog. Hist.*

Phil. consilio et arte, Diss. Leipzig 1913, 54 ff.; H. Fuchs, *Der geistige Widerstand gegen Rom*, 1938, 42 n. 41). As for the sources used by Pompeius Trogus, it is difficult to ascertain anything concrete. The "Timagenes thesis" once advanced by A. v. Gutschmid, *Kl. Schr.* V, 1894, 218 ff., and to which even F. Jacoby (*FgrHist.* no. 88, Comm.) still subscribed, must be abandoned, since there is too little that has survived from the work *Concerning Kings* by Timagenes of Alexandria to attain any certainty about the composition of the work or the political views of the author. To assume that Timagenes was one of the chief sources used by Livy, Strabo, Appian and Plutarch (thus, initially, G. Schwab, *De Livio et Timagene, historiarum scriptoribus aemulis*, Stuttgart 1834) is nothing less than unauthorised use of an unknown individual.

Material handed down from Polybius and Poseidonius is to be found not only in Diodorus (v. *supra*) but also in Appian's Roman History (written about 160 A.D.), namely the *Civil Wars*; in addition the *Macedonian War*, the *Illyrian War* and the *Syrian War*, reflect Polybian transmission, but by no means in unadulterated form (E. Schwartz, *RE* II, 219 ff.). The nature of the sources in Appian's *Mithradatic War* is even more impenetrable, for which "neither Poseidonius, nor Sallust nor Livy were used directly or exclusively" (E. Schwartz, *op. cit.*, 222). There are many particulars on late Hellenistic history in Plutarch's *Vitae* (T. Quinctius Flamininus, Philopoemen, Aemilius Paullus, Sulla, Lucullus, Pompey, Crassus, Caesar, Antony, *et al.*), some also in the Roman History of Cassius Dio (he wrote in the time of the Severi) Books XVIII ff. (only in excerpts and in the extract of Zonaras; the extant part of Dio's work begins in 68 B.C. with Book XXXVI). For the chronology of the Hellenistic dynasties Porphyry's *Chronicle* (F. Jacoby, *FgrHist.* no. 260) should be consulted.

DOCUMENTS: The inscriptions, papyri and ostraca, which are steadily increasing in number, furnish scholars with much information, but since this is scattered in an almost unlimited number of publications a survey is made difficult. The most important collections have been cited above 531, while particularly important specific documents will be referred to below in the surveys of the sources on pp. 575-583. On the coins v.s.p. 531; further, for instance, E. A. Sydenham, *The Coinage of the Roman Republic*, London 1952.

BIBLIOGRAPHY: The following provide an overall history of the Mediterranean world: K. J. Neumann, "Die hellenistischen Staaten u. die röm. Republik," in *Weltgeschichte*, ed. Pflugk-Harttung, Bd. I, 1909, 432 ff.; G. De Sanctis, in *Propyläen-Weltgeschichte*, ed. W. Goetz, II, 1931; further, H. E. Stier and W. Weber, in *Neue Propyläen-Weltgeschichte des Mittelmeerraumes*, ed. by W. Andreas, I, 1940; and, finally, E. Kornemann, *Weltgeschichte des Mittelmeerraumes*, I, 1948. New points of view are put forward by H. E. Stier, *Roms Aufstieg zur Weltmacht und die griechische Welt*, Cologne and Opladen 1957, a work which, with its actualisation of the past, has assumed somewhat the character of a political tract. The accounts in Vols. VIII to X of the *Cambridge Ancient*

History are excellent. On the history of later Hellenism: B. Niese, *Mak.* II, 577 ff.; III, 1 ff. (down to 120 B.C.); M. Cary, *A History of the Greek World from 323 to 30 B.C.*, London ^{2}1972 (with a select bibliography by V. Ehrenberg) (first published 1932); also Berve, *GG* II^{2}, 325 ff., as well as the works cited above 540 f., by E. Bevan, A. Bouché-Leclercq and P. Jouguet. Hellenistic developments are dealt with more or less in detail in the general histories of the Roman Republic, thus, for instance, in the extensively documented *Storia dei Romani*, Vol. IV 1, by G. De Sanctis ("Dalla battaglia di Naraggara [= Zama] alla battaglia di Pidna"), 1923; in the first two volumes of *Histoire romaine* (within the framework of the *Histoire Générale*, edited by G. Glotz), Vol. I: *Des origines à l'achèvement de la conquête*, by E. Pais, revised by J. Bayet; Vol. II: *La République romaine de 133 à 44*, Ier section: "Des Gracches à Sulla," by G. Bloch and J. Carcopino, 1935; IIe section: "César," by J. Carcopino, 1936; and in *Historie de Rome*, ^{5}1962, by A. Piganiol, although in fact brief, is nevertheless indispensable on account of its outstanding bibliography and list of sources. Valuable is E. Will, *Histoire politique du monde hellénistique (323-30 av. J.-C.)*, Vol. II, Nancy 1967 [from Antiochus III to the end of the Ptolemaic kingdom]. On the Greek attitude towards the Romans see B. Forte, *Rome and the Romans as the Greeks saw Them* (Papers and Monographs of the American Academy in Rome, 24), Rome 1972; J. Deininger, *Der politische Widerstand gegen Rom in Griechenland 217-86 v. Chr.*, Berlin 1971 (cf. G. W. Bowersock, *Gn.* 45, 1973, 576 ff.).

On the history of Greece: G. Colin, *Rome et la Grèce de 200 à 146 av. J.-C.*, Paris 1905 (partly out of date); Ferguson, *Ath.*; F. Münzer, *Die politische Vernichtung des Griechentums* (Das Erbe der Alten, 2. Reihe, Bd. 9), Leipzig 1925; F. W. Walbank, *Phil. V*; *idem*, "Alcaeus of Messene, Philip V, and Rome," *CQ* 36, 1942, 134 ff.; 37, 1943, 1 ff. (with correction, *CQ* 38, 1944, 87 f.); cf. also Ch. Edson, *CP* 43, 1948, 116 ff.; E. S. Gruen, "The Last Years of Philip V," *GRBS* 15, 1974, 221 ff.; Accame, *Dom.*; cf. also *RF* NS 24, 1946, 104 ff. (on the Koinon of Lesbos in Roman times).

On the history of the Iranian and Indian regions of the East: A.v. Gutschmid, *Geschichte Irans u. seiner Nachbarländer von Alexander d. Gr. bis zum Untergang der Arsaciden*, Tübingen 1888 (of lasting value); Debevoise, *Parth.*; Tarn, *Bact.*; Altheim, *As.*, who was unaware, however, of recent studies by Russian scholars on Iran (cf. E. Bickerman, *Bibliotheca Orientalis*, Leiden 1949, 68 ff.); cf. F. Altheim, *Saeculum* 1, 1950, 280 ff.

ROME IN CONFLICT WITH PHILIP V AND ANTIOCHUS III. THE END OF THE MACEDONIAN MONARCHY

PRINCIPAL SOURCES: (Cf. the survey in CAH VIII, 736 ff.; 758 f.): Polyb. XVI-XXIX; Livy XXXI-XLV; Diod. XXVIII-XXX; Appian, *Makedonike* 4-19; *Syriake* I-44; Cassius Dio XVIII-XX (partly in excerpts of Zonaras); Justin, *Epit.* of Pompeius Trogus XXX-XXXIII (with the *Pro-*

logi of Pompeius Trogus); Plutarch, *Lives* of Flamininus (on his sources see R. E. Smith, *CQ* 38, 1944, 89 ff.), Cato Maior (12-14), Aemilius Paullus, Philopoemen (on the *Life* of Aemilius Paullus see W. Schwarze, *Quibus fontibus Plutarchus in vita L. Aem. Paulli usus sit*, Leipzig 1891; also the special edition by C. Liedmeier, *Plutarchus' biographie van Aemilius Paullus*, Nijmegen 1935). From the great number of inscriptions (cf. the survey by M. Holleaux, *CAH* VIII, 730 ff.), the following may be stressed: the letter of Philip V to the Athenians in Hephaestia on Lemnos, published by S. Accame, "Una lettera di Filippo V ed i primordi della seconda guerra macedonica," *RF* NS 19, 1941, 179 ff.; cf. P. M. Fraser and A. H. McDonald, *JRS* 42, 1952, 81 ff.; the inscription from Stymphalus with references to the banishment of the inhabitants of Elateia, probably in 198 B.C., published by M. Mitsos, *REG* 59-60, 1946-47, 150 ff.; cf. S. Accame, *RF* NS 27, 1949, 217 ff.; and G. Klaffenbach, *BCH* 92, 1968, 257 ff.; the honorary decree for Hegesias of Lampsacus, *Syll.* II^3, 591; cf. E. Bickermann, "Rom u. Lampsakos," *Ph.* 87, 1932, 277 ff.; the accusation of Perseus by the Romans in the Delphic Amphictyons, *Syll.* II^3 643 (171 B.C.); the *senatus consultum* concerning Thisbe in Boeotia, *Syll.* II^3 646 (Oct. 170 B.C.); (cf. R. M. Errington, *RF* 102, 1974, 79-86, who argues that the decree is to be dated to the end of 171/0 B.C.; see also Sherk, *Docs.* no. 2) (cf. the decree of the Senate on Coronea, published by L. Robert, *Et. épig. et phil*, 1938, 287 ff.; cf. Sherk, *Docs.* no. 3); the inscription from Argos honouring the Roman envoy Cn. Octavius (P. Charneux, *BCH* 81, 1957, 181 ff.), from the autumn of 170 B.C.; the inscription of the victor L. Aemilius Paullus from the base of the Perseus monument in Delphi, *Syll.* II^3 652a (168/7 B.C.) (cf. the Plate in Rostovtzeff, *SEHHW* II, 740). A number of important Macedonian inscriptions are cited in Rostovtzeff, *SEHHW* III, 1470 f. From Egypt we have the decree issued by the priests at Memphis from 196 B.C. (OGI I 90; a parallel text [fragment] published by P. M. Fraser, *Bull. Soc. Arch. d'Alexandrie* no. 41, 1956, 57 ff.), that is, the so-called Rosetta Stone (in hieroglyphic, Demotic and Greek), by means of which Champollion deciphered the Egyptian hieroglyphics; from Anatolia the inscriptions connected with the declaration of *Asylia* of Teos (c. 200 B.C.) deserve emphasis, published by P. Hermann, *Anadolu* (*Anatolia*) 9, 1965, 29-159; cf. F. Sokowlowski, "Divine Honours for Antiochus and Laodike at Teos and Iasos," *GRBS* 13, 1972, 171 ff.; also the inscription of Corragus, *SEG* II 663, from 186 B.C. (cf. M. Holleaux, *Et. ép.* II, 73 ff.; and Bengtson, *Strat.* II, 212 ff.) (from Apollonia on the Rhyndacus [?]); and the highly interesting inscription from Lycian Araxa (G. E. Bean, *JHS* 68, 1948, 46 ff.; cf. J. and L. Robert, *REG* 63, 1950, Bull. épig. no. 183), which should, however, probably be dated in the period after 189 B.C. From Palestine there is a Greek inscription with letters of Antiochus III, addressed to, *inter al.*, the *strategos* Ptolemaeus of Syria and Phoenicia, from 202/1 or 201/0 B.C.; the inscription was found at Hefzibah (north-west of Beth Shean) and published by J. H.

Landau, *Israel Exploration Journal* 16, 1966, 54 ff., and J. and L. Robert, *REG* 83, 1970, Bull. épigr. no. 627, 469-473.

Greek inscriptions from Istrus (Histria) and Apollonia on the Pontus have furnished valuable information on the civilisation of the cities on the west Pontus and their relations to the native peoples; see H. Bengtson, *H.* 11, 1962, 18 ff. = *KS*, 377 ff. (inscription from Istrus c. 200 B.C.); *H.* 12, 1963, 96 ff. = *KS*, 389 ff. (Apollonia); on these see J. and L. Robert, *REG* 74, 1961, Bull. épigr. no. 419, 187-201.

On the coins cf. the references in *CAH* VIII, 734 ff.; also Rostovtzeff, *SEHHW* III, 1471 n. 40.

In addition to the studies cited above 574 f. the following works may be stressed: On the history of Hellas (200-168 B.C.): W. Schorn, *Gesch. Griechenlands von der Entstehung des ätol. u. achäischen Bundes bis auf die Zerstörung Korinths*, Bonn 1833; G. F. Hertzberg, *Gesch. Griechenlands unter der Herrschaft der Römer* I, 1866, 53 ff. (both works are naturally out of date); G. Daux, *Delphes au IIème et au Ier siècle*, 1936, 213 ff. (cf. G. Klaffenbach, *Gn.* 14, 1938, 6 ff.); A. Aymard, *Les premiers rapports de Rome et de la conféd. achaienne (198-189 av. J.-C.)*, Bordeaux 1938; J. A. O. Larsen, "Roman Greece," in Tenney Frank, *ESAR* IV, 266 ff.; Walbank, *Phil. V* (with a survey of the sources on the history of the ruler, 278 ff.); Rostovtzeff, *SEHHW* II, Chap. V; III, 1458 ff. (also on the history of the East); L. de Regibus, *La repubblica romana e gli ultimi re di Macedonia*, Genoa 1951 (cf. K.-E. Petzold, *Gn.* 25, 1953, 399 ff.); P. Meloni, *Perseo e la fine della monarchia macedone*, Rome 1953 (a valuable and well-documented work); J. P. V. D. Balsdon, "Rome and Macedon 205-200 B.C.," *JRS* 44, 1954, 30 ff. On the history of Antiochus III: E. L. Heyden, *Res ab Antiocho III Magno Syriae rege praeclare gestae, 223-192*, Diss. Göttingen, published Münster 1877; *Beitr. z. Gesch. Antiochus d. Gr.*, Emmerich 1873; E. Degen, *Kritische Ausf. z. Gesch. Antiochus' d. Gr.*, Diss. Zurich, published Basle 1918; O. Leuze, "Die Feldzüge Ant. d. Gr. nach Kleinasien u. Thrakien," *Hermes* 58, 1923, 190 ff.; 241 ff.; E. Bickermann "Bellum Antiochicum," *Hermes* 87, 1932, 47 ff.; "Notes sur Polybe I," *REG* 50, 1937, 217 ff.; M. Holleaux, *Et. ép.* III; V; Schmitt, *Ant.*; A. H. McDonald and F. W. Walbank, "The Treaty of Apamea (188 B.C.): the Naval Clause," *JRS* 59, 1969, 30 ff.; V. Polacek, "La paix d'Apamée" *Listy filologické* 92, 1969, 1 ff.; W. E. Thompson, "Philip and the Islanders." *TAPA* 102, 1971, 615 ff.; E. S. Gruen, *CQ* 25, 1975, 58 ff. From the articles in *RE* the following, in addition to many others, deserve particular mention: *Antiochos III., RE* I, 2459 ff. s.v. no. 25 (U. Wilcken); *Attalos I., RE* II, 2159 ff. s.v. no. 9 (U. Wilcken); *Eumenes II., RE* VI, 1091 ff. s.v. no. 6 (H. Willrich); *Makedonia, RE* XIV, 751 ff. (F. Geyer); *Philipp V., RE* XIX, 2312 ff. s.v. no. 10 (F. Geyer); *Perseus, RE* XIX, 996 ff. s.v. no. 5 (F. Geyer); *Rhodos, RE* Suppl. V, 788 ff. (F. Hiller v. Gaertringen); *Sparta, RE* III A, 1438 ff. (V. Ehrenberg); *Nabis, RE* XVI, 1471 ff. (V. Ehrenberg); *Prusias, RE* XXIII, 1086 ff. s.v. nos. 1 and 2 (C. Habicht); *T. Quinctius Flamininus, RE* XXIV, 1047-1100 s.v. no. 45 (H. G.

Gundel). On Philip V see also Bengtson, *Herrs.*, 211 ff.; and on Eumenes II, *ibid.*, 235 ff.

On the civilisation of the cities on the west Pontus see above all the very valuable studies by D. M. Pippidi, for instance, "Istros et les Gètes au IIIe siècle av. notre ère," *Studii Clasice* 3, 1961, 53-66; *Epigraphische Beiträge zur Geschichte Histrias in hellenistischer und römischer Zeit*, Berlin 1962; *Din istoria Dobrogei*, Bucarest 1965 (together with D. Berciu), especially Chap. 4; *Contributii la istoria veche a României*, Bucarest 1967, with a French summary.

THE DECLINE OF THE HELLENISTIC STATES IN THE EAST AND THE RISE OF THE PARTHIAN KINGDOM. THE FIRST PERIOD OF ROMAN RULE IN HELLAS AND ASIA MINOR

Surveys of the principal sources may be found in *CAH* VIII, 758 ff.; 778; IX 924 ff.; in Rostovtzeff, *SEHHW* III, 1490 ff.; 1501 ff.; 1533 ff.; 1541 ff.; and in A. Piganiol, *Histoire de Rome*, [5]1962, 130 ff.; 160 ff.

LITERARY SOURCES: a) Contemporary: Polybius, *Hist.* XXX-XXXIX (extant only in fragments; noteworthy is the account of the Achaean War, 146 B.C.: XXXVIII 9-18; XXXIX 1-6); Poseidonius, *Hist.* (in Jacoby, *FgrHist.* no. 87.1-27, *et al.*); *Maccabees* I and II (cf. the survey and bibliography cited by E. Bickermann, *RE* XIV, 779 ff.; also E. Cavaignac, *Rev. d'hist. des rélig.* 130, 1945, 42 ff. [on Book II]); P. Desideri, "Posidonio e la guerra mitridatica," *Ath.* 51, 1973, 3-29; 237-269. b) Secondary: Diod., *Bibl. hist.* XXXI-XXXIV/V (fragments); Strabo, *Hist.* (in Jacoby, *FgrHist.* no. 91); and *Geog.*; Pompeius Trogus, *Hist. Philipp.* (in the *Epitome* of Justin) XXXIV-XLII, and the corresponding *Prologi*; the *Epitomes* of Livy and the *Periochae*, Bks. XLVI ff.; Josephus, *Ant. Jud.* XII 237 ff.; Pausanias VII 7-17 (an account of the Achaean War); Appian, *Syriake* 46 ff.; Porphyry, *Chron.* (in Jacoby, *FgrHist.* no. 260.32).

From the sources in non-classical languages the report of the envoy Tsan K'ien on conditions in Bactria in the year 128 B.C. is especially valuable (cf. the studies cited by Tarn, *Bact.*, 513 f., also 280 ff.).

Of the large number of inscriptions stress falls on the following groups: the Delian inscriptions from the time after 166 B.C. (*Inscr. de Délos* nos. 1400-2879); the inscriptions from Anatolia (the most important are printed in Dittenberger's collection *OGI* I nos. 217 ff.; II nos. 751 ff.; a number of recent additions in *SEG* II); cf. also the documents from Susa (*SEG* VII nos. 1 ff.). The dedications of the Roman generals in Greece have been assembled by M. Guarducci, *Le offerte dei conquistatori romani ai santuari della Grecia*, Rend, Pontif. Accad., 1938, 41 ff.; the *senatus consulta* and *epistulae* may be found in Sherk, *Docs.* Instructive for internal conditions in Greece, above all in the Peloponnesus at the close of the second century B.C., are the "documents from Messene" discussed by A. Wilhelm, *Öst. Jh.* 17, 1914, 1 ff. (with valuable references for the history of the period from about 130 to 80 B.C., 97 ff.). Important specific documents: The testament inscription of the "younger Ptolemy" (the later Ptolemy VIII Euergetes II), from 155 B.C., the first testament of a Hellenistic ruler in favour of the Romans (*SEG* IX no. 7); the popular decree of Pergamum mentioning the testament of Attalus III († 133 B.C.) (*OGI* I 338); the Cyprian amnesty decree of Ptolemy VIII, from the year 145/4 B.C. (published by T. B. Mitford, *Actes du V*[ème] *Congr. intern. de papyr.*, Oxford 1937, 291 ff.; and *AfP* 13, 1938, 24 ff.; cf. A. Wilhelm, *Griech. Königsbriefe*, 48. Klio-Beih., 1943, 48 ff.; A. Rehm, *Ph.* 97, 1948, 267 ff.; 369; M. Th. Lenger, *BCH* 80, 1956, 437 ff.); the Delphic copy of a Roman *lex de piratis persequendis* from about 100 B.C. (*SEG* III no. 378 = S. Riccobono, *FIRA* I², 121 ff. no. 9; cf. the copy from Cnidus, published by M. Hassal, M. Crawford, J. Reynolds, "Rome and the Eastern Provinces at the End of the Second Century B.C.," *JRS* 64, 1974, 195 ff. Papyri of note: The edict of the *Dioiketes* Herodes from 164 B.C., which reflects the bleak lot of the Egyptian *Chora* (*UPZ* II, 110; cf. Rostovtzeff, *SEHHW* II, 719 ff.); the great amnesty decree of Ptolemy VIII from 118 B.C. (*P. Teb.* I 5, bibliography in Rostovtzeff, *SEHHW* III, 1543); the so-called 'Memmius papyrus', with references to the anticipated visit of a Roman senator to the Fayum in 112 B.C. (*P. Teb.* I 33).

Numismatic Material: On the Ptolemaic and Seleucid empires see the works cited above 531; for the Iranian and Indian regions: A.v. Sallet, *Die Nachfolger Alexanders in Baktrien und Indien*, Berlin 1879; Gardner and Poole, *The Coins of the Greek and Scythic Kings of Bactria and India*, London 1886. A new work is lacking, but urgently required. Important for the chronology of the Parthian coins is the work by Le Rider on Susa (v.s.p. 555). In Qunduz in Afghanistan a hoard of over 600 Bactrian silver tetradrachms was found, chiefly of Eucratides II and of Heliocles I (R. Curiel et G. Fussman, *Le trésor monétaire de Q., Mém. Délég. archéol. franç. en Afghan.*, Vol. 20, Paris 1965). On the *Cistophoroi* see the bibliography survey by D. Kienast, "Cistophoren," *JNG*. 11, 1961, 159 ff.

BIBLIOGRAPHY: On the history of the Ptolemaic empire: Otto, 6. *Ptol.*; Otto-Bengtson, *Ptol.* [cf. H. Heinen, *Les mariages de Ptolémée VIII. Euergete et leur chronologie*, (Münch. Beitr. 66), 1974, 147-155]; H. Winkler, *Rom. u. Ägypten im 2. Jahrh. v. Chr.*, Diss. Leipzig 1933. On Seleucid history: U. Mago, *Antioco IV Epifane re di Siria*, Sassari 1907; Ed. Meyer, *Ursprung und Änfänge des Christentums* II, Berlin 1921; E. Bickermann, *Die Makkabäer. Eine Darstellung ihrer Gesch. von den Änfängen bis z. Untergang des Hasmonäerhauses*, Berlin 1935; *Der Gott der Makkabäer*, Berlin 1937; F. Reuter, *Beiträge zur Beurteilung des Königs Antiochos Epiphanes*, Diss. Münster 1938 (cf. F. Hampl, *Gn.* 15, 1939, 619 ff.); O. Mørkholm, *Anticohos IV of Syria*, Copenhagen 1966. On the history of the later Seleucids: A. R. Bellinger, "Hyspaosines of Charax," *YCS* 8, 1942, 53 ff.; H. Volkmann, "Demetrios I. u. Alexander Balas," *Klio* 19, 1925, 373 ff.; *idem*, "Zur Münzprägung des Demetrios I. und Alexander I. von Syrien," *Z. f. Num.* 34, 1923, 51 ff.; U. Wilcken, "Ein

Beitrag z. Seleukidengesch., *Hermes* 29, 1894, 436 ff.; A. Kuhn, *Beitr. z. Gesch. d. Seleukiden vom Tode Antiochos' VII. Sidetes bis auf Antiochos XIII. Asiatikos*, Diss. Strassburg, Altkirch 1891; A. R. Bellinger, *The End of the Seleucids*, Transactions of the Connecticut Academy of Arts and Sciences 38, 1949, 51 ff. (on the basis of the coins from 129 to 64 B.C.); J. Briscoe, "Eastern Policy and Senatorial Politics 168-146 B.C.," *H.* 18, 1969, 49 ff.; and on various questions of detail see L. Robert, *Etudes anatoliennes*, 1937; [2]1970. Also the articles: *Antiochos, RE* I, 2470 ff. s.v. nos. 26 to 33 (U. Wilcken); *Demetrios, RE* IV, 2795 ff. s.v. nos. 40-42 (H. Willrich): *Hasmonäer, RE* VII, 2491 ff. (W. Otto); *Kleopatra, RE* XI, 785 ff. s.v. nos. 24 and 25 (F. Stähelin); *Ptolemaios, RE* XXIII, 1702 ff. s.v. nos. 24-31 (H. Volkmann); *Syria, RE* IV A, 1618 ff. (E. Honigmann); *Tryphon, RE* VII A, 715 ff. (W. Hoffmann). On the history of the Iranian East see, in addition to the works cited above 575 by A.v. Gutschmid, N. C. Debevoise, W. W. Tarn, F. Altheim: J. Dobias, "Les premiers rapports des Romains avec les Parthes," *Arch. Orientàlní* 3, 1931, 244 ff.; F. Altheim and A. Szabo, "Eine Vorläuferin der grossen Völkerwanderung," *WG* 2, 1936, 314 ff.; the articles: *Mithridates, RE* XV, 2208 ff. s.v. nos. 21 and 22 (F. Geyer); *Parthia, RE* XVIII, 1968 ff. (P. J. Junge), where, however, the references to the new views are missing. On Greece and Asia Minor: In addition to the works by Colin and Accame (v.s.p. 575): J. A. O. Larsen, "Roman Greece," and T. R. S. Broughton, "Roman Asia," in Tenney Frank, *ESAR* IV; Ferguson, *Ath.*, 312 ff.; P. Roussel, *Délos colonie athénienne*, 1916; G. Daux, *Delphes au IIe et au Ier siècle depuis l'abaissement de l'Etolie jusqu'à la paix romaine, 191-31 av. J.-C.*, Paris 1936 (cf. G. Klaffenbach, *Gn.* 14, 1938, 6 ff.); T. Schwertfeger, *Der achaische Bund von 146 bis 27 v. Chr.*, Munich 1974; J. Hatzfeld, *Les trafiquants italiens dans l'Orient hellénique*, Paris 1919; F. Stähelin, *Gesch. der kleinasiat. Galater*, [2]1907; L. Robert, *Etudes anatoliennes*, 1937; [2]1970 (many contributions to inscriptions from Asia Minor); *idem, Villes d'Asie Mineure*, 1935; [2]1962; V. Chapot, *La province romaine proconsulaire d'Asie*, 1904; P. Bernhardt, *Imperium und Eleutheria. Die röm. Politik gegenüber den freien Städten des griechischen Ostens*, Diss. Hamburg 1971; the articles: *Aristonikos, RE* II, 962 ff. s.v. no. 14 (U. Wilcken); *Attalos, RE* II, 2168 ff. s.v. nos. 10 and 11 (U. Wilcken); *Mummius, RE* XVI, 1195 ff. s.v. no. 7a (F. Münzer); *Asia, RE* II, 1538 ff. (C. Brandis); *Nikomedes, RE* XVII, 494 ff. s.v. nos. 4-6 (F. Geyer); *Prusias, RE* XXIII, 1107 ff. s.v. no. 2 (C. Habicht). On the decline of the Hellenistic world: C. Préaux, *Atti dell' XI Congr. Intern. di Papirologia 1965* (published 1966), 475-498.

THE GREEKS IN THE TIME OF MITHRADATES. THE REORGANISATION OF THE NEAR EAST BY POMPEY. THE END OF THE PTOLEMAIC KINGDOM

SURVEY OF THE PRINCIPAL SOURCES: Although it has now been rendered out of date on certain details, an excellent survey of the sources for the era of the Pontic king Mithradates VI Eupator has been given by T.

Reinach, *Mith.*, 413 ff. More recent surveys: M. Rostovtzeff and H. A. Ormerod, *CAH* IX, 924 f.,; W. W. Tarn, *CAH* IX, 947 ff. (on the Parthians): Rostovtzeff, *SEHHW* III, 1556 ff. (notes to Chap. VII); cf. further, the relevant volumes of Tenney Frank, *ESAR*, namely "Syria," by F. Heichelheim; "Greece," by J. A. O. Larsen; "Roman Asia," by T. R. S. Broughton.

The majority of literary primary sources have been lost or exist only in a fragmentary state. Specific reference may be made to the following: the *Histories* of Poseidonius (most important is the fragment relating to the Athenian tyrant Athenion: Jacoby, *FgrHist.* no. 87.36); Metrodorus of Scepsis, the historian of Mithradates (Jacoby, *FgrHist.* no. 184; on the historians of Mithradates see further, H. Fuchs, *Der geistige Widerstand gegen Rom*, 1938, 43 f. n. 43); Theophanes of Mytilene, the minion of Pompey (Jacoby, *FgrHist.* no. 188, cf. Rostovtzeff, *SEHHW* III, 1528, and L. Robert, *CRAI* I, 1969, 42-647); the *Histories* of Sallust, encompassing the time from 78-67 B.C. (edition by B. Maurenbrecher, Leipzig 1891-93; cf. K. Bauhofer, *Die Komposition der Hist. Sallusts*, Diss. Munich 1935); and finally, Strabo's *Histories* (cf. *supra* 572 f.; the fragments are in Jacoby, *FgrHist.* no. 91). Strabo's work on Geography is only partly extant (17 Books; edition by A. Meineke; cf. also the Budé ed., by G. Aujac and F. Lasserre, 1966-1975) with particularly valuable references to the history and geography of his homeland, Pontus. Among Cicero's speeches the following particularly contain information on the history of the East and Macedonia: *In Verrem; De imperio Cn. Pompeii; Pro Flacco; Pro Sestio; De provinciis consularibus; In Pisonem; Pro rege Deiotaro;* and his *Letters*, above all those from his Cilician proconsulate (interpreted, for instance, by Debevoise, *Parth.*, 96 ff.). Of primary relevance from the *Corpus Caesarianum* are the *Bellum civile* and the *Bellum Alexandrinum*; and for conditions in Asia Minor after Caesar's death the *Brutus Letters* (*Epistologr. Graeci*, ed. R. Hercher, 177 ff.), which are to be regarded as authentic; cf. the edition by L. Torraca, *Marco Giunio Bruto, Epistole greche*, Naples (no year) [1959] (with a lengthy Introduction); cf. H. Bengtson, *Zur Geschichte des Brutus*, SB.M, 1970, Heft 1, 37-38, who argues for their authenticity. The Munich treatise by Karin Huber (not published as yet) reaches an essentially positive conclusion. Of a different view is J. Deininger, "Brutus und die Bithynier," *RhM* 109, 1966, 356-372; cf. the bibliography in *CAH* X, 900; Rostovtzeff, *SEHHW* III, 1528 n. 98; D. Magie, *Roman Rule in Asia Minor* II, 1950, 1274 n. 54.

From the large number of inscriptions (see, for instance, Reinach, *Mith.*, 456 ff.; *OGI* I nos. 367 ff.; Sherk, *Docs.*), only the following may be cited here as particularly important: the letter of Mithradates to the Satrap Leonippus (*Syll.* II³ 741); the important Ephesian inscription from 85 B.C. (*Syll.* II³ 742; cf. J. H. Oliver, *AJP* 60, 1939, 467 ff.; Rostovtzeff, *SEHHW* III, 1559 n. 14); two letters of Sulla, one to Cos, the other to the Artists, from the end of the eighties (M. Segre, *RF* 66, 1938, 253 ff.; cf. Sherk *Docs.*, no. 49); the last decree of the Ptolemies, from 41 B.C.

(*SB* 7337; cf. G. Lefebvre, *Mélanges M. Holleaux*, 1913, 103 ff.; Marie-Thérèse Lenger, *Corpus des ordonn. des Ptolémées*, Brussels 1964, 210 ff.; also H. Volkmann, *RE* XXIII, 1761 s.v. *Ptolemaios* n. 37). For Thasos: Christiane Dunant and J. Pouilloux, *Recherches sur l'histoire et les cultes de Thasos* II, 1958, especially 26 ff.; of greatest importance is a letter of Sulla (37 ff.), and another of Cn. Cornelius Dolabella (45 ff.)—both from 80 B.C. Also valuable is the collection of Greek inscriptions honouring Caesar: A. E. Raubitschek, *JRS* 44, 1954, 65-75. Of the papyri, special emphasis falls on the important late Ptolemaic group, *BGU* VIII, from Herakleopolites (cf. W. Otto, *HZ* 152, 1934, 539 ff.); and, finally, the letter of Antony from 33/2 B.C. to the *Koinon* of Asia, explained by C. G. Brandis, *Hermes* 32, 1897, 509 ff.; cf. *SB* I 4224; and L. Robert, *Hel.* 7, 1949, 122; cf. also Sherk, *Docs.*, no. 57.

BIBLIOGRAPHY: Besides the relevant works and handbooks on Roman history, in which developments in the Greek East are for the most part taken into account, the following may be cited here: Reinach, *Mith.*; *CAH* IX, Chaps. V and VIII, by M. Rostovtzeff, H. A. Ormerod and M. Cary; Rostovtzeff, *SEHHW* II, 934 ff.; M. Gelzer, *RE* XIII, 376 ff. s.v. *Licinius* (Lucullus) (cf. M. Villoresi, *Lucullo*, Florence 1939); F. Geyer *RE* XV, 2163 ff. s.v. *Mithridates* (VI) no. 12; VI A, 970 ff. s.v. *Tigranes* no. 1; C. F. Lehmann-Haupt, *RE* VI A, 981 ff. s.v. *Tigranokerta*. On Mithradates, see further, Bengtson, *Herrs.*, 251 ff.

On the history of Greece and the neighbouring countries to the north: G. F. Hertzberg, *Gesch. Griechenlands unter d. Herrschaft d. Römer* I, 1866, 340 ff.; G. Finlay, *Greece under the Romans* I, 1844 (both works are naturally very much out of date); Ferguson, *Ath.*, 440 ff.; D. J. Geagan, *The Athenian Constitution after Sulla* (Hesp. Suppl. 12), Princeton 1967; G. Daux, *Delphes* 1936, 392 ff.; Accame, *Dom.*; C. Patsch, *Beitr. z. Völkerkunde von Südosteuropa* V, SB.W 214, 1, Vienna 1932 (cf. M. Rostovtzeff, *Gn.* 10, 1934, 1 ff.).

On the history of Asia Minor, Syria and Palestine: Ed. Meyer and C. Brandis, *RE* III, 520 ff. s.v. *Bithynia*; C. Brandis, *RE* II, 1538 ff. s.v. *Asia* (the Roman Province); V. Chapot, *La province romaine proconsulaire d'Asie*, Paris 1904; F. Geyer, *RE* XVII, 496 ff. s.v. *Nikomedes* nos. 5 and 6 (on the Bithynian rulers of this name cf. the copious notes by Rostovtzeff, *SEHHW* III, 1529 f.; see also A. Wilhelm, "Eine Inschrift des Königs Nikomedes Epiphanes," *Öst. Jh.* 11, 1908, 75 ff.); D. Magie, *Roman Rule in Asia Minor*, 2 vols., Princeton 1950. On Syria *et al.*: W. Otto, *Herodes*, Stuttgart 1913 (an essentially unaltered reprint of the article in *RE* Suppl. II); H. Buchheim, *Die Orientpolitik des Triumviren M. Antonius*, Abh. Heidelberg, 1960, H. 3; H. Bengtson, *Marcus Antonius. Triumvir und Herrscher des Orients*, Munich 1977; A. Dobias, *Gesch. d. röm. Provinz Syrien* I, 1924 (Czech., with a French summary); E. M. Sandforth, "The Career of Aulus Gabinius," *TAPA* 70, 1939, (published 1940) 64 ff.; 82 ff.

On the history of the Parthian Kingdom: Tarn, *CAH* IX, 574 ff.; Debevoise, *Parth.*; P. J. Junge, *RE* XVIII 4, 1983 ff. s.v. *Parthia*.

On the end of the Ptolemaic Empire: V. Gardthausen, *Augustus u. seine Zeit* I, 1891; A. Bouché-Leclercq, *Hist. des Lagides* II, 1904, 177 ff.; IV, 1907, 328 f. (also the other relevant works on Ptolemaic history by E. Bevan, P. Jouguet, in Hanotaux, *Hist. de la nation égypt.* III); F. Stähelin, *RE* XI, 750 ff. s.v. *Kleopatra* no. 20; W. W. Tarn, *CAH* X, 35 ff. (with bibliography, *ibid.*, 910 ff.); *JRS* 26, 1936, 187 ff. (cf. Otto-Bengtson, *Ptol.*, 149 n. 2); H. Volkmann, *RE* XXIII, 1738 ff. s.v. *Ptolemaios* nos. 30 ff.; also his book *Kleopatra*, Munich 1953; further: E. Olshausen, *Rom und Ägypten von 116 bis 51 v. Chr.*, Diss. Erlangen-Nürnberg 1963 (contains little that is new); E. Bloedow, *Beiträge zur Gesch. des Ptolemaios XII.*, Diss. Würzburg 1963; H. Heinen, *Rom und Ägypten von 51 bis 47 v. Chr.*, Diss. Tübingen 1966; Michael Grant, *Cleopatra*, London 1972. Basic for the policy of Antony is J. Kromayer, "Kleine Forsch. z. Gesch. d. 2. Triumvirats," *Hermes* 29, 1894, 556 ff.; 31, 1896, 70 ff.; 33, 1898, 1 ff.; 34, 1899, 1 ff.; cf. 68, 1933, 361 ff.; the extensive bibliography on the battle of Actium may be found in W. W. Tarn, *CAH* X, 912; on the last events of Egypt before the death of Cleopatra: A. Stein, *Untersuch. z. Gesch. u. Verwaltung Ägyptens unter röm. Herrschaft*, Stuttgart 1915, 39-74; cf. Bengtson, *Herrs.*, 279 ff.

1. Holleaux, "La chronologie de la cinquième guerre de Syrie," *Et. ép.* III, 317 ff.; cf. O. Leuze, *Hermes* 58, 1923, 192 n. 2. On the administration of the newly-won territory, Coele Syria and Phoenicia, see E. Bikerman, *Rev. bibl.* 54, 1947, 262; cf. R. M. Errington, "The Alleged Syro-Macedonian Pact and the Origins of the Second Macedonian War," *Ath.* 49, 1971, 336 ff.

2. Cf. Schmitt, *Staatsv.* III, no. 549.

3. Holleaux, "L'expédition de Philippe V en Asie," *Et. ép.* IV, 211-335, and *CAH* VIII, 153 ff.; Bengtson, *Strat.* II, 369 ff.

4. That an Athenian embassy also arrived in Rome at the time (thus Livy XXX 1.10 ff., on the basis of an annalistic source), has been exposed as spurious by Holleaux, (*Et. ép.* V, 9 ff.). Indeed, the Athenian envoy Cephisodorus did not arrive in Rome until after the Comitia had decided on war (July 200 B.C.); see also Walbank, *Phil. V*, 312 f.

5. Thus A. Heuss, "Die römische Ostpolitik und die Begründung d. röm. Weltherrschaft," *NJb.* 1, 1938, 337 ff., esp. 344; similarly M. Holleaux, *CAH* VIII, 156 ff.; and G. T. Griffith, "An Early Motive of Roman Imperialism (201 B.C.)," *Cambr. Hist. Journ.* 5, 1935, 1 ff., who lays particular stress on Rome's alleged fear at the growing strength of Macedonia.

6. Cf., for instance, M. Gelzer, *Arch. f. Kulturgesch.*, 1935, 262; "Die Anfänge des röm. Weltreiches," in *Das Reich, Idee und Gestalt* (*Festschr. f. J. Haller*), 1940, 1 ff.; A. Heuss, *NJb.* 1, 1938, 337 ff.; H. Haffter, "Polit. Denken im alten Rom," in *Röm. Politik und röm. Politiker*, Heidelberg 1967, 39 ff. (first published 1940); H. E. Stier, "Roms Aufstieg zur Vormacht im Mittelmeer," *WG* 7, 1941, 9 ff., *et mult. al.* See, on the other hand, for instance, F. Münzer, *Die politische Vernichtung des Griechentums*, 1925, 37 ff.; T. Frank, *Roman Imperialism*, New York 1929, 138 ff.; Otto, *6. Ptol.*, 38 ff.; SB.M, 1940, Schlussheft 21 f. (obituary of E. Pais). As compared with H. E. Stier, *Roms Aufstieg zur Weltmacht und die griech. Welt*, 1957, 14, I might add parenthetically, that I have *not* altered my view since 1939. I continue to regard 201 B.C. as the crucial turning point in Rome's eastern policy.

7. Cf. already R. Heinze, "Von den Ursachen der Grösse Roms," in *Vom. Geist des Römertums*, ed. 3 by E. Burck, Darmstadt 1960, 15 (first published 1921).

8. P. Culmann, *Die römische Orientgesandtschaft v. J. 201-200*, Diss. Giessen 1922; H. Winkler, *Rom und Ägypten im 2. Jahrh. v. Chr.*, Diss. Leipzig 1933, 14 ff.; Walbank, *Phil V*, 128 f.; 311 ff.

9. On the negotiations in Abydos see the controversy between E. Bickerman, *CP* 40,

1945, 137 ff., and F. W. Walbank, *CP* 44, 1949, 15 ff., esp. 17 ff. The latter appears, in my view, to have shown that the meeting in Abydos ended in the *denuntiatio belli* by Lepidus.

10. That M. Aemilius Lepidus was at the time appointed tutor of Ptolemy V, then a minor, is a family legend of the Aemilii from the sixties of the first century B.C.; cf. H. Winkler, *op. cit.*, 16; and Otto, *6. Ptol.*, 27 f.

11. On operations in the Second Macedonian War see Kromayer, *Schl.* II, 3-115; Kromayer-Veith, *Atlas* II, *Röm. Abt.* II, Blatt 9 1-4; cf. the bibliography in *CAH* VIII, 751; Walbank, *Phil V*, 138 ff. (a thorough discussion); N. G. L. Hammond, *JRS*, 56, 1966, 39 ff. (on the opening campaign of the Romans and the battle of the Aous Straits); F. M. Wood, *AJP* 62, 1941, 277 ff.; cf. also *TAPA* 70, 1939, 93 ff. (on the tradition relating to Flamininus).

12. On T. Quinctius Flamininus see E. Badian, *Titus Quinctius Flamininus. Philhellenism and Realpolitik*, University of Cincinnati 1973.

13. Holleaux, "Les conférences de Locride et la politique de Flamininus," *Et. ép.* V, 29 ff.

14. Cf. Kromayer, *Schl.* II, 57 ff.; also F. Stähelin, *Das hellenische Thessalien*, 1924, 108 ff.; Pritchett, *Top.* II, 133 ff.; M. Holleaux, *CAH* VIII, 174 f.; Walbank, *Phil. V*, 167 ff. On the chronology see Polyb. XVIII 20.3; cf. K. J. Beloch, *Klio* 15, 1918, 382 ff. (opposed to Varese, *Cronologia romana* I, 1908, who attempts to date the battle in 196 B.C.).

15. *Syll.* II³ 591; cf. Holleaux, *Et. ép.*, V, 141 ff.; M. Clerc, *Massalia* I, Marseille 1927, 296 Fig. 75; cf. E. Bickermann, "Rom und Lampsakos," *Ph.* 87, 1932, 227 ff.

16. The senatorial decree (not the peace treaty) has been transmitted by Polybius XVIII 44; Livy XXXIII 30, etc.; cf. E. Täubler, *Imperium Romanum* I 28 ff.; 432 ff.; Walbank, *Phil. V*, 178 ff. On the treaty see Polyb. XVIII 48.3 ff.

17. Polyb. XVIII 46; Livy XXXIII 32; Plut., *Tit.* 10; *Philop.* 15.

18. V. Ehrenberg, *RE* XVI, 1477 ff. s.v. *Nabis*; cf. the inscription published by A. Wilhelm, *Anz.*W, 1921, no. 18. On the extent of the liberation of the helots by Nabis see B. Shimron, *CP* 61, 1966, 1-7; on his view Nabis did not abolish the *heloteia*.

19. *Syll.* II³ 592; paean to Flamininus in Chalcis: Plut., *Tit.* 16 (the evidence for his cult may be found in H. Seyrig, *Rev. arch.*, 1929, I 94 f.); cf. the references in Nilsson, *Gr. Rel.* II, 178.

20. On the date see O. Leutze, *Hermes* 58, 1923, 211 ff. That Cleopatra received the revenue from Coele Syria as a dowry is an invention of Josephus (*AJ* XII 154 f.); cf. Bengtson, *Strat.* II, 161 n. 2 (with the earlier bibliography); a different view is held by M. Holleaux, *CAH* VIII, 199.

21. M. Holleaux, *Et. ép.* V, 180 ff. The alleged meeting of Hannibal and Scipio in Ephesus in 193 B.C. is legendary; see O. Leutze, *op. cit.*, 247 ff.

22. On the strategic-political situation before Antiochus began the war see Kromayer, *Schl.* II, 127 ff., who is no doubt correct in representing Antiochus as adopting a 'limited offensive'. Cf. also J. Kromayer, "Hannibal u. Antiochos d. Gr.," *NJb.*, 1907, 681 ff.; A. Passerini, "L'ultimo piano di Annibale e una testimonianza di Ennio," *Ath.* NS 11, 1933, 10 ff.

23. After the Roman victory, however, matters changed. Thus the marvellous story recounted by Phlegon, *Mirab.* (Jacoby, *FgrHist.* 257, 36 III), is certainly to be traced back to Syrian propaganda; cf. Holleaux, *Et. ép.* V, 244 ff.; H. Fuchs, *Der geistige Widerstand gegen Rom*, 1938, 5 ff.; 29 n. 16.

24. That this was a goal difficult to realise has been correctly stressed by A. Heuss, *NJb.* 1, 1938, 350. On the other hand, it was not utopian.

25. On the battle of Magnesia see Livy XXXVII 38 ff.; Appian, *Syr.* 31 ff. (= Polybius); cf. Kromayer, *Schl.* II, 158 ff.; Kromayer-Veith, *Atlas* II, *Röm. Abt.* II, 9 nos. 7 and 8; Delbrück, *Krieg.* I³ 426 ff.; De Sanctis, *Rom.* IV 1, 182 ff.; M. Holleaux, *CAH* VIII, 222 ff.

26. Livy XXXVII 45.

27. Polyb. XXI 34 ff.; Livy XXXVIII 12 ff. Cf. T. Mommsen, "Der Friede mit Antiochos und die Kriegszüge des Cn. Manlius Volso," *Röm. Forsch.* II, 538 ff.; Niese, *Mak.* II, 751 ff.; F. Stähelin, *Gesch. der kleinasiat. Galater*, ²1907, 39 ff.; De Sanctis, *Rom.* IV 1, 218 ff.; F. Münzer, *RE* XIV, 1217 ff. s. v. *Cn. Manlius Vulso* (no. 91).

28. Polyb. XXI 46 = Livy XXXVIII 39; cf. P. Ghione, "I comuni del regno di

Pergamo," *Mem. Acc, Torino*, 1905, 72 f.; G. Cardinali, *Il regno di Perg.*, 1906, 218 ff.; E. Bikerman, "Notes sur Polybe I. Le statut des villes d'Asie après la paix d'Apamée," *REG* 50, 1937, 217 ff.

29. Polyb. XXI 46.10 = Livy XXXVIII 39. Information on the attitude of the cities handed over to Eumenes II is evidently contained in an inscription, found in Brussa, perhaps stemming from Apollonia on the Rhyndacus (?); *SEG* II 663; cf. Holleaux, *Et. ép.* II, 73 ff.; Bengtson, *Strat.* II, 212 ff.

30. The possession of Pamphylia was a matter of dispute between Eumenes and Antiochus; see Ernst Meyer, *Die Grenzen der hellenist. Staaten*, 1925, 146 ff.; Holleaux, *Et. ép.* V, 208 ff.

31. On the war of Eumenes II against Prusias of Bithynia and the Galatian prince Ortiagon (184 B.C.) see Th. Lenschau, *RE* XVIII, 1505 f. s.v. *Ortiagon*; and especially the decree from Telmessus from 184 B.C., published by M. Segre, *RF* 60, 1932, 446 ff.; cf. L. Robert, *Rph.* 60, 1934, 284; *Etud. anatol.* 73 n. 1; Bengtson, *Strat.* II, 215 n. 2.

32. For a different view see M. Segre, "L'institution des Niképhoria de Pergame," in L. Robert, *Hel.* 5, 1948, 102 ff., esp. 122, whose views, however, are contested by G. Klaffenbach, *Mitt. Deutsch. Arch. Inst.* 3, 1950, 99 ff. See, on the other hand, J. and L. Robert, *REG* 65, 1952, Bull. épigr. no. 127.

33. E. Cavaignac, "Fulvius Nobilior en Grèce (189 av. J.-C)," *Mélanges P. Thomas*, 1930, 120 ff. (cf. the contribution by Holleaux, *Et. ép.* V, 249 ff.).

34. H. Horn, *Foederati*, Diss. Frankfurt 1930, 28 ff.; M. Holleaux, *CAH* VIII, 227.

35. On Philopoemen see A. Neumeyer, *Philopoemen, der letzte der Hellenen*, Progr. Amberg 1879; W. Hoffmann, *RE* XX, 76 ff. A good assessment by P. V. M. Benecke, *CAH* VIII, 299; see also R. M. Errington, *Philopoemen*, Oxford 1969; and R. Ranaud, "Philopoimen," *LEC* 39, 1971, 427 ff.

36. Cf. C. Habicht, *Hermes* 84, 1956, 90 ff.

37. Tarn, *Bact.*, 129 ff.; Altheim, *As.* I, 323 ff.

38. H. Bengtson, *HZ* 166, 1942, 337; Altheim, *As.* I, 307.

39. Interesting are the Greek words in the Indian language, especially in the military sphere: B. Liebich, *Bulletin Society of Oriental Studies* 6, 1931, 431 ff. (Studies Presented to E. J. Rapson). New aspects have been brought to light on Graeco-Bactrian culture by the excavations at Begram, north-east of Cabul; cf. R. Ghirshman, *Begram*, Cairo 1946; see also F. Altheim, *Saec.* 1, 1950, 295 ff.

40. Tarn, *Bact.*, 414 ff.: The Milindapañha and Pseudo-Aristeas; on Menander's empire, *ibid.*, 225 ff.

41. P. Heiland, *Untersuchungen zur Gesch. d. Königs Perseus*, Diss. Jena 1913; F. Geyer, *RE* XIX, 996 ff. s.v. *Perseus* (the characterisation is incorrect); P. Meloni, *Perseo e le fine della monarchia macedone*, Rome 1953; E. Bikerman, "Initia belli Macedonici," *REG* 66, 1953, 479 ff.

42. Cf. Livy XLII 47; cf. C. Peter, *Studien z. röm. Gesch.*, 1863, 125; F. Münzer, *RE* XIV, 1574 f. s.v. *Marcius* (79) *Philippus*; F. W. Walbank, *JRS* 31, 1941, 82-93; J. Briscoe, *JRS* 54, 1964, 66 ff.; also A. Giovannini, *BCH* 93, 1969, 853 ff.

43. Cf. J. M. F. May, "Macedonia and Illyria (217-167)," *JRS* 36, 1946, 48 ff.

44. Whether the Roma-hymn of the poetess Melinno from Locri is linked with this event, is not completely certain; concurring: H. Hommel, *Ant.* 18, 1942, 155 ff.; J. Vogt, *Vom Reichsgedanken der Römer*, 1943, 137; cf., of a different opinion, C. M. Bowra, *JRS* 47, 1957, 21-28.

44a. G. A. Lehmann, "Die Endphase des Perseuskrieges im Augenzeugenbericht des P. Cornelius Scipio Nasica," in *Beiträge zur Alten Geschichte, Festschrift f. F. Altheim*, 1969, 387-412.

45. The date is certain, on the basis of the eclipse of the moon during the night before the battle (despite K. J. Beloch, *Klio* 15, 1918, 142 f.; *GG* IV 2, 114); cf. De Sanctis, *Rom*, IV 1, 369 ff.; Otto, *6. Ptol.*, 32 n. 3.

46. Livy XLIV 37 ff. (with a major lacuna); Polyb. XXIX 17; Plut., *Aemil.* 18 ff.; Justin XXXIII 2; cf. above all Kromayer, *Schl.* II, 310 ff.; Ed. Meyer, *Kl. Schr.* II, 463 ff.; Pritchett, *Top.* II, 145 ff.

47. Livy XLV 18; 19; Diod. XXXI 8; Strabo fr. VII 48; Plut., *Aemil.* 28; Justin XXXIII

2.7; cf. Niese, *Mak.* III, 179 ff.; T. Frank, *CP* 9, 1914, 49 ff.; J. A. O. Larsen, in Tenney Frank, *ESAR*, IV, 298 f.; P. V. M. Benecke, *CAH* VIII, 273; J. Vogt, *Vom Reichsgedanken der Römer*, 1943, 95 ff.; Rostovtzeff, *SEHHW* II, 758; Bengtson, *Strat.* II, 323 and 326. Additional bibliography in Rostovtzeff, *SEHHW* III, 1509.

48. M. Feyel, "Paul-Emile et le synedrion macédonien," *BCH* 70, 1946, 187 ff., has admittedly attempted to show that a Macedonian *Synedrion* was created as a central organisation in which envoys from all four zones met together. But see, on the other hand, correctly, J. A. O. Larsen, "*Consilium* in Livy XLV 18.6-7 and the Macedonian *Synedria,*" *CP* 44, 1949, 73 ff., and A. Aymard, "L'organisation de la Macédoine et le régime représentatif dans le monde grec," *CP* 45, 1950, 96 ff.

48a. According to L. Perelli, *RF* 30, 1975, 403-412, the Romans wanted to forestall further growth in precious metals.

49. According to H. Küthmann, *AA*, 1966, 407-410, the ban was introduced to prevent the salt from being used for refining raw metals.

50. Rostovtzeff, *SEHHW* II, 739; H. H. Scullard, "Charops and Roman Policy in Epirus," *JRS* 35, 1945, 58 ff. (a defense of Aemilius Paullus); S. I. Oost, *Roman Policy in Epirus and Acarnania in the Age of the Roman Conquest of Greece*, Dallas 1954, 84 ff., chiefly also 134 f. n. 112.

51. According to P. Meloni, *Perseo*, 1953, 438 f., much more in 162 B.C. (on the basis of Porphyry, cf. Jacoby, *FgrHist.* no. 260 F 3,18).

52. Cf. Otto, *6. Ptol.*, 23 ff. (with earlier bibliography, 23 n. 3); further: A. Passerini, "Roma e Egitto durante la terza guerra macedonica," *Ath.* NS 13, 1935, 317 ff.; P. Jouguet, "Les débuts du règne de Ptolémée Philométor et la sixième guerre syrienne, d'après un mémoire de M. Walter Otto," *Rev. de phil.* 63, 1937, 193 ff.; "Eulaios et Lénaios," *Bull. de l'Inst. de l'Egypte* 19, 1937, 157 ff.; (the numerous reviews of Otto's study have been assembled by H. Bengtson, "Walter Otto," *Burs. Jahrb.* 284 [necrology], 1944, 31 n. 2 = *KS*, 607 n. 12); J. W. Swain, "Antiochus Epiphanes and Egypt," *CP* 39, 1944, 73 ff. On the basis of the *P. Ryl.* cited in the following note the chronology of the three (?) campaigns of Antiochus IV now requires reinvestigation. The first invasion of Antiochus IV must, on the basis of this papyrus, have taken place at the latest in the spring of 170 B.C., not as late as 169 B.C. (W. Otto). See on this question (and on the following note) T. C. Skeat, *JEA* 47, 1961, 107-112.

53. To wit, if the dating of *P. Ryl.* IV 583 from Philadelphia in the Fayum is correct (12 Nov. 170 B.C.), already *before* the first of Thoth, namely before 5 Oct. 170 B.C. According to this Papyrus, the sister of the two Ptolemies, Cleopatra II, shared in the regency from the very outset. E. Bikermann, *Cd'E* 27, 1952, 396 ff., thinks that the official Ptolemaic chronology (accession of the Younger Ptolemy 169 B.C.) is to be traced back to the deliberate forgery of the Ptolemaic court.

54. Otto, *6. Ptol.*, 81.

55. Polyb. XXX 31.12; cf. Schmitt, *Rom und Rhodos*, 1957, 160 ff.

56. Inscription, published by D. M. Pippidi, *Studii Clasice* 3, 1961, 56 ff.

57. *Syll.* I^3 495. The dating of the inscription ("c. 230 B.C.") is not certain; it could equally be placed at the end of the third or the beginning of the second century B.C.

58. Polyb. IV 45.

59. See the inscription from the first half of the second century discussed by H. Bengtson, *H.* 12, 1963, 100 ff. = *KS*, 393 ff.

60. Otto-Bengtson, *Ptol.*, 38 (with bibliography).

61. Some scholars admittedly deny the inner transformation of Antiochus IV after Eleusis.

62. Cf. the collection of relevant texts by T. Reinach, *Textes grecques et latines relatifs au Judaisme*, Paris 1896 (revision necessary).

63. Thus Rostovtzeff, *SEHHW* II, 703 ff.; III, 1492 f.; cf. also *idem*, *Mél. syriens off. à M. Dussaud*, 1939, 294.

64. R. Koldewey, *Das wiedererstehende Babylon*, ^{2}1925, 293 ff.; also B. Haussoullier, *Klio* 9, 1909, 352 ff.; cf. *SEHHW* II, 1049. In the Babylonian inscription OGI I 253 from 166 B.C. Antiochus is called "Saviour of Asia and founder of the city". (On the inscription cf. the far-reaching combinations by Tarn, *Bact.*, 194 ff.; differently, M. Zambelli, *RF* NS 38, 1960, 374 ff.)

65. See the document transmitted by Josephus, *AJ* XII 138 ff., an edict of Antiochus III which, published between 200 and 197 B.C., confirmed former privileges to the Jews: E. Bikerman, "La charte séleucide de Jerusalem," *Rev. ét. juives* 100, 1935, 4 ff.; Bengtson, *Strat.* II, 166 f.; 396 f.

66. Otto, *6. Ptol.*, 66 f.; 77 f.

67. Macc. II 4.9; cf. E. Bickermann, *Gott der Makk.*, 1937, 59 ff.; Bengtson, *Strat.* II, 175.

68. Macc. II 4.13.

69. See, in addition to the concise but essentially inclusive survey by W. Otto, *RE* VII, 2494 ff. s.v. *Hasmonäer*, the detailed study by E. Schürer, *Gesch. d. jüd. Volkes* I[3] and [4], 1901, 165 ff.; Meyer, *Christ.* II, 205 ff.; E. Bevan, *CAH* VIII, 495 ff.; see also A. Ben-David, "When did the Maccabees Begin to Strike their First Coins," *Pales. Explor. Quart.*, July-Dec. 1972, 93 ff.; W. Wirgin, "Maccabaean History from Coins," *ibid.*, 103 ff.

70. U. Wilcken, *RE* I, 2479 s.v. *Antiochos* (VII) no. 30; Niese, *Mak.* III, 295 f.; Meyer, *Christ.* II, 267 ff. (with the correct chronology, 268 n. 1).

71. I Macc. 8. 23-30. See B. Niese, *Orientalist. Studien für Th. Nöldeke* 817 ff.; E. Täubler, *Imp. Rom.* I, 1913, 240 ff.; Accame, *Dom.*, 79 f. (with additional bibliography). On relations between Rome and Judaea in general see M. S. Ginsburg, *Rome et la Judée*, Paris 1928, and now D. Timpe, *Ch.* 4, 1974, 133 ff., who argues for an allied treaty based on Roman formula.

72. F. Altheim, *WG* 2, 1936, 314 f.; *As.* I, 59.

73. On the Tochari see Tarn, *Bact.*, 285 ff. (partly out of date); G. Haloun, *ZDMG* 91, 1937, 243 ff.; F. Altheim (and P. Schnabel), *As.* I, 51 ff.; II, 88 ff.; A. Herrmann, *RE* VI A, 1632 ff.

74. The most recent study is that of P. J. Junge, *RE* XVIII 4, 1974 ff. The conclusions, however, in part still require verification.

75. Holleaux, *Et. ép.* III, 255 ff. On the chronology see H. Bengtson, *H.* 4, 1955, 113 f. = *KS*, 343 ff.

76. The best study is by Meyer, *Christ.* II, 270 ff.; cf. further, Debevoise, *Parth.*, 31 ff.; Altheim, *As.* II, 95 ff.; cf. now also T. Fischer, *Untersuchungen zum Partherkrieg Antiochos VII. im Rahmen der Seleukidengesch.* (Münchener Diss.), Tübingen 1970 (cf. E. Will, *REG* 84, 1971, 179).

77. U. Kahrstedt, *Syr. Territorien in hellenist. Zeit*, 1926, 73 ff.; Bikerman, *Sél.*, 149 ff.; 153; Rostovtzeff, *SEHHW* II, 842 ff.; III, 1533 f.

78. On Petra cf. C. Watzinger and T. Wiegand, *Petra, Wiss. Veröff. d. deutsch-türk. Denkmalsschutzkommission* 3, 1921; additional bibliography in A. Piganiol, *Hist. de Rome*, 1954, 387 f. See also *Petra und das Königsreich der Nabatäer. Lebensraum, Gesch. u. Kultur eines arabischen Volkes der Antike*, ed. by M. Lindner, Munich [2]1974. On the organisation of the Nabataean empire: Bengtson, *Strat.* II, 271 ff.; see also P. C. Hammond, *The Nabataeans,*, Göteborg 1973.

79. E. H. Minns, "Parchments of the Parthian Period from Avroman in Kurdistan," *JHS* 35, 1915, 22 ff. (cf. F. Heichelheim, *Burs. Jb.* 150, 1935, 280 f.; Rostovtzeff, *SEHHW* III, 1423 n. 221).

80. On the organisation of the Parthian kingdom cf. M. Rostovtzeff and C. B. Welles, *YCS* 2, 1931, 1 ff.; 45 ff.; W. W. Tarn, *CAH* IX, 588 ff.; M. Rostovtzeff, *CAH* XI, 113 ff.; Bengtson, *Strat.* II, 277 ff.

81. The evidence has been assembled by Bengtson, *Strat.* II, 297 ff.; and J. Johnson, *Dura-Studies*, Thesis Philadelphia 1932, 17 ff. (The Hereditary Strategos).

82. See above all the investigations of S. P. Tolstov on the culture of ancient Chorasmenia, and also B. Spuler, *H.* 1, 1950, 601 ff.

82a. See D. Schlumberger and P. Bernard, *BCH* 89, 1965, 590-657.

83. J. E. van Lohuizen-De Leeuw, *The Scythian Period. An Approach to the History, Art, Epigraphy and Palaeography of North India from the First Century B.C. to the Third Century A.D.*, Leiden 1949.

84. A. Grünwedel, *Buddh. Kunst in Indien*, [2]1919; A.v. Le Coq, *Die buddh. Spätantike in Mittelasien* I-VII, 1922-1933; R. Fick, *Die buddh. Kultur u. das Erbe Alex. d. Gr.*, Morgenland, Heft 25, 1933; A. Ippel, "Wirkungen griech, Kunst in Asien," *AO* 39, 1-2, Leipzig 1940.

85. Cf. Rostovtzeff, *SEHHW* II, 715 ff.

86. See the decree of the *dioiketes* Herodes from 164 B.C., in U. Wilcken, *UPZ* I no. 110; cf. Rostovtzeff, *SEHHW* II, 717; 719 ff.

87. *SEG* IX 7 (with bibliography). From the large number of studies, the following may be cited: G. Oliverio, *Doc. ant. dell'Africa ital.* I. *Cirenaica* I, Bergamo 1932 [first publication]; G. De Sanctis, *RF* NS 10, 1932, 59 ff.; U. Ratti, *RF* NS 10, 1932, 375 ff.; U. Wilcken, *Das Testament des Ptolemaios von Kyrene v. J. 155 v. Chr.*, SB.B, 1932, 317 ff.; W. Schubart, "Parakatatithesthai in der hellenistischen Amtssprache," *PhW*, 1932, 1077 ff. (with an incorrect explanation of the term); E. Bickermann, *Gn.* 8, 1932, 424 ff.; P. Roussel, *REG* 45, 1932, 286 ff.; L. Wenger, "Zum Test. des Ptolemaios Neoteros von Kyrene," in *Studi in onore di S. Riccobono* I, 1932, 527 ff. Further studies are cited and discussed in Otto, *6. Ptol.*, 97 n. 2; in V. Arangio-Ruiz, *Studia et documenta hist. et iuris* 2, 1936, 428 ff.; and in L. Wenger, *AfP* 13, 1939, 297 ff. That the testament was issued already in 162/1 B.C. has been shown by Otto, *6. Ptol.*, 107 ff. Otto, *6. Ptol.*, 102 f., has also rejected as unfounded the view held by G. Oliverio and W. Schubart, that Cyrenaica was to become a gift to Rome in the event of death (so-called *donatio mortis causa*).

88. See Otto, *6. Ptol.*, 117 ff.; 123.

89. Otto, *6. Ptol.*, 123 ff.

90. I Macc. II.13; Jos., *AJ* XIII 113; cf., again, Otto, *6. Ptol.*, 126 n.1. For a different view see L. S. Amantini, *Ist. Lombardo, Rendiconti Classe di Lettere*, Vol. 108, 1974, 511 ff, who maintains that Ptolemy VI wanted only to conquer Coele Syria.

91. Ptolemy VII Neos Philopator was murdered a short time later (in 145 or at the latest 144 B.C.); see Otto-Bengtson, *Ptol.*, 28.

92. For a detailed discussion see Otto-Bengtson, *Ptol.*, 23 ff. (with the sources); a summary in Rostovtzeff, *SEHHW* II, 873 ff.; III, 1541 ff. (with the most important sources). On the marriages of Ptolemy VIII see H. Heinen, "Les mariages de Ptolémée VIII Euergète et leur chronologie. Etude comparative de papyrus et d'inscriptions grecs, démotiques et hiéroglyphiques," *Akten XIII. internat. Papyrologenkongr. Marburg/Lahn, 2-6 Aug. 1971* (Münch. Beitr. 66), Munich 1974, 147 ff.

93. Otto-Bengtson, *Ptol.*, 194 ff.; J. H. Thiel, *Eudoxus of Cyzicus*, Groningen 1966 [first published in Dutch, in 1939]; Rostovtzeff, *SEHHW* II, 926 ff.; III, 1556. The intervention of L. Mooren, *Ancient Society* 3, 1972, is not (thanks to Strabo) convincing.

94. Otto-Bengtson, *Ptol.*, 121 ff., on the basis of Justin XXXIX 3.2 and Paus. I 9.1 f.

95. *SEG* III 378 from 100 B.C. (*Lex de piratis persequendis*); cf. Otto-Bengtson, *Ptol.*, 187.

96. Otto, *6. Ptol.*, 109 n. 1; and S. I. Oost, "Cyrene 96 to 74 B.C.," *CP* 58, 1963, 11-25.

97. Athen. IV 184 C. The linguist Aristarchus was also among the banished; he died in Cyprus in 144 B.C.

98. Cf. now, however, M. G. Morgan, *H.* 18, 1969, 422 ff.

99. On the revolt of Andriscus see in particular Diod. XXXI 40a; XXXII 15; Livy, *Per.* 49 f.; cf. U. Wilcken, *RE* I, 2441 ff. s.v. *Andriskos*; G. Cardinali, "Lo Pseudo-Filippo," *RF* 39, 1911, 1 ff.; P. V. M. Benecke, *CAH* VIII, 276 f.; U. Wilcken in particular has correctly stressed that there can be no question of a national revolt.

100. C. I. Makaronas, *Mnemosynon Pappadakis*, Saloniki 1948, 293 ff.; cf. J. and L. Robert, *REG* 62, 1949, Bull. épigr. no. 92.

101. Cf. Niese, *Mak.* III, 337 ff.; cf. A. Fuks, "The Bellum Achaicum and its Social Aspect," *JHS* 90, 1970, 78 ff.; Th. Schwertfeger, *Der achaiische Bund von 146 bis 27 v. Chr.* (Vestigia 19), Munich 1973.

102. Cf. the excavation publications: *Corinth* I-XII and XIV-XV, Cambridge, Mass., 1932 ff.; cf. the remark by R. Herzog, *HZ* 165, 1942, 350.

103. The old controversy whether all Hellas became a Roman province in 145 B.C. (thus inceptively C. Sigonius, *De antiquo iure populi Romani* II cap. 9, 63-72), or retained its freedom in the greater part of the country up to the time that Augustus established the province of Achaea (K. F. Hermann, "Die Eroberung von Korinth und ihre Folgen für Griechenland," in *Verh. d. Philologenversammlung zu Basel*, 1847, 32 ff., = *Ges. Abh. u. Beitr. z. klass. Lit.-und Altertumskd.*, Göttingen 1849, 356 ff.), now appears to have been resolved through the fortunate restoration of the inscription *IG* VII 2413/4 (from 112/11 B.C.), by Accame, *Dom.*, 2 ff. Accordingly, part of Hellas was under the Macedonian governor, while the remainder of Hellas was "free".

104. U. Kahrstedt, *GGA*, 1926, 124 ff., who exaggerates, however, when he characterises the disturbances as distinctly communistic; see, on the other hand, F. Oertel, *Klassenkampf, Sozialismus und organischer Staat im alten Griechenland*, 1942, 39 ff.

105. *Syll.* II[3] 684; cf. Rostovtzeff, *SEHHW* II, 757; Accame, *Dom.*, 149 ff.

106. The most important source: OGI I 138: a Pergamene inscription which confirms the references in our literary sources. Niese, *Mak.* III, 365 ff.; G. Cardinali, "La morte di Attalo III e la rivolta di Aristonico," in *Saggi di Storia Antica e di Archeologia off. a G. Beloch*, Rome 1910, 269 ff.; H. Last, *CAH* IX, 102 ff.; Broughton, *As.*, 505 ff.; M. Segre, *Ath.* NS 16, 1938, 123 f.; J. Vogt, *Ancient Slavery and the Ideal of Humanity*, Cambridge, Mass. 1975, 93 ff.

107. See E. S. G. Robinson, *Num. Chron.*, 1954, 1-8; L. Robert, *Villes d'Asie Mineure*, [2]1962, 252 ff., and the dissertation by J. Hopp, *Untersuch. z. Gesch. d. letz. Attaliden*, Munich 1976, who rightly places the uprising before the death of Attalus III.

108. On the war of Aristonicus see, in addition to the studies cited above n. 106, further, U. Wilcken, *RE* II, 962 ff.; Broughton, *As.*, 505 ff.; Rostovtzeff, *SEHHW* II, 807 ff. (with the most important epigraphical sources, III, 1522 f. n. 80, of which the decree from Bargylia for Poseidonius, discussed by Holleaux, *Et. ép.* II, 179 ff., deserves emphasis); on the Stoic Blossius of Cumae and his part in the revolt, lastly, D. R. Dudley, *JRS* 31, 1941, 94 ff., esp. 98 f. J. Fontenrose, "The Crucified Daphidas," *TAPA* 91, 1960, 83 ff.; this, he argues, was an episode from the Aristonicus War.

109. On the dating of Iambulus (probably in the third century B.C.) see Tarn, *Alex.* II, 411 ff.; further, Altheim, *As.* II, 155 ff.; 181 ff.

110. Thus, following Mommsen, Rostovtzeff, *SEHHW* II, 808, who denies the alleged Stoic influence of Aristonicus. On the Hellenistic utopias, especially the "sun state", see W. W. Tarn, *Alexander the Great and the Unity of Mankind*, Proc. Brit. Acad. 19, 1933, 9 ff.; J. Bidez, "La cité du monde et la cité du soleil chez les stoïciens," *Bull. de l'Acad. Royale de Belgique*, 5 sér., 18, 1932, 244 ff.

111. On the position of the Greek cities, which were indeed free but not exempt from tribute, see Rostovtzeff, *SEHHW* II, 812 ff.; cf. the inscription of Diodorus Pasparus (IGR IV 292; cf. A. Wilhelm, SB. W 214,4, 1932, 21 ff.; L. Robert, *Etud. anatol.*, 1937. 45 ff.), from approximately 125 B.C., and the so-called *senatus consultum* from Adramyttium dated 129 B.C., in truth a decision of a *praetor de consilii sententia*, with a newly discovered copy from Smyrna, published by A. Passerini, *Ath.* NS 15, 1937, 252 ff., cf. M. Segre, *Ath.* 16, 1938, 119 ff.; also Rostovtzeff, *SEHHW* III, 1522 f.; 1525; and G. Tibiletti, *JRS* 47, 1957, 136-8. The oft-cited inscription of Diodorus Pasparus belongs *not* in the Aristonicus war but in the time of Mithradates VI Eupator: see C. P. Jones, *Ch.* 4, 1974, 183-205; cf. J. and L. Robert, *Bull. épigr.* 1974, no. 466.

112. On Q. Mucius Scaevola and the festival of *Moukieia* see F. Münzer, *RE* XVI, 438 f.; E. Badian, *Ath.* NS 34, 1956, 104 ff.; on Rutulius Rufus, F. Münzer, *RE* I A. 1273 ff.; and the bibliography cited in Rostovtzeff, *SEHHW* III, 1527 n. 94.

113. See the inscription in L. Robert, *La Carie* II, 1954, 97 ff. no. 5.

114. Poseidonius (no. 87) fr. 36 Jacoby. The prevailing view ever since Casaubonus, that Athenion is to be equated with the Ariston who appears in Appian (*Mithr.* 28) and on coins (R. Weill, "Das Bündnis der Athener mit Mithradates," *AM*, 1881, 315 ff.) and who later played a leading rôle in Sulla's siege of Athens, has been refuted by B. Niese, *RhM* 42, 1887, 574 ff.; cf. also U.v. Wilamowitz-Moellendorff, *Athenion und Aristion*, SB. B, 1923, no. VII, 39 ff. (=*Kl. Schr.* V 1, 204 ff.). See the bibliography in F. Geyer, *RE* XV, 2171; and in Rostovtzeff, *SEHHW* III, 1557 n. 4. Finds of Mithradates coins with a new era beginning in Athens, namely Piraeus, in 88/7 B.C.: W. Schwabacher, *Num. Chron.*, 1939, 162 ff.

115. Mithradates was still elected as *stephanephoros* in Miletus in February-March 86 B.C., cf. A. Rehm, *Milet* I 3 No. 125; SB. Bay, 1939, Heft 8, 6 ff.

116. On the transplanting of peoples under Mithradates, in particular in the Bosporic kingdom, see Rostovtzeff, *SEHHW* II, 943; III, 1559 n. 13 (with reference to the important inscription from Olbia: B. Latyschev, *Inscript. ant. orae sept. Ponti Euxini gr. et lat.*, I[2], 1916, no. 35; and also A. Wilhelm, *Klio* 29, 1936, 50 ff.). On the treatment of Chios: F. Koepp, *RhM* 39, 1884, 216; Th. Reinach, *Mithr. Eupator*, 1895, 173 f.; F. Geyer, *RE* XV, 2174 f.

117. U. Kahrstedt's view, expressed in various places (*GGA*, 122 ff.; "Das Zeitalter des antiken Sozialismus," *Hellas-Jb.*, 1929, 105 ff.), that the measures of Mithradates are to be regarded as the attempt at a general "world revolution," is misleading. See, opposed to this, inter al., J. Vogt, *Slavery and the Ideal of Humanity*, Cambridge, Mass. 1975, 83 ff.

118. Appian, *Mithr.* 62 f.; Plut., *Sulla* 25; *Luc.* 4; 20; cf. in particular A. Momigliano, *Atti IV Congr. naz. di Studi rom* I, 1938, 280 ff.; Rostovtzeff, *SEHHW* III, 1560, n. 17.

119. *IG* IV^2 1,66 (Epidaurus) cf. K. Latte, *Gn.* 7, 1931, 128 n. 1; *Syll.* II^3 748; *IG* V 1, 1145 (Gythium); cf. Rostovtzeff, *SEHHW* II, 951 ff.; III, 1563 n. 27 (bibliography).

120. Cic., *ad Quint. fratr.* I 1.8; 24 f.; cf. Rostovtzeff, *SEHHW* II, 973 f.; also F. Münzer, *RE* VII A, 1290 f.; further, Drumann-Groebe, *Gesch. Roms* VI 640 ff.; and the special edition of the letter by Atzert, *Ausgewählte Briefe Ciceros* II, Münster 1929.

121. M. Cary, *CAH* IX, 392 ff.; Broughton, *As.*, 530 ff.; M. Gelzer, *Pompeius*, 1949, 123 ff. Additional bibliography in F. E. Adcock, *JRS* 40, 1950, 136.

122. The *Lex Pompeia* was still the basis of administration in Bithynia and Pontus in the time of Pliny the Younger; cf. Pliny, *ad Traianum imperatorum* (X), 79; 80; 112; 114; 115.

123. Cf. R. Syme, "Observations on the Province of Cilicia," *Studies Buckler*, 1939, 299 ff.

124. Bengtson, *Strat.* II, 251 ff.; 257 ff. On Commagene, see further: *Commagene, Geschichte und Kultur einer antiken Landschaft*, ed. F. K. Dörner, Küsnacht-Zürich 1975.

125. Strabo XII 539.

126. *SEG* I 466.

127. Remzi Oguz Arik and J. Coupry, "Les tumuli de Karalar et la sépulture du roi Déiotaros II," *Rev. arch.*, 1935, II, 133 ff.; Rostovtzeff, *SEHHW* II, 837.

128. *OGI* I 383 = Jalabert and Mouterde, *Inscript. gr. et lat. de la Syrie* I no. 1. On the inscription cf H. Dörrie, *Der Königskult des Antiochos von Kommagene im Lichte neuer Inschriftenfunde*, Abh. Göttingen, phil.-hist. Kl., 3. Folge, Nr. 60, 1964, [with bibliography]. In addition, there are the results of more recent investigations by F. Dörner in Arsameia; cf. the "Sammelwerk": *Neue deutsche Ausgrabungen im Mittelmeergebiet und im Vorderen Orient*, 1959, 71 ff.; and above all F. K. Dörner and T. Göll, *Arsameia am Nymphaios. Die Ausgrabungen im Hierothesion des Mithradates Kallinikos von 1953 bis 1956*, Istanbuler Forschungen 23, Berlin 1963.

128a. Cf. in regard to him the inscription published by J. Keil and A. Wilhelm, *Mon. Asiae Min. Antiqua* III, Manchester 1931, 64 ff. no. 62; also P. Treves, *RE* XIX, 2554 ff. On the last Seleucids see, otherwise, the works cited above 580 by A. Kuhn, E. R. Bevan (*The House of Seleucus*, Vol. II), Bouché-Leclercq (*Hist. des Séleucides*) and A. R. Bellinger.

129. Cic., *pro Sestio* § 93; cf. Rostovtzeff, *SEHHW* II, 981.

130. Survey in C. Patsch, *Beitr.* V 34 ff.; Rostovtzeff, *SEHHW* II, 985 ff.

131. Eutrop. VI 10; Ruf. Fest. 9.2-4; Appian III. 30; cf. C. Patsch, *Beitr.* V, 1932, 36 ff. Perhaps to be considered in this connection is the treaty between Rome and Callatis: S. Lambrino, *CRAI*, 1933, 278 ff.; A. Passerini, *Ath.* NS 13, 1935, 57 ff.; D. S. Marin, *Epigraphica* 10, 1948 (published 1950), 103 ff. Cf. also the decree from Mesembria for a Roman officer from 71 B.C.: G. Mihailov, *Inscr. Graecae in Bulgaria repertae* I, Sofia 1955, no. 314.

132. From 57 to 55 B.C. L. Calpurnius Piso Caesoninus was governor there with special plenary powers; cf. F. Münzer, *RE* III, 1387 ff. s.v. no. 90; Rostovtzeff, *SEHHW* II, 986 ff.; III, 1574 f.; H. Bloch, *AJA* 44, 1940, 485 ff.; Piso owned the Villa dei papiri in Herculaneum. The Epicurean Philodemus was a friend of his.

133. Dio Chrys. XXXVI 4 f. (H. v. Arnim); see also C. Patsch, *op. cit.*, 46 ff. (with additional references); further: M. Rostovtzeff, *Gn.* 10, 1934, 6; A. Alföldi, *Z. Gesch. d. Karpathenbeckens im 1. Jahrh. v. Chr.*, 1942.

134. Inscriptions from Pergamum, Ephesus, Aegae, Magnesia on the Maeander honour the memory of the proconsul of Asia (46-44 B.C.), P. Servilius Isauricus; cf. L. Robert, *Hel.* 6, 1948, 37 ff.

135. M. Rostovtzeff, "Caesar and the South of Russia," *JRS* 7, 1917, 27 ff.

136. See R. Herzog, "Nikias und Xenophon von Kos," *HZ* 125, 1922, 189 ff., esp. 206 ff.; R. Syme, *JRS* 51, 1961, 26 ff.

137. Noteworthy is the influence which the orator Hybreas wielded among Romans and

Parthians on behalf of his native city Mylasa (reference from L. Robert; cf. *REG* 72, 1959, Bull. épigr. no. 107a), and *idem*, *AC* 35, 1966, 419-420, 421.

138. Thus the senator L. Memmius appeared in Egypt in 112 B.C., certainly on a diplomatic mission; cf. *P. Teb.* I 33; see Otto-Bengtson, *Ptol.*, 159 f.

139. Otto-Bengtson, *Ptol.*, 191.

140. Paus. I 9.3, and the so-called letters of Plato (*P. Bour.* 10-12; *P. Ross Georg.* II 10); cf. Rostovtzeff, *SEHHW* III, 1542.

141. The view held by former scholars, primarily on the basis of Trog., *Prol.* 39, that Ptolemy XII was illegitimate, is contested by Otto-Bengtson, *Ptol.*, 192 n. 2.

142. Cf. Otto-Bengtson, *Ptol.*, 192 n. 2. New views on the testament in E. Badian, *RhM* 110, 1967, 178-192; cf., on the other hand, E. Bloedow, *Beiträge zur Gesch. des Ptolemaios XII.*, Diss. Würzburg 1963, 26 ff.

143. S. I. Oost, *CP* 50, 1955, 98 ff.

144. P. Graindor, "La guerre d'Alexandrie," *Recueil de trav. publ. par la fac. des lettres de l'Univ. égypt.* fasc. 7, Cairo 1931; and H. Heinen, *Rom und Ägypten von 51 bis 47 v. Chr.*, Diss. Tübingen 1966, 69 ff.

145. J. Carcopino, "Etud. d'archéol. rom.," *Ann. de l'école des hautes étud. de Gand*, I 1 ff.

146. Plut., *Ant.* 26; Appian V 1.8; Athen. IV 147f-148c; Cass. Dio XLVIII 24.2; Zon. X 22. Cf. the famous lines of Shakespeare in Antony and Cleopatra.

147. On the economic conditions see F. Stähelin, *RE* XI, 779; Rostovtzeff, *SEHHW* II, 108 ff. (There is evidence for famines in 48, 42 and 41 B.C.). On Cleopatra's attitude to things Egyptian see W. W. Tarn, *JRS* 26, 1936, 187 ff. (cf. Otto-Bengtson, *Ptol.*, 131 n. 1; 149 n. 2); *CAH* X, 35 ff. (cf. the reservations of Rostovtzeff, *SEHHW* III, 1551 n. 190).

148. The importance of the gift of 37/6 B.C. is emphasised by the fact that Cleopatra adopted a new dating by regnal years alongside the old (year 16 = year 1); see U. Wilcken, on *P. Würzburg* 5; Otto-Bengtson, *Ptol.*, 5 n. 3; 52 n. 6. According to A. Dobiaš, "La donation d'Antoine à Cléopâtre en l'an 34 av. J.-C.," *Ann. de l'Inst. de Phil. et d'Hist. orient.* II (*Mél. Bidez*), 1933/34, 287 ff., there were *two* different donations; in 37/6 B.C. Cleopatra received only Chalcis and Damascus, while the other regions were presented to her in 34 B.C. See also H. U. Instinsky, in *Studies Presented to D. M. Robinson* II, 1955, 975 ff.

149. Plut., *Ant.* 54; Cass. Dio XLIX 41; cf. W. W. Tarn, *CAH* X, 80 f.; A. E. Samuel, *Etud. papyr.* 9, 1971, 73 ff.

150. W. W. Tarn, "Alexander Helios and the Golden Age," *JRS* 22, 1932, 135 ff. (cf. *CAH* X, 82), has attempted to link far-reaching theories with the name of Alexander Helios, but they are not sound. The attempt to connect *Orac. Sibyll.* III 350 ff. with Cleopatra has been rejected by H. Fuchs, *Der geistige Widerstand gegen Rom in der antiken Welt*, 1938, 36; cf. also F. Oertel, *Klassenkampf, Sozialismus und organischer Staat im alten Griechenland*, 1942, 65 f. ns. 133-135. On the religious policy of Antony see the bibliography in J. L. Tondriau, *Symbolae Osloenses* 27, 1949, 129 n. 2.

151. W. Spiegelberg, SB.M, 1925, 2 no. 1, 3 ff.; W. W. Tarn, *CAH* X, 110; M. A. Levi, *PP* 42, 1952, 293 ff. On the chronology: T. C. Skeat, *JRS* 43, 1955, 98-100.

152. On the era (beginning 1 Thoth 30 B.C.): U. Wilcken, "Octavian after the Fall of Alexandria," *JRS* 27, 1937, 138 ff. (chiefly on the basis of R. Mond and O. H. Meyers, *The Bucheum*, 1934, Stele no. 13).

15 THE GREEKS IN THE ROMAN EMPIRE

THE GREEK WORLD FROM AUGUSTUS TO MARCUS AURELIUS

SOURCES AND BIBLIOGRAPHY: Due to their unusual fragmentary character the sources for Greek history in the first two centuries of the Roman Empire are even more difficult to grasp and survey than those of the Hellenistic period. The primary sources are abundant but vary as to historical content: they are comprised of decrees *(constitutiones, edicta, rescripta)* issued by the Roman emperors (the most important are assembled in S. Riccobono, *FIRA* I²); ordinances of the Roman governors, countless documents of a municipal and private character, including a vast number of honorary decrees; an unlimited amount of numismatic information on the Imperial coins and local issues, especially from Asia Minor, Syria and Egypt. Of literary documents the correspondence of the Younger Pliny with the emperor Trajan (Pliny *ep.* X) is of exceptional importance.

Of the inscriptions, chiefly the following collections may be cited: *Inscriptiones Graecae*, with the important Attic inscriptions of the Roman Imperial era in Vol. II/III² by Joh. Kirchner; Dittenberger's *Orientis Graeci Inscriptiones Selectae* and *Sylloge Inscriptionum Graecarum*³; Dessau's *Inscriptiones Latinae Selectae; Inscriptiones Graecae ad res Romanas pertinentes* by R. Cagnat, *et al.*; *Monumenta Asiae Minoris Antiqua*; *Tituli Asiae Minoris; Inscriptiones Creticae* by M. Guarducci; *Inscriptions grecques et latines de la Syrie* by L. Jalabert et R. Mouterde; *Supplementum Epigraphicum Graecum* by J. J. E. Hondius; and, finally, a large number of local editions, a good survey of which has been given by J. J. E. Hondius, *Saxa loquuntur*, Leiden 1938. Useful are the collections: *Documents Illustrating the Reigns of Augustus and Tiberius* (edited by V. Ehrenberg and A. H. M. Jones, Oxford 1949; ²1955); *Documents Illustrating the Reigns of Claudius and Nero* (edited by M. P. Charlesworth, Cambridge 1939); *Select Documents of the Principate of the Flavian Emperors, Including the Year of Revolution* (edited by M. McCrum and A. G. Woodhead, Cambridge 1961); *Documents Illustrating the Principates of Nerva, Trajan and Hadrian* (edited by E. Mary Smallwood, Cambridge 1966); translations of many important inscriptions and papyri are available in N. Lewis, *Greek Historical Documents: The Roman Principate*, Toronto, 1974. New inscriptions from Delphi: *Fouilles de Delphes* III. *Epigraphie*, fasc. IV, Paris 1970, nos. 300 ff. (by A. Plassart): letters of Roman emperors (fragmentary) from Claudius to Caracalla. On Hadrian and Delphi: R. Flacelière, *CRAI* I, 1971, 168-185. The additional new epigraphical material is reported annually in the Bulletin épigraphique of *REG* by J. and L. Robert.

The papyri which are historically of greatest importance have been collected by U. Wilcken, *Chrestomathie der Papyruskunde*, 1912, and discussed by him in *Grundzüge der Papyruskunde*. More recent finds are dealt with in U. Wilcken's *Urkundenreferate* in *AfP* (down to Vol. XV, 1953, inclusive, published posthumously); for everything subsequent see M. Hombert, "Bulletin papyrologique," *REG* 59-60, 1946/47, 373 ff., and subsequent years. Of the papyri which are historically of great importance, only the following are cited here (a good survey may be found in *CAH* X, 922 ff.; cf. also Piganiol, *HR*, 390 ff.): *P. London* 1912, published by Bell, *Jews* (with a letter of Claudius to the Alexandrians); the extensive bibliography may be found in Stephan Lösch, *Epistula Claudiana*, Rottenburg a.N. 1930; see also W. Seston, *Rev. d'hist. et de philosophie* 11, 1931, 275 f.; the so-called *Acts of the Pagan Martyrs:* cf. U. Wilcken, *Zum alexandrinischen Antisemitismus*, Abh. S 27, 1900, 800 ff.; a new edition by H. A. Musurillo, *The Acts of the Pagan Martyrs*, Oxford 1954; cf. also the lecture by H. I. Bell, *JJP* 4, 1950, 19 ff.; the *Gnomon* of *the Idios Logos*, published by W. Schubart, *BGU* V 1, 1919; the commentary written by W. Graf Uxkull-Gyllenband, *BGU* V 2, 1934; cf. M. Rostovtzeff, *Gn.* 11, 1935, 522 ff.; see also the partial printing in S. Riccobono, *FIRA* I², 469 ff. The *Gnomon* probably stems from the time of Marcus Aurelius. For the administration of taxes in Egypt, S. L. Wallace, *Taxation in Egypt from Augustus to Diocletian*, Princeton 1938, is still indispensable, while important supplementary information for the early Roman period may be found in G. Mattha, *Demotic Ostraca from the Collections at Oxford, Paris, Berlin, Vienna and Cairo*, Cairo 1945.

Important works on numismatics: J. P. Shear, "Athenian Imperial Coinage," *Hesp.* 5, 1936, 285 ff.; F. Münzer and M. L. Strack, *Die antiken Münzen von Thrakien* I, 1912; W. H. Waddington, E. Babelon, Th. Reinach, *Recueil général des monnaies grecques d'Asie Mineure* I 1-4, Paris 1904-12 (I 1 published in a second edition, 1925); C. Bosch, *Die kleinasiatischen Münzen der römischen Kaiserzeit*, Bd. I, 1, 1: *Bithynien*, Stuttgart 1935 (no more have been published); an introduction is provided by P. R. Franke, *Kleinasien zur Römerzeit. Griechisches Leben im Spiegel der Münzen*, Munich 1968. For Syria cf. the catalogues of the British Museum; and W. Wruck, *Die syrische Provinzialprägung von Augustus bis Trajan*, Stuttgart 1931. For Egypt: J. Vogt, *Die alexandrinischen Münzen*, Stuttgart 1924; and J. G. Milne, *Catalogue of Alexandrian Coins, University of Oxford. Ashmolean Museum*, Oxford 1933.

Contemporary oratory is of great importance. The speeches by Dion of Prusa are accordingly an important source for the history of the Greek East about 100 A.D. (edition by G. de Budé, 1916-19; cf. the basic work by H. v. Arnim, *Leben und Werke des Dio von Prusa*, Berlin 1898). The same applies to the speeches of Aelius Aristides (117-189 A.D.), a native of Hadrianutherae in Mysia. With the sole exception of the oration *To*

Rome (no. 26, Keil; cf. the edition, with commentary, by J. H. Oliver, *The Ruling Power. A Study of the Roman Empire in the 2nd Century A.D. through the Roman Oration of Aelius Aristides*, Philadelphia 1953, and the Loeb edition, by C. A. Behr, 1973 ff.; cf. H. Bengtson, *Gym.* 71, 1964, 160 ff. = *KS*, 549-567; J. Bleicken, *NGG*, 1966, no. 7), only those speeches which are of importance for the history of religion have hitherto claimed the attention of scholars. The ethical writings by Plutarch of Chaeroneia (c. 46-123 A.D.) are also only in the early stages of being assessed in so far as their historical and political content is concerned (cf. above all the *Praecepta ger. rei publ.*; cf. Bengtson, *WG* 10, 1950, 93 ff. = *KS* 231 ff., R. Flacelière, "Rome et ses empereurs vus par Plutarque," *AC* 32, 1963, 28-47), and in this regard there is still much work that remains to be done on Lucian of Samosata (cf. nevertheless A. Perretti, *Luciano, un intellettuale greco contro Roma*, Florence 1946, whose judgment, however, is one-sided in describing Lucian as a sworn enemy of Rome). Valuable is J. Delz, *Lukians Kenntnis der athenischen Antiquitäten*, Diss. Basle, published Freiburg (Switzerland) 1950. Strabo's *Geography* (from the time of Augustus) is of principal importance for the geography of the East. The chapters on Greece are admittedly the weakest, whereas most successful is his description of his homeland, Pontus, then also of Anatolia and Egypt, primarily Alexandria. Strabo's description of Greece is supplemented by that of the *Periegetes* Pausanias, stemming from the middle of the second century A.D. On the description of Delphi by Pausanias see G. Daux, *Pausanias à Delphes*, Paris 1936; cf. otherwise, the references by E. Pernice, *Hdb. Arch.* I, 1939, 244 n. 3. On relations between the Greek world, especially Egypt, and India in the time of the Roman Empire the *Periplous Maris Erythraei* is important, the handbook on sailing by a Greek merchant, probably from the second half of the first or the beginning of the second century A.D.: edition of the *Periplous* by H. Frisk, *Göteborgs Högskolas Arsskrift*, 1927, 1; on the date see the references in Otto-Bengtson, *Ptol.*, 197 n. 3 and 203; further, A. Grohmann, *RE* XVI, 1459 s.v. *Nabataioi* (between 38 and 75 A.D.); also R. Güngerich, *Die Küstenbeschreibung in der griech. Lit.*, 1950, 29 n. 47; and M. P. Charlesworth, in *Studies in Roman Economic and Social History in Honor of A. C. Johnson*, Princeton 1951, 129 ff., especially 132. Valuable is E. Kornemann, "Die historischen Nachrichten des Periplus maris Erythraei über Arabien," *Janus I (Festschr. f. C.F. Lehmann-Haupt)*, 1921, 55 ff.; and A. Dihle, *Umstrittene Daten. Untersuchungen zum Auftreten der Griechen am Roten Meer*, Cologne and Opladen 1965, who dates the *Periplous* in the first and not in the third century A.D. (as Jacqueline Pirenne and F. Altheim). In this connection reference should be made to the excavations in Arikamedu near Pondicherry on the east coast of India; cf., for instance, R. E. M. Wheeler, A. Gosh, Krishna Deva, *Ancient India* 2, 1946, 17-124.

The information on Hellas and the Greek East in the historians of the Roman Empire, chiefly in Cornelius Tacitus and Suetonius, must in part be regarded as secondary material; the same applies to the *Vitae sophis-*

tarum of Philostratus, from the end of the Severan period, of such exceptional value for the history of education and civilisation; moreover his work on the miracle-working Apostle Apollonius of Tyana is, despite the romantic elaboration on points of detail, a highly interesting sidelight on the history of Hellenism during the Roman Empire (cf. Ed. Meyer, *Hermes* 52, 1917, 371 ff.; concise, F. Solmsen, *RE* XX, 139 ff.; cf. also the references in Piganiol, *HR*, 419.

BIBLIOGRAPHY: A general account of the history of Hellenism during the Roman Empire continues to be a desideratum as much as ever. A valuable monograph is G. W. Bowersock, *Augustus and the Greek World*, Oxford 1965 (with, *inter al.*, references on Greeks in the service of Augustus, 30 ff.; on the eastern colonies, 62 ff.); cf. *idem*, *Greek Sophists in the Roman Empire*, Oxford 1969. A survey: R. Syme, *The Greeks under Roman Rule*, Proc. of the Massachusetts Hist. Soc. 72, 1957-1960, 3-20. What is cited below is no more than some leading features which need to be supplemented and expanded throughout. Among earlier studies, which are partly out of date and antiquated on many points of detail, the following may be cited here: for Greece: G. F. Hertzberg, *Die Geschichte Griechenlands unter der Herrschaft der Römer*, II. Teil: *Von Augustus bis auf Septimius Severus*, Halle 1868 (out of date, but still worth reading); U. Kahrstedt, *Das wirtsch. Gesicht Griechenlands in der Kaiserzeit*, Bern 1954 [a wealth of material, but the conclusions need to be scrutinised]; for Asia Minor: V. Chapot, *La province romaine proconsulaire d'Asie*, Paris 1904; for Egypt: J. G. Milne, *Egypt under Roman Rule*, London ^{3}1924; P. Jouguet, *La domination romaine en Egypte aux deux premiers siècles après J.-C.*, Alexandria 1947; F. Zucker, *Ägypten im röm. Reich*, SB. Leipzig 104 7, 1958. For Southern Italy: U. Kahrstedt, *Die wirtschaftliche Lage Grossgriechenlands in der Kaiserzeit* (H.-Einzelschr. 4), Wiesbaden 1960. The classic survey which Th. Mommsen gave in Vol. V of his *Römische Geschichte* on the Greek regions in the Roman Empire still deserves close attention (cf. the excellent remarks by Th. Nöldeke, *ZDMG* 39, 1885, 331 ff.: "Über Mommsens Darstellung der römischen Herrschaft u. röm. Politik im Orient"). A reading of H. Dessau's relevant chapters in his *Geschichte der römischen Kaiserzeit* II 2, 1930, makes the uniqueness of Mommsen's art of delineation all the more pronounced. The chapters in the *Cambridge Ancient History* are excellent: XI, Chap. XIV: "The Greek Provinces" (by J. Keil); and Chap. XV: "The Frontier Provinces of the East" (by Fr. Cumont); basic for social history is Rostovtzeff, *SEHRE*. Indispensable for the material culture and economic life is *ESAR*, edited by Tenney Frank, as follows: Vol. II: *Roman Egypt to the Reign of Diocletian*, by A. C. Johnson (predominantly a textbook); from Vol. IV the following sections: "Roman Syria" (by F. Heichelheim); "Roman Greece" (by J. A. O. Larsen); and "Roman Asia" (by T. R. S. Broughton), the last named is a particularly impressive achievement (cf. M. Rostovtzeff, *AJP* 60, 1939, 363 ff.; 373 ff.). For the rest, reference must be made to the extensive bibliographies in *CAH*: Vol. X, 922 ff.; Vol. XI, 927 (on Roman Egypt; more recent works are cited by Bell, *Eg.*, 161 f.); *ibid.*, 914 ff.; 918 ff. (on Hellas, Asia Minor and the Middle East); to the bibliographical survey in E. Gren, *Kleinasien und der Ostbalkan in der wirtschaftlichen Entwicklung der röm. Kaiserzeit*, Uppsala 1941, XII ff.; and to the references by Piganiol, *HR*, 381 ff.; 575 ff. Useful is J. Palm, *Rom, Römertum und Imperium in der griechischen Literatur*, Lund 1959; see also G. W. Bowersock, "Syria under Vespasian," *JRS* 63, 1973, 133 ff.

From the vast number of specialised studies only the following are selected here: For the history of Greece: P. Graindor, *Athènes sous Auguste*, Cairo 1927; *Athènes de Tibère à Trajan*, Cairo 1931; *Athènes sous Hadrien*, Cairo 1934; also the earlier investigations by B. Keil, *Beitr. z. Gesch. des Areopags*, SB Sächs. Ak. 71 Heft 8, 1920, is still valuable; on economic history see J. Day, *An Economic History of Athens under Roman Domination*, New York 1942: Chap. V, 177 ff. Valuable are the works by J. A. O. Larsen, for instance: "A Thessalian Family under the Principate," *CP* 48, 1953, 86-95 (a family from Hypata); *Rep. Govt.*, especially 106 ff. For Asia Minor: The many epigraphical studies by Louis Robert are also of great importance for historians: *Villes d'Asie Mineure*, Paris 1935; [2]1962 (brilliant examples of combined epigraphical, numismatic and philological investigations); *Etudes anatoliennes*, 1937; [2]1970; *Etudes épigraphiques et philologiques*, 1938; *Hel.*, 1940 ff. (to date 13 vols.); *Les gladiateurs dans l'Orient grec*, Paris 1940; and many articles which are analysed in the *Index*, 1937, edited by L. Robert, as well as in Bulletin épigraphique of *REG*. Important contributions have been made by Sir William Ramsay in the study of Phrygia and Galatia (cf. *Cities and Bishoprics of Phrygia* I-II, Oxford 1895-97; *Historical Commentary on St. Paul's Epistle to the Galatians*, London [2]1900; *The Social Basis of Roman Power in Asia Minor*, Aberdeen 1941 [published posthumously], is unfortunately not on the same level as the former works; cf. the remarks by L. Robert, *REG* 57, 1944, 223). Indispensable is D. Magie, *Roman Rule in Asia Minor to the End of the Third Century A.D.*, 2 vols., Princeton 1950, a regular thesaurus for all questions relating to Roman Anatolia. Also valuable for the Roman period of Anatolian history are the *Anatolian Studies Presented to Sir William Ramsay*, Manchester 1923, and *Anatolian Studies Presented to W. H. Buckler*, Manchester 1939—both volumes with contributions by many eminent scholars; see also C. H. Emilie Haspels, *The Highlands of Phrygia. Sites and Monuments*, Vol. I, Princeton 1971, 153 ff. (with bibliography). Penetrating studies on the importance of Hellenism for Syria and Mesopotamia are lacking, since scholars, under the strong impulse of the life work carried out by Franz Cumont, occupied themselves predominantly with the other great problem, namely the question of the orientalisation of the Eastern Greeks. What is greatly needed now is a comprehensive study of the epigraphical finds and the excavation reports from the East (Dura-Europus, Gerasa, Petra, Palmyra, Susa *et al.*), to determine the extent to which Hellenism subsisted here from Hellenistic times on. As preparatory collections of evidence we may refer to the books by A. H. M. Jones, *The Cities of the*

Eastern Roman Provinces, Oxford 1940 [^{2}1971], and *The Greek City from Alexander to Justinian*, Oxford 1940. Cf. Further, O. Eissfeldt, *Tempel und Kulte syr. Städte in hellenist. u. röm. Zeit* (AO 40), 1939. B. P. Reardon, *Courants littéraires grecs des IIe et IIIe siècles après J.-C.* (Annales littéraires de l'Université de Nantes 3), Paris 1971 (cf. M. D. MacLeod, *JHS* 95, 1975, 223-225); and D. M. Pippidi, "Les villes de la côte de la Mer Noire d'Auguste à Dioclétien," in *Akten des VI. Intern. Kongr. für Griechische u. Lateinische Epigraphik*, Munich 1972, 99 ff.

THE GREEKS FROM MARCUS AURELIUS TO THE END OF THE THIRD CENTURY A.D.

PRIMARY SOURCES: What is necessary to a discussion on the editions and collections of inscriptions, papyri and coins has been stated above 592. Of the large number of documents from the time of Marcus Aurelius to Diocletian the following are stressed as particularly instructive: the letter of Commodus to the Eumolpids of Eleusis (*Syll.* II^{3} 873 [cf. a new fragment in A. E. Raubitschek, *Hesp.* Suppl. 8, 1949, 285]); the edict by a Proconsul of Asia, C. Gabinius Barbarus Pompeianus, for the community of Euhippe in Caria, from the years 212-217 (L. Robert, *CRAI*, 1952, 589 ff.; *Centennial Volume of the American Numismatic Society*, New York, 1958, 582 ff.); the complaints by an inhabitant of the Thracian district of Scaptopara about oppression at the hands of travelling officials in the form of a petition to the emperor Gordian, from 238 A.D. (*Syll.* II^{3} 888); the inscription of the emperor Claudius II Gothicus on the rebuilding of the walls of the Bithynian city Nicaea, from 269 A.D. (*Syll.* II^{3} 895); the petition of the league of the Aragoueni from 246/7 A.D., with important evidence on internal conditions in the province of Asia (*OGI* II 519); the inscription from Kula in Lydia, published by P. Hermann, *Denkschr. Akad. Wien, phil.-hist. Kl.* 80, 1962, 26-27, from 247-248 A.D., which mentions, *inter al.*, the *collectiones* and contains complaints of the inhabitants, directed against the emperor Philip the Arab. Information on the development of the institution of *dekaproteia* in Asia Minor comes from —besides other documents—inscriptions from Prusias ad Hypium (*IGR* III 60-67), and from Thyateira (*IGR* IV 1248; 1261; 1265; 1273). A decree from Chalcis on Euboea (*IG* XII 9, 906 = *Syll.* II^{3} 898) contains evidence for the functioning of the *Boule* and the *Ekklesia* in the third century A.D. From the large number of papyri only the following are cited here: *P. Giss.* I 40 (the *Constitutio Antoniniana*; cf. the text in S. Riccobono, *FIRA* I^{2}, 445 ff.; cf. Chr. Sasse, *Die Constitutio Antoniniana*, Wiesbaden 1958, with bibliography). Instructive for conditions in Egypt about the turn of the third century A.D. is the edict of Subatianus Aquila (*BGU* 484, from 201/2 A.D.; cf. U. Wilcken, *Chrestomathie d. Papyruskunde* no. 202, Einleitung; and Rostovtzeff, *SEHRE*, 418 ff., II, 719 f. n. 38). The council records from Hermopolis (*P. Ryl.* 77, bibliography in A. H. M. Jones, *The Greek City from Alexander to Justinian*, 1940, 343 n.

58), and from Oxyrhynchus (*P. Oxy.* 1414 and 1415) provide interesting sidelights on the problem of *leitourgia.* The oration *To the King* transmitted under the name of the Sophist Aelius Aristides (no. 35 Keil), is instructive for the spirit of the times. But in actual fact it belongs to an orator of the third century and is directed towards the emperor Philip the Arab, as has been shown by E. Groag, *Wiener Stud.* 40, 1918, 20 ff. The intervention by C. P. Jones, *JRS* 62, 1972, 134 ff., is not convincing.

HISTORIOGRAPHY: From the great *Roman History* by Cassius Dio Cocceianus (c. 155-235 A.D.) only the extract of the Byzantine monk Johannes Xiphilinos 11th century) has survived for the period in question. The *History* of the Syrian Herodianus, written about 240 A.D. and covering the period after Marcus Aurelius (180-238 A.D.), is only a compendium. Only fragments have survived from the *Chronicle* and the *Skythika* by the admirable P. Herennius Dexippus of Athens (Jacoby, *FgrHist.* no. 100; cf. F. Millar, *JRS* 59, 1969, 12-29; C. Habicht, *Ch.* 2, 1972, 129 ff.). The imperial history from the beginning of the fourth century A.D., written in Latin, is lost (A. Enmann, *Eine verlorene Geschichte der röm. Kaiser,* Philologus Suppl. Bd. 4, 1884, 340 ff.). The *Epitomes* of the fourth century which were culled from it (Aurelius Victor, Eutropius, Rufius Festus, the *Epitome de Caesaribus*) are only sparse interspersions. The *Scriptores Historiae Augustae*, which cover an imperial history from Hadrian to Carus and his sons (117-285) are open to much doubt in regard to their detailed value as a source; they are probably a work which was written by some writer from the time of Theodosius. For details reference may be made to Bengtson, *Einf.* 98; 11 f. with additional references (cf. English translation, *Anc. Hist.*, 11 ff.). Details on specific evidence dealing with historians (as well as on the whole subject of sources) may be found in the bibliographies of *CAH* XI and XII, and in *Histoire de Rome*, [5]1962, by A. Piganiol (especially 410 ff.; 429 ff.; 451 ff.). It would be desirable to have a work compiling the principal sources for the history of the Hellenic East.

BIBLIOGRAPHY: A historical narrative of the Greek region of the Empire in the third century A.D. which incorporates recent finds and the results of modern scholarship has not as yet been written; it is an urgent desideratum. A question that is particularly ripe for investigation is the extent to which there are, besides the doubtless existing Hippocratic features, also brighter and more positive elements, which for the most part have not been sufficiently appreciated in previous surveys because of the influence exerted by Rostovtzeff's standard work, *SEHRE.* A good beginning has been made, especially for Asia Minor, by C. Bosch, "Die kleinasiastischen Münzen der römischen Kaiserzeit," *AA*, 1931, 422 ff. (see also his book of the same title, but of which only Bd. I 1,1 [Bithynia] has been published, Stuttgart 1935). Further reference may be made to V. Schultze, *Altchristl. Städte u. Landschaften* II. *Kleinasien*, Gütersloh 1922 and 1926; to T. R. S. Broughton, "Roman Asia" (in T. Frank, *ESAR*); and to E. Gren, *Kaiserzeit*, Uppsala 1941. Cf. for the rest the bibliography cited above 592 ff.; cf. also P. Brown, *The World of Late Antiquity from Marcus Aurelius to Muhammed*, London 1971.

1. Thus in 7/6 B.C. Augustus was able to ascertain the presence of only 215 Romans of every age in Cyrenaica (with a census of at least 2500 drachms) (*SEG* IX 8 I)—and this after two full generations of Roman administration! It was not until the reign of Trajan that the picture changed in this country.
2. P. Graindor, *Athènes sous Auguste*, 1927, 180 ff.; W. Judeich, *Top.*, 99.
3. M. P. Nilsson, *Ant.* 18, 1942, 227.
4. M. Rostovtzeff, "Augustus und Athen," *Festschrift f. Otto Hirschfeld*, Berlin 1903, 303 ff.; J. A. O. Larsen "The Policy of Augustus in Greece," *Acta Classica* I, 1958, = *Roman Life and Letters. Studies Presented to T. I. Haarhoff*, Capetown 1959, 123-130; G. W. Bowersock, *Augustus and the Greek World*, 1965, 95.
5. W. Kolbe, *IG* V 1, 307; E. Kjellberg, "C. Iulius Eurykles," *Klio* 17, 1920, 44 ff.; L. Ross Taylor and A. B. West, *AJA* 30, 1926, 389 ff.; H. Box, *JRS* 21, 1931, 200 ff.; cf. also 22, 1932, 165 ff.; G. W. Bowersock, *JRS* 51, 1961, 112-118.
6. Cf. A. Gitti, "I perieci di Sparta e le origini del *koinon ton Lakedaimonion*," *RALinc.*, Ser. VI, Vol. 17, 3-4, 1939, 189 ff.; "La condizione delle città della Laconia e l'opera di Augusto," *Atti V Congr. naz. di Studi Romani*, 1939, 3 ff.
7. Strabo IX p. 420.
8. Paus. X 8; cf. Fr. Frhr. Hiller von Gaertringen, *RE* IV, 2578; J. A. O. Larsen, *CP* 47, 1952, 14; *Rep. Govt.*, 111.
9. W. Dörpfeld, *Olympia in röm. Zeit*, Berlin 1914.
10. *IG* IX 2, 415b; on the dating: A. S. Arbanitopulos, *Arch. Ephem.*, 1917, 149. E. Groag, *Die röm. Reichsbeamten von Achaia bis auf Diokletian*, Schrift. der Balkan-Komm. der Akad. d. Wiss. Wien, Antiqu. Abt., Vienna and Leipzig, 1939; cf. J. H. Oliver, *GRBS* 14, 1973, 389 ff.
11. Cf. M. Grant, *From imperium to auctoritas. A Historical Study of Aes Coinage in the Roman Empire 49 B.C.-A.D. 14*, Cambridge 1946, 11 ff.
12. See the outstanding study by L. Robert, "Le culte de Caligula à milet et la province d'Asie," *Hel.* 7, 1949, 206 ff. (on the basis of an inscription from the Milesian Didymaeum).
13. Buckler-Robinson, *Sardis* VII 1 no. 8.
14. H. Dessau, *Gesch. d. röm. Kaiserzeit* II 2, 1930, 592 n. 1. See Octavian's letter to the city of Rhossus in Syria, published by H. Seyrig and P. Roussel, *Syria* 15, 1934, 33 ff., also in S. Riccobono, *FIRA* I², 308 ff. no. 55; cf. above all E. Schönbauer, *AfP* 13, 1939, 177 ff.
15. *Editio princeps* by G. Oliverio, "La stele di Augusto rivenuta nell'Agora di Cirene," *Ministero delle Colonie, Notiziario archeologico*, fasc. 4, 1927, 13 ff. From the extensive literature which has since accrued on the edicts, cited in SEG IX 8 and in Riccobono, *FIRA* I², 403 ff. no. 68, the following studies may be mentioned as particularly useful: A.v. Premerstein, "Die 5 neugefundenen Edikte des Augustus aus Kyrene," *ZSS Röm.* 48, 1928, 419 ff.; J. Stroux and L. Wenger, *Die Augustusinschrift auf dem Marktplatz von Kyrene*, Abh. Bay. 34,2, 1928; the survey in A.v. Premerstein, "Zu den kyrenäischen Edikten des Augustus," *ZSS Röm.* 51, 1931, 431 ff.; F. de Visscher, *Les édits d'Auguste découverts à Cyrène*, Univ. Louvain. Rec. de trav. d'hist. et phil., 3 sér., fasc. 1, Louvain 1940.
16. Cf. J. P. Thrige, *Res Cyrenensium*, Hafniae 1828 (reprint prepared by S. Ferri, Verbania 1940); P. Romanelli, *La Cirenaica romana*, Verbania 1943.
17. J. Stroux and L. Wenger, *op. cit.*, 45 ff.; 53 ff. For a different view see W. Otto, *ibid.*, 48 n. 5, who interprets the term Hellenes in the sense of constitutional law and restricts it to the inhabitants of Pentapolis. The issue cannot be resolved with complete certainty.
18. P. M. Fraser, *JRS* 40, 1950, 77 ff.; J. A. O. Larsen, "Cyrene and the Panhellenion," *CP* 47, 1952, 7-16.
19. W. Capelle, *RhM* 97, 1954, 185 ff.
20. An inscription from Adalia in Pamphylia attests the settling of 3000 veterans from *Legio III Cyrenaica* in Cyrene in the reign of Trajan; cf. J. and L. Robert, *REG* 61, 1948, 201.

21. P. Romanelli, *CAH* XI, 670.
22. L. Robert, *Hel.* 1, 1940, 7 ff.
23. P. Romanelli, *Storia delle provincie romane dell'Africa*, Rome 1959.
24. It was definitely transformed into a Roman province in the reign of Claudius.
25. De la Blanchère, *De rege Iuba*, Paris 1883; W. Thieling, *Der Hellenismus in Kleinafrika*, Leipzig and Berlin 1911, 19 f.; 153 f.; etc.; F. Jacoby, *RE* IX, 2384 ff. s.v. *Juba* no. 2; also the fragments of Juba's writings in *FgrHist.* III no. 275. Greek inscriptions in Volubilis: L. Robert, *REG* 1936, 8 ff. (third century A.D.).
26. On the administration of Egypt under the Romans see A. Stein, *Untersuch. z. Gesch. u. Verwaltung Ägyptens unter röm. Herrschaft*, Stuttgart 1915; *Die Präfekten von Ägypten in der röm. Kaiserzeit*, Bern 1950.
27. See the excellent survey by Bell, *Eg.*, 65 ff.
28. M. Rostovtzeff, "Roman Exploitation of Egypt in the First Century A.D.," *Journ. of Economic and Business History* I, 1929, 337 ff. The picture is delineated in somewhat more positive terms by the study of H. I. Bell, "Philanthropia in the Papyri of the Roman Period," in *Hommages à Joseph Bidez et à Franz Cumont*, Coll. Latomus II, Brussels 1949, 31 ff.
29. V. Martin, *Les épistratèges*, Geneva 1911; cf. the restoration of the list of *epistrategoi*, *AfP* 6, 1913, 216 ff.; and H. Henne, *Liste des stratèges*, 1935,; and the supplement to this by G. Mussies, in *Papyrologica Lugduno-Batava* XIV, Leiden 1965.
30. Basic on local administration is P. Jouguet, *La vie municipale dans l'Egypte romaine*, Paris 1911; additional bibliography in Piganiol, *HR*, 391 f.
31. Strabo XVII 798.
32. The question which for many years was a subject of controversy, whether Jews possessed Alexandrian citizenship or not, has finally been settled, in the negative, by *P. Lond.*, 1912, published by Bell, *Jews*. A good bibliography may be found in Bell, *Jud.*, Leipzig 1926, 49 ff.
33. F. Oertel, *Die Liturgie*, Leipzig 1917. For new points of view on the early Roman period of Egypt see H. Metzger, *MusHelv* 2, 1945, 54 ff. (cf. A. Kränzlein, *JJP* 6, 1952, 195 ff.).
34. F. Zucker, "*Gymnasiarchos komes*," *Aeg.* 11, 1930, 485 ff.
35. G. Plaumann, "Die *en Arsinoïte andres Hellenes* 6475," *AfP* 6, 1913, 176 ff.
36. A.v. Premerstein, "Alexandrinische Geronten vor Kaiser Gaius" (P. Bibl. Univ. Giss. 46), *Mitt. aus der Papyrussamml. d. Giessner Univ.-Bibl.* V, 1939, 40 ff.
37. See, for instance, F. Kenyon, "The Library of a Greek at Oxyrhynchus," *JEA* 8, 1922, 129 ff.; C. H. Oldfather, *The Greek Library Texts from Graeco-Roman Egypt*, Univ. of Wisconsin Stud. on the Social Sciences and History 9, 1923; B. Olsson, *Papyrusbriefe aus der frühsten Römerzeit*, Diss. Uppsala 1925; J. G. Winter, *Life and Letters in the Papyri*, Ann Arbor 1933 [[2]1965]. The latest catalogue of literary papyri: R. A. Pack, *The Greek and Latin Literary Texts from Graeco-Roman Egypt*, Ann Arbor 1952.
38. See Nilsson, *Sch.*, 85 ff.
39. On Clement, for instance, see R. C. Lilla Salvadore, *Clement of Alexandria. A Study in Christian Platonism and Gnosticism*, London and New York 1971.
40. On the Hellenistic elements in the rule of Gaius (Caligula) see, for instance, H. Willrich, *Klio* 3, 1903, 85 ff.; 288 ff.; 397 ff.; and J. P. V. D. Balsdon, *The Emperor Gaius*, Oxford 1934; on Claudius: A. Momigliano, *L'opera dell'imperatore Claudio*, Florence 1932, available in an English translation: *Claudius the Emperor and his Achievement*, Oxford 1934; V. M. Scramuzza, *The Emperor Claudius*, Cambridge, Mass., 1940; on Nero: G. Schumann, *Hellenistische u. griechische Elemente in der Regierung Neros*, Diss. Leipzig 1930. On women see the older Dissertation of E. Sandel, *Die Stellung der kaiserlichen Frauen im iul.-claud. Hause*, Giessen 1912; cf. Kornemann, *Fr.* 221 ff. (on Julia Agrippina).
41. Cf. the references above 593, in particular the book by H. A. Musurillo, also, for instance, Meyer, *Christ*, III, 539 ff.; Bell, *Jud.*, 15 f.; 28 f.; 34 ff.; also the bibliography in *CAH* X, 929; and in H. Fuchs, *Der geistige Widerstand gegen Rom*, 1938, 57 f.; H. I. Bell, *JRS* 31, 1941, 11 ff. More recent research in D. Henning, *Ch* 4, 1974, 425 ff.
42. M. Rostovtzeff was the first to recognise that the *Acts of Pagan Martyrs* reflect the political opposition of the Alexandrians to Rome, in which the lawsuits against the leaders

of Alexandrian Hellenism acted as a foil in the struggles against the Jews of the city; see his remark in *SEHRE* II, 587 n. 19, with the reference to a work published by him in the Russian monthly *Mir Božij*, 1901.

43. The extant *Acts* extend from the time of Gaius (Caligula) to Commodus.

44. Cf. the edicts of Germanicus in Egypt, published by U.v. Wilamowitz-Moellendorff and F. Zucker, SB.B, 1911, 794 ff., also in V. Ehrenberg and A. H. M. Jones, *Documents Illustrating the Reigns of Augustus and Tiberius*, Oxford 1949, no. 320; cf., *inter al.*, E. Hohl, "Ein röm. Prinz in Ägypten," Preuss. Jahrb. 182, 1920, 344 ff.; U. Wilcken, *Hermes* 63, 1928, 48 ff.; in great detail, D. G. Weingärtner, *Die Ägyptenreise des Germanicus*, Bonn 1969 (with extensive bibliography).

45. See Cass. Dio LI 17.2; cf. M. Engers, *Klio* 20, 1925, 168 ff.; and W. Otto, *PhW*, 1926, 9 f. On the controversial problem of the Alexandrian Council see from the great number of recent works cited above: H. I. Bell, *Aeg.* 12, 1932, 173 ff.; P. Viereck, *Aeg.* 12, 1932, 210 ff.; U. Wilcken, *AfP* 10, 1932, 255 f. A number of modern scholars hold the view that the Alexandrians lost their Council already in the Ptolemaic period: cf. P. Jouguet, *Bull. Soc. Arch. Alex.* no. 37, 1948, 8 f.

46. See the letter of the emperor Claudius to the Alexandrians, preserved in *P. Lond.* 1912, published by Bell, *Jews.*

47. E. Groag, *Wien. Stud.* 50, 1932, 204 n. 11.

48. Evidence of this in the "decree of the governor of Asia, Paullus Fabius Persicus," found in Ephesus, from the time of Claudius (see the Dissertation bearing the same title by F. K. Dörner, Greifswald 1935). See further, V. M. Scramuzza, "Claudius Soter Euergetes," *HSCP* 51, 1940, 261 ff.; and his book *The Emperor Claudius*, Cambridge, Mass., 1940.

49. Basic on this subject is the edict of Tiberius Julius Alexander (on his personality see E. G. Turner, *JRS* 44, 1954, 54 ff.; and V. Burr, *Tiberius Julius Alexander*, Bonn 1959); *OGI* II 669 (see also the more recent edition by H. G. E. White and J. H. Oliver, *The Temple of Hibis in El Khargen Oasis* II, New York 1939, nos. 3 and 4; further, S. Riccobono, *FIRA*, I², 318 ff. no. 58); cf. H. I. Bell, "The Economic Crisis in Egypt Under Nero," *JRS* 28, 1938, 1 ff.; *idem, Eg.*, 77 ff.; and G. Chalon, *L'édit de Tiberius Julius Alexander*, Olten and Lausanne 1964 [cf. D. Nörr, *ZSS Röm.* 83, 1966, 431-436]). On Nero and Egypt see O. Montevecchi, *PP* 30, 1975, 48-58.

50. See the address of Nero delivered before the Greeks, preserved in an inscription from Acraephia (*Syll.* II³ no. 814); further, Plut., *Tit.* 12; Suet., *Nero* 24; Cass. Dio LXIII 11; cf. in particular Holleaux, *Et. ép.* I, 1938, 165 ff. The dating of the declaration of freedom in 66 A.D. (J. Vogt, *Die alexandrinischen Münzen*, 1924, 34 f.; also A. Momigliano, *CAH* X, 735 n. 2) is, as A. Stein, *Gn.* 1, 1925, 342 f., has shown, untenable.

51. *Syll.* II³ 814,9.

52. *Ibid.*, lines 48 ff.; cf. G. Schumann, *Hellenist. u. griech. Elemente in der Regierung Neros*, 1930, 76.

53. If *P. Fouad* I 8 is connected with this event, remains disputed; that it is, see, for instance, P. Jouguet, "L'arrivée de Vespasian à Alexandrie," *Bull. de l'Inst. d'Egypte* 24, 1941/42, 21 ff.; *Bull. Soc. Arch. Alex.* no. 37, 1948, 23; that it is not, E. G. Turner, *Gn.* 27, 1955, 461 f. See R. Merkelbach, *AfP* 16, 1958, 111 ff., and A. Henrichs, *ZPE* 3, 1968, 59.

54. Suet., *Vesp.* 19.2; Dio Chrysos. XXXII 71 f.

55. Suet., *Vesp.* 8.2 and 4: *provinciae civitatesque liberae, nec non et regna quaedam tumultuosius inter se agebant... Achaiam. Lyciam, Rhodum, Byzantium, Samum libertate adempta, item Trachiam Ciliciam et Commagenen dicionis regiae usque ad id tempus, in provinciarum formam redegit (sc. Vespasianus).*

56. Cass. Dio LXV (LXVI) 13 and 13a (Vol. III 146 f. Boissevain), cf. 15 (Vol. III 149 Boissevain); Suet., *Vesp.* 15; cf. Rostovtzeff, *SEHRE* I, 114 ff., ns. 12 and 13; also R. Weynand, *RE* VI, 2661.

57. It is correctly stressed by Rostovtzeff, *SEHRE* II, 586 n. 14; that the *political* side of Cynic propaganda has for the most part been overlooked, also by P. Wendland, *Die hellenistisch.-römische Kultur*, ²⁻³1912, 75 ff.

58. See above all H.v. Arnim, *Leben und Werke des Dio von Prusa*, 1898, 223 ff.; W. Schmid, *RE* V, 852 ff.; *GGL*, 361 ff.

59. Dio Chrysos., *or.* XXXVI.

60. R. Herzog, *Urkunden zur Hochschulpolitik der röm. Kaiser*, SB.B,1935, no. 32, 967 ff. (cf. W. Hartke, *Gn.* 14, 1938, 507 ff., who is, however, incorrect in rejecting Herzog's emendations and the interpretation of the Pergamene inscriptions); it is also printed in Riccobono, *FIRA* I², 420 ff. no. 73.

61. On the activities of Pliny the Younger in Bithynia see above all his letters to Trajan (Bk. X); cf. M. Rostovtzeff, *BSA* 22, 1916-1918, 1 ff.; O. Cuntz, *Hermes* 61, 1926, 192 ff.; 352.

62. According to M. N. Tod, "The Corrector Maximus," in *Studies Buckler*, 333 ff., in 108/9 A.D.; cf. E. Groag (v.s.p. 599 n. 10) 125 ff.

63. F. Zucker, "Plinius ep. VIII 24, ein Denkmal antiker Humanität," *Ph.* 84, 1928, 209 ff.

64. See P. Graindor, *Ath.*; J. H. Oliver, "The Athens of Hadrian," in *Les empereurs romains de l'Espagne*, 1965, 123 ff.; idem, *Hesp.* 39, 1970, 332-336 (appeal procedure).

65. Judeich, *Top.*, 100 ff.; P. Graindor, *Ath.*, 214 ff.

66. See the inscription from Thessalonike, published by M. N. Tod, *JHS* 42, 1922, 173 ff.; cf. Graindor, *Ath.*, 102 ff.

67. See M. P. Nilsson, "Die eleusinische Religion," *Ant.* 18, 1942, 227.

68. L. Robert, *Hel.* 3, 1946, 89.

69. On the *Mouseion* of Ephesus: J. Keil, *Öst. Jh.* 8, 1905, 128; 135 f.; *Ephesos* III 68; of Smyrna: L. Robert, *Etud. anatol.*, 1937, 146 ff.

70. E. Kühn, *Antinoopolis*, Diss. Göttingen 1913; H. I. Bell, *CAH* XI, 650 f.; *JRS* 30, 1940, 133 ff.

71. H.v. Arnim, *Leben und Werke des Dio von Prusa*, 1898, 492 ff.; Ed. Meyer, *Kl. Schr.* I², 1924, 164 ff.; J. A. O. Larsen, "Roman Greece," in Tenny Frank, *ESAR*, 479 f.; cf. the Dissertation by D. Reuter, *Untersuch. z. Euboikos des Dion von Prusa*, Diss. Leipzig (published Weida i. Th. 1932); J. Day, in *Studies in Roman Economic and Social History in Honor of A. Ch. Johnson*, 1951, 209-235; also D. Kienast, "Ein vernachlässigtes Zeugnis für die Reichspolitik Trajans. Die zweite tarsische Rede des Dion von Prusa," *H.* 20, 1971, 62 ff.

72. Hadrian's *Lex* on oil: IG II/III² 1100 (cf. B. D. Meritt, *Hesp. Suppl.* 8, 1949, 221 ff.); the ordinance on fish and trade: A. Wilhelm, *Öst. Jh.* 12, 1909, 146 ff.; also Rostovtzeff, *SEHRE* II, 700 n. 21; Graindor, *Ath.*, 74 ff.

73. Rostovtzeff, *SEHRE* II, 698 ff.

74. P. Münscher, *RE* VIII, 921 ff. s.v. *Herodes* no. 13; P. Graindor, *Un miliardaire antique, Hérode Attique et sa famille*, Cairo 1930; cf. K. Gerth, *Burs. Jb.* 272, 1941, 159 ff.

75. A. Boulanger, *Aelius Aristide et la sophistique dans la province d'Asie au IIe siècle de notre ère*, Bibl. des Ecoles franç. d'Athènes et de Rome 126, Paris 1923: U.v. Wilamowitz-Moellendorff, *Der Rhetor Aristeides, SB.B*, 1925, 333 ff.; L. Robert, *Etud. anatol.*, 1937, 207 ff. (property of Aelius Aristides).

76. See Lucian's treatise on "How to Write History"; cf. the edition with German translation by H. Homeyer, Munich 1965. Also valuable is G. Avenarius, *Lukians Schrift zur Geschichtsschreibung*, Diss. Frankfurt a.M. 1954 (published Meisenheim a.d. Glan 1956).

77. Rostovtzeff, *SEHRE* I, 130 ff.; cf. W. Hüttl, *Antoninus Pius* I, 1936, 327 ff.; and in particular the works cited above 594 by J. H. Oliver and J. Bleiken. "Der Preis (sic) des Aelius Aristides auf das römische Weltreich," *NGG*, 1966, no. 7.

78. See the evidence in W. Liebenam, *Städteverwaltung im römischen Kaiserreiche*, Leipzig 1900, 165 ff. (for the entire empire, partly out of date); B. Laum, *Stiftungen in der griechisch-römischen Antike* I/II, 1914; a great amount of evidence has been assembled by T. R. S. Broughton in his contribution on Asia Minor in Tenney Frank, *ESAR* IV; cf. also Rostovtzeff, *SEHRE* I, 601 n. 13.

79. The relevant inscription has been published by G. Pugliese Carratelli, in *Studi di antichità class. off. a E. Ciaceri*, 1940; cf. J. and L. Robert, *REG* 59-60, 1946-1947, Bull. épigr. no. 156.

80. K. A. Neugebauer, "Herodes Atticus, ein antiker Kunstmäzen," *Ant.* 10, 1934, 92 ff.

81. J. Keil, *CAH* XI, 588 n. 1.

82. R. Heberdey, *Opramoas*, Vienna 1897; E. Ritterling, *RhM* 73, 1920, 35 ff.; E. S. Walton, *JRS* 19, 1929, 54 ff. The inscriptions are assembled in *Tituli Asiae Minoris* II 3, 1944, see Rhodiapolis.

83. The study on Ephesus in the second century A.D. by O. Benndorf, *Ephesus* I, 1906, 92 ff., is in itself excellent, but unfortunately fails to touch on any of the negative aspects of the period.

84. L. Robert, *Rev. arch.*, 1934, I 48 ff.; *Hel.* 7, 1949, 74 ff.; 8, 1950, 76 f.

85. On *leitourgiai* see F. Oertel, *Liturgie*, 1917; further, Rostovtzeff, *SEHRE* I. 380 ff.

86. Cf., for instance, the *curatores rei publicae*, an institution which goes back at least to the time of Trajan; cf. W. Liebenam, *Städteverwaltung*, 1900, 480 f.; E. Kornemann, *RE* IV, 1806 ff.; O. Seeck, *Gesch. des Unterganges d. antiken Welt* II, 1901, 170 ff.

87. Pliny, *epist.* X 33 and 34.

88. For details see the studies by Ed. Meyer, *Christ.;* A.v. Harnack, *Mission und Ausbreitung des Christentums in den ersten drei Jahrh.*, [4]1924; H. Lietzmann, *Gesch. der Alten Kirche* I-IV 1, 1932-1944; Vol. I, [2]1937. Most excellent is the Chapter, "Das Christentum in der antiken Welt," in J. Vogt, *Constantin d. Gr. und sein Jahrhundert*, 1949, 74 ff.; 282 f. (with the most important bibliography); in many instances I agree with his views. See also J. Molthagen, *Der römische Staat und die Christen im zweiten und dritten Jahrh.* (Hypomnemata 28), Göttingen 1970; and *Kirchengeschichte als Missionsgeschichte.* 1. *Die alte Kirche*, ed. H. Frohnes and V. W. Knorr, Munich 1974.

89. Cf. W. H. C. Frend, *Martyrdom and Persecution in the Early Church. A Study of a Conflict from the Maccabees to Donatus*, Oxford 1965 (cf. G. Anderson, *Gn.* 45, 1973, 691 ff.).

90. On Celsus: L. Rougier, *Celse*, Paris 1925; P. de Labriolle, *La réaction païenne*, Paris 1934.

91. Cf. *Kirchengeschichte als Missionsgeschichte.* 1. *Die alte Kirche*, ed. H. Frohnes and V. W. Knorr, Munich 1974.

92. The influence of Christianity on the senatorial class may be taken as symbolic, cf. W. Eck, *Ch.* 1, 1971, 381 ff.

93. R. Heberdey, *Öst. Jh.* 7, 1904, *Beiblatt*, 53 ff.; 157 f.; F. Eichler, "Das sog. Parther-denkmal von Ephesos," in *Bericht über den VI. Kongress f. Archäologie*, 1939 (published Berlin 1940), 488 ff. The monument is, accordingly, to be dated to the end of the sixties, namely still before the death of Lucius Verus (169 A.D.).

94. A.v. Premerstein, *Klio* 12, 1912, 145 ff.; *RE* XI, 1504 ff. s.v. *Kostoboken*; Plassart, *Mél. G. Glotz* II, 731 ff.

95. Cf. the inscription from Thyateira in Lydia, Fiebiger-Schmidt, *Inschriften z. Gesch. d. Ostgermanen*, 1917, no. 15.

96. A.v. Premerstein, *Der Protest des Gymnasiarchen Appianos gegen seine Verurteilung durch Commodus,* Ph. Suppl. 16, 1928, 23 ff. A more recent fragment of the *Acts* of Appian: C. B. Welles, "A Yale Fragment of the Acts of Appianus," *TAPA* 67, 1936, 7 ff.; the entire evidence may now be found in Musurillo [v.s.p. 593] 65 ff.; 205 ff.

97. According to A. E. Raubitschek, *Hesp. Suppl.* 8, 1949, 281 ff., in 188-189 A.D.

98. L. Robert, *Hel.* 8, 1950, 75. A list (which now needs to be supplemented) of the Roman emperors as *Eponymoi* has also been drawn up by L. Robert. *Etud. épigr. et phil.*, Paris 1938, 145 ff.

99. See the letter of Septimius Severus to Nicopolis, published by M. Britschkoff, *AM* 48, 1923, 99 ff. no. 7.

100. L. Robert, *Hel.* 1, 1940, 58 f.

101. That Athens lost her foreign holdings is contested by A.v. Premerstein, *Öst. Jh.* 16, 1913, 269.

102. J. Hasebroek, *Untersuch. z. Gesch. des Kaisers Septimius Severus*, Heidelberg 1921, 11, regards this as strictly conjectural.

103. A.v. Premerstein, "Athenische Kultehren für Kaiserin Julia Domna," *Öst. Jh.* 16, 1913, 249 ff.; J. H. Oliver, "Julia Domna as Athena Polias," *Studies Ferguson,* 521 ff.

104. This is the view held by Rostovtzeff, *SEHRE* I, 407 f.; II, 706 n. 47; 715 n. 19. L. Robert (by correspondence), on the other hand, on the basis of the epigraphical evidence, regards precisely the period of the Severii as a time of prosperity. For parts of Asia Minor this may be so; cf. *supra* 343.

105. *P. Oxy.* XII 1477.

106. The importance of the *Constitutio Antoniniana*, especially for the regions of the Greek East, to a large degree still remains shrouded in darkness. Only comprehensive

studies in social history and on the leading personalities can shed more light on it. Rostovtzeff, *SEHRE* II, 719 n. 38, has correctly drawn attention to the levelling effect ensuing from the *Constitutio*. On the problems posed by *P. Giss.* I 40, see E. Bickermann, *Das Edikt des Kaisers Caracalla in P. Giss. 40,* Diss. Berlin 1926; Riccobono, *FIRA* I², 445 f. (with the more recent bibliography); cf. also E. Meyer, *Röm. Staat und Staatsgedanke*, 1948, 456 n. 26; and Chr. Sasse, *Die Constitutio Antoniniana*, 1958.

107. *Script. Hist. Aug. Caracalla* 6.2-3; P. Benoit and J. Schwartz, "Caracalla et les troubles d'Alexandrie en 215 après J.-C.," *Etudes de Papyr.* 7, 1948, 17 ff. (according to a papyrus from Hermopolis Magna); J. Schwartz, "Notes sur le séjour de Caracalla en Egypte," *Cd'E* 34, 1959, 120 ff.

108. Cass. Dio LXXVII 7.3.

109. Instructive is *P. Oxy.* XVIII 2186; the subject is the admission of an ephebe from approximately 260 A.D., who was able to trace his Greek ancestry back to the time of Vespasian or even to the time of Augustus.

110. See above all M. N. Tod, "An Ephebic Inscription from Memphis" (from 220 A.D.), *JEA* 37, 1951, 86 ff.; cf. J. and L. Robert, *REG* 65, 1952, Bull. épigr. no. 180; 66, 1953, no. 235; Nilsson, *Sch.*, 93 f.

111. Herodian VII 3.3 ff.

112. Rostovtzeff, *SEHRE* I, 143 ff.

113. [Aelius Aristides] *Eis Basilea* § 21.

114. H. Kortenbeutel, *Der ägypt. Süd- und Osthandel in der Politik der Ptolemäer und römischen Kaiser,* Diss. Berlin 1931, 72.

115. M. Rostovtzeff, *Monuments Piot* 26, 1923, 1 ff.; *SEHRE* I, 259 ff.

116. C. Bosch, *AA*, 1931, 431 ff.; D. Kienast, *Jb. f. Num. u. Geldegesch.* 14, 1964, 51 ff.

117. B. Rappaport, *Die Einfälle der Goten in das Röm. Reich*, Leipzig 1899; A. Alföldi, *CAH* XII, 141 ff.; L. Schmidt, *Gesch. der deutschen Stämme bis zum Ausgang der Völkerwanderung. Die Ostgermanen*, Munich ²1941, 209 ff.

118. The principal source is the pastoral letter by Bishop Gregorius Thaumaturgus of Neo-Caesarea, *Migne, Patr. Graec.* X 1037 ff.; cf. J. Dräseke, *Jahrb. f. protest. Theologie* 7, 1881, 724 ff.; A. Alföldi, *CAH* XII, 148.

119. On the date of the great invasion by the Goths into Asia Minor (262 and not 267 A.D.), see L. Robert, *Hel.* 6, 1948, 117 ff. (on the basis of an inscription from the region of Daldis, or Iulia Gordus).

120. Herenn. Dexipp. (in Jacoby, *FgrHist.* no. 100) fr. 28a; cf. Zosim. I 39.1; Syncell. p. 717.9, cf. Jacoby, *FgrHist.* no. 100 Test. 3. On buried coins in Laconia see M. Karamesini-Oikonomidou, in *Chasisterion K. Orlandos* I, Athens 1966, 376 ff. On destruction in Athens, see H. A. Thompson, *JRS* 49, 1959, 61 ff., esp. 61 n. 5. A. Alföldi, *CAH* XII, 721 ff., cf. *ibid.*, 149, transfers the invasion of the Herulians in 268 A.D., but this is a view which does not appear to be sufficiently substantiated; see also E. Kornemann, *Weltgesch.* II, 1949, 230 n. 2.

121. J. Liegle, "Architekturbilder auf antiken Münzen," *Ant.* 12, 1936, 217 and 227.

122. Basic is A. Alföldi, "Die Vorherrschaft der Pannonier im Römerreiche und die Reaktion des Hellenentums unter Gallienus," in *Fünfundzwanzig Jahre Röm.-German. Kommission*, Berlin and Leipzig 1930, 11 ff., esp. 18 ff., 21 ff.; E. Kornemann, *Weltgeschichte* II, 227 ff.; more cautious regarding the relationship between Gallienus and Plotinus is E. Manni, *L'impero di Gallieno*, Rome 1949, 62 ff.

123. Cf. *Script. Hist. Aug., Gall.* 11.3; Gallienus was, accordingly, not only Athenian archon but also had himself admitted into the Areopagus.

124. Illustrated in, for instance, *CAH* Volume of Plates V 236 K; cf. A. Alföldi, *Zeitschr. f. Num.* 38, 1928, 174 ff.; *CAH* XII, 189.

125. On Plotinus see the studies by R. Harder, printed in his *Kleine Schriften*, 1960, 256 ff.; cf., further, his translations *Plotins Schriften* I-V, Leipzig 1930-1937, which have inaugurated a new era in Plotinian studies; see also the article in *RE* XXI, 471-592 s.v. *Plotinos*, by H.-R. Schwyzer. A new edition by P. Henry-H.-R. Schwyzer has been in process since 1951.

126. Cf. W. den Boer, *CP* 69, 1974, 198 ff.

127. On him see *RE* XIII, 1401 ff. (by Aulitzky).

128. A. Stein, "Kallinikos von Petrai," *Hermes* 58, 1923, 448 ff.

129. Basic on this subject is A. Alföldi, in *Fünfundzwanzig Jahre Röm.-German. Kommission*, 1930, 23 ff.

130. H. H. Schaeder, *Zeitschr. f. Kirchengesch.*, 1932, 21 ff.; H. Lietzmann, *Geschichte der alten Kirche* II, 1936, 267 ff.

130a. H. Lietzmann, *op.cit.*, 275.

131. *The excavations at Dura-Europos VI, Preliminary Report* (published 1936) 309 ff. (with excellent photographs in the Appendix); Du Mesnil de Buisson, *Les peintures de la Synagogue de Doura-Europus 245-256 après J.-C.*, Rome 1939; A. Perkins, *The Art of Dura-Europos*, Oxford 1973.

132. See the excellent remarks by Rostovtzeff, *SEHRE*, I, 433 ff.; 504 ff. To date a monograph is lacking. W. Liebenam, *Städteverwaltung im röm. Kaiserreiche*, Leipzig 1900, is out of date.

133. K. Holl, "Das Fortleben der Volkssprachen in Kleinasien in nachchristlicher Zeit," *Hermes* 43, 1908, 240 ff.

134. J. H. W. G. Liebeschutz, *Antioch. City and Imperial Administration in the Later Roman Empire*, Oxford 1971.

135. See the orations of Libanius: *On Behalf of the Council; Against Besieging Magistrates; Against Market Clerks.*

136. A. Schulten, *Öst. Jh.* 9, 1906, 40 ff.; R. Heberdey, *Öst. Jh.* 9, 1906, 182 ff.; the document is printed in Riccobono, *FIRA* I², 511 ff. no. 108 (with additional bibliography).

137. This must have occurred in the first half of the fourth century, at the latest under Constantius II; see A. Piganiol, *L'empire chrétien*, 1947, 281.

137a. See H. Bengtson, *Die Olympischen Spiele in der Antike*, Zurich-Stuttgart ²1972, 91 ff.

138. P. Petit, *Libanius et la vie municipale à Antioche au IVme siècle apr. J.-C.*, Paris 1956; *Les étudiants de Libanius*, Paris 1956.

139. V. Stegemann, *RE* V A, 1642 ff. s.v. no. 2.

140. R. Laqueur, in *Probleme der Spätantike*, Stuttgart 1930, 27 ff.; J. Straub, *Vom Herrscherideal in der Spätantike*, 1939.

141. Cf. on this term L. Robert, *Hel.* 4, 1948, 95 f. Already Herodes Atticus was thus named.

142. Basileius, *Logos pros tous neous, hopos an ex Hellenikon opheleointo logon*. Editions are cited in Schmid-Stählin, *GGL* II⁶ 2, 1409 n. 6; there is also the edition of the Collection G. Budé by F. Boulanger, Paris 1935.

143. The sources in A. Piganiol, *L'empire chrétien*, 1947, 259; cf. also the illustrated Chronicle of *Papyrus Golenischew*, published by A. Bauer and J. Strzygowski, *Denkschr. Ak. Wien* 51, 1905, Tafel 6. Cf. further, R. Herzog, "Der Kampf um den Kult von Menuthis," in *Pisciculi, Franz Joseph Dölger dargeboten*, Münster i.W., 1939, 117 ff.

144. J. Maspero, "Un dernier poète grec en Egypte: Dioscore fils d'Apollos," *REG* 24, 1911, 426 ff.; H. J. M. Milne, *Cat. of the Literary Papyri in the British Museum*, 1927, 68 ff.; H. I. Bell, "An Egyptian Village in the Age of Justinian," *JHS* 64, 1944, 21 ff.; *Eg.*, 127 f.

145. Cf. De Lacy O'Leary, *How Greek Science Passed to the Arabs*, London 1949; also the bibliography cited by W. Kutsch, *Gn.* 24, 1952, 53 f.

146. A. Grohmann, "Griech. und lateinische Verwaltungstermini im arabischen Ägypten, *Cd'E* 13-14, 1932, 275 ff.

147. Cf. in particular F. Fuchs, "Die höheren Schulen von Konstantinopel," *Byz. Arch.* 8, 1926, 1 ff.; the older bibliography in W. Schmid-O. Stählin, *GGL* II⁶ 2, 949 n. 4; cf. L. Bréhier, *Rev. d'hist. et de philos. relig.* 21, 1941, 34 ff.; H. I. Marrou, *Histoire de l'éducation dans l'antiquité*, ²1950, 408 ff. On the arrival of Greek culture in the West see P. Courcelle, *Les lettres grecques en Occident, de Macrobe à Cassiodore*, Paris ²1948.

Research: 1976-1987

Note: In the citation of new research, the same format is adopted as that used above. In addition, to simplify this section for the reader, works are arranged for the most part in chronological order of publication. Occasionally, however, a work of later date is cited immediately in conjunction with an earlier study when it is directly relevant. Selection is concentrated chiefly on those studies which advance a subject and/or foster debate and contain additional bibliography.

INTRODUCTION: MODERN RESEARCH IN THE FIELD OF GREEK HISTORY

363 The second volume of Nilsson's *Geschichte der griechischen Religion* is also available in a third edition (1974).
On research in Ancient History in the USSR, see H. Heinen, *Die Geschichte des Altertums im Spiegel sowjetischen Forschung* (Erträge der Forschung 146), Darmstadt 1980.

364 n. 16 See also E. Meyer, *Heinrich Schliemann aus dem Nachlass in Auswahl*, 2 vols., Berlin 1953 and 1958. On Schliemann, cf. further below, under "8. Western Asia Minor" (pp. 376-377).

365 n. 29 See also E.M. Jansen, *Jacob Burckhardt und die Griechen. Jacob Burckhardt-Studien. 2. Teil*, Aspen 1979.

n. 38 See also L. Robert, *A travers l'Asie Mineure. Poètes et prosateurs, monnaies grecques, voyageurs et géographie* (Bibl. des Éc. franç. d'Athènes et de Rome, 239), Paris 1980; J. and L. Robert, *Fouilles d'Amyzon en Carie I. Exploration, histoire, monnaies et inscriptions*, Paris 1983.

n. 41 A.W. Gomme, A. Andrewes and K.J. Dover, *A Historical Commentary on Thucydides* V, Oxford 1981. F.W. Walbank, *A Historical Commentary on Polybius III (Bks. XIX-XL)*, Oxford 1979.

n. 42 N.G.L. Hammond, *A History of Greece*, Oxford [3]1986 (essentially a reprint).

1. THE EARLY AGES OF GREECE

368 On **Linear A:** J. Raison and M. Pope, *Index transnuméré du Linéaire A* (Bibl. des Cahiers de l'Institut de Ling. de Louvain 11), Louvain 1977.

Y. Duhoux (ed.), *Études minoennes I: Le linéaire A* (Bibl. des Cahiers de l'Institut de Ling. de Louvain 14), Louvain 1978.
E. Hallager, "The Linear A Tablets from the Greek-Swedish Excavations, Kastelli Khania," *SMEA* 19, 1978, 35-48.
L. Godart, "Le linéaire A et son environnement," *SMEA* 20, 1979, 27-42.
S. Hiller, "Forschungsbericht. Linear A und die semitischen Sprachen," *AfO* 26, 1978-1979, 221-235.
F. Vandenabeele, "La chronologie des documents en linéaire A," *BCH* 109, 1985, 3-20.
A. Karetsou, L. Godart and J.-P. Olivier, "Inscriptions en linéaire A du sanctuaire de sommet minoen du mont Iouktas," *Kadmos* 24, 1985, 89-147.
E. Hallager and M. Vlasakis, "New evidence of Linear A archives from Khania," *Kadmos* 25, 1986, 108-118.

On **Linear B:** J. Chadwick, J.T. Killen and J.-P. Olivier, *The Knossos Tablets. A Translation*, Cambridge [4]1971.
E.L. Bennett and J.-P. Olivier, *The Pylos Tablets, I. Texts and Notes* (Incunabula Graeca 51), Rome 1973.
Iidem, ibid. II: Hands, Concordances, Indices (Incunabula Graeca 59), Rome 1976.
A. Sacconi, *Corpus delle Iscrizioni Vascolari in Linear B*, 2 vols. (Incunabula Graeca 57 and 58), Rome 1974.
T. Spyropoulos and J. Chadwick, *The Theban Tablets* II (Minos Suppl. 4), Salamanca 1975.
L. Godart and A. Sacconi, *Les Tablettes en linéaire B de Thèbes* (Incunabula Graeca 71), Rome 1978.
J. Chadwick, "Evidence after 25 Years," *SMEA* 20, 1979, 11-14.
Idem, "Twenty-Seven Years of Linear B," in J. Harmatta (ed.), *Actes du XIIe Congrès de la Fédération Internationale des Associations d'Études Classiques* II, Budapest 1984, 451-459.
J. Chadwick, "The Use of Mycenaean Documents as Historical Evidence," in E. Risch and H. Muehlestein (eds.), *Colloquium Mycenaeum. Actes du VIe Colloque intern. sur les textes mycéniens et égéens tenu à Chaumont sur Neuchâtel du 7 au 13 septembre 1975*, Geneva 1979, 21-33.
J.-P. Olivier, "Éditions, index, dictionnaires; état des questions," *ibid.*, 35-42.
A. Sacconi, "Les éditions de textes 25 ans après," *SMEA* 20, 1979, 15-26.
J.-P. Olivier, "L'origine de l'écriture Linéaire B," *ibid.*, 43-52.
J.T. Hooker, *The Origin of the Linear B Script* (Suppl. a Minos 8), Salamanca 1979.
A. Heubeck, "L'origine della Lineare B," *SMEA* 23, 1982, 195-207.
E. Risch, "Die griechischen Dialekte im 2. vorchristlichen Jahrtausend," *SMEA* 20, 1979, 91-111.

J.T. Hooker, *Linear B. An Introduction*, Bristol 1980.
L. Godart, J.T. Killen and J.-P. Olivier, "Eighteen more Fragments of Linear B Tablets from Tiryns. Ausgrabungen in Tiryns 1981," *AA* 1983, 413-426.
C.J. Ruijgh, "Problèmes de philologie mycénienne," *Minos* 19, 1985, 105-167.
A. Morpurgo-Davies and Y. Duhoux (eds.), *Linear B: A Survey. Proceedings of the Mycenaean Colloquium of the VIIIth Congress of the International Federation of the Society of Classical Studies (Dublin, 27th August-1st September 1984)*, Louvain-La-Neuve 1985.
L. Godart, J.T. Killen, C. Kopaka and J.-P. Olivier, "Quarante-trois raccords et quasi-raccords de fragments inédits dans le volume I du 'Corpus of Mycenaean Inscriptions from Knossos'," *BCH* 110, 1986, 21-39.
A. Etter (ed.), *-o-o-pe-ro-si. Festschrift für Ernst Risch zum 75. Geburtstag*, Berlin and New York 1986.
J. Chadwick, *Linear B and Related Scripts*, Berkeley and Los Angeles 1987.
J.T. Killen, J.L. Melena and J.-P. Olivier (eds.), *Studies in Mycenaean and Classical Greek Presented to John Chadwick*, Salamanca 1987.

370 Add to Schachermeyr's reviews on research: F. Schachermeyr, "Ausgrabungen in Thera, Kythera, Nichoria, Pylos, Orchomenos," *AfO* 25, 1971-1974, 280-287; *idem*, *AnzAltWiss* 35, 1982, 1-38.

371 **General Works:** Taylour's *The Mycenaeans* is now available in a second edition, London 1983.
F. Schachermeyr, *Die ägäische Frühzeit I. Forschungsbericht über die Ausgrabungen im letzten Jahrzehnt und über ihre Ergebnisse für unser Geschichtsbild: Die vormykenischen Perioden des griechischen Festlandes und der Kykladen* (Mykenische Studien III) (SAWW 303), Vienna 1976 (also contains an extensive section on the Neolithic period).
Idem, *Griechische Frühgeschichte. Ein Versuch, frühe Geschichte wenigstens in Umrissen verständlich zu machen* (SAWW 425), Vienna 1984.
S. Hood, *The Arts in Prehistoric Greece* (Pelican History of Art), Harmondsworth 1978.
R.H. Simpson and O.T.P.K. Dickinson, *A Gazetteer of Aegean Civilization in the Bronze Age I: The Mainland and Islands* (SIMA 52, 1), Göteborg 1979.
G.A.S. Snyder, *Minoische und mykenische Kunst. Aussage und Deutung*, Munich 1980 (cf. S. Hiller, *AnzAltWiss* 39, 1986, 237-242).
N. Platon, *La civilisation égéenne I: Du néolithique au bronze récent; II: Le bronze récent et la civilisation mycénienne*, Paris 1981.
R. Higgins, *Minoan and Mycenaean Art*, London [2]1981 (cf. W. Schiering, *Gnomon* 58, 1986, 163-164).

R. Treuil, *Le Néolithique et le Bronze Ancien égéens: Les problèmes stratigraphiques et chronologiques, les techniques, les hommes*, Paris 1983 (cf. J.D. Evans, *JHS* 106, 1986, 244).
H. van Effenterre, *Les Égéens. Aux origines de la Grèce, Chypre, Cyclades, Crète et Mycène*, Paris 1986.
H.-G. Buchholz *et al.*, *Ägäische Bronzezeit*, Darmstadt 1987.

Studies on Specific Subjects: Muhly's Doctoral Thesis on *Copper and Tin* is published under the same title as Vol. 43 of the Transactions of the Connecticut Academy of Sciences, Hamden, Conn., 1973; cf. *idem*, *Supplement to Copper and Tin* (Transactions of the Connecticut Academy of Sciences, Vol. 46), Hamden, Conn., 1976, 77-136.
On **metallurgy**, see, further, A.D. Franklin, J.S. Olin and T.A. Wertime, *The Search for Ancient Tin*, Washington 1978.
T.S. Wheeler, J.D. Muhly and R. Maddin, "Mediterranean Trade in Copper and Tin in the Late Bronze Age," *Annali dell'Istituto Italiano Numismatica* 26, 1979, 139-152.
H. Matthäus, "Die Amphora von Skopelos. Zur kretisch-mykenischen Metallindustrie des 15. und 14. Jahrhunderts v. Chr.," *MDAI(A)* 97, 1982, 1-16.
N.H. Gale and Z.A. Stos-Gale, "Bronze and Copper Sources in the Mediterranean: A New Approach," *Science* 216, 1982, 11-19.
S. Iakovidis, "The Mycenaean Bronze Industry," in J.D. Muhly, R. Maddin and V. Karageorghis (eds.), *Acta of the International Archaeological Symposium 'Early Metallurgy in Cyprus, 4000-500 B.C.' Larnaca, 1-6 June 1981*, Nicosia 1982 [1983], 213-231.
V. McGeehan-Liritzis, "The relationship between metalwork, copper sources and the evidence for settlement in the Greek neolithic and early bronze age," *OxfJournArch* 2, 1983, 299-337.
J.D. Muhly, "Beyond Typology: Aegean Metallurgy in its Historical Context," in N.C. Wilkie and W.D.E. Coulson (eds.), *Contributions to Aegean Archaeology: Studies in Honor of William A. McDonald*, Dubuque, Iowa, 1985, 109-141 (with bibliography).
Idem, "Sources of Tin and the Beginning of Bronze Age Metallurgy," *AJA* 89, 1985, 275-291.
K.A. Yener and H. Ozbal, "Tin in the Turkish Taurus mountains: the Bolkardağ mining district," *Antiquity* 61, 1987, 220-226.
V. McGeehan-Liritzis and J.W. Taylor, "Yugoslavian Tin Deposits and the Early Bronze Age Industries of the Aegean Region," *OxfJournArch* 6, 1987, 287-300.
Z.A. Stos-Gale and N.H. Gale, "Metal Sources and the Metal Trade in the Bronze Age Aegean—the Isotope Evidence," *BICS* 32, 1985, 157-158.
N.H. Gale and Z.A. Stos-Gale, "Oxhide Copper Ingots in Crete and Cyprus and the Bronze Age Metals Trade," *BSA* 81, 1986, 81-100.
T. Stech and V.C. Pigott, "The metals trade in southwest Asia in the third millennium B.C.," *Iraq* 48, 1986, 39-64.

In connection with Bronze Age **Glyptic**, a mine of information is contained in the *Corpus der minoischen und mykenischen Siegel*, Berlin 1965 ff. (to date, 16 vols.): initially edited by F. Matz, now continued by I. Pini.

W.-D. Niemeier (ed.), *Studien zur minoischen und helladischen Glyptik. Beiträge zum 2. Marburger Siegel-Symposium 26.-30. September 1978* (Corpus der minoischen und helladischen Siegel. Beiheft 1), Berlin 1981.

I. Pini, "Neue Beobachtungen zu den töneren Siegelabdrücken von Zakros," *AA* 1983, 559-572.

J.C. Younger, "Aegean Seals of the Late Bronze Age: Stylistic Groups IV," *Kadmos* 24, 1985, 34-73.

Idem, "Aegean Seals of the Late Bronze Age: stylistic groups V. Minoan groups contemporary with LM III AI," *Kadmos* 25, 1986, 119-140.

Idem, "Aegean seals of the Late Bronze Age VI. Fourteenth-century mainland and later fourteenth-century Cretan workshops," *Kadmos* 26, 1987, 44-73. See also below (381).

On the so-called **'Barbarian' Pottery**, which has recently received much attention, see J.B. Rutter, "Ceramic Evidence for Northern Intruders in Southern Greece at the Beginning of the Late Helladic IIIC Period," *AJA* 79, 1975, 17-32.

S. Deger-Jalkotzy, *Fremde Zuwanderer in spätmykenischen Griechenland. Zu einer Gruppe handgemachter Keramik aus den Myk. III C Siedlunsschichten von Aigeira* (SAWW 326), Vienna 1977.

H.W. and E.A. Catling, "'Barbarian' Pottery from the Mycenaean Settlement at the Menelaion, Sparta," *BSA* 76, 1981, 71-82.

K. Kilian, "Ausgrabungen in Tiryns 1978, 1979," *AA* 1981, 170, 180-181; *idem*, "Ausgrabungen in Tiryns 1980," *AA* 1982, 399.

B. Palsson Hallager, "A New Social Class in Late Bronze Age Crete: Foreign Traders in Khania," in O. Krzyszowska and L. Nixon (eds.), *Minoan Society. Proceedings of the Cambridge Colloquium 1981*, Bristol 1983, 111-119.

E.F. Bloedow, "Handmade Burnished Ware or 'Barbarian' Pottery and Troy VIIb," *PP* 40, 1985 [1986], 161-199.

Other Aspects: E.N. Davis, *The Vapheio Cups and Aegean Gold and Silver Ware*, New York 1977.

J. Schaeffer, "Zur kunstgeschichtlichen Interpretation altägäischer Wandmalerei," *JDAI* 92, 1977, 1-23.

L. Vagnetti and P. Belli, "Characters and Problems of the Final Neolithic in Crete," *SMEA* 19, 1978, 125-163.

K.P. Foster, *Aegean Faience of the Bronze Age*, New Haven 1979.

Cf. *eadem* and A. Kaczmarczyk, "X-ray fluorescence analysis of some Minoan faience," *Archaeometry* 24, 1982, 143-157.

W. Helck, *Die Beziehungen Ägyptens und Vorderasiens zur Ägäis bis ins 7. Jahrhundert v. Chr.* (Erträge der Forschung 120), Darmstadt 1979.

R. Higgins, *The Aegina Treasure. An Archaeological Mystery*, London 1979.
R.B. Edwards, *Kadmos the Phoenician. A Study in Greek Legends and the Mycenaean Age*, Amsterdam 1979.
M. Sakellariou, *Le Peuplement de la Grèce et du basin égéen aux haute époques*, 2 vols., Athens 1971 and 1980.
J.C. van Leuven, "Economic Determinism and Bronze Age Greece," *Historia* 29, 1980, 129-141.
B.J. Kemp and R.S. Merrillees, *Minoan Pottery in Second Millennium Egypt*, Mainz 1980.
P. Åström and S.A. Erikson, *Fingerprints and Archaeology* (SIMA Pocket Book 28), Göteborg 1980.
K.-E. Sjöqvist and P. Åström, *Pylos: Palmprints and Palmleaves* (SIMA Pocket Book 31), Göteborg 1985 (cf. I. Pini, *Gnomon* 58, 1986, 427-431).
R. Hägg and N. Marinatos (eds.), *Sanctuaries and Cults in the Aegean Bronze Age. Proceedings of the First International Symposium at the Swedish Institute in Athens, 12-13 May, 1980*, Stockholm 1981.
S. Wachsmann, "The Ships of the Sea Peoples," *IJNA* 10, 1981, 187-220.
J.F. Cherry, "Pattern and process in the earliest colonisation of the Mediterranean islands," *PPS* 47, 1981, 41-68.
O.T.P.K. Dickinson, "Parallels and Contrasts in the Bronze Age of the Peloponnesus," *OxfJournArch* 1, 1982, 125-138.
B. Hänsel (ed.), *Südosteuropa zwischen 1600 und 1000 v. Chr.* (Prähistorische Archäologie in Südosteuropa 1), Berlin 1982.
P. Yule, "Notes on Scarabs and Aegean Chronology," *BSA* 78, 1983, 359-367.
J.B. Rutter, "Fine Gray-Burnished Pottery of the Early Helladic III Period: The Ancestry of Gray Minyan," *Hesp.* 52, 1983, 327-355.
J.L. Melena, "Olive Oil and Other Sorts of Oil in the Mycenaean Tablets," *Minos* 18, 1983, 89-123.
D.N. Konsola, "Beobachtungen zum Wegenetz in frühhelladischen Siedlungen," *AA* 1984, 197-210.
J.F. Cherry, "The Emergence of the State in the Prehistoric Aegean," *ProceedCambPhilolSoc* N.S. 30, 1984, 18-48.
P. Themelis, "Early Helladic Monumental Architecture," *MDAI(A)* 99, 1984, 335-351.
K.O. Pope and T.H. van Andel, "Late Quaternary Alluviation and Soil Formation in the Southern Argolid: its History, Causes and Archaeological Implications," *JArchSc* 11, 1984, 281-306.
N.C. Wilkie and W.D.E. Coulson (eds.), *Contributions to Aegean Archaeology: Studies in Honor of William A. McDonald*, Dubuque, Iowa, 1985.
G. King and E. Bailey, "The Palaeoenvironment of Some Archaeological Sites in Greece: The Influence of Accumulated Uplift in a Seismically Active Region," *PPS* 51, 1985, 273-292.

A. Knapp and T. Stech (eds.), *Prehistoric Production and Exchange: The Aegean and Eastern Mediterranean* (Institute of Archaeology, University of California, Monograph 25), Los Angeles 1985.
B. Otto, *Die verzierte Keramik der Sesklo- und Diminikultur Thessaliens* (Keramik Forschungen 6), Mainz 1985.
E.M. Melas, *The Islands of Karpathos, Saros and Kasos in the Neolithic and Bronze Age* (SIMA 68), Göteborg 1985 (cf. J.T. Hooker, *JHS* 107, 1987, 244-245).
J. Rutter, "Some Comments on the Nature and Significance of the Ceramic Transition from Early Helladic III to Middle Helladic," *Hydra. Working Papers in Middle Bronze Age Studies* 2, 1986, 29-57.
G. Cadogan, *The End of the Early Bronze Age in the Aegean* (Cincinnati Classical Studies 6), Leiden 1986.
R. Hägg and D. Konsola (eds.), *Early Helladic Architecture and Urbanization. Proceedings of a Seminar held at the Swedish Institute in Athens, June 8, 1985*, Göteborg 1986.
R. Torrence, *Production and Exchange of Stone Tools: Prehistoric Obsidian in the Aegean*, Cambridge 1986 (cf. C. Perlès, *Antiquity* 61, 1987, 336-337).
E.F. Bloedow, "Aspects of Ancient Trade in the Mediterranean: Obsidian," *SMEA* 26, 1987, 59-124.
G.C. Nordquist, *A Middle Helladic Village. Asine in the Argolid* (Acta Universitatis Upsaliensis. Boreas 16), Uppsala 1987.
R. Laffineur (ed.), *Thanatos. Les coutumes funéraires en Égée à l'âge du Bronze: Burial Customs in the Aegean Bronze Age. Actes du colloque de Liège (21-23 avril 1986)*, Liège 1987.
J.W. Shaw, "The Early Helladic II Corridor House: Development and Form," *AJA* 91, 1987, 59-79.
J.M. Hansen, "Agriculture in the Prehistoric Aegean: Data versus Speculation," *AJA* 92, 1988, 39-52.

1. Northern Greece

Macedonia: M. Gimbutas (ed.), *Neolithic Macedonia: as Reflected by the Excavations at Anza, Southeast Yugoslavia* (Monumenta Archaeologica 1), Los Angeles 1976.
Of considerable importance are the excavations at Assiros: see K.A. Wardle, "Excavations at Assiros, 1975-1979," *BSA* 75, 1980, 229-269.
Idem, in C. Svolopoulos (ed.), *Papers read at the Third International Symposium held in Thessaloniki, Sept. 21-25, 1977*, Thessaloniki 1983, 291-305.
G. Jones, K. Wardle, P. Halstead and D. Wardle, "Crop Storage at Assiros," *Scientific American* 254,3, 1986, 96-103.
K.A. Wardle, *ArchRep* 33, 1986-87, 34-36.
D.K. Washburn, "A Study of the Red on Cream and Cream on Red Designs on Early Neolithic Ceramics from Nea Nikomedeia," *AJA* 88, 1984, 305-324.

H.J. Kroll, *Kastanas. Ausgrabungen in einem Siedlungshügel der Bronze- und Eisenzeit Makedoniens: Die Pflanzenfunde* (Prähistorische Archäologie in Südosteuropa 2), Berlin 1983.
I. Aslanis, *ibid.*, *Die frühbronzezeitlichen Funde und Befunde* (PAS 4), Berlin 1985.
C. Becker, *ibid.*, *Die Tierknochenfunde* (PAS 5), Berlin 1986.
A. Hochstetter, *ibid.*, *Die Kleinfunde* (PAS 6), Berlin 1987.

Thrace: G. Bakalakis and A. Sakellariou, *Paradimi* (Heidelberger Akademie der Wissenschaften, Internationale Interakademische Kommission für die Erforschung der Vorgeschichte des Balkans, Monographien 2), Mainz 1981 (cf. C. Renfrew, *BonJahrb* 183, 1983, 723-724, and S. Hiller, *AnzAltWiss* 39, 1986, 224-227).
M. Sèfèriadès, "Dikili-Tash. Introduction à la préhistoire de la Macédoine occidentale," *BCH* 107, 1983, 635-677.
B. Brukner, "Die Vinca-Gruppe und ihr Verhältnis zu den spätneolithischen Kulturen in Nord-Ost-Griechenland," *Archaeologia Iugoslavica* 22-23, 1982-1983, 1-14.
S. Hiller and G.I. Georgiev, *Tell Karanovo, 1984. Vorläufiger Ausgrabungsbericht*, Salzburg 1984.
Iidem, *Tell Karanovo, 1986. Vorbericht über die dritte Kampagne der Österreichisch-Bulgarischen Ausgrabungen am Tell von Karanovo*, Salzburg 1986.
A.C. Renfrew, M. Gimbutas and E.S. Elster (eds)., *Excavations at Sitagroi* I, Los Angeles 1986.
P. Hellström *et al.*, *Paradeisos: A Late Neolithic Settlement in Aegean Thrace* (Medelhavsmuseet, Memoir 7), Stockholm 1987.

372 **Thessaly:** E. Hanschmann, *Die deutschen Ausgrabungen auf der Argissa-Magula in Thessalien IV. Die mittlere Bronzezeit* (Beiträge zur ur- und frühgeschichtlichen Archäologie des Mittelmeerkulturraumes 23 und 24), bearbeitet von P. Bayerlein, Bonn 1981 (cf. S. Hiller, *BonJahrb* 183, 1983, 729-730).
Y. Mottier, *Die deutschen Ausgrabungen auf der Otzaki-Magula in Thessalien, II. Das mittlere Neolithikum*; H. Hauptmann, *ibid. III. Das späte Neolithikum und das Chalkolithikum* (Beiträge zur ur- und frühgeschichtlichen Archäologie des Mittelmeerkulturraumes 22 und 21), Bonn 1981 (cf. B. Jovanović, *PZ* 59, 1984, 94-97).
V. Milojčić, *Otzaki-Magula II. Das mittlere Neolithikum: Die mittelneolithische Siedlung*, Bonn 1983.
V. Milojčić, *Otzaki-Magula III. Das späte Neolithikum und das Chalkolithikum: Stratigraphie und Bauten*, Bonn 1983.
B. Otto, *Die verzierte Keramik der Sesklo- und Diminikultur Thessaliens*, Mainz 1985.
C.G. Gallis, "Cremation Burials from the Early Neolithic in Thessaly," in B. Helly (ed.), *La Thessalie. Actes de la Table-Ronde 21-24 Juillet 1975*, Lyons and Paris 1979, 65-73.

Cf. *idem*, *Kausis Nekron apo te Neolithike Epoche ste Thessalia*, Athens 1982.
G. Ch. Chourmoudziadis, *To Neolithiko Dimini. Prospatheia gia mia nea prosengise tou neolithikou hylikou*, Volos 1979.
M.-H.J.M.N. Wijnen, *The Early Neolithic I Settlement at Sesklo: An Early Farming Community in Thessaly, Greece*, Leiden 1982.
R. Avila, "Das Kuppelgrab von Volos-Kapakli," *PZ* 58, 1983, 15-60.
G. Freund, "Zur Silexindustrie der Samari-Magula (Boibe-See)," *PZ* 58, 1983, 94-105.
B. Feuer, *The Northern Mycenaean Border in Thessaly* (BAR Intern. Ser. 176), Oxford 1983.
H.-J. Weisshaar, *Die deutschen Ausgrabungen auf der Pevkakia-Magula in Thessalien I. Spätes Neolithikum und Kupferzeit* (Beiträge zur ur- und frügeschichtlichen Archäologie des Mittelmeerkulturraumes 28), Bonn 1987.

2. Central Greece

Boeotia: H.W. Catling and A. Millett, "A study of the inscribed stirrup jars from Thebes," *Archaeometry* 8, 1975, 3-85.
P.A. Mountjoy, "Some Early and Middle Helladic Pottery from Boeotia," *BSA* 75, 1980, 139-149.
D.N. Consola, *Promykenaïki Thiva*, Athens 1981.
A. Sampson, *He Neolithike kai he Protoelladike I sten Euboia*, Athens 1981.
J. Knauss *et al.*, *Die Wasserbauten der Minyer in der Kopaïs: die älteste Flussregulierung Europas* (Institut für Wasserbau und Wassermengenwirtschaft und Versuchsanstalt für Wasserbau, Bericht 50), Munich 1984.
P.A. Mountjoy, *Mycenaean Pottery from Orchomonos, Eutresis and other Boeotian Sites* (Orchomenos 5) (Bay. Akad. d. Wiss., phil.-hist. Kl. Abh. N.F. 89), Munich 1985.
A. Sampson, "La destruction d'un atelier palatial mycénien à Thebes," *BCH* 109, 1985, 21-29.
H. Tzavella-Evjen, *Lithares. An Early Bronze Age Settlement in Boeotia* (Institute of Archaeology, University of California. Occasional Paper 15), Los Angeles 1985.
S. Lauffer, *Kopaïs. Untersuchungen zur historischen Landeskunde Mittelgriechenland* I, Frankfurt am Main 1986.

Euboea: M.R. Popham and L.H. Sackett, *Excavations at Lefkandi, Euboea 1964-1966*, London 1968.
J.B. Rutter, *Ceramic Change in the Aegean Early Bronze Age. The Kastri Group, Lefkandi I, and Lerna IV: A Theory Concerning the Origin of Early Helladic III Ceramics* (Institute of Archaeology, University of California, Los Angeles, Occasional Paper 5), Los Angeles 1979.

Sporades: N. Efstratiou, *Agios Petros. A Neolithic Site in the Northern Sporades. Aegean Relationships during the Neolithic of the 5th Millennium* (BAR Intern. Ser. 241), Oxford 1985.

373 **Attica:** U. Knigge, "Eine prähistorische Siedlung am Hymettos," *AA* 1977, 137-141.
P.A. Mountjoy, *Four Early Mycenaean Wells from the South Slope of the Acropolis at Athens*, with an Appendix by R.D.G. Evely, "The 'Bellow's Nozzle'," Gand 1981.
N. Lambert, *La Grotte Préhistorique de Kitsos (Attique). Missions 1968-1978. L'occupation néolithique, les vestiges des temps paléolithiques, de l'antiquité et de l'histoire récent*, 2 vols., Paris 1981.
P. Spitaels (ed.), *Studies in South Attica* I, Ghent 1982.

Aegina: S. Hiller, *Alt-Aigina IV 1: Mykenische Keramik*, Mainz 1975.
H. Walter and F. Felten, *Alt-Aigina: Die vorgeschichtliche Stadt. Befestigungen, Häuser, Funde*, Mainz 1981.
I. Pini, "Aigina, Aphaia-Tempel X. Die Steinsiegel," *AA* 1987, 413-433.

3. North-West Greece and the West Coast of the Peloponnesus

North-West Greece: G.N. Bailey, P.L. Carter, C.S. Gamble and H.P. Higgs, "Epirus revisited: seasonality and inter-site variation in the Upper Palaeolithic of North-West Greece," in G.N. Bailey (ed.), *Hunter-Gatherer Economy in Prehistory*, Cambridge 1983, 64-78.
G.N. Bailey, P.L. Carter, C.S. Gamble and H.P. Higgs, "Asprochaliko and Kastritsa: Further Investigations of Palaeolithic Settlement and Economy in Epirus (North-West Greece)," *PPS* 49, 1983, 15-42.
G.N. Bailey *et al.*, "Palaeolithic Investigations in Epirus: The Results of the First Season's Excavations at Klithi," *BSA* 79, 1984, 7-22.
G.N. Bailey *et al.*, "Palaeolithic Investigations at Klithi: Preliminary Results of the 1984 and 1985 Field Seasons," *BSA* 81, 1986, 7-35.
G. King and G. Bailey, "The Palaeoenvironment of Some Archaeological Sites in Greece: The Influence of Accumulated Uplift in a Seismically Active Region," *PPS* 51, 1985, 273-282.
T.I. Papadopoulos, "Das mykenische Kuppelgrab von Kiperi bei Parga (Epirus)," *MDAI(A)* 96, 1981, 7-24.
S. Brodbeck-Jucker, *Mykenische Funde von Kephallenia* (Archaeologica 42), Rome 1986.

Achaea: A.J. Papadopoulos, *Excavations at Aigion 1970* (SIMA 46), Göteborg 1976.
W. Alzinger, "Aigeira-Achaia," *JÖAI* 51, 1976-1977, 30-34.
Idem et al., "Griechenland, Aigeira (Achaia), Elis, Lousoi," *ibid.* 53, 1981-1982, 8-24.
W. Alzinger, S. Deger-Jalkotzy and E. Alram-Stern, "Aigeira-Hyperesia und die Siedlung Phelloë in Achaia. Österreichische Ausgrabungen auf der Peloponnes," *Klio* 67, 1985, 389-426.

S. Deger-Jalkotzy, *Fremde Zuwanderer im spätmykenischen Griechenland. Zu einer Gruppe handgemachter Keramik aus den Myk. III C Siedlungsschichten von Aigeira* (SAWW 326), Vienna 1977.
T.J. Papadopoulos, *Mycenaean Achaea* (SIMA 55, 1-2), 2 vols., Göteborg 1979.

Elis: K. Koumouzelis, *The Early and Middle Helladic Periods in Elis*, Diss. Brandeis Univ., Waltham, Mass., 1980.
W. Alzinger *et al.*, "Griechenland, Aigeira (Achaia), Elis, Lousoi," *JÖAI* 53, 1981-1982, 8-24.

Messenia: M. Lindgren, *The People of Pylos. Prosopographical and Methodological Studies in the Pylos Archives. I: A Prosopographical Catalogue of Individuals and Groups; II: The Use of Personal Designations and their Interpretation* (Boreas 3, 1-2), Stockholm 1973.
G. Rapp and S.E. Aschenbrenner, *Excavations at Nichoria in Southwest Greece I: Site, Environs, and Techniques*, Minneapolis 1978.
J.C. Kraft, G.R. Rapp and S.E. Aschenbrenner, "Late Holocene Palaeogeomorphic Reconstructions in the Area of the Bay of Navarino. Sandy Pylos," *JArchSc* 7, 1980, 187-210.
K. Kilian, "Pylos. Funktionsanalyse einer Residenz der späten Palastzeit," *Archäologisches Korrespondenzblatt* 14, 1984, 37-48.
C.W. Shelmerdine, *The Perfume Industry of Mycenaean Pylos* (SIMA Pocket Book 34), Göteborg 1985.

4. Corinth and Environs

J.B. Rutter, *The Late Helladic III B and III C Periods at Korakou and Gonia in the Corinthia*, Diss. Univ. of Penn. 1974, Ann Arbor 1975.
J.C. Lavezzi, "Prehistoric Investigations at Corinth," *Hesp.* 47, 1978, 402-451.
J.B. Rutter, "The Last Mycenaeans at Corinth," *Hesp.* 48, 1979, 348-392.

5. The Peloponnesus

Argolid: The excavations which were resumed at both Mycenae and Tiryns have produced important results. For preliminary reports, see, on **Mycenae**: G.E. Mylonas, "Hoi Periboloi tes Akropolis," *Arch Ephem.* 1962, 167-185; *idem*, "Anaskaphe Mykenon," *Praktika* 1958 to 1975; W. Taylour, "Mycenae 1968," *Antiquity* 43, 1969, 91-97; *idem*, "New Light on Mycenaean Religion," *ibid.* 44, 1970, 270-280. On **Tiryns**: K. Kilian, "Ausgrabungen in Tiryns," *AA* 1978, 449-470; 1979, 379-411; 1981, 149-194; 1982, 393-430; 1983, 277-328.

The results have contributed in particular to our understanding of the Late Helladic period, namely, the latter part of it. The newly discovered pottery, for instance, has made it possible to establish a much more reliable chronology, especially for the LH III B and the

LH III C periods, and above all for the early phases of the latter. On the *LH III A* and *III B*, see, in particular, E. French, "Pottery Groups from Mycenae," *BSA* 58, 1963, 44-52; "Late Helladic III A1 Pottery from Mycenae," *BSA* 59, 1964, 241-261; "Late Helladic III A2 Pottery from Mycenae," *BSA* 60, 1965, 159-202; "A Group of Late Helladic IIIB 1 Pottery from Mycenae," *BSA* 61, 1966, 216-238; "Pottery from Late Helladic IIIB 1 Destruction Contexts," *BSA* 62, 1967, 149-193; "A Group of Late Helladic IIIB 2 Pottery from Mycenae," *BSA* 64, 1969, 71-93; K.A. Wardle, "A Group of Late Helladic IIIB 1 Pottery from within the Citadel at Mycenae," *BSA* 64, 1969, 261-292; *idem*, "A Group of Late Helladic IIIB 2 Pottery from within the Citadel at Mycenae: 'The Causeway Deposit'," *BSA* 68, 1973, 297-353; P.A. Mountjoy, "Late Helladic IIIB 1 Pottery Dating the Construction of the South House at Mycenae," *BSA* 71, 1976, 77-111. On **LH III C**: E. Wace French, "The First Phase of LH IIIC," *AA* 1969, 133-136; and (for Tiryns) especially Ch. Podzuweit, "Bericht zur spätmykenischen Keramik," *AA* 1978, 471-498; 1979, 412-440; 1981, 194-220; 1983, 359-402.

Also important is the evidence for earlier periods, such as the Early Helladic (cf. [on the pottery at Tiryns], H.-J. Weisshaar, "Bericht zur frühhelladischen Keramik," *AA* 1981, 220-256; 1982, 440-466; 1983, 329-358); and especially evidence for the first habitation at Tiryns, namely as early as (if not earlier than) the Middle Neolithic period (cf. K. Kilian, "Ausgrabungen in Tiryns," *AA* 1983, 326-327); but above all, the first indication of the existence of lions in Greece, in the Late Bronze Age—at Tiryns (cf. J. Boessneck and A. von den Driesch, "Ein Löwenknochenfund aus Tiryns," *AA* 1979, 447-449; *iidem*, "Ein Beleg für das Vorkommen des Löwen auf der Peloponnesos in 'Herakleischer' Zeit," *ibid.*, 1981, 257-258). Meanwhile more lion bones seem to keep turning up (cf. I. Pini, in P. Darcque and J.-C. Poursat [eds.], *L'iconographie minoenne* [BCH Suppl. 11], Paris 1985, 156 n. 12).

Not even this, however, exhausts the results: cf. E. Havernick, "Kleinfunde aus Glas, Fayence, Fritte, Karneol und Bernstein," *AA* 1979, 440-447; G. Hiesel, "Bericht zur unbemalten mykenischen Keramik von Tiryns," *AA* 1982, 431-439; and H. Kroll, "Kulturpflanzen von Tiryns," *AA* 1982, 467-485.

For summaries of the results, see G.E. Mylonas, *Mycenae and the Mycenaean Age*, Princeton, N.J., 1966; *idem*, *Mycenae's Last Century of Greatness*, Sydney 1968; S.E. Iakovidis, "The Present State of Research at the Citadel of Mycenae," *BIAL* 14, 1977, 99-141; *idem*, "A Hundred Years of Mycenaean Archaeology," *Antiquaries Journal* 58, 1978, 13-30; R. Laffineur, "Un siècle de fouilles à Mycène," *Revue belge de philologie et d'histoire* 55, 1977, 5-20; K. Kilian, "Zum Ende der mykenischen Epoche in der Argolis," *JRGZM* 27, 1980, 166-195; *idem*, "Neue historische Aspekte des Spätmykenischen. Ergebnisse der Grabungen in Tiryns," *Jb. der Heidelb. Akad. der Wiss.* 1981, 76-83. Meanwhile, at least three fascicules of the final publication on Mycenae (38 are envisaged [cf. W. Taylour, "A Note on the Recent Excavations at Mycenae and the Scheme Proposed for their Publication," *BSA* 64, 1969, 259-260]) have appeared: cf., for instance, W.D. Taylour, E.B. French and K.A. Wardle, *Well Built Mycenae: the Helleno-British Excavations within the Citadel at Mycenae 1959-1969*, Fasc. 1: *The Excavations*, Warminster 1981. As a convenient publication for the earlier period, see *Excavations at Mycenae 1939-1955*, by A.J.B. Wace and others. Reprinted from the Annual of the British School at Athens Vols. 45-56, Edited and Indexed by E. French (BSA Suppl. Vol. No. 12), London 1980.

In the meantime, at Tiryns excavation has been shifted to the *Oberburg* (palace) (cf. H.W. Catling, *ArchRep* 32, 1985-86, 26-27), and continued at Mycenae (*ibid.*, 27).

Elsewhere in the Argolid: I. and R. Hägg (eds.), *Excavations in the Barbouna Area at Asine 2: Finds from the Levendis Sector, 1970-1972*, Uppsala 1978.

S. Dietz *et al.*, *Asine II. Results of the Excavations East of the Acropolis 1970-1974*. Fasc. 1: *General Stratigraphical Analysis and Architectural Remains*, Stockholm 1982.

S. Dietz, *ibid. II* Fasc. 2: *The Middle Helladic Cemetery, The Middle Helladic and Early Mycenaean Deposits*, Stockholm 1980.

B.S. Frizell, *ibid. II* Fasc. 3: *The Late and Final Mycenaean Periods*, Stockholm 1986.

S. Dietz, "Kontinuität und Kulturwende in der Argolis von 2000-700 v. Chr. Ergebnisse der neuen schwedisch-dänischen Ausgrabungen in Asine," in *Kleine Schriften aus dem vorgeschichtlichen Seminar Marburg 17: Ägäische Frühzeit*, Marburg 1984, 23-52.

J.B. Rutter, "A Group of Distinctive Pattern-decorated Early Helladic III Pottery from Lerna and its Implications," *Hesp.* 51, 1982, 459-488.

E.J. Holmberg, *A Mycenaean Chamber Tomb near Berbati in Argolis*, Göteborg 1983.

C. Runnels, "The Bronze-Age Flaked-Stone Industries from Lerna: A Preliminary Report," *Hesp.* 54, 1985, 357-391.

On **Franchthi Cave**: S. Payne, "Faunal Change at Franchthi Cave from 20,000 to 3,000 B.C.," in A.T. Classon (ed.), *Archaeological Studies*, Amsterdam and New York 1975, 120-131.

T.W. Jacobsen, "17,000 Years of Greek Prehistory," *Scientific American* 234, 1976, 76-87.

Idem, "Franchthi Cave and the Beginning of Settled Village Life in Greece," *Hesp.* 50, 1981, 303-319.

J.A. Gifford, "Core Sampling of a Holocene marine sequence and underlying Neolithic cultural material off Franchthi cave," in P.M. Masters and N.C. Flemming (eds.), *Quaternary Coastlines and Marine Archaeology*, New York 1983, 269-281.

C. Perlès, "Étude Préliminaire des Industries Paléolithiques de Grotte Franchthi, Argolide, Grèce," in J.K. Kozlowski and S.K. Kozlowski (eds.), *Advances in Palaeolithic and Mesolithic Archaeology* (Archaeologia Interregionalis), Warsaw 1984, 151-171.
T.W. Jacobsen and W.R. Farrand, *Excavations at Franchthi Cave, Greece*. Fasc. 1: *Franchthi Cave and Paralia: Maps, Plans, and Sections*, Bloomington, Ind., 1988.
T.H. van Andel and S.B. Sutton, *Excavations at Franchthi Cave, Greece*. Fasc. 2: *Landscape and People of the Franchthi Region*, Bloomington, Ind., 1988.
C. Perlès, *Excavations at Franchthi Cave, Greece*. Fasc. 3: *Les Industries lithiques taillées de Franchthi: Tome I, Présentation générale et Industries Paléolithiques*, Bloomington, Ind., 1988.
J.C. Shackleton, *Excavations at Franchthi Cave, Greece*. Fasc. 4: *Marine Molluscan Remains from Franchthi Cave*, Bloomington, Ind., 1988.

Other Aspects: G. Graziadio, "Le influenze minoiche e cicladiche sulla cultura Tardo Medio-Elladica del Peloponneso," *SMEA* 19, 1978, 165-204.
K.O. Pope and T.H. van Andel, "Late Quaternary alluviation and soil formation in the southern Argolid: Its history, causes and archaeological implications," *JourArchSc* 11, 1984, 281-306.
C. Gates, "Rethinking the Building History of Grave Circle A at Mycenae," *AJA* 89, 1985, 263-274.
D. Kaza-Papageorgiou, "An Early Mycenaean cist grave from Argos," *AM* 100, 1985, 1-21.
S. Payne, "Zooarchaeology in Greece: A Reader's guide," in N.C. Wilkie and W.D. Coulson (eds.), *Contributions to Aegean Archaeology: Studies in Honor of William A. McDonald*, Dubuque, Io., 1985, 211-244.
T.H. van Andel, C.N. Runnels and K.O. Pope, "Five Thousand Years of Land Use and Abuse in the Southern Argolid, Greece," *Hesp*. 55, 1986, 103-128.
T.H. van Andel and C. Runnels, *Beyond the Acropolis: A Rural Greek Past*, Stanford 1987, 3-75.
J.F. Cherry *et al.*, "Archaeological Survey in an Artifact-Rich Landscape: A Middle Neolithic Example from Nemea, Greece," *AJA* 92, 1988, 159-176.
For a comprehensive synthesis, see F. Schachermeyr, *Die ägäische Frühzeit I. Forschungsbericht über die Ausgrabungen im letzten Jahrzehnt und über ihre Ergebnisse für unser Geschichtsbild: Die vormykenischen Perioden des griechischen Festlandes und der Kykladen* (Mykenische Studien III) (SAWW 303), Vienna 1976.

375 **6. The East Greek Islands**

Cyprus: Under the dynamic aegis of Professor Karageorghis, archaeological activity on Cyprus continues with an impressive momentum, affecting every era. For the prehistoric period, the following may be cited:

Excavations: J.-C. Courtois *et al.*, *Mission archéologique d'Alasia V: Alasia, II. Les tombes d'Enkomi: Le mobilier funéraire* (*Fouilles C.F.A. Schaeffer 1947-1965*), Paris 1981.
Iidem, *ibid.* VI. *Alasia III: Les objets des niveaux stratifiés* (*Fouilles C.F.A. Schaeffer 1947-1970*), Paris 1984.
P. Åström, D.M. Bailey and V. Karageorghis, *Hala Sultan Tekke I. Excavations 1897-1971* (SIMA 45, 1), Göteborg 1973.
O.T. Engvig and P. Åström, *Hala Sultan Tekke II. The Cape Keti Survey* (SIMA 45, 2), Göteborg 1975.
P. Åström, G. Hult and M. Strandberg Olofsson, *Hala Sultan Tekke III. Excavations 1972* (SIMA 45, 3), Göteborg 1977.
G. Hult, *Hala Sultan Tekke IV. Excavations in Area 8 in 1974 and 1975*, and D. McCaslin, *The 1977 Underwater Report* (SIMA 45, 4), Göteborg 1978.
U. Åbrink, *Hala Sultan Tekke V. Excavations in Area 22, 1971-1973 and 1975-1978* (SIMA 45, 5), Göteborg 1979.
U. Åbrink, *Hala Sultan Tekke VI. A Sherd Deposit in Area 22* (SIMA 45, 6), Göteborg 1979.
G. Hult, *Hala Sultan Tekke VII. Excavations in Area 8 in 1977* (SIMA 45, 7), Göteborg 1981.
P. Åström *et al.*, *Hala Sultan Tekke VIII. Excavations 1971-1979* (SIMA 45, 8), Göteborg 1983.
P. Åström, "Hala Sultan Tekke—An international harbour town of the Late Cypriote Bronze Age," *OpAth* 16, 1986, 7-17.
V. Karageorghis *et al.*, *Excavations at Kition II: Objets égyptiens et égyptisants, scarabées, amulettes et figurines en pate de verre et faience, vase plastique en faience. Sites I et II, 1959-1975*, Nicosia 1976.
V. Karageorghis, M. Demas and B. King, "Excavations at Maa-Palaeokastro, 1979-1982. A Preliminary Report," *RDAC* 1982, 86-108.
S.F. Kromholz, *The Bronze Age Necropolis at Ayia Paraskevi (Nicosia): Unpublished Tombs in the Cyprus Museum* (SIMA Pocket Book 17), Göteborg 1982.
E.J. Peltenburg, *Vrysi. Subterranean Settlement in Cyprus. Excavations at Prehistoric Ayios Epiktitos Vrysi 1969-73*, Warminster 1982.
A. Le Brun *et al.*, *Fouilles Récentes à Khirokitia (Chypre), 1977-1981*, 2 vols., Paris 1984; cf. *RDAC 1986*, 1-11.
V. Karageorghis and M. Demas, *Pyla-Kakkinokremos: a Late 13th Century B.C. Fortified Settlement in Cyprus*, Nicosia 1984 (cf. E. Goring, *JHS* 107, 1987, 247-248).
E.J. Peltenburg, *Lemba Archaeological Project I: Excavations at Lemba Lakous, 1976-1983* (SIMA 70), Göteborg 1985.
V. Karageorghis and M. Demas, *Excavations at Kition V. The Pre-phoenician Levels. Areas I and II. Part I.* With Appendices by H. Frost *et al.*, Nicosia 1985.

J.-C. Courtois and J. and E. LaGrace, *Enkomi et le bronze récent à Chypre*, Nicosia 1986.

General Works: R.S. Merrillees, *Introduction to the Bronze Age Archaeology of Cyprus* (SIMA 9), Göteborg 1978.
V. Karageorghis, *Cyprus. From the Stone Age to the Romans*, London 1982.
F.G. Maier, *Cypern. Insel am Kreuzweg der Geschichte*, Munich [2]1982.
V. Karageorghis, *Archaeology in Cyprus 1960-1985*, Nicosia 1985.

Studies on Specific Questions: V. Karageorghis (ed.), *Acts of the International Archaeological Symposium "The Mycenaeans in the Eastern Aegean," Nicosia 27th March-2nd April 1972*, Nicosia 1973.
D. Frankel, *Middle Cypriot White Painted Pottery: an Analytical Study of the Decoration* (SIMA 42), Göteborg 1974.
V. Karageorghis, *Mycenaean and Phoenician Discoveries in Cyprus*, London 1976.
D.L. Saltz, "The Chronology of the Middle Cypriote Period," *RDAC 1977*, 51-70.
R.S. Merrillees, "The Absolute Chronology of the Bronze Age in Cyprus," *RDAC 1977*, 33-50.
P. Åలin, "Idalion Pottery from the Excavations of the Swedish Cyprus Expedition," *OpAth* 12, 1978, 91-109.
H.W. Catling, R.E. Jones and A. Millet, "Composition and Provenance Problems in some Late Bronze Age Pottery found in Cyprus," *RDAC 1978*, 70-90.
E.D.T. Vermeule and F. Wolsky, "New Aegean Relations with Cyprus: The Minoan and Mycenaean Pottery from Toumba tou Skourou, Morphou," *ProcAmerPhilosSoc* 122, 1978, 294-317.
H.W. Catling, "Reflections upon the Interpretation of the Archaeological Evidence for the History of Cyprus," in *Studies in Memory of Porphyrios Dikaios*, Nicosia 1979, 194-205.
V. Karageorghis *et al.* (eds.), *Acts of the International Archaeological Symposium "The Relations between Cyprus and Crete, ca. 2000-500 B.C.," Nicosia, 16-22 April 1978*, Nicosia 1979.
H.W. Catling, *Cyprus and the West 1600-1050 B.C.* (Ian Sanders Memorial Lecture, 1979), Sheffield 1980.
P. Åström, "Cyprus and Troy," *OpAth* 13, 1980, 23-28.
E. Gjerstad, "The Phoenician Colonisation and Expansion in Cyprus," *RDAC 1979*, 230-254.
Idem, "The Origin and Chronology of the Early Bronze Age in Cyprus," *RDAC 1980*, 1-16.
N.P. Stanley Price, *Early Prehistoric Settlement in Cyprus: A Review and Gazetteer of Sites c. 6500-3000 B.C.* (BAR Intern. Ser. 65), Oxford 1980.
J. Reade, *Chalcolithic Cyprus and Western Asia* (British Museum Occasional Paper 26), London 1981.

E.J. Peltenburg, *Recent Developments in the Later Prehistory of Cyprus* (SIMA Pocket Book 16), Göteborg 1982.
J.D. Muhly, R. Maddin and V. Karageorghis (eds.), *'Early Metallurgy in Cyprus, 4000-500 B.C.' Acta of the International Archaeological Symposium, Larnaca, Cyprus, 1-6 June 1981*, Nicosia 1982 [1983].
G. Hult, *Bronze Age Ashlar Masonry in the Eastern Mediterranean. Cyprus, Ugarit and Neighboring Regions* (SIMA 66), Göteborg 1983.
S.S. Weinberg, *Bamboula at Kourion: The Architecture* (Univ. Mus. Monographs 42), Philadelphia 1983.
V. Karageorghis and J.D. Muhly (eds.), *Cyprus at the End of the Bronze Age*, Nicosia 1984.
S. Hiller, "Die Kyprominoischen Schriftsysteme," *AfO* 20, 1985, 61-93.
I.A. Todd, "The Vasilikos Valley and the Chronology of Neolithic/Chalcolithic Periods in Cyprus," *RADC 1985*, 1-15; *RDAC 1986*, 12-27.
A. Nibbi, *Wenamun and Alashiya Reconsidered*, Oxford 1985.
W. Helck, "Zur Keftiu-, Alasia- und Ahhijawa-Frage," in H.-G. Buchholz *et al.*, *Ägäische Bronzezeit*, Darmstadt 1987, 218-226.
H.-G. Buchholz, "Alaschia-Zypern (Literaturbericht)," *ibid.*, 227-236.
O. Negbi, "The Climax of Urban Development in Bronze Age Cyprus," *RDAC 1986*, 97-121.
Z.A. Stos-Gale, N.H. Gale and U. Zwicker, "The Copper Trade in the South-East Mediterranean. Preliminary Scientific Evidence," *RDAC 1986*, 122-144.
P.M. Fisher, *Prehistoric Cypriot Skulls. A Medicoanthropological, Archaeological and Microanalytical Investigation* (SIMA 75), Göteborg 1986.
V. Karageorghis (ed.), *Acts of the International Archaeological Symposium "Cyprus between the Orient and the Occident," Nicosia, 8-14 September 1985*, Nicosia 1986.
A.B. Knapp, *Copper Production and Divine Protection: Archaeology, Ideology and Social Complexity on Bronze Age Cyprus* (SIMA Pocket Book 42), Göteborg 1986.

Rhodes: C. Mee, *Rhodes in the Bronze Age. An Archaeological Survey*, Warminster 1982 (cf. Ch.G. Doumas, *Gnomon* 59, 1987, 182-183).
S. Dietz, *Lindos IV, 1: Excavations and Surveys in Southern Rhodes. The Mycenaean Period*, Copenhagen 1984.

Samos: R. Felsch, *Die prähistorischen Funde vom Kastro Tigani* (Samos II), Mainz 1987.

376 **Chios:** S. Hood, *Excavations in Chios 1938-1955: Prehistoric Emporio and Ayio Gala*, 2 vols., London 1981 and 1982.

Dodecanese: A. Sampson, "The Neolithic of the Dodecanese and Aegean Neolithic," *BSA* 79, 1984, 239-249.

C. Macdonald, "Problems of the Twelfth Century BC in the Dodecanese," *BSA* 81, 1986, 125-151.

7. The Cyclades

Keos: J.L. Caskey, *Hesperia* 31, 1962, 263-283; 40, 1971, 359-396; 41, 1972, 357-401; *AJA* 83, 1979, 412.
J.E. Coleman, *Keos. Results of Excavations Conducted by the University of Cincinnati I: Kephala. A Late Neolithic Settlement and Cemetery*, Princeton, N.J., 1977.
K. Abramovitz, "Frescoes from Ayia Irini, Keos, II-IV," *Hesp.* 49, 1980, 57-85.
W.W. Cummer and E. Schofield, *Keos. Results of the Excavations Conducted by the University of Cincinnati under the Auspices of the American School of Classical Studies at Athens III: Ayia Irini: House A*, Mainz 1984.
A. Halepa Bikaki, *ibid. IV: Ayia Irini: The Potters' Marks*, Mainz 1984.
J.L. Davis, *ibid. V: Ayia Irini: Period V*, Mainz 1986.
H.S. Georgiou, *ibid. VI: Ayia Irini: Specialized Domestic and Industrial Pottery*, Mainz 1986 (cf. H. Lohmann, *Gnomon* 59, 1987, 565-566).
M.E. Caskey, *Keos II; The Temple at Ayia Irini I: the Statues*, Princeton, N.J., 1986.

Delos: J.A. MacGillivray, *Early Cycladic Pottery from Mt. Kynthos in Delos*, Edinburgh 1979.
Idem, "Mount Kynthos in Delos. The Early Cycladic Settlement," *BCH* 104, 1980, 3-45.

Melos: C. Renfrew and M. Wagstaff (eds.), *An Island Polity: The Archaeology of Exploitation in Melos*, Cambridge 1982.
C. Renfrew *et al.*, *The Archaeology of Cult. The Sanctuary at Phylakopi* (The British School of Archaeology at Athens Supplementary Vol. 13), London 1985 (cf. E. Vermeule, *AJA* 92, 1988, 293-294).

Naxos: Evidence for Mycenaean occupation, namely from LH III B to LH III C, is turning up (cf. H.W. Catling, *ArchRep* 32, 1985-86, 75).

Paros: The site of **Koukounaries** continues to yield late Mycenaean material (cf. D. Schilardi, *Ergon* 1984 [1985], 69-72, *Ergon* 1985 [1986], 51-56, and H.W. Catling, *ArchRep* 32, 1985-86, 76-78).

General Works: For a synthesis, see F. Schachermeyr, *Die ägäische Frühzeit I: Die vormykenischen Perioden des griechischen Festlandes und der Kykladen* (Mykenische Studien III) (SAWW 303), Vienna 1976.
J. Thimme (ed.), *Art and Culture of the Cyclades: Handbook of an Ancient Civilisation*, Karlsruhe 1977.

Ch. Doumas, *Cycladic Art: Ancient Sculpture and Pottery from the N. P. Goulandris Collection*, London 1983.
W. Ekschmitt, *Kunst und Kultur der Kykladen 1: Neolithikum und Bronzezeit* (Kulturgeschichte der Antiken Welt 28,1), Mainz 1986.

Studies on Specific Subjects: Ch. Doumas, *Early Bronze Age Burial Habits in the Cyclades* (SIMA 48), Göteborg 1977.
E. Sapouna-Sakellarakis, *Die Fibeln der griechischen Inseln* (Prähistorische Bronzefunde, Abt. XIV, 4), Munich 1978.
J.L. Davis and J.F. Cherry (eds.), *Papers in Cycladic Prehistory*, Los Angeles 1979.
P. Getz-Preziosi, "The Male Figure in Early Cycladic Sculpture," *Metropolitan Museum Journal* 15, 1980, 5-33.
N.H. Gale and Z.A. Stos-Gale, "Cycladic Leads and Silver Metallurgy," *BSA* 76, 1981, 169-224.
R.N.L. Barber, "The Late Cycladic Period: a Review," *BSA* 76, 1981, 1-21.
E. Schofield, "The Western Cyclades and Crete: a 'special relationship'," *OxfJournArch* 1, 1982, 9-25.
Ch. Doumas, "The Minoan Thalassocracy and the Cyclades," *AA* 1982, 5-14.
R.L. Barber, "The Definition of the Middle Cycladic Period," *AJA* 87, 1983, 76-81.
J.A. MacGillivray and R.L.N. Barber (eds.), *The Prehistoric Cyclades: Contributions to a Workshop on Cycladic Chronology. London, 10th-11th, 13th, June 1983 in Memorium of J.L. Caskey*, Edinburgh 1984.
J.L. Fitton (ed.), *Cycladica: Studies in Memory of N. P. Goulandris: Proceedings of the Seventh British Museum Classical Colloquium, June 1983*, London 1984 (cf. O. Höckmann, *Gnomon* 58, 1986, 425-427).
J.E. Coleman, "'Frying Pans' of the Early Bronze Age Aegean," *AJA* 89, 1985, 191-219.
P. Getz-Preziosi, *Early Cycladic Sculpture. An Introduction*, Malibu, Ca., 1985.
O. Höckmann, "Frühbronzezeitliche Kulturbeziehungen im Mittelmeergebiet unter besonderer Berücksichtigung der Kykladen," in H.-G. Buchholz *et al.*, *Ägäische Bronzezeit*, Darmstadt 1987, 53-87.

8. Western Asia Minor

Troy and Environs: J.W. Sperling, "Kum Tepe in the Troad. Trial Excavation, 1934," *Hesp.* 45, 1976, 305-364.
D.F. Easton, "Towards a Chronology of the Aegean Early Bronze Age," *AnatSt* 28, 1976, 145-172.
P.Z. Spanos, "Zur absoluten Chronologie der zweiten Siedlung in Troja," *ZeitschrAssyriol* 67, 1977, 85-107.

J. Yakar, "Troy and Anatolian Early Bronze Age Chronology," *AnatSt* 29, 1979, 51-67.

H. Quitta, "Radiokarbondaten und die Zeitstellung der 'verbrannten Stadt' von Troja," in H.W. Coblenz and F. Horst (eds.), *Mitteleuropäische Bronzezeit*, Berlin 1979, 112-118.

R. Maxwell-Hyslop and S. Hood, "Dating Troy II," *BICS* 26, 1979, 125-129.

T.R. Bryce, "Ahhiyawa and Troy—a Case of Mistaken Identity?," *Historia* 26, 1977, 24-32.

Ch. Podzuweit, *Trojanische Gefässformen der Frühbronzezeit in Anatolien, der Ägäis und angrenzenden Gebieten. Ein Beitrag zur vergleichenden Stratigraphie*, Mainz 1979 (cf. S. Hiller, *BonJahrb* 182, 1982, 590-592).

Idem, "Neue frühtrojanische Funde in Nordwestanatolien und Griechenland," *JRGZM* 26, 1979, 131-153.

Idem, "Die mykenische Welt und Troja," in B. Hänsel (ed.), *Südosteuropa zwischen 1600 und 1000 v. Chr.* (Prähistorische Archäologie in Südosteuropa 1), Berlin 1982, 65-88.

D.H. French, "Mycenaeans in the Black Sea," in *Thracia Pontica* I, Sofia 1982, 19-30.

G. Rapp, Jr., and J. Gifford (eds.), *Troy. The Archaeological Geology* (Supplementary Monograph 4), Princeton, N.J., 1982.

Z.A. Stos-Gale, N.H. Gale and G.R. Gilmore, "Early Bronze Age Trojan Metal Sources and Anatolians in the Cyclades," *OxfJournArch* 3,3, 1984, 23-44.

E. Pernicka *et al.*, "Archäometallurgische Untersuchungen in Nordwestanatolien," *JRGZM* 31, 1984, 533-599.

T.C. Seeliger *et al.*, "Archäometallurgische Untersuchungen in Nord- und Ostanatolien," *JRGZM* 32, 1985, 597-659.

G.A. Wagner *et al.*, "Geochemische und isotopische Charakteristika früher Rohstoffquellen für Kupfer, Blei, Silber und Gold in der Turkei," *JRGZM* 33, 1986, 723-752.

M. Korfmann, "Beşik-Tepe. Vorbericht über die Ergebnisse der Grabung von 1982. Die Hafenbucht vor Troja (Hisarlık), Grabungen am Beşik-Yassıtepe," *AA* 1984, 165-176; *idem*, "Beşik-Tepe 1983 Grabungen an Beşik-Yassıtepe und Beşik-Sivritepe," *AA* 1985, 157-182; *idem*, "Beşik-Tepe. Vorbericht über die Ergebnisse der Grabungen von 1984. Grabungen am Beşik-Yassıtepe, Beşik-Sivritepe und Beşik-Gräberfeld," *AA* 1986, 303-363.

E. French, "Who were the Mycenaeans in Anatolia?," in E. Akurgal (ed.), *Proceedings of the Xth International Congress of Classical Archaeology, Ankara-Izmir 23.IX.1973* I, Ankara 1978, 165-168.

There is at the moment vigorous 'psychological warfare' being waged against Schliemann, spearheaded by Calder and Traill; cf., however, D.F. Easton, "Priam's Treasure," *AnatSt* 34, 1984, 141-169, and E.F. Bloedow, "Schliemann on his Accusers," *Tyche* 1, 1986, 30-40.

Further, W.M. Calder III and D.A. Traill (eds.), *Myth, Scandal, and History. The Heinrich Schliemann Controversy and a First Edition of the Mycenaean Diary*, Detroit 1986.
Cf. E.F. Bloedow, "Schliemann on his Accusers II: A Study on the Reuse of Sources," *AC* [in press].
For already a more correct view of Schliemann's contribution, see H. Kyrieleis, "Schliemann in Griechenland," *JRGZM* 25, 1978, 74-91, and H. Döhl, *Heinrich Schliemann. Mythos und Ärgernis*, Munich 1981.
M. Séfériadès, *Troie I: Matériaux pour l'étude des sociétés du Nord-Est-Égéen au début du Bronze Ancien* (Recherches sur des Civilisations. Cahiers 15), Paris 1985.
J. Yakar, "Regional and Local Schools of Metalwork in Early Bronze Age Anatolia: Part II," *AnatSt* 35, 1985, 25-38.
N.H. Gale, Z.A. Stos-Gale and G.R. Gilmore, "Alloy Types and Copper Sources of Anatolian Copper Alloy Artifacts," *AnatSt* 35, 1985, 143-173.
J. Mellaart, "Some Reflections on the History and Geography of Western Anatolia in the Late Fourteenth and Thirteenth Centuries B.C.," *Anadolu Araştırmaları* 10, 1986, 215-230.
J. Seeher, "Prähistorische Funde aus Gülpinar/ Chryse. Neue Belege für einen vor-trojanischen Horizont an der Nordwestküste Kleinasiens," *AA* 1987, 533-556.

377 **Asia Minor:** M. Korfmann *et al.*, "Demircihüyük. Eine vorgeschichtliche Siedlung an der phrygisch-bithynischen Grenze. Vorbericht über die Ergebnisse der Grabung von 1975," *IstMitt* 27/28, 1977/1978, 1-59; cf. *ibid.* 29, 1979, 9-64; 30, 1980, 5-21.
M. Korfmann, *Demircihüyük. Die Ergebnisse der Ausgrabungen 1975-78 I. Architektur, Stratigraphie und Befunde*, Mainz 1983.
M. Korfmann *et al.*, *Demircihüyük II. Naturwissenschaftliche Untersuchungen*, Mainz 1987.
J. Seeher, *Demircihüyük III, 1. Die Keramik 1: A. Die neolitische und chalkolitische Keramik; B. Die frühbronzezeitliche Keramik der älteren Phasen bis Phase G*, Mainz 1987.
L.A. Bordaz, *Metal Artifacts from Bronze Age Excavations at Karataş Semayük, Turkey, and their Significance in Anatolia, the Near East, and the Aegean*, Diss. Bryn Mawr College 1978.
W. Voigtländer, "Frühe Funde vom Killiktepe bei Milet," *IstMitt* 33, 1983, 5-39.
I. Singer, "Western Anatolia in the Thirteenth Century B.C. according to the Hittite Sources," *AnatSt* 33, 1983, 205-217.
P.E. Pecorella *et al.*, *Missione arceologica italiana di Iasos I: cultura preistorica di Iasos in Caria*, Rome 1984.
M. Sharp Joukousky *et al.*, *Prehistoric Aphrodisias: An Account of the Excavations and Artifact Studies*, 2 vols., Providence, R.I., and Louvain-La-Neuve 1986.

9. Crete

Excavations: S. Hiller, *Das minoische Kreta nach den Ausgrabungen des letzten Jahrzehnts* (SAWW 330. Mykenische Studien 5), Vienna 1977.
Idem, "Kreta," *AfO* 29-30, 1983-1984, 307-320.

Knossos: E.A. Catling, H.W. Catling and D. Smyth, "Knossos 1975. Middle Minoan III and Late Minoan I Houses by the Acropolis," *BSA* 74, 1979, 1-80.
M.R. Popham *et al.*, *The Minoan Unexplored Mansion at Knossos* (BSA Suppl. Vol. 17), London 1984 (cf. D.J.I. Begg, *JHS* 107, 1987, 245-246, and L.V. Watrous, *AJA* 91, 1987, 197-198).

Phaistos: D. Levi, *Festos e la Civiltà Minoica*, I,i and I,ii and II (Incunabula Graeca 60 and 77), Rome 1976 and 1981.

Mallia: H. and M. van Effenterre, *Fouilles exécutées à Mallia. Exploration des maisons et quartiers d'habitation (1956-1960)* (Ét. Crét. 22), Paris 1976.
J.-C. Poursat, L. Godart and J.-P. Olivier, *Fouilles exécutées à Mallia. Le quartier MU I: Introduction générale. Écriture hiéroglyphique crétoise* (Ét. Crét. 23), Paris 1978.
F. Vandenabeele and J.-P. Olivier, *Fouilles exécutées à Mallia. Les idéogrammes archéologiques du linéaire B* (Ét. Crét. 24), Paris 1979.
O. Pelon, E. Andersen and J.-P. Olivier, *Fouilles exécutées à Mallia. Le palais de Malia 5* (Ét. Crét. 25), Paris 1980.
B. Detournay, J.-C. Poursat and F. Vandenabeele, *Fouilles exécutées à Mallia. Le quartier MU, II: Vases de pierre et de métal, vannerie, figurines et reliefs d'applique, éléments de parure et de décoration, armes, sceaux et empreintes* (Ét. Crét. 26), Paris 1980.
M.-E. Schmid, "Les portes multiples au 'Megaron' du Palais de Malia," *BCH* 107, 1983, 705-716.
O. Pelon, "Un dépôt de fondation au palais de Malia," *BCH* 110, 1986, 3-19.

Khania: Y. Tzedakis and E. Hallager, "The Greek-Swedish Excavations at Kastelli, Khania (1976 and 1977)," *AAA* 11, 1978, 31-46.
E. Hallager and Y. Tzedakis, "The Greek-Swedish Excavations at Kastelli, Khania (1978 and 1979)," *AAA* 15, 1982, 21-30.
Y. Tzedakis and E. Hallager, "The Greek-Swedish Excavations at Kastelli, Khania 1980," *AAA* 16, 1983, 3-17.
E. Hallager, "The Greek-Swedish Excavations at Kastelli, Khania 1980. The Linear B Inscriptions," *ibid.*, 58-73.
E. Hallager and Y. Tzedakis, "The Greek-Swedish Excavations at Kastelli, Khania 1982-1983," *AAA* 17, 1984, 3-20.

Kommos: J.W. Shaw, P.P. Betancourt and V. Watrous, "Excavations at Kommos (Crete) during 1976," *Hesp.* 46, 1977, 199-240; see also

47, 1978, 111-170; 48, 1979, 145-173; 49, 1980, 207-250; 50, 1981, 211-251; 51, 1982, 164-195; 53, 1984, 251-287; 55, 1986, 219-269.

Hagia Triada: F. Halbherr, E. Stefani and L. Banti, "Haghia Triada nel periodo tardo palaziali," *ASAtene* 39, 1977 [1980], 9-296 (cf. L. Watrous, *AJA* 88, 1984, 123-134, and S. Hiller, *AnzAltWiss* 39, 1986, 234-237).
V. La Rosa, "La ripressa dei lavori ad Haghia Triada: realazione preliminare sui saggi del 1977," *ASAtene* 39, 1977 [1980], 297-342.
Idem, "Haghia Triada, II: Relazione preliminare sui saggi del 1978 e 1979," *ASAtene* 41-42, 1979-80 [1986], 49-164.
D. Levi and C. Laviosa, "Il forno minoico da vasio di Haghia Triada," *ibid.*, 7-47.

Pyrgos: G. Cadogan, "Pyrgos, Crete 1970-7," *ArchRep* 24, 1978, 70-81.

Archanes: H.W. Catling, *ArchRep* 32, 1986, 85-86.

Ayia Photia: An Early Minoan settlement has been discovered here, with possibly a fortification enclosure-wall, which would be the first of its kind on Crete (cf. H.W. Catling, *ArchRep* 32, 1986, 94).

Mt. Iouktas: This highly interesting site, originally investigated by Sir A. Evans, has been excavated again, between 1974 and 1981 (cf. A. Karetsou, *Praktika* 1974, 228-239; 1975, 330-342; 1976, 408-418; 1977, 419-420; 1978, 232-258; 1979, 280-281; 1980, 337-353; 1981, 405-408; cf. *eadem*, "The Peak Sanctuary of Mt. Juktas," in R. Hägg and N. Marinatos [eds.], *Sanctuaries and Cults in the Aegean Bronze Age. Proceedings of the First International Symposium at the Swedish Institute in Athens, 12-13 May, 1980*, Stockholm 1981, 137-153). Meanwhile, the excavations have been resumed (cf. H.W. Catling, *ArchRep* 32, 1986, 86; 33, 1987, 55).

Kavousi: G. Gesell, L. Day and W. Coulson, "Excavations and Survey at Kavousi, 1978-1981," *Hesp.* 52, 1983, 389-420; *ibid.*, 54, 1985, 327-355.

Palaikastro: J.A. MacGillivray *et al.*, "An Archaeological Survey of the Russolakkos Area at Palaikastro," *BSA* 79, 1984, 129-159.
L.H. Sackett and J.A. MacGillivray, *ArchRep* 33, 1986-87, 59-60.

Rethymnon: W. Schiering and W.-D. Niemeier, "Landbegehungen in Rethymnon und Umgebung," *AA* 1982, 15-54.

378 **10. Thera**

For a brief survey, see F. Schachermeyr, *Die ägäische Frühzeit II: Die mykenische Zeit und die Gesittung von Thera* (Mykenische Studien IV) (SAWW 309), Vienna 1976.

For further discussion of the **volcanic eruption**, see Ch. Doumas (ed.), *Thera and the Aegean World. Papers Presented at the Second International Scientific Congress, Santorini, Greece, August 1978*, 2 vols., London 1978 and 1980.
W.-D. Niemeier, "Die Katastrophe von Thera und die spätminoische Chronologie," *JDAI* 95, 1980, 1-76.
H. Pichler and W. Schiering, "Der spätbronzezeitliche Ausbruch des Thera-Vulkans und seine Auswirkungen auf Kreta," with an Excursus by H.H. Schock and H. Pichler, "Identifizierung von Bimsstein- und Obsidian-Artefakten mittels der Neutronenaktivierungs-Analyse," *AA* 1980, 1-37.
V. Francaviglia, "The Eruption of the Thera Volcano and the Mallia Pumices," *Archeologia Classica* 34, 1982, 196-198.
O. Longo, "Thera (Santorini) e l'eruzione del 1500 a.C.," *A & R* 30, 1985, 115-136.
C.U. Hammer *et al.*, "The Minoan eruption of Santorini in Greece dated to 1645 BC?," *Nature* 328, 1987, 517-519; cf. G. Cadogan, *ibid.*, 473.
Otherwise: P. Warren, "The Miniature Fresco from the West House at Akrotiri, Thera, and its Aegean Setting," *JHS* 99, 1979, 115-129.
L. Morgan, "Theme in the West House Paintings at Thera," *Archaiologike Ephemeris* 1983 [1985], 85-105.
N. Marinatos, "The West House at Akrotiri as a Cult Center," *MDAI(A)* 98, 1983, 1-19.
Ch.G. Doumas, *Thera. Pompeii of the Ancient Aegean. Excavations at Akrotiri 1967-1979*, London 1983. Cf. H.W. Catling, *ArchRep* 32, 1985-86, 74.
N. Marinatos, *Art and Religion in Thera. Reconstructing a Bronze Age Society*, Athens 1984.
C. Palyvou, "Notes on the Town Plan of Late Cycladic Akrotiri, Thera," *BSA* 81, 1986, 179-194.
P. Sotirakopoulou, "Early Cycladic Pottery from Akrotiri," *BSA* 81, 1986, 297-312.
J. Vanschoonwinkel, "Thera et la jeune civilisation mycénienne," *AC* 55, 1986, 5-41.
M. Marthari, "The Local Pottery Wares with Painted Decoration from the Volcanic Destruction Level of Akrotiri, Thera. A Preliminary Report," *AA* 1987, 359-399.
See also the contributions by S. Marinatos, S. Sinos and W. Schiering in H.-G. Buchholz *et al.*, *Ägäische Bronzezeit*, Darmstadt 1987, 275-328.

379 **11. Eastern Frontier Regions**

Cape Gelidonya: G.F. Bass *et al.*, *Cape Gelidonya: A Bronze Age Shipwreck* (Trans. Amer. Phil. Soc. 57/8), Philadelphia 1967.
J.D. Muhly, T. S. Wheeler and R. Maddin, "The Cape Gelidonya Shipwreck and the Bronze Age Metals Trade in the Eastern Mediterranean," *JFA* 4, 1977, 353-362.

Kaş: G.F. Bass, "A Bronze Age Shipwreck at Ulu Burun (Kaş): 1984 Campaign," *AJA* 90, 1986, 269-296, cf. *IJNA* 13, 1984, 271-279.
C. Pulak, "The Bronze Age Shipwreck at Ulu Burun, Turkey: 1985 Campaign," *AJA* 92, 1988, 1-37.

Cilicia: E.S. Sherratt and J.H. Crouwel, "Mycenaean Pottery from Cilicia in Oxford," *OxfJournArch* 6, 1987, 325-352.

Ugarit: J. Margueron, "Ras Shamra 1975 et 1976. Rapport préliminaire sur les campagnes d'automne," *Syria* 54, 1977, 152-188, cf. *CRAI* 1977, 303-319.
Mission de Ras Shamra, XVIII: Ugaritica VII, Paris 1978.
J.-C. Courtois, "Ras Shamra: Archéologie du site," in *Supplément au Dictionnaire de la Bible*, Fasc. 52-53, 1979, 1126-1295.
H. de Contenson, "Nouvelles données sur la chronologie du Bronze Ancien de Ras Shamra," *Ugarit-Forschungen 11. Festschrift für Claude Schaeffer zum 80. Geburtstag am 6. März 1979*, Neukirchen 1979, 857-862.
Mission archéologique de Ras Shamra. Ras Shamra, 1929-1979, Lyon 1980.
M. Yon, A. Caubet and J. Mallet, "Ras Shamra-Ougarit, 38e, 39e et 40e campagnes (1978, 1979 et 1980)," *Syria* 59, 1982, 169-192.
M. Yon *et al.*, "Fouilles de Ras Shamra-Ougarit 1981-1983 (41e, 42e & 43e campagnes)," *Syria* 60, 1983, 201-224.
C.F.A. Schaeffer *et al.*, *Corpus des cylindres-sceaux de Ras Shamra-Ugarit et d'Enkomi-Alasia* I, Paris 1983.
D. Pardée, *Les textes hippiatriques. Ras Shamra-Ougarit* II (Éditions Recherches sur les Civilisations, Mémoire 53), Paris 1985.
J.-C. Courtois, "Enkomi und Ras Schamra, zwei Aussenposten der mykenischen Kultur," in H.-G. Buchholz *et al.*, *Ägäische Bronzezeit*, Darmstadt 1987, 182-217.

381 **Minoan Culture**

General Works: F. Schachermeyr, *Die ägäische Frühzeit III. Die Ausgrabungen und ihre Ergebnisse für unser Geschichtsbild: Kreta zur Zeit der Wanderungen vom Ausgang der minoischen Ära bis zur Dorisierung der Insel* (Mykenische Studien VII) (SAWW 355), Vienna 1979.
R.F. Willetts, *The Civilisation of Ancient Crete*, London 1977.
S. Hood, *The Arts in Prehistoric Greece*, Harmondsworth 1978.
F. Schachermeyr, *Die minoische Kultur des alten Kreta*, Stuttgart ^{2}1979.

Studies on Specific Subjects: S. Hood, "Minoan Town Shrines," in K.H. Kinzl (ed.), *Greece and the Eastern Mediterranean in History and Prehistory. Studies... Fritz Schachermeyr*, Berlin 1977, 156-172.
M.A.S. Cameron, R.E. Jones and S. Philippakis, "Scientific Analysis of Minoan Fresco Samples from Knossos," *BSA* 72, 1977, 121-184.

J. Killen, "The Knossos Texts and the Geography of Mycenaean Crete," in J. Bintliff (ed.), *Mycenaean Geography. Proceedings of the Cambridge Colloquium, September 1976*, Cambridge 1977, 40-54.
E. Hallager, *The Mycenaean Palace at Knossos: Evidence for Final Destruction in the IIIB Period* (Medelhavsmuseet, Memoir 1), Stockholm 1977 (cf. M. Popham, *JHS* 99, 1979, 202-203, S. Hood, *CR* 29, 1979, 283-284, and S. Hiller, *Gnomon* 51, 1979, 768-773).
P.A. Mountjoy, R.E. Jones and J.F. Cherry, "Provenance Studies of LM I B/LH II A Marine Style," *BSA* 73, 1978, 143-171.
J.W. Graham, "Further Notes on Minoan Palace Architecture I: West Magazines and Upper Halls at Knossos and Mallia," *AJA* 83, 1979, 49-63.
S. Merié, *Das Thronraumareal des Palastes von Knossos. Versuch einer Neuinterpretation seiner Entstehung und seiner Funktion* (Saarbrücker Beiträge zur Altertumskunde 26), Bonn 1979.
M. Aposkitou, "*Minos Kalokairinos, ekato chronia apo proti anaskaphi tis Knosou*," *Kritologia* 8, 1979, 81-94.
J. Coulomb, "Le 'Prince aux Lis' de Knossos reconsidéré," *BCH* 103, 1979, 29-50.
Idem, "Les boxeurs minoens," *BCH* 105, 1981, 27-40.
H.W. Catling, J.F. Cherry, R.E. Jones and J.T. Killen, "The Linear B inscribed stirrup jars and West Crete," *BSA* 75, 1980, 49-113.
N. Platon, I. Pini and G. Salies, *Corpus der minoischen und mykenischen Siegel II, 2: Iraklion, Archäologisches Museum. Die Siegel der Altpalastzeit*, Berlin 1977.
J.H. Betts, *CMS X. Die schweizer Sammlungen*, Berlin 1980.
J.A. Sakellarakis, *CMS I 1: Athen. National Museum*, Supplementum, Berlin 1982.
N. Platon and I. Pini, *CMS II 3: Iraklion, Die Siegel der Neupalastzeit*, Berlin 1984.
Iidem, *CMS II 4: Iraklion, Die Siegel der Nachpalastzeit und undatierte spätminoische Siegel*, Berlin 1985.
A. Onassoglou, *CMS Beiheft II: Die "Talismannischen" Siegel*, Berlin 1985.
P. Yule, *Early Cretan Seals: A Study of Chronology* (Marburger Studien zur Vor- und Frühgeschichte 4), Mainz 1980.
B.J. Kemp and R.S. Merrillees, *Minoan Pottery in Second Millennium Egypt*, Mainz 1980.
I. Strøm, "Middle Minoan Crete. A Reconsideration of Some of its External Relations," in J.G.P. Best and N.M.W. de Vries (eds.), *Interaction and Acculturation in the Mediterranean*, Amsterdam 1980, 105-123.
P. Yule, "Early and Middle Minoan Foreign Relations: the Evidence from the Seals," *SMEA* 26, 1987, 161-173.
A. Kanta, *The Late Minoan III Period in Crete. A Survey of Sites, Pottery and their Distribution* (SIMA 58), Göteborg 1980.

J. Strange, *Caphtor-Keftiu. A New Investigation* (Acta Theologica Danica 14), Leiden 1980.

W. Helck, "Zur Keftiu-, Alasia- und Ahhijawa-Frage," in H.-G. Buchholz *et al.*, *Ägäische Bronzezeit*, Darmstadt 1987, 218-222.

L.R. Palmer, "The First Fortnight at Knossos," *SMEA* 21, 1980, 273-301.

S. Hiller, "The South Propylaeum of the Palace at Knossos, some Reflections on its Reconstruction," in *Pepragmena tou Delta Diethnous Kritologikou Synedriou* A1, Athens 1980, 216-232.

L.R. Palmer, "The Khyan Lid Deposit at Knossos," *Kadmos* 20, 1981, 108-128.

S. Hood and D. Smyth, *Archaeological Survey of the Knossos Area*, second ed., rev. and expanded (BSA Suppl. Paper 14), London 1981.

J.K. McArthur, "The textual evidence for location of place-names in the Knossos tablets," *Minos* 17, 1981, 147-210.

Eadem, *The Place-Names of the Knossos Tablets*, in J.L. Melena (ed.), *A Tentative Lexicon of Mycenaean Place-Names*: Part One (Preliminary Issue) = Annex to *Minos* 19, 1985.

K.P. Foster, *Minoan Ceramic Relief* (SIMA 64), Göteborg 1982.

W.-D. Niemeier, "Mycenaean Knossos and the Age of Linear B," *SMEA* 23, 1982, 219-287. [There is also a German version of this study.]

L.V. Watrous, *Lasithi: A History of Settlement on a Highland Plain in Crete* (Hesp. Suppl. 18), Princeton, N.J., 1982.

J.L. Davis, "The Earliest Minoans in the South-East Aegean: a Reconsideration of the Evidence," *AnatSt* 32, 1982, 33-41.

O. Pelon, "L'épée à l'acrobate et la chronologie maliote (I)," *BCH* 106, 1982, 165-190.

Idem, *ibid.* "(II)," *BCH* 107, 1983, 679-703.

J. Weingarten, *The Zakro Master and his Place in Prehistory* (SIMA Pocket Book 26), Göteborg 1983.

O. Krzyszkowska and L. Nixon (eds.), *Minoan Society. Proceedings of the Cambridge Colloquium 1981*, Bristol 1983.

D. Preziosi, *Minoan Architecture. Design, Formation and Significance* (Approaches to Semiotics 63), Berlin, New York, Amsterdam 1983.

R. Hägg and N. Marinatos (eds.), *The Minoan Thalassocracy. Myth and Reality. Proceedings of the Third International Symposium at the Swedish Institute in Athens, 31 May-5 June, 1982*, Stockholm 1984 (cf. J. Bouzek, *Gnomon* 59, 1987, 71-73).

R. Hägg and Y. Lindau, "The Minoan 'Snake-Frame' reconsidered," *OpAth* 15, 1984, 67-77.

N. Marinatos, "The Date-Palm in Minoan Iconography and Religion," *ibid.*, 115-122.

W.-D. Niemeier, "Zum Problem von Import und Imitation minoischer Keramik in frühmykenischer Zeit," in *Aux origines de l'hellénisme: La Crète et la Grèce. Hommage à Henri van Effenterre* (Histoire ancienne et médiévale 15), Paris 1984, 111-119.

O. Pelon, "Le palais minoen en tant que lieu de culte," in G. Roux (ed.), *Temples et sanctuaires. Séminaire de recherche 1981-1983*, Paris 1984, 61-79.

L.V. Watrous, "Ayia Triada. A new Perspective on the Minoan Villa," *AJA* 88, 1984, 123-134.

P. Warren, "Circular Platforms at Minoan Knossos," *BSA* 79, 1984, 307-323.

C. Verlinden, *Les statuettes anthropomorphes crétoises en bronze et en plomb du IIIe millénaire au VIIe siècle av. J.-C.* (Archaeologia Transatlantica 4), Providence, R.I., and Louvain-La-Neuve 1984.

P.P. Betancourt *et al.*, *East Crete White-on-Dark Ware. Studies on a Handmade Pottery of the Early to Middle Minoan Periods* (University Monographs 51), Philadelphia 1984.

P.A. Mountjoy, "The Marine Style Pottery of LM I B/LH II A: Towards a Corpus," *BSA* 79, 1984, 161-219.

I. Kilian-Dirlmeier, "Noch einmal zu den 'Kriegergräbern' von Knossos," *JRGZM* 32, 1985, 196-214.

J.M. Driessen, "Quelques remarques sur la 'Grande Tablette' (AS 1516) de Cnossos," *Minos* 19, 1985, 169-193.

P.P. Betancourt, *The History of Minoan Pottery*, Princeton, N.J., 1985.

G.C. Gesell, *Town, Palace, and House Cult in Minoan Crete* (SIMA 67), Göteborg 1985.

P. Darcque and J.-C. Poursat (eds.), *L'iconographie minoenne: Actes de la Table Ronde d'Athènes (21-22 avril 1983)* (BCH Suppl. 11), Paris 1985.

E. Hallager, *The Master Impression: A Clay Sealing from the Greek-Swedish Excavations at Kastelli, Khania* (SIMA 69), Göteborg 1985.

W.-D. Niemeier, *Die Palastkeramik von Knossos. Stil, Chronologie und historischer Kontext* (Archäologische Forschungen Bd. 13), Berlin 1985.

B. Palsson Hallager, "Crete and Italy in the Late Bronze Age III Period," *AJA* 89, 1985, 293-305.

D.E. Wilson, "The Pottery and Architecture of the EM IIA West Court House at Knossos," *BSA* 80, 1985, 281-364.

J. Bennet, "The Structure of the Linear B Administration at Knossos," *AJA* 89, 1985, 231-249.

A. Pilali-Papasteriou, *Die bronzenen Tierfiguren aus Kreta* (Prähistorische Bronzefunde 1, III), Munich 1985.

R. Hägg, "Die göttliche Epiphanie im minoischen Ritual," *AM* 101, 1986, 41-62.

N. Marinatos, *Minoan Sacrificial Ritual. Cult Practice and Symbolism*, Stockholm 1986.

E. Karantzali, "Une tombe du Minoen Récent III B à La Canée," *BCH* 110, 1986, 53-87.

G. Walberg, *Tradition and Innovation. Essays in Minoan Art*, Mainz 1986.

S.M. Wall, J.H. Musgrave and P.M. Warren, "Human Bones from a Late Minoan Ib House at Knossos," *BSA* 81, 1986, 333-388.

W.-D. Niemeier, "Zur Deutung des Thronraumes im Palast von Knossos," *AM* 101, 1986, 63-95.

E. Hallager, "The Inscribed Stirrup Jars: Implications for Late Minoan IIIB Crete," *AJA* 91, 1987, 171-190.

B.J. Hayden, "Crete in Transition: LM IIIA-IIIB Architecture. A Preliminary Study," *SMEA* 26, 1987, 199-234.

E. Lévy (ed.), *Le système palatial en Orient, en Grèce et à Rome. Actes du colloque de Strasbourg 19-22 juin 1985*, Leiden 1987.

F. Schachermeyr, "Kreta und Mykene, ein Vergleich ihres Kulturcharakters," in H.-G. Buchholz *et al.*, *Ägäische Bronzezeit*, Darmstadt 1987, 379-387.

E.F. Bloedow and C. Björk, "The Mallia Insect Pendant: A Study in Iconography and Minoan Religion," *SMEA* 27 [in press].

Mycenaean Culture

General Works: J.T. Hooker, *Mycenaean Greece*, London and Boston 1976.

F. Schachermeyr, *Die ägäische Frühzeit II. Die mykenische Zeit und die Gesittung von Thera* (Mykenische Studien IV) (SAWW 309), Vienna 1976.

Idem, *Die ägäische Frühzeit IV. Griechenland im Zeitalter der Wanderungen vom Ende der mykenischen Ära bis auf die Dorier* (SAWW 372), Vienna 1980.

S. Hood, *The Arts in Prehistoric Greece*, Harmondsworth 1978.

For a **survey within the context of the Linear B Tablets**, see S. Hiller, "Mykenische Archäologie," *SMEA* 20, 1979, 183-197.

Studies on Specific Subjects: P. Faure, *La vie quotidienne en Grèce au temps de la guerre de Troie (1250 avant Jesus-Christ)*, Paris 1975.

J.A. Sakellarakis, "Mycenaean Stone Vases," *SMEA* 17, 1976, 173-187.

A. Strobel, *Die spätbronzezeitliche Seevölkersturm. Ein Forschungsüberblick mit Folgerungen zur biblischen Exodusthematik* (Zeitschr. für Alttestamentliche Wissenschaften Beiheft 145), Berlin 1976.

C.G. Thomas, "The Nature of Mycenaean Kingship," *SMEA* 17, 1976, 93-116.

J.B. and S.H. Rutter, *The Transition to Mycenaean. A Stratified Middle Helladic II to Late Helladic II A Pottery Sequence from Ayios Stephanos in Lakonia* (Monumenta Archaeologica 4), Los Angeles 1976.

O.T.P.K. Dickinson, *The Origins of Mycenaean Civilization* (SIMA 49), Göteborg 1977.

K. Kilian, "Nordgrenze des ägäischen Kulturbereiches in mykenischer und nachmykenischer Zeit," *Jahresbericht des Instituts für Vorgeschichte der Universität Frankfurt a. M.*, 1976 [1977], 112-129.

J.-C. Poursat, *Les ivoires mycéniens. Essai sur la formation d'un art mycénien* (Bibl. des Éc. fr. d'Athènes et de Rome 230), Paris 1977.
Idem, *Catalogue des ivoires mycéniens du Musée National d'Athènes* (Bibl. des Éc. fr. d'Athènes et de Rome 230 bis), Paris 1977.
R. Laffineur, *Les vases en métal précieux à l'époque mycénienne*, Göteborg 1977.
J.B. Rutter, "Late Helladic IIIC Pottery and Some Historical Implications," in E.N. Davis (ed.), *Symposium on the Dark Ages in Greece, Sponsored by the Archaeological Institute of America and Hunter College, City University of New York, April 30, 1977*, New York 1977, 1-20.
J. Bintliff (ed.), *Mycenaean Geography. Proceedings of the Cambridge Colloquium. September 1976*, Cambridge 1977.
P. Åström, *The Cuirass Tomb and Other Finds at Dendra. I: The Chamber Tombs; II: Excavations in the Cemeteries, Lower Town and* Citadel (SIMA 4, 1-2), Göteborg 1977 and 1983.
A. Åkerström, "Mycenaean Problems," *OpAth* 12, 1978, 19-86.
S. Deger-Jalkotzy, *E-qe-ta. Zur Rolle des Gefolgschaftswesens in der Sozialstruktur mykenischer Reiche* (Mykenische Studien VI) (SAWW 344), Vienna 1978.
S. Iakovides, "Chronologies in Old World Archaeology. The Chronology of LH IIIC," *AJA* 83, 1979, 454-462.
L. Baumbach, "The Mycenaean Contribution to the Study of Greek Religion in the Bronze Age," *SMEA* 20, 1979, 143-160.
K. Kilian, "Zur Darstellung eines Wagenrennens aus spätmykenischer Zeit," *MDAI(A)* 95, 1980, 21-31.
B. Kaiser, "Mykenische Steingefässe und Verwandtes im Magazin zu Nauplia," *MDAI(A)* 95, 1980, 1-19.
O. Höckmann, "Lanze und Speer im spätminoischen und mykenischen Griechenland," *JRGZM* 27, 1980, 13-158.
J.C. Wright, "Mycenaean palatial terraces," *MDAI(A)* 95, 1980, 59-86.
A. Heubeck and G. Neumann (eds.), *Res Mycenaeae. Akten des VII. Internationalen Mykenologischen Colloquiums in Nürnberg vom 6.-10. April 1981*, Göttingen 1983.
S. von Reden and J.G.P. Best, *Auf der Spur der ersten Griechen. Woher kammen die Mykener? Neue archäologische Erkentnisse über die Herkunft der Griechen*, Cologne 1981.
E. Vermeule and V. Karageorghis, *Mycenaean Pictorial Vase Painting*, Cambridge, Mass., 1982.
R. Hägg, "On the Nature of the Minoan Influence in Early Mycenaean Messenia," *OpAth* 14, 1982, 27-37.
S.E. Iakovidis, *Late Helladic Citadels on Mainland Greece* (Monumenta Graeca et Romana 4), Leiden 1983.
O.T.P.K. Dickinson, "Cist Graves and Chamber Tombs," *BSA* 78, 1983, 55-67.

N. Sandars, "North and South at the End of the Mycenaean Age: Aspects of an Old Problem," *OxfJournArch* 2, 1983, 43-68.

E. Holmberg, *A Mycenaean Chamber Tomb near Berbati in Argolis*, Göteborg 1983.

J.L. Melena, "Olive Oil and other Sorts of Oil in the Mycenaean Tablets," *Minos* 18, 1983, 89-123.

H. Kroll, "Zum Ackerbau gegen Ende der mykenischen Epoche in der Argolis," *AA* 1984, 211-222.

I. Kilian-Dirlmeier, *Nadeln der frühhelladischen bis archaischen Zeit von der Peloponnes* (Prähistorische Bronzefunde Abt. 13, VIII), Munich 1984.

C.B. Mee and W.G. Cavanagh, "Mycenaean tombs as evidence for social and political organisation," *OxfJournArch* 3, 1984, 45-64.

A. Uchitel, "Women at Work. Pylos and Knossos, Lagash and Ur," *Historia* 33, 1984, 257-282.

J. Driessen and C. Macdonald, "Some Military Aspects of the Aegean in the Late Fifteenth and Early Fourteenth Centuries B.C.," *BSA* 79, 1984, 49-74.

A. Heubeck, "Zu einigen Problemen der pylischen Tafel An 607," *Minos* 19, 1985, 61-90.

C. Gates, "Rethinking the Building History of Grave Circle A at Mycenae," *AJA* 89, 1985, 263-274.

J. Bouzek, *The Aegean, Anatolia and Europe: Cultural Interrelations in the Second Millennium B.C.* (SIMA 29), Göteborg and Prague 1985 (cf. N.K. Sandars, *JHS* 107, 1987, 241).

K. Kilian, "Civiltà micenea in Grecia. Nuovi aspetti storici ed interculturali," in *Magna Grecia e mondo Magna Grecia, Taranto, 7-11 ottobre 1982*, Taranto 1983 [1985], 53-96.

Idem, "La caduta dei palazzi micenei continentali: aspetti archeologici," in D. Musti (ed.), *Le origini dei Greci. Dori e mondo egeo*, Rome 1985, 73-115.

Idem, "Violinbogenfibeln und Blattbügelfibeln des griechischen Festlandes aus mykenischer Zeit," *PZ* 60, 1985, 145-203.

A. Xenake-Sakellariou, *Hoi Thalamotoi Taphoi ton Mykenon. Anaskaphes Chr. Tsountas (1887-1898), Les Tombs à Chambre de Mycènes. Fouilles de Chr. Tsountas (1887-1898)*, Paris 1985 (cf. E. French, *JHS* 107, 1987, 249-250, and I. Kilian, *Gnomon* 59, 1987, 376-378).

I. Kilian-Dirlmeier, "Beobachtungen zu den Schachtgräbern von Mykenai und zu den Schmuckbeigaben mykenischen Männergräber. Untersuchungen zur Sozialstruktur in späthelladischer Zeit," *JRGZM* 33, 1986, 159-198.

P.A. Mountjoy, *Mycenaean Decorated Pottery: A Guide to Identification* (SIMA 73), Göteborg 1986.

J. Boardman and C.E. Vaphopoulou-Richardson (eds.), *Chios: A Conference at the Homereion in Chios 1984*, Oxford 1986.

E. Lévy (ed.), *Le système palatial en Orient, en Grèce et à Rome. Actes du colloque de Strasbourg 19-22 juin 1985*, Leiden 1987.

H. Gallet de Santerre, "Les statuettes de bronze mycéniennes au type du 'dieu Reshef' dans leur contexte égéen," *BCH* 111, 1987, 7-29. N.H. Gale, H.C. Einfalt, H.W. Hubberten and R.E. Jones, "The sources of Mycenaean gypsum," *JournArchSc* 15, 1988, 57-72. For additional bibliography, see *Nestor*, originally edited by E.L. Bennett, Jr., but meanwhile by T.W. Jacobsen and W.W. Rudolph, 1978 ff., pp. 1178 ff.

384 n. 41 More recent attempts are: L. Pomerance, *The Phaistos Disc. An Interpretation of Astronomical Symbols*, Göteborg 1976; L. Delekat, "Der Diskos von Phaistos. Entwurf einer Textlesung und -deutung," *Ugarit-Forschungen. Festschrift für Claude Schaeffer zum 80. Geburtstag am 6. März 1979*, Neukirchen 1979, 165-178; W. Nahm, "Zum Diskos von Phaistos II," *Kadmos* 18, 1979, 1-25; V.I. Georgiev, "Le disque de Phaistos. Un essai de déchiffrement (Information préliminaire)," in E. Risch and H. Muehlestein (eds.), *Colloquium Mycenaeum. Actes du VIe Colloque international sur les textes mycéniens et égéens tenu à Chaumont sur Neuchâtel du 7 au 13 septembre 1975*, Geneva 1979, 387-395; A. Kaulins, *The Phaistos Disc. Hieroglyphic Greek with Euclidean Dimensions*; *The Lost Proof of Parallel Lines* (Studies in the History of Mankind and its Languages 1), Darmstadt 1980; R. Hoschek, "Zur Schriftrichtung beim Diskos von Phaistos," *Kadmos* 20, 1981, 85-93; Y. Duhoux, "Les langues du linéaire A et du disque de Phaestos," *Minos* 18, 1983, 33-68; P. Gorissen, *Le disque de Phaistos. Voorafgegaan door en biografische en bibliografische nota*, Louvain 1983; O.S. Amundsen, *Le disque de Phaistos. Essai de déchiffrement*, Brussels 1985; H.-J. Haecker, "Neue Überlegungen zu Schriftrichtung und Textstruktur des Diskos von Phaistos," *Kadmos* 25, 1986, 89-96.

n. 48 See also S. Iakovidis, *He Mykenaïke Akropolis ton Athenon*, Athens 1962, 177-199; 231-235; L. Beschi, *ASAtene* 29/30, 1967-1968, 390-397; and J. McK. Camp II, "Water and the Pelargikon," in K.J. Rigsby (ed.), *Studies Presented to Sterling Dow on his Eightieth Birthday*, Durham, N.C., 1984, 37-41.

385 n. 53 M.A. Littauer and J. Crouwel, "The origin and diffusion of the cross-bar wheel?," *Antiquity* 51, 1977, 95-105; J.H. Crouwel, *Chariots and Other Means of Land Transport in Bronze Age Greece*, Amsterdam 1981; M.A. Littauer and J.H. Crouwel, "Chariots in late bronze age Greece," *Antiquity* 57, 1983, 187-192; S. Piggott, *The Earliest Wheeled Transport: From the Atlantic Coast to the Caspian Sea*, London 1983; P.R.S. Moorey, "The emergence of the light, horse-drawn chariot in the Near-East c. 2000-1500 B.C.," *World Archaeology* 18, 1986, 196-215. See also following note.

n. 69 For the West: W. Taylour, *Mycenaean Pottery in Italy and Adjacent Areas*, Cambridge 1958; M. Marazzi and S. Tusa, "Die mykenische Penetration im westlichen Mittelmeerraum," *Klio* 61, 1979, 309-351; H. Matthäus, "Italien und Griechenland in der ausgehenden Bronzezeit. Studien zu einigen Formen der Metallindustrie beider Gebiete," *MDAI(A)* 95, 1980, 109-139; E. Peruzzi and L. Vagnetti, *Mycenaeans in Early Latium* (Incunabula Graeca 75), Rome 1980; R.R. Holloway, *Italy and the Aegean 3000-700 B.C.*, Louvain-La-Neuve 1981; see also B. Palsson Hallager, "A New Social Class in Late Bronze Age Crete: Foreign Traders in Khania," in O. Krzyszkowska and L. Nixon (eds.), *Minoan Society. Proceedings of the Cambridge Colloquium 1981*, Bristol 1983, 111-119; *eadem*, "Italians in Late Bronze Age Khania," in *Atti XXII Convegno di studi sulla Magna Grecia, Taranto 1982*, Taranto 1982, 358-363; P. Schauer, "Spuren minoisch-mykenischen und orientalischen Einflusses im atlantischen Westeuropa," *JRGZM* 31, 1984, 137-186; G. Bergonzi, "Southern Italy and the Aegean during the Late Bronze Age: economic strategies and specialised craft products," in C. Malone and S. Stoddart (eds.), *Papers in Italian Archaeology* IV, Vol. 3, Oxford 1985, 355-387; A.F. Harding, *The Mycenaeans and Europe*, London and Toronto 1985 (cf. J. Bouzek, *Gnomon* 59, 1987, 181-182); C. Pare, "Wheels with thickened spokes, and the problem of cultural contact between the Aegean World and Europe in the Late Bronze Age," *OxfJournArch* 6, 1987, 43-61.

n. 71 Since the introduction of radiocarbon dating, a number of changes have, of course, taken place in the study of Aegean chronology, chiefly during the last few decades. Some very basic problems, however, still remain. Cf., for instance, S. Hood, "Discrepancies in ^{14}C Dating as illustrated from the Egyptian New and Middle Kingdoms and from the Aegean Bronze Age and Neolithic," *Archaeometry* 20, 1978, 197-199; P.P. Betancourt, H.N. Michael and G.A. Weinstein, "Calibration and the radiocarbon chronology of Late Minoan IB," *ibid.*, 200-203; G.A. Weinstein and H.N. Michael, "Radiocarbon dates from Akrotiri, Thera," *ibid.*, 203-209; G. Walberg, "The Tod Treasure and Middle Minoan Absolute Chronology," *OpAth* 15, 1984, 173-177; M.K.H. Eggert, S. Kurz and H.-P. Wotzka, "Historische Realität und archäologische Datierung. Zur Aussagekraft der Kombinationsstatistik," *PZ* 55, 1980, 110-145. For the latest developments, as well as problems, see *Radiocarbon* 26 A-B, 1986, 177-1030, and B.S. Ottaway (ed.), *Archaeology, Dendrochronology and the Radiocarbon Calibration Curve* (Edinburgh, Department of Archaeology, Occasional Paper No. 9) Edinburgh 1983; P.P. Betancourt, "Dating the Aegean Late Bronze Age with radiocarbon," *Archaeometry* 29, 1987, 45-49; *idem* and H.N. Michael, *ibid.*, 212-213; P.M. Warren, "Absolute dating of the Aegean Late Bronze Age," *ibid.*, 205-211; P. Åström (ed.), *High, Middle or Low? Acts of an International Colloquium on Absolute Chronology held at the University of Gothenburg, 20-22 August, 1987*, Göteborg 1987; C.U. Hammer *et al.*, "The Minoan eruption of Santorini in Greece dated to 1645 BC?," *Nature* 328, 1987, 517-519; cf. G. Cadogan, *ibid.*, 473; M.J. Aitken, "The Thera eruption: Continuing discussion of the dating I: Résumé of dating," *Archaeometry* 30, 1988, 165-169; H.N. Michael and P.P. Betancourt, "The Thera eruption II: Further arguments for an early date," *ibid.*, 169-175; P.M. Warren, "The Thera eruption III: Further arguments against an early date," *ibid.*, 176-182; H.N. Michael and P.P. Betancourt, "The Thera eruption IV: Addendum," *ibid.*, 180-183. See also O. Montelius, *Dating in the Bronze Age*, new ed., Stockholm 1986.

386 n. 75 W. Schiering, "Zu den Beziehungen zwischen der ältesten Siedlung von Milet und Kreta," in W. Müller-Wiener (ed.), *Milet 1899-1980* (IstMitt Beiheft 31), Tübingen 1986, 11-15.

n. 77 J.L. Huxley, *Achaeans and Hittites*, Oxford 1960; I. Singer, "Western Anatolia in the Thirteenth Century B.C. according to the Hittite Sources," *AnatSt 33*, 1983, 205-217; H. Güterbock, "The Hittites and the Aegean World: Part 1. The Ahhiyawa Problem Reconsidered," *AJA* 87, 1983, 133-138; M.J. Mellink, "The Hittites and the Aegean World: Part 2. Archaeological Comments on Ahhiyawa-Achaians in Western Anatolia," *AJA* 87, 1983, 138-141; E.T. Vermeule, "Response to Hans Güterbock," *AJA* 87, 1983, 141-143; H. Güterbock, "Hittites and Akhaeans. A New Look," *ProcAmerPhilosSoc* 128, 1984, 114-122; J.G. MacQueen, *The Hittites and their Contemporaries in Asia Minor*, revised and enlarged ed., London 1986; F. Schachermeyr, *Mykene und das Hethiterreich* (SAWW 472), Vienna 1986, *passim*.

2. MIGRATION AND TRANSITION

388 **The Dorians:** Interesting is J. Chadwick, "Who were the Dorians?," *PP* 31, 1976, 103-117, *idem*, "Der Beitrag der Sprachwissenschaft zur Rekonstruktion der griechischen Frühgeschichte," *Anzeiger der phil.-hist. Klasse der Österreichischen Akademie der Wissenschaften* 113, 1976, 183-198, who argues that the Dorians were always in Greece, i.e., they formed a lower social class among the original Indo-European immigrants, but cf. E. Risch, "Die Griechischen Dialekte im 2. Vorchristlichen Jahrtausend," *SMEA* 20, 1979, 91-111. There has since been a tendency in some circles to reject the idea of a Dorian Invasion altogether (cf., for instance, J.T. Hooker, "New Reflexions on the Dorian Invasion," *Klio* 61, 1979, 353-360, and A. Schnapp-Gourbeillon, "Le mythe dorien," in *Archeologia e storia antica* I, Naples 1979, 1-11), but see now E.F. Bloedow, "Handmade Burnished Ware or 'Barbarian' Pottery and Troy VIIb," *PP* 40, 1985 [1986], 161-199 (with extensive bibliography). See also H.J. Diesner, *The Great Migration*, Leipzig 1978; P.G. van Soesbergen, "The coming of the Dorians," *Kadmos* 20, 1981, 38-51; and G. Bockisch,

"Die Dorier: Autochthone oder Zuwanderer?," in P. Oliva and A. Frolikova (eds.), *Concilium Eirene. Proceedings of the 16th International Eirene Conference, Prague 31.8-4.9. 1982*, III, Prague 1983, 63-68; furthermore, D. Musti (ed.), *Le origini dei Greci. Dori e mondo egeo*, Rome 1985.

The Trojan War: On the question of the Trojan War, see now E.F. Bloedow, "The Trojan War and Late Helladic III C," *PZ* [in press]. See meanwhile, L. Foxhall and J.K. Davies (eds.), *The Trojan War. Its Historicity and Context: Papers of the first Greenbank Colloquium, Liverpool, 1981*, Bristol 1985.
M. Wood, *In Search of the Trojan War*, London 1985.
M.J. Mellink (ed.), *Troy and the Trojan War. A Symposium held at Bryn Mawr College October 1984*, Bryn Mawr, Pa., 1986.

General Works on the so-called Dark Age: J.N. Coldstream, *Geometric Greece*, London 1977.
J. Boardman, I.E.S. Edwards, N.G.L. Hammond and E. Sollberger (eds.), *CAH* III ^{2}1: *The Prehistory of the Balkans; and the Middle East and the Aegean World, tenth to eighth centuries B.C.*, Cambridge 1982.
J. Boardman (ed.), *The Cambridge Ancient History. Plates to Volume III*, Cambridge 1984.
F. Schachermeyr, *Die ägäische Frühzeit IV. Die Ausgrabungen und ihre Ergebnisse für unser Geschichtsbild: Griechenland im Zeitalter der Wanderungen vom Ende der mykenischen Ära bis auf die Dorier* (Mykenische Studien VIII) (SAWW 372), Vienna 1980.
Idem, *Die ägäische Frühzeit V: Die Levant im Zeitalter der Wanderungen vom 13. bis zum 11. Jahrhundert v. Chr.* (SAWW 387), Vienna 1982.
Idem, *Die griechische Rückerinnerung im Lichte neuer Forschungen* (SAWW 404), Vienna 1983.
Idem, *Griechische Frühgeschichte. Ein Versuch, frühe Geschichte wenigstens in Umrissen verständlich zu machen* (SAWW 425), Vienna 1984.

Studies on Specific Subjects: R. Hägg, *Die Gräber der Argolis in submykenischer, protogeometrischer und geometrischer Zeit I. Lage und Form der Gräber* (Boreas 7,1), Uppsala 1974.
Idem, "Some Aspects of Burial Customs of the Argolid in the Dark Ages," *AAA* 13, 1980, 119-126.
K. Kilian, *Fibeln in Thessalien von der mykenischen bis zur archaischen Zeit* (Prähistorische Bronzefunde 14, II), Munich 1975.
B. Wells, *Asine II. Results of the Excavations East of the Acropolis 1970-1974*. Fasc. 4: *The Protogeometric Period*, Part 1: *The Tombs*, Stockholm 1976.
Eadem, *ibid.*, Fasc. 4: *The Protogeometric Period*, Part 2: *An Analysis of the Setting*. With an Appendix by B. Hulthen and S. Olsson,

Stockholm 1983. Part 3: *Catalogue of the Pottery and Other Artefacts*, by B. Wells, Stockholm 1983.
M. Sakellariou, "La situation politique en Attique et en Eubée de 1100 à 700 avant J.C.," *REA* 78-79, 1976-1977, 11-21.
E.N. Davis (ed.), *Symposium on the Dark Ages in Greece, Sponsored by the Archaeological Institute of America and Hunter College, City University of New York, April 30, 1977*, New York 1977.
J.C.L. Waldbaum, *From Bronze to Iron: The Transition from the Bronze Age to the Iron Age in the Eastern Mediterranean*, Göteborg 1978.
A.W. Johnston and R.E. Jones, "The 'SOS' Amphora," *BSA* 73, 1978, 103-141.
I. Kilian-Dirlmeier, *Anhänger in Griechenland von der mykenischen Zeit bis zur spätgeometrischen Zeit (griechisches Festland, Ionische Inseln, dazu Albanien und Jugoslavien, Mazedonien)* (Prähistorische Bronzefunde Abt. 11, II), Munich 1979.
A.M. Snodgrass, "Iron and Early Metallurgy in the Mediterranean," in T.A. Wertime and J.D. Muhly (eds.), *The Coming of the Age of Iron*, New Haven and London 1980, 335-374.
M. Popham, L.H. Sackett and P.G. Themelis (eds.), *Lefkandi I: The Iron Age. The Settlement and the Cemeteries* (BSA Suppl. 11), 2 vols., London 1980 [1981] and 1979 (cf. A.M. Snodgrass, *JHS* 102, 1982, 279-280); cf. M. Popham *et al.*, *BSA* 77, 1982, 213-248.
M. Popham, E. Touloupa and L.H. Sackett, "The hero of Lefkandi," *Antiquity* 56, 1982, 169-174.
S. Dietz, *Asine II. Results of the Excavations East of the Acropolis 1970-1974*. Fasc. 1: *General Stratigraphical Analysis and Architectural Remains*, Stockholm 1982.
M. Fortin, "Fondation de villes grecques à Chypre: Légendes et découvertes archéologiques," in J.B. Caron, M. Fortin and G. Maloney (eds.), *Mélanges d'Études Anciennes offerts à Maurice Lebel*, Québec 1980, 25-44.
V. Karageorghis, *Cyprus, from the Stone Age to the Romans*, London 1982, 114-127.
Idem, *Ausgrabungen in Alt-Paphos auf Cypern 3. Palaepaphos-Skales: An Iron Age Cemetery in Cyprus I*, Konstanz 1983.
J. Matthers *et al.*, "Black-on-Red Ware in the Levant," *JArchSc* 10, 1983, 369-382.
W.A. McDonald, W.D.E. Coulson and J. Rosser (eds.), *Excavations at Nichoria in Southwest Greece, III: Dark Age and Byzantine Occupation*, Minneapolis 1983.
R. Hägg (ed.), *The Greek Renaissance of the Eighth Century B.C. Tradition and Innovation: Proceedings of the Second International Symposium at the Swedish Institute in Athens, 1-5 June, 1981*, Stockholm 1983.
S. Deger Jalkotzy (ed.), *Griechenland, die Ägäis und die Levante während der "Dark Ages" vom 12. bis zum 9. Jh. v. Chr. Akten des Symposions von Stift Zwettl (NÖ) 11.-14. Oktober 1980*, Vienna 1983.

W.D.E. Coulson, "The Dark Age Pottery of Sparta," *BSA* 80, 1985, 29-84.
Idem, The Dark Age Pottery of Messenia (SIMA Pocket Book 43), Göteborg 1986.
J. Boardman and C.E. Vaphopoulou-Richardson (eds.), *Chios: A Conference at the Homereion in Chios, 1984*, Oxford 1986.
G. Wickert-Micknat, *Die Frau* (Archaeologia Homerica III R), Göttingen 1982.
Eadem, Unfreiheit im Zeitalter der homerischen Epen (Forschungen zur antiken Sklaverei im Auftrag der Kommission für Geschichte des Altertums der Akademie der Wissenschaften und der Literatur 16), Wiesbaden 1983, cf. *eadem*, "Unfreiheit in der frühgriechischen Gesellschaft: Schwierigkeiten bei der Beschreibung des Phänomens," *Historia* 35, 1986, 129-146.
O.T.P.K. Dickinson, "Homer, the Poet of the Dark Age," *G & R* 33, 1986, 20-37.

390 n. 12 On the influence which the names of these tribes had subsequently among Dorians, see N.F. Jones, "The Order of the Dorian Phylai," *CP* 75, 1980, 197-215.

n. 19 H. Otten, "Zum Ende des Hethiterreiches auf Grund der Boğazköy-Texte," *Jahresbericht des Instituts für Vorgeschichte der Universität Frankfurt a. M.*, 1976 [1977], 22-35.
K. Bittel, "Das Ende des Hethiterreiches auf Grund archäologischer Zeugnisse," *ibid.*, 36-56.

391 n. 22 See also A. Strobel, *Der spätbronzezeitliche Seevölkersturm*, Berlin 1976; G.A. Lehmann, "Die 'Seevölker'-Herrschaften an der Levantküste," *Jahresbericht des Instituts für Vorgeschichte der Universität Frankfurt a. M.*, 1976 [1977], 78-111; cf. W. Helck, "Die Seevölker in den ägyptischen Quellen," *ibid.*, 7-21; and especially N.K. Sandars, *The Sea Peoples: Warriors of the Ancient Mediterranean 1250-1150 B.C.*, London 1978 (cf. S. Hood, *JHS* 99, 1979, 200-201) [[2]1985]; cf. also G.A. Lehmann, "Die Sikalaju—ein neues Zeugnis zu den 'Seevölker'-Herrschaften im späten 13. Jh. v. Chr. (RS 34.129)," *Ugarit-Forschungen 11. Festschrift für Claude Schaeffer zum 80. Geburtstag am 6. März*, Neukirchen 1979, 481-494; *idem*, *Die mykenisch-frühgriechische Welt und der östliche Mittelmeerraum in der Zeit der 'Seevölker'-Invasionen um 1200 v. Chr.*, Opladen 1985 (cf. W. Helck, *Gnomon* 58, 1986, 626-629).

n. 26 A. Wertime and J.D. Muhly (eds.), *The Coming of the Age of Iron*, New Haven and London 1980.

n. 33 See also now, in particular, H.G. Niemeyer (ed.), *Phönizier im Westen* (Madrider Berträge 8), Mainz 1982; *idem*, "Die Phönizier und die Mittelmeerwelt im Zeitalter Hermes," *JRGZM* 31, 1984, 3-94;

J.D. Muhly, "Phoenicia and Phoenicians," in J. Amitas (ed.), *Biblical Archaeology Today: Proceedings of the International Congress on Biblical Archaeology Jerusalem, April 1984*, Jerusalem 1985, 177-191 (cf. the remarks by M. Bietak, *ibid.*, 215-216, as well as by O. Negbi, *ibid.*, 221-222).

392 n. 39 B.S.J. Isserlin, "The Antiquity of the Greek Alphabet," *Kadmos* 22, 1983, 151-163.
M. Bernal, "On the Transmission of the Alphabet to the Aegean Before 1400 B.C.," *BASOR* 267, 1987, 1-19.

n. 44 See also J.V. Luce, *Homer and the Heroic Tradition*, London 1975 (which is, however, too optimistic on the reliability of the epic tradition).

393 n. 46 See also S. Hiller, "Der Becher des Nestor," *Antike Welt* 7,1, 1976, 22-31.

n. 54 C.G. Thomas, "From Wanax to Basileus: Kingship in the Greek Dark Age," *Hispania Antiqua* 6, 1978, 187-206. R. Drews, *Basileus. The Evidence for Kingship in Geometric Greece*, New Haven and London 1983, raises many pertinent questions in his highly critical study, but he does not explain how the Greek tradition about kings and kingship in early times arose. For instance, if kingship never existed at the time, why did the Greeks create the legends of it? Cf. P. Carlier, *La royauté en Grèce avant Alexandre* (Études et travaux publiés par le Groupe de recherche d'histoire romaine, Strasbourg 6), Strasbourg 1984; and D. Knoepfler, "La royauté grecque," *REG* 99, 1986, 332-341.

3. THE GREEK COLONISATION (800-500 BC)

395 The Beginning of Greek Individualism

Sources: See the helpful discussions in M. Crawford (ed.), *Sources for Ancient History*. With contributions by E. Gabba, F. Millar and A. Snodgrass, Cambridge 1983, covering the topics Literature, Epigraphy, Archaeology and Numismatics.
For a selection of sources in translation, see C.W. Fornara (ed.), *Archaic Times to the End of the Peloponnesian War* (Translated Documents of Greece and Rome 1), Baltimore, Ma., and London 1977 [[2]1983].

Delphi: G. Roux, *Delphes. Son oracle et ses dieux*, Paris 1976.
J. Fontenrose, *The Delphic Oracle. Its Response and Operations, with a Catalogue of Responses*, Berkeley, Los Angeles, London 1978 (cf. J. Pollard, *JHS* 101, 1981, 182-183).

397 **The Orient and the Rise of Greek States**

Tyrtaeus: W.K. Pritchett, "The Topography of Tyrtaios and the Messenian Wars," in *idem*, *Studies in Ancient Greek Topography* V, Berkeley, Los Angeles, London 1985, 1-68.

398 **Al Mina:** M. Popham *et al.*, "Al Mina and Euboea," *BSA* 75, 1980, 151-161.

399 Very useful as a general survey is L. Jeffery, *Archaic Greece. The City-States, c. 700-500 B.C.*, London 1976.
Also worth consulting is R.J. Hopper, *The Early Greeks*, London 1976.
A. Snodgrass, *Archaic Greece. The Age of Experiment*, London 1980.
M. Sordi, *Storia politica del mondo greco*, Milan 1982.
C.G. Starr, *The Economic and Social Growth of Early Greece, 800-500 B.C.*, New York 1977.
Idem, *Individual and Community: the Rise of the Polis 800-500 B.C.*, New York 1986.
M. Sakellariou, "La Grecia continentale ed insulare nei secoli VIII e VII a.C.," *ASAtene* 43 1981 [1983], 17-26.
G. Wickert-Micknat, *Unfreiheit im Zeitalter der homerischen Epen* (Forschungen zur antiken Sklaverei, im Auftrag der Kommission für Geschichte des Altertums der Akademie der Wissenschaften und der Literatur herausgegeben von J. Vogt und H. Bellen Bd. 16), Wiesbaden 1983.
See also H. van Effenterre, *La cité grecque*, Paris 1985.

Argos: T. Kelly, *A History of Argos to 500 B.C.* (Minnesota Monographs in the Humanities 9), Minneapolis 1976.

The Expansion of the Greeks in the Mediterranean World: There are a number of useful general surveys:
L. Jeffery, *Archaic Greece. The City-States, c. 700-500 B.C.*, London 1976.
A. Snodgrass, *Archaic Greece: The Age of Experiment*, London 1980.
There are also the numerous contributions in J. Boardman and N.G.L. Hammond (eds.), *CAH* III ^{3}2, *The Expansion of the Greek World, Eighth to Sixth Centuries B.C.*, Cambridge 1982, with extensive bibliography (471-512).
P. Oliva, "Kolonisation als Phänomen der frühgriechischen Geschichte," *Eirene* 19, 1980, 5-16.
W. Leschhorn, *'Gründer der Stadt': Studien zu einem politisch-religiösen Phänomen der griechischen Geschichte* (Palingenesia 20), Stuttgart 1984, 6-117.

400 On **Eusebius**, see A.A. Mosshammer, *The Chronicle of Eusebius and Greek Chronographic Tradition*, Lewisburg and London 1979.

401 **The Scythians:** A.P. Smirnov, *Die Skythen*, Dresden 1979.
A.M. Khazanov, "The Dawn of Scythian History," *Iranica Antiqua* 17, 1982, 49-63.

A. Häusler, "Zur Sozialstruktur der Skythen, Forschungsbericht," *Ethnographisch-archäologische Zeitschrift* 25, 1984, 437-444.
T. Sulimirski, "The Scyths," in I. Gershevitch (ed.), *The Cambridge History of Iran 2: The Median and Achaemenian Periods*, Cambridge 1985, 149-199.
B. Isaac, *The Greek Settlements in Thrace until the Macedonian Conquests* (Studies of the Dutch Archaeological and Historical Society 10), Leiden 1986.

Phrygian Connections: K. DeVries, "Greeks and Phrygians in the Early Iron Age," in K. DeVries (ed.), *From Athens to Gordion. The Papers of a Memorial Symposium for Rodney S. Young, held at the University Museum, May 3, 1975* (University Museum Papers 1), Philadelphia 1980, 33-49.
C. Brixhe and M. Lejeune, *Corpus des inscriptions paléophrygiennes* (Recherches sur les Civilisations Mémoire 45), 2 vols., Paris 1984.

North Africa: J. Boardman and J. Hayes, *Excavations at Tocra 1963-1965. The Archaic Deposits, II and Later Deposits* (The Society for Libyan Studies, Suppl. 10), London 1973.
G. Barker, J. Lloyd and J. Reynolds (eds.), *Cyrenaica in Antiquity* (Society for Libyan Studies, Occasional Papers 1) (BAR Intern. Ser. 236), Oxford 1985.

402 **Greeks on the Black Sea:** D.M. Pippidi, *Scythica minora. Recherches sur les colonies grecques du littoral roumain de la Mer Noire*, Bucharest 1975.
A.X. Kocybala, *Greek Colonization on the North Shore of the Black Sea in the Archaic Period*, Diss. Univ. of Pennsylvania 1978.
J. Vinogradov, "Griechische Epigraphik und Geschichte des nördlichen Pontosgebietes," in D.M. Pippidi (ed.), *Actes du VIIe Congrès intern. d'épigraphie grecque et latine, Constantza, 9-15 septembre 1977*, Bucharest 1979, 293-316.

Southern Italy: S.C. Bakhuizen, *Chalcis-in-Euboea. Iron and the Chalcidians Abroad* (Chalcidian Studies 3), Leiden 1976.
Idem, "Le nom de Chalcis et la colonisation chalcidienne," in *Nouvelle contribution à l'étude de la société de la colonisation eubéennes* (Cahiers du Centre Jean-Bérard 6), Naples 1981, 161-174.
M.R. Popham, "Why Euboea?," *ASAtene* 43, 1981 [1983], 237-239.
G. Buchner, "Pithekoussai: alcuni aspetti peculiari," *ibid.*, 263-273.
H. van Effenterre, "La fondation de Paestum," *PP* 35, 1980, 161-175.
G. Pugliese Carratelli, "Magna Grecia e Sicilia nei secoli VIII e VII a.C.," *ASAtene* 43, 1981 [1983], 29-42.
A. Di Vita, "L'urbanistica più antica delle colonie di Magna Grecia e di Sicilia: problemi e reflessioni," *ibid.*, 63-78.
G. Nenci and G. Vallet (eds.), *Bibliografia topografica della colonizzazione greca in Italia e nelle isole tirreniche, II. Opere di carattere generale (1976-1980), Addenda (1537-1980)*, Pisa 1981.

C. Sabbione, "Le aree di colonizzazione di Crotone e Locri Epizefiri nell'VIII e VII sec. a.C.," *ASAtene* 44, 1982 [1984], 251-298.
R. Bosi, *Magna Graecia. Die griechischen Städte in Spanien, Frankreich, Italien, Jugoslavien, Albanien*, Freiburg, Basle, Vienna 1982 (cf. S. Steingräber, *BonJahrb* 184, 1984, 720-722).
G. de Sensi Sestito, *La Calabria in età arcaica e classica. Storia—Economia—Società*, Rome and Reggio di Calabria 1984.
D. Musti, "Città di Magna Grecia II: L'idea de *megale Hellas*," *RivFil* 114, 1986, 286-319.
A useful survey covering both southern Italy and Sicily is provided by F. Cordano, *Antiche fondazioni greche. Sicilia e Italia meridionale*, Palermo 1986 (cf. B.E. McConnell, *AJA* 92, 1988, 296-298).

Sicily: N. Allegro, *Himera II. Campagne di scavo 1966-1973*, Rome 1976.
G. Fiorentini and E. De Miro, "Gela protoarcaica," *ASAtene* 45, 1983 [1984]: ("Dati, topografici, archeologici e cronologici": 53-73; "Dati storico-artistici": 73-106).
As a general survey, Boardman's study is available in a new edition: J. Boardman, *The Greeks Overseas: Their Early Colonies and Trade*, London [3]1980.

Spain: P. Cabrera and R. Olmos, "Die Griechen in Huelva. Zum Stand der Diskussion," *Madrider Mitteilungen* 26, 1985, 61-74.
Y.B. Tsirkin, "The Greeks and Tartessos," in I. Hahn *et al.* (eds.), *Oikumene. Studia ad Historiam Antiquam Classicam et Orientalem Spectantia* 5, Budapest 1986, 163-171.

The West: W. Kimming, "Die griechische Kolonisation im westlichen Mittelmeergebiet und ihre Wirkung auf die Landschaften des westlichen Mitteleuropa," *JRGZM* 30, 1983, 3-78.

403 n. 2 See the first volume of the final publication: R.S. Young *et al.*, *The Gordion Excavations. Final Reports I: Three Great Early Tumuli* (Univ. Mus. Monogr. 43), Philadelphia 1981.

n. 5 A. Spalinger, "The Death of Gyges and its Historical Implications," *JAOS* 98, 1978, 400-409.

n. 6 Very useful information on the capital, Sardis, is emerging from the extensive American investigations. Cf., for instance, J.G. Pedley, *Archaeological Exploration of Sardis. Report II: Ancient Literary Sources on Sardis*, Cambridge, Mass., 1972; G.M.A. Hanfmann and J.C. Waldbaum, *Archaeological Exploration of Sardis I: A Survey of Sardis and the Major Monuments outside the City Walls*, Cambridge, Mass., 1975; G.M.A. Hanfmann and N.H. Ramage, *Archaeological Exploration of Sardis II: Sculpture from Sardis. The Finds through 1975*, Cambridge, Mass., 1978, 1-52; A. Ramage, *Archaeological Exploration of Sardis V: Lydian Houses and Architectural Terracottas*,

Cambridge, Mass., 1978 (cf. M.F. Billot, *RevArch* 1982, 263-294); G.M.A. Hanfmann, "On Lydian Sardis," in K. DeVries (ed.), *From Athens to Gordion. The Papers of a Memorial Symposium for Rodney S. Young, held at the University Museum, May 3, 1975*, Philadelphia 1980, 99-131; J.C. Waldbaum, *Archaeological Exploration of Sardis VIII: Metalwork from Sardis. The Finds through 1974*, Cambridge, Mass., 1983; see also the excellent synthesis: G.M.A. Hanfmann, *Sardis from Prehistoric to Roman Times. Results of the Archaeological Exploration of Sardis 1958-1975*, Cambridge, Mass., 1983; and the more recent preliminary reports by C.H. Greenwalt, Jr., *BASOR* 228, 1977, 47-59; 233, 1979, 1-32; 249, 1983, 1-44; G.M.A. Hanfmann, "Les nouvelles fouilles de Sardes," *CRAI* 1985, 497-519. C.H. Greenwalt, Jr., *et al.*, *The Sardis Campaign of 1984* and *The Sardis Campaign of 1985* (BASOR Suppl. 25), Baltimore, Md., 1987.

n. 8 I.M. Diakonoff, "The Cimmerians," *Acta Iranica* 21, 1981, 103-140, denies that the Cimmerians were an ethnic entity, preferring to see them as a military grouping; cf. I.V. Kuklina, "The Early Evidence on the Scythians and Cimmerians," *VDI* 156, 1981, 162-173 [Russ., with an Eng. summary].

n. 10 J.M. Cook, "On the Date of Alyattes' Sack of Smyrna," *BSA* 80, 1985, 25-28.

n. 12 J. Elayi and A. Cavigneaux, "Sargon II et les Ioniens," *OpAth* 18, 1979, 59-75.

n. 16 A. Spalinger, "Psammetichus, King of Egypt, I," *Journal of the American Research Center in Egypt* 13, 1976, 133-147.

n. 18 J. Boardman, *The Greeks Overseas*, London [3]1980, 117-135. See also W.D.E. Coulson and A. Leonard, Jr., "A preliminary survey of the Naukratis region in the western Nile Delta," *JFA* 6, 1979, 151-168; *iidem*, *Cities of the Delta, Part I: Naukratis* (American Research Center in Egypt Reports 4), Malibu, Ca. 1981.

405 n. 58 The War is contested by N. Robertson, "The Myth of the First Sacred War," *CQ* 28, 1978, 38-73, but cf. E.W. Kase and G.J. Szenler, "The Amphiktyonic League and the First Sacred War: a New Perspective," in J. Harmatta (ed.), *Actes du VIIe congrès de la Fédération Internationale des Associations d'Études classiques* I, Budapest 1984, 107-116. See also G.A. Lehmann, "Der 'erste Heilige Krieg'—eine Fiktion?," *Historia* 29, 1980, 242-246.

406 n. 60 Of some use are M.I. Finley and H.W. Pleket, *The Olympic Games: The First Thousand Years*, London 1976, and E.J. Holmberg, *Delphi and Olympia* (SIMA Pocket Book 10), Göteborg 1979.

n. 63 R. Martin, "Relations entre métropoles et colonies. Aspects institutionnels," in *Studi di storia antica offerti dagli allievi a Eugeno Manni* IV, Rome 1976, 1433-1445.

n. 70 M. Popham, "Al Mina and Euboea," *BSA* 75, 1980, 151-161; M. Popham, A.M. Pollard and H. Hatcher, "Euboean Exports to Al Mina, Cyprus, and Crete: a Reassessment," *BSA* 78, 1983, 281-290. See also the discussion by E.D. Francis and M. Vickers, "Greek Geometric Pottery at Hama and its Implications for Near Eastern Chronology," *Levant* 17, 1985, 131-138.
M. Frederiksen, *Campania*, London 1984, 54-116, esp. 54-84. On **Neapolis**, see E. Rozzi (ed.), *Napoli antica*, Naples 1985.

n. 72 On **Megara Hyblaea**, see G. Vallet, "Bilan des recherches à Megara Hyblaea," *ASAtene* 44, 1982 [1984], 173-181.

n. 73 See also D. Ridgway, "The foundation of Pithekoussai," in *Nouvelle contribution à l'étude de la société et de la colonisation eubéennes* (Cahiers du Centre Jean-Bérard 6), Naples 1981, 45-59; *idem*, "The Eighth Century Pottery at Pithekoussai: An Interim Report," in *La céramique grecque ou de tradition grecque en Italie centrale et méridionale* (Cahiers du Centre Jean-Bérard 3), Naples 1982, 69-101; *idem*, *L'Alba della Magna Grecia* (Archeologia 7), Milan 1984. Cf. M.R. Popham, "Why Euboea?," *ASAtene* 43, 1981 [1983], 237-239.

n. 76 Cf. P. Pelagatti, "Siracusa. Elementi dell'abitato di Ortigia nell'VIII e VII secolo a.C.," *Cranache di archeologia e di storia dell'arte* 17, 1978, 119-133; *idem*, "Siracusa: Le ultimi ricerche in Ortigia," *ASAtene* 44, 1982 [1984], 117-162.

n. 78 On a specific aspect of the War, see S.D. Lambert, "A Thucydidean Scholium on the 'Lelantine War'," *JHS* 102, 1982, 216-220. See also C. Bearzot, "La guerra lelantea e il *koinon* degli Ioni d'Asia," in M. Sordi (ed.), *Santuari e politica nel mondo antico*, Milan 1983, 57-81.

407 n. 82 On **Tarentum**, see G. Bauer, Jr., *Taras: Its History and Coinage*, New Rochelle and New York 1986.
On **Locri Epizephyrii**, see R. van Compernolle, "Le tradizioni sulla fondazione e sulla storia arcaica di Locri Epizefiri e la propaganda politica alla fine del V e nel IV secolo av. Cr.," *Annali della Scuola Normale Superiore di Pisa* 6, 1976, 329-400; D. Musti, "Problemi della storia di Locri Epizefiri," in *Locri Epizefiri. Atti del XVI Convegno di studi sulla Magna Grecia, Taranto 3-8 ottobre 1976*, Naples 1977, 23-146; and C. Sabbione, "Le aree di colonizzazione di Crotone e Locri Epizefiri nell' VIII e VII sec. a.C.," *ASAtene* 44, 1982 [1984], 251-298. On **Sybaris**, see P.G. Guzzo, "La Sibaritide e Sibari nell' VII sec. a.C.," *ibid.*, 237-250. On **Metapontum**, see G.F. Lo Porto, "Metaponto (Matera), Nuovi 'scavi nella città' e nella sua necropoli," *Notizie degli Scavi di Antichità* 35, 1981, 289-391; D. Musti, "Città di Magna Grecia: I. Metaponto: note sulla tradizione storica," *RivFil* 111, 1983, 265-291; and S.P. Noe, *The Coinage of Metapontum*, Parts

1 and 2, with additions and corrections by A. Johnston (The American Numismatic Society Notes and Monographs, Nos. 32 and 47), New York 1984. On **Croton**, see W. Goegebeur, "Hérodote et la fondation achéenne de Crotone," *AC* 54, 1985, 116-151.

n. 90 J.G. Chamorro, "Survey of Archaeological Research on Tartessos," *AJA* 91, 1987, 197-232.

n. 91 Of great interest is the discovery of a Phocaean 1/24 electrum stater ca. 7 km north of Seville, near the site of El Carambolo, dating from ca. the middle of the sixth century BC—the first Greek coin known from southern Spain (cf. A.E. Furtwängler, "Auf den Spuren eines ionischen Tartessos-Besuchers. Bemerkungen zu einem Neufund," *MDAI(A)* 92, 1977, 61-70).

n. 92 M. Clavel-Lévêque, *Marseille grecque. La dynamique d'un impérialisme marchand*, Marseille 1977.

n. 94 On **Maenace**, see H.G. Niemeyer, "Auf der Suche nach Mainake. Der Konflikt zwischen literarischer und archäologischer Überlieferung," with an Addendum by B.W. Treumann, "Mainake—Originally a Phoenician Placename?," *Historia* 29, 1980, 165-189.

408 n. 95 Cf. N. Ehrhardt, *Milet und seine Kolonien. Vergleichende Untersuchung der kultischen und politischen Einrichtungen*, Frankfurt a. M. and Bern 1983; cf. *idem*, "Probleme der griechischen Kolonisation am Beispiel der milesischen Gründungen," *Eos* 73, 1985, 81-99.

n. 96 R. Drews, "The Earliest Greek Settlements on the Black Sea," *JHS* 96, 1976, 18-31, plausibly argues that the first colonising activity on the Black Sea was designed to gain access to the metals of the Pontic region.

n. 97 I.V. Kuklina, "The Early Evidence on the Scythians and Cimmerians," *VDI* 156, 1981, 162-173 [Russ., with an Eng. summary].

n. 98 L.V. Kopejkina, "The Peculiarities of the Development of the Berezan Settlement of the Archaic period," *Sovietskaja Archeologija* [Moscow] 1981, 1, 193-208 [Russ. with an Eng. summary].

n. 99 A. Wasowicz, *Olbia pontique et son territoire. L'aménagement de l'espace* (Annales Littéraires de l'Université de Besançon 13), Paris 1975; and S.D. Kryzickij and A.S. Rus'ajeva, "Les plus anciennes habitations d'Olbia," *Dialogue d'histoire ancienne* 6, 1980, 73-100; J. Vinogradov, *Olbia. Geschichte einer altgriechischen Stadt am Schwarzen Meer* (Xenia 1), Konstanz 1981.

n. 102 On **Heracleia**, see S.M. Burnstein, *Outpost of Hellenism: The Emergence of Heracleia on the Black Sea* (Univ. of Calif. Clas. Stud. 14), Berkeley 1976.

n. 105 See also R. Martin, "Thasos colonie de Paros," *ASAtene* 45, 1983 [1984], 171-177.

n. 111 See also L.J. Bartson, *Cyrenaica in Antiquity*, Diss. Harvard University, Cambridge, Mass., 1982; and R.G. Goodchild, J.G. Pedley and D. White, *Apollonia, the Port of Cyrene: Excavations by the University of Michigan 1965-1967*, with contributions by T.V. Buttrey, R.M. Harrison, J. Reynolds, J.B. Ward-Perkins and G.R.H. Wright (The Society for Libyan Antiquities Suppl. 4), Tripoli 1978; cf. R.G. Goodchild, *Kyrene und Apollonia*, Feldmeilen 1978.

4. POLITICS AND SOCIETY IN THE COLONISATION PERIOD

410 See also H. Qviller, "The Dynamics of the Homeric Society," *SO* 56, 1981, 109-155.
A useful background to an important aspect of the rise of the Greek states is provided by R. Osborne, *Classical Landscape with Figures. The Ancient Greek City and Its Countryside*, Dobbs Ferry, N.Y., 1987. For a selection of sources in translation, see C.W. Fornara (ed.), *Archaic Times to the End of the Peloponnesian War* (Translated Documents of Greece and Rome 1), Baltimore, Ma., and London, 1977 [^{2}1983].

411 On the **Great Rhetra**, see E. Levy, "La Grande Rhetra," *Ktema* 2, 1977, 85-103.
F. de Polignac, *La naissance de la cité grecque: cultes, espace et société VIIIe-VIIe siècle avant J.-C.*, Paris 1984 (cf. I. Malkin, *JHS* 107, 1987, 227-228).
See also H. van Effenterre, *La cité grecque*, Paris 1985.
W.R. Connor, "Tribes, festivals and processions: civic ceremonial and political manipulation in archaic Greece," *JHS* 107, 1987, 40-50.

412 **The Spartan Constitution:** K.-W. Welwei, "Die spartanische Phylenordnung im Spiegel der Grossen Rhetra und des Tyrtaios," *Gymnasium* 86, 1979, 178-196.
D.M. MacDowell, *Spartan Law* (Scottish Classical Studies 1), Edinburgh 1986.

The *Boulé démosié* at Chios: C. Ampolo, "La BOULE DEMOSIE di Chio: un consiglio 'popolare'?," *PP* 38, 1983, 401-416.

413 **Coinage:** H.A. Cahn, "Asiut: kritische Bemerkungen zu einer Schatzfundpublikation," *SNR* 56, 1977, 279-287.
J.H. Kroll, "From Wappenmünzen to Gorgoneia to Owls," *AmerNumSoc Notes* 26, 1981, 1-32 (represents the new orthodoxy viewpoint). Meanwhile, Kagan, building on the study of Lieselotte Wei-

dauer, *Probleme der frühen Elektronprägung*, Friburg 1975, has argued for more traditional dates: D. Kagan, "The Dates of the Earliest Coins," *AJA* 86, 1982, 343-360. Cf. the reply of J.H. Kroll and N.M. Waggoner, "Dating the Earliest Coins of Athens, Corinth and Aegina," *AJA* 88, 1984, 325-340; R.R. Holloway, "The Date of the First Greek Coins," *RevBelNum* 130, 1984, 5-17; and the study of M. Vickers, "Early Greek Coinage, a Reassessment," *NumChron* 145, 1985, 1-44, who adopts an even more radical point of view, cf. *idem*, "Persépolis, Athènes et Sybaris: questions de monnayage et de chronologie," *REG* 99, 1986, 239-270.

P. Spahn, "Die Anfänge der antiken Ökonomik," *Chiron* 14, 1984, 301-323, discusses the theoretical framework.

See also R. Carson, P. Berghaus and N. Lowick (eds.), *A Survey of Numismatic Research 1972-1977*, Bern 1979.

W. Gentner, O. Müller, G.A. Wagner and N.H. Gale, "Silver Sources of Archaic Greek Coinage," *Die Naturwissenschaften* 64, 1978, 273-284.

C. Boehringer, "Die frühen Bronzemünzen von Leontini und Katane," in *Le origini della monetazione di bronzo in Sicilia e in Magna Grecia. Atti del VI Convegno del centro internazionale di studi numismatici (Napoli 17-22 aprile 1977)*, Rome 1979 [1980], 145-176.

F. Bodenstedt, *Die Elektronmünzen von Phokaia und Mytilene*, Tübingen 1981.

Hoards: M. Thompson, O. Mørkholm and C.M. Kraay, "An Inventory of Greek Coin Hoards. A Discussion," *Annali dell'Istituto Italiano di Numismatica* 23-24, 1976-1977 [1979], 319-323.

C.M. Kraay and P.R.S. Moorey, "A Black Sea Hoard of the Late Fifth Century B.C.," *NumChron* 21, 1981, 1-19.

414 **Sparta:** See also D.M. Lewis, *Sparta and Persia. Lectures delivered at the University of Cincinnati, Autumn 1976 in Memory of Donald W. Bradeen*, Leiden 1977, 27-49.

P. Cartledge, *Sparta and Laconia. A Regional History 1300-362 B.C.*, London 1979 (cf. F. Kiechle, *CR* 31, 1981, 79-81).

K. Bringmann, "Die soziale und die politische Verfassung Spartas—ein Sonderfall der griechischen Verfassungsgeschichte?," *Gymnasium* 87, 1980, 465-484.

G.L. Huxley, "Problems in the Chronography of Eusebius," *Proc. Royal Irish Acad.* 81, C. No. 7, 1982, 183-196.

J.F. Lazenby, *The Spartan Army*, Warminster 1985.

Athenian Constitution: Valuable is P.J. Rhodes, *A Commentary on the Aristotelian 'Athenaion Politeia,'* Oxford 1981 (cf. M.H. Hansen, "The History of the Athenian Constitution. A Review Article," *CP* 80, 1985, 51-66).

See also P.J. Rhodes, *'The Athenian Constitution.' Translation with Introduction and Notes*, Harmondsworth 1984.

For a new edition of the text (Teubner), see M. Chambers, *Aristoteles' ATHENAION POLITEIA*, Leipzig 1986.
E. Ruschenbusch, *Untersuchungen zu Staat und Politik in Griechenland vom 7.-4. Jh. v. Chr.*, Bamberg 1978 (cf. D.M. Lewis, *CR* 30, 1980, 77-78).
R.T. Ridley, "The Hoplite as Citizen. Athenian Military Institutions in their Social Context," *AC* 48, 1979, 508-548.
W. Gawantka, *Die sogenannte Polis. Zur Entstehung, Geschichte und Kritik der modernen althistorischen Grundbegriffe, der griechische Staat, die griechische Staatsidee, die Polis*, Wiesbaden and Stuttgart 1985 (cf. K.-W. Welwei, *Gymnasium* 94, 1987, 267-269).
K.-W. Welwei, *Die griechische Polis. Verfassung und Gesellschaft in archaischer und klassischer Zeit*, Stuttgart 1983.
R.W. Wallace, *The Areopagus, from the Origins to 307 B.C.*, Diss. Harvard University, Cambridge, Mass., 1984.
See also J.D. Mikalson, *The Sacred and Civil Calendar of the Athenian Year*, Princeton, N.J., 1975.
R. Sealey, *The Athenian Republic. Democracy or the Rule of Law?*, University Park, Pa., 1987.

Tyrannis: See also K.H. Kinzl, "Betrachtungen zur älteren Tyrannis," in K.H. Kinzl (ed.), *Die ältere Tyrannis bis zu den Perserkriegen: Beiträge zur griechischen Tyrannis* (Wege der Forschung DX), Darmstadt 1979, 298-325.
K. Raaflaub, "Zum Freiheitsbegriff der Griechen. Materialen und Untersuchungen zur Bedeutungsentwicklung von eleutheros/eleutheria in der archaischen und klassischen Zeit," in E.C. Welskopf (ed.), *Soziale Typenbegriffe im alten Griechenland und ihr Fortleben in den Sprachen der Welt, IV: Untersuchungen ausgewählter altgriechischen Typenbegriffe und ihr Fortleben in Antike und Mittelalter*, Berlin 1981, 180-405.
P. Oliva, "The Early Tyranny," *Dialogues d'histoire anciennes* 8, 1982, 363-380.
W. Leschhorn, *'Gründer der Stadt': Studien zu einem politisch-religiösen Phänomen der griechischen Geschichte* (Palingenesia 20), Stuttgart 1984, 118-128.
R. Bernhardt, "Die Entstehung der Legende von der tyrannenfeindlichen Aussenpolitik Spartas im sechsten und fünften Jahrhundert v. Chr.," *Historia* 36, 1987, 257-289.

416 **Sparta:** W.G. Forrest, *A History of Sparta 950-192 B.C.*, London ^{2}1980.
J.T. Hooker, *The Ancient Spartans*, London 1980.
K.L. Noethlichs, "Bestechung, Bestechlichkeit und die Rolle des Geldes in der spartanischen Aussen- und Innenpolitik vom 7.-2. Jh. v. Chr.," *Historia* 36, 1987, 129-170.

Megara: R.P. Legon, *Megara. The Political History of a Greek City-State to 336 B.C.*, Ithaca and London 1981.

Other Districts: H.-J. Gehrke, *Jenseits von Athen und Sparta. Das Dritte Griechenland und seine Staatenwelt*, Munich 1986.

n. 2 J. Vogt, "Die Sklaverei im antiken Griechenland," *Antike Welt* 9,2, 1978, 49-56. Vogt's *Ancient Slavery and the Ideal of Humanity* is available in a second edition, in German: *Sklaverei und Humanität. Studien zur antiken Sklaverei und ihrer Erforschung, Ergänzungsheft zur 2. erweiterten Auflage*, Wiesbaden 1983. Vogt's first edition is attacked by M.I. Finley, *Slavery and Modern Ideology*, New York 1980.
On **slavery**, see also Y. Garlan, *Les Esclaves en Grèce ancienne*, Paris 1982; J. Vogt and H. Bellen (eds.), *Bibliographie zur Antiken Sklaverei*. Revised by E. Herrmann in cooperation with N. Brockmeyer, two parts, Bochum 1983; and the relevant sections in G.E.M. de Ste. Croix, *The Class Struggle in the Ancient Greek World from the Archaic Age to the Arab Conquests*, London 1981.

417 n. 4 N.T.W. Arnheim, *Aristocracy in Ancient Greek Society*, London 1977.
Cf. K.-W. Welwei, "Adel und Demos in der frühen Polis," *Gymnasium* 88, 1981, 1-23.

n. 7 C. Bearzot, "La guerra lelantea e il koinon degli Ioni d'Asia," *Contributi dell'Istituto di Storia antica* (Milan) 9, 1983, 57-81.

n. 19 R. van Compernolle, *Gründung und frühe Gesetzgebung von Lokroi Epizephyrioi* (Xenia 2), Konstanz 1982.
See also M. Gagerin, *Early Greek Law*, Berkeley, Los Angeles, London 1986.
R. Garner, *Law and Society in Classical Athens*, London 1987.

418 n. 29 See M. McGregor, "Cleisthenes of Sicyon and the Panhellenic Festivals," *TAPA* 72, 1941, 266 ff., who contests Bury's thesis that the tyrants were the founders of the major Panhellenic games. See also M. Sordi, "Clistene di Sicione e Delfi," *Aevum* 53, 1979, 5-10.

n. 31 M. Stahl, "Tyrannis und das Problem der Macht. Die Geschichten Herodots über Kypselos und Periander von Korinth," *Hermes* 111, 1983, 202-220.

n. 33 J.B. Salmon, *Wealthy Corinth: A History of the City to 338 B.C.*, Oxford 1984.

419 n. 49 See also P.A. Rahe, "The Selection of Ephors at Sparta," *Historia* 29, 1980, 385-401; cf. P.J. Rhodes, "The Selection of Ephors at Sparta," *Historia* 30, 1981, 498-502.

420 n. 68 M. Gagarin, *Drakon and Early Athenian Homicide Law*, New Haven and London 1981. On Draco's Law on Homicide, cf. *SEG* 32, 1982, no. 14.

n. 70 H. van Effenterre, "Solon et la terre d'Eleusis," *Revue Intern. des Droits de l'Antiquité* 24, 1977, 91-130; J. Bleicken, *Die athenische Demokratie*, Paderborn, Munich, Vienna, Zurich 1985, 17-21 and 318-320.

n. 74 J.C. Billigmeier and M.S. Dusing, "The Origin and Function of the Naukraroi of Athens. An Etymological and Historical Explanation," *TAPA* 111, 1981, 11-16.

n. 76 On the date, see R.W. Wallace, "The Date of Solon's Reforms," *AJAH* 8, 1983, 81-95.

421 n. 84 See also M.H. Hansen, "The Athenian Heliaia from Solon to Aristotle," *ClMed* 33, 1981-82, 9-47.

422 n. 94 See also R. Stroud, *The Axones and Kyrbeis of Drakon and Solon*, Berkeley, Los Angeles, London 1979; P.J. Rhodes, *A Commentary on the Aristotelian Athenaion Politeia*, Oxford 1981, 131-135; and N. Robertson, "Solon's Axones and Kyrbeis, and the Sixth-Century Background," *Historia* 35, 1986, 147-176. On the **Stoa Basileios**, see T. Leslie Shear, Jr., *Hesp*. 40, 1971, 243-255.

n. 98 A second edition of Lauffer's study was published in 1979.

5. THE GROWTH OF POWER

423 On **Samos**, see also H.J. Kienast, *Die Stadtmauer von Samos* (Samos 15), Bonn 1978.

424 **The Achaemenid Empire**

Sources: E.N. von Voigtländer, *The Besitun Inscription of Darius the Great: Babylonian Version (Corpus Inscriptionum Iranicarum Part 1: Inscriptions of Ancient Iran Vol. II: The Babylonian Versions of the Achaemenian Inscriptions. Text 1)*, London 1978.
R. Schmitt, "Zur babylonischen Version der Besitun-Inschrift," *AfO* 27, 1980, 106-126.
J.C. Greenfield and B. Porten, *The Bisitun Inscription of Darius the Great. Aramaic Version. Text, Translation and Commentary (Corpus Inscriptionum Iranicarum, Part 1: Inscriptions of Ancient Iran, Vol. V: The Aramaic Versions of the Achaemenian Inscriptions, Text 1)*, London 1982.
R. Borger and V. Hinz, "Die Behistun-Inschrift Darius' des Grossen," in O. Kaiser (ed.), *Texte der Umwelt des Alten Testaments* I, Gütersloh 1984, 419-450.
Cf. R. Borger, *Die Chronologie des Darius-Denkmals am Behistun-Felsen* (Nachrichten der Akademie der Wissenschaften in Göttingen 1. Phil.-hist. Kl. 3), Göttingen 1982.
W. Vogelsang, "Four Short Notes on the Bisutun Text and Monument," *Iranica Antiqua* 21, 1986, 121-140.

R.N. Frye, "The 'Aramaic' Inscription on the Tomb of Darius," *Iranica Antiqua* 17, 1982, 85-90.
P. Calmeyer, "Zur Genese altiranischen Motive VII. Die 'statistische Landcharte des Perserreiches'—I," *ArchMitt aus Iran* 15, 1982, 105-187; "II," *ibid.* 16, 1983, 141-222.
R.T. Hallock, "The Evidence of the Persepolis Tablets," in I. Gershevitch (ed.), *The Cambridge History of Iran* 2, Cambridge 1985, 588-609.
M. Mayrhofer, *Supplement zur Sammlung altpersischen Inschriften*, Berlin 1978
See also C.W. Fornara (ed.), *Archaic Times to the End of the Peloponnesian War* (Translated Documents of Greece and Rome 1), Baltimore, Ma., and London 1977 [²1983].

Bibliography

General Works: Olmstead's *History of the Persian Empire* is now superseded by J.M. Cook, *The Persian Empire*, London 1983, specifically designed to bring *History of the Persian Empire* up to date (cf. A. Kuhrt, *JHS* 105, 1985, 211-212).
Burn's *Persia and the Greeks* is now available in a second edition (London 1984) (actually a reprint, but with a valuable "Postscript" by D.M. Lewis, 587-609).
A very useful survey is also provided by R.N. Frye, *The History of Ancient Iran* (Handbuch der Altertumswissenschaft III,7), Munich 1983 (cf. J. Duchesne-Guillemin, *Gnomon* 58, 1986, 133-136).
There are also the various contributions, with bibliographies, in I. Gershevitch (ed.), *The Cambridge History of Iran 2. The Median and Achaemenian Periods*, Cambridge 1985 (cf. J. Wiesehöfer, *Gnomon* 59, 1987, 313-316), which include:
J.M. Cook, "The Rise of the Achaemenids and the Establishment of their Empire," 200-291.
A.R. Burn, "Persia and the Greeks," 292-391.
See, further, D. Stronach, *Pasargadae: A Report of the Excavations Conducted by the British Institute of Persian Studies from 1961 to 1963*, Oxford 1978.
See also A. Kuhrt, "A Brief Guide to Some Recent Work on the Achaemenid Empire," *LCM* 8,10, 1983, 146-153.

Studies on Specific Subjects: M.A. Dandamayev, *Persien unter den ersten Achämeniden* (Beiträge zur Iranistik 8), Wiesbaden 1976.
Idem, *Politticeskaja Istorija Achemenidskoj Derzavy*, Moscow 1985.
D.M. Lewis, *Sparta and Persia*, Leiden 1977, 1-26.
F. Gschnitzer, *Die sieben Perser und das Königtum des Dareios. Ein Beitrag zur Achaimenidengeschichte und zur Herodotanalyse* (SHAW phil.-hist. Klasse 1977,3), Heidelberg 1977.
D. Metzler, "Reichsbildung und Geschichtsbild bei den Achämeniden," in H.G. Kippenberg (ed.), *Seminar 'Die Entstehung der antiken Klassengesellschaft,' Frankfurt 1977*, Frankfurt 1977, 279-312.

J. Hofstetter, *Die Griechen in Persien. Prosopographie bei Griechen im persischen Reich vor Alexander*, Diss. Bern (ArchMitt aus Iran. Ergänzungsband 5), Berlin 1978.
C. Nylander, "Achaemenid Imperial Art," in N.T. Larsen (ed.), *Power and Propaganda: A Symposium in Ancient Empires*, Copenhagen 1979, 345-359.
I. Hoffmann and A. Vorbichler, "Das Kambysesbild bei Herodot," *AfO* 27, 1980, 86-105.
H. Witzel, "Early Eastern Iran and the Atharvaveda," *Persica* 9, 1980, 86-128.
N.G.L. Hammond, "The Extent of Persian Occupation of Thrace," *Chiron* 10, 1980, 53-61.
A. Heuss, "Weltreichbildung im Altertum," *HZ* 232, 1981, 265-326.
P. Briant, *Rois, tributs et paysans. Études sur les formations tributaires du Moyens-Orient ancien* (Centre de Recherches d'Histoire ancienne 43), Paris 1982.
Cf. G. Walser, "Der Tod des Kambyses," in H. Heinen (ed.), *Althistorische Studien Hermann Bengtson zum 70. Geburtstag dargebracht von Kollegen und Schülern* (Historia-Einzelschriften 40), Wiesbaden 1983, 8-23.
G. Walser, *Hellas und Iran. Studien zu den griechisch-persischen Beziehungen vor Alexander* (Erträge der Forschung 209), Darmstadt 1984.
J.M. Balcer, *Sparda by the Bitter Sea: Imperial Interaction in Western Anatolia*, Chico, Ca., 1984.
P. Briant, "La Perse avant l'empire (un état de la question)," *Iranica Antiqua* 19, 1984, 71-118.
Idem, *L'Asie central et les royaumes Proche-Orientaux du premier millénaire (c. VIIIe-IVe siècles avant notre ère)* (Éditions Recherches sur les Civilisations, Mémoire no. 42), Paris 1984.
P. Frei and K. Koch, *Reichsidee und Reichsorganisation im Perserreich* (Orbis Biblicus et Orientalis 55), Freiburg [Switzerland] and Göttingen 1984 (cf. J. Wiesehöfer, *Gnomon* 57, 1985, 565-567).
D.F. Graf, "Greek Tyrants and Achaemenid Politics," in J.W. Eadie and J. Ober (eds.), *The Craft of the Ancient Historian. Essays in honor of Chester G. Starr*, Lanham, New York, London, 1985, 79-123.
H. Koch and D.K. MacKenzie (eds.), *Kunst, Kultur und Geschichte der Achämenidenzeit und ihr Fortleben* (ArchMitt aus Iran Ergänzungsband 10), Berlin 1983, 169-189.
W.M. Sumner, "Achaemenid Settlement in the Persepolis Plain," *AJA* 90, 1986, 3-31.
J.M. Balcer, *Herodotus and Bisutun: Problems in Ancient Persian Historiography* (Historia-Einzelschriften 49), Stuttgart 1987.

425 **Peisistratidae:** K.H. Kinzl (ed.), *Die ältere Tyrannis bis zu den Perserkriegen. Beiträge zur griechischen Tyrannis* (Wege der Forschung DX), Darmstadt 1979.

F. Kolb, "Die Bau-, Religions- und Kulturpolitik der Peisistratiden," *JdAI* 92, 1977, 99-138.
F.J. Frost, "Toward a History of Peisistratid Athens," in J.W. Eadie and J. Ober (eds.), *The Craft of the Ancient Historian. Essays in honor of Chester G. Starr*, Lanham, New York, London, 1985, 57-78.

Cleisthenes: H. van Effenterre, "Clisthène et les mesures de mobilisations," *REG* 89, 1976, 1-17.
A. Andrewes, "Cleisthenes' Reform Bill," *CQ* 27, 1977, 241-248.
R.D. Cromey, "Kleisthenes' Fate," *Historia* 28, 1979, 129-147.
E. Kluwe, "Nochmals zum Problem: Die soziale Zusammensetzung der athenischen Ekklesia und ihr Einfluss auf politische Entscheidungen," *Klio* 59, 1977, 45-81.
M. Osborne, *Naturalization in Athens*, Brussels 1981.
F. Gschnitzer, *Griechische Sozialgeschichte von der mykenischen bis zum Ausgang der klassischen Zeit*, Wiesbaden 1981.
Ch. Meier, *Die Entstehung des Politischen bei den Griechen*, Frankfurt a. M. 1980 (cf. W. Schuller, *Gnomon* 55, 1983, 769-773).
M. Ostwald, *Autonomia: its Genesis and Early History*, Chico, Ca., 1982 (cf. W. Gawantka, *Gnomon* 57, 1985, 563-565).
P. Siewert, *Die Trittyen Attikas und die Heeresreform des Kleisthenes* (Vestigia 33), Munich 1982 (cf. P.J. Rhodes, *JHS* 103, 1983, 203-204, and K.H. Kinzl, *Gymnasium* 93, 1986, 556-558).
G.R. Stanton, "The Tribal Reform of Kleisthenes the Alkmeonid," *Chiron* 14, 1984, 1-41.
R. Osborne, *Demos: The Discovery of Classical Attica*, Cambridge 1985.
E. Kearns, "Change and Continuity in the Religious Structures after Cleisthenes," in P.A. Cartledge and F.D. Harvey (eds.), *Crux. Essays in Greek History presented to G.E.M. de Ste. Croix on his 75th Birthday*, London 1985, 189-207.
W. Gawantka, *Die sogenannte Polis*, Wiesbaden and Stuttgart 1985.
E. David, "A Preliminary Stage of Cleisthenes' Reforms," *Classical Antiquity* 5, 1986, 1-13.
D. Whitehead, *The Demes of Attica 508/7–ca. 250 B.C. A Political and Social Study*, Princeton, N.J., 1986 (cf. M. Errington, *Gnomon* 59, 1987, 712-716).
J.S. Traill, *Demos, and Trittys: Epigraphical and Topographical Studies in the Organisation of Attica*, Toronto 1986.
Meanwhile, Kinzl has mounted a fundamental challenge to the authority of Aristotle's *Ath. Pol.*: K.H. Kinzl, "On the Consequences of Following AP 21.4 (On the Trittyes of Attika)," *The Ancient History Bulletin* 1, 1987, 25-33.

Polycrates: H.J. Kienast, *Die Stadtmauer von Samos* (Samos 15), Bonn 1978.

J. Labarbe, "Polycrate, Amasis et l'anneau," *AC* 53, 1984, 15-34.
G. Shipley, *A History of Samos 800-188 B.C.*, Oxford 1987.

n. 2 J. Cargill, "The Nabonidus Chronicle and the Fall of Lydia," *AJAH* 2, 1977, 97-116, attempts to challenge the date of 547. W. Burkert, "Das Ende des Kroisos: Vorstufen einer herodoteischen Geschichtserzählung," in Chr. Schäublein (ed.), *Catalepton. Festschrift für Bernhard Wyss zum 80. Geburtstag*, Basle 1985, 4-15.

426 n. 6 E.J. Bickerman and H. Tadmor, "Darius I, Pseudo-Smerdis and the Magi," *Athenaeum* 56, 1978, 239-261.
J. Wiesehöfer, *Der Aufstand Gaumatas und die Anfänge Dareios' I.*, Bonn 1978.

427 n. 22 See also J. Bleicken, *Die athenische Demokratie*, Paderborn, Munich, Vienna, Zurich 1985, 21-28 and 320-332.

n. 27 For the new orthodoxy point of view, cf. J.H. Kroll, "From Wappenmünzen to Gorgoneia to Owls," *AmerNumSocNotes* 26, 1981, 1-32.

n. 28 J. Perreault, "Céramique et échanges: les importations attiques au Proche-Orient du VIe au milieu du Ve siècle avant J.-C.—Les données archéologiques," *BCH* 110, 1986, 145-175.

n. 34 B. Fehr, *Die Tyrannentöter: Kann man der Demokratie ein Denkmal setzen?*, Frankfurt am Main 1984.

n. 38 A. Sh. Shabazi, "Darius in Scythia and Scythians in Persepolis," *ArchMitt aus Iran*, 15, 1982, 189-255.

428 n. 41 N.G.L. Hammond, "The Extent of Persian Occupation in Thrace," *Chiron* 10, 1980, 53-61.

429 n. 50 A. Andrewes, "Kleisthenes' Reform Bill," *CQ* 27, 1977, 241-248. On the Eponymous heroes after whom the tribes were named, see U. Kron, *Die zehn attischen Phylenheroen. Geschichte, Mythos, Kult und Darstellungen* (MDAI[A] Beiheft 5), Berlin 1976. For an idea of life on one of the notable demes, see J. Labarbe, *Fouilles de Thorikos I. Les Testimonia*, Ghent 1977. See also J. Bleicken, *Die athenische Demokratie*, Paderborn, Munich, Vienna, Zurich 1985, 28-32 and 321-323.

n. 58 On the Prytaneion, see S.G. Miller, *The Prytaneion: Its Function and Architectural Form*, Berkeley 1978.

n. 59 See also R. Develin, "Cleisthenes and Ostracism: Precedents and Intentions," *Antichthon* 11, 1977, 10-21; C.P. Longo, "La bulé e la procedura dell'ostracismo; considerazioni su Vat. Gr. 1144," *Historia* 29, 1980, 257-281; G.A. Lehmann, "Der Ostrakismos-Entscheid in Athen: von Kleisthenes zur Ära des Themistokles," *ZPE* 41, 1981,

85-99; J. Bleicken, *Die athenische Demokratie*, Paderborn, Munich, Vienna, Zurich 1985, 32-33 and 323-324.

6. THE PERSIAN WARS

432 **Sources**

Herodotus: J.G. MacQueen, "The Assyrioi Logoi of Herodotus and their Position in the Histories," *CQ* 28, 1978, 284-291.
S. Zawadzki, "Herodotus' Assyrian History," *Eos* 72, 1984, 233-267.

433 Fornara's date for Herodotus' publication is opposed by J. Cobet, "Wann würde Herodots Darstellung der Perserkriege publiziert?," *Hermes* 105, 1977, 2-27, as well as by J.A.S. Evans, "Herodotus' Publication Date," *Athenaeum* 57, 1979, 145-149; cf. C.W. Fornara, "Herodotus' Knowledge of the Archidamian War," *Hermes* 109, 1981, 149-156.

435 R. Toelle-Kastenbein, *Herodot und Samos*, Bochum 1976.
P. Hohti, *The Interrelation of Speech and Action in the Histories of Herodotus*, Helsinki 1976.
M.L. Lang, *Herodotean Narrative and Discourse*, Cambridge, Mass., and London 1984.
G.E.M. de Ste. Croix, "Herodotus," *G & R* 24, 1977, 130-148.
As introductions to Herodotus, the following may be consulted:
J. Hart, *Herodotus and Greek History*, New York 1982.
J.A.S. Evans, *Herodotus*, Boston 1982.
G. Bockisch, "Herodot. Geschichten- und Geschichtsschreiber," *Klio* 66, 1984, 488-501.
The book by K.H. Waters, *Herodotus the Historian: his Problems, Methods and Originality*, Norman, Okl., 1985, is less satisfactory (cf. K.H. Kinzl, *Classical Views* 30, 1986, 305-306, and J. Cobet, *Gnomon* 58, 1986, 545-546).
W. Nicolai, *Versuch über Herodots Geschichtsphilosophie*, Heidelberg 1986.
For a recent brief synthesis on Herodotus, with a limited bibliography, see H.R. Immerwahr, "Herodotus," in P.E. Easterling and B.M.W. Knox (eds.), *The Cambridge History of Classical Literature* I, Cambridge 1985, 426-441.
D.M. Lewis, "Persians in Herodotus," in M.H. Jameson (ed.), *The Greek Historians: Literature and History: Papers Presented to A.E. Raubitschek*, Saratoga, Ca., 1985, 101-117.
S. West, "Herodotus' Epigraphical Interests," *CQ* 35, 1985, 278-305.

Ktesias: F.W. König, *Die Persika des Ktesias von Knidos* (*AfO* Beiheft 18), Graz 1972.

436 **Plutarch:** F.W.J. Frost, *Plutarch's Themistocles: A Historical Commentary*, Princeton, N.J., 1980 (cf. H.-J. Gehrke, *Gnomon* 54, 1982, 494-496).

For a selection of sources, see also C.W. Fornara (ed.), *Archaic Times to the End of the Peloponnesian War* (Translated Documents of Greece and Rome 1), Baltimore, Ma., and London 1977 [²1983].

437 D. Gillis, *Collaboration with the Persians* (Historia-Einzelschriften 34), Wiesbaden 1979.

438 **The Ionian Revolt:** P. Tozzi, *La rivolta ionica*, Pisa 1978; cf. H.T. Wallinga, "The Ionian Revolt," *Mnemosyne* 37, 1984, 401-437.

439 **Xerxes' Campaign against Greece**

Themistocles Inscription: M.M. Henderson, "The Decree of Themistocles," *Acta Classica* 20, 1977, 85-103.
H.B. Mattingly, "The Themistocles Decree from Troizen; Transmission and Status," in G.S. Shrimpton and D.J. McCargar (eds.), *Classical Contributions. Studies in honour of Malcolm Francis McGregor*, Locust Valley, N.Y., 1981, 79-87.
N.G.L. Hammond, "The Narrative of Herodotus VII and the Decree of Themistocles of Troezen," *JHS* 102, 1982, 75-93.
N. Robertson, "The Decree of Themistocles in its Contemporary Setting," *Phoenix* 36, 1982, 1-44.
N.G.L. Hammond, "The Meaning of the Fleet in the Decree of Themistocles," *Phoenix* 40, 1986, 143-148.
P.B. Georges, "Saving Herodotus' Phenomena: The Oracles and the Events of 480 B.C.," *Classical Antiquity* 5, 1986, 14-59.

Themistocles: A.J. Podlecki, *The Life of Themistocles: A Critical Survey of the Literary and Archaeological Evidence*, Montreal 1975.
R.J. Lenardon, *The Saga of Themistocles*, London 1978.
H. Bengtson, *Griechische Staatsmänner des 5. und 4. Jahrhunderts v. Chr.*, Munich 1983, 109-146.

440 **The Western Greeks from 500 to 480 B.C.:** G. de Sensi Sestito, "I Dinomenidi nel basso e medio Tirreno fra Imera e Cuma," *Mélanges d'Archéologie et d'Histoire de l'École française de Rome* 93, 1981, 617-642.
L.-M. Hans, *Karthago und Sizilien. Die Entstehung und Gestaltung der Epikratie auf Hintergrund der Beziehungen der Karthager zu den Griechen und den nichtgriechischen Völkern Siziliens (VI.-III. Jahrhundert v. Chr.)*, Hildesheim 1983.

441 n. 8 E. Lanzilotta, "Milziade nel Chersoneso e la conquista di Lemno," *Misc. greca e romana* 5, 1977, 65-94; and H. Bengtson, *Griechische Staatsmänner des 5. und 4. Jahrhunderts v. Chr.*, Munich 1983, 21-45.

n. 23 See also H. Bengtson, *ibid.*, 46 ff.; D.M. Lewis, "Themistocles' Mother," *Historia* 32, 1983, 245.

442 n. 26 See also I.H.M. Hendriks, "The Battle of Sepeia," *Mnemosyne* 33, 1980, 340-346. On political life at Sparta, cf. P. Carlier, "La vie

politique à Sparte sous le règne de Cléomène Ier. Essai d'interprétation," *Ktema* 2, 1977, 65-84.

n. 32 For possibly earlier activity by Datis in the region, see D.M. Lewis, "Datis the Mede," *JHS* 100, 1980, 194-195.

n. 39 H.Y. McCulloch, Jr., "Herodotus, Marathon and Athens," *SO* 57, 1982, 35-55.
E.D. Francis and M. Vickers, "The Oenoe Painting in the Stoa Poikile, and Herodotus' Account of Marathon," *BSA* 80, 1985, 99-113.

443 n. 40 See also G. Shrimpton, "The Persian Cavalry at Marathon," *Phoenix* 34, 1980, 20-37.

n. 45 R. Develin, "Miltiades and the Parian Expedition," *AC* 46, 1977, 571-577, has attempted to show that this expedition was not directed against Paros.

n. 46 On **Xanthippus**, see T.J. Figueira, "Xanthippos, Father of Perikles, and the Prutaneis of the Naukraroi," *Historia* 35, 1986, 257-279, with additional bibliography.

n. 47 J. Bleicken, *Die athenische Demokratie*, Paderborn, Munich, Vienna, Zurich 1985, 331 and 324-325.

n. 49 See also A.J. Podlecki, "Athens and Aegina," *Historia* 25, 1976, 396-413; T.J. Figueira, *Aegina. Society and Politics*, New York 1981; *idem*, "Aeginetan Membership in the Peloponnesian League," *CP* 76, 1981, 1-24; *idem*, "Herodotus on the Early Hostilities between Aegina and Athens," *AJP* 106, 1985, 49-74.

n. 51 H. Kalcyk, *Untersuchungen zum attischen Silberbergbau. Gebietsstruktur, Geschichte und Technik*, Frankfurt a. M. and Bern 1982; cf. J. Ellis Jones, "Laurion: Agrileza, 1977-1983: Excavations at a Silver-Mine Site," *ArchRep* 31, 1984-85, 106-123; J. Wolski, "Thémistocle, la construction de la flotte athénienne et la situation internationale en Méditerannée," *RivstorAnt* 13-14, 1983-1984, 179-192; Ch. Haas, "Athenian Naval Power before Themistocles," *Historia* 34, 1985, 29-46.

444 n. 54 J. Bleicken, *Die athenische Demokratie*, Paderborn, Munich, Vienna, Zurich 1985, 33-36 and 325.

445 n. 76 W.K. Pritchett, *Studies in Greek Topography* IV, Berkeley, Los Angeles, London 1982, 176-210. On **Persian movements after Thermopylae**, see *ibid.*, 211-233, cf. also 123-175.
A.R. Burn, "Thermopylai Revisited; and some Topographical Notes on Marathon and Plataia," in K.H. Kinzl (ed.), *Greece and the Eastern Mediterranean in History and Prehistory. Studies... Fritz Schachermeyr*, Berlin 1977, 89-105; J.F. Lazenby, *The Spartan Army*, War-

minster 1985, 83-96; and see now, in particular, J.C. Kraft *et al.*, "The Pass at Thermopylae, Greece," *JFA* 14, 1987, 181-198.

n. 77 P.W. Wallace, "The Anopaia Path at Thermopylae," *AJA* 84, 1980, 15-23; cf. W.K. Pritchett, "In Defense of the Thermopylae Pass," in *idem*, *Studies in Ancient Greek Topography* V, Berkeley, Los Angeles, London 1985, 190-216.

n. 80 See also J. Elayi, "Le rôle de l'oracle de Delphes dans le conflit gréco-perse d'après 'les Histoires' d'Hérodote," *Iranica Antiqua* 14, 1979, 67-151.

n. 81 P.B. Georges, "Saving Herodotus' Phenomena: The Oracles and Events of 480 B.C.," *Classical Antiquity* 5, 1986, 14-59. See also J.S. Morrison and J.F. Coates, *The Athenian trireme. The history and reconstruction of an ancient Greek warship*, Cambridge 1986, 49-60; and J.S. Morrison, "The Athenian Trireme," *IJNA* 16, 1987, 168-170, cf. P.F. Laures, *loc. cit.*; J. Morrison, "The British sea trials of the reconstructed trireme, 1-15 August 1987," *Antiquity* 61, 1987, 455-459.

446 n. 84 J. Delorme, "Deux notes sur la bataille de Salamine," *BCH* 102, 1978, 87-96.

n. 88 Cf. M.P. Milton, "The Second Message to Xerxes and Themistocles' View of Strategy," *ProcAfrClassAssoc* 17, 1983, 22-52.

n. 97 P.W. Wallace, "The Final Battle at Plataia," in *Studies in Attic Epigraphy, History and Topography Presented to Eugene Vanderpool* (Hesp. Suppl. 19), Princeton, N.J., 1982, 183-192; W.K. Pritchett, "The Site of Skolos near Plataiai," in *idem*, *Studies in Ancient Greek Topography* III, Berkeley, Los Angeles, London 1980, 289-294; *idem*, "The Roads of Plataiai," in *ibid.* IV, 1982, 88-102; and *idem*, "The Strategy of the Plataiai Campaign," in *ibid.* V, 1985, 92-137; J.F. Lazenby, *The Spartan Army*, Warminster 1985, 97-111.

n. 99 On **Pausanias**, see H. Bengtson, *Griechische Staatsmänner des 5. und 4. Jahrhunderts v. Chr.*, Munich 1983, 77-93.

447 n. 113 R. Bichler, "Der Synchronismus von Himera und Salamis. Eine Quellenkritische Studie zu Herodot," in E. Weber and G. Dobesch (eds.), *Römische Geschichte, Altertumskunde und Epigraphik. Festschrift für Artur Betz zur Vollendung seines 80. Lebensjahres*, Vienna 1985, 59-74.

7. FIFTY CRUCIAL YEARS

448 **Sources:** C.W. Fornara (ed.), *Archaic Times to the End of the Peloponnesian War* (Translated Documents of Greece and Rome 1), Baltimore, Ma., and London 1977 [[2]1983].

On the **hellenotamiai**, namely the duration of their office, see W.K. Pritchett, "The Hellenotamiai and Athenian Finance," *Historia* 26, 1977, 295-306.

452 **Bibliography:** R.K. Unz, "The Chronology of the Pentecontaetia," *CQ* 36, 1986, 68-85, is inconsequential.
B. Jordan, *The Athenian Navy in the Classical Period: A Study of Athenian Naval Administration and Military Organisation in the Fifth and Fourth Centuries B.C.*, Berkeley, Los Angeles, London 1975 (cf. F.D. Harvey, *CR* 31, 1981, 83-87).
Idem, *Servants of the Gods: A Study in the Religion, History and Literature of Fifth-century Athens* (Hypomnemata 55), Göttingen 1979.
D.M. Lewis, *Sparta and Persia*, Leiden 1977, 50 ff.
F. Gschnitzer, *Ein neuer spartanischer Staatsvertrag und die Verfassung des peloponnesischen Bundes* (Beiträge zur Klassischen Philologie 93), Meisenheim am Glan 1978.
N.H. Demand, *Thebes in the Fifth Century: Heracles Resurgent*, London, Boston, Melbourne 1982.
Ch. W. Clairmont, *Patrios Nomos: Public Burial in Athens during the Fifth and Fourth Centuries B.C. The Archaeological, Epigraphic-Literary and Historical Evidence* (BAR Intern. Ser. 161, i-ii), Oxford 1983.
R. Sealey, *The Athenian Republic: Democracy or the Rule of Law?*, University Park, Pa., 1987.

453 **The Founding of the Attic Maritime League:** C.G. Starr, "Thucydides on Sea Power," *Mnemosyne* 31, 1978, 345-350.
For yet another interpretation of the League, see N.D. Robertson, "The True Nature of the 'Delian League,' 478-461 B.C.," *AJAH* 5, 1980, 64-96 (Athens' design in founding the League was to punish medisers: an ingenious hypothesis, but one that does not appear to be convincing).
Nor does the equally novel thesis advanced by A. Giovannini and G. Gottlieb, *Thukydides und die Anfänge des athenischen Arche* (SHAW 1980,7), Heidelberg 1980, that the Alliance did not have any real existence, seem to be compelling.
See also A.G. Woodhead, "The Founding Fathers of the Delian Confederacy," in G.S. Shrimpton and D.J. McCargar (eds.), *Classical Contributions. Studies in honour of Malcolm Francis McGregor*, Locust Valley, N.Y., 1981, 179-190.
E. Ruschenbusch, "Tribut und Bürgerzahl im ersten athenischen Seebund," *ZPE* 53, 1983, 125-148.
M. Steinbrecher, *Der delisch-attische Seebund und die athenisch-spartanischen Beziehungen in der Kimonischen Ära (ca. 478/7-462/1)* (Palingenesia 21), Stuttgart 1985.
A brief introduction: P.J. Rhodes, *The Athenian Empire*, Oxford 1985.
M.F. McGregor, *The Athenians and their Empire*, Vancouver 1987.

The End of Pausanias and Themistocles: H.D. Westlake, "Thucydides on Pausanias and Themistocles. A Written Source?," *CQ* 27, 1977, 95-110.
H. Bengtson, *Griechische Staatsmänner des 5. und 4. Jahrhunderts v. Chr.*, Munich 1983, 77-93 (Pausanias).
L. Schumacher, "Themistokles und Pausanias. Die Katastrophe der Sieger," *Gymnasium* 94, 1987, 218-246.

454 **Themistocles:** J.F. Barrett, "The Downfall of Themistocles," *GRBS* 18, 1977, 291-305.
J. Seibert, *Die politischen Flüchtlinge und Verbannten in der griechischen Geschichte. Von den Anfängen bis zur Unterwerfung durch die Römer*, Darmstadt, 1979, 40-43 (with bibliography).
L. Piccirilli, "Artemide e la metis di Temistocle," *Quaderni di Storia* 7, 1981 No. 13, 143-166, claims to find a significant connection between Themistocles and Artemis.
H. Bengtson, *Griechische Staatsmänner des 5. und 4. Jahrhunderts v. Chr.*, Munich 1983, 46-76.
L. Bracesi (ed.), *Tre studi su Temistocle*. Contributi dei F. Ravioli, G. Cresci Marrone, E. Culasso Gastaldi, Padua 1986.
L. Schumacher, "Themistokles und Pausanias. Die Katastrophe der Sieger," *Gymnasium* 94, 1987, 218-246.
A.J. Holladay, "The Forethought of Themistocles," *JHS* 107, 1987, 182-187.

Athens in the Time of Pericles: G. Wirth (ed.), *Perikles und seine Zeit* (Wege der Forschung CDXII), Darmstadt 1979 (with extensive bibliography, 535-559).
M.A. Levi, *Pericle. Un uomo, un regime, una cultura*, Milan 1980 (cf. J.D. Smart, *JHS* 102, 1982, 268-269).
H. Bengtson, *Griechische Staatsmänner des 5. und 4. Jahrhunderts v. Chr.*, Munich 1983, 109-146.
R.E. Wycherly, *The Stones of Athens*, Princeton, N.J., 1978.
D.M. MacDowell, *The Law in Classical Athens*, Ithaca, N.Y., 1978 (cf. D. Lotze, *Gnomon* 55, 1983, 172-174).
D. Lotze, "Zwischen Politen und Metöken. Passivbürger im klassischen Athen?," *Klio* 63, 1981, 159-178.
M.J. Osborne, *Naturalization in Athens*, Brussels 1981.
C. Patterson, *Pericles' Citizenship Law of 451-50 B.C.*, Salem, N.H., 1981.
C.W. Weber, *Perikles; das goldene Zeitalter von Athen*, Munich 1985.
D. Whitehead, "The Ideology of the Athenian Metic," *ProcCambPhilSoc* 212, 1986, 145-158.

455 T. Linders, *The Treasurers of the Other Gods in Athens and their Functions* (Beiträge zur Klassischen Philologie 62), Meisenheim am Glan 1975.

A. Corso, *Monumenti Periclei. Saggio critico sulla attività edilizia di Pericle* (Memorie Classe di Scienze, Lettera ed Arte 40, 1), Venice 1986.

456 **The Attic Maritime League and Spartan Hegemony up to the Eve of the Peloponnesian War:** On **Athenian foreign policy**, see W.R. Connor, "Tyrannis Polis," in J.H. D'Arms and J.W. Eadie (eds.), *Ancient and Modern: Essays in Honor of Gerald F. Else*, Ann Arbor, Mich., 1977, 95-109.
C.W. Fornara, "IG I^2, 39.52-57 and the 'Popularity' of the Athenian Empire," *CSCA* 10, 1977, 39-55.
M.I. Finley, "The Fifth-Century Athenian Empire. A Balance-Sheet," in P.D.A. Garnsey and C.R. Whittaker (eds.), *Imperialism in the Ancient World: The Cambridge University Research Seminar in Ancient History*, Cambridge 1979, 103-126.
C.G. Starr, "Athens and its Empire," *CJ* 83, 1988, 114-123.
J.M. Balcer, *The Athenian Regulations for Chalcis. Studies in Athenian Imperial Law* (Historia-Einzelschriften 33), Wiesbaden 1978 (cf., however, M. Moggi, *Gnomon* 54, 1982, 448-453).
H.B. Mattingly, "Coins and Amphoras—Chios, Samos and Thasos in the Fifth Century B.C.," *JHS* 101, 1981, 78-86.
See also the contributions by Balcer, Gehrke, Raaflaub and Schuller, in W. Schuller (ed.), *Studien zum attischen Seebund* (Xenia 8), Konstanz 1984 (cf. N. Robertson, *Gnomon* 57, 1985, 657-659).
G.L. Huxley, "Thucydides on the Growth of Athenian Power," *Proc. Royal Irish Academy* 83, C, 6, 1983, 191-204 (argues for a significant increase in Athenian power in the last years of the Pentecontaetia).
K.-W. Welwei, "'Demos' und 'Plethos' in athenischen Volksbeschlüssen um 450 v. Chr.," *Historia* 35, 1986, 177-191.

The Western Greeks in the Pentecontaetia: U. Westermark, "The Fifth Century Bronze Coinage of Akragas," in *Le origini della monetazione di bronzo in Sicilia e Magna Grecia. Atti del VI Convegno del centro internazionale di studi numismatici (Napoli 17-22 aprile 1977)*, Rome 1979, 3-17.
U. Westermark and K. Jenkins, *The Coinage of Kamarina* (Numismatic Society Special Publication 9), London 1980.
G. De Sensi Sestito, "Contrasti etnici e lotte politiche a Zancle-Messene e Reggio alla caduta della tirannide," *Athenaeum* 61, 1981, 38-55.

457 n. 14 On **Cimon**, see H. Bengtson, *Griechische Staatsmänner des 5. und 4. Jahrhunderts v. Chr.*, Munich 1983, 94-108.

458 n. 20 Cf. also W.A.P. Childs, "Lycian Relations with Persians and Greeks in the Fifth and Fourth Centuries Re-examined," *AnatSt* 31, 1981, 55-80; O. Mørkholm and J. Zahle, "The Coinage of Kuprilli. A Numismatic and Archaeological Study," *Acta Archaeologica* 43,

1972, 57-113; O. Mørkholm, "The Coinages of the Lycian Dynasts Kheriga, Kherêi and Erbinna. A Numismatic and Archaeological Study," *ibid.* 47, 1976, 47-90.

n. 30 On **eisangelia**, see P.J. Rhodes, "Eisangelia in Athens," *JHS* 99, 1979, 103-114.

n. 35 See also J. Ducat, "Le tremblement de terre de 464 et l'histoire de Sparte," in B. Helly and A. Pollino (eds.), *Tremblements de terre: histoire et archéologie. Actes du colloque des IVèmes rencontres internationales d'archéologie et d'histoire d'Aibes 2.3.4. novembre 1983*, Valbonne 1984, 73-85.

459 n. 37 L. Boffo, "L'intervento di Efialte di Sofonide sull'Areopago nell'interpretazione del IV secolo," *Rendiconti della Classe di Scienze morali, storiche e filologiche dell'Accademia dei Lincei* 31, 1976, 435-450; E. Ruschenbusch, "Ephialtes und der Areopag," in *idem*, *Athenische Innenpolitik im 5. Jahrhundert v. Chr. Ideologie oder Pragmatismus?*, Bamberg 1979, 57-65; W. Schuller, "Neue Gedanken zur Entstehung der athenischen Demokratie," *Siegener Hochschulblätter* 6, 1983, 16-29; J. Bleicken, *Die athenische Demokratie*, Paderborn, Munich, Vienna, Zurich 1985, 36-38 and 325-326; D. Lotze, "Die Teilhabe des Bürgers an Regierung und Rechtssprechung in den Organen der direkten Demokratie des klassischen Athen," in E. Kluwe (ed.), *Kultur und Fortschritt in der Blütezeit der griechischen Polis*, Berlin 1985, 52-76; L.A. Jones, "The Role of Ephialtes in the Rise of Athenian Democracy," *Classical Antiquity* 6, 1987, 53-76.

460 n. 58 M.H. Hansen, "Demographic Reflections on the Number of Athenian Citizens 451-309 B.C.," *AJAH* 7, 1982, 172-189.

n. 59 Ch. Triebel-Schubert, "Zur Datierung der Kallias-Dekrete," *Qaderni Catanesi di studi classici e medievali* 6, 1984, 355-375.

461 n. 68 See also A.J. Holladay, "Sparta's Role in the First Peloponnesian War," *JHS* 97, 1977, 54-63; D.M. Lewis, "The Origins of the First Peloponnesian War," in G.S. Shrimpton and D.J. McCargar (eds.), *Classical Contributions. Studies in honour of Malcolm Francis McGregor*, Locust Valley, N.Y., 1981, 71-78; M. Piérart, "Note sur l'alliance entre Athènes et Argos au cours de la première guerre du Péloponnèse. A propos de Thucydide I 107-108," *MH* 44, 1987, 175-180.

n. 69 K.R. Walters, "Diodorus 11.82-84 and the Second Battle of Tanagra," *AJAH* 3, 1978, 188-191.
C. Clairmont, "Sparta's 'Golden Phiale' at Olympia," *ZPE* 48, 1982, 79-85; A. Andrewes, "Diodorus and Ephorus: One Source of Misunderstanding," in J.W. Eadie and J. Ober (eds.), *The Craft of the Ancient Historian. Essays in honor of Chester G. Starr*, Lanham, New York, London, 1985, 189-197.

n. 73 B.D. Meritt, "The Alliance between Athens and Egesta," *ProcAmerPhilosAssoc* 121, 1977, 437-447; H.B. Mattingly, "The Alliance of Athens with Egesta," *Chiron* 16, 1986, 167-170.

462 n. 81 The authenticity of the treaty is also contested by K. Meister, *Die Ungeschichtlichkeit des Kalliasfriedens und deren historischen Fragen* (Palingenesia 18), Wiesbaden 1982.
See also J. Walsh, "The Authenticity and the Dates of the Peace of Callias and the Congress Decree," *Chiron* 11, 1981, 31-63; cf. A.J. Holladay, "The Détente of Kallias?," *Historia* 35, 1986, 503-507, who adopts a *via media*, whereas E. Badian, "The Peace of Callias," *JHS* 107, 1987, 1-39, argues vigorously for its authenticity.

n. 85 M. Philippides, "King Pleistonax and the Spartan Invasion of Attica in 446 B.C.," *The Ancient World* 11, 1985, 33-41.

n. 93 C.W. Fornara, "On the Chronology of the Samian War," *JHS* 99, 1979, 7-19; cf. A.P. Bridges, "The Athenian Treaty with Samos, ML 56," *JHS* 100, 1980, 185-188; T.J. Quinn, *Athens and Samos, Lesbos and Chios*, Manchester 1981, 10-23; B.D. Meritt, "The Samian Revolt from Athens in 440-439 B.C.," *ProcAmerPhilosSoc* 128, 1984, 123-133; P. Karavites, "Enduring Problems of the Samian Revolt," *RhM* 128, 1985, 40-56.
On **Miletus**, see H.-J. Gehrke, "Zur Geschichte Milets in der Mitte des 5. Jahrhunderts v. Chr.," *Historia* 29, 1980, 17-31.

n. 94 P. Krentz, "The Ostracism of Thoukydides, son of Melesias," *Historia* 33, 1984, 499-504, argues for a later date.

n. 95 C. Triebel-Schubert, "Zur Datierung des Phidiasprozesses," *AM* 98, 1983, 101-112.
W. Ameling, "Zu einem neuen Datum des Phidiasprozesses," *Klio* 68, 1986, 63-66.

463 n. 96 See, on the other hand, L. Prandi, "I processi contro Fidia, Aspasia, Anassagora e l'opposizione a Pericle," *Aevum* 51, 1977, 10-26; and A. Andrewes, "The Opposition to Pericles," *JHS* 98, 1978, 1-8; also R. Klein, "Die innenpolitische Gegnerschaft gegen Perikles," in G. Wirth (ed.), *Perikles und seine Zeit* (Wege der Forschung CDXII), Darmstadt 1979, 494-533.

8. THE PELOPONNESIAN WAR

464 **Sources:** H.B. Mattingly, "The Tribute Quota Lists from 430 to 425 B.C.," *CQ* 28, 1978, 83-88.

465 **The Pseudo-Xenophontic *Constitution of Athens*:** C. Leduc, *La Constitution d'Athènes attribuée à Xenophon* (Annales littéraires de l'Université de Besançon 192), Paris 1976; cf. Ed. Will, "Un nouvel essai d'interprétation de *l'Athénaion Politeia* pseudo-xénophontique," *REG* 91, 1978, 77-95.

L. Canfora, *Studi sull'Athenaion Politeia Pseudosenofontea* (Memorie della Academia delle Scienze di Torino, classice di scienze morali, storiche e filologiche, serie 5,IV,1), Turin 1980.
S. Cataldi, *La democrazia ateniese e gli alleati (Ps.-Senofonte, Athenaion Politeia, I, 14-18)* (Saggi e materiali Universitari, I, Serie di antichità e tradizione classica), Padua 1984.

466 **Thucydides:** K.J. Dover, "Strata of Composition" = Appendix 2 in A.W. Gomme, A. Andrewes and K.J. Dover, *A Historical Commentary on Thucydides* V, Oxford 1981, 384-444.
F. Ferlauto, *Il secondo proemio tucidideo e Senofonte* (Suppl. V al BollClass), Rome 1983.

467 See also A. Andrewes, "Indications of Incompleteness" = Appendix 1 in A.W. Gomme, A. Andrewes and K.J. Dover, *A Historical Commentary on Thucydides* V, Oxford 1981, 361-383.

468 M. Tulli, "Cleone in Tucidide," *Helikon* 20-21, 1980-1981 [1983], 249-255.
H.R. Rawlings III, *The Structure of Thucydides' History*, Princeton, N.J., 1981 (cf. J.R. Ellis, *JHS* 103, 1983, 167-168).
N. Marinatos, *Thucydides and Religion* (Beiträge zur Klassischen Philologie 129), Königstein 1981 (cf. A. Rengakos, *Gnomon* 56, 1984, 365-366).
F. Egermann, "Zu den Grundbegriffen der thukydideischen Geschichtsschreibung," in H. Heinen (ed.), *Althistorische Studien Hermann Bengtson zum 70. Geburtstag dargebracht von Kollegen und Schülern*, Wiesbaden 1983, 44-55.
K.J. Dover, "Thucydides 'as History' and 'as Literature'," *History and Theory* 22, 1983, 54-63.
W.R. Connor, *Thucydides*, Princeton, N.J., 1984; cf. *idem*, "Narrative Discourse in Thucydides," in M.H. Jameson (ed.), *The Greek Historians: Literature and History. Papers Presented to A.E. Raubitschek*, Saratoga, Ca., 1985, 1-17; cf. R. Robinson, *ibid.*, 19-23.
Also R. Leimbach, *Militärische Musterrhetorik. Eine Untersuchung zu den Feldherrnreden des Thukydides*, Wiesbaden 1985.
For a recent synthesis on Thucydides, with a limited bibliography, see H.R. Immerwahr, "Thucydides," in P.E. Easterling and B.M.W. Knox (eds.), *The Cambridge History of Classical Literature* I, Cambridge 1985, 441-456.
The Gomme Commentary on Thucydides is now complete, with A.W. Gomme, A. Andrewes and K.J. Dover, *A Historical Commentary on Thucydides [HCT]* V, Oxford 1981.

Xenophon: L. Canfora, "Storia antica del testo di Tucidide," *Quaderni di storia* 3, 1977, No. 6, 3-39, has attempted to argue that Thucydides' *History* does not break off in 411, but continues in Xenophon's *Hellenica* and, vice versa, some of Xenophon's account can be detected in that of Thucydides—a view that is probably wide of the mark.

469 W.E. Higgins, *Xenophon the Athenian: The Problem of the Individual and the Society of the Polis*, Albany, N.Y., 1977.
R. Nickel, *Xenophon* (Erträge der Forschung CXI), Darmstadt 1979.
J.D. Smart, "Thucydides and Hellanicus," in J.S. Moron, J.D. Smart and A.J. Woodman (eds.), *Past Perspectives: Studies in Greek and Roman Historical Writing. Papers Presented at a Conference in Leeds, 6-8 April 1983*, Cambridge 1986, 19-35.
See also C.W. Fornara (ed.), *Archaic Times to the End of the Peloponnesian War* (Translated Documents of Greece and Rome 1), Baltimore, Ma., and London 1977 [21983].

470 **Bibliography**

Specific Aspects: B. Jordan, *The Athenian Navy in the Classical Period*, Berkeley, Los Angeles, London 1975.
S. Cataldi, "La restituzione della terra ai Mitilenesi e le rinnovale *xumbolai* tra Atene e Mitilene," *Annali della Scuola Normale Superiore di Pisa* 6, 1976, 15-33.
D.M. Lewis, *Sparta and Persia*, Leiden 1977, 63 ff.
W.K. Pritchett, *The Greek State at War III: Religion*, Berkeley 1980.
M. Piérart, "Deux notes sur la politique d'Athènes en mer Égée (428-425)," *BCH* 108, 1984, 161-176.

Events Leading up to the Peloponnesian War: T.E. Wick, "Thucydides and the Megarian Decree," *AC* 46, 1977, 74-99.
M. Sordi, "Il decreto di Pericle contro Megara, un decreto ragionevole e umano?," in P. Maggi (ed.), *Studi in onore di Ferrante Rittatore Vonwiller II: Archeologia italica classica medievale. Diritto. Letteratura. Linguistica. Storia. Varie*, Como 1980, 507-511.
P.A. Stadter, "Plutarch, Charinus, and the Megarian Decree," *GRBS* 25, 1984, 351-372.
K. Kiechle, "Korkyra und der Handelsweg durch das Adriatische Meer im 5. Jh. v. Chr.," *Historia* 28, 1979, 173-191.
E.F. Bloedow, "The Speeches of Archidamus and Sthenelaidas at Sparta," *Historia* 30, 1981, 129-143.
Idem, "Sthenelaidas the Persuasive Spartan," *Hermes* 115, 1987, 60-66.
P.J. Rhodes, "Thucydides on the Causes of the Peloponnesian War," *Hermes* 115, 1987, 154-165.

The Archidamian War: J.-P. Vernant, *Myth and Society in Ancient Greece*, Brighton 1979.
N. Loraux, *L'invention d'Athènes. Histoire de l'oraison funèbre dans la cité classique*, Paris 1981.
Eadem, "Le lit, la guerre,", *L'homme* 21, 1981, 37-67.
Ch.W. Clairmont, *Patrios Nomos. Public burial in Athens during the fifth and fourth centuries B.C. The archaeological, epigraphic-literary and historical evidence* (BAR Intern. Ser. 16, 1-2), Oxford 1983.

T.J. Quinn, *Athens and Samos, Lesbos and Chios*, Manchester 1981, 24-38.
E.F. Bloedow, "Archidamus the 'Intelligent' Spartan," *Klio* 65, 1983, 27-49.
B. Jordan, "Religion in Thucydides," *TAPA* 116, 1986, 119-147.
J.S. Rusten, "Structure, Style, and Sense in Interpreting Thucydides: the Soldier's Choice (Thuc. 2.42.4)," *HSCP* 90, 1986, 49-76.
E. Bloedow, "Pericles' Powers in the Counter-Strategy of 431," *Historia* 36, 1987, 9-27.
O. Andersen, "The Widows, the City, and Thucydides (II 45.2)," *SO* 62, 1987, 33-49.

471 **The Peace of Nicias and the Great Sicilian Expedition of Athens:** R. Seager, "After the Peace of Nicias: Diplomacy and Policy 421-416 B.C.," *CQ* 70, 1976, 249-269.
Also useful on **Sicily** is M. Finley, *Ancient Sicily*, London ²1979.
Likewise, some relevant sections in E. Gabba and G. Vallet (eds.), *La Sicilia antica*, Naples 1980.
G.B. Sunseri, "Instabilità politica in città siceliote durante la Grande Spedizione ateniese," *Kokalos* 28-29, 1982-83, 53-70.
For a monograph on the subject, see D. Kagan, *The Peace of Nicias and the Sicilian Expedition*, Ithaca, N.Y., 1981 (cf. B. Jordan, *CP* 80, 1985, 74-78).
D.H. Frank, "The Power of Truth. Political Foresight in Thucydides' Account of the Sicilian Expedition (6. 32-42)," *Prudentia* 16, 1984, 99-107.
K. Rutter, "Sicily and South Italy: The Background to Thucydides Books 6 and 7," *G & R* 33, 1986, 142-155.

472 **The Decelian and the Ionian War:** D.M. Lewis, *Sparta and Persia*, Leiden 1977, 75 ff.
M. Amit, "The Disintegration of the Athenian Empire in Asia Minor (412-405 B.C.E.)," *Scripta classica Israelica* 2, 1975, 38-72.
W. Gawantka, *Isopolitie. Ein Beitrag zur Geschichte der zwischenstaatlichen Beziehungen in der griechischen Antike* (Vestigia 22), Munich 1975.
H.D. Westlake, "Ionians in the Ionian War," *CQ* 29, 1979, 9-44.
B. Smarczyk, *Bündnerautonomie und athenische Seebundspolitik im Dekeleischen Krieg* (Beiträge zur Klass. Phil. 177), Frankfurt a. M. 1986.
On the death of Artaxerxes, see M.T. Stolper, "The Death of Artaxerxes I," *ArchMitt aus Iran* 16, 1983, 223-236.

473 D. Flach, "Der oligarchische Staatsstreich in Athen vom Jahre 411," *Chiron* 7, 1977, 9-33.
Fundamental for the events of 411 is the discussion in A.W. Gomme, A. Andrewes and K.J. Dover, *HCT* V, Oxford 1981.
See also W.J. McCoy, "Thrasyllus," *AJP* 98, 1977, 264-289.

H.D. Westlake, "Abydos and Byzantium: The Sources for Two Episodes in the Ionian War," *MH* 42, 1985, 313-327.
V.J. Gray, "The Value of Diodorus Siculus for the Years 411-386 BC," *Hermes* 115, 1987, 72-89.
On the **chronology** of the period, for another attempt, see N. Robertson, "The Sequence of Events in the Aegean in 408 and 407 B.C.," *Historia* 29, 1980, 282-301.

474 n. 5 On **Potidaea**, G.S. Shrimpton, "Strategy and Tactics in the Preliminaries to the Siege of Potidaea (Thuc. 1.61-65)," *SO* 59, 1984, 7-12.

n. 9 M.H. Hansen, "The Number of Athenian Hoplites in 431 B.C.," *SO* 56, 1981, 19-32.

n. 13 See also A.J. Holladay, "Athenian Strategy in the Archidamian War," *Historia* 27, 1978, 399-427.

n. 14 On the **plague**, see also R. Seitschek, *Die Pest in Athen. Eine medizinhistorische und philologische Studie*, Vienna 1976; S.L. Radt, "Zu Thukydides' Pestbeschreibung," *Mnemosyne* 31, 1978, 233-245; A.J. Holladay and J.C.F. Poole, "Thucydides and the Plague of Athens," *CQ* 29, 1979, 282-300; *iidem*, *CQ* 34, 1984, 483-485; J. Seibert, "Heeresseuchen und Kriegsverlauf," in H. Heinen (ed.), *Althistorische Studien Hermann Bengtson zum 70. Geburtstag dargebracht von Kollegen und Schülern*, Wiesbaden 1983, 78 ff.; A.D. Lanmuir, "The Thucydides Syndrome: A New Hypothesis of the Cause of the Plague," *New English Journal of Medicine* 313, 1985, 1027-1030.

475 n. 19 P. Krentz and Ch. Sullivan, "The Date of Phormion's First Expedition to Akarnania," *Historia* 36, 1987, 241-243.

n. 21 F. Bourriot, "La famille et le milieu social de Cléon," *Historia* 31, 1982, 404-435.

n. 25 On the campaign: J. Wilson, "Strategy and Tactics in the Mytilene Campaign," *Historia* 30, 1981, 144-163.

n. 28 D.M. Lewis, "The Treaties with Leontini and Rhegion (Meiggs-Lewis 63-64)," *ZPE* 22, 1976, 223-225 (in opposition to Ruschenbusch).

n. 29 See, especially, J.B. Wilson, *Pylos 425 B.C. A Historical and Topographical Study of Thucydides' Account of the Campaign*, Warminster 1979; also M.H.B. Marshall, "Cleon and Pericles: Sphacteria," *G & R* 31, 1984, 19-36; J.F. Lazenby, *The Spartan Army*, Warminster 1985, 113-123; D. Babut, "L'épisode de Pylos-Sphactérie chez Thucydide: L'agencement du récrit et les intentions de l'historien," *RevPhil* 60, 1986, 59-79.

476 n. 30 B.D. Meritt, "Kleon's Assessment Tribute to Athens," in G.S. Shrimpton and D.J. McCargar (eds.), *Classical Contributions: Studies in honour of Malcolm Francis McGregor*, Locust Valley, N.Y., 1981, 89-93.

n. 31 A.L. Boegehold, "Thucydides' Representation of Brasidas before Amphipolis," *CP* 74, 1979, 148-152.

n. 35 F.T. Hinrichs, "Hermokrates bei Thukydides," *Hermes* 109, 1981, 46-59.

n. 38 J.R. Ellis, "Thucydides at Amphipolis," *Antichthon* 12, 1978, 28-35; cf. *idem*, *Quaderni di storia* 5, 1979, 39-69 (Thucydides' account is misleading, intended to present Thucydides' failure in a more favourable light).

n. 40 On the death of Artaxerxes I, see H.W. Stolper, "The Death of Artaxerxes I," *ArchMitt aus Iran* 16, 1983, 223-236.

n. 42 See also R. Meiggs, *Trees and Timber in the Ancient Mediterranean World*, Oxford 1982, 121-131 and 188-217.

n. 43 N. Jones, "The Topography and Strategy of the Battle of Amphipolis in 422 B.C.," *CSCA* 10, 1977, 71-104; D. Lazaridis, "La cité grecque d'Amphipolis et son système de défense," *CRAI* 1977, 194-214; W.K. Pritchett, "Amphipolis Restudied," in *idem*, *Studies in Ancient Greek Topography III: Roads*, Berkeley, Los Angeles, London 1980, 298-346.

477 n. 49 P. Bicknell, "Alcibiades and Kleinias: A Study in Athenian Genealogy," *Museum Philologum Londoniense* 1, 1975, 51-64; G. Giuliani, "Problemi Tucididei. Il giudizio su Alcibiade," *Nuova Rivista Storica* 61, 1977, 356-366. Highly apologetic is M. Delaunois, "Les leçons d'Alcibiade," *Les Études Classiques* 46, 1978, 113-126. See also H. Bengtson, *Zu den strategischen Konzeptionen des Alkibiades* (SBAW 1979,3), Munich 1979; and *idem*, *Griechische Staatsmänner des 5. und 4. Jahrhunderts v. Chr.*, Munich 1983, 147-183.

n. 55 For another attempt at a complete reinterpretation of the Melian Dialogue, alleging that it is anti-Athenian and belongs to a period of a decade earlier, see S. Cagnazzi, *La spedizione ateniese contro Melo del 416 a.C. Realtà e propaganda*, Bari 1983 (cf. D. Lotze, *Gnomon* 57, 1985, 476-477); see also H. Goergemanns, "Macht, Moral und Psychologie bei Thukydides. Spielarten der Macht," *Humanistische Bildung* 1, 1977, 64-93.

n. 61 On the nature of Athenian power, cf. K. Bayer, "Athenische Realpolitik. Zu Thuk. VI, 76-88," in W. Sürbaum and F. Maier (eds.), *Festschrift für Franz Egermann zu seinem 80. Geburtstag am 13. Februar 1985*, Munich 1985, 57-65.

478 n. 62 R. Osborne, "The erection and mutilation of the Hermai," *ProcCambrPhilSoc* 31, 1985, 47-73.

n. 73 See also P. Krentz, "SEG XXI, 80 and the Rule of the Thirty," *Hesp.* 48, 1979, 54-63; *idem*, "Foreigners Against the Thirty. *IG* 2^2 *10* again," *Phoenix* 34, 1980, 298-306.

n. 74 See also J.S. Morrison and J.F. Coates, *The Athenian trireme: The history and reconstruction of an ancient Greek warship*, Cambridge 1986, 83-87; and J.S. Morrison, "The Athenian Trireme," *IJNA* 16, 1987, 168-170, cf. F.F. Laures, *loc. cit.*; and J. Morrison, "The British sea trials of the reconstructed trireme, 1-15 August 1987," *Antiquity* 61, 1987, 455-459; see also O. Höckmann, *Antike Seefahrt*, Munich 1985; and F. Meijer, *A History of Seafaring in the Classical World*, London and Sydney 1986.

479 n. 88 J.-F. Bommelaer, *Lysandre de Sparte. Histoire et traditions* (Bibl. Éc. franç. d'Athènes et de Rome 240), Paris 1981.

n. 88a See L. Robert, "Le lieu de la mort d'Alcibiade," in *A travers l'Asie Mineure, Poètes et prosateurs grecques, voyageurs et géographie* (Bibl. Éc. fr. d'Athènes et de Rome 239), Paris 1980, 257-299; cf. J. and L. Robert, *REG* (Bull. epigr.) 94, 1981, 462-463.

n. 90 M. Sordi, "Teramene e il processo delle Arginuse," *Aevum* 55, 1981, 3-12; G. Németh, "Der Arginusen-Prozess: Die Geschichte eines politischen Justizmordes," *Klio* 66, 1984, 51-57.

n. 92 B.S. Straus, "Aegospotami Reexamined," *AJP* 104, 1983, 24-35.

9. THE DECLINE OF THE GREEK POLIS

480 **Sources**

Maussolleum of Halicarnassus: K. Jeppesen, "Neue Ergebnisse zur Wiederherstellung des Maussolleions von Halikarnassos. 4. vorläufiger Bericht der dänischen Halikarnassosexpedition," *MDAI(I)* 26, 1976, 47-99; *idem*, "Zur Gründung und Baugeschichte des Maussolleions von Halikarnassos," *ibid.* 27/28, 1977/1978, 169-211; K. Jeppesen, F. Höjlund and K. Aaris-Sorensen, *The Maussolleion at Halikarnassos: Reports of the Danish Archaeological Expedition to Bodrum I: The Sacrificial Deposit, The Deposit of Sacrificial Animals, A Zoological Analysis* (Jutland Archaeological Society Publications 15,1), Copenhagen 1981.
K. Jeppesen, *The Maussolleion at Halikarnassos: Reports of the Danish Archaeological Expedition to Bodrum 2: The Written Sources and their Archaeological Background i: The Ancient Greek and Latin Writers*, Hojbjerg 1986.

A. Luttrell, *ibid. ii: The Later History of the Maussolleion and its Utilization in the Hospitaller Castle at Bodrum*, Hojbjerg 1986.

481 **Isocrates:** H.-G. Kleinow, *Die Überwindung der Polis im frühen 4. Jahrhundert v. Chr. Studien zum epitaphischen Tatencatalog und zu den panhellenischen Reden bei Lysias, Platon und Isokrates*, Diss. Erlangen-Nürnberg 1981.
P.G. van Soesbergen, "Colonisation as a Solution to Social-Economic Problems in Fourth-Century Greece. A Confrontation of Isocrates with Xenophon," *AncSoc* 13, 1983, 131-145.

483 For a selection of sources in translations, see P. Harding (ed.), *From the End of the Peloponnesian War to the Battle of Ipsus* (Translated Documents of Greece and Rome 2), Cambridge 1985.

Bibliography: On Maussollus, see S. Hornblower, *Mausolus*, Oxford 1982 (cf. Ch.G. Starr, *JHS* 103, 1983, 206, and F.G. Maier, *Gnomon* 59, 1987, 169-170).
On **internal conditions in Athens**: M.H. Hansen, *Eisangelia. The Sovereignty of the People's Court in Athens in the Fourth Century B.C. and the Impeachment of Generals and Politicians* (Odense University Classical Studies 6), Odense 1975; cf. *idem*, *JHS* 100, 1980, 89-95; and *idem*, *The Athenian Ecclesia: A Collection of Articles 1976-1983*, Copenhagen 1983.
Also H. Stier, "Zum Problem des Untergangs der klassischen Demokratie," in P. Funke and G.A. Lehmann (eds.), *H.E. Stier, Kleine Schriften* (Beiträge zur Klassischen Philologie 109), Meisenheim am Glan 1979, 345-354.
P. Funke, *Homonoia und Arche. Athen und die griechische Staatenwelt vom Ende des Peloponnesischen Kriegs bis zum Königsfrieden (404/3-387/6 v. Chr.)* (Historia-Einzelschriften 37), Wiesbaden 1980.
G.E.M. de Ste. Croix, *The Class Struggle in the Ancient Greek World from the Archaic Age to the Arab Conquests*, London 1981.
J. Ober, *Fortress Attica: Defense of the Athenian Land Frontier, 404-322 B.C.*, Leiden 1985 (cf. H. Lohmann, *Gymnasium* 94, 1987, 270-274).
P.J. Rhodes, "Political activity in classical Athens," *JHS* 106, 1986, 132-144.
B.S. Strauss, *Athens after the Peloponnesian War: Class, Faction, and Policy 404-386 B.C.*, Ithaca, N.Y., London, Sydney 1986.
J. Bleicken, "Die Einheit der athenischen Demokratie in Klassischer Zeit," *Hermes* 115, 1987, 257-283.
Th.C. Loening, *The Reconciliation Agreement of 404/02 B.C.*, Stuttgart 1987.

484 **The Expedition of Cyrus the Younger. The Spartan-Persian War in Western Asia Minor:** S. Hurter, "Der Tissaphernes-Fund," in O. Mørkholm and N.M. Waggoner (eds.), *Greek Numismatics and Ar-*

chaeology: Essays in Honor of Margaret Thompson, Wetteren 1979, 97-108.
H.D. Westlake, "Decline and Fall of Tissaphernes," *Historia* 30, 1981, 257-279.
On **Agesilaus**: C.D. Hamilton, "Étude chronologique sur le règne d'Agésilas," *Ktema* 7, 1982, 281-296.
H. Bengtson, *Griechische Staatsmänner des 5. und 4. Jahrhunderts v. Chr.*, Munich 1983, 184-198.
P. Cartledge, *Agesilaos and the Crisis of Sparta*, Baltimore 1987.
H.D. Westlake, "Spartan Intervention in Asia, 400-397 B.C.," *Historia* 35, 1986, 405-426.

485 **The Revolt of the Greeks against Sparta, and the King's Peace:** G.A. Lehmann, "Spartas *arché* und die Vorphase des Korinthischen Krieges in der Hellenica Oxyrhyncia (II)," *ZPE* 30, 1978, 73-93.
R. Seager and C. Tuplin, "The Freedom of the Greeks of Asia: On the Origins of a Concept and the Creation of a Slogan," *JHS* 100, 1980, 141-154.
C.D. Hamilton, *Sparta's Bitter Victories. Politics and Diplomacy in the Corinthian War*, Ithaca, N.Y., 1978.
B.A. Strauss, "Thrasybulus and Conon: A Rivalry in Athens in the 390s B.C.," *AJP* 105, 1984, 37-48.
H.D. Westlake, "The Sources for the Spartan Debacle at Haliartus," *Phoenix* 39, 1985, 119-133.
Idem, "Spartan Intervention in Asia, 400-397 B.C.," *Historia* 35, 1986, 405-426.

486 **Sparta and Thebes in the Struggle for Supremacy. The Second Athenian Maritime League:** V.J. Gray, "The Years 375 to 371 B.C.: A Case Study in the Reliability of Diodorus Siculus and Xenophon," *CQ* 30, 1980, 306-326.
B. Jordan, *The Athenian Navy in the Classical Period*, Berkeley, Los Angeles, London 1975.
G.T. Griffith, "Athens in the Fourth Century," in P.D.A. Garnsey and C.R. Whittaker (eds.), *Imperialism in the Ancient World: Cambridge University Research Seminar in Ancient History*, Cambridge 1979, 127-144.
S. Dušanić, "L'Académie de Platon et la Paix Commune de 371 av. J.-C.," *REG* 92, 1979, 319-347.
G.L. Cawkwell, "Notes on the failure of the Second Athenian Confederacy," *JHS* 101, 1981, 40-55.
Idem, "Athenian naval power in the fourth century," *CQ* 34, 1984, 334-345.
See also J. Cargill, *The Second Athenian League: Empire or Free Alliance*, Berkeley, Los Angeles, London 1981 (cf. S. Hornblower, *CR* 32, 1982, 235-237).
T.V. Buttrey, "The Athenian Currency Law of 375-374 B.C.," in O. Mørkholm and N.M. Waggoner (eds.), *Greek Numismatics and Ar-*

chaeology: Essays in Honor of Margaret Thompson, Wetteren 1979, 33-45.
O. Mørkholm, "More on the Athenian Coinage Law of 375/4 B.C.," *Numismatica e antichità classiche* 10, 1981, 71-94.
F. Mitchel, "The Assessment of the Allies in the Second Athenian League," *Classical Views* 28, 1984, 23-37.
R.M. Kallet-Marx, "Athens, Thebes, and the Foundation of the Second Athenian League," *Classical Antiquity* 4, 1985, 127-151.
H.M. Hack, "Thebes and the Spartan Hegemony, 386-382 B.C.," *AJP* 99, 1978, 210-227.
P. Cartledge, *Agesilaos and the Crisis of Sparta*, Baltimore 1987.
On **Euboea**: O. Picard, *Chalcis et la confédération eubéenne. Étude de numismatique et d'histoire (IVe-Ier siècle)* (Bibl. Éc. franç. d'Athènes et de Rome 234), Paris 1979 (cf. F.W. Walbank, *JHS* 101, 1981, 202).

The Era of the Theban Hegemony: J. Buckler, "Plutarch on the Trials of Pelopidas and Epameinondas (369 B.C.)," *CP* 83, 1978, 36-42.
Idem, *The Theban Hegemony, 371-362 B.C.*, Cambridge, Mass., and London 1980.
Idem, "The Alleged Achaian Arbitration after Leuktra," *SO* 53, 1978, 85-96.
Idem, "Epameinondas and the *Embolon*," *Phoenix* 39, 1985, 134-143.
So far as Boeotia is concerned, of some relevance is the size of the population. Although the large-scale, long-term survey being conducted over the entire country (cf. J.L. Bintliff and A.M. Snodgrass, "The Cambridge/Bradford Boeotian Expedition: the First Four Years," *JFA* 12, 1985, 123-161, cf. *ArchRep* 32, 1986, 40-41) is very hypothetical in respect of its results to date, it has none the less essentially corroborated the figures reached by Beloch a century ago.
On the question of **Spartan imperialism**, see A. Andrewes, in P.D.A. Garnsey and C.R. Whittaker (eds.), *Imperialism in the Ancient World: The Cambridge University Research Seminar in Ancient History*, Cambridge 1978, 91-102. Andrewes argues that Sparta lacked a genuine determination to establish an empire.
S. Dušanić, "Plato's Academy and Timotheus' Policy, 365-359 B.C.," *Chiron* 10, 1980, 111-144.
Idem, "Athens, Crete and the Aegean after 366/5 B.C.," *Talanta* 12-13, 1980-1981, 7-29.
J. Mandel, "Jason. The Tyrant of Pherae, Tagus of Thessaly as Reflected in Ancient Sources and Modern Literature. The Image of the New Tyrant," *Rivista storica dall'Antichità* 10, 1980, 47-77.

488 **The Empire of Dionysius I and his Successors in Sicily**

Timoleon: L.J. Sanders, "Plato's First Visit to Sicily," *Kokalos* 25, 1979, 207-219.
M. Sordi, "Dionigi I e gli Italioti," *Aevum* 52, 1978, 1-16.
C. Boehringer, "Zur Finanzpolitik und Münzprägung des Dionysios von Syrakus," in O. Mørkholm and N.M. Waggoner (eds.), *Greek Numismatics and Archaeology: Essays in honor of Margaret Thompson*, Wetteren 1979, 9-32.
H. Bengtson, *Griechische Staatsmänner des 5. und 4. Jahrhunderts v. Chr.*, Munich 1983, 228-259 (Dionysius I); *ibid.*, 260-271 (Timoleon).
M. Sordi, "Timeo e Atanide, fonti per le ricende di Timoleonte," *Athenaeum* 55, 1977, 239-249.
Eadem, *La Sicilia dal 368/7 al 337/6 a.C.*, Rome 1983.
E. Manni *et al.*, "I Cartaginesi in Sicilia nell'epoca dei due Dionisi," *Kokalos* 28-29, 1982-1983, 127-277.
L.J. Sanders, *Dionysius I of Syracuse and Greek Tyranny*, London 1988.

n. 5 See also I.A.F. Bruce, "Theopompus, Lysander and the Spartan Empire," *The Ancient History Bulletin* 1, 1987, 1-5.

n. 6 D. Whitehead, "The Tribes of the Thirty Tyrants," *JHS* 100, 1980, 208-213 (a critical discussion of Loeper's theories); *idem*, "Sparta and the Thirty Tyrants," *AncSoc* 13/14, 1982/1983, 105-130.

489 n. 21 J.M. Bigwood, "The Ancient Accounts of the Battle of Cunaxa," *AJP* 104, 1983, 340-357.

n. 26 V.J. Gray, "Two Different Approaches to the Battle of Sardes in 395 B.C. Xenophon *Hellenica* 3.4.20-24 and *Hellenica Oxyrhynchea* III (6). 4-6," *CSCA* 12, 1979, 183-200.

490 n. 30 On Agesilaus, see C.D. Hamilton, "The Generalship of King Agesilaus of Sparta," *The Ancient World* 8, 1983, 119-127.

n. 39 J.G. DeVoto, "Agesilaus, Antalcidas, and the Failed Peace of 392/91 B.C.," *CP* 1986, 191-202.

n. 45 See also G.L. Cawkwell, "The King's Peace," *CQ* 31, 1981, 69-83.

491 n. 61 J. Buckler, "The Re-establishment of the *Boiotarchia* (378 B.C.)," *AJAH* 4, 1979, 50-64.

492 n. 72 H. Bengtson, *Griechische Staatsmänner des 5. und 4. Jahrhunderts v. Chr.*, Munich 1983, 199-227; see also P. Roesch, "Un décret inédit de la ligue thébaine et la flotte d'Epaminondas," *REG* 97, 1984, 45-60.

n. 77 J. Buckler, "Plutarch on Leuktra," *SO* 55, 1980, 75-93; C.J. Tuplin, "The Leuctra Campaign: Some Outstanding Problems," *Klio* 69, 1987, 108-121.

493 n. 95 On Antalkidas, see J. Buckler, "Plutarch and the Fate of Antalkidas," *GRBS* 18, 1977, 139-145.

494 n. 112 L.-M. Hans, *Karthago und Sizilien. Die Entstehung und Gestaltung der Epikratie auf dem Hintergrund der Beziehungen der Karthager zu den Griechen und den nichtgriechischen Völkern Siziliens (VI.-III. Jahrhundert v. Chr.)*, Hildesheim, Zurich, New York 1983.

n. 118 B.S.J. Isserlin and J. Du Plat Taylor, *Motya. A Phoenician and Carthaginian City in Sicily I: Fieldwork and Excavation*, Leiden 1974.

10. PHILIP II OF MACEDONIA

495 **Sources:** One of the most dramatic recent developments has been the discovery of the 'royal tombs' by Greek archaeologists at Vergina (cf. M. Andronikos, "The Royal Graves in the Great Tumulus," *AAA* 10, 1977, 40-72 [also published separately as *The Royal Graves at Vergina*, Athens 1980], cf. *idem*, "The Royal Tomb of Philip II. An Unlooted Tomb at Vergina," *Archaeology* 31,5, 1978, 33-41; *idem*, "The Royal Tombs at Aigai [Vergina]," in M.B. Hatzopoulos and L.D. Loukopoulos [eds.], *Philip of Macedon*, Athens 1980, 188-231; and *idem*, "The Finds from the Royal Tombs at Vergina," *ProcBritAcad* 65, 1981, 355-367). In the absence of any inscriptions or similar data in the tombs, and in the absence of a definitive publication of the results to date, an equally dramatic controversy has developed over the attribution of the tombs (Tombs I, II, III) and their contents (cf., however, M. Andronikos, *Vergina. The Royal Tombs and the Ancient City*, Athens 1984).

On three points, however, there seems to be broad agreement: 1) The identification of Vergina as Aegae (first demonstrated by N.G.L. Hammond, "The Archaeological Background of the Macedonian Kingdom," in *Archaia Makedonia I. Diethnes Symposion, 26-29 Aug. 1968*, Thessaloniki 1970, 65; cf. *idem*, *History of Macedonia* I, Oxford 1972, 56-58). 2) That the Great Tumulus constitutes the royal Macedonian necropolis. 3) That the finds are to be dated to the second half of the fourth century B.C.

On the other hand, there has been vigorous debate over the individuals who were interred in these tombs, especially in Tomb II. The chief contenders are Philip II and Philip III Arrhidaeus. For the former: M. Andronikos, *The Royal Graves at Vergina*, Athens 1978; N.G.L. Hammond, "'Philip's Tomb' in Historical Perspective," *GRBS* 19, 1978, 331-350; R.L. Fox, *The Search for Alexander*, Boston 1980, 81-89; W.L. Adams, "The Royal Macedonian Tomb at Vergina: An Historical Interpretation," *The Ancient World* 3, 1980, 67-72; M. Andronikos, "The Royal Tombs at Vergina and the Problem of the Dead," *AAA* 13, 1980, 168-178; E.A. Fredricksmeyer, "Again the So-called Tomb of Philip II," *AJA* 85, 1981, 330-334; W.M. Calder III, "Diadem and Barrel-Vault: a Note," *AJA* 85, 1981, 334-335; P. Green, "The Royal Tombs at Vergina: A Historical Analysis," in W.L. Adams and E.N. Borza (eds.), *Philip II, Alexander the Great and the Macedonian Heritage*, Washington 1982, 129-151; E.A. Fredricksmeyer, "Once more the Diadem and Barrel-Vault at Vergina," *AJA* 87, 1983, 99-102. For Philip III Arrhidaeus: P. Williams Lehmann, "The So-Called Tomb of Philip II: a Different Interpretation," *AJA* 84, 1980, 527-531; A. Prestianni Giallombardo and B. Tripodi, "Le Tombe regale di Vergina: quale Filippo?," *Annali della Scuola Normale Superiore di Pisa, clas. lett. fil.* 10, 1980, 989-1001; P. Williams Lehmann, "Once again the Royal Tomb at Vergina," *AAA* 14, 1981, 134-144; *eadem*, "The So-Called Tomb of Philip II: An Addendum," *AJA* 86, 1982, 437-442; cf. E.N. Borza, "The Macedonian Royal Tombs at Vergina: Some Cautionary Notes," *ArchNews* 10, 1981, 73-87; 11, 1982, 8-10.

Meanwhile, the debate has entered a new phase with the scientific analysis of the skeletal remains, in which, however, slightly differing conclusions appear to have been reached, but essentially in favour of Philip II. Thus, N.I. Xirotiris and F. Langenscheidt, "The Cremations from the Royal Macedonian Tombs of Vergina," *Archaiologike Ephemeris* 1981, 142-160, cf. A.J.N.W. Prag, J.H. Musgrave and R.A.H. Neave, "The Skull from Tomb II at Vergina: King Philip II of Macedonia," *JHS* 104, 1984, 60-78.

No less controversial, it seems, is the question of the artistic style represented by the contents of the tombs, culminating in the small ivory bust of Alexander the Great from Tomb II (cf. M. Andronikos, N. Yalouris, and K. Rhomiopoulou, *The Search for Alexander: An Exhibition*, New York 1980, 187 Fig. 171 and Colour Pl. 34). If a date of 336 B.C. is accepted for this piece, it threatens to stand some of the fundamental views concerning late Classical–early Hellenistic art on their heads. According to one study, "Either the tomb is that of Philip and we must re-think the development of portraiture in the time of Alexander, or its presence is an indication that the attribution of the tomb is in error" (R.W. Hartle, "The Search for Alexander's Portrait," in W.L. Adams and E.N. Borza [eds.], *Philip II, Alexander the Great and the Macedonian Heritage*, Washington 1982, 174).

The controversy over identification of the individuals buried in these tombs has, however, tended to obscure their real significance. These tombs incontrovertibly afford us a new insight into Macedonian wealth and royal burial habits at this time.

Meanwhile, however, the focus of attention has shifted from Vergina to Pella, where the excavations of Maria Karamanoli-Siganidou have disclosed the gigantic size of the palace, namely, covering an area of five to six hectares, raising, among other things, the question of whether Alexander the Great may have been born here (cf. M.

Karamanoli-Siganidou, *ArchDelt* 32, 1977 [1984] Chron. P. 213-216; 33, 1978 [1985], Chron. P. 259-263; H.W. Catling, *ArchRep* 32, 1985-86, 61-62; 33, 1986-87, 39).

Coins: G. Le Rider, *Le monnayage d'argent et d'or de Philippe frappé en Macédoine 351 à 294*, Paris 1977.

496 **Isocrates:** On his *Philippos*, see M.M. Markle, "Athenian Intellectuals and the Support for Philip," *JHS* 96, 1976, 80-99.

499 **Demosthenes:** H. Wankel, *Rede für Ktesiphon über den Kranz*, 2 vols., Heidelberg 1976.
M.R. Dilts (ed.), *Scholia Demosthenica I: Scholia in orationes 1-18 continens*, Leipzig 1983.
L. Pearson, *The Art of Demosthenes* (Beiträge zur Klassischen Philologie 68), Meisenheim am Glan 1976.
U. Schindl, *Demosthenes* (Wege der Forschung 350), Darmstadt 1982.
H. Bengtson, *Griechische Staatsmänner des 5. und 4. Jahrhunderts v. Chr.*, Munich 1983, 272-306.

Diodorus: Useful for Diodorus is J.I. McDougall, *Lexicon in Diodorum Siculum. Pars I: Alpha-Kappa; Pars II: Lamda-Omega*, Hildesheim and New York 1983.
For a selection of sources in translation, see P. Harding, *From the End of the Peloponnesian War to the Battle of Ipsus* (Translated Documents of Greece and Rome 2), Cambridge 1985.

Bibliography

General Works: N.G.L. Hammond and G.T. Griffith, *A History of Macedonia II: 550-336 B.C.*, Oxford 1979 (Hammond: 550-359 [1-202]; Griffith: 359-336 [203-731]) (cf. M. Zahrnt, *Gnomon* 55, 1983, 36-46).
Ed. Will, *Histoire politique du monde hellénistique (323-30 av. J.-C.)*, Nancy, I, 1979; II, 1982.
M. Errington, *Geschichte Makedoniens. Von den Anfängen bis zum Untergang des Königreiches*, Munich 1986.

Studies on Specific Subjects: M. Opitz, *Das Bild Philipps II. von Makedonien bei den attischen Rednern im ersten Jahrzehnt seiner Herrschaft*, Diss. Düsseldorf 1976.
J.R. Ellis, *Philip II and Macedonian Imperialism*, London 1976.
G.W. Cawkwell, *Philip of Macedon*, London 1978.
K. Rosen, "Die Gründung der makedonischen Herrschaft," *Chiron* 8, 1978, 1-27.
R.M. Errington, "The Nature of the Macedonian State under the Monarchy," *Chiron* 8, 1978, 77-133.
M.H. Hansen, *Die athenische Volksversammlung im Zeitalter des Demosthenes* (Xenia 13), Konstanz 1984.

H. Bengtson, *Philipp und Alexander der Grosse. Die Begründer der hellenistischen Welt*, Munich 1985, 52-117.
H. Montgomery, "The Economic Revolution of Philip II—Myth or Reality?," *SO* 60, 1985, 37-47.

501 **Macedonia before Philip II:** On Vol. I of Hammond's *History of Macedonia*, see the review by M. Zahrnt, *Gnomon* 55, 1983, 36-46.
M. Zahrnt, "Die Entwicklung des makedonischen Reiches bis zu den Perserkriegen," *Chiron* 14, 1984, 325-368.

The First Years of Philip's Reign: M.B. Hatzopoulos, "The Oleveni Inscription and the Dates of Philip's Reign," in W.L. Adams and E.N. Borza (eds.), *Philip II, Alexander the Great and the Macedonian Heritage*, Washington 1982, 21-42.

502 **Greece and Macedonia in the Time of the Third Sacred War:** E.W. Marsden, "Macedonian Military Machinery and its Designers under Philip and Alexander," in K. Metsakas (ed.), *Ancient Macedonia II: Papers read at the Second International Symposium held in Thessaloniki, 19-24 August 1973*, Thessaloniki 1977, 211-223.
M.M. Markle III, "Use of the Sarissa by Philip and Alexander of Macedon," *AJA* 82, 1978, 483-497.
J.R. Ellis, "Philip's Thracian Campaign of 352-351," *CP* 72, 1977, 32-39.
G. Roux, *L'amphictionie, Delphes et le temple d'Apollon au IVᵉ siècle*, Paris 1979.
D.H. Kelley, "Philip II of Macedon and the Boeotian Alliance," *Antichthon* 14, 1980, 64-83.
H. Wankel, "Philipp II. an den Thermopylen 346," *ZPE* 39, 1980, 57-62.
J.R. Ellis, "Philip and the Peace of Philocrates," in W.L. Adams and E.N. Borza (eds.), *Philip II, Alexander the Great and the Macedonian Heritage*, Washington 1982, 43-59.
C.D. Hamilton, "Philip II and Archidamus," *ibid.*, 61-83.
J. Buckler, "Thebes, Delphoi and the Outbreak of the Third Sacred War," in *La Béotie antique. Lyon-Saint-Étienne, 16-20 mai 1983*, Paris 1985, 237-246.
W. Unte, "Die Phoker und der Philokratesfrieden," *Hermes* 115, 1987, 411-429.

503 **From the Peace of Philocrates to the Death of Philip II**

Studies on Specific Subjects: S.M. Burnstein, "I.G. II^2 653, Demosthenes and Athenian Relations with the Bosporus in the Fourth Century," *Historia* 27, 1978, 428-436.
G.L. Cawkwell, "Euboea in the Late 340's," *Phoenix* 32, 1978, 42-67.
On **Philip's ultimate plans**, see E.A. Fredricksmeyer, "On the Final Aims of Philip II," in W.L. Adams and E.N. Borza (eds.), *Philip II*,

Alexander the Great and the Macedonian Heritage, Washington 1982, 85-98.

n. 7 Meanwhile, more final reports on Labraunda have appeared: *I, 3: The Temple of Zeus*, by P. Hellström and Th. Thieme, Stockholm 1982; *II, 4: Die karischen Inschriften*, by M. Meier-Brüger, Stockholm 1983. On Amyzon, see now J. and L. Robert, *Fouilles d'Amyzon en Carie I: Exploration, histoire, monnaies et inscriptions*, Paris 1983. And on Stratoniceia, see M.C. Şahin, *The Political and Religious Structure in the Territory of Stratonikeia in Caria*, Ankara 1976; *idem*, *Die Inschriften von Stratonikeia* (Inschriften griechischer Städte aus Kleinasien 21 and 22, 1-2), Bonn 1981, 1982.

n. 9 R. Bichler, '*Hellenismus*'. *Geschichte und Problematik eines Epochenbegriffs* (Impulse der Forschung 41), Darmstadt 1983 (cf. S. Hornblower, *CR* 34, 1984, 245-247).

505 n. 48 F. Papazoglou, "Le territoire de la colonie de Philippes," *BCH* 106, 1982, 89-106.

507 n. 77 See also G. Cawkwell, "The Peace of Philocrates Again," *CQ* 28, 1978, 93-104.

n. 80 I. Prunner, *Die Rolle Delphis in der griechischen Geschichte des 4. und 3. Jahrhunderts*, Diss. Vienna 1981.

508 n. 110 H. Wankel, "Die athenischen Strategen der Schlacht bei Chaironeia," *ZPE* 55, 1984, 45-53.
M.A. Kondrat'uk, "The League of Corinth and its Role in the Political History of Greece in the Thirties and Twenties of the Fourth Century B.C.," *VDI* 140, 1977, 25-42 [Russ., with Eng. summary]; R. Urban, "Das Verbot innenpolitischer Umwälzungen durch den Korinthischen Bund (338/37) in antimakedonischer Argumentation," *Historia* 30, 1981, 11-21.
S. Perlman, "Greek Diplomatic Tradition and the Corinthian League of Philip of Macedon," *Historia* 34, 1985, 153-174.

509 n. 115 Cf. J.R. Ellis, "The Assassination of Philip II," in H.J. Dell (ed.), *Ancient Macedonia: Studies in honor of Charles F. Edson*, Thessaloniki 1981, 99-137.

11. ALEXANDER THE GREAT

510 **Sources**

Portraits: R. Leimbach, "Plutarch über das Aussehen Alexanders des Grossen," *AA* 1979, 213-220.
W. Radt, "Der 'Alexanderkopf' in Istanbul. Ein Kopf aus dem grossen Fries des Pergamon-Altars," *AA* 1981, 583-596.

Coins: M.J. Price, "In Search of Alexander the Great," *NomChron* 5-6, 1978, 27-34.
Idem, "Alexander's Reform of the Macedonian Royal Coinage," *NC* 22, 1982, 180-190.
Idem, "The Porus Coinage of Alexander the Great. A Symbol of Concord and Community," in *Studia Paulo Naster oblata I: Numismatica Antiqua*, Louvain 1982, 75-88.
O.H. Zervos, "The Earliest Coins of Alexander the Great," *NumChron* 142, 1982, 166-194.

511 **Documentary Evidence:** L.L. Gunderson, *Alexander's Letter to Aristotle about India* (Beiträge zur Klassischen Philologie 110), Meisenheim am Glan 1980.
On **the letter of Aristotle to Alexander**, see also A.J. Heisserer, *Alexander the Great and the Greeks: The Epigraphic Evidence*, Norman, Okl., 1980.
M. Sordi, "La lettere di Aristotele ad Alessandro e i raporti tra Greci e Barbari," *Aevum* 58, 1984, 3-12.
Important, although of only indirect significance for Alexander, is **the trilingual inscription** (Greek, Lycian, Aramaic) discovered in 1963 during the excavations at Xanthos. See H. Metzger, E. Laroche, A. Dupont-Sommer and M. Mayerhofer, *Fouilles de Xanthos VII: La stèle trilingue du Létoon*, Paris 1979 (cf. A. Heubeck, *Gnomon* 52, 1980, 560-561).

513 **Aristobulus:** P. Pédech, *Historiens compagnons d'Alexandre: Callisthène, Onésicrite, Néarcque, Ptolémée, Aristobule* (Collection d'Études Anciennes), Paris 1984.

514 **Q. Curtius Rufus:** J.E. Atkinson, *A Commentary on Q. Curtius Rufus' Historiae Alexandri Magni Books 3 and 4* (London Studies in Classical Philology 4), Amsterdam and Uithoorn 1980.
L.L. Gunderson, "Quintus Curtius Rufus: On his Historical Methods in the *Historiae Alexandri*," in W.L. Adams and E.N. Borza (eds.), *Philip II, Alexander the Great and the Macedonian Heritage*, Washington 1982, 177-196.
On the Vulgate historians see also N.G.L. Hammond, *Three Historians of Alexander the Great. The So-called Vulgate Authors, Diodorus, Justin and Curtius. A Collection of Articles 1976-1983*, Copenhagen 1983 (cf. C. Reid Rubincam, *Phoenix* 40, 1986, 208-211).
J. Yardley and W. Heckel, *Quintus Curtius Rufus: The History of Alexander* (translation by J. Yardley, Introduction and Notes by W. Heckel), Harmondsworth 1984.

Flavius Arrianus: For an edition of Arrian, see now, in particular, P.A. Brunt, *Arrian*. With an English Translation, in two vols. I: *Anabasis Alexandri* (*Bks. I-IV*); II: *Indica* (*Bks. V-VII*) (Loeb), Cambridge, Mass., and London 1983.

Equally valuable is A.B. Bosworth, *A Historical Commentary on Arrian's History of Alexander I: Commentary on Books I-III*, Oxford 1980.
And for a good monograph on Arrian, cf. P.A. Stadter, *Arrian of Nicomedia*, Chapel Hill, N.C., 1980.
J.H. Olivier, "Arrian in two Roles," in *Studies in Attic Epigraphy, History and Topography Presented to Eugene Vanderpool* (Hesp. Suppl. 19), Princeton, N.J., 1982, 122-129.
G. Wirth, "Ephemeridenspekulationen," in H. Kalcyk, B. Gullath and A. Graeber (eds.), *Studien zur Alten Geschichte. Siegfried Lauffer zum 70. Geburtstag am 4. August 1981 dargebracht von Freunden, Kollegen und Schülern* III, Rome 1986, 1049-1075.
See also P. Pédech, "Les historiens d'Alexandre," in T. Reekmans, E. van't Dack and H. Verdin (eds.), *Historiographia Antiqua. Commentationes Lovanienses in honorem W. Peremans septuagenarii editae*, Louvain 1977, 119-138.

515 **The Alexander Romance:** U. Wilcken, *Alexander der Grosse und die indischen Gymnosophisten*, SB Berlin 1923 No. XXIII, 150 ff., provides some observations on a number of papyrus fragments which contain legendary details on Alexander; Wilcken also provides information on the Metzer Epitome, p. 159. On the whole question see now R. Merkelbach, *Die Quellen des griechischen Alexanderromans* (Zetemata 9), Munich [2]1978. Also F. Pfister, *Der Alexanderroman. Mit einer Auswahl aus den verwandten Texten* (Beiträge zur Klassischen Philologie 92), Meisenheim am Glan 1978.
For a selection of documents in English, see P. Harding, *From the End of the Peloponnesian War to the Battle of Ipsus* (Translated Documents of Greece and Rome 2), Cambridge 1985.

517 **Bibliography**

General Assessments: P. Briant, *Alexandre le Grand*, Paris 1974.
M.A. Levi, *Alessandro Magno*, Milan 1977.
S. Laufer, *Alexander der Grosse*, Munich 1978 [[2]1981].
A. Jähne, "Alexander der Grosse. Persönlichkeit, Politik, Ökonomie," *Jahrb. für Wirtschaftsgesch.* 1978, Teil I, 245-261.
N.G.L. Hammond, *Alexander the Great: King, Commander and Statesman*, London 1981.
P. Faure, *Alexandre*, Paris 1985.
H. Bengtson, *Philipp und Alexander. Die Begründer der hellenistischen Welt*, Munich 1985, 125-267.
W. Will, *Alexander der Grosse. Geschichte Makedoniens*, 2, Stuttgart, Berlin, Cologne, Mainz 1986.
M. Errington, *Geschichte Makedoniens. Von den Anfängen bis zum Untergang des Königreiches*, Munich 1986.

Studies on Specific Aspects: C.G. Starr, "Greeks and Persians in the Fourth Century B.C. A Study in Cultural Contacts before Alexander II: The Meeting of Two Cultures," *Iranica Antiqua* 12, 1977, 49-115.

A. Heuss, "Alexander der Grosse und das Problem der historischen Urteilsbildung," *HZ* 225, 1977, 29-64.
D.W. Engels, *Alexander the Great and the Logistics of the Macedonian Army*, Berkeley 1978.
D. Engels, "Alexander's Intelligence System," *CQ* 30, 1980, 327-340.
N.M. Waggoner, "Tetradrachms from Babylon," in O. Mørkholm and N.M. Waggoner (eds.), *Greek Numismatics and Archaeology: Essays in Honor of Margaret Thompson*, Wetteren 1979, 269-280.
M.J. Price, "On Attributing Alexanders—Some Cautionary Tales," *ibid.*, 241-246; cf. O.H. Zervos, *ibid.*, 295-305.
P. Goukowsky, *Essai sur les origines du mythe Alexandre (336-270 av. J.-C.)*, I: *Les origines politiques*, Nancy 1978; II: *Alexandre et Dionysos*, Nancy 1981.
W.E. Higgins, "Aspects of Alexander's Imperial Administration: Some Modern Methods and Views Reviewed," *Athenaeum* 58, 1980, 129-152.
B. Gullah, *Untersuchungen zur Geschichte Boiotiens in der Zeit Alexanders und der Diadochen*, Frankfurt am Main and Berlin 1982.
P. Faure, *La vie quotidienne des armées d'Alexandre*, Paris 1982.
W. Will, *Athen und Alexander. Untersuchungen zur Geschichte der Stadt von 338 bis 322 v. Chr.* (Münchener Beiträge zur Papyrusforschung und antiken Rechtsgeschichte 77), Munich 1983 (cf. A.B. Bosworth, *Gnomon* 57, 1985, 431-436).
M. Sordi (ed.), *Alessandro Magno tra storia e mito* (Ricerche dell'Istituto di Storia Antica del Università Cattolica di Milano), Milan 1984.
J. Seibert, *Die Eroberung des Perserreiches durch Alexander den Grossen auf kartographischer Grundlage* (Beih. zum Tübinger Atlas des Vorderen Orients R.B., Geisteswiss. 68), Wiesbaden 1985.
C.J. Schwenk, *Athens in the Age of Alexander. The Dated Laws and Decrees of the 'Lykourgan Era,' 338-322 B.C.*, Chicago 1985.
B.M. Kingsley, "Harpalos in the Megarid (333-331 B.C.) and the Grain Shipments from Cyrene (S.E.G. IX 2 + = Tod, Greek Hist. Inscr. II no. 196)," *ZPE* 66, 1986, 165-177.
A.B. Bosworth, "Alexander the Great and the decline of Macedon," *JHS* 106, 1986, 1-12.
A.E. Samuel, "The Earliest Elements in the Alexander Romance," *Historia* 35, 1986, 427-437.
J.S. Morrison, "Athenian sea-power in 323/2 BC: dream and reality," *JHS* 107, 1987, 88-97.
W. Will (ed.), *Zu Alexander d. Gr. Festschrift G. Wirth zum 60. Geburtstag am 9.12.86*, Amsterdam 1988.

518 **From the Hellespont to Persepolis:** E.W. Marsden, "Macedonian Military Machinery and its Designers under Philip and Alexander," in K. Metsakas (ed.), *Ancient Macedonia II: Papers read at the Second International Symposium held in Thessaloniki, 19-24 August 1973*, Thessaloniki 1977, 211-223.

M.M. Markle III, "Macedonian Arms and Tactics under Alexander the Great," in B. Barr-Sharrar and E.N. Borza (eds.), *Macedonia and Greece in Late Classical and Early Hellenistic Times*, Washington 1982, 87-112.
G. Wirth, "Erwägungen zur Chronologie des Jahres 333 v. Chr.," *Helikon* 17, 1977, 23-55.
E.I. McQueen, "Some Notes on the Anti-Macedon Movement in the Peloponnese in 331 B.C.," *Historia* 27, 1978, 40-64.
P. Högemann, *Alexander der Grosse und Arabien*, Munich 1985 (cf. G.W. Bowersock, *Gnomon* 59, 1987, 508-511).

519 **The Conquest of East Iran and North-West India:** P.H.L. Eggermont, *Alexander's Campaigns in Sind and Baluchistan and the Siege of the Brahmin Town of Harmatelia*, Louvain 1975.
A.B. Bosworth, "A Missing Year in the History of Alexander the Great," *JHS* 101, 1981, 17-39 (C. Rufus is to be preferred to Arrian, who contains major distortions).
Idem, "The Indian Satrapies under Alexander the Great," *Antichthon* 17, 1983, 37-46 (the Indian provinces were reorganised under Alexander and not under his successors).
W. Vogelsang, "Early Historical Arachosia in South-East Afghanistan: Meeting-place between East and West," *Iranica Antiqua* 20, 1985, 55-99.
E. Badian, "Alexander in Iran," in I. Gershevitch (ed.), *The Cambridge History of Iran* 2, Cambridge 1985, 420-501 (with extensive bibliography: 897-903).
Idem, "Alexander at Peucelaotis," *CQ* 37, 1987, 117-128.

Alexander's Last Years: See the important study by S. Jaschinski, *Alexander und Griechenland unter dem Eindruck der Flucht des Harpalos*, Bonn 1981.
U. Hackl, "Die sogenannten Weltreichspläne Alexanders des Grossen," *WürzbJahrb* N.F. 12, 1986, 105-124.

520 n. 14 See also W. Rutz, "Das Bild des Dareios bei Curtius Rufus," *WürbJahrb* N.F. 10, 1984, 147-159.
J. Seibert, "Dareios III," in W. Will (ed.), *Zu Alexander d. Gr. Festschrift G. Wirth zum 60. Geburtstag am 9.12.86*, Amsterdam 1988, 437-448.

n. 18 N.G.L. Hammond, "The Battle of the Granicus River," *JHS* 100, 1980, 73-88; cf., however, E. Badian, "The Battle of the Granicus: a New Look," in K. Metsakas (ed.), *Ancient Macedonia II: Papers read at the Second International Symposium held in Thessaloniki, 19-24 August 1973*, Thessaloniki 1977, 271-293, and C. Foss, "The Battle of the Granicus: a New Look," *ibid.*, 495-502; and especially A.B. Bosworth, *A Historical Commentary on Arrian's History of Alexander* I, Oxford 1980, s.v. Bk. I, 13-16.

Otherwise, A.M. Devine, "Demythologising the Battle of the Granicus," *Phoenix* 40, 1986, 265-278.

521 n. 37 B.R. Brown, "Deinokrates and Alexandria," *BullAmerSocPapyr* 15, 1978, 39-42; R.S. Bagnall, "The Date of the Foundation of Alexandria," *AJAH* 4, 1979, 46-49.

522 n. 46 G. Wirth, "Zwei Lager bei Gaugamela. Zur grossen Konfrontation 331 v. Chr.," *Quaderni Catanesi di studi classici e medievali* 2, 1980, 51-100; *idem*, *ibid*. 3, 1981, 5-61.

523 n. 52 The view adopted by J.M. Balcer, "Alexander's Burning of Persepolis," *Iranica Antiqua* 13, 1978, 119-133, is not compelling.

n. 59 N.G.L. Hammond, "The Campaign of Alexander against Cleitus and Glaucias," in K. Metsakas (ed.), *Ancient Macedonia II: Papers read at the Second International Symposium held in Thessaloniki 19-24 August 1973*, Thessaloniki 1977, 503-509; E. Carney, "The Death of Clitus," *GRBS* 22, 1981, 149-160.

524 n. 73 S. Jaschinski, *Alexander und Griechenland unter dem Eindruck der Flucht des Harpalos*, Bonn 1981; cf. I. Worthington, "The Flight of Harpalus Reconsidered," *G & R* 21, 1984, 161-169.

n. 79 Also D.S. Potter, "IG II^{2} 399: Evidence for Athenian Involvement in the War of Agis III," *BSA* 79, 1984, 229-235.

525 n. 89 J. Coulomb, "La mort d'Alexandre le Grand," *Histoire des sciences médicales* 18, 1984, 137-145.

526 n. 96 A.B. Bosworth, "Alexander and the Iranians," *JHS* 100, 1980, 1-21.

n. 100 An illuminating instance of city foundations is illustrated by the recent excavations at Aï Khanoum in Bactria. See, for instance, for final reports, P. Bernard, *Fouilles d'Aï Khanoum 1. Campagnes 1965, 1966, 1967, 1968* (Mémoires de la délégation archéologique française en Afghanistan 21), Paris 1973 (cf. K. Fischer, *Gnomon* 48, 1976, 290-295); O. Guillaume, *Fouilles d'Aï Khanoum 2. Les propylées de la rue principale* (Mém. de la déleg. arch. franç. en Afgh. 26), Paris 1983; H.P. Francfort, *Fouilles d'Aï Khanoum III: Le sanctuaire du temple à niches indentés 2: Les trouvailles* (Mém. de la déleg. arch. franç. en Afgh. 27), Paris 1984. P. Bernard, *Fouilles d'Aï Khanoum IV: Les monnaies hors trésors. Questions d'histoire grèco-bactrienne* (Mém. de la déleg. arch. franç. en Afgh. 28), Paris 1985 (cf. S. Sherwin-White, *JHS* 107, 1987, 238-239). P. Leriche, *Fouilles d'Aï Khanoum V. Les remparts et les monuments associés* (Mém. de la déleg. arch. franç. en Afgh. 29), Paris 1986 (cf. R.A. Tomlinson *JHS* 107, 1987, 251-252). For preliminary reports: P. Bernard, *CRAI* 1970, 301-349; 1971, 385-453; 1974, 280-308; 1975, 167-197; 1976, 287-322; 1978, 421-463; 1980, 435-459; *idem*, "Campagne de fouilles

1978 à Aï Khanoum (Afghanistan)," *Bull. Éc. fr. Extrême-Orient* 68, 1980, 1-75; and on special aspects, *idem*, "Alexandre de Aï Khanoum," *Journal des Savants* 1982, 125-138 (takes issue with A.B. Bosworth, *JHS* 101, 1981, 17-39, and *idem*, *JHS* 100, 1980, 1-21); P. Bernard and O. Guillaume, "Monnaies inédites de la Bactriane grecque à Aï Khanoum (Afghanistan)," *RevNum* 22, 1980, 9-32; S. Veuve, "Cadrans solaires greco-bactriens à Aï Khanoum (Afghanistan)," *BCH* 106, 1982, 23-51; C. Rapina, "Les textes littéraires grec de la Trésorerie d'Aï Khanoum," *BCH* 111, 1987, 225-266. See also W. Leschhorn, *'Gründer der Stadt': Studien zu einem politisch-religiösen Phänomen der griechischen Geschichte* (Palingenesia 20), Wiesbaden and Stuttgart 1984, 203-233; and P.M. Fraser, "The Son of Aristonax at Kandahar," *Afghan Studies* 2, 1979 [1980], 9-21.

n. 102 P. Briant, "Colonisation hellénistique et populations indigènes. La phase d'installation," *Klio* 60, 1978, 57-92. Cf. J. Wolski, "Le problème de la fondation de l'état greco-bactrien," *Iranica Antiqua* 17, 1982, 131-146.

n. 108 And on the **apotheosis** of Alexander, see E. Badian, "The deification of Alexander the Great," in H.J. Dell (ed.), *Ancient Macedonia: Studies in honor of Charles F. Edson*, Thessaloniki 1981, 27-71; also E.A. Fredericksmeyer, "On the background to the Ruler Cult," *ibid.*, 145-156; and J.R. Hamilton, "The Origins of Ruler-Cult," *Prudentia* 16, 1984, 3-15.

12. THE HELLENISTIC MONARCHIES

527 **Sources**

Hieronymus of Cardia: J. Hornblower, *Hieronymus of Cardia*, Oxford 1981 (cf. A.B. Bosworth, *JHS* 103, 1983, 209-210).

Diodorus: R.M. Errington, "Diodorus Siculus and the Chronology of the Early Diadochoi, 320-311 B.C.," *Hermes* 105, 1977, 478-504 (Diodorus' statements on chronology are not reliable).

528 **Polybius:** H. Labuske, "Zur geschichtsphilosophischen Konzeption des Polybios," *Klio* 59, 1977, 403-413.
For further volumes in the Budé edition, see P. Pédech, livre V, 1977; R. Weil, livre VI, VII-IX, 1977 and 1982.
S. Mohm, *Untersuchungen zu den historiographischen Anschauungen des Polybios*, Diss. Saarbrücken 1977.
See also F.W. Walbank, "Polybius' Last Ten Books," in T. Reekmans, E. van't Dack and H. Verdin (eds.), *Historiographica Antiqua. Commentationes Lovanienses in honorem W. Peremans septuagenarii editae*, Louvain 1977, 139-162.
For a collection of studies on Polybius, see K. Stiewe and N. Holzberg (eds.), *Polybios* (Wege der Forschung CCCXLVII), Darmstadt 1982.

See also M.M. Austin (ed.), *The Hellenistic World from Alexander to the Roman Conquest: A Selection of Ancient Sources in Translation*, Cambridge 1981.
R.S. Bagnall and P. Derow (eds.), *Greek Historical Documents: The Hellenistic Period*, Chico, Ca., 1981.
P. Harding (ed.), *From the End of the Peloponnesian War to the Battle of Ipsus* (Translated Documents of Greece and Rome 2), Cambridge 1985.

Bibliography: F.W. Walbank, "Polybius," *CAH* VII 1², 1984, 1-22 [= F.W. Walbank, A.E. Astin, M.W. Frederiksen and R.M. Ogilvie (eds.), *The Cambridge Ancient History VII 12: The Hellenistic World*, Cambridge 1984 (cf. M.M. Austin, *JHS* 107, 1987, 229-230)].
E. Ling (ed.), *CAH: Plates to Volume VII Part 1*, Cambridge 1984.

530 K. Sacks, *Polybius on the Writing of History* (University of California Publications in Classical Studies 24), Berkeley and Los Angeles 1981.

531 **Demetrius of Phalerum:** H.-J. Gehrke, "Das Verhältnis vom Politik und Philosophie im Wirken des Demetrios von Phaleron," *Chiron* 8, 1978, 149-193.

Inscriptions: Very useful in connection with *Syll.* I³ and *OGI* I is W. Gawantka, *Aktualisierende Konkordanzen zu Dittenbergers Orientis Graeci Inscriptiones Selectae (OGIS) und zur dritten Auflage der von ihm begründeten Sylloge Inscriptionum Graecarum (Syll.³)* (Subsidia Epigraphica 8), Hildesheim and New York 1977.
E. Bernand, "Le corpus des inscriptions grecques de l'Égypte," *ZPE* 26, 1977, 95-117.

Coinage: O. Mørkholm, "Cyrene and Ptolemy I: Some Numismatic Comments," *Chiron* 10, 1980, 145-159.

532 **Chronology:** A.A. Mosshammer, *The Chronicle of Eusebius and the Greek Chronographic Tradition*, Lewisburg and London 1979 (cf. W.G. Forrest, *CR* 31, 1981, 77-79).

Bibliography: A new contribution in prosopography is (the first of three planned volumes) E. Olshausen, *Prosopographie der hellenistischen Königsgesanten I: Von Triparadeisos bis Pydna* (Studia Hellenistica 19), Louvain 1974 (cf. S.M. Sherwin-White, *JHS* 96, 1976, 232-233).
For a review of the literature on the whole period, see J. Seibert, *Das Zeitalter der Diadochen* (Ertäge der Forschung 185), Darmstadt 1983.
H.H. Schmitt and E. Vogt (eds.), *Kleines Wörterbuch des Hellenismus*, Wiesbaden [in press].

534 **The Struggle for Alexander's Empire:** Ed. Will, "The Succession to Alexander," *CAH* VII 1², 1984, 23-61.
H.-J. Gehrke, *Phokion. Studien zur Erfassung seiner historischen Gestalt* (Zetemata 64), Munich 1976.

R.M. Errington, "An Inscription from Beroia and the Alleged Co-Rule of Demetrius II," in K. Metsakas (ed.), *Ancient Macedonia II: Papers Read at the Second International Symposium Held in Thessaloniki, 19-24 August 1973*, Thessaloniki 1977, 115-122.

K. Buraselis, *Das hellenistische Makedonien und die Ägäis. Forschungen zur Politik des Kassandros und der drei ersten Antigoniden (Antigonos Monophthalmos, Demetrios Poliorketes und Antigonos Gonatas) im Ägäischen Meer und in Westkleinasien* (Münchener Beiträge zur Papyrusforschung und antiken Rechtsgeschichte 73), Munich 1982 (cf. P.M. Fraser, *CR* 34, 1984, 259-261).

B.Z. Wachholder, "The Beginning of the Seleucid Era and the Chronology of the Diadochoi," in F.E. Greenspahn *et al.* (eds.), *Nourished with Peace: Studies in Hellenistic Judaism in Memory of Samuel Sandmel*, Chico, Ca., 1984, 183-211.

B. Gullath and L. Schober, "Zur Chronologie der frühen Diadochenzeit. Die Jahre 320 bis 315 v. Chr.," in H. Kalcyk, B. Gullath and A. Graeber (eds.), *Studien zur Alten Geschichte Siegfried Lauffer zum 70. Geburtstag am 4. August 198l dargebracht von Freunden, Kollegen und Schülern* I, Rome 1986, 329-378.

J. Seibert, "Demographische und wirtschaftliche Probleme Makedoniens in der frühen Diadochenzeit," *ibid.* III, 835-851.

A. Mehl, *Seleukos Nikator und sein Reich. I. Teil: Seleukos' Leben und die Entwicklung seiner Machtposition* (Studia Hellenistica), Louvain 1986.

H. Bengtson, *Die Diadochen. Die Nachfolger Alexanders des Grossen (323-281 v. Chr.)*, Munich 1987.

U. Hackl, "Die Aufhebung der attischen Demokratie nach dem Lamischen Krieg 322 v. Chr.," *Klio* 69, 1987, 58-71.

535 **The Consolidation of the Hellenistic Territorial States:** On **Demitrias**, see V. Milojčić *et al.*, *Demitrias 1* (Die deutschen archäologischen Forschungen in Thessalien. Beiträge zur ur- und frühgeschichtlichen Archäologie des Mittelmeerkulturraumes 12), Bonn 1976.

S.C. Bakhuizen, F. Gschnitzer, Ch. Habicht and P. Marzolff, *Demetrias* 5 (Die deutschen archäologischen Forschungen in Thessalien. Beiträge zur ur- und frühgeschichtlichen Archäologie des Mittelmeerkulturraumes 27), Bonn [in press].

U. Kron and A. Furtwängler, "Demetrios Poliorketes, Demetrias und die Magneten. Zum Bedeutungswandel von Siegel- und Münzbild einer Stadt," in C. Svolopoulos (ed.), *Ancient Macedonia III: Papers read at the Third International Symposium held in Thessaloniki, September 21-25, 1977*, Thessaloniki 1983, 147-168.

M. Wörrle, "Epigraphische Forschungen zur Geschichte Lykiens I," *Chiron* 7, 1977, 43-66.

See also S.M. Burnstein (ed.), *The Hellenistic Age from the Battle of Ipsos to the Death of Kleopatra VII* (Translated Documents of Greece and Rome 3), Cambridge 1985.

Bibliography: F.W. Walbank, "Monarchies and Monarchic Ideas," *CAH* VII 1^{2}, 62-100.
Ed. Will, "The Formation of the Hellenistic Kingdoms," *ibid.*, 101-117.
E.S. Gruen, "The Coronation of the Diadochoi," in J.W. Eadie and J. Ober (eds.), *The Craft of the Ancient Historian. Essays in honor of Chester G. Starr*, Lanham, New York, London 1985, 253-271, attempts a new interpretation of the assuming of the royal title.
H.W. Ritter, "Die Bedeutung des Diadems," *Historia* 36, 1987, 290-301.
H. Bengtson, *Die Diadochen. Die Nachfolger Alexanders des Grossen (323-281 v. Chr.)*, Munich 1987.
On **Aetolia**, see A.B. Bosworth, "Early Relations between Aetolia and Macedon," *AJAH* 1, 1976, 164-181.
On **Antigonid Sea-Power**: F.W. Walbank, "Sea-Power and the Antigonids," in W.L. Adams and E.N. Borza (eds.), *Philip II, Alexander the Great and the Macedonian Heritage*, Washington 1982, 213 ff.
On **Delos**: C. Vial, *Délos indépendante (314-167 avant J.-C.). Étude d'une communauté vivique et de ses institutions* (BCH Suppl. 10), Paris 1984.

537 **The Western Greeks in the Time of Agathocles and Pyrrhus**

Bibliography: K. Meister, "Agathocles," *CAH* VII 1^{2}, 1984, 384-411.
R.R. Holloway, "The Bronze Coinage of Agathocles," in O. Mørkholm and N.M. Waggoner (eds.), *Greek Numismatics and Archaeology. Essays in Honor of Margaret Thompson*, Wetteren 1979, 87-95.
S.N. Consolo Langher, "La politica di Agatocle e i caratteri della tradizione dal conflitto con Messana alla battaglia presso il fiume Himera (315-310 a.C.)," *Arch. Stor. Messinese* 26-27, 1975-1976, 29-89.
Idem, "Agatocle: Il colpo di Stato. Quellenfrage e ricostruzione storica," *Athenaeum* 54, 1976, 382-429.
Idem, "Agatocle: Il colpo di Stato. Quellenfrage e ricostruzione storica," in *Scritti in onore di Salvatore Pugliatti*, Milan 1978, 349-396.
Idem, "La Sicilia dalla scomparsa di Timoleonte alla morte di Agatocle. La introduzione della Basileia," in E. Gabba and G. Vallet (eds.), *La Sicilia antica* II 1, Naples 1980, 291-342.
G. de Sensi Sestito, "La Sicilia dal 289 al 210 a.C.," *ibid.*, 345-370.
Idem, "La strategato di Agatocle e l'imperialismo siracusano sulla Sicilia greca nelle tradizioni diodorea e trogiana (316-310 a.C.)," *Kokalos* 25, 1979 [1981], 117-187.
G. Marasco, "Agatocle e la politica siracusana agli inizi del III secolo a.C.," *Prometheus* 10, 1984, 97-113.

538 **The Balance of Power in the Hellenistic States**

Sources

Inscriptions: Add the following: in particular, the inscription found recently on a stele in the Athenian Agora, constituting a long honorary decree for Kallias of Sphettus: see T. Leslie Shear, Jr., *Kallias of Sphettos and the Revolt of Athens in 286 B.C.* (Hesperia Suppl. 17), Princeton, N.J., 1978 (cf. below, 546 n. 63); also the Greek inscription discovered north of Lattakia in Syria in 1975, bearing a list of Ptolemaic mercenaries: see J.-P. Rey-Coquais, "Inscription grecque découverte à Ras Ibn Hani," *Les annales archéologiques arabes syriennes* 26, 1976, 51-60.
M. Wörrle, "Epigraphische Forschungen zur Geschichte Lykiens, II: Ptolemaios II. und Telmessos," *Chiron* 8, 1978, 201-246.
Idem, "Epigraphische Forschungen zur Geschichte Lykiens, III: Ein hellenistischer Königsbrief aus Telmessos," *Chiron* 9, 1979, 83-111; cf. the remarks by J. and L. Robert, *REG* (Bull. épigr.) 92, 1979, 498-300, and 93, 1980, 455-458.
R.K. Sherk (ed.), *Rome and the Greek East to the Death of Augustus* (Translated Documents of Greece and Rome 4), Cambridge 1984, Nos. 1 and 2.
For further details, see also *CAH* VII 1^2, 1984, 513-602.

Non-Greek Inscriptions: U. Schneider, *Die grossen Felsen-Edikte Asokas. Kritische Ausgabe, Übersetzung und Analyse der Texte* (Freiburger Beiträge zur Indologie 2), Wiesbaden 1978.
See also S.M. Burnstein (ed.), *The Hellenistic Age from the Battle of Ipsos to the Death of Kleopatra VII* (Translated Documents of Greece and Rome 3), Cambridge 1985.

540 **Bibliography**

General Works: See the new edition of *CAH* VII 1^2, 1984 (*The Hellenistic World to the Coming of the Romans*), 513 ff.

Ptolemaic and Seleucid History: E.G. Turner, "Ptolemaic Egypt," *CAH* VII 1^2, 1984, 118-174.
D. Musti, "Syria and the East," *ibid.*, 175-220.
R.S. Bagnall, *The Administration of the Ptolemaic Possessions Outside Egypt*, Leiden 1976 (cf. H. Heinen, *Gnomon* 52, 1980, 386-387).
Ph. Gauthier, "EXAGOGE SITOU: Samothrace, Hippomédon et les Lagides," *Historia* 28, 1979, 76-89.
J. Wolski, "L'Iran dans la politique des Séleucides," *AAntHung* 25, 1977, 149-156.
K.-W. Welwei, *Unfreie im antiken Kriegsdienst II: Die kleineren und mittleren griechischen Staaten und die hellenistischen Reiche* (Forschungen zur antiken Sklaverei 8), Wiesbaden 1977.

G. Herman, "The 'Friends' of the Early Hellenistic Rulers. Servants or Officials?," *Talanta* 12-13, 1980-1981, 103-149.
E. Laroche and A. Davesne, "Les fouilles de Meydandjik près de Gülnar (Turquie) et le trésor monétaire hellénistique," *CRAI* 1981, 356-371.
See also the brief survey by E. Bickerman, "The Seleucid Period," in E. Yashater (ed.), *The Cambridge History of Iran* 3,1, Cambridge 1983, 3-20.
G. Le Rider, "L'enfant-roi Antiochos et la reine Laodice," *BCH* 110, 1986, 409-417.

541 **The Hellenistic East:** J. Wolski, "Le problème de la fondation de l'état gréco-bactrien," *Iranica Antiqua* 17, 1982, 131-146.

The Parthian Kingdom: P. Lozinski, "The Parthian Dynasty," *Iranica Antiqua* 19, 1984, 119-139.

The Attalids: R.E. Allen, *The Attalid Kingdom: A Constitutional History*, Oxford 1981.
H. Heinen, "The Syrian Egyptian Wars and the New Kingdoms of Asia Minor," *CAH* VII 1^2, 1984, 412-445.
H.-J. Scholles, *Untersuchungen zur Kulturpolitik der pergamenischen Herrscher im dritten Jahrhundert vor Christus* (IstForsch 36), Tübingen 1985 (cf. Ch. Habicht, *Gnomon* 59, 1987, 138-141, and E.E. Rice, *AJA* 92, 1988, 142-143).

The Hellenistic East: F.L. Holt, "Discovering the Lost History of Ancient Afghanistan. Hellenistic Bactria in Light of Recent Archaeological and Historical Research," *The Ancient World* 9, 1984, 3-11.
Idem, "Select Bibliography of Recent Research and Studies on Hellenistic Bactria (Afghanistan)," *ibid.*, 13-28 (cf. above, 524 n. 100).
Ch. Roueché and S.M. Sherwin-White, "Some Aspects of the Seleucid Empire: Greek Inscriptions from Failaka, in the Persian Gulf," *Chiron* 15, 1985, 1-39.

542 **The Antigonids:** F.W. Walbank, "Macedonia and Greece," *CAH* VII 1^2, 1984, 221-256 (applies also to the following section).

Greece in the Third Century: Ch. Habicht, "Aristeides, Sohn des Mnesitheos, aus Lamptrai: Ein athenischer Staatsmann aus der Zeit des Chremonideischen Krieges," *Chiron* 6, 1976, 7-10.
Idem, *Untersuchungen zur politischen Geschichte Athens im 3. Jahrhundert v. Chr.* (Vestigia 30), Munich 1979 (cf. M.J. Osborne, *JHS* 102, 1982, 273-274).
Idem, *Studien zur Geschichte Athens in hellenistischer Zeit* (Hypomnemata 73), Göttingen 1982.
B.D. Meritt, "Athenian Archons 347/6-48/7 B.C.," *Historia* 26, 1977, 161-191.
Idem, "Mid-Third Century Athenian Archons," *Hesp.* 50, 1981, 78-99.

Ph. Gauthier, "Le réunification d'Athènes en 281 et les deux archontes Nicias," *REG* 92, 1979, 348-399.
A.S. Henry, "Athenian Financial Officials after 303 B.C.," *Chiron* 14, 1984, 49-92.
R. Etienne and D. Knoepfler, *Hyettos de Béotie et la chronologie des archontes fédéreaux entre 250 et 171 av. J.-C.* (BCH Suppl. 3), Paris 1976.
D. Henning, "Der Bericht des Polybios über Boiotien und die Lage von Orchomenos in der 2. Hälfte des 3. Jahrhunderts v. Chr.," *Chiron* 7, 1977, 119-148 (inscriptions correct the bleak picture painted by Polybius).

The Achaean League: R. Urban, *Wachstum und Krise des Achäischen Bundes: Quellenstudien zur Entwicklung des Bundes von 280 bis 222 v. Chr.* (Historia-Einzelschriften 35), Wiesbaden 1979.

Boeotia: P. Roesch, *Études béotiennes* (Centre de recherches archéologiques. Institut Fernand-Courby, Lyon. URA 15), Paris 1982 (cf. F.W. Walbank, *JHS* 104, 1984, 243-244).

Rhodes: R.M. Berthold, *Rhodes in the Hellenistic Age*, Ithaca, N.Y., and London 1984.

n. 7 N.G. Ashton, "The Lamian War—A False Start?," *Antichthon* 17, 1983, 47-63.

543 n. 13 H.-J. Gehrke, *Phokion. Studien zur Erfassung seiner historischen Gestalt* (Zetemata 64), Munich 1976.

544 n. 44 L. Schober, *Untersuchungen zur Geschichte Babyloniens und die oberen Satrapien von 323-303 v. Chr.*, Frankfurt a. M. and Bern, 1981.

546 n. 63 For the year 286/5 B.C., see also T.L. Shear, Jr., *Kallias of Sphettos and the Revolt of Athens in 286 B.C.* (Hesp. Suppl. 17), Princeton, N.J., 1978, *passim*, but for 287, Ch. Habicht, *Untersuchungen zur politischen Geschichte Athens im 3. Jahrhundert v. Chr.* (Vestigia 30), Munich 1979, 45-67; see also M.J. Osborne, "Kallias, Phaidros and the Revolt of Athens in 287 B.C.," *ZPE* 35, 1979, 181-194; and the comments by J. and L. Robert, *REG* (Bull. épigr.) 94, 1981, 394-400; also Ph. Gauthier, "Notes sur trois décrets honorant les citoyens bienfaiteurs: La fortune de Kallias de Sphettos," *RevPhil* 56, 1982, 221-226.

n. 68 H. Müller, *Milesische Volksbeschlüsse. Eine Untersuchung zur Verfassungsgeschichte der Stadt in hellenistischer Zeit* (Hypomnemata 47), Göttingen 1976.

548 n. 115 E.E. Rice, *The Grand Procession of Ptolemy Philadelphus*, Oxford 1983.

n. 119 See also S.M. Burnstein, "Arsinoe II Philadelphos: A Revisionist View," in W.L. Adams and E.N. Borza (eds.), *Philip II, Alexander the Great and the Macedonian Heritage*, Washington 1982, 197-212; and H.A. Troxell, "Arsinoe's Non-Era," *AmerNumSocNotes* 28, 1983, 35-70.

n. 121 Ch. Habicht, *Untersuchungen zur politischen Geschichte Athens im 3. Jahrhundert v. Chr.* (Vestigia 20), Munich 1979, 95-112; see also J.J. Gabbert, "The Grand Strategy of Antigonos II Gonatas and the Chremonidean War," *The Ancient World* 8, 1983, 129-136; *eadem*, "The Anarchic Dating of the Chremonidean War," *CJ* 82, 1987, 230-235.

n. 125 See also Ch. Habicht, *Untersuchungen zur politischen Geschichte Athens im 3. Jahrhundert v. Chr.* (Vestigia 30), Munich 1979, 113-166.

549 n. 133 H. Herrli, "Die Silberdrachmen der kappadokischen Könige Ariarathes IV. und V.," *Numismatische Nachrichten* 32, 1983, 162-175.

550 n. 152 R. Wenning, *Die Galateranatheme Attalos I. Eine Untersuchung zum Bestand zur Nachwirkung pergamenischer Skulptur* (Pergamenische Forschungen 4), Berlin 1978; K. Bittel, "Die Galater, archäologisch gesehen," in E. Akurgal (ed.), *Proceedings of the Xth International Congress of Classical Archaeology, Ankara-Izmir 23-30. IX. 1973*, I, Ankara 1978, 169-174.

n. 157 See also W. Huss, "Der 'König der Könige' und der 'Herr der Könige'," *Zeitschrift des Deutschen Palestinavereins* 93, 1977, 131-140.

n. 158 E. Galli, "Raphia, 217 B.C.E. Revisited," *Scripta classica Israelica* 3, 1977, 52-126.

n. 159 On **Achaeus**, see also W. Huss, "Eine ptolemäische Expedition nach Kleinasien," *AncSoc* 8, 1977, 187-193.

551 n. 168 D. Mendels, "Polybius and the Socio-Economic Reforms of Cleomenes III Reexamined," *Gräzer Beiträge* 10, 1981 [1983], 95-104.

n. 172 J.D. Morgan, "Sellasia Revisited," *AJA* 85, 1981, 328-330.

n. 173 U. Bernini, "Studi su Sparta ellenistica. Da Leonida II a Cleomene III," *QuadUrbCulClas* 27, 1978, 29-59; *idem*, "Archidamo e Cleomene III. Politica interna ed estera a Sparta (241-227 a.C.)," *Athenaeum* 59, 1981, 439-458.

13. HELLENISTIC CIVILISATION

554 In the second edition of *CAH* VII 1, 1984, see: J.K. Davies, "Cultural, Social and Economic Features," 257-320.
G.E.R. Lloyd, "Hellenistic Science: Its Application in Peace and War," 321-383.
Idem, "Physics, Mathematics and their Application, Geography and Astronomy, Medicine and Life Sciences," 321-352.
V. Garlan, "War and Siegecraft," 353-362.
D.J. Thompson, "Agriculture," 363-370.
F.W. Winter, "Building and Townplanning," 371-383.
Rich as always, with many penetrating insights, is L. Robert, *A travers l'Asie mineur. Poètes et prosateurs, monnaies grecques, voyageurs et géographie* (Bibl. des Éc. franç. d'Athènes et de Rome 239), Paris 1980.
See also Ed. Will, "Pour Une 'Anthropologie Coloniale' Du Monde Hellénistique," in J.W. Eadie and J. Ober (eds.), *The Craft of the Ancient Historian. Essays in honor of Chester G. Starr*, Lanham, New York, London 1985, 273-301.
Ph. Gauthier, *Les cités grecques et leurs bienfaiteurs (IVe-Ier siècle avant J.-C.): contribution à l'histoire des institutions* (BCH suppl. 12), Paris 1985 (cf. E.S. Gruen, *JHS* 107, 1987, 230).
M.M. Austin, "Hellenistic kings, war and economy," *CQ* 36, 1986, 450-466.

556 G.M. Cohen, *The Seleucid Colonies: Studies in Founding, Administration and Organisation* (Historia-Einzelschriften 30), Wiesbaden 1978, does not mark any progress (cf. S.M. Sherwin-White, *JHS* 100, 1980, 259-260).
See, on the other hand, H. Kreissig, "Tempelland, Katoiken, Herodulen im Seleukidenreich," *Klio* 59, 1977, 375-380.
Idem, *Wirtschaft und Gesellschaft im Seleukidenreich. Die Eigentums- und die Abhänigkeitsverhältnisse* (Schriften zur Geschichte und Kultur der Antike 16), Berlin 1978.
W. Leschhorn, *'Gründer der Stadt': Studien zu einem politisch-religiösen Phänomen der griechischen Geschichte* (Palingenesia 20), Wiesbaden and Stuttgart 1984, 229-245.
I. Hahn, "Königsland und königliche Besteuerung im hellenistischen Osten," *Klio* 60, 1978, 11-34.
W. Orth, *Königlicher Machtanspruch und städtische Freiheit: Untersuchungen zu den politischen Beziehungen zwischen den ersten Seleukidenherrschern (Seleukos I., Antiochos I., Antiochos II.) und den Städten des westlichen Kleinasien* (Münchener Beiträge zur Papyrusforschung und antiken Rechtsgeschichte 71), Munich 1977.
Ph. Gauthier, "Les honneurs de l'officier séleucide Larichos à Priène," *Journ. des Savants* 1980, 35-50.
V.M. Masson, *Das Land der tausend Städte. Baktrien, Chorismien, Margiane, Parthien, Sogdien. Ausgrabungen in der südlichen Sowjetunion*, Wiesbaden and Berlin 1987.

557 On **Zenon**, see P.W. Pestman *et al.*, *A Guide to the Zenon Archive I: Lists and Surveys; II: Indexes and Maps* (Papyrologica Lugduno-Batava 21A and 21B), Leiden 1981 (cf. J.D. Thomas, *CR* 34, 1984, 154-155, and J. and L. Robert, *REG* [Bull. épigr.] 94, 1981, 478-479).
C. Orrieux, *Les papyrus de Zenon: L'horizon d'un grec en Égypte au IIIe siècle avant J.-C.*, Paris 1983.
On **Tebtunis**, see J.G. Keenan and J.C. Shelton, *The Tebtunis Papyri* IV (Egyptian Exploration Society Graeco-Roman Memoires 64), London 1976.
W. Huss, "Staat und Ethos nach den Vorstellungen eines ptolemäischen Dioiketes des 3. Jh. Bemerkungen zu P. Teb. III 1, 703," *Archiv für Papyrologie und verwandte Gebiete* 27, 1980, 67-77.
On **inscriptions in Egypt**: L. Könen, *Eine agonistische Inschrift aus Ägypten und frühptolemäische Königsfeste* (Beiträge zur Klassischen Philologie 56), Meisenheim am Glan 1977.
For **Egypt**: E. Bernand, "Le corpus des inscriptions grecques de l'Égypte," *ZPE* 26, 1977, 95-117.
On a small, but illuminating, collection of **Demotic papyri**, see P.W. Pestman *et al.*, *Recueil de textes démotiques et bilingues* I-III, Leiden 1977 (cf. H. Heinen, *Gnomon* 53, 1981, 289-291).

558 J.W.B. Barns, *Egyptians and Greeks* (Papyrologica Bruxellenisia 14), Brussels 1978.
Under **General Bibliography**, see *CAH* VII 1^2, 1984, 563.
See also W.M. Brashear, *Ptolemäische Urkunden aus Mumienkartonage* (Ägyptische Urkunden aus der Staatlichen Museen Berlin) (= BGU 14), Berlin 1980.
D.J. Crawford, J. Quaesebeur and W. Clarysse, *Studies on Ptolemaic Memphis* (Studia Hellenistica 24), Louvain 1980.

559 L. Mooren, *La hiérarchie de cour ptolémaïque. Contribution à l'étude des institutions et des classes dirigeantes à l'époque hellénistique* (Studia Hellenistica 23), Louvain 1977.
H.J. Wolff, *Das Recht der griechischen Papyri Ägyptens in der Zeit der Ptolemäer und des Prinzipats, II: Organisation und Kontrolle des privaten Rechtsverkehrs* (Handbuch der Altertumswissenschaft X 5,2), Munich 1978.
H. Mähler and V.M. Strocka (eds.), *Das ptolemäische Ägypten. Akten des internationalen Symposions 27.-29. September 1976 in Berlin*, Mainz 1978.
L.C. Youtie, D. Hagedorn and H.C. Youtie, *Urkunden aus Panopolis*, Bonn 1980.
W. Peremans, "Un groupe d'officiers dans l'armée des Lagides," *AncSoc* 8, 1977, 175-185.
Idem, "Les indigènes égyptiens dans l'armée de terre des Lagides. Recherches anthroponymiques," *ibid.* 9, 1978, 83-100.
Idem, "Les Égyptiens dans l'armée de terre des Lagides," in H. Heinen (ed.), *Althistorische Studien Hermann Bengtson zum 70. Ge-*

burtstag dargebracht von Kollegen und Schülern, Wiesbaden 1983, 92-102.
R.S. Bagnall, "The Origin of Ptolemaic Cleruchs," *BullAmerSocPap* 21, 1984, 7-20.
R.A. Hazzard and I.D. Brown, "The Silver Standard of the Ptolemaic Coinage," *RevNum* 26, 1984, 231-239.
P.W. Pestman *et al.*, *Vreemdelingen in het land van Pharao. Een bundel artikelen samengesteld ter gelegenheid van het vijftigjarig bestaan van het Papyrologisch Insituut van de Rijksuniversiteit van Leiden*, Zutphen 1985.
On **Administration in Egypt**, cf. *CAH* VII 1^2, 1984, 566-571.
G.F. Seibt, *Griechische Söldner im Achaimenidenreich*, Bonn 1977.
On the **rôle of women**, see S.B. Pomeroy, *Women in Hellenistic Egypt: From Alexander to Cleopatra*, New York 1984.

560 H. Heinen, "Aspects et problèmes de la monarchie ptolemaïque," *Ktema* 3, 1978, 177-199.
F. Dunand, "L'exode rural en Egypte à l'époque hellénistique," *Ktema* 5, 1980, 137-150.
N. Lewis, *Greeks in Ptolemaic Egypt. Case Studies in the Social History of the Hellenistic World*, Oxford 1986.
On **Ptolemaic city foundations**, see W. Leschhorn, *'Gründer der Stadt': Studien zu einem politisch-religiösen Phänomen der griechischen Geschichte* (Palingenesia 20), Wiesbaden and Stuttgart 1984, 223-228.

561 On the **Attalid Kingdom**, see also H. Heinen, "The Syrian-Egyptian Wars and the New Kingdoms of Asia Minor," *CAH* VII 1^2, 412-445. Likewise, on the Greek Federal Leagues, F.W. Walbank, "Macedonia and the Greek Leagues," *ibid.*, 446-481.
On **Rhodes**, see V. Kontorini, *Rhodiaka I: Inscriptions inédites relatives à l'histoire et aux cultes de Rhodes au IIᵉ et au Iᵉʳ siècle av. J.-C.* (Archaeologia Transatlantica 6), Louvain-la-Neuve and Providence, R.I., 1983.
R.M. Berthold, *Rhodes in the Hellenistic Age*, Ithaca and London 1984 (cf. J. Deininger, *Gnomon* 58, 1986, 412-417); also H. Heinen, *CAH* VII 1^2, 1984, 412-445.
J.-H. Michel, "Rhodes ou le dynamisme de l'État-cité à l'époque hellénistique," *CE* 60, 1985, 204-213.
P. Brulé, *La piraterie crétoise hellénistique* (Centre de Recherches d'Histoire Ancienne 27), Paris 1978.
On the **Syracusan kingdom**: G. de Sensi Sestito, *Gerone II. un monarca ellenistico in Sicilia*, Palermo 1977 (cf. R.J.A. Talbert, *JHS* 100, 1980, 258-259).
On **Civic Organisation in Asia Minor**, see C. Şahin, *The Political and Religious Structure in the Territory of Stratonikeia in Caria*, Ankara 1976, cf. the remarks by J. and L. Robert, *REG* (Bull. épigr.) 92, 1979, 495-497.

562 **The Universal Sovereignty of the Greek Mind**

General Surveys: A. Barigazzi, P. Lévêque and D. Musti, *La società ellenistica Quadro politico* (Storia e civiltà dei Greci 7), Milan 1977.
F.W. Walbank, *The Hellenistic World*, Atlantic Highlands, N.J., 1981.
See also, and in particular, the outstanding synthesis by Claire Préaux, *Le monde hellénistique. La Grèce et l'Orient de la mort d'Alexandre à la conquête romaine de la Grêce (323-146 avant J.C.)* (Collection Nouvelle Clio. L'histoire et ses problèmes VI et VI bis), Paris 1978.
M. Grant, *From Alexander to Cleopatra. The Hellenistic World*, New York 1982.
L. Canfora, *Ellenismo*, Rome and Bari 1987.
H.H. Schmitt and E. Vogt (eds.), *Kleines Wörterbuch des Hellenismus* [in press].

Studies on Specific Aspects: A. Momigliano, *Alien Wisdom. The Limits of Hellenisation*, Cambridge 1975.
J. Hengstl *et al.*, *Griechische Papyri aus Ägypten als Zeugnisse des öffentlichen und privaten Lebens*, Munich 1978.
H. Kreissig, "Zum Problem der Landvergabe im hellenistischen Orient," in J. Harmatta (ed.), *Actes du VIIe congrès de la Fédération Internationale des Associations d'Études classiques* I, Budapest 1984, 313-321.
A.E. Samuel, *From Athens to Alexandria: Hellenism and Social Goals in Ptolemaic Egypt* (Studia Hellenistica 26), Louvain 1983 (cf. P.M. Fraser, *Phoenix* 40, 1986, 100-102, and D.J. Thompson, *JHS* 107, 1987, 240-241).

563 On **city foundations**, see also the references to Aï Khanoum above, 526 n. 100.
On **slavery**: H. Heinen, "Zur Sklaverei in der hellenistischen Welt I," *AncSoc* 7, 1976, 127-149; *ibid.* "II," *ibid.* 8, 1977, 121-154 (a critical review of publications on slavery in the USSR); cf. *idem*, *Historia* 28, 1979, 125-128.
See also the relevant sections in G.E.M. de Ste. Croix, *The Class Struggle in the Ancient Greek World from the Archaic Age to the Arab Conquests*, London 1981.
On **Judaism**: E. Will and C. Origeux, *Ioudaïsmos-hellénismos: essai sur le judaïsme judéen à l'époque hellénistique*, Nancy 1986.
On **Public Finance**: L. Migeotte, *L'Emprunt public dans les cités grecques. Recueil des documents et analyse critique*, Québec and Paris 1984 (cf. R. Osborne, *JHS* 107, 1987, 225-226).

564 Y. Garlan, *Recherches de poliorcétique grecque* (Bibl. des Éc. franç. d'Athènes et de Rome 223), Paris 1974.
S.M. Sherwin-White, *Ancient Cos: An Historical Study from the Dorian Settlement to the Imperial Period* (Hypomnemata 51), Göttingen 1978.

566 On **Greek relations with the distant East**, see J.W. Sedlar, *India and the Greek World: A Study in the Transmission of Culture*, Totowa, N.J., 1980 (cf. F.F. Schwarz, *Gnomon* 58, 1986, 510-515).

567 C. Préaux, "L'image du roi de l'époque hellénistique," in *Images of Man in Ancient and Medieval Thought. Studia Gerardo Verbeke ab amicis et collegis dicta*, Louvain 1977, 53-75.

n. 17. E. Winter, "Der Herrscherkult in den ägyptischen Ptolemäertempeln," in H. Mähler and V.M. Strocka (eds.), *Das ptolemäische Ägypten. Akten des internationalen Symposions 27-29. September 1976 in Berlin*, Mainz 1978, 147-160.

n. 18. W. Cheshire, "Zur Deutung eines Zepters der Arsinoe II. Philadelphos," *ZPE* 48, 1982, 105-111.

568 n. 30 W. Orth, *Königlicher Machtanspruch und städtische Freiheit. Untersuchungen zu den politischen Beziehungen zwischen den ersten Seleukidenherrschern (Seleukos I., Antiochos I., Antiochos II.) und den Städten des westlichen Kleinasiens* (Münchener Beitr. zur Papyrusforsch. und antiken Rechtsgesch. 71), Munich 1977.

n. 34 C. Hopkins, *The Discovery of Dura-Europos*, New Haven 1979.

570 n. 90a See the additional reports cited above, 526 n. 100.

14. THE HELLENISTIC STATES UNDER ROMAN SUPREMACY

572 **Poseidonius:** K.v. Fritz, "Poseidonios als Historiker," in T. Reekmans, E. van't Dack and H. Verdin (eds.), *Historiographica Antiqua. Commentationes Lovanienses in honorem W. Peremans septuagenarii editae* (Ser. A VI), Louvain 1977, 163-193.
J. Malitz, *Die Historien des Poseidonios* (Zetemata 79), Munich 1983 (cf. M.T. Griffin, *Gnomon* 57, 1985, 568-570).
See also S.M. Burnstein (ed.), *The Hellenistic Age from the Battle of Ipsos to the Death of Cleopatra VII* (Translated Documents of Greece and Rome 3), Cambridge 1985.
R. Sherk (ed.), *Rome and the Greek East to the Death of Augustus* (Translated Documents of Greece and Rome 4), Cambridge 1984.

575 **Bibliography:** For a general survey, see Ed. Will, *Histoire politique du monde hellénistique (323-30 av. J.C.) II. Des avènements d'Antiochos III et de Philip V à la fin des Lagides*, Nancy [2]1982.

Greek-Roman Relationships: W.V. Harris, *War and Imperialism in Republican Rome, 327-70 B.C.*, Oxford 1979 (cf. W. Eder, *Gnomon* 54, 1982, 549-554).
E.S. Gruen, *The Hellenistic World and the Coming of Rome*, 2 vols., Berkeley, Los Angeles, London 1984 (cf. Ed. Will, *Phoenix* 40, 1986, 212-214).

A.C. Scafuro, "Prusias II of Bithynia and Third Party Arbitration," *Historia* 36, 1987, 28-38.

Greece: O. Mørkholm, "The Chronology of the New Style Coinage of Athens," *AmerNumSocMusNotes* 29, 1984, 29-42.

577 V. Kontorini, "Rome et Rhodes au tournant du IIIe s. av. J.-C. d'après une inscription inédite de Rhodes," *JRS* 73, 1983, 24-32.
On **coins**, see, further, O. Mørkholm, "The Portrait of Ptolemy V. The Main Series," in O. Mørkholm and N.M. Waggoner (eds.), *Greek Numismatics and Archaeology. Essays in Honor of Margaret Thompson*, Wetteren 1979, 203-214.
B. Deppert-Lippitz, *Die Münzprägung Milets vom vierten bis ersten Jahrhundert v. Chr.* (Typos 5), Aarau, Frankfurt am Main, Salzburg 1984.
On **conditions following the accord of Apameia**: S.M. Burnstein, "The Aftermath of the Peace of Apameia: Rome and the Pontic War," *AJAH* 5, 1980, 1-12.
On **the Third Macedonian War**: F.W. Walbank, "The Causes of the Third Macedonian War: Recent Views," in K. Metsakas (ed.), *Ancient Macedonia II: Papers read at the Second International Symposium held in Thessaloniki 19-24 August 1973*, Thessaloniki 1977, 81-94.
On **the war between Perseus and Rome**: R. Werner, "Quellenkritische Bemerkungen zu den Ursachen des Perseuskrieges," *Gräzer Beiträge* 6, 1977, 149-216.
On **Epirus**: P. Cabanes, *L'Épire de la mort de Pyrrhos à la conquête romaine (272-167)* (Annales littéraires Univ. de Besançon 186), Paris 1976.
On **Thessaly**: H. Kramolisch, *Die Strategen des thessalischen Bundes vom Jahre 196 v. Chr. bis zum Ausgang der römischen Republik* (Die deutschen archäologischen Forschungen in Thessalien. Beiträge zur ur- und frühgriechischen Archäologie des Mittelmeerkulturraumes für das Institut für Ur- und Frühgeschichte der Universität Heidelberg 18) (= Demetrias 2), Bonn 1978.
On **the acquisition of Delos by L. Aemilius Paulus after the Third Macedonian War**: S.V. Tracy, *I.G. II[2] 2336: contributors of 'first fruits' for the Pythaïs* (Beiträge zur Klassischen Philologie 139), Meisenheim am Glan 1982.
On **developments following Pydna**: E.S. Gruen, "Rome and the Seleucids in the Aftermath of Pydna," *Chiron* 6, 1976, 73-95.

578 **The Decline of the Hellenistic States in the East and the Rise of the Parthian Kingdom. The First Period of Roman Rule in Hellas and Asia Minor:** A. Momigliano, "The Date of the First Book of Maccabees," in *idem*, *Sesto contributo alla storia degli studi classice e del mondo antico* (Storia e Letteratura. Raccolta di Studie e Testi 150) II, Rome 1980, 561-566.
Idem, "The Second Book of Maccabees," *ibid.*, 567-578.

579 **Numismatic Material:** I. Nicolaou and O. Mørkholm, *Paphos I: A Ptolemaic Coin Hoard*, Nicosia 1976 (cf. M.H. Crawford, *Gnomon* 53, 1981, 401).
C.M. Kraay, "Demetrius in Bactria and India," *Numismatica e Antichità* 10, 1981, 219-233.

Bibliography: P. Aupert, "Une donation lagide et chypriote à Argos (170-164 av. J.-C.)," *BCH* 106, 1982, 263-280.
H. Heinen, "Die Tryphe des Ptolemaios VIII. Euergetes II. Beobachtungen zum ptolemäischen Herrschaftsideal und zu einer römischen Gesandschaft in Ägypten (140/39 v. Chr.)," in H. Heinen (ed.), *Althistorische Studien Hermann Bengtson zum 70. Geburtstag dargebracht von Kollegen und Schülern*, Wiesbaden 1983, 116-130.
P. Roesch, "Les Lagides à Salamine: épigraphie et administration," in V. Karageorghis (ed.), *Salamine de Chypre, Histoire et archéologie. États des recherches, Lyon 13-17 mars 1978*, Paris 1980, 249-256.
O. Mørkholm, "The Last Ptolemaic Silver Coinage in Cyprus," *Chiron* 13, 1983, 69-79.

Seleucids: O. Mørkholm, "Sculpture and Coins. The Portrait of Alexander Balas of Syria," *NumAntClass* 10, 1981, 235-245.
Idem, "A Posthumous Issue of Antiochus IV of Syria," *NumChron* 143, 1983, 57-63 [by Alexander Balas].
Idem, "The Attic Coin Standard in the Levant during the Hellenistic Period," in *Studia Paulo Naster oblata I: Numismatica Antiqua*, Louvain 1982, 139-149.
D. van Berchem, "Le port de Séleucie de Piérie et l'infrastructure logistique des guerres parthiques," *BonJahrb* 185, 1985, 47-87.
F. Piejko, "Antiochus Epiphanes Savior of Asia," *RivFil* 114, 1986, 425-436.

Parthians: B.P. Lozinski, "The Parthian Dynasty," *Iranica Antiqua* 19, 1984, 119-139.

580 **Bibliography:** H. Köhler, *Die Nachfolge in der Seleukidenherrschaft und die parthische Haltung im römisch-pontischen Konflikt* (Bochumer historische Studien. Alte Geschichte 3), Bochum 1978.
H. Kyrieleis, *Ein Bildnis des Königs Antiochos IV. von Syrien*, Berlin 1980.
W. Vogelsang, "Early Historical Arachosia in South-East Afghanistan. Meeting-place between East and West," *Iranica Antiqua* 20, 1985, 55-99.
J. Hopp, *Untersuchungen zur Geschichte der letzten Attaliden* (Vestigia 25), Munich 1977.
L. Robert, "Un décret de Pergame," *BCH* 108, 1984, 472-489; *idem*, "Le décret de Pergame pour Attale III," *BCH* 109, 1985, 468-481.
S.M. Sherwin-White, *Roman Foreign Policy in the East 168 B.C. to A.D. 1*, London 1984.

On **Greece:** H. Kramolisch, "Das Ende des perrhäbischen Bundes," in B. Helly (ed.), *La Thessalie. Actes de la Table-Ronde 21-24 Juillet 1975, Lyon* (Collection de la Maison de l'Orient Méditerranéen No. 6, sér. arch. 5), Paris 1979, 201-220.
B. Helly, "Une liste des cités de Perrhébie dans la première moitié du IVe siècle avant J.-C.," *ibid.*, 165-200.
S.V. Tracy, "Athens in 100 B.C.," *HSCP* 83, 1979, 213-236.
F. Papazoglou, "Quelques aspects de la province de Macédoine," in H. Temporini (ed.), *Aufstieg und Nidergang der römischen Welt* II 7, 1, Berlin and New York 1979, 302-369.
R. Bernhardt, *Polis und römische Herrschaft in der späten Republik (149-31 v. Chr.)*, Berlin and New York 1985 (cf. F.W. Walbank, *Gnomon* 58, 1986, 515-518).
Ch. Habicht, "The Role of Athens in the Reorganization of the Delphic Amphictiony after 189 B.C.," *Hesp.* 56, 1987, 59-71.

582 **The Greeks in the Time of Mithradates. The Reorganisation of the Near East by Pompey. The End of the Ptolemaic Kingdom:**
S.M. Burnstein (ed.), *The Hellenistic Age from the Battle of Ipsos to the Death of Cleopatra VII* (Translated Documents of Greece and Rome 3), Cambridge 1985.
R. Sherk (ed.), *Rome and the Greek East to the Death of Augustus* (Translated Documents of Greece and Rome 4), Cambridge 1984.
On **Mithradates**: D.G. Glew, "Between the Wars: Mithridates Eupator and Rome, 85-73 B.C.," *Chiron* 11, 1981, 109-130.
M.-F. Baslez, "Delos durant le Première Guerre de Mithridate," in F. Coarelli, D. Musti and H. Solin (eds.), *Delo e l'Italia* (Opuscula Instituti Romani Finlandiae II), Rome 1982, 51-66.
N.N. Zalesskij, "Les Romains à Délos (de l'histoire du capital commercial et du capital usuraire romain)," *ibid.*, 21-49.
X. McGing, *The Foreign Policy of Mithridates VI Eupator King of Pontus*, Leiden 1986.
F.W. Walbank, "Via illa nostra militaris: Some Thoughts on the Via Egnatia," in H. Heinen (ed.), *Althistorische Studien Hermann Bengtson zum 70. Geburtstag dargebracht von Kollegen und Schülern*, Wiesbaden 1983, 131-147.

Greece: Ch. Habicht, "Zur Geschichte Athens in der Zeit des Mithridates' VI.," *Chiron* 6, 1976, 127-142.

Asia Minor and Palestine: S.M. Burnstein, *Outpost of Hellenism. The Emergence of Heracleia on the Black Sea*, Berkeley 1976.
U. Baumann, *Rom und die Juden. Die römish-jüdischen Beziehungen von Pompeius bis zum Tode des Herodes (63 v. Chr.-4 v. Chr.)* (Studia Philosophica et Historica 4), Frankfurt am Main, Bern, New York 1983.
O. Mørkholm, "The Coinages of Ariarathes VI and Ariarathes VII of Cappadocia," *Schweizerische Numismatische Rundschau* 57, 1978, 144-163.

Idem, "The Parthian Coinage of Seleucia on the Tigris, c. 90-95 B.C.," *NumChron* 20, 1980, 33-47.

Egypt: E. van't Dack, "L'armée lagide 55 à 30 av. J.C.," *JournJurPap* 19, 1983, 77-86.

583 n. 5 That Rome consciously intervened in the politics of the Eastern Mediterranean is also disputed by P.S. Derow, "Polybius, Rome and the East," *JRS* 69, 1979, 1-15 (cf. above, 575).

584 n. 17 See also D. Baronowski, "A Reconsideration of the Roman Approval of Peace with Macedonia in 196 B.C.," *Phoenix* 37, 1983, 218-233 (see also below, 586 n. 48).

585 n. 44a B. Schleussner, "Die Gesandtschaftsreise P. Scipio Nasicas im Jahre 133/2 v. Chr. und die Provinzialisierung des Königreichs Pergamon," *Chiron* 6, 1976, 97-112.

n. 46 For another attempt, see N.G.L. Hammond, "The Battle of Pydna," *JHS* 104, 1984, 31-47.

586 n. 48 Otherwise, E.S. Gruen, "Macedonia and the Settlement of 167 B.C.," in W.L. Adams and E.N. Borza (eds.), *Philip II, Alexander the Great and the Macedonian Heritage*, Washington 1982, 257-267.

n. 60 H.B. Mattingly, "Scipio Aemilianus' Eastern Embassy," *CQ* 36, 1986, 491-495.

587 n. 65 See also E. Bickerman, *The God of the Maccabees: Studies on the Meaning and Origin of the Maccabean Revolt* (Studies in Judaism and Late Antiquity 32), Leiden 1979; and K. Bringmann, *Hellenistische Reform und Religionsverfolgung in Judäa. Eine Untersuchung zur jüdisch-hellenistischen Geschichte (175-163 v. Chr.)*, Göttingen 1983.

n. 70 Th. Fischer, *Silber aus dem Grab Davids? Jüdisches und Hellenistisches auf Münzen des Seleukidenkönigs Antiochos' VII. 132-130 v. Chr.* (Abh. Akad. der Wiss. Göttingen, phil.-hist. Kl., Folge 3,132), Bochum 1983.

n. 78 Hammond's *Nabataeans* is now available in a fourth edition, published in 1984.
See also A. Negev, "The Nabataeans and the Province of Arabia," in H. Temporini and W. Haase (eds.), *Aufstieg und Niedergang der römischen Welt. Prinzipat* II 8, Berlin and New York 1977, 520-686.

n. 80 See also K.W. Dobbins, "Vonones, Maues and Hermaios. The Imperial Coinage of Mithradates II," *East and West* 30, 1980, 31-53.

588 n. 101 E.S. Gruen, "The Origins of the Achaean War," *JHS* 96, 1976, 46-69 (characterised by a low opinion of Polybius and over-subtle arguments).

589 n. 108 See also C. Delplace, "Le contenu social et économique du soulevement d'Aristonicos: opposition entre riches et pauvres," *Athenaeum* 56, 1978, 20-53.

n. 114 E. Salomone Gaggero, "La propaganda antiromana di Mithridate VI Eupatore in Asia Minore e in Grecia," in *Contributi di storia antica in onore di Algino Garzetti*, Genoa 1977, 89-123.

590 n. 121 G. Wirth, "Pompeius—Armenien—Parther: Mutmassungen zur Bewältigung einer Krisensituation," *BonJahrb* 183, 1983, 1-60.

n. 127 See also S. Mitchell, "Population and Land in Roman Galatia," in H. Temporini (ed.), *Aufstieg und Niedergang der römischen Welt, Prinzipat* II 7, 2, Berlin and New York 1980, 1053-1081.

591 n. 140 L. Mooren and E. van't Dack, "Le stratège Platon et sa famille," *AC* 50, 1981, 535-544.

15. THE GREEKS IN THE ROMAN EMPIRE

592 **Sources:** A. Balland, *Fouilles de Xanthos, 7. Inscriptions d'époque impériale du Létoon* (Inst. franç. d'Ét. anatoliennes), Paris 1981.
J. Reynolds, *Aphrodisias and Rome: Documents from the Excavation of the Theatre Conducted by Professor Kenan T. Erim together with Some Related Texts* (JournRomStud Monograph No. 1), London 1982 (cf. J. and L. Robert, *REG* [Bull. épigr.] 96, 1983, 149-158).
R. Hodot, "Décret de Kyme en l'honneur du prytane Kléanax," *The J. Paul Getty Museum Journal* 10, 1982, 165-180, cf. the comments by J. and L. Robert, *REG* (Bull. épigr.) 96, 1983, 132-138.

593 On **Dion of Prusa**, see G. Salmeri, *La politica e il potere saggio su Dione di Prusa* (Quaderni del Sicolorum Gymnasium 9), Catania 1982.

595 **Bibliography:** For **Greece**, see M. Woloch, *Roman Citizenship and the Athenian Elite A.D. 96-161. Two Prosopographical Catalogues*, Amsterdam 1973.
J.H. Oliver, "Roman Emperors and Athens," *Historia 30*, 1981, 412-423.
D.J. Geagan, "Roman Athens: Some Aspects of Life and Culture I, 86 B.C.–A.D. 267," in H. Temporini (ed.), *Aufstieg und Niedergang der römischen Welt. Prinzipat* II 7,1, Berlin and New York 1979, 371-437.
J. Wiseman, "Corinth and Rome I: 228 B.C.–A.D. 267," *ibid.*, 438-535.
T.L. Shear, Jr., "Athens: From City-State to Provincial Town," *Hesp.* 50, 1981, 356-377.
Recent excavations in **Patras** have begun to give a highly informative picture of a Greek urban centre under Roman rule (cf. H.W. Catling, *ArchRep* 32, 1985-86, 31-38).

D. Samaris, "Les mines et la metallurgie de fer et le cuivre dans la province romaine de Macedoine," *Klio* 69, 1987, 152-162.

597 S. Follet, *Athènes au IIe et IIIe siècle. Études chronologiques et prosopographiques*, Paris 1977.

Elsewhere: A wealth of information may be found in the series, *Inschriften griechischer Städte aus Kleinasien* I ff., 1972 ff. (over 30 volumes to date).

J.-L. Ferrary, "Recherches sur la législation de Saturninus et de Glaucia I, La lex de pirates de Delphes et de Cnide," *MEFR* 89, 1977, 619-660.

L. Robert, "La titulature de Nicée et de Nicomédie, la gloire et la haine," *HSCP* 81, 1977, 1-39.

J. Bregman, *Synesius of Cyrene: Philosopher-Bishop*, Berkeley, Los Angeles, London 1982.

N.A. Frolova, *The Coinage of the Kingdom of Bosporus A.D. 69-238* (BAR Intern. Ser. 56), Oxford 1979.

K. Ziegler, "Münzen Kilikiens als Zeugnis kaiserlicher Getreidespenden," *Jahrb. f. Num. u. Geldgesch*, 27, 1977, 29-67.

J. Geiger, "The Last Jewish Revolt," *Scripta classica Israelica* 5, 1979-1980, 250-257.

S. Applebaum, "The Second Jewish Revolt (AD 131-135)," *Palestine Exploration Quarterly* 116, 1984, 35-41.

K.T. Erim, *Aphrodisias. City of Venus Aphrodite*, London 1986.

E. Gibson, *The "Christians for Christians." Inscriptions of Phrygia* (Harvard Theological Studies 32), Missoula, Mon., 1979.

M. Hengel and H. Lichtenberger, "Die Hellenisierung des antiken Judentums als Praeparatio Evangelica," in E. Olshausen (ed.), *Das Christentum in der Antiken Welt*, Stuttgart 1981, 1-30.

G.H.R. Horsely (ed.), *New Documents Illustrating Early Christianity 1-3. A Review of the Greek Inscriptions and Papyri Published in 1976, 1977, 1978*, North Ryde, N.S.W., 1981, 1982, 1983.

W.H.C. Frend, *The Rise of Christianity*, London 1984.

A. Effenberger, *Frühchristliche Kunst und Kultur. Von den Anfängen bis zum 7. Jahrhundert*, Munich 1986.

R.L. Fox, *Pagans and Christians in the Mediterranean World from the Second Century AD to the Conversion of Constantine*, London and New York 1986.

598 **Bibliography:** J.H. Oliver, *Marcus Aurelius: Aspects of Civic and Cultural Policy in the East* (Hesp. Suppl. 13), Princeton, N.J., 1970.

S. Mitchell, "Iconium and Ninica. Two Double Communities in Roman Asia Minor," *Historia* 28, 1979, 409-438.

Idem et al., *Regional Epigraphical Catalogue of Asia Minor II. The Ankara District: The Inscriptions of North Galatia* (BAR Intern. Ser. 135), Oxford 1982.

Illuminating is L. Robert, *A travers l'Asie Mineur. Poètes et prosateurs, monnaies grecques, voyageurs et géographie* (Bibl. des Éc. franç. d'Athènes et de Rome 239), Paris 1980.
L. de Blois, "The Third Century Crisis and the Greek Elite in the Roman Empire," *Historia* 33, 1984, 358-377.
I. Browning, *Palmyra*, London 1979.
Ch. Roueché, "Rome, Asia and Aphrodisias in the Third Century," *JRS* 71, 1981, 103-120.
M. Sartre, *Trois études sur l'Arabie romaine et byzantine* (Coll. Latomus 178), Brussels 1982.
J. Wagner, "Neue Denkmäler aus Doliche. Ergebnisse einer archäologischen Landesaufnahme im Ursprungsgebiet des Iupiter Dolichenus," *BonJahrb* 182, 1982, 133-166.
R.K. Sherk, "A Chronology of the Governors of Galatia A.D. 112-285," *AJP* 100, 1979, 166-175.
S. Mitchell, "Galatia under Tiberius," *Chiron* 16, 1986, 17-33.
Les provinces hellénophones de l'empire romain: de Pompée au milieu du IIIe siècle ap. J.-C. Recueil bibliographique à partir des analyses du BAHR (1962 à 1974), Strasbourg 1986.

602 n. 74 W. Ameling, *Herodes Atticus I: Biographie*; *II: Inschriftenkatalog* (Subsidia Epigraphica 2), Hildesheim, Zurich, New York 1983 (cf. L. Schumacher, *Gnomon* 57, 1985, 35-42).

603 n. 90 C.T.H.R. Ehrhardt, "Eusebius and Celsus," *Jahrbuch für Antike und Christentum* 22, 1979, 40-49.

605 n. 131 S. James, "Dura-Europos and the Chronology of Syria in the 250s AD," *Chiron* 15, 1985, 111-124; see, further, the "nouvelles recherches à Dura-Europos," by E. Will *et al.*, in *Syria* 63, 1986, 3-155.
See also I. Weiler, "Der 'Niedergang' und das Ende der antiken olympischen Spiele in der Forschung," *Gräzer Beiträge* 12/13, 1985/1986, 235-263.

Appendix

I. KING LISTS

All dates are B.C.

1. THE ACHAEMENIDAE

Cyrus II, the Great	559-530
Cambyses	530-522
Darius I, the Great	522-486
Xerxes I	486-465/4
Artaxerxes I	465/4-425
Xerxes II and Sogdianus	425-424
Darius II	424-404
Artaxerxes II	404-359/8
Artaxerxes III Ochus	359/8-338
Arses	338-336
Darius III Codomannus	336-330

2. THE KINGS OF MACEDONIA UP TO ALEXANDER THE GREAT

The reignal periods for the first kings of Macedonia from the house of the Argeadae are uncertain. We do not reach relatively solid footing until we come to Amyntas I

Amyntas I	Second half of the sixth century
Alexander I Philhellene	c. 495-c. 450/40
Perdiccas II	c. 450/40-413
Archelaus	413-399
Orestes	399-396
Aëropus	396-393
Amyntas the 'Minor' (II) / Pausanias	393-392
Amyntas III	393-370
Alexander II	370-369/8
Ptolemy	369/8-365

Perdiccas III	365-359
Philip II	359-336
Alexander III, the Great	336-323

3. THE PTOLEMIES

The numbering is taken from T. C. Skeat, *The Reigns of the Ptolemies*, Münch. Beitr. 39, 1954

Ptolemy I Soter	-283
Ptolemy II Philadelphus	285-246
Ptolemy III Euergetes I	246-221
Ptolemy IV Philopator	221-204
Ptolemy V Epiphanes	204-180
Ptolemy VI Philometor	180-145
Ptolemy VII Neus Philopator	145-144
Ptolemy VIII Euergetes II (Physcon)	145-116
Ptolemy IX Soter II	116-107 and 88-80
Ptolemy X Alexander I	107-88
Ptolemy XI Alexander II	80
Ptolemy XII Neus Dionysus (Auletes)	80-51
Ptolemy XIII Cleopatra VII	51-48
Ptolemy XIV Cleopatra VII	47-44
Cleopatra VII Caesarion	-30

4. THE SELEUCIDS

For the dates cf. R. A. Parker and W. H. Dubberstein, *Babylonian Chronology 626 B.C. - A.D. 75*, Providence, R. I., 1956

Seleucus I Nicator	312-281
Antiochus I Soter	281-261
Antiochus II Theus	261-246
Seleucus II Callinicus	246-225
Seleucus III Soter	225-223
Antiochus III, the Great	223-187
Seleucus IV Philopator	187-175
Antiochus IV Epiphanes	175-164 (?)
Antiochus V Eupator	164 (?)-162
Demetrius I Soter	162-150
Alexander Balas	150-145
Demetrius II Nicator	145-140 and 129-125
Antiochus VI Epiphanes	145-142/1
Antiochus VII Sidetes	139/8 -129

Cleopatra Thea Antiochus VIII Grypus	125-121
Seleucus V	125
Antiochus VIII Grypus	121-96
Antiochus IX Cyzicenus	115-95
Seleucus VI Epiphanes Nicator	96-95
Antiochus X Eusebes Philopator	95-83
Demetrius III Eucaerus	95-88
Antiochus XI Philadelphus	94
Philippus I Philadelphus	94-83
Antiochus XII Dionysus	87-84
Antiochus XIII Asiaticus	69-64
Philippus II	65-64

From 83 to 69 Syria was a province of the Armenian empire of Tigranes I

5. THE ANTIGONIDS

Antigonus Monophthalmus	-301
Demetrius Poliorcetes	306-283
(king of Macedonia:	294-287)
Antigonus Gonatas	283-239
(king of Macedonia:	276-239)
Demetrius II, king of Macedonia	239-229
Antigonus Doson	229-222/1
Philip V	222/1-179
Perseus	179-168

On the date of the reignal period for Antigonus Gonatas see M. Chambers, *AJP* 75, 1954, 385 ff.

6. THE ATTALIDS OF PERGAMUM

Philetaerus	283-263
Eumenes I	263-241
Attalus I Soter	241-197
Eumenes II Soter	197-160/59
Attalus II	160/59 -139/8
Attalus III	139/8-133

The first two Attalids did not adopt the royal title

II. STEMMATA

1. THE ROYAL HOUSE OF MACEDONIA UP TO PHILIP II

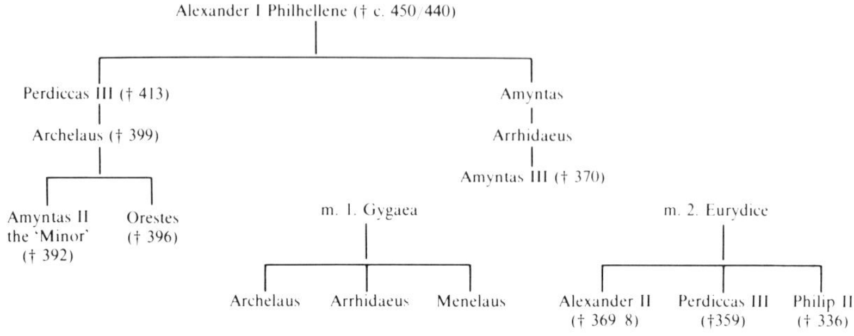

2. PHILIP II AND ALEXANDER THE GREAT

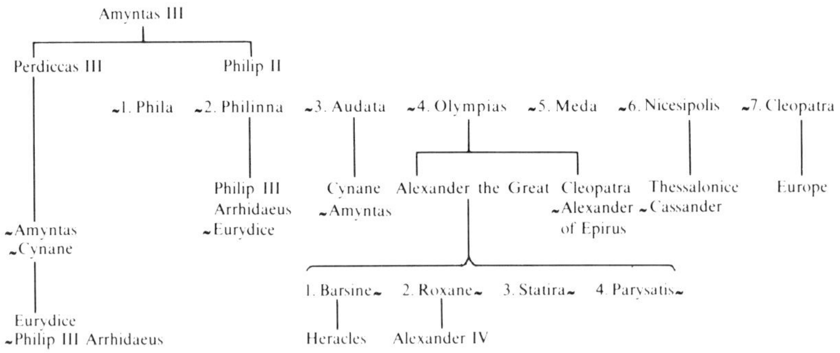

3. THE FAMILY OF ANTIPATER

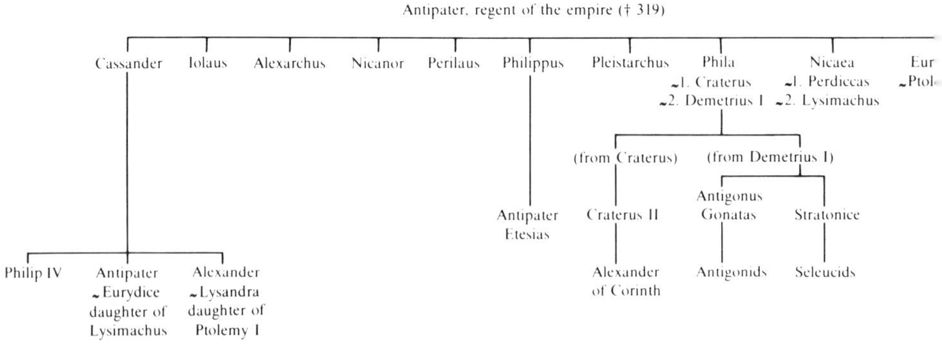

4. THE FAMILY OF LYSIMACHUS

Agathocles of Crannon
- Lysimachus
  - ∞1. Nicaea
    - Agathocles ∞m. Lysandra
    - Eurydice ∞Antipater son of Cassander
    - Arsinoe I ∞Ptolemy II
  - ∞2. Amastris
  - ∞3. Arsinoe II
    - Ptolemy
    - Lysimachus
    - Philip
  - ∞Odrysian concubine
    - Alexander
- Autodicus
- Philippus

5. THE ANTIGONIDS

Antigonus I the 'One Eyed' (Monophthalmus) († 301)
- Demetrius (Poliorcetes)(† 283)
  - ∞1. Phila I
    - Antigonus II Gonatas († 239) ∞Phila (II)
      - Demetrius II († 229) ∞1. Stratonice II ∞2. Phthia ∞3. Chryseis
        - (from Phthia) Philip V († 179)
          - Perseus
            - Philip
            - Alexander
            - Daughter
          - Demetrius
          - Daughter ∞Prusias II
          - Daughter ∞Teres of Thrace
    - Stratonice ∞1. Seleucus I ∞2. Antiochus I
  - ∞2. Eurydice (Athenian)
  - ∞3. Deidameia
  - ∞4. Lanassa
  - ∞5. Ptolemaïs
    - Demetrius the 'Handsome' ∞Olympias (Thessalian)
      - Antigonus III Doson († 221) ∞Chryseis

6. THE FAMILY OF PTOLEMY I

Lagus m. Arsinoe
- Ptolemy I ∞Eurydice (Daughter of Antipater)
  - Ptolemy Ceraunus
  - Meleager
  - Lysandra ∞1. Alexander son of Cassander ∞2. Agathocles son of Lysimachus
  - Ptolemaïs ∞Demetrius Poliorcetes
- Ptolemy I ∞Berenice
  - Arsinoe (II) ∞1. Lysimachus ∞2. Ptolemy Ceraunus ∞3. Ptolemy II Philadelphus
  - Philotera
  - Theoxene ∞Agathocles of Syracuse
  - Ptolemy II (later Philadelphus) ∞1. Arsinoe I (daughter of Lysimachus) ∞2. Arsinoe II
    - Ptolemy III Euergetes ∞Berenice, daughter of Magas I
      - Ptolemy IV Philopator ∞Arsinoe III (sister)
      - Magas II
      - Arsinoe III
    - Lysimachus
    - Berenice ∞Antiochus II
- Menelaus (Strategos of Cyprus)

7. THE LATER PTOLEMIES

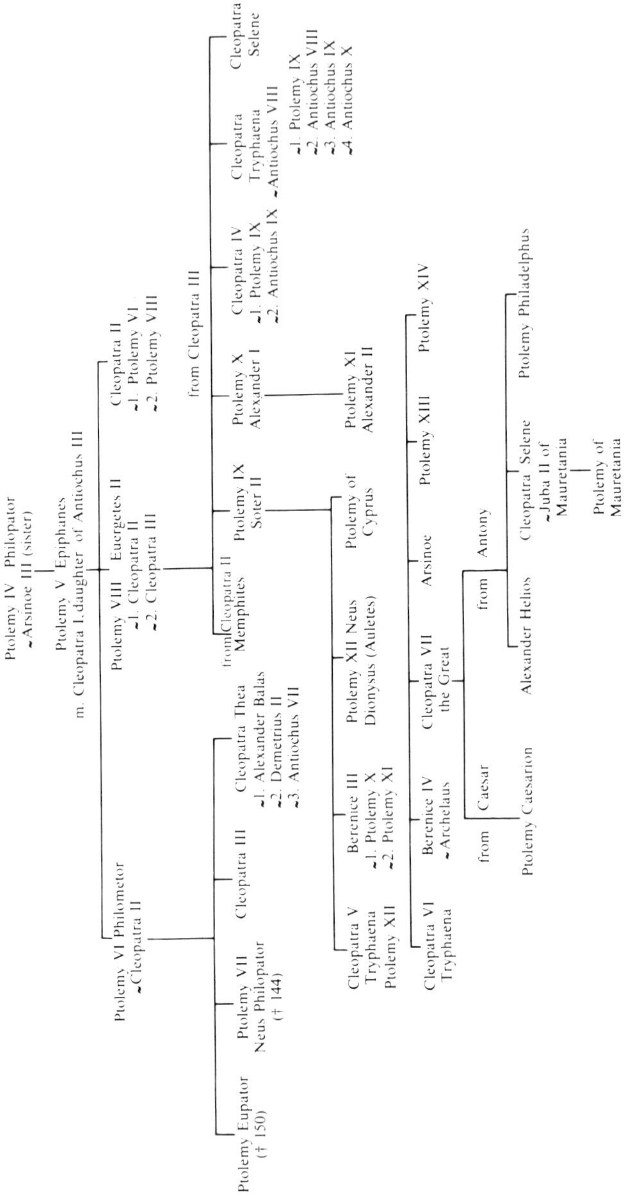
Ptolemy IV Philopator
~Arsinoe III (sister)
Ptolemy V Epiphanes
m. Cleopatra I, daughter of Antiochus III
Ptolemy VI Philometor
~Cleopatra II
Ptolemy VIII Euergetes II
~1. Cleopatra II
~2. Cleopatra III
Cleopatra II
~1. Ptolemy VI
~2. Ptolemy VIII
Ptolemy Eupator
(† 150)
Ptolemy VII
Neus Philopator
(† 144)
Cleopatra III
Cleopatra Thea
~1. Alexander Balas
~2. Demetrius II
~3. Antiochus VII
from Cleopatra II
Memphites
from Cleopatra III
Ptolemy IX
Soter II
Ptolemy X
Alexander I
Cleopatra IV
~1. Ptolemy IX
~2. Antiochus IX
Cleopatra
Tryphaena
~Antiochus VIII
Cleopatra
Selene
~1. Ptolemy IX
~2. Antiochus VIII
~3. Antiochus IX
~4. Antiochus X
Cleopatra V
Tryphaena
Ptolemy XII
Berenice III
~1. Ptolemy X
~2. Ptolemy XI
Ptolemy XII Neus
Dionysus (Auletes)
Ptolemy of
Cyprus
Ptolemy XI
Alexander II
Cleopatra VI
Tryphaena
Berenice IV
~Archelaus
Cleopatra VII
the Great
Arsinoe
Ptolemy XIII
Ptolemy XIV
from
Caesar
Ptolemy Caesarion
from
Antony
Alexander Helios
Cleopatra Selene
~Juba II of
Mauretania
Ptolemy Philadelphus
Ptolemy of
Mauretania

8. THE FAMILY OF SELEUCUS I

Apame I (daughter of Spitamenes) ~ Seleucus I Nicator ~ Stratonice (daughter of Demetrius Poliorcetes)

Antiochus I ~Stratonice (stepmother)

Achaeus the Elder

Phila II ~Antigonus Gonatas

Seleucus

Antiochus II Theus ~1. Laodice I (daughter of Achaeus' parents) ~2. Berenice (1 son)

Apame II ~Magas of Cyrene

Stratonice II ~Demetrius II of Macedonia

(from Laodice)

Seleucus I Callinicus ~Laodice II (sister of Achaeus the younger)

Antiochus Hierax ~Daughter of Ziaelas of Bythinia

Stratonice III ~Ariarathes III of Cappadocia

Laodice ~Mithradates II of Pontus

Seleucus III Soter

Antiochus III, the Great ~1. Laodice III, daughter of Mithradates II of Pontus ~2. Euboea of Chalcis

9. THE LATER SELEUCIDS

Antiochus († 193 B.C.)

Antiochus III, the Great

Seleucus V Philopator

Antiochus V Epiphanes

Antiochus (eliminated 170 B.C.)

Demetrius I Soter

Antiochus V Eupator

(Alexander Balas) Cleopatra Thea (first marriage)

Antiochus VI Epiphanes Dionysus

Demetrius II Nicator ~1. Cleopatra Thea (second marriage) ~2. Rhodogune, daughter of Mithradates I of Parthia

Antiochus VII Euergetes (Sidetes)

(from Cleopatra)

Seleucus V

Antiochus VIII Philometor (Grypus)

Antiochus IX Philopator (Cyzicenus)

Seleucus VI Epiphanes

Antiochus XI Philadelphus

Philip I Philadelphus

Demetrius III (Eucaerus)

Antiochus XII Dionysus

Laodice ~ Mithradates I of Commagene

Antiochus X Eusebes

Philip II

Antiochus I of Commagene

Antiochus XIII (Asiaticus)

10. THE ATTALIDS[1]

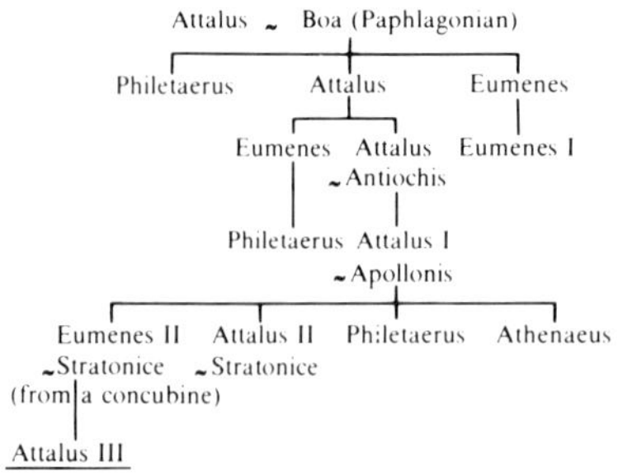

1. Taken from G. Cardinali et M. Holleaux, *Etudes d'épigr. et d'hist. gr.* II, 1938, 16; different is Strabo XIII 624.

III. CHRONOLOGICAL TABLE

Dates B.C.	
Second half of the fourth millennium to the first half of the third millennium	Neolithic culture in Greece (so-called Sesklo culture), especially in Thessaly and in the district of Corinth
Middle of the third millennium	So-called Dimini phase
c. 2300-1900	Early Helladic culture ("Urfirnis" pottery), especially in Thessaly, central Greece and the northern Peloponnesus
2200	Beginning of Early Minoan III; first flowering of Cretan art
c. 2000	Beginning of Middle Minoan I; court culture in central Crete
c. 1900 (at the latest c. 1600)	Immigration of the Indo-Europeans into Greece
c. 1900-1550	Middle Helladic culture in Greece (Minyan pottery)
c. 1700	Hammurabi of Babylon; establishment of Hyksos rule in Egypt; decline of the first flowering in Cretan culture (by an earthquake?)
Sixteenth century	Great new efflorescence in Cretan culture (Cnossus, Phaestus, Mallia)
c. 1550	Beginning of the so-called Late Helladic (Mycenaean) period in Greece: the shaft graves

Fifteenth century	Static period of culture in Hellas
From c. 1500 onwards	Beginning of the vaulted tombs
c. 1400	Overthrow of the Minoan thalassocracy
c. 1350	"Treasury of Atreus"; Lion Gate of Mycenae;
Fourteenth and thirteenth century	Expansion of the Mycenaean Greeks, especially in the eastern Mediterranean (finds in Ras Shamra, Minet el Beïda, Byblus), encroachment on Crete
Middle of the fourteenth century	Ahhiyawa in Hittite cuneiform tablets
1200	Beginning of the Great Migration (Aegean or Dorian Migration), precipitated by the Illyrians; the Dorians and North-West Greeks arrive in Greece
c. 1200	Destruction of Troy VII A (by the Thracians?); overthrow of the Hittite empire
Twelfth century (end)	Establishment of the Middle Assyrian empire (Tiglathpilesar I) and the Phrygian kingdom; rise of the Phoenician cities (climax c. 1000-800)
c. 1100	Beginning of the Iron age in Hellas
c. 1000 (?)	First expeditions of the Etruscans reach Italy
Before 1000	Colonisation of the west coast of Asia Minor by the Greeks (Ionians, Aeolians)
Tenth (or ninth) century	Phoenician alphabet taken over by the Greeks
Ninth or eighth century	Creation of the Homeric poems
883-859	Assurnasirpal, king of Assur: first climax in Assyrian power
Second half of the ninth century	Rise of Urartu (between Lakes Van and Urmia)
814/13	Founding of Carthage
800 at the latest	Origin of Sparta by *synoikismos*
Eighth century	Union of Attica completed; formation of the Thessalian Tetrarchy

776	Beginning of the Olympian victor lists
754	Beginning of the Spartan ephor lists
Middle of the eighth century	Beginning of the great Hellenic colonisation; founding of Cumae (Cyme) in Campania, of Sinope and Trapezus on the Pontus
c. 735	Founding of Naxos at Mount Aetna
Eighth century (end)	First Messenian War: helotisation of the Messenians by the Spartans
711	First reference to the Greeks (Iamâni = Ionians) in Assyrian documents
c. 700	Founding of Tarentum
700	Hesiod of Ascra
Seventh century (beginning)	From the mountainous regions the Macedonians penetrate the plain of the Haliacmon (King Perdiccas I)
First half of the seventh century	Rise of the Lydian kingdom under the Mermnad dynasty (Gyges); Lelantine War in Greece.
c. 688	Foundation of Gela by Rhodians; c. 680 Thasos settled by Parians; Cimmerian incursions into Asia Minor; first naval battle between Greeks (Corinth and Corcyra)
From c. 650 onwards	Rise of *tyrannis*: Cypselus of Corinth
From 650 onwards	Finds of Greek pottery in the Nile Delta
Seventh century middle	Great Helot revolt in Messenia: so-called Second Messenian War. Pheidon of Argos
Seventh century second half	Foundation of Naucratis; voyage of Colaeus of Samos to Tartessus
636 or 632	Coup d'état of Cylon in Athens
c. 630	Founding of Cyrene
c. 624	Dracon, the first lawgiver of Athens
612	Fall of Nineveh, end of the Assyrian empire
Towards 600	Foundation of Olbia on the Hypanis (Bug);
c. 600	Founding of Massalia by Phocaeans; Alcaeus of Lesbos; Periander tyrant of Corinth

594/3	Solon arbiter between the classes in Athens: implementation of his reforms ("freeing of the farmers"); establishment of the timocracy
582-580	Damasias, archon of Athens
561/60	Beginning of the *tyrannis* of Peisistratus
559-530	Cyrus II, the Great
547	Fall of Sardis; end of the Lydian kingdom; Croesus taken prisoner by Cyrus
after 540	Naval battle of Alalia off Corsica (Carthaginians and Etruscans against the Phocaeans); foundation of Phanagoreia
539	Cyrus II conquers Babylon
530-522	Cambyses, king of Persia
528/7	Death of Peisistratus of Athens; beginning of the *tyrannis* of Hippias and Hipparchus
525	Cyme at war with Etruscans, Umbrians and Daunians; *tyrannis* of Aristodemus
c. 522	End of the tyrant Polycrates of Samos
522-486	Darius I, king of Persia
514	Hipparchus murdered at the Great *Panathenaea* in Athens
513/12 (?)	Scythian expedition of Darius I
511/10	Complete destruction of Sybaris by Croton
510	Overthrow of Hippias in Athens
508/7	Beginning of Cleisthenes' reforms in Athens
506	Athenian victory over the Boeotians and Chalcidians
From c. 505 onwards	Cleander, tyrant of Gela in Sicily
500 (or 499) - 494	The Ionian revolt
498	Capture of Sardis by the Ionians
497	Reconquest of Cyprus by the Persians
494	Fall of Miletus; battle of Sepeia (defeat of the Argives in conflict with Sparta)
494-476	Anaxilaus, tyrant of Rhegium

493	Themistocles, archon in Athens
492	Expedition of Mardonius to Thrace
From 491 (?) onwards	Gelon, tyrant of Gela
490	Expedition of Datis and Artaphernes by sea against Eretria and Athens; destruction of Eretria; battle of Marathon (September)
489 (spring)	Abortive expedition of Miltiades against Paros
488(?)	Death of the Spartan king, Cleomenes I; his successor: Leonidas
488/87	War between Athens and Aegina
487/86	Constitutional reform in Athens: archons chosen by lot; rise of the *strategia*
486	Death of Darius I, king of Persia; his successor: Xerxes (to 465/64)
From 483 onwards	Persian mobilisation for the campaign against Greece
482	Beginning of construction on Themistocles' fleet
481	Proclamation of a general peace throughout Greece
480 (high summer)	Battles of Thermopylae and Artemisium
480 (end of Sept.)	Battle of Salamis Battle of Himera
479	Revolt in Babylonia; inhabitants of Athens evacuated for the second time (summer); battles of Plataea and Mycale (autumn); defection of the Ionians from Persia
479/78	Construction of fortifications at Athens
478	Death of Gelon; Hieron, tyrant of Syracuse (-466) Pausanias on Cyprus and before the gates of Byzantium (recalled 477)
478/77	Beginnings of the Attic Maritime League
477	Leotychidas in Thessaly
476	Pausanias driven out of Byzantium

476/75	Elimination of the Persian base Eion (on the Strymon)
475	Scyros and Carystus conquered by Cimon
474	Victory of Hieron over the Etruscans at Cumae (Cyme)
473	Defeat of Tarentum and Rhegium in conflict with the Iapygians
472	The *Persae* of Aeschylus
471	Ostracism of Themistocles
Beginning of the sixties	Battle at the Eurymedon
467 (?)	Death of Pausanias
465	Cimon's expedition against the Thracian Chersonese; defection of Thasos
464	Athenian defeat at Drabescus; earthquake at Sparta; capitulation of Thasos; beginning of the Third Messenian War
462 (summer)	Constitutional reform of Ephialtes († 461) in Athens; Cimon in Messenia; termination of the Spartan-Athenian Alliance (autumn)
461	End of *tyrannis* in Sicily (Messana-Rhegium)
460	Athenian expedition against Egypt: capture of Memphis
c. 460	In the Peloponnesus: battle of Oenoe Hippocrates born in Cos
459 (spring)	Aegina invested by Athenian forces
459/58	End of the Third Messenian War
457	Battles of Tanagra and Oenophyta
456	Aegina capitulates; Persian victory of Megabyzus over the Egyptians and Athenians besieged on Prosopitis in the Nile
455	Height of Athenian power in the entire Pentecontaetia
454	End of the Athenian expedition in Egypt; the treasury of the Maritime League transferred from Delos to Athens (summer)

453 (?)	Truce (for five years) between Athens and Sparta
451 (?)	Thirty Years' Peace between Argos and Sparta
451/50	Ducetius, leader of the Sicels
450	Athenian naval victory over the Persians at Salamis (Cyprus)
449 (spring)	Athenian-Persian treaty: so-called Peace of Callias
448-447 (or after 446)	Panhellenic congress planned by Pericles
447 (summer ?)	Defeat of the Athenians at Coroneia; creation of the Boeotian League
446/45	Thirty Years' Peace between Athens and Sparta
444	Foundation of Thurii
443	Ostracism of Thucydides (son of Melesias)
440-439	Revolt of Samos
435	Naval battle of Leucimme: the Corinthians defeated by the Corcyraeans
434	Financial decree of Callias
433 (high summer)	Naval battle off the islands of Sybota: Corinthians victorious over the Corcyraean fleet; Pericles demands that Potidaea hand over the *epidamiourgoi*
432	Megarian *psephisma*
431-421	The Archidamian War
431	Theban surprise attack on Plataea; first invasion of Attica by the Spartans under King Archidamus; expulsion of the Aeginetans by Pericles; treaty between Athens and Sitalces.
430	The Plague in Athens (summer); deposition of Pericles (autumn)
429 (spring)	Capitulation of Potidaea; Pericles reinstated; dies in autumn
(summer)	Defeat of the Athenians at Spartolus
(autumn)	Expedition of Phormion

428	Lesbos defects from Athens
428/27	Mission of Gorgias of Leontini in Athens
427 (summer)	Capitulation of Mytilene; oligarchic revolution on Corcyra suppressed with Athenian aid; Plataea capitulates (autumn); Laches despatched to Sicily with a fleet (so-called First Sicilian Expedition of Athens)
426	Foundation and occupation of Heracleia in Trachis by the Peloponnesians
425	Landing of Demosthenes in Messenian Pylos; capitulation of the Spartans beleaguered on Sphacteria (August)
424	Reorganisation of the tribute assessment among the members of the Maritime League by Cleon (so-called Cleon assessment); occupation of Cythera by Nicias; Brasidas' march to Chalcidice (autumn); defeat of the Athenians at Delium; Congress of Gela
424/23	Peace of Callias renewed between Athens and Persia (treaty of Epilycas)
423	Truce of Laches
422	Cleon and Brasidas slain at Amphipolis
421 (April)	Fifty Years' Peace between Athens and the Lacedaemonians: Peace of Nicias
421-414	The era of the Peace of Nicias
421	Attic-Spartan defensive alliance for fifty years
420 (spring)	Treaty concluded between Sparta and Boeotia
420 (summer)	Athenian defensive treaty with Argos, Mantineia and Elis
418	Battle of Mantineia: defeat of the Argives and the Peloponnesian special alliance against the Spartans (King Agis)
417	Ostracism of Hyperbolis; Nicias in Thrace
416	The Athenians subjugate neutral Melos; Alcibiades at Olympia; envoys of Segesta (Sicily) in Athens
415 (summer)	Departure of the Athenian fleet for Sicily under Nicias, Lamachus and Alcibiades
(autumn)	Initial struggles for Syracuse

414 (May)	Beginning of the siege of Syracuse
(summer)	Resumption of the war between Athens and Sparta (so-called Deceleian War and Ionian War down to 404)
413 (spring)	Occupation of Deceleia by the Spartans (King Agis)
(high summer to autumn)	Destruction of the Sicilian expedition of Athens
412 (summer)	Treaty between Sparta and Persia; collapse of Athenian sovereignty on Chios, Lesbos (Mytilene, Methymna) and Miletus; financial straits in Athens
411	Renewal of the Spartan-Persian treaty by Tissaphernes and Pharnabazus
(May-June)	Abolition of Athenian democracy, establishment of an extreme oligarchy (dictatorship of the Four Hundred)
(summer)	Constitution of Theramenes: compromise between the democratic and oligarchic factions; the government in the hands of the Five Thousand
(end)	Naval battles of Cynossema and Abydus
410 (May)	Naval victory of Alcibiades at Cyzicus
(July)	Collapse of the rule of the Five Thousand in Athens, restoration of the former democracy; resolution to codify current law
409	Armistice between Athens and Pharnabazus; Selinus and Himera destroyed by the Carthaginians
408 (June)	Alcibiades' entry into Athens; his appointment as generalissimo; Cyrus the Younger, vice-regent in Sardis
407 (spring)	Naval victory of Lysander at Notium; fall of Alcibiades
406 (summer)	Conon invested in the harbour of Mytilene; naval battle of Arginusae (August); Arginusae lawsuit (autumn); height of Carthaginian power in Sicily; Athenian embassy despatched to the Carthaginians in Sicily; Dionysius I *strategos autokrator* in Syracuse (406/5)
405 (mid-summer)	Battle of Aegospotami
405/4	Peace between Syracuse and Carthage

404 (March or April)	Capitulation of Athens, (summer); subjugation of Samos by Lysander
404-403	Rule of the Thirty in Athens
404 (end)	Thrasybulus in Phyle; revolt of Egypt from the Persian empire
403	General amnesty in Athens (archonship of Eucleides; (end) fall of Lysander
402-400	Spartan-Elian War
401/00	Eleusis reunited with Athens
401	The March of the Ten Thousand; battle of Cunaxa (autumn): death of Cyrus the Younger
400-394	The Spartan-Persian War: Thibron in Asia Minor (-399)
399	Death of Socrates
397	Beginning of the Second Carthaginian War in Sicily; truce in Asia Minor
396	Agesilaus crosses to Asia Minor; Conon blockaded in Caunus; crisis of the Sicilian War: landing of Himilco in Panormus, siege of Syracus
395	Encounter at Sardis; Timocrates as Persian envoy in Hellas; outbreak of the Corinthian War; battle of Haliartus (autumn): death of Lysander
394	Battles of Nemea and Coroneia; naval battle of Cnidus: end of Spartan sovereignty on the seas
393	Conon in Athens
392	Peace concluded between Dionysius I and Carthage
392-386	Corinthian-Argive double state
392	Peace negotiations between Athens and Sparta; Antalcidas despatched to Sardis: peace congress under the superintendence of Tiribazus
389	Successes of Thrasybulus in the region of the former Maritime League

388	Death of Thrasybulus; victory of Dionysius at the Eleporus river
387	Peace negotiations in Susa
386	The King's Peace (so-called Peace of Antalcidas); capitulation of Rhegium: Dionysius I in possession of the Sicilian straits
385	*Dioikismos* of Mantineia
382	Spartan-Olynthian War: occupation of the Cadmeia in Thebes by Phoebidas of Sparta; Greece divided into military zones by the Spartans
380	*Panegyrikos* of Isocrates
379	Capitulation of Olynthus, the Chalcidian state dissolved; liberation of Thebes, the Spartan garrison forced to withdraw
378/77	Founding of the Second Attic Maritime League
377 and 376	Spartan army under Agesilaus and Cleombrotus in Boeotia
376	Naval victory of Chabrias of Athens over the Peloponnesians at Naxos
375/4	Peace Congress in Sparta
374/73 (or 373/72)	Theban destruction of Plataea
372	Union of Thessaly by Jason of Pherae († 370)
371-362	Theban hegemony
371 (summer)	Peace between Athens and Sparta; battle of Leuctra; second Peace Congress at Sparta
370	Foundation of the Arcadian League; first campaign of Epameinondas in the Peloponnesus (second campaign: 369, third: 367, fourth: 362)
369 (spring)	Creation of a separate Messenian state; occupation of Thessalian Larisa by King Alexander II of Macedonia (murdered 369/68)
368	Peace Congress of Delphi
367-357	Dionysius II, ruler of Syracuse
367	Negotiations in Susa: treaty between Persia and Boeotia (Pelopidas)

367/66	The Aetolian League mentioned for the first time
366	Special peace concluded in Thebes between the Boeotians and the states of the northern Peloponnesus
365	Timotheus conquers Samos for Athens
364	Voyage of Epameinondas; death of Pelopidas in the encounter at Cynoscephalae
362	Battle of Mantineia: death of Epameinondas
362/61	General peace in Greece (Sparta excluded)
361/60	Callistratus of Athens in Macedonia
359	Perdiccas III, king of Macedonia, slain in battle against the Illyrians
358	Philip II conquers the Illyrians
357	*Areiopagitikos* of Isocrates; Philip takes Amphipolis and (winter 357/56) Pydna
357-355	Athenian Social War
356	Potidaea conquered and destroyed by Philip; birth of Alexander (the Great); accusation launched in Delphi against the Phocians
354	Methone conquered by Philip; battle of Neon (Philomelus †); Eubulus of Athens superintendent of the Theoric Fund
353	Victory of Phocian Onomarchus over Philip of Macedonia
352 (spring)	Philip defeats Onomarchus on the Crocus *campus*; the Macedonian king at Thermopylae; Chares restores Attic sovereignty in the Thracian Chersonese; (end of 362 or 351): Philip's Thracian campaign as far as Heraion Teichos
350	Stageira captured and destroyed
349-348	Olynthian War (Olynthus destroyed 348)
349 (spring)	Demosthenes' *First Philippic*
347	Death of Plato
346	Peace of Philocrates; end of the Third Sacred War; Isocrates' *Philippos*

344	Philip in Illyria (battles against Pleuratus); Philip archon of the Thessalians (perhaps not until 342); Timoleon in Sicily
343 (summer)	Treaty of friendship and non-aggression between Macedonia and Persia
343/42 (winter)	Artaxerxes III Ochus reconquers Egypt
342	Creation of the Thessalian tetrarchy and the "province" of Thrace
341	Demosthenes' *Third* and *Fourth Philippics*; Timoleon's victory over the Carthaginians at the Crimisus
340 (beginning)	Formation of a Hellenic alliance on the initiative of Demosthenes; Athens declares war against Philip (autumn)
339	Scythian campaign of Philip II; Philip invested with the supreme command in conducting the Amphictyonian War (late autumn); Philip in Elateia (year-end); Timoleon's peace with the Carthaginians; the *Panathenaikos* of Isocrates
338	Death of Archidamus III in Italy (Mandonium); battle of Chaeroneia (2 August); constitutional congress of the Panhellenic League in Corinth (establishment of a general peace) (winter); death of Artaxerxes Ochus, king of Persia
337 (spring)	"War session" of the Corinthian Congress: resolution carried to conduct the war against Persia
336 (spring)	Parmenion and Attalus in Asia Minor: launching of the Persian War
(summer)	Philip II assassinated in Aegae
336	Renewal of the Corinthian League by Alexander
335	Alexander on the Lower Danube; disturbances in Hellas; destruction of Thebes (autumn)
334 (spring)	Alexander crosses the Hellespont; Alexander's victory at the Granicus (May/June); Alexander the Molossian crosses to Italy

334/33	Alexander in winter quarters at Gordium
333 (spring)	Death of Memnon at the siege of Mytilene
(November)	Battle of Issus
332 (August)	Capture of Tyre
331 (beginning)	Foundation of Alexandria in Egypt; expedition to the Oasis of Siwah (spring); battle of Gaugamela (1 October); Alexander adopts the title: "King of Asia"
331/30	Alexander of the Molossians assassinated at Pandosia
331	King Agis of Sparta defeated by Antipater at Megalopolis
330 (spring)	Burning of Persepolis: end of the Panhellenic "war of revenge"; discharge of the Greek contingents; death of the Achaemenid Darius III (July)
330-327	Battles in East Iran against Bessus and Spitamenes
330 (autumn)	Catastrophe of Philotas, death of Parmenion
327-325	Alexander's Indian campaign
326 (May/June)	Battle with Porus at the Hydaspes
325 (July)	Alexander in Pattala (Hyderabad)
(September)	Departure of Nearchus from the Indus Delta; meeting of Nearchus and Alexander in the vicinity of Hormuz (December)
324 (beginning)	Alexander in Pasargadae; mass wedding in Susa (spring and summer); Alexander demands apotheosis from the Greeks; decree concerning the restoration of the Greek exiles; mutiny of Opis; Harpalus in Athens
323 (10 June)	Death of Alexander
323 (summer)	Resolutions passed in Babylon: redistribution of the satrapies under the direction of Perdiccas
323/22	The Lamian War; naval battle of Amorgus (summer 322); death of Demosthenes (winter 322)
321	Perdiccas assassinated during the Egyptian

	campaign; Craterus slain in Asia Minor; reorganisation of the empire at Triparadeisus: Antipater "regent," Antigonus Monophthalmus *strategos* of Asia
319 (summer)	Death of Antipater; Polyperchon proclaimed "regent"
318-316	Eumenes supreme commander in Asia († 316)
317	Athens changes sides in favour of Cassander; Polyperchon deposed; Agathocles seizes power in Syracuse as plenipotentiary *strategos*
317-307	Demetrius of Phalerum as deputy of Cassander in Athens
316	Execution of Olympias
315	Antigonus Monophthalmus in Tyre proclaims his assuming of the regency; establishment of the Island League
315-311	First Coalition War (Cassander, Lysimachus, Ptolemy and Seleucus against Antigonus)
312	Battle of Gaza: Demetrius son of Antigonus defeated by Ptolemy; Seleucus returns to Babylon
311	Conclusion of peace (Seleucus excluded)
310	Agathocles lands in Africa
310/9	Cassander has Alexander IV and Roxane eliminated
309	Death of Ophellas, governor of Cyrene
307	Demetrius Poliorcetes gains control of Athens
307-304	"Four-Year War" in Hellas; successes of Cassander
306	Naval victory of Demetrius over Ptolemy at Salamis (on Cyprus); Antigonus and Demetrius adopt the royal title; peace between Agathocles and Carthage
305	Ptolemy, Cassander, Lysimachus and Seleucus assume the royal title
305/4	Agathocles Basileus; siege of Rhodes by Demetrius

302 (spring)	Panhellenic League of Corinth; Antigonus and Demetrius *hegemones*
301 (summer)	Battle of Ipsus: death of Antigonus Monophthalmus
299/98	Wedding of Rhossus: Seleucus I marries Stratonice (daughter of Demetrius Poliorcetes)
298 (?)	Death of Cassander; Agathocles gains possession of Corcyra
294 (spring)	Demetrius Poliorcetes captures Athens (defected from 301 onwards) and becomes king of Macedonia (294-287)
292	Demetrius gains control of Boeotia
289	Death of Agathocles
287	Pyrrhus and Lysimachus divide Macedonia between them; liberation of Athens by Olympiodorus (summer); Demetrius in Asia Minor
286	Demetrius taken prisoner by Seleucus I
285	Ptolemy I appoints his son, Ptolemy II, as coregent
283	Death of Demetrius and Ptolemy I; Lysimachus has his son Agathocles executed
282	Roman occupation of Thurii
281	Curupedion: death of Lysimachus
281 (late summer)	Seleucus I assassinated by Ptolemy Ceraunus
280 (beginning)	Pyrrhus crosses to Italy
280 (summer)	Pyrrhus victorious over the Romans at Heraclea on the Siris; formation of the Achaean League
280-279	Battles between Ptolemy II and Antiochus I: so-called Syrian War of Succession
279	Ausculum; Celtic invasion into Macedonia and Greece; death of Ptolemy Ceraunus
278	Pyrrhus lands in Sicily (Tauromenium); the Celts cross the Hellespont
277	Victory of Antigonus Gonatas over the Celts at Lysimacheia

276	Antigonus Gonatas king of the Macedonians (to 239)
275	Battle of Maleventum (later called Beneventum); Pyrrhus returns to Epirus
275/74-215 (214)	King Hieron II of Syracuse
274-271	First Syrian War: Ptolemy II against Antiochus I
272	Death of Pyrrhus in Argos; Tarentum taken by the Romans
271/70	Triumphal celebrations in Alexandria: *pompe* of Ptolemy II; death of Epicurus
270	Rhegium under Roman control; death of Arsinoe II (9 July)
267-261 (?)	Chremonideian War (Ptolemy II, Areus of Sparta and Athens against Antigonus Gonatas)
263/62	Athens capitulates and receives a Macedonian garrison (to 229); death of Zenon of Citium
c. 260	Formation of the Cappadocian empire under Ariarathes
260-253	Second Syrian War (Ptolemy II against Antiochus II and Antigonus Gonatas)
255	Separate peace between Ptolemy II and Antigonus Gonatas
253	Peace between the Ptolemaic and Seleucid empires
253/52 (?)	The vice-regent Alexander defects from Antigonus Gonatas
251	Aratus liberates Sicyon
247 (spring)	Beginning of the Parthian era
246-241	Third Syrian War (Ptolemy III against Seleucus II): Laodice War
243	Aratus takes Acrocorinth
242-228/27	Antiochus Hierax in Asia Minor
241	Death of the reformer, Agis IV, king of Sparta; Carthaginian Sicily falls to Rome

240	First performance of a Greek drama in Rome (Livius Andronicus)
239	Death of Antigonus Gonatas
229-228	First Illyrian War of Rome against Teuta
c. 228-223	Temporary expansion of Attalus I over the whole of Seleucid Asia Minor this side of the Taurus; height of Aetolian power in Greece
227	Sicily becomes a Roman province; naval expedition of Antigonus Doson to Caria; coup d'état of Cleomenes III in Sparta
227 (or 226)	Earthquake on Rhodes
224	Hellenic alliance of Antigonus Doson
223	Mantineia destroyed by Antigonus Doson; accession of Antiochus III to the throne of the Seleucid empire (to 187)
222 (summer)	Battle of Sellasia
222/1-179	Philip V king of Macedonia
221-217	Fourth Syrian War: Antiochus III against Ptolemy IV Philopator
220-217	The Social War in Hellas
220	Revolt of Molon suppressed by Antiochus III
219	Antiochus III takes Seleuceia in Pieria; Second Illyrian War of Rome
217	Battle of Raphia
215	Treaty between Hannibal and Philip V
215-205	First Macedonian War
213	Achaeus taken prisoner and executed in Sardis
212-206	The Aetolians at war with Philip V
212-205	The "Anabasis" of Antiochus III in the East
212	Conquest of Syracuse by the Romans (M. Marcellus); death of Archimedes
205	Peace of Phoenice (in Epirus)
204	Death of Ptolemy IV Philopator

203/2 (winter)	Secret treaty between Philip V and Antiochus III on the partition of the Ptolemaic empire
202	Philip V takes Lysimacheia
201	Antiochus III invades South Syria (so-called Fifth Syrian War); naval battle of Chios: Philip V against Attalus I, the Rhodians, Byzantium and Cyzicus; embassy of the Rhodians and Attalus I in Rome
200-197	Second Macedonian War of the Romans
197	Battle of Cynoscephalae
196	Declaration of freedom by T. Quinctius Flamininus; Antiochus III in Europe: Lysimacheia built up
195 (?)	Peace concluded between Antiochus III and Ptolemy V Epiphanes
195 (summer)	Hannibal meets with Antiochus III in Ephesus
192-188	War of the Romans against Antiochus III
190 (end) or 189 (beginning)	Battle of Magnesia (at Mount Sipylus)
189	Ambracia taken by M. Fulvius Nobilior; peace concluded between the Romans and Aetolians
188	Peace of Apameia
187	Death of Antiochus III at Susa
after 184	Establishment of Greek sovereignty in North-West India by Demetrius, son of Euthydemus
183	Death of Philopoemen (and Hannibal)
179	Death of Philip V; Perseus king of Macedonia (-168)
175-164 (?)	Antiochus IV ruler of the Seleucid empire
171-168	War of the Romans against Perseus
170 (?)-168	Sixth Syrian War
168 (22 June)	Battle of Pydna; humiliation of Antiochus IV by the Romans before the gates of Alexandria

167	The "height of Hellenism" in Jerusalem (December)
From 166 onwards	Wars of the Maccabaeans
164	Conquest of Jerusalem by Judas Maccabaeus
164 (?)	Death of Antiochus IV in Gabae (Isfahan)
163	Partition of the Ptolemaic kingdom: Ptolemy Philometor receives Egypt and Cyprus, the younger Ptolemy obtains Cyrenaica
155	Publication of the testament of the "younger" Ptolemy, in which Rome is declared official heir
c. 150	First great victory of the Parthians under Mithradates I: annexation of Media
149-148	Revolt of Andriscus ("Pseudo Philip") in Macedonia
148	Macedonia becomes a province; beginning of the Macedonian era
146	The Achaean War; destruction of Corinth
145	Ptolemy VI Philometor proclaimed "king of Asia"; his death in Syria
145-116	Ptolemy VIII Euergetes II
145/44	Expulsion of the Greek scholars and savants from Alexandria
141	Advance of the Parthians as far as Mesopotamia
140/39	Demetrius II Nicator taken prisoner by the Parthians
133	Death of Attalus III of Pergamum; in his testament Rome declared heir
132-129	Revolt of Aristonicus in western Asia Minor
131	Ptolemy VIII Euergetes II forced to leave Alexandria
130/129	Fall of Antiochus VII Sidetes in the Parthian campaign; end of the Seleucid empire as a major power
127	Ptolemy VIII regains control of Alexandria
121/20-63	Mithradates VI Eupator, king of Pontus

117 (or 116)	Discovery of the direct sea route from Egypt to India with the aid of the monsoons
116	Death of Ptolemy VIII; new throne disputes in Alexandria
104 and 100	Slave disturbances in Attica
c. 100	The former Ptolemaic empire partitioned into three separate states: Egypt, Cyprus, Cyrenaica
96	Death of Apion of Cyrene: the Romans declared heirs
88	Ephesian massacre: slaughter of 80,000 Italics; outbreak of a revolt by the indigenous population in Thebes
86	Sulla's victories at Chaeroneia and Orchomenus over Archelaus, the commander of Mithradates VI; capture of Athens by Sulla
83-69	Syria (and east Cilicia) become a province of the Armenian empire under Tigranes I
80	Throne disturbances in Egypt engineered by Sulla
80-51	Ptolemy XII Neus Dionysus ("Auletes") king of Egypt
75-73	C. Scribonius Curio advances as far as the Lower Danube
74	Expedition of M. Antony the elder against the pirates; Bithynia bequeathed to Rome by Nicomedes IV
74-67	Third Mithradatic War: the Greek cities on the Pontus seriously affected
72-70	Conquest of the Greek cities on the Pontus by Lucullus
67-49	Time of peace for the Greek world
67	Cilicia organised into a province by Pompey
63	End of the Seleucid dynasty in Syria, Pompey establishes the province of Syria
61	Defeat of C. Antonius Hybrida against the Bastarnae at the Istrus
58	Romans take control of Cyprus
49	Massalia loses its autonomy

48	Battle of Pharsalus; Pompey assassinated in Egypt
48/47	Caesar's Alexandrine War
47	Embassy from Chersonesus (Crimea) in Rome
42	Battle of Philippi
41	Cleopatra VII in Tarsus before Antony
41/40-33	Nicias tyrant of Cos through the good-will of M. Antony
37/36	Antony presents Cleopatra VII with the kingdom of Chalcis in the Lebanon
36	Antony's abortive Parthian campaign
34	The Alexandrine gifts
31 (2 September)	Battle of Actium
30 (1 August)	Fall of Alexandria; death of Cleopatra
27	Greece constituted as senatorial province *Achaea*
25 B.C. - 23 A.D.	King Juba II of Mauretania
7/6 and 5/4	The Cyrenaic edicts of Augustus

Dates A.D.

17-19	Germanicus general governor of the Orient with headquarters in Antioch
67 (28 November)	Achaea declared free by Nero
69	Vespasian in Alexandria
74	Philosophers expelled from Rome by Vespasian
(27 December)	Vespasian's "charter of the ancient universities"
101-102 105-106	Trajan's Dacian Wars
106	Nabataea reorganised into the province of Arabia
108/109	Maximus *corrector* of Achaea
110-112 or 111-113	The Younger Pliny governor of Bithynia and Pontus
114-117	Trajan's Parthian War

c. 120	Death of Dio Chrysostom of Prusa
124/125 128/29 131/32	Hadrian in Athens
130	Foundation of Antinoöpolis in Egypt
135	Hadrian establishes the Athenaeum in Rome
143	*Eulogy of Rome* by Aelius Aristides
c. 150	Pausanias' *Periegesis* of Hellas
165	The Plague dragged in from the East into the Roman Empire
170	Invasion of the Costoboci into Hellas; the *Eleusinios* of Aelius Aristides
175	The usurper Avidius Cassius in the Orient
177	Herodes Atticus †
c. 180	*True Doctrine* of Kelsos (Celsus)
189	Death of Aelius Aristides
195 (end)	Byzantium capitulates; deprived of its privileges
199/200	Emperor Septimius Severus (193-211) grants Alexandria a Council
212	The *Constitutio Antoniniana* of the emperor Caracalla
215	Disturbances in Alexandria: Caracalla intervenes against the *epheboi*
235-238	Emperor Maximinus Thrax: the affliction of the cities at its height
c. 236	Death of Bishop Hippolytus of Rome (the last Roman bishop who used Greek)
From 253 onwards	Invasions of Germanic tribes into the Empire (Asia Minor and Greece)
256	The Bithynian cities plundered
260-268	Renaissance of Hellenic culture under the emperor Gallienus
262	Goths invade Asia Minor
267	Herulians invade Greece; victory of Herennius Dexippus of Athens

270	Death of Plotinus
284-305	Reign of the emperor Diocletian; end of the old autonomous Greek community-states
323	An *agon* of the *epheboi* of Oxyrhynchus mentioned for the last time
324	Construction begins on Constantinople
373	Death of Athanasius of Alexandria
383-84	Themistius city prefect of Constantinople
391	Destruction of the Alexandrian Sarapeum
c. 393	Death of Libanius of Antioch
393	The last Olympian games
395-396	Devastation of Greece by Alarich
529	Justinian closes down the University of Athens
636	The Arabs in Syria
639	Beginning of the Arab conquest of Egypt

Abbreviations

AA	*Archäologischer Anzeiger*
Abh. B	Abhandlungen der Berliner Akademie der Wissenschaften, philologisch-historische Klasse
Abh.Bay	Abhandlungen der Bayerischen Akademie der Wissenschaften, philologisch-historische Klasse
Abh.S	Abhandlungen der Königlichen sächsischen Gesellschaft der Wissenschaften, philologisch-historische Klasse
Accame, *Dom.*	S. Accame, *Il dominio romane in Grecia*, Rome 1946
Accame, *Lega*	S. Accame, *La Lega ateniese*, Rome 1941
Aeg.	*Aegyptus*
AfO	*Archiv für Orientforschung*
AfP	*Archiv für Papyrusforschung*
AHR	*American Historical Review*
AJA	*American Journal of Archaeology*
AJP	*American Journal of Philology*
Altheim, *As.*	F. Altheim, *Weltgeschichte Asiens im griechischen Zeitalter*, 2 vols., Halle 1947 & 1948
AM	*Mitteilungen des Deutschen Archäologischen Instituts, Athenische Abteilung*
Amit, *GSP*	M. Amit, *Great and Small Poleis. A Study in Relations Between the Great Powers and the Small Cities in Ancient Greece* (Collection Latomus, 134), Brussels 1973
Ann	*Annuario, Annuaire*

Ant.	*Die Antike*
Ant. Journ.	*Antiquarians Journal*
Anz.Alt.	*Anzeiger für die Altertumswissenschaft*
Anz.W	*Anzeiger der Akademie der Wissenschaften in Wien, philologisch-historische Klasse*
AO	Der Alte Orient
Arch.	*Archaeologia*
AR	*Atene et Roma*
ARW	*Archiv für Religionswissenschaft*
Ath.	*Athenaeum*
ATL	B. D. Meritt, H. T. Wade-Gery, M. F. McGregor (eds.), *The Athenian Tribute Lists*, 4 vols., Cambridge, Mass., 1939-1953
AW	*Antike Welt*
AZ	*Zeitschrift für ägyptische Sprache*
Baloch, *Ref.*	E. Baloch, *Political Refugees in Ancient Greece*, Johannesburg 1943
BASOR	*Bulletin of the American Schools of Oriental Research*
BCH	*Bulletin de Correspondence Hellénique*
Bell, *Eg.*	H. I. Bell, *Egypt from Alexander the Great to the Arab Conquest*, Oxford 1948
Bell, *Jews*	H. I. Bell, *Jews and Christians in Egypt*, London 1924
Bell, *Jud.*	H. I. Bell, *Juden und Griechen im römischen Alexandreia*, 9. Beih. z. Alt. Orient, Leipzig 1926
Beloch, *AP*	K. J. Beloch, *Die attische Politik seit Perikles*, Leipzig 1884
Beloch, *GG*	K. J. Beloch, *Griechische Geschichte*, ed. 1, 3 vols., Strassburg 1893-1904; ed. 2, 4 vols., Strassburg–Berlin 1912-1927 [down to 217 B.C.]
Bengtson, *Anc.Hist.*	H. Bengtson, *Introduction to Ancient History*, Univ. California Press 1970, transl. by R. I. Frank and F. D. Gilliard of Bengtson, *Einf.*^{6}

Bengtson, *Einf.*	H. Bengtson, *Einführung in die Alte Geschichte*, [7]1975
Bengtson, *Einz.*	H. Bengtson, *Einzelpersönlichkeit und athenischer Staat zur Zeit des Peisistratos und des Miltiades*, SB.M, 1939, Heft 1
Bengtson, *Herrs.*	H. Bengtson, *Herrschergestalten des Hellenismus*, Munich 1975
Bengtson, *KS*	H. Bengtson, *Kleine Schriften*, Munich 1974
Bengtson, *Labr.*	H. Bengtson, *Die Inschriften von Labranda und die Politik des Antigonos Doson*, Munich 1971
Bengtson, *Staatsv.*	H. Bengtson, *Die Verträge der griechisch-römischen Welt, von 700–338 v. Chr.*, Vol. II, Munich 1962
Bengtson, *Strat.*	H. Bengtson, *Die Strategie in der hellenistischen Zeit. Ein Beitrag zum antiken Staatsrecht*, 3 vols., Münch. Beitr. 26, 1937; 32, 1944; 36, 1952; reprint: I & II, 1964; III, 1967
Berve, *Alex.*	H. Berve, *Das Alexanderreich auf prosopographischer Grundlage*, 2 vols., Munich 1926
Berve, *GG*	H. Berve, *Griechische Geschichte*, 2 vols., Freiburg i. Br. 1931 & 1933; [2]1950, [2]1951
Berve, *Milt.*	H. Berve, Miltiades, *Studien zur Geschichte des Mannes und seiner Zeit*, Hermes–Einzelschr., 2, Leipzig 1937
Berve, *Tyr.*	H. Berve, *Die Tyrannis bei den Griechen*, 2 vols., Munich 1967
BGU	*Ägyptische Urkunden aus den Staatlichen Museen zu Berlin*, Berlin 1895 ff.
Bikerman, *Sél.*	E. Bikerman, *Institutions des Séleucides*, Paris 1938
Bilabel, *Kleinform*	F. Bilabel, *Die Kleineren Historikerfragmente auf Papyrus*, Bonn 1923
Bittel, *KS*	K. Bittel, *Kleinasiatische Studien*; Istanbul, 1942
Bittel, *EF*	K. Bittel, *Etruskische Frühgeschichte*, Berlin 1929

Bloedow, *Alc.*	E. Bloedow, *Alcibiades Reexamined*, H.-Einzelschr. 21, Wiesbaden 1973
Bossert, *Kr*:	H. T. Bossert, *Altkreta*, Berlin ³1937
Broughton, *As.*	T. R. S. Broughton, "*Roman Asia*," in T. Frank (ed.), *An Economic Survey of Ancient Rome*, Vol. IV, Baltimore 1938, 499 ff.
BSA	*Annual of The British School at Athens*
Burn, *Pers.*	A. R. Burn, *Persia and The Greeks. The Defense of The West c. 546-478 B.C.*, London 1962
Burs. Jb.	*Bursians Jahresberichte über die Fortschritte der klassischen Altertumswissenschaft*
Busolt, *GG*	G. Busolt, *Griechische Geschichte bis zur Schlacht bei Chäroneia* [goes down only to 404 B.C.], 3 vols., Gotha ²1893–1904
Busolt, *Gr.St.*	G. Busolt, *Griechische Staatskunde,* 2 vols. [Vol. II by H. Swoboda], in Hdb. Alt. IV 1, 1; IV 1, 2, Munich 1920 & 1926
CAH	*Cambridge Ancient History*, ed. by J. B. Bury, S. A. Cook, F. E. Adcock, M. P. Charlesworth, N. H. Baynes, 12 vols., Cambridge 1924-1939; ed. 3, ed. by I. E. S. Edwards, C. J. Gadd, N. G. L. Hammond, I 1, 1970; I 2, 1971; II 1, 1973, II 2, 1975
Cahn, *Knid.*	H. A. Cahn, Knidos, *Die Münzen des sechsten und des fünften Jahrhunderts vor Chr.*, Berlin 1970
Callmer, *Ark.*	C. Callmer, *Studien zur Geschichte Arkadiens*, Lund 1943
Cassola, *Ion.*	F. Cassola, *La Ionia nel Mondo Miceneo*, Naples 1957
Cd'E	*Chronique d'Egypte*
Ch.	*Chiron*
Ciaceri, *St.MGr.*	E. Ciaceri, *Storia della Magna Grecia*, 2 vols., Milano–Rome–Naples ²1928 ²1940
CIG	*Corpus Inscriptionum Graecarum*. Started and organised by A. Böckh in the Preusische Akademie 1825-1859; Index published in 1877. Since 1873 the *CIG* has been replaced by *IG*

CIL	*Corpus Inscriptionum Latinarum*. Begun under the direction of Th. Mommsen in 1893 (I^2, Mommsen, Henzen, Hülsen, Lommatzsch, 1893-1943)
CP	*Classical Philology*
CQ	*Classical Quarterly*
Cornelius, *Tyr. Ath.*	F. Cornelius, *Die Tyrannis in Athen*, Munich 1929
CR	*Classical Review*
CRAI	*Comptes rendus de l'Académie des inscriptions et Belles Lettres*
CSCA	*California Studies in Classical Antiquity*
CW	*Classical World*
Debevoise, *Parth.*	N.C. Debevoise, *A Political History of Parthia*, Chicago 1938
Delbrück, *Krieg.*	H. Delbrück, *Geschichte des Kriegskunst*, Berlin 1920
Delbrück, *Pkr.*	H. Delbrück, *Die Perserkriege und die Burgunderkriege*, Berlin 1887
den Boer, *Lac.*	W. den Boer, *Laconian Studies*, Amsterdam 1954
De Sanctis, *Att.*	G. De Sanctis, *Atthis. Storia della repubblica ateniese dalle origini all' eta di Pericle*, Turin ^{2}1912, new edition, Florence 1975
De Sanctis, *Per.*	G. De Sanctis, *Pericle*, Milan-Messina 1944
De Sanctis, *Rom.*	G. De Sanctis, Storia dei Romani, 4 vols., 1907 ff.; ^{2}1956 ff.
De Sanctis, *St. Gr.*	G. De Sanctis, *Storia dei Greci dalle origini alla fine del secolo V*, 2 vols., Florence 1939; ^{6}1961
De Sanctis, *St. Sic.*	G. De Sanctis, *Ricerche sulla storiographia siceliota*, Palermo 1958
Desborough, *GrDA*	V. R. d'A. Desborough, *The Greek Dark Ages*, London 1972
Desborough, *Last M*,	V. R. d'A. Desborough, *The Last Mycenaeans and their Successors*, Oxford 1964
Diss.	Dissertation

DLZ	*Deutsche Literature Zeitung*
Droysen, *GH*	J. G. Droysen, *Geschichte des Hellenismus*, 3 vols., Gotha ²1877-1878
Dunbabin, *West.*	T. J. Dunbabin, *The Western Greeks. The History of Sicily and South Italy from the Foundation of the Greek Colonies to 480 B.C.*, Oxford 1948
Ebert, *Südr.*	M. Ebert, *Südrussland im Altertum*, Berlin 1921
Ehrenberg, *Al. Aeg.*	V. Ehrenberg, *Alexander und Aegypten*, Beitr. z. Alten Orient 7, Leipzig 1926
Ehrenberg, *Alex.*	V. Ehrenberg, *Alexander and the Greeks*, Oxford 1938
Ehrenberg, *AW*	V. Ehrenberg, *Aspects of The Ancient World*, Oxford 1946
Ehrenberg, *Neugr.*	V. Ehrenberg, *Neugründer des Staates. Ein Beitrag zur Geschichte Spartas und Athens im 6. Jahrhundert*, Munich 1925
Ehrenberg, *OW*	V. Ehrenberg, *Ost und West*, Brunn 1935
Ehrenberg, *State*	V. Ehrenberg, *The Greek State*, London ²1969, transl. of *Der Staat der Griechen*, Zurich and Stuttgart 1965
Et. class	*Etudes classiques*
Evans, *Knossos*	Sir. Arthur Evans, *The Palace of Minos at Knossos*, 4 vols., London 1921-35
Ferguson, *Ath.*	W. S. Ferguson, *Hellenistic Athens*, London 1911
Feyel, *Pol.*	M. Feyel, *Polybe et l'histoire de Béotie au IIIe siècle av. notre ère*, Paris 1942
FgrHist	F. Jacoby, *Die Fragmente der griechischen Historiker*, 15 vols., Berlin 1923 ff.
FHG	*Fragmenta Historicorum Graecorum*, ed. by C. and Th. Müller, Paris 1841-70
Fimmen, *KM*	D. Fimmen, *Die kretisch-mykenische Kultur*, ed. 2 by G. Karo, Leipzig 1924
Flacelière, *Ait.*	R. Flacelière, *Les Aitoliens à Delphes*, Paris 1937

Fornara, *Gen.*	C. W. Fornara, *The Athenian Board of Generals from 501 to 404*, H.-Einzelschr. 16, Wiesbaden 1971
Fraser, *PA*	P. M. Fraser, *Ptolemaic Alexandria*, 3 vols., Oxford 1972
Friedel, *Tmord.*	H. Friedel, *Der Tyrannenmord in Gesetzgebung und Volksmeinung der Griechen*, Würzburger Stud. 11, 1937
Furumark, *Myc. Pot.*	A. Furumark, *The Mycenaean Pottery*, Stockholm 1941, repr. 1972
Gercke-Norden, *Einl.*	A. Gercke and E. Norden, *Einleitung in die Altertumswissenschaft*, 3 vols., Leipzig & Berlin 1910-1912
Geyer, *Mak.*	F. Geyer, *Makedonien bis zur Thronbesteigung Philipps II*, HZ Beih. 19, Munich 1930
GG	*Griechische Geschichte*
GGA	*Göttingische Gelehrte Anzeigen*
GGM	*Geographi Graeci minores*, ed. by C. Müller
GHD 5C	N. Lewis, *Greek Historical Documents, The 5th Century*, Toronto 1971
Glotz, *Cité Gr.* or *Gr. City*	G. Glotz, *La cité grecque*, Paris 1928, and English transl., *The Greek City*, Paris 1929
Glotz (Glotz-Cohen), *HG*	G. Glotz (and R. Cohen), *Histoire grecque*, 4 vols., Paris 1925-38, in *Histoire Générale*, publ. sous la direction de Gustave Glotz
Gn.	*Gnomon*
Götze, *Heth.*	A. Götze, *Hethither, Churriter und Assyrer, Hauptlinien der vorderasiatischen Kulturentwicklung im 2. Jahrtausend v. Chr.*, Oslo 1936
Göetze, *KAO*	A. Goetze, "Kleinasien," in *Kulturgeschichte des alten Orients*, Hdb. Alt. III 1, 3, Munich ²1957
Gomme, *Comm. Thuc.*	A. W. Gomme, *A. Historical Commentary on Thucydides*, I-III, Oxford, 1945-56; IV with A. Andrewes, K. J. Dover, Oxford 1970
Gomme, *Essays*	A. W. Gomme, *Essays in Greek History and Literature*, Oxford 1938

Gomme, *Pop.*	A. W. Gomme, *The Population of Athens in the Vth and IVth Centuries B.C.*, London 1933
Graham, *Pal.*	J. W. Graham, *The Palaces of Crete*, Princeton ²1969
Graindor, *Ath.*	P. Graindor, *Athènes sous Hadrien*, Cairo 1934
GRBS	*Greek, Roman and Byzantine Studies*
Grundy, *PW*	G. B. Grundy, *The Great Persian War and its Preliminaries*, London 1901
Gym.	*Das Gymnasium*
H.	*Historia*
Habicht, *Gott.*	C. Habicht, *Gottmenschentum und griechische Städte*, *Zetemata* 14, 1956, ²1970
Hammond, *HG*	N. G. L. Hammond, *A History of Greece to 322 B.C.*, Oxford ²1967
Hammond, *Studies*	N. G. L. Hammond, *Studies in Greek History*, Oxford 1973
Hampl, *KM*	F. Hampl, *Der König der Makedonien*, Diss. Leipzig 1934
Hampl, *Staatsv.*	F. Hampl, *Die griechische Staatsverträge des 4. Jahrhunderts v. Chr. Geb.*, Leipzig 1938
Hanell, *Meg.*	K. Hanell, *Megarische Studien*, Lund 1934
Hasebroek, *Gr. Wirt.-Ges.*	J. Hasebroek, *Griechische Wirtschafts- und Gesellschaftsgeschichte bis zur Perserzeit* I, Tübingen 1931
Hdb. Alt.	Handbuch der Altertumswissenschaft
Hdb. Arch.	Handbuch der Archäologie, in Hdb. Alt.
Head, *HN*	B. V. Head, *Historia Numorum, a Manual of Greek Numismatics*. New and enlarged ed., by B. V. Head, assisted by G. F. Hill, George Macdonald & W. Wroth, London 1963
Heichelheim, *Wirts. Alt.*	F. M. Heichelheim, *Wirtschaftsgeschichte des Alterums vom Paläolithikum bis zur Völkerwanderung*, 2 vols. Leiden 1938; also in English transl., *Ancient Economic History*, I, Leiden 1958 (²1965); II, 1964
Heinen, *Hell.*	H. Heinen, *Untersuchungen zur hellenistischen*

	Geschichte des 3. Jahrhunderts v. Chr., H.-Einzelschr. 20, Wiesbaden 1972
Hel.	*Hellenica* H. Einzelschr. Historia-Einzelschriften
Herzfeld, *Altp.I.*	E. Herzfeld, *Altpersische Inschriften*, Berlin 1938
Hesp.	*Hesperia*
HG	see Glotz, *HG*
Highby, *ED*	L. I. Highby, *The Erythrae Decree, A Contribution to the Early History of the Delian League and the Peloponnesian Confederacy*, Klio Beih. 36, Leipzig 1936
Hignett, *Const.*	C. Hignett, *A History of The Athenian Constitution to the End of the 5th Century B.C.*, Oxford 1952
Hignett, *Inv.*	C. Hignett, *Xerxes' Invasion of Greece*, Oxford 1963
HM	*Historia Mundi*, Handbook of World History in 10 vols., founded by F. Kern, ed. by F. Valjavec. Relevant for Greek History are: Vol. II, 1953: "Grundlagen und Entstehung der ältesten Hochkulturen", Vol. III, 1954: "Der Aufstieg Europas."
Holleaux, *Et. ép.*	M. Holleaux, *Etudes d'épigraphie et d'histoire grecques*, 5 vols., 1938-57
Holleaux, *Rome*	M. Holleaux, *Rome, la Grèce, et les monarchies hellénistiques au IIIe siècle av. J.-C., (273-205)*, Paris 1921
Hood, *Mins.*	M. S. F. Hood, *The Minoans. Crete in The Bronze Age*, London 1971
HSCP	*Harvard Studies in Classical Philology*
Jacoby, *Att.*	F. Jacoby, *Atthis, The Local Chronicles of Ancient Athens*, Oxford 1949
Jacoby, *FgrHist*	F. Jacoby, *Die Fragmente der griechischen Historiker*, 15 vols., Berlin 1923 ff.
Jaeger, *Paid.*	W. Jaeger, *Paideia. Die Formung des griechischen Menschen*, 3 vols., ^{2}I, Berlin 1936; ^{2}II, 1944; ^{2}III, 1947, trans. *Paideia: The Ideals of Greek Culture*, by G. Highet, Oxford 1946-1947

JdI	*Jahrbuch des Deutschen Archäologischen Instituts*
JEA	*Journal of Egyptian Archaeology*
Jh	*Jahresheft*
Jhs	*Journal of Hellenic Studies*
JJP	*Journal of Juristic Papyrology*
JNES	*Journal of Near Eastern Studies*
JNG	*Jahrbuch für Numismatik und Geldgeschichte*
JRS	*Journal of Roman Studies*
Judeich, *KS*	W. Judeich, *Kleinasiatische Studien*, Marburg 1892
HVSchr.	*Historische Vierteljahrschrift*
HZ	*Historische Zeitschrift*
IG	*Inscriptiones Graecae*
IGR	*Inscriptiones Graecae ad res Romanas pertinentes*, ed. by R. Cagnat et al.
Istanbuler Mitt.	*Istanbuler Mitteilungen*
Jb(b)	*Jahrbuch* (*Jahrbücher*)
Judeich, *Top.*	W. Judeich, *Topographie von Athen*, (Hdb. Alt. III 2, 2), Munich [2]1931
Junge, *Dar.*	P. J. Junge, *Dareios I, König der Perser*, Leipzig 1944
Kaerst, *GH*	J. Kaerst, *Geschichte des Hellenismus*, 2 Vols., Leipzig & Berlin, [3]I, 1927; [2]II, 1926
Kaerst, *Mon.*	J. Kaerst, *Studien zur Entwicklung und theoretischen Begründung der Monarchie im Altertum*, Munich & Leipzig 1899
Kahrstedt, *Stsr.*	U. Kahrstedt, *Griechische Staatsrecht*. I: *Sparta und seine Symmachie*, Göttingen 1922
Karo, *Sch.*	G. Karo, *Die Schachtgräber von Mykenai*, Munich 1930-33
Kiechle, *Messen.*	F. Kiechle, *Messenische Studien*, Diss. Erlangen 1957
Klaffenbach, *Gr.Ep.*	G. Klaffenbach, *Griechische Epigraphik*, Studien zur Altertumswissenschaft, 6, Göttingen 1957; [2]1966

Kl. Schr. (KS)	*Kleine Schriften*
Köster, *Seewesens*	A. Köster, *Studien zur Geschichte des antiken Seewesens*, Klio Beih. 32, Leipzig 1934
Kolbe, *Thuk.*	W. Kolbe, *Thukidides im Lichte der Urkunden*, Stuttgart 1930
Kornemann, *Fr.*	E. Kornemann, *Grosse Frauen des Altertums*, Wiesbaden ^{2}1947
Krahe, *Ant.*	K. Krahe, "Die Indogermanisierung Griechenlands", *Antike, Alte Sprachen und Deutsche Bildung*, 1943
Kretschmer, "Sprache"	P. Kretschmer, "Sprache," in Gercke-Norden, *Einl.* I^{3}, Leipzig & Berlin 1927
Kromayer-Veith, *Schl.*	J. Kromayer and G. Veith, *Antike Schlachtfelder*, 4 vols., Berlin 1903-1931
Kromayer-Veith, *Atlas*	J. Kromayer and G. Veith, *Schlachtenatlas zur antiken Kriegsgeschichte*, Leipzig 1922 ff.
Kromayer-Veith, *Heerw.*	J. Kromayer and G. Veith, *Heerwesen und Kriegführung der Griechen und Römer*, (Hdb. Alt. IV 3, 2), Munich 1928; reprint: 1963
Kroymann, *Paus.*	J. Kroymann, *Pausanias und Rhianos*, Berlin 1943
KZ	*Kuhns Zeitschrift für vergleichende Sprachwissenschaft*
Larsen, *Gr.Fed. S.*	J. A. O. Larsen, *Greek Federal States*, Oxford 1968
Larsen, *Rep. Govt.*	J. A. O. Larsen, *Representative Government in Greek and Roman History*, Berkeley 1955
Ledl, *Verf.*	A. Ledl, *Studien zur älteren athenischen Verfassungsgeschichte*, Heidelberg 1914
Lévêque, *Pyr.*	P. Lévêque, *Pyrrhus*, Paris 1957
Lotze, *Met.*	D. Lotze, *Metaxu eleutherion kai doulon. Studien zur Rechtsstellung unfreier Landbevölkerung in Griechenland bis zum 4. Jahrhunderts vor Chr.*, Berlin 1959
Matz, *Ägäis*	F. Matz, *Die Ägäis* (in Hdb. Alt. VI 2), Munich 1950
Mazzarino, *Fr.OO*	B. Mazzarino, *Fra Oriente e Occidente*, Florence 1947

MDOG	*Mitteilungen der Deutschen Orient-Gesellschaft*
Mederer, *A.leg.*	E. Mederer, *Die Alexanderlegenden bei den ältesten Alexanderhistorikern*, Würzburger Studien zur Altertumswissenschaft, 8, Stuttgart 1936
Meier, *Sp.St.*	T. Meier, *Das Wesen der spartanischen Staatsordnung nach ihren lebensgesetzlichen und bodenrechtlichen Voraussetzungen*, Klio Beih. 42, Leipzig 1939; reprint: Aalen 1967
Meiggs-Lewis	R. Meiggs, D. M. Lewis (eds.), *A Selection of Greek Historical Inscriptions to the End of the Fifth Century B.C.*, Oxford 1969 (unless preceded by p., numbers refer to numbered texts)
Mél	*Mélanges*
Meritt-West, *Ath.A*	B. D. Meritt & A. West, *The Athenian Assessment of 425 B.C.*, Ann Arbor 1934
Meyer, *Christ*,	Ed. Meyer, *Ursprung und Anfang des Christentums*, 3 vols., Berlin 1921-1923
Meyer, *Forsch.*	Ed. Meyer, *Forschungen zur alten Geschichte*, 2 vols., Halle 1892 & 1899
Meyer, *GdA*	Ed. Meyer, *Geschichte des Altertums*, 5 Vols., Stuttgart 1884-1902; Vol. ^{3}I, 1910-13 ^{2}II 1 & ^{2}II 2, 1928, 1931; ^{3}III & ^{3}IV, 1 & 2, ^{4}V, ed. by H. E. Stier, 1939-1958
Min.	*Minoica, Festschrift zum 80. Geburtstag von J. Sundwall*, Berlin 1958
Mn.	*Mnemosyne*
Momigliano, *Fil.*	A. Momigliano, *Filippo il Macedone. Saggio nella storia greca del IV secolo av. Chr.*, Florence 1934
Müller, *GGM*	C. Müller (ed.), *Geographi Graeci minores*
MVAG	*Mitteilungen der Vorderasiatische Ägyptischen Gesellschaft*
Münch. Beitr.	Münchener Beiträge zur Papyrusforschung und antiken Rechtsgeschichte
NBAnt.	*Das Neue Bild der Antike*, ed. H. Berve, 2 vols., I: Hellas; II: Rome, Leipzig 1942

Nesselhauf, *Symm.*	H. Nesselhauf, *Untersuchungen zur Geschichte der delische-attischen Symmachie*, Klio-Beiheft 30, Leipzig 1933; reprint: Aalen 1963
NF	*Neue Folge*
NGG	*Nachrichten der Göttinger Gesellschaft der Wissenschaften*
Niese, *Mak.*	B. Niese, *Geschichte der griechischen und makedonischen Staaten seit der Schlacht bei Chäroneia*, 3 vols., Gotha 1893-1903
NJb	*Neue Jahrbücher*
Nilsson, *Gr. Rel.*	M. P. Nilsson, *Geschichte der griechischen Religion*, 2 vols. (Hdb. Alt. V 2, 1; V 2, 2), Munich 1941 & 1950; ^{3}I, 1967; ^{2}II 1961
Nilsson, *Gr.Tyr.*	M. P. Nilsson, *The Age of the Early Greek Tyrants*, Dill Memorial Lecture, Univ. Belfast 1936
Nilsson, *Hom.*	M. P. Nilsson, *Homer and Mycenae*, London 1933; reprint: New York 1968
Nilsson, *MMRel.*	M. P. Nilsson, *The Minoan-Mycenaean Religion and its Survival in Greek Religion*, Lund 1927
Nilsson, *OS*	M. P. Nilsson, *Opuscula Selecta*
Nilsson, *Sch.*	M. P. Nilsson, *Die hellenistische Schule*, Munich 1955
NS	*Neue Serie*
NJb	*Neue Jahrbücher*
NPhU	*Neue Philologische Untersuchungen*
Num. Chron.	*Numismatic Chronicle*
Obst, *Xerx.*	E. Obst, *Der Feldzug des Xerxes*, Klio Beih. 12, Leipzig 1914
OGI	*Orientis Graeci Inscriptiones Selectae*, ed. by W. Dittenberger, Leipzig 1903-5
Olmstead, *HPE*	A. T. Olmstead, *A History of The Persian Empire*, Chicago 1948
OLZ	*Orientalistische Literaturzeitung*
Opusc. Arch.	*Opuscula Archaeologica*

Öst. Jh.	*Jahreshefte des Österreichischen Archäologischen Instituts*
Otto, *Kulturg.*	W. Otto, *Kulturgeschichte des Altertums. Ein Überlick über neue Erscheinungen*, Munich 1925
Otto, *6. Ptol.*	W. Otto, *Zur Geschichte der Zeit des 6. Ptolemäers. Ein Beitrag zur Politik und zum Staatsrecht des Hellenismus*, Abh. Bay, NF 11, Munich 1934
Otto, *Sel.*	W. Otto, *Beiträge zur Seleukidengeschichte des 3. Jahrh. v. Chr.*, Abh. Bay 34, 1, Munich 1928
Otto-Bengtson, *Ptol.*	W. Otto & H. Bengtson, *Zur Geschichte des Niederganges des Ptolemäerreiches. Ein Beitrag zur Regierungszeit des 8. und 9. Ptolemäers*, Abh. Bay, NF 17, Munich 1938
Parke-Wormell, *Or.*	H. W. Parke & E. W. Wormell, *The Delphic Oracle*, Oxford 1956
Pendlebury, *Cr.*	J. D. S. Pendlebury, *The Archaeology of Crete*, London 1939, reprint: 1965
Persson, *Dend.*	A. W. Persson, *The Royal Tombs at Dendra Near Midea*, Skrivter utg. av. Hum. Vetenskapssamfundet i Lund 15, Lund 1931
Persson, *Dend.New*	A. W. Persson, *New Tombs at Dendra Near Midea*, Skrifter utg. av. Hum. Vetenskapssamfundet i Lund 34, Lund 1942
Ph.	*Philologus*
Phil.	*Philology*
PhU	*Philologische Untersuchungen*
PhW	*Philologische Wochenschrift*
Piganiol, *HR*	A. Piganiol, *Histoire de Rome*, Paris [5]1962
Pohlenz, *Hdt.*	M. Pohlenz, *Herodot, der erste Geschichtsschreiber des Abendlandes*, Wege zur Antike II, 7-8, Leipzig 1937; Stuttgart 1961
Pöhlmann, *GG*	R. v. Pöhlmann, *Griechische Geschichte und Quellenkunde*, in Hdh. Alt. III, 4, Munich [5]1914
Pokorny, *St.*	E. Pokorny, *Studien zur griechischen Geschichte im 6. und 5. Jahrzehnt des 4. Jahrhundert vor Chr.*, Diss. Griefswald 1913

Poulson, *Frühgr.*	F. Poulson, *Der Orient und die frühgriechische Kunst*, Leipzig 1912
P. Oxy.	*The Oxyrhynchus Papyri*, London 1898 ff.
PP	*La Parola del Passato*
Pr.Br.Ac.	*Proceedings of The British Academy*
Préaux, *Econ.*	*C. Préaux, L'économie royale des Lagides,* Brussels 1939
Prestel, *Antidem.*	G. Prestel, *Die antidemokratische Strömung in Athen des 5. Jahrhunderts bis zum Tode des Perikles*, Breslauer Historische Forschungen 12, 1939
PSI	*Papiri della Società Italiana*, Florence 1912 ff.
Pritchett, *Top.*	W. K. Pritchett, *Studies in Ancient Greek Topography*, 2 vols., Berkeley 1965 & 1969
P.Teb.	*The Tebtunis Papyri*, 3 vols., London, New York, California 1902-1938
Px.	*Phoenix*
QUUC	*Quaderni Urbinati di Cultura classica*
RALinc.	*Accademia dei Lincei, Rendiconti della Classe de Scienze Morali*
RE	*Realencyclopädie der classischen Altertumswissenschaft*
Reinach, *Mith.*	T. Reinach, *Mithridates Eupator, König von Pontos* (German by A. Götz), Leipzig, 1895
REA	*Revue des Etudes anciennes*
REGr.	*Revue des Etudes grecques*
Rev. arch.	*Revue archéologique*
Rev. hist.	*Revue historique*
Rend.	*Rendiconti*
Rev. de phil.	*Revue de Philologie*
RF	*Rivista di Filologia*
RhM	*Rheinisches Museum*
Riccobono, *FIRA*	S. Riccobono, *Fontes Iuris Romae Antejustinianae*
RIL	*Rendiconti dell'Istituto Lombardo, Classe de Lettere, Scienze morali e storiche*

RLVorg.	*Reallexikon der Vorgeschichte*, ed. by M. Ebert
RM	*Mitteilungen des Archäologischen Instituts, Römische Abteilung*
Rodenwaldt, *Fries*	G. Rodenwaldt, *Der Fries des Megarons von Mykenai*, Halle 1921
Rph.	*Revue de Philologie*
Rostovtzeff, *SEHHW*,	M. Rostovtzeff, *Social and Economic History of The Hellenistic World*, 3 vols., Oxford 1941
Rostovtzeff, *SEHRE*	M. Rostovtzeff, *Social and Economic History of the Roman Empire*, 2 vols., ed. 2 revised by P. M. Fraser, Oxford 1957
RSA	*Rivista storica dell'Antichità*
Ruschenbusch, *SN*	E. Ruschenbusch, *Solons nomoi. Die Fragmente des solonischen Gesetzwerkes mit einem Textund Überlieferungs geschichte*, H.-Einzelschr., 9, 1966
RVV	*Religionsgeschichtliche Versuche und Vorarbeiten*
Saec.	*Saeculum*
Sakellariou, *MG*	M. B. Sakellariou, *La migration grecque en Ionie*, Athens 1958
SB	*Sammelbuch der griechischen Papyrusurkunden*, ed. by Preisigke-Bilabel-Kiessling
SB.B	*Sitzungsberichte der Deutschen Akademie der Wissenschaften zu Berlin, Klasse für Philosophie, Geschichte, Staats-, Rechts- und Wirtschaftswissenschaften*
SB.Bay	Sitzungsberichte der Bayerischen Akademie der Wissenschaften, philosohisch-historische Klasse
SB.H	Sitzungsberichte der Heidelberger Akademie der Wissenschaften, philosophisch-historische Klasse
SB.M	Sitzungsberichte der Münchener Akademie der Wissenshaften, philosophisch-historische Klasse

SB.Ö	Sitzungsberichte der Österreichen Akademie der Wissenschaft in Wien, philosophisch-historische Klasse
SB.W	Sitzungsberichte der Akademie der Wissenschaft in Wien, philosophisch-historische Klasse
SJ	*Schmollers Jahrbuch*
Schachermeyr, *EF*	F. Schachermeyr, *Etruskische Forschungen*
Schachermeyr, *GRG*	F. Schachermeyr, *Forschungen und Betrachtungen zur griechischen und römischen Geschichte*, Vienna 1974
Schachermeyr, *Griech.*	F. Schachermeyr, *Die ältesten Kulturen Griechenlands*, Stuttgart 1955
Schachermeyr, *H.U.A.*	F. Schachermeyr, *Hethiter und Achäer*, (Mittilungen der Altorientalischen Gesellschaft 9, 1-2), Leipzig 1935
Schachermeyr, *Min.*	F. Schachermeyr, *Die minoische Kultur des alten Kreta*, Stuttgart 1964
Schachermeyr, *Rasse*	F. Schachermeyr, *Zur Rasse und Kultur im minoischen Kreta*, Heidelberg, 1939, also in *Wörter und Sachen* NF 2, 1939, 97 ff.
Schaeder, *PW*	H. H. Schaeder, *Das persische Weltreich*, Breslau 1941
Schaefer, *Staats.*	H. Schaefer, *Staatsform und Politik. Untersuchungen zur griechischen Geschichte des 6. und 5. Jahrhunderts*, Leipzig 1932
Scheele, *Str.*	M. Scheele, *Strategos Autokrator*, Diss. Leipzig 1932
Schmid, *GGL*	W. Schmid & O. Stählin, *Geschichte der griechischen Literatur*, 3 vols. (Hdb. Alt. VII 1,1; VII 1,2,; VII 1,3), Munich 1929-1940
Schmitt, *Ant.*	H. H. Schmitt, *Untersuchungen zur Geschichte Antiochos der Grosse und seiner Zeit*, H.-Einzelschr. 6, Wiesbaden 1964
Schmitt, *Staatsv.*	H. H. Schmitt, *Die Verträge der griechisch-römischen Welt von 338 bis 200 r.Chr*, Vol. III, Munich 1969
Schuchhardt, *Alt.*	G. Schuchhardt, *Alteuropa*, Berlin [3]1935

Schwyzer, *Gramm.*	E. Schwyzer, *Griechische Grammatik, auf der Grundlage von Karl Brugmanns Griechischer Grammatik*, (Hdb. Alt. II 1,1) Munich 1950-1953
SEG	*Supplementum Epigraphicum Graecum*, Leiden 1923 ff.
Sherk, *Docs.*	R. K. Sherk, *Roman Documents from the Greek East, Senatus Consulta and Epistulae to the Age of Augustus*, Baltimore 1969
Skeat, *Reigns*,	T. C. Skeat, *The Reigns of the Ptolemies*, Münch. Beitr. 39, [3]1969
SIMA	*Studies in Mediterranean Archaeology*
Snodgrass, *DA*	A. M. Snodgrass, *The Dark Age of Greece. An Archaeological Survey of the Eleventh to the Eighth Centuries B.C., Edinburgh* & Chicago 1971
Stroux-Wenger, *A. Insch.*	J. Stroux & L. Wenger, *Die Augustus-inschrift auf dem Marktplatz von Kyrene*, Abh.Bay, phil-hist. Kl. 34,2, Munich 1928
Studies Buckler	*Anatolian Studies Presented to W. H. Buckler*, Manchester 1939
Studies Ehrenberg	*Ancient Society and Institutions, Studies Presented to Victor Ehrenberg*, Oxford 1966
Studies Ferguson	*Athenian Studies Presented to W. S. Ferguson*, HSCP, Suppl. I, Cambridge, Mass., 1940
Studies Goldman	*The Aegean and the Near East. Studies Presented to Hetty Goldman on the Occasion of her Seventy-Fifth Birthday*, ed. by S. Weinberg, Locust Valley, New York 1956
Syll.	*Sylloge Inscriptionum Graecarum*, ed. 3, by W. Dittenberger, Leipzig 1915-24
TAPA	*Transactions of the American Philological Association*
Tarn, *Alex.*	W. W. Tarn, *Alexander the Great*, 2 vols., Cambridge 1948
Tarn, *Antig.*	W. W. Tarn, *Antigonos Gonatas*, Oxford 1913
Tarn, *Bact.*	W. W. Tarn, *The Greeks in Bactria and India*, Cambridge 1938, [2]1951; reprint: 1966

Tenney Frank, *ESAR*	Tenney Frank, *Economic Survey of Ancient Rome*, 5 vols., Baltimore 1933-41
Theunissen, *Ar.*	W. P. Theunissen, *Ploutarchos Leven van Aratos*, Nijmegen 1935
Tod	M. N. Tod, *A Selection of Greek Historical Inscriptions*, I, Oxford [2]1946, II, Oxford, [2]1948 (unless preceded by p., numbers refer to numbered inscriptions [cf. Meiggs-Lewis, p. 75])
Toepffer, *B.gr.Alt.*	J. Toepffer, *Beiträge zur griechischen Altertumswissenschaft*, Basle 1897
Toynbee, *Pr.*	A. J. Toynbee, *Some Problems of Greek History*, Oxford 1972
Triepel, *Heg.*	H. Triepel, *Die Hegemonie, ein Buch von führenden Staaten*, Stuttgart 1938
UPZ	*Urkunden der Ptolemäerzeit*, ed. by U. Wilcken, 2 vols., Berlin 1922 & 1935
Ure, *Or.*	P. N. Ure, *The Origin of Tyranny*, Cambridge 1922
Vallet, *Rhég.*	G. Vallet, *Rhégion et Zanclé, Histoire, commerce et civilization des cités chalcidiennes du détroit de Messine*, Paris 1958
VDI	*Vestnik Drevnej Istorii*
Wade-Gery, *Essays*	H. T. Wade-Gery, *Essays in Greek History*, Oxford 1958
Walbank, *Comm. Polyb.*	F. W. Walbank, *An Historical Commentary on Polybius*, to date, 2 vols., Oxford 1957 & 1967
Walbank, *Phil.V*	F. W. Walbank, *Philip V of Macedon*, Cambridge 1940
Welles, *RC*	C. B. Welles, *Royal Correspondence in the Hellenistic Period, a Study in Greek Epigraphy*, New Haven 1934; reprint: Rome 1966
West, *IEG*	(*OCT*) M. L. West (ed.), *Iambi et Elegi Graeci*, 2 vols., Oxford 1971
Westlake, *Essays*	H. D. Westlake, *Essays on Greek Historians and Greek History*, Manchester & New York 1969

WG	*Die Welt als Geschichte*
Wk/Ph	*Wochenschrift für klassische Philologie*
Wilamowitz, *Arist.*	U. v. Wilamowitz-Moellendorff, *Aristoteles und Athen*, 2 vols., Berlin 1893; reprint: Berlin 1966
Wilcken, *GSoph.*	U. Wilcken, *Alexander der Grosse und die indische Gymnosophisten*, SB.B, 1923, 23
Wilamowitz, *Gl.*	U. v. Wilamowitz-Moellendorff, *Der Glaube der Hellenen*, 2 vols., Berlin 1931 & 1932; reprint: Darmstadt 1959
Wilcken, *Alex.*	U. Wilcken, *Alexander the Great*, New York 1967, transl. of *Alexander der Grosse*, Leipzig 1931
Wilcken, *Kult.*	U. Wilcken, *Zur Entstehung des hellenistischen Königskultes*, SB. B, 1938, 28
Wilcken, *Ent.*	U. Wilcken, *Über Entstehung und Zweck des Königsfriedens*, Abh. B, phil,-hist. Kl. 15, 1942
Wilcken, *Phil.*	U. Wilcken, *Philipp II. von Makedonien und die panhellenische Idee*, SB. B, 1929, XVIII
Ad. Wilhelm, *Att. Urk.*	Ad. Wilhelm, *Attische Urkunden*, Sitzungsberichte der Weiner Akademie, 5 Hefte, 1911-1942
Will, *MGr.*	Ed. Will, *Le monde grec et l'Orient*, I, Paris 1972
Will, *Korinthiaka*	Ed. Will, *Korinthiaka Recherches sur l'histoire et la civilisation de corinthe des origines aux guerres médiques*, Paris 1955
Woodhouse, *Solon*	W. J. Woodhouse, *Solon the Liberator, A Study in the Agrarian Problem in the 7th Century*, Oxford & London 1938
Wüst, *Phil.*	F. R. Wüst, *Philipp II. von Makedonien und Griechenland in den Jahren von 346 - 338 v. Chr.*, Münchener Historische Abhandlungen I, 14, Munich 1938
WZKM	*Wiener Zeitschrift für die Kunde des Abendlandes*
YCS	*Yale Classical Studies*
ZAss.	*Zeitschrift für Assyriologie*

ZDMG	*Zeitschrift der Deutschen Morgenländischen Gesellschaft*
ZDPV	*Zeitschrift des Deutschen Palästina-Vereins*
Z.f. Num.	*Zeitschrift für Numismatik*
ZPE	*Zeitschrift für Papyrologie und Epigraphik*
ZSS Röm.	*Zeitschrift der Savignystiftung für Rechtsgeschichte, Römische Abteilung*

Index

B

C

E

F

G

H

I

J

K

L

M

N

O

P

Q

R

T

U

V

W